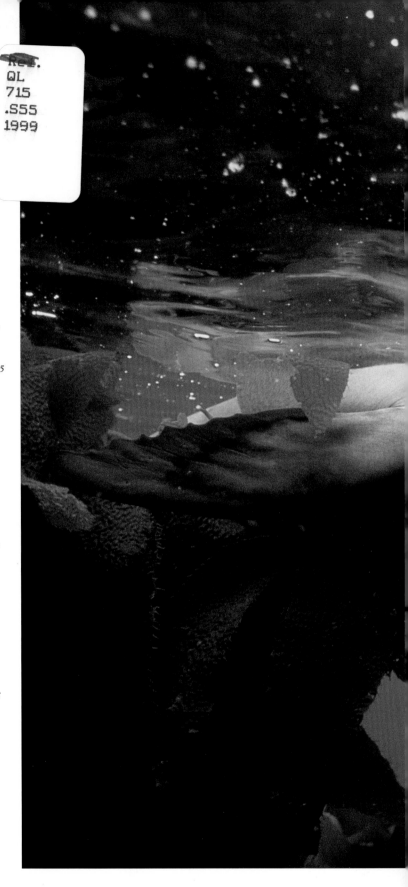

PRODUCTION EDITOR: Duke Johns
EDITORIAL PROOFREADER AND INDEXER: Barry R. Koffler
DESIGNER: Janice Wheeler
PRODUCTION MANAGER: Martha Sewall
TYPESETTER AND LAYOUT: Blue Heron Typesetters, Inc.

Library of Congress Cataloging-in-Publication Data
The Smithsonian book of North American mammals / edited by
    Don E. Wilson and Sue Ruff.
      p.   cm.
    "In association with the American Society of Mammalogists."
    Includes bibliographical references (p.   ) and index.
    ISBN 1-56098-845-2 (alk. paper)
    1. Mammals—North America.   I. Wilson, Don E.   II. Ruff, Sue.
III. American Society of Mammalogists.
    QL715.S55   1999
    599.097—dc21   98-43735

British Library Cataloguing-in-Publication Data available

Manufactured in Singapore, not at government expense
06 05 04 03 02 01 00   5 4 3 2

♾   The paper used in this publication meets the minimum requirements of the American National Standard for Information Sciences—
Permanence of Paper for Printed Library Materials ANSI Z39.48-1984.

For permission to reproduce illustrations appearing in this book, please
correspond directly with the owners of the works, as listed in the photo
credits. The Smithsonian Institution Press does not retain reproduction
rights for these illustrations individually, or maintain a file of addresses
for photo sources.

FRONT-MATTER PHOTOS: p. i: Townsend's big-eared bat *(Corynorhinus
townsendii);* pp. ii–iii: elk *(Cervus elaphus);* pp. iv–v: California sea lion
(Zalophus californianus); p. vi: snowshoe hare *(Lepus americanus);*
p. x: nine-banded armadillo *(Dasypus novemcinctus);* p. xii: raccoons
(Procyon lotor); pp. xiv–xv: humpback whale *(Megaptera novaenangliae);*
p. xvi: Cascade golden-mantled ground squirrel *(Spermophilus saturatus);*
p. xxiv: black bear *(Ursus americanus)*

Contents

Preface   ix

Acknowledgments   xiii

Contributors   xvii

Plan of the Book   xxiii

Order Didelphimorphia
Family Didelphidae: Opossums   3

Order Xenarthra
Family Dasypodidae: Armadillos   9

Order Insectivora
Shrews and Moles

Family Soricidae: Shrews   15

Family Talpidae: Moles   56

Order Chiroptera
Bats

Family Mormoopidae: Ghost-faced Bats   71

Family Phyllostomidae: Leaf-nosed Bats   73

Family Vespertilionidae: Vesper Bats   82

Family Molossidae: Free-tailed Bats   127

Order Carnivora
Carnivores

Family Canidae: Dogs   139

Family Ursidae: Bears   157

Family Mustelidae: Weasels, Badgers, and Otters   165

Family Mephitidae: Skunks   183

Family Odobenidae: Walrus   193

Family Otariidae: Fur Seals and Sea Lions   195

Family Phocidae: Earless Seals   203

Family Procyonidae: Ringtail, Raccoon, and Coati   219

Family Felidae: Cats   226

Order Cetacea
Whales and Dolphins

Family Balaenidae: Right Whales   241

Family Balaenopteridae: Rorquals   246

Family Eschrichtiidae: Gray Whale   259

Family Delphinidae: Dolphins   262

Family Monodontidae: Beluga and Narwhal   291

Family Phocoenidae: Porpoises   295

Family Physeteridae: Sperm Whales   299

Family Ziphiidae: Beaked Whales   304

Order Sirenia
Family Trichechidae: Manatees   319

Order Artiodactyla
Even-toed Hoofed Mammals

Family Tayassuidae: Peccaries   325

Family Cervidae: Deer   327

Family Antilocapridae: Pronghorn   339

Family Bovidae: Bison, Sheep, and Goats   342

Order Rodentia

Rodents

Family Aplodontidae: Mountain Beaver   355

Family Sciuridae: Squirrels   357

Family Geomyidae: Pocket Gophers   466

Family Heteromyidae: Pocket Mice, Kangaroo Rats,
     and Kangaroo Mice   494

Family Castoridae: Beaver   548

Family Muridae: Rats, Mice, Voles, and Lemmings
     553

Family Dipodidae: Jumping Mice   665

Family Erithizontidae: Porcupines   671

Order Lagomorpha

Pikas, Rabbits, and Hares

Family Ochotonidae: Pikas   677

Family Leporidae: Rabbits and Hares   681

Appendix: Common and Scientific Names of
     Plants Cited   707

Glossary   711

Literature Cited   715

Photography Credits   737

Index to Scientific Names   743

Index to Common Names   747

Preface

North America north of Mexico is home to more than 400 species of mammals, each of which is treated in considerable detail in the pages that follow. The accumulation of knowledge about North American mammals has been growing for at least 10,000 years, since early humans took the first tentative footsteps across the Bering Strait and opened a whole new world to the eyes of an important addition to that mammal fauna, *Homo sapiens.* However, it is only within the past three centuries that a new wave of immigrants has systematically documented that knowledge.

One of the earliest publications on North American mammals was *The Natural History of Carolina, Florida, and the Bahamas,* written by Mark Catesby in 1748. This was a groundbreaking volume, providing the world with the first comprehensive view of New World mammals. In 1799, one of our more accomplished early naturalists, Thomas Jefferson of Virginia, published a paper describing fossil ground sloths in the *Transactions of the American Philosophical Society.* He was serving as Vice President of the United States at the time, and when he later assumed the presidency, he was in a position to advance our knowledge of North American mammals on a broader front. Jefferson's breadth and depth of knowledge of natural history has remained unmatched by later presidents, although some, such as Theodore Roosevelt, also contributed directly to our knowledge of mammals.

Jefferson's personal contributions on mammals were not nearly so important as his sponsorship of numerous expeditions that opened up the western half of the continent and led to the first descriptions of many species of North American mammals. The first and undoubtedly most significant of these was the 1804 journey of Meriwether Lewis and William Clark. This expedition, to find a route across the continent to the Pacific Ocean, was also tasked to report on geology, geography, mineral resources, climate, zoology, and botany, and particularly to look for large mammals. An additional charge involved making recommendations on how to interact with both peaceful and hostile groups of indigenous people.

The Lewis and Clark Expedition set a standard for all other such journeys of exploration to follow. It produced a wealth of information about the natural resources of this continent. Much of that information was due to the dedication of Meriwether Lewis, an accomplished naturalist and competent collector, who recorded his observations in a series of journals, most of which have remained available for study by subsequent scholars. Although Lewis intended to edit the journals into publishable form, he did not live to see that happen. This means that although he is not credited with the scientific names, he did provide the first descriptions of a variety of mammals such as the black-tailed prairie dog, bushy-tailed woodrat, eastern woodrat, grizzly bear, kit fox, mountain goat, mule deer, pronghorn, and white-tailed jackrabbit.

Describing a new species of mammal involves not only an accurate description of the animal, but the collection and deposition of an actual specimen in a museum collection. Specimens from the Lewis and Clark expedition were deposited in the Peale Museum in Philadelphia, where they were available for other naturalists to study and describe formally. Unfortunately, when that private museum fell on hard times, the specimens were auctioned off to P. T. Barnum and subsequently lost in a fire.

Jefferson continued his sponsorship of exploration by sending Lieutenant Zebulon Pike to the headwaters of the Mississippi River and subsequently, to the Indian Territory between the Arkansas and Red rivers. Pike provided additional descriptions of mammals. Although the war of 1812 slowed the westward push of exploration, it continued apace in the 1820s. Major Stephen Long led field parties to the Rocky Mountains and along the Canadian border. Thomas Say served as zoologist on these expeditions, and he zealously collected specimens of many kinds of animals, and provided detailed descriptions of them. Another scientist who accompanied early expeditions, the geologist William Keating, sounded an early warning about human impact on wildlife by complaining about the adverse effects of military camps and human settlement on the vast bison herds—herds that were soon to disappear.

A European naturalist, Maximilian, the Prince of Wied-Neuwied, also contributed to our knowledge of North American mammals through an expedition up the Missouri River. On this journey, in the 1830s, he was accompanied by Carl Bodmer, an artist who produced an atlas of paintings that added greatly to the specimens that were ultimately purchased by the American Museum of Natural History in New York. British naturalists continued to explore the continent, especially the northern regions, in an attempt to find a northwest passage to the Pacific Ocean. Sir John Richardson's volume on mammals in his important *Fauna Boreali Americana* was published in 1829. Several species of mammals were named after early British explorers: for example, *Spermophilus franklinii, S. parryii,* and *S. richardsonii.* As you use this volume, you will notice scientific names that honor some of the other early explorers and naturalists mentioned in this preface.

The western half of the continent continued to draw attention from the United States government as well. Officers of the U.S. Topological Survey, such as John C. Fremont, led expeditions that collected mammals. Mountain men and fur trappers also contributed to our knowledge during this period.

Probably the next most significant compilation of information on North American mammals was that produced by John James Audubon and John Bachman over the course of a decade beginning in 1846. Their work, *The Viviparous Quadrupeds of North America,* provided a complete atlas of color plates of North American mammals, with descriptions of each and much new information on their natural history. Audubon conducted his own field expeditions and set a high standard of accuracy with his descriptions and paintings of mammals and birds. He was an influential figure for an entire generation of naturalists.

That same year, 1846, saw the establishment of the Smithsonian Institution in Washington, D.C. The Smithsonian has been a strong supporter of North American mammalogy throughout the 150 years of its existence, and continues that tradition with this volume. One of Audubon's protégés, Spencer Fullerton Baird, was an early Assistant Secretary of the Smithsonian, and was responsible for the founding of the National Museum of Natural History as part of the Institution. Baird's tenure coincided with the massive national effort to construct a transcontinental railroad. Potential routes across the continent were surveyed by teams from the U.S. Army Medical Corps, whose surgeons were also naturalists and collected many specimens and much data about mammals. This flurry of activity ultimately involved more than 100 naturalists, either

collecting specimens and data in the field, or describing the material once it reached the museums in the East. The geological surveys resulted in three volumes on zoology, one of which was on mammals. That book, the first *Mammals of North America,* was edited by Baird and published in 1859. It contained accounts of the 256 species of mammals then recognized from the region, and the specimens on which it was based formed the nucleus of what was to become the largest mammal collection in the world, housed at the National Museum of Natural History.

Dr. Elliot Coues was appointed the first curator of mammals at the National Museum of Natural History, which was established as a separate entity within the Smithsonian in 1879. Coues made enormously important contributions to both mammalogy and ornithology in North America. He drew upon his two decades of experience as an Army Medical Corps naturalist and his position as Secretary of the Geological and Geographical Survey of the Territories to publish 15 volumes on early explorations of the West. In addition to publishing more than 500 papers and helping to found the American Ornithologists' Union, Coues was the biological supervisor for the Century Dictionary. His monographs on fur-bearers and rodents are classics in the literature of North American mammals.

The Army Medical Corps provided another pioneering North American mammalogist in the person of surgeon-naturalist Dr. Edgar Alexander Mearns. Mearns served as the naturalist and medical officer for the Mexico–United States International Boundary Commission, where he collected more than 30,000 specimens for the National Museum. Later, he accompanied President Theodore Roosevelt on an African collecting expedition. Additional trips to Africa under the sponsorship of Childs Frick added a wealth of specimens to the collections of the American Museum of Natural History in New York. Mearns also completed the first comprehensive assessment of the mammals of the Philippines, published 125 papers, and in 1907 produced a monumental work, *The Mammals of the Mexican Boundary of the United States.*

Museums and universities have traditionally housed scientists involved in the study of mammals. In a tradition begun in Europe, knowledge was frequently acquired by field naturalists who collected specimens, and enhanced by museum-based curators who identified the material using research collections and a rapidly accumulating literature. Naturally, many individuals combined these talents and were able to study the animals both in the field and in the museum.

The museum tradition began early in North America, with the establishment of the Charleston Museum in Charleston, South Carolina, in 1773. In addition, many talented and knowledgeable amateur collectors accumulated material. Charles Wilson Peale's collections, established with the American Philosophical Society in Philadelphia, provided an early repository for many important collections. Their subsequent loss due to economic difficulties pointed to the need for more secure facilities and reinforces the case today for strong support of our research institutions.

Natural history museums that developed as research arms of major universities combined research and training in a most advantageous fashion. Harvard University's Museum of Comparative Zoology (MCZ), established in 1860, was an early supporter of rigorous research and carefully curated collections, under the supervision of Professor Louis Agassiz. Several mammalogists trained at the MCZ were instrumental in the establishment of the American Museum of Natural History (AMNH) in New York. The AMNH, along with its metropolitan counterpart in Chicago, has contributed a great deal to our understanding of North American mammals.

Other universities developed strong programs in research and training in the field of mammalogy. The University of California at Berkeley's Museum of Vertebrate Zoology, under the direction of Joseph Grinnell, spawned an entire generation of competent mammalogists, who in turn produced most of the practitioners in North America today. Grinnell's students went on to establish strong programs at many universities, including Kansas and Michigan, both of which have major collections of mammals.

The U.S. government also recognized the value of studying mammals, by establishment of the National Museum within the Smithsonian Institution, and also by expanding the Division of Economic Ornithology to include mammals in 1886. Dr. C. Hart Merriam converted that early Division of Economic Ornithology and Mammalogy into the Bureau of Biological Survey, an agency that played a major role in inventorying our biological resources around the turn of the century. Merriam demonstrated convincingly the value of understanding the interplay between mammals and the environment.

This long history of involvement with the study of mammals in North America sets the stage for the current volume. The authors of the individual species accounts are mammalogists who have studied their subjects in some detail. The information they have summarized is drawn from a rich published literature produced by both previous and current mammalogists. The work itself stems from a decision by the American Society of Mammalogists to produce such a volume. Additional inspiration came from our Australian colleagues and their excellent volume *Mammals of Australia,* edited by Ronald Strahan.

Acknowledgments

This volume began at a meeting of the Board of Directors of the American Society of Mammalogists (ASM), when Dr. J. Mary Taylor, then Director of the Cleveland Museum of Natural History, lamented the fact that a book of this type did not exist. Dr. Taylor, like many of the rest of us, was impressed by a book on the mammals of Australia, compiled by our Australian mammalogist colleagues. The assembled group reached a consensus that such a volume was worthwhile, and then-President Dr. James L. Patton asked Wilson to undertake the editorial effort. The goal was to produce the first comprehensive account of the biology of the mammals of North America north of Mexico on a species-by-species basis.

Having just published *Mammal Species of the World* as a collaborative effort with the ASM and the Smithsonian Institution Press, we were able to organize the effort fairly quickly. We began by contacting just over 200 mammalogists, each a specialist on a species or group, and asking them to participate in the effort. They responded with great good will and provided us the requested information, along with a range map and color photograph, if available.

The individual accounts were edited for style and consistency, but the content is that provided by the authors, listed in each account. Most of these professional mammalogists have studied the animals first-hand, and many have done extensive field work on their subjects.

Daniel Cole, a computer cartographer with the National Museum of Natural History (NMNH), transformed the range maps drawn by the authors into the finished maps you see in the pages that follow, and his colleague Kurt Luginbyhl provided crucial computer support throughout the project.

Spurred on and aided by Smithsonian Institution Press photo editor Anne DuVivier, we then began the protracted process of filling in the photographic gaps. We are truly grateful to a huge segment of the natural history photography community for making their work available, in many cases without charge, and helping us network our way to other photographers.

Although all the contributing photographers are listed in the credits, we would like particularly to thank Mrs. Roger Barbour, who graciously made available the excellent collection of mammal photographs taken by her late husband. Dr. Richard B. Forbes was also extremely helpful in providing photographs and helping us reach other photographers. Professional photographers J. Scott Altenbach, Bob Gress, B. Moose Peterson, and Robert L. Pitman made enormous contributions. Ronn Altig, Russell Benedict, Troy L. Best, John Bickham, Harold Broadbooks, Mark Chappell, Robert Dowler, Brock Fenton, Kathy Frost, Kenneth and Keith Geluso, John D. Haweeli, Thomas E. Lee, Jr., Robert Rausch, Lynn and Donna Rogers, John and Gloria Tveten, Merlin Tuttle, Wayne Van Devender, and many others, all gave generously of their time and talent to make the volume a success.

Many other people aided in this project. Dr. Peter Cannell of the Smithsonian Institution Press has been helpful at every step of the process. His colleague Heidi Lumberg read all of the species accounts and made helpful suggestions. Kay Kenyon, former librarian at the National Zoo, helped bring the list of Literature Cited under control. Meridel Jellifer and Abelardo Sandoval of the Office of Biodiversity Programs in the National Museum of Natural History provided valuable support, Meridel on the clerical front and Abelardo with the maps. Dr. Stanwyn Shetler of the NMNH Department of Botany gave generously of his time in helping us with the names of plants. Dr. Robert S. Hoffmann of the NMNH Division of Mammals provided help and encouragement from the inception to the completion of the project. Dr. James G. Mead and Dr. Philip Clapham greatly improved the section on Cetaceans, and also wrote the ordinal and family accounts for that section. The Division of Mammals provided us with an intellectual home for the project, and the NMNH collection of mammals and library resources were invaluable.

Financial support was obtained from the Molson Brewing Co. at a critical juncture. This provided another happy coincidence with the previous effort of our Australian colleagues, who were also supported by a brewery. Given the long tradition of mutual support between hardworking field mammalogists and the brewing industry, we are happy to acknowledge this patronage.

Contributors

A. Abend
Zoo New England
Boston, MA

L. F. Alexander
University of Nevada
Las Vegas, NV

J. S. Altenbach
University of New Mexico
Albuquerque, NM

C. G. Anderson
University of Tennessee
Knoxville, TN

F. I. Archer, II
Southwest Fisheries Science Center
La Jolla, CA

H. T. Arita
Universidad Nacional Autonoma de Mexico
Morelia, Michoacan, Mexico

D. M. Armstrong
University of Colorado
Boulder, CO

J. Arroyo-Cabrales
Instituto Nacional de Anthropologia y
    Historia
Mexico City, Mexico

G. Bachman
University of Nebraska
Lincoln, NE

R. J. Baker
Texas Tech University
Lubbock, TX

R. H. Baker
Eagle Lake, TX

G. O. Batzli
University of Illinois
Champaign, IL

G. D. Baumgardner
Nevada State Museum
Carson City, NV

M. Bekoff
University of Colorado
Boulder, CO

P. Beier
Northern Arizona University
Flagstaff, AZ

R. A. Benedict
University of Nebraska State Museum
Lincoln, NE

B. J. Bergstrom
Valdosta State University
Valdosta, GA

T. L. Best
Auburn University
Auburn, AL

B. Birchler
National Museum of Natural History
Washington, DC

D. E. Birkenholz
Illinois State University
Normal, IL

E. C. Birney
University of Minnesota
St. Paul, MN

J. A. Bissonette
Utah State University
Logan, UT

A. Bixler
University of Missouri
St. Louis, MO

H. L. Black
Brigham Young University
Provo, UT

B. H. Blake
Bennett College
Greensboro, NC

D. J. Blankenship
University of Great Falls
Great Falls, MT

M. A. Bogan
U.S. Geological Survey
Albuquerque, NM

D. J. Boness
National Zoological Park
Washington, DC

R. T. Bowyer
University of Alaska
Fairbanks, AK

R. D. Bradley
Texas Tech University
Lubbock, TX

J. K. Braun
University of Oklahoma
Norman, OK

H. E. Broadbooks
Thousand Oaks, CA

P. Brown
Brown-Berry Biological Consulting
Bishop, CA

R. L. Brownell
Marine Mammal Science Center
La Jolla, CA

W. Caire
University of Central Oklahoma
Edmond, OK

G. N. Cameron
University of Cincinnati
Cincinnati, OH

A. B. Carey
Forestry Sciences Laboratory
Olympia, WA

G. Ceballos-G
Universidad Nacional Autonoma de Mexico
Mexico City, Mexico

B. R. Chapman
University of Georgia
Athens, GA

J. A. Chapman
North Dakota State University
Fargo, ND

S. S. Chapman
University of Georgia
Athens, GA

I. Christensen
Institute of Marine Research
Bergen, Norway

C. S. Churcher
University of Toronto
Toronto, Ontario, Canada

P. Clapham
Northeast Fisheries Science Center
Woods Hole, MA

T. W. Clark
Northern Rockies Conservation
    Cooperative
Jackson, WY

H. J. Cleator
Freshwater Institute
Winnipeg, Manitoba, Canada

R. E. Cole
University of California, Davis
Davis, CA

J. A. Cook
University of Alaska
Fairbanks, AK

J. B. Cope
Earlham College
Richmond, IN

J. E. Cornely
U.S. Fish and Wildlife Service
Denver, CO

R. Cosgriff
Brigham Young University
Provo, UT

J. A. Cranford
Virginia Polytechnic Institute and State
    University
Blacksburg, VA

M. Crête
Ministère de l'Environnement et de la Fauna
Québec, Canada

K. Crooks
University of California, Santa Cruz
Santa Cruz, CA

N. J. Czaplewski
University of Oklahoma
Norman, OK

R. Davis
University of Arizona
Tucson, AZ

R. C. Dowler
Angelo State University
San Angelo, TX

J. W. Dragoo
University of New Mexico
Albuquerque, NM

R. Dueser
Utah State University
Logan, UT

J. L. Eger
Royal Ontario Museum
Toronto, Ontario, Canada

C. L. Elliott
Eastern Kentucky University
Richmond, KY

L. S. Ellis
Northeast Missouri State University
Kirksville, MO

L. H. Emmons
National Museum of Natural History
Washington, DC

M. D. Engstrom
Royal Ontario Museum
Toronto, Ontario, Canada

K. Ernest
Central Washington University
Ellensburg, WA

J. A. Estes
U.S. Geological Survey
Santa Cruz, CA

F. H. Fay
University of Alaska
Fairbanks, AK

G. A. Feldhamer
Southern Illinois University
Carbondale, IL

M. B. Fenton
York University
North York, Ontario, Canada

M. Festa-Bianchet
University of Sherbrooke
Sherbrooke, Quebec, Canada

J. S. Findley
Universty of New Mexico,
Albuquerque, NM

J. T. Flinders
Brigham Young University
Provo, UT

V. Flyger
University of Maryland
College Park, MD

P. W. Freeman
University of Nebraska State Museum
Lincoln, NE

A. R. French
State University of New York
Binghamton, NY

T. W. French
Natural Heritage and Endangered Species
    Program
Commonwealth of Massachusetts
Westborough, MA

J. K. Frey
Eastern New Mexico University
Portales, NM

E. K. Fritzell
University of Missouri
Columbia, MO

J.-P. Gallo-Reynoso
Centro de Investigacion en Alimentacion y
    Desarrollo
Guaymas, Sonora, Mexico

W. L. Gannon
University of New Mexico
Albuquerque, NM

A. L. Gardner
National Museum of Natural History
Washington, DC

D. E. Gaskin
University of Guelph
Guelph, Ontario, Canada

K. N. Geluso
University of Nebraska
Omaha, NE

H. H. Genoways
University of Nebraska
Lincoln, NE

S. B. George
University of Utah
Salt Lake City, UT

B. M. Gharaibeh
Texas Tech University
Lubbock, TX

J. R. Goetze
Texas Tech University
Lubbock, TX

B. A. Gower
University of Alabama at Birmingham
Birmingham, AL

D. K. Grayson
University of Washington
Seattle, WA

I. F. Greenbaum
Texas A&M University
College Station, TX

D. J. Hafner
New Mexico Museum of Natural History
Albuquerque, NM

J. G. Hallett
Washington State Unversity
Pullman, WA

C. O. Handley, Jr.
National Museum of Natural History
Washington, DC

A. H. Harris
University of Texas
El Paso, TX

G. D. Hartman
McNeese State University
Lake Charles, LA

J. P. Hayes
Oregon State University
Corvallis, OR

V. Hayssen
Smith College
Northhampton, MA

L. R. Heaney
Field Museum of Natural History
Chicago, IL

J. W. Hermanson
Cornell University
Ithaca, NY

E. Heske
Illinois Natural History Survey
Champaign, IL

J. E. Heyning
Natural History Museum of Los Angeles
    County
Los Angeles, CA

R. S. Hoffmann
National Museum of Natural History
Washington, DC

N. R. Holler
Auburn University
Auburn, AL

R. L. Honeycutt
Texas A&M University
College Station, TX

F. A. Iwen
University of Wisconsin
Madison, WI

F. J. Jannett, Jr.
St. Paul, MN

S. H. Jenkins
University of Nevada
Reno, NV

C. Jones
Texas Tech University
Lubbock, TX

C. A. Jones
Denver Museum of Natural History
Denver, CO

L. Jones
Northwest Fisheries Science Center
Seattle, WA

D. A. Kelt
University of California, Davis
Davis, CA

K. W. Kenyon
Seattle, WA

G. L. Kirkland, Jr.
Shippensburg University
Shippensburg, PA

M. Kiser
University of New Mexico
Albuquerque, NM

D. R. Klein
University of Alaska
Fairbanks, AK

E. Kritzman
Slater Museum
Takoma, WA

T. H. Kunz
Boston University
Boston, MA

A. Kurta
Eastern Michigan University
Ypsilanti, MI

J. A. Lackey
State University of New York
Oswego, NY

J. Laerm
University of Georgia
Athens, GA

J. N. Layne
Archbold Biological Station
Lake Placid, FL

D. M. Leslie, Jr.
Oklahoma State University
Stillwater, OK

W. Z. Lidicker, Jr.
University of California, Berkeley
Berkeley, CA

B. K. Lim
Royal Ontario Museum
Toronto, Ontario, Canada

A. V. Linzey
Indiana University of Pennsylvania
Indiana, PA

C. A. Long
University of Wisconsin, Stevens Point
Stevens Point, WI

W. Longland
USDA/Agricultural Research Service
Reno, NV

T. R. Loughlin
National Marine Mammal Laboratory
Seattle, WA

D. R. Ludwig
Forest Preservation District of
    Dupage County
Wheaton, IL

M. R. Lynch
Texas Tech University
Lubbock, TX

J. A. MacMahon
Utah State University
Logan, UT

R. E. MacMillen
Talent, OR

P. Majluf
Wildlife Conservation Society
San Juan, Peru

J. E. Maldonado
National Zoological Park
Washington, DC

M. A. Mares
University of Oklahoma
Norman, OK

R. E. Marsh
University of California, Davis
Davis, CA

C. Mauk-Cunningham
Texas Tech University
Lubbock, TX

K. McBee
Oklahoma State University
Stillwater, OK

D. K. McClearn
Organization for Tropical Studies
San Jose, Costa Rica

G. F. McCracken
University of Tennessee
Knoxville, TN

D. R. McCullough
University of California, Berkeley
Berkeley, CA

J. G. Mead
National Museum of Natural History
Washington, DC

L. D. Mech
U.S. Geological Survey
St. Paul, MN

R. Medellín
Universidad Nacional Autonoma de Mexico
Mexico City, Mexico

J. F. Merritt
Powdermill Biological Station
Rector, PA

G. R. Michener
University of Lethbridge
Lethbridge, Alberta, Canada

J. O. Murie
University of Alberta
Edmonton, Alberta, Canada

D. Murray
University of Idaho
Moscow, ID

D. Nagorsen
Royal British Columbia Museum
Victoria, British Columbia, Canada

T. R. Nagy
University of Alabama at Birmingham
Birmingham, AL

M. W. Newcomer
Los Altos, CA

G. J. North
University of California, Davis
Davis, CA

R. M. Nowak
Falls Church, VA

M. A. O'Connell
Eastern Washington University
Cheney, WA

D. K. Odell
Sea World Research Institute
Orlando, FL

M. J. O'Farrell
O'Farrell Biological Consulting
Las Vegas, NV

B. O'Gara
University of Montana
Missoula, MT

T. J. O'Shea
U.S. Geological Survey
Fort Collins, CO

J. F. Pagels
Virginia Commonwealth University
Richmond, VA

D. A. Parish
Texas Tech University
Lubbock, TX

B. D. Patterson
Field Museum of Natural History
Chicago, IL

D. L. Pattie
Northern Alberta Institute of Technology
Edmonton, Alberta, Canada

J. L. Patton
University of California, Berkeley
Berkeley, CA

J. M. Peek
University of Idaho
Moscow, ID

W. F. Perrin
Southwest Fisheries Science Center
La Jolla, CA

E. Perry
National Zoological Park
Washington, DC

R. O. Peterson
Michigan Technological University
Houghton, MI

J. V. Planz
Biosynthesis, Inc.
Lewisville, TX

D. Post
University of Texas of the Permian Basin
Odessa, TX

C. W. Potter
National Museum of Natural History
Washington, DC

R. A. Powell
North Carolina State University
Raleigh, NC

M. V. Price
University of California, Riverside
Riverside, CA

J. Rappole
National Zoological Park
Front Royal, VA

R. R. Reeves
Okapi Wildlife Associates
Hudson, Quebec, Canada

P. E. Reynolds
University of Alaska
Fairbanks, AK

D. W. Rice
National Marine Mammal Laboratory
Seattle, WA

E. A. Rickart
University of Utah
Salt Lake City, UT

B. R. Riddle
University of Nevada
Las Vegas, NV

D. S. Rogers
Brigham Young University
Provo, UT

L. L. Rogers
North Central Forest Experiment Station
St. Paul, MN

R. K. Rose
Old Dominion University
Norfolk, VA

S. Ruff
Washington, DC

D. Rugh
National Marine Mammal Laboratory
Seattle, WA

D. J. Schmidly
Texas Tech University
Lubbock, TX

D. F. Schmidt
National Museum of Natural History
Washington, DC

J. Seidensticker
National Zoological Park
Washington, DC

J. H. Shaw
Oklahoma State University
Stillwater, OK

S. R. Sheffield
Clemson Unversity
Pendleton, SC

K. E. W. Shelden
National Marine Mammal Laboratory
Seattle, WA

H. S. Shellhammer
San Jose State University
San Jose, CA

P. Sherman
Cornell University
Ithaca, NY

K. A. Shump, Jr.
Durham, NH

R. Sidner
University of Arizona
Tucson, AZ

R. S. Sikes
University of Minnesota
Minneapolis, MN

L. H. Simons
Shasta Natural History Foundation
Yreka, CA

A. T. Smith
Arizona State University
Tempe, AZ

D. W. Smith
University of Nevada
Reno, NV

H. D. Smith
Brigham Young University
Provo, UT

M. F. Smith
University of California, Berkeley
Berkeley, CA

M. J. Smolen
World Wildlife Fund
Washington, DC

D. T. Stalling
Northwestern State University of Louisiana
Nachitoches, LA

B. S. Stewart
Hubbs-Sea World Research Institute
San Diego, CA

R. E. A. Stewart
Freshwater Institute
Winnipeg, Manitoba, Canada

I. Stirling
Canadian Wildlife Service
Edmonton, Alberta, Canada

D. A. Sutton
California State University
Chico, CA

G. E. Svendsen
Ohio University
Athens, OH

R. H. Tamarin
University of Massachusetts
Lowell, MA

J. M. Taylor
Portland, OR

R. K. Thacker
Brigham Young University
Provo, UT

S. C. Trombulak
Middlebury College
Middlebury, VT

R. Tumlison
Henderson State University
Arkadelphia, AR

F. Van Dyke
Northwestern College
Orange City, IA

C. G. van Zyll de Jong
North Augusta, Ontario, Canada

A. M. Wallace
Texas Tech University
Lubbock, TX

W. D. Webster
University of North Carolina
Wilmington, NC

S. D. West
University of Washington
Seattle, WA

J. O. Whitaker, Jr.
Indiana State University
Terre Haute, IN

J. S. Whitman
Alaska Department of Fish and Game
Sitka, AK

D. F. Williams
California State University, Stanislaus
Turlock, CA

L. R. Williams
University of Houston
Houston TX

S. L. Williams
Baylor Universty
Waco, TX

D. E. Wilson
National Museum of Natural History
Washington, DC

J. O. Wolff
University of Memphis
Memphis, TN

C. A. Woods
University of Florida
Gainesville, FL

F. D. Yancey, II
Texas Tech University
Lubbock, TX

T. L. Yates
University of New Mexico
Albuquerque, NM

E. Yensen
Albertson College of Idaho
Caldwell, ID

P. J. Young
University of Arizona
Tucson, AZ

E. Zimmerman
North Texas State University
Denton, TX

Plan of the Book

This book includes a species account for each of the native species known to occur in North America north of the U.S.—Mexico border. Although such artificial political boundaries in no way reflect the distribution of naturally occurring populations of mammals, there is considerable precedence for considering the mammal fauna of the United States and Canada as a distinct North American unit. Biogeographically, most of Mexico is part of Middle America. We also include species found on offshore islands, and those marine mammals whose distributions include the offshore waters of the region. We have not included accounts of introduced species, as drawing the line between which of the many exotics are established and which are not becomes difficult.

We have followed Wilson and Reeder's *Mammal Species of the World* in deciding which species to recognize. Exceptions include recognition of the Mephitidae as a family distinct from Mustelidae; the genus *Dicrostonyx,* with fewer species currently accepted; the recognition of *Geomys knoxjonesi* as a species distinct from *G. bursarius;* the inclusion of *Sorex alaskanus* as a subspecies of *S. palustris;* and the recognition of *Microtus mogollonensis* as distinct from *M. mexicanus.* Mammalian taxonomy is a dynamic science, and some of the arrangements used herein will surely change in the coming years, as we continue to add to our knowledge of the evolutionary relationships of these animals. (For those interested in a more detailed update of recent taxonomic changes, we recommend Jones et al., 1997.)

The orders and families are arranged phylogenetically, or according to their evolutionary relationships. This is the sequence preferred by professional mammalogists, and it provides some information, as closely related groups tend to be near each other, and more distant ones farther apart. However, the evolutionary history of these groups more closely resembles a branching tree than a straight line, so the sequence can also be a bit deceiving. For this reason, we have not followed phylogenetic order in arranging the species within each genus, but rather have ordered them alphabetically, an arrangement that should also facilitate finding a particular species. A list of North American genera follows each family account.

Each species account contains one or more common names as available. Standard information on size and weight of each species is also included. An identification section gives diagnostic characters for the species and includes information on how to distinguish it from similar species. Recent synonyms of the scientific name are also listed. Some indication is given of the current status of the animal. Currently recognized subspecies, if any, are listed, along with some indication of their geographic distribution.

Each account summarizes what is known about the species, and includes information on behavior, diet, habitat preferences, reproduction, growth and development, longevity, and predation. For some species, there is also information on the fossil record and evolutionary history. Additional information on population densities, diseases, parasites, and changes in status or distribution due to human impact is provided if applicable.

The references listed in each account provide additional information on each species. Although each account should be easily accessible to readers of all levels, a glossary of technical terms has been added. The author of each account is identified, and a complete list of contributors is also included. When no information is available or relevant regarding recent synonyms, other common names, or subspecies, those headings do not appear in a given account.

Common Names

The common names used for each species of mammal are drawn from a list of common names compiled by Don E. Wilson and F. Russell Cole as a supplement to Wilson and Reeder (1993). For the most part, the names chosen also conform to those used by Jones et al., in the *Revised Checklist of North American Mammals North of Mexico,* published by Texas Tech University.

Scientific Names

Scientific names are used universally by biologists to identify organisms. Latinized in form, they provide a standard way to refer to each species in all countries and all languages. The scientific name consists of two words—the genus and the specific

epithet. Most scientific names have Latin or Greek roots, and frequently convey additional information about the species.

Size
Some indication of the size of each species is given by listing weight ranges and the range of total lengths of adults, usually followed by an average in parentheses. If significant sexual dimorphism occurs, separate figures are given for males and females. If appropriate, length of tail is also included, and for bats, forearm length is given, as it is often used as a standard measure of size. These data are uniformly expressed in the metric system, as used by scientists worldwide.

Identification
This volume is not intended to be a field guide, but some indication is given of how to distinguish each species from other similar species. If such differentiation can be done based on external characters of size, color, and shape, they are used. If detailed characters of the skull, teeth, or other parts are necessary for identification, they are mentioned as well. These characters, and additional descriptive information given in each account, combined with the color photographs, will allow iden-

tification of most North American mammals. Many species of small mammals are difficult to distinguish externally, and much of our recent understanding of their relationships comes from new methods that allow direct comparison of DNA "fingerprints" and other molecular systematic techniques.

Recent Synonyms
Because of the dynamic nature of our system of scientific nomenclature, the name used to describe a given species may change through time. We include other scientific names that may refer to the species in question in order to simplify use of earlier literature. The list of recent synonyms includes only those names that might prove confusing, and is by no means a complete synonymy of each species.

Other Common Names
Although the common name given at the beginning of each account is the one we recommend using for each species, we have included other common names that have been applied in the past or are used locally or regionally. These other common names are similar to the scientific synonyms, except that there is no standard system of common names. This frequently leads

to the same common name being used for different species in different parts of the range. To unequivocally refer to a given species, the scientific name is preferable.

Status

Each account contains a summary of the current population status of the species. For those that are widespread and common, no additional information is given. Some species are naturally rare and limited in distribution, and others may be so poorly known that we are unable to give accurate information about their current status. Still others have clearly been adversely affected by the continuing encroachment of humans and their associated habitat destruction. This listing is not meant to be authoritative, but rather indicative. The International Union for the Conservation of Nature (IUCN) regularly publishes "red lists" of threatened and endangered mammals of the world.

Subspecies

The subspecies category is used to describe distinct geographic variants of species. Such variation may occur in external characters such as size or color, or less obvious features such as chromosomes or molecular characters. If such subspecies are currently recognized, they are listed, along with a description of their ranges. For more detailed information on subspecific ranges, Hall's (1981) two-volume classic technical treatise *The Mammals of North America* is the standard reference.

References

Each account contains additional references, many of which were used in assembling the information provided in the account. Others may provide additional reading about the species in question. The American Society of Mammalogists publishes a series called *Mammalian Species,* each of which provides a complete summary of the biology of one species of mammal. About 600 such accounts have been produced to date, and many North American species are included. If a *Mammalian Species* account exists, it is listed by number under References; the full citation can be found in the the Literature Cited section of this volume, where they are listed at the end in numerical order.

Maps

Distribution maps are included to give an indication of the general part of North America from which the species is known. Some additional detail can be obtained from the text of each account, and from the subspecies ranges, if any.

Photographs

We attempted to include a color photograph of each species. This proved impossible, and we urge both mammalogists and photographers to attempt to obtain high-quality, color photographs of the species for which no photo is included. Any such photos sent to the editors will be considered for possible future editions of this book.

Order Didelphimorphia

This taxon traditionally was grouped into the single order Marsupialia, but the current consensus among taxonomists favors treating Marsupialia as a subclass of the class Mammalia, and dividing it into seven separate orders. Only one of these orders, Didelphimorphia, occurs in North America. The single family, Didelphidae, includes 15 genera and 63 species and is split into two subfamilies, Caluromyinae and Didelphinae. Didelphimorphs extend from southern Canada to northern Argentina, and reach their greatest species diversities in tropical regions. Body sizes range from 75 mm head and body length (HBL) in tiny species of *Monodelphis* to more than 500 mm in the largest *Didelphis*. There are both terrestrial and arboreal species, and even an aquatic form, the yapok or water opossum, *Chironectes minimus*.

Opossums occur in a variety of habitats including forests and grasslands, often near lake shores or stream banks; the yapok inhabits freshwater streams and lakes in tropical and subtropical areas. Species in the Didelphimorphia are mostly nocturnal or crepuscular, and solitary. Although some are primarily insectivorous or carnivorous, most are omnivorous. Opossums have short gestation periods and long post-natal developmental times. Some species have an external pouch, which the young occupy during early post-natal development.

References

Mammalian Species 40; *Mammalian Species* 109,
  Mammalian Species 190; Gardner, 1993a

Virginia opossum *(Didelphis virginiana)*

Family Didelphidae

Didelphids are the most common representatives of the subclass Marsupialia in the Western Hemisphere. Marsupials are much more diverse and common in Australia, but the New World species represent a distinctive and very old lineage of mammals. Most members of this family live south of the U.S.–Mexico border. The single exception is *Didelphis virginiana,* the Virginia opossum.

With 15 genera and 63 species, the family Didelphidae is a distinctive component of the New World mammal fauna. They are all small to medium in size, and the Virginia opossum is the largest species. Although clearly related to other marsupial orders, not all of the genera have a marsupium, or pouch, in which the young are carried. The genus *Didelphis* does have the pouch, and Virginia opossums carry their young in the pouch for the first two months or so.

This is an ancient family, with fossils known from North America as long ago as the middle Cretaceous period, roughly 100 million years ago. Although such animals are commonly known as primitive forms, perhaps they are better described as successful survivors. Members of this family effectively occupy a variety of niches throughout the tropical and subtropical regions of Central and South America.

References
Eisenberg, 1989; Gardner, 1993a

North American Genera
Didelphis

Virginia opossum | *Didelphis virginiana*

The only living marsupial north of Mexico, the Virginia opossum is instantly recognizable by its large whitish to pale gray head and narrow snout, black leathery ears with white or flesh-colored tips, an opposable big toe on the hind foot, white toes on both fore- and hind feet, and its long, scaly, nearly naked, prehensile tail. Females have an abdominal, fur-lined pouch containing teats. The body fur is usually gray, with long white and gray guard hair (gray phase) or, rarely north of Mexico, the guard hair and underfur may be predominantly black (black phase). True albinos, albinotic individuals (which have white fur, but normally pigmented skin), and cinnamon-colored variants are known.

Virginia opossums are found from southern Canada (Ontario and British Columbia) through most of the non-arid United States and Mexico, and into northwestern Costa Rica. A non-hibernator that may lose its ear tips and the end of its tail from frostbite, its northern distribution is limited by average snow depth and days of freezing temperatures. Far western populations, including those in Idaho, western Colorado, British Columbia, and Baja California, resulted from introductions. Reports from Arizona and New Mexico may represent either introductions or native populations having geographic affinities with Mexican forms, but specimens are lacking. Western introduced populations belong to the white-faced, short-tailed, eastern nominate subspecies. A second subspecies, *D. v. pigra,* occurs in Georgia, Florida, and the Gulf coastal states. Middle American *D. v. californica* occurs in extreme southern Texas and may have been in Arizona, but specimens that would prove this are lacking. A fourth subspecies, *D. v. yucatanensis,* occurs in Mexico. The species is known from mid-Pleistocene (Sangamon Interglacial) fossils; post-Wisconsin remains are common in and north of Mexico.

A nocturnal, terrestrial, and arboreal omnivore that prefers deciduous-forest habitat with permanent water, the Virginia opossum also does well in urban and suburban environments. It is most famous for "playing possum," a temporary state of catatonia in response to perceived imminent danger that has high survival value. Another behavior, inhibition under bright light, has low survival value when the opossum freezes in the headlights of a vehicle. Den sites include caves, hollow logs and trees, burrows dug by woodchucks (*Marmota monax*) and skunks (*Mephitis*), and a variety of man-made structures. Foraging is localized around a den, which may be changed every few days. Foods range from fruits, nuts, and grains to earthworms, arthropods, and vertebrates, including carrion. Opossums actively prey on snakes, seem immune to pit-viper venoms, and show high resistance to rabies and plague, as may be expected in scavengers.

Reproductive potential is high, longevity short, and population turnover is rapid (less than 3 years). Breeding usually commences during the first two weeks of January, or late December in the South, and may extend into September, followed by

a 2- to 3-month nonbreeding period. Gestation is about 12.5 days. Neonates are in an embryonic state and use their fore-limbs to travel from vulva to pouch, where each attaches to a nipple. If the number of neonates exceeds the number of available nipples (normally there are 13 nipples, and litters usually average fewer), those that do not attach die. Snow and cold weather can inhibit successful reproduction in northern states and Canada, where pouch young may not be found before March or April. Females are polyestrous and reenter estrus within 8 days of unsuccessful breeding or loss of young. The young remain attached to nipples for the first 55–60 days; weaning occurs at 95–105 days. Normally only two litters can be weaned each season. Virginia opossums are short-lived. Females are 6 to 12 months old when reproduction begins and usually have only one successful reproductive season. Some may breed during a second reproductive season, but few successfully rear second-season young to weaning age. The oldest known Virginia opossum, a male from Maryland, was 36 months old when last captured.

The only member of its family to store fat, Virginia opos-

Didelphis virginiana

sums are hunted and trapped for food and fur. Their bad reputation as destroyers of poultry is largely undeserved, but they can be serious predators of waterfowl and other ground-nesting birds. Eaten by a variety of carnivores, dogs and large owls are their most effective natural predators, but most mortality probably is caused by motor vehicles. *A. L. Gardner*

Size

Males are usually slightly larger and much heavier than females, with significantly longer canine teeth.

Total length: 350–940 (740) mm

Length of tail: 216–470 (319) mm

Weight: 0.8–6.4 kg (males); 0.3–3.7 kg (females)

Identification

Distinguished north of Mexico by large size, white toes, almost all-white head, white-tipped, leathery ears, and long, scaly, naked tail. In Mexico and south to limit of range in Costa Rica, distinguished from common opossum *(D. marsupialis)* by white cheeks and shorter tail (always shorter than head and body), and from gray four-eyed opossum *(Philander opossum)* by larger size, longer fur, and lack of prominent white spots above eyes.

Other Common Names

Opossum, possum

Status

Common

Subspecies

Didelphis virginiana californica, extreme southern Texas

Didelphis virginiana pigra, Georgia, Florida, and the Gulf Coast states

Didelphis virginiana virginiana, eastern United States; introduced into Idaho, western Colorado, British Columbia, and Baja California

Didelphis virginiana yucatanensis, Mexico

References

Mammalian Species 40; Gardner, 1973; Gardner, 1982

Order Xenarthra

Representatives of this order are found exclusively in the New World, from the southern United States to South America. They comprise four families, 13 genera, and 29 species and fall into three distinct and highly specialized subgroups: sloths, armadillos, and anteaters. Sloths (families Bradypodidae and Megalonychidae) are exclusively arboreal and inhabit subtropical and tropical forests. These herbivorous animals spend much of their life hanging from branches and move very slowly along branches using a hand-over-hand motion. They venture to the ground only occasionally to urinate or defecate. They are active primarily at night. Armadillos (Dasypodidae) and one anteater (Myrmecophagidae), the giant anteater, are ground dwellers and powerful diggers. Armadillos and the giant anteater are active day or night, and inhabit savannas, grasslands, and forests. Lesser and silky anteaters are found in tropical forests and savannas where they are usually nocturnal and arboreal. Anteaters and some armadillos are insectivorous; other armadillos are more omnivorous. Xenarthrans are generally solitary animals, but individuals of some species may form loose associations.

The name Xenarthra is from two Greek words meaning "strange joint." It refers to a peculiar type of vertebral articulation that this group has in common.

References
Gardner, 1993b; Montgomery, 1985; Nowak,
    1991

Nine-banded armadillo *(Dasypus novemcinctus)*

Family Dasypodidae

This group of 8 genera and 20 species is primarily limited to tropical regions in the New World. The single exception is the nine-banded armadillo, *Dasypus novemcinctus,* which extends into the southern United States. Armadillos are covered with a shell-like series of skutes and plates that resemble armor; hence the name, which in Spanish means "little armored one." This bone-like covering is interspersed with more flexible skin that allows the animals to move about in normal mammalian fashion.

Armadillos tend to be fairly heavy-bodied for their size, at least partly due to the increased weight of the hardened epidermis. The giant armadillo of South America weighs up to 60 kg, and head and body lengths for the family range from 125 mm to almost a meter. Most armadillos have small ears and relatively long snouts, with a protrusible tongue and small, peg-like teeth.

These animals are all terrestrial, and may be solitary or sometimes forage in small groups. They are found both in grasslands and in forested habitats. They tend to dig and root around in the ground for insects, bulbs, invertebrates, and some plant material. Their dens tend to be in underground burrows.

Nine-banded armadillos give birth to identical young that are produced from a single ovum. Some other species have delayed implantation, which may result in gestation periods of up to 4 months or so. The young are flexible and supple at birth, but the outer shell quickly hardens into the armorlike substance found in adults.

References
Mammalian Species 162; Nowak, 1991

North American Genera
Dasypus

Nine-banded armadillo │ *Dasypus novemcinctus*

The nine-banded armadillo's turtle-like appearance and slow, shuffling gait make it unique among North American mammals. The most widely distributed xenarthran, it occurs from northwestern Argentina and Uruguay through Central America and Mexico and into the southern United States as far north as Kansas and Nebraska and east to Florida. *Dasypus novemcinctus* has shown remarkable range expansion during the last 100 years; it was first recorded in the Rio Grande Valley of southern Texas in the mid-1800s and had moved northward into Oklahoma, Kansas, Missouri, and Tennessee by the 1970s. Possible reasons for its northward expansion include progressive changes in climate, overgrazing, and removal of large predators. Drought and cold temperatures are probably the factors most limiting its continued movement northward.

Nine-banded armadillos are typically nocturnal or crepuscular, but they may forage actively during daylight when it is cold or cloudy for extended periods of time. *D. novemcinctus* relies on its keen sense of smell when searching for food. It shuffles along, nose to the ground, stopping to root with its nose and dig a small, conical hole with its forefeet when a food

Dasypus novemcinctus

item is found. Insects make up more than 75 percent of the nine-banded armadillo's diet. Occasionally worms, snails, birds' eggs, small amphibians, and berries also are eaten. During periods of foraging, the nine-banded armadillo periodically rears up on its hind legs, using its strong, thick tail as a brace, and turns its head slowly from side to side, sniffing the air.

Burrows are constructed by digging with the nose and forefeet and kicking loosened soil out of the burrow with the hind feet. To bring nest material, including leaves, dead grass, and twigs, into the burrow, the armadillo rakes a pile of vegetation beneath the body with its forefeet and then shuffles backwards into the burrow with the vegetation clamped between forefeet and hind feet.

In spite of their heavily armored bodies, nine-banded armadillos are strong swimmers and can even walk across the bottoms of streams for extended distances because of their ability to accumulate a large oxygen debt. When startled, or pressed by predators, armadillos can jump straight up, and move remarkably quickly. The short tapered tail is also difficult for a predator to grasp.

First breeding occurs at about one year of age; *D. novemcinctus* breeds between June and August. Five to seven days after fertilization, development of the fertilized egg ceases. The long period of delayed implantation can last four months. Each litter consists of a set of identical quadruplets, which develop from a single fertilized egg: members of a litter are always of the same sex. Young are born fully formed and with their eyes open, in March or April. Within a few hours they are able to walk. They begin accompanying their mother on foraging expeditions within a few weeks.

Nine-banded armadillos are the only mammals other than humans in which lepromatid leprosy can occur naturally, making these small, armored tanks invaluable contributors to medical research. *K. McBee*

Size

Males tend to be slightly heavier than females.
Total length: 615–800 mm
Length of tail: 245–370 mm
Weight: 5.5–7.7 kg (males); 3.6–6.0 kg (females)

Identification

Armadillos are distinguished from all other living mammals by the presence of bony skin plates. *Dasypus novemcinctus* is distinguished from other armadillos by the presence of 8 to 11 (usually 9) movable bands across the dorsum. The ears are longer than in *Dasypus hybridus* and *D. sabanicola*, which may be sympatric south of Mexico.

Other Common Names

Long-nosed armadillo

Status

Abundant

Subspecies

Dasypus novemcinctus aequatorialis, western Ecuador and possibly into Colombia and Peru

Dasypus novemcinctus davisi, from the Balsas Basin to the mountains of northern Morelos, Mexico

Dasypus novemcinctus fenestratus, Oaxaca, Mexico, and Panama

Dasypus novemcinctus hoplites, Trinidad, Tobago, and Grenada

Dasypus novemcinctus mexicanus, southern United States into southern Mexico

Dasypus novemcinctus novemcinctus, east of the Andes from Colombia and Venezuela to Paraguay and northern Argentina

References

Mammalian Species 162; Freeman and Genoways, 1998; Montgomery, 1985

Order Insectivora

This relatively large order comprises 7 families, 66 genera, and 428 species. Most are found in the Palearctic, Ethiopian, and Oriental regions, but a few also occur in the New World. These mouse-like animals are generally small (head and body length less than 180 mm) and most inhabit terrestrial, often moist habitats. More than 70 percent (312 species) of the Insectivora are shrews (Family Soricidae). Larger terrestrial members of this order include the hedgehogs of Eurasia and Africa (Erinaceidae), the solenodons (Solenodontidae) of the West Indies, and the tenrecs (Tenrecidae) of Madagascar and Africa. Only two families are represented in North America: shrews (Soricidae) and moles (Talpidae).

Insectivora inhabit a diverse assortment of habitats. Terrestrial species are found in grasslands, scrub, forests, and on cultivated lands. They often shelter in and under logs, branches, and leaf litter, among rocks and roots of trees, in burrows, and under dense vegetation. Some species, such as the desmans (Talpidae) and the water or otter shrews (Tenrecidae) are semiaquatic or aquatic, seeking protection in the water or in burrows located in banks above the high water level of streams, ponds, and lakes. Other species, such as the moles (Talpidae) of the Palearctic and Nearctic and the golden moles (Chrysochloridae) of the Ethiopian region, are fossorial and spend most of their life underground. These species frequent areas where the soil is loose and often sandy.

Many Insectivora are nocturnal, but some shrews and aquatic forms may be active day or night. Insectivores are generally solitary, but individuals of some species occur in small groups. Members of this order generally feed on immature or adult insects, other invertebrates, and small vertebrates that they encounter while moving over the ground or through their burrows, or while digging or swimming.

References
Hutterer, 1993; Nowak, 1991

Desert shrew *(Notiosorex crawfordi)*

Family Soricidae

Shrews are known from Eocene fossils in North America, but probably have been around even longer. The first mammals to begin to flourish after the age of reptiles may have been small, shrew-like forms that probably followed a lifestyle not unlike that of modern day shrews.

Shrews combine a small body size with a high metabolic rate that forces them to spend much of their time actively foraging. This has given them the reputation of being aggressive, constantly hungry, predators. They tend to be mainly insectivorous, owing primarily to their small size, but they are active hunters willing and able to take down whatever small prey they encounter. Some species have poisonous salivary secretions that help to subdue prey. Some also employ echolocation, to aid in navigation and perhaps in prey capture as well.

These tiny nocturnal creatures tend to live in leaf litter or in burrows and runways constructed by rodents. They are mainly solitary, getting together only during breeding seasons. They breed actively from early spring to late fall, and population sizes increase greatly during the summer months. Gestation periods of 2–4 weeks combined with litter sizes of 2–10 can result in burgeoning populations in some areas where several litters per year are possible.

Shrews tend to be rather nervous and flighty, moving at a rapid pace even when foraging. Although most are terrestrial, some are aquatic, and most species are found more commonly in moist habitats. These habitat requirements may be dictated at least partly by their small size and susceptibility to high temperatures and evaporative water loss because of their high activity level.

References

Mammalian Species 337; Nowak, 1991

North American Genera

Sorex
Blarina
Cryptotis
Notiosorex

Arctic shrew | *Sorex arcticus*

The present distribution of the arctic shrew is largely limited to the region of boreal coniferous forests that crosses Canada in a broad band south of the tundra from the Northwest Territories to the Gulf of St. Lawrence. The arctic shrew does not occur in southern Quebec and Ontario but does extend southward in the Upper Midwest into North and South Dakota, Minnesota, Wisconsin, and the Upper Peninsula of Michigan. An isolated population occurs in eastern New Brunswick and Nova Scotia.

The range of this boreal species encompasses areas that were extensively glaciated during the Pleistocene. Fossils from late Pleistocene cave deposits have been reported from Arkansas, Kansas, Missouri, Pennsylvania, Tennessee, Virginia, and West Virginia, indicating that the arctic shrew's range once extended considerably southward of its present range.

Although confined in distribution to regions of boreal coniferous forest, the arctic shrew nevertheless appears to prefer nonforested habitats. This shrew has been taken in a variety of habitats, but populations generally are highest in marshes and grassy clearings in forests.

Relatively little is known about the biology of the arctic shrew. This reflects the fact that few mammalogists work in the boreal latitudes where this species occurs. What we know about the biology of this species comes principally from research carried out in the southern portions of its range, principally in Wisconsin, Minnesota, and southern Manitoba.

At the southern limits of its distribution in Wisconsin the breeding season extends from February to August. The length of the breeding season appears to decrease with increasing latitude. Average litter size ranges from 6.0 to 7.7 in different portions of the range. Individual litters range from 5 to 9 young. *S. arcticus* appears to occur in only modest numbers, with estimated densities of 4–5 per hectare in July, increasing to 7–9 per hectare in September and October.

Arctic shrews experience high mortality early in life. An estimated one in seven individuals dies within one month of leaving the nest, and 80 percent of arctic shrews die before reaching sexual maturity. Nevertheless, individuals may live as long as 18 months.

Observations of hunting behavior suggest that this species uses vision in hunting insects and that its vision may be acute. Like other species of shrews, *S. arcticus* feeds principally on small insects. During late summer and autumn (August to November) it may be an important predator on pupae of the larch sawfly *(Pristiphora erichsonii).*

Like other soricids, arctic shrews are active throughout the 24-hour day in order to satisfy their high energy requirements. There are alternating periods of resting and activity, during which feeding takes place. Activity is greater at night and lowest between 6 and 10 in the morning.

Arctic shrews are unusual in possessing trivalent sex chromosomes. The three sex chromosomes in males are X, Y1, and Y2. Females are XX. The diploid number is 29 in males and 28 in females. Two closely related species, the European common shrew *(S. araneus)* and the tundra shrew *(S. tundrensis),* whose range includes both the northwestern Nearctic and eastern Palearctic, also have trivalent sex chromosomes. *G. L. Kirkland, Jr.*

Sorex arcticus

Size
No significant sexual dimorphism
Total length: 100–124 (114.7) mm
Length of tail: 36–45 (41.0) mm
Weight: 5–13.5 (8.1) g

Identification
The medium-sized arctic shrew is distinctive among North American shrews for its tricolored pelage. In adults the dorsum is very dark brown to black, the sides are paler brown, and the underparts are grayish-brown. The tail is indistinctly bicolored, brown to brownish-black above and paler below. Young-of-the-year are bicolored, brownish above with a paler brown venter.

Recent Synonyms
Sorex maritimensis

Other Common Names
Black-backed shrew, saddle-back shrew, musaraigne nordique

Status
Common

Subspecies
Sorex arcticus arcticus, southern and central Canada from Yukon and Northwest Territories to the Gulf of St. Lawrence; absent from southern Ontario and Quebec

Sorex arcticus laricorum, largely confined to upper midwestern United States, including eastern North and South Dakota, Minnesota, Wisconsin, and the Upper Peninsula of Michigan

Sorex arcticus maritimensis, eastern New Brunswick and mainland Nova Scotia. Disjunct from *S. a. arcticus* and may represent a separate species

References
Mammalian Species 524; Clough, 1963

Arizona shrew | *Sorex arizonae*

Arizona's namesake shrew was not recognized until the late 1970s, when shrewologists compared skulls of the few specimens available from the southwestern United States. All darker shrews from higher elevations in southern Arizona had been thought to represent the widespread *Sorex vagrans,* but another form was found mixed in with genuine *Sorex vagrans.* This new shrew was more closely related to the arid-adapted

Sorex merriami, and was given the name *Sorex arizonae* in deference to its only known place of occurrence.

Sorex arizonae's original description was based on only 10 specimens, and additional records accrued slowly. Two *Sorex arizonae* were subsequently found at a single site in the Animas Mountains of southwestern New Mexico, and a single specimen was obtained from the Sierra Madre Occidental of Chi-

Sorex arizonae

huahua, Mexico. Although *Sorex arizonae* was the only shrew inhabiting higher elevation forests of the zoologically famous Huachuca and Santa Rita mountains, and coinhabiting (with *Sorex vagrans)* the equally famous Chiricahua Mountains, only a handful of additional specimens were reported from Arizona until the 1990s. In 1992 and 1993 the Arizona Game & Fish Department (AGFD) initiated surveys for the shrew, prompted by concern that the species may be at risk of extinction based on its sporadic records.

AGFD found 30 *Sorex arizonae,* increasing substantially the number of specimens known to science (from about 22 to 52). Both historic localities assessed by AGFD continued to support *Sorex arizonae,* and 7 of the 11 new sites surveyed also supported the shrew. Surveys in mountain ranges not known to harbor *Sorex arizonae* revealed no additional populations, but

these efforts were not extensive and many other seemingly suitable areas remain to be surveyed. AGFD's unprecedented success implies that the shrew is more abundant and widespread than earlier records suggest. Although important questions remain, such as the long-term trends of populations, the species may not be in trouble at this time.

Arizona shrews occupy forested slopes from about 1,575 meters to at least 2,590 meters elevation. These shrews often live near springs or other water sources where considerable cover exists in the form of logs and dense vegetation. Dominant vegetation at these sites includes pines *(Pinus),* walnut *(Juglans),* oaks *(Quercus),* maples *(Acer),* Douglas fir *(Pseudotsuga),* aspen *(Populus),* madrone *(Arbutus),* junipers *(Juniperus),* and sycamore *(Platanus).* Although *Sorex arizonae* also occurs away from water, often in association with large boulders or rocky outcrops, it nearly always remains beneath a thick canopy of vegetation.

Details of *Sorex arizonae's* diet are unknown, but cursory observations suggest that, as with many other shrews that have been studied, arthropods (insects, spiders, and relatives) seem to form the bulk of its diet. Shrews do not hibernate, and they have very high metabolic rates—hence a need for large quantities of food. These furry bundles of energy seem to spend all of their time either finding food, eating, or resting. Probably because their tiny stomachs cannot process enough food at one time to last very long, shrews tend to be active both night and day. Their secretive habits and quick, dashing movements undoubtedly help protect them from many predators. In *Sorex arizonae's* mountain home these threats probably include owls, cats, gray foxes, ringtails, coatis, and several species of snakes. Although *Sorex arizonae* may be active at any time, one situation that seems to stimulate activity is rainfall. At this point one can only speculate on the reasons. The noise and moisture of falling rain may muffle the shrew's activities from predators, may make food easier to secure, may ameliorate the dessicating costs of surface activity, or the explanation may involve a combination of these or other factors. *L. H. Simons*

Size
Sexual dimorphism unknown
Total length: 79–114 (101) mm
Length of tail: 37–55 (43) mm
Weight: 1.9–5.2 (3.3) g

Identification
The Arizona shrew is distinguished from other shrews in the United States by a combination of cranial and dental characteristics, and in some locations by its sole representation of the genus *Sorex.* It may eventually prove to be synonymous with some Mexican shrews.

Recent Synonyms
Sorex emarginatus (hypothetical conspecific)
Sorex vagrans (in part)
Sorex vertralis (hypothetical conspecific)

Status
Uncertain (limited records available)

References
Diersing and Hoffmeister, 1977; Hoffmeister, 1986

Baird's shrew | *Sorex bairdi*

Sorex bairdi lives in the moist coniferous forests of the Pacific coast and Coast Range of northwestern Oregon, and in the Cascade Range of Oregon from the Columbia River south to southern Lane County. In the Coast Range, the conifer forests include Douglas fir *(Pseudotsuga menziesii)*, western hemlock *(Tsuga heterophylla)*, Pacific yew *(Taxus brevifolia)*, Sitka spruce *(Picea sitchensis)*, lodgepole pine *(Pinus contorta)*, western red cedar *(Thuja plicata)*, incense cedar *(Calocedrus decurrens)*, bigleaf maple *(Acer macrophyllum)*, red alder *(Alnus rubra)*, Pacific madrone *(Arbutus menziesii)*, Pacific dogwood *(Cornus nuttallii)*, rhododendron *(Rhododendron macrophyllum)*, salal *(Gaultheria shallon)*, and salmonberry *(Rubus spectabilis)*. On the west slope of the Cascade Range, *Sorex bairdi* occurs in Douglas fir forests that include conifers such as Douglas fir, western hemlock, western red cedar, silver fir *(Abies amabilis)*, and grand fir *(Abies grandis)*, and understory vegetation such as mountain Oregon grape *(Berberis nervosa)*, salal, vine maple *(Acer circinatum)*, wild blackberry *(Rubus macropetalus)*, huckleberry *(Vaccinium parvifolium)*, rhododendron, and sword fern *(Polystichum munitum)*. No fossils of *Sorex bairdi* have been found.

Sorex bairdi

Baird's shrews live and forage near logs and rocks, where they feed on insects, snails, worms, and arachnids. The specific diet of *Sorex bairdi* is unknown. Like all shrews, *S. bairdi* feeds throughout the 24-hour day and remains active all year.

In the summer, Baird's shrews are brownish-chestnut to olive-brown on the dorsum; the sides and belly are slightly paler, buffy-brown or tawny-olive. The pelage is darker brown during the winter. The tail is indistinctly bicolored.

Other small mammals that live in the forest with Baird's shrews include six other species of shrews, six species of voles, the coast and shrew moles, one species of jumping mouse, one species of deer mouse, two species of woodrats, Townsend's chipmunk, Douglas's and western gray tree squirrels, the northern flying squirrel, the mountain beaver, and one species of pocket gopher. *L. F. Alexander*

Size
No significant sexual dimorphism
Total length: 100–143 mm
Length of tail: 32–64 mm
Weight: 5.5–11.2 (7.6) g

Identification
Baird's shrew is distinguished from sympatric shrews as follows: from *Sorex trowbridgii* by brownish pelage, unicuspids wider than long, and tail not sharply bicolored; from *S. bendirii* by smaller size, brownish pelage, and unicuspids wider than long; from *S. vagrans* by slightly larger size and the medial tine on first upper incisors well within pigment; from *S. pacificus* by darker brown pelage and small tine on anteriomedial edge of first upper incisors; from *S. sonomae* by smaller size and presence of a medial tine on the first upper incisors; and from *S. monticolus* by larger body

size and slightly smaller medial tine on the first upper incisors.

Recent Synonyms
Sorex monticolus bairdi

Sorex monticolus permiliensis
Sorex obscurus bairdi
Sorex obscurus permiliensis
Sorex vagrans bairdi
Sorex vagrans permiliensis

Status
Unknown

Subspecies
Sorex bairdi bairdi, Pacific coast and Coast Range of northwestern Oregon
Sorex bairdi permiliensis, the Cascade Range of Oregon from the Columbia River south to southern Lane County

References
Alexander, 1996; Carraway, 1990; Jackson, 1918; Merriam, 1895

Marsh shrew | *Sorex bendirii*

Although the name "shrew" suggests small size, the marsh shrew is as large as many mice. It and the water shrew, which it closely resembles and part of whose range it shares, are the largest members of the genus *Sorex* in North America. The marsh shrew occupies part of the coastal rain forest extending from extreme southwestern British Columbia to just north of San Francisco Bay. The eastern limit of its range approaches the sagebrush deserts east of the Cascade Mountains. Within this range, marsh shrews are associated closely with western skunk cabbage marsh, riparian alder, small stream habitats, and beach debris. During the winter rainy season they may extend their range about a kilometer beyond their traditional habitats.

Marsh shrews have uniformly velvety, brownish-grayish-black backs throughout the year. The bellies are nearly as dark on the subspecies *S. b. bendirii* and *S. b. palmeri*. The subspecies *S. b. albiventer,* of Washington's Olympic Peninsula, may have whitish underparts, as does the water shrew, which shares its range. The single specimen of *S. b. bendirii* that has been examined was found to have a diploid chromosome number of 54.

The hind toes of the marsh shrew are not abundantly fringed with stiff hairs like those of the water shrew, and this feature is useful in distinguishing between the two species. The marsh shrew's tail is long and its ears do not project noticeably above the fur. The eyes are small but visible. They may be of limited capability, as wild shrews have been seen to run to the edge of and fall off logs a meter above the substrate, and captive shrews ran off tables or desks without hesitation. However, this may be more of a predator-avoidance response than lack of visual acuity.

Frenetic feeders, marsh shrews dive to search for the aquatic insect larvae that make up nearly half the diet. The shrew may actually run over the surface of the water for three seconds or so before submerging. Away from water, the nose, with its abundant vibrissae, is in constant motion as the shrew seeks slugs, snails, spiders, sowbugs, termites, and earthworms, which supplement the aquatic invertebrates in the diet. Unlike the northern water shrew, which frequently dines on fish, there is no evidence that marsh shrews consume vertebrates. Regardless of where prey is captured, eating takes place out of the water. After feeding, the shrew squeezes through narrow spaces in dry vegetation or bark to extract moisture from its fur before curling up and sleeping, sometimes for more than half an hour.

Little is known about the natural history of the marsh shrew. *Sorex bendirii* is thought to breed in late January or February, as does the northern water shrew. The gestation period, molt pattern, and litter size are unknown. By late March, the young are capable of finding their own food. Males do not ap-pear to mature sexually during their first summer. Only one nest has been described. It was constructed of shredded bark and was located beneath the loose bark of a fallen Douglas fir, above a small stream that the fallen tree spanned. In late March, that nest was occupied by at least five juvenile marsh shrews.

Other insectivores that share at least part of the range of the marsh shrew include the cinereus shrew, Pacific shrew, montane shrew, vagrant shrew, Trowbridge's shrew, water shrew, shrew mole, Townsend's mole and the coast mole. Because it is larger than most of the other shrews and because moles have enlarged hands directed toward the sides, the only species it might be confused with within its range and habitat is the water shrew. *D. L. Pattie*

Sorex bendirii

Size
No significant sexual dimorphism
Total length: 128–174 (156) mm
Length of tail: 58–80 (70) mm
Weight: 7.5–21 (15.4) g

Identification
The marsh shrew is the only large, velvety, brownish-grayish-black shrew within its range. The underparts are usually as dark, or almost as dark, as the upperparts and there is only a slight fringe of stiff hairs on the hind toes. Individuals on the Olympic Peninsula of Washing-

ton may have whitish underparts; here *S. bendirii* is distinguished from the sympatric water shrew, *S. palustris,* by the noticeable fringe of stiff hairs on the hind toes of the latter.

Other Common Names
Bendire's water shrew, Bendire's shrew, Pacific water shrew

Status
Common, limited

Subspecies
Sorex bendirii albiventer, peninsular Washington
Sorex bendirii bendirii, Cascade Mountains from southern British Columbia south to northern California
Sorex bendirii palmeri, Oregon west of the Cascade Mountains and extreme northwestern California

References
Mammalian Species 27; Brown, 1974; Cowan and Guiguet, 1965; Dalquest, 1948; Merriam, 1895; Pattie, 1969

Cinereus shrew | *Sorex cinereus*

The cinereus shrew is widely distributed and common in the coniferous and northern deciduous forest biomes up to timberline. It is found in a variety of habitats ranging from wet to quite dry, including forests, shrub thickets, and grassy and herbaceous areas. Its diet consists of insects and other invertebrates.

This species is most active at night. Because of its predominantly nocturnal activity and its habit of staying under cover, it is rarely seen.

The cinereus shrew lacks distinctive markings. It is brown on the back and has grayish-white underparts. Its tail is brown

above and paler below, with a blackish tip. In winter the pelage is darker overall. It molts from April to June, depending on latitude.

Sorex cinereus starts breeding in spring (April) and continues into the fall. The length of gestation is not known. Litter size varies from 4 to 10, averaging about 7. The neonates are approximately 15 to 17 mm long, hairless, and their eyelids are fused. The eyes open after 17 or 18 days and the young are weaned when they are approximately 20 days old. *C. G. van Zyll de Jong*

Sorex cinereus

Size
No significant sexual dimorphism
Total length: 75–125 (96.6) mm
Length of tail: 28–50 (39.9) mm
Weight: 2.2–5.4 g

Identification
This shrew is distinguished from similar shrews in its range as follows: from *Sorex haydeni* by the ventral coloration of the tail being darker and the terminal tuft black; from *Sorex ugyunak* by its longer tail and lack of pale coloration on the sides of the body; from *Sorex hoyi* by its longer tail (more than 40 percent of the total length) and longer rostrum, with a series of five unicuspid teeth showing a gradual reduction in size from front to back; and from *Sorex vagrans* and *Sorex monticolus* by longer rostrum and the possession of a third unicuspid that is not reduced.

Other Common Names
Masked shrew, common shrew

Status
Common, widespread

Subspecies
Sorex cinereus acadicus, Cape Breton Island, Nova Scotia, and New Brunswick
Sorex cinereus cinereus, Alaska and Canada from the Yukon and British Columbia to Quebec and Ontario
Sorex cinereus fontinalis, Maryland, southeastern Pennsylvania, and extreme eastern West Virginia
Sorex cinereus hollisteri, Alaska
Sorex cinereus lesueurii, southern Michigan, Indiana, Illinois, southern Wisconsin, Iowa, South Dakota, Nebraska, and northernmost Kansas
Sorex cinereus miscix, Labrador
Sorex cinereus ohionensis, Ohio (probably intergrade of *cinereus* and *lesueurii*)
Sorex cinereus streatori, coastal British Columbia and Washington

References
van Zyll de Jong, 1983

Long-tailed shrew | *Sorex dispar*

Sorex dispar is a species of the mountains of eastern North America, where it occurs in suitable habitat from mainland Nova Scotia and southeastern New Brunswick southward through the Appalachians and adjacent ranges, such as the Catskills and Adirondacks in New York, to North Carolina and Tennessee.

Two of the common names of this species, rock and long-tailed shrew, aptly describe its habitat and appearance. This shrew is almost invariably associated with rocky habitats and has an exceptionally long tail for a shrew (about half of the total length). Although long-tailed shrews have been taken in a variety of rocky habitats, including rocky forests and along small rocky streams, this species is most abundant in the glaciated portions of its range where boulders have accumulated at the base of steep-sided mountains. Here, in cool, moist northern hardwood and boreal coniferous forests, this species carries on its activities in the maze of passages below the surface. The long-tailed shrew spends so much time foraging in its rocky labyrinths and so little time aboveground that mammalogists once considered it among the rarest of North American mammals—until they discovered that traps placed at arm's length or more below the surface in rocky or boulder-strewn habitats frequently yielded this species. Even today, there are relatively few specimens of the long-tailed shrew in museum collections. A substantial number of these have been taken in rocky habitats immediately adjacent to cool, fast-flowing mountain streams, often in traps set specifically to capture the semi-aquatic water shrew *(Sorex palustris).* S. *dispar* has even been collected in two man-made rocky habitats: artificial talus created by road-building in Great Smoky Mountains National Park and open-pit mines in New York's Adirondack Mountains.

The long tail of this species is viewed as an adaptation to climbing, presumably serving as a counterbalance in much the same way that some arboreal mammals use their tails. The ecologically and morphologically convergent European alpine shrew *(Sorex alpinus)* often stands upright on its hind legs, us-

Sorex dispar

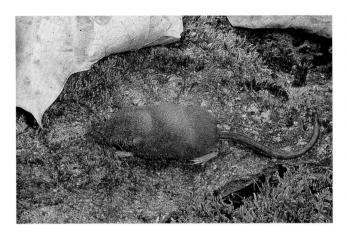

ing its tail as a counterbalance. It is believed that long-tailed shrews exhibit this same behavior, although it has never been observed.

Compared to most other shrews in eastern North America, the skull of *S. dispar* is very slender, with a long rostrum and somewhat buck-toothed upper and lower incisors. The slender rostrum may allow the long-tailed shrew to exploit food resources in narrow crevices in the rocks, and the procumbent incisors may further aid by acting as forceps to extract small prey items, which are a specialty.

Because so few long-tailed shrews have ever been collected by mammalogists, we know relatively little about the biology of this species other than its preferred habitats and largely subterranean habits. Its food includes insects (coleopterans, orthopterans, and adult dipterans), spiders, and centipedes. The reproductive season appears to extend from April through August, and known litter size ranges from 2–5.

The long-tailed shrew is significantly smaller in northern latitudes and larger in the southern part of its range. This is the reverse of Bergmann's Rule, which states that in warm-blooded vertebrates there is an increase in body size with increasing latitude. Populations in the southern Appalachians, represented by *S. d. blitchii,* are considerably larger than populations to the north, which tend to decrease in size from Pennsylvania northward to the Canadian Maritime Provinces. *G. L. Kirkland, Jr.*

Size
No significant sexual dimorphism
Total length: 103–136 (119.5) mm
Length of tail: 46–67 (56.3) mm
Weight: 3.1–8.3(4.9) g

Identification
The long-tailed shrew is medium-sized, slender, slate-gray, and has a long tail, generally longer than 48 mm. Among eastern North American shrews, only the water shrew *(Sorex palustris)* possesses a longer tail (57–89 mm). The water shrew is considerably larger (total length more than 130 mm and weight greater than 8 g), and has denser fur and a distinctive fringe of hairs on the feet. Generally its belly is noticeably paler than its dorsum; the belly of *S. dispar* is only slightly paler than the dorsum. The other medium-sized (4–8 g) soricid that inhabits the mountains of eastern North America is the smoky shrew *(Sorex fumeus).* Long-tailed shrews may be confused with smoky shrews when the latter are in gray winter pelage. The smoky shrew has a shorter tail (generally less than 48 mm), paler gray dorsal pelage, and is more robust; especially the skull, which is not slender and delicate like that of the long-tailed shrew. The range of the Gaspé shrew *(S. gaspensis)* approaches that of *S. dispar* in New Brunswick and Nova Scotia. Both are slender and slate gray with long tails, but *Sorex dispar* is considerably larger.

Recent Synonyms
Sorex blitchii
Sorex macrurus

Other Common Names
Rock shrew, gray long-tailed shrew, musaraigne longicaude

Status
Uncommon to rare

Subspecies
Sorex dispar blitchii, central and southern Appalachian Mountains from West Virginia southward to North Carolina and Tennessee
Sorex dispar dispar, mountainous regions of the mid-Atlantic states, New England, southeastern New Brunswick and adjacent mainland Nova Scotia

References
Mammalian Species 155; Kirkland and Van Duesen, 1979

Smoky shrew | *Sorex fumeus*

The smoky shrew is often common in moist woods in its range, living in both conifers and hardwoods. It runs about in the labyrinth of tunnels under logs and under the bed of leaves on the forest floor, and in runways under overhangs of banks along woodland roads or creeks.

Sorex fumeus is primarily nocturnal and is active throughout the year, even on the coldest nights. Shrews often live in size-ranked communities. Such a community might include large, medium, and small shrews such as short-tailed, smoky, and cinereus shrews, which feed respectively on large, medium, and small invertebrates. The smoky shrew feeds heavily on small earthworms, centipedes, insects and their larvae, sowbugs, and other small invertebrates, consuming up to about half its weight in food per day. It also eats salamanders, severing the spinal cord with its enlarged, protruding first incisors, which are efficient pinchers. Shrews echolocate, and smoky shrews constantly twitter as they forage, probably as part of their echolocation repertoire. They also produce a high-pitched grating note when disturbed, similar to that of bats.

Smoky shrews do not breed in the year of their birth, but produce two or sometimes three litters of three to seven young in their second year. Young are born from April through July, and rarely in August, in a nest of shredded vegetation in or under a log or stump or under a rock. Young shrews apparently stay in the nest until they are nearly full size. They are gray, and change to the brownish adult coloration in the summer after their birth. Few adults are found in winter, as maximum life expectancy is about 14 to 17 months. Most adult females apparently die soon after giving birth in their second year.

The principle predators on smoky shrews are owls, hawks, foxes, weasels, and other opportunistic mammalian predators. A wide array of ectoparasites is found on this host, the most

Sorex fumeus

abundant being five species of mites, including two chiggers and two hypopial (immature transport stage) mites.

Shrews are important in maintaining the balance of nature because of their predation on small invertebrates. *J. O. Whitaker, Jr.*

Size
No significant sexual dimorphism
Total length: 110–127 (117) mm
Length of tail: 37–49 (44) mm
Weight: 6–11 g

Identification
The smoky shrew is all gray or grayish-brown, medium-sized, and long-tailed. It is often common and is most similar to the long-tailed shrew, *Sorex dispar,* and the water shrew, *Sorex palustris,* the other large gray, long-tailed shrews in its range, both of which are usually uncommon. The water shrew's tail is longer than 60 mm and its hind feet are conspicuously fringed with stiff hairs. The smoky shrew is most similar to *Sorex dispar,* which has a longer tail (usually over 50 mm), slimmer body, and more nearly uniform darker colora-

tion above and below. The smoky shrew is gray above, paler below in winter, but is much browner in summer.

Status
Often fairly common in moist woods

Subspecies
Sorex fumeus fumeus, Ontario and western Quebec south to Georgia and South Carolina
Sorex fumeus umbrosus, eastern Quebec to Vermont and New Hampshire

References
Mammalian Species 215; Hamilton, 1940; Whitaker and Cudmore, 1987

Gaspé shrew | *Sorex gaspensis*

The Gaspé shrew is known from three apparently disjunct populations. It is found in the Gaspé Peninsula region of Quebec, on Cape Breton Island, Nova Scotia, and in north-central and western New Brunswick. In these locations, *S. gaspensis* has been taken in rocky boreal (spruce) and mixed deciduous forests. Rocks or talus represent an important habitat component, and *S. gaspensis* may confine much of its activity to rocky galleries below the surface. Many specimens have been trapped along the edges of cool, rocky streams at sites that would appear to be ideal habitat for the water shrew *(Sorex palustris)*. In its affinity for rocky forests and streamside habitats *S. gaspensis* is similar in ecological niche to the closely related *S. dispar.*

For many years the Gaspé shrew was considered to be one of the rarest mammals in North America, because only about two dozen specimens were collected in the 66 years following its description in 1924. However, in 1980 65 specimens of this species were caught in pitfall and snap traps in New Brunswick's Mount Carleton Provincial Park and one specimen was trapped on Moose Mountain in western New Brunswick, near the Maine border.

Almost nothing is known about the biology of the Gaspé shrew. Only three pregnant females have been collected. These had a mean of 5.7 embryos (range 5–6). Analysis of the stomach contents of two individuals indicates that beetles and spiders may be important dietary items for this species.
G. L. Kirkland, Jr.

Sorex gaspensis

Size
No significant sexual dimorphism
Total length: 95–127 (105) mm
Tail length: 45–55 (49.7) mm
Weight: 2.2–4.4 (2.9) g

Identification
The Gaspé shrew is a smaller version of the rock shrew, *Sorex dispar,* to which it is obviously closely related. Both are slate-gray with slender bodies and very long tails, which are about half of the total length. The venter is only slightly paler than the dorsum and the tail is not distinctly bicolored. The skull is slender and delicate. These traits easily distinguish the Gaspé shrew from all sympatric shrews. *Sorex dispar* is not sympatric, but its range in Quaggy Joe Mountain, Maine and that of *S. gaspensis* in Moose Mountain, New Brunswick, are only 45 km apart.

Other Common Names
Musaraigne de Gaspé

Status
Uncommon to rare

References
Mammalian Species 155; French and Kirkland, 1983; Kirkland and Van Duesen, 1979

Prairie shrew | *Sorex haydeni*

Sorex haydeni lives on the northern Great Plains from southern Manitoba, Alberta, and Saskatchewan south to the Black Hills of northeastern Wyoming and east to northwestern Iowa. It is found in grassland habitats on the prairies, parklands in the northern plains, and in the Black Hills it is locally abundant in wet areas and is found occasionally in rocky, drier pine habitats.

Little is known of the behavior of the prairie shrew, although adults, like most shrews, are believed to be solitary. It uses runways under leaf litter, and nests resembling birds' nests can be found under logs and in rock crevices. The diet is thought to be similar to that of other shrew species, consisting primarily of small invertebrates, including beetles, earthworms, larvae, spiders, and grasshoppers. The prairie shrew probably requires open ground water.

Pregnancy does not occur until the second year of life, and it has been observed from early spring through July. Gestation is 19–22 days, and litter size is 4–10. Occasionally, two or three

Sorex haydeni

litters are produced in one year. Young reach adult size and leave the nest at 20–30 days of age. *Sorex haydeni* has only recently been distinguished from *Sorex cinereus,* on the basis of morphometric studies. Fossils identified as *S. cinereus* have been identified from the Pleistocene in the southern Great Plains. These might actually be *S. haydeni,* given the southward compression of prairie habitat during the Pleistocene, but studies to determine which species the fossils represent have not yet been undertaken. *S. B. George*

Size
No significant sexual dimorphism
Total length: 88–99 mm (Wyoming); 77–101 (87) mm (Canada)
Length of tail: 34–40 mm (Wyoming); 25–38 (32) mm (Canada)
Weight: 3–5 g (Wyoming); 2–5 (3) g (Canada)

Identification
A small brown shrew, *Sorex haydeni* is distinguished by a relatively shorter tail lacking a terminal tuft of dark hairs, and by dental charac-

ters: the fourth upper unicuspid is smaller than the third and reddish pigmentation on the lower incisor is divided into two distinct areas, one including the tip and first two cusps, the second on the third cusp only.

Recent Synonyms
Sorex cinereus

Other Common Names
Hayden's shrew

Status
Uncommon, but may be locally abundant in appropriate habitat

References
Clark and Stromberg, 1987; Van Zyll de Jong, 1983

Pygmy shrew | *Sorex hoyi*

The pygmy shew's geographic range crosses the continent in a giant, circular pattern south of the tundra from central Alaska to eastern Quebec, extending southward through New England and New York. Specimens are unknown between New York and the Maryland-Virginia area, a 200–250 mile gap. From there the range continues through the Allegheny Mountains into northern Georgia, and westward through Tennessee, Kentucky, southern Indiana, and into southern Illinois. Unknown farther south or on the arid prairies and plains of the west, relict populations are found in Colorado and Wyoming. Pgymy shrews also occur in Montana and the northern Rocky Mountains. From there the distribution continues northward with the Alaskan race, *S. h. eximius,* completing a great circle

made up of interbreeding, but diverse, subspecies. These subspecies differ in weight by a factor of three, and some of them may eventually be shown to represent distinct species. Distributions like this, known scientifically by the German word "Rassenkreis," usually reflect the climatic effects of past glaciations.

Pygmy shrews are most abundant in boreal latitudes. They occupy forests, marshes, swamps, disturbed habitats, wet-dry soils, boreal habitats, and grassy and herbaceous understory. They are associated with a variety of vegetation types, including paper birch, aspen, jack pine, blackberry, raspberry, blueberry, oak, hazelnut, and alder. These shrews exhibit wide tolerance for wet, dry, cold, and warm environments, regardless

Sorex hoyi

of vegetation type and ground cover. The southern subspecies inhabits relatively moist, cool microhabitats. It is remarkably smaller in size and apparently differs somewhat in breeding pattern (winter breeding, multi-litters).

Like other shrews, the pygmy shrew feeds on small arthropods (larchfly larvae, lepidopteran larvae, grasshoppers, crane flies, beetles, probably spiders), worms, and on limited amounts of vegetation (such as seeds or berries and trap bait). Occasionally they eat carrion. They often stand on their hind limbs in kangaroo fashion and run quickly with the extended tail slightly curved. They climb with agility and bound as high as 110 mm. Their calls are sharp squeaks, low purrs, or high-pitched whistling and whispering. There is a strong musk.

The den may be a burrow or a shelter under a log, or may be located in the roots of old stumps. In captivity, pygmy shrews repeatedly made nests of cotton with openings at both ends. Predators include snakes *(Thamnophis),* hawks *(Buteo),* domestic cats, and foxes *(Vulpes).* Doubtless other shrews, owls, and other carnivores occasionally eat them. Parasites include fleas, mites, a tick, and intestinal hymenolepidid tapeworms.

Studies based on tooth-wear suggest an extended breeding season, with births in every month of the year. Actual collections of pregnant animals, however, suggest a more restricted breeding season, especially in northern parts of the range. Females likely produce more than one litter per year in favorable areas, and litter size ranges from 2 to 8. Most shrews captured are in the earlier age classes, and reproductively active individuals are less common.

As in other shrews, *S. hoyi* diminishes in size in winter. One old Wisconsin shrew found frozen in ice (9 March), with teeth greatly worn, and obviously over a year old, weighed only 1.85 g, which is comparable to the smallest *S. h. winnemana.* The young attain adult size by winter, and older shrews have tooth wear, a more exposed root of the upper bicuspid, and shorter, flattened skulls. Dental abnormalities are uncommon, except in *S. h. winnemana,* where the frequency may be as high as 8–9 percent.

Classification of the pygmy shrew remains a matter of controversy. V. E. Diersing placed them in the the genus *Sorex,* considering them to belong to an Holarctic array of species with a given number of teeth, variable tine development, and more or less reduction of the third unicuspid. Others hold to the use of *Microsorex* as a genus with a long fossil history, which has been differentiated into five or six taxa. Diersing suggests using *Microsorex* as a subgenus; some others prefer the subgenus *Otisorex.* C. A. Long

Size

Total length: 62–106 mm (mean length, Ontario: 98.2 mm)

Length of tail: 21–39 mm (mean tail length, Ontario: 34.9 mm)

Weight: 2.1 g to as much as 7.3 g (some Alaskan specimens)

Identification

S. Hoyi is tiny, with small, bright black eyes and obscure ear pinnae. Its long snout, which is constantly in motion, has conspicuous vibrissae. Each foot has five toes. The color varies from coppery brown to grayish above. The underparts are paler, grayish brown or drab white, often tinged with copper or tan. The tail

is dark brown above, much paler below, and the muzzle is paler than the crown and back. The tail is long. Females have six mammae; breeding males have a prominent, slit-like scent gland on each flank. Small body size is often diagnostic of *S. hoyi* in southern latitudes, but in northern latitudes pygmy shrews are usually as large as *S. cinereus* or even larger.

Although the snout or muzzle is a little broader and the felt-like pelage a little grayer than in *S. cinereus,* the most reliable characters for identifying *S. hoyi* are the five crowded upper unicuspate teeth. They include a small, peg-like posterior unicuspid (typical in this genus) and a third unicuspid that is a tiny disk, barely visible to the naked eye.

Recent Synonyms

Microsorex hoyi
Microsorex thompsoni (part)

Status

Usually rare and sparsely distributed. Uncommon except locally throughout the Rocky Mountains. Relatively rare in Canada. The subspecies *S. h. winnemana* is considered rare or threatened.

Subspecies

Sorex hoyi alnorum, northeastern Manitoba, northern Ontario, and northern Quebec in an arc around Hudson Bay
Sorex hoyi eximius, Alaska and Yukon Territory
Sorex hoyi hoyi, northeastern British Columbia, north into Northwest Territory, and east to Labrador; south into North and South Dakota, northern Iowa, and the Great Lakes region
Sorex hoyi montanus, north-central Colorado and southern Wyoming
Sorex hoyi thompsoni, northeastern states and north to the Gaspé Peninsula
Sorex hoyi winnemana, Maryland, Georgia, Virginia, Tennessee, Southern Indiana, and Illinois

References

Mammalian Species 33; Diersing, 1980; Feldhamer et al., 1993; Long, 1972a, 1972b

Pribilof Island shrew | *Sorex hydrodromus*

The Pribilof Island shrew is one of the least known of all North American mammals. Its other common name, the Unalaska Island shrew, may be a misnomer, because no one knows for certain that the shrew actually lives (or lived) on Unalaska Island, one of the Aleutian Islands in the Bering Sea west of the Alaskan mainland. The species was described from two specimens reported to have been collected from "Unalaska" in the 1840s by Russian explorers. Some biologists interpreted "Unalaska" to mean Unalaska Island, but attempts since then to collect additional specimens have failed. When Russia occupied Alaska, "Unalaska" also referred to a much larger region that included the islands in the Bering Sea. On one of these islands, St. Paul Island in the Pribilof island group northwest of Unalaska Island, a small shrew was found by American biologists after Russia's sale of Alaska to the United States. This shrew was given the name *Sorex pribilofensis,* the Pribilof Island shrew. A number of specimens of this shrew have been taken from St. Paul Island over the years, in contrast to the apparent absence of shrews on Unalaska Island, suggesting that the two Russian specimens might actually have been taken on St. Paul Island. The Russian and American specimens are quite similar in most respects, supporting this interpretation. However, Russian biologists report that the structure of the penis of the two shrews is different. This raises the possibility that a species of shrew once lived on Unalaska Island, where it was found by early Russian explorers, but has now become extremely rare or even extinct, and that another, closely related species continues to survive on St. Paul Island.

Another species of shrew, the St. Lawrence Island shrew (*Sorex jacksoni),* is closely related to the shrew on St. Paul Island. Both belong to the *cinereus* shrew group, which includes species occurring both in North American and eastern Siberia.

Sorex hydrodromus

During the Ice Age, many sorts of mammals that are today separated by the waters of the Bering Strait ranged widely across a continuous land area that encompased Unalaska and the other islands throughout the region. It is likely that all of the areas that now form islands in the Bering Sea once had populations of shrews, and that as the sea level rose with the melting of the great ice sheets, populations were isolated on what eventually became the Bering Sea islands. This isolation then gave rise to the species we see today. However, not all of the islands now have shrew populations; shrews that may have occupied Unimak, Nunivak, St. Matthew, and St. George Island appear to have become extinct with the rising sea level and restriction of their ranges. Insular populations are more likely to go extinct than mainland ones because of lower population sizes and restricted gene flow from surrounding populations.

Virtually nothing is known of the biology of *S. hydromus* on St. Paul Island. It lives in maritime tundra habitats, and at least occasionally is abundant enough that a number of individuals have been collected in short periods of time. Its habits are presumably quite similar to those of the cinereus shrew and the St. Lawrence Island shrew, but no specific information is available concerning its diet, behavior, reproduction, or seasonal cycle. All that is known is that one of the two Russian specimens, an adult female, contained six embryos. *R. S. Hoffmann*

Size
No significant sexual dimorphism
Total length: 88–97 mm
Length of tail: 32–37 mm
Weight: unknown but probably 3–4 g

Identification
The only shrew found on St. Paul Island in the Pribilof Islands and on Unalaska Island in the state of Alaska.

Other Common Names
Unalaska Island shrew

Status
Apparently not uncommon on St. Paul Island, but may be extinct (if it ever occurred) on Unalaska Island.

Subspecies
Sorex hydrodromus hydrodromus, Unalaska Island, Alaska
Sorex hydrodromus pribilofenis, St. Paul Island, Alaska

References
Murie, 1959; Hoffmann and Peterson, 1967; Van Zyll de Jong, 1991

St. Lawrence Island shrew | *Sorex jacksoni*

The St. Lawrence Island shrew is found only on St. Lawrence Island in the Bering Sea. The island is a remnant of a land bridge that connected Siberia and Alaska during the Ice Age. The St. Lawrence Island shrew is a member of the *cinereus* group, an essentially North American group of closely related shrews, which is also represented in eastern Siberia by several species. Like other tundra-dwelling shrews in this group, the St. Lawrence Island shrew is characterized by a bi-colored pattern of the pelage, a brown back and pale buffy or grayish sides. Its biology is virtually unknown. *C. G. van Zyll de Jong*

Size
No significant sexual dimorphism
Total length: 94–107 (100) mm
Length of tail: 32–37 (34) mm
Weight: 4–5 g

Identification
It is the only shrew in its range.

Other Common Names
St. Lawrence shrew

Status
Common in its limited range

References
Hall and Gilmore, 1932

Sorex jacksoni

Southeastern shrew | *Sorex longirostris*

Although first described in 1837 by the Reverend John Bachman, a contemporary and friend of the well-known American bird and mammal painter John James Audubon, even a century later fewer than 100 individuals had been collected or reported. In spite of its widespread distribution this small shrew remained very poorly known until the use of pitfall traps became more common. In the 1970s and 1980s their use revealed that in some habitats this shrew was actually quite common. Even today, however, few people have seen a southeastern shrew alive.

The southeastern shrew is now known to inhabit a wide variety of habitats ranging from wooded swamps, marshes, and river floodplain forests to oldfields, upland hardwood forests, and even loblolly pine plantations. In Florida, *S. longirostris* has been found in the same wide range of wet to bone-dry habitats, including cypress swamps, bay swamps, palmetto thickets, slash pine and longleaf pine flatwoods, longleaf pine sandhills, and sand pine scrub. However, most specimens have come from moist to wet sites with a dense ground cover of plants such as grasses, sedges, rushes, blackberry, or the exotic and aggressive Japanese honeysuckle vine.

Like most shrews, *S. longirostris* is active both day and night, spending most of its time in the underground burrows of other animals and rooting under the leaf litter. Here it hunts at a seemingly frantic pace for small invertebrates. Its most important prey is small spiders. Other frequently taken foods include small moth caterpillars, small crickets, harvestmen, small beetles (both adults and larvae), and centipedes.

Young are born as early as April and as late as October, with females giving birth to two or more litters of one to six (average about 4) young per litter. By the time the young leave the nest at between three and four weeks of age, they are practically the size of adults. Females born early in the breeding season give birth to their own litters before summer's end. For this diminutive shrew there is little time to waste: they are born, produce and raise several litters, and die of old age, assuming a predator does not get them first, all in about 14 months. *T. W. French*

Sorex longirostris

Size
No significant sexual dimorphism, but subspecies vary in size; *S. l. longirostris* is smallest and *S. l. fisheri* largest.
Total length: 77–102 mm
Length of tail: 27–40 mm
Weight: 2–5.8 (3.25) g *(S. l. longirostris)*

Identification
Throughout most of its range this is the only long-tailed shrew. Near the northern limits of its range and at higher elevations it may be found with or near *Sorex cinereus* and *Sorex hoyi*, with which it can easily be confused. *Sorex cinereus* can be distinguished by its slightly larger overall size when compared to *S. l. longirostris,* by its relatively longer and heavier tail, longer and narrower face, and usually by the upper third and fourth unicuspid teeth being about equal in size (the third upper unicuspid is usually smaller than the fourth in *S. longirostris). Sorex hoyi* is distinguished by its upper tooth row having only three unicuspid teeth easily visible when viewed from the side; the third and fifth being greatly reduced in size. Young, brown-colored *Sorex fumeus* can be distinguished by their overall larger size. No other species of small, brown, long-tailed shrew occurs within the geographic range of *S. longirostris.*

Other Common Names
Dismal Swamp southeastern shrew *(S. l. fisheri)*

Status
Sorex longirostris is fairly common but secretive throughout most of its range. *S. l. fisheri* was listed by the U.S. government as a threatened "species" in 1986, largely because of its restricted range. More recent research has shown that *S. l. fisheri* is more geographically widespread than previously known, is relatively abundant and secure in a variety of habitat types, and is unlikely to be genetically swamped by surrounding populations of *S. l. longirostris.* As a result, it is being considered for delisting.

Subspecies
Sorex longirostris eonis, northern two-thirds of peninsular Florida
Sorex longirostris fisheri, restricted to the region of the Great Dismal Swamp in Virginia and nearby North Carolina; recent specimens suggest that this subspecies may be more widespread in the coastal plain of North Carolina and possibly even South Carolina
Sorex longirostris longirostris, most of the southeastern United States

References
Mammalian Species 143; French, 1980; Jones et al., 1991; U.S. Fish and Wildlife Service, 1994

Mt. Lyell shrew │ *Sorex lyelli*

This rare species has been found only at elevations above 2,000 meters in the central Sierra Nevada Mountains of California. *Sorex lyelli* is very closely related to *Sorex cinereus,* which it resembles closely. The Mt. Lyell shrew may have evolved from a population of *S. cinereus* that became isolated on an ecological "island" when the distributional range of that species shifted northward at the end of the last ice age. Nothing is known about the life history of the Mt. Lyell shrew. *C. G. van Zyll de Jong*

Size
No significant sexual dimorphism
Total length: 88–108 (100) mm
Length of tail: 38–43 (40) mm
Weight: 4–5 g

Identification
Distinguished from similar shrews in its range, *Sorex ornatus, S. vagrans,* and *S. monticolus,* by having the third upper unicuspid tooth larger than the fourth.

Other Common Names
Lyell shrew

Status
Rare

References
Grinnell and Storer, 1924; Williams, 1984

Sorex lyelli

Merriam's shrew │ *Sorex merriami*

Sorex merriami is a shrew of relatively dry habitats across a broad geographic range in interior western North America. The most commonly reported habitat is sagebrush steppe, but the animals also have been taken in semiarid grasslands, pinyon-juniper woodland, montane brushlands, and even rather mesic mixed woodlands of ponderosa pine, Douglas fir, and cottonwood. Elevations of capture range from 200 m in Washington to over 2,900 m in Colorado and nearly that high in California.

Information on reproduction is minimal. Pregnant females

have been reported from mid-March to July. Embryo counts range from five to seven. Flank glands are large and quite prominent in spring, especially on adult males, suggesting that these may function to facilitate the breeding biology of the species.

Merriam's shrew occupies habitats drier than most of the several species of shrews with which it is broadly sympatric, except for the dwarf shrew *(Sorex nanus)* and Preble's shrew *(Sorex preblei)*. Therefore, competition with other shrews probably is minimal. Further, ground-foraging insectivorous birds are diurnal and hence isolated temporally from the generally nocturnal shrews. White-footed mice *(Peromyscus)* often are insectivorous in summer, but the prey base of insects usually is large and competition with shrews has not been demonstrated. Several studies have found Merriam's shrew to be associated with runways of arvicoline rodents, especially the sagebrush vole *(Lemmiscus curtatus),* but also species of *Microtus.* No direct dependence is implied, although these runways may form relatively safe and energy-efficient routes through the habitat, and they may be favored habitat of potential prey.

Reported foods include spiders, beetle adults and larvae, cave crickets, caterpillars, and wasps. Shrews tend not to have specialized food habits, and probably most terrestrial invertebrates are captured and eaten as available.

The only documented predators on Merriam's shrews are owls; one would assume that any other carnivorous vertebrates capable of capturing the animals would also kill them

Sorex merriami

(although shrews have a pungent odor and sometimes are not eaten, especially by provisioned predators like house cats). Known parasites include nematodes, cestodes, and fleas.

D. M. Armstrong

Size
Sexual dimorphism has not been documented.
Total length: 88–107 (96.3) mm
Length of tail: 33–42 (36.2) mm
Weight: 4–7 (5.9) g

Identification
This shrew's pelage is grayish-brown above, paler on the flanks, and nearly white below; the tail is strongly bicolored, grayish-brown above and white below. The unicuspid teeth are notably crowded; the rostrum is broad and abruptly truncated anteriorly; the braincase is flattened, and little elevated above the rostrum; the flank glands are large (to 3 by 7 mm)

and prominent (especially in males during the breeding season in spring). Dental and cranial details separate Merriam's shrew from the Arizona shrew *(Sorex arizonae)* of the mountains of southeastern Arizona. *S. merriami* is relatively larger than any other North American shrew except the desert shrew *(Notiosorex crawfordi).*

Status
Unknown; records of occurrence are scattered widely and based mostly on opportunistic captures or retrieval from owl pellets; few studies have documented absolute or relative abundance.

Subspecies
None (Some authors recognize two subspecies: *Sorex merriami leucogenys,* Colorado westward across much of Utah and Nevada and south on the Colorado Plateau to Arizona and New Mexico, and *Sorex merriami merriami,* South Dakota to Washington, southward to northeastern California, northern Nevada and Utah, and Wyoming.)

References
Mammalian Species 2; Armstrong et al., 1973; Diersing and Hoffmeister, 1977

Montane shrew | *Sorex monticolus*

The montane shrew is one of the most widespread and common species of the genus *Sorex.* It is distributed from Alaska in the north almost continuously through the Rocky Mountains. It is found in the Blue Mountains of Oregon and the Sierra

Nevada of California, on mountaintops in Utah, Arizona, and New Mexico, and through the Sierra Madre Occidental of Mexico in the south. The species also inhabits many coastal islands of the Pacific Northwest, including the Alexander Archi-

Sorex monticolus

pelago, the Queen Charlotte Islands, and Vancouver Island. In the Cascade Mountains, *Sorex monticolus* is not found south of the Columbia River, except for disjunct populations in a few counties in north-central Oregon, which are thought to be there as the result of a transfer of shrews from Washington via a massive landslide that temporarily blocked the Columbia River 1,700 years ago. In New Mexico, the species is not found east of the Rio Grande River, except for disjunct populations in the Sacramento Mountains of New Mexico.

Brownish dorsally in summer, with the underside washed with silver, the montane shrew molts into a darker, longer coat in September or October. Musk glands on the flanks are insignificant in juvenile males, but are strongly defined in breeding males, as is true of most shrews. Glands also are found in about 30 percent of breeding females. Spring molt takes place in late March and early April for females, but from late May to August for males. Molting begins on the rump and nose and spreads outward, finishing in the area between the ears.

Montane shrews are found in a variety of habitats, but their environment is always mesic, and the species is often (although not always) associated with water. In the tundra and taiga to the north, the species is found in willow and alder thickets along streams. In central Canadian grasslands, it is associated with thick, grassy, riparian habitats. In the mountains of California, the Southwest, and Mexico, it is found in meadows and in leaf litter in canyons of coniferous forest, often along streams. In the Rocky Mountains, it occurs in spruce-fir forests and alpine tundra.

Sorex monticolus often is found in association with as many as four other species of *Sorex*. At such sites, it is usually the most commonly caught species. One reason for this is that *S. monticolus* is more of a generalist in its diet, and thus able to maintain higher population density. Like all other long-tailed shrews *(Sorex)*, *S. monticolus* subsists on a diet of insects, earthworms, and other invertebrates. It also tends to be the largest shrew in such associations (with the exception of the water

shrew, *S. palustris,* which is much larger but narrowly restricted to stream banks and pools of water). There often are microhabitat differences among the species that can be detected only with detailed study; for example, in British Columbia, where *S. monticolus* and *S. vagrans* are sympatric, the former species is found more often on acidic soils under leaf litter, whereas the latter is found more often on richer soils in grassier openings. These differences were not initially detected in a gross survey of the area.

Activity tends to occur in peak periods, two in the night and one in the early morning, with shorter activity periods interspersed throughout the day. *Sorex monticolus* does not hibernate, but remains active all year.

Young individuals are somewhat territorial, not only with conspecifics, but also with other members of the genus. Home ranges of nonbreeding individuals in Canada are about 1,200 square meters; however, breeding montane shrews range far more widely, covering up to 4,000 square meters. Males have larger home ranges during breeding than females, and each male home range can encompass up to five females' home ranges.

The breeding season lasts from February to August; births have been noted as early as March. Females may produce two litters per year, each of 2 to 9 (average 5 to 6) young. Usually females do not breed until after their first winter, but a few individuals born early in the year may produce a litter late in the summer before their first winter. Few individuals live through two winters—normal life span does not exceed 16 to 18 months.

Fossils of *S. monticolus* have been identified from as early as the late Pleistocene. *S. B. George*

Size

No significant sexual dimorphism

Total length: 95–139 (119) mm (Canada); 95–116 (107) mm (Colorado)

Length of tail: 30–62 (51) mm (Canada); 40–49 (44.5) mm (Colorado)

Weight: 4.4–10.2 g (5 g in nonbreeding season, on average, in Canada; 7.5 g in breeding season)

Identification

This shrew is distinguished by a combination of dental characters: the third upper unicuspid is smaller than the fourth and the red tooth pigmentation extends above the notch on the front of the first incisor. *Sorex monticolus* is part of a large complex of closely related species, including *S. bairdii, S. ornatus,* and *S. vagrans.* Where *S. monticolus* and *S. vagrans* are sympatric, they can be distinguished by the degree to which the front incisors are pigmented: the first incisors have more color in *S. monticolus* and the rusty-colored pigmentation extends high on the tooth, above the middle tine. Also, the hind feet of *S. monticolus* have more (more than four) paired digital callosities (callouses) than do the feet of *S. vagrans.*

Recent Synonyms

Sorex obscurus

Sorex vagrans

Other Common Names

Dusky shrew

Status

Common

Subspecies

Sorex monticolus alascensis, eastern Kodiak Peninsula, Alaska, south along coast to the Sheslay River of British Columbia

Sorex monticolus calvertensis, Calvert and Banks islands, British Columbia

Sorex monticolus elassodon, Admiralty and Baranof islands south through the Alexander Archipelago to the Queen Charlotte Islands

Sorex monticolus insularis, Bardswell Island Group, British Columbia

Sorex monticolus isolatus, Vancouver Island

Sorex monticolus longicauda, Port Snettisham, Alaska, south along coast to River Inlet, British Columbia

Sorex monticolus malitiosus, Warren and Coronation islands, Alaska

Sorex monticolus monticolus, mountainous regions of Arizona and New Mexico, south through the Sierra Madre Occidental of Mexico

Sorex monticolus neomexicanus, Sacramento Mountains region of New Mexico

Sorex monticolus obscurus, Brooks Range, Alaska, inland and south through the Rocky Mountains to northern New Mexico; disjunct population in the Sierra Nevada of California

Sorex monticolus setosus, coastal British Columbia south through Washington west of the crest of the Cascade Range

Sorex monticolus shumaginensis, Alaska south of the Brooks Range, inland through the Wrangell Mountains, westward to the coast at Kodiak Island, through the Alaska Peninsula

Sorex monticolus soperi, northern Saskatchewan and west-central Manitoba

References

Clark and Stromberg, 1987; van Zyll de Jong, 1983

Dwarf shrew | *Sorex nanus*

The dwarf shrew is well named: it is among the smallest shrews in North America. Only the pygmy shrew is definitely smaller, although Preble's and southeastern shrews average only slightly larger. The dwarf shrew has an extensive distribution throughout the central and southern Rocky Mountains, and extends both eastward onto the Great Plains and southwestward onto isolated "sky island" mountains in Arizona and New Mexico. Because of its small size, it is very unlikely to trigger conventional snap or box traps, and prior to 1966, only 18 specimens had been collected. However, at that time mammalogists began to use "pitfall" traps. These consist of a can or other container sunk flush into the ground, so that very small animals such as these shrews do not have to trigger the trap: instead, they tumble in and are unable to jump out. Because it requires this special trapping technique, the actual range of the dwarf shrew may be wider than is indicated by published records and range maps.

The dwarf shrew occurs in a variety of habitats, from alpine tundra through subalpine forests and rock slides, and, at lower elevations, from montane forests and foothills to arid short-grass prairie. Dwarf shrews appear to be relatively tolerant of

Sorex nanus

arid situations and often occur at greater distances from permanent water than do other small shrews such as the pygmy shrew and the cinereus shrew. Rocky situations such as talus slopes at any elevation seem to be favorite habitat, but especially in alpine and subalpine situations. Pitfall traps placed at some distance from the talus capture fewer dwarf shrews than do those placed immediately adjacent to or buried under the slide-rock. Apparently the cover afforded by the rocks, among which the dwarf shrews can move easily, is important in providing protection from climatic extremes, and perhaps also from predators. However, the species also occurs in environments lacking such piles of rocks, such as on the arid Great Plains; the elevational range of the species is from about 600 to over 4,300 meters.

The dwarf shrew takes advantage of its very small size to live within a micro-environment where it can exploit small, soft-bodied invertebrates such as insect larvae and spiders, as well as adult small insects. Such potential prey organisms are often abundant in talus, and are themselves caught in pitfall traps. Because of its small body size, the dwarf shrew has a very high metabolic rate, and must remain active in order to capture sufficient prey to sustain its metabolism. If provided with excess food, captive dwarf shrews exhibit caching behavior, piling up uneaten prey in a corner of their cage. Caching has also been observed in other small shrews. This behavior increases the efficiency of prey utilization by taking advantage of locally or temporarily abundant food for later use.

Information on the breeding and life cycle of the dwarf shrew is scarce, but reproduction probably begins in the alpine zone in late June to early July, before the snow melts. In the central Rocky Mountains first litters are produced from late July to early August and may be followed immediately by a second breeding and a second summer litter. In contrast to other, slightly larger shrews, dwarf shrews may have a shorter breeding season that is restricted to the brief summer, particularly at high elevations. Both adult males and females may breed twice in a season, in contrast to some other species of small shrews, such as the ornate shrew, in which adult females are unlikely to produce a second litter, although some early-born females may produce a late summer litter. The litter size is usually between 6 and 7; there is no information on the development of the young or on the length of gestation, but these are likely to be similar to other small *Sorex*. At lower elevations, and particularly in grassland habitats, reproductive patterns may be different, but have not been investigated.

Information on behavior, territoriality, and home range in the dwarf shrew has not yet been gathered, nor are there good estimates of population density. However, capture rates indicate that the species may be common in certain places. Although data are yet incomplete, what is known concerning their habitat preferences suggests that populations in the central Rocky Mountains (Montana, Wyoming) may be broadly contiguous from the mountains to the adjacent plains, but there may be a gap in distribution between dwarf shrews in northern and southern Wyoming. Toward the south of the southern Rocky Mountains, the distribution of dwarf shrews may become more fragmented, and populations occurring at high elevations in the mountains of northern and central Arizona and New Mexico are almost certainly isolated from other populations by expanses of desert and semi-desert. The fossil record of the dwarf shrew supports this interpretation. The species occurred in the Guadalupe Mountains of southern New Mexico a few thousand years ago, but does not occur there today. It also occurred in northwestern Kansas south of its present known range. The species was probably more widespread in the southern Rocky Mountains and Great Plains at the end of the Ice Age; as the glaciers melted, the cool-adapted biota retreated northward, leaving small, isolated populations where suitable islands of habitat remained. The only reported instance of predation upon a dwarf shrew was a jaw recovered from an owl pellet. *R. S. Hoffmann*

Size
No significant sexual dimorphism
Total length: 82–105 mm
Length of tail: 27–45 mm
Weight: 1.8–3.2 g

Identification
Sorex nanus is restricted to the Rocky Mountain region and adjacent plains. It can be distinguished from cinereus, Hayden's, and Preble's shrews by dental characters: its third upper unicuspid tooth is smaller than the second and fourth teeth. It is also distinguished from the pygmy shrew by its teeth: *S. nanus* has four upper unicuspids, which are easily seen in side view, instead of three. Montane and vagrant shrews are larger.

Other Common Names
Rocky Mountain dwarf shrew

Status
Widespread but usually uncommon

References
Mammalian Species 131; Brown, 1967; Spencer and Pettus, 1966

Ornate shrew | *Sorex ornatus*

The ornate shrew bears a rather grandiose name when in fact, like most small shrews, it is quite inconspicuous. This general characteristic is what makes many small shrews quite difficult to tell apart, particularly where they occur together with other species of about the same size and coloration. The ornate shrew is restricted to the southern Pacific coast region, where it occurs both in upland habitats and marshlands, both near inland freshwaters and along the seacoast.

These small shrews weigh about five grams. *S. ornatus* has a relatively short tail, the dorsal surface of the body is grayish-brown, and the ventral surface is paler grayish in color. Shrews from populations in the northern part of the range are somewhat smaller than those from farther south. Particularly interesting are two populations occurring in Baja California, Mexico. One occurs in salt marshes along the northwestern Baja California coast, and the other occurs in uplands at the southern tip of the peninsula. These populations and one found on Santa Catalina Island, in the Channel Islands group, are isolated from the remainder of the species. Such small, isolated populations are vulnerable both to human encroachment and to environmental fluctuation, and more vulnerable to extinction than are continental populations.

Throughout its range the ornate shrew occupies a Mediterranean climate, characterized by long, dry summers and shorter, rainy winters. In the San Francisco Bay region rain falls mainly from November to April, but the timing and duration of the winter rainy season is variable, and ornate shrews can suffer stress if the onset of the rainy season is delayed and/or the summer is unusually long and hot. This is true not only of salt marsh populations, but also of populations inhabiting freshwater marshes and stream-side vegetation. These shrews seem to prefer habitats with low, dense vegetation that provides cover from the hot sun or drenching rains and harbors abundant invertebrates, which they hunt for their food.

Sorex ornatus

Such a vegetative structure is found in both marshes and stream-sides, and also in the drier upland habitats of the Coast ranges and at lower elevations (below 1,670 m) on the western slope of the Sierra Nevada range in central California (but to 2,400 m in the San Jacinto Mountains). Here home ranges may extend out into grassy hillsides and dry, brush-covered areas (called chaparral), and even into woodlands and open forests.

The ornate shrew, like other small shrews, has a relatively high metabolic rate. Its small size means it has a relatively large surface area, and its rather thin fur leads to more rapid heat loss than larger, better-furred mammals experience. To replace the lost heat and maintain their body temperatures, small

shrews are active both day and night, especially during the breeding season, which imposes additional energy demands. Periods of intense activity, ranging from a few minutes to as much as an hour, alternate with periods of inactivity throughout the 24-hour period. During active periods ornate shrews forage vigorously for food in the vegetation litter covering the ground, taking all sorts of invertebrates. They probably are willing scavengers of any dead animals they encounter, even including other small mammals and birds. They actively defend their nest sites against other shrews, and probably an area around those nests, but this has not been directly documented.

The main breeding period for the ornate shrew is in the early spring (April–May) in the San Francisco Bay area, although some breeding may occur as early as late February. With the onset of the summer dry season, reproduction decreases, but it may increase again in late summer; this renewed breeding may be restricted to young animals born earlier in the year. Only a few females produce two litters; these are females in their second year of life who have bred in the spring and may live long enough to produce a second, late summer litter. Four to six young are born after a gestation period of about 21 days. The life span of the ornate and other small shrews is rarely more than 12–18 months. The mortality of shrews born in one season is moderate over the first non-breeding (fall–winter) season, but after being reproductively active in their second year of life, mortality among these adult shrews is very high, and there is virtually a total turnover in the population each year. The young are born in a quite well-developed state and grow rapidly while in the nest, so that when they emerge from the nest they are only slightly smaller than their parents. However, they may be distinguished by their unworn teeth, well-furred tails, and subtle differences of pelage.

Shrews have two molts a year, in spring and fall. The summer pelage is brownish dorsally and somewhat paler and grayer ventrally. Following the fall molt, the winter pelage is somewhat darker dorsally and paler ventrally; the spring molt produces the adult summer pelage, which appears somewhat "rougher" and more grizzled than that of juveniles. The ornate shrew shows some geographic variation in color, those populations farther south having somewhat darker ventral fur. In addition, some salt marsh populations are very dark, and the population living around San Francisco Bay is almost black. This phenomenon of "salt marsh melanism" is also known in certain other small shrews. *R. S. Hoffmann*

Size
No significant sexual dimorphism
Total length: 80–110 mm
Length of tail: 28–46 mm
Weight: 2.9–8.7 g

Identification
The ornate shrew is restricted to the Pacific coastal region from California south to southern Baja California, where it is the smallest shrew, except for the vagrant shrew. Both species occur in the San Francisco Bay region; there they can be separated on the basis of tooth characters. Other shrews occurring in the region are much larger and usually have distinctive color patterns or specializations (water shrew, fog shrew, Trowbridge's shrew).

Recent Synonyms
Sorex sinuosus

Other Common Names
Suisun shrew

Status
Formerly common and widespread, and remaining so in some parts of its range, but populations in coastal salt marshes, freshwater swamps and marshes, and the now highly agricultural Central Valley of California have been greatly reduced or eliminated.

Subspecies
Sorex ornatus juncensis, vicinity of San Quitín, northern Baja California, Mexico

Sorex ornatus lagunae, southern tip of Baja California, Mexico
Sorex ornatus ornatus, southern California and northern Baja California, Mexico
Sorex ornatus relictus, vicinity of Buena Vista Lake, Kern County, California
Sorex ornatus salarius, coastal Monterey County, California
Sorex ornatus salicornicus, coastal Los Angeles and adjacent counties, California
Sorex ornatus sinuosus, coastal north San Francisco Bay, California
Sorex ornatus willeti, Santa Catalina Island, California

References
Mammalian Species 212; George, 1988; Rudd, 1955

Pacific shrew | *Sorex pacificus*

Pacific shrews are commonly found in moist areas containing fallen decaying logs and thickets of brushy vegetation, often in association with alder *(Alnus),* salmonberry *(Rubus spectabilis),* or yellow skunk cabbage *(Lysichiton americanum).* An Oregon species, the Pacific shrew usually prefers habitats along streams in shady areas, in moist ditches, and in damp grasses beneath alder thickets.

The Pacific shrew's diet includes slugs and snails, centipedes, amphibians, insect larvae, and a variety of other invertebrates. Other items found in their stomachs include insects such as beetles and flies, ant eggs, and vegetation, including fungi. The internal organs of invertebrates comprised roughly one-third of the total volume of stomach contents.

Pacific shrews are found in association with other species of shrews, including Trowbridge's, fog, montane, and marsh shrews. Other small mammals within the range of this species include northern flying squirrels, deer mice, three species of moles, four species of voles, Townsend's chipmunks, Pacific jumping mice, bushy-tailed woodrats, and Botta's pocket gophers. The Pacific shrew, like other species of shrews, is preyed upon by carnivorous mammals and birds.

Male Pacific shrews are reproductively active primarily from February to August, although sexually mature males may be encountered throughout the year. Females are reproductively active from March to August and bear two to six young per litter; the usual number is four or five.

Three captive individuals were mostly inactive during the day, but awakened periodically to eat food items stored near their nests. During periods of inactivity these shrews used nest boxes or nests they constructed themselves with materials they carried in their mouths. Nests were built of natural materials provided, but wood, string, and paper were not utilized. Nighttime activities were characterized by sudden movements, frequent vocalizations, and constant sniffing of the air.

Captive Pacific shrews were observed to hunt their prey through smell and hearing; terrestrial prey appeared to be located by scent, but flying prey was located by sound and was occasionally caught in flight. When several prey items were

Sorex pacificus

presented to them, the shrews commonly immobilized and stored some but not all; crickets were immobilized by biting at the junction of the head and thorax, beetles by biting near the attachment of the wings, and, on rare occasions, ants were bitten through the thorax. Other prey was eaten where it was encountered. When shrews were not hungry they ignored prey even when it moved near them. They maintained a midden for deposit of excretory material separate from the nest area.

J. E. Maldonado

Size

No significant sexual dimorphism
Total length: 134–154 (143.1) mm
Length of tail: 59–72 (65.5) mm
Weight: 10–18 g

Identification

Sorex pacificus is a large shrew, distinguishable by its pale reddish-brown color. It has five sets of friction pads on the second to fourth digits of the hind feet. It can be differentiated from *Sorex sonomae* by the proturberance on the medial edge of the first upper incisors, more superficial coronoid processes, and a shorter unicuspid tooth row, and from *Sorex bairdi* by its larger size and darker pelage, unicuspids that are longer than wide, and by the shape and position of the protuberance on the medial edge of the first upper incisors.

Recent Synonyms

Sorex vagrans pacificus
Sorex yaquinae

Status

Common, limited

Subspecies

Sorex pacificus cascadensis, northeastern Linn County southward to southern Jackson County, Oregon
Sorex pacificus pacificus, Cascade Head, Tilamook County, Coos County, eastward to Philomath, Benton County, Cottage Grove, Lane County, and northwest of Sutherlin, Douglas County; all in Oregon

References

Mammalian Species 231; Carraway 1990

Water shrew | *Sorex palustris*

Water shrews are aptly named, as they are almost invariably found in the vicinity of streams or other bodies of water. Heavy vegetative cover and plentiful logs, rocks, crevices, or other sources of shelter that offer high humidity and overhead protection are common habitat attributes. Water shrews are typical animals of northern forests or of Canadian or Hudsonian life-zone montane forests to the south. In much of the southern portion of the range, populations are isolated on montane islands, separated from other populations by semi-arid, inhospitable habitat. These populations may have been in contact as recently as 10 to 15 thousand years ago. Fossil water shrews of Pleistocene age have been identified from elevations below 1,300 meters as far south as Trans-Pecos Texas.

The water shrew uses its aquatic habitat to find food and to escape from predators. These shrews readily dive to stream bottoms, paddling furiously to keep from bobbing to the surface. Their fur, full of trapped air, makes them buoyant. Aquatic predators range from trout to garter snakes; water shrews also face predation from hawks, owls, and weasels. The shrews appear even more at home on top of the water, skittering across the surface like water striders (courtesy of air bubbles clinging to the fringes of hair on either side of the feet).

Foraging in water provides food in the form of insect larvae, adult aquatic invertebrates, and even small fish. In addition, much food is gathered from the near-water larder, including terrestrial insects, snails, earthworms, and even appreciable amounts of fungi and green plant material (perhaps ingested accidentally while feeding on other matter). Food frequently is cached, to be retrieved at a later date. The voracious appetites of shrews are legend, and captive animals have been observed eating small meals at about 10-minute intervals during active periods. The daily intake seems to be about 5–10 percent of body weight (about 1 g) per day.

Sorex palustris

Shrews are active throughout the year. Although some activity may occur during daylight hours, they are active primarily at night, particularly shortly after dusk. During inactive phases, when energy husbanding is desirable, self-constructed nests in protected areas are used.

The life of a shrew is not a long one. Their maximum life span is about 18 months. Births occur in spring or summer, and males usually attain sexual maturity the following winter. Rarely, females may be reproductively active during their first summer, but most do not breed until late winter or early spring. Between this time and their death during late summer or fall, they may produce two to three litters of 3 to 10 offspring (average about 6). Gestation is estimated at about 3 weeks.

Sorex alaskanus is considered a subspecies of the water shrew, although some studies have suggested it might be a distinct species. Known only from Glacier Bay, Alaska, it is, on average, slightly smaller than *S. palustris* and has a somewhat more ridged skull. *A. H. Harris*

Size
Males average slightly heavier and longer than females.
Total length: 130–170 (151.4) mm

Length of tail: 57–89 (72.5) mm
Weight: 8–18 (13.8) g

Identification
The water shrew's dorsal pelage is black or black frosted with gray, never distinctly brownish. The hind foot is longer than 18 mm, there

are distinct fringes of stiff hairs on the toes and on the sides of the feet, and the snout is not greatly down-turned.

Other Common Names
American water shrew, northern water shrew

Status
Widespread but captured infrequently

Subspecies
Sorex palustris alaskanus, Glacier Bay, Alaska
Sorex palustris albibarbis, New England and New York to James Bay and central Quebec, eastern Ontario
Sorex palustris brooksi, Vancouver Island
Sorex palustris gloveralleni, Nova Scotia and Cape Breton Island northwest to central Quebec
Sorex palustris hydrobadistes, northeastern Nebraska and central Minnesota east through northern Michigan
Sorex palustris labradorensis, southern Labrador and adjacent Quebec
Sorex palustris navigator, near Anchorage, Alaska, east to northwestern Northwest Territories, south to highlands of south-central California, southern Utah, and northern New Mexico; isolated population in the White Mountains of Arizona
Sorex palustris palustris, central Alberta and Northwest Territories east and south to northern Minnesota and eastern Ontario
Sorex palustris punctulatus, Appalachian Mountains from southern Pennsylvania to just north of Georgia
Sorex palustris turneri, northeastern Quebec

References
Mammalian Species 296; Conaway, 1952

Preble's shrew | *Sorex preblei*

The very small, gray Preble's shrew has been reported from widely separated localities in the western states of Washington, Oregon, California, Idaho, Nevada, Montana, Wyoming, Utah, Colorado, and New Mexico. Additional investigations will probably fill in some of the distributional gaps. Its known elevational range is from 1,280 m in Oregon to 2,750 m in New Mexico. Fossil remains of Preble's shrew have been found in southern New Mexico, over 400 km south of the nearest recent records.

Preble's shrew has a long, pointed snout, small eyes, somewhat conspicuous ears, and plantigrade feet with five toes. The back is grayish and the underside silvery. The tail is bicolored, olive brown above and hazel below, darkening toward the tip. Preble's shrew is among the smallest members of the genus in North America and appears to be most closely related to *Sorex cinereus, S. haydeni,* and *S. longirostris.*

Little is known of the biology and natural history of this uncommon mammal. No published information is available concerning its reproduction, development, or behavior, and there is no published karyotype. Most of these shrews have been collected in arid or semiarid shrub-grass associations or openings in coniferous forest dominated by sagebrush *(Artemisia tridentata).* However, they are known from marsh, wet meadow, and riparian habitats as well. In Washington, they have been found in fir and pine forests, in Utah in wet alkaline habitat with salt grass *(Distichlis),* pickleweed *(Salicornia),* iodine bush *(Allenrolfea),* and greasewood *(Sarcobatus).* The only known Colorado locality was a habitat of Gambel's oak *(Quercus gambelii)* and sparse grass, and the only recent New Mexico site was an open stand of ponderosa pine with an understory of Gambel's oak and grass. Fossils of Preble's shrews have been found only

Sorex preblei

in southern New Mexico, in Dry Cave in Eddy County and U-Bar Cave in Hidalgo County. Both sites date from the late Pleistocene.

Other mammals associated with Preble's shrews include Merriam's, montane, cinereus, Hayden's, dwarf, and vagrant shrews; yellow-pine chipmunks; northern pocket gophers; deer, northern rock, and western harvest mice; and southern red-backed, sagebrush, montane, water, and long-tailed voles.

J. E. Cornely

Size
Total length: 77–95 m
Length of tail: 28–38 mm
Weight: 2.1–4.1 g

Identification
This species is distinguished from closely re-lated shrews with overlapping distribution as follows: from *S. merriami* by the presence of a tine on the first upper incisor, a shorter and narrower skull, a grayish dorsum, and a silvery-colored venter; from *S. cinereus* by a shorter skull; from *S. hayden* by a shorter toothrow; and from other *Sorex* by the third unicuspid being as large as or larger than the fourth and by the foramen magnum, or large opening that allows the spinal cord to attach to the brain, being lower on the back of the skull.

Other Common Names
Malheur shrew

Status
Uncommon

References
Mammalian Species 416; Long and Hoffmann, 1992

Fog shrew | *Sorex sonomae*

This large brown shrew is restricted primarily to the fog belt of the California and Oregon coastlines, thereby giving rise to its common name, the fog shrew. This species is more widely distributed than previously considered; therefore the vernacular name "Sonoma shrew," for Sonoma County, California, is no longer used.

In California, this shrew was trapped in redwood or dense spruce forests, under old logs or stumps in dense chaparral, in marshes, and near muddy stream bottoms. In Oregon, fog shrews were collected within 15 m of a stream in areas dominated by red alder *(Alnus rubra)* in the overstory, with occasional big-leafed maple *(Acer macrophyllum)*, Douglas fir *(Pseudotsuga menziesii)*, western hemlock *(Tsuga heterophylla)*, Sitka spruce *(Picea sitchensis)*, and western red cedar *(Thuja plicata)*. Shrub layer at these sites was dominated by salmonberry *(Rubus spectabilis)* and vine maple *(Acer circinatum)*.

Fog shrews obtain much of their food by foraging on the ground, where a process of random but thorough searching is used to locate food, largely with the help of olfactory and tactile cues. They probe amid vegetation, leaf litter, and surface soil for the invertebrates that constitute the majority of their diet. Among the items found in the stomachs of *S. sonomae* from western Oregon were slugs and snails, centipedes, insects (Coleoptera, Hemiptera, and Diptera), ants (Hymenoptera), ticks, and earthworms.

Fog shrews are found in association with Trowbridge's shrews, Pacific shrews, montane shrews, and marsh shrews. Other small mammals within the range of this species include northern flying squirrels, deer mice, three species of moles, four species of voles, Townsend's chipmunks, Pacific jumping mice, bushy-tailed woodrats, and Botta's pocket gophers.

Investigators of the food habits of carnivorous mammals and raptors within the range of the fog shrew did not distinguish among soricids, but *S. sonomae* was probably included in the diet of some of those predators.

Sorex sonomae

Fog shrews are reproductively active primarily from early spring to late summer. Females have litters that range in size from two to six young.

It is difficult to obtain information on the activity of shrews in the field since most of their movements take place under dense cover and in the dark. However, captive fog shrews have been observed to remain inactive during the day except for brief periods of activity to obtain food. At night the intervals of activity are greater. The fog shrew, like many species of shrews maintained in captivity, will readily hoard prey when presented with surplus food, although the extent to which this occurs in the wild is not known. Grooming was frequently observed in captive shrews. Except when cleaning the urogenital area, it was performed in a crouched position; scratching with a hind foot after stretching the skin by bowing the body to spread the hairs was the usual mode of grooming. The face was cleaned by licking the forefeet and rubbing them over the face. The tail was held by the forefeet and cleaned in the mouth. The urogenital area was cleaned by licking while the shrews lay on their sides; they spent a few moments licking up fluid from the everted rectum. This activity, known as refection, has been likened to the coprophagous feeding habits of rabbits and, although shrews do not appear actually to eat their feces, refection may have a similar function in helping to extract further nutrients from food. *J. E. Maldonado*

Size
No significant sexual dimorphism
Total length: 105–180 (137.25) mm
Length of tail: 36–85 (60.75) mm
Weight: 5.5–15 g

Identification
Sorex sonomae is the largest of the Pacific Coast brown shrews. In adults the dorsal pelage is dark grayish-brown. *S. sonomae* is distinguished from *Sorex pacificus* by the absence of medial projections on the edge of the first upper incisors. It has a broad and deep coronoid process and the unicuspids are large and robust.

There are four pairs of digital friction pads on the second to fourth toes of the hind feet.

Recent Synonyms
Sorex pacificus sonomae
Sorex vagrans sonomae

Other Common Names
Sonoma shrew

Status
Common, limited

Subspecies
Sorex sonomae sonomae, Pacific coast from Newport, Lincoln County, east to Corvallis, Ben-

ton County, Oregon, and then southward to Crescent City, Del Norte County, and Inverness, Marin County, California
Sorex sonomae tenelliodus, Oregon from Taft and Newport, Lincoln County, southeastward to Coberg Hills, Lane County, and Eastern Linn County, and then southward on the west slope of the Cascade Mountains to Hilt, Siskiyou County, California

References
Mammalian Species 231; Carraway, 1990

Inyo shrew | *Sorex tenellus*

The Inyo shrew is so similar to the dwarf shrew that the mammalogist who described both, C. Hart Merriam, considered them to be subspecies of the same species. Because of this, the Inyo shrew is sometimes called the Great Basin dwarf shrew, to distinguish it from *Sorex nanus,* the Rocky Mountain dwarf shrew. Although both species occur in the southwestern United States, their ranges are not known to overlap or come into contact. The Inyo shrew is slightly larger than the dwarf shrew and has a relatively longer tail. Moreover, the Inyo shrew is paler and grayer in color both dorsally and ventrally, particularly in winter pelage. As in other small shrews, there are two molts, to summer pelage in mid- to late July, and back to winter pelage probably in October.

Like the dwarf shrew, the Inyo shrew is primarily montane in its distribution, occurring above 2,300 meters. Its general distribution, in the arid mountain ranges of the southern Great Basin and westward along the arid eastern slope of the Sierra Nevada, suggests that this shrew, like the dwarf shrew, may be tolerant of relatively arid situations. One specimen from south-

Sorex tenellus

ern Nevada appears to have come from a semi-arid shrub steppe. However, most of the few dwarf shrews that have been captured were trapped in shaded, moist micro-habitats such as along the bottoms of canyons and the bases of cliffs. Until recently the Inyo shrew was known from only four localities. It has now been discovered to occur not only on the arid eastern slope, but also on the moist western slope of the Sierra Nevada, as well as in the Sweetwater Mountains. In both of these newly-discovered localities, Inyo shrews occur with such other mesic shrews as the Mt. Lyell shrew, the vagrant shrew, the montane shrew, Trowbridge's, and the water shrew. Like dwarf shrews, Inyo shrews are difficult to trap because of their small size. The shrews caught in these new localities were trapped with pitfalls. More extensive use of this device might extend the known range of the Inyo shrew.

Because this species is so poorly known, virtually nothing is known of its reproduction, ecology, or behavior. Evolutionary relationships with its two similar, more common neighboring species, the dwarf shrew to the east and the ornate shrew to the west, are equally obscure. Ornate and Inyo shrews, although both occurring on the western slope of the Sierra Nevada, are elevationally separated and are not known to come into contact or overlap, although the distance between them is not great. The closest known localities of occurrence of the Inyo shrew and the dwarf shrew are nearly 300 miles apart, but the intervening area has been poorly surveyed, and pitfall trapping there might extend the range of either or both species. This is of particular interest since the Inyo shrew appears to be intermediate in size and form between the somewhat larger ornate shrew and the smaller dwarf shrew. It is possible that all three may form a single, variable, hybridizing species, but until much more is known about them it is preferable to retain them as separate species. *R. S. Hoffmann*

Size
No significant sexual dimorphism
Total length: 85–103 mm
Length of tail: 36–48 mm
Weight: 3.4–4.1 g

Identification
The Inyo shrew is restricted to a limited area in southern and western Nevada and eastern California; all but one record, from the western slope of the Sierra Nevada, are within the arid Great Basin. Here, this small shrew can be distinguished from the even smaller Preble's shrew by its third upper unicuspid tooth, which is smaller than either the second or fourth unicuspids. Preble's shrew has a third unicuspid smaller than the second, but larger than the fourth. In the Sweetwater Mountains, an eastern extension of the Sierra Nevada, the Inyo shrew occurs with the somewhat larger Mt. Lyell shrew. This shrew has the same upper unicuspid pattern as Preble's shrew. The vagrant shrew, which resembles the Inyo shrew in tooth pattern, also occurs there. Vagrant and Inyo shrews are differentiated on the basis of the pigmentation pattern on the anterior face of the upper incisor teeth. On the western slope of the Sierra Nevada, the Inyo shrew has been found in high elevation red fir forest, together with the much larger water shrew and Trowbridge's shrew. Also occurring there are montane shrews, which are generally larger than the Inyo shrew, and have darker dorsal pelage.

Recent Synonyms
Sorex myops

Other Common Names
Great Basin dwarf shrew

Status
Local, often rare

References
Burt, 1934; Hall, 1946; Williams, 1991

Trowbridge's shrew | *Sorex trowbridgii*

Sorex trowbridgii is found from coastal southwestern British Columbia through western Washington and Oregon, and south through the coast ranges of California to Santa Barbara. It also occurs in the mountains ringing the Sacramento and San Joaquin valleys of Calfornia south to Santa Barbara, and along the western slope of the Sierra Nevada to Kern County. Common characteristics of the preferred habitat throughout the range of the species are a relatively thick organic layer, low water table, and a large amount of ground cover or canopy. In Washington and Oregon, *S. trowbridgii* tends to occur in uncut, mature forest with abundant ground litter or in riparian (but not stream-side) habitat. On Destruction Island, Trowbridge's

Sorex trowbridgii

tends to be found in surface debris (*S. trowbridgii* burrows in deeper, organic layers of soil), whereas *S. vagrans,* a nonburrower, is displaced by *S. trowbridgii* in drier, more friable soils. In wet, mossy, "shrewy" habitats such as ravine bottoms in the Cascade Mountains, *S. vagrans* tends to displace *S. trowbridgii*. *Sorex trowbridgii* also is often found in loose association with the water shrew and the marsh shrew, *S. palustris* and *S. bendirii*. In the habitats it prefers, *S. trowbridgii* is usually the most common shrew.

Sorex trowbridgii tends to be active in one-hour cycles that consist of short bursts at regular intervals followed by quiescent periods. Activity is greatest at night, though individuals are active at all times. Activity also is correlated with breeding status: breeding individuals are more active than nonbreeding individuals.

The breeding season in the northern part of the range is from March to May, and in the southern part of the range, from February to June. Females tend to mature about two weeks earlier than males. The onset of sexual maturity is accompanied by a significant increase in weight. Approximately 12 percent of females breed twice during a season. The gestation period and age at weaning are not known, but litter size is three to six.

Eighteen months is probably the maximum life span of *Sorex trowbridgii,* as most adults that survive a winter disappear early the following spring. All over-wintering adults have disappeared by the following November. Populations in the autumn are usually double the size of spring populations because of the high spring and summer recruitment.

There are two seasonal molts each year. All animals molt in the autumn, sometime between August and November, to a

shrews are found in grass and tall brush. In California, they are found most commonly in drier woods such as Ponderosa pine, mixed conifer and red fir forests, or, at the southern end of the range, in moist canyon bottoms and even under chaparral.

Some of this variability in habitat preference may be the result of complex relationships with other shrew species sharing the same habitat. Trowbridge's shrews are strong burrowers, stronger than either *Sorex monticolus* or *S. vagrans*. *S. monticolus* thicker, longer, grayer, and paler coat. Some molt again, to a brown summer coat, sometime between April and August. Juveniles are more brownish than adults before molting to their adult coat. The tail is hairy in young animals and becomes naked as they age; the ears are almost hidden by the pelage. The teeth of *S. trowbridgii* are pigmented a dark reddish-brown, as are the teeth of some other members of the genus.

Trowbridge's shrews tend to be generalists with respect to diet. They eat insects, arachnids, worms, molluscs, conifer seeds, and fungi. Plant material can comprise up to 60 percent of the diet, and hoarding of seeds has been observed. Predators include owls and Pacific giant salamanders; domestic cats will kill shrews but usually refuse to eat them.

Only one fossil has been described, from a late Pleistocene "tar pit" at Carpinteria, California, at the southern end of the species' current range. Based on protein data, it is thought that the species may date from the Pliocene. However, there are few terrestrial fossil deposits within the range of the species dating from the Pliocene and Pleistocene, so the potential for finding additional fossils seems low. *S. B. George*

Size
No significant sexual dimorphism
Total length: 104–124 (113) mm (British Columbia); 114–131 (122.5) mm (California)
Length of tail: 50–59 mm (British Columbia); 48–56 (52) mm (California)
Weight: 3.8 g (nonbreeding); 5 g (breeding)

Identification
This shrew can be distinguished by its nearly uniform dark gray fur, whitish feet, and a tail that is paler on the underside. *Sorex trowbridgii* is the only shrew in its range that does not have a belly significantly paler than the back but has a strongly bicolored tail.

Recent Synonyms
Sorex montereyensis

Status
Common

Subspecies
Sorex trowbridgii destructioni, Destruction Island, Washington
Sorex trowbridgii humboldtensis, northern California in the vicinity of Humboldt Bay
Sorex trowbridgii mariposae, Sierra Nevada in California through Cascades in southern Oregon
Sorex trowbridgii montereyensis, central California coast
Sorex trowbridgii trowbridgii, southwestern British Columbia to the Klamath Mountains of northern California

References
Mammalian Species 337; Maser et al., 1981; van Zyll de Jong, 1983

Tundra shrew | *Sorex tundrensis*

This distinctively marked shrew is found only in Alaska, including Kodiak Island, and extreme northwestern Canada Its nearest relatives live in Siberia and have a similar appearance, but there are significant differences in the chromosomes of the Eurasian and North American species. The evidence suggests that the ancestor of the tundra shrew entered North America from Asia during the last Ice Age, when Alaska and Siberia were connected. The tundra shrew inhabits the dense vegetation composed of grasses, shrubs, and dwarf trees such as alder, dwarf birch, and dwarf willow that grow on hillsides and other well-drained sites.

Little is known about the habits of this shrew, but they are probably not very different from those of other species of shrews.

The tundra shrew is strikingly patterned. In summer the pelage is distinctly tricolored: dark brown on the back, pale-brown or brownish-gray on the sides, and pale-grayish on the underparts. In winter the pelage is longer and bicolored, with the sides and underparts grayish and the back brown. The winter fur molts in April and May, continuing into June. Winter fur begins to grow in late August to September and the molt is complete by November.

Sorex tundrensis

Little is known about the breeding biology of this species. Pregnant females have been recorded in June, July, and September. Males in breeding condition are common in summer, but their numbers decrease rapidly as fall approaches. This suggests a breeding season from spring (May) to late summer or fall (September). The number of young in a litter is not known, but embryo counts in a small sample of pregnant females ranged from 8 to 12 and averaged 10. A female probably produces several litters in a season. There is also little information on food habits. Insects, earthworms, and the floral parts of a small grass were found in the digestive tracts of some shrews from Alaska. *C. G. van Zyll de Jong*

Size
No significant sexual dimorphism
Total length: 83–120 (94.9) mm
Length of tail: 22–36 (28.6) mm
Weight: 5–10 g

Identification
The tundra shrew can be distinguished from other shrews in its range, except *Sorex ugyunak,* by its distinct coloration (brown back contrasting with pale brown or grayish sides). *Sorex arcticus,* found in the boreal forest to the east and south, is similarly patterned, but has a darker, blackish back and a longer tail. *Sorex ugyunak* is smaller than *S. tundrensis.*

Recent Synonyms
Sorex arcticus tundrensis

Status
Common, limited

References
van Zyll de Jong, 1983

Barren ground shrew | *Sorex ugyunak*

The barren ground shrew occurs on the vast tundra that stretches from the western shore of Hudson Bay to Point Barrow in Alaska. Similar-looking and closely related shrews, *Sorex hydrodromus* and *Sorex jacksoni,* live on St. Paul and St. Lawrence islands in the Bering Sea and in eastern Siberia. These shrews probably evolved from an ancestor closely related to *Sorex cinereus* that became isolated during the last glaciation in Beringia, a region comprising present day Yukon, Alaska, and eastern Siberia.

The barren ground shrew is small and distinctively colored, with pale underside and sides. Its brown back forms a well-defined dorsal stripe. Its tail is pale brown above; below it is whitish, with the terminal tuft pale buff to light brown. In summer (June–September) the fur is short, brown on the back and buffy on the sides and belly. Juveniles are somewhat darker than adults and the demarcation between dark back and pale sides is less distinct. The winter pelage (October–May) is much longer, brownish on the back, and gray on the sides and underparts.

We know nothing of the life history of this species. It appears to favor low sedge-grass meadows and thickets of dwarf willow and birch. *C. G. van Zyll de Jong*

Sorex ugyunak

Size
No significant sexual dimorphism
Total length: 74–103 (82) mm
Length of tail: 22–31 (26) mm
Weight: 2.9–5.2 (3.6) g

Identification
The barren ground shrew is distinguished from *Sorex cinereus,* the only shrew of similar size in its range, by the pale color of the underside extending far up on the sides and by the distinct demarcation between the dark fur on the back and the pale fur on the sides. *Sorex tundrensis,* which has a similar color pattern, is much larger.

Status
Widespread north of treeline; abundance appears to fluctuate over time

References
van Zyll de Jong, 1983

Vagrant shrew | *Sorex vagrans*

Vagrant shrews live in moist habitats throughout their range. They are often common in lakeside or streamside communities of sedges, grasses, and willows, and in coastal salt marshes. They also occur in mesic forests. In southern British Columbia, where *S. vagrans* and *S. monticolus* occur in the same forests, *S. vagrans* is most often found in moister soils supporting western red cedar, red alder, vine maple, and sword fern, whereas *S. monticolus* occupies drier sites supporting western hemlock and moss.

Vagrant shrews construct globular nests of plant material that are used as shelters, and wherein the young are born. Females bear litters of 1–9 young in spring. There is a postpartum estrus, and an individual animal may bear up to three litters a year. Newborn young weigh about half a gram, have their eyes closed, and are hairless. The youngsters develop rapidly, are weaned in about three weeks, and reach 5–6 g in about a month, after which their weight drops to 4–5 g. They stay at this weight until late winter, at which time an increase to 7–8 g accompanies the onset of reproductive readiness. The maximum life span is about 16 months. By autumn most animals in the population are 3–6 months old, having been born that spring.

Young shrews quickly settle into an exclusive home range of about 0.1 to 0.2 hectares. With the approach of the breeding season the home range increases to as much as 0.5 hectares or more.

The vagrant shrew's food consists chiefly of invertebrates, but some plant material is consumed as well. Much foraging is done during the day. Other kinds of *Sorex* are known to follow learned paths to cover their foraging areas, and like some other shrews, *S. vagrans* uses high frequency vocalizations (echolocation) to orient itself. Some shrews possess toxic saliva, but this has not been shown for *S. vagrans*. *J. S. Findley*

Sorex vagrans

Size

No significant sexual dimorphism
Total length: 100–115 (107) mm
Tail length: 38–48 (43) mm
Weight: about 3–8 g, depending on age and
    reproductive condition

Identification

Most American shrews of the genus *Sorex* are superficially similar, being very small, brownish or grayish, mouse-like mammals with minute eyes, short ears, and a long, flexible, pointed snout. Distinguishing between the species usually requires examination of the skull and teeth under magnification. *Sorex vagrans* is identified as a member of the subgenus *Otisorex* because it lacks a postmandibu-

lar foramen (a tiny hole on the inside of each jaw bone, toward the rear), and has a medially-directed, pigmented ridge running from the apex of each unicuspid tooth, usually ending in a pigmented cusplet. Among *Otisorex* shrews, *S. vagrans* is unique in possessing small, pigmented medial tines on each upper incisor that are usually separated from the pigmented tips of the incisors by a pale-colored or white line; the upper level of the pigment of the incisors is usually at or below the top of the pigment of the medial tines. This character can be seen with a 10X hand lens on an intact shrew, and is thus a reasonable field mark. Other shrews occurring in the range of *S. vagrans* either lack the medial tine on the incisors or have one that is enclosed within the pigmented portion of

the tooth with the pigment of tine and tooth-tip continuous. The third unicuspid tooth is generally seen to be smaller than the fourth when the upper tooth-row is viewed laterally with a hand lens. The above notwithstanding, in southwestern British Columbia and Vancouver Island, where *S. vagrans* and *S. monticolus* occur together, there is sufficient variation in the configuration of the incisor tines to cause some confusion. However, in this region *S. monticolus* is absolutely larger than *S. vagrans* in several skull measurements, and breeding males of the two species are said to have distinctively different odors.

Recent Synonyms

Sorex trigonirostris

From 1955 until 1977 *Sorex monticolus* (then known as *S. obscurus*) and its subspecies were considered to belong to the species *S. vagrans*, as was *Sorex pacificus*.

Other Common Names
Wandering shrew

Status
Abundant

Subspecies
Sorex vagrans halicoetes, southern San Francisco Bay and the Monterey Bay region
Sorex vagrans orizabae, transverse volcanic belt of Mexico
Sorex vagrans paludivagus, Monterey Bay north to San Gregorio, California
Sorex vagrans vagrans, Pacific northwest to southern British Columbia and Vancouver Island, south to San Francisco Bay, east

across the Great Basin and Columbia Plateau to western Montana, Idaho, and northern Utah. *Sorex vagrans vancouverensis* is considered inseparable from *Sorex vagrans vagrans*.

References
Buchler, 1976; Carraway, 1990; George and Smith, 1991; Junge and Hoffmann, 1981

Northern short-tailed shrew | *Blarina brevicauda*

Northern short-tailed shrews occur throughout much of the north-central and northeastern United States and the southern regions of adjacent Canadian provinces. In southern Iowa, northern Missouri, northeastern Kansas, and the Ozarks of Missouri and Arkansas, the range of *Blarina brevicauda* overlaps with *B. hylophaga*, but the former can be distinguished by its slightly larger size and by its distinctive karyotype. Individuals of the two western subspecies, *B. b. brevicauda* and *B. b. manitobensis*, are significantly larger than individuals of the eastern subspecies.

Blarina brevicauda is found in areas with good cover, which may be tall, dense grass in the western portion of its range or deep woods with thick ground litter in the east. It is semifossorial, foraging for invertebrates through burrows in leaf litter or fallen grass or herbs, generally within 10 cm (5 inches) of the surface. Digging generally is done with the front feet and the dirt is kicked out of the tunnel with the hind feet. The tunnels of this shrew can literally honeycomb an area. Nests are underground and often lined with vegetation or even fur.

Although northern short-tailed shrews are rarely found on the surface, it has been noted that they are more active on cloudy days than on sunny or rainy days. Because of its high energy requirements, *Blarina brevicauda* is active for short periods (average 4.5 minutes) separated by periods of inactivity (average 24 minutes). There is a distinct tendency for these shrews to be more active in the early morning. *Blarina brevicauda* does not hibernate.

The saliva of *Blarina brevicauda* is poisonous, and is both a neurotoxin and hemotoxin, much as is snake venom. Short-tailed shrews cannot inject the poison; rather it is "chewed" into a wound and is used to subdue and kill mice and other larger prey. It also is used to paralyze invertebrates such as snails; the prey is then cached and the shrews return repeatedly to the cache to consume the relatively fresh food and replenish

Blarina brevicauda

their supply. This behavior is most common in winter but has been observed in summer when there has been a sudden abundance of prey.

Northern short-tailed shrews are generally solitary. Once the young are weaned, all maternal behavior ceases and the young separate from the mother. The degree of sociability of *Blarina brevicauda* is highly variable, however; males and older individuals tend to be less sociable than females and younger individuals.

Density of shrew populations varies from year to year (from extremes of 1.6 per hectare to 121 per hectare) and populations occasionally even crash, requiring several years to recover. Winter mortality can reach as high as 90 percent, and is thought to be related to cold stress. Individuals avoid areas with little cover and those with extremes of temperature and moisture. Home ranges average about 2.5 hectares, and individuals' ranges overlap. Northern short-tailed shrews are not thought to be territorial. They possess a repertoire of behavioral patterns and postures that are probably used in species recognition, thus minimizing the amount of energy wasted in competition for food, space, and social position.

Invertebrates (earthworms, millipedes, insects, arachnids, molluscs) make up the majority of the diet of *Blarina brevicauda,* but a variety of vertebrates and even plants and fungi are eaten as well. Northern short-tailed shrews eat an average of half their weight daily, with significantly more (43 percent) food required in the winter than in the summer. They require a great deal of free water because of their high evaporative water loss, but are capable of deriving some metabolic water from the oxidation of food.

There are a variety of predators of *B. brevicauda,* owls being the most common. Many mammalian predators will not consume shrews they have killed because of their musky odor and (presumably) taste. Northern short-tailed shrews have scent glands on their flanks and belly that produce a strong odor. The size and musk production of the glands varies with the sex and reproductive status of the individual; breeding males have the largest and most productive glands. It is thought that the musk is produced as a defense mechanism when individuals are stressed rather than as an attractant or to mark territories, as the northern short-tailed shrew has a poorly developed sense of smell.

Blarina brevicauda uses ultrasonic "clicks" (echolocation) to detect objects and openings and even to distinguish among materials blocking openings. Its vision is probably limited to the perception of light.

The breeding season lasts from early February to September, and females enter estrus before males enter breeding condition. During copulation, the shrews are locked together for about 5 minutes; the female usually is active and drags the inactive male behind her. At least six matings per day are required to induce ovulation. There are two peaks of breeding, one in spring and a second in late summer or early autumn. Gestation lasts 21 or 22 days and litters usually consist of 4 to 7 young. The neonates are are dark pink, "honeybee size," and have closed eyes and ears; they are hairless except for 1-mm-long whiskers. After 25 days, the young are weaned, and females can breed as early as 47 days of age. Spring young tend to mature more rapidly than autumn young and may breed in late summer or autumn. Although *B. brevicauda* may live up to 30 months, generally only 11 percent live more than a year. Only 73 percent of young survive to weaning, and thus average survival is about 4.5 months.

The molt from summer to winter pelage occurs in October and November and moves in a tail-to-head direction. The spring molt can occur at any time between February and July; in females it proceeds in a head-to-tail direction, and in males it is irregular. The winter pelage is long (for shrews) and mole-like. Summer pelage is short and slightly paler. The teeth are pigmented to a deep chestnut color from iron deposits; it is thought that this deposit confers some degree of protection from wear to the teeth, which are subjected to a diet that contains a lot of grit.

The genus *Blarina* has a rich fossil record and *B. brevicauda* first appeared in the middle or late Pliocene. It is considered to be the ancestor of its southern relatives, *B. carolinensis* and *B. hylophaga,* which diverged in isolation during the middle and late Pleistocene, respectively. The southern species are distinguished from *B. brevicauda* most strongly by chromosomal differences (*B. brevicauda:* 2N=48–50, due to a polymorphic Robertsonian fusion, FN=48; *B. carolinensis:* 2N=37–46, due to polymorphic Robertsonian fusions, FN=44, 45, due to a polymorphic loss of chromosomal arms; *B. hylophaga:* 2N=52, FN=60–62, due to polymorphic loss of chromosomal arms). The large western forms of *B. brevicauda (B. b. brevicauda* and *B. b. manitobensis)* can be distinguished from the smaller eastern forms (all other subspecies) in the fossil record in the early Pleistocene. However, no chromosomal differences have been established and thus the two forms are considered to be "semi-species" by some paleontologists. *S. B. George*

Size

Males are sometimes slightly larger than females

Total length: 118–139 mm (northern Great Plains); 95–126 (113) mm (Indiana)

Length of tail: 23–32 mm (northern Great Plains); 17–28 (23) mm (Indiana)

Weight: 18–30 g (northern Great Plains); 11–26 (17) g (Indiana)

Identification

This shrew is distinguished by nearly uniform silver to black fur, often with brown tips on the hairs; it is significantly larger and has a relatively shorter tail than other shrews in its range.

Recent Synonyms
Blarina telmalestes

Other Common Names
Short-tailed shrew, mole shrew

Status
Common

Subspecies
Blarina brevicauda aloga, Martha's Vineyard, Massachusetts

Blarina brevicauda angusta, Gaspé Peninsula and northern New Brunswick, Canada
Blarina brevicauda brevicauda, northern Great Plains of the United States
Blarina brevicauda churchi, Appalachian Mountains
Blarina brevicauda compacta, Nantucket Island, Massachusetts
Blarina brevicauda hooperi, Green Mountains, Vermont
Blarina brevicauda kirtlandi, Pennsylvania south to northern Georgia and west to eastern Wisconsin

Blarina brevicauda manitobensis, southern Saskatchewan and Manitoba
Blarina brevicauda pallida, northern Maine to Nova Scotia
Blarina brevicauda talpoides, southeastern Ontario, southern Quebec, southern Maine south to New Jersey
Blarina brevicauda telmalestes, southeastern Virginia, northeastern North Carolina

References
Mammalian Species 261; Jackson, 1961

Southern short-tailed shrew | *Blarina carolinensis*

Prior to the late 1970s, all short-tailed shrews were considered one species, *Blarina brevicauda*. Currently three, and possibly four, species are recognized, based upon morphological and chromosomal differences. Much of the information in the literature pertaining to this species is still found under the name *B. brevicauda*.

The southern short-tailed shrew is a highly active predator that occupies a crescent-shaped geographic range through the southeastern United States from southern Illinois to south-central Virginia. The northernmost record in Illinois is a speci-

men from near Wilsonville in southern Macoupin County. The distribution of the species is south of a line from this locality through Wayne County. Southward the distribution of *B. carolinensis* is confined primarily to the lowlands along the Mississippi River and its major tributaries. In Kentucky the southern short-tailed shrew occurs west of the Tennessee River, and in Tennessee the contact zone with *B. brevicauda* is slightly to the east of the Tennessee River. In Missouri the species is definitely known only from the Mississippi lowlands in the boot-heel area. The range of the species then expands to

Blarina carolinensis

captured in dry grassy upland fields, weedy fields, *Lespedeza* fields, palmetto groves, and honeysuckle thickets. Because they spend substantial amounts of time underground, southern short-tailed shrews avoid poorly drained sites, which usually have saturated soils. There is good evidence that these shrews are more active during and immediately following rainy periods. *B. carolinensis* is often abundant in good habitats; densities of 6.1 to 16.2 individuals per hectare have been found in Tennessee and South Carolina. An estimate of minimum home range size of this species along the Savannah River in South Carolina was 0.959 hectare.

The nests of these shrews are composed of shredded grass, roots, dry leaves, and other vegetable fibers. Some nests reach 15 to 20 centimeters in diameter. These nests may be located under decaying logs and stumps or in burrows that may reach a depth of 35 centimeters.

Southern short-tailed shrews feed on a variety of soil invertebrates. They are not known to feed on small vertebrates, as does the northern short-tailed shrew, and the experiment to test for venom as is found in their northern cousins has not been performed. In western Tennessee, this species was found to be feeding on land snails, true bugs, lepidoptera larvae, both adult and larval beetles, and ants. Adult and larval beetles appeared to be the most commonly taken food items, being found in nearly 60 percent of the stomachs examined. Several authors have mentioned earthworms as a common food item of these shrews, but this statement does not seem to have been confirmed by actual dietary studies.

Like most small mammals, southern short-tailed shrews are important prey items for a variety of other animals. Raptors, including several species of hawks and owls, seem to be the most common predators; this shrew is one of the principal food items of the barn owl. Some mammals, such as the coyote and red fox, take these shrews in low numbers, as do some of the large snakes, including the cottonmouth moccasin, black rat snake, and copperhead. Some predators may not eat large numbers of short-tailed shrews due to their unpleasant odor.

In South Carolina, where the most extensive study of reproduction of this species has been undertaken, a distinctly bimodal yearly reproductive cycle was documented. Pregnant females were found from March through June with a peak in April and again from September through November with a peak in October. Litter size varied from 2 to 6 young, with a mean of 4.

There are at least three species of short-tailed shrews, which are essentially identical in external appearance except for size. Generally the southern short-tailed shrew is the smallest of the three, but all three species show size variation throughout their geographic ranges, so size alone cannot be used to separate them. Little overlap in their geographic ranges has been

include all but northwestern Arkansas, one locality in extreme southeastern Oklahoma, the eastern quarter of Texas, and most of Louisiana, Mississippi, and Alabama. In Florida, the southern short-tailed shrew definitely occupies the northern half of the peninsula, but the relationship with the taxon *peninsulae* in the southern half of the peninsula is unclear at the present time. The boundary of distribution between northern and southern short-tailed shrews in Georgia is still unclear. Specimens from the southern half of the state, below the Fall Line, are southern short-tailed shrews, and those from the southern limit of the Appalachian Mountains, in northern Georgia, are northern short-tailed shrews, but the populations on the intervening Piedmont Plateau need additional study. The southern short-tailed shrew occupies the Piedmont Plateau and coastal plain in South and North Carolina, extending to south-central and portions of eastern Virginia. The northern limit of contiguous populations of the species appears to be along the Appomattox River to the north and west of Chesterfield Court House, Chesterfield County, although there appear to be isolated populations farther to the north on the islands and peninsulas along the eastern shore of Chesapeake Bay.

Like most small mammals, the southern short-tailed shrew is primarily nocturnal. It is a habitat generalist, but tends to be most abundant in moist habitats, especially well-drained sites dominated by hardwoods. These areas offer deep vegetative ground litter that makes easy burrowing and harbors food items. Pine stands also appear to be relatively good habitat. These shrews are frequently taken in association with fallen logs or heavy pieces of bark. Less frequently they have been documented, so one of the easiest ways to identify a species is to know where it came from. Experts rely on counting chromosomes: populations of the southern short-tailed shrew have between 36 and 46 chromosomes, as compared with the northern short-tailed shrew, which possesses 48 to 50, and Elliot's short-tailed shrew, which has 52. Populations of shrews in the southern half of Florida have 50 to 52 chromosomes. These southern peninsular populations are morphologically quite distinct from both northern and Elliot's short-tailed shrews, and they are geographically in contact only with the southern short-tailed shrew, which is quite distinct in its chromosome numbers. Therefore, some experts believe that populations in south Florida represent a distinct species—the Everglades short-tailed shrew. *H. H. Genoways and R. A. Benedict*

Size
No significant sexual dimorphism
Total length: 72–107 (90) mm
Length of tail: 12–26 (18.7) mm
Weight: 5.5–13 g

Identification
Blarina carolinensis is the smallest member of the genus *Blarina*. Areas of overlap in members of the genus are extremely limited, so geographic location is an excellent way to identify species. Where it is found in contact with other *Blarina*, *B. carolinensis* is usually obviously smaller than *B. brevicauda* and slightly but noticeably smaller than *B. hylophaga*. For positive identification the number of chromosomes must be known. In *B. carolinensis* the chromosome count varies from 36 to 46.

Recent Synonyms
Blarina brevicauda

Status
Locally common, occurring in most available habitats

Subspecies
Blarina carolinensis carolinensis, Atlantic coastal states from southern Virginia south through the northern half of the Florida peninsula and west into most of Alabama and Mississippi
Blarina carolinensis minimia, extreme western Mississippi, all of Louisiana, eastern Texas, one locality in southeastern Oklahoma, the southeastern three quarters of Arkansas, extreme southeastern Missouri, and Tennessee west of the Tennessee River
Blarina carolinensis peninsulae, southern half of the Florida peninsula (may represent a distinct species)

References
George et al., 1982; Hoffmeister, 1989

Elliot's short-tailed shrew | *Blarina hylophaga*

Elliot's short-tailed shrews occur throughout much of the central Great Plains from west of the Mississippi floodplain to western Kansas. An isolated population appears to live in Aransas County, Texas. *Blarina hylophaga* is best distinguished from its congeners by karyotype (see the species account for *Blarina brevicauda),* but where it overlaps with *B. brevicauda, B. hylophaga* is slightly smaller, and where it overlaps with *B. carolinensis, B. hylophaga* is slightly larger. Individuals in the isolated population in Aransas County, Texas, which has tentatively been called *B. hylophaga plumbea,* are larger than those in surrounding populations. The identification of this isolated population has not yet been confirmed by karyotypic data.

Blarina hylophaga has only recently been recognized as a species distinct from *B. carolinensis* and *B. brevicauda.* It is found in moist areas with good cover, most commonly tall, dense grass in ditches, riparian habitats, and along roadsides, habitat similar to that preferred by western populations of *Blarina brevicauda.*

Invertebrates, including earthworms, insects, and other arthropods, make up the bulk of the diet of Elliot's short-tailed shrew. It also feeds on small mammals, amphibians, and rep-

tiles when the opportunity arises. *Blarina hylophaga* has submaxillary glands that produce venomous saliva, which probably has the same structure and function as the venom of other *Blarina* species. Owls are a significant predator on *Blarina hylophaga,* but because of its abdominal musk glands, it has few mammalian predators.

Elliot's short-tailed shrew is thought to be very similar to other species of short-tailed shrews in its habits. It is semi-fossorial, using tunnels of other animals or rooting in leaf litter on its own. It does not hibernate, and has been captured year-round. Population size varies widely from year to year, and it is thought that the western edge of the species' range fluctuates from year to year, particularly after very cold winters with little snow cover, when populations have been noted to crash. Individuals are solitary in nature, but are not thought to be territorial.

Elliot's short-tailed shrews breed as early as February and as late as September. One or two litters are produced annually; after a three-week gestation period, a litter of six to seven young (on average) is born. Young are extremely altricial, but grow rapidly, reaching adult size at approximately one month after birth. At this point they are weaned and leave the nest. The average life span is eight months, with few individuals living through two winters.

Fossils of *B. hylophaga* are known from the very latest Pleistocene of Missouri and Texas.   *S. B. George*

Blarina hylophaga

Size
Males are sometimes slightly larger than
  females
Total length: 92–121 mm
Length of tail: 19–25 mm
Weight: 13–16 g

Identification
Distinguished by nearly uniform brownish-gray fur, often with brown tips on hairs; larger

and with a relatively shorter tail than other shrews in its range.

Recent Synonyms
Blarina brevicauda
Blarina carolinensis

Status
Common in the northern part of its range, uncommon to the south

Subspecies
Blarina hylophaga hylophaga, northwestern
  Louisiana to southwestern Iowa, west
  across southern Nebraska and south to
  south-central Oklahoma
Blarina hylophaga plumbea, Aransas County,
  Texas

References
Schmidly, 1983

Least shrew | *Cryptotis parva*

The least shrew occurs in grassy, weedy, and brushy fields in the northern part of its range, but has been found in marshes on the East Coast and is found in a greater variety of habitats, including wooded habitats, in the south. In Florida it lives in marshy areas among cabbage palms and in pine woods as well as in dry fields.

Most shrews are solitary and presumably intolerant of one another. However, there are records of several individuals of this species occupying the same nest. Twelve and at least 31 individuals were reported in two nests in Texas, and 25 in a nest in Virginia.

Nests are of leaves or grasses in some hidden place, such as on the ground under a cabbage palm leaf or in brush. Least

shrews have a repertoire of tiny calls, audible to human ears up to a distance of only 20 inches or so.

Least shrews eat caterpillars and other insect larvae, slugs, snails, spiders, crickets, and other insects. This species has been reported in captivity to eat more than its own weight in food in a 24-hour period. The shrews subdue crickets and grasshoppers by biting them in the head. Only the internal organs of larger insects are eaten, and excess insects are stored in the burrow. This species has been called the bee shrew because of its supposed habit of entering beehives. However, I could not find beekeepers in Indiana who had ever heard of this, although *Peromyscus* frequently nests in beehives in the winter.

Least shrews produce young from March to November in

Cryptotis parva

the north, but reproduction may occur throughout the winter in the south. Litters, consisting of two to seven young (averaging about 5), are born after a gestation of 21 to 23 days. A litter of six young found in a nest in Kentucky in mid-April weighed 17.5 g, whereas the female weighed but 5.4 g. The combined weight of six newborn shrews found in Virginia did not exceed 2 g. These neonates were 22 mm long, with tails 3 mm long and hind feet that measured 2.5 mm. Young are weaned at about three weeks.

Owls appear to be a chief predator on this species, and least shrews often make up a large percentage of their food. For example, 171 least shrew skulls comprised 41 percent of the remains of prey found in the pellets of barn owls in Texas. Hawks, snakes, and many predatory mammals also prey on least shrews. One species of flea and four species of mites were the most abundant ectoparasites on this species in Indiana.
J. O. Whitaker, Jr.

Size
No significant sexual dimorphism
Total length: 61–89 (75) mm
Length of tail: 19–37 (28) mm
Weight: 3–10 g

Identification
The least shrew is a tiny shrew with a very short tail, less than 45 percent of the head and body length. The animal's total length usually does not exceed 95 mm. The only other short-tailed shrews of North America (other than some larger species of least shrews in Central America) are the short-tailed shrews in the genus *Blarina,* which have a minimum total length in adults of about 95 mm and are much grayer than least shrews, ranging from a very pale, almost silvery color to almost black. Least shrews are brownish in summer, grayish in winter.

Recent Synonyms
Cryptotis celatus
Cryptotis exilipes
Cryptotis eximius
Cryptotis micrurus
Cryptotis pergracilis

Other Common Names
Small short-tailed shrew, little short-tailed shrew, bee shrew

Status
Common (based partly on evidence of skulls found in owl pellets), but often hard to find

Subspecies
Cryptotis parva berlandieri, southern Texas south into Mexico

Cryptotis parva ellason, much of Ohio
Cryptotis parva floridana, most of Florida
Cryptotis parva harlani, eastern Illinois and much of Indiana
Cryptotis parva parva, southeastern United States except Florida

Four other subspecies occur in Central America: *C. p. orophila, C. p. pueblenis, C. p. soricina,* and *C. p. tropicalis*

References
Mammalian Species 43; Davis, 1941; Davis and Joeris, 1945; Hamilton, 1944

Desert shrew | *Notiosorex crawfordi*

The natural history of the desert shrew is rather poorly known. Typical habitat is desert shrub, including plant communities dominated by mesquite, agave, cholla, and oakbrush. However, the animals also have been captured in riparian woodlands, pinyon-juniper and ponderosa pine woodlands, and grassy or gravelly desert washes. These shrews usually are located under cover that provides a relatively mesic microhabitat in the desert, including brushpiles, rubbish, and fallen logs; there are a number of reports from beehives. Golfball-sized nests of fine fibers (web-silk, plant fibers) frequently have been reported from both occupied and abandoned houses of woodrats (especially the white-throated and southern plains woodrats, *Neotoma albigula* and *N. micropus),* from both stick nests and dens built of cactus joints. The desert shrew's elevational range is from sea level along the Pacific Ocean and the Gulf of California to above 2,000 m in Colorado and Durango.

The diet in the wild has not been studied in detail. Foods accepted by captives have included mealworms, cutworms, cockroaches, crickets, earwigs, sowbugs, moths, beetles, centipedes, and carrion of mammals, birds, and lizards. Live rodents, salamanders, earthworms, and scorpions were refused. Captives immobilized live prey by removing limbs or crushing the head.

The details of this shrew's reproductive biology are unknown. Based on specimen records, desert shrews breed through the warmer months of the year, with records of pregnant females from April to November. The gestation period is unknown; a typical litter is 3 to 5 young. Neonates are blind and the pinnae are not open, but development is rapid, and hair is evident within a week. The young leave the nest by 6 weeks of age.

Mammals as tiny as desert shrews live seemingly frantic lives. The behavior of captives has been described as "nervous." Movements are rapid, erratic, seemingly sometimes along runways of other animals. Between bouts of activity the animals enter a deep sleep from which they are difficult to arouse, suggesting an energy-saving period of torpor. Tiny, elongate feces often are deposited in conspicuous places, such as on a leaf or piece of debris; this hints at territorial marking, although that possibility has not been investigated.

Notiosorex crawfordi

Over most of its wide range, the desert shrew does not share its semiarid habitat with other shrews. Several broadly sympatric species of shrews are restricted mostly to mesic habitats, often on mountain "islands" in a "sea" of desert. Most of the other nocturnal insectivorous mammals of the desert habitat are bats, and the only species of bat likely to forage in the same space as the desert shrew is the pallid bat *(Antrozous pallidus)*, a widespread animal that forages on or near the ground. Many mice of the genus *Peromyscus* are highly insectivorous during the warmer months and share the desert shrew's habitat then. Birds that feed on insects in leaf litter in desert shrublands (towhees, for example) and a number of species of lizards are also in a broad foraging guild with the desert shrew. The structure of this guild has not been detailed, however.

Predation by great-horned and barn owls has been reported, and owl pellets have been a principal source of information on the distribution of the animals, but doubtless numerous other predators take desert shrews as opportunity allows. Known parasites include nematodes and flatworms.

D. M. Armstrong

Size
Total length: 77–98 (87.6) m
Length of tail: 24–32 (28.1) mm
Weight: 2.9–6.3 (4.3) g

Identification
The tail of the desert shrew is short (less than one-third total length) and unicolored; the ears are conspicuous, extending beyond the fur; the dorsum is silvery to brownish-gray, the venter paler; there are 28 teeth. This is the only shrew of arid and semi-arid environments of the southwestern United States and Mexico, although a number of species of *Sorex* (especially *S. merriami, S. nanus,* and *S. preblei*) have been taken in semi-desert environments in the western states.

Other Common Names
Gray shrew

Status
Difficult to ascertain; specimens are from widespread localities and generally have been taken opportunistically; the few intensive local studies suggest that the animals are common in suitable habitat.

Subspecies
Notiosorex crawfordi crawfordi, southern California eastward to Arkansas and southward to Baja California Sur, Sonora, Durango, Nuevo Leon, and Tamaulipas
Notiosorex crawfordi evotis, western Mexico: Sinaloa, Nayarit, Michoacan, Jalisco, Zacatecas

References
Mammalian Species 17; Hoffmeister and Goodpaster, 1962

Family Talpidae

Moles are known from the Oligocene in North America, but European fossils date back to Eocene times. This suggests that they have enjoyed a long evolutionary history along with their close relatives, the shrews.

Although there are 42 species in 17 genera worldwide, only 7 species in 5 genera are known from North America. All are small, although most are slightly larger than even the largest shrews. They have long, tubular bodies that are well adapted for their burrowing lifestyle. The eyes are tiny, also in keeping with their fossorial tendencies. They lack external ears, and the limbs are modified into efficient digging tools.

The fur of most moles is unique in being very uniform in length, and quite soft and flexible. This allows the fur to be smoothed in both directions, also an adaptation for moving both forwards and backwards in burrows. The shallow burrows most often associated with moles are used for foraging and resting. During the winter months, they use deeper tunnels that provide better protection from the elements.

All species are insectivorous, although some also consume some plant material. Their presence in lawns and gardens is actually probably salutary in that they may consume harmful soil insects and grubs. In addition, they play an important role in aerating and loosening the soil in many areas.

References
Mammalian Species 253; Hutterer, 1993

North American Genera
Neurotrichus
Scapanus
Parascalops
Scalopus
Condylura

American shrew mole | *Neurotrichus gibbsii*

The American shrew mole is restricted to the northwestern portion of North America, with populations occurring in British Columbia and the states of Washington, Oregon, and California. A small population of shrew moles is also known from Destruction Island, Washington. Like their more fossorial relatives, shrew moles prefer soils where digging is easy, but they show a preference for areas with substantial leaf litter or shrub or bunch grass cover. The species ranges in elevation from sea level to 2,500 meters.

North American shrew moles are the smallest talpids in the New World. They are not as well adapted for subterranean life as are other North American moles, but they still show significant modifications for burrowing. The forepaws are slightly broadened, the external ears are absent, and the eyes are greatly reduced. The tail in this species is rather thick and is approximately half as long as the head and body. Some of the hairs of shrew moles are longer and coarser than in their subterranean relatives, giving the pelage a less velvety appearance. Color ranges from gray to black. Morphologically, this species exhibits relatively little variation across its rather extensive geo-

Neurotrichus gibbsii

works of tunnels beneath leaf litter. These resemble shallow troughs. More complex tunnels similar to those made by other moles are also constructed. They are never more than 30 cm below the surface and mole hills are not formed. There are more openings in these tunnels than is characteristic of the tunnels of other species. Shrew moles can place their forepaws flat on the ground, which gives them more agility than other species of moles possess. They spend considerable time aboveground, are known to climb small bushes, and appear to be gregarious.

Shrew moles are the only moles known to nest aboveground. Breeding appears to occur throughout the year, and it is possible that more than one litter may be born annually. Each litter consists of from one to four young. The young are born blind and helpless and weigh less than a gram.

Shrew moles, like their relatives, eat large quantities of food daily and do not hibernate. Earthworms appear to be preferred food items, but the diet is extremely varied. Insects, larvae, isopods, and plant material have been reported in the shrew mole diet, as have miscellaneous items such as salamanders. *T. L. Yates*

graphic range. Maximum sizes occur around the San Francisco Bay region and slightly decrease from there to the south.

The shrew mole is active both day and night. It is described as semifossorial because it most commonly constructs net-

Size
No significant sexual dimorphism
Total length: 92–132 (114) mm
Length of tail: 12–19 (16) mm
Weight: 9–11 g

Identification
Distinguished from other North American moles by much smaller size and the presence of two premolars per quadrate. From shrews, it differs in the presence of broad forepaws and lack of pigmentation on the teeth.

Recent Synonyms
Urotrichus gibbsii

Other Common Names
Gibb's shrew mole, least shrew mole

Status
Common

Subspecies
Neurotrichus gibbsii gibbsii, southern British Columbia, central Washington east of the Cascade Mountains, central and southern Oregon, western California south to Sonoma County, northern and eastern California south to Plumes County

Neurotrichus gibbsii hyacinthinus, from north of San Francisco Bay south through Santa Cruz, San Benito, and Monterey Counties, California

Neurotrichus gibbsii minor, Washington west of the Cascade Mountains south to Tillamook County, Oregon

References
Mammalian Species 387; Dalquest and Orcutt, 1942; Dalquest and Scheffer, 1944; Yates, 1982

Broad-footed mole | *Scapanus latimanus*

The broad-footed mole is found west of the Rocky Mountains from Oregon south along the Pacific coast to the Sierra San Pedro Martír, Baja California, Mexico. Its range also extends throughout much of northern California, eastward into western Nevada, and south in California east of the central valley. This species appears to prefer moist soils and can be found from low elevations in valleys to elevations as high as 3,000

meters. In northern Baja California, broad-footed moles occur exclusively in and around mountain ranges.

These moles exhibit classic adaptations to a subterranean lifestyle. Like other western moles, they have reduced eyes and lack external ears. Their bodies are torpedo-shaped and each hair is almost equal in length, which reduces drag as the animals move through the soil. The forefeet are almost as wide as they are long and the pectoral girdle is highly modified for lateral-stroke burrowing. The species is relatively more variable than are Townsend's mole or the coast mole. Although the almost black coloration remains fairly uniform throughout the broad-footed mole's range, other morphological features change geographically. In general, there is a gradual decrease in size from north to south, with the largest individuals in northern California and southern Oregon and the smallest in Mexico. Local exceptions to this rule occur on islands in San Francisco Bay. As individuals become smaller to the south the normal complement of four unicuspid teeth may be reduced to three or even two.

The tunnels constructed by broad-footed moles are similar to those dug by coast moles. They are basically of two types: a temporary network near the surface used in foraging for food, and a deeper, more permanent system used for nest building and resting. This species also forms molehills on the surface of the ground when excavating deep tunnels, but to a lesser degree than Townsend's mole. *S. latimanus* also occurs across a wider array of habitat types and may be found living among large boulders in relatively dry areas in addition to its preferred moist habitats.

Broad-footed moles have a distinct breeding season. They breed once per year, in January or February, and give birth to from two to five young in March or April. The young are born

Scapanus latimanus

in a nest chamber in one of the deep tunnels and remain in the mother's tunnel system until June or July. These moles prefer earthworms as food but take other species of invertebrates as they are encountered. *T. L. Yates*

Size
Males average larger than females
Total length: 136–193 mm
Length of tail: 21–45 mm
Weight: 39–55 (46) g

Identification
This mole is distinguished from other species in the genus by the uneven spacing of the unicuspid teeth and by having a shorter and broader rostrum.

Recent Synonyms
Scalops latimanus

Other Common Names
Topociego

Status
Common throughout most of range, except rare in the San Pedro Martír Mountains of Baja California, Mexico

Subspecies
Scapanus latimanus anthonyi, San Pedro Martír Mountains, Baja California, Mexico

Scapanus latimanus campi, east of California's central valley, from north of Sanger to Dunlap and Minkler
Scapanus latimanus caurinus, western third of California from north of San Francisco Bay to the Oregon border
Scapanus latimanus dilatus, from Fremont, Oregon south through northwestern California to near Auburn, east from there to the Nevada line, then north in a narrow band in Nevada to the Oregon border

Scapanus latimanus grinnelli, a small region of southeastern California around Lone Pine and Owens Lake
Scapanus latimanus insularis, known only from Angel Island in San Francisco Bay, California
Scapanus latimanus latimanus, western California from San Francisco Bay south to San Benito Mountain
Scapanus latimanus minusculus, restricted to the area around Placerville, California
Scapanus latimanus monoensis, from near Mono Lake in eastern California north to near Wabuska, Nevada
Scapanus latimanus occultus, south-central and southwestern California from near Sequoia National Park and the San Bernadino Mountains south to the Sierra Juarez, Baja California, Mexico
Scapanus latimanus parvus, restricted to Alameda Island, San Francisco Bay, California
Scapanus latimanus sericatus, east-central California from Twain Harte and Coulterville east to Tuolumne Meadows

References
Palmer, 1937; Yates, 1982

Coast mole | *Scapanus orarius*

These industrious little diggers occur from extreme south-western British Columbia south through the western portions of Washington and Oregon to coastal northern California. The range extends eastward into much of eastern Washington, northeastern Oregon, and a relatively small area in extreme west-central Idaho. The western portion of the range overlaps extensively with that of the coast mole's nearest relative, *Scapanus townsendii* (Townsend's mole). In a small portion of northwestern California, the range also overlaps with that of the broad-footed mole, *Scapanus latimanus*.

The pelage is dark gray, velvety, and is easily moved in any direction. There are two molts each year: one usually begins in March and another in October. Unlike some other moles, differences in color, length, and texture of old and new pelage usually are not pronounced. Specimens sometimes have patches of white, cream, yellow, or orange fur on their belly, sides, wrists, or head. The tail is short (less than one-fourth of the total length), somewhat fleshy, scantily haired, slightly tapered at the end, and slightly constricted at its base. The eyes and ears are very small and concealed in the fur. The unicuspid teeth appear evenly spaced and uncrowded. This mole can be difficult to distinguish from Townsend's mole, and although the two species usually differ in their habitat preferences, both can occur in the same field. Specimens should be taken to a professional at a museum or university for identification. Coast moles are about the same size as broad-footed moles; however, broad-footed moles have distinctly hairy tails and unicuspid teeth that are unevenly spaced and crowded together.

Coast moles are active year-round and at all times of the day and night. Although most of their lives are spent underground, the presence of coast mole remains in owl pellets indicates that some aboveground activity occurs; this appears to be especially true of young individuals dispersing from the maternal home range during summer and autumn months. Individuals of *Scapanus orarius* can be found in a wide variety of habitats including coastal sand dunes, grassy meadows, sagebrush-grass, deciduous forest, and pine, fir, redwood, spruce, and hemlock woodlands. Specimens have been taken from elevations up to 1,676 m. Known predators include barn owls, long-eared owls, and rubber boas. Dogs and cats frequently catch and kill coast moles, but seldom eat them. Humans also kill large numbers of these moles each year.

Tunnels of *Scapanus orarius* usually range in depth from just a few centimeters to about 90 cm under the soil surface; however, during dry periods, tunnels may be constructed that reach depths of 1 to 2 meters. The presence of shallow tunnels usually is evidenced by characteristic ridges along the surface of the soil. These tunnels are excavated using dorso-lateral thrusts of the large, spade-like forefeet: a digging mole looks

Scapanus orarius

somewhat like a swimmer doing the breaststroke. The tunnels are used for foraging, dispersing, or finding mates; such tunnels often may be used only once. As they dig deeper, it becomes more difficult for the animals to compress the soil, and soil excavated from deep tunnels is brought to the surface and deposited in mounds ("molehills"). Mounds constructed by coast moles tend to be smaller than those of Townsend's moles and average about 30 cm in diameter and 15 cm in height. During autumn and winter, when soil moisture is higher, tunnel systems are extended and there is an increase in the frequency of mound construction. A single coast mole may construct from 200 to 400 molehills from October to March.

Members of this species are solitary except during the annual breeding season; during this time, males enlarge their ranges in search of females. Mating occurs in late winter or early spring; the length of the gestation period is unknown. An average of four young are born in March or April. As is the case in other species of mole, the young grow rapidly and probably are ready to wean and leave the nest at about four weeks of age. Nests usually have multiple entrances, are lined with coarse grass, average about 20 cm across, and are situated about 15 cm below the soil surface. Unlike Townsend's mole, there rarely if ever is a mound of soil over the nest.

Coast moles prefer better drained and more sandy soils than do Townsend's moles, and generally avoid soils that are subject to flooding. Earthworms, insects, and insect larvae usually form the bulk of the diet, but slugs, centipedes, millipedes, small vertebrates, and subterranean fungi also are eaten. This mole is economically neutral in most areas, but tunneling and mound building activities can cause damage to lawns, golf courses, and gardens. The mounds also can be a nuisance by clogging hay-cutting equipment. Coast moles occasionally consume some plant material, but much of the damage to gardens ascribed to them is actually caused by mice and voles that travel through and forage in the moles' tunnels.

The generic name, *Scapanus*, is derived from the Greek and refers to a digger or digging tool, and the specific epithet, *orarius*, comes from the Latin, meaning "belonging to the coast." No fossils of *Scapanus orarius* are known. G. D. Hartman

Size

Males average larger than females.

Total length: 136–190 mm (males); 133–168 mm (females)

Length of tail: 30–45 mm (males); 21–46 mm (females)

Weight: 64–91 g (males); 61–79 g (females)

Identification

In *Scapanus orarius,* the palmar surface of the forefoot is wider than it is long; the animal's total length is less than 200 mm; the tail less than 25 percent of the total length; and the hind foot is less than 24 mm long. *Scapanus orarius* can be distinguished from the broad-footed mole *(Scapanus latimanus)* by its evenly-spaced unicuspid teeth (upper teeth just posterior to canines) and scantily-haired tail. Adult coast moles can be distinguished from adult Townsend's moles *(Scapanus townsendii)* on the basis of total length (*S. townsendii* is longer than 200 mm) and hind foot length (more than 24 mm in *S. townsendii*). They can be distinguished from the shrew mole *(Neurotrichus gibbsii)* by size of the forefeet and length of the tail.

Other Common Names

Pacific mole, red-footed mole

Status

Locally common

Subspecies

Scapanus orarius orarius, coastal northern California from Mendocino north through the western half of Oregon to the Olympic Peninsula of Washington, then east to the Cascade Mountains in Washington

Scapanus orarius schefferi (yakimensis is a synonym), extreme southwestern British Columbia, northwestern Washington, central and western Washington east of the Cascade Mountains, extreme northeastern Oregon, and a small portion of west-central Idaho

References

Mammalian Species 253; Glendenning, 1959

Townsend's mole | *Scapanus townsendii*

Townsend's mole has a limited distribution, occurring only on the west side of the Cascade Mountains from northwestern California to extreme southwestern British Columbia. Primarily a lowland animal, these moles are seldom found above 700 meters. One population, however, occurs in the Olympic Mountains of Washington in alpine meadows at elevations ranging from 1,500 to 1,900 meters, where suitable habitat is covered with snow for much of the year. Throughout the rest of its range Townsend's mole seems to prefer deep loamy soils in meadows and adjacent areas. It is rare in the sandy soils along the beach preferred by the coast mole, *Scapanus orarius.*

Townsend's moles are the largest moles in North America. They show very little morphological variation throughout

Scapanus townsendii

wide as they are long and are also ringed with stiff tactile vibrissae. The pectoral girdle is highly modified for lateral-stroke burrowing and the humerus is almost square in shape and articulates directly with the clavicle.

Townsend's mole constructs both deep and surface tunnels. It excavates two types of deep tunnels. The most extensive type is permanent and is located 15–20 cm below the surface. The other kind of deep system is often located beneath fencerows, building foundations and roadways, and may be up to 3 meters deep. These extensive, deep excavations generate large amounts of dirt, which the moles deposit on the surface. As many as 805 molehills per hectare have been reported for this species. Surface tunnels are also used in foraging, but to a lesser extent than in other species.

Townsend's mole appears to be the most advanced nest builder of North American talpids, and often constructs a large nest chamber 15–20 cm below the surface. Its location can be surmised by the appearance in early spring of an extremely large (51–76 cm or larger) mound or a large aggregation of small mounds. The nest chamber may have as many as 11 exits and is lined with an outer layer of green grass and an inner layer of dry grass that is periodically replaced as long as the nest is occupied. Two to five young are born in March or April.

Like other mole species, Townsend's mole consumes large quantities of food and does not hibernate. Earthworms and other soil invertebrates are preferred food items, although this species appears to have a greater fondness for plant material than other moles. Earthworms, insects, and vegetation comprise by far the bulk of the diet. Commercial bulb growers and cattle ranchers sustain considerable loss to this species each year, although much of the damage is the incidental result of burrowing activities or is caused by the use of mole tunnels by rodents. *T. L. Yates*

their range. Only two geographic races are recognized and one of these has a distribution restricted to a small area in the Olympic Mountains of Washington. The species is well adapted to life underground and has many morphological features associated with this lifestyle. The soft, velvety pelage is designed to reduce friction as the mole travels through its tunnel system and is resistant to becoming matted with soil; the animals were once collected commercially for their fur. External ears are absent and the eyes are reduced to tiny dots. The body is streamlined and the snout is elongated and ringed with stiff vibrissae that serve a tactile function. The forepaws are as

Size

Males average larger than females.
Total length: 207–237 (225) mm (males); 183–209 (196) mm (females)
Length of tail: 35–56 (46) mm (males); 29–51 (38) mm (females)
Weight: 100–171 (142) g (males); 50–110 (87) g (females)

Identification

Townsend's mole can be distinguished from other species in the genus by much larger size. From sympatric moles in the genus *Neurotrichus*, it differs in much larger size, more

premolars, and shorter tail relative to head and body length.

Recent Synonyms

Scalops townsendii
Scapanus tow[n]sendii

Other Common Names

Snow mole

Status

Locally common to abundant

Subspecies

Scapanus townsendii olympicus, known only from the Olympic Mountains, Clallam County, Washington
Scapanus townsendii townsendii, northwestern California from Ferndale north through Oregon and Washington (excluding the Olympic Mountains) west of the Cascade Mountains, to extreme southwestern British Columbia, Canada

References

Mammalian Species 434; Johnson and Yates, 1980; Yates, 1982

Hairy-tailed mole | *Parascalops breweri*

The hairy-tailed mole is broadly distributed in eastern North America from southern Ontario and Quebec south to central Ohio and Connecticut, and in the Appalachian Mountains as far south as the northeastern corner of Georgia. Its range overlaps those of the star-nosed mole *(Condylura cristata)* and the eastern mole *(Scalopus aquaticus)*. Although hairy-tailed moles are often captured in the same area as star-nosed moles, they rarely co-occur with eastern moles.

Parascalops has a number of external and anatomical characteristics associated with digging and living in underground tunnels. The body is thick, tapering at each end, and the head is triangular and depressed. The legs are short, but the feet are large and fleshy, with sparse hair only on the upper surface. The claws of the forefeet, which are used for digging, are broad, flat, and heavy. The outer end of the upper foreleg (humerus) points forward and upward, so that the thumb side of the forefoot points down and the palm faces out or back. The shoulder girdle is modified and is located in the neck region rather than in the anterior thorax. Unusual in mammals is the keeled sternum, to which the powerful muscles of the foreleg are attached. External ears are absent and the eyes are very small (less than 1 mm in diameter). *Parascalops* has vibrissae on the snout, stiff hairs on the upper surface of the head behind the eyes, and a dense fringe of vibrissae on the edge of the palms of the forefeet. These hairs are all believed to have a tactile function.

As in other moles, the fur of the hairy-tailed mole is very dense, soft, and silky. Its hairs are short and about equal in length—suitable for traveling in underground tunnels. The pelage is grayish-brownish-black on the back, and slightly paler and grayer on the underparts. The tail, feet, and base of the snout are dark brown, but become progressively whiter with age. Adults molt in spring from late March to late May and in autumn from September to mid-October. Immature moles usually start molting in late August and have their new pelage by late October. Molt spreads from the breast to the tail and sides, and from the lower back towards the head.

Mating occurs in late March and early April. Females typically produce one litter of four or five young after a gestation estimated at 4 to 6 weeks. At birth, hairy-tailed moles are naked except for short vibrissae on the snout and facial hairs near the eyes and lips. The forelimbs are similar to those of the adult, but the claws are short, soft, and blunt. Young moles remain in the nest for about four weeks, by which time they are eating solid food. By the time they abandon the nest, the young moles have reached at least 67 percent of adult weight. Postnatal pelage is much shorter and slightly grayer than that

Parascalops breweri

of adults in summer. Hairy-tailed moles can be aged by the degree of tooth wear. The maximum life span is about four years, by which time the teeth are worn to the level of the gums.

Hairy-tailed moles are active throughout the year. Most of their time is spent underground in extensive tunnel systems that they construct both near the surface and at depths of 25–45 cm. The ridges of the near-surface tunnels are not as pronounced as those made by eastern moles, and may go unnoticed unless they are in hard-packed soils with little vegetation. These tunnels branch irregularly. The main routes, which are permanent structures that can remain in use for several years, are large, well-packed, and smooth. Occasional openings to the surface are present. The moles repair any artificial breaks that appear. They hunt in existing tunnels or forage by digging smaller branch tunnels. In one study area in Ontario, 24.7 km of near-surface tunnels per hectare was reported.

The deeper tunnels are less extensive and are used when the soil freezes in winter. These tunnels are enlarged in the fall, which results in the creation of many mole hills. Individuals winter separately in areas about 15–24 m in diameter. Winter nests are ovoid (200 by 150 mm) and may be lined with leaves and grass. In spring, when activity in surface tunnels resumes, females stay near their winter ranges; males leave their winter ranges in search of mates. Females remain solitary after mating and construct spherical nests (160 mm) about 25 cm below the surface that they line with dried leaves. Males freely associate in spring, and by late summer tunnels are shared by males, females, and young. Average densities are probably about three

moles per hectare, with highs of 25–30 per hectare in very favorable sites. Many other species of small mammals, including shrews, deer mice, voles, and jumping mice, utilize the tunnels of *Parascalops*.

Parascalops occupies a variety of habitat types including hardwood, coniferous, and mixed coniferous and hardwood forests, as well as open fields, roadsides, and cultivated fields. This mole is most abundant in light soils (e.g., sandy loam) with good surface cover and sufficient moisture. Soils that have high clay or moisture content, or that are dry and hard, are avoided. The suitability of the soil for burrowing and for providing food probably limits the distribution of this species. Common foods include earthworms and various insects (larval, pupal, and adult stages), but especially beetles. Known predators on *Parascalops* include red foxes, barn owls, opossums, and copperhead snakes. *J. G. Hallett*

Size
Males are slightly larger than females.
Total length: 151–173 (163) mm
Length of tail: 26–33 (31) mm
Weight: 41.0–62.8 g

Identification
The fleshy tail is densely haired, slightly con-

stricted at its base, and less than one-fourth of total length. The snout, which extends about 9 mm beyond the incisors, is shorter than in *Scalopus* and lacks the fleshy, tentacle-like appendages of *Condylura*.

Other Common Names
Brewer's mole

Status
Locally common

References
Mammalian Species 98; van Zyll de Jong, 1983

Eastern mole | *Scalopus aquaticus*

The eastern mole has the widest range of any North American mole. The species is distributed from northern Tamaulipas, Mexico to southern South Dakota, eastward to Massachusetts, and south to the southernmost tip of Florida. It is common throughout most of the eastern United States where soils are favorable. However, its actual distribution is far more patchy than this would suggest. This mole prefers moist loamy or sandy soils. It is scarce or absent in heavy clay, stony, or gravelly soils, and avoids otherwise suitable soil types that are too wet or too dry. Populations of eastern moles are, therefore, often separated spatially by intervening sections of unsuitable habitat. Human activities such as the building of roads and golf courses often prove beneficial to eastern moles by providing high quality soils and adequate moisture.

The extensive geographic distribution of the eastern mole

has resulted in a corresponding degree of variation in color and size. Color ranges from almost black in subspecies in the northern part of the range to silver or gold in southern races.

Scalopus aquaticus

their relatives, the shrews, eastern moles lack external ears, and their eyes are completely covered with skin. The forepaws are broader than they are wide and the fingers and toes are partially webbed. Early biologists noted this webbing, thought the mole was aquatic, which it is not (although it is a good swimmer), and named it *aquaticus*.

Eastern moles spend 99 percent of their lives underground in tunnels of their own construction. They are solitary except during the breeding season. Males construct more extensive tunnel systems than females. The tunnels are of two basic types: deep, more permanent ones and shallow surface runways that are used primarily for feeding. Many of the latter may be used only once; others may be used frequently and for many years. Eastern moles will not tolerate breaks in their tunnels and repair them as soon as the break is discovered. Deep tunnels are used for nest construction and for foraging when the surface of the ground is frozen. Dirt excavated from these deep tunnels may be deposited in mounds (mole hills) or in abandoned surface runways.

The eastern mole has a voracious appetite. Captives consume from 31 to 55 percent of their weight in food daily. The moles are active year-round and do not hibernate. They eat invertebrates of many types, but in most localities earthworms are preferred. Ant larvae are eaten frequently in some localities.

Breeding occurs once a year, usually in late winter or early spring. Litter sizes range from 2 to 5. The exact gestation period is not known. The young share the tunnel system of the mother until they are old enough to forage on their own. At this stage they establish their own tunnel systems outside the home range of the mother. *T. L. Yates*

Size also varies from north to south: northern individuals are considerably larger than their southern conspecifics. Males tend to be larger than females in most characters in all populations. Despite considerable geographic variation in size and color, all eastern moles look very much alike. They are well adapted for a fossorial lifestyle. The body is streamlined and covered with thick velvety fur that is, in essence, hinged so that it can bend forward and backward with little friction. Unlike

Size
Males are larger, on average, than females.
Total length: 103–208 (151) mm (males); 129–168 (149) mm (females)
Length of tail: 16–38 (25) mm (males); 20–28 (24) mm (females)
Weight: 40–140 (90) g (males); 32–90 (70) g (females)

Identification
The eastern mole can be distinguished from other North American moles by the possession of three premolars in each jaw quadrant and by having webbing between the foretoes. Its tail is shorter and not as hairy as those of other moles in its range.

Recent Synonyms
Scalopus inflatus
Scalopus montanus

Other Common Names
Topos

Status
Common with the exception of populations in Mexico and Presidio County, Texas, which are extremely rare and possibly extinct.

Subspecies
Scalopus aquaticus aereus, the Texas Panhandle, Oklahoma, southern Kansas, Arkansas, Louisiana, and extreme eastern Texas
Scalopus aquaticus alleni, southern Texas west of the Brazos River, from Mason County south to Padre Island near Corpus Christi
Scalopus aquaticus anastasae, restricted to Anastasae Island, Florida
Scalopus aquaticus aquaticus, eastern United States from west-central Massachusetts and southeastern New York south through eastern Pennsylvania, West Virginia, Virginia, extreme eastern Tennessee, and western North Carolina
Scalopus aquaticus australis, southern Georgia to east-central Florida near Lake Okeechobee

Scalopus aquaticus bassi, Englewood, Sarasota County, Florida
Scalopus aquaticus caryi, extreme southern South Dakota and southeastern Wyoming, central and western Nebraska, northeastern Colorado, and northwestern Kansas
Scalopus aquaticus cryptus, central and eastern Texas from Grayson County south to Montgomery County; from the Brazos River eastward to Tyler County
Scalopus aquaticus howelli, from eastern and central North Carolina across northern Georgia and west to the Mississippi River
Scalopus aquaticus inflatus, extreme southern Texas and northern Tamaulipas, Mexico
Scalopus aquaticus machrinoides, west of the Mississippi River from southwestern Minnesota south through Missouri, then westward to northeastern Kansas, eastern Nebraska, and southeastern Iowa

Scalopus aquaticus machrinus, between the Mississippi River and the Appalachian Mountains from southwestern Wisconsin south to Mississippi

Scalopus aquaticus montanus, near Piedra Blanca, Coahuila, Mexico

Scalopus aquaticus parvus, west coast of Florida north of Tampa Bay in Hillsboro, Pinellas, and Pasco Counties

Scalopus aquaticus porteri, extreme southern tip of Florida

Scalopus aquaticus texanus, Presidio County, Texas

References

Mammalian Species 105; Yates, 1982; Yates and Schmidly, 1977

Star-nosed mole | *Condylura cristata*

Named for its peculiar snout, which has 22 fleshy, finger-like appendages surrounding the nostrils, the star-nosed mole is a denizen of moist fields, meadows, woods, and marshy areas. This mole occurs from extreme eastern Manitoba and Minnesota to Labrador and Nova Scotia; the range extends southward through most of Wisconsin, northern Indiana and Ohio, along the Appalachian mountains to northern Georgia and South Carolina, and along the Atlantic coast as far as southeastern Georgia. Distribution records are rather poor for the southern part of the range, and much of our current knowledge of star-nosed moles is based on individuals and populations occurring at the mid- and upper latitudes of the range.

Star-nosed moles are active year-round, both day and night. Their presence usually can be detected by ridges resulting from their tunneling activities near the surface of the soil, and by the mounds of soil ("molehills") pushed up during the construction of deep tunnels. Tunnels made by this mole are approximately 4 cm in diameter and range in depth from about 3 to 60 cm. The animals also use runs on the surface of the ground, and in some areas, this mole may be present even when molehills or surface ridges are lacking; this appears to be the case quite often in the more southern portions of the range. Some authors consider this mole to be gregarious or possibly colonial. Star-nosed moles spend less time under-

ground than do some other moles, often foraging above-ground at night; they also frequently forage in water. They are accomplished swimmers and divers, and tunnels often can be found that open underwater. During winter, star-nosed moles have been seen traveling on the surface or just under the surface of snow, and in some cases, even swimming under ice. Although they most often are found in wet places, they sometimes occur at well-drained sites. Eastern moles *(Scalopus aquaticus)* occasionally have been captured from the same tunnels as star-nosed moles, but *Scalopus* usually avoids the moister habitats preferred by *Condylura*.

The pelage is dense, relatively coarse, and ranges from blackish-brown to black; the belly may appear somewhat paler than the back. There are two molts: the spring molt occurs as early as May and as late as July, and the autumnal molt usually takes place in September or October. The scaly tail is about as long as the head and body, is covered rather sparsely with dark hair, and is constricted at its base. During winter and spring, the tails of both sexes thicken as the result of fat deposition, presumably an energy store for the coming breeding season. The eyes are extremely small and probably useful only for detecting light from dark; the ears are only barely discernible externally. The palms of the forefeet are about as wide as they are long. As in all members of the family Talpidae, the upper forelimb articulates with the collarbone rather than with the shoulder blade as seen in most mammals. When swimming (as well as digging), lateral thrusts of the forefeet are used rather than a 'dog-paddle' type of motion.

The nasal rays contain large numbers of highly sensitive tactile organs called Eimer's organs. For many years, these rays were believed to be strictly tactile in function. However, recent research has shown that the nasal rays also are used to manipulate objects, and may allow the animal to detect electrical fields that are given off by prey in the water. The diet varies according to habitat, but generally consists of terrestrial and aquatic invertebrates, especially annelids, insects, and insect larvae. Small crustaceans, molluscs, and fish also are eaten. A variety of predators have been reported, including owls, hawks, skunks, house cats, snakes, largemouth bass, and mink; there is one report of an eastern chipmunk *(Tamias striatus)* eating a star-nosed mole! For the most part this mole is economically neutral, although it occasionally may cause disturbance to lawns and golf courses.

Females produce a single litter each year. Litter sizes range from 3 to 7, and average about 5. The majority of pregnancies occur in April and May, but newborn litters have been reported

Condylura cristata

as early as March and as late as August. The exact gestation period is unknown. Nests are roughly spherical, about 15 cm in diameter, lined with dead leaves and grasses, and are excavated under stumps, logs, or fallen trees, above high-water level. Nests for rearing the young generally are larger and more elaborate than are those used during the rest of the year. Newborn moles are hairless except for short vibrissae (whiskers) on their snouts; their feet are well developed, and the nose "star" is present, enclosed within a thin, translucent membrane. The young grow rapidly, and are covered with fine hair at about ten days of age; by three to four weeks they leave the nest. Sexual maturity is attained at about 10 months, and both males and females are able to breed during the first breeding season following their birth.

The name *Condylura* is derived from Greek words meaning "knobby tail," and has its origin in an early and inaccurate drawing of the animal that showed the tail as being constricted at intervals, like a string of beads. *Crista* is a Latin root meaning "crest" or "tuft" and refers to the "star" of the nose. Fossils of *Condylura cristata* are known from numerous Pleistocene sites in North America. Two fossil species, *Condylura kowalskii* and *C. izabellae,* have been described from Middle and Late Pliocene deposits in Poland. *G. D. Hartman*

Size

No significant sexual dimorphism, but individuals are typically larger in the north and smaller in the south.

Total length: 132–230 mm

Length of tail: 48–99 mm

Weight: 40–85 g

Identification

The presence of 22 fleshy appendages surrounding the nostrils distinguishes the star-nosed mole from every other mammal in the world

Status

Locally abundant in northern portions of range; status uncertain in more southern portions of range

Subspecies

Condylura cristata cristata, New Brunswick, Newfoundland, Nova Scotia, all except southwestern and southern Ontario, Quebec, Connecticut, Maine, Massachusetts, Michigan (part), New Hampshire, New Jersey, New York (part), Pennsylvania (part), and Wisconsin (part)

Condylura cristata parva (nigra is a synonym), remainder of range, from southeastern Georgia north to Vermont and northwest to southeastern Manitoba

References

Mammalian Species 129; Gould et al., 1993

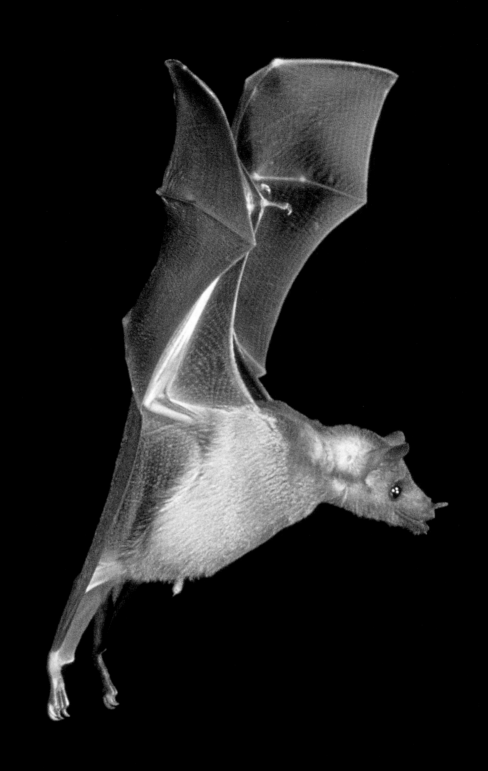

Order Chiroptera

Bats comprise the second largest order of mammals, with 177 genera and 925 species. This diverse group of mammals is divided into two suborders: the Megachiroptera (one family of Old World fruit bats containing 166 species) and the Microchiroptera (the remaining 16 families and 756 species). Chiroptera occur throughout the temperate and tropical regions of both hemispheres, and on all but the most isolated oceanic islands. Bats are the only true flying mammals, and they occupy a wide array of ecological niches.

Bats shelter in tree cavities, crevices, caves, and buildings, and some rest exposed on trees. Bats in temperate regions may hibernate or migrate to warmer regions during the cold seasons.

The majority of microchiropteran bats are insectivorous, using echolocation while flying to catch insects. Other species of microchiropteran bats feed on mammal blood, fishes, or other small vertebrates. However, some Microchiroptera and the Megachiroptera feed on plant materials, including pollen, nectar, and particularly fruits.

Microchiroptera are renowned for their ability to orient and hunt using echolocation. Fruit-eating or blood-eating bats appear to use vision and olfaction in addition to echolocation to find prey.

Three families of microchiropteran bats—Vespertilionidae, Molossidae, and Emballonuridae—occur in both the Old and New Worlds. The insectivorous vespertilionids (little brown bats) occur throughout temperate and tropical areas and comprise the largest and most widely distributed family of bats (318 species). Many species living in temperate regions hibernate during the winter, often migrating long distances to their hibernation caves.

The free-tailed bats (Molossidae) are generally limited to subtropical and tropical environments. They extend into the southern United States during the summer months when insect populations are high. They use these abundant resources to support huge colonies that serve as maternity roosts for females producing young.

Six families of microchiropteran bats are restricted to the New World. The American leaf-nosed bats (Phyllostomidae) occur in subtropical and tropical areas from the southern United States to Argentina.

Southern long-nosed bat *(Leptonycteris curasoae)*

These bats number 142 species and dominate the bat fauna in the Neotropical region. They are the most diverse family of bats and have exploited the widest variety of food types. They range from small insectivores through the blood-feeding vampires to large carnivorous species. Only five species of this family are known from North America.

The remaining bat families endemic to the New World are primarily tropical in distribution. Ghost-faced bats (Mormoopidae) are among the most abundant chiropterans in the New World tropics. These bats are exclusively insectivorous and gregarious cave dwellers. Only a single species has been recorded from North America, and it barely penetrates into our region, in south Texas.

References
Eisenberg and Wilson, 1978; Fenton, 1983; Koopman, 1993; Nowak 1991; Wilson, 1973, 1989

Family Mormoopidae

The family Mormoopidae has only two genera and is limited to the New World. One genus, *Pteronotus,* has several species, two of which are naked-backed bats, so called because the wing membranes meet and fuse in the middle of the back, giving the bats a smooth, naked-backed appearance. Underneath these membranes, the bats have a normally furry body. None are very large; *Pteronotus parnellii* is the largest, with a forearm length of about 60 millimeters .

These bats have no noseleaf, but the lips are wrinkled up and modified into a strange sort of funnel-shape. The eyes are small and quite inconspicuous. The ears are short and pointed, and the tragus is not only present, but quite distinctive in comparison to that of other bats. The interfemoral membrane is well-developed, and the tail extends out through the dorsal surface of the uropatagium.

These bats are agile flyers, and are strictly aerial insectivores. They occur in a variety of habitats, ranging from dry savannahs to tropical rainforest. Most roost in caves or tunnels, although they have been found in houses on occasion. They produce a single young per year, at a time that depends on the local climate.

References

Mammalian Species 209; Smith, 1972; Wilson, 1997

North American Genera

Mormoops

Ghost-faced bat | *Mormoops megalophylla*

The ghost-faced bat is distributed from southwestern Texas and southern Arizona southward through Baja California and mainland Mexico into eastern Honduras and El Salvador. There are no records of *M. megalophylla* from Nicaragua, Costa Rica, or Panama. Records resume in Columbia and Venezuela, the Netherlands Antilles, and Trinidad, and the Pacific coasts of Columbia, Ecuador, and northern Peru.

Ghost-faced bats from South America are deep cinnamon red in color, with an iridescent, purplish frost over the back and rump and a pinkish, fan-shaped cape over the shoulders, formed by relatively long, stiff hairs. This cape and the rich cinnamon red coloration are absent in individuals from North America. The dorsal pelage of the ghost-faced bat is long and lax, with four zones of coloration on each hair. As individuals age the second zone gains a reddish tinge, which makes the entire animal appear reddish. The pelage fades in adults, and patches of different hues occur on the body. Molts, which occur from June through September, begin dorsally in patches on the shoulders and sides and expand over the back. Ventrally, molts begin under the wings and on the chin and neck, spread across the abdomen, and join molt areas on the chin and neck.

Unlike bats in the closely-related family Phyllostomidae, *M. megalophylla* does not have a well-developed nose leaf, but instead has wart-like protuberances. Its lip and chin have leaflike appendages, giving rise to the name leaf-chinned bat.

Mormoops megalophylla

The tragus, with its large secondary fold of skin at right angles to the longitudinal axis and its heavily swollen cranial ridge, is the most complex described in mormoopid bats.

Mormoops megalophylla inhabits humid, semi-arid, and arid

brasiliensis, Myotis velifer, Pteronotus parnellii, P. personatus, P. davyi, and *Leptonycteris curasoae* share roosting caves with *M. megalophylla. M. megalophylla* feeds exclusively on large-bodied moths. Pregnant females have been taken from February through June and lactating females from June through August. Females usually have one embryo.

Ghost-faced bats spend the day in caves or abandoned mine shafts and emerge soon after dark. Once out of the roost, individuals fly quickly to foraging sites along arroyos and canyons. Ghost-faced bats are relatively strong, fast flyers and travel at high altitudes to foraging areas. Foraging may occur over standing water. Colonies may contain more than 500,000 individuals, and are spatially isolated from colonies of other species roosting in the same caves. The bats begin returning to their caves seven hours after they first leave them. Nursing females roost separately from males and nonreproductive females, choosing areas that minimize ventilation and maximize retention of heat from their metabolism and from reactions occurring in the guano. The temperature in these sites is usually 36° C.

Mormoops megalophylla contains 18 pairs of autosomal chromosomes and a pair of sex chromosomes. *G. N. Cameron*

regions below 3,000 m in elevation. Mixed boreal-tropical forest (transition zone between pine-oak forest and tropical deciduous forest between 1,500 and 2,200 m in elevation), tropical rain forest, and riparian areas with mature cottonwood, sycamore, and willow in oak-woodlands are commonly used. In Peru, the species inhabits arid coastal regions with rock outcrops where there are caves or abandoned mines suitable as roosting sites, stands of *Acacia* and *Prosopis,* orchards, and large stands of *Acacia* forest. A number of other bat species occur in association with the ghost-faced bat in these habitats. *Tadarida*

Size

No significant sexual dimorphism
Total length: 78–98 mm
Length of tail: 19.5–28.3 mm
Length of forearm: about 54.5 mm
Weight: 15–16 g

Identification

Mormoops megalophylla is larger than the only other ghost-faced bat, the Caribbean species *Mormoops blainvillii.* They can be distinguished as follows: the forearm of *M. megalophylla* is longer than 50 mm, whereas that of *M. blainvillii* is shorter than 41 mm. The rostrum of *megalophylla* is extremely upturned and broad and the braincase is squared and flattened dorsally; the rostrum of *blainvillii* is upturned and

narrow. The ears of *megalophylla* are rounded and connected by two high bands that fuse on top of the rostrum, whereas the ears of *blainvillii* are rounded and the dorsal portion is inconspicuous, short, and pointed. The tragus of *megalophylla* has a prominent secondary fold; there is a lanceolate flap above the secondary fold in *blainvillii.* Each nostril of *megalophylla* is surrounded by a separate pad, the margin above and between the nostrils contains several wart-like tubercules, and a long, prominent ridge separates the nostrils.

Other Common Names

Leaf-chinned bat, old man bat, Peter's ghost-faced bat

Status

Not abundant, localized

Subspecies

Mormoops megalophylla carteri, Columbia, Ecuador, northern Peru
Mormoops megalophylla intermedia, Netherlands Antilles, Trinidad
Mormoops megalophylla megalophylla, southwestern Texas, southern Arizona, Baja California and Mexico, eastern Honduras, El Salvador
Mormoops megalophylla tumidiceps, Columbia, Venezuela

References

Mammalian Species 448; Davis and Schmidly, 1994; Matson and Baker, 1986; Schmidly, 1991; Smith, 1972

Family Phyllostomidae

This enormously diverse group of leaf-nosed bats is basically tropical, with only five species extending into the southwestern United States. The family is so large and diverse that division into subfamilies facilitates discussion of the natural history of the individual species.

Macrotus californicus is a member of the subfamily Phyllostominae. This group of 11 genera and 33 species represents a relatively old lineage of bats that share the general characteristics of large ears and noseleaves, broad wings that produce slow, maneuverable flight, and a propensity for life in old, well-developed forests. They tend to prey on larger insects that they frequently take from the surface of the vegetation, a foraging strategy known as foliage gleaning.

The phyllostomid subfamily Glossophaginae includes 10 genera and 22 species. Most are highly specialized for feeding on nectar. They tend to have elongated snouts, long, extrusible tongues, and reduced dentition. The ears are short, the wings are broad, and most are capable of very maneuverable, even hovering, flight. The two genera with three species that occur in North America, *Leptonycteris* and *Choeronycteris,* have interesting lifestyles. These bats are known from the southwestern United States, where they are summertime residents only, to northern Central America. The northern populations are migratory and appear to follow the flowering cycles of large *Agave,* or century plants, and some species of cactus.

Probably no other bat carries as much name recognition as the vampire, yet most people understand little about the real vampire bats. Actually, there are three species of vampires in the phyllostomid subfamily Desmodontinae, although only one, *Desmodus rotundus,* is common and widespread. All three are limited to the New World Tropics, with only *Diphylla ecaudata* extending into the United States.

The dentition is reduced to only 20 teeth, and the only really functional ones are the two chisel-shaped upper incisors and the greatly enlarged upper canines. The wings are broad and the animals are capable of taking flight from the ground by leaping high into the air. They frequently fly low to the ground and are able to maneuver easily through the understory.

Roosts are found in caves, mines, hollow trees, and occasionally in abandoned buildings. Vampire roosts are easily recognizable by the dark stains of digested and excreted blood on the walls and floor. This results in a characteristic pungent odor as well.

Vampires forage early in the evening, usually traveling no farther than 5–8 km from the roost in search of prey. Once a prey item is located, the bat may spend some time approaching it, often from the ground or along a tree branch. Next, a particular site is selected, and the bat begins by licking the site with its tongue. In addition, feathers *(Diphylla* feeds primarily on birds) may be removed, and a bite is made, either by a slash with the upper teeth or by nipping off a small piece of skin.

How did such a curious habit come into existence? No one knows for sure, but various theories have been suggested. Vampires are closely related to the basically frugivorous phyllostomids, so one theory would have them originating from fruit-eating ancestors. The strong dentition of phyllostomids could certainly be modified through evolution to produce the specialized feeding mechanism of vampires, but the intermediate steps between biting into a fruit and biting into a bird are a bit more difficult to imagine.

Another theory likens them to tick-feeding birds that developed a taste for blood by feeding on insects that were themselves blood-feeders. This would derive them from insectivorous ancestors, and would require an equally difficult transition from feeding on blood-engorged insects like ticks to tapping the source itself.

The third theory suggests that the bats began by feeding on insects and larvae, such as screwworms, that develop in the wounds of large animals. This would also require the well-developed anterior dentition that could logically be derived from phyllostomid-like ancestors. It also presents a somewhat easier to imagine intermediate scenario of moving from feeding on the insect larvae to feeding on the wounds themselves, and eventually to inflicting the wounds in order to feed on the blood alone.

Regardless of the ultimate origin, the bats today present a fantastic example of the wonderful specializations provided by evolutionary process over a long period of time. Even without the vampire legends from the Old World, these animals are truly amazing in their own right.

References
Arita and Wilson, 1987; Wilson, 1989, 1997

North American Genera
Macrotus
Choeronycteris
Leptonycteris
Diphylla

California leaf-nosed bat | *Macrotus californicus*

Macrotus is the most northerly representative of the Phyllostomidae (a predominantly Neotropical family), occurring in the Lower Sonoran life zone in the deserts of California, southern Nevada, Arizona, and south into Baja California and Sonora, Mexico. This species neither hibernates nor migrates, and it is incapable of lowering its body temperature to become torpid. Although longevity in this species does not approach the 30 or more years of temperate zone vespertilionid bats, banded *Macrotus* in California have been recaptured after 14 years. *Macrotus* has a relatively narrow thermal-neutral zone, with the lower critical temperature near 34° C and the upper near 37° C. No special physiological adaptations occur in *Macrotus* for desert existence. Behavioral adaptations such as foraging methods and roost selection contribute to its successful exploitation of the temperate zone desert.

Macrotus feeds at night primarily on moths and immobile diurnal insects such as butterflies and katydids, which it locates by vision, even at low ambient light levels. The culled remains of these prey items can be found beneath night roosts. This strategy of gleaning larger prey from the substrate as compared to aerial insectivory appears to reduce the total time and energy necessary for foraging. In total darkness, *Macrotus* utilizes echolocation, an energetically more costly method of

Macrotus californicus

finding its food. Radio-telemetry studies of *Macrotus* in the California desert show that the bats forage almost exclusively among desert wash vegetation within 10 km of their roost. The bats emerge from their roosts 30 or more minutes after sunset, and fly near the ground or vegetation in slow, maneuverable flight. Shallow caves and short mine prospects are used by both sexes as night roosts between foraging bouts at all seasons except the coldest winter months.

To remain active yearlong in the temperate deserts of California, Arizona, and southern Nevada, *Macrotus* uses warm diurnal roosts in caves, mines, and buildings with temperatures that often exceed 28° C. Depending on the season, the bats roost singly or in groups of up to several hundred individuals, hanging separately from the ceiling rather than clustering. Often the bats hang from one foot, using the other to scratch or groom themselves. Most diurnal winter roosts are in warm mine tunnels at least 100 meters long. At this season, the large colonies of more than 1,000 bats may contain both males and females, although the sexes may also roost separately. The areas in the mines used by the bats are always warm and humid and have no circulating air currents. The mines appear to be located in geothermally heated rock formations and are usually warmer than the annual mean temperature. Except for the approximately 2-hour-nightly foraging period, in winter *Macrotus* inhabits a stable, warm environment.

Females congregate in large maternity colonies of about 100–200 individuals in the spring and summer, utilizing different mines or different areas within mines from those occupied

in the winter. A few males are found in these colonies, although large male-only roosts also form. The single young is born between mid-May and early July, following a gestation of almost nine months. Development of the fetus is delayed following ovulation, insemination, and fertilization in September. Males attract females through wing-flapping and vocalizations, often at mine sites that are only used for these displays. In March, with increased temperatures and insect availability, embryonic development accelerates. Since the newborn bats are unable to warm themselves, maternity colonies are located fairly close to entrances, where temperatures exceed 30° C and daytime outside temperatures can reach 50° C in the summer. The bats sometimes use shallow natural rock caves that would be too cold for a winter roost. *P. Brown*

Size
No significant sexual dimorphism
Total length: 85–99 (94.3) mm
Length of tail: 28–41 (36.3) mm
Length of forearm: 46–52 (49.3) mm
Weight: 12–22 g

Identification
M. californicus has large ears (longer than 25 mm), gray pelage, and a distinct leaflike projection from the tip of the nose; the tail extends slightly beyond the tip of the interfemoral membrane.

Recent Synonyms
Macrotus waterhousii californicus

Status
Locally common in restricted localities; more information is needed to determine its status.

References
Mammalian Species 1; Barbour and Davis, 1969; Bell, 1985; Bell and Fenton, 1986, Bell et al., 1986

Mexican long-tongued bat | *Choeronycteris mexicana*

Choeronycteris mexicana is a medium-sized member of the family Phyllostomidae, with grayish to brownish pelage, an elongated muzzle, and a prominent nose leaf. The tail is short and extends about one-third the length of the naked uropatagium. The species is restricted to Central America, Mexico, and a small region within the southwestern United States, where it occurs only as a summer resident of southern California and Arizona, southwestern New Mexico, and extreme southern Texas.

Mexican long-tongued bats are known to inhabit deep canyons in small, insular mountain ranges, where they use caves and mine tunnels as day roosts, and also may be found in buildings and culverts; complete darkness seems not to be required. They have been taken in a wide variety of habitat associations ranging from arid thorn scrub to tropical deciduous forest and mixed oak-conifer forest.

These bats feed on fruits, pollen, nectar, and probably insects. Because of their longer tongues, they may be able to recover nectar from a greater variety of night-blooming plants than the other nectar-feeding bats *(Leptonycteris)* occurring in the United States.

Parturition occurs from June to early July in Arizona and New Mexico, and earlier to the south. Litter size is one. Pregnant females have been reported from March through September in different parts of this bat's range, indicating an extended breeding season for this species.

Parturition usually lasts about 15 minutes, resulting in the birth of a neonate in a remarkably advanced state of development. The newborn bat is surprisingly well furred on the dor-

Choeronycteris mexicana

sum with a dense, dark pelage; the venter is scantily furred with silvery hair. Mothers seem to carry their babies while they are feeding, and are not impaired in their flight.

This species is known to occur in the United States most commonly during the warmer months of the year when blooming plants provide pollen and nectar for its consumption. The bats leave New Mexico in August, Arizona in October, and California in December. *J. Arroyo-Cabrales*

Size

No significant sexual dimorphism
Total length: 81–103 mm
Length of tail: 6–10 mm
Weight: 10–25 g

Identification

Choeronycteris mexicana is similar to the Mexican long-nosed bat *(Leptonycteris nivalis)*, but differs in having a short, conspicuous tail and a well-developed interfemoral membrane. The Mexican long-tongued bat also lacks both lower incisors and has an incomplete zygomatic arch.

Other Common Names

Hog-nosed bat

Status

Common, limited

References

Mammalian Species 291; Herly, 1979; Schmidly, 1991

Southern long-nosed bat | *Leptonycteris curasoae*

One subspecies of the southern long-nosed bat is found from the southwestern United States and northern Mexico to El Salvador. Another occurs in northern South America, inhabiting arid portions of Colombia, Venezuela, and the island of Curacao. In the United States this bat is found only in southernmost Arizona and New Mexico. Its presence there is seasonal, and individuals migrate each fall to northern Mexico. *Leptonycteris curasoae* is found from sea level to about 2,400 meters, but is most abundant below 1,700 meters.

In southern Arizona and northern Mexico, the southern long-nosed bat is found mainly in arid grassland and scrub land, but it has been observed also in oak forests. Typical plants in its habitat in Arizona include the saguaro, ocotillo, palo verde, prickly pear, and agaves.

In central and southern Mexico, this bat inhabits tropical deciduous and thorn forests, but individuals are frequently observed in pine-oak forests and arid grassland. In northern South America, the southern long-nosed bat is strongly associated with tropical dry forest.

Leptonycteris curasoae

During the day these bats roost mainly in caves and abandoned mines, forming colonies that range in size from a few individuals to more than 10,000 bats. At night, between their foraging activity periods, individuals use small caves and old structures as roosts. North American populations are migratory and travel each year from Arizona and New Mexico to northern and central Mexico, probably following a "nectar trail" of plants of different species that provide food for the bats along their migratory route.

At the local scale, individuals can also travel great distances. In Mexico, long-nosed bats fly up to 30 km each night from their roosts on Isla Tiburón in the Sea of Cortés to their feeding grounds in mainland Sonora. Apparently the large body size and the particular morphology of the wing are adaptations to long-distance flying over the sea and the desert.

In northern Mexico and the southern United States, *L. curasoae* breeds at the end of spring or the beginning of summer. Females form huge maternity colonies from May to August in caves and tunnels in Sonora and Arizona. In contrast, males spend the summer in groups of only a few individuals. A single juvenile is born to each female between early May and late June. Parturition occurs in the maternity colonies. Copulation probably takes place in northern Mexico before the females

migrate north. Juveniles start flying at the age of one month, and venture outside caves about two to three weeks later.

Southern long-nosed bats feed mainly on the nectar and pollen of tropical and subtropical plants such as silk trees *(Ceiba, Pseudobombax)*, agaves and related forms *(Agave, Manfreda brachystachya)*, and several species of columnar cacti, especially saguaro, Mexican cardon, and organ pipe. In Arizona there is a shift in the diet from cactus pollen and nectar in May and June to agave nectar and pollen in July and August. Long-nosed bats complement their diet with some insects and fruits from cacti.

Bats of this species frequently form flocks to forage. When the group finds a suitable plant, each individual feeds on the flowers for less than a second, then returns to the flock. After a feeding period of about 20 minutes, the bats take a rest of about equal duration. Several times during the night, individuals gather in a small cave or human-built structure to roost and groom.

There is a close symbiotic relationship between *L. curasoae* and some species of plants. In Arizona, several species of agaves apparently depend completely on long-nosed bats for pollination. In Sonora, Mexico, seed production by cardon and organ pipe cacti occurs only where pollinating long-nosed bats are present. In central Mexico, a decline in the population of long-nosed bats apparently caused a 75 percent decrease in the fecundity of *Manfreda brachystachya,* a bat-pollinated plant.

It has been suggested that bats of the genus *Leptonycteris* might be the main pollinators of certain commercially important plants such as the mezcal and tequila agaves. However, recent studies have shown that cultivated populations of these plants are only distantly related to natural populations, so their pollination by bats seems to be of minor importance.

A similar species, the Mexican long-tongued bat *Choeronycteris mexicana,* is also a seasonal inhabitant of southern Arizona. It is never found in groups as large as those of the long-nosed bats. In a large part of its range in Mexico, *L. curasoae* is sympatric with the Mexican long-nosed bat *(Leptonycteris nivalis).* In the United States, however, the two species do not normally overlap; *L. nivalis* occurs regularly only in the southern tip of Texas. Recently, however, two individuals of *L. nivalis* were collected in New Mexico, suggesting that it may co-occur with the southern long-nosed bat much farther west than previously thought.

The southern long-nosed bat is considered threatened by the governments of Mexico and the United States, and vulnerable by the International Union for the Conservation of Nature, based on evidence of population declines in both countries. Recent research suggests that populations may not be as threatened as previously thought. However, its migratory behavior, specialized diet, and roost specificity make the southern long-nosed bat a fragile species that deserves protection.
H. T. Arita

Size
No significant sexual dimorphism
Total length: 75–85 mm (81)
Length of tail: external tail is inconspicuous
Length of forearm: 51–54 mm
Weight: 15–25 g

Identification
Leptonycteris curasoae is one of only four North American bats with a noseleaf. It can be distinguished from *Macrotus californicus* and *Choeronycteris mexicana* by the lack of a conspicuous external tail; its tail consists of three vertebrae that are not externally visible. *Leptonycteris nivalis* is larger, with grayish (instead of brownish) pelage, and has a narrower uropatagium (tail or interfemoral membrane) and longer wings.

Recent Synonyms
Leptonycteris nivalis nivalis
Leptonycteris sanborni
Leptonycteris yerbabuenae

Other Common Names
Sanborn's long-nosed bat, little long-nosed bat, lesser long-nosed bat

Status
Threatened

Subspecies
Leptonycteris curasoae curasoae, Colombia, Venezuela, and adjacent Caribbean islands
Leptonycteris curasoae yerbabuenae, southwestern United States and northern Mexico to El Salvador

References
Arita and Humphrey, 1988; Hoffmeister, 1986

Mexican long-nosed bat | *Leptonycteris nivalis*

The Mexican long-nosed bat ranges mainly at middle elevations in the mountains of northern Mexico. In the United States, large populations of this bat are found only in Brewster and Presidio counties, in Trans-Pecos Texas. A new locality was recently reported in Hidalgo County, New Mexico. In Mexico, these long-nosed bats inhabit deserts, pine-oak forests, and the transition zone between these forests and tropical dry areas. Most localities for this species are between 1,000 and 2,200 meters. Two records, however, indicate that Mexican long-nosed bats can reach higher elevations. In 1860, the French naturalist Saussure described the species from the snow line of the Orizaba Volcano in Veracruz, Mexico. Similarly, Koestner, in 1941, found a colony of these bats at 3,780 meters in the Cerro Potosí in northeastern Mexico.

Mexican long-nosed bats feed mainly on the nectar and pollen of the flowers of century plants *(Agave)* and other plants such as some species of morning-glories *(Ipomoea),* silk trees *(Ceiba),* and columnar cacti *(Myrtillocactus geometrizans).* The presence of this bat in Texas is seasonal and coincides with the blooming of agaves in June and July. This bat might be the main pollinator of the pulque plant *(Agave salmiana),* a plant of some economic importance in the highlands of central Mexico.

Mexican long-nosed bats roost mainly in caves and abandoned mines. In the southern part of their range, they form small colonies of 500 or fewer individuals. In contrast, the colony in Emory Peak Cave in Texas can number more than 10,000 bats. In tropical areas this long-nosed bat shares the roost with as many as 12 other bat species. In temperate zones, it is frequently found sharing caves with big-eared bats *(Corynorhinus).*

Leptonycteris nivalis

The reproductive pattern of *L. nivalis* is poorly known. In Texas, lactating females have been found in June and July, but pregnant females have never been observed there. This suggests that copulation and parturition occur in Mexico during the spring and that females migrate to the caves in Texas to form maternity colonies. In northern Mexico, pregnant females have been seen in March and April, and lactating females and juveniles in July, which coincides with the cycle in Texas. However, in central Mexico, pregnant and lactating females have been collected in January, suggesting that reproductive patterns might be different in the southern part of the distribution of this species.

The Mexican long-nosed bat co-occurs in large areas of Mexico with the southern long-nosed bat *(Leptonycteris curasoae)* and the long-tongued bat *(Choeronycteris mexicana)*. In some cases they even share the same roost. However, in the United States *L. nivalis* occurs regularly only in far southwest-ern Texas, where the southern long-nosed bat is not found. It is possible that the long-tongued bat occurs in Texas, but records there are based only on field observations, with no museum specimen to corroborate them.

The species is considered threatened by the governments of Mexico and the United States. This bat has a restricted distributional range and seems to be uncommon in most places where it occurs. Its migratory habits and specialized feeding habits make it particularly vulnerable. *H. T. Arita*

Size
No significant sexual dimorphism
Total length: 76–88 (83) mm
Length of tail: tail is not externally visible
Length of forearm: 56.6–59.5 mm
Weight: 18–30 g

Identification
Leptonycteris nivalis is the only leaf-nosed bat with confirmed records in Texas. It can be distinguished from *Macrotus californicus* and *Choeronycteris mexicana* by the lack of a conspicuous external tail. *Leptonycteris curasoae* is smaller, has a more brownish pelage, and has a wider uropatagium and shorter wings.

Other Common Names
Big long-nosed bat

Status
Threatened

References
Mammalian Species 307; Arita and Humphrey, 1988; Schmidly, 1991

Hairy-legged vampire bat | *Diphylla ecaudata*

Vampire bats are restricted to the warmer regions of the Americas. The hairy-legged vampire bat is known from the United States only by a single female obtained in 1967 in an abandoned railroad tunnel near Comstock in Val Verde County, Texas. This specimen, now in The Museum at Texas Tech University, extended the known distribution of the species north-northwest by more than 700 km (from southern Tamaulipas, Mexico) and is the only record of a vampire bat in the U.S. in recent times. The absence of corroborative evidence that the species is present elsewhere in or near Texas suggests that this individual might have been a wanderer from a breeding population far to the south.

Despite the existence of fossilized specimens of an extinct species of *Desmodus, D. stocki,* from Pleistocene deposits in several U.S. states, and the abundance and extensive distribution of *D. rotundus* in Mexico, living examples of the common vampire bat have not been encountered in the United States. The northernmost record of the white-winged vampire bat, *Diaemus youngii,* is near El Encino, in southern Tamaulipas, Mexico. Pleistocene fossils of *Diphylla* are known from only two caves, one in Yucatan, Mexico, and the other in Distrito Caripe, Estado Monagas, Venezuela. In both cases, the specimens appear to be of *D. ecaudata.* It has been suggested that vampire bats are absent from cooler portions of both North and South America because their food source, vertebrate blood, cannot be transported by the bats in adequate quantities for them to maintain a high body temperature in the cooler caves of higher latitudes. Certainly there is no shortage of potential mammalian and avian prey beyond the present distributional limits of vampires either to the north or the south of their present distribution.

The intergeneric relationships of the three vampires have been debated, but most investigators, including those employing molecular techniques, favor the hypothesis that *Desmodus* and *Diaemus* are more closely related to each other than either is to *Diphylla.* Although *Diphylla* and *Diaemus* both have diploid (2n) chromosome numbers of 32 and an Fn (number of autosomal arms) of 60 and *Desmodus* has a diploid number of 28 and an Fn of 52, the chromosomal banding patterns of *Diphylla* and *Diaemus* reveal important differences. Chromosomal change in vampires appears to have involved both translocations and inversions. Recent work suggests that *Diphylla* is the most evolutionarily primitive of the three vampire genera.

Like the other two species of vampires, *Diphylla* is a sanguinivore, feeding on the blood of other animals. *Desmodus* feeds primarily on mammals, *Diaemus* utilizes blood of both birds and mammals, and *Diphylla* specializes on avian hosts. *Diphylla* has been maintained in captivity when allowed to feed regularly from roosting chickens. Field observations reveal that *Diphylla* usually lands near a target host or on the host's back and then crawls to its legs or cloacal region and feeds from a hanging position. A shallow wound is made with the sharp incisors on the lower legs or around the cloacal region of the host bird. *Desmodus* produces a salivary anticoagulant that functions to prevent clotting and maintain blood flow while the bat feeds from the wound. A similar adaptation of the

Diphylla ecaudata

saliva presumably exits for all vampires, but its presence in *Diphylla* awaits investigation.

There is some speculation that the broad, flexible lips, nonprotruding lower jaw, and absence of a lower lip cleft in *Diphylla* might allow this bat to form a seal over the wound and actually suck blood (Dracula style!) from the host rather than using the "drinking straw" formed by grooves on the lower side of the tongue as in *Desmodus* and *Diaemus*. Regardless of the feeding method, hosts are often not greatly disturbed by a vampire's activities. Several theories have been advanced to explain the evolution of sanguinivory. One suggests that dental preadaptations resulted from teeth used to cut the hard rinds of fruit, and another theory is that feeding on blood-eating ectoparasites may have led to feeding directly on blood. A third argument is that the intermediate stage involved feeding on insect larvae and body fluids at wounds on large mammals and thence to feeding directly on blood. The most recent hypothesis involves the highly arboreal feeding behavior observed in the most closely related nonsanguinivorous phyllostomid bats and in *Diphylla*. Morphological adaptations of the hind limbs, shared by *Diphylla* and some arboreal frugivorous bats, may aid in climbing. The other two vampire genera, which feed on the ground, lack these adaptations.

Vampires may act as vectors for various viral, bacterial, and fungal pathogens (including the rabies virus) that affect humans and other species. Some harm to the host may result simply from the wound made during feeding. Repeated bleeding can debilitate the host animal, and a single feeding may cause small hosts, such as chickens, to bleed to death. Wounds produced by vampires also provide a source of entry for other pathogens unrelated to the bats.

All vampire bats have a highly modified alimentary canal.

The stomach wall is thin and capable of expanding to hold up to 30 ml of blood. The caecum of *Diphylla* is much shorter than that of *Desmodus,* but the reasons for the difference are unknown. Vampires have a high degree of vascularization around the stomach and efficient kidneys. These adaptations allow them to shed water as soon as they begin feeding, through the excretion of very dilute urine, significantly reducing body mass prior to the return flight to the roost.

Hairy-legged vampires typically have only a single young, which weighs about 4.5 g, per litter. Although it has been suggested that *Diphylla* has a well-defined breeding season, the accumulation of breeding records to date suggests that aseasonal polyestry better defines the breeding habits of this species. Although little is known about the length of gestation and development in *Diphylla,* gestation lengths of 210 to 220 days are known for *Desmodus.*

In contrast to the highly social common vampire, *Diphylla* is usually solitary, although an adult female often roosts with a juvenile or young adult, presumably her own offspring. When more than a single hairy-legged vampire or a presumed family is found in a roost site (usually a cave or tunnel, but occasionally a hollow tree) they do not cluster together. Curiously, however, individuals have been observed in clusters of mixed species. Females are highly protective of their young, and the family appears to remain together for several months, probably until the offspring is capable of selecting a host, making an incision, and feeding alone. Blood sharing, in which females regurgitate blood for other females, especially relatives, who have stayed at the roost to take care of young, is common in *Desmodus,* but owing to the solitary life style of the species such complex social interactions probably are absent in *Diphylla.*

E. C. Birney and R. S. Sikes

Size

No significant sexual dimorphism
Head and body length: 67–93 (83) mm
Forearm length: 50–56 (53) mm
Weight: 24–43 (31) g

Identification

Like the other two genera of vampire bats, *Diphylla ecaudata* has no tail, the noseleaf is greatly reduced, and the front teeth are prominent, with curved, razor-sharp cutting edges.

The hairy-legged vampire bat differs from *Desmodus* in having hairy legs and no pads under its thumbs; it differs from *Diaemus* by lacking white wing tips. The second lower incisor is seven-lobed and comblike only in *Diphylla,* and the total number of teeth is 26, as compared to 20 in *Desmodus* and 22 in *Diaemus.* The dorsal fur is dark brown, the venter slightly paler, and the ears are more rounded than in other vampires.

Recent Synonyms

Diphylla centralis

Status

Rare in the United States but common over most of its range

References

Mammalian Species 227; Greenhall and Schmidt, 1988

Family Vespertilionidae

If you live in North America, chances are pretty good that you have seen a member of the family Vespertilionidae. This widespread and diverse family includes the most common species of bats foraging for insects on summer evenings throughout North America. They have also adapted readily to the tendency of human beings to build houses, barns, and other structures that the bats assume were meant to be bat roosts. If you have a colony of bats in your attic, it is likely to be a member of this family.

Most are small, brownish, and rather nondistinctive, even for bats. In the summer, they roost in a variety of natural and artificial refuges, including buildings of all types, caves, hollows, and mines, as well as in trees and other foliage roosts in the case of some migratory species. In winter, they hibernate in cold caves in the northern part of the range, or migrate south to more hospitable climes. Their preferred feeding areas include a wide variety of habitats, where they feed on insects. Their prowess for catching small, mosquito-sized prey enables them to take up to several hundred insects per hour.

These bats are frequently the cause of complaints from householders, as they tend to deposit guano in the attic, and an occasional individual may stray into the living quarters. However, they are superb insect control devices, and people who understand and appreciate them are willing to put up with the inconvenience of sharing their buildings with them.

References

Tuttle, 1988; Wilson, 1997

North American Genera

Myotis
Lasiurus
Lasionycteris
Pipistrellus
Eptesicus
Nycticeius
Euderma
Corynorhinus
Idionycteris
Antrozous

Southwestern myotis | *Myotis auriculus*

Myotis auriculus is a bat of the southwestern mountains. It occurs from desert grassland up into pine and mixed coniferous forests. Pine forest is probably the most frequently chosen habitat. The subspecies *M. a. auriculus* may occur in tropical deciduous forest. Although range maps show this species as continuous over broad areas of desert and grassland in Mexico, probably most of the records of its occurrence are from mountains. The species has been taken from 366 meters up to 2,226 meters. Probably some of this elevational variation is seasonal. In the Southwest many kinds of montane bats are taken at lower elevations during migration or during their movement to winter quarters.

The southwestern myotis belongs to a hovering-gleaning group of bats that also includes *M. evotis* and *M. thysanodes*. This group is characterized by large, forward-directed ears, broad wing membranes, somewhat reduced tail membranes, relatively large brains, and a fundamental chromosome number of 52 (rather than 50 as in other species of *Myotis* that have been examined). Southwestern myotis have been observed to pick insects from the surface of tree trunks and buildings.

Myotis auriculus

Moths seem to constitute the chief prey species. Unlike bats that engage in aerial pursuit of insects, the cries of *M. auriculus* are short and of low intensity, with no increase in repetition rate as the prey is approached.

Females bear a single young, usually in June. Pregnant females have been observed frequenting caves occurring in habitats from mixed coniferous forest to desert grassland in New Mexico. Probably the maternity roosts are in these caves, as are the maternity roosts of the closely related big-eared myotis, *M. thysanodes. Myotis auriculus* has not been found in its hibernaculum. *J. S. Findley*

Size
Total length: 85–101 m
Tail length: 34–49 mm
Weight: 6–8 g; pregnant females to 10 g

Identification
M. auriculus is medium-sized, with long, brownish ears. Among long-eared species of *Myotis* only *M. thysanodes* and *M. evotis* are likely to be found within its range. *M. auriculus* can be distinguished from *M. thysanodes* by lacking a visible fringe of hairs on the rear edge of the tail membrane (*M. auriculus* may have a

fringe that is visible with magnification). It can be distinguished from *M. evotis* by its shorter ears (usually shorter than 21 mm), paler colored flight membranes, and by its dorsal hairs, which are brownish, rather than blackish, at the base. *M. evotis* lacks even a microscopic fringe of hairs on the tail membrane.

Recent Synonyms
Myotis evotis apache
Myotis evotis auriculus
Myotis keenii apache
Myotis keenii auriculus

Status
Common in appropriate habitat

Subspecies
Myotis auriculus apache, Jalisco, Mexico, northward to the mountains of southwestern New Mexico, southeastern Arizona, and northern Coahuila, Mexico
Myotis auriculus auriculus, Tamaulipas, Nuevo Leon, and Vera Cruz, Mexico

References
Mammalian Species 191; Reduker et al., 1983

Southeastern myotis | *Myotis austroriparius*

The southeastern myotis occurs from the southern part of North Carolina south to the northern half of the Florida peninsula West of the Appalachian Mountains, its range extends north into southern Illinois and Indiana, and westward to northeastern Texas and southeastern Oklahoma. *M. austroriparius* is not

known to migrate. In the northern reaches of its distribution, it hibernates almost all winter. In Florida, these bats change roosting sites seasonally and are intermittently active throughout winter.

Myotis austroriparius lives in close association with water.

These bats use caves as their primary roosts, and prefer caves that contain pools of water. Trees and man-made structures also are used as roosts in areas that lack caves. These bats emerge from their roosts late in the evening and fly directly to water to drink and forage for insects. They usually fly close to the surface of the water while feeding. Rat snakes, corn snakes, opossums, and owls prey heavily on *M. austroriparius.* Cockroaches have been known to feed on young that fall from their roosts.

The southeastern myotis is a small bat with a dull, woolly pelage. The most common color is dull gray to gray-brown, but some individuals are a bright orange-brown. The fur on the underside is dark brown to black at the base, with contrasting white at the tip. Males, which are slightly smaller than females, often are not as brightly colored.

In Florida, newborn *M. austroriparius* begin appearing in late April; the majority of births occur in the second week of May. Most females give birth to twins. The southeastern myotis is unique in this: all other members of this genus in the United States normally produce only one offspring. The female uses her interfemoral membrane to form a birthing pocket. Parturition is by breech presentation and occurs while the female hangs by her feet and thumbs. The mother bites the umbilical cord in two and may assist the young in finding the nipples. The young bats are nearly naked at birth. The skin is fairly transparent and has a pinkish hue. The eyes and ears are closed at the time of parturition, but the tips of the ears become erect when the animals are 1 to 2 days old. Young bats can fly at 5 to 6 weeks of age and reach sexual maturity before the end of their first year.

Myotis austroriparius

Myotis is derived from two Greek words, *mys,* meaning mouse, and *otis,* meaning ear. The specific name, *austroriparius,* is of Latin origin, from the words meaning southern and bank of a stream, and is descriptive of this bat's choice of habitat.
C. Mauk-Cunningham and C. Jones

Size
Females are larger than males.
Total length: 77.0–89.0 (83.7) mm (males);
80.0–97.0 (87.2) mm (females)
Length of forearm: 33.0–39.0 (36.0) mm
(males); 33.5–40.0 (38.6) mm (females)
Length of tail: 26.0–44.0 (36.8) mm (males);
29.0–42.0 (38.0) mm (females)

Weight: 5.1–6.8 (5.9) g (males); 5.2–8.1 (6.9) g
(females)

Identification
Myotis austroriparius can be distinguished from
Myotis septentrionalis by its relatively smaller
ears. *Myotis lucifugus* has glossy, dark brown
fur; in contrast, the fur of *M. austroriparius* is
dull and woolly in appearance.

Other Common Names
Mississippi myotis

Status
Common

References
Mammalian Species 332; Schmidly, 1991

California myotis | *Myotis californicus*

Throughout much of its range, *M. californicus* is a bat of deserts
and arid interior basins, where it frequently occurs with the
pallid bat *(Antrozous pallidus)* and the western pipistrelle *(Pipistrellus hesperus).* The California myotis uses small waterholes
to obtain needed moisture and its kidneys are adapted for water conservation in an arid environment. It is a slow, acrobatic
flyer, often appearing early in the evening and foraging less
than 3 meters above the ground, over and near water, along
the edges of forests and tree canopy, and in open areas. It de-
tects its prey at close range (less than 1 m) and eats moths, flies,
beetles, and other insects. Its diet likely varies from area to area
and depending upon the presence of its close relative, *M. ciliolabrum.* Where the two species occur together, they are believed to partition food resources spatially: *M. californicus* forages over water and *M. ciliolabrum* over rocky areas. The two
species may also specialize on different prey in such areas, one
eating more moths and the other more beetles.

During warmer months, the California myotis roosts alone
or in small groups in caves, mines, rocky hillsides, under tree
bark, occasionally on shrubs and on the ground, and especially
in buildings. In the winter, solitary individuals and small
groups have been found in caves, mines, and buildings. This
bat is active in the winter, even at temperatures below freezing,
but at low temperatures it is active for shorter periods. At high
elevations and latitudes it hibernates, and small groups of hibernating *M. californicus* have been found in caves and mines in
Arizona, Nevada, and Utah.

Like most north temperate bats, the California myotis
mates in the fall and females store sperm in the uterus; fertilization follows ovulation in the spring. In California, mating
may also occur in the spring. The single young, born in June or
July, develops rapidly and is able to fly about one month after
birth. Females may reside in small maternity colonies during
pregnancy, birth, and lactation. Individuals are known to live as
long as 15 years, but the average life span is undoubtedly
shorter.

Myotis californicus

In arid areas *M. californicus* is adaptively colored and typically is a pale yellowish-orange; the fur often appears tricolored when compared to that of *M. ciliolabrum*. In the Colorado Plateau, adjacent Great Basin, and lower Colorado River, the California myotis occupies low-elevation areas and is especially small and pale in color. In the Pacific Northwest, where it lives in forests, it, like other *Myotis,* is darker in color. Similarly, in the forested highlands of Mexico the species is dark and often richly colored; some individuals there appear auburn in color. Elsewhere, the species occupies both low-elevation and montane areas up to at least the level of ponderosa pine. Variation in color is great in southeastern Arizona and western New Mexico, where dark-colored populations live in the mountains and pale-colored bats occur at low elevations.

Despite considerable information on variation within the species in southwestern North America, no one has satisfactorily dealt with relationships among the various subspecies nor explained the bewildering color variation. Several recent studies have shown that what had been classified as subspecies of some species of *Myotis* are full species (e.g., *M. keenii* and *septentrionalis; M. leibii* and *ciliolabrum)* and such a possibility exists within *M. californicus* as well.

Although much remains to be learned of this widespread and adaptable bat, there seems to be no reason to be concerned about its welfare. With increasing concern for the welfare of all bats, and now that special care is being taken to assess the status of abandoned mines as potential bat habitats before the mine entrances are sealed, the California myotis should continue to be secure. *M. A. Bogan*

Size
Females average larger than males in most characters.
Total length: 70–94 mm
Length of forearm: 30–35 mm
Weight: 3.3–5.4 g

Identification
Myotis californicus shares its combination of short ears (shorter than 15 mm), relatively short hind feet (shorter than 6–9 mm), and an obviously keeled calcar with only two other western *Myotis, M. ciliolabrum* and *M. volans.* From *M. volans,* the California myotis is distinguished by shorter forearm (less than 35 mm), shorter tibia (less than 15 mm), usually paler pelage, and ventral surface of wing membrane from elbow to knee not densely furred. The California myotis can easily be confused with the western small-footed myotis, *M. ciliolabrum,* from which it differs in more subtle characters: cranium globose with a distinct "forehead," rostrum shorter and more delicate, pelage often tricolored, and overall more delicate form in *M. californicus.*

Other Common Names
California bat

Status
Common

Subspecies
Myotis californicus californicus, New Mexico, eastern Arizona, northern Mexico, Baja California, and northward through interior California to southeastern British Columbia
Myotis californicus caurinus, Pacific coast of California, Oregon, Washington, British Columbia, and southeastern Alaska; also reported from the Northern Channel Islands (California)
Myotis californicus mexicanus, central and southern Mexico, Guatemala
Myotis californicus stephensi, Colorado Plateau (including southeastern Wyoming), Great Basin, and Colorado River country of Arizona, California, and Baja California

References
Mammalian Species 428; Bogan, 1975

Western small-footed myotis | *Myotis ciliolabrum*

The western small-footed myotis is widespread in western North America and is absent only from the west coast. In the high plains grasslands of the west, it is a denizen of rocky outcrops in short-grass ecosystems and is pale in color. Farther west and in more mountainous areas, it is larger and more richly colored and is an inhabitant of rocky areas in yellow pine and mixed coniferous forests. In Arizona, it is known from deserts, chaparral, riparian areas, and oak-juniper forests. It is one of two small-sized, small-footed bats in western North America, the other being *M. californicus*. Unlike the California myotis, the western small-footed myotis has a flattened braincase, perhaps indicative of a proclivity to roost in crevices.

Scientists have had a difficult time determining the correct name of this species. It was known for years as *Myotis keenii* and was believed to occur throughout much of the United States and Canada. Later, it was called *M. subulatus,* and was divided into three races: *leibii, subulatus,* and *melanorhinus*. In the 1960s the name *subulatus* was replaced by the name *ciliolabrum*. Subsequently, van Zyll de Jong showed that there were two species of small-footed bats: *Myotis leibii* in eastern North America and *M. ciliolabrum* in the west. *M. ciliolabrum* is divided into two subspecies: *ciliolabrum* and *melanorhinus*. Because of this confusion, one must be careful to determine whether a given author is discussing eastern or western small-footed myotis.

These little bats follow a typical pattern of mating in the fall, sperm storage in winter, and fertilization following ovulation in the spring. The single young is born in May, June, or July and begins to fly about one month later. Known maximum life span is about 12 years, with an average life span of around 5 to 7 years. Adults molt in June or July; males molt before reproductively-active females.

This species roosts singly or in small groups in cracks and crevices in rocks, caves, mines, under tree bark, in abandoned swallow nests, and in buildings. In California, a small maternity colony was found beneath the wallpaper of an abandoned house. In the winter it hibernates; single individuals and small groups have been found hibernating in cracks and crevices in mines and caves. Unlike *M. californicus,* which often is active at low temperatures, *M. ciliolabrum* does not appear to be active in winter. *M. leibii*, the eastern small-footed myotis, is also more active in winter than its western relative, and is known to enter hibernation late and emerge relatively early.

Myotis ciliolabrum occurs in moister areas than *M. californicus,* and its kidney morphology and urine concentrating ability reveal that it is not a true arid land dweller. Indeed, it is more common in montane and coniferous forest. Rarely does it occur below the level of ponderosa pine. It eats moths, flies, beetles,

Myotis ciliolabrum

bugs, and ants, and where it occurs with the California myotis, it tends to forage in different areas, often over rocky areas, and on different species of prey.

This species recently was listed as a Category 2 Candidate Species by the U. S. Fish and Wildlife Service and is a species of concern in some western states. However, little information is available on its status and more data on population status and trends are needed. There appear to be few specific threats to its existence, although closure of abandoned mines could threaten some roosting sites. It continues to be fairly common in sites where it has been found historically. Given its similarity to *M. californicus,* identification of either species in capture and release records should be accepted cautiously. *M. A. Bogan*

Size

Females tend to average larger than males in most characters.

Total length: 76–90 mm

Length of forearm: 30–34 mm

Weight: 2.8–7.1 g

Identification

This species, *M. californicus,* and *M. volans* share similar characteristics of short ears (less than 15 mm), relatively short hind foot length (less than 9 mm), and an obviously keeled calcar. From *M. volans,* the western small-footed myotis is distinguished by shorter forearm (less than 35 mm), shorter tibia (less than 15 mm), paler pelage, and ventral surface of wing membrane from elbow to knee not densely furred. From *M. californicus* the western small-footed myotis differs more subtly: its cranium is flattened; it lacks a distinct "forehead"; its rostrum is longer and more robust; its pelage is often bicolored rather than tricolored, and has a glossy sheen; and its overall appearance is more robust.

Recent Synonyms

Myotis leibii

Myotis subulatus

Other Common Names

Small-footed myotis, western small-footed bat

Status

Common, limited; more information is needed to determine its status.

Subspecies

Myotis ciliolabrum ciliolabrum, east of the Continental Divide and in the high plains from the Canadian prairie provinces, Montana, and North Dakota southward to northeastern New Mexico, the panhandle of Texas, and western Oklahoma

Myotis ciliolabrum melanorhinus, Continental Divide westward to British Columbia, Washington, Oregon, and California, northern Baja California, and northern Mexico; not known from the Pacific Coast

References

Bogan, 1974; van Zyll de Jong, 1984, 1985

Long-eared myotis | *Myotis evotis*

This species, perhaps the most striking of North American *Myotis* with its large dark glossy ears and often contrasting pale pelage, is a member of a group of long-eared *Myotis* that includes *M. auriculus, M. keenii, M. septentrionalis,* and *M. thysanodes.* The range of *M. evotis* overlaps portions of the ranges of these species, but the long-eared myotis can be distinguished from them by its larger size and longer ears. Some individuals of *M. evotis* have small scattered hairs along the trailing edge of the uropatagium, but a distinct fringe of hairs, as in *M. thysanodes,* is lacking. The pelage is long and glossy and varies from dark brown *(M. e. pacificus)* to pale yellow *(M. e. milleri, evotis, chrysonotus).* Two disjunct subspecies, their distinctness the subject of some debate, occur on the Baja California peninsula.

Like most North American *Myotis,* this species is insectivorous. It is often seen flying in dense vegetation, from which it is thought to glean insects. Lepidoptera (moths) and Coleoptera (beetles) are particularly important as food items, but long-eared myotis also feed on flies, lacewings, wasps, bees, and true bugs. When *M. evotis* occurs with a close relative such as *M. auriculus,* it consumes more beetles and the other

Myotis evotis

species eats more moths. When other long-eared *Myotis* are absent, male *M. evotis* eat more moths and females eat more beetles. Recent studies have shown that at times this species "turns off" its sonar and listens passively for sounds made by potential prey. It appears to adjust its echolocation behavior to meet the demands of individual foraging situations. The species forages over and drinks from small bodies of water, frequently attaining considerable speed when it flies over water.

The reproductive pattern is similar to other north temperate *Myotis*. Mating occurs in the fall, ovulation and fertilization in spring, followed by development of the single embryo. The testis length of males increases in late summer and fall in preparation for breeding. Pregnant long-eared myotis have been found as early as 19 May (southern California) and as late as 7 July (British Columbia). Lactation occurs into late July, at which time the young begin to fly. Females are known to form small maternity colonies; males and nonreproductive females occur singly or in small groups. Individuals have been known to live 22 years, but the average life span is considerably shorter. Molting occurs in July and August, with males molting before females. A snake, the yellow-bellied racer, is a known predators of these bats in British Columbia.

Within its known range, and depending upon the site, the species varies from moderately common to scarce. It seems to prefer coniferous vegetation, but occurs as low as pinyon-juniper forests and sagebrush steppe in the western United States and riparian desert scrub vegetation in Baja California. It has been collected in areas containing deciduous trees, particularly where streams or reservoirs are present. The presence of broken rock outcroppings and tree snags, where roosts can be located, is likely more important in determining habitat suitability than the actual type or species of vegetation. *M. evotis* is known to roost in lava tubes in Idaho.

In warmer months, the long-eared myotis has been found singly or in small groups (of 12 to 30 individuals) using day roosts in buildings, railroad trestles, sink holes, crevices, caves,

abandoned mines, behind slabs of bark, under rocks, and in hollow trees. Little is known of its winter habits; it presumably migrates short distances to suitable quarters where it spends the winter in hibernation or in short bouts of torpor. It has been found hibernating in an abandoned mine in Montana.

The long-eared myotis recently was listed as a Category 2 Candidate Species by the U.S. Fish and Wildlife Service, but lit-

tle is known about the status and population trends of this species. Presumably the major threat to its existence is destruction of roosting sites in abandoned mines, caves, and trees. Although it is not common everywhere in its range, it is usually moderately common in areas where its habitat requirements are met. *M. A. Bogan*

Size
Significant sexual dimorphism in some
    characters
Total length: 87–100 mm
Length of forearm: 36–41 mm
Weight: 5–8 g

Identification
Myotis evotis can be distinguished from other North American long-eared *Myotis* by its larger body size, longer, glossy dark brown to black ears (longer than 19–23 mm), and by its lack of an obvious fringe of hairs on the posterior border of the uropatagium.

Other Common Names
Long-eared bat, little big-eared bat

Status
Widespread, limited; more data are needed for its status to be determined.

Subspecies
Myotis evotis chrysonotus, northern and interior parts of western North America
Myotis evotis evotis, inland areas surrounding San Francisco Bay and southward along the coastal ranges to San Diego County

Myotis evotis jonesorum, northern and eastern Arizona (Kaibab Plateau, Mogollon Rim) and west-central New Mexico
Myotis evotis micronyx, known only from Comondu, Baja California Sur, Mexico
Myotis evotis milleri, Sierra San Pedro Martir, Baja California, Mexico
Myotis evotis pacificus, northwestern North America (British Columbia, Washington, Oregon, California, Idaho, and Montana)

References
Mammalian Species 329; Faure and Barclay, 1994; Manning, 1993

Gray myotis | *Myotis grisescens*

The gray myotis occurs in the south-central and southeastern United States, primarily in karst areas with underlying limestone caverns. It is known from Illinois, Indiana, Kansas, Missouri, Kentucky, Oklahoma, Arkansas, Tennessee, Virginia, North Carolina, Alabama, Georgia, and Florida; current populations are found primarily in Alabama, Tennessee, Kentucky, and Missouri. Most of our understanding of this species comes from studies in caves used as roosts.

In summer, females locate their maternity colonies in warm (13–26° C) caves that usually have large streams running through them; the streams prevent predators from entering and serve as protection for the bats. The caves are usually within 1–2 km of a major river or lake. In winter, virtually the entire species hibernates in nine major caves with temperatures ranging from 6–11° C. This dependence on particular caves that meet specific roosting requirements has placed the species in jeopardy as historically-used caves have been developed for tourism, flooded by reservoirs, vandalized, or closed without benefit of "bat-friendly" gates.

Gray myotis typically mate in the fall and females store the sperm during hibernation. In spring, fertilization occurs, and the single young is born in May or June. Maternity colonies, where females and young cluster on the ceilings of caves, dis-

perse in July when the young become volant. Historically, these nursery colonies contained 4,000 to 200,000 individuals, but they declined in size to 1,900 to 127,500; current protective measures are allowing some colonies to recover. The bats are sensitive to intrusions and repeated disturbance may lead them to abandon the cave or may cause females to drop their non-flying young to the floor. Colonies of males and nonreproductive females typically use separate caves, but sometimes occur with reproductively active females. Unlike some other *Myotis,* male and female gray myotis do not breed until their second year. Gray myotis have been known to live 18 years, but the average life span is closer to 5 years, as juvenile mortality is high.

Gray myotis are believed to do most of their foraging over water and are known to eat mayflies and other aquatic insects, although a wide array of insects may be eaten. Foraging bats have been found as far as 25 km from their summer roost. Young bats grow faster when roosting in caves near water. Indeed, the use of warm caves located near sources of water with rich food supplies is a strategy that promotes the rapid growth of young and fat deposition prior to hibernation.

Gray myotis travel hundreds of kilometers in September to reach the few caves suitable for hibernation. Stress from migratory flights is an important mortality factor, especially for

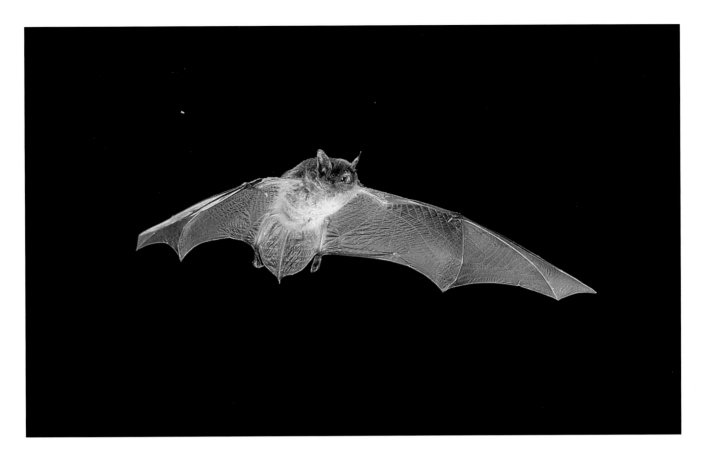

young born that year. The bats do not normally leave the cave once in hibernation, but repeated disturbances can cause them to arouse and expend energy stored as fat. Once an individual's fat stores are depleted, it may be forced out to forage at a time when no food is available, and therefore it may die. Emergence from hibernation usually begins in late March, and migration to summer roosts reaches a peak in April.

The gray myotis was one of the first species of North American bats to be recognized as vulnerable to population declines. As early as 1962, Manville noted how vulnerable these bats were to vandalism and disturbance, and in 1969 Barbour and Davis predicted that the species seemed likely to continue a rapid decline in numbers and probably faced extinction. Merlin Tuttle and his co-workers documented declines in this species, detailing vandalism, shooting, and frequent disturbance of bats in roosts. In 1976 the gray myotis was listed by the United States government as endangered. The species is vulnerable to factors such as land clearing, stream impoundment, and pesticide poisoning, but human disturbance of critically important roosting caves has been the key factor affecting its numbers.

Current population size is believed to be about 1.6 million in the nine largest hibernacula; it has been estimated that populations have declined about 50 percent since 1965. Most authorities believe the population is still declining but that recent conservation measures have slowed the rate of decline. Probably the most significant conservation measure has been the

Myotis grisescens

protection, by gating or purchase, of several significant nursery and hibernation caves. Continued public awareness of the plight of this species, and of other cave-dwelling bats, combined with measures to prevent disturbance of roosting colonies, will aid their recovery. *M. A. Bogan*

Size

Sexual dimorphism unstudied but may occur
Total length: 80–96 mm
Length of forearm: 40–46 mm
Weight: 7–16 g

Identification

This bat can be distinguished from other *Myotis* in eastern North America by overall larger size and uniformly colored pelage; hairs gray from base to tip rather than bi- or tricolored. Other distinguishing characters include a distinct sagittal crest on the skull, attachment of wing membrane to hind feet on the ankle rather than at the base of the toes (as in other *Myotis),* and no keel on the calcar.

Other Common Names

Gray bat, cave bat, Howell's bat

Status

Endangered (U.S. Fish and Wildlife Service)

References

Mammalian Species 510; Gore, 1992; Tuttle, 1976, 1979

Keen's myotis | *Myotis keenii*

Myotis keenii is very similar to other small bats of the same genus. It is medium-sized, with a long tail and short forearm and hind foot. The pelage is brown, darker on the back than on the underside. The ear is fairly long for a *Myotis,* extending slightly beyond the tip of the nose when laid forward. The tragus is long and pointed.

Myotis keenii

Keen's myotis roosts in a variety of shelter types from caves to trees, where it can sometimes be found under the bark. It occasionally occurs in small colonies. Daytime and night roosts may differ in the summer. Foraging activities occur just after dark and again just prior to dawn. *M. keenii* is a colonial hibernator and may be associated with other bats in the hibernaculum.

Little information on reproduction is available, although it is probably similar to that of the little brown bat, *M. lucifugus.* Breeding occurs in the fall, just before hibernation, but fertilization does not occur until spring. Small maternity colonies are usually separate from the summer roosting sites used by males. *K. A. Shump*

Size
Head and body length: 40.4–55.0 mm
Length of ears: 18.0–19.0 (18.6) mm
Length of forearm: 34–39 mm
Weight: 4–6 (5) g

Identification
The ear extends noticeably beyond the muzzle
when laid forward, but not as far as in the long-
eared myotis or northern long-eared bat. The
pelage is dark brown.

Recent Synonyms
Vespertilio subulatus keenii

Other Common Names
Keen's bat

Status
Uncommon, restricted

References
Mammalian Species 121; Barbour and Davis,
1969; Fenton, 1983; Kunz, 1982; Wimsatt,
1977

Eastern small-footed myotis | *Myotis leibii*

This is one of the two smallest bats in eastern North America, the other being the eastern pipistrelle. The thick fur is soft and glossy, and has been described as yellowish-tan to blackish-brown; typically it is a variable shade of brown and the individual hairs have a golden sheen. Some of the described variation may be because the hair becomes worn between annual molting sequences. Males and females likely molt at different times during the summer, thus causing variation in color within single populations. The ears and face are black, and the membranes are dark brownish-black.

Myotis leibii occurs from Maine, Quebec, and Ontario southwestward through the Appalachian region to Arkansas and eastern Oklahoma. It seems to be uncommon in most localities and some authorities consider it to be one of the rarest bats in the eastern United States. The U.S. Fish and Wildlife Service lists it as a Category 2 Candidate Species; in Pennsylvania, the species is listed as threatened. However, recent work in Arkansas suggests that it occupies a somewhat larger distribution than previously thought. Historically, this species is best known from studies of wintering concentrations in Pennsylvania, New York, Vermont, and Ontario.

In the winter, the eastern small-footed myotis hibernates singly or in small groups in narrow cracks and crevices in walls, floors, or roofs of caves and mines. It enters hibernation later than other eastern *Myotis,* often not until November or December, and becomes active as early as March. It tolerates colder temperatures than the little brown myotis, and this tolerance may account for its being found near the entrances of caves and mines, where the conditions are more variable and extreme. It sometimes arouses during hibernation and flies about the cave. Weight loss during hibernation averaged 16 percent in a combined sample of both sexes. Two banded individuals were found in summer 16 and 20 km (10 and 12 miles) from their hibernation site, suggesting that they may spend much of their lives within a relatively restricted area.

Myotis leibii

Habitat requirements are poorly known, although the species seems limited to eastern deciduous and coniferous forests. Summer roosts have been found in buildings, swallow nests, bridge expansion joints, behind doors, and under rocks, as well as in caves and mines. Individuals of this species have been found under loose tree bark and it is possible that the paucity of known records in summer is related to use of trees as roosts. Radiotracking of these small bats might shed important new light on their habits.

Little is known of this bat's reproductive habits. Mating occurs in autumn before hibernation and sperm is stored in the female until fertilization of the ovum in the spring. Females give birth to a single young between late May and July, depending upon latitude. Embryos were found in females captured on 17 and 24 June, and a pregnant female was caught on 12 July in New England. A maternity colony of about 12 females was found behind a door in a barn in Ontario and maternity colonies of 12 to 20 have been found in other buildings. One individual is known to have lived 12 years.

This little bat emerges at dusk, flying slowly and somewhat erratically at heights of 1–6 m while foraging over bodies of water and over land. We know little of its food habits, but eastern small-footed myotis undoubtedly take small insects, especially flies, beetles, and moths. Although they can be captured in mist nets, some investigators report they are more easily captured in hand nets. Their flight is characteristic and with practice these bats can be identified in flight.

This species was known for many years as *Myotis subulatus* and then, more recently, as *M. leibii,* with three races recognized: *M. l. leibii, M. l. ciliolabrum,* and *M. l. melanorhinus.* In 1984 van Zyll de Jong showed that *M. leibii* in eastern North America and *M. ciliolabrum* (with two subspecies) in the west are as distinct from one another as either is from *M. californicus.*

More information is needed on this species, especially information on population trends. Data should be gathered prior to the closing of abandoned mines, and known roosts should be closed with "bat-friendly" gates. Frequent disturbance of hibernating colonies should be avoided as this causes the bats to arouse and deplete stored fat too rapidly to survive hibernation. *M. A. Bogan*

Size
Sexual dimorphism is unstudied but may occur.
Total length: 73–82 mm
Length of forearm: 30–35 mm
Weight: 3–7 g

Identification
This bat is distinguished from other *Myotis* in eastern North America by its overall smaller size, shorter ears (less than 15 mm), shorter hind feet (less than 8 mm in length), obviously keeled calcar, and small, flattened skull. *M. leibii* is isolated from the other keeled, small-footed *Myotis, M. californicus* and *M. ciliolabrum,* which occur in western North America. The eastern pipistrelle, *Pipistrellus subfavus,* which is of similar size, can be distinguished by its blunt, rather than pointed, tragus.

Recent Synonyms
Myotis subulatus

Other Common Names
Small-footed myotis, least myotis, Leib's myotis

Status
Uncommon, limited. Listed as threatened by the state of Pennsylvania; more information is needed before its status can be determined elsewhere.

References
Mammalian Species 547; Godin, 1977; van Zyll de Jong, 1984, 1985

Little brown bat | *Myotis lucifugus*

Small and brown and often exploiting buildings as roosts, little brown bats are widespread in North America. They occur over a wide range of latitude and elevation, tending to be more abundant in areas with suitable hibernation sites. Little brown bats spend the winter hibernating in underground sites such as caves or abandoned mines, and may make lengthy migrations (up to 1,000 km) between summer and winter roosts.

Little brown bats are nocturnal and depend upon echolocation to orient themselves and locate, track, and evaluate their insect prey. When hunting, these bats typically produce echolocation calls that last about 4 milliseconds, sweeping from about 80 kiloHertz to 40 kHz. Cruising little brown bats produce echolocation calls about 20 times per second (50 ms between calls), but when attacking airborne prey, increase

their pulse repetition rates to 200 per second (5 ms between calls).

Little brown bats often forage near or over water and, not surprisingly, feed mainly on aquatic insects such as caddis flies, mayflies, and midges. They sometimes eat mosquitoes. Like other insectivorous bats, they have voracious appetites, typically eating half of their body weight in insects each night they are active. Lactating females eat even more, up to 110 percent of their body weight each night.

Mating occurs in the late summer, at night, in hibernation sites. Males mate with different females and females mate repeatedly with different males. Females store sperm in their uteri through the winter, and ovulation and fertilization take place when they leave hibernation. Females tend to congregate

Myotis lucifugus

in nursery colonies, where each bears a single young about 60 days after fertilization. The actual timing of birth varies widely from north to south and from higher to lower elevations. Early to mid June is the typical birth time for little brown bats in the northeastern United States.

The newborn pup weighs about 25 percent of its mother's body mass. Females nurse their own young, each mother bat recognizing her pup by its distinctive calls and odors. For the first 18 days or so after birth, the young ingest only milk. By then, their permanent teeth are fully erupted and they begin to feed on insects. We do not know if mother bats bring their young their first insects, but for a few days both insects and milk are included in the young's diet.

Female little brown bats return to the same nursery colonies year after year. This strong site fidelity makes them vulnerable to eviction by humans. Although little brown bats quickly exploit artificial structures as roosts, they do not necessarily occupy bat houses installed for them. In an effort to make these bats more attractive as household residents, they often are identified as major predators of mosquitoes. This claim remains unverified.

Little brown bats are the bats that most Canadians and Americans encounter flying around in their homes at night. Although bats, like other mammals, are susceptible to rabies, the incidence of this disease is very low in this species. *M. B. Fenton*

Size
Females are slightly larger than males; there is a significant difference in winter mass.
Total length: 60–102 (87) mm
Length of forearm: 33–41 (38) mm
Weight: 7–13 (10) g

Identification
Myotis lucifugus can be distinguished from *M. yumanensis* by its glossy versus dull fur, and from *M. sodalis* by its unkeeled calcar and long toe hairs. Differences in bacular shape distinguish *M. lucifugus* from the neotropical *M. fortidens,* and the length of the tibia and the extent of fur on the underside of the wing membranes distinguish it from *M. volans.*

M. lucifugus differs from *M. septentrionalis, M. evotis, M. keenii,* and *M. auriculus* by the size of the ears and the shape of the tragus.

Other Common Names
Little brown myotis

Status
Common, widespread, but vulnerable

Subspecies
Myotis lucifugus alascens, Alaska through British Columbia and southward into the Pacific Northwest
Myotis lucifugus carissima, central and western United States except for coastal regions

Myotis lucifugus lucifugus, throughout the eastern seaboard, from northern Florida to the Northwest Territories, and where other subspecies do not occur
Myotis lucifugus occultus, restricted distribution in Texas, New Mexico, and Arizona
Myotis lucifugus pernox, restricted distribution in middle of the border between Alberta and British Columbia
Myotis lucifugus relictus, very restricted distribution in the mountains of California

References
Mammalian Species 142; Kurta et al., 1989; Neilson and Fenton, 1994

Northern long-eared myotis | *Myotis septentrionalis*

Relatively little is known about the roosting habits of northern long-eared myotis. In winter they are often found hibernating in caves and mines throughout their range. At most sites they are much less common than other species (such as the little brown bat). There are few banding records and little is known about their longevity. Most of the records of nursery roosts are of bats found under pieces of loose tree bark, but northern long-eared myotis sometimes form nursery roosts in buildings.

Like other *Myotis,* female northern long-eared myotis bear a single young each year. Data on other species of *Myotis* suggests that newborn young weigh about 25 percent of their mother's mass and that females nurse their own young. Mating presumably occurs in the late summer and early fall, with females storing sperm through the winter. Ovulation and fertilization take place after the females leave hibernation.

The echolocation calls of northern long-eared myotis are short (1–2 milliseconds long), broadband (sweeping from about 120 to 40 kiloHertz), and relatively low in intensity. With most bat detectors, the echolocation calls of these bats are typically detectable at distances of about 2 meters (compared to 10 or more meters for the calls of little brown bats). Together, the short duration and low intensity make the echolocation calls of northern long-eared myotis all but inaudible to most moths.

Foraging northern long-eared myotis find their prey by homing in on the sounds the insects produce by moving or fluttering their wings. These bats are gleaners, typically taking insects from the ground, branches, or foliage rather than catching them on the fly. Northern long-eared myotis usually carry their catches to perches and eat them there. This method of feeding enables the bats to eat larger insects than those eaten by little brown bats. *M. B. Fenton*

Myotis septentrionalis

Size
Females are slightly larger than males; there is
  a significant difference in winter mass.
Total length: 80–96 (86) mm
Forearm length: 35–40 (36.4) mm
Weight: 4.3–10.8 (7.4) g

Identification
This is a long-eared myotis with a long, sharply pointed tragus. Until 1979 the northern long-eared myotis was considered a subspecies of Keen's myotis *(Myotis keenii).* Differences in distribution (Keen's myotis is restricted to the northwest coast) and morphology (Keen's myotis has darker shoulder spots and few scat-

tered hairs on the surface of the uropatagium) were used to justify recognizing the two taxa as distinct species. The northern long-eared myotis can be distinguished from *Myotis evotis* by the latter's black, longer ears.

Other Common Names
Northern long-eared bat

Status
Widespread and locally common

References
Mammalian Species 121; Faure et al., 1993;
  van Zyll de Jong, 1979

Indiana bat | *Myotis sodalis*

The Indiana bat, an insect feeder, is primarily known from its winter range in well-developed limestone caverns where it hibernates; abandoned mines are also often used. The summer range is less well known, as only a few nursery colonies have been discovered. *Myotis sodalis* occurs from Oklahoma, Iowa, Wisconsin, and Michigan east to Vermont and Massachusetts, and south to northwestern Florida.

Caverns where the temperature remains cool (3–6° C) and the humidity is high (66–90 percent) from November to mid-March are optimal for hibernation. The bats congregate by the thousands in dense clusters, hanging by their toes from the ceiling with their wings and forearms pressed against their bodies. These clusters are so dense—they can contain 300–450 individuals per square foot—that only the ears, noses, mouths and wrists are visible from below. Droplets of moisture do not

Myotis sodalis

form on the fur as noted in other species. There is some evidence that the bats arouse from their torpor every 10–20 days, fly to a warmer part of the cave, and return shortly to the original or to another cluster. If the hibernating bats are disturbed, they move to another cave where the temperature and humidity are suitable, if one is nearby. The sex ratio is near parity.

The bats start to move out of the hibernaculum between the middle and the end of March; the females are the first to leave. They forage in the vicinity for several days before they start their migration to their summer haunts. Most of the males scatter throughout the range near the hibernaculum. Our knowledge of their movements is very sparse. Mist-netting of foraging sites in the vicinity of maternity colonies typically produces only one or two adult males.

Understanding of the natural history of the Indiana bat was enhanced in 1974 (46 years after it was first described), when the first active nursery colony, containing 30 individuals, was found. It was located under the loose bark of a dead bitternut hickory (*Carya cordiformis*). Some of the spaces behind patches of bark were interconnected; others were isolated. Most of the bats roosting under the bark had east-southeast and south-southwest exposures, thus appearing to take advantage of solar heat. Occasionally part of the population used an alternate roost, a living shagbark hickory (*Carya ovata*) with naturally exfoliating bark, which was thirty meters away from the dead bitternut hickory. The live tree seemed to afford better protectiom from wet and cold, particularly in the spring and fall.

Females and young start their migration south around the last week in August, although a few remain in and around maternity colonies even after the first frost in mid-September. The latest departures are in the first week of October. As the bats arrive in the cave region, from early September to mid-October, a phenomenon called swarming occurs: large numbers of bats fly in and out of cave entrances from dusk to dawn. Presumably this enables individuals that are widely dispersed during the summer to come together to breed. The 2- to 3-week swarming period also gives the bats time to forage extensively and accumulate a fat reserve of 1 to 2 g to see them through the long period of hibernation, which lasts from November until mid-March. *J. B. Cope*

Size
No significant sexual dimorphism
Total length: 73–99 mm (86.30; n=99)
Length of tail: 29–43 mm (36.39; n=100)
Length of forearm: 31–40 mm (37.26; n=76)
Weight: 3.5–10 g (6.39; n=74)

Identification
Myotis sodalis is a small bat that resembles and is often confused with *Myotis lucifugus*. The best characteristic to use in distinguishing *M. sodalis* from *M. lucifugus* is the length and density of hairs on the toes. The hairs on the toes of *M. sodalis* are sparse, 1–3 on each toe, and extend only to the base of the toenail. The hairs on the toes of *M. lucifugus* are not so sparse; there are 5–7 hairs on each toe, and each extends to the end of the toenail or beyond. The hind foot of *M. sodalis* averages 1 to 1.5 mm. shorter than that of *M. lucifugus*. The general color of *M. sodalis* is dull gray to brown, with a pinkish cast; *M. lucifugus* is light to dark brown and glossy. An inconspicous keel on the calcar is visible on fresh specimens of *M. sodalis*. There is no keel on the calcar of *M. lucifugus*.

Other Common Names
Social bat, social myotis, Indiana myotis

Status
Classified as endangered by the United States government under the federal endangered species act

Reference
Mammalian Species 163; Barbour and Davis, 1969; Cope and Humphrey, 1977; Hall, 1962; Humphrey et al., 1977

Fringed myotis | *Myotis thysanodes*

The distribution of the fringed myotis encompasses most of western North America from British Columbia to southern Mexico. Over much of its range, *M. thysanodes* occupies middle elevations through a variety of desert, grassland, and woodland habitats. Coastal populations occur in low-elevation woodlands and some records indicate forays into high-elevation forests.

The fringed myotis belongs to the long-eared myotis group, all of which tend to be high-elevation forest bats. *Myotis thysanodes* has the shortest ears and occupies the lowest elevations in this group. Its wings are short and broad, indicating maneuverable, low-speed flight. The wing membranes are thick and very resistant to punctures, which further suggests a foraging strategy of flying within the vegetation canopy and gleaning insects from plant surfaces. Physiological studies indicate that *M. thysanodes* has a great deal of control over body temperature regulation and can fly at low ambient and body temperatures.

The fringed myotis forms maternity colonies in caves, mine tunnels, and buildings. These are occupied solely by females and their young. Males appear to roost alone. Females enter the maternity colony in late April and leave by late September. Fat deposition prior to the autumn exodus suggests that the

Myotis thysanodes

colony moves to a hibernaculum. Presumably these hibernation sites are at lower elevations; individuals probably hibernate for short periods interspersed with some nights of activity. Within a roost, individuals select sites in the open, rather than crevices. Clusters of individuals tend to shift sites within the roost periodically in response to temperature changes or disturbance. Human disturbance can cause abandonment of the roost site.

The summer colony of fringed myotis exits the roost at sunset and returns at dawn. During lactation, two to ten adults are always present in the roost to care for the young. Although a variety of insect species are eaten, small beetles are selected more than 70 percent of the time. These insects appear to be gleaned from vegetation surfaces, a highly specialized foraging behavior.

Copulation begins in late April. Pregnancy lasts between 50 and 60 days, and a single young is born between late June and early July. The neonate is huge in proportion to the mother, at 22 percent of her body mass and 54 percent of her total length. Females deposit newborns in a separate roost site and only visit them to nurse or to assist young in distress. Juveniles grow rapidly and are capable of flight at 16.5 days of age. Body measurements of young are indistinguishable from those of adults

by 21 days of age. Banding studies indicate life spans of up to 11 years.

Fringed myotis live in a wide range of habitats and elevations. Common co-existing bats include the southwestern myotis, California myotis, western small-footed myotis, long-eared myotis, little brown bat, cave myotis, long-legged myotis, Yuma myotis, western red bat, hoary bat, silver-haired bat, western pipistrelle, big brown bat, spotted bat, Townsend's big-eared bat, Allen's big-eared bat, pallid bat, Brazilian free-tailed bat, and big free-tailed bat. *M. J. O'Farrell*

Size
Females have longer heads, bodies, and
    forearms than males.
Total length: 80–99 (89) mm
Length of tail: 35–45 (39) mm
Length of forearm: 40.3–45.3 (42.8) mm
Weight: 6.0–11.8 (8.8) g

Identification
This species can be distinguished by its large ears (16–20 mm) and the well-developed fringe

of hairs on the posterior edge of the tail membrane.

Status
Common

Subspecies
Myotis thysanodes aztecus, Oaxaca, Mexico
Myotis thysanodes pahasapensis, Black Hills,
    South Dakota

Myotis thysanodes thysanodes, central Mexico to
    British Columbia, and through most of the
    western United States including Washington, Oregon, Idaho, California, Nevada,
    Utah, Wyoming, Colorado, Arizona, New
    Mexico, and west Texas

References
Mammalian Species 137; Paradiso and
    Greenhall, 1967; Reduker et al., 1983

Cave myotis | *Myotis velifer*

Myotis velifer, as the common name cave myotis suggests, usually inhabits caves. There it exists in colonies that may number in the thousands. This bat occurs at lower elevations in the southwestern United States from Kansas to southern Nevada and southeastern California southward through Mexico to Honduras.

The cave myotis is light brown to nearly black, with bicolored and sometimes tricolored body hairs. The fur may be bleached if the bats roost where humidity and ammonia (from guano) are high. One annual molt occurs during July and August. The males molt first and the females molt after weaning their young.

Populations in Kansas and Texas appear to be permanent residents, hibernating in caves during the winter. Few seem to overwinter to California and Arizona, suggesting they may move south. Populations in Mexico move to higher elevations in winter to hibernate.

Like most North American bats, *M. velifer* is insectivorous. Its diet changes with the season and habitat, but moths and beetles seem to be eaten most often. The cave myotis normally

Myotis velifer

feeds twice a night during the summer, once soon after sunset and again just before sunrise. The cave myotis has a much stronger and less erratic foraging flight than most species of *Myotis*.

Mating occurs in the fall, but the sperm are stored in the uterus and fertilization does not occur until spring. Gestation is about 60–70 days, with a single young being born at the end of June or early July. Neonates weigh about 3 g and reach adult weight (about 12 g) by week 9 or 10. The females leave their young clustered in nursery roosts when they forage and seem to be able to recognize their own young when they return. Young bats begin to forage by 4 weeks of age. Weaning occurs at about 6 weeks and by 13 weeks young and adults cannot be distinguished from each other. *K. A. Shump*

Size

Females have significantly longer forearms than males, but are comparable in other measurements.

Length of head and body: 44.2–55 (56.7) mm

Length of tail: 39–47 (42.8 mm)

Length of forearm: 40.1–44.2 (42.0) mm

Weight: about 9–14 (12) g

Identification

This light brown to nearly black bat is one of the larger *Myotis*. It has a stubby-nosed appear-

ance. The ears reach only to the end of the nose when bent forward.

Recent Synonyms

Vespertilio incautus

Vespertilio velifer

Status

Common

Subspecies

Myotis velifer grandis, southern Kansas into Oklahoma and northern Texas

Myotis velifer incautus, southern Texas into northwestern Mexico

Myotis velifer velifer, southern Arizona into Central America

References

Mammalian Species 149; Babour and Davis, 1969; Hill and Smith, 1984; Kunz, 1973, 1974, 1982

Long-legged myotis | *Myotis volans*

Myotis volans is a rather large western myotis with short, rounded ears. Its belly fur extends out onto the underside of the wing to a line joining the elbow and the knee. Although a few other kinds of *Myotis* have hair on the underwing, it is usually not as long, dense, or extensive as in the long-legged myotis. The color of the fur on the back varies geographically; most mainland individuals are a rich, dark, slightly reddish- or yellowish-brown, but the small subspecies occurring in Baja California is reddish-buff dorsally. The ventral fur ranges from pale buffy to smoky brown.

The peninsular subspecies is poorly known and distinctive. If it is found, on further study, to be a distinct species separate from the mainland races, it alone would be called *Myotis volans*. The mainland bats would then take the name of the earliest-named subspecies, becoming known as *Myotis longicrus*.

Long-legged myotis typically occupy mountainous or relatively rugged areas. They occur across an elevational range

from 60 to 3,770 m, most often between 2,000 and 3,000 m. They inhabit primarily coniferous forest, although they may sometimes be found in oak or riparian woodlands and even desert areas. For example, the distinctive Baja California subspecies utilizes low desert habitats. By migrating locally, these bats may shift habitat seasonally. They use a variety of roosts including large ponderosa pine snags, crevices in cliffs, cracks in the ground, caves, and abandoned buildings. They are able to fly at relatively cool temperatures, with a body temperature as low as 25° C (77° F). This probably enables them to extend their period of activity before going into hibernation. In winter, they hibernate in caves and mine tunnels.

These bats are strong, direct fliers, capable of speeds up to 15–17 km per hour. They feed mainly upon moths but have been known to eat a variety of other, mostly soft-bodied, insects such as flies, termites, lacewings, wasps, true bugs, leafhoppers, and small beetles. Like many insectivorous bats,

Myotis volans

they are opportunistic foragers, catching appropriate prey approximately in proportion to its availability in the environment. They pursue their prey over relatively long distances around, over, under, and sometimes through the forest canopy, especially in open areas within the forest. They often also forage over open water. There is some evidence that an individual bat will follow a similar foraging route night after night.

The typical echolocation calls of long-legged myotis are relatively short (1–10 milliseconds long) and intense, beginning with a brief frequency-modulated (FM) sweep from 89 down to 40 kHz and ending with a constant frequency (CF) portion at the latter frequency. The CF portion of the calls is shortened during the final phases of pursuit of an insect. When several bats of the same species are feeding in the same area, it may at times be difficult for them to distinguish the echoes of their own calls from the calls of a neighbor. As a result, when they seem to be on a collision course they may "honk" at each other by lowering the frequency in the terminal portion of an FM sweep.

The timing of reproductive activity in this species seems to vary extensively, probably partly in relation to climatic factors. Copulation occurs in late summer. Females store sperm in their reproductive tracts over winter while in hibernation. Then they ovulate in spring (March through May), fertilization occurs, and young may be born as early as May or (depending on the location) as late as August. Based on the recapture of marked individuals, the life span is at least 21 years. *N. J. Czaplewski*

Size
The peninsular (Baja California) subspecies is smaller than mainland subspecies.
Total length: 76–106 mm
Length of tail: 29–49 mm
Length of forearm: 35–42 mm
Weight: 5–10 (7.5) g

Identification
Myotis volans has longer, denser fur on the underside of the wing membrane between the elbow and the knee than have other species of *Myotis* in North America. Its calcar is keeled and short and its ears are rounded. The dorsal fur varies from dark brown to reddish buff; the ears and wing membranes are blackish.

Recent Synonyms
Leuconoe volans

Other Common Names
Hairy-winged myotis

Status
Common, widespread in the west

Subspecies
Myotis volans amotus, Sierra Volcánica Transversal, Mexico
Myotis volans interior, United States between 100th and 120th meridians and uplands of northwestern Mexico
Myotis volans longicrus, southeastern Alaska, British Columbia, and Alberta southwestward to western California
Myotis volans volans, Baja California peninsula

References
Mammalian Species 224; Barbour and Davis, 1969

Yuma myotis | *Myotis yumanensis*

Typically seen at dusk cruising back and forth a few inches above water, the Yuma myotis almost always occurs near ponds and rivers, avoiding regions where open water is rare. Although often common within valleys and mountain waterways in the West, much of the arid Great Basin is devoid of this small bat. Although many colonies are at relatively low elevations in desert or semi-desert habitats, they are always near watercourses, and the Yuma myotis shows no particular adaptations for an arid climate. Unlike bats characteristically found in desert environments far from water, this bat has little ability to concentrate urine and succumbs to dehydration quickly if barred from access to water.

As with other *Myotis,* feeding activity is mostly nocturnal, commencing at about dusk, usually peaking within a short time, and then dwindling, sometimes with a secondary pulse before dawn. Skull and jaw morphology indicate particular dependence on relatively soft insects such as moths and diptera, and the little dietary information available supports this. This fits well with the bat's habit of foraging mainly over water, where moths, diptera, and other soft-bodied insects tend to be more common than the beetles preferred by many bats. In common with other species of mouse-eared bats, ultrasonic sound waves are used to detect and home in on suitable prey.

Buildings, the undersides of bridges, vertical crevices in cliffs, and mines and caves are favored places for communal summer roosts. Man-made structures are not the only artificial

Myotis yumanensis

shelters utilized, however; nests of mud abandoned by cliff swallows seem to be viewed as high-class day-time residences. Little is known about the bats' winter range, but presumably they move to cool caves and mines for hibernation in most of

their range; some winter activity is known from coastal California and the lower Colorado River region.

Breeding occurs predominantly in fall, and sperm is retained within the female reproductive tract until spring, when fertilization occurs. A single offspring is born between late May and mid-July, timing depending largely on local climate. Maternal colony sites, sometimes shared with *Myotis lucifugus,* usually consist entirely or mostly of females and their young; males scatter to live as solitary bachelors, though at times associated with other species of bats.

The little brown bat seems to be the closest relative of the Yuma myotis. In some areas where both occur, identification is easy; in other situations, however, the line between the species blurs and some individuals appear intermediate. This has led to speculation that occasional hybridization between the spe-

cies may occur. Investigation at the biochemical level in one such area of supposed hybridization in British Columbia, however, showed genetic distinctiveness with no hint of gene exchange. Probably the two species are so similar overall, and individual variation within each species is so great, that overlap in morphological characters is inevitable.

The Yuma myotis shows considerable geographic variation. Color tends to be light in the arid portions of its range and darker in forested areas, such as the Northwest Coast. Nevertheless, populations in Sonora and southeastern Arizona buck the trend by being relatively dark. Size varies from small in northern Mexico to relatively large in northern Utah and Colorado. As the size in the northern areas approaches that of *M. lucifugus,* discrimination between the two species becomes more difficult. *A. H. Harris*

Size

No sexual dimorphism
Total length: 75–89 (80.6) mm
Length of forearm: 30.4–37.9 (34.107) mm
Length of tail: 29–43 (35.9) mm
Weight: 4.7–7.1 (5.9) g

Identification

The Yuma myotis *(Myotis yumanensis)* and little brown bat *(M. lucifugus)* both have ears that are shorter than 16 mm and extend less than 2 mm beyond the nose if held forward, no obvious keel on the calcar, and no pronounced saggital crest on the skull. This combination of traits separates these two species from other *Myotis.* Distinguishing *M. yumanensis* from *M. lucifugus* is difficult, but *M. yumanensis* usually is slightly smaller, usually lacks burnished tips on the

dorsal hair, and its ears are pale brown, as opposed to dark brown or black. In addition, the skull of *M. yumanensis* has a relatively abrupt increase in forehead height, not a gradually ascending forehead.

Status

Common but scattered in occurrence; probably decreasing numbers

Subspecies

Myotis yumanensis lambi, known only from San Ignacio, Baja California
Myotis yumanensis lutosus, Mexico from Morelos north to southern Zacatecus and northern Sinaloa
Myotis yumanensis oxalis, Central Valley of California

Myotis yumanensis saturatus, coast and central mountains of West Coast from Mexican border north to central British Columbia
Myotis yumanensis sociabilis, southeastern British Columbia and western Montana west to central Washington and Oregon, and then south to northeastern California
Myotis yumanensis yumanensis, extreme western and southern Nevada, portions of Utah and Colorado, south through most of Baja California and to central Durango, east to panhandle of Oklahoma and south to Del Rio, Texas

References

Barbour and Davis, 1969; Black, 1974; Herd and Fenton, 1983; Hoffmeister, 1986

Red bat | *Lasiurus borealis*

Lasiurus borealis is found from southern Canada southward throughout the United States, Mexico, Central America, and into South America. It has also been found on several Caribbean Islands (Cuba, Jamaica, Hispaniola, Puerto Rico, and the Bahamas). It is common in the midwestern and east-central states and wherever there are trees in the prairie and Great Plains states.

Red bats are solitary and roost mostly in trees or shrubs, and sometimes near or even on the ground. During the day they often roost in edge habitats adjacent to streams, open fields, and in urban areas. They appear to have a preference for the south side of trees and for sites bordering dense leafy crops such as corn or beans.

Lasiurus borealis generally begins to forage 1 to 2 hours after sunset, later than most other bats found in the same localities except for the hoary bat, *Lasiurus cinereus*. Red bats probably feed primarily on moths, but also consume flies, beetles, and even ground-dwelling insects such as crickets and cicadas.

The fur of the red bat is dense and soft all over the body, including the uropatagium. Its upperparts are brick red to rusty red, washed with white. The underparts are slightly paler. Males are usually more brightly colored than females. The way the tail, which is fairly long, extends straight behind the body distinguishes the red bat from other bats in its range.

Red bats are migratory and seem to migrate in groups even though they are normally solitary. Males and females appear to migrate at different times and to different summer ranges. They are sometimes found at the mouths of caves in the sum-

Lasiurus borealis

mer, but seem to prefer trees, and those that do not migrate hibernate in trees.

The red bat breeds in August and September, but fertilization does not occur until spring. Gestation is estimated to be 80–90 days and the birth of 1–5 young usually occurs in June. Very young bats cling to the fur of their mother, but the mother usually leaves them at the roost when she forages for food in the evening. Young are born completely hairless, with their eyes closed, and weigh about 0.5 g each. They grow quickly, and by 4 weeks the eyes are open, the body is covered with short dense fur, and they weigh nearly half of the mother's weight. They can fly between 3 and 6 weeks and are weaned between 4 and 6 weeks. *K. A. Shump*

Size
Females are larger than males.
Total length: 95–126 (112.3) mm
Length of tail: 45–62 (49) mm
Length of forearm: 37.5–42 (40) mm
Weight: 7–16 g

Identification
Reddish color, furred interfemoral membrane, and long tail set this species apart from relatives. The ears are low, broad, and rounded; the tragus is triangular. Distinguished from other bats in its range by the way its fairly long tail extends straight behind the body.

Recent Synonyms
Atalapha frantzii
Atalapha teliotis
Lasiurus enslenii
Nycticeius varius
Vespertilio borealis (part)

Status
Common, widespread

Subspecies
Lasiurus borealis blossevillii, South America
Lasiurus borealis borealis, southernmost Canada and eastern two-thirds of the United States into northeastern Mexico
Lasiurus borealis frantizii, Panama and southern Costa Rica
Lasiurus borealis teliotis, western United States into western and southern Mexico and Central America
Lasiurus borealis varius, Chile and extreme western Argentina

References
Mammalian Species 183; Babour and Davis, 1969; Fenton, 1983; Hill and Smith, 1984; Kunz, 1982

Hoary bat | *Lasiurus cinereus*

Lasiurus cinerus is the most widespread of all American bats, ranging from near the northern limit of trees in Canada south throughout the United States and Mexico and into Guatemala. This bat is also found in Hawaii and South America.

The hoary bat is mixed dark brownish and grayish tinged with white, producing a frosted or hoary effect. This is a large bat (20–35 g), with the females larger than the males. The interfemoral membrane is heavily furred. The ears are thick, rounded, edged with black, and short: they do not reach as far as the nostrils when laid forward.

Lasiurus cinereus is solitary and roosts mainly in the foliage of trees. During the day the bats usually roost 3–5 m above the ground, well-hidden from above but visible from below. It is believed that this species migrates, although some of them do hibernate. They have a swift, direct flight that makes them easy to identify on the wing anywhere in the United States except where the largest free-tailed bats occur. They seem to prefer moths, but also are known to eat beetles, flies, grasshoppers, dragonfiles, and wasps.

Except during the mating season, males and females are seldom found together. Mating occurs during the autumn migra-

Lasiurus cinereus

tion but implantation is delayed until spring. The birth of 1–4 (average 2) young occurs between mid-May and early July. Newborn hoary bats are covered with fine, silvery-gray hair except on the belly, and the eyes and ears are closed. The ears

open by the third day, the eyes by day 12, and by day 33 they can fly. The young cling to the mother during the day, but are left hanging from a twig or leaf while she forages at night. *K. A. Shump*

Size
Females are larger than males.
Length of head and body: 77–87 [80.5 mm
(males); 83.6 mm (females)]
Length of forearm: 46–55 [52.6 mm (males);
54.2 mm (females)]
Weight: 20–35 g

Identification
The hoary bat is fairly easily distinguished from other bats in its range by its large size and mixed brownish and grayish fur, which is tinged with white to produce a frosty or hoary effect. The interfemoral membrane is heavily furred, the ears are thick, short, and rounded, and the tragus is short and broad.

Recent Synonyms
Atalapha mexicana
Vespertilio cinereus

Vespertilio pruinosus
Vespertilio villosissimus

Status
Common, widespread

Subspecies
Lasiurus cinereus cinereus, northern Canada,
throughout the United States, and south
into Mexico and Guatemala
Lasiurus cinereus semotus, Hawaii
Lasiurus cinereus villosissimus, South America

References
Mammalian Species 185; Barbour and Davis,
1969; Fenton, 1983; Hill and Smith, 1984;
Kunz, 1982

Southern yellow bat | *Lasiurus ega*

The southern yellow bat is found throughout much of South America and ranges northward through Central America and Mexico into the southern United States. There it is found in southern California and Arizona, southwestern New Mexico, and extreme southern Texas along the Gulf Coast. Although it is a strong flier and occasionally is captured well out to sea, the species has only managed to colonize Trinidad, which is near the coast of South America, and not any other Caribbean islands. The southern yellow bat is basically a lowland species, yet some individuals wander into the mountains to elevations as high as 2,300 m. The only North American fossils are specimens of late Pleisotcene age from the Yucatan Peninsula.

This bat is small-bodied, with a short broad muzzle, short, rounded ears, and long narrow wings. Its body fur is soft and silky, pale yellow to a dull sooty yellow in color, and may be washed with flecks of gray, brown, or black. Fur extends onto the wing along the forearm and as much as halfway onto the tail membrane.

The southern yellow bat occupies a range of habitats from extremely arid areas to lush tropical forests; this adaptable spe-

Lasiurus ega

cies inhabits savannas, secluded woodlands, regions dominated by pasture or cropland, and even tolerates residential areas. The southern yellow bat occasionally roosts within thatched roofs in tropical climates, but it most often is found in trees, where it generally hangs from the midrib of a leaf using its hind claws and possibly its thumbs. It has a weakness for palm trees, particularly fan palms *(Washingtonia)*, and the widespread planting of trees of this genus in the southwestern United States may be allowing this bat to expand its range northward. Coconut, mango, banana, and hackberry *(Celtis reticulata)* are other known roost trees. Most often, only a single southern yellow bat occupies a roost tree, but on occasion, two or more cling to the same tree. The southern yellow bat and the northern yellow bat sometimes find shelter in the same palm.

This fast-flying bat leaves its roost shortly after sunset and is active until midnight and perhaps beyond. It is most often captured while flying over streams, rivers, ponds, and swimming pools, and occasionally two or three individuals appear to fly together. Other species that fly or forage in the same areas include the Brazilian free-tailed bat *(Tadarida brasiliensis)*, big brown bat *(Eptesicus fuscus)*, cave bat *(Myotis velifer)*, and pallid bat *(Antrozous pallidus)*. Diet has not been studied in detail, but one biologist states that this aerial insectivore prefers beetles to anything else. At one time, mammalogists believed that the southern yellow bat migrated southward for the winter, but it is now apparent that some of these bats are present in the United States year-round. There is no annual cycle of fat stor-

age. This bat does not hibernate, although it does use daily torpor on occasion.

Mating probably occurs in autumn. Females store the sperm over winter inside the uterus, ovulate in spring, and then carry the developing fetus for an additional 3–3.5 months. The single annual birth occurs between May and July, with the timing somewhat dependent on latitude—as early as 1 May in Costa Rica and as late as 14 July in northern Mexico and the United States. Although most bats have only a single pair of nipples, members of the genus *Lasiurus,* including the southern yellow bat, have four. Not surprisingly, litter size in this species varies from one to four, with three being most common. The youngsters subsist on milk for about two months before learning to fly and forage on their own. Young bats probably breed in their first year.

Little is known concerning mortality factors in this species. A few succumb to the rabies virus, and house cats, domestic dogs, and barn owls are known predators.

Based on chromosomal, genetic, and molecular evidence, some biologists have proposed that the subspecies *L. e. xanthinus* actually represents a distinct species, namely *L. xanthinus,* although structural differences among the subspecies are extremely minor. The distribution of the subspecies *L. e. panamensis* also is in dispute. Some mammalogists state that it only occurs as far north as Costa Rica, others claim the Yucatan Peninsula as its northern limit, and some believe that it ranges along the Gulf Coast all the way to Texas. *A. Kurta*

Size
Females are slightly larger than males.
Total length: 102–118 (115.1) mm
Length of tail: 38–56 (49) mm
Length of forearm: 43–52 mm
Weight: 10–14 (11.9) g

Identification
The southern yellow bat can be distinguished from other bats by its short rostrum and yellowish fur, its tail membrane, which is furred on the proximal one-third to one-half, and its single upper incisor and premolar. The northern yellow bat, *Lasiurus intermedius,* generally is larger, exceeding 120 mm in total length.

Recent Synonyms
Dasypterus ega

Other Common Names
Western yellow bat, tropical yellow bat

Status
Common

Subspecies
Lasiurus ega argentinus, eastern Brazil to northern Argentina
Lasiurus ega ega, central Brazil to central Colombia

Lasiurus ega fuscatus, Ecuador and western Colombia
Lasiurus ega panamensis, northern Venezuela to Yucatan Peninsula, perhaps farther north
Lasiurus ega xanthinus, California to Yucatan Peninsula

References
Mammalian Species 515; Baker et al., 1972, 1988; Hall and Jones, 1961; Morales and Bickham, 1995

Northern yellow bat | *Lasiurus intermedius*

The northern yellow bat is a denizen of forested habitats and is never far from permanent sources of water and open areas over which it feeds. This tropical species is less migratory than temperate species of *Lasiurus,* except in the northernmost part of its range, where it normally migrates and if it does not, becomes torpid when exposed to cool temperatures. There are extralimital records from southeastern Virginia and northern New Jersey.

As with other lasiurines, the northern yellow bat seldom roosts in man-made structures. Daytime roosts include dead palm fronds and clumps of Spanish moss *(Tillandsia usneoides)* in both coniferous and deciduous forests. This somewhat gregarious bat typically roosts in small, loosely-organized groups that sometimes include its closest relative, the southern yellow bat *Lasiurus ega.* There is sexual segregation during much of the year, however, with males congregating in smaller numbers than females. One relatively large nursery colony of approximately 45 female and juvenile northern yellow bats was found roosting among dried corn stalks hanging in a large open tobacco shed. Nursery colonies are especially noisy.

This handsome bat forages above the treetops, along forest edges, and over open areas such as golf courses, pastures, lake edges, and coastal beaches for mosquitos, flies, dragonflies, leafhoppers, ants, beetles, and diving beetles. Females do not carry their newborn offspring on nightly foraging expeditions, but they will carry their young if flushed from daytime roosts. Females and offspring that can fly forage in relatively large groups, whereas males tend to forage singly or in small groups.

Northern yellow bats apparently mate in autumn and winter, and 2 to 4 offspring are born in May and June. Females have but 2 nipples, and litters of 4 seldom survive intact. The young become volant in June and July, but they may continue to nurse until late July.

Lasiurus intermedius

Recent ribosomal RNA analyses indicate that *Lasiurus intermedius* likely consists of two species. Bats from mainland North America *(L. i. intermedius* and *L. i. floridana)* comprise one species, whereas bats from Cuba *(L. i. insularis)* comprise the second. Detailed chromosomal and protein comparisons of all yellow bat taxa are warranted.

Given its widespread distribution, relatively little is known about the northern yellow bat. The barn owl is the only known predator and only one parasite, a macronyssid mite *(Steatonyssus radovskyi),* has been reported. This bat is known to carry rabies. *D. Webster*

Size

Females are larger than males; both sexes are smallest in Florida and largest in Cuba.

Total length: 121–131.5 (126.8) mm (males from Florida); 150–164 (158.3) mm (females from Cuba)

Length of tail: 51–60 (54.2) mm (males from Florida); 68–77 (73.7) mm (females from Cuba)

Length of forearm: 46.7–50.0 (48.1) mm (males from Florida); 61.2–62.6 (61.9) mm (females from Cuba)

Weight: 14–20 (17.0) g

Identification

Lasiurus intermedius is distinguished by yellowish-gray to yellowish-brown pelage, with no whitish patches on the shoulder or wrist. Only the basal half of the upper surface of the interfemoral membrane is furred. The ears are pointed; there is one upper premolar. This bat is much larger than sympatric *Lasiurus ega*.

Recent Synonyms

Dasypterus floridanus

Dasypterus intermedius
Lasiurus insularis
Nycteris intermedia

Other Common Names

Eastern yellow bat, Florida yellow bat, greater yellow bat, big yellow bat

Status

Uncommon to common in suitable habitat

Subspecies

Lasiurus intermedius floridana, southeastern United States (South Carolina southwestward to southern Texas)

Lasiurus intermedius insularis, Isla de Pinos and mainland Cuba

Lasiurus intermedius intermedius, southern Texas, Mexico (excluding Baja and the Mexican Plateau), Belize, Guatamala, El Salvador, Honduras

References

Mammalian Species 132; Barbour and Davis, 1969; Schmidly, 1991

Seminole bat | *Lasiurus seminolus*

Seminole bats range throughout all portions of the southeastern states along the Gulf of Mexico and the southern Atlantic seaboard. These medium-sized bats are described as tree bats because they are found in woodland habitats. Their geographical distribution is thought to be closely associated with the occurrence of Spanish moss *(Tillandsia usneoides),* a favored daytime roost for this bat. However, Seminole bats also are found beyond the range of Spanish moss, where they roost beneath loose bark, in clumps of foliage, and occasionally in caves. Adult bats are solitary and rarely are more than two bats found roosting together.

The flight of Seminole bats is swift and direct. The bats drop from their daytime roosts in early evening to forage for insects (true bugs, flies, and beetles) among or above the crowns of trees and over watercourses and clearings. They have also been observed foraging on insects attracted to street lights. Occasionally, Seminole bats forage close to the ground and may even alight to capture flightless insects such as crickets.

Seminole bats are active throughout the year when evening temperatures permit, and probably do not hibernate in the true sense. They are reported to make a definite shift southward in fall, suggesting migration. Most tree bats are migra-

Lasiurus seminolus

tory, but there is no conclusive evidence that Seminole bats migrate, although they have been collected outside their breeding range. Young Seminole bats tend to wander extensively after they have been weaned. This and storm winds may account for the extralimital records of individuals collected in autumn.

Little information is available concerning reproduction in Seminole bats. Like the red bat, *Lasiurus seminolus* may breed in autumn and sperm may be stored in the female's reproductive tract through the winter. Female Seminole bats give birth to 1 to 4 (usually 2 or 3) young in late May or June. Few litters have been found in Spanish moss, suggesting that Seminole bats may select other sites to rear their young. Young bats grow quickly and are capable of flight at 3 to 4 weeks of age.

Like red bats, Seminole bats have broad rounded ears, long pointed wings, and a densely furred interfemoral membrane. Both males and females are a deep mahogany color with pale frosting. Red bats range in color from brick red (males) to rusty red with frosting (females), and Seminole bats are often mistaken for female red bats. The best way to distinguish the two species is to examine the lacrimal shelf (a cranial feature), which is poorly developed in the Seminole bat and well developed in the red bat.

Predators of the Seminole bat probably include blue jays, snakes, and raptors. However, a greater threat to this tree bat may be the commercial collection of Spanish moss. Rabies has been detected in Seminole bats in Florida, but reported infection is apparently low (0.6 percent). *S. S. Chapman and B. R. Chapman*

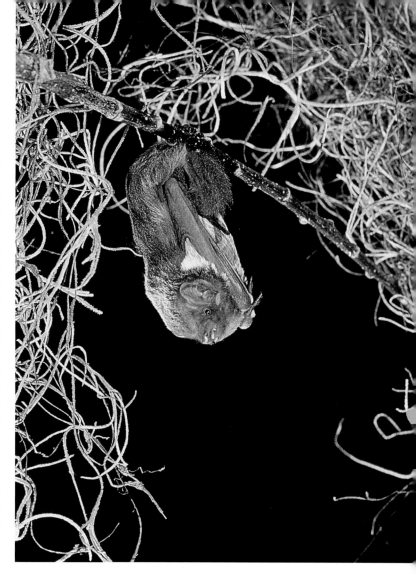

Size
Total length: 89–114 [97.7 mm (males); 103.5 mm (females)]
Length of tail: 35–50 [39.7 mm (males); 45.5 mm (females)]
Length of forearm: 37–43 [39.7 mm (males); 40.7 mm (females)]
Weight: 9.3–13.8 g

Identification
Lasiurus seminolus can accurately be distinguished from *Lasiurus borealis,* which is similar in size and appearance, by a poorly-defined lacrimal shelf. The lacrimal shelf is well developed in *Lasiurus borealis.*

Recent Synonyms
Atalapha borealis seminola
Nycteris seminola

Other Common Names
Mahogany bat

Status
Common locally, but listed as a species of special concern in Oklahoma

References
Mammalian Species 280; Barbour and Davis, 1969; Hill and Smith, 1984; Kunz, 1982

Silver-haired bat | *Lasionycteris noctivagans*

The silver-haired bat occurs throughout most of the contiguous United States and southern Canada, but is uncommon in the Gulf States, Texas, and southern California. Throughout its range, it is associated with forest and grassland habitats, and it is often abundant in old-growth forests. In warm months, individuals and small groups can be found roosting in hollow trees, beneath exfoliating bark, in abandoned woodpecker holes, and sometimes beneath rocks. Females are known to form small maternity colonies, mostly in hollow trees. The sexes are segregated during the summer, with males predominating in western North America and females in the midwest and east. Although considered to be relatively common

Lasionycteris noctivagans

throughout its range in summer months, relatively few individuals have been observed in winter.

The silver-haired bat is thought to be migratory, based on conspicuous changes in its seasonal abundance. Northward shifts in spring and southward shifts in autumn have been noted. In parts of its range, this bat has been observed only during migration, but no direct information is available on the movements of individuals. During presumed migratory periods in spring and autumn, silver-haired bats have been found roosting on the sides of buildings, beneath exfoliating bark, in tree cavities, and occasionally in caves. Because this bat is capable of entering torpor to conserve energy, some individuals may overwinter in colder regions where protected shelters are available.

Mating presumably occurs during autumn, when the bats are migrating, and females presumably store sperm in their reproductive tracts during the winter. Following a gestation period of 50–60 days, twin pups are born during June. Newborn pups grow rapidly and are weaned in about 3–4 weeks.

Silver-haired bats become active shortly after sunset, foraging at tree-top level in wooded areas and over small ponds and streams and feeding largely on small flying insects. Nightly foraging activity is generally bimodal, with one peak of activity before midnight and another before sunrise. The diet consists mostly of moths, although beetles, leaf hoppers, true bugs, midges, flying ants and termites, and small flies are also taken.
T. H. Kunz

Size
Females are slightly larger than males.
Total length: 90–117 mm
Length of tail: 31–50 mm
Length of forearm: 37–47 mm
Weight: 9–12 g

Identification
Silver-haired bats are distinguished by their dark brown to black pelage and frosted dorsal hairs. The upper surface of the tail membrane is furred near the body. The ears are blunt and rounded and the tragus is short and curved forward. The silver-haired bat is similar in appearance to the larger and more colorful hoary bat *(Lasiurus cinereus)*.

Status
Common in the northern part of its range during summer but winter habits poorly known.

Probably not threatened or endangered, but may be at risk due to loss of roosting habitat.

References
Mammalian Species 172; Barbour and Davis, 1969; Nagorsen and Brigham, 1993

Western pipistrelle | *Pipistrellus hesperus*

A tiny bat with slow, erratic, fluttering flight, the western pipistrelle is sometimes mistaken for a late-flying butterfly. Its body hairs are black at the base and smoky gray to buff brown at the ends. *Pipistrellus hesperus* often shows a yellowish-gray-brown body color that contrasts sharply with its dark face and ears, making it appear to have a black face mask.

Abundant and most common at low elevations in desert scrub and arid grassland habitats, the western pipistrelle is also found consistently in adjacent woodlands. It occurs from near sea level to 2,825 m elevation and is typically found along canyon drainages and cliff faces. It roosts in small crevices in rocky outcrops near permanent sources of water, including natural waterways and artificial sites like stock tanks and swimming pools. Its day roosts are usually not the same as those used for night roosting. Buildings and even vegetation as unlikely as sedges are sometimes used for roosting, as are mine tunnels (although less frequently). In the Tucson, Arizona, area, this species commonly roosts in the exterior crevices of homes with swimming pools. Many homeowners have been amazed and fascinated by the small size and delicate features of the western pipistrelle when live bats have been extracted from crevices in joints on patio ceilings. *Pipistrellus hesperus* is not a strong flier, which contributes to its always being found near a source of water. Predictably, it is also nonmigratory.

The western pipistrelle is often visible in flight before sundown. It can commonly be observed in its erratic feeding flight as much as an hour before dark when the sun is behind canyon walls. This bat is most often netted during the first hour or two after sunset and then not again until near dawn. It is one of the most common bats seen over waterholes and streams in arid habitats. In 1890, the famous ecologist, C. Hart Merriam, wrote that western pipistrelles were found in swarms in the Grand Canyon of the Colorado River (Arizona), an observation that attests to their abundance and prominence in canyon environments for many years.

Pipistrellus hesperus

Unlike most species of bats, and interesting especially because of its tiny size, the western pipistrelle gives birth to two young in its annual litter. This species is only modestly colonial; solitary individuals are typical. Maternity colonies are small, with 12 individuals, including adults and juveniles, the largest reported. Young are born in June and by July they are flying independently.

Like many species of insectivorous bats, the western pipistrelle eats many kinds of insects, varying its diet with the insect species that are available by season. Usually only one kind of insect is found in a full stomach at any one time. The most common prey items are small moths, leafhoppers, and during the rainy season in the Southwest, flying ants.

The western pipistrelle shares the record with some shrews for being the smallest mammal in North America. It is not uncommon to capture subadults of this species at desert waterholes in July that weigh less than 3 grams. This diminutive size is impressive when one considers that this bat has the same complement of bones and body organs as an elephant! *R. Sidner*

Size
Females are significantly larger than males, and the subspecies *Pipistrellus hesperus maximus* is larger than *Pipistrellus hesperus hesperus*.

Total length: 60–86 mm
Length of tail: 25–36 mm
Length of forearm: 26–33 mm
Weight: 2.0–6.0 g

Identification
This bat is distinguished by its small size, a tragus that is blunt and slightly curved, and a hind foot less than half as long as the tibia.

Other Common Names
Canyon bat

Status
Common, abundant

Subspecies
Pipistrellus hesperus hesperus, coastal states from Washington to Guerrero, Mexico, eastward to western Colorado and New Mexico, and south to Zacatecas and Morelos, Mexico
Pipistrellus hesperus maximus, southern Colorado, New Mexico, western Oklahoma, and Texas south to Hidalgo, Mexico.

References
Findley and Traut, 1970; Hayward and Cross, 1979; Hoffmeister, 1986

Eastern pipistrelle | *Pipistrellus subflavus*

The eastern pipistrelle occurs throughout the eastern United States, extending westward to southeastern Minnesota, Iowa, Kansas, Oklahoma, and east Texas. It is locally abundant in caves during winter but its summer habits are poorly known. Small maternity colonies have been observed roosting in the darkened attics of houses and in the lofts of old barns, but these bats also roost in trees under dense foliage and may occupy tree hollows. In late summer and early autumn they may migrate several hundred miles from their maternity roosts to hibernating sites. In winter, both sexes roost deep in caves and mines, either alone or in small, dense clusters. Hibernating colonies can consist of several thousand individuals; sometimes eastern pipistrelles share a hibernaculum with other local species. In winter, solitary pipistrelles are often covered with condensation, giving them a glistening, whitish appearance when a light is shined on them.

Beginning in late April and early May, female eastern pipistrelles form maternity colonies ranging from a few dozen up to 50 individuals. Maternity colonies consist of females and their young; the roosting behavior of males in summer is largely unknown, although some have been observed roosting in caves and mines at this time. Females and grown young in maternity colonies become active shortly after sunset, when they emerge to feed. The diet consists mostly of small flying insects, including moths, beetles, leafhoppers, and small flies. While foraging this bat can be recognized by its small size and weak, erratic flight. These bats commonly forage over open pasture and adjacent to vegetation. Two to three feeding bouts are often interrupted by periods of night roosting. Pipistrelles are most active in their day roost right after they return from feeding and again prior to nightly emergence; during these pe-

Pipistrellus subflavus

riods grooming activity is most intense. Most of the day is spent resting, but this is sometimes interrupted by short bouts of grooming and movements in the roost associated with increasing temperatures.

During late summer and early autumn eastern pipistrelles store fat, which they mobilize during hibernation. Mating occurs in autumn before entry into hibernation. Females store sperm in their reproductive tracts over the winter and ovulate in early spring, at the time of arousal from hibernation. Following a gestation period of about 60 days, twin pups are born during June. Pups are hairless at birth, and each weighs about 20 percent of its mother's weight. Nursing pipistrelle pups grow rapidly and begin to fly between the ages of 14 to 21 days. Young pipistrelles are weaned at about 4 weeks. They usually make practice flights for two or three nights before venturing out to feed on insects; early foraging flights are most common in the vicinity of the natal roost. Females and young begin to disperse from maternity roosts in late July and August. Adults and young of both sexes engage in swarming activity in late summer and early autumn, as individuals seek suitable hibernacula and potential mates. The highest mortality occurs during the first year of life. Maximum longevity is 10 years for females and 15 years for males. *T. H. Kunz*

Size
Females are slightly larger than males.
Total length: 75–90 mm
Length of tail: 33–45 mm
Length of forearm: 31–35 mm
Weight: 6–10 g

Identification
The eastern pipistrelle is distinguished from other species that share its range by having yellowish-brown to grayish-brown pelage; the venter is somewhat paler. The dorsal hairs are tri-colored, darkest at the base, pale in the middle, and dark at the tip. The membranes are dark brown. The dorsal third of the uropatagium is lightly furred.

Other Common Names
Pipistrelle

Status
Locally common in caves and mines during winter but summer habits are poorly known.

References
Mammalian Species 228; Barbour and Davis, 1969; Hoying and Kunz, 1998; Kunz and Hoying, 1995; Winchell and Kunz, 1996

Big brown bat | *Eptesicus fuscus*

This common bat inhabits rural areas, towns, and cities throughout temperate North America and follows the western mountains southward through Central America into Colombia. In addition, the big brown bat has colonized many Caribbean islands, including Cuba, Puerto Rico, Jamaica, and Hispaniola.

The face, ears, and wing and tail membranes are black and essentially naked, whereas the husky body is covered by long, lax fur that is soft and somewhat oily. Along the back, the fur color is brownish, but it varies greatly with subspecies, ranging from pinkish tans to rich chocolates. Belly hairs are distinctly paler. The large head is marked by a broad nose, bright eyes, and thick rounded ears that are rather short and barely reach the nostrils when laid forward.

Throughout spring and summer, males generally are solitary, whereas females gather in maternity colonies that contain 20–75 adults. Maternity colonies are found in hollow trees, especially in western North America, but these bats frequently roost in barns, churches, and houses, often inside outer walls or in an enclosed eave. Unlike the little brown bat *(Myotis lucifugus)*, another common building-dwelling species, the big brown bat does not relish a hot roost and generally moves when air temperature exceeds 32–35° C. Females are quite loyal to their roosts and often return year after year.

Each day, colony members begin leaving the roost about 20 minutes after sunset and travel 1–2 km to their foraging grounds, flying at speeds up to 33 km per hour. Foraging is most intense during the second and third hours after sunset, although activity occurs at any time of night. Like most bat species, the big brown bat prefers to forage on dry nights when the air is warmer than 10–12° C. On rainy or cold evenings, it often remains in the roost, lowers its body temperature, and subsists on fat reserves until conditions improve. This species may use a night roost; between bouts of foraging, it may hang under a nearby porch awning or behind a shutter to rest and digest its dinner. Before dawn, it returns to the day roost, leaving behind a small pile of fecal pellets as the only evidence of its nighttime visit.

This species forages in a variety of habitats—over rivers, at forest-field edges, above cropland, and along city streets. Flying beetles are preferred prey. The bat locates its quarry by emitting high-frequency (27–48 kHz) sounds and listening for the returning echos. Under good conditions, a big brown bat attacks an insect every three seconds and consumes 2.7 grams per hour. During July, when hungry young demand ever-increasing amounts of milk, an adult female ingests 17 g of insects each night—an amount equal to her own body mass.

In most areas, females probably mate in September, store sperm inside the uterus throughout winter, and do not ovulate until arousing from hibernation in spring. The breech birth occurs about 60 days later, sometime between late May and early July. Eighty percent or more of the females in eastern North America produce twins, but litter size in the West is generally one. Each pinkish pup is essentially hairless at birth and has tightly closed eyes and floppy ears. The average weight of a newborn is 3.3 g. When separated from its mother, the young bat produces a persistent chirping noise that humans often mistake for a bird. Mother bats do not carry their young on foraging trips, and as the adults are leaving to feed, the combined cries of the anxious pups may be audible to humans 10–20 meters from the roost. Youngsters learn to fly in 18–35 days.

Maternity colonies disband in August and September, and most bats migrate a short distance (less than 80 km) to winter quarters. Although many spend the winter in mines or caves, this bat frequently hibernates inside the walls or attic of a heated building, where air temperatures remain cool but above freezing. Dramatic changes in outside temperature cause the bats to arouse and search for a more suitable site, often coming into contact with humans in the process. When hibernating in caves, big brown bats select locations that are drier and more exposed to air currents than the sites chosen by such other species as the Indiana bat *(Myotis sodalis)* or little brown bat *(Myotis lucifugus)*. The big brown bat most often hangs alone while hibernating, although small clusters of fewer than 20 bats also occur. Big brown bats enter hibernation weighing about 21 g, lose 0.03–0.04 g of fat per day, and weigh 16 g or less by the end of hibernation. In far northern regions, hibernation may last from October to May. In tropical areas, this bat apparently does not hibernate but may use daily torpor.

Secluded roosts protect big brown bats from many predators, although snakes, owls, domestic cats, and raccoons *(Procyon lotor)* take a few. As in other hibernating bats, failure to accumulate sufficient fat for hibernation is a major mortality

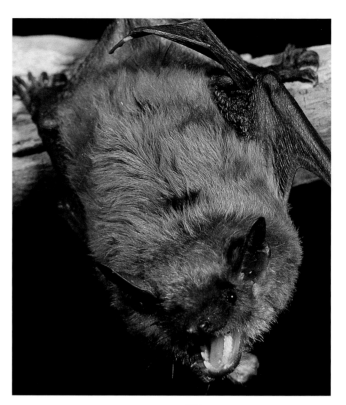

Eptesicus fuscus

factor, especially for youngsters. Many big brown bats are needlessly killed by humans unwilling to share their homes. The best solution to this intolerance is to force the bats to move by blocking their entrance holes after the bats have left the building to forage, either early or late in the year when flightless young are not inside. The evicted animals will move to nearby alternate roosts. The big brown bat lives up to 19 years in the wild. *A. Kurta*

Size

Females are slightly larger than males.
Total length: 87–138 (112) mm
Length of tail 34–56 (43) mm
Length of forearm: 39–54 mm
Weight 11–23 (16) g

Identification

The big brown bat differs from most bats by this combination of characters: overall brown color, naked membranes, tail vertebrae mostly enclosed by tail membrane, ear height less than 21 mm, keeled calcar, forearm length longer than 40 mm, and two incisors and single premolar on each side of the upper jaw.

Other Common Names

Brown bat

Status

Abundant

Subspecies

Eptesicus fuscus bahamensis, Bahama Islands
Eptesicus fuscus bernardinus, coastal regions from central California to British Columbia
Eptesicus fuscus dutertreus, Bahama Islands and Cuba
Eptesicus fuscus fuscus, most of eastern North America
Eptesicus fuscus hispaniolae, Hispaniola and Jamaica

Eptesicus fuscus miradorensis, Colombia to southern Texas
Eptesicus fuscus osceolae, peninsular Florida
Eptesicus fuscus pallidus, Alberta and Manitoba to western Texas, northwestern Mexico, and southern California
Eptesicus fuscus peninsulae, southern Baja Peninsula
Eptesicus fuscus petersoni, Isle de Pinos (Cuba)
Eptesicus fuscus wetmorei, Puerto Rico

References

Mammalian Species 356; Brigham and Fenton, 1991; Kalcounis and Brigham, 1998; Kurta et al., 1990; Whitaker and Gummer, 1992

Evening bat | *Nycticeius humeralis*

The evening bat, *Nycticeius humeralis,* occurs throughout much of the southeastern United States, extending westward to southeastern Nebraska and northward to central Iowa and southern Michigan; it is absent from the Allegheny Mountains.

Maternity colonies of the evening bat are known from attics, the lofts of old barns, and hollow trees. In autumn the females and young are thought to migrate several hundred miles from summer quarters to warmer latitudes. Although there are few records of individual movements, one marked evening bat was captured in autumn about 520 km south of its summer habitat. In Florida, these bats have been observed roosting beneath palm fronds in winter, suggesting that they may overwinter in warmer climates. Evening bats do not roost in caves either in summer or winter. Female migrants arrive at maternity roosts in late April and early May. Males do not accompany females on northward migrations; instead, they remain in southern latitudes during the summer months.

Female evening bats typically form maternity colonies ranging from 30 to several hundred individuals. They become active shortly after sunset and feed largely over clearings, farm ponds, and openings in trees along watercourses. A relatively slow and deliberate flier, this bat eats mostly beetles, moths, and leaf hoppers, although true bugs, small flies, caddis flies, and flying ants are also sometimes consumed. The most important insect it eats from the farmer's perspective is the spotted cucumber beetle (the adult form of the southern corn rootworm). Evening bats that roost together seem to share information about the location of rich foraging patches and alternative roosting sites.

Nycticeius humeralis

In late summer and early autumn evening bats store fat, and later mobilize these reserves during migration, to sustain hibernation, or perhaps to supplement food when shortages occur during winter months in warmer climates. Although evening bats are capable of entering torpor, the extent to which they hibernate is unknown. In the southeastern United States, evening bats may be active year-round. The testes of males undergo enlargement in autumn, suggesting that mating occurs near this time, although most aspects of their reproduction are unknown.

Females give birth to one to three pups (usually twins) during June. Each females usually suckles her own young, although communal nursing has been observed near the time of weaning in about 20 percent of the nursing bouts. Communal nursing appears to increase near the time of weaning, when the young bats began to feed on insects. The young initiate nursing by forcing their heads beneath the wings of females, and the female responds to this action by lifting her wing to allow the pup access to a nipple. The sex ratio of young evening bats is equal at birth, but young males experience higher postpartum mortality. Young females are allowed to nurse communally more often than young males, which may contribute to their higher survival rate. Young evening bats grow rapidly, begin to feed on insects at 24 days of age, and are weaned by the age of 4 weeks. Both females and young begin to disperse from maternity roosts in late July and August. *T. H. Kunz*

Size
Females are slightly larger than males.
Total length: 83–96 mm
Length of tail: 35–40 mm
Length of forearm: 34–37 mm
Weight: 9–14 g.

Identification
Evening bats are similar in appearance to big brown bats, but smaller. They can be distinguished by their reddish to dark brown fur above and tawny color below. The ears are blunt and rounded; the tragus is short and curved forward. The calcar is not keeled. Only one pair of upper incisors is present.

Status
Relatively common throughout its summer range, but not often observed in winter; probably not threatened or endangered, but may be at risk from loss of roosting and foraging habitats.

References
Mammalian Species 23; Barbour and Davis, 1969; Whitaker and Clem, 1992; Wilkinson, 1992a, 1992b

Spotted bat | *Euderma maculatum*

With three white spots on a black background on its back, disproportionately large ears, echolocating calls that are audible to humans, and a small mouth for its size, the spotted bat is among the most distinctive of North American mammals. When released by researchers in daylight, they are more than conspicuous; this would suggest that nocturnality is a must. Spotted bats are distributed over much of western North America from southern British Columbia into central Mexico, but they are only irregularly caught in mist-nets or heard as they forage overhead.

Spotted bats, like most insectivorous bats that feed on the wing, regularly catch and eat a variety of moths and other insects. Moths that are able to detect the ultrasonic foraging calls of many species of bats seem unable to detect the calls of spotted bats. The bats are believed to capture about one insect every 45 seconds, which is not an especially high rate and may indicate that they feed primarily on solitary prey. Spotted bats use habitual feeding grounds, but tolerate considerable overlap between individuals; they vocalize to communicate their positions and achieve spacing while foraging. Early studies suggested that spotted bats effectively gleaned insects from surfaces, but this does not seem to be the case. They appear to have a somewhat more direct and rapid flight than the morphology of their wings and ears would predict.

Euderma maculatum has been found in lowland habitats of the Chihuahua Desert in Texas and in coniferous forests in the western United States. One bat was caught above 3,000 meters (10,000 feet) in New Mexico; others are known from below sea level in California. They are often caught in open ponderosa pine woodlands. Rocky outcrops, associated with many of the habitats where spotted bats are caught, can provide crevices for day roosts, but few roosts have been found. Four bats were found hibernating in a cave in southern Utah and others have been mist-netted in mid-winter over water at low elevations in the same part of the state.

Young are born in June and can weigh 20 percent of their mothers' nonpregnant weight. They are altricial and do not show the color pattern characteristic of adults. The ears of

Euderma maculatum

newborns are large and floppy and not fully developed. Juveniles were netted in Texas in early July. Lactating females have been caught as late as mid-August.

In the 74 years between 1891, when spotted bats were first discovered, and 1965, only 35 specimens were reported. By 1985, a total of 73 specimens existed in private and institutional collections. Several of these were obtained in urban settings: for example, the first *Euderma* from Nevada was found alive in a zoological laboratory on the University of Reno campus, and in Utah two of the early specimens were found in Provo and Salt Lake City. Because most biologists in the 1960s and 70s were reluctant to collect these rarely-caught bats, more bats have probably been released than retained. As the use of bat detectors becomes more widespread and as field biologists become better at recognizing the calls of spotted bats, we may be able to document range extensions and a less spotty distribution. A recent study in California, from 1992 to 1997, added 23 more localities to the 14 known prior to 1992. *H. Black and R. Cosgriff*

Size
No sexual dimorphism
Total length: 107–125 mm
Length of tail: 47–55 mm
Length of forearm 48–54 mm
Weight: 15–22 g

Identification
The spotted bat is easily identified by three white spots on the back and enormous, pinkish-white ears.

Other Common Names
Pinto Bat

Status
Widespread in western North America but not abundant

References
Mammalian Species 77; Best, 1988; Easterla, 1973; Leonard and Fenton, 1984; Navo et al., 1992; Wai-Ping and Fenton, 1989

Rafinesque's big-eared bat | *Corynorhinus rafinesquii*

This medium-sized, large-eared bat is found mainly in the southeastern United States, where it occurs along the east coast from the tip of Florida as far north as southern Virginia. Its range extends westward and northward through central Indiana and Illinois. Its western boundary includes parts of southeastern Missouri and far eastern portions of Oklahoma and Texas. Although documentation of its local distribution is somewhat patchy, it is believed to inhabit forested areas and riparian associations throughout its range.

Rafinesque's big-eared bat is an agile flyer, capable of mov-

ing swiftly and then hovering for a time as it acquires food. It emerges from its roost later at night than many other bats, beginning to forage for insects after dark rather than at twilight. It returns to its roosting site before dawn.

Roosts occupied by *C. rafinesquii* vary from man-made structures such as abandoned buildings or culverts to various kinds of natural shelters, including caves, hollow trees, and crevices behind loose tree bark. It is often found in colonies ranging in size from several to 100 bats, although it may occasionally be found singly. *C. rafinesquii* prefers to occupy partially lighted regions within its roost, and ambient temperatures are a factor in roost site selection.

There are differences in seasonal activity patterns throughout the range of this bat. In harsher northern climes, it is known to hibernate in caves and similar shelters during the winter. In the warmer southern parts of its range, its winter habits have not been well documented, although some period of torpor is believed to occur.

C. rafinesquii is smoky-gray on its back, with distinctly bicolored hairs, which have a dark blackish base and a white or pale tip, on its venter. Its unusually large ears generally exceed 2.5 cm in length. Two fleshy, lumpy facial glands are present on either side of the snout. Two cusps on the first upper incisor also help to distinguish this bat from other members of its genus.

Close observation reveals two long toe hairs that extend beyond the tips of the claws. As in other vespertilionids, the membrane attached to the legs and caudal region completely encloses the tail.

Corynorhinus rafinesquii

As with most bats that hibernate, copulation takes place in autumn and winter. Females congregate in nursery colonies after emerging from the hibernaculum, and give birth to a single young in late May or early June. At birth, the newborns are naked and their eyes are closed. A few days after birth the dark juvenile pelage appears. This remains for approximately three months, at which time molting to adult coloration occurs. The young are very vulnerable until they can fly, and therefore they remain close to the adult females for roughly three weeks. By this time they are almost fully grown, their eyes have opened, they have their permanent teeth, and they are capable of flight.

Because the range of Rafinesque's big-eared bat is relatively extensive, it occurs in sympatry with many woodland dwellers, including several other species of bats. In roosts that are shared with other bats, *C. rafinesquii* is found most often with the eastern pipistrelle *(Pipistrellus subflavus),* and occasionally with the big brown bat *(Eptesicus fuscus),* various members of the genus *Myotis,* and another member of its own genus, Townsend's big-eared bat *(C. townsendii).* In shared roosting sites such as caves, *C. rafinesquii* is usually spatially separated from other bat species, preferring areas closer to the entrances. This preference tends to expose *C. rafinesquii* to increased predation by snakes, raccoons, opossums, and cats and make it more susceptible than the other species of bats to human disturbances.
M. R. Lynch and C. Jones

Size
Females can weigh more than males.
Total length: 80–110 (95) mm
Length of tail: 42–54 (45) mm
Length of forearm: 38.8–43.5 mm
Weight: 7.9–9.5 g (males); 7.9–13.6 g (females)

Identification
Rafinesque's big-eared bat is distinguished from other medium-sized bats within its range by considerably larger ears, long toe hairs that extend beyond the tips of the claws, distinctly bicolored ventral hairs (black at the base and whitish at the tip), and the presence of two large, fleshy lumps on each side of the snout.

Recent Synonyms
Plecotus rafinesquii
Plecotus leconteii
Plecotus macrotis

Other Common Names
Eastern big-eared bat, southeastern big-eared bat, eastern lump-nosed bat, eastern long-eared bat

Status
Limited

Subspecies
Corynorhinus rafinesquii macrotis, eastern North Carolina, South Carolina, Georgia, Florida, Alabama, Mississippi, Louisiana, eastern edge of Texas, and southwestern corner of Arkansas
Corynorhinus rafinesquii rafinesquii, Kentucky, western North Carolina, Tennessee, southern Indiana, eastern edge of Illinois, eastern edge of Minnesota, and eastern edge of Arkansas

References
Mammalian Species 69; Schmidly, 1991

Townsend's big-eared bat | *Corynorhinus townsendii*

Townsend's big-eared bat is known from the western United States, where it occurs northward to southern British Colombia and eastward through Idaho, Wyoming, Colorado, New Mexico, southern Kansas, Oklahoma, and Texas, with scattered populations (subspecies) in Arkansas, Missouri, Kentucky, Virginia, and West Virginia. Isolated populations are also known from the gypsum cave regions of south-central Kansas, northern Oklahoma, and Texas. Townsend's big-eared bat is uncommon throughout its range in summer, but is more often observed in caves and mines during the winter months.

Female big-eared bats form maternity colonies in caves and sometimes in buildings, especially in the west, ranging from several hundred to a thousand or more individuals. They arrive at maternity roosts from mid-March to early April. Early in spring, females may become torpid during the day, but by late April and early May they are usually active within the roost throughout the day. Maternity colonies are found mostly in the warmer parts of caves and in buildings from mid-April through late July. The length of gestation can vary from 56 to 100 days, depending on ambient temperature and the extent of daily torpor experienced by the bats. A single pup is born each year, usually during June. Pups grow rapidly and are weaned in about 4–5 weeks. Most maternity colonies are abandoned by mid-September. In autumn these big-eared bats typically seek

Corynorhinus townsendii

shelter in small caves and mines, where the air temperature is buffered from the colder outdoor environment. This bat may use the same cave in winter as in summer. Little is known about the summer habits of males, although a few individuals have been observed roosting singly in caves, rock crevices, or beneath overhanging cliffs.

Female Townsend's big-eared bats emerge nightly to feed beginning about 45 minutes after sunset. Individuals often circle inside a cave entrance before departing. Because of their relatively late departure in the evening, big-eared bats are seldom seen foraging even in areas where they are thought to be common. One to three foraging periods per night have been reported. Unimodal foraging bouts are characteristic of this species once colonies have formed in spring, but a progressive shift from bimodal to trimodal foraging has been observed from late pregnancy through lactation. Presumably this shift occurs in response to increased energy demands associated with feeding and lactation. Similarly, nightly foraging distances increase from about 1.0 km during early days of lactation to 4.2 km during late lactation. The big-eared bat feeds mostly on moths, although beetles, leaf hoppers, and small flies are also taken. Moths comprise up to 85 percent of the volume of prey consumed. Edge habitat between forested and open areas is preferred for foraging. Individuals typically feed low over open pastures or high in the crowns of trees. During nightly feeding, big-eared bats often use caves and buildings as night roosts, where they cull the wings of moths and other insects before consuming their abdomens.

During the winter months, both sexes hibernate in caves and mines at relatively cold and moderately humid locations. Hibernation sites range from areas of twilight near cave entrances to areas of total darkness deep within caves. If cave temperatures become too extreme, the bats move to more thermally stable areas within the cave. Big-eared bats may hibernate in tightly-packed clusters ranging from a few to 100 or more individuals, although most appear to roost singly or in small clusters. A cluster of about 1,100 *C. townsendii virginianus* was observed, although clusters of 25 or fewer are more common.

Townsend's big-eared bats sometimes awaken during the winter and move both within and among caves, often during periods of freezing temperature. In winter, the large ears are often curled like a ram's horns, especially on a bat in deep torpor. This species is relatively sedentary, often using the same cave in summer and winter. The longest reported movement of a banded individual was 64 kilometers. Maximum recorded longevity for this species is 16 years, based on recaptured individuals.

The greatest threats to local populations are human disturbance and vandalism at maternity and hibernating sites, and loss of roosting (mine closures) and foraging habitats (deforestation). Efforts to protect big-eared bats include the installation of gates at the entrances to caves and mines, regular monitoring of population trends, and the identification and characterization of alternative and artificial roosts. Presently, cave gating appears to be the most effective way to protect big-eared bats whose populations are at high risk of disturbance by humans, although this approach may not be effective or desired at all locations. *T. H. Kunz*

Size

Females are slightly larger than males.
Total length: 89–116 mm
Length of tail: 35–54 mm
Length of forearm: 39–47 mm
Weight 9–12 g

Identification

Townsend's big-eared bat is distinguished by its pale- to reddish-brown upperparts and pale buff underparts, large ears nearly half the length of the body, and two prominent glandular lumps on the nose. It is similar in appearance to Rafinesque's big-eared bat *(Corynorhinus rafinesquii)* in the east, which has white underparts, and Allen's big-eared bat *(Idionycteris phyllotis)* in the west, which has a pair of leaf-like flaps projecting forward from the base of its ears.

Recent Synonyms

Plecotus townsendii

Other Common Names

Western long-eared bat, western big-eared bat, western lump-nosed bat, mule-eared bat, Townsend's big-eared bat, Mexican big-eared bat, Ozark big-eared bat, Virginia long-eared bat

Status

Relatively uncommon. Local populations of *Corynorhinus townsendii* are threatened throughout most of its range; small isolated populations (subspecies) are especially vulnerable to disturbance at roosts and loss of foraging habitats. Two subspecies *(C. t. ingens* and *C. t. virginianus)* are listed as endangered under the U.S. Endangered Species Act, and two western subspecies *(C. t. townsendii* and *C. t. pallescens)* have been listed as endangered or sensitive by state and regional governments in the western United States.

Subspecies

Corynorhinus townsendii australis, highlands of central Mexico southward to the Isthmus of Tehuantepec

Corynorhinus townsendii ingens, an isolated population in the Ozark Highlands of southwestern Missouri, northwestern Arkansas, and eastern Oklahoma

Corynorhinus townsendii pallescens, central highlands of northern Mexico and southern California to the Edwards Plateau of Texas, with isolated populations in the Black Hills of South Dakota and the Gypsum Hills of south-central Kansas, western Oklahoma, and northwestern Texas

Corynorhinus townsendii townsendii, principally in the coastal range from southern California northward to British Colombia

Corynorhinus townsendii virginianus, an isolated population in limestone caves in Kentucky, West Virginia, and Virginia

References

Mammalian Species 175; Barbour and Davis, 1969; Clark et al., 1993; Handley, 1990; Humphrey and Kunz, 1976; Pierson et al., 1991

Allen's big-eared bat | *Idionycteris phyllotis*

Although this bat was first discovered in San Luis Potosí, México, in 1878, only three specimens had been collected by the time the species was first found in the United States in 1955. Its geographical distribution is better known today, yet it remains a species whose biology is poorly understood. It is most closely related to the spotted bat *(Euderma maculatum)* and big-eared bats in the geneus *Plecotus*. The distinctive, horizontal lappets over the forehead are similar to fleshy flaps beneath the front bases of the ears in closely related Eurasian bats of the genus *Plecotus*. Allen's big-eared bats are able to make these lappets

Idionycteris phyllotis

slide over one another as they rotate their ears sideways. Although they give this species one of its common names, the function of the lappets is unknown.

The dorsal fur of this species is long and soft, blackish or dark brown at the base. The tips of the hairs are a contrasting yellowish-gray, bronze, cinnamon, or dark brown. There is a patch of white hairs behind the base of each ear. As in other big-eared bats, the huge ears can be curled back along the sides of the neck so that they resemble a ram's horns. When its ears are tucked out of the way in this manner, the large tragus (14–16 mm long) remains erect and can appear to be a small ear, sometimes making identification of roosting bats difficult.

Most of what is known about Allen's big-eared bats comes from individuals that were netted at night while flying; few have actually been observed in their roosts. Most have been caught at elevations above 900 m, and in a variety of wooded habitats including especially ponderosa pine forest, pinyon-juniper woodland, riparian woodland, encinal (oak woodland), pine-oak woodland, and fir forest. Others come from more arid habitats; in the northwestern portion of their range this includes Mojave Desert scrub, and in Mexico, mesquite-

grassland with scattered oaks, xeric scrub, and tropical deciduous forest. Rock outcroppings were present at almost all the sites of capture; the rocks sometimes serve as roost sites for the bats. Maternity roosts have been discovered in a pine snag, in a pile of boulders beneath a rock shelter, and in mine entrances. Single individuals have been observed in hibernation in northern Arizona, one in a cave in pinyon-juniper woodland and one in a mine entrance in Mojave Desert scrub.

The species is a highly adapted insect predator using a sophisticated combination of sonar signals and flight maneuvers to forage for and intercept its nocturnal prey. Although it is somewhat opportunistic in the kinds of insects it eats, it usually selects small moths (Microlepidoptera). Other known prey include soldier beetles, dung beetles, leaf beetles, roaches, and flying ants; these include both flying insects that could be taken in flight and nonflying insects that are gleaned from surfaces such as tree bark or foliage. The sonar sounds it uses for orientation and for the echolocation of insects seem to be flexible and encompass the range of signal types used by nearly all bat species. This allows Allen's big-eared bats considerable versatility for orienting and hunting in diverse situations. This ability is complemented by flight movements that are equally flexible; in close quarters the species flies slowly, is highly maneuverable, able to hover, and can even fly vertically, whereas in open-air situations it uses fast, more direct flight from one place to another. For example, while foraging within the echo-filled, complex acoustical environment of the forest canopy, the species uses slow, maneuverable, searching flight and cries that combine long-constant frequency (CF) with modulated frequency (FM) components (called long-CF/FM sounds), but the bats may switch to swift, direct movements and FM signals to quickly locate and reach another patch of trees in which to forage. Such adaptable modes of flight and echolocation ap- parently enable it to forage between, within, and even below forest canopies. During open-air direct flight, these bats are au- dible to humans: they emit rather loud peeps at about one-second intervals, rather like those of spotted bats but lower in pitch. *N. J. Czaplewski*

Size

Sexual dimorphism is minor and varies geo- graphically; females are about 5 percent longer than males.

Total length: 103–135 (110) mm

Length of tail: 40–53 (48) mm

Length of forearm: 41.8–49.0 mm

Weight: 8–16 g

Identification

A lappet projects from front base of each ear over the muzzle; the ears are huge, nearly two-thirds of the body length; dorsal fur varies from yellowish-gray to blackish-brown.

Recent Synonyms

Euderma phyllote

Plecotus phyllotis

Other Common Names

Mexican big-eared bat, lappet-browed bat

Status

Uncommon

Subspecies

Idionycteris phyllotis hualapaiensis, southern Utah, southern Nevada, and northwestern Arizona

Idionycteris phyllotis phyllotis, central and south-eastern Arizona, southwestern New Mex-ico, and mountainous regions of Mexico to central Oaxaca

References

Mammalian Species 208; Barbour and Davis, 1969

Pallid bat | *Antrozous pallidus*

The pallid bat is gregarious and locally common throughout the western United States and northern Mexico. It frequents arid or semi-arid locations. The prominent ears and bright eyes make this rather docile bat one of the more attractive North American bats.

The diet of pallid bats includes a significant proportion of beetles, grasshoppers, and moths. Pallid bats are notorious for their consumption of scorpions and flightless arthropods such as Jerusalem crickets, both groups that are capable of deliver-ing painful stings or bites. Lizards have also been reported as prey items. Pallid bats are not specialized aerial insectivores, feeding on small flying insects, as are many of the other North American vespertilionid bats. Instead, they often use passive sound (in addition to echolocation) to home in on their slow-moving targets. With their large ears, they detect prey items on the desert floor or in low brush. Pallid bats are known to visit flowers and are pollinators of several species of cactus. The bats do not appear to be feeding on pollen or nectar, how-ever. Rather, they seem to be opportunistic visitors to flowers and fruits, feeding on insects found within these structures.

Pallid bats generally occur in groups larger than 20. In Ari-zona, pallid bats were observed using separate day and night roosts, with site preference based on thermal factors. Night roosts were selected for a stable temperature that remained warmer than the ambient temperature. Day roosts were se-lected for high temperatures by pregnant females in maternity colonies, and for stable daytime temperatures that were cooler than the hot ambient temperature of the desert in midsum-

Antrozous pallidus

mer. Roost switching, while predominantly driven by thermal considerations, probably serves also to lower exposure to predators.

Mating takes place in late autumn or early winter. Female pallid bats store sperm in the reproductive tract until ovulation takes place in the spring. Births generally occur in large mater-

nity colonies in May and June. Males are generally absent from these maternity colonies. Yearling females have single offspring, whereas older females may have twins annually.

The winter habits of pallid bats are poorly known. In most parts of their range, their winter roosts have not been described. Although several books have described pallid bats as migratory, they probably migrate on a limited basis and move locally to deep recesses of mine shafts or caves to avoid cold winter weather. Pallid bats readily go into hibernation when maintained at low ambient temperatures.

Pallid bats emit "directive" calls, a series of clear, high-pitched notes that are audible to humans. Although the major components of their vocalizations are ultrasonic and used for orientation, prey detection, and identification, the directive call appears important in social behavior. Bats entering a night roost often use the directive call as if to assess whether other pallid bats are present. Bats already settled within a night roost

also emit directive calls when other pallid bats are flying outside the roost, as if to alert the bats to their presence. Directive calls are commonly heard along rocky desert outcrops whenever large numbers of pallid bats are present. *J. W. Hermanson*

Size
Total length: 92–135 m
Length of tail: 35–53 mm
Weight: 13.6–24.1 g (males); 13.9–28.9 g
    (females)

Identification
The pallid bat is distinguished from other vespertilionid bats by its large separate ears, large eyes, and large bare muzzle. Glands on the muzzle emit a strong odor.

Status
Locally common

Subspecies
Antrozous pallidus bunkerii, Kansas and
    Oklahoma
Antrozous pallidus koopmani, Cuba
Antrozous pallidus minor, Baja California, southern California, and southwestern Arizona
Antrozous pallidus pacificus, Pacific coast of the
    United States

Antrozous pallidus packardi, central and northern Mexico
Antrozous pallidus pallidus, southwestern
    Canada, United States, and Mexico

References
Mammalian Species 213; Martin and Schmidly,
    1982

Family Molossidae

If you have been to Carlsbad Caverns or other large caves in the southwestern U.S., you have probably seen the spectacular exit flight of the Mexican free-tailed bat, *Tadarida brasiliensis*. These animals, members of the widespread family Molossidae, form some of the largest colonies of vertebrates on earth, up to 20 million individuals in a single cave. Such large colonies play an important role in insect control over a large area of countryside. They also require constant, high population levels of insects in order to feed so many individuals. Therefore, the six species of molossids known from North America migrate southward in the winter, where they spread out and form smaller colonies over a very wide area.

These bats are aerial insectivores, and they tend to forage high above the forest canopy, or in open desert areas. They have long, narrow wings that lend themselves to fast flight and somewhat lower maneuverability. Their sleek fur and flattened ears all contribute to this image of speed.

Their migratory lifestyles dictate that young must be produced and reared to sufficient size to undertake their initial migratory flight in a fairly short period of time during the summer when insect populations are high.

This family is one of the few families of bats found around the world, although the bulk of the diversity is limited to tropical regions, as with most kinds of bats. Most of the North American species occur only in the Southwest, and there only in summer.

References
Tuttle, 1988; Wilson, 1997

North American Genera
Tadarida
Nyctinomops
Eumops

Brazilian free-tailed bat | *Tadarida brasiliensis*

Brazilian free-tailed bats are among the most abundant and conspicuous bats in North America. In the southwestern United States and northern Mexico, *T. b. mexicana* forms the largest colonies that have been reported for any mammal, with the colony in Bracken Cave, Texas, estimated at 20 million individuals. Another dozen or so caves in the region harbor other colonies of a million or more. On summer evenings, the departure of free-tailed bats from a large colony provides the spectacular impression of thick clouds of black smoke emanating from the cave's mouth.

One of the most widely distributed mammal species in the Western Hemisphere, Brazilian free-tailed bats also show substantial diversity in behavior. *T. b. mexicana* is typically migratory, spending winter months in central and southern Mexico, where it roosts primarily in caves and man-made structures in colonies of a few hundred to many thousand. Mating occurs in January or February. Northward migration of up to 1,300 km occurs between February and April. The largest cave colonies are occupied between May and October, mostly by pregnant females and their offspring. Other populations of *T. b. mexicana*

Tadarida brasiliensis

in California and southern Oregon, and those of *T. b. cyno-cephala* in the southeastern United States, are year-round, apparently nonmigratory residents of those regions. Brazilian free-tailed bats in these populations hibernate during cold weather and roost in much smaller colonies, mostly in manmade structures. Little has been reported regarding the behavior or natural history of the other subspecies, and most information concerns *T. b. mexicana.*

Their long, narrow wings allow Brazilian free-tailed bats to fly at high speed for long distances. They tend to feed in habitats that are relatively uncluttered by vegetation and often at high altitudes. During a single night, individuals fly to foraging sites 50 km or more from their roost, often at altitudes above 3,000 m. Moths are their major food, but they also eat beetles, flying ants, and a variety of other insects. Lactating females eat an amount equal to more than 50 percent of their own body mass during a single night's feeding. Their high energetic demands and huge populations make them major insect predators. Isotopic studies of their feces indicate that they consume large numbers of insects that are agricultural pests.

Most females give birth to a single pup, in early-mid June. During the approximately 6-week period from birth to weaning, pups are massed together in large "creches" in densities that, for *T. b. mexicana,* can exceed 5,000 pups per square meter of cave surface. Mothers roost apart from the pups but visit the creche for nursing two or more times daily. They locate their own pup using a combination of locational, vocal, and olfactory information.

Although they are abundant, their long life spans (the average life span of adults may exceed 10 years, and during a bat's lifetime its body accumulates organochlorine hydrocarbons from pesticides), low rates of reproduction, and habits of aggregating in a limited number of very large colonies for reproduction raise serious concerns for the conservation of Brazilian free-tailed bat populations. Declines and extirpations of several formerly large colonies have been documented in recent years, both in the United States and Mexico. Poisoning by agricultural pesticides may have a role in the decline of Brazilian free-tailed bat populations, but the major factor is the disturbance and destruction of roost sites by humans. *G. F. McCracken*

Size

Males are about 5 percent longer than females; females weigh about 5 percent more than males.

Total length: 85–109 (95) mm
Length of forearm: 36–46 (42) mm
Weight: 10–15 g

Identification

Molossids are distinguished from other families of bats by the conspicuous projection of the tail beyond the limits of the short uropatagium. *Tadarida brasiliensis* is distinguished from other North American molossids, except *Mormopterus minutus* of Cuba, by deep vertical grooves on the upper lip. It is larger than *M. minutus,* and can be distinguished from other *Tadarida* by ears not joined at the midline and a nearly uniform brown pelage.

Recent Synonyms

Nyctinomus brasiliensis

Other Common Names

Guano bat, Mexican free-tailed bat

Status

Common

Subspecies

Tadarida brasiliensis antillularum, Puerto Rico, windward islands of the Lesser Antilles
Tadarida brasiliensis bahamensis, Bahama Islands
Tadarida brasiliensis brasiliensis, Costa Rica, Panama, South America
Tadarida brasiliensis constanzae, Haiti, Dominican Republic
Tadarida brasiliensis cynocephala, southeastern United States
Tadarida brasiliensis intermedia, southern Mexico, Guatemala
Tadarida brasiliensis mexicana, western United States, northern and central Mexico
Tadarida brasiliensis murina, Jamaica
Tadarida brasiliensis muscula, Cuba, Grand Cayman Island

References

Mammalian Species 331; Davis et al., 1962; McCracken and Gustin, 1991

Pocketed free-tailed bat | *Nyctinomops femorosaccus*

Nyctinomops femorosaccus is a small to medium-sized free-tailed bat with deep vertical grooves along its upper lip, ears that are joined at the basal midpoint and that extend noticeably beyond the nostrils when laid forward, and forearms measuring 45.4–49.2 mm long. Its body color is brown to grayish-brown, although sometimes with a reddish hue, and its hairs are whitish at the base. The ventral surface of the body is slightly paler in color. The pocket for which this bat is named is an inconspicuous fold of membrane near the knee.

The pocketed free-tailed bat reaches the northern edge of its distribution in desert scrub and arid lowland habitats in southern California and southern Arizona, with two additional localities known in New Mexico and one in Big Bend, Texas. In Mexico this species occurs in Baja California and the western coastal states as far south as Guerrero, extending northeastward to Nuevo Leon. In Arizona it is restricted in distribution from near sea level up to 1,250 m elevation in desert riparian corridors and up to 2,250 m elsewhere in its range. Although it is limited in overall distribution, this freetail occurs consistently at certain netting localities in southern Arizona and probably elsewhere within its range.

Like most large molossids, during dry seasons it utilizes water sources with open access and a large available surface area from which to drink. It leaves its roosts after dark and is usually not taken in mistnets until two or three hours after sunset. It

Nyctinomops femorosaccus

roosts in caves, rock crevices in cliff faces, and man-made structures. Colonies usually number fewer than 100 individuals.

The pocketed free-tailed bat gives birth to only one young per year, usually in early July, and the young are flying in mid-to late August. This long-winged, rapid-flying bat generally pursues insects on the wing. A variety of insect orders (Lepidoptera, Hymenoptera, Homoptera, Coleoptera, Hemiptera, Orthoptera, Diptera, and Neuroptera) are represented among its prey. Stomach analyses show a higher percentage of moths eaten than any other insects.

These are audibly vocal bats. When they hit a net, they chirp loudly, and continue to emit squeaks and chirps while being handled. A rehabilitated *N. femorosaccus* kept in captivity for several years chirps loudly and impatiently for its evening meal whenever its keeper is not on time or quick enough with its mealworms. *R. Sidner*

Size
No significant sexual dimorphism
Total length: 99–118 (109) mm
Length of tail: 34–45 mm
Length of forearm: 45.4–49.2 mm
Weight: 13.8–17.0 g

Identification
Distinguished from *N. macrotis* by shorter forearms, from *N. laticaudatus* in Mexico by longer ears (22–24 mm), from *N. aurispinosa* in Mexico by shorter length of skull (less than 20.0 mm) and shorter maxillary toothrow (less than 7.5 mm). Distinguished from *Tadarida brasiliensis*

by its ears: the ears of *T. brasiliensis* are not joined at their basal midpoint, as they are in *N. femorosaccus.*

Recent Synonyms
Nyctinomops femorosacca
Tadarida femorosacca

Status
Limited and uncommon

References
Mammalian Species 349; Freeman, 1981; Hoffmeister, 1986

Big free-tailed bat | *Nyctinomops macrotis*

The big free-tailed bat lives in the southwestern United States. It inhabits mostly rugged, rocky country, and migrates seasonally from the U.S. to Mexico. It ranges from southern and western Texas to southern California and southeastern Nevada, and north to central Colorado and western Utah. It is known to occur primarily at elevations from near sea level to about 1,800 m.

Nyctinomops macrotus roosts in buildings, caves, and occasionally in holes in trees. These bats are nocturnal and do not leave their day roosting sites to forage until after dark. They feed mainly on large moths (Lepidoptera). Occasionally, however, big free-tailed bats eat crickets, grasshoppers, flying ants, stinkbugs, froghoppers, and leafhoppers. They pursue and capture prey using echolocation. Most of their echolocation emissions are of frequencies below 20 kHz, and are therefore audible to humans, often sounding like loud clicks.

As is the case with other species of *Nyctinomops,* the wings of *N. macrotus* are long and narrow, especially at the tips. The wingspan ranges from 417 to 436 mm. This wing design allows for rapid, enduring, although not extremely maneuverable, flight.

The pelage of the big free-tailed bat is glossy. The juvenile pelage is darker than that of the adult. Each individual hair is bicolored, with a nearly white base, which distinguishes *N. macrotis* from *Tadarida brasiliensis.* The large, broad ears are joined basally at the midline of the head and extend beyond the tip of the snout when laid forward. The upper lip is deeply furrowed by vertical wrinkles and the muzzle is slender. The large size of this bat distinguishes it from both *T. brasiliensis* and *N. femorosaccus.*

Female big free-tailed bats usually give birth to one young in late spring or early summer. They form maternity colonies and separate themselves from the males throughout the summer, while the young are being raised. Juveniles begin flying by late August. The only known nursery colony of this bat in the United States is in the Chisos Mountains in Big Bend National Park, in Texas. Approximately 130 bats occupied the colony in May and October.

Nyctinomops macrotis is usually easy to handle and fairly docile. However, some investigators have found that temperament of individual bats can vary considerably. Some of them, when captured, readily bite and vocalize loudly. Two big free-tailed bats have been reported to the Texas Department of Health; both proved to be nonrabid.

The genus name, *Nyctinomops,* is compounded from Greek words that mean "resembling a night feeder." The species name, *macrotis,* is from the Greek *macros* and *otos,* or "long ear." *D. A. Parish and C. Jones*

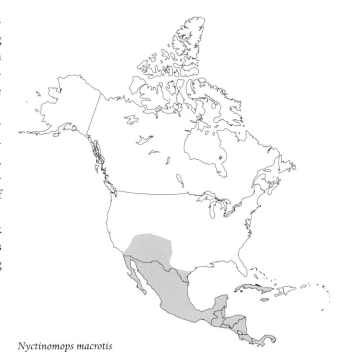

Nyctinomops macrotis

Size

Males tend to be slightly larger than females.
Total length: 145–160 mm (males); 120–139 (131.8) mm (females)
Length of tail: 40–57 (50.45) mm
Weight: 22.0–30.0 g

Identification

Nyctinomops macrotis is the largest member of the genus. Its dorsal pelage ranges from pale reddish-brown to dark brown and blackish, with individual hairs white at the base. The ears are large and joined basally at the midline of the head. The sides of the lips are wrinkled.

Recent Synonyms

Tadarida macrotis
Tadarida molossa

Status

Common

References

Mammalian Species 351; Schmidly, 1991

Wagner's mastiff bat | *Eumops glaucinus*

Wagner's mastiff bat, *Eumops glaucinus,* is an uncommon species but is widely distributed in the Neotropics. In the United States it is found in the Miami / Coral Gables area of southern Florida, and has been recorded once in Charlotte County in western Florida. Fossils from the late Wisconsin period have been found in Brevard, Dade, and Indian River counties. This bat is considered to be endangered by the state of Florida because of habitat destruction and the use of insecticides. *Eumops glaucinus* is found in Mexico as far north as Jalisco and the Yucatan Peninsula. Normally it is found from sea level to 900 meters elevation, and has been reported as high as 2,750 meters.

The mastiff bat is a medium-sized brown bat with a white band at the base of each hair. The ventral pelage is paler than the dorsal.

Like most bats, *Eumops glaucinus* is nocturnal, leaving the roost after dark. These bats fly high, generally above 10 meters, producing recognizable calls—audible to humans—as they fly. *Eumops glaucinus* has long, narrow wings, enabling it to fly long distances quickly. Unlike other species of free-tailed bats, which need to drop from a roost to launch into flight, *Eumops glaucinus* can take off from a horizontal surface.

In Florida this species has been seen foraging high, feeding on insects. It feeds primarily on coleopteran, dipteran, and hemipteran insects, but its diet probably varies with the insects available. Because of their size and speed, these bats can forage in open spaces. They use echolocation to detect prey at relatively long range (3–5 m).

Based on information from Cuba and Florida, *Eumops glaucinus* appears to be polyestrous. The female gives birth to a single young. These bats are known to roost singly as well as in groups of up to 32 individuals. There is some evidence to suggest that the social groups might be breeding colonies of a mature male and his harem.

Eumops uses both buildings and tree hollows as diurnal roosts. Known to occur in cities as well as in forested areas, *Eumops glaucinus* has been found roosting in attics, under Spanish tile roofs, in shafts of royal palm *(Roystonea regia)* leaves, in the foliage of the palm *Copernicia vespertilionum,* and in cavities in longleaf pine *(Pinus palustris),* royal palm, dagame trees *(Cattycophyllum candidissimum),* and mastic trees *(Bursera simaruba).* In forested areas, old, mature trees are essential roosting sites for this species. *J. Eger*

Eumops glaucinus

Size

Males are significantly larger than females.
Total length: 123–165 (139.7) mm (males); 117–156 (138) mm (females)

Length of tail: 40–64 (50.2) mm (males); 40–61 (49.4) mm (females)
Length of forearm: 56.6–67.7 (60.5) mm (males); 55.7–62 (59.2) mm (females)

Weight: 25–47 (34.1) g (males); 28.2–55.4 (36.1) g (females)

Identification

This bat is distinguished from other free-tailed bats by smooth (rather than wrinkled) lips and large, joined ears; it is distinguished from *Eumops auripendulus,* which occurs from Mexico southward, and is the only other species of *Eumops* of similar size, by paler color, white basal band on the fur, and a square, broad tragus.

Recent Synonyms

Eumops floridanus
Eumops orthotis

Other Common Names

Florida mastiff bat

Status

Considered endangered by the state of Florida; uncommon elsewhere

Subspecies

Eumops glaucinus floridanus, southern Florida
Eumops glaucinus glaucinus, Cuba, Jamaica, and central Mexico south to northwestern Argentina and southeastern Brazil

References

Mammalian Species 551; Bellwood, 1992; Eger, 1977

Western mastiff bat | *Eumops perotis*

Western mastiff bats are found from San Francisco Bay across southern California, Nevada, Arizona, and New Mexico to just east of Big Bend National Park in Texas, and in northern Mexico, into Sonora and as far south as Coahuila. These large bats live in rugged, rocky canyons typical of the arid southwest, where they inhabit crevices in vertical cliffs. Records from earlier in the century show that they were once common in buildings in southern California, but this may not be the case today.

Western mastiff bats prefer deep crevices that are at least 5 or 6 meters (15 or 20 feet) above the ground, and will usually wedge themselves into the narrowest part of a crack so that both back and stomach are in contact with the rock. Roosting sites have moderately large openings that can be entered from below in a place where the approach is unobstructed. Unlike other molossids in North America, these bats do not migrate, but they do move to different sites, depending on the season, in the northern part of their range. Males and females are found in the same roost, unlike their smaller cousin, the Mexican free-tailed bat, *Tadarida brasiliensis,* which has large nursery colonies of adult females and young only.

The need for roosts with unobstructed approaches is easy to understand given the weight of the body and the nature of the wings. Western mastiff bats are large, with long, narrow wings (the wingspan measures 530–570 mm), and cannot take flight from a flat surface. Instead they must free-fall from a height to achieve enough lift for successful flight. From the ground, they will scramble to an object or tree to gain the height needed for a launch. The long, narrow wings, while not good for takeoffs from the ground, are well-adapted for rapid and enduring flight. Besides being large and having long, narrow wings, mastiff bats have large ears (32–47 mm long) that reach over the face like a bonnet. Bats in the genus are sometimes called bonneted bats. One author speculated that because the ear is shaped like an airfoil in side view, it may play a role in creating extra lift for the large head. Unlike some of its wrinkled-lipped smaller relatives, western mastiffs have smooth lips that are maneuverable and expandible and useful for manipulating and consuming large insect prey. Wings, heads, and thoracic segments of the insects are clipped off and only the abdomens are consumed.

Reproductive activity is consistent with a nonmigrating, nonhibernating mammal in the temperate zone and occurs in the spring. Ovulation in females is thought to occur soon after copulation, but the exact time is variable. The length of gesta-

tion is unknown and the time of birth is the most variable of any bat in the United States. Babies have been born as early as April, as late as August, and a very young individual was found as late as November. Males have a well-developed throat gland that enlarges and produces a thick and particularly odiferous secretion during the breeding season. The location of this gland and its unique odor are typical of molossid bats.

Western mastiff bats have unusually long foraging periods and have been estimated to stay out 6.5 hours each night. This supports the theory that large insectivorous bats eating large insects need longer periods of time to find them. Food items for these bats include large moths (up to 60 mm), crickets, grasshoppers, dragonflies, cicadas, beetles, and bees. The bats often forage as high as several hundred to two thousand feet above the ground, and foraging can occur as far as 24 km (15 miles) from the nearest roost. *Eumops perotis* has an audible, high pitched, piercing "chip" of great intensity that can be heard readily if it is foraging nearby.

The ranges of the western mastiff and the slightly smaller Underwood's mastiff overlap slightly in the United States, and more so in Mexico. The exact requirements of habitat are unknown for the two species, but both seem to like rocky desert environments. *P. W. Freeman*

Eumops perotis

Size
Males are larger than females.
Total length: 159–187 (175) mm
Length of tail: 55–72 (60) mm
Length of forearm: 72–83 (78) mm
Weight: 45.5–73.0 g

Identification
The western mastiff is larger than *Eumops underwoodi,* making it the largest bat in North America. It is also darker than *E. underwoodi* and has no long guard hairs on the rump.

Other Common Names
Greater mastiff bat, bonnetted bat

Status
Not common

Subspecies
Eumops perotis californicus, southern California, Arizona, New Mexico, Texas, and northern Mexico
Eumops perotis perotis, northern Venezuela, Paraguay, northern Argentina, southern Brazil, Bolivia, and east of the Andes in Ecuador and Peru

References
Mammalian Species 534; Barbour and Davis, 1969; Eger, 1977; Hoffmeister, 1986

Underwood's mastiff bat | *Eumops underwoodi*

The southern subspecies of Underwood's mastif bat, *Eumops u. underwoodi,* occurs from Chihuahua, Mexico south to Honduras, Belize, and Nicaragua, and is associated with pine-oak forests or tropical deciduous forest with some areas converted to grassland. Its habits are poorly known, but it has been captured at night over pools of water where it apparently comes to drink. It has been observed roosting in hollow trees and beneath the leaves of a royal palm. *Eumops u. sonoriensis* occurs from Sonora, Mexico to southern Arizona. In the warm season in southern Arizona both males and females of this species

are captured in mist nets set over pools of water in the desert, where they apparently come to drink. Nothing is known of its diurnal roosts and nothing is known of its cold season distribution. *Eumops perotis*, which is similar in size and form to *Eumops underwoodi*, commonly roosts in high rock crevices from which it free-falls into flight. It is likely that *Eumops u. sonoriensis* uses similar roost sites. Although individuals may roost in the vicinity of the Baboquivari Mountains of southern Arizona, where they are commonly captured over bodies of water, it is likely that many roost sites are in Mexico. Individuals captured in September at Quitobaquito Tank in Organ Pipe Cactus National Monument circled to a height of several hundred feet above the ground and flew out of sight to the south, over Mexico, when released in the early morning. *Eumops perotis, Nyctinomops femorosacca, Nyctinomops macrotus,* and several species of common vespertilionid bats are captured in the same mist nets that catch *Eumops u. sonoriensis.*

Like other large molossid bats, *Eumops underwoodi* has long, narrow wings (its wingspan is 500–540 mm) and shoulder musculoskeletal anatomy that suit it for rapid, prolonged, and efficient flight. A reported maximum flight speed of more than 43 km per hour is probably an underestimate. High-pitched "chips" repeated several times a minute typically announce the presence of this species, although the calls are not always heard when the bats approach the bodies of water where they are captured. The bats apparently leave their roosts well after dark and probably stay airborne all night.

Eumops underwoodi

Eumops underwoodi is a large and formidable-looking bat but is typically gentle when captured. Although some individuals will bite, complete docility is more common. If strongly provoked, a gape of the huge mouth and simultaneous, high-pitched pulse of sound is directed toward the source of annoyance. The sound is louder than that of *E. perotis* and is so intense that it is painful to persons close by. The jaws are thicker and more massive than those of *E. perotis* and suitable to a diet of hard items such as beetles and grasshoppers. The upper pelage of *Eumops u. sonoriensis* varies from cinnamon to mummy brown and the underparts are hazel. *Eumops u. underwoodi* varies from light yellowish- to grayish-brown dorsally and is paler ventrally.

As with much of the rest of the biology of this species, little is known of its reproduction. A single pup is born in late June or early July. *M. Kiser and J. S. Altenbach*

Size
Total length: 160–165 m
Length of forearm: 65–77 mm
Weight: 40–65 g

Identification
The lips of *Eumops underwoodi* are not wrinkled. This bat is distinguished from *E. perotis*, the only other bat of comparable size in North America, by having shorter ears (reaching the tip of the nose when laid forward), being slightly smaller, and having a distinct fringe of bristle-like guard hairs on the rump that project 7–10 mm beyond the rest of the pelage.

Recent Synonyms
Eumops sonoriensis

Status
Southern subspecies poorly known, limited; northern subspecies locally common, limited

Subspecies
Eumops underwoodi sonoriensis, Sonora, Mexico to southern Arizona
Eumops underwoodi underwoodi, Chihuahua, Mexico to Honduras, Belize, and Nicaragua

References
Mammalian Species 516; Cockrum and Gardner, 1960

Order Carnivora

This order is native to all continents, except Australia and Antarctica, and to the world's oceans. The Order Carnivora encompasses 12 families, 129 genera, and 271 species. Although most species are terrestrial, the otters frequent freshwater habitats; others, such as sea otters, seals, sea lions, and walruses are marine organisms. Most species have well-developed senses of smell, sight, and hearing. Typically, these animals eat vertebrate prey.

Canidae, Felidae, and Mustelidae are found naturally from the Arctic to the tropics on most large land masses. They feed primarily on freshly killed vertebrate prey. Canids are the most cursorial of the carnivores and frequently travel in packs. Canids may be active anytime during the day and have excellent sight, smell, and hearing. Cats (Felidae) are also excellent hunters and may stalk prey until moving close enough for a brief dash and the kill. Many species are nocturnal but some are diurnal. Most mustelids search aggressively for prey in burrows or dense cover. Others, such as the mink and otter, are good swimmers and hunt in aquatic environments.

Bears (Ursidae) occur worldwide from the Arctic to the tropics. In colder regions, bears enter a deep sleep during winter. Bears may shelter in holes they dig, in caves or crevices, in tree hollows, or in dense vegetation. Most bears are omnivorous, but the polar bear takes little other than fish and seals, and the panda feeds primarily on bamboo. Procyonids are also omnivorous, typically are active at night, and all species appear to be good climbers.

Carnivora includes approximately 37 species of marine mammals within five families: Phocidae (earless seals), Otariidae (eared seals and sea lions), Odobenidae (walrus), Mustelidae (two species of marine otter), and Ursidae (the polar bear). They are well-adapted for life in aquatic environments and are excellent swimmers and divers. Most species are solitary while at sea but form large colonies during the breeding season, usually on isolated islands. Marine Carnivora consume invertebrate and vertebrate prey.

References
Bueler, 1973; Grzimek, 1975; Nowak, 1991;
    Riedman, 1990; Wozencraft, 1993

American marten *(Martes americana)*

Family Canidae

This family includes 14 genera and 34 species, worldwide. The nine species known from North America are divided into four genera: *Canis, Alopex, Vulpes,* and *Urocyon.* The largest species, the wolf *(Canis lupus),* ranges up to a meter and a half in head and body length, with another half-meter of tail, and may weigh up to 80 kg. In general, males tend to be larger than females in this family. Like wolves, domestic dogs are in the genus *Canis.*

Canids have been an important part of the predator guild in North America since Eocene times. Some species, especially the larger ones like wolves, form large packs of up to 30 animals, which allows them to hunt prey larger than themselves. Wolves have fallen on hard times in North America, owing to their propensity to come into conflict with humans, especially ranchers, in the western part of the continent. However, recent reintroduction efforts may once again lead to viable populations in some protected areas.

Most of the smaller species are much more solitary in their foraging habits, although some may hunt in pairs. These smaller forms tend to prey on rodents and small birds, rather than larger game. Nevertheless, they have also been persecuted as "varmints" throughout much of North America in the past two centuries. This persecution probably has hastened natural selection to sharpen many species into wily, vigilant, nocturnal or crepuscular predators.

Canids are found in almost every habitat, from hot southwestern deserts to Arctic glaciers. They frequent home ranges that may include actively defended territories, and have evolved complex and varied social systems. They den in burrows, caves, hollow trees, and other such out-of-the-way places. They tend to be active year-round, but females generally give birth only once per year. Litter sizes range from 2–13, and gestation lengths average about two months. Young are born altricial, and considerable parental care is required.

Foraging strategies have favored long-distance movements, and they tend to be cursorial (adapted for running), moving lightly on the digits at a tireless trot, but capable of short bursts of considerable speed. Most are strictly terrestrial, although gray foxes *(Urocyon cinereoargenteus)* occasionally climb trees.

References
Nowak, 1991; Wilson and Reeder, 1993

North American Genera
Canis
Alopex
Vulpes
Urocyon

Coyote | *Canis latrans*

References to the way "the" coyote lives can be misleading: coyotes are incredibly adaptable and behaviorally variable as a species. Coyotes are mobile (they can run as fast as 48 km per hour) and opportunistic. They thrive in diverse habitats ranging from warm deserts to wet grasslands and plains, to colder climates at high elevations (up to about 3,000 m), to large cities such as Los Angeles, California. They are found between about 10° north latitude (northern Alaska) and 70° south latitude (Costa Rica), and throughout the United States and Canada. Coyotes enjoy a catholic diet including plant and animal matter and occasionally even inanimate objects (such as leather boots); their diet varies greatly seasonally and geographically, as do the methods by which they acquire prey. Coyotes are successful scavengers. They are frequently portrayed as cunning tricksters, gluttons, outlaws, spoilers, and survivors in American mythology and in Native American tales. These characterizations are based mainly on this ma-

ligned predator's uncanny ability to survive and reproduce successfully in diverse locations and under extremely harsh conditions, even in the face of onslaughts (including brutal planned community hunts) by humans.

Coyotes are usually monogamous, and pair bonds between a male and female can last for years. In a pack, there is usually only one mated pair per season. Both males and females are able to breed during their first year of life, usually when they are about 9–10 months of age. Coyotes typically breed once a year, in early- to mid-winter, depending on locale. Males appear to go through an annual cycle of spermatogenesis. The female's annual estrus lasts about 2–5 days; ovulation occurs about 2–3 days before the end of estrus. Courtship can last for as long as 2 or 3 months before copulation. The gestation period averages 63 days (58–65) and mean litter size is about six pups, with an even sex ratio at birth; litter size can vary with population and prey density. Pups are born blind and helpless,

Canis latrans

are about 4–5 months of age and continues until they are about 10 months old. Some individuals disperse after they are a year old, although only rarely will an entire litter remain intact longer than a year. Males and females seem to disperse in equal numbers and travel the same distances and for the same amount of time before they settle down (if they do settle down). Sex and age at dispersal do not appear to be linked. Mortality is higher for dispersers than for those young who remain in their natal group. The causes of dispersal are unknown, although there appears to be an association between food availability and dispersal. When there is enough food to feed more than just the mated pair, competition is reduced, social bonds are more likely to form among at least some group members, and the likelihood of dispersal is reduced. It is unclear whether aggression among young or between adults and young also plays a role. Some dispersing individuals continue to live as transients, whereas some join up with one or more other coyotes, associating with them for varying periods of time. It has been suggested, but not proved, that coyotes who disperse are more likely to breed than are those who do not.

Coyotes show great variation in their social organization. Some live singly, others in pairs (usually mates), and some live in packs. Coyote packs resemble wolf packs in many ways, and, as in other canids, are usually composed of the mated pair, young-of-the-year, and some of their nondispersing offspring from previous years. Defense of food and territory is shared by pack members. One study found that it usually took more than a mated pair to deter intruders. Packs are often observed around dead deer, elk, and moose. Coyotes will kill these ungulates, but this has seldom been seen happening; of-

usually in an excavated den, emerge from the den at about 2–3 weeks of age, and are weaned at about 5–7 weeks of age. Parents often receive help from other group members in rearing young and in defending the group's territory both during and outside of the breeding season. Mortality typically is highest during the first year of life, but depends greatly on the level of exploitation to which populations are exposed, and generalizations are of questionable validity. Coyotes can live as long as 18 years in captivity, but in the wild few live longer than about 6–10 years. Coyotes can produce fertile hybrids when they mate with gray and red wolves, domestic dogs, and golden jackals.

Dispersal of young-of-the-year usually begins when the pups

ten packs congregate around the carcasses of animals that died of other causes.

Some studies indicate that food supply is a major factor influencing social organization and the use of space. Home ranges of coyotes can be as large as 50–70 square km, and there are no consistent sex differences. Ranges differ regionally and seasonally (with variations in temperature, food supply, the reproductive status of the female, the presence of pups). They also vary according to the age and habits of the individual (transient or more sedentary pack member), mortality rate, which might be related to food supply, the presence of other coyotes or other potential competitors, intensity of exploitation for their fur, and the amount of population control to which they are subjected.

Coyotes communicate using a rich repertoire of olfactory, tactile, vocal, and visual signals. Many of their social signals are common to other canids. Coyotes, usually males, scent-mark in and around territorial boundaries. Coyotes do not groom one another very often, but they will often rest in contact with one another, and tactile contact may be important for reinforcing social bonds. They are vocal animals and may howl following a reunion of two or more individuals, to announce their location or territorial occupancy, or possibly because they enjoy howling. They display a wide variety of facial expressions, and by combining these expressions with different vocalizations and various gaits, postures, and ear and tail positions, they are able to send a wide variety of subtle messages to other individuals.

Coyotes have shown themselves to be great survivors, a skill they do not appear to be losing. In many ways they are victims of success, as their range expands and they come into increasing conflict with humans. *M. Bekoff*

Size
Males are typically heavier, taller, and longer than females, but there is significant geographic and subspecific variation.
Length of head and body: 750–1,000 mm
Length of tail: 300–400 mm
Weight: 8–20 kg (males); 7–18 kg (females)

Identification
Coyotes at higher elevations tend to be gray and black, whereas those in the desert are more reddish-brown. The hair is generally longer and coarser in northern subspecies. The belly and throat are paler than the rest of the body. Melanistic coyotes are rare. Coyotes are usually lighter in weight and shorter at the shoulder than gray wolves (*Canis lupus*), but overlap in size with red wolves (*C. rufus*). *C. latrans* has a smaller nose pad and hind foot pad than *C. lupus*, but its ears are longer and its stride is shorter than that of either *C. lupus* or *C. rufus*. *Canis latrans* can be differentiated from both by cranial measurements and brain morphology. Coyotes are typically more aggressive as infants than wolves.

Status
Common

Subspecies
Canis latrans cagottis, east-central Mexico
Canis latrans clepticus, southern California and northern Baja California
Canis latrans dickeyi, El Salvador to Costa Rica
Canis latrans frustror, eastern Kansas, Oklahoma, and Texas through Missouri, Arkansas, and Louisiana to western Mississippi
Canis latrans goldmani, Oaxaca and Chiapas, Mexico
Canis latrans hondurensis, Honduras
Canis latrans impavidus, southern Sonora and Chihuahua through Sinaloa and Durango to Zacatecas, Mexico
Canis latrans incolatus, central Alberta and British Columbia through Alaska
Canis latrans jamesi, Tiburon Island, Gulf of California
Canis latrans latrans, southern Alberta and Saskatchewan south to Texas Panhandle

Canis latrans lestes, intermontane west from southern British Columbia and Alberta to northern New Mexico
Canis latrans mearnsi, southwestern U.S. and northwestern Mexico
Canis latrans microdon, Nuevo Leon and Tamaulipas, Mexico, to Rio Grande Valley, Texas
Canis latrans ochropus, western California
Canis latrans peninsulae, Baja California, Mexico
Canis latrans texensis, western Texas and eastern New Mexico to Tamaulipas, Coahuila, and Chihuahua, Mexico
Canis latrans thamnos, southern Manitoba to New Brunswick, southwards to northern Missouri and Massachusetts
Canis latrans umpquensis, Oregon and Washington west of the Cascade Mountains
Canis latrans vigilis, Colima and Jalisco, Mexico

References
Mammalian Species 79; Bekoff, 1978; Bekoff and Wells, 1986; Bright, 1993

Gray wolf | *Canis lupus*

Formerly distributed throughout the Northern Hemisphere north of 20° N latitude, deliberate extermination has restricted the wolf's current North American range to Canada, Alaska, Montana, northern Minnesota, Wisconsin, and Michigan (including Isle Royale in Lake Superior). Washington, Idaho, Wyoming, and North and South Dakota support sporadic individuals, and Mexico may have a few. The wolf is on the federal Endangered Species List in the 48 contiguous states, but will probably be delisted by 2001.

The wolf is a social animal, usually living in packs of 5–10

members, although packs of up to 36 have been reported. Generally wolf packs contain a set of parents (the "alpha pair") and some of the offspring of their past 2–3 litters; in some areas, about 25 percent of the packs also include an unrelated immigrant. Packs are held together by strong affectional ties that develop, are reinforced, and become fixed during courtship between two mature adults and between them and their pups. The alpha pair leads the pack in its travel and activities.

After a courtship that may last from days to months, wolves copulate during estrus, which occurs once per year and lasts 5–14 days. Blood may flow from the female's vagina for a few days to a few weeks before estrus. The receptive period may be as early as January in low latitudes or as late as April in high latitudes. During copulation the pair remains coupled, back to back, for as long as 30 minutes, during which ejaculation occurs many times. Gestation lasts 63 days, and litters average six young (extremes, 1 to 11). The young are born blind and helpless, usually in a hole in the ground or other place of quiet and shelter; sometimes just a depression in the ground is used. The same den may be used year after year.

The female usually stays near the young for at least three weeks. During this time, the male and other pack members hunt and feed her and later the pups. The pups' eyes open at days 11–15, most milk teeth are present by about week 3, and weaning takes place at about week 9. After about 8–10 weeks, the pups move to a ground nest known as a "rendezvous site," where they romp and play over an area of a hectare or more.

Healthy pups join adults in their travels as early as October, when they may be almost adult size. Adult canine teeth usually replace deciduous teeth by week 26. The cartilage between the long bones calcifies when the pups are about a year old. Most wolves disperse from their natal packs when they are 1–3 years old, and may travel to new areas more than 800 km away. Although a few may gain sexual maturity in their first year, in the wild they do not breed until they are 2, 3, or 4 years of age. Both sexes may continue to breed through at least 10 years of age and can live to be about 16 years old.

Wolves are primarily predators on ungulates, beavers (Castor canadensis), and hares (Lepus), although almost any species of animal may be eaten, including any type of domestic animal. Young, old, and otherwise inferior prey constitute most of the animals killed by wolves. Average estimated consumption rates are 2.5–6.3 kg per wolf per day.

Mortality factors include diseases, parasites, starvation, intraspecific strife, injuries by prey, and exploitation and persecution by human beings.

Wolves travel a great deal, and territory sizes range from 130 to 13,000 square km. Daily travels within territories vary from a few km per day to up to 72 km, at speeds of about 8 km per hour. The wolf's running speed is about 70 km per hour.

Few other species have had such a variety of relationships with humans as has the wolf. Early humans tamed and domesticated wolves, eventually selectively breeding them and finally developing the domestic dog. More recently, humans have poisoned, persecuted, and exterminated wolves from many areas.

Wolves have three main methods of communication: howling and other vocalizations; postural and visual displays involving especially the face; and scent-marking.

Individual wolves have distinctive howls. The howling of pups is usually high-pitched, with considerable yapping, whereas the pitch of adults is much lower. One function of howling is in assembling the pack, and territory advertisement is another. Coarse barking, whining, and growling are alarm and threat vocalizations.

Body positions and facial expressions primarily show social status. Inguinal presentation and sniffing are also involved in status demonstrations, but probably also serve in individual identification. Scent-marking involves deposition of urine and/or feces on conspicuous objects along trails and intense scraping of the ground. Scent-marking is usually performed by high-ranking adults, often at trail intersections.

Wolves are good swimmers and do not hesitate to wade or swim across rivers and lakes; they sometimes follow prey into water even in winter. *L. D. Mech*

Canis lupus

Size

Length of head and body: 1,000–1,300 (1,100) mm (males); 870–1,170 (1,050) mm (females)
Length of tail: 350–520 (450) mm
Weight: 30–80 (55) kg (males); 23–55 (45) kg (females)

Identification

The largest wild dog, the wolf is usually mottled gray but may be black or white or any grade between. It is distinguished from its nearest relative, the red wolf *(Canis rufus),* by being 10–50 percent larger and having a broader snout and proportionately shorter ears, and from the coyote *(Canis latrans)* by being 50–100 percent larger and having a broader snout and proportionately larger feet.

Other Common Names

Wolf, timber wolf, tundra wolf, lobo, prairie wolf, Mexican wolf, arctic wolf

Status

Common in about two-thirds of its original circumpolar range; extinct, endangered, or threatened in the other third. Listed as endangered except in Alaska by the United States government.

Subspecies

Canis lupus arctos, northern and northeastern Greenland Queen Elizabeth Islands, Parry Islands, Banks Island, and Victoria Island of Northwest Territories
Canis lupus baileyi, Mexico, southwestern Texas, southwestern New Mexico, southeastern Arizona
Canis lupus lycaon, lower Michigan northeast to southeastern Canada and northeastern United States; south to Tennessee and North Carolina; west to southwestern Illinois
Canis lupus nubilus, Pacific Coast east to Wisconsin; Arizona and New Mexico to southern Montana; eastern Canada; and western Greenland
Canis lupus occidentalis, Alaska, Yukon Territory, western Northwest Territories, eastern British Columbia, Alberta, Saskatchewan, southwestern Manitoba, northern Montana

References

Mammalian Species 37; Mech, 1981

Red wolf | *Canis rufus*

A zoological and conservation dilemma, the red wolf survives today only as a small captive/reintroduced population. Formerly found in most habitats of the Southeast—mountains, lowland forests, and wetlands—it was steadily eliminated by settlers, ranchers, and government trappers, who blamed it for depredations on livestock and game. At some point in the 19th century, after the wolf had been largely extirpated east of the Mississippi and greatly reduced elsewhere, remnant groups ap-

parently began to hybridize with the coyote *(Canis latrans),* which was moving eastward to fill the predatory niche. By 1967, when the red wolf was recognized officially as an endangered species, the only population that seemed predominantly like the original was that of extreme southeastern Texas and southwestern Louisiana. The U.S. Fish and Wildlife Service, leading a major salvage effort, live-captured and studied many animals from this area, 14 of which eventually became the

Canis rufus

vated in stream banks or sand knolls, or taken over from some other animal; they average about 2.4 meters in length. The home range, a portion of which is the exclusive territory of the pack, usually covers about 50 to 100 square kilometers. Packs consist of a mated pair, the pups of the year, and sometimes earlier offspring up to two years old. Members generally have a harmonious relationship, but may be highly aggressive towards other packs. Historically, the red wolf has not been compatible with intensive human activity, but there are no well-documented cases of attacks on people.

The red element of the fur is sometimes pronounced, particularly in winter, but the upperparts are usually a mixture of cinnamon buff, cinnamon, or tawny, with gray or black; the dorsal area is generally heavily overlaid with black. The muzzle, ears, and outer surfaces of the limbs are usually tawny. The underparts are whitish to pinkish buff, and the tip of the tail is black. There is an annual molt during the summer. There were reported to be locally common dark or fully black animals in heavily forested areas. Trip-wire photographs of such wolves were made in northeastern Louisiana in 1934 by Tappan Gregory, for whom the surviving subspecies is named.

Mating occurs from January to March and pups are born in the spring. The gestation period is 60–63 days, and litters contain up to 12 young, usually about 3–6. Dispersal and formation of new family groups commonly occurs at 15–22 months of age, but has been reported earlier if the natal pack is disrupted. Few individuals survive more than 5 years in the wild but potential longevity is at least 14 years. The reintroduced

founders of the current population. Practice reintroduction began on coastal islands in 1976, and an attempt to establishment a permanent, viable population started in 1987 at Alligator River National Wildlife Refuge in eastern North Carolina. Releases also have been made in Great Smoky Mountains National Park. As of late 1997, there were about 50 animals at Alligator River, 30 at other field sites, and 160 in captive-breeding facilities.

Like most large carnivores, the red wolf is primarily nocturnal, but may increase its daytime activity during the winter. It hunts over a relatively small part of its home range for about 7–10 days and then shifts to another area. Dens, used only for rearing young, are located in the trunks of hollow trees, exca-

animals in coastal North Carolina prey mainly on white-tailed deer, raccoons, and swamp rabbits.

Fossil cranial material identical to that of modern *C. rufus* has been recovered from Irvingtonian and Wisconsinan sites in Florida (roughly 750,000 to 10,000 years old). The early Irvingtonian *C. edwardii* of the western United States closely resembles *C. rufus,* and similar material has been found in the Pleistocene of the Old World. *C. rufus* appears to be a surviving line of small, primitive wolves that once occurred throughout the Holarctic and that formed an evolutionary stage between the coyote and the modern gray wolf. The latter species appears to have originated in Eurasia and subsequently invaded North America, displacing the smaller wolves from most of their range.

Specimens confirm that the red wolf was a species distinct from the coyote, but its relationship with the gray wolf remains in question. Because wolves were extirpated so early, few specimens from areas of range overlap are known. Those available show a close morphological approach between *C. rufus* and the small *C. lupus lycaon* of southeastern Canada. Mitochondrial DNA studies have found no definitive features of *C. rufus*. These studies support its being a subspecies of *C. lupus* that hybridized with *C. latrans*. In contrast, early 20th century specimens of *C. lupus* from central Texas are completely distinct from the hybrid *C. rufus-C. latrans* population that then had formed in the same area. Hybrids or fully coyotelike animals eventually occupied most of the Southeast and now have even reached the North Carolina reintroduction sites. The trials of the red wolf are far from over. *R. M. Nowak*

Size

Males average about 10 percent larger than females.
Total length: 1,300–1,700 mm
Length of tail: 300–420 mm
Weight: 20–38 kg (males); 18–30 kg (females)

Identification

Distinguished from North American subspecies of *Canis lupus* by usually smaller size, narrower proportions of body and skull, shorter fur, and relatively longer legs and ears and from *C. latraus* by usually larger size, broader snout, and relatively larger feet.

Recent Synonyms

Canis niger

Other Common Names

Southern wolf, timber wolf

Status

Extremely rare, classified as critically endangered by World Conservation Union and as endangered by the United States government

Subspecies

Canis rufus floridanus, Pennsylvania to Florida (extinct)
Canis rufus gregoryi, southern Missouri and Ohio Valley to southeastern Texas and

Mississippi (no longer extant in wild; reintroduced in North Carolina)

Canis rufus rufus, southeastern Kansas to central and southern Texas [probably extinct, although wolf-coyote *(Canis latrans)* hybrids are present on the Texas coast].

References

Mammalian Species 22; Nowak, 1979, 1991; Phillips and Parker, 1988; Wayne and Jenks, 1991

Arctic fox | *Alopex lagopus*

The arctic fox is one of the best-adapted of all terrestrial mammals for living in the extremely cold, harsh Arctic environment. It has several morphological characters that enable it to withstand cold temperatures for extended periods of time. The ears are much shorter that those of any other fox, which reduces the amount of body heat lost by minimizing the surface area exposed to the cold. The muzzle and limbs are also reduced in size to prevent heat loss from the extremities, and the soles of the feet are covered with fur to insulate the foot pads from the frigid Arctic substrate. One of its best, and best-known, adaptations is the thick, luxurious fur, which provides an enormous amount of insulation. In winter the fur is several inches thick. Long guard hairs and a dense undercoat that accounts for about 70 percent of the fur insulate the fox so efficiently that it does not begin to shiver until temperatures reach an incredible –70° C.

The color of the coat changes seasonally, a feature that is unique in the canids. There are two winter color phases, white and blue. The normal or white phase is, as its name implies, white in winter, changing to a grayish-brown in summer. The blue phase is a steely bluish-gray in winter, changing to a dark chocolate brown or darker bluish-gray in summer. Blue phase foxes are found largely on islands in the North Atlantic and Bering Sea, and on the Aleutian Islands in Alaska, and occur rarely in white phase populations in eastern Canada. White phase foxes are largely continental in distribution, occasionally occurring in blue phase populations in Greenland, apparently moving across the Davis Strait in Canada when food is scarce. Litters of arctic foxes may contain both color forms. Breeding experiments have shown that the darker phase is dominant to the white phase.

Arctic fox pelts are in great demand for commercial purposes and are an important part of the fur trade in regions

Alopex lagopus

where foxes are abundant. Arctic foxes are commonly raised on fur farms, and have been introduced onto small remote islands, where they are allowed to roam freely until they are harvested. This practice has been extremely detrimental to seabird populations on the islands where the foxes have been released.

The arctic fox has a circumpolar distribution, primarily above 60° N latitude, but extending southward in central and eastern Canada, the Aleutian Island chain in Alaska, and the Kamchatka Peninsula in Russia. In North America the range lies along the coastal areas of the polar seas and inland across western and northern Alaska. It extends eastward through Canada's Yukon and Northwest Territories and into the northern portions of the lower tier of provinces (extreme northeastern Saskatchewan, northern Manitoba, northern Ontario, western and northern Quebec, northern Newfoundland, and northern Newfoundland Island).

Like most other solitary canids, this fox is usually found alone or in pairs, although it is occasionally found in larger groups when feeding on a sizable prey item such as a stranded whale, or while scavenging from a wolf or polar bear kill. Male-female pairs form during the breeding season and raise the litter together, but the female provides most of the care. There have been occasional reports of additional young adult "helpers" at the den, presumably offspring from the previous litter, but this varies with geographic location.

Arctic foxes are bold considering their small size, and there are many reports of their running up to people and nipping and barking like small dogs, and even entering tents at night to harass the occupants and steal camping gear or food. Primarily nocturnal in nature, these foxes normally hunt from sundown to sunrise, except during the Arctic summer, when the extended period of light (up to 24 hours) forces them to forage in daylight.

The prey of arctic foxes varies with both season and locality. Lemmings and voles are the main items taken during summer. Ground nesting birds and seabirds, their fledglings and eggs, ground squirrels, and young arctic hares make up the remainder of the diet. Lemmings and voles both have periodic population fluctuations, rising to huge numbers and then crashing. Arctic fox populations closely follow these fluctuations, rising when prey is plentiful and falling off sharply when prey is less abundant. During summer, when prey is more plentiful, arctic foxes bury or "cache" excess food items for use in winter or at other times when food is scarce.

During the harsh Arctic winter the foxes rely heavily on carrion, often following wolves on land and polar bears over the pack ice to clean up the remains of caribou and seal kills. Since wolves and polar bears occasionally prey on arctic foxes, they usually keep a safe distance when following these large predators. Whales occasionally get trapped in the pack ice and die, providing a huge windfall of meat during the hard winter. Voles, lemmings, and ptarmigan are hunted in winter, but form a smaller percentage of the diet than scavenged carrion and cached food. Ringed seal pups are occasionally taken from their subnivean (snow) lairs, after the fox has dug through the snow to reach them. Fish are sometimes caught by stirring the water with a paw to attract them, then catching the fish with the jaws when they come within reach. Along the coasts, mollusks, crabs, sea urchins, and fish trapped in tidal pools are also taken. During years when food is scarce arctic foxes are known to range widely in search of it: one marked individual travelled a straight line distance of more than 1,120 km over a two-year period. Foxes that travel with the current on ice floes also cover great distances, and have been found as far north as 140 km from the true North Pole.

Arctic foxes prefer to den in light, sandy soil along river banks, on small hillocks, and occasionally in talus (rock slide) fields. Den entrances usually face south to take advantage of the sun's warmth, and slope downward towards the permafrost. The average number of entrances is 12. Most dens are used by successive generations, being expanded and enlarged each year. An old, much-used den can have as many as 60 entrances. The average litter of 6–10 pups is born after a gestation period of about 53 days. The size of the litter is quite variable, ranging from 3 to 25 young, depending on the vole and lemming population. The life expectancy of the arctic fox is very short due to the extreme conditions under which it lives. Most young die before they are six months old, and few adults live longer than 3–4 years. One individual lived a record 15 years in captivity.

The only other canids found within the range of the arctic fox are gray wolves, and in areas where they have been introduced for the fur trade, red foxes. In areas where the red fox occurs, it often harasses and dominates the arctic fox. Wolves, polar bears, and snowy owls are the fox's only predators besides humans, their main predator. *C. G. Anderson*

Size
Males average about 10–20 percent larger than females.
Total length: 830–1,100 (853) mm (males); 713–850 (821) mm (females)
Length of tail: 280–425 (303) mm (males); 255–320 (289) mm (females)
Weight: 3.2–9.4 (3.5) kg (males); 1.4–3.3 (2.9) kg (females)

Identification
This fox is easily distinguished from other canids by its distinctive coloration, reduced limb size, short snout, rounded head, short, rounded ears, and dense winter fur that also covers the foot pads. The eyes have golden yellow irises and the call is a bark-like yap. The pelage is long and thick in winter, short and thinner in summer. There are two winter color phases, white and so-called blue, both of which change to shades of brown in summer.

Recent Synonyms
Vulpes lagopus
Recent genetic studies suggest that *Alopex* is closely related to *Vulpes velox*, the swift fox, and *Vulpes vulpes*, the red fox, and should not be given generic status based solely on morphological adaptations to living the Arctic. It has been proposed that it should be included in the genus *Vulpes*, to which most other North American foxes belong.

Other Common Names
Polar fox, white fox, blue fox

Status
Stable, but variable with food availability

Subspecies
Alopex lagopus groenlandicus, Ellesmere Island, Canada
Alopex lagopus hallensis, Hall and St. Matthew Islands, Bering Sea, western Alaska
Alopex lagopus pribilofensis, St. George and St. Paul Islands, Pribilof Islands, western Alaska
Alopex lagopus ungava, Quebec, Newfoundland, Labrador, Nova Scotia (Linguan Bay)

References
Banfield, 1974; Geffen et al., 1992; Nowak, 1991; Underwood and Mosher, 1982

Kit or swift fox | *Vulpes velox*

Kit and swift foxes are the smallest wild canids in North America. There is considerable disagreement about whether they should be considered two distinct species or whether they differ only at the subspecific level. Traditional skull and other morphological measurements support separate species status. The existence of hybrids and some recent genetic evidence indicates only subspecific differences; however, a 1993 mitochondrial DNA study supports their separation into two species. In this account they are treated as one species and distinct populations of kit and swift foxes are distinguished as subspecies.

Kit foxes are found from northern Mexico to the southeastern corner of Oregon, including Utah, Nevada, southern California, Arizona, New Mexico, southwestern Colorado and western Texas. Swift foxes, which inhabit short, medium, and mixed grass prairies, were once found from the Canadian prairies in the north, south through Montana, North and South Dakota, Nebraska, eastern Wyoming, eastern Colorado, the Oklahoma Panhandle, and into northwest Texas. Habitat destruction, trapping, and poisoning for predator control has greatly reduced populations of both subspecies, and the swift

Vulpes velox

fox is now extremely rare or extinct in the northern half of its former range. A reintroduction program is underway to restore the swift fox to its former range in the Canadian prairie provinces. In the United States, the California San Joaquin kit fox was listed as an endangered species as *V. v. mutica*. It is still managed under that status.

Kit foxes are found in shrub-steppe, arid, and semiarid desert habitat. Typically, each established family group of kit foxes utilizes a cluster of 7 to 17 dens. Each den site may have from one to 25 entrances, which are often keyhole-shaped. Entrances are connected by spiraling tunnels. In the dens, there are separate chambers for sleeping and caching of food. The

vast system of subterranean tunnels in a cluster of dens serves as habitat for potential prey such as fossorial rodents, insects, and reptiles.

Males seem to rotate use of dens within clusters more often than females. The load of ectoparasites such as fleas and ticks carried by an individual fox (and in the empty den) usually decreases following a change from one den site to another. Moving to a new den not only helps control parasites, it also allows the foxes to rotate hunting to different portions of their home range. Kit foxes are not considered strongly territorial outside the whelping season, and it is not uncommon to find a member of a mated pair in a den site with another adult. These foxes may have an expanded social system based on a dominance hierarchy, which serves to parcel out acceptable habitat for home ranges and whelping areas.

Swift and kit fox are primarily nocturnal, spending the day in the cool security of their dens. Occasionally they will sit by a den entrance and sun themselves during warm weather. They leave the den after sunset, hunting sporadically until sunrise. Both kit and swift foxes are carnivorous. Their diets consist primarily of lagomorphs and rodents, but also include birds, lizards, and insects. Kit foxes often inhabit arid regions where water is not readily available, and survive on the moisture derived from their prey. The foxes play important roles in their respective ecosystems as predators on small mammals and as architects of subterranean burrows used by many other species.

Adult foxes usually hunt alone but live in mated pairs throughout the year. The home ranges of males almost completely overlap those of females. Occasionally an adult male will share a den and home range with two adult females, with one female acting as a helper with the pups. Kit and swift foxes breed once a year, between late December and early February, depending on latitude. After a gestation period of approximately 49–55 days, litters of three to six pups are born in late February through early April. Pups emerge from the den after one month and begin accompanying adults on hunting trips after 3 months. Young disperse during August and September.

The curious and somewhat unwary nature of swift and kit foxes has contributed to their decline in much of their range. Populations have been severely affected by poisons, traps, and other measures intended to control coyotes or other "nuisance" animals. Shootings and vehicle-caused mortalities also contribute to their decline. Natural causes of mortality include disease, den cave-ins, starvation, and predation. Coyotes are the most common predators of the foxes throughout most of their range.

Swift and kit foxes are easily distinguished from other North American foxes. Red foxes are larger, with white-tipped tails. The gray fox is also larger and has gray fur and a black dorsal streak on the tail. Adult coyotes are much larger, and young coyotes are stockier and have shorter faces than those of kit or swift foxes. *R. K. Thacker and J. T. Flinders*

Size
Males are usually larger than females.
Total length: 740–820 mm (males); 680–750 mm (females)
Length of tail: 270–330 mm (males); 230–300 mm (females)
Weight: 1.4–3.0 kg

Identification
Vulpes velox is yellowish-tan, with a gray tint along the back and white undersides. It has distinctive, large ears, a slender body, and a long, bushy, black-tipped tail. The kit fox has larger ears, a longer tail, and a narrower snout than the swift fox. *Canis latrans, Vulpes vulpes,* and

Urocyon cinereoargenteus are all larger. *V. vulpes* has a white-tipped tail; *U. cinereoargenteus* is gray, with a black streak on the top of the tail.

Other Common Names
Northern kit fox, prairie kit fox, swift kit fox

Status
Locally common but rare in much of its range. The San Joaquin kit fox is protected as an endangered species, and in Canada, the swift fox is protected as an endangered species.

Subspecies
Vulpes velox macrotis (kit fox), northern Mexico

to southeastern Oregon, including Utah, Nevada, southern California, Arizona, New Mexico, southwestern Colorado, and western Texas
Vulpes velox velox (swift fox), Canadian prairies south through Montana, North and South Dakota, Nebraska, eastern Wyoming, eastern Colorado, the Oklahoma Panhandle and into northwest Texas

References
Mammalian Species 122; *Mammalian Species* 123 *(Vulpes macrotis);* Mercure et al., 1993; O'Farrell, 1987; O'Neal et al., 1987; Scott-Brown et al., 1987

Red fox | *Vulpes vulpes*

The red fox is the most widely distributed wild carnivore in the world, occurring in North America, Asia, Europe, and northern Africa. They were also introduced into Australia in about 1850 for fox hunting, and they are now widely distributed there. European red foxes were introduced into the eastern

United States around 1790, and there is some confusion regarding the original distribution of the native red fox before this time. Red foxes prefer habitats with great diversity, such as intermixed crop lands, brush, and pastures. They use edges heavily; they do not use dense, extensive forests. The pervasive

Vulpes vulpes

landscape change from forest to agriculture following the European settlement of North America, together with the extirpation of the gray wolf *(Canis lupus)* and red wolf *(C. rufus)*, resulted in the expansion of red fox range in eastern North America. More recently, expanding coyote *(C. latrans)* numbers and more intensive agricultural practices in the Midwest have been linked with red fox population declines in that region of the United States.

Red foxes are opportunistic hunters and scavengers. Their diet varies between areas and seasons. Voles (most often *Microtus pennsylvanicus)*, rabbits *(Sylvilagus)*, and hares *(Lepus)* are often reported as the primary prey species, supplemented by other small mammals, birds, fruits, and invertebrates, including beetles and earthworms. To catch a rodent, the red fox uses a floating "mouse leap," a strong spring that propels the fox toward and above its prey. By beating its tail to steer in midair, a fox can land directly on a target as far as five meters away. Red foxes also scavenge on carrion from white-tailed deer *(Odocoileus virginianus)* and livestock. These are important overwintering food sources in some regions, as is garbage for foxes living in suburban areas. Red foxes frequently cache excess food items and are proficient at relocating these caches.

The core of the red fox mating and rearing system is the mated pair living on a territory. Older, usually female, offspring may serve as helpers in provisioning the young. Most male offspring disperse from their parents' territories before they are a year old. Mean dispersal distance for male offspring in the Midwest was 29 kilometers; for dispersing females it was 8 kilometers. Foxes usually forage independently on territories

that may vary from 20 to 40 hectares in suburban areas in England, to 500 to 2,000 hectares on Ontario farmland, to 3,400 hectares in the Arctic. Territories are smallest where food availability is greatest. Territories are defended by scent-marking and through direct, overt challenges to intruding neighboring resident and itinerant foxes.

Mating extends from late December through late March, being later at higher latitudes. Estrus lasts from 1–6 days, fol-

lowed by a gestation period of 51–53 days. Vixens can breed before their first birthday, but the actual number that breed and give birth varies greatly between regions and is governed by fox density, food supplies, and mortality (population turnover) rates.

Where density is low and mortality (through trapping, hunting, and rabies) high, such as in Ontario, 80–90 percent of the yearling vixens give birth. Where population turnover is low, as many as 20 percent of all vixens fail to produce litters. Mean litter size varies between regions roughly from 4 to 7, with 5 being the most common number. Young are born in dens that are dug by the foxes or in reworked dens of other burrowing mammals such as groundhogs *(Marmota)* or badgers *(Taxidea taxus)*. A pup's weight at birth is about 100 g; the

eyes open at 11–14 days; lactation lasts from 56 to 70 days. The male and the helpers (if present) provision the female and pups. Later, the female takes the pups with her when she forages.

The red fox is a principal vector and victim of rabies in the Northern Hemisphere. Once infected, usually through a bite from another infected fox, most foxes incubate the disease for about 20 days. The fox can remain infectious for up to six days before it dies. About 11 percent of foxes show the "furious" form of rabies and attack other animals and objects before succumbing. The others suffer progressive paralysis but lose their fear of humans. The red fox's social and territorial system is particularly well suited to the spread of the rabies virus through encounters between family members and territory defenders and intruding foxes. *J. Seidensticker*

Size
Size varies according to locality but within an area males average about 5 percent longer and 15–25 percent heavier than females. Northern foxes tend to be larger than southern forms.
Total length: 827–1,097 mm
Length of tail: 291–455 mm
Weight: 3–7 kg

Identification
Red foxes are small-dog sized. This fox has a slender muzzle; triangular, erect ears, often trimmed in black; variable black triangular face marks between the eyes and nose; a rust to flame-red coat (with black, silver and cross color phases); white belly and chin; long bushy tail, usually with a white tip; and moderately long legs with black "stockings."

Recent Synonyms
The North American red fox was formerly considered a separate species, *Vulpes fulva* or *Vulpes fulvus.*

Other Common Names
Common names often describe or refer to color phases: black fox, silver fox (black with white-tipped guard hairs), cross fox (dark cross on shoulders), bastard fox (bluish gray), and Sampson fox (no guard hairs).

Status
Common

Subspecies
Vulpes vulpes abeitorum, western Canada
Vulpes vulpes alascensis, Alaska
Vulpes vulpes bangsi, northern Quebec and Labrador

Vulpes vulpes cascadensis, coastal northwestern United States
Vulpes vulpes deletrix, Island of Newfoundland
Vulpes vulpes fulva, eastern United States
Vulpes vulpes harrimani, Kodiak Island, Alaska
Vulpes vulpes kenaiensis, Kenai Peninsula, Alaska
Vulpes vulpes macroura, Rocky Mountains
Vulpes vulpes necator, California and Nevada
Vulpes vulpes regalis, plains, United States and Canada
Vulpes vulpes rubricosa, southern Quebec and Nova Scotia

References
Mammalian Species 537; Macdonald, 1987; Samuel and Nelson, 1982; Storm et al., 1976; Voigt, 1987

Common gray fox | *Urocyon cinereoargenteus*

The secretive and beautiful gray fox can be found in wooded, brushy, and rocky habitats from southern Canada to northern Venezuela and Colombia, excluding parts of the mountainous western United States and the Great Plains. This fox is an important member of deciduous woodland communities, from expansive hardwood forests in the East to linear, brushy riparian communities in the semiarid West.

The pelage of the gray fox is grizzled on its upperparts, because individual guard hairs there are banded with white, gray, and black. A prominent dark stripe extends down the back and into a black mane of coarse hair along the top of the black-tipped tail. Portions of the neck, sides, and legs are cinnamon-

colored and the belly is pale tan. White shows on the ears, throat, chest, belly, and hind legs. Black, white, and rufous facial markings provide distinctive accents, but in brushy shadows the fox is well concealed.

Gray foxes are nocturnal or crepuscular. They are seldom seen during daylight hours, when they rest in dense vegetation or in rugged, inaccessible topography. When active, gray foxes typically range over 2–5 square km, although home range sizes may vary among different types of habitat. Movement patterns also vary with the status of an individual fox. For example, when females are nursing small pups they typically stay within a few hundred meters of their dens—which may be located in burrows, hollow logs or trees, rock outcroppings, abandoned buildings, or just in a dense clump of brush. Protection from potential predators and the elements is key to a secure whelping den—one fox whelped her pups in a discarded milk can!

An adult male and female and their offspring likely comprise the typical gray fox social unit. This family unit maintains a range separate from other such family groups, but unpaired foxes may be present. Mating occurs from early January through March in the northern half of the range, and typically 4 pups are born about 59 days later. The uniformly dark-gray pups weigh about 85 g at birth, but grow to 2 kg in about 4

Urocyon cinereoargenteus

months, when they begin to forage on their own. Maternal–offspring bonds last for about 7 months. Then some pups, mainly males, disperse from the natal area, traveling as far as 84 km. Most males and females mature sexually at about 10 months and reproduce annually for the rest of their lives.

Gray foxes eat a wide variety of plant and animal matter and are considered the most omnivorous of the North American canids. Although they are efficient predators, it is not unusual for a gray fox to stuff itself with apples or corn. The diet varies with the locale, but small mammals, invertebrates, and fruits are staples. Cottontails and rodents are eaten year-round but are especially important in winter. Insects such as grasshoppers and crickets assume greater importance in summer, when they become abundant. And when fruits such as persimmons, wild grapes, and apples ripen in the fall, they too are relished by foxes. In the arid southwest, cactus fruit and juniper berries are important seasonal foods.

Gray fox population densities typically range from 1 to 2 adults per square km in good habitat. Over large areas with varying habitat quality, densities are lower. Reliable estimates of home range size range from 30 hectares for a female in California during summer to 2,755 hectares for a barren female in Alabama throughout the year. Gray foxes in western North America appear to travel over smaller areas (usually less than 200 hectares) than those in the East (usually more than 200 hectares). Harvest by humans is the most important source of mortality in most regions, and is closely regulated. Populations of gray foxes can be reduced temporarily by infectious diseases, especially rabies and canine distemper, but outbreaks are confined to relatively small areas.

Gray foxes are well known for their tree-climbing abilities and have been seen in trees at heights up to 18 m. They can shinny a vertical tree trunk by pushing with their hind feet while grasping with their forefeet; among their anatomical adaptations for climbing are forelegs that can rotate more than those of other canids. They may jump from branch to branch, and they descend by backing down or by running headfirst down a sloping tree. They often climb to escape or to forage on fruits. *E. K. Fritzell*

Size
No significant sexual dimorphism
Total length: 800–1,130 mm
Length of tail: 275–433 mm
Weight: 3.0–7.0 kg

Identification
Urocyon cinereoargenteus is equal in size to but more robust than *Vulpes vulpes*. It is grizzled gray above, with pale underparts, and has white, black, and cinnamon markings. The black dorsal stripe on the black-tipped tail is distinctive.

Recent Synonyms
Canis (Vulpes) cinereoargenteus
Vulpes cinereoargenteus

Other Common Names
Zorra; zorra gris; gato de monte

Status
Common

Subspecies
Urocyon cinereoargenteus borealis, New England
Urocyon cinereoargenteus californicus, southern California
Urocyon cinereoargenteus cinereoargenteus, east of Mississippi River north of Georgia and Alabama
Urocyon cinereoargenteus costaricensis, Costa Rica
Urocyon cinereoargenteus floridanus, southeastern United States from Georgia and Florida to eastern Texas
Urocyon cinereoargenteus fraterculus, Yucatan Peninsula
Urocyon cinereoargenteus furvus, Panama
Urocyon cinereoargenteus guatemalae, Costa Rica to southern Mexico, except Yucatan Peninsula

Urocyon cinereoargenteus madrensis, north-central Mexico
Urocyon cinereoargenteus nigrirostris, central Mexico
Urocyon cinereoargenteus ocythous, midwestern United States
Urocyon cinereoargenteus orinomus, southern Mexico
Urocyon cinereoargenteus peninsularis, Baja California
Urocyon cinereoargenteus scottii, southwestern United States and northern Mexico
Urocyon cinereoargenteus townsendi, central California to the Columbia River

References
Mammalian Species 189; Fritzell, 1987

Island gray fox | *Urocyon littoralis*

The diminutive island gray fox is about one-half to two-thirds the size of its mainland cousin, the common gray fox *(Urocyon cinereoargenteus)*. Otherwise, *Urocyon littoralis* closely resembles the mainland gray fox in having salt-and-pepper colored fur, rufous or buffy underfur, and a dorsal median black stripe ending in the black tip of the tail.

Island foxes occur only on the six largest of the eight California Channel Islands. They are thought to have first arrived on the northern Channel Islands, Santa Cruz, Santa Rosa, and San Miguel, about 16,000 years ago by swimming or by rafting on floating debris. Foxes therefore pre-date the arrival of the Chumash, Native Americans who colonized the islands ap-

Urocyon littoralis

proximately 9,000 to 10,000 years ago and who subsequently transported foxes to the southern islands, Santa Catalina, San Nicolas, and San Clemente.

Foxes are habitat generalists. They are distributed over most of the islands on which they occur. However, their abundance varies with habitat type and may be related to habitat productivity. Overall, island foxes generally occur at higher densities (2.4–14.3 per square km) than do gray foxes on the mainland (1.2–2.1 per square km). Island foxes maintain home ranges of approximately 20–40 hectares, depending on habitat and season. Their home ranges are considerably smaller than those of mainland gray foxes, even after accounting for body size differences between the two species. The relatively small home ranges of island foxes may be related to their high densities on the islands.

Island gray foxes are active both day and night, unlike their mainland cousins, which are most active at night and relatively sedentary during the day. The increased daytime activity may partially result from their freedom from predation. Golden eagles and red-tailed hawks are potential predators, but they are relatively uncommon and only occasionally prey on foxes. Indeed, island foxes are highly inquisitive and remarkably docile, a phenomenon characteristic of other insular animals and attributable to the lack of predatory pressures in species-poor island ecosystems.

Island foxes forage on a wide assortment of both plant and animal matter. A substantial portion of the diet consists of seasonally available fruits and berries, including toyon, manzanita, and prickly pear. They frequently consume deer mice and a va-riety of insects, including Jerusalem crickets, grasshoppers, and beetles, and also occasionally prey on lizards and birds.

The social structure of *Urocyon littoralis* primarily consists of male and female mated pairs, with high spatial overlap between members of a pair and relatively little overlap with adjacent pairs. Courtship activities occur from January to March. In April or May, following a gestation of approximately 50 days, young are born in a simple den. Unlike many other canids, island foxes do not excavate their own dens. They use any available sheltered site, such as brush piles, bushes, rock outcroppings, or human-made structures. On average, two young are raised to maturity by each pair. The young reach adult weight and achieve independence during their first winter.

Overall, fox populations on the six islands are generally considered stable. Nevertheless, several factors support their classification as threatened by the State of California. Their numbers are small, their distribution is limited, and there is recent evidence of a lack of genetic variability and susceptibility to canine diseases. Specific threats to *Urocyon littoralis* include competition with feral cats, risk of exposure to canine diseases, extensive road systems on some islands, and habitat loss or degradation by humans and exotic species. *K. Crooks*

Size
Total length: 625–790 (716) mm (males);
   590–787 (689) mm (females)
Length of tail: 140–290 (242) mm (males);
   110–287 (231) mm (females)
Weight: 1.6–2.5 (2.00) kg (males); 1.5–2.3 (1.88)
   kg (females)

Identification
The island gray fox is about one-half to two-thirds the size of its closest mainland relative, the common gray fox *(Urocyon cinereoargen-teus),* but is otherwise similar in proportions and external appearance.

Other Common Names
Island fox, Channel Island fox

Status
Threatened

Subspecies
Urocyon littoralis catalinae, Santa Catalina Island
Urocyon littoralis clementae, San Clemente Island
Urocyon littoralis dickeyi, San Nicolas Island
Urocyon littoralis littoralis, San Miguel Island
Urocyon littoralis santacruzae, Santa Cruz Island
Urocyon littoralis santarosae, Santa Rosa Island

References
Mammalian Species 489; Crooks and Van Vuren, 1994, 1995, 1996; Grinnell et al., 1937; Roemeret et al., 1994; Wayne et al., 1991

Family Ursidae

There are 9 species in 6 genera of bears in the world, and the 3 species in North America all belong to the nominate genus *(Ursus)*. Bears occur worldwide from the Arctic to the tropics. In colder regions, they enter a deep sleep during winter. Bears may shelter in holes they dig, in caves or crevices, in tree hollows, or in dense vegetation. Most bears are omnivorous, but the polar bear takes little other than fish and seals, and the panda feeds primarily on bamboo.

Bears are large, highly variable animals, which has led to considerable taxonomic uncertainty, especially regarding subspecies recognition. Reproductive systems are complicated by hibernation, but all three North American species breed in the spring, and have a 6–7 month delay in implantation. Young are born in the hibernaculum or in maternity dens, and are relatively tiny and altricial at birth. Mother and cubs stay together during the cubs' first year. Although cubs survive quite well while they are with their mothers, the mortality rate rises during the second year, when they strike out on their own. Bears have a relatively low reproductive rate, owing to small litter sizes (1–3), 2–3 year intervals between litters, slow growth rates with consequent delay in sexual maturity (5–7 years), and climatic uncertainties and resultant stress that may affect reproductive physiology.

Social heirarchies develop when bears come into close contact, but social interactions are much more common in brown bears *(Ursus arctos)* than in the other two species. Some tolerance to other individuals develops at important communal feeding sites. Daily activity cycles are tied to temperature regimes, with foraging frequently limited to cooler periods of the day. Some seasonal movements of populations occur in response to food availability, especially in polar bears.

Black and brown bears tend to be strongly herbivorous, although they will take fish and occasionally scavenge on other available animal food. Polar bears depend heavily on seals for food, but take vegetative matter and other animal foods as well. They spend large amounts of time on open pack ice, but brown and black bears favor areas with denser cover.

Fossil are known from the late Miocene to Recent in North America, but extend back to the late Eocene in Europe.

References
Cole and Wilson, 1996; Jonkel, 1978

North American Genera
Ursus

American black bear | *Ursus americanus*

Black bears are the bears people most often encounter. Numbering more than 600,000 across North America, they are 12 times more abundant than grizzly/brown bears. They are the only bears in eastern forests. Highly adaptable, they live in habitats as varied as Louisiana bayou, Pacific Northwest rain forest, and Labrador tundra. Where people are tolerant, they even live in urban housing developments. A housing development in Pennsylvania with more than a thousand people per square mile has a denser black bear population than is found in any national forest or national park.

The greatest threat to the black bear is its own exaggerated reputation for ferocity, which has led to many unnecessary shootings. Black bears almost always retreat from people unless lured with food. Unlike grizzly bear mothers, black bear mothers rarely attack people. When threatened, they send their cubs up trees and either bluff or retreat. The timid nature of the black bear probably stems from its having evolved with such powerful predators as short-faced bears and sabre-toothed cats (both now extinct), and more recently with grizzly/brown bears, gray wolves, and humans. Only about three dozen human deaths from black bears have occurred across North America in this century, despite millions of encounters. To put this figure in perspective, for each person killed by a black bear in the United States and Canada, more than 60 people are killed by domestic dogs, 180 are killed by bees, 350 are killed by lightning, and 90,000 are murdered, according to data from the National Center for Health Statistics.

Black bears come in more colors than any other carnivore. In dense forests in eastern and northern North America, most are black with a brown muzzle, and some individuals have a white chest patch. In the more open forests of the West, most are brown, cinnamon, or blond. In coastal British Columbia and southern Alaska, a few are creamy white (Kermode bears) or bluish gray (Glacier bears).

Although black bears eat some meat and insects, most of their diet is fruit, nuts, and vegetation. Consequently, their an-

nual behavioral and physiological cycle is tied to the annual cycle of plant growth and fruiting, and the abundance and distribution of this food determines social order. Where abundant food is clumped in a central location, bears congregate and form social hierarchies, and unrelated bears of the same sex frequently travel together to wrestle and play. In most areas, food is dispersed in patches too small to support groups and hierarchies, and the bears are solitary. If the dispersed food is abundant enough to warrant it, females defend territories (average 10 square km) that they share with their independent offspring. Mother bears recognize their offspring year after year and behave toward them in ways consistent with kinship theory. They allow their offspring to take over portions of their territories, but exclude strange bears and attempt to usurp adjacent territories from unrelated females. Only daughters remain in their mothers' territories until adulthood. Young males voluntarily disperse at 1–3 years of age and travel up to 219 km (average 61 km) or more before establishing adult ranges.

Males establish ranges large enough to secure mates as well as food. A male range averages 81 square km and typically encompasses 7–15 female territories. Male ranges are too large to defend, so they overlap, and the males compete. Females mate every other year after producing their first cubs at 2–9 years of age, depending on food, so only about half the females are receptive each year. Old males carry many scars from mating season fights. Males reach sexual maturity at 3–4 years of age, but continue to grow until they are 10–12 years old, becoming large enough to dominate most younger males without fighting. Males take no direct role in raising cubs, but help indirectly by aggressively deterring immigrant males from settling, thereby reducing future competition among all resident bears. Old males are 2–3 times the size of immigrant males and approximately twice the size of adult females; females stop growing at around 6 years of age. Maximum weights reported for wild males and females are 409 and 236 kg (902 and 520 pounds), respectively, but most adults weigh less than half that much.

Black bears communicate with vocalizations, body language, and scent. Sociability is expressed with grunts, fear with moans and huffs, pain with screams and bellows, anger with a pulsing voice, and pleasure with a motorlike hum. Both sexes drip urine to mark their ranges. "Bear trees" are rubbed and scent-marked by both sexes but especially by adult males before and during the mating season.

In spring, black bears eat newly sprouting plants, leaves, and flowers. They also raid ant colonies for pupae and find a few newborn mammals and birds. They usually ignore adult mammals and birds. Their ability to run at a speed of up to 50 km per hour (30 mph) is more useful for escape than predation. The black bear's blocky body is built more for strength, storing fat, and conserving heat than for agility. Fish and carrion are not available in significant quantities over most of the black bear's range.

Black bears accumulate most of their fat during summer and fall, eating fruit, nuts, and (in many areas) acorns. Their short, curved claws make them expert tree climbers, and their powerful front legs enable them to bend food-laden branches to their nimble lips, or to turn over rocks and tear apart logs to reach ant colonies. They have color vision and feed mainly in daylight , but some become nocturnal around campgrounds and human residences. In late summer and fall, many forage up to 200 km (126 miles) outside their usual ranges before returning for hibernation. Cubs remember distant feeding locations their mothers showed them and return to the best of them as adults. The remarkable navigation ability of bears is poorly understood.

Mating occurs in early summer before most berries and nuts ripen. This timing minimizes interference with the feeding that is critical for overwinter survival and reproduction. Implantation of the fertilized eggs is delayed until November, which means that birth also occurs at a time that does not interfere with feeding. Well-fattened mothers give birth to 1–6 cubs (usually 2–3) in dens, in January.

Newborn cubs weigh only 200–450 grams each, which is approximately 1/250th of the mother's weight, compared to 1/20th for humans. No other placental mammal gives birth to relatively smaller young. Short gestation and small cub size are adaptations for reproducing during hibernation. Fasting involves a switch in energy base from glucose to fatty acids, which are difficult for fetuses to utilize in utero. The early birth enables the mother to nourish the (nonhibernating) cubs with milk in what is sometimes termed an external pregnancy. Even in hibernation the mother is alert to her cubs' needs, responding to vocal demands for warmth, comfort, and suckling. Linking reproduction with hibernation is adaptive in the north, where hibernation is necessary, but this linkage probably limits the southward expansion of the species into areas where the mothers' obligate period of inactivity would put the bears at a competitive disadvantage against nonhibernating omnivore species.

When black bear families emerge from dens in spring, the cubs weigh 2–5 kg each. They remain with their mothers through the next winter, until they are about 17 months of age, when the mothers approach estrus and force them away. By that time, the yearlings can weigh as much as 49 kg (109 pounds) or as little as 7 kg (15 pounds), depending on food. This plasticity in growth rate is part of the adaptability that enables black bears to survive in high or low quality habitat.

Ursus americanus

In southern states where food is available year-round, only pregnant females hibernate. In the north, both sexes hibernate up to seven months. Where they hibernate longest, they also hibernate more deeply, to ration fat over the longer period. Black bears differ from smaller hibernators, which wake up every few days to eat, move around, and pass wastes. The bears hibernate continuously without eating, drinking, urinating, or exercising. They produce small amounts of feces from dead cells sloughed from the digestive tract, a phenomenon also seen in starving humans. Weight loss is up to 40 percent in lactating females. In the north, their metabolic rate is reduced 50 percent. Heart rate drops from summer rates of 66 (sound sleep) to 140 (exertion) beats per minute to winter sleep rates of between 8 and 22 beats per minute. Body temperature drops 1 to 7° C but remains high enough to maintain mental function for tending cubs and reacting to danger, but reactions to danger are often slow, because circulation to the limbs is so reduced that the hibernating bears cannot immediately get up and run. Some become active only after several minutes of prodding and handling. Even so, fewer than one percent of bears die during hibernation, although some yearlings starve following emergence in spring.

Native Americans called bears "keepers of the medicine" and revered them for their ability to survive for months without eating. Researchers are studying the metabolic pathways bears use to cope with hibernation and are gaining insights into new ways to treat kidney failure, gallstones, severe burns, and other ailments.

Black bears can live more than 30 years, but they seldom live a third that long, mostly because of their encounters with humans. More than 90 percent of the deaths of black bears older than 18 months of age are from gunshots, trapping, motor vehicle accidents, or other human involvement. Bears also face a rising threat of habitat reduction: vacation homes and retirement homes are being built in bear country at an unprecedented rate. Landowners can reduce the threat to bears by adopting a more tolerant attitude based on a more realistic assessment of the danger, or lack of it, from black bears. *L. L. Rogers*

Size
Length of head and body: 1,400–2,000 mm (males); 1,200–1,600 mm (females)
Length of tail: 80–140 mm
Weight: 47–409 (120) kg (males); 39–236 (80) kg (females)

Identification
Ursus americanus is distinguished from *Ursus arctos,* which is sympatric in northwestern North America, by ears that are longer, more tapered, and less heavily furred; by a smaller shoulder hump; by a convex rather than concave profile; by shorter, more tightly curved front claws; by a furred rear instep; and by a contrasting pale muzzle on most dark-furred individuals.

Recent Synonyms
Euarctos americanus

Other Common Names
See subspecies

Status
Ursus americanus luteolus is listed as threatened under the federal Endangered Species Act.

Subspecies
Further study is needed to resolve the validity of these classifications:

Ursus americanus altifrontalis (Olympic black bear), coastal California, western Oregon, western Washington, and southern British Columbia
Ursus americanus amblyceps (New Mexico black bear), New Mexico, southern Arizona, and western Colorado
Ursus americanus americanus (American black bear), forested portions of the coast of southwestern and northwestern Alaska; and extensively forested regions in Canada and the eastern and central United States
Ursus americanus californiensis (California black bear), interior California
Ursus americanus carlottae (Queen Charlotte black bear), Queen Charlotte Islands of British Columbia
Ursus americanus cinnamomum (cinnamon bear), Wyoming, western Montana, Idaho, eastern Colorado; and in Canada, the vicinity of Waterton, Banff, and Jasper National Parks
Ursus americanus emmonsii (Glacier bear), coastal Alaska from Glacier Bay north to Prince William Sound
Ursus americanus eremicus (East Mexico black bear), mountains of northeastern Mexico and the Big Bend area of Texas
Ursus americanus floridanus (Florida black bear), small enclaves in Florida and southernmost Georgia and Alabama

Ursus americanus hamiltoni (Newfoundland black bear), Newfoundland
Ursus americanus hunteri, southeastern Yukon and a small portion of southwestern Northwest Territory
Ursus americanus kermodei (Kermode's bear), British Columbia
Ursus americanus luteolus (Louisiana black bear), small portions of Louisiana and southern Mississippi, with some populations mixed with introduced bears from Minnesota
Ursus americanus machetes (West Mexico black bear), mountains of western Mexico
Ursus americanus perniger (Kenai black bear), Kenai Peninsula of Alaska
Ursus americanus pugnax (Dall black bear), southeastern Alaska north to Chichagof Island
Ursus americanus randi, central Yukon Territory
Ursus americanus vancouveri (Vancouver black bear), Vancouver Island

References
Bauer and Bauer, 1996; Pelton, 1982; Rogers, 1987

Grizzly or brown bear | *Ursus arctos*

Large, impressive, and powerful, grizzly or brown bears once inhabited much of northern and central Europe and Asia, the Atlas Mountains of Morocco and Algeria in North Africa, and northwestern North America. Historically the North American population occupied most of Alaska, the Yukon, and the Canadian Barrens (tundra). The bear's range extended eastwards to Hudson Bay, southeast through the Cordillera and Rocky mountains into the Canadian Prairies and the U.S. Great Plains west of the Mississippi River, and as far south as northern Mexico. The last Mexican population was probably extirpated in the 1960s.

Grizzlies are generally solitary, except for females with cubs or when breeding. They are wide-ranging, powerful predators, and space themselves within overlapping territories, which reduces aggression. Dominant males are highest in rank. Females with young are dominant over young males and females without cubs. When a dominant bear is present, subordinate animals feed only with its permission.

The grizzly bear can be recognized by its massive head, rounded, inconspicuous ears, small eyes, short tail, and powerful body of great size and strength. The claws on the forepaws are pale yellow or brown, slender, recurved, and twice as long

Ursus arctos

as those on the hind paws. The third upper incisors are canine-like and the third molars are elongate. The grizzly's coat color varies from pale tan, blond, gold, gray, silver, cinnamon, and all shades of brown to nearly black. The head and shoulder cape are generally paler and the flanks darker. Interior Alaskan and Canadian animals usually have pale tipped guard hairs, hence the name "grizzly." The bears lose their underfur in late spring or early summer and replace it and the guardfur from mid-August to October.

Adults den in well-drained sites in chambers that are about 1.5 m in diameter and 1.0 m high. Some dens have entrance tunnels. South-facing sites are favored in Alaska and northern Canada, but southern grizzlies choose north-facing slopes to avoid sudden thaws and floods. The den may have a plain dirt floor or a bed of bear grass or spruce or fir boughs; gestating females make beds of mosses.

Grizzlies usually breed between mid-May and July. Estrus lasts 10–30 days, with much individual variation within a 2–4 year reproductive cycle. The female copulates with one or two males each day during the receptive period. Implantation of the blastocyst occurs some five months later, in November, after the female enters winter sleep, and gestation continues for 6–8 weeks. Two or three young (range 1–4) are born between January and March. They are small (230–280 mm long), helpless, sightless, and weigh 340–680 g (500). At three months of age, young weigh approximately 15 kg and have fully developed milk teeth. The head is round; it grows longer as the animal matures. At six months the average weight is about 25 kg. At a year, weights range from 9–37 kg. Lactation lasts 18–30 months. Cubs remain with their dam for 2–3 years, until they are chased away when she enters a new estrous cycle. Young bears frequently socialize with their littermates for months or even years after leaving the mother, but females become solitary upon being bred and young males are solitary when they enter competition for mates. Grizzlies may live for 20–30 years in the wild.

Like most bears, grizzlies are omnivorous and will eat nearly any nutritious matter, including a wide variety of herbage (e.g., mosses, fungi, grasses, herbs, new shoots, leaves, buds, flowers, roots, bulbs, tubers, fruits, nuts, berries) and animals (e.g., insects, larvae, birds and fish and their eggs, small mammals, winter-killed big game, and carrion). They prey on larger ungulates that are sick, infirm, injured, or disabled by deep snow or mud, on fish during spawning runs, and on burrowing mammals, which they excavate. Juvenile ungulates, both wild and domestic, are favored prey. Grizzlies are good swimmers. They have poor sight but excellent hearing and smell. They are normally active at night and during twilight hours, and tend to be shy unless they are surprised. However, they are often ill-tempered and dangerous and will attack without provocation. Mother bears with cubs will attack other bears or intruders preemptively. Males will attack aggressively in defense of living space or food resources, or to obtain mates.

The grizzly can adapt to a wide range of climate and habitat, from Arctic tundra to the margins of deserts in Asia and North Africa, and from open plains to mountainous forests with icefields. It can stand considerable heat and it copes with extreme winter cold, usually by denning. All bears of the genus *Ursus* are descended from the Eurasian Pliocene forest-dwelling *U. minimus* through the Pleistocene *U. etruscus*. The earliest record of *U. arctos* is from Choukoutien, China, about 500,000 years ago. It entered North America about 25,000 years ago, at the beginning of the last major glacial event, and is known from fossils found in Illinois, Kentucky, Ohio, Ontario, and West Virginia.

The black bear, *U. americanus,* which is descended from the European cave bear, *U. spelaeus,* is similar to the grizzly but is smaller and lacks the dished profile and paler head and cape. The polar bear, *U. maritimus,* is as large as the grizzly but is rangier and has a convex profile and a distinctive all-white coat.
C. S. Churcher

Size

Males are 8–10 percent larger than females.

Total length: 1–2.8 m (North American populations); mean lengths, Yellowstone National Park: 1.64 m (males); 1.51 m (females)

Length of tail: 65–210 mm; mean lengths, Yellowstone National Park: 43 mm (males); 40 mm (females)

Weight: 80 to more than 600 kg (North American populations); mean weights, Alaska: 389 kg (males), 207 kg (females); mean weights, Siberia:140–320 kg (males), 100–200 kg (females)

Identification

The brown or grizzly bear is distinguished from the black bear, *Ursus americanus,* by its dished (concave) facial profile, large, robust body with prominent shoulder hump, and long, slightly curved foreclaws that are about twice the length of those on the hind feet. The pelage varies from almost yellow to almost black; guard hairs are long and often white-tipped.

Recent Synonyms

Ursus horribilis

Other Common Names

"Grizzly" is applied to bears living in the interior of North America and "brown" to North American west coast and Eurasian populations. Also Old Ephraim, Moccasin Joe, range bear, grisly, roach back, and silver tip.

Status

Once common in northern Eurasia, the North African Atlas Mountains, and northwestern North America in tundra, forests, mountains, and grasslands; now generally reduced by humans. *U. a. horribilis,* the Great Plains grizzly, is endangered.

Subspecies

The taxonomy of this bear is formidable and confused. At least 100 species and subspecies have have been named, with 16 subspecies currently generally recognized, 8 or 9 in North America. Hall (1981) considered the North American brown and grizzly bears to form a species group with 10 species and 3 indigenous subspecies, based on the last published revision by Merriam (1918) and his unpublished 1941 notes. Hall lists *Ursus absarokus* from Little Bighorn, Ranch, Montana; *U. alascensis* from Unalaklik River, Alaska; *U. alexandrae* from Kasilov Lake, Kenai Peninsula, Alaska; *U. andersoni* from Dease River, Great Bear Lake, MacKenzie District; *U. apache* from the White Mountains, Arizona; *U. arctos beringianus* from Great Shantar Island, Sea of Okhotsk, Siberia; *U. arizonae* from the Escudilla Mountains, Arizona; *U. atnarko* from the Atnarko and Bella Coola Rivers, British Columbia; *U. californicus* from Monterey, California; *U. c. canadensis* from Mount Robson, British Columbia; *U. c. rungiusi* from the headwaters of the Athabaska River, Alberta; *U. c. sagittalis* from Champaigne Landing, southwestern Yukon; and *U. horribilis* from the Great Plains.

No subspecific distributions are available and named taxa are lacking only from Coahila, Durango, North and South Dakota, Manitoba, Minnesota, Nebraska, Nevada, Oklahoma, Saskatchewan, and the District of Franklin.

References

Mammalian Species 439; Banfield, 1974; Merriam, 1918

Polar bear | *Ursus maritimus*

Polar bears are distributed throughout the coastal areas and islands of the circumpolar Arctic. Few are found in the multiyear ice of the polar basin. The water below this thick multiyear pack ice is biologically less productive, so there are fewer seals to hunt there. During the winter, when the seasonal pack ice drifts south, polar bears are found in the northern Bering Sea and off the coast of Newfoundland. In areas such as the Bering and Chukchi seas, where polar bears must travel extensively to remain with the ice to hunt seals, some bears have annual home ranges that exceed 300 square km.

Female polar bears have their first cubs at five or six years of age. They mate in April or May and apparently ovulation is induced by mating. Once the egg is fertilized, implantation and the onset of development are delayed until the following September or October. The cubs are born in December, weighing only about 0.6 kg. By March or April the cubs weigh 10–12 kg and the female takes them from the den onto the sea ice to hunt seals. The cubs stay with their mother, learning how to hunt and where to go at different seasons, for 2.5 years, after which they are weaned and she mates again. In most areas, maternity denning is widely spread at low density. However,

Ursus maritimus

three large concentrated denning areas are known: Kong Karl's Land in the Svalbard Island group (Norway), Wrangell Island in Russia, and northeastern Manitoba, Canada, on the western Hudson Bay coast.

Only pregnant females spend the winter in dens. Bears of all other age and sex classes hunt seals throughout the winter, except during brief periods of especially cold or inclement weather, when any bear may dig a temporary den in the snow and occupy it for a few days or up to a few weeks at a time.

Polar bears prey mainly on ringed seals and to a lesser degree on bearded seals. They prefer to eat the fat. In spring, they particularly hunt ringed seal pups, which are hidden in birth lairs dug in the snow that covers the seal's breathing hole in the ice. Polar bears are also known to prey upon harp seals, hooded seals, walruses, white whales, narwhals, and sea ducks. On land, they occasionally eat berries, grass, and kelp washed up along the shore.

One of the most remarkable adaptations of the polar bear is its ability to fast, depending on its stored fat reserves for long periods of time. Unlike brown or black bears, which can do this only during the winter denning period, polar bears are capable of prolonged fasting at any season if food becomes unavailable. For example, in Hudson Bay, the ice melts completely by late July, so the entire population fasts for four months until freeze-up in early November. However, pregnant females cannot return to the ice to feed, because they must enter their dens to give birth to their cubs, so they go for eight full months without eating, living only on their fat. While fasting, whether in dens or on land waiting for freeze-up, polar bears do not drink water or urinate. They are capable of meeting their body requirements for water by metabolizing fat and recycling the waste products.

Polar bears are a very recent species, having evolved from brown bears less than a million years ago. In zoos, polar and brown bears have mated and produced fertile offspring. The oldest male and female polar bears known from the wild were 29 and 32 years of age respectively. They have no natural predators except for other polar bears and humans. *I. Stirling*

Size
Males are about twice the size of females.
Total length: 2,300–2,600 mm (males);
   1,900–2,100 mm (females)
Length of tail: 75–125 mm
Weight: 400–600 kg (males; exceptional individuals may exceed 800 kg); 175–300 kg (females; 350–500 kg when pregnant)

Identification
Ursus maritimus is a large, distinctly white bear with black skin, a longer neck than that of other bears, and no marked shoulder hump; it cannot be confused with any other bear.

Recent Synonyms
Thalarctos maritimus

Other Common Names
White bear, ice bear, nanuk

Status
Worldwide population estimated to exceed 25,000

References
Mammalian Species 145; Stirling, 1988

Family Mustelidae

With 24 genera and 54 species worldwide, mustelids are the most diverse group of carnivores. The 6 genera and 11 species in North America range in size from the world's smallest carnivore, the 25–50 g least weasel *(Mustela nivalis)* to sea otters *(Enhydra lutris)* that are a meter long and weigh 45 kg. In most species, males are larger than females. Most mustelids search aggressively for prey in burrows or dense cover. Others, such as the mink *(Mustela vison)* and otter *(Lontra canadensis),* are good swimmers and hunt in aquatic environments. Mustelids have been in North America since Oligocene times.

The fur industry took a heavy toll on many mustelid populations, especially during the 19th century and the early part of the 20th century. The dense pelts, with a heavy insulating layer of underfur, were prized for coats and hats. Some populations have also been considered pests, especially on poultry, and their numbers have been controlled by agricultural interests.

However, they also play an important role as major predators of rodents, so healthy populations of mustelids may prove more beneficial than harmful in many areas.

In some species, like the ermine *(Mustela erminea),* the coat color changes from brown in the summer to white in the winter. Most mustelids are built low to the ground, with short legs, and long, slender bodies adapted to foraging in the burrows of their prey. Others, like badgers *(Taxidea taxus)* and wolverines *(Gulo gulo),* are stocky and powerfully built. Badgers are adapted for digging prey out of the ground rather than entering the burrows proper.

Most species are nocturnal, although some are diurnal. They may dig their own burrows in the ground, or shelter in trees or rock crevices. They are active hunters, and most take a wide variety of prey items. The sense of smell is well developed, and both hearing and vision are used as well.

References
Gittleman, 1989; MacDonald, 1984

North American Genera
Martes
Mustela
Gulo
Taxidea
Lontra
Enhydra

American marten | *Martes americana*

American martens occur across most of North America from Alaska through much of forested Canada, into the northeastern United States, and south along the major mountain ranges in the western United States. The marten still occurs throughout most of its former range, but because of loss of habitat, it has been eliminated from many southeastern areas where it was abundant in colonial times. A number of reintroduction programs and natural reinvasions have been made in recent years, and some are still underway (e.g., in the Black Hills of South Dakota and northeastern Minnesota and adjacent Ontario).

The marten is closely associated with boreal forest, including mature spruce and fir, Douglas fir, old lodgepole pine, various deciduous forests, and other similar, structurally complex forests. It can occur at all elevations in the mountains. Use of habitat is related to food availability, especially in winters with deep snows.

Martens are active year-round and may be active at any time of the day or night. They are at home in the trees or on the ground. Most hunting is done at ground level in early morning and near sunset, when their prey is most active. Martens can swim, even underwater. They are inquisitive, agile, and fast.

Martens can live to 15 years. They are solitary except during the breeding season, and tend to be territorial. They communicate by scents and vocalizations, including various huffs, chuckles, and screams.

American martens generally breed at about 15 months of age. During estrus the female scent-marks extensively. Courtship may last two weeks or more, and there is much playing and wrestling. Copulation usually occurs on the ground, may last 1.5 hours, and several matings may occur in a single day. The polygamous marten mates in mid to late summer. Delayed implantation is characteristic, and gestation is 220–276 days, although the period of active pregnancy is about 27 days.

Martes americana

Litter sizes average 3 (range 1–5). Young are born between mid-March and late April, and by about 90 days, they are nearly adult size.

Martens are extremely diverse in their diets; more than 100 different food items have been recorded, including small mammals, birds, insects, fruits, and seeds. Red-backed voles and other voles and mice are a major staple. Chipmunks, ground squirrels, pocket gophers, flying squirrels, and snowshoe hares are also eaten. *T. W. Clark*

Size

Total length: 560–680 mm (males); 500–600 mm (females)

Length of tail: 200–230 mm (males); 180–200 mm (females)

Weight: 470–1,250 g (males); 280–850 g (females)

Identification

The American marten is densely furred, long, and slender-bodied. It is slightly larger than a mink, with relatively rounded ears, short limbs, and bushy tail. The thick fur can range in color from tawny brown to almost black to a pale yellowish buff; the throat and chest bib range in color from vivid orange to pale straw.

Other Common Names

Pine marten, marten

Status

Common to rare, secretive

Subspecies

Two subspecies groups: The *americana* group includes:

Martes americana abietionoides, central British Columbia

Martes americana actuosa, Alaska, Yukon Territory, Northwest Territory, northern British Columbia, east to Manitoba

Martes americana americana, Ontario, southern Quebec, Maritime Provinces

Martes americana atrata, Newfoundland, Labrador

Martes americana kenaiensis, Kenai Peninsula

The *caurina* group includes:

Martes americana caurina, Rocky Mountains from Montana to New Mexico and west to eastern Oregon

Martes americana humboldtensis, northern coastal California

Martes americana nesophila, Queen Charlotte Islands

References

Mammalian Species 289; Buskirk et al., 1994

Fisher | *Martes pennanti*

Sometimes called American sables because of their lustrous fur, fishers occur only in North America. Their present range is reduced from what it was before the European settlement of North America, but most of this reduction has occurred in the United States. Once fishers ranged as far south as central California in the Pacific coastal mountains, into Wyoming in the Rocky Mountains, into southern Illinois in the Midwest, and into the southern Appalachians. This range nearly coincided with the combined distributions of northern hemlock-hardwood, western mountain, and boreal forests. The northern limit to the species' range is approximately 60° N latitude in the west and somewhat south of the southern tip of James Bay in the east.

Fishers may be active both day and night. Each day they have a small number of activity periods that last 2–5 hours. Activity appears to be stimulated more by hunger than by time of day. Weather influences where fishers rest. They are most likely to rest in holes in the ground or holes in trees during cold weather and usually rest on tree branches during warm weather. Fishers are largely solitary. Members of each sex generally defend territories only against members of their own sex. Territories of males range in size from 20 to 80 square km and overlap one or more of the smaller territories of females, which range in size from 4 to 35 square km. Territory size for each sex depends on habitat quality and prey availability.

The fisher is a medium-sized mammal and the largest member of the genus *Martes*. Fishers have the general body build of stocky weasels; they are long, thin, and set low to the ground. Their muzzles are more elongate than those of weasels but less pronounced than those of canids. Their ears are large but rounded and are set close to their heads. The fur of fishers differs between the sexes and changes with the seasons, but is generally deep brown in color. During winter especially, the tail, rump, and legs are glossy black. Fishers' faces, necks, and shoulders usually have a hoary gold or silver color that comes from tricolored guard hairs. The fur of females is glossier and finer than that of males, which can be coarse. Fishers molt in late summer and autumn, and the molt is finished by early winter.

Fishers are generalized predators. They eat any animals they can catch, and readily eat carrion. Most prey are medium- to small-sized rodents such as mice and squirrels. Hares, rabbits, porcupines, and birds are also eaten. Few predators other than fishers are able to kill porcupines consistently. The fisher does this, when it finds a porcupine on the ground in the open, by attacking the porcupine's face, which is not protected with quills. After half an hour or more, it may have bitten the face several times, weakening the porcupine sufficiently to turn it over and begin eating from its ventrum, where there are few quills.

Fishers breed in March or April, but implantation of fertilized ova is delayed for about 11 months, until the following February or March, after which an approximately 30-day active gestation ensues. Parturition occurs in March or early April, and females breed again within 10 days. An adult female is pregnant almost all the time, except for a brief period following parturition. Healthy females breed for the first time when they are a year old, produce their first litters when they are two years old, and breed every year thereafter as long as they are healthy. The testicles of male fishers produce sperm in February and males are ready to breed by early March. They will travel long distances to find receptive females.

Martes pennanti

The now-extinct *M. divuliana* was the first true fisher in North America and apparently came to North America via the Bering Strait. *M. pennanti* is closely related to *M. divuliana* but is probably not a direct descendant. The fossil record of *M. pennanti* is largely confined to eastern North America; fisher distribution in the West may have been limited through the Pleistocene by competition with the now-extinct marten *M. nobilis.* The division of *M. pennanti* into subspecies is probably not warranted. *R. A. Powell*

Size

Males are larger and heavier than females.
Total length: 900–1,200 mm (males); 750–950 mm (females)
Length of tail: 370–410 mm (males); 310–360 mm (females)
Weight: 3,500–5,500 g (males); 2,000–2,500 g (females)

Identification

The fisher is larger and darker in color than the marten and can be distinguished from it by the lack of a pale chin/chest patch. Its fur is long, except on the face; the legs, tail, and rump are black. Tri-colored guard hairs give the face, neck, and shoulders a hoary gold or silvery appearance.

Other Common Names

Pekan, fisher cat, black cat, wejack, American sable

Status

Populations have recovered from extreme lows in early to mid-1900s. Harvested in some states and provinces; listed as endangered in others.

Subspecies

Martes pennanti columbiana, northern Manitoba to eastern British Columbia and south to Idaho and Utah
Martes pennanti pacifica, coastal British Columbia south through California
Martes pennanti pennanti, northeastern Quebec, south to southern Appalachian Mountains, northwest to southern Manitoba and southern Alberta, and south from Alberta to northern Wyoming

References

Mammalian Species 156; Powell, 1993

Ermine | *Mustela erminea*

Mustela erminea is a mid-sized weasel with the most widespread distribution of all mustelid species. It occurs throughout Canada, including the Arctic islands, and in the northeastern and northwestern United States, extending from Maine to Virginia in the east and into California and New Mexico in the west. It is found in a variety of habitats such as Arctic tundra, coniferous forests, and parklands, and occurs from sea level to an elevation of 3,500 meters.

Mustela erminea breeds in mid to late summer, but development of the embryo is delayed until the following March. Gestation is approximately 27 days, and 4–9 young are born in a well-formed nest often located in a rodent burrow or hollow log. Females usually rear young alone, although male assistance has been reported. Young ermine are quite helpless at birth. Their eyes and ears are sealed and their bodies are naked. The female can be remarkably aggressive in her defense of the young. The young grow rapidly, and by 6 weeks of age males are as heavy as their mothers. They reach adult size shortly thereafter. The mother plays an active role in teaching the young how to hunt, and family groups can sometimes be seen travelling together in search of prey. Ermine actively defend their territories from other, trespassing ermine.

Mustela erminea is primarily nocturnal and has well developed senses of sight and smell. It is a quick and agile predator,

Mustela erminea

using its slender body to enter small burrows and crevices in search of mice, voles, and young rabbits. Squirrels, frogs, and earthworms also may be taken. Ermine are found wherever prey are abundant, and in winter their presence can often be

inferred from trails and tunnels left in the snow. Although primarily terrestrial, they sometimes swim or climb trees. Ermine populations are dependent on those of their prey, and for that reason their numbers vary where rodent numbers fluctuate from year to year. *Mustela erminea* is itself preyed upon by a number of birds and mammals.

The ermine posesses a coat of fine, soft fur that in summer is light to dark brown on the back and shoulders and whitish or yellow on the belly and throat. In winter, the fur is pure white, although the tail tip remains black year-long. It usually has little fear of humans and readily approaches in search of food, but this courageous little creature cannot easily be tamed. *D. Murray*

Size
Males are approximately twice the size of females.
Total length: 219–343 (272) mm (males); 190–292 (240) mm (females)
Length of tail: 65–90 (75) mm (males); 42–70 (55) mm (females)
Weight: 67–116 (80) g (males); 25–80 (54) g (females)

Identification
The ermine is a long, slender weasel with a small head and oval ears. The body is light brown with whitish underparts in summer, and pure white in winter. The tail is approximately a third of the total length and has a distinct black tip. Two other species of weasel occur in North America, and in some regions their distributions overlap with that of the ermine. *Mustela erminea* is sometimes mistaken for the larger *M. frenata*, although the two species differ on the basis of size and tail length. *Mustela erminea* is also similar to *M. nivalis,* which is smaller and lacks a black tip on its tail.

Other Common Names
Short-tailed weasel, stoat

Status
Common, widespread

Subspecies
Mustela erminea alascensis, mainland of Alaskan Panhandle
Mustela erminea anguinae, Vancouver Island, British Columbia
Mustela erminea artica, northern Canada and Alaska
Mustela erminea bangsi, western Great Lakes, North Dakota, Iowa
Mustela erminea celenda, Prince of Wales Island, Alaska
Mustela erminea cicognanii, southern Quebec and Ontario, northeastern United States
Mustela erminea fallenda, southwestern British Columbia
Mustela erminea gulosa, eastern Oregon and Washington

Mustela erminea haidarum, Queen Charlotte Islands, British Columbia
Mustela erminea initis, Baranof Island, Alaska
Mustela erminea invicta, Idaho, Montana, Alberta
Mustela erminea kadiacensis, Kodiak Island, Alaska
Mustela erminea muricus, northern California, Utah, New Mexico, Nevada, Oregon, Idaho, Wyoming
Mustela erminea olympica, Olympic Mountains, Washington
Mustela erminea polaris, northwestern Greenland
Mustela erminea richardsonii, Newfoundland to British Columbia
Mustela erminea salva, Admiralty Island, Alaska
Mustela erminea seclusa, Suemez Island, Alaska
Mustela erminea semplei, northwestern Hudson's Bay

References
Mammalian Species 195; Banfield, 1974

Long-tailed weasel | *Mustela frenata*

The long-tailed weasel has the largest range of any mustelid in the Western Hemisphere. It inhabits all life zones, from alpine to tropical, except desert areas of the southwestern United States and northwestern Mexico. It is found in a wide variety of habitats, but usually near water. Favored habitats include brushland and open timber, brushy and grassy field edges, grasslands along creeks and lakes, swamps, and cattail marshes. *M. frenata* is usually most abundant in late seral stages or eco-

tones where prey diversity is greatest. Dens are located in dense brushy vegetation in or around dry creeks and drainage ravines. Waterways are a natural avenue for dispersal, particularly in areas that otherwise are unsuitable.

Typical of weasels, the long-tailed weasel has a long, thin body, short legs, a long neck, and a flattened, triangular head. The ears are rounded and there are long vibrissae. The fur is short and soft, and during summer is a rich brown on the back

By five weeks, the eyes and ears open, nursing ceases, and the pelage is nearing adult summer coloration. Adult body size is attained by 5–6 weeks. By 11–12 weeks, the permanent teeth are present, the young have achieved their adult weight, and dispersal occurs. The sex ratio in long-tailed weasels is equal; the age at sexual maturity is one year in males and 3–4 months in females.

Except during breeding, long-tailed weasels are thought to lead a solitary existence. When prey is readily available, males normally maintain home ranges of 10–24 hectares, but when prey is scarce, home ranges may increase to 80–160 hectares. Home ranges for females usually are smaller and are included within male home ranges. Residents maintain intrasexual territories, but transient individuals do not maintain intrasexual territories. Territories are staked out and marked by chemical scent excreted from paired anal glands. Males defend territories against other males and females defend against other females. In favorable habitats, population densities may reach 6–7 per square kilometer; however, densities fluctuate with annual changes in small mammal abundances. Densities as low as 0.4 per square km and as high as 38 per square km are known.

The long-tailed weasel actively searches its range day and night for prey and is a fearless, curious predator. It runs in a series of bounds, with its back bent and its tail elevated. It is an able swimmer, readily climbs trees in pursuit of prey, and often tunnels under snow to search out prey during winter. It normally hunts in an elliptical route from the den and back again. Prey is detected primarily by scent and hearing prior to its being seen. Small and medium prey are easily killed with a few rapid bites to the nape of the neck. Large prey are attacked

and sides. The neck is pale and the underside is whitish tinged with yellow. The tail is brown and tipped with black. Annual molts occur in spring and autumn. Northern subspecies acquire a white winter pelage, whereas southern subspecies have the characteristic brown dorsum all year. Subspecies inhabiting the southwestern United States, Florida, Mexico, and Central America have distinctive white or yellowish facial markings. The teeth of long-tailed weasels are highly specialized for a diet of flesh.

Breeding occurs in July and August. After fertilization, the ova develop for 8 days, then cease all development until spring, about 7.5 months later, when they implant in the uterus. Average gestation, including this period of delayed implantation, is 279 days (range 205–337 days). A single litter, usually of 4–5 young, but ranging from 1–9, is born in a den between mid-April and early May. The young are born blind and have only a few long, white hairs, but postnatal development is rapid. By three weeks, the canines and carnassial teeth erupt and the young begin to feed on meat and crawl outside the nest. By four weeks, the upper incisors erupt, the young walk long distances from the nest, and trill and squeal vocalizations begin.

Mustela frenata

from the side repeatedly until they are disabled. Aboveground, the weasel wraps its body around its prey and holds it with all four feet, biting the nape of the neck. Underground, a throat bite is used, causing death by suffocation.

Mustela frenata is a generalist, preying on a wide variety of small vertebrates, but concentrating on rodents and immature rabbits. Shrews, moles, bats, birds and their eggs, snakes, invertebrates, and carrion are consumed as alternative prey when favored prey are scarce. *M. frenata* also is known to kill and sometimes consume its close relatives, *M. erminea* and *M. nivalis,* on occasion. Males generally select larger prey than do females. Frequency of occurrence of a prey species in the diet varies seasonally and geographically as well as between the sexes. Captive adult long-tailed weasels consume 17–33 percent of their body weight in 24 hours, but growing young can consume much more. Caching of food is common, either in a side burrow of the main burrow or at a site located near a kill, including arboreal sites. Long-tailed weasels drink about 25 cubic centimeters of water daily. The main predators of the long-tailed weasel are foxes and raptors, but they are also taken by coyotes, domestic dogs and cats, and rattlesnakes.

Two closely related but smaller species of weasels, *Mustela erminea* and *Mustela nivalis,* occur in sympatry with *Mustela frenata*. *M. frenata* occurs primarily in the southern parts of the ranges of the other two weasels. In the area surrounding the Great Lakes in the U.S. and Canada, where all three species occur, habitat and dietary overlap is high, and competition significantly influences weasel population dynamics. *S. R. Sheffield*

Size

Males are significantly larger than females.
Total length: 330–420 mm (males); 280–350 mm (females)
Length of tail: 132–294 mm (males); 112–245 mm (females)
Weight: 160–450 g (males); 80–250 g (females)

Identification

Where sympatric, *Mustela frenata* can be distinguished from *M. erminea* by its larger body size and longer tail (more than 44 percent the length of head and body), and from *M. nivalis* by larger body size, longer tail, and black tip on the tail.

Other Common Names

Bridled weasel (southern portion of range)

Status

Generally low densities throughout its large range; uncommon to rare. Owing to the low densities and periodic fluctuations of North American *M. frenata* populations, this species is listed as endangered, threatened, rare, or as a species of special concern in many states and provinces. *M. f. longicauda* is listed as threatened in Canada.

Subspecies

(north of Mexico; 15 other subspecies occur from Mexico south into Bolivia and Peru)
Mustela frenata alleni, southwestern South Dakota and northeastern Wyoming
Mustela frenata altifrontalis, Pacific coast of Oregon and western third of Washington, into southwestern corner of British Columbia
Mustela frenata arizonensis, north-central Arizona into southwestern corner of New Mexico
Mustela frenata arthuri, southeastern Texas and along Gulf Coast into Mississippi
Mustela frenata effera, southeastern corner of Washington and most of the northern half of Oregon (except coast)
Mustela frenata frenata, southern Texas and most of eastern and central Mexico
Mustela frenata inyoensis, Inyo County, California
Mustela frenata latirostra, coastal southern California into northwestern corner of Baja California
Mustela frenata longicauda, central Alberta, Saskatchewan, and southern Manitoba south through the northern Great Plains (eastern Montana, most of North Dakota, South Dakota, Nebraska) into western Kansas and eastern Colorado
Mustela frenata munda, coastal northern California
Mustela frenata neomexicana, southeastern corner of Colorado, western Oklahoma, western third of Texas, eastern and southern New Mexico, and south into most of western Mexico
Mustela frenata nevadensis, south-central British Columbia and eastern two-thirds of Washington south through most of the Rocky Mountain states (Idaho, Nevada, Utah, most of Wyoming, western two-thirds of Colorado, northern New Mexico, and northeastern corner of Arizona) into northeastern California and southern and eastern Oregon
Mustela frenata nigriauris, coastal central California
Mustela frenata noveboracensis, southern Ontario and Quebec south through New York, Vermont, New Hampshire, Rhode Island, Connecticut, Pennsylvania, Ohio, New Jersey, Maryland, West Virginia, Virginia, Kentucky, Tennessee, Michigan, Wisconsin, Illinois, Indiana, and the northern two-thirds of North Carolina, into northern South Carolina, Georgia, and Alabama
Mustela frenata occisor, Maine, southeastern corner of Quebec, and southern New Brunswick
Mustela frenata olivacea, northern half of Mississippi, southern two-thirds of Alabama and Georgia, and southern half of South Carolina, south into northern half of Florida
Mustela frenata oregonensis, narrow strip from northern Oregon to coast of southern Oregon and northern California
Mustela frenata oribasus, most of southern British Columbia into west-central Alberta, south to western Montana and northwestern corner of Wyoming
Mustela frenata peninsulae, southern half of Florida
Mustela frenata primulina, eastern and southern Iowa and southeastern corner of Nebraska, south through Missouri, eastern half of Kansas, eastern two-thirds of Oklahoma, Arkansas, northeastern corner of Texas, and northern Louisiana
Mustela frenata pulcra, small portion of south-central California
Mustela frenata saturata, small portion of north-central California and southwestern Oregon
Mustela frenata spadix, southeastern corner of Manitoba, south through Minnesota, northern Iowa, small portions of eastern North and South Dakota, and northeastern Nebraska
Mustela frenata texensis, southwestern Oklahoma south into central Texas
Mustela frenata washingtoni, small portion of southwestern Washington south into northwestern Oregon
Mustela frenata xanthogenys, narrow strip of north-central California

References

Mammalian Species 570; Fagerstone, 1987; Hall, 1951; King, 1979; Svendsen, 1982

Black-footed ferret | *Mustela nigripes*

Black-footed ferrets were probably once common throughout the grasslands and basins of interior North America from southern Canada to northern Mexico. About two dozen fossils of ferrets are known. Apparently extinct in the wild by 1987, today they are known from three locations—northeastern Montana, western South Dakota, and southeastern Wyoming —all three populations reintroduced since 1991. Seven zoos and breeding facilities also have ferrets.

Ferrets are found almost exclusively in prairie dog colonies. No breeding ferrets have been found independent of prairie dogs, but single individuals have. Ferrets live in prairie dog tunnels and eat prairie dogs and other animals resident in the colonies. They are alert, agile, and curious animals. Black-footed ferrets are mostly nocturnal, but may be active aboveground at any hour. Peak activity is near dusk, for a few hours after dusk, and again for a few hours before dawn. In winter, they may remain belowground for up to a week at a time.

Because of their rarity and nocturnal, ground-dwelling habits, ferrets are hard to locate. Even in areas where they are known to occur, finding them aboveground is challenging. However, their tracks in snow and their unique diggings are easily located if they are present. Diggings, which originate from prairie dog burrow openings and may require 2 to 3 hours to produce, are thought to be related to prey acquisition. Subsoil is thrown out onto the surface of the ground in piles that average about a meter long, 40 cm wide, and 10 or more cm deep; most have a trough down the center, and some are multi-lobed. Early mornings from December through March when there is light snow cover are the best times to find these distinctive signs. At night, observers in vehicles with high-powered spotlights can sometimes see the ferrets themselves, systematically surveying prairie dog colonies. They are most likely to be spotted this way in mid- to late summer, when litters are active aboveground and before the young disperse.

Black-footed ferrets breed at one year of age. Breeding occurs from mid-March through early April, and gestation is about 42–45 days. Litter sizes average about 3.5. The young remain in the nest burrow for about 42 days before coming aboveground. When they first venture out of the burrow, the young ferrets are nearly adult size. Females and young stay together throughout July and early August and then begin to separate as the young become independent. Young may disperse in September and throughout the fall. *T. W. Clark*

Mustela nigripes

Least weasel | *Mustela nivalis*

The least weasel favors meadows, marshes, and grassy fields, and avoids woodland. Even where it is locally abundant, it is rarely noticed. Population density fluctuates in relation to prey abundance. Day and night, the least weasel alternates bouts of hunting and feeding with sleeping; it is active both in winter and summer. *Mustela nivalis* darts erratically from side to side when hunting, and when prey is encountered, rushes to catch it. The weasel wraps its body and limbs around the victim and kills with a bite to the base of the skull. Males and females have body diameters no larger than the mice and voles they eat, allowing them to follow their prey into underground burrows and through tunnels in snow and matted grass.

The senses of sight, hearing, and smell are acute. Adults use a variety of postural, vocal, and olfactory cues in communication. The exudate from the anal glands is pungent and is emitted when the weasel is excited. The sexes remain separate except during breeding. Individuals defend an exclusive central home area from others of their sex. The home ranges of males are larger (7 to 15 hectares) and overlap the smaller home ranges of females (1 to 4 hectares).

Males are sexually active in all months except December and January, and litters may occur throughout the year. Unlike the long-tailed weasel and ermine, both of which have delayed implantation, prolonged gestation, and one litter per year, female least weasels have more than one litter per year, implantation is not delayed, and gestation is 35 days. One to six young are born naked, blind, and helpless. At 11 days they are covered with a fine, white body hair. At 18 days young have brown hair on their backs and white hair on their bellies, and they are eating solid food. By 40 days they can kill prey. Females reach sexual maturity at four months, males at eight months.

The least weasel has short, fine underfur and longer guard hairs. The pelage fluoresces, producing a lavender color under ultra-violet light. The pelages of the long-tailed weasel and ermine do not fluoresce. In summer, the least weasel's upperparts are chocolate brown, and the underparts are white from the lower lip to the base of the tail. The brown tail does not

Mustela nivalis

have a black tip. In winter, the pelage is totally white in northern parts of its distribution, but remains brown in the southern parts.

The food of the least weasel consists chiefly of small rodents. Captive individuals were found to require one gram of food per hour in order to survive. That means that this small carnivore must consume half its body weight—about two deer mice or one meadow vole—every day to survive. When the least weasel kills more food than it can consume, it stores the surplus in its burrows for future meals. *G. E. Svendsen*

Size
Males are larger than females.
Total length: 180–205 mm (males); 165–180 mm (females)
Length of tail: 25–40 mm (males); 22–30 mm (females)
Weight: 40–55 g (males); 30–50 g (fenales)

Identification
Mustela nivalis has a long, slender body; the tail is short and lacks a black terminal brush. In summer the upperparts are rich, chocolate brown, and the underparts are white. In winter the pelage is completely white in northern regions but remains brown in southern regions.

M. nivalis can be distinguished from *M. erminea* by its small body size and short tail that lacks a black terminal brush, and from *M. frenata* by total length less than 300 mm and tail length less than 100 mm.

Other Common Names
Weasel, dwarf weasel, pygmy weasel, mouse weasel

Status
Common

Subspecies
Mustela nivalis allegheniensis, southern Great Lakes states from Wisconsin and Illinois east through Pennsylvania, and in Appalachian Mountains south to North Carolina
Mustela nivalis campestris, South Dakota, Nebraska, Iowa, northern Nebraska, and Arkansas
Mustela nivalis eskimo, Alaska and Yukon Territories
Mustela nivalis rixosa, Mackenzie Delta across Canada and south into northern Montana, North Dakota, and Minnesota

References
Svendsen, 1982

American mink | *Mustela vison*

Mustela vison dens near water, preferring the banks of lakes, marshes, and rivers, especially if they are forested or brushy. Mink are primarily nocturnal, with peak activity at dawn and dusk. They travel by a series of bounds on land and swim rapidly when in water. The den may be a hole under tree roots, in a hollow log, or in a muskrat house. The female's den has a nest lined with grass, plant fibers, feathers, and fur, whereas the den of the male does not. Mink are solitary except for females with their young.

Males have large home ranges that extend for a half mile or more along waterways and overlap with the smaller home ranges of several females. Mink are polygynous: during the mating season a male mates with several females. Breeding begins in January and extends through spring. Gestation is variable, depending on variation in delayed implantation. The average gestation period is 51 days, but the embryo is attached to the uterine wall for only 30 to 32 days. One litter of three to six young is produced per year. Growth is rapid and young are weaned at 5 to 6 weeks.

The rich brown pelage consists of a thick underfur and long stiff guard hairs. Demand for the lush pelts of wild mink has been high, but now ranched mink provides the fur industry

Mustela vison

with most pelts. Mink farmers have produced many mutants with colors ranging from white and buff to nearly black. These have descriptive trade names such as Aleutian, amber gold, blue iris, pastel, platinum, sapphire, and winter blue.

Mink eat mainly crayfish, mammals, and frogs in summer and mammals, fish, frogs, and birds in winter. Muskrats are the chief prey items in many areas. However, mink are opportunistic hunters and will include snakes, insects, bats, tree squirrels, moles, and varying hares in their diet. Unlike weasels, mink do not cache food. Sometimes they kill several animals and eat only part of each victim, however. Very few animals prey on mink, but red foxes, bobcats, and owls are known to kill them. *G. E. Svendsen*

Size

Males are about 10 percent longer and 20 percent heavier than females.

Total length: 550–700 mm (males); 470–600 mm (females)

Length of tail: 190–220 mm (males); 150–190 mm (females)

Weight: 550–1,250 g (males); 550–1,000 g (females)

Identification

The mink is semiaquatic, with a long, slender, weasel-like body and a tail that is bushy at the tip. The fur is dark brown except for white blotches on the chin, throat or chest. The rich brown color and large size distinguish it from *Mustela frenata* and *M. erminea*.

Status

Common along the edges of streams, lakes, and marshes

Subspecies

Mustela vison aestuarina, northern California

Mustela vison aniakensis, southwestern Alaska

Mustela vison energumenos, western Canada and United States from Yukon Territory to Arizona

Mustela vison evagor, Vancouver Island

Mustela vison evergladensis, Everglades, southern Florida

Mustela vison ingens, Alaska

Mustela vison lacustris, central Canada

Mustela vison letifera, north-central United States

Mustela vison lowii, northeastern Canada

Mustela vison lutrensis, Florida and coastal Georgia

Mustela vison melampeplus, Prince William Sound, Alaska

Mustela vison mink, eastern and midwestern United States

Mustela vison nesolestes, Sitka and surrounding islands, Alaska

Mustela vison vison, southeastern Canada to southern Appalachian Mountains

Mustela vison vulgivaga, Alabama and Arkansas

References

Linscombe et al., 1982

Wolverine | *Gulo gulo*

Throughout their range, wolverines exist at relatively low densities in comparison to other large carnivores. They are generally solitary wanderers, able to travel great distances for extended periods of time. Their habitats range from high, remote mountainous areas in the southern portion of their range to Arctic coastal tundra in the far north. In Alaska and northwestern Canada, the densest populations are probably found in terrain that includes both mountains and lowland areas.

Wolverines are usually solitary animals. Pairs and threesomes are seen on occasion, and these are probably either family units (females with dependent young) or breeding pairs. Breeding has been reported from early spring through late fall, with kits being born between February and April following a period of delayed implantation of the blastocyst. Although two or three is the mean litter size, one to five young may be born. Natal dens can be snow caves or tunnels, uprooted trees, or rock dens. Wolverines are largely nocturnal, but have been observed to copulate during bright March afternoons. Despite their relatively low reproduction rate, on average, wild wolverines live only about five years.

Annual home ranges of wolverines are large, ranging from about 100 square km to more than 600 square km. Females generally range over much smaller areas than males. Established adults of both sexes appear to maintain territories that exclude conspecifics of the same sex. However, one male territory may overlap several female home ranges. Dispersal of

Gulo gulo

subadult animals often occurs, with one documented movement of 378 km. Where the animals are trapped for their fur, males generally outnumber females in the harvest. This is probably because males have larger home ranges and are more likely to remain transients for longer periods, thus traveling more than females and increasing their chances of encountering traps. Females' movements are inhibited by the need to care for kits during the late spring.

Throughout their range, wolverines are famous for disturbing traplines and associated cabins and equipment. Most of their food is probably made up of carrion. Large ungulates that have succumbed to winter starvation or predation by wolves or bears are often utilized extensively, and anecdotal information indicates they often defend these food bonanzas from other predators and scavengers. Wolverines are also accomplished predators. Animals as large as caribou *(Rangifer tarandus)* are known to be taken, but more often, they prey on ground squirrels, ptarmigan, and snowshoe hares. Musk is often deposited from the anal glands or ventral glands near food caches or other "property," probably to advertise to other wolverines that the property has been claimed. Wolverines are known to consume fish and berries when other, more desirable menu items are limited.

Wolverine behavior is similar to that of other mustelids in many respects. They are seemingly inexhaustible in their search for prey or carrion. Their reputation as insatiable northern "demons" probably stems from their propensity to wreak havoc on remote cabins and food caches and their aggressiveness when caught in traps. Evidence at trap sites points to a struggling wolverine's impressive ability to claw, scratch, chew, or remove dirt, shrubs, trees, and boulders.

Scientifically-based management of wolverine populations has been limited. Their low density even during population "highs" and their wide-ranging habits make obtaining data difficult and expensive. Of the medium to large predators in North America, the wolverine is probably less understood than any other species. Density estimates based on aerial track counts have been done in Alaska and northwestern Canada, but the methods used have not been thoroughly tested. Although populations in Alaska and the Yukon and Northwest Territories appear quite healthy, more data are needed on almost all aspects of wolverine ecology to ensure the species' continued viability. *J. S. Whitman*

Size
Males are generally 25–30 percent heavier and about 10 percent greater in most standard body measurements than females of the same age class, and northern wolverines tend to be heavier than those from the southern part of the range.

Total length: 650–1,050 mm
Length of tail: 170–260 mm
Weight: 12.7–14.1 kg (males); 8.3–9.9 kg (females)

Identification
Wolverines have been likened to small bears,

but can readily be distinguished by their longer, bushier tails and smaller size. Often, too, they are active during winter, when black bears are usually hibernating. They differ from North American badgers by having longer pelage and usually much darker coloration.

Other Common Names
Glutton, stink-bear, little bear, carcajou
(French-Canadian)

Status
Generally rare in the southern portion of its range, with isolated populations usually found only in remote, mountainous terrain. More northern subpopulations are variable, with densities of one wolverine per square km considered normal.

Subspecies
Gulo gulo gulo, Eurasia
Gulo gulo luscus, North America

References
Mammalian Species 499; Hash, 1987; Whitman et al., 1986

American badger | *Taxidea taxus*

In contrast to its boldly marked head, the fur of the badger's body is usually drab grayish-brown mixed with whitish, brown, buff, rust, creamy buff, or even orange. There is a great deal of individual and microgeographic variation. Its feet are dark brown, and the short tail resembles the dorsal fur, but is paler. Coarse, bristly fur protects the short ears, and the shaggy dorsal fur fluffs out and rotates about when the badger hisses, grunts, and threatens. Young badgers are pale buff in color. Badgers molt once each year. The molt commences in the mid-dorsal white band, with prime fur growing out before winter. *Taxidea* differs from other North American carnivores in its wedge-shaped skull and in certain dental characters. It has anal scent glands, which are used in defense, mating, and possibly in other functions. The scent is not very powerful to the human nose.

Some of the morphological peculiarities of the badger are adaptations to its underground lifestyle. A large nictitating membrane, or third eye-lid, protects each eye. Badgers have partially webbed toes, and Pacinian corpuscles (nerve endings) in the foreclaws suggest that they may be organs of

Taxidea taxus

touch, but this has not been investigated. Its teeth are self-sharpening.

Badgers occur from alpine meadows to elevations as low as Death Valley, California, which is below sea level. In its remote desert, treeless pasture, drained marsh, or grassy meadow, the badger wanders about making its conspicuous excavations. Abundant diggings and den entrances, often large and with characteristic ellipsoid shape, reveal its presence on road embankments, weedy dikes, or grassy hillsides. Besides digging dens for hibernation and rearing young, badgers usually lay up during the day in temporary dens. Their digging contributes to soil development, and badgers are important in controlling rodent populations. They also provide ready-made dens for many other furbearers, kill venomous snakes, and eat carrion and insects.

Although fierce and formidable when cornered or attacked, the American badger is secretive and solitary. It is so fossorial that one was seen digging itself underground through an asphalt road. An unwilling mascot taken to a Wisconsin high school football game escaped and meandered under the sod of the playing field, raising up many humps and ridges. Badgers dig into rodent burrows, and feed extensively on pocket gophers, ground squirrels and other sciurids, mice and rats, and a great variety of other small vertebrates, including birds, snakes, toads, and frogs. They eat insects and their grubs, wasps and bees, and worms, but only occasionally feed on seasonal vegetal foods such as corn or oats. One was seen catching fish in a shallow stream, and another feeding on crayfish.

Badgers sleep through most of the winter, but are active on warm days. Torpor cycles last about 29 hours. In torpor, the body temperature falls about 9° C and the heartbeat is about half the normal rate. This torpor, called *Winterschlaf* by German naturalists, is not true hibernation. Body fat stored for the winter is seldom used up by spring.

Badgers breed in the summer or fall. Implantation is delayed until February. About five weeks later, in March or April, the young are born, furred but helpless. They are born in a specially prepared natal den with one or two, occasionally three brothers and sisters. Their eyes open after four to six weeks. By summer (six weeks after birth) the young emerge from the den to play, usually in the evenings. The mother brings dead rodents for them to eat. She fiercely protects her young. The male goes his own way except during pair bonding leading up to copulation. The young are weaned after attaining their permanent teeth at about two-thirds growth. Young-of-the-year females occasionally breed at about this time, and young of both sexes must fatten themselves and find a winter den, often the re-worked den of a fox or woodchuck.

The home ranges of males are larger than those of females. Young-of-the-year do not maintain a territory or home range. The area in which the badger wanders shrinks between the summer or fall mating period and winter. In areas of abundance, badgers reach densities of 3–5 per square kilometer.

Although badgers can live 12–14 years, few live longer than two years, and about 80 percent are yearlings or young. Natural predation on badgers is probably never common, and mostly affects the young. The young and the very old are most likely to die of starvation. Diseases in badgers have not been investigated much, but badgers are known to harbor many internal and external parasites. Unfortunately, humans are the badger's greatest enemy, responsible for the destruction of habitats and heavy mortality from trapping, hunting, and automobiles. Government agencies have poisoned badgers intentionally or incidentally (in eradicating wolves and coyotes). Bounties have been paid for badger carcasses, badgers are shot for sport, and others are killed incidentally in traps set for other furbearers. However, unlike the European badger, *Meles meles,* the American species was seldom "badgered" with dogs in the pit.

Although the Israelites' holy tabernacle was tented with badger fur, the fur of most badgers, including *Taxidea,* is not much prized. Badger fur is occasionally used for shaving and paint brushes, but most of these are made from the pelage of *Meles.* The states and provinces where most pelts have been taken are Minnesota, North and South Dakota, and Saskatchewan. The badger is given full protection now in British Columbia, Wisconsin, Illinois, and Michigan. *C. A. Long*

Size

Males are significantly larger than females, and northern subspecies are significantly heavier than southern populations.

Total length: 600–790 mm

Length of tail: 105–135 mm

Weight: up to 12 kg in northern adults, nearly 18 kg in captives

Identification

Resembling a short-legged, shaggy, medium-sized dog, the badger can be identified by its huge foreclaws (up to 5 cm in length) and prominent head markings. The so-called "badges" are brown or blackish patches on the cheeks. A bold median white stripe on the black head continues onto the neck, and as far as the base of the tail in *T. t. berlandieri*.

Other Common Names

North American badger, tlalcoyote (Mexico), blaireau or siffleur (French Canadian)

Status

Uncommon to rare. Rare in British Columbia, Ontario, Michigan, Indiana, Arkansas, Missouri, and Illinois, and in most Mexican states. Protected by law in British Columbia, Wisconsin, Illinois, and Michigan.

Subspecies

Taxidea taxus berlandieri, grasslands and deserts of Puebla, Mexico, northward into low valleys of California, where it meets the geographic range of *T. t. jeffersonii;* northeastward to the range of *T. t. taxus.* These subspecies intergrade in a wide zone from northern Texas to northern Oklahoma and northwest Arkansas.

Taxidea taxus jacksoni, sandy soils and drained marshes in the Great Lakes region, including southernmost Ontario

Taxidea taxus jeffersonii, friable soils in western mountains and deserts from British Columbia south to California, southern Nevada, and Utah, and eastward into Montana, Wyoming, and Colorado

Taxidea taxus taxus, prairie provinces in southern Canada and Great Plains in the United States as far south as northern Oklahoma

References

Mammalian Species 26; Long, 1992; Long and Killingley, 1983; Messick, 1987; Messick and Hornocker, 1981

Northern river otter | *Lontra canadensis*

The geographic range of the river otter once extended throughout Canada and the United States, with the exception of the Mohave Desert in Nevada and Colorado and the southern regions of California, New Mexico, and Texas. In Mexico, river otters were found only near the deltas of the Grande (=Bravo) and Colorado rivers. Now, however, they are extirpated or rare throughout most of the central and eastern United States.

River otters are semiaquatic, slender, long-bodied mammals. They are specialized for aquatic life with thick guard hair, dense oil under the fur, webbed toes, and small ears. They can live in any marine (coastal) or freshwater habitat with a permanent food and water supply. Rivers, streams, lakes, reservoirs, marshes, swamps, and estuaries all provide potential habitat. They are abundant in coastal areas and some large rivers; however, river otters are very sensitive to pollution and have disappeared from heavily polluted waters.

Their dens are located in shelters dug by other mammals or in natural hollows under logs, trees, rock piles, thickets, or on river banks. Each den has an underwater entrance with a tunnel leading to a nesting chamber, where the otters build a nest of plant material, using leaves, grasses, mosses, pieces of bark, and some hair. Otters have both permanent and temporary nests.

River otters breed once a year, in late winter or early spring. During the breeding season a male can copulate with several females, and mating usually occurs in the water. The pregnancy period is estimated to be around 2 months, but because

otters employ delayed implantation, gestation can last up to a year. Parturition takes place from November to May, with a peak in March and April. Litter size varies from 1 to 6, but it usually consists of 2 or 3. The young are fully-furred, but helpless, at birth. Young otters open their eyes after one month and are weaned at about three months. Dispersal from the natal area probably begins about three months after weaning. They reach sexual maturity after 2 or 3 years and can live up to 21 years in captivity.

Lontra canadensis

River otters feed mainly on fish, crayfish, frogs, crabs, birds and birds' eggs, and turtles. They occasionally prey upon muskrats and other small mammals or feed on aquatic plants. They are very skillful swimmers and divers and can remain submerged for up to eight minutes. In most regions, they hunt in the water at night. They can cover several kilometers in a hunting foray, searching for prey under logs, rocks, and in the mud. Large prey are often eaten on land. River otters have few natural enemies, but they are sometimes attacked by bobcats, coyotes, or other mammalian predators, by some birds of prey, or by alligators.

Adult males are generally solitary. Females live with their young until dispersal. Densities and home range sizes are quite variable, depending on habitat quality, but some reports from good habitat indicate densities of one otter per 2 or 3 km of waterway. Male otters mark and defend territories within their home ranges.

The river otter is an important furbearer in North America, and 20,000 to 30,000 individuals are harvested annually in Canada and the United States. *G. Ceballos-G.*

Size
Males average larger than females.
Total length: 889–1,300 mm
Length of tail: 300–507 mm
Weight: 5–14 kg

Identification
The only river otter north of Mexico, *Lontra canadensis* is distinguished from *Lontra longicaudis,* a river otter found in Mexico, by less hair on the side of the nose, a dorsally flattened skull, and tufts of hair under the toes.

Recent Synonyms
Lutra canadensis

Other Common Names
River otter, common otter

Status
Common in some areas of Canada and the United States, but extirpated or rare in Arizona, Colorado, Indiana, Iowa, Kansas, Kentucky, Nebraska, New Mexico, North Dakota, Ohio, Oklahoma, South Dakota, Tennessee, Utah, and West Virginia. Endangered in Mexico, and extirpated or rare in the states of Sonora and Tamaulipas. Included in Appendix II of CITES.

Subspecies
Lontra canadensis canadensis, northeastern United States (Connecticut, Maine, Massachusetts, New York) and Canada (Ontario, Quebec, Labrador, Newfoundland, Nova Scotia), Labrador Peninsula, and the Great Lakes region (Michigan, Wisconsin)
Lontra canadensis kodiacensis, Kodiak Islands, Alaska
Lontra canadensis lataxina, central, eastern, and southeastern United States, south of the Great Lakes region and east of the Rocky Mountains, and northern Mexico in the Rio Grande (=Bravo) near Brownsville

Lontra canadensis mira, along the coast and offshore islands of southeastern Alaska and British Columbia
Lontra canadensis pacifica, Alaska, central and western Canada, and central and western United States
Lontra canadensis periclyzomae, Queen Charlotte Islands and other nearby islands off British Columbia
Lontra canadensis sonora, major rivers in Colorado, Nevada, Arizona, and New Mexico, and the Colorado River in Sonora, Mexico

References
Mammalian Species 587; Toweill and Tabor, 1982; van Zyll de Jong, 1972

Sea otter | *Enhydra lutris*

Enhydra lutris is the only fully aquatic species in the Order Carnivora; it is also one of the largest species in the Family Mustelidae, and one of the smallest marine mammals. Sea otters are identifiable by their habit of floating back-down and their use of rocks and other hard objects as tools to open prey. They are readily observed from shore, and their unique behavior and appealing appearance have made them a popular attraction to coastal visitors in many areas.

Sea otters live in shallow coastal waters. They once ranged from central Baja California across the Pacific rim to northern

Japan. Hunted to the verge of extinction during the 18th and 19th centuries, the species recovered following protection in 1911. Most of the historic range westward from about Prince William Sound is now recolonized, although populations have declined in the 1990s. These recent declines have likely been caused by increased killer whale predation, which in turn is linked to oceanic ecosystem shifts. Isolated but growing populations occur in southeastern Alaska, British Columbia, Washington, and central California. In contrast with population growth rates of 17–20° per year for Alaska, British Columbia, and Washington, the California population has grown at about 5° per year. Other than humans, predators include white sharks, bald eagles, brown bears, coyotes, and killer whales.

Sea otters feed mainly on marine invertebrates, and in some areas, fish. Foraging dives usually last just over a minute, but can range from several seconds to about 4 minutes in duration. Prey are consumed at the surface while the otter floats on its back. Numerous prey species are consumed in most areas. However, individual otters in California tend to specialize on 2–3 prey types. The dietary patterns of individuals appear to be matrilineally inherited and persist for many years (perhaps throughout life). Sea otters use their powerful forelimbs and tools (rocks and other hard objects) to dislodge and open hard-

shelled invertebrate prey, which they crush with their broad, flattened molars.

Females become sexually mature at 3–5 years of age, after which they usually give birth to a single young annually. Males reach sexually maturity at about 5–7 years, but probably are unable to establish territories until several years later. Length of gestation is about 6 months. The interval from birth to weaning averages another 6 months, but may vary from 4–9 months in California and 2–11 months in Alaska. Breeding and pupping occur throughout the year. Pupping is less seasonal in California than in Alaska. Parturition peaks during late winter/early spring in California and early summer in Alaska. Maximum longevity in the wild is estimated to be about 10–15 years for males and 15–20 years for females. Mortality is typically highest in young and very old individuals, although this pattern appears to vary by sex and among populations.

Sea otters are polygynous. Adult males defend territories against other males. Females appear to move freely among these territories. Females enter estrus soon after weaning or losing their pup, and form brief, sequential pair-bonds with 1–3 males, during which mating takes place repeatedly.

As with many other carnivores, post-weaning males tend to disperse widely. Females often remain near the area of their birth as juveniles and adults. Sea otters are nonmigratory. Seasonal movements may occur, especially among males, although these seem to vary greatly among locations as well as in relation to sex, age, and social status. Sea otters rest and interact in groups called "rafts," although they tend to forage and mate away from other otters. Rafts are small in California (2–12 animals), but in Alaska males may congregate in groups of hundreds of individuals. Although sea otters spend most of their time in the water, they sometimes haul out on land or ice. They segregate by sex. Female areas comprise females, pups, and territorial males. Male areas, consisting of young and nonterritorial males, are often located at population range peripheries or exposed points.

The effectiveness with which sea otters limit the abundance and distribution of their invertebrate prey is well known. For this reason, and because some of these prey also have important ecological functions, sea otters have been referred to as a "keystone species." The limiting influence of sea otter predation on prey types such as abalone, crabs, clams, and sea urchins has led to conflicts with recreational and commercial shellfisheries, but in many areas lacking sea otters, herbivorous sea urchins have destructively overgrazed kelp forests, and kelp is the base of an important coastal food web, ultimately providing habitat and nutrition for a myriad of species. There is growing evidence that sea otters and their recent ancestors have substantially influenced the character of marine plant/herbivore interactions over evolutionary time. By maintaining

Enhydra lutris

an environment in which the influence of herbivores on marine plants was minimal, the sea otter may actually have promoted selection for the absence of significant chemical defenses in marine plants of the North Pacific Ocean. *J. A. Estes*

Size
Total length: 1,260–1,450 mm (males);
    1,070–1,400 mm (females)
Length of tail: one-third total length
Weight: 18–45 kg (males); 11–33 kg (females)

Identification
The sea otter can be distinguished from other otters by large, flipper-like hind limbs, flattened molars, tail flattened dorso-ventrally; distinguished from pinnipeds by paw-like forelimbs.

Status
Threatened (California); abundant (elsewhere)

Subspecies
Enhydra lutris kenyoni, Washington, British Columbia, coastal Alaska through Aleutian Islands

Enhydra lutris lutris, Commander Islands, Pacific coast of Asia to northern Japan
Enhydra lutris nereis, California

References
Mammalian Species 133; Kenyon, 1969; Riedman and Estes, 1991

Family Mephitidae

Long considered a subfamily of Mustelidae, the skunks were raised to the familial level based on molecular systematic studies by Dragoo and Honeycutt (1997). This arrangement had been hinted at by earlier works, and the molecular evidence seems quite convincing. In addition to the nine species in three genera found in the New World, the two species of Oriental stink badgers, genus *Mydaus,* are included in the family Mephitidae.

North American skunks are familiar animals, particularly known for their anal scent glands. These glands emit a powerful secretion that can be actively sprayed by the animals as an antipredator device. All skunks have also developed a striking black-and-white color pattern that helps to serve as a warning to predators. Behavioral displays help to emphasize the color pattern when the animals are threatened. The spray itself is used as a defense of last resort, if the color pattern and threat displays are ineffective in discouraging a potential predator.

Skunks are omnivorous foragers, most active at night but occasionally out at any time of day. They have adapted to rural human activities, and are common in parks and farmland throughout their ranges. Their susceptibility to the rabies virus has kept many populations under control and poses a health risk to humans from time to time.

References

Dragoo and Honeycutt, 1997

North American Genera

Spilogale
Mephitis
Conepatus

Western spotted skunk | *Spilogale gracilis*

North American spotted skunks are generally separated into two species, *Spilogale putorius* and *Spilogale gracilis.* The western form, *S. gracilis,* had been considered a subspecies of the eastern skunk, but the presence of delayed implantation in the western form and its absence in the eastern form have persuaded taxonomists to classify it as a separate species. *Spilogale gracilis* occurs from northern Mexico to southwestern British Columbia, meeting the range of the eastern skunk along the central Great Plains.

The western spotted skunk is an interesting and beautiful

Spilogale gracilis

it stands on its front feet in a "handstand," directing its anal sphincter at its adversary and prominently displaying its white-tipped tail. This acrobatic display is a clear warning of imminent chemical defense. Spraying usually is used as a last resort.

Spilogale gracilis has a prolonged delay of implantation of the fertilized egg. The skunk breeds in late September and early October, following which the fertilized egg remains in a state of arrested development for approximately 200 days. The embryo is activated in March or April, and two to six young are born roughly one month later. Their pelage is well developed by three weeks, the eyes are open at one month, the young are weaned at two months, and by three months they are nearly full grown.

Western spotted skunks readily excavate dens in a variety of substrates; dens may be located in shrubs, trees, cavities in rocks, open grassy areas, road cuts, human-made structures, and abandoned burrows of other animals. Individual spotted skunks on the California Channel Islands utilize several dens distributed throughout their home ranges, which average approximately 25 hectares and overlap those of other skunks. Several individuals may use the same den, either simultaneously or at different times. Dens occurring in an area do not necessarily belong to an individual skunk but rather may be available to the whole population.

The western spotted skunk is nocturnal, with activity beginning around dusk and continuing on and off until dawn. The diet is largely carnivorous. Small mammals, especially mice, and a wide variety of insect prey including Jerusalem crickets, grasshoppers, beetles, caterpillars, earwigs, and ants are consumed. Other items in the diet include lizards, birds, carrion, and occasionally vegetable matter.

Little is known about the natural predators of the spotted skunk. Great horned owls are generally listed as their primary predator; bobcats, foxes, coyotes, and domestic dogs and cats are additional threats. Not surprisingly, humans have had a large impact on spotted skunks; the animals are poisoned, trapped, or shot as pests or for their pelts. Road kills are another major mortality factor. The status of *Spilogale gracilis* is currently unknown, but there is growing concern that the species is becoming increasingly uncommon. *K. Crooks*

little carnivore about which surprisingly little is known. The limited ecological information available for the species comes mainly from research on the insular subspecies *(S. g. amphiala)* that occurs on two of the California Channel Islands. Generally, spotted skunks, the smallest skunks, can be described as having weasel-like habits. Compared to their larger and more conspicuous relative, the striped skunk, spotted skunks are faster, more agile, and highly carnivorous.

The pelage of both male and female western spotted skunks is jet black and generally softer and glossier than that of the striped skunk. White markings occur as a broad triangular nose patch, one spot under each ear, and four to six broken stripes along the neck, back, and sides. The end of the tail is also tipped with white. Relative proportions of black and white vary considerably among individuals and populations.

The spotted skunk has a pair of scent glands under the base of the tail from which pungent fluid, called musk, can be sprayed through the anus. When threatened, the skunk stamps its front feet on the ground in warning. If further aggravated,

Size
Males are 7–10 percent larger than females.
Total length: 350–581 (425) mm (males);
   320–470 (383) mm (females)
Length of tail: 100–210 (149) mm (males);
   85–203 (135) mm (females)
Weight: 500–900 (700) g (males); 200–600
   (400) g (females)

Identification
Spilogale gracilis can be distinguished from other skunks in its range by its small size, broken white stripes and white spots on jet black fur, and white-tipped tail

Recent Synonyms
Spilogale putorius gracilis

Other Common Names
Civet cat, hydrophobia cat, polecat

Status
Unknown: widespread distribution but locally uncommon and may be declining

Subspecies

Spilogale gracilis amphiala, two California Channel Islands, Santa Cruz and Santa Rosa

Spilogale gracilis gracilis, Great Basin, western United States

Spilogale gracilis latifrons, Pacific Northwest

Spilogale gracilis leucoparia, southwestern United States, northern Mexico

Spilogale gracilis martirensis, central Baja California

Spilogale gracilis phenax, western California

Spilogale gracilisl ucasana, southern Baja California

References

Crooks and Van Vuren, 1994, 1995, 1996; Howard and Marsh, 1982; Van Gelder, 1959

Eastern spotted skunk | *Spilogale putorius*

Spotted skunks are the smallest and most weasel-like in appearance of the three genera of skunks. Their fur is finer and denser than that of *Conepatus* and *Mephitis.* The spotted color pattern occurs because six white stripes along the back and sides break into spots at the middle of the back. *Spilogale putorius* also has a small white spot in the middle of the forehead. The eastern spotted skunk is larger than the pygmy spotted skunk, *Spilogale pygmea,* a Mexican species, a .d, with the exception of the subspecies that occurs on the Florida peninsula, larger than *Spilogale gracilis* and its allies.

The eastern spotted skunk has a patchy distribution from south of Canada in Minnesota to Tamaulipas, Mexico. It occurs as far west as eastern Wyoming and Colorado and can be found in northern and eastern Texas. It also occurs in Florida, throughout the Appalachians, and in Pennsylvania.

Spotted skunks forage primarily at night. They are secretive and not often seen. These skunks are exceptional "mousers" and do farmers a great service when they forage around barns and buildings. They are rarely found in the open, preferring either forested areas or habitats containing significant vegetative cover. In the plains states, eastern spotted skunks inhabit riparian woodlands and areas of vegetation along fences. They den in protected, dark, dry holes including natural crevices in trees, in dens previously occupied by other mammals, in haystacks, under houses or rocks, and in the walls of houses or barns. Spotted skunks also dig their own burrows. They usually den alone, but in cold winter months several skunks may bed down together. They usually use more than one den site within their home range.

Eastern spotted skunks are omnivorous, but tend to be more carnivorous than striped or hog-nosed skunks. The diet consists mainly of insects, small mammals, birds, and birds' eggs. Like a center hiking a football, the skunk uses its front paws to hike an egg through its back legs in order to crack the shell. These skunks also eat fruits and vegetables in the summer and fall, when they are available. Natural predators of

spotted skunks include larger carnivores such as canids (domestic dogs, foxes, and coyotes), cats (feral and bobcats), and birds of prey (owls). Human activities also are a major source of mortality, and in many states there is concern that the species is on the decline.

Reproduction in the eastern spotted skunk is different from that in the western spotted skunk. The main breeding season for this species is during March and April, although some individuals may breed again in July and September to produce a second litter. Gestation is estimated to be from 50 to 65 days, with only a two-week period of delayed implantation. First season litters are produced in late May and early June, and litter size averages five but ranges from two to nine kits.

Spotted skunks are agile climbers and can scurry squirrel-like up and down trees. This agility also is seen in their threat behavior. Spotted skunks can do front handstands. When faced with an enemy, the skunk rushes forward, then stands on its forepaws with its hind end elevated off the ground. A spotted skunk was observed using this threat against a hog-nosed skunk; neither skunk sprayed. Spotted skunks also stomp with their front paws as a warning behavior, yet these threats do not

Spilogale putorius

always lead to spraying. When it does spray, however, the skunk is agile enough to face the predator while twisting its rump to direct the spray toward its enemy.

During the early part of this century (and still today) it was believed that a bite from this skunk would transmit the rabies virus. These animals can transmit rabies *only* if they carry the disease. Multiple incidents of bizarre behaviors in these skunks prior to a person's being bitten have been recorded, and in most cases the skunk was not rabid. Around 1915 a famous naturalist, Joseph D. Mitchell, offered an alternative explanation for the madness often observed in these skunks. He wrote, "During the mating season, the male sometimes has spells of 'temporary insanity,' and runs amuck. During these spells he travels usually in a gallop, and will attack anything in his path." While Mitchell's rationalization that the "violent frenzy" was brought on by "unsatisfied sexual desires" may not be accurate, he offered evidence that the majority of spotted skunks do not carry rabies. In fact, these animals are a benefit to humans because they prey on rodent pests and insects harmful to agriculture. *J. W. Dragoo and R. L. Honeycutt*

Size

Total length: 310–610 (459) mm (males);
  270–544 (422) mm (females)
Length of tail: 80–280 (164) mm (males);
  85–210 (154) mm (females)
Weight: 276–885 g (males); 207–475 g
  (females)

Identification

Where populations of eastern spotted skunks approach or overlap those of western spotted skunks *(Spilogale gracilis),* eastern spotted skunks can be distinguished by a smaller white spot between the eyes, narrower stripes down the back and sides, and a small tuft of white hairs on the tip of the tail. *Spilogale putorius* also is larger than *Spilogale gracilis* in these areas.

Other Common Names

Civet-cat, little spotted skunk, hydrophoby cat, little pole-cat, four-striped skunk

Status

Currently this species is listed as Category 2 by the U. S. Fish and Wildlife Service; that is, more information on population density is required before a determination of its status can be made.

Subspecies

Spilogale putorius ambarvalis, peninsular Florida
Spilogale putorius interrupta, Canadian border in Minnesota, central North Dakota, eastern Wyoming, eastern Colorado, western Oklahoma, northwestern Texas, south to central Texas and to Tamaulipas, Mexico, and east to the Mississippi River and St. Croix County, Wisconsin
Spilogale putorius putorius, southeastern United States from Alabama, Mississippi, and northern Florida northward through western and central Georgia and South Carolina, and northward through the Appalachian Mountains to south-central Pennsylvania

References

Mammalian Species 511; Nowak, 1991; Van Gelder, 1959

Hooded skunk | *Mephitis macroura*

The hooded skunk, *Mephitis macroura,* occurs at low elevations (below 2,500 m) in desert areas. It prefers rugged, rocky canyons or heavily vegetated stream edges and valleys. In southwestern desert habitats in the United States, it has been reported in association with mesquite *(Prosopis),* pine-oak *(Pinus-Quercus)* woodland, and other shrubs and grasses. In these areas, three other species of skunks share its range. The striped skunk, *M. mephitis,* the spotted skunk, *Spilogale gracilis,* and the hog-nosed skunk, *Conepatus mesoleucus,* coexist with the hooded skunk by adopting different behavioral and ecological strategies.

The hooded skunk is more secretive than the striped skunk, and prefers to den away from man-made structures. However, dens have been found at the edges of grain fields and under

concrete irrigation canals. *Mephitis macroura* is nocturnal and spends almost all nighttime hours foraging. The animal retires to its den at dawn, where it spends the daytime in slumber. It has been observed at night digging for its favorite foods, beetles and other insects. The diet of the hooded skunk also includes small rodents and ground-dwelling birds. Some plant materials, mainly prickly pear cactus fruits, are also consumed.

The body of *M. macroura* is black, with one, two, or three white stripes running down the back and sides of the body and tail. A short, thin, white stripe is present between the eyes. Three color phases have been recorded: a black-backed phase with two narrow lateral white stripes, a white-backed phase with one wide mid-dorsal white stripe, and a combination black and white-backed phase. The latter phase is the least common.

The reproductive biology of the hooded skunk is poorly known. The information available about its breeding season and gestation period is based upon data from only a few specimens. Males and females apparently are reproductively active from mid-February to the end of March. A neonate was reported in mid-May. Females seem to nurse their young until mid-August.

Like all skunks, this skunk defends itself with a powerful scent squirted from two glands located near the base of the tail. When threatened, the animal stamps its front feet as a warning. If it is further provoked, it turns its back, raises its tail, and contracts the muscles around the scent glands, discharging the secretion. *B. M. Gharaibeh and C. Jones*

Mephitis macroura

Size

Males are usually larger than females.

Total length: 560–790 mm

Length of tail: 350–400 mm

Weight: 820–1,200 g

Identification

The pelage is black, usually with two widely separated white stripes on the back and one thin white stripe on the head. Another common color phase has one wide stripe on the back and one thin white stripe on the head. The hooded skunk can be distinguished from the striped skunk, *Mephitis mephitis*, which shares its range, by having longer, softer fur, and by the presence of a hood of longer hairs, usually white, on the upper neck and head.

Other Common Names

White sided skunk, southern skunk, zorrillo (in Mexico)

Status

Uncommon in the United States, common in Mexico

Subspecies

Mephitis macroura eximius, Veracruz, Mexico

Mephitis macroura macroura, central and southern Mexico, Guatemala, El Salvador, Honduras, and Nicaragua

Mephitis macroura milleri, southwestern United States and northern Mexico

Mephitis macroura richardsoni, northwestern Nicaragua

Mephitis macroura vittata, southern Mexico, Guatemala, El Salvador, and Honduras

References

Davis and Schmidly, 1994; Olin, 1975; Schmidly, 1984

Striped skunk │ *Mephitis mephitis*

The striped skunk is probably the best-known small carnivore in North America because of both its odor and its coloration. People who know nothing else about this animal know that it is capable of producing a nauseating spray. Even the Latin name of the skunk reflects this fact: *Mephitis* means "bad odor." When threatened, a striped skunk will raise its tail and repeatedly stamp its forefeet on the ground in warning. If this is ineffective, it curves its body into a U so that it can see its target as it expels a yellowish spray from muscular sacs on either side of the anus. Skunks can aim reliably at a distance of 4 m or more and can spray several times in quick succession. Holding the animal off the ground by its tail does not always prevent it from spraying. The spray, or musk, is composed of several volatile sulphur compounds. It has been likened in smell to everything from garlic to sewage, but all descriptions pale in comparison with close exposure to the real thing. The musk causes extreme pain and temporary blindness if it enters the eyes and it is harmful if ingested. It is almost impossible to remove from clothing and fur because of its oily nature; a dilute solution of chlorine bleach works best. With such a superb defense mechanism, it is not surprising that skunks are not noted for the intelligence, strength, speed, or stamina that other animals depend upon.

The skunk's distinctive black-and-white markings include a white blaze on the nose, a white hood, and white stripes that extend from the hood to or onto the tail. The tail may be tipped with white, and there may be additional spots on the legs and around the ears. The stripes on the back vary from one skunk to another in length and width, so that an individual may appear all white, all black, or anything in between. Most skunks that appear all white are not albino, although albinism does occur in this species.

The striped skunk is found throughout southern Canada, the United States, and northern Mexico. It occurs in all habitat types except the driest, and is most common along forest-field edges. In the summer, skunks use aboveground dens such as hollow logs or rock piles. In the winter, although they do not hibernate, they den for extended periods of time in underground burrows, usually dens excavated by woodchucks or badgers. They can also make nuisances of themselves denning in or under buildings. As many as 20 skunks (one male plus a group of females) have been known to den communally in the winter. Communal denning is more common in the northern part of their range.

Mephitis mephitis

The diet of the striped skunk is extremely variable, including insects (up to 70 percent), small rodents, rabbits, birds and their eggs, carrion, fruit, and other vegetable matter. Although they are often accused of destroying crops, bees, and poultry, less than 5 percent of the striped skunk's diet is composed of foods that are of value to people. This cost is far outweighed by their consumption of harmful pests such as grasshoppers, beetle grubs, and mice.

Skunks are preyed upon primarily by great horned owls and some other raptors, although many predators will kill a skunk if they are hungry enough to ignore the musk. Skunks are also killed in large numbers by vehicles. They are probably attracted to roadsides in their search for food, including carrion, and sometimes attempt to drive off the oncoming threat by standing their ground and spraying. The most common cause of mortality in this animal is disease. Striped skunks are susceptible to pneumonia, distemper, and leptospirosis, and they are among the most important vectors of rabies in North America. Rabid skunks exhibit "furious" symptoms including high levels of activity and aggression. Contrary to popular belief, it is impossible to contract rabies from skunk spray.

Striped skunks breed in February and March. Litters of 1–10 kits are born 59–77 days after conception (the variability is due to delayed implantation). Color patterns are apparent on the skin of kits at birth, although they are virtually hairless. They are capable of emitting musk as early as 8 days of age, but they cannot aim until their eyes open at around 24 days of age. Their ears open soon thereafter. Juveniles are weaned at 2 months; details of their dispersal from the natal range are not known. Overwinter mortality of juveniles is extremely high (up to 90 percent) but those that survive are capable of mating the following spring (at approximately 10 months of age). Most skunks do not live more than 2–3 years in the wild but they may survive 5 years in captivity.

Very little is known of the natural behavior of striped skunks. They are solitary except for a mother and her kits, and nocturnal, except in unusual circumstances (for instance, after an extreme cold spell, or if ill). Most information about the species is from captive animals because striped skunks were commonly bred for the fur industry in the early 1900s. The white stripes were excised and the black furs were sold, often under a different name, such as "sable." Subsequently, skunks became popular as pets, again under a different name, this time "sachet kitten." In most states it is now illegal to own pet skunks for fear of transmission of rabies. *A. Bixler*

Size
Females are 15 percent smaller than males but have longer tails; both sexes are heavier in the fall and in the northern part of their range.
Total length: 575–800 mm
Length of tail: 173–307 mm
Weight: 1,200–5,300 g

Identification
Mephitis mephitis is the most common skunk in North America. It can be extremely variable in stripe pattern. The dorsal stripes can be so short that the animal appears nearly black, so wide that the animal appears nearly white, or broken so that they look like spots. Even with that color pattern, *M. mephitis* is easily distinguished from the spotted skunks (*Spilogale*). *Spilogale* is smaller and has at least four horizontal stripes on the upper back in addition to several vertical stripes across the hindquarters. *M. mephitis* can be distinguished from *M. macroura*, the hooded skunk, in having a shorter tail and dorsal stripes that converge to a V at the nape. Hog-nosed skunks *(Conepatus)* have elongated, hairless noses.

Other Common Names
Skunk, big/large skunk, polecat

Status
Abundant

Subspecies
Mephitis mephitis avia, central Illinois, northern Missouri, northeastern Kansas
Mephitis mephitis elongata, southwestern Virginia, North and South Carolina, eastern Georgia, Florida, southern Alabama, Mississippi, and Louisiana
Mephitis mephitis estor, eastern and southern Utah, western Colorado and Arizona, New Mexico; eastern Sonora and western Chihuahua, Mexico
Mephitis mephitis holzerni, southwestern California
Mephitis mephitis hudsonica, eastern British Columbia, Alberta, Saskatchewan, southern Manitoba, and southwestern Ontario, Canada, through northern Colorado and the southern borders of Nebraska, Iowa, and Wisconsin
Mephitis mephitis major, eastern Washington, southern Idaho, northern Nevada, northwestern Utah
Mephitis mephitis mephitis, northeastern

Manitoba, Ontario, southern Quebec to the
Hudson River
Mephitis mephitis mesomelas, southwestern
Missouri, western Oklahoma, eastern
Arkansas, western Texas, Louisiana
Mephitis mephitis nigra, from New Brunswick
and Nova Scotia south to northern Virginia,
west through Michigan, Indiana, eastern
Missouri and Arkansas, south through

most of Mississippi and Alabama, western
Georgia
Mephitis mephitis notata, central Washington.
Mephitis mephitis occidentalis, southwestern
Oregon, northern California
Mephitis mephitis spissigrada, west coast of
Washington
Mephitis mephitis varians, western Kansas,
southeastern Colorado, eastern Ariaona,

western and central Texas, and eastern
Chihuahua, northern Coahuila, Nuevo
Leon, and Tamaulipas, Mexico

References
Mammalian Species 173; Rosatte, 1987; Verts,
1967

Eastern hog-nosed skunk | *Conepatus leuconotus*

Skunks of the genus *Conepatus* occur from Argentina northward through South America and Mexico, and into the United States as far north as Colorado. However, *Conepatus leuconotus* has one of the smallest distributions of any North American skunk. Much of its geographic range is in Mexico along the Gulf coastal plain from central Veracruz north to the Rio Grande River. Its distribution in the United States is restricted to southern Texas, including the Gulf coastal plains. It is presumed to be geographically isolated from the closely-related and widely distributed western hog-nosed skunk, *Conepatus mesoleucus,* although from a taxonomic standpoint, several researchers have suggested that *C. leuconotus* is conspecific with *C. mesoleucus. C. leuconotus* can be distinguished from *C. mesoleucus* by its size (it is 20–25 percent larger) and by differences in the dorsal white stripe, which is much narrower or absent near the rump in *C. leuconotus.* In addition, the underside of the tail in *C. leuconotus* is black basally and white toward the tip. In *C. mesoleucus* the tail is predominantly white.

Little is known about the basic biology of *Conepatus leuconotus.* Most information about the species comes from records of capture, with associated habitat descriptions, and specimen records are from biological surveys of the mid-1800s to the mid-1900s. The most recent records from Texas are from Kingsville and were collected in 1966. Because few sightings or specimens have been reported in recent years, there is a growing consensus among mammalogists that the population level of this species in Texas may have declined during the past few decades. As a result of this decline, photographs of live eastern hog-nosed skunks are harder to come by than pictures of Big Foot or the Loch Ness Monster.

A medium-sized carnivore, this hog-nosed skunk is the largest of all North American skunks. The snout is relatively long and wide, and the naked nose pad resembles that of a small hog. Hog-nosed skunks can be readily distinguished from other skunks by the lack of a white dot or medial bar near the eyes and by their primarily black body fur with a single white stripe of varying width that extends down the back and onto the tail.

Conepatus leuconotus

The hog-nosed skunk's body generally is larger, and the tail is shorter in proportion to the body, than in other skunks.

In Mexico, these skunks are found mainly in the tropical parts of San Luis Potosi, although they also occur in the mountains and coastal plains. They have been found in cornfields surrounded by low brushland, in grassy plains, and in scattered thickets of bull-horn acacia and other thorny plants in Veracruz. In Tamaulipas they have been found in thorn woodland, riparian forest, and the Tamaulipan plain, which consists of low scrub and cacti. In the United States, *C. leuconotus* has been found in live oak brush habitat, mesquite-brushland, improved pasture habitat, and areas of semi-open native grassland. Thorny brush and cactus are the predominant vegetation in the region of southern Texas where it occurs. Degradation of its habitat in southern Texas began in the 1700s and increased notably in the mid-1800s. In the past 65 years, 95 percent of the land once covered by native vegetation has been converted to agriculture.

Hog-nosed skunks are more insectivorous than striped or spotted skunks, and have been observed eating insects in cornfields in Mexico. Their forelimbs and claws are well developed for digging in extremely rough terrain, and they are especially adept at digging up beetles and larvae, thus earning the name rooter skunk. When insects are not plentiful, however, they tend to be more opportunistic feeders and will eat small vertebrates and fruits.

No direct information on the reproductive biology of *C. leuconotus* is available, but it is probably similar to that of *C. mesoleucus,* which breeds in February and March and produces a litter of two to four kits in late April or early May. By late August the young of *C. mesoleucus,* and presumably also of *C. leuconotus,* begin to disperse.

Hog-nosed skunks are nocturnal and more solitary than striped skunks. Much of their known behavior revolves around their food habits. There has been an abundance of research on the striped skunk because of its commensal relationship with man and its potential to carry rabies. However, to the average person a skunk is just a skunk, and skunks are (in)famous because of their noxious odor. Hog-nosed skunks avoid contact with humans whenever possible, and when they are observed they are considered "odd." Like all skunks, they are beneficial in agricultural areas because they destroy crop-damaging insects. *J. W. Dragoo and R. L. Honeycutt*

Size
Total length: 560–920 (709.49) mm (males); 580–740 (673.65) mm (females)
Length of tail: 224–410 (295.39) mm (males); 192–340 (260.26) mm (females)
Weight: 2,300–4,500 g

Identification
Conepatus leuconotus is larger than *C. mesoleucus,* and the dorsal stripe is much narrower and is reduced (or entirely absent) on the rump. The underside of the tail is black basally and white toward the tip. *C. leuconotus* can be distin-

guished from Mexican *C. semistriatus,* the striped hog-nosed skunk, which has a double white stripe, by stripe pattern.

Other Common Names
Gulf Coast hog-nosed skunk, white backed skunk, rooter skunk

Status
Currently being considered for endangered status by the U.S. Fish and Wildlife Service and the Texas Parks and Wildlife Department

Subspecies
Conepatus leuconotus leuconotus, southern Veracruz, Mexico
Conepatus leuconotus texensis, coastal plain of the Gulf of Mexico from Veracruz to the southern tip of Texas

References
Nowak, 1991

Western hog-nosed skunk | *Conepatus mesoleucus*

Although the western hog-nosed skunk's distribution once extended from Nicaragua to Colorado, today these skunks are common in the United States only in southern Arizona and New Mexico and western Texas. Specimens were collected in Colorado and Oklahoma during the 1920s and 30s, but in recent years no western hog-nosed skunks have been seen north of southern New Mexico. One subspecies, *Conepatus mesoleucus telmalestes,* from the Big Thicket of eastern Texas, is presumed extinct, and populations in Mexico and Central America probably are in decline.

Conepatus mesoleucus is about the same size as the striped skunk, *Mephitis mephitis,* but differs in appearance. *C. mesoleucus* has a long, naked nose pad and long claws. Typically, a single white stripe starts at the forehead, widens at the shoulders, and continues down the back to the tail, which is predominantly white. There is no white marking between the eyes. *C. mesoleucus* is smaller than *C. leuconotus,* the white stripe is broader on the rump, and the tail has little or no black coloration.

C. mesoleucus inhabits canyons, stream beds, and rough, rocky terrain in desert-scrub and mesquite-grasslands. Where these skunks are common, they can be seen foraging along highway shoulders. With the exception of the Big Thicket hog-nosed

Conepatus mesoleucus

The western hog-nosed skunk's mating season reportedly occurs from late February through early March. Gestation usually lasts for 60 days, with parturition occurring in April and May. Usually, two to four kits are produced per litter and by early August the young begin to disperse. Captive males have exhibited breeding behavior as early as late November, and females as early as mid-January. A gestation period of about 70 days has been recorded for a captive hog-nosed skunk. In the other two genera of skunks, *Mephitis* and *Spilogale,* variation in gestation period is attributed to delayed implantation, but little is known about the reproductive biology of hog-nosed skunks, especially with respect to delayed implantation.

When hog-nosed skunks are faced with danger they, like all skunks, can squirt a noxious liquid from their anal scent glands. However, this skunk's first response is to run into brush or under cactus for cover. It may then turn to face the pursuer and, depending on the size and threat of the predator, may stand on its hind legs and even take two or three steps forward. Then it will come down hard on its front paws and exhale a burst of air in a loud hiss. Finally, it will draw its paws under its body, flinging dirt backwards. A defensive, frightened skunk will crouch, stomp its front paws, raise its tail and hold it flat against its back, and bare its teeth. The animal then is in a position to bite and spray a predator, and will do both.

Hog-nosed skunks are adapted for digging in rough, rocky terrain and resemble badgers rather than other species of skunks with respect to this ability. They have tremendous strength in the forearms. As a result, these skunks are capable climbers, though not as agile as spotted skunks *(Spilogale).* Hog-nosed skunks have short, coarse fur, which is of little value commercially. They are beneficial to agriculture because they destroy harmful insect pests. *J. W. Dragoo and R. L. Honeycutt*

skunk, which occurs in the most humid and densely forested area of Texas, this skunk prefers desert climates and vegetation.

Hog-nosed skunks have been observed attacking and devouring small rodents. However, this species is more insectivorous by nature and will spend hours digging for grubs and larvae. Many naturalists have been unable to find a bait suitable for trapping these "carnivores" and have had to capture individuals by hand. Captive hog-nosed skunks, unlike striped skunks, have to be trained to eat dog food. However, they instinctively eat pears, raisins, zucchini, squash, green beans, radishes, green peppers, and a variety of other fruits and vegetables.

Size
Total length: 400–838.2 (626.4) mm (males); 452–725 (590.23) mm (females)
Length of tail: 127–351 (242.47) mm (males); 122–372 (236.36) mm (females)
Weight: 1,135–2,725 g

Identification
The western hog-nosed skunk is smaller than the eastern hog-nosed skunk, *Conepatus leuconotus,* and its tail is predominantly white underneath. The white color pattern continues as a single stripe on the back from the rump to the head. There is no white marking between the eyes and the nose pad is long and naked.

Other Common Names
White backed skunk, Texan skunk, badger skunk, conepate, rooter skunk

Status
Some subspecies of *Conepatus mesoleucus* may be endangered or extinct. Other subspecies are common, but patchily distributed, throughout the range.

Subspecies
Conepatus mesoleucus figginsi, western Baca County, Colorado
Conepatus mesoleucus filipensis, Oaxaca, Mexico
Conepatus mesoleucus fremonti, El Paso and Fremont counties, Colorado, and Black Mesa, Oklahoma
Conepatus mesoleucus mearnsi, southeastern New Mexico, western Texas south to Tamaulipas, San Luis Potosi, and Jalisco in central Mexico
Conepatus mesoleucus mesoleucus, Hidalgo to Chiapas, Mexico

Conepatus mesoleucus nelsoni, Colima, Michoacan, and Guerrero, Mexico
Conepatus mesoleucus nicaraguae, Honduras, Nicaragua, and El Salvador
Conepatus mesoleucus sonoriensis, Sonora and Sinaloa, Mexico
Conepatus mesoleucus telmalestes, Big Thicket of eastern Texas
Conepatus mesoleucus venaticus, southern Arizona, southwestern New Mexico, and Sonora and Chihuahua in north-central Mexico

References
Nowak, 1991

Family Odobenidae

The family Odobenidae contains only the single species *Odobenus rosmarus,* the walrus. This animal is well-adapted for life in Arctic seas and is an excellent swimmer and diver. It has a rotund body with a relatively small and stout head supported by a massive neck. The distinctive upper canine teeth form large, ever-growing tusks in both males and females.

Males are larger than females, with large adults ranging up to 3.5 m in length and weighing up to 1,700 kg. Both sexes are slow growing, with females reaching full adult size at about 10–12 years, and males at 15–16 years. Short, tawny brown hairs covering the thick (2–4 cm) skin give a chestnut to cinnamon color to the animals.

Walruses occur discontinuously across the Arctic, with a large gap between the Chukchi Sea and the central Canadian Arctic. They have traditionally been split into two subspecies, a Pacific and an Atlantic form, with a somewhat intermediate population occurring in the Laptev Sea of Russia.

The fossil history of walruses and their ancestral relatives is relatively well known, and can be traced back to at least Miocene times, some 22 million years ago. Pleistocene specimens resembling modern forms are known from Quebec southward to North Carolina, and in Europe from Scandinavia to France. Although earlier, ancestral walruses disappeared from the north Pacific a couple of million years ago, the modern forms probably re-invaded during the last interglacial period.

References
Mammalian Species 238

North American Genera
Odobenus

Walrus | *Odobenus rosmarus*

Walruses are ponderous and clumsy when out of the water, but they are adept swimmers, completely at home in Arctic seas. They spend about a third of their time sleeping on ice floes or on shore when ice is absent. Though circumpolar in distribution, they are limited to continental shelves and shoals, for they feed at depths of 100 m or less. To maintain access both to their food supply and to the air they breathe, they reside mainly in areas where the sea ice is unstable and some leads and channels are always present. When necessary, they can break through ice as thick as 20 cm and can maintain holes in heavier ice by chopping and abrading it with their tusks, but they tend to avoid such areas when possible.

Atlantic walruses, which occur from Hudson Bay to the Kara Sea, are smaller than Pacific walruses and have smoother skin and more rounded snouts. Pacific walruses reside principally in the Bering and Chukchi seas. A small population with somewhat intermediate physical characters inhabits the Laptev Sea, in Russia's central Arctic. The Laptev walruses are thought by some Russian scientists to be different enough from both the Atlantic and Pacific populations to merit subspecific status, but this has not yet been demonstrated to the satisfaction of the rest of the scientific community.

The most distinctive physical attributes of walruses are their tusks, which are greatly enlarged upper canine teeth. These

teeth have evolved primarily as "social organs." That is, their most important function is in behavioral displays by males, in which one animal attempts to dominate another by posturing with his tusks raised high, showing off their size to the opponent. If display alone is not sufficient, the tusks are used as weapons to strike, point-first, and injure the opponent. Tusks are present in both sexes but are much larger in males than in females. They grow most rapidly in young animals (4–8 cm per year), more slowly in adults (1–2 cm per year), and slowest in old age (as little as 1 or 2 mm per year). As they increase in length, they also increase in basal girth.

Odobenus rosmarus

Walruses are known to feed on more than 60 different kinds of prey, most of which are bottom-dwelling invertebrates that range in size from tiny crustaceans weighing less than 0.1 gram to various kinds of worms, clams, shrimps, snails, holothureans, octopuses, anemones, tunicates, and large crabs weighing up to 1,000 g. In addition, they occasionally prey on vertebrates, including some fishes and seals. They apparently locate and uncover their prey pig-fashion, using their snouts rather than their tusks for digging. They are able to extract the meat from clams and snails by means of powerful oral suction, ingesting the meat and rejecting the shells. As many as 6,000 prey can be consumed in a single feeding bout.

Walruses have been hunted for thousands of years, mainly for their meat, hides, oil, and the ivory in their tusks. The walrus's only enemies other than humans are killer whales and polar bears, which prey mainly on the very young. The adult walrus's hide, which is 2–3 cm thick, is comparable to that of elephants and rhinoceroses in being extremely effective armor, not only against the attacks of predators but also against blows inflicted by other walruses with their tusks. The hide is cov-

ered by a short (1 cm), coarse coat of reddish-brown to tawny hair that is shed and replaced during the summer and autumn. Calves-of-the-year molt first, followed by the older animals. In adult males, especially, the molt may be so complete that they become entirely naked for a time before any of the new pelage appears.

In adulthood male walruses develop local thickenings of their hide, mainly on the neck and shoulders, where they receive the most tusk-strikes in battle. Whether these bosses are the result of scarring or some other condition is unknown. Their absence in females, who also bear the scars of battle, suggests that they are a secondary sexual character, perhaps genetically or hormonally induced.

Walruses breed mainly in February, in the darkness of the Arctic winter and deep within the pack ice. Because of their remoteness and the unfavorable conditions for observation at that time, little is known of their breeding behavior. During the winter, adult females and their young tend to congregate in groups of 5–30 animals. Each such group is attended by one or more adult males, which engage in both visual and vocal displays in the water nearby. Presumably, females are attracted to the displaying males and copulation takes place in the icy water. Females generally breed for the first time at 6 or 7 years of age; males become capable of breeding by 9 or 10 years but are not able to compete for mates until they are about 15 years old. Each impregnated female gives birth to a single calf about 15 months after mating. Because of the long pregnancy, females breed at intevals of two years or longer. *F. H. Fay*

Size
Total length: 2.5–3.5 m (males); 2.3–3.1 m (females)
Weight: 590–1,656 kg (males); 400–1,250 kg (females)

Identification
Distinguished from all other pinnipeds by its broad, deep snout covered with short stiff vibrissae and the presence of long, whitish tusks descending from the upper jaw.

Recent Synonyms
Odobenus obesus (Pacific)

Other Common Names
Morse, avik, ayveq, amak

Status
Common

Subspecies
Odobenus rosmarus divergens, Pacific Arctic
Odobenus rosmarus rosmarus, Atlantic Arctic

References
Mammalian Species 238; Fay, 1981

Family Otariidae

There are 7 genera and 14 species of eared seals found worldwide. Four species in four separate genera inhabit the shores and offshore waters of North America. Members of this family, which includes the sea lions and fur seals, more closely resemble land mammals than do those in the Family Phocidae. There are Miocene fossils from the North Pacific.

Eared seals range in length from about 1–3.5 meters, and weights vary from 25–1,100 kg. In this group, males are always larger than females. The body shape is the familiar fusiform body of seals and sea lions, and a tail is always present. Although the common name would imply large ears, they are in fact rather small, but distinct. Locomotion is primarily by use of the front flippers in water, but these animals can move adroitly on land by using both front and hind flippers. The flippers are cartilaginous, thickest at the leading edge, and bear rudimentary nails.

The shape of the head is somewhat variable, with sea lions having shorter, blunter snouts than fur seals, in general. The pelage is also variable: sea lions tend to have rather coarse guard hairs covering only a small amount of underfur, whereas the fur seals have a thick, luxurious underfur, the commercial value of which greatly jeopardized their existence at various times in the past.

Eared seals are found on rocky islands and in sheltered bays along the Pacific Coast of North America. They are active both day and night, and have well-developed senses of vision, hearing, and olfaction. They feed mainly on fish and small marine invertebrates like squid and crustaceans.

During the breeding season these animals are highly gregarious. Males establish territories, and females join them as the season progresses. A single bull may control up to 50 females in some species. After a year-long gestation period that may include some interval of delayed implantation, the females give birth, enter post-partum estrus, and breed again in quick succession. The young normally do not swim for the first couple of weeks, and may remain with the mother up to 3 years in some species.

References
Nowak, 1991; Scheffer, 1958

North American Genera
Callorhinus
Arctocephalus
Eumetopias
Zalophus

Northern fur seal | *Callorhinus ursinus*

North American populations of the northern fur seal breed on the Pribilof Islands, on Bogoslof Island in the Aleutians, and on San Miguel Island in the Channel Islands of southern California. Northern fur seals also breed in Russia on the Commander and central Kuril islands and on Roben Island. During the fall-winter nonbreeding season the Pribilof seals range widely for five to eight months in the Gulf of Alaska and North Pacific. In the eastern Pacific a few seals range as far south as the U.S.-Mexican border and in the western Pacific, as far south as southern Japan. Seals tagged as pups on their islands of birth have been recorded as adult breeding females on different breeding grounds. Because there is no separation of breeding populations, all northern fur seals are classified as *Callorhinus ursinus*.

San Miguel Island was colonized in the late 1950s and early 1960s. Since then the population has steadily increased. In 1992 1,837 pups were counted and the total population was estimated at more than 8,000.

On Bogoslof Island immature and adult males were first observed in 1976 and 1977, and in 1980 the first two pups were observed there. By 1988 about 80 pups were found and the total population had grown to more than 400. By 1992 about 500 pups were observed and the total population was estimated at about 2,235 seals.

At sea the seals are widely scattered except in areas of plentiful food. They leave their breeding islands in late fall and rarely, unless sick or injured, come ashore. Adult males are the last to leave and seldom migrate south of Alaskan waters.

Adult females and immature animals of both sexes travel farthest south during the fall and winter nonbreeding season.

Adult males establish their territories on island breeding grounds (rookeries) in late May or June. The females come ashore, join a territorial bull, and give birth to a single pup in late June or July. Several days after the pup's birth the cow becomes receptive to her harem master and mating takes place. The fertilized egg undergoes delayed implantation in the female's uterus; the fetus does not develop until late in the winter and the new pup is born approximately a year after mating took place.

Newborn male pups weigh about 5.4 kg and females weigh about 4.5 kg. The pups are born with black fur; during the late summer and fall the black pelage is shed and replaced by silver-gray guard hair, which covers the soft insulating underfur. While the seals are at sea during their first winter, the pelage becomes golden brown. Females remain in various shades of brown throughout their lives, but males become darker, some almost black, as they mature. When their fur is wet all seals appear almost black. On land, when the fur dries, the various shades of brown appear. On breeding rookeries the pelage color may appear to change when the seals become soiled with mud and fecal matter.

The Pribilof Islands were discovered by a Russian fur seal hunter, Gerasim Pribilof, in 1786. The fur seal population remained prosperous under Russian control, particularly from 1835 to 1867. After the United States purchased Alaska in 1867, unmanaged hunting of seals at sea (pelagic sealing) began and continued uncontrolled through the early 1900s. The pelagic

harvest consisted mostly of females. After as many as 800,000 seals had been taken at sea it is estimated that the Pribilof population dropped to between 200,000 and 300,000 seals.

In 1911 the United States, Great Britain (for Canada), Russia, and Japan signed an international treaty to stop North Pacific pelagic sealing. Both Russian and U.S. breeding populations of fur seals had declined drastically. Under U.S. government management, only immature (nonbreeding) males were allowed to

Callorhinus ursinus

decline. These nets are made of plastic (nondegradable) fibers. Floating, damaged net scraps, discarded at sea, are mistaken for floating kelp by fur seals, who climb onto floating kelp to survey their surroundings. Many seals have been found entangled in net scraps. Many others have undoubtedly perished and never been found.

The fur seal population declined alarmingly between the 1960s and the late 1980s. The major cause of the decline has not been pinpointed. Is it the annual commercial harvest of millions of tons of food fish? Is it mortality caused by entanglement in discarded net scraps? Or is it a change in management of the commercial seal harvest, which permitted the taking of 300,000 female seals between 1956 and 1968?

All of these factors have contributed to the Pribilof seal population decline, but the major cause has not yet been defined. Surprisingly, the fur seal populations of the Russian islands have not shown a similar decline. Also, the small populations on Bogoslof and San Miguel islands have grown during recent years.

Natives of the Pribilof Islands are permitted a small annual subsistence harvest, but no fur seals have been commercially harvested since 1984, when the Fur Seal Convention lapsed. Because it was determined that the Pribilof fur seal population had declined to less than 50 percent of its Optimum Sustainable Population (OSP) as observed in the 1950s, this population was designated as depleted under the Marine Mammal Protection Act on 17 June 1988. No commercial harvesting has been permitted since that date. *K. W. Kenyon*

be harvested, in late June and July, on the Pribilof Islands. The population prospered and reached a high of 1.5 to 2 million seals in the late 1940s and 1950s.

Large scale pelagic fishing with deepwater trawls and 30-mile-long gillnets began in the North Pacific and Bering sea in the middle 1950s, and the Pribilof seal population began to

Size
Length: up to 2.1 m (males); 1.2–1.5 m
 (females)
Weight: 136–279 kg (males); 30–50 kg (females)

Identification
The northern fur seal is distinguished from the Guadalupe fur seal, *Arctocephalus townsendi*, which shares the southern tip of its breeding and winter range off southern California, by having a more sharply pointed nose, and by its

pelage forming a straight line at the base of the foreflipper, rather than extending into a point.

Recent Synonyms
Callorhinus alascanus

Other Common Names
Alaska fur seal

Status
The Pribilof population declined in recent

years to less than 50 percent of its 1950s size and was designated as depleted under the Marine Mammal Protection Act in June, 1988. Small new colonies on Bogoslof Island (in the Aleutians) and San Miguel Island (Channel Islands, California) are increasing in size.

References
Gentry, 1981; Haley, 1986; Reeves et al., 1992; Scheffer, 1970

Guadalupe fur seal | *Arctocephalus townsendi*

During the 19th century an unknown type of fur seal was hunted nearly to extermination off the coast of Baja California, Mexico. In 1892 the U.S. Department of State sent Charles Haskins Townsend, then with the U.S. Fish Commission, to Isla de Guadalupe, Mexico, to identify the fur seal reported on

islands in this region. Townsend sighted seven live fur seals in the water but none were observed on land. He collected four weathered skulls from an old killing ground on Guadalupe and deposited them at the Smithsonian Institution. In 1897 Dr. C. H. Merriam described the specimens as a new species of

fur seal. The Guadalupe fur seal is the only member of the genus *Arctocephalus* that occurs in the Northern Hemisphere. At the turn of the century the species was feared by some to be extinct. In 1975 the Mexican government declared Guadalupe Island a sanctuary for pinnipeds, and today, these fur seals are slowly increasing. Today they breed and pup only at Guadalupe and Islas San Benito, Baja California, Mexico.

Rookeries were originally found from San Miguel and San Nicolas islands, off southern California, south to the Mexican islands of Isla de Guadalupe and Isla Cedros. The seals may also have bred on Isla Socorro in the Revillagigedo Archipelago, Mexico, but that is questionable. At present, these fur seals land and breed regularly only along the precipitous, rocky coast of Guadalupe, using the various caves and recesses along the narrow lava shoreline, and on the rocky coastline of Isla Benito del Este, one of the Islas San Benito. Occasionally fur seals are sighted in the Gulf of California, Mexico, the Channel Islands off southern California, and off central California.

Field identification characters that may be useful in distinguishing Guadalupe fur seals from other Northern Hemisphere otarriids include the shape of the head and hind flippers and the appearance of the pelage. Adult males do not have a pronounced head crest, and the muzzle is narrow, pointed, and upcurved. The flippers are conspicuously larger and the hind flippers have a distinctive shape. The pelage has a thick, grizzled

appearance, especially when dry, compared to the coarser hair of sea lions.

The most unusual behavior of the Guadalupe fur seal is that males defend territories that include recesses and caves. These areas provide important shade from the direct exposure to sunlight of hot afternoons. Guadalupe fur seals are commonly observed floating on the surface of the water with their hind flippers or a pectoral flipper exposed to the air. This behavior is highly correlated with the increase of air temperature during the day.

Guadalupe fur seals give birth and copulate in May, June, and July. Age at sexual maturity is unknown for both sexes. Territorial bulls are usually observed in or near a cave or recess where there are tide pools or access to the sea. This allows the bulls to be relatively isolated from each other. Females generally aggregate in harems during the breeding season. The length of newborn pups is about 0.66 m.

Little is known about their feeding behavior or food habits, but scats from a few fur seals contained remains of various types of squid and fish. Fish remains included frigate mackerel, Pacific mackerel, and Pacific sardine. Both jumbo and nail squid were also identified.

Townsend observed seven live fur seals during his visit to Guadalupe in 1892. In 1926 about 60 animals were observed on the island. Most of these were killed by fishermen in 1928. The San Diego Zoo collected two live animals in 1928, and no others were seen until 1949, when a single bull was spotted on San Nicolas Island, off southern California. In 1954 only 14 animals were found on Guadalupe. Since that time the population has

Arctocephalus townsendi

been slowly increasing. A survey in 1987 counted 3,259 fur seals, including 998 pups. In the early 1990s, the total island population was estimated at 7,348 individuals. Compared to other recovering species of *Arctocephalus,* the growth rate of the Guadalupe fur seal population was lower. The population size decreased in 1992 as a result of an El Niño event and Hurricane Darby. Population growth has probably been adversely affected a number of times in the 20th century by El Niño events, and the seals will remain vulnerable to El Niño conditions and hurricanes until the population grows to a much larger size. *R. L. Brownell, Jr., and J. P. Gallo-Reynoso*

Size
Males are larger than females.
Total length: 1.9–2.4 (2.2) m (males); 1.4–1.9 (1.5) m (females)
Weight: 150–220 (190) kg (males); 40–55 (50) kg (females)

Identification
Like other fur seals, these animals have a thick pelage, with dense underfur. Both sexes are dark brown or dusky black. Only the adult male Guadalupe fur seal is readily distinguishable from other North Pacific otariids. Adult males have a large head with a long, pointed muzzle.

Other Common Names
Foca fina, lobo fino de Guadalupe

Status
Vulnerable (IUCN)

References
Fleischer, 1987; Reeves et al., 1992

Steller sea lion | *Eumetopias jubatus*

Steller sea lions occur throughout the North Pacific rim from Japan to southern California. They abound on numerous breeding sites (rookeries) in California, Oregon, British Columbia, and Alaska; Washington is the only western coastal state that does not contain a Steller sea lion rookery. Unlike their more gregarious cousin, the California sea lion, Steller sea lions tend to avoid people and prefer isolated offshore rocks and islands to breed and rest. Although rookeries and resting (haulout) sites occur in many areas, the locations used are specific and change little from year to year. Steller sea lions tend to return to their birth island as adults to breed, but they range widely during their first few years and during the non-breeding season.

They are attractive animals. Pups are born with a wavy, chocolate brown fur that molts after they are about 3 months of age. Adult fur varies from pale buff to reddish-brown, with most of the underparts and flippers a dark brown to black. Both sexes become blonder with age. Adult males have long, coarse hair on the chest, neck, and shoulders, which are massive and muscular. A thick blubber layer retains body heat; the fur is not a thermoregulatory mechanism in adults. The species is rarely seen in aquaria because of its large size and generally pugnacious nature. Steller sea lions are an important subsistence resource for Alaskan natives, who hunt them for food and other uses. Three hundred or more are taken annually in Alaska.

Sea lions probably evolved in temperate waters of the North Pacific Ocean; the earliest known remains of a sea lion ancestor are between 10 and 12 million years old. Fossil remains of Steller sea lions three to four million years old were found in California.

Steller sea lion population numbers have declined by more than 90 percent in the last 20 years in most of Alaska and southern California. Populations in Oregon and southeastern Alaska have remained stable. The worst declines occurred in the Aleutian Islands and Gulf of Alaska, areas that historically were the centers of abundance. Causes for these declines have not been identified, but may be related to disease or to reduced food availability, because of natural changes in the ocean or because of commercial fishing. The large population declines resulted in the species being listed as "threatened" by the United States in 1992. A survey in 1989 provided an estimate of about 116,000 Steller sea lions range-wide, of which about 15 percent

Eumetopias jubatus

were in Russia, 70 percent in Alaska, 9 percent in British Columbia, and 6 percent in Oregon and California.

Rookeries and haulout sites are a cacophony, with animals of both sexes and all ages vocalizing throughout the day and night. Territorial male sounds are low frequency. They signal threats to other males and are used for courting females or for comfort. Females vocalize less and at a higher frequency. Pups have a bleating, sheep-like cry; their voices deepen with age.

Grooming is performed by bending the head and neck backward and scratching with the claws of the hind flippers. Sea lions also rub themselves on rocks or on each other. While swimming, the foreflippers are used primarily for movement and the rear flippers for braking and turning. On land the rear flippers are turned forward to walk, with the animal balancing on the tarsal region of the rear flippers and on the foreflippers.

Females reach sexual maturity between 3 and 8 years of age and may breed into their early 20s. Males reach sexual maturity at about the same age, but do not have the size or skill to obtain and keep a breeding territory until they are 9 years of age or older. Males may return to the same territory for up to 7 years, but usually not beyond 3 years. While they are on the territory during the breeding season, they sometimes fast for 1–2 months. The rigors of fighting to obtain and hold a territory and the physiological stress during the mating season reduces their life expectancy. Males rarely live beyond their mid-teens; females may live as long as 30 years. Males establish territories in May in anticipation of the arrival of females. Copulations may occur in the water but most are on land.

Viable births begin at the rookeries in late May and continue through early July. Like most pinnipeds, Steller sea lions give birth to a single pup each year; twinning is rare. The sex ratio at birth is slightly in favor of males. The mother nurses the pup during the day and goes to sea on nightly feeding trips. Pups generally are weaned before the next breeding season, but it is not unusual for a female to nurse her offspring for a year or more. During the breeding period, females swim only about 30 km from the rookery to feed. Later, feeding trips tend to go farther offshore and last longer. A typical feeding dive is usually less than 50 m deep. Their food includes most schooling fish, squid, and octopus found in continental shelf waters to 900 km or more offshore, but also includes an occasional fur seal or other small seal. In Alaska the most common prey is walleye pollock. *T. R. Loughlin*

Size

Males are larger than females.

Total length: 2.8 m (males); 2.3 m (females) (maximums about 3.25 m and 2.9 m)

Weight: 566 kg (males); 263 kg (females) (maximums about 1,120 kg and 350 kg)

Identification

Eumetopias jubatus has a distinctive, conspicuous space between the upper fourth and fifth post-canine teeth. It is the largest member of the family Otariidae, and can be distinguished from the California sea lion (*Zalophus californianus*) by paler color and larger size. Underwater, *E. jubatus* appears blond and *Z. californianus* appears darker.

Recent Synonyms

Eumetopias jubata

Other Common Names

Northern sea lion, seevitchie (Aleut)

Status

Eastern stock (east of 144° W) classified by the United States government as threatened; western stock classified as endangered

References

Mammalian Species 283; Loughlin et al., 1993; National Marine Fisheries Service, 1992

California sea lion | *Zalophus californianus*

California sea lions are now restricted to breeding mostly on remote or protected islands off the west coast of North America. The largest breeding populations are found in the Channel Islands and other islands along the coast of Baja California. Smaller breeding colonies are found on South Farallon and Año Nuevo islands and off the Gulf of California. The largest breeding colony is found on San Miguel Island. Females and juveniles are found within their breeding range throughout the year. Adult males move north in autumn and winter, ranging as far north as Vancouver Island, Canada. Galapagos sea lions are restricted to the Galapagos Archipelago. *Z. c. japonicus* was formerly abundant in the Sea of Japan, but by 1950 only 50–60 individuals were left on Takeshima Island. Since then, no confirmed observation of the species in the northeastern Pacific has been reported.

California sea lions are perhaps the most familiar species of pinniped because of their popularity in zoos, aquaria, and circuses. They breed on land, gathering once a year in large, noisy aggregations in rocky or sandy beaches. The breeding season extends from May through July in California. Ninety percent of all births occur in June. In the Galapagos the breed-

Zalophus californianus

ing season is much longer, extending from May to January, with 90 percent of pupping occurring over 120 days with a shifting peak in births.

Females give birth on land to a single pup in a season and nurse it for up to two years. Most pups are weaned by one year of age, but when prey is scarce, a greater proportion of yearlings continues suckling for a second year. Females remain with their pups continuously through the first week postpartum. After this period on land, and throughout the entire lactation period, females divide their time between foraging trips to sea and visits to the breeding rookery to nurse their young. Estrus occurs 3–4 weeks after parturition. Mating takes place in the water or in intertidal areas.

Because mating takes place long after pupping occurs and females move freely across territory boundaries, males are not able to control access to females, and this affects mating behavior. In some areas females form "milling" groups and wander around the rookery choosing mates. In other areas, females also form groups, but mate with the male nearest the tide pool they use for thermoregulation. In other cases, females do not form groups, but still choose their mates. The form of mating system may be determined by the type of habitat, environmental temperature ranges, and foraging conditions.

Adult males defend territories on land or in shallow water along the coast. Throughout their period of tenure (27 to 45 days), the males fast and patrol their territories continuously, barking to advertise their presence. Males may hold territories for up to six consecutive years.

All foraging occurs at sea. California sea lions in southern California feed mostly on northern anchovy (Engraulis mordax), Pacific mackerel (Scomber), jack mackerel (Trachurus symmetricus), rock fish (Sebastes) and market squid (Loligo opalescens). In the Galapagos they feed mainly on sardines (Sardinops sagax). Sea lions are opportunistic feeders, so their diet changes according to seasonal and annual variations in local prey availability. Most foraging occurs in shallow waters (30–80 m), but in El Niño years, when fish disperse and migrate to greater depths, the animals have to dive deeper, longer, and spend more time at sea to catch their prey. As a result, pups grow more slowly and, in extreme cases, die when their mothers are away for too long. In severe El Niño years, even adults, both females and males, may starve to death.

California sea lions suffer little predation while at sea. Some are eaten by great white, blue, or hammerhead sharks, or by killer whales, with little effect on the populations. At present the main cause of mortality is entanglement and drowning in monofilament gill nets and illegal killing by commercial fishermen (about 1,500 per year in the 1980s). California sea lions are now legally protected throughout their range, except in Japan. *P. Majluf*

Size

Males are about four times larger than females. Galapagos sea lions (Z. c. wollebaeki) are smaller than those from California and Mexico (Z. c. californianus).

Total length: 2–2.5 (2.14 m) (males); 1.6–1.8 (1.64 m) (females)

Weight: 350–400 (375 kg) (males); 90–120 (94 kg) (females)

Identification

Adult males are usually dark brown, almost black, but can be as pale in color as females and juveniles, which are generally tawny brown. Pups are dark brown or black from birth to about 4–6 months, when they molt and attain the juvenile coloration. Adult males also have a thick neck and a prominent sagittal crest that is paler in color than the rest of the body.

Other Common Names

Galapagos sea lion

Status

The Z. c. californianus population (United States and Mexico) was estimated at about 160,000 individuals in 1989 and is assumed to be increasing. The Z. c. wollebaeki population was estimated in 1979 at 30,000 individuals; Z. c. japonicus is probably extinct.

Subspecies

Zalophus californianus californianus, southern California and Baja California

Zalophus californianus japonicus, Sea of Japan

Zalophus californianus wollebaeki, Galapagos Archipelago

References

Gentry and Kooyman, 1986; Peterson and Bartholomew, 1967; Reeves et al., 1992; Reijnders et al., 1993; Renouf, 1991; Riedman, 1990; Trillmich and Ono, 1991

Family Phocidae

Earless seals belong to 19 species in 10 genera, with 9 species in 5 genera represented in North America. They occur generally in polar to temperate seas, with isolated monk seal species found farther south. They tend to occur both in land-fast and pack ice, and on offshore islands and rocks. The size range is from just over a meter in ringed seals to almost 5 meters in the largest southern elephant seal bulls. Weights range from 45–2,400 kilograms.

Unlike eared seals, phocids are much less adept at moving on land, and are specialized for deep dives and long underwater stays. Their limbs are much more anatomically adapted for swimming and steering in the water than for locomotion on land. Nevertheless, they remain tied to the land for the parturition and early development of the young. The gestation period is 10–11 months, including a 3-month period of delayed implantation. These animals are quite long-lived, with records up to 56 years.

This group originated in the North Atlantic region in Miocene times. It seems most likely that they were derived from otter-like ancestors in Europe or Western Asia. Subsequent specialization for life in the sea included a shift in dentition from the variable array of cutting and slicing teeth found in terrestrial carnivores to a uniform row, usually of five teeth, adapted for relatively small, soft foods. Food items include fish, squids, shrimps, and a variety of other crustaceans and mollusks. One exception is the leopard seal, which is a skillful predator on other seals and penguins.

All of the North American species mate in the water except the gray and elephant seals. Much more is known about the social behavior of the highly territorial, land-breeding species, as they are much easier to observe. However, underwater territoriality is probably the norm in the water-breeding species as well. Males may restrict access to females by controlling breathing holes in the ice, for example.

Although many species suffered from overharvesting in the past, most are strictly regulated at present. Populations of most species are stable or increasing, suggesting that current management strategies are effective.

References
Macdonald, 1984

North American Genera
Phoca
Halichoerus
Erignathus
Cystophora
Mirounga

Ribbon seal | *Phoca fasciata*

Ribbon seals are found mainly in the Okhotsk Sea (Russia) and in the Bering Sea. Occasionally they are found in the Chukchi Sea, south of the Aleutian Islands in the northern Pacific Ocean, or in the Beaufort Sea. During the pupping, mating, and molting periods in late winter and spring, these seals are concentrated in heavy pack ice 100–200 km offshore. They are almost never seen on land. In the late spring and summer, when the northern seas are free of ice, it is presumed that ribbon seals are pelagic, living in the open sea. Few seals are seen then and their distribution is poorly known. It is unclear to what extent the seals in the Okhotsk and Bering seas intermingle, and whether they should be treated as one population or two. Present estimates are that the Bering Sea population (60,000–90,000) is about half the size of that of the Okhotsk Sea (130,000–140,000).

Male ribbon seals become sexually mature between 3 and 5 years of age and females between 2 and 4 years. Mature females give birth to a single young on pack ice once each year, in the spring (most births occur from 5–15 April), as do many other ice-breeding phocid seals. The ice floes they use are a relatively long distance from shore, which probably removes the threat of predators such as foxes, polar bears, or even humans. Females apparently leave their pups on the ice and disappear for hours at a time, perhaps to feed, although feeding

Phoca fasciata

during lactation has not been confirmed in this species. Most phocids fast throughout their short lactation. Lactation in the ribbon seal is thought to be 3–4 weeks long. This is similar to harbor seals, and as female harbor seals and ribbon seals are about the same size and harbor seal females need to feed to sustain lactation, it is plausible to think that ribbon seal females feed while they are away from their pups.

Unlike other seals, ribbon seals have an inflatable air sac extending from the posterior end of the trachea over the ribs on the right side. This air sac is better developed in males, although it is also present in adult females. Its function is unknown, but the difference in the degree to which it is developed in the two sexes suggests that it may be used by males to produce underwater vocalizations in competition for mates. Vocal communication may be more useful than visual or chemical communication for animals that interact mostly in

water. Recordings of underwater vocalizations in ribbon seals have been made during the presumed mating period. Particularly distinctive are a long sweeping sound that declines in frequency and a short puffing noise.

Ribbon seals appear to be primarily fish eaters, although samples of their diets are available only from the springtime. Their spring diet in the Okhotsk Sea is mostly pollock *(Theragra chalcograma),* with some cephalopods (squid and octopus), shrimp (mostly *Pandalus goniurus),* and Pacific cod *(Gadus macrocephalus).* In the Bering Sea it is mainly pollock, eelpout *(Lycodes)* and capelin *(Mallotus villosus).*

The unusually pelagic nature of this species makes it a difficult one for biologists to study. The use of new technology such as satellite telemetry and molecular genetic techniques will undoubtedly help. *D. J. Boness*

Size
Total length: 1.55–1.65 m
Weight: about 70–80 kg

Identification
Adult males are dark brown to black with white to yellowish bands around the neck, flippers, and rear flanks. Adult females have similar coloration, but there is less contrast between the background and bands or ribbons than in the males. Pups are born with a white

coat (lanugo) that is shed at about five weeks of age; for the remainder of first year the coat is blue-gray dorsally and silver-gray ventrally.

Recent Synonyms
Histriophoca fasciata

Other Common Names
Banded seal

Status
Good population surveys are not available, but the most recent estimates (1979–1982) suggest a world population of between 193,000 and 240,000 animals.

References
Lentfer, 1988; Reeves et al., 1992; Reijnders et al., 1993

Harp seal | *Phoca groenlandica*

The public has a love-ignore relationship with harp seals. For a few weeks each spring, the media focus on the harp seals born on the pack ice of the Gulf of St. Lawrence (the "Gulf") and off the coast of Newfoundland and Labrador (the "Front") during the annual hunt. Then harp seals fade from the public mind for another 11 months, just when they start a fantastic journey that will take them to the far corners of their Arctic range and back again—more than 5,000 km.

In North America, harp seals range from Nova Scotia up the Canadian east coast and into the Arctic, including Foxe Basin and Hudson Bay, and as far north as Ellesmere Island. Their range extends west to the central Arctic archipelago and east to Greenland. This population, named for its pupping area, is known as the Northwest Atlantic stock. There are two other stocks, the Jan Mayen stock, which pups northeast of Iceland, and the White Sea stock, which pups north of Russia.

Throughout much of their range, harp seals are associated with sea ice; their annual migration corresponds closely with the seasonal limits of pack ice. This association is most apparent during the spring pupping season, when harp seals haul out in expansive herds on the pack ice of the Gulf and Front to produce and nurse their pups. Each female gives birth to a single pup that she nurses on fat-rich milk for about 10 days. The mother does not feed during this time and may lose 30 kg or 25 percent of her weight. The pup grows from about 10 kg to 35 kg, a weight gain of approximately 2.5 kg per day!

The white coat of the pup insulates it from the cold and traps heat from the sun, much as a greenhouse does. As weaning approaches, the white hair starts to shed and within a couple of weeks, the weaned "beater" has a new silver-gray coat with black blotches. It lives off blubber stored during nursing and loafs on the ice and learns to swim. The adults mate to produce next year's pup and then move to ice farther north to molt in the warm spring sun. Through successive molts, the spots of the beater and bedlamer are replaced by the harp pattern of the fully mature animals. Some males develop a dark coat, referred to as "sooty," at about four years of age. By June, most harp seals are moving to Arctic waters of Canada and Greenland. Harp seals spend about six months in the north, consuming fish and invertebrates to meet about 54 percent of their annual energy needs. Although conception occurs in the spring, implantation of the fertilized ovum is delayed until early August. This allows the females time to restore their energy reserves and synchronizes pupping for early the following March.

Harp seals seem to change their personalities between the ice in spring and the Arctic in summer. Thousands of harp seals are present on the ice during pupping and molting. They crawl about, spend much of their time sleeping, and the younger ani-

mals are somewhat solitary. At sea the quintessential harp seal charges about with several to hundreds of its kind, porpoising, leaping, and swimming on its back to peer over its stomach or below. They look like herds of aquatic mustangs, surrounded by froth and foam instead of dust. Aboriginals from Canada and Greenland hunt these herds, but much less than before

Phoca groenlandica

Europe banned the importation of products from seal pups. The major hunt remains in the south during the pupping and molting periods, although this hunt has also declined. In some areas, it has been replaced economically, but not culturally, by a growing tourist industry that shows harp seals to visitors from around the world. *R. E. A. Stewart*

Size
Total length: 1.68–1.9 (1.8) M
Weight: 115–140 (130) kg

Identification
Adults are identified easily by a black lyre-shaped marking on the back and by the black face. Their white color and general appearance distinguishes very young harp seal pups from those of other seal species in the range. Hooded seal *(Cystophora cristata)* pups have blue backs; gray seal *(Halichoerus grypus)* pups are larger and have darker faces with "Roman" noses. Juvenile and younger adult harp seals may be confused with other spotted seals. Harp seals have fewer spots than do harbor seals *(Phoca vitulina)* and hooded seals. The spots on ringed seals *(Phoca hispida)* form rings, giving that seal its common name.

Recent Synonyms
Pagophilus groenlandicus

Other Common Names
Greenland seal, saddle-backed seal, jumping seal, beater (a weaned young-of-the-year), bedlamer (a harp seal with spots, before the mature harp pattern appears)

Status
Abundant

References
Lavigne and Kovacs, 1988; Reeves et al., 1992

Ringed seal | *Phoca hispida*

The ringed seal is the smallest of the northern phocids, or true seals, and the most common seal of the Arctic. Its range is circumpolar in both the Arctic and subarctic, and it is most often found in association with ice throughout the year. Ringed seals range as far south as Newfoundland and as far east as the Baltic Sea in the North Atlantic Ocean. In the Pacific they range throughout the Bering Sea and as far south as the Sea of Japan. Ringed seals are also found in several freshwater lakes, including Ladoga and Saimaa, near the Gulf of Finland, and Nettilling Lake, Baffin Island. In part owing to their wide distribution, ringed seals have been subdivided into five subspecies. Three subspecies have been placed on the IUCN (International Union for Conservation of Nature and Natural Resources) Red List of Threatened Animals: *P. h. botnica* and *P. h. ladoga* are listed as vulnerable, and *P. h. saimensis* is listed as endangered. Both *P. h. hispida* and *P. h. ochotensis* populations are abundant and relatively stable, although there are annual fluctuations in abundance that depend on ice conditions in different areas.

Ringed seals are unique among seals in their use of lairs under ice and snow. These are most often constructed around ice hummocks, along pressure ridges, and in snow accumulations or drifts. Lairs can vary in size, shape, and number of chambers, but the most common birth lairs have an elongated chamber that is about 2.5 m by 3.0 m in size. Ringed seals maintain a hole to the water within their lairs by using the strong nails on their foreflippers to scratch away newly formed ice. Lairs used by rutting adult males can usually be distinguished from other lairs by a strong, pungent odor associated with oily secretions from the males' facial skin glands.

The mating system of the ringed seal is incompletely known, although some evidence, such as increased underwater vocalizations, strong site fidelity, incidence of wounds on adult males, and the strong odor of adult males during the breeding season, suggests that males are at least slightly polygynous. Females become sexually mature between four and eight years of age and males mature at five to seven years. Ringed seals mate in the water shortly after the female gives birth. Following a period of delayed implantation of approximately 2.5 months, gestation lasts about 9 months.

Pupping occurs between mid-March and mid-April. The female gives birth to a single, white-coated pup that weighs 4.5 to 5.0 kg and measures 0.6 to 0.65 m in length. Pups more than double their birth weights over the course of lactation, which appears to vary from 3 to 7 weeks across the ringed seal's range. At the time that pups are weaned, they have shed their white coats and replaced them with a silvery coat that lacks the

Phoca hispida

rings characteristic of the adult ringed seal, and they and their mothers have abandoned the birth lairs. In June and July, when the ice is breaking up, and after the pups have been weaned, the ringed seals gather on the ice to molt.

The diet of ringed seals varies with time of year and location. Fish species such as Arctic cod *(Boreogadus saida)* and saffron cod *(Eleginus)* are common prey items during the fall, winter, and spring, whereas euphausiids (for example, *Thysanoessa),* shrimp (for example, *Crangon* and *Pandalus),* and other crustaceans (for example, *Mysis)* predominate in the late spring and early summer. Ringed seals appear to eat less during the summer, while they are molting, which might be because of the amount of time the seals spend out of the water, or could reflect changes in prey availability.

There are many potential ringed seal predators, of which the most significant seem to be polar bears, arctic foxes, wal-

rus, and humans. Arctic foxes are known to take pups from birth lairs, and polar bear predation on all ages of seals is heavy. The incidence of walrus predation on ringed seals appears to be quite low.

Exploitation of ringed seals by humans probably has the greatest impact on *P. hispida.* Native peoples of the Arctic traditionally depended on ringed seals as a source of clothing, food for themselves and their dogs, and oil for lamps and stoves, and still hunt the seals for those purposes. Recently there have also been shore-based and ship-based hunts by non-indigenous people, which take a significant number of animals. Despite hunting pressure, the world population of *P. h. hispida* is not in danger.

Pollution appears to be having a major impact on the subspecies that inhabit lakes Ladoga and Saimaa and the Baltic Sea. The Lake Saimaa population is also suffering mortality as a result of entanglement in fishing gear. In these areas, efforts are being made to help the populations recover, and hunting has either been prohibited or greatly reduced. *E. Perry*

Size
There is considerable geographic variation in the size of ringed seals; females tend to be slightly smaller than males.
Total length: 1–1.5 (1.3) m
Weight: 45–107 (68) kg

Identification
Ringed seals have dark gray to black coats with oval white or pale gray rings across the back and sides.

Other Common Names
Jar, silver jar

Status
The world population of ringed seals is estimated at 6–7 million animals, including a probable minimum of 2.5 million *P. h. hispida.* Two subspecies are classified as vulnerable, and one as endangered, by the IUCN.

Subspecies
Phoca hispida botnica, Baltic Sea, with largest populations in the Gulf of Bothnia, Finland, and Riga

Phoca hispida hispida, Arctic coasts of Alaska, Canada, Greenland, and Europe (including the Svalbard Islands and Russia)
Phoca hispida ladogensis, Lake Lagoda, Russia
Phoca hispida ochotensis, Okhotsk Sea from Kamchatka south to Pacific coast of Japan
Phoca hispida saimensis, Lake Saimaa in southeastern Finland

References
Kelly, 1988b; Reeves et al., 1992; Reijnders et al., 1993; Renouf, 1991

Spotted seal | *Phoca largha*

Spotted seals are mid-sized northern phocids, or true seals. They are sometimes confused with harbor seals *(Phoca vitulina)* as the two species overlap in range and are somewhat similar in appearance. Until recently, the spotted seal was thought to be a subspecies of the harbor seal; however, based on DNA analysis, the spotted seal is now considered a separate species. Spotted seals breed in isolated pairs on pack ice, where they give birth to and care for a single, white-coated pup. In contrast, harbor seals gather in dense aggregations on beaches and rocky outcroppings for pupping and their pups have a dark pelage. Furthermore, where the two species overlap in range, their breeding seasons differ by about two months.

During the open water season, from early summer to autumn, spotted seals are found in coastal waters of the Bering and Chukchi seas, along the entire northwestern coast of Alaska, as far east as Herschell Island, Beaufort Sea, and as far south as the Pribilof Islands, Bristol Bay, and the eastern Aleutian Islands. In the west, spotted seals range as far north as Chaun Bay, the Chukchi Sea, and as far south as the Yellow Sea. The greatest densities of spotted seals are found during the winter and spring in close association with the southern edge of the pack ice, on which they give birth to and nurse their young, mate, and molt. There are eight known breeding concentrations, of which three occur in the Bering Sea. One is between Bristol Bay and the Pribilof Islands, one is farther west, between the Pribilof Islands and Kamchatka, and the third is in the Gulf of Anadyr. The remaining breeding sites are in the Sea of Okhotsk, the Sea of Japan, and the Yellow Sea.

Phoca largha

Spotted seals are among the few seals that are thought to be seasonally monogamous. During the breeding season, family groups consisting of an adult female, adult male, and pup are found spaced approximately 0.2 kilometers apart. Males tend to pair with females about 10 days before parturition and remain with them until the pups are weaned and the females become receptive.

Parturition occurs after a gestation period of about 10.5 months, including a delayed implantation. The female gives birth to a single, white-coated pup in late April to early May, and remains with her pup for the three to four week nursing period, during which time the pup more than doubles its birth weight. Pups remain on the ice for most of the nursing period and do not venture into the water until close to weaning. The pups are not proficient swimmers. A month after weaning they can only attain depths of 80 meters, in comparison to the adult's dive capacity of at least 300 metres.

Females are sexually mature at three to four years of age and males mature when they are about four to five years of age. Copulation occurs underwater. Following mating, in May and June, when the Bering Sea ice is breaking up, the adult seals gather on the ice in small herds for their annual molt.

The diet of spotted seals varies with age, time of year, and location. Weaned pups eat euphausids *(Thysanoessa),* amphipods, a variety of shrimp *(Pandalus, Sclerocrangon, Crangon, Argis),* sand lance *(Ammodytes hexapterus)* and crabs *(Pagurus).*

The relative proportion of different food items varies with location. Seals from one to four years of age eat predominantly fish and some cephalopods. Animals more than five years old eat primarily fish and secondarily shrimp, cephalopods, and crustaceans. During the summer months, when the seals are in coastal waters, the diet is made up of smaller schooling fish, in contrast to the deeper water species taken during the winter months.

Spotted seals can live to the age of 35 years, although few live to be older than 25. Mortality is approximately 45 percent in the first year of life, and drops significantly to between 5 and 8 percent after about four years of age. Predators, environmental factors, and hunting pressures all contribute to mortality in this species. Predators include sharks *(Somniosus pacificus)*, killer whales, walruses, bears *(Ursus maritimus* and *U. arctos)*, arctic foxes, eagles *(Haliaeetus)*, ravens *(Corvus corax)*, and gulls *(Larus)*. Generally pups are most susceptible to predation, as a result of their reduced mobility. In addition to predators, environmental factors can cause some mortality. For example, during the breeding season pups and adults can be crushed by ice as it shifts with winds and currents.

The Commonwealth of Independent States has set total allowable annual catches for spotted seals in the Bering Sea to control hunting pressure on the population. The shore-based hunt limit has been set at 2,000 animals and the ship-based hunt has been set at 5,000 animals. There has been no recent monitoring of the Alaskan native harvest. Currently the annual catches seem to be below the total allowable, and hunting does not appear to be a threat to the population. However, oil and gas development in the Bering Sea may pose a threat to spotted seal habitat, and competition with commercial fisheries has the potential to impact on the population directly, because the seals become entangled in nets, and indirectly, through competition for prey species. Currently the world population of spotted seals appears stable. *E. Perry*

Size
Males and females are similar in size.
Total length: 1.4–1.7 m
Weight: 81–109 kg

Identification
Spotted seals have many irregularly-shaped, dark spots over their backs and upper flanks, on a generally brownish-yellow background, although background color can vary. The underside is paler. Spotted seals are sometimes confused with harbor seals *(Phoca vitulina)* as the two species overlap in range, but behavioral, ecological, and morphological differences distinguish them.

Recent Synonyms
Phoca vitulina largha

Other Common Names
Larga seal

Status
The world population is estimated at 335,000–400,000 animals, including approximately 200,000–250,000 in the Bering-Chukchi Sea population.

References
Quakenbush, 1988; Reeves et al., 1992; Reijnders et al., 1993; Renouf, 1991

Harbor seal | *Phoca vitulina*

Atlantic harbor seals inhabit islands and inshore coastal waters from Long Island (New York) north to Davis Strait. Pacific harbor seals occur from San Quintín Bay, Baja California, north to western Alaska. Although they are known to travel long distances (more than 1,000 km), particularly as juveniles, harbor seals apparently do not make annual long-distance migrations as do some other phocids. In many areas they are present year-round.

Harbor seals have been recorded to dive to depths of 450 m and stay submerged for periods of nearly half an hour. Most dives, however, are to depths of 30–100 m and last about six minutes. The diet of the species as a whole is extremely diverse and includes many pelagic and benthic fishes, cephalopods, and crustaceans. In a given area and season, they tend to specialize on a few prey species. For example, they eat large quantities of herring *(Clupea)* and sand lance *(Ammodytes)* in New England waters. In Prince William Sound, Alaska, they eat pollock *(Theragra chalcogramma)* in fall and winter, herring in winter and spring, and salmon *(Oncorhynchus)* in summer. In Netarts Bay, Oregon, a large part of their diet is chum salmon *(Oncorhynchus keta)*. Spawning runs of eulachon *(Thaleichthys pacificus)* attract large numbers of harbor seals to Washington's lower Columbia River and Alaska's Copper River delta each spring.

Groups of harbor seals routinely use particular haul-out sites, which can be intertidal ledges, rocky islets, reefs, mud flats, log rafts, piers, or remote sand or cobble beaches. In some areas they haul out on glacial or sea ice. Their daily pattern of hauling out or swimming is governed by tidal and weather conditions, season, time of day, and disturbance. Har-

bor seals are vigilant while hauled out, and they usually flee into the water when approached by boats or by people and pets walking along the beach. In a few exceptional areas such as near Santa Barbara and in La Jolla Cove, California, the seals are fairly tolerant of approaches by humans.

The harbor seal's body is covered with short, bristly guard hairs up to 9 mm long. Pups usually molt in utero, but occasionally individuals are born in the soft white to pale gray lanugo. There are two basic color patterns, or phases, one a dark background with irregularly shaped, pale-colored rings superimposed; the other a pale background with dark splotches. Various intermediate patterns are observed as well.

Harbor seals have an annual reproductive cycle, and females generally give birth to a single pup. The main birth season in the western Atlantic is May–July. In the eastern Pacific the timing of births varies widely, from a peak season in February–March in Baja California to June–September in Washington and British Columbia. The precocial pups, which are often born in the intertidal zone, are nursed for three to six weeks. Mating generally takes place in the water within two weeks after the pups are weaned. Implantation of the embryo is delayed for 1.5 to 3 months, so gestation lasts 8–9 months. Adult

females molt in late spring or summer, whereas males and juveniles molt somewhat later in summer.

Males and females become sexually mature when they are 3–7 years old. First-year mortality is high (close to 25 percent), and fewer than half the pups survive long enough to reproduce. Harbor seals fall prey to large sharks, killer whales, and northern sea lions (in the Pacific). Pups are sometimes taken by eagles and coyotes. Although the life span can be about 30 years, few harbor seals live longer than 25 years.

Harbor seals in parts of North America and Europe have a high incidence of heartworm. Occasionally, large numbers die from viral outbreaks. One recent epizootic, involving a newly discovered virus, phocine distemper, killed more than 18,000 harbor seals in Europe during 1988. A substantial decline in the number of harbor seals in Alaskan waters during the 1980s and early 1990s remains unexplained.

Bounty programs, which were justified as measures to protect fisheries from competition, were formerly used in Canada and the United States to reduce populations of harbor seals. A commercial hunt, involving mainly pups, annually removed 40,000–60,000 harbor seals in Alaska during the mid-1960s. This was in addition to the kill by native hunters for food and

Phoca vitulina

household use. In recent years, these seals have been protected in much of North America, and some populations have made strong recoveries. In British Columbia, for example, the population had reached 100,000 by the early 1990s and was still growing at about 12 percent per year. California had an esti-mated 30,000 harbor seals, and Oregon and Washington an estimated 43,000, in the mid-1990s. The total population off eastern North America was more than 40,000 in the early 1990s, with at least 28,000 in Maine alone. *R. R. Reeves*

Size

Males are slightly larger than females; harbor seals in the Pacific typically grow 100–250 mm longer and weigh 10–20 kg more than those in the Atlantic.

Total length: (Atlantic) 1.8 m (males); 1.5 m (females)

Weight: (Atlantic)130 kg (males); 105 kg (females)

Identification

In the Bering Sea, *P. vitulina* can be distinguished from the closely-related spotted seal (*P. largha*) mainly by cranial features and habitat differ-ences. Spotted seals inhabit areas with open pack ice, and harbor seals generally occur in ice-free areas. The gray seal (*Halichoerus grypus*) is sympatric in the North Atlantic: *P. vitulina* is smaller, has a more rounded, cat-like face, and has "V"-shaped (rather than parallel) nostrils.

Other Common Names

Common seal (in Europe)

Status

Common on undisturbed tidal flats, beaches, ledges, and tidally exposed rocks along east and west coasts of North America

Subspecies

Phoca vitulina concolor, western Atlantic

Phoca vitulina mellonae, freshwater lake system of northern Quebec

Phoca vitulina richardsi, eastern Pacific

Phoca vitulina stejnegeri, western Pacific

Phoca vitulina vitulina, eastern Atlantic (including Iceland)

References

Hoover-Miller, 1994; Reeves et al., 1992; Reijnders et al., 1993

Gray seal | *Halichoerus grypus*

The gray seal is found in the northwest Atlantic Ocean, the northeast Atlantic, and the Baltic Sea. The largest breeding colony in the northwest Atlantic is found on Sable Island, a 25-mile-long sand bar 150 miles off the coast of Nova Scotia, where approximately 15,000 pups are born each year. The southernmost breeding site of North American gray seals is Monomoy Island off Cape Cod, Massachusetts. This is near Nantucket, where gray seals used to breed; they abandoned that traditional rookery after being disturbed frequently and even killed by fisherman because the seals damaged fishing gear. The gray seal is one of the few seals that gives birth both on island beaches and on ice floes. Ice-breeding populations

are found in the Gulf of St. Lawrence and St. Georges Bay, Newfoundland.

The North American gray seal population is larger than the European population. The British Isles population has been estimated to be about 85,000. Populations in other countries in the eastern Atlantic are much smaller. Estimates include 11,500 in Iceland, 3,000 in Norway, 2,000 in Ireland, 1,500 in the White Sea, and 2,500 in the Baltic Sea.

Like all seals, gray seals are semi-aquatic. They find their food in the sea, but need land or ice on which to give birth and care for their young. They breed once a year, producing their pups and then mating within a matter of about a month in most locations. The timing of the breeding season is variable. Land-breeding populations in North America breed in January; ice-breeding populations breed from late February to early March. In the British Isles, the breeding season can start as

early as August in southern Wales or as late as November on the Farne Islands off the coast of Northumberland. The Baltic seals, which breed mainly on ice floes, do so in February–March like their Canadian counterparts.

A female gives birth to a single offspring each season. Because of the large separation between feeding and breeding grounds, both males and females fast during the reproductive period. Consequently, females have evolved a short lactation period of 16–18 days, during which their pups gain about 2 kg per day. Most of the pups' weight gain from the high-fat milk produced by their mothers takes the form of subcutaneous blubber. The fat content of gray seal milk ranges from 40 percent at parturition to 60 percent by day 15. The blubber of pups not only serves to keep them warm; it also serves as their main source of energy during a 3–4 week fast following weaning. The reason for this fast is not yet understood.

The clustering of females on land or ice enables some males to monopolize mates through aggressive competition. Males expend a lot of energy jostling and fighting for mating opportunities, and lose about 2.5 kg of weight per day. Those males that can remain among the female herd for the longest period of time are able to mate with the most females. Large size is in part responsible for their success. The most successful males mate with about 5–7 females. By comparison, a successful male elephant seal *(Mirounga angustirostris* or *M. leonina)* may mate with 60 or more females, and a territorial northern fur seal *(Callorhinus ursinus)* can control access to more than 100 females. These differences among species are primarily due to the degree to which females cluster.

The only time other than the breeding period that gray seals spend significant amounts of time on land is during the annual shedding (molting) of their coats. Molting takes place in the summer, after the animals have had an extended period of feeding following the energy-consuming reproductive period. Both males and females fast during the molt. Pups molt their white natal coat, called "lanugo," just after they are weaned; some pups start the molt while they are still nursing. The

Halichoerus grypus

lanugo serves to keep the pups warm until they have built up a layer of blubber, but because it consists of long hairs, it would interfere with effective swimming.

Gray seals are primarily fish eaters. The type of fish they eat varies by location. In Canada the principal fish eaten near Sable Island, Nova Scotia, is cod *(Gadus morhua)*, but in the Gulf of St. Lawrence, capelin *(Mallotus vollosus)* is the predominant food. In the British Isles, gray seals eat mostly sand eels *(Ammodytidae)* at the Farne Islands and in Orkney Scotland, but in the Outer Hebrides and at the Isle of May a fish known as ling *(Molva molva)* is most commonly eaten. Some of these fish species are caught commercially, and consequently there are conflicts between the fish industry and preservationists. An important fish industry concern in North America is that the gray seal is the primary host for a parasitic worm, sealworm *(Pseudoterranova decipiens)*, which invades the muscle tissue of fish. Sealworm is not harmful to humans, nor are humans infected if the parasite is eaten. However, consumers will not buy fish if they can see worms in it or if they think they are there, so it costs the industry millions of dollar to pick worms from fish fillets before they are sold.

Molecular genetic studies are currently addressing the question of whether gray seals in North America and Europe should be considered separate subspecies. There is no evidence that seals cross the Atlantic and intermingle, and the frequency with which different coat pattern types occurs differs in the two locations. In addition, adult females are about 40 percent larger and adult males are about 30 percent larger in North America than in the British Isles. *D. J. Boness*

Size

Males are 15 percent longer and 30 percent heavier than females.

Total length: 2–2.7 (2.3) m (males); 1.6–2.2 (2) m (females)

Weight: 240–320 (271) kg (males); 150–260 (207) kg (females)

Identification

Males can be solid black, dusky gray-green, or mottled with a dark background and silvery patches. Females are usually silvery-gray with dark patches, although a few are solid black. Males have particularly long, broad, curved snouts. The gray seal is not easily confused with any other species sharing its range.

Other Common Names

Atlantic seal, horsehead seal

Status

Population estimated to be 80,000–110,000 in 1987 and increasing by more than 10 percent per year

References

Boness and James, 1979; Iverson et al., 1993; Reeves et al., 1992; Reijnders et al., 1993

Bearded seal | *Erignathus barbatus*

Bearded seals are large phocids that reside in arctic and subarctic waters year-round. In the Pacific Ocean their distribution extends as far south as Hokkaido, Japan (45° N) and in the Atlantic as far south as northeastern Newfoundland (approximately 50° N). Bearded seals typically occur alone or in small groups and are patchily distributed at relatively low densities throughout their range. They prefer areas of moving ice and open water that is less than 150–200 meters deep. Although they tend to avoid thick shorefast ice, in a few areas they maintain breathing holes in such ice throughout the winter. This probably occurs in areas where the ice freezes late and breaks up early, and where there is abundant prey. In the Bering and Chukchi seas, bearded seals move seasonally to maintain contact with ice. Over much of their range, however, they appear to make only local movements in response to variation in ice conditions. In areas where the annual ice melts in summer, they haul out on land. Bearded seals feed primarily at the bottom of the sea, and consume a broad range of food items, although their diet typically consists of only a few species of crustaceans, mollusks, and fish.

Adults are typically gray in color and unpatterned, although some individuals have a brownish or reddish coloration, especially on the face and foreflippers. Newborn pups have a dark birth coat with some white patches, especially around the face, mid-back, and hind flippers. Bearded seals can be distinguished from other northern pinnipeds by the small size of the head relative to the length of the body and by the numerous long mystacial vibrissae (whiskers). The sexes cannot be distinguished at a distance. On warm, calm days in late spring when bearded seals haul out on the ice to bask and molt, they are relatively undisturbed by human activity. In contrast, they are quite wary when hauled out in the winter.

Most females become pregnant for the first time at 5 or 6 years of age and reproduce annually thereafter, except perhaps during years when food resources are limited. Ovulation and mating occur between mid-April and late May. After a delay of

approximately two months, the blastocyst implants on the uterine wall; active gestation lasts 9 months. Females bear a single pup sometime between mid-March and early May; seals at the more southern end of the range whelp earlier than those farther north. At birth, the sex ratio is close to even, but females are often more numerous in older age classes. Pups are able to swim shortly after birth. They spend approximately half of their time diving and resting at the surface and half hauled out on ice. Lactation lasts only 24 days, by which time the pup has shed its natal coat and acquired its adult pelage. Longevity in the wild ranges between 23 and 31 years.

In the spring, during the breeding season, bearded seals produce trill-like calls that last as long as 30 seconds. These can be heard underwater for distances of 25 km or more. Limited evidence suggests that only males call and that while calling they remain relatively stationary. Call repertoire varies geographically. These warbling sounds may be produced to advertise breeding condition, territoriality, or both. Bearded seals appear to be polygynous and may use lek-display (males congregate and vocalize on communal display grounds).

Recent analyses of mitochondrial DNA sequences indicate that bearded seals are more closely related to the tropical and warm-temperate monk seals *(Monachus)* and the Antarctic Weddell seal *(Leptonychotes weddelli)* than they are to other Arctic phocids.

Polar bears are the chief predators of bearded seals. Occasionally, parts of young bearded seals have been found in the stomachs of walruses and killer whales. Historically, this species was a valuable resource to the Inuit for food, fuel, and gear that required strength and durability (e.g., dog-team traces). More recently, in most communities, the importance of bearded seals to local northern economies has declined. *H. J. Cleator and I. Stirling*

Erignathus barbatus

Size

Females may be slightly longer than males. Weight varies seasonally (the seals are leanest in summer, heaviest in late winter-spring).

Total length: 2–2.6 m

Weight: 225–300 kg; maximum weight 350–360 kg.

Identification

The bearded seal is distinguished from other northern phocids by large size, gray color, square-shaped foreflippers, a disproportionately small head, numerous long whiskers, and four teats (instead of two). In the water, the head and back are often exposed.

Other Common Names

Squareflipper

Status

Bearded seals are distributed widely at low densities; population sizes are unknown.

Subspecies

Two subspecies have been suggested: *Erignathus barbatus barbatus* (central Canadian Arctic east to the Laptev Sea, north of Siberia) and *Erignathus barbatus nauticus* (central Canadian Arctic west to the Laptev Sea). However, the basis for this division is questionable.

References

Burns, 1981; Kelly, 1988a; Reeves et al., 1992

Hooded seal | *Cystophora cristata*

The hooded seal derives its name from the nasal sac that can be inflated on the dorsal rostrum of the male. This sac, absent in females, is developed early in the life of a male and increases in size with age. Another male-only structure is an inflated nasal septum that looks like a large red balloon extending from the nose. This balloon is made by closing one nostril and forcing air into the septum between the nostrils, causing it to expand and extrude from the nose. Why do these structures exist? They are probably secondary sexual characteristics, structures that have evolved either for attracting mates or fighting or threatening other males. This inference is drawn because females lack these features, and the structures are inflated mostly during the mating period. It is not clear whether the hood and balloon serve mainly to attract females or to threaten other males.

The mating system of hooded seals is not well understood, because mating occurs off the ice and males and females are relatively dispersed. Sometimes the nearest females are a kilometer or more from each other. Sometimes a male apparently stays with a particular female until she weans her pup, fighting off or threatening other males that approach. The same male may be seen later with another female. This suggests a system known as female-defense polygyny, where a male defends different females sequentially, moving from one to another after he has mated with them.

The hooded seal, like many of its phocid cousins, gives birth and cares for its single young on pack ice. The pupping season is later in spring than is the case for most other ice-breeding seals, and ice conditions are much less stable. Perhaps in part because of this late pupping, the hooded seal has the shortest known lactation period of any mammal. Hooded seal mothers nurse their pups for just under four days. An array of unusual behavioral and physiological traits is associated with this remarkably short lactation period. Females arrive at the breeding grounds with almost 50 percent of their weight in stored fat (blubber). They fast during the four days of nursing, turning much of their blubber into a very fat-rich milk. Hooded seal milk contains nearly twice as much fat (about 60 percent) as there is in whipping cream. Not only are pups consuming an energy-dense milk, they are also nursed more frequently than are other phocid pups. Pups more than double their birth weight (20 kg) in the four days of nursing, gaining an astounding average of 7 kg per day.

Most of the weight gained by the pups during lactation takes the form of subcutaneous blubber. The blubber helps the pup stay warm in the subzero temperatures to which it is exposed, and provides a source of energy for the pup as it fasts until it can forage for its food, a period that lasts for several weeks after the mother leaves it. The reasons for this delay are not known, but such a delay in independent foraging is typical of phocid seals.

Cystophora cristata

The hooded seal has a specialized digestive system to accomplish the feat of putting on 7 kg of fat a day. In most animals digestion of milk fats occurs primarily in the small intestine. In the hooded seal, there are lipase enzymes that break down fat in the milk itself that are activated by the saliva of the pup. Lipase is released in the mouth and stomach of the pup, so the digestive process begins earlier than it would in most mammals.

Hooded seals are considered migratory. They move from areas around Greenland, where they feed for most of the year, to the pack ice regions around Labrador and Davis Strait where they breed in late March. Little is known about their feeding habits because of the difficulty of finding them at sea when they are foraging. Ongoing research involves attaching satellite transmitters to the seals so they can be located by satellites while they are foraging. Food samples taken from the stomachs of dead seals indicate that adults feed on halibut *(Reinhardtius hippoglossoides),* redfish *(Sebastes marinus),* and polar cod *(Arcogadus glacialis).* Weaned pups feed mainly on capelin *(Mallotus villosus).*

The hooded seal has few predators besides humans, although polar bears kill both adults and young on the ice during breeding and molting. Polar bear predation may, in fact, have contributed to the evolution of the extremely short lactation period in this species. Seals generally are not well equipped either to fend off polar bears on the ice or to escape from them. *D. J. Boness*

Size

Males are about 1.8 times heavier and 1.2 times longer than females.

Total length: 2.3–2.85 m (males); 2.0–2.3 m (females)

Weight: average 250 kg, maximum 435 kg (males); average 180 kg, maximum 350 kg (females)

Identification

Both males and females have silvery-gray coats with irregularly-shaped black patches. Adult males can inflate an air sac on the dorsal surface of the rostrum to form a bi-lobed "hood," and can inflate the nasal septum through one nostril, producing a large, red, balloon-like structure. Pups have very dark, round faces and are born with a coat that is silvery blue-gray dorsally and creamy white ventrally.

Other Common Names

Crested seal, bladder seal

Status

World population is estimated at 500,00–600,000 (1991). The Atlantic population numbers about 325,000 seals and the Jan Mayen group about 200,000.

References

Mammalian Species 258; Boness et al., 1988; Bowen et al., 1985; Lavigne, 1988; Oftedal et al., 1988

Northern elephant seal | *Mirounga angustirostris*

Third largest of all pinnipeds, northern elephant seals haul out onto land seasonally to breed, molt, or rest on islands and on a few mainland beaches from Cedros Island off Baja California north to Vancouver Island off British Columbia. Northern elephant seals have also gone ashore on Midway Island in the northern Hawaiian islands and on Nijiima Island near Japan.

The earliest fossils of *Mirounga* in the North Pacific are from Pleistocene rocks in southern California. Northern elephant seals evidently evolved from an ancestral group that entered the Pacific Ocean from the Caribbean through the Central American Seaway around 5 million years ago. The generic name is derived from *miouroung,* the Australian aboriginal name for the southern elephant seal, *Mirounga leonina.*

Northern elephant seals were intensively hunted in the 1800s for their blubber, which was rendered into oil for lighting and lubrication. They were extirpated from California waters by the mid-1800s and reduced to a remnant population of a few dozen to a few hundred at Isla de Guadalupe, Baja California, by the turn of the century. Since then the population has grown substantially and also steadily expanded its breeding range northward. The population was estimated to be 110,000–125,000 in 1992. Genetic studies have detected little variability, perhaps because of the population reduction in the 1800s.

At birth, northern elephant seals have a black pelage, which is replaced by silverish hair soon after weaning. After their first year they molt every year in spring (females and juveniles) or summer (adult males); the new pelage is silvery-gray but fades quickly. During most of the year northern elephant seals appear uniformly brownish dorsally and yellowish-blond ventrally; this countershading is evidently an evolutionary adaptation for escaping detection by predators and prey while at sea.

Mirounga angustirostris is polygynous and breeds from December through late February. Males compete for access to estrous females. They establish dominance hierarchies with sterotyped visual and vocal threats, occasionally resorting to phsyical combat. Groups of breeding females can be quite large, depending on beach topography. Male hierarchies generally develop among groups of 25 to 50 females, with the most dominant male in the hierarchy mating with most of the females. Adult males sometimes remain ashore fasting for up to three months during the breeding season. Females give birth to a single pup and suckle it for 24–28 days. They stay on shore continuously and fast during this period, losing about 42 percent of their body mass, primarily blubber, which is converted to milk. Pups weigh about 47 kg at birth and about 147 kg when weaned. Lactating females are mated near the end of the nurs-

Mirounga angustirostris

Adult males spend about 8–9 months and females about 10 months each year at sea. They make two annual migrations covering about 18,000 to 21,000 km all told. They dive, and evidently forage, continuously while migrating and spend about 90 percent of their time submerged. Most dives are to depths of 350–650 meters and last for 18–25 minutes, though a few exceed 1,500 meters and last up to 2 hours. Adults segregate by sex when migrating and foraging; males forage substantially farther north (in the Gulf of Alaska and near the Aleutian Islands) than females. Development of these patterns of differential migration and sexual segregation correlates with accelerated growth in males during puberty. Elephant seals appear to be solitary when at sea.

Northern elephant seals prey mostly on mesopelagic, bioluminescent squid. In coastal waters they also eat small sharks and sedentary fish. They are occasionally attacked and eaten by killer whales *(Orcinus orca)* and great white sharks *(Carcharodon carcharias),* particularly near the Farallon Islands off San Francisco, California, but that predation has evidently had little effect on the demography of the northern elephant seal.

Juveniles, adult females, and subadult males haul out to molt for 3–4 weeks in April, May, and June, respectively, and adult males molt in July and August. The old hair and upper layer of skin are shed in large patches. In recent years, some molting seals on southern Vancouver Island were killed by local game wardens because they thought that the sloughing pelage was a sign of disease.

Aborigines on the California Channel Islands hunted elephant seals from as early as 10,000 years ago through the early 1800s, and they may have had substantial effects on some colonies. Aborigines along the mainland coast of California, Oregon, Washington, and British Columbia also traditionally hunted elephant seals when the seals migrated through those areas in spring, summer, and autumn. *B. S. Stewart*

ing period. Attachment of the fertilized egg (blastocyst) to the uterine wall is delayed for 2–3 months; attachment is followed by an 8–9 month gestation period. Within a few days after mating, females abandon their pups and depart the rookeries to feed at sea for about 2.5 months. The pups remain ashore for another 4–6 weeks, fasting and molting, before they enter the water and embark on their first independent foraging efforts.

Most females first give birth when they are 4–6 years old, though some reproduce as early as 2 years of age. They can live for 18–20 years. Males are sexually mature when they are 5–6 years old, but few begin breeding before they are 8, and most males die before they are 12 years old.

Size
Substantial sexual dimorphism in size, cranial morphology, and external physical characteristics
Total length: 3.6–4.2 (3.8) m (males); 2.2–3 (2.45) m (females)
Weight: 1,500–2,300 (1,800) kg (males); 400–800 (650) kg (females)

Identification
The northern elephant seal is distinguished from all other North Pacific phocids by its large size, long proboscis, the calloused neck shield of adult males, and (except from Hawaiian monk seals) by uniform brownish dorsal and yellowish ventral pelage color and incisor formula (2/1). There is virtually no overlap in the geographic distributions of northern elephant seals and Hawaiian monk seals, though a few juvenile northern elephant seals have been found to wander to the Hawaiian Islands. Northern elephant seals are distinguishable from Hawaiian monk seals by the single pair of abdominal teats in elephant seals compared with two pairs in monk seals, and by the shape of the head and muzzle, particularly the location of the external nares, which are at the tip of the snout in elephant seals and more dorsal in monk seals, and by various differences in cranial and dental morphology.

Recent Synonyms
Cystophora angustirostris
Macrorhinus angustirostris
Mirounga leonina leonina
Morunga angustirostris

Other Common Names
Sea elephant, elefante marino

Status
Recovering from overhunting and near extinction in late 1800s; breeding range limited to islands between central Baja California and central California and a few mainland sites in central California; foraging range extensive in the eastern and central North Pacific

References
Mammalian Species 449; Le Boeuf and Laws, 1994; Reeves et al., 1992; Stewart, 1997; Stewart and DeLong, 1995; Stewart et al., 1994

Family Procyonidae

This exclusively New World family contains 18 species in 6 genera, including 3 species in 3 genera in North America. Procyonids are omnivores and forage actively both as predators and scavengers. They move about alone, in small family groups, or in large bands in species like coatis *(Nasua narica)*. All are arboreal to a certain extent, or at least all are capable of climbing trees

Procyonids move along with shuffling, bear-like gaits that belie their ability to move quickly when necessary. Although most den in trees, raccoons *(Procyon lotor)* frequently den in the ground as well. Raccoons are hunted as game animals in some areas, usually by running them with dogs. They do have edible flesh and useful fur, but are not really important economic commodities at present.

Although all species are capable of making sounds, they use vocalizations much less frequently than many other carnivores. Social systems are highly developed in some species (coatis) and reproductive patterns tend towards a single litter per year. Gestation periods average around two months, and litter sizes range from one to six.

Procyonids occupy almost all terrrestrial and arboreal habitats, but all need access to water. They are most diverse in tropical regions, but raccoons range northward into southern Canada. Fossils are known from the Early Oligocene to Recent in North America.

References
Stains, 1984

North American Genera
Bassariscus
Procyon
Nasua

Ringtail | *Bassariscus astutus*

The ringtail occurs in mountainous terrain, eroded badlands, and forested lowlands and highlands in the southwestern United States and in northern, central, and western Mexico southward to the Isthmus of Tehuanatepec, and including all of Baja California plus some of its offshore islands. Perhaps the most colorful of procyonids, this lithe, graceful, long-tailed mammal features a conspicuous, sooty-gray, fox-like face adorned with soft round ears and big chestnut-brown eyes. The eyes are enhanced by being ringed with blackish hair and bounded above, below, and laterally by patches of white to pale buff. The upperparts of the ringtail's house-cat-sized body are pale-yellowish to tawny-reddish in color and washed on nape, shoulders, and the dorsal midline with a tinge of black-tipped guard hairs. In contrast, the underparts and feet are white to slightly buff. The flashy, fully-haired tail features 14 to 16 alternating black and white rings and has a black tip.

In favorable habitat ringtails may be common. In the northern Central Valley of California, for example, ringtails occur in densities as high as one individual per 12 acres (5 hectares); in juniper-oak woodland of central Texas, density may be one per 62 acres (25 hectares). Unfortunately, outdoor enthusiasts rarely see ringtails. Inconspicuous and almost strictly nocturnal, they leave few tracks or other obvious signs. They are sometimes spotted at night crossing roads or in trees or along rocky ledges.

Ringtails are agile climbers, using canyon sides, ledges in rimrock, talus, other piled rocks, or woodlands, including montane pine-oak, chaparral, riparian growth along desert watercourses, and the arid tropical shrublands of western Mexico. For daytime retreats and for nurseries, ringtails use openings in rock crevices, boulder piles, and rock slides, or tree hollows, ground dens under brush piles, or tree-root-based burrows (often dug by other mammals). They sometimes even use human-made structures. Rarely do ringtails construct or modify nests and except during inclement weather usually spend only a few days in any one harborage. Ringtails are generally solitary and territorial, marking their haunts with urine scent and fecal deposits to announce their presence to same-sex ringtail intruders. Home ranges may shift seasonally and include areas, at least in Texas, as large as 128 acres (52 hectares)

Bassariscus astutus

for males and 69 acres (28 hectares) for females. The ranges of males may overlap those of females but usually not those of other males. Active courtship chases and other rousing and vocal male/female foreplay culminate in matings in early spring (April) in northern sectors of the ringtail's range. Apparently some mated pairs remain associated during the female's gestation period of approximately seven weeks, after which time 1 to 4 young are born in a sheltered den. At 2–3 months of age, littermates are mature enough to follow their mothers on foraging trips.

Much like its relative, the raccoon, the ringtail eats both animal and plant materials, preferring small mammals, grasshoppers, beetles, moths, arachnids, other arthropods, and fruits. Acorns, lizards, birds and their eggs, carrion, and other such edibles also attract ringtails. Afflictions include rabies and an assortment of fleas, ticks, mites, and lice externally, and cestodes and nematodes internally. Coyotes, bobcats, great horned owls and other sizeable carnivores prey on ringtails. These procyonids may invade human habitations, both rural and urban, sometimes becoming nuisances by preying on poultry. Captives are easily tamed and can make desirable pets.
R. H. Baker

Size
Little significant sexual dimorphism
Total length: 616–811 mm (males, 793; females, 756)
Length of tail: 310–438 mm (males, 387; females, 383)
Weight: 0.87–1.43 kg

Identification
Bassaricus astutus is a small, almost cat-like carnivore with long, pale fur and a long tail with 14 to 16 contrasting dark bands. The ringtail differs from the raccoon *(Procyon lotor)* in lacking a distinctive facial mask and in having a longer, furrier tail. Coatis *(Nasua narica)* are larger, have longer noses, longer, nonretractable claws, shorter tails with fewer contrasting bands, and tend to be darker in color.

Other Common Names
Babisuri, bandtailed cat, basaride, bassarisk, cacomistle, cacomixtle, civet cat, comandreja, guayanoche, mico de noche, mico rayado, onza, pintorabo, ring-tailed cat, rintel, sal coyote

Status
Common in rocky and mountainous terrain; less so in nonmontane forested habitat

Subspecies
Bassariscus astutus arizonensis, parts of Colorado, Utah, Arizona, and New Mexico
Bassariscus astutus astutus, southeastern Mexico from San Luis Potosi to Veracruz and Oaxaca
Bassariscus astutus bolei, southern Mexico in Guerrero and Oaxaca
Bassariscus astutus consitus, western Mexico from Sinaloa and western Durango south to Jalisco and Michoacan
Bassariscus astutus flavus, south-central United States and northeastern Mexico from Colorado, Oklahoma, southwestern Arkansas, Louisiana, Texas, New Mexico, and southeastern Arizona south to Sonora, Chihuahua, Durango, Coahuila, northern San Luis Potosi, Nuevo Leon, and western Tamaulipas
Bassariscus astutus insulicola, Isla San José, Gulf of California, Baja California
Bassariscus astutus macdougalli, Istmo de Tehuanatepec, Oaxaca
Bassariscus astutus nevadensis, Nevada, Utah, and Arizona
Bassariscus astutus octavus, southwestern California
Bassariscus astutus palmarius, Baja California
Bassariscus astutus raptor, southwestern Oregon and northern California
Bassariscus astutus saxicola, Isla Espiritu Santo, Gulf of California, Baja California
Bassariscus astutus willetti, southeastern California
Bassariscus astutus yumanensis, extreme southeastern California and southwestern Arizona

References
Mammalian Species 327; Grinnell et al., 1937; Kaufmann, 1982; Toweill and Teer, 1980

Northern raccoon | *Procyon lotor*

Raccoons range from the tropics to the cold temperate regions of North America and they have been introduced to and are now widely distributed in Asia and Europe. They differ from the other procyonids in their thermoregulatory ability, extraordinarily diverse diet, and high reproductive potential. These differences have enabled the raccoon to become a highly successful climate generalist and have allowed it to break out of the tropical, warm-adapted mode of the other procyonids. The cornerstone of this success was the evolution of a high basal metabolic rate together with well-defined cyclic changes in body fat and heat regulation, a high level of heat tolerance, and a high capacity for evaporative cooling.

Within their range raccoons are found nearly everywhere there is water. They reach densities of about 50 per square kilometer in swamps, mangroves, flood plain forests, and fresh and salt marshes. The highest density ever recorded (400 per square kilometer) was in a Missouri marsh. They are common in well-watered hardwood stands, cultivated and abandoned farmland (up to 20 raccoons per square kilometer), and in suburban residential areas (up to 69 per square kilometer). Raccoons reach these densities where they have no major preda-

Procyon lotor

were present in the population for at least three years. Both males and females dispersed from the population, with a maximum movement of 4.7 km per year.

Raccoon home-range diameters commonly vary from 1 to 3 km and up to 10 km on western prairies. During spring, summer, and fall, raccoons forage at night and spend their days in tree dens; they frequently shift dens. During winter, they will remain in dens for weeks at a time if the temperature does not rise above freezing. In a Virginia mountain hollow, raccoons shifted from tree dens to ground dens during very cold winter weather. In the same hollow, they traveled between 0.75 and 2.5 km per night, depending on the season. Males traveled farther than females each night during the fall, winter, and spring; females traveled farther each night when the cubs were first out of the den in late summer. The raccoon is a carnivore, granivore, frugivore, and insectivore in its terrestrial foraging and crustacivore, molluscivore, insectivore, piscevore, and carnivore in its semiaquatic foraging. Raccoons make long, direct-line movements from their dens to foraging areas and rapid direct movements between rich food patches.

The raccoon mating season extends from February to June, with peak activity in March; mating occurs earlier in the northern regions of their range than in the south. During the mating season, some adult males temporarily expand their home range, presumably to increase the number of females encountered. In the Virginia study mentioned above, each of the seven radio-tagged females was found in a den with each of the two radio-tagged adult males at some time during the mating season. Estrus lasts from 3 to 6 days, followed by a gestation period of 63 to 65 days. Females can breed before their first birthday and in some populations 60 percent do. Litter size is 3 to 7, usually 4. Young weigh 62–98 grams at birth and are usually born in tree dens. The female raises the cubs alone. The eyes of the cubs open at 18–24 days; the duration of lactation is 70 days. Cubs take their first short excursions from the den with their mother at week 9 or 10; by week 12 they travel with her nightly and bed with her during the day. By week 20, siblings may forage alone at night or with other siblings, and may bed together or alone during the day. In winter, mother and young frequently den together or close by. *J. Seidensticker*

tor. Usually there is no exclusive male-male, male-female, or female-female use of space, but territoriality has been reported among males living in the harsh environs of the western prairies at the northern edge of their range, where they occur at low densities (0.5–3 per square kilometer). In a Virginia mountain hollow, there were 7.4 raccoons per square kilometer during a rabies outbreak; density doubled when rabies was not present. In this population at its higher density, there were equal numbers of males and females; 52 percent were immigrants, 25 percent had been born in the hollow, and 23 percent

Size
Males are 10–30 percent heavier than females. Body size correlates with severity of climate, from smallest in the subtropical Florida Keys to largest in areas with 100 or more days of snow cover. All raccoons may be able to fatten to 50 percent body fat, but only the large northern animals achieve this level of obesity.
Total length: 603–950 mm

Length of tail: 192–405 mm
Weight: 1.8–10.4 kg

Identification
The raccoon is distinguished by a stout but cat-like build; fox-like face; brown-black facial mask around black eyes, sharply delineated by adjacent areas of whitish hairs; rounded, pale-tipped ears; and a bushy tail with 4–7 alternating brown and black rings. The pelage is grizzled or silvered in appearance and varies from iron-

gray to blackish with a yellowish or reddish tinge, especially on the nape of the neck as the winter progresses. Other color phases include albino, fisher (dark brown lacking in silver), and cinnamon. The soles of the feet are bare; the feet have five digits with short, compressed, recurved claws and no webbing between the digits. The front feet are adapted for manipulating objects while the hind feet support the weight of the body.

Other Common Names

'Coon. The name raccoon is from a Native American word, *aroughcan* or *arakua*, roughly meaning "he who scratches with his hands."

Status

Abundant

Subspecies

Procyon lotor auspicatus, Key Vaca, Florida
Procyon lotor crassidens, Hondurus to Costa Rica
Procyon lotor dickeyi, southeastern Guatemala, southwestern El Salvador
Procyon lotor elucus, peninsular Florida and southern Georgia
Procyon lotor fuscipes, Texas, northern Louisiana, and northeastern Mexico
Procyon lotor grinnelli, Baja California, Mexico
Procyon lotor hernandezii, southern Mexico
Procyon lotor hirtus, plains from Oklahoma to Alberta, Canada

Procyon lotor incautus, Big Pine Key to Key West, Florida
Procyon lotor inesperatus, Lower Matecumbe Key to Virginia Key, Florida
Procyon lotor litoreus, Atlantic barrier islands and coastal Georgia
Procyon lotor lotor, northeastern United States to Lake Michigan and southeastern Canada
Procyon lotor marinus, Ten Thousand Islands and southern coastal Florida
Procyon lotor megalodous, coastal Louisiana
Procyon lotor mexicanus, Rio Grande drainage from southern Colorado to Big Bend National Park and northwestern Mexico
Procyon lotor pacificus, western Oregon and Washington and southwestern British Columbia, Canada
Procyon lotor pallidus, Colorado River drainage and northwestern Sonora, Mexico
Procyon lotor psora, California
Procyon lotor pumilus, Panama

Procyon lotor shufeldti, Yucatan Peninsula, Tabasco, and Chiapas, Mexico; Guatemala; Belize
Procyon lotor simus, South Carolina
Procyon lotor vancouverensis, Vancouver Island, British Colombia, Canada
Procyon lotor varius, Tennessee south to Gulf of Mexico
Several insular forms are considered conspecific with *Procyon lotor* by recent authors: *Procyon insularis* (Marias Islands, west coast of Mexico), *Procyon gloveralleni* (Barbados), *Procyon maynardi* (New Providence Island, Bahamas), *Procyon minor* (Guadeloupe Island, French Antilles), and *Procyon pygameus* (Cozumel Island, Quintana Roo, Mexico).

References

Mammalian Species 119; Kaufmann, 1982; Mugaas and Seidensticker, 1993; Mugaas et al., 1993; Sanderson, 1987

White-nosed coati | *Nasua narica*

The geographic range of the white-nosed coati extends from the southernmost portions of Texas, New Mexico, and Arizona south through Mexico and Central America. The southern extent of the range is considered to be northern Columbia by some authors and the west coast of Ecuador and northern Peru by others. The elevational range of these animals extends from sea level to over 2,400 meters; coatis are found at these higher elevations in both tropical cloud forests and temperate montane woodlands. In dry, lowland areas their distribution is generally confined to riparian habitat.

Coatis are diurnal, in contrast to other members of the family Procyonidae (raccoons, ringtails and cacomistles, olingos, kinkajous). They may shift to a more nocturnal activity pattern in areas where they are hunted heavily or if they are close to a human settlement (for example, a research station) where artificial light and food are available in the evening. In tropical forests they spend the night in trees and descend to the ground at first light. In the southwestern United States, coatis have been seen curled up asleep in oak, pinyon, and palo verde trees and on rocky ledges. Most studies of coati behavior have been conducted in forested regions of Mexico and Central America; consequently the natural history of coatis at the extreme northern end of their range and in the less forested habitats is largely anecdotal.

Coatis are the most social of the procyonids. Adult females travel and live in bands that may include subadults, juveniles, and young of both sexes. Males leave the natal band when they are about 24 months of age. Adult males are usually solitary and were considered by some local people to represent a distinctly different animal (gato solo) from the females (gato social). Band size varies considerably depending on habitat, resource availability, and reproductive status. In the tropical

Nasua narica

moist forest on Barro Colorado Island in Panama, a band with more than a dozen adults and subadults would be considered large; however, bands as large as 40 individuals have been reliably reported in dryer areas in the southwestern United States.

Coatis are robust, with a flat-footed (plantigrade) stance. They employ a rocking pacing gait, rather than a trot, at intermediate speeds of locomotion, as do raccoons. Their limbs are muscular; this characteristic, as well as their long, curved claws and interdigital webbing, have been considered adaptations for the digging and shredding behaviors employed in finding food. Coatis are also talented, although not graceful, climbers. They climb vertical supports from 2 to about 50 cm in diameter, leap distances of several meters within the forest canopy, and use their long tails for balance and direct contact with tree branches. Coatis can descend head-first from trees with a partial reversal of the hind feet that permits them to grip the substrate with the soles of their feet.

Much of the white-nosed coati's day is spent foraging for food on the ground, interspersed with resting and napping periods. Band members engage in social interactions, including mutual grooming, throughout the day. In a band of foraging coatis, members are often spread out over a moving front several meters wide; they may also travel in roughly single-file or-

der. On level ground, typically an animal has its nose to the ground and its tail straight up in the air. Band members often emit a series of high-pitched chirping sounds as they move. Small leaf-litter invertebrates are snapped up as they are encountered. Coatis also chase and nab small vertebrates such as lizards. Coatis dig in the soil to root out tarantulas and shred dead logs to obtain insect larvae. They also eat the fruits of many trees, either on the ground or in the trees, sometimes splitting up so that some animals in the band are feeding in the canopy while others are on the ground. Although band members may feed in close proximity to one another, food is neither obtained cooperatively nor shared. In tropical forests with large-diameter canopy trees, coatis gain access to tree crowns by climbing the smaller understory trees and lianas.

White-nosed coati bands are composed primarily of closely related females and their young. In cases in which relatedness of the band members has been determined, it is clear that an unrelated female may also occasionally join a band. Female coatis generally stay with their natal group, although some emigration has been documented. Large bands may split into two, usually with adjacent home ranges; the remaining members of a band that has been greatly reduced in size may join with another band.

Band members join together to face off intruders (often an adult male coati) and have been reported to attack a predator that has captured one of their members. They respond to the squeak/snort alarm calls of other band members, usually by dashing a few meters away and then turning to identify the source of alarm. Frequently a startled coati will climb a couple of meters into a tree, look back over its shoulder, then jump from the tree and move out of range. If coatis in trees are alarmed by an observer on the ground, they descend from the trees and gallop away.

During the breeding season the band is usually joined by one adult male for a few weeks. Adult males have been known to join bands at other times of the year as well. Recent work on the paternity of young coatis on Barro Colorado Island indicated that an adult male associated with a band during the breeding season sires some but by no means all of the litters from that band. In at least one case, the consort male was not the father of any offspring in the band.

Gestation lasts ten to eleven weeks. Pregnant females leave their band toward the end of gestation to select a nesting site in a tree. One to six young are born in an altricial state and the mother cares for the young in the nest for approximately four or five weeks. The mother forages alone during this time and returns to nurse the young and sleep with them at night. All the coati mothers in a given area bring their young out of the nests at roughly the same time, and social bands are reconstituted at this time.

Mortality for young coatis can be quite high, with the period of greatest risk apparently the first few weeks after leaving the nest. Young coatis are known to be vulnerable to predation by large cats, white-faced monkeys, boa constrictors, and even adult male coatis. They may also succumb to various diseases and the aftereffects of accidents. As with most other aspects of coati natural history, the foregoing information is largely based on studies of white-nosed coatis in tropical forests.

White-nosed coatis are hunted as favored food by some indigenous peoples and largely ignored by others throughout Mexico and Central America. They are considered pests on agricultural lands, in orchards, and where chickens are raised. Their fur is not particularly valuable. Young coatis are occasionally kept as pets. Hand-raised coatis, male and female, may remain tame into adulthood, but their behavior can be unpredictable and their large canine teeth are formidable weapons.

D. K. McClearn

Size

Males are significantly larger than females.
Total length: 750–1,350 mm
Length of tail: 350–680 mm
Weight: 2.5–5.5 kg

Identification

The white-nosed coati is similar to the South American coati, *Nasua nasua*, but the ranges of the two species probably do not overlap. Captive (e.g., zoo) specimens may be difficult to distinguish because there is a wide variation in coat color in both species; *N. narica* is generally more brown whereas *N. nasua* is more reddish. *N. narica* also has a white muzzle and a series of white marks around the eye not seen in *N. nasua*. Characters of the palate, nasal bones, second lower molar, and os penis also differ in the two species. White-nosed coatis are readily distinguished from other medium-sized mammals in their range by the long, mobile snout that extends beyond the lower jaw and by the long, slender tail with incomplete dark rings.

Recent Synonyms

At times in recent decades considered a subspecies of *N. nasua*

Other Common Names

Coatimundi, gato solo, pizote

Status

Common throughout Mexico and Central America; restricted in the United States to southern Texas, New Mexico, and Arizona. Listed as endangered in Texas since 1987 under the name *Nasua nasua;* completely protected in New Mexico; hunted in Arizona. Little is known of population sizes in the United States.

Subspecies

Nasua narica molaris, Arizona north to the Gila River, New Mexico in Hidalgo and Grant counties, Texas along the Rio Grande to Big Bend, and south throughout Mexico

Nasua narica narica, Nicaragua south to Panama and northern South America

Nasua narica nelsoni, Yucatan Peninsula along Caribbean coast

Nasua narica yucatanica, central Yucatan Peninsula

References

Mammalian Species 487; Decker, 1991; Kaufmann, 1962

Family Felidae

Worldwide, there are 36 species of cats, divided into 18 genera. In North America, there are 7 species in 5 genera. North American cats occur from the Arctic to the Mexican border (and beyond), in virtually all available natural habitats, and fossils are known from as far back as the Eocene. Cats are excellent hunters and may stalk prey until moving close enough for a brief dash and the kill. Many species are nocturnal but some are diurnal.

Cats range in size from just over 300 mm to almost 3 m, with tails adding another 50 mm to over a meter. Weights range from 1.5 kg in the smallest species to 300 kg in tigers. In North America, the margay, *Leopardus wiedii,* is the smallest, and the jaguar, *Panthera onca,* the largest. Colors range from black in the jaguarundi, *Herpailurus yagouarondi,* through shades of gray and brown in bobcats *(Lynx rufus)* and lynxes, *(Lynx canadensis)* to reddish in pumas *(Puma concolor).* Additional markings like the rosettes of jaguars, and spots of margays and ocelots *(Leopardus pardalis),* are common, as are stripes in the young of several species.

Cats are built for stealthy stalks and quick bursts of speed. They are muscular and lithe, with heavy chest musculature and long, sinewy limbs. The forefeet have five digits and the hind feet have four, all with retractable claws. The head is shortened and compact, with strong dentition supported by powerful jaw muscles for handling vertebrate prey.

Most cats are adept at climbing and quite capable of swimming to cross rivers and lakes. They rely heavily on both vision and hearing in foraging. They shelter in trees, caves, burrows, hollow logs, dense vegetation, or occasionally in burrows of other animals. Most are solitary, with the sexes getting together only to breed. Females usually produce only a single litter of 1–6 kittens per year. The young are born helpless and rely on the mother until they are old enough to hunt on their own. Most cats are fairly long-lived, with individuals surviving for 15–30 years in the wild.

References
Nowak, 1991

North American Genera
Puma
Leopardus
Herpailurus
Lynx
Panthera

Cougar | *Puma concolor*

The cougar has the widest distribution of any mammal in the western hemisphere, extending from southeastern Alaska to southern Argentina and Chile. It uses many habitats, including desert scrub, chaparral, swamps, and forests, but avoids agricultural areas, flat shrubless deserts, and other habitats that lack topographic or vegetative cover. Cougars live at low density (0.9 to 4.9 cougars per 100 square km), with an adult sex ratio of about 2 females per male. Home ranges of females average 140 square km (26–350) and overlap extensively, whereas male home ranges average 280 square km (140–760), with minimal overlap between adjacent adult males. Male home ranges may overlap those of several females.

Puma concolor is strongly nocturnal and crepuscular, and hunts by slow stalking or by springing from cover at close range. When hunting, a cougar travels about 10 km per night in 6 travel bouts averaging 1.2 hours each, alternating with shorter periods of stasis (presumably stalking or waiting in ambush). When feeding on a large mammal, cougars minimize spoilage and loss to scavengers by dragging the kill up to 350 m to a secluded cache site, burying the carcass under leaves and debris, and feeding only at night. During the day they bed an average of 400 m (0–4200 m, mode 0–50 m) from the carcass. Except when feeding on a large mammal (about 3 nights per carcass), an individual rarely beds in the same location on successive days. Throughout its range, ungulates are the cougar's primary prey; each cougar kills about 48 ungulates per year. In North America, cougars also feed on coyotes, bobcats, porcupines, lagomorphs, beavers, opossums, raccoons, skunks, and other cougars. Domestic livestock, especially sheep, goats, and young calves, are also taken.

The specific epithet *concolor* refers to pelage that does not vary in color over the back, sides, limbs, and tail (except the tip) of adult cougars. The shade of brown varies geographically and seasonally from gray to reddish-brown. The monotone col-

oration and long tail, which is usually held close to the ground when walking, are the best field marks. Individual cougars vary in facial color patterns, and black-tipped tails are common.

Both males and females are solitary except for breeding associations lasting 1–6 days. Cougars breed throughout the year; a weak summer peak in births is more pronounced at higher latitudes. After a 90-day gestation period, the female gives birth, usually to 3 (1–6) cubs. Each blind neonate weighs about 500 g and has a spotted pelage. The parturition site, usually in nearly impenetrable vegetation, is kept free of feces and prey remains, lacks any nest-like modifications, and is abandoned when the cubs are about 40–70 days old. Cubs accompany their mother until dispersal at 10–26 months of age (mean 15 months), at which time juvenile females disperse net distances of 9–140 km (mean 32 km) and juvenile males 23–274 km (mean 85 km). Dispersers may take more than a year to integrate themselves into the breeding population; during the transition they may sequentially occupy 1–5 small transient home ranges. The interval between births is usually about 24 months, but decreases when a litter is lost or disperses early.

To protect livestock, until the 1960s the cougar was persecuted by professional government hunters and was subject to state bounties. Since 1970, control efforts in the United States and Canada have focused on known stock-killers, and most states and provinces manage cougar populations for sustained sport hunting. Although the cougar is threatened by habitat fragmentation in southern California and other urbanizing areas, habitat connectivity can be maintained by protecting habitat corridors, which dispersers readily find and use. Although cougars are elusive and usually avoid humans, they attack about four humans per year (averaging about one fatality a year) in the United States and Canada. Most victims are children or adults traveling alone. *P. Beier*

Puma concolor

Size

Head and body length: 1,020–1,540 (1,270) mm
(males); 860–1,310 (1,140) mm (females)
Tail length: 680–960 (760) mm (males);
630–790 (710) mm (females)
Weight: 36–120 (62) kg (males); 29–64 (42) kg
(females)

Identification

The cougar is distinguished from the jaguar,
the only other large New World cat, by
unspotted pelage, and from the bobcat and
lynx by its much longer tail.

Recent Synonyms

Felis concolor

Other Common Names

Mountain lion, puma, Florida panther
(*P. c. coryi*), catamount (archaic)

Status

Populations in western North America are
stable except in areas of urban growth.

P. c. schorgeri is probably appropriate for listing
under the U.S. Endangered Species Act, but
conclusive data on biological vulnerability and
threat are not currently available. Except for
the endangered population in Florida, the
cougar is extinct in the eastern United States
and Canada, with extinctions since 1950 in
Arkansas, Louisiana, Tennessee, and West
Virginia. It is present in unknown numbers
throughout Central and South America.

Subspecies

Puma concolor azteca, Arizona, New Mexico,
western Mexico
Puma concolor browni, lower Colorado River
(probably not a valid taxon)
Puma concolor californica, California
Puma concolor coryi, Florida (endangered as *Felis
concolor coryi*)
Puma concolor costaricensis, Nicaragua, Costa
Rica, Panama (endangered, extant)
Puma concolor couguar, northeastern United
States (endangered, probably extinct)
Puma concolor hippolestes, Colorado, Wyoming
Puma concolor improcera, Baja California
Puma concolor kaibabensis, Utah, Nevada
Puma concolor mayensis, southern Mexico to
Honduras
Puma concolor missoulensis, Montana, Alberta,
Saskatchewan, northern British Columbia
Puma concolor oregonensis, Oregon, Washington,
southern British Columbia (except Vancou-
ver Island)
Puma concolor schorgeri, Kansas and Missouri to
Minnesota and Wisconsin (probably extinct)
Puma concolor stanleyana, Texas, Oklahoma,
northeastern Mexico
Puma concolor vancouverensis, Vancouver Island

References

Mammalian Species 200; Anderson, 1983; Beier
et al., 1995; Hansen, 1992

Ocelot | *Leopardus pardalis*

The ocelot is a strikingly beautiful animal. Its subtle gray and
brown coat dappled with dark spots and streaks renders the cat
nearly invisible in the shadowy dense thickets where it sleeps
through most of the daylight hours. Found from southern
Texas and Arizona south through the lowlands and mid-
elevations of Mexico, Central, and South America to northern
Argentina, the ocelot occurs in a wide range of habitats from
rainforest, gallery, and tropical deciduous forest to savanna and
xeric scrub. Principally nocturnal, the cats travel as much as
6 km on a night's hunt in search of food, alternating active
hunting with rest stops at favorite denning sites. Prey consists
of a wide variety of small vertebrates and large invertebrates,
including mammals, birds, reptiles, amphibians, fish, insects,
and land crabs. The proportions vary according to seasonal
availability, but rodents are generally the principal food item.

Adult males occupy territories of 4–18 square km; their territories vary in size by habitat and season. Other males are apparently excluded from these territories, though one or more
females often occupy smaller home ranges (2–11 square km)
within the territory of a single male. Adult males are solitary
except for a few hours during mating. Seasonality of ocelot

Leopardus pardalis

breeding is not known, and newborn kittens have been reported from every month of the year. Ocelots bear 1–2 young, 3 exceptionally. The natal den is usually a bare area in a dense thicket, though dens have also been reported in caves, logs, and hollow trees. Gestation is 70–80 days, and the young are born fully furred, with their eyes closed. Offspring remain on the mother's home range for the first year. Young males often disperse at this age, probably forced out by the resident adult male. Females linger on and may settle on a portion of the mother's home range or on a neighboring site after reaching sexual maturity at 15–22 months.

Threats to the species include habitat loss and hunting for the fur trade (ocelot coats sell for as much as $40,000 in Europe). *J. Rappole*

Size
Total length: 950–1,367 (1,078) mm (males);
    920–1,209 (1,022) mm (females)
Length of tail: 280–400 (350) mm (males);
    270–371 (322) mm (females)
Weight: 7.0–14.5 (10.0) kg (males); 7.0–10.8
    (8.8) kg (females)

Identification
The ocelot is comparable in size to the bobcat *(Lynx rufus)*, from which it is easily distinguished by its long tail and grayish or tawny coat covered with numerous dark spots and streaks. The only other spotted cat found in North America north of Costa Rica is the margay *(Leopardus wiedii)*, which is roughly half the size of the ocelot and lacks the two prominent black cheek stripes.

Recent Synonyms
Felis pardalis

Other Common Names
Ocelote, tigrillo

Status
"Endangered," U.S. Department of the Interior, 1982; "Vulnerable," IUCN 1982; rare, local

Subspecies (North America)
Leopardus pardalis albescens, eastern Texas (extirpated) south through the Mexican state of Tamaulipas
Leopardus pardalis mearnsi, Nicaragua, Costa Rica, Panama, and perhaps neighboring Colombia
Leopardus pardalis nelsoni, Mexican states of Sinaloa, Colima, and Guerrero

Leopardus pardalis pardalis, Mexican states of Veracruz, Tabasco, Yucatan, Campeche, Quintana Roo, and Chiapas; also Guatemala, Belize, Honduras, and El Salvador
Leopardus pardalis sonoriensis, Arizona (extirpated?) and the Mexican state of Sonora

References
Mammalian Species 548; Emmons, 1988; IUCN, 1982; Laack et al., 1987; Mondolfi, 1986; Tewes and Schmidly, 1987

Margay | *Leopardus wiedii*

One of the least studied members of the family Felidae, the margay is an arboreal, forest-dwelling cat ranging, in North America, from northeastern Mexico to southern Panama. In South America, its range continues south to northern Argentina. Also known as the margay cat, caucel, tiger cat, or tigrillo, the margay resembles a smaller, thinner version of its close relative the ocelot *(Leopardus pardalis).* Early investigators reported that natives in southern Mexico and Venezuela did not distinguish the margay from the ocelot.

Coloration varies from pale gray to yellow-brown to deep brown, overlaid with variable combinations of darker spots, blotches, stripes, and streaks, with the streaks normally ar-

ranged in longitudinal rows. Margays normally possess a black eye ring and cinnamon-colored cheeks and have a narrow area of white between the cheek and eye. The fur is short, soft, dense, and silky.

Though the margay is often listed as occurring as far north as the Rio Grande Valley of southeastern Texas, its past occurrence there has been rare at best and it is questionable whether viable populations ever existed in the United States. The so-called Texas margay, the subspecies *F. w. cooperi,* which gave rise to such later listings, is based on a single specimen taken at Eagle Pass, Texas, and catalogued in the U.S. National Museum in 1852. Eagle Pass is more than 300 miles north of

Leopardus wiedii

the most northerly known margay populations today, and the subspecies based on this single specimen is almost certainly spurious.

The margay is listed as endangered, but the actual status of its total population is unknown. It is reported to avoid open country and prefer wet savanna, tropical rain forest, and deciduous tropical forest from sea level to elevations above 3,050 m (10,000 feet), but there have been no systematic studies of its home ranges, movement patterns, or habitat preferences. The margay's increasing scarcity has been attributed to the clearing of tropical and subtropical forests and their replacement by pastures and commercial plantations. Official reports from Central American governments describe margay populations as scattered and localized, and report that it is one of the mammals most negatively affected by human populations and associated development.

Limited studies of captive margay activity patterns suggest that the margay is nocturnal, but this also has not been well investigated. One of the most agile and acrobatic of all the cats, it is an outstanding climber and jumper, leading some to dub it the "tree ocelot." The margay's ankle joint is sufficiently mobile to permit supination through 180 degrees, permitting it to grasp a branch equally well with either front or hind paws. Captive margays have been seen to jump nearly 2.5 m vertically and nearly 4 m horizontally, to make nearly instantaneous changes in direction or orientation in mid-jump, to run along a clothesline less than a centimeter in diameter, and to hang by their hind legs while manipulating objects with their front paws.

The margay is reported to use these abilities to its advantage in taking monkeys, tamarins, sloths, squirrels, opossums, birds, rats and smaller mammals, and various species of reptiles and amphibians. Margays are also known to raid chicken coops, and have been observed plucking chickens and other birds before eating them. Captive margays have also been seen eating certain fruits and vegetables, including figs. In controlled experiments, cotton-top tamarins *(Saguinus oedipus)* and red-bellied tamarins *(S. labiatus)* exhibit anxiety or give alarm calls when presented with margay scent, indicating their recognition of the margay as a natural predator.

Margays mature physically and sexually at 6–12 months of age. The estrous cycle has been measured at 32 days, and the period of heat from 4–10 days. Gestation is approximately 9–12 weeks. Litters normally consist of only one or two kittens. Margays can be bred in captivity, though often not without difficulty and they have been known to cannibalize the litters.

Vocalizations include hissing, spitting, growling, snarling, moaning, purring, meowing, and a "barking meow" that is initiated and terminated by an abrupt, hollow-sounding vocalization somewhat similar to a normal meow.

Despite their desirability as pets, the margay's present endangered status makes commercial trade in this species illegal. Indeed, commercial dealers may have contributed to population declines of the species in the past by stimulating private demand and providing financial incentive for the capture of both adults and kittens. *F. Van Dyke*

Size

Total length: 862–1,300 (931) mm (males); 805–1,029 (907) mm (females)

Length of tail: 331–510 (394) mm (males); 324–440 (410) mm (females)

Weight: 3–7 kg (males); 3–5 kg (females)

Identification

Leopardus wiedii is distinguished from *Leopardus pardalis* (ocelot), the other small spotted cat that shares its range, by smaller size, less distinctive spots, slimmer build, fuller face, larger eyes, and longer tail.

Recent Synonyms

Felis wiedii

Other Common Names

Caucel, cunaguaro, margay cat, tiger cat, tigrillo

Status

Endangered

Subspecies (North America)

Leopardus wiedii glaucula, west-central Mexico (Sonora) to southwestern Mexico (Guadalajara)

Leopardus wiedii nicaraguae, Honduras and Nicaragua

Leopardus wiedii oaxacensis, northeastern Mexico (Tamaulipas) to south-central Mexico (Oaxaca)

Leopardus wiedii pirrensis, Panama to northwestern Columbia

Leopardus wiedii salvinia, southwestern Mexico to El Salvador

Leopardus wiedii yucatanica, Yucatan

References

Mammalian Species 579; Koford, 1983; Petersen, 1979; Tewes and Schmidly, 1987

Jaguarundi | *Herpailurus yaguarondi*

Jaguarundis live from Texas and Arizona south to Brazil and northern Argentina. These small cats can be found in tropical and subtropical habitats, almost always in forests and thickets. Their distribution in the United States is restricted to two small, low, semitropical areas, one in Texas and one in Arizona. In the extreme southern corner of Texas along the Rio Grande Valley, jaguarundis inhabit mesquite thickets with dense undergrowth in a region that is an extension of the Tamaulipas coastal plain. In extreme southeastern Arizona they inhabit the densest desert scrub, but there is no recent confirmation of the species' presence in that state. U.S. populations of *Herpailurus*

yaguarondi are marginal extensions of the distribution in Mexico, which covers both coastal lowlands.

The jaguarundi is the least nocturnal wild cat in the United States. It tends to be active primarily in the morning and before dusk, but where it has been hunted, it becomes partially nocturnal. Jaguarundis move alone or in pairs along watercourses, cliff bases, or thickets, mostly under the protection of thick vegetation, boulders, or other cover. Their preference for dense, brushy cover has been noted in several different major habitats: in mesquite woodlands in the north, in pine and oak forests, and in dry and wet tropical forests, where they are

Herpailurus yaguarondi

most frequently seen in secondary vegetation that is a result of disturbance.

Its secretive nature, sensitive senses of smell, hearing, and sight, and its quick reflexes make the jaguarundi difficult to detect in the wild. Typically, an observer sees only a long, slender, cinnamon or dark gray shape darting across a path or small clearing among the bushes. However, its curiosity sometimes betrays it into full view. A camouflaged photographer stalking wildlife in the cloud forests of Mexico was approached by a jaguarundi, which sniffed at his equipment and clothes. At the photographer's slightest movement, the cat jumped backwards and disappeared in the undergrowth.

Two color phases (independent of sex) occur in this uniformly-colored cat. One is reddish brown; the other is dark gray. The venter is slightly paler, and young individuals frequently have whitish patches around the mouth. The ears are short, triangu-

lar, and pointed, the neck is relatively long, the hind legs are longer than the front legs, and the tail is relatively long.

In the southern part of its distribution the young are born at the end of the dry season or the beginning of the rainy season, but there are records of reproduction throughout the year. Gestation lasts 60 to 70 days, and there can be from two to four kittens in a litter. Both color phases can be represented in a litter. The den can be located under the bulky roots of large trees, in fallen hollow logs, or in rock crevices.

The jaguarundi's diet seems to vary regionally; they eat reptiles, including whip-tail lizards and small snakes; small birds, including quail, chachalacas, ducks, and nestlings; and mammals such as rats, mice, squirrels, and rabbits. They also frequently eat arthropods, but the bulk of their energy needs seem to be met by vertebrates. They hunt primarily by stalking, and attack by surprise. They are agile both on the ground, where they are most frequently seen, and in trees. Sometimes jaguarundis become accustomed to hunting in the vicinity of farms and ranches, quickly becoming used to preying on poultry and other farm animals. This behavior frequently ends with the death of the jaguarundi at the hands of the farmer. Some captive jaguarundis eat fruit as part of their regular diet, and relish bananas and grapes.

Jaguarundis have a whistle-like call that resembles that of a small bird. They are sometimes tamed as pets, and behave much like house cats, but their hunting instincts are not easy to control; they will readily jump on chickens or songbirds if given the chance. Jaguarundis are not hunted for their pelts, which are of low quality and lack the fine colors of the coats of mottled cats, but their numbers are decreasing due to habitat destruction and because they are purposefully or opportunistically killed by hunters pursuing other prey.

The fossil record indicates that jaguarundis were present in the United States along the Gulf of Mexico some three million years ago. There is some anecdotal evidence that populations of this species may have become established again in Florida and some other southeastern states. *R. A. Medellín*

Size
No significant sexual dimorphism
Total length: 888–1,372 mm
Length of tail: 320–609 mm
Weight: 4.5–9.0 kg

Identification
The jaguarundi is the only wild cat of its size with a unicolored coat. Cougars are much larger, and ocelots and margays have mottled fur. In tropical areas the jaguarundi can be confused with the tayra *(Eira barbara),* but this mustelid is black with a pale head and a bushier tail.

Recent Synonyms
Felis jaguarundi

Other Common Names
Onza, gato moro, leoncillo, yaguarundi

Status
Rare, widespread; listed as threatened by the government of Mexico and included on Appendix I of CITES

Subspecies
Two subspecies occur in the United States:
Herpailurus yaguarondi cacomitli, extreme

southern Texas along the Rio Grande Valley; most of the range is in Mexico
Herpailurus yaguarondi tolteca, extreme southeastern Arizona; most of the range is in Mexico

References
Mammalian Species 578; Eisenberg, 1989; Nowak, 1991

Canada lynx | *Lynx canadensis*

One of only two species of spotted cats that are not on endangered species lists, the Canada lynx lives in the boreal forests of North America from Alaska to Newfoundland, with some extensions into the northern United States. During population peaks, the range extends into the northern Great Plains states. Habitats include rocky outcrops, bogs, and thickets that may be characterized in winter by deep snow and low temperatures.

Both sexes have similar coloration. The lynx's winter fur is long, thick, and fluffy, with the upperparts grizzled grayish-brown. The ears are buffy brown to blackish with a central white spot, and long black hairs extend from each ear to form a tuft. Longer hairs on the head form a facial ruff. The underparts are whitish with scattered blackish spots, especially on the legs. An annual molt begins in late spring, and gradual replacement of guard hairs accounts for differences in winter and summer coats.

The Hudson Bay Company, along with other European fur interests, began commercial exploitation of the lynx in North America about 200 years ago. Company harvest records provide evidence that lynx populations increase and decline about every 10 years. The cause of the cycle is debated, but remains unresolved.

A predator-prey relationship often is used to explain the population cycles of the Canada lynx, based on similar cycles in its primary food, the snowshoe hare. Like the lynx, it is adapted for life in deep snow by having large, spreading, well-furred paws, and it may constitute more than 80 percent of the lynx's diet. Other foods include squirrels and other small mammals, beaver, deer, and birds. The lynx's hunting techniques include following game trails, focusing on areas of high prey activity, or waiting to ambush passing prey from a "hunting bed." Hunting activity peaks at dawn and dusk, and some food may be cached (stored under snow or debris for later use). Attacks on humans are very rare, but may occur during prey scarcity or when the human wears or carries animal hides or carcasses.

Except for females with young, lynxes are usually solitary animals. Puberty is attained at one year, but may be delayed during periods of low prey availability. Breeding may occur from February through May, but is most common in March and April. Altricial young are born after a gestation period of about 60–70 days. Birth, usually of three young (the range is 1–5) occurs in a den in a hollow log, stump, clump of timber, or in a tangle of roots. The pelage of neonates is well developed, with dark longitudinal streaking apparent on the upperparts. Juveniles may remain with the female until the next breeding season, and probably learn how to capture prey by imitating her. Cooperative hunting is observed occasionally, often involving adult and young lynxes.

Home ranges overlap, but the ranges of females overlap one another more than those of males. Solitary behavior, therefore, is maintained through mutual avoidance. Adults scent-mark their ranges by urinating and defecating frequently on logs, stumps, and bushes located along their travel routes. Cues in the urine are used to avoid contact or to attract mates during the breeding season. Kittens, who share the range of their mother, bury their feces and cover urination sites unless the snow is too hard to allow it.

Individual home ranges vary from 11 to 300 square km. Daily movement distance within the range averages 5–10 km, but varies depending on hunting conditions. The maximum dispersal distance recorded was from Minnesota to Ontario—a distance of 483 km. *R. Tumlison*

Lynx canadensis

Size
Males average slightly larger than females.
Total length: 670–1,067 mm
Length of tail: 50–130 mm
Weight: 4.5–17.3 kg

Identification
Distinguished from the bobcat *(Lynx rufus)*, the
only other spotted cat found within its range,
by slightly larger size, larger paws (an adaptation for walking on snow), and tail having a
black tip that completely encircles the tail
(bobcats have white underneath). The tail is

short, the rostrum is abbreviated, the ears ter-
minate in a tuft of black hairs, the claws are
retractile, and the eyes have an ovoid pupil.
The teeth are reduced in number to 28 in
adults and are highly specialized for carnivory.

Recent Synonyms
Felis canadensis
Felis lynx
Lynx lynx

Other Common Names
Wildcat, loup-cervier (French Canadian)

Status
Common but cyclical, threatened by over-
trapping

Subspecies
Lynx canadensis canadensis, boreal North
    America
Lynx canadensis subsolanus, Newfoundland

References
Mammalian Species 269; McCord and Cardoza,
    1982

Bobcat | *Lynx rufus*

The bobcat is the most widely distributed native cat in North
America. It is a habitat generalist, occurring in almost every
terrestrial habitat type from deserts to swamps to mountains.
Even within a local area, individual bobcats usually use a variety of habitats. Rocky outcrops with ledges are favored for
the den site, but bobcats also use brush piles, hollow logs,
caves, fallen trees, and dense bushes for shelter. In the Southeast, dens are often located in dense clumps of saw palmetto
(Serenoa repens).

There is considerable individual variation in coloration, as
well as seasonal and geographic differences. The upperparts
vary from yellowish- to reddish-brown, with streaks and spots

of dark brown or black, and the underparts are white with
prominent black spots. Occasional melanistic individuals have
been recorded in Florida. The ears have a prominent white
spot on the back and a tuft of black hairs at the tip. Bobcats often walk with the short tail curled upwards, exposing the white
tip on the underside.

Bobcats are primarily nocturnal, but may be abroad at any
time of day. They are largely opportunistic in their choice of
prey, taking mammals ranging in size from mice to deer, as
well as fishes, amphibians, reptiles, birds, and insects. Over
their range, rabbits of different species predominate in the diet;
rat-sized rodents are also an important component. Bobcats
also eat carrion and frequently consume grass or other vegetation, perhaps as a purgative. A bobcat may cover a large kill
such as a deer with debris and return to feed on it.

Estimates of bobcat numbers in different parts of the range
vary from 4 to 274 individuals per 100 square km. Adult bobcats resident in an area occupy home ranges that have been estimated to range from 0.6 to 201 square km. Males generally
have larger home ranges than females; other factors influencing home range size include habitat, season, population density, and prey abundance. Generally home ranges of individuals of the same sex do not overlap appreciably, but male and
female home ranges usually overlap extensively. In addition to
established adults and dependent young, bobcat populations
usually include transient individuals or "floaters," most of
whom are dispersing immature animals. Marking behavior in
the form of exposed feces, urine deposits, and scrapes made
with the hind feet into which urine or feces are deposited play
an important role in bobcat social organization.

Female bobcats reach breeding age at 1 to 2 years, but males
do not normally become fertile until their second year. Breeding usually occurs in winter and spring, but over the entire
range breeding has been reported from August to July. Gesta-

Lynx rufus

tion is about 62 days, and the average number of young is 3, with a range of 1 to 8. A single litter a year appears to be the rule, although a semi-wild free-ranging female in Florida produced two litters in one year. Newborn kittens are reported to weigh from 200 to 800 grams. Their eyes are closed but they are relatively well haired. The eyes open at about 10 days of age, and by 4 weeks of age the young begin to explore their surroundings and require solid food. They are weaned by the 7th or 8th week and begin to accompany the mother on short excursions. Kittens over 4 months of age move around the home range with the mother, as well as on their own, and from about 7 months until they disperse from the natal range become increasingly independent of her.

Little is known about the longevity of wild bobcats. The maximum life span has been estimated to be from 10 to 14 years. A wild female in Florida was known to be approximately 9 years, 10 months old when last observed. Natural mortality factors include starvation, injuries incurred in capturing prey, and predation on kittens by owls, foxes, dogs, and adult male bobcats and on adults by mountain lions and coyotes. Diseases, including notoedric mange, rabies, and feline panleucopenia also cause deaths. *J. N. Layne*

Size
Total length: 475–1252 (869) mm (males);
   610–1219 (786) mm (females)
Length of tail: 108–201 (148) mm (males);
   90–171 (137) mm (females)
Weight: 7.2–31.0 (12) kg (males); 3.8–24.0 (9)
   kg (females)

Identification
The bobcat is distinguished from the Canada lynx *(Lynx canadensis),* the only other short-tailed cat in North America, by a longer tail (more than half the length of the hind foot) that is tipped with black above and white below rather than being all black on the tip.

Recent Synonyms
Felis rufus

Other Common Names
Wildcat, bay lynx, barred bobcat, pallid bobcat, red lynx

Status
Rare to common, depending on geographic region

Subspecies
Lynx rufus baileyi, southwestern United States and northwestern Mexico
Lynx rufus californicus, most of California west of the Sierra Nevada
Lynx rufus escuinapae, central Mexico, with a northern extension along the west coast to southern Sonora
Lynx rufus fasciatus, northwestern California, Oregon, and Washington west of the Cascade Range, and southwestern British Columbia
Lynx rufus floridanus, southeastern United States and north in the Mississippi Valley to southeastern Missouri and southern Illinois
Lynx rufus gigas, northern New York to Nova Scotia and New Brunswick

Lynx rufus oaxacensis, Oaxaca, Mexico
Lynx rufus pallescens, northwestern United States and southern British Columbia, Alberta, and Saskatchewan
Lynx rufus peninsularis, Baja California
Lynx rufus rufus, eastern and midwestern United States
Lynx rufus superiorensis, western Great Lakes area, including southern Ontario, Upper Michigan, Wisconsin, and most of Minnesota
Lynx rufus texensis, western Louisiana, eastern three-fourths of Texas, and south-central Oklahoma, south into Tamaulipas, Nuevo Leon, and Coahuila, Mexico

References
Mammalian Species 563; McCord and Cardoza, 1982; Wassmer et al., 1988; Young, 1958

Jaguar | *Panthera onca*

Jaguars are the largest cats in the New World, but they vary so much in body size, both among individuals within the same population and between average populations in different habitats, that smaller jaguars (e.g. from Belize) weigh less than large pumas (from Wyoming), and female jaguars are outweighed by large male pumas. The differences between our two great cats thus involve lifestyle more than body size.

Jaguars are solitary hunters of the warmer forests where daytime temperatures rarely drop below freezing. Their primary habitat is now the evergreen tropical forest that flanks the Equator, but they were once common in subtropical dry forests, and higher into the desert scrubs that border these to the north (Sonoran Desert canyons, California to Texas), and south (Chaco of Argentina to Uruguay). Sadly for the jaguar, these drier habitats are excellent for cattle ranching, and as cattle have spread, jaguar have dwindled or been locally extirpated because of hunting by ranchers or because they have lost their natural prey. It has been 134 years since the last California jaguar was shot, and there have been only 16 verified records from Arizona in the past 150 years, the most recent in 1997, when one jaguar was photographed and another was seen. However, anecdotal claims of sightings persist in Arizona. The last breeding populations in the United States were probably eliminated shortly after the turn of the century, and all more recent records are likely to have been of lone wanderers that dispersed many kilometers from the nearest viable populations in Mexico. We know little of jaguar ecology in northern Mexico or the United States: the few ecological studies of jaguars have been made in evergreen tropical rainforests of Central and South America and in the flooded grasslands of the Brazilian Pantanal.

Jaguars take a great variety of prey, from tapirs to turtles, and seem to concentrate their diet on the commonest larger mammal species that occur wherever they live. Thus, in some regions they prey largely on peccaries (javalina), in others, on capybaras, and, where large prey is scarce, on armadillos. Jaguars have a strong predilection for water and wet habitats such as flooded grasslands, river floodplains, or lakeshores, and they travel the water's edge to hunt water-dependent prey such as caimans, turtles, capybaras, and fish. They seem to hunt at any hour of the day or night that suits them, perhaps mirroring the activity of their local prey. Where they come into contact with livestock, a minority of individuals become cattle-killers, usually with fatal repercussions for all.

Home ranges vary from 10 to 170 square km, with smaller ranges reported from rain forest and larger ones from open habitats. In the Pantanal, home areas were found to be smaller in the wet season and larger during dry months. Jaguars are not strictly territorial, because a few adults of both sexes share the same area, but they appear to avoid each other. Rarely is more than one adult jaguar at a time found in the same geographic sector, and the number of individuals that can coexist is limited. To signal each other from afar, jaguars sometimes call with a repeated series of deep, resonant grunts, like a bow being rasped across the strings of a bass fiddle. Indeed, hunters sometimes call them in with stringed gourds or hollow kettles that mimic this sound. Jaguars scratch trees and logs, and leave their scats prominently in the middle of trails, behaviors that may serve for remote communication. Only rarely do they scratch the ground, a behavior frequently seen in pumas. There is little data for the wild, but litter size in captivity is usually two, rarely three or four, and females can first breed as two-year-olds. Wild young have been recorded remaining with their mother until they were about 18 months old, which suggests that females may give birth at intervals of two or more years. *L. H. Emmons*

Panthera onca

Size

Males are 10–25 percent larger than females.
Length of head and body: 1,110–1,850 mm
Length of tail: 440–750 mm
Weight: 31–158 kg

Identification

Jaguars are the only very large cats in the
Americas that are spotted with black rosettes;
all other cats with spotted backs are much
smaller. The dorsal surface of the neck is spotted; in ocelots and margays the top of the neck
has strong, longitudinal black stripes. Bobcats
and lynx have short tails; adult puma are
unspotted. Occasional individual jaguars are
black, with visible rosettes.

Other Common Names

Tigre (in Mexico)

Status

Classified as endangered by the United States
government; CITES–Appendix I. Extirpated
(no breeding population) in the United States;
greatly reduced throughout Mesoamerica and
reduced in northern and southern South
America, but still abundant in many parts of
the Amazonian rainforest.

Subspecies

Panthera onca arizonensis, southwestern United
   States and northwestern Mexico
Panthera onca centralis, Panama to southern
   Mexico

Panthera onca goldmani, Yucatan Peninsula
Panthera onca hernandesii, southwestern Mexico
Panthera onca onca, Amazon Basin
Panthera onca paraguensis, Paraguay
Panthera onca peruviana, Peru
Panthera onca veraecrucis, Texas and northeast-
   ern Mexico

References

Mammalian Species 340; Crawshaw and Quigley,
   1991; Seidensticker and Lumpkin, 1991;
   Tewes and Schmidly, 1987

Order Cetacea

Of all mammals, cetaceans are the most completely adapted to life in an aquatic environment. They inhabit all the world's oceans, and are found in a wide range of habitats from coastal and estuarine to highly pelagic. The range of one family, the platanistiids (river dolphins), is confined to several of the world's major rivers and some freshwater lake systems. Cetaceans comprise 10 families, 41 genera, and 78 species. However, it is considered likely that one group, the ziphiids (beaked whales), harbors yet-undiscovered species. One beaked whale species *(Mesoplodon peruvianus)* was described as recently as 1991, and another *(M. pacificus)* has never been observed alive in the field.

The Cetacea are subdivided into two suborders. The Odontoceti (toothed whales) include six families: Delphinidae (oceanic dolphins), Phocoenidae (porpoises), Physteridae (sperm whales), Monodontidae (beluga and narwhal), Platanistidae (river dolphins), and Ziphiidae (beaked whales). The Mysticeti (baleen whales) comprises four families: Balaenopteridae (rorquals), Balaenidae (right whales), Eschrichtiidae (the gray whale), and Neobalaenidae (the pygmy right whale). Representatives of 8 families, 27 genera, and 47 species are found in the waters off North America.

All odontocetes possess teeth, although the number varies by species from one to more than two hundred. Toothed whales generally feed on fish and invertebrates, notably cephalopods and crustaceans. A primary feature of most species is the use of sophisticated echolocation for orientation and prey detection. One form of odontocete, the killer whale *(Orcinus orca),* is the only species known to regularly consume warm-blooded prey, including penguins, seals, and other cetaceans. The mysticetes have no teeth, but instead employ an elaborate filtration system known as baleen (also called whalebone). The keratinous baleen plates hang in large racks from each upper jaw, and these huge screens are fringed on the inside with hair that acts to filter prey from the water. The prey of mysticetes varies by species and includes zoöplankton, amphipods and a variety of small schooling fish.

Dolphins are perhaps the fastest and most agile of the cetaceans; they often are observed following ships. Whales are also strong swimmers and may travel long distances during migrations between feeding and breeding areas; indeed, the humpback *(Megaptera novaeangliae)* and gray whale *(Eschrichtius robustus)* un-

Beluga *(Delphinapterus leucas)*

dertake the longest migrations of any mammal. Generally, the smaller species of the Odonticeti are shallow divers, but sperm whales and beaked whales are known to be capable of extraordinarily deep dives. Although they are sometimes found in deep water, mysticetes generally forage in the upper 200 meters of the water column. While many cetaceans can be found in coastal waters, others are exclusively deep water inhabitants, often occurring near cold-water upwellings where food is abundant. Cetaceans communicate by producing a variety of underwater sounds. Most species of toothed whales are gregarious; however, the social organization of baleen whales is generally characterized by small, unstable groups or solitary individuals. Cetaceans evolved from terrestrial ancestors, who returned to the sea some 50–70 million years ago. Fossils of both surviving suborders are known from the Middle Oligocene; a third suborder, the Archaeoceti, is long extinct. *P. Clapham*

References
Gaskin, 1982; Mead and Brownell, 1993

Family Balaenidae

With only two genera, the balaenids represent one of the smaller families of cetaceans. Indeed, there is strong pressure to revise the taxonomy of this group and re-erect a single genus, *Balaena,* for all three currently recognized species: the northern right, southern right, and bowhead whale. Balaenids are the most robust and massive of all whales for their length: the largest specimens are less than 20 meters in length, yet can attain weights of perhaps 100 tons. All are characterized by a broad back, huge tail, and the absence of a dorsal fin.

Both genera of balaenids occur in North American waters, but one species (the southern right whale) is not found here. Bowheads are the most adapted of all whales to life among ice, and have more than half a meter of blubber to insulate themselves from the cold. Their present range encompasses high-Arctic areas as well as the Okhotsk Sea. Right whales are not quite as fat, but are nonetheless very robust animals. They frequent coastal and shelf waters, although they can also be found far from continental land masses around remote islands.

Balaenids have huge mouths that represent more than one third of the body size, and all species have very long baleen. The baleen is fringed with much finer hair than that of other whales, since it must filter the smallest prey of any mysticete. Right whales feed primarily on copepods; bowheads have a broader diet that includes numerous small invertebrates. Un-like the rorquals, balaenids do not feed in discrete "gulping" events, but instead move through prey patches continually filtering as they swim, a behavior that is known as skim-feeding.

Bowheads undertake limited migrations that are closely associated with sea ice. Right whales make much more extensive seasonal movements into warm water. Females of both species breed every three to five years, but maturity in bowheads occurs much later than in right whales, perhaps as late as 15–20 years of age. All three species are known to be long-lived.

Right whales were so named because they were considered the "right" whales to hunt during the days of early whaling. Indeed, northern rights were probably the first whales to be taken commercially on a systematic basis. Being slow and often coastal, they were easy to capture; furthermore, they floated when killed, and yielded a large quantity of oil and high-quality baleen. These characteristics almost led to their demise, and right whales today include some of the world's most critically endangered mammal populations. The bowhead whale was similarly overexploited, and all but one population of this species is considered close to extinction. Western Arctic bowheads remain the target of subsistence hunting by the Inuit, but this well-managed hunt has little impact on what appears to be a growing population. *P. Clapham*

References
Brownell et al., 1986; Burns et al., 1993

North American Genera
Eubalaena
Balaena

Northern right whale | *Eubalaena glacialis*

Right whales were so called because they were the "right" whales to hunt. Their historic range encompassed much of the North Atlantic and North Pacific oceans; they are now among the rarest mammals on earth. They were targeted by whalers because of their slow swimming speed, high yield in oil and whalebone (baleen), and because their carcasses floated, or "righted," themselves.

Northern right whales were hunted from the onset of whaling in the North Atlantic at least 800 years ago until their commercial extinction at the height of Yankee whaling in the 18th and 19th centuries. No reliable pre-exploitation population estimates exist, but accounts of 19th-century whalers indicate that the right whale was once extremely abundant in the North Pacific. In both oceans, eastern and western stocks have been recognized, and in each case, the eastern stock is virtually extinct. Early exploitation by Basques and other whalers wiped out this species in the eastern North Atlantic. Intensive 19th-century hunting, followed by probable illegal Soviet catches after World War II, reduced the eastern North Pacific stock to a remnant group, a small population that may become extinct when its remaining members die in the next century. No reproduction has been observed in this stock in this century. The western North Atlantic population probably consists of fewer than 350 individuals, and the population in the western North

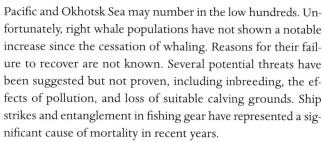

Eubalaena glacialis

Pacific and Okhotsk Sea may number in the low hundreds. Unfortunately, right whale populations have not shown a notable increase since the cessation of whaling. Reasons for their failure to recover are not known. Several potential threats have been suggested but not proven, including inbreeding, the effects of pollution, and loss of suitable calving grounds. Ship strikes and entanglement in fishing gear have represented a significant cause of mortality in recent years.

In the North Atlantic, right whales summer in the Gulf of Maine and on the Scotian shelf. In late fall or early winter the whales begin their southerly migration. Some are observed at what has recently been recognized as a calving ground off the coasts of Georgia and Florida. Calving has been reported in this area from December through March. A few juveniles and males have been seen in this area, but most sightings have been of cow/calf pairs. The wintering grounds for the rest of the population are unknown. Recently cow/calf pairs that were not seen in the Georgia–Florida area have been observed in feeding grounds. This may reflect incomplete surveys of the Georgia and Florida area, but it raises the possibility that other, unidentified calving grounds or summer nursery grounds exist.

In the eastern North Pacific, the distribution of right whales is poorly known. They were once abundant in the Gulf of Alaska, and have been reported from Baja California to the Bering Sea, but is it doubtful that the west coast of the United States ever represented a significant habitat for the species. It is assumed that the whales migrate from higher latitudes to lower latitudes (or to deep water far offshore) in the fall and return in the spring, as do the North Atlantic populations. In the western North Pacific, they occur from the Aleutian Islands and Kamchatka to Japan, with significant concentrations in the

Kuril Islands and the Okhotsh Sea. Recently there have been two sightings of right whales off Hawaii, the first sightings of right whales in these waters in this century, but this area is probably not commonly part of their range.

Male right whales are reported to be sexually mature at a length of 15 m and females at a length of 15.5 m; estimates of the age at sexual maturity range from 5–10 years. An individual female mates with multiple males. It is likely that sperm competition is a major feature of the mating system, because the males have the largest testes of any species: the testes can weigh a ton. Gestation lasts a year. Because most calves are born in winter, it is assumed that mating leading to conception also takes place in winter, although sexual activity has been observed year-round. Females give birth every 3–4 years. Calves are 4.5 to 6 m long at birth and, like other baleen whales, grow rapidly, attaining a length of 12 m by the age of 18 months.

The food of right whales consists primarily of small marine crustaceans, mostly copepods and occasionally euphausiids and other zooplankton. There have been reports of their feeding on small fish, but only rarely. Researchers have also reported right whales feeding below the surface on zooplankton, avoiding nearby schools of fish. Right whales are skim feeders, moving slowly through the water with their mouths partially open, continuously straining the food items with their long baleen. This feeding mechanism contrasts with that of other baleen whales such as humpback whales, which are gulp feeders.

Right whales are known to be long-lived. They are individu-

ally identifiable by the pattern of callosities on the head. A mature female that was photographed when her calf was killed off Florida in 1935 was identified in the Gulf of Maine in 1992, when she was at least 67 years old (assuming that she was at least 10 years old when she calved). Much has been learned about the behavior and biology of this species in the North Atlantic from long-term studies of individuals.

Mature right whales probably have few predators other than humans, although on rare occasions they may be attacked by killer whales. *C. W. Potter and B. Birchler*

Size
Total length: 17 m (maximum recorded 18 m)
Weight: 60,000–100,000 kg

Identification
Right whales can easily be distinguished from the other great whales by their lack of a dorsal fin or dorsal ridge, their stout, robust stature, and the presence of distinctive growths on the head known as callosities. Only the bowhead is similar in overall shape and size, and it lacks the right whale's characteristic callosities. The right whale often raises its huge, all-black tail in the air before a dive. Its baleen, which is black, can be up to 2,440 mm (8 feet) in length.

Other Common Names
Biscayan right whale

Status
Endangered

References
Cummings, 1985; Ellis, 1980; Leatherwood and
    Reeves, 1983

Bowhead whale | *Balaena mysticetus*

Bowhead whales are found only in the far north and are generally associated with sea ice. Their original distribution was more circumpolar, but following intense harvesting by whalers in the 19th century, remnant stocks are now more isolated. Whales of the largest remaining stock, currently estimated at 8,000 (6,900–9,200) animals, migrate around Alaska between the Bering and Beaufort seas. Smaller stocks occur in the Okhotsk Sea of Russia (approximately 300), Davis Strait between northeast Canada and Greenland (approximately 350), Hudson Bay in northeastern Canada (at least 100), and Spitsbergen in the North Atlantic (only "in the tens"). These population estimates are very sketchy due to the logistical challenges of research in the Arctic seas where these whales live and due to the small size of most stocks.

The only other ice-associated whales commonly found in the far north are belugas *(Delphinapterus leucas)* and narwhals *(Monodon monoceros)*. Because bowheads evolved as air-breathing mammals in a sea partially covered with ice, they have developed adaptations such as a smooth back without a dorsal fin, a blow hole situated in a high crown on top of the head, a thick insulating layer of blubber (up to 28 cm thick), and an ability to make long dives, in some cases for more than an hour. Also, bowheads can break through ice as thick as 60 cm.

Bowheads have thick (up to 2.4 cm) black skin with various amounts of white on the chin, ventral surfaces, and tail stock. The patterns of white and black are genetically endowed and are to some degree unique. In addition, wounds that penetrate their black skin result in white marks that may last a lifetime. These wounds are so common and visible that individuals can be identified in aerial photographs, and certain whales have been seen several times over many years. The cause of the wounds is unknown but they are probably most often due to contact with sea ice.

Bowheads of the western Arctic stock apparently do most of their feeding during the four months they are in the Beaufort Sea. Feeding occurs in the water column, sometimes at or near the bottom (as evidenced by mud plumes) or on the surface (described as skimming). The cavernous mouth opens, taking in volumes of water including prey items; then the tongue rises, pushing out the water but trapping particles on the frilled inside surface of the baleen plates. The tongue then sweeps the prey into the whale's digestive tract. More than 60 species of animals—tiny crustaceans from several different families—

Balaena mysticetus

were found in the stomachs of 35 whales killed by Eskimos in their subsistence hunt. Copepods and euphausiids predominated both in terms of volume and number of species (11 copepod species and 2 euphausiid species). Mysids and gammarid amphipods were dominant in only a few stomach samples.

The bowhead breeding period is probably in late winter or early spring, but sexual activity has been observed during most

months of the year. Mating occurs in pairs or in groups consisting of several males and one or more females. Active vocalizations in the spring suggest that acoustics play a role in reproduction, allowing bowheads to interact across distances of 5–10 km. Aerial displays, such as breaching and fluke-slapping, are sometimes conducted with such persistence that it appears they have a role in demonstrating reproductive dominance. Following a gestation period of 13–14 months, most calves are born from April to early June, during the spring migration. Females give birth to a single calf, which measures 4.0–4.5 m in length, every three or four years. Weaning probably occurs during the following year's spring migration, when most yearlings are 6.6–8.2 m long. Subsequent growth is slower than for other baleen whales. Females become sexually mature when they are 12.5–14.0 m long, presumably at 15 years. Very few data are available for males, but they apparently become sexually mature when they are 12–13 m long. With a calving inter-

val of 3–4 years (longer than for most other cetaceans), a slow growth rate, and a persistent harvest, the bowhead population has been slow to recover from the heavy depletion it suffered during years of commercial whaling. *D. Rugh*

Size

Total length: 14–17 m (males); 16–18 m (females)

Width of fluke: 2–6 m (one-third of body length)

Length of baleen: up to 4 m (longest of all whales)

Weight: 7,500–10,000 kg

Identification

Bowhead whales are large black cetaceans with various amounts of white on their chins and ventral surfaces. When a mature animal is at the surface, its profile often consists of a triangular head and smooth, round back with the neck below the water line.

Recent Synonyms

Balaena borealis

Other Common Names

Arctic right whale, Greenland right whale, polar whale

Status

Endangered

References

Braham et al., 1980; Burns et al., 1993; Sheldon and Rugh, 1995

Family Balaenopteridae

This family contains 2 genera and 6 species, all of which occur in North American waters. Balaenopterids are known as "rorquals," from a Danish word meaning "tubed whale," because of the ventral pleats that distinguish all members of this family. Rorquals range in size from moderate to enormous; in the latter category is the blue whale, which, at more than 30 m in length and almost 200 tons, is the largest animal known ever to have inhabited the earth.

These whales are capable of opening their mouths very wide. By expanding their pleats, they distend a huge ventral pouch that can accommodate an enormous quantity of water and prey. The water is then squeezed out, with the small fish or crustaceans trapped by the fringe of hair that lines the inner surface of the baleen plates. All rorquals feed on krill, which is the primary prey of this group in the Southern Ocean. However, all but the blue whale also feed extensively on small schooling fish, and some occasionally take other prey. Most rorquals migrate to low-latitude waters in winter to mate and calve. During this time, they feed little or not at all, subsisting instead on the vast stores of fat accumulated during the summer feeding season in high latitudes. The Bryde's whale (*B. edeni*) is an exception: at least one form of this species remains in warm water all the time, and is the only mysticete that breeds year-round.

Gestation lengths are around 11–12 months for all species, and the foetal growth rate is the fastest of any mammal. Age at weaning varies by species from a few months to a year. Although at least the humpback whale is capable of annual reproduction, the most common interbirth interval in all rorquals is two or three years. The young are large (3–7 m) at birth, and range in size at weaning from 5 to 16 m.

Most populations of rorquals were devastated by whaling this century, and some (notably minke whales) are still taken commercially today. Balaenopterids are known from mid-Miocene to Pleistocene and Recent in North America. *P. Clapham*

Reference
Rice, 1984

North American Genera
Balaenoptera
Megaptera

Minke whale | *Balaenoptera acutorostrata*

Along the western coast of North America, minke whales range from Point Barrow, Alaska, south to Baja California, Mexico, in both shallow coastal waters and deep waters far offshore. Most minke whales evidently migrate north through coastal waters in spring and summer and then migrate south, farther offshore, in autumn and winter. Some, however, may reside year-round in a few areas, particularly in northern Puget Sound. In the northwest Atlantic, minke whales range from the Gulf of Mexico and the Antilles in winter to Davis Strait and Baffin Bay in summer. During the northward migration in spring and summer, most of them appear to travel in nearshore waters. The southward migration in fall and winter appears to be farther offshore. Minke whales are common in the Gulf of Maine and along the Newfoundland and Labrador coasts during summer. Some whales reach Baffin Bay by late summer, and some may reside year-round in the Gulf of St. Lawrence, St. Lawrence River, and Hudson Strait. However, little is known about population structure or additional movements within this overall range, and there is evidence that the whales may segregate by age.

Along the coast of western North America, breeding appears to occur year-round, but most calves are born in January and June. In waters off eastern North America, minke whales mate from October to March and calves are born about 10 months later. Neonates are about 2.4–2.8 m long; the calves are nursed for about 4–5 months. About half of all females are sexually mature when they are about 6 to 7 years old, and 86–97 percent of the mature female population gives birth each year. About 50 percent of females are physically mature when 30 years old, compared to about 22 years for males.

Minke whales generally occur alone or in groups of two or three, although larger aggregations have been observed on some summer feeding grounds. The whales approach boats in some areas, evidently attracted by motor noise. When travel-

Balaenoptera acutorostrata

ing, minke whales usually surface only a few times before diving, and because their blows are not visible, the whales are not easily seen even in calm conditions.

Minke whales are not particularly vocal, although some low-frequency grunts and thumps and some higher frequency pings and clicks have been recorded in the St. Lawrence River and off Newfoundland. These vocalizations are evidently used for intraspecific communication.

In the North Atlantic, commercial whalers began hunting minke whales in the 1920s, mostly near Norway, Greenland, and Iceland; small numbers were killed in eastern North American waters, mostly in the bays of northeastern Newfoundland, where a small land-based fishery operated from 1947–1972. In the Pacific, small numbers of minke whales were killed historically by natives of the Pacific Northwest, particu-larly those at Cape Flattery, Washington. A few minke whales were killed by commercial whalers near British Columbia and near Akutan, Alaska, in the early 1900s, but otherwise this species was never actively hunted along the western coast of North America. Minke whales in those waters may be a stock distinct from those in the Okhotsk Sea, Sea of Japan, East China Sea, and Yellow Sea in the western North Pacific.

In the North Pacific minke whales eat euphausiids, copepods, sand lance, and herring. In the North Atlantic they prey on euphausiids, copepods, sand lance, capelin, cod, whiting, pollack, and herring. Cod, before stocks declined, and capelin have been reported as dominant prey in waters off Newfoundland. Killer whales (*Orcinus orca*) occasionally attack and kill minke whales. *B. S. Stewart*

Size

Females are somewhat larger than males.
Total length: 6.7–8.4 m (maximum about 9.8 m, males); 7.3–8.8 m (maximum about 10.7 m, females)
Weight: 20,000–40,000 kg

Identification

B. acutorostrata is the smallest member of the genus *Balaenoptera* and the second smallest of all baleen whales. The rostrum is very pointed and narrow, with a single prominent ridge along its dorsal midline. There are 50–70 ventral grooves along the throat, chest, and belly to just behind the flippers, in front of the umbilical scar. The dorsal fin is relatively tall, strongly back-curved, and located about two-thirds of the way back from the tip of the snout. The body is black to dark gray dorsally and white ventrally, with some gray extending onto the sides just behind the flippers and below the dorsal fin. Some individuals have a pale dorsal chevron behind the head, and most minke whales in the northern hemisphere have a distinct white band across the dorsal surface of each flipper. There are 230–360 yellowish-white baleen plates hanging from the upper gums. The minke whale's size, head shape, and body coloration distinguish it from other rorquals (sei, Bryde's, fin, and blue whales); the most reliable and obvious diagnostic feature is the white stripe on the flippers. Minkes rarely have a visible blow.

Recent Synonyms

Agaphelus gibbosus
Balaenoptera bonaerensis
Balaenoptera huttoni
Balaenoptera rostrata

Other Common Names

Sharp-headed finner, lesser rorqual, piked whale, little piked whale

Status
Relatively common in coastal waters of the
western North Atlantic; relatively common
seasonally in coastal waters of the eastern
North Pacific

Subspecies
Some authors have recognized three sub-
species based on geographic distribution:
B. a. acutorostrata in the North Atlantic,
B. a. davidsoni in the North Pacific, and
B. a. bonaerensis in the Southern Hemisphere.

Recent molecular data support this division,
but the issue remains unresolved.

References
Horwood, 1990; Leatherwood et al., 1987;
  Stewart and Leatherwood, 1985

Sei whale | *Balaenoptera borealis*

The distribution of sei whales is poorly known. Like the other rorquals, sei whales are thought to undertake a summer migration to higher latitudes and a winter migration towards more temperate or equatorial waters. Sei whales can be found in the North Pacific from California to the Gulf of Alaska in the summer, migrating as far south as 20° north latitude during the winter months. Sightings have been reported in the western North Atlantic, most from north of the mid-Atlantic region. There are some accounts, however, of sei whales off Maryland, North Carolina, and Florida. Although strandings of Brydes whales and sei whales have been confused in the literature, there are valid records from Massachusetts, North Carolina, South Carolina, Louisiana, and Mississippi. Two of these strandings involved the same whale and may be indicative of normal migratory patterns. In July, 1974, a live sei whale was found stranded in a boat harbor in Eastham, Massachusetts. The Coast Guard attempted to tow the animal to sea by tying a heavy nylon line around the caudal peduncle. The tow

had to be abandoned when the whale became active. The line was cut at the boat, leaving the whale with the line still attached. The following April, the whale washed ashore freshly dead at Corolla, North Carolina, with the line still attached.

In the Northern Hemisphere, female sei whales reach a maximum length of 18.6 m. Adult males are slightly smaller at 17.7 m. Sexual maturity is attained between eight and ten years of age, when the whales are 12.7 to 13.7 m in length. Calves are born during the fall-spring mating season of September to March. They are typically 4.5 to 4.8 m long and about 65 kg at birth. The calving interval is thought to be 2–3 years, with a gestation period of approximately one year and a lactation period of 6 to 9 months.

The name "sei," pronounced "sigh," comes from the Norwegian word for codfish, which sei whales have been known to prey upon. These whales feed primarily on copepods, but are also known to consume euphausiids, squid, and small schooling fish. They are unique feeders in that they both gulp, like

Balaenoptera borealis

blue and fin whales, and skim, like right, bowhead, and gray whales. When feeding, sei whales may be found in fairly large numbers, but generally they are seen in small groups of six or fewer. They are known for sudden influxes into particular feeding areas, followed by their disappearance, sometimes for years. This is assumed to be related to fluctuations in prey abundance, but it is not clear why other baleen whales do not show similar dramatic movements and disappearances.

As early as the 17th century, Japanese whalers were catching sei whales in their net fisheries. However, large-scale commercial harvesting was not possible until the 1800s, with the invention of the explosive harpoon gun and steam-driven whaling ships. At first modern whalers concentrated on the larger rorquals, but as those stocks began to thin, efforts to take sei whales increased. In the North Pacific the take of sei whales peaked in the mid-1960s and 1970s. By the mid-1980s North Pacific sei whale populations were reduced to the point where they received protection by the International Whaling Commission. Except for a limited take in Iceland, sei whales have not been hunted in the western North Atlantic since the 1970s. In the North Pacific, pre-exploitation population levels were probably around 63,000, but today there are estimated to be only 14,000 sei whales. An estimated 12–13,000 remain in the North Atlantic. Data are not adequate to make an accurate estimate of the North Atlantic pre-exploitation population.
C. W. Potter and B. Birchler

Size
Total length: 14–18.6 m
Weight: 8,500–11,300 kg (males); 8,600–15,600 kg (females)

Identification
The sei whale can be distinguished from the other rorquals by its large, prominent, dolphin-like dorsal fin and by its uniformly dark gray coloration. Sei whales frequently have round or oval scars, which can give them a mottled appearance superficially resembling that of the blue whale. Bryde's whale is very similar to the sei whale in size and appearance, but has ridges on the rostrum; the sei whale does not have rostral ridges. (The latitudinal range of the two species is different, but does overlap in some areas.) At close range, sei whales are distinguishable from fin whales by the color of the lower right jaw,which is black in the sei whale and white in the fin whale. The sei whale's baleen is typically gray-black, with a paler fringe that is almost the same texture as human hair.

Status
Endangered

Subspecies
Balaenoptera borealis borealis, Northern Hemisphere
Balaenoptera borealis schlegelii, Southern Hemisphere

References
Ellis, 1980; Evans, 1987; Gambell, 1985; International Whaling Commission, 1977; Leatherwood and Reeves, 1983

Bryde's whale | *Balaenoptera edeni*

Bryde's whales look so much like sei whales that they were not generally recognized until 1908, when Johan Bryde (rhymes with Frieda), a pioneer of the Norwegian whaling industry, set up the first whaling station in South Africa. The Norwegian whalers working there began killing fair numbers of a kind of rorqual that they had never before encountered, so Bryde commissioned Orjan Olsen, a zoologist at Kristiania (= Oslo) University, to spend the 1912/1913 whaling season in South Africa studying them. Once Olsen had pointed out the diagnostic features of this new species, which he named *Balaenoptera brydei,* whalers and biologists identified them in many other parts of the world. Shortly thereafter, most cetologists decided that Bryde's whale was the same species as *Balaenoptera edeni,* a somewhat smaller rorqual from Burma, which had been given the name *Balaenoptera edeni* by John Anderson, Superintendent of the Indian Museum in Calcutta, in 1879. However, molecular studies now indicate that *B. edeni* and *B. brydei* may not be conspecific, and the scientific name of this species may again become *Balaenoptera brydei.*

Balaenoptera edeni

In contrast with most of their congeneers, Bryde's whales are confined to tropical and warm temperate waters. Many of them are year-round local residents of shallow coastal waters, whereas others lead a pelagic life far from land, and migrate north and south with the seasons. In the central North Pacific, some of the pelagic individuals move north in late summer as far as the Subarctic Boundary—the convergence between the cold Aleutian Current and the warmer Kuroshio Extension, or North Pacific Current—which crosses the western and central Pacific at roughly 42° N. In the eastern North Pacific, because of the cold southward-flowing California Current, these whales usually do not go above 26° N on the west coast of Baja California, but at least two vagrants have been sighted off southern California. In the western North Atlantic, Bryde's whales range in the Caribbean Sea, the Gulf of Mexico, and along the east coast of the United States as far north as the Chesapeake Bay (37° N). On the eastern side of the Atlantic they range north to the Strait of Gibraltar (36° N).

At sea, the pair of lateral ridges on their rostrum is the only field mark by which Bryde's whales can be separated with certainty from sei whales and young fin whales. Nevertheless, experienced observers become aware of other distinctive physical and behavioral attributes that are useful clues. The dorsal fin of Bryde's whale is intermediate in shape and relative size between those of sei and fin whales. In color, they are indistinguishable from sei whales, but can be separated from fin whales by the lack of white on the right lower lip. A fresh carcass presents another distinction: Bryde's whales are recognizeable by their black baleen plates, the fringe of which is pale gray and coarse, not white and silky as in the sei whale. They

also differ from sei (and minke) whales in that their throat grooves extend posteriorly beyond the umbilicus, as do those of fin and blue whales. When surfacing to blow, Bryde's whales usually rise obliquely, so that the head is the first part of the body to break the surface, and the dorsal fin does not clear the water until after the whale has inhaled and is rolling forward to submerge; in this habit they resemble fin whales rather than sei whales. Dives may last from 1 to 11 minutes, and are interspersed with a series of 1 to 7 blows at 15-second intervals—again, a pattern much more like that of fin whales than sei whales. When chased by a vessel, Bryde's whales characteristically swim close to the surface and attempt to elude the vessel by frequently changing course, rather than by increasing their speed and fleeing, as fin and sei whales tend to do.

Bryde's whales eat a greater variety of organisms than the other kinds of large rorquals do, and they are the only ones that routinely take more fishes than crustaceans. The whales that live along the Pacific coast of Mexico have been seen preying on schools of northern anchovies *(Engraulis mordax)* and on swarms of epipelagic red crabs *(Pleuroncodes planipes)*. In the Gulf of California they subsist on Pacific sardines *(Sardinops sagax),* deepbody thread herrings *(Opisthonema libertate),* and the euphausiid *Nyctiphanes simplex.* The stomachs of animals taken on the high seas in the central Pacific contained eight species of fishes and ten species of crustaceans, but the predominant items were oceanic lightfish *(Vinciguerria nimbaria),* found in 55 percent of the stomachs, and two kinds of euphausiids *(Euphausia similis* and *Nematoscelis difficilis)* in 36 percent.

The reproductive cycle of these whales has been little studied. Their age at sexual maturity has not been determined. The migratory, pelagic individuals are seasonal breeders. They mate mostly in the winter, give birth to their calves 12 months later, and wean them the following summer when they are about six months old. The resident coastal animals, on the other hand, seem to mate at any time of the year. Each mature female bears a calf only once every two or three years. Young calves accompanied nine percent of the older Bryde's whales seen in the equatorial eastern Pacific from February to April.

The only times that Bryde's whales were ever exploited in the eastern North Pacific were in 1913/14, from 1925 to 1929, and in 1935, when Norwegian whalers killed a total of 116 along the west coast of Mexico. In the western Pacific, Japanese whalers were catching Bryde's whales as long ago as 1910, but the species was confounded with the sei whale in the official statistics. There were so many around the Ogasawara Gunto (Bonin Islands) that one to three Japanese floating factories were sent there each spring from 1946 to 1952. These fleets caught a total of 1,342 "sei" whales, all of which were probably Bryde's whales. In addition, shore-based whalers in Japan killed 4,241 Bryde's whales between 1945 and 1986, after which a worldwide moratorium on whaling went into effect.

Meanwhile, because of the increasing scarcity of fin and sei whales, Soviet and Japanese pelagic whaling expeditions shifted their hunting grounds farther south and redirected their effort toward Bryde's whales. From 1970 until 1979, the two to five fleets that operated in the North Pacific each season took a total of 6,815 Bryde's whales, after which pelagic whaling was banned. This exploitation reduced the North Pacific population (north of 20° N), which originally numbered 23,000 or more, to about 18,000 animals. Bryde's whales fared better in the North Atlantic, where the only known catches were ten animals that were landed at the shore station in Ceuta (Spanish Morocco) in 1948. *D. W. Rice*

Size
Total length: 11.9–14.6 m (males); 12.2–15.6 m (females)
Weight: 11,300–16,200 kg

Identification
At sea, Bryde's whale can be distinguished from *Balaenoptera borealis* by the presence of a lateral ridge along each side of the rostrum, in addition to the medial ridge.

Recent Synonyms
Balaenoptera brydei

Other Common Names
Roqual

Status
Common

References
Best, 1977; Mead, 1977; Omura, 1966; Rice, 1977, 1979; Tershy et al., 1993

Blue whale | *Balaenoptera musculus*

Blue whales are the largest animals ever to exist on our planet, with some females in the Southern Hemisphere reaching lengths of 33.58 m and weighing up to 190,000 kg—as much as 30–40 African elephants. Animals off the North American coasts are thought to be slightly smaller on average than their counterparts in southern waters.

In the North Pacific, one population of blue whales spends the summer months off California. In the fall these whales migrate south to winter in the warmer waters off southern California and Baja California, where they are thought to calve and mate. An apparently separate population summers in the Gulf of Alaska and along the Aleutian Islands; the migratory destination of this population is less clear. The North Atlantic population feeds in the summer months as far north as Davis Strait, Baffin Bay, and southwestern Greenland. Where the whales migrate for the winter is not as well known as for the North Pacific population; there are records from Long Island, New York, Ocean City, New Jersey, and even as far south as Florida. In all populations, it is likely that much mating and calving takes place offshore, far from the coast.

Calves are 6–7 m in length when they are born, in late fall and winter. They nurse for approximately seven to eight months, by which time they are 16 m long. During this period of nursing, a calf's weight increases an average of 90 kg per day and its length an average of 4.2 cm. Females reach sexual maturity in five years at lengths of 21–23 m. Males mature in slightly less time at just under five years and at slightly shorter lengths of 20–21 m. Their testes are surprisingly small for the size of the animal, suggesting that sperm competition does not

Balaenoptera musculus

occur in this species. Once mature, females give birth to one calf every 2–3 years. The gestation period is 10–11 months. Longevity in blue whales has been difficult to determine, in part due to the limited data. Various techniques of estimating age include counting the number of corpora albicantia (ovarian scars caused by ovulation in sexually mature females), eye lens coloration, and counting the number of ridges on baleen plates

two species are known to hybridize, albeit rarely. Blue whales rank among the fastest of the whales, with feeding speeds of 2–6.5 km per hour and cruising speeds of 5–33 km per hour. When chased, they can reach speeds as high as 48 km per hour.

Blue whales have the deepest voices in the animal kingdom, vocalizing as low as 14 Hz (well below the range of human hearing) at a volume of almost 200 decibels. These sounds can travel thousands of miles in deep water, leading to speculation that the whales may be able to communicate across oceans. They may also use regularly-spaced low-frequency pulses to navigate by "imaging" distant land masses or islands from hundreds of miles away.

In part because of their swiftness and large size, blues were not often hunted by whalers before the invention of the harpoon gun and steam-driven whaling ships, which signaled the advent of modern whaling in the mid-1800s. These changes in technology, coupled with over-fishing of the whalers' more traditional quarry (sperm, right, and bowhead whales), focused the attention of the whaling industry on blue whales and the other rorquals. In the North Pacific, pre-exploitation values for blue whales are estimated at 4,500–6,000 animals, although any population figure for such a wide-ranging, deep-diving species is at best an educated guess. Today the population is estimated at only 1,400–1,900 animals. Early population levels in the northwest Atlantic are estimated to have been 1,100 whales, but today that number has been reduced to only a few hundred. Blue whales have been protected by the International Whaling Commission (IWC) since 1966. Unfortunately, their populations are still not showing signs of recovery. *C. W. Potter and B. Birchler*

(although these chip and wear off with age). In 1955 British zoologist Peter Purves introduced the now widely used method for age determination in some baleen whale species of counting annual layers in the whale's waxy ear plug. Maximum age estimates for blue whales range up to 80–90 years.

Blue whales feed almost exclusively on euphausiids, which are small, shrimplike zooplankton commonly known as krill, and may consume up to six or seven tons of food a day. Characterized as "gulp feeders," they have long throat grooves that allow the throat to expand. Huge amounts of water and krill are taken into the mouth. When the mouth closes, the water is forced out through the baleen and the food remains on the bristles of the baleen.

Observations of blue whales are usually of solitary individuals or small groups of two or three animals. Occasionally, mixed schools of blue and fin whales have been seen, and the

Size

Females are larger than males.
Total length: 22–28 m (Northern Hemisphere)
Weight: 64,000 kg (average for 22.4 m whale)

Identification

The blue whale is easily distinguished by its huge, mottled, bluish-gray body, its broad, U-shaped head, and its very small dorsal fin, located on the posterior quarter of the back. Unlike the fin whale, the only roqual of comparable size, the blue whale often raises its tail prior to a dive.

Other Common Names

Sulphur-bottom

Status

Endangered

Subspecies

Balaenoptera musculus brevicauda (pygmy blue whale), known from Southern Hemisphere; extent of range unclear
Balaenoptera musculus intermedia, Southern Hemisphere
Balaenoptera musculus musculus, Northern Hemisphere

References

Evans, 1987; Leatherwood and Reeves, 1983; Yochem and Leatherwood, 1985

Fin whale | *Balaenoptera physalus*

The fin whale is the second-largest of all the cetaceans (after the blue whale) and thus probably the second largest animal ever to have lived on earth. In the Southern Hemisphere, the largest recorded individual was a female slightly more than 27 m (89 feet) in length, weighing more than a hundred tons. The finback (as it is commonly known) is a vast, sleek animal that is among the fastest of all the great whales, and is probably capable of reaching burst speeds of 25 knots. Found in all the world's oceans, fin whales were probably among the most abundant large whales before whaling devastated many populations.

In light of the fact that hundreds of thousands of fin whales were slaughtered this century, our knowledge of this species remains surprisingly poor in many respects. Like many baleen whales, finbacks undertake long seasonal migrations. In summer they are found feeding in cold productive waters in high and temperate latitudes. In winter they migrate to warm waters; although specific wintering grounds have yet to be clearly identified, fin whales probably mate and calve in tropical or subtropical waters offshore. Unlike humpback and right whales, they do not appear to aggregate during the winter, and are not commonly observed around islands or close to the coast. Thus, they have been historically inaccessible and difficult to study at this time of year.

Fin whales are distributed widely in coastal, shelf, and pelagic waters. In the North Atlantic, they are found feeding from the mid-Atlantic states of the U.S. to Greenland, Iceland, Norway, and to the ice-edge in Arctic waters. A similarly broad distribution prevails in the North Pacific, where they feed from the Chuckchi Sea south to California. The migration is not straightforward. There is evidence that some populations move latitudinally with the seasons, with some whales moving south in winter to occupy the summering ranges of others. Other data suggest that many animals do not undertake the winter migration every year. Furthermore, it has been sug-

Balaenoptera physalus

gested that some finback populations are structured by sex or age class, although recent data indicate that such structuring, if it exists, may be quite loose. Several stocks are recognized in the North Atlantic and North Pacific, although it is likely that our view of the population structure of this species will change with more information, notably from ongoing genetic studies. It is possible that some populations of fin whales remain associated with locally-productive tropical areas year-round; for example, this has been suggested for the Gulf of California.

From research based upon radio telemetry, we know that fin whales are capable of extensive movements. One tagged individual travelled 1,700 km across the Irminger Sea in nine days. Discovery tags (uniquely-marked stainless steel cylinders that

were shot into whales and sometimes recovered when the whale was killed and butchered) indicate that some Antarctic fin whales have feeding ranges that encompass as much as 90 degrees of longitude over several seasons. In contrast to this, some radio tag studies have shown very limited movement over periods of up to a month. Studies based upon the identification of individual fin whales have demonstrated long-term fidelity (up to 20 years) by some animals to specific feeding grounds such as the Gulf of Maine. This fidelity is maternally directed, with fin whales returning to the areas to which they were brought by their mothers in their calf year.

Fin whales feed on a variety of prey, including euphausiids (krill) and several species of small schooling fish such as herring, capelin, and sand lance. They feed by lunging, often with astonishing turns of speed, into schools of prey, frequently rolling onto one side as they engulf a vast quantity of water and food. The water is exhausted through the baleen, leaving the prey trapped on the fringe of hair on the inner surface of the baleen plates. Like the five other species of rorqual (a Danish word meaning "tubed whale"), fin whales possess a series

of ventral pleats running longitudinally from the tip of the lower jaw to the umbilicus. These expand like an accordian when the whale engulfs water and prey, increasing the volume of the mouth, and then contract to aid in the expulsion of water through the baleen. As with other balaenopterids, it is estimated that fin whales eat the equivalent of three or four percent of their own weight each day; thus a typical adult finback of 23 meters and 60 tons might consume two or three tons of fish or krill daily.

As in most baleen whales, reproduction in the fin whale is strongly seasonal, with mating taking place in mid-winter. Gestation is approximately one year, and calves are probably born offshore either in the tropics or in warm temperate waters. Calves are on average about 6.5 meters in length at birth, and nurse for perhaps six or eight months before being weaned. Energetic studies have shown that the cost to the mother of producing a fat-rich milk are considerable: while she is nursing, she will lose one-third of her body weight (as much as 15–20 tons for a large female). Calves leave their mothers towards the end of their natal year. Both males and females are sexually mature between six and ten years. Some scientists have claimed that the average age at sexual maturity in some populations declined after whaling, but there is considerable dispute regarding the validity of the data used to support this assertion. Females give birth on average every two years.

Little is known of the mating system; anecdotal observations suggest that intrasexual competition among males for females may occur, but the frequency of this behavior is unknown. As with all baleen whales, the social organization of the finback is highly fluid, with short-term associations between individuals. Interestingly, social behavior appears to vary considerably with location. In the Gulf of Maine, single animals are common, and associated groups of more than three are quite rare. By contrast, in the Gulf of St. Lawrence, large groups of fifteen or more whales are sometimes observed. Whether this is a function of different foraging strategies, or a reflection of structuring of the population by age class, is presently unknown. It is unclear whether long-term bonds are ever established; calves do not appear to reassociate with their mothers after independence, and it seems unlikely that kinship plays a significant role in fin whale society.

Together with blue whales, fin whales have the deepest voices in the animal kingdom, vocalizing at frequencies far below the range of human hearing (sometimes below 20 Hz). These sounds, which are often of great intensity, can be detected by naval listening stations over hundreds or even thousands of miles in deep water. Whether fin whales utilize this long-range communication capability is unknown, but the ability to detect a conspecific over great distance may partly explain the lack of aggregation during the winter breeding season.

The fin whale's lower jaw coloration (white on the right, black on the left, a distinction that is also reflected in different baleen color) is noteworthy since such asymmetry is so rare among mammals. Several explanations have been advanced for this feature, but none are based on much more than conjec-

ture. The most popular theory revolves around the fact that fin whales are often observed circling prey. It is suggested that when the circling movement is clockwise, the white right lower jaw will scare fish into a tighter aggregation, thus facilitating capture. By contrast, a fin whale circling prey counterclockwise will present its black left lower jaw, which potentially acts as camouflage. However, this intriguing hypothesis lacks convincing supporting data.

Human exploitation of the fin whale is a relatively recent phenomenon, a function of the fact that early whalers simply could not catch this fast, sleek animal, and, when killed, the body sinks (unlike that of the right whale and some humpbacks). As late as 1851, Herman Melville noted that "there is no means known by which to catch the fin whale." This changed not long afterwards with two inventions: the explosive harpoon, introduced in 1868, provided whalers with a means to rapidly dispatch an animal, and the steam engine permitted the protracted chasing of even the fastest rorquals. The problem of the carcass sinking was overcome by pumping compressed air into it, so it floated. Exploitation began at low levels in the late nineteenth century. In 1906, with the opening of the world's richest whaling grounds in the Antarctic, a slaughter of unparalleled dimensions began. This century, in the Southern Hemisphere alone, some three quarters of a million fin whales have been killed. How many exist in the world's oceans today is unclear, reflecting the great difficulty of counting a wide-ranging, diving animal whose habitat is often inhospitable to humans. Nonetheless, the finback is clearly not among the world's most endangered whales. Although the great Southern Ocean populations of this species were reduced to a fraction of their original size, there are strong indications that this resilient species is doing well in most areas despite the slaughter to which it was once subject. *B. Birchler, C. W. Potter, and P. Clapham*

Size
Total length: 17.7–22 m (males); 18.3–24 m (females)
Weight: 45,000–70,000 kg

Identification
Adult fin whales are larger than any other balaenopterids except the blue whale. Fin whales can be easily distinguished from blue whales by their coloration, which is black or dark gray, with none of the mottling that characterizes the blue whale's body. The fin whale's dorsal fin, which is prominent and often falcate, is much larger than that of the blue whale. More confusion is likely to occur with sei or Bryde's whales, and the inexperienced observer will have difficulty separating the three species. At close range, the fin whale's asymmetric coloration (unique among large whales) can be seen: the lower right jaw is white or ivory, and the lower left jaw is black. This difference is diagnostic of the species. The fin whale has a chevron pattern across the back posterior to the blowholes, and a pale-colored wash of pigment on the right side of the head (the "blaze"). Both blaze and chevron patterns vary considerably in intensity and form from whale to whale, and these differences are used by scientists to identify individuals. Unlike blue whales, fin whales very rarely raise their tails prior to diving.

Other Common Names
Finback, razorback, common rorqual

Status
Endangered

References
Ellis, 1980; Leatherwood and Reeves, 1983

Humpback whale | *Megaptera novaeangliae*

The humpback whale is among the most familiar and best-studied of all the great whales. Once heavily exploited by the whaling industry, the humpback is today the subject of considerable popular interest and is the mainstay of many commercial whale-watching businesses in North America and elsewhere. Although listed as endangered, the species appears to be making a strong recovery in much of its historic range. Much of what is known of the humpback has come from long-term studies of identified individuals in North American waters: the ventral tail pattern is individually distinctive, and animals can also be recognized by the shape, size, and scarring of the dorsal fin.

The humpback whale has a cosmopolitan distribution, and is found in all the oceans of the world. Like many baleen whales, humpbacks are highly migratory. In spring, summer, and autumn they feed in the cold, productive waters of high latitudes. In late fall they migrate to the tropics to mate and give birth. This distinct geographic partitioning of the humpback's year is reflected in a similar division of behavior. During summer, the whales feed, and engage in virtually no sexual activity. In winter, by contrast, they do not eat for up to several months, and it is at this time that most courtship and mating behavior occurs. Recent studies have challenged the widespread belief that all humpback whales migrate every year, and a population in the Arabian Sea appears to be unique in that it remains in tropical waters year-round.

In the Northern Hemisphere, humpbacks return each spring to specific high-latitude feeding grounds. In the North Atlantic, they feed off the northeastern United States (from the Gulf of Maine to the mid-Atlantic States), Newfoundland and Labrador, Greenland, Iceland, and Norway. Each of these subpopulations is relatively discrete, with regional fidelity determined matrilineally. However, whales from all North Atlantic feeding grounds migrate to common breeding areas in the West Indies (the most important of which are off the Dominican Republic), where they mix both spatially and genetically. A similar situation exists in the North Pacific: humpbacks feed in Alaskan waters and migrate to the Hawaiian Island chain to mate and calve. A second, largely separate Pacific population summers along the coast from California to British Columbia and migrates to breeding grounds in the Mexican Pacific. However, identified individuals have sometimes been observed in widely separated locations: one individual was sighted in both Hawaii and Japan, and another was recorded off both Japan and British Columbia. Although it is generally thought that there is little mixing between the eastern and western North Pacific, some exchange between these regions clearly occurs.

Megaptera novaeangliae

Humpbacks are commonly found in coastal or shelf waters in summer and around islands or reef systems in winter. They feed upon a variety of small schooling fish, including herring *(Clupea harengus),* sand lance *(Ammodytes),* capelin *(Mallotus villosus)* and mackerel *(Scomber scombrus),* as well as on euphausiid crustaceans (krill). Humpbacks are probably unique among baleen whales in their use of large nets or clouds of bubbles to trap or concentrate schooling fish. Bubble nets consist of a series of columns blown at intervals to form a circle or spiral around a school of prey; the effect is to force the prey into a confined area within the bubble "net," so that when the whale lunges into the net's center it can engulf as much of the school as possible. A bubble cloud—which seems to be unique to the North Atlantic population—is a single burst of bubbles up to 20 m across which presumably functions to trap prey between the rising cloud and the surface. Humpback whales usually have individually specific bubble-feeding behavior (either clouding or netting), and may also add a variety of refinements to the technique. The baleen is generally black, and the inner surface is fringed with coarse hair. Humpbacks are "gulp-feeders." They feed in discrete events, rather than continuously filtering their prey as do some balaenids, such as the right whale. Typically, they lunge into prey schools and engulf a huge volume of water and food; this process is aided by the ventral pleats, which expand during a feeding lunge and thus greatly increase the capacity of the whale's mouth.

Breeding is strongly seasonal. Females come into estrus in mid-winter, and testosterone production and spermatogenesis peak at that time in males. The gestation period is approximately 11 months. It is worth noting that fetal growth in baleen whales is the fastest of any mammal, being some twenty times that of primates. The majority of calves are born between January and March, and are typically 4 m long and weigh about three-quarters of a ton at birth. Humpback calves nurse for up to ten months, taking an estimated 50 gallons of milk a day. The milk is approximately one-third fat, and its production is thus energetically very expensive for the mother: it is estimated that a female humpback will lose up to one-third of her body weight over the period of lactation. Most calves separate from their mothers after one year, and both males and females attain sexual maturity at an average age of five years. Mature females give birth most commonly at intervals of two years, although consecutive-year calving is not uncommon. Although multiple fetuses have been recorded in a few females killed by whaling, twins have never been observed in the field.

Unlike many mammals (including some toothed whales), baleen whales are rarely found in long-term stable groups. The social organization of the humpback is characterized by fluid and constantly changing associations with many individuals. Feeding behavior is often coordinated, but the size and stability of a foraging group appears to be related to the dimensions of the prey patch. Territoriality has not been observed.

The mating system is largely promiscuous, and there is no male parental investment. During the winter breeding season, males fight aggressively for access to estrous females; these "competitive groups" may last for hours, with one or more challengers attempting to displace a principal escort from his key position next to the nuclear female. Agonistic interactions during this time can include ramming, tail slashing, and head butting. Fights are rarely serious, but the dorsal fins, tubercles, and caudal peduncles of participating males are often bloody and raw. In many respects, the mating system resembles a lek. (Although there is disagreement among behavioral biologists, a lek can be broadly defined as a system involving a traditional area to which males come to display, and which females visit for the purpose of selecting mates.) However, unlike in classical leks, male humpbacks do not appear to establish territories. Nonetheless, males sing long songs, which probably function primarily as a breeding display to attract females, but which may also serve to maintain spacing between males.

The song of the humpback is among the most complex in the animal kingdom, containing up to nine themes, which are sung in a generally invariant order. Males sing continuously for hours or even days. Both the structure and the content of the song change over time: two songs recorded from the same breeding range several years apart will be unrecognizably different. Despite these changes, all of the males within one population continue to sing the same song; the mechanism by which this exchange occurs is unclear. It appears likely that males remain in breeding areas longer than females and probably attempt to mate repeatedly. Whaling data show that the migration is staggered, with newly pregnant females among the first to leave the tropics.

More than any other whale, the humpback engages in often spectacular aerial behaviors. These include breaching (the whale jumps headfirst out of the water), lobtailing (the tail is repeatedly slammed down), and flippering (one flipper slaps the surface). These displays are seen at all times of year and among all age classes, and it is clear that they have multiple functions.

Despite the breadth of our knowledge of the humpback whale, many mysteries remain regarding its biology and behavior. Among the most perplexing is the reason for the long seasonal migration. The most popular of many hypotheses concerns the supposed advantages of calving in warm water. However, a convincing explanation remains elusive. *P. Clapham*

Size
Females are typically up to one meter longer than males.
Total length: 14–15 m (maximum recorded 17 m)
Weight: 25,000–45,000 kg

Identification
At close range, humpback whales are easily distinguished from other baleen whales by their remarkably long flippers, which are approximately one third of the body length. The dorsal surface of the flipper is generally white in the North Atlantic, black in the North Pacific. The body color is black. Humpbacks have a small dorsal fin, which varies in shape from low and stubby to high and falcate, and which is often scarred. The head possesses numerous small bumps called tubercles, each of which contains a single vibrissa. Like all balaenopterid ("rorqual") whales, humpbacks have a series of ventral pleats that run longitudinally from the head to the umbilicus. The ventral surface of the tail ranges in color from all white to all black; the posterior margin is distinctively serrated. The tail is generally raised in the air prior to a deep dive.

Recent Synonyms
Megaptera nodosa

Status
Endangered

References
Mammalian Species 604 (in press); Clapham, 1996; Leatherwood and Reeves, 1983; Winn and Winn, 1985

Family Eschrichtiidae

The family Eschrichtiidae contains only a single species, *Eschrichtius robustus,* the gray whale. The gray whale is often considered the most primitive of the baleen whales, although recent molecular analysis has suggested otherwise. Like other large whales, this species was threatened with extinction about a century ago. Gray whales did become extinct in the North Atlantic only a few centuries ago, although the reason for their demise is unknown and may not have been related to whaling. The North Pacific population is split into two subpopulations with sharply contrasting recovery histories: the eastern group, which migrates from Baja California and the Bering/Chukchi Seas, numbers more than 21,000 animals and is thriving. The western stock, inhabiting the Okhotsk Sea and other areas of the Far East, is thought to be in the low hundreds and is critically endangered.

As the only species readily observed from shore, gray whales were in the forefront of the "whale-watching" movement. This species is also among the cetaceans best known to science, with many studies conducted during the past century, beginning with Scammon's 1874 account of marine mammals off the northwestern coast of North America.

These animals annually perform one of the longest migrations of any mammal, travelling over 10,000 kilometers between summer feeding grounds in the Arctic seas and winter calving areas in shallow-water lagoons off the coast of Baja California. This movement exposes them to a wide range of water temperatures and day lengths during the course of the year. When migrating, they move more or less continuously, night and day.

Gray whales, unlike other baleen whales, are primarily bottom feeders. They selectively specialize on gammaridean amphipods, which they likely filter from sediments that they disturb from the bottom. In the process, they tend to accumulate sand, silt, and gravel in their stomachs. After spending the summer feeding and laying down blubber, they do not feed while migrating, and likely feed little or not at all while on the winter grounds.

Calves are born in January after a 13-month gestation, and grow from 5 m and 500 kg at birth to about 8 m and 7,000 kg by weaning in August. Such rapid growth in the first year is common in marine mammals that rely on size both for thermoregulation and for protection from predators. The only known predators of gray whales are killer whales. Gray whales reach sexual maturity somewhere between 5 and 11 years, by which time they have attained a length of about 11 m.
P. Clapham

References
Jones et al., 1984; Leatherwood and Reeves, 1983

North American Genera
Eschrichtius

Gray whale | *Eschrichtius robustus*

The sole species of the family Eschrichtiidae, the gray whale differs in many respects from all other baleen whales. Gray whales are the only mysticetes that habitually feed on the bottom. Their baleen plates are small, thick, widely-spaced, and have a coarse fringe. The gray whale's tongue is heavy and muscular, and functions somewhat like a piston. When feeding, this whale rolls so that one side of its head is parallel to the bottom. It then lowers the lip on that side and moves across the sea-floor like a giant vacuum cleaner, sucking up the abundant invertebrates that live on or just above the bottom or burrow in the sediments. In most areas amphipods—tiny crustaceans sometimes known as "sand fleas"—comprise the bulk of the whales' food, but in some areas polychaete worms or mysids (another family of small crustaceans) predominate, and in Puget Sound the whales even forage on ghost shrimps *(Callianassa californiensis)* in the intertidal zone.

Gray whales are now endemic to the North Pacific Ocean, but a number of intriguing published records suggest that they also inhabited the North Atlantic well into historical times. An early 17th century account of Icelandic mammals includes a description of a whale called the "sandloegja" ("sand-lier"), and in the early 18th century, New England whalers hunted animals that they called "scrag whales." Descriptions of both of these whales include features diagnostic of the gray whale. Lending substance to these accounts are a number of subfossil specimens of gray whales, some dated as recently as the year 1675, that have been unearthed along the eastern seaboard between New York and Florida. Similar remains have been found in Sweden, the Netherlands, and England—one estimated to be only about 1,400 years old.

Famed as long-distance migrants, gray whales exceed even humpbacks in distance travelled each year. Most of the eastern Pacific population of gray whales spends the summer feeding season in the shallow waters over the continental shelf in the northern Bering Sea, the southern Chukchi Sea, and the southwestern Beaufort Sea near Alaska. A few, however, summer along the coasts of Vancouver Island, Washington, Oregon, and California. In November they exit the Bering Sea through Unimak Pass and swim southward, usually keeping within about 5 km of the beach, until they reach their winter quarters in Mexico—mostly along the west coast of the Baja California peninsula. The few survivors of the western Pacific population spend the summer in the shallow western and northern parts of the Sea of Okhotsk, then migrate south along the mainland coast of Asia, probably to winter grounds in southern China, along the coast of Guangdong Province and around Hainan Island (not southern Korea, as previously supposed).

Both sexes of gray whales attain sexual maturity at an age of 5 to 11 years. Estrus and mating take place mostly in late November and early December, but the few females that fail to conceive during their first ovulation may ovulate again and mate as late as January. At other times of the year, the whales may engage in much ineffectual mating behavior. The fetus grows exponentially during the following summer and reaches its full length of about 4.6 m by December, after which further growth is arrested during the final month or so of pregnancy. In January almost all of the pregnant females aggregate in certain shallow, nearly-locked lagoons, notably Laguna Guerrero Negro, Laguna Ojo de Liebre (or "Scammon's Lagoon"), Laguna San Ignacio, and Bahia Magdalena. There they give birth to their calves and nurse them during the first few weeks of their lives. In May, after all the other whales have departed, the females with nursing calves begin their northward journey. Back on the summer grounds, the calves begin to feed on their own, and are completely weaned by the age of about seven months. Most of their mothers conceive again the following winter, thus producing one calf every two years.

Within days of birth, every calf begins to acquire a load of ectoparasites and epizoites that will burden it for life. Most obvious is a host-specific barnacle, *Cryptolepas rhachianecti,* which can grow in clusters anywhere on the whale's body but is most numerous on the rostrum and back. These barnacles breed when the whales are concentrated on the calving grounds, so their free-swimming cypris larvae have a high chance of finding a whale to settle on. Other ubiquitous parasites are three species of amphipod crustaceans called "whale-lice," two of which are host-specific. These creatures never leave their host and can be transferred from whale to whale only when the latter make body contact, such as during mating or nursing. Each

Eschrichtius robustus

species has its own "habitat" on the whale's body—*Cyamus ceti* mainly in skin folds such as the throat grooves and the crease at the corner of the mouth, *C. scammoni* around the barnacle clusters, and *C. kessleri* in the genital and anal grooves. Endoparasites, by contrast, are sparse in gray whales. The stomach worms *(Anisakis)* that burden all fish- and squid-eating cetaceans are absent. The only frequent helminth parasites are two species of anal flukes, one of which, *Ogmogaster pentalineatus,* is host-specific to the gray whale.

Killer whales are the only animals seen attacking and killing gray whales. Parallel tooth scars on the flukes of many gray whales attest to frequent unsuccessful attacks by these predators.

The Inuit of the Bering Strait region—especially those on the Siberian side—and several Indian tribes in the eastern Aleutians, on Kodiak Island, and along the coasts of British Columbia, were renowned for their skill in harpooning gray and other whales from skin-covered umiaks or from large dugout canoes. In the middle and late 19th century, the aggregations of females and their calves in the Mexican lagoons became easy prey for American open-boat whalers. Shore-based whalers killed others as they migrated along the coast of California. The population was drastically depleted by the turn of the century.

Beginning in 1905, many shore whaling stations were established along the west coast of Canada and the United States; the last one closed in 1971. They operated mainly in the summer, when most gray whales had already moved into the Arctic, so their catches included only 15 gray whales, all taken between 1913 and 1928. In the winters of 1913/14 and 1924/25

through 1928/29, 200 gray whales were taken by Norwegian whalers who operated from one or two floating factory ships anchored in Bahia Magdalena and at other points along the coast of Mexico. During the summer of 1925, one of these Norwegian vessels, the *Kommandören I,* shifted operations to the Bering Sea, where 33 gray whales were taken; she returned there in 1926, but took no more grays. A Soviet floating factory ship, the *Aleut,* was the first pelagic floating factory with a stern slipway to operate on the high seas in the North Pacific. Between 1933 and 1947, catches by the *Aleut* fleet included a total of 624 gray whales from the Bering and Chukchi seas. A further 58 grays were taken from there by the Japanese floating factory *Tonan Maru* in 1940. Since 1947, the International Whaling Commission (IWC) has prohibited the killing of gray whales for commercial purposes. The Russian government takes most of an annual quota of 179 gray whales allotted by the IWC to the aborigines of the Chukotski Peninsula and Alaska. Under Special Scientific Permits, 10 gray whales were killed in British Columbia in 1953, and 326 more in California between 1959 and 1969. Despite these catches, the eastern Pacific population continues to multiply. By 1988, it had reached an estimated total of 21,000 animals—probably as many as were present prior to commercial exploitation—so in 1994 the species was deleted from the endangered list under the U.S. Endangered Species Act. Gray whales are now the object of a large and lucrative whale-watching industry. *D. W. Rice*

Size
Total length: 11.1–14.3 m (males); 11.7–15.0 m (females)
Weight: 15,700–33,800 kg.

Identification
The gray whale is readily recognized by its mottled gray color, the presence of a low rounded hump in place of a dorsal fin, and by a series of knobs or knuckles along the dorsal ridge of the caudal peduncle between the hump and the flukes.

Recent Synonyms
Eschrichtius gibbosus
Rhachianectes glaucus

Other Common Names
California gray whale, Korean gray whale

Status
Abundant in the eastern North Pacific; very rare in the western North Pacific; extinct in the North Atlantic

References
Buckland et al., 1993; Jones et al., 1984; Rice and Wolman, 1971; Scammon, 1968

Family Delphinidae

Worldwide, there are 17 genera and 32 species in this widespread family, with 12 genera and 19 species known from North America. These oceanic dolphins include species that range in size from just over a meter to the 9-m killer whale. This is the largest and most diverse family of cetaceans, and its taxonomic affinities are still undergoing active revision. Dolphins are united in having numerous conical teeth, compression and fusion of neck vertebrae, and a variety of anatomical specializations associated with their well-developed echolocation systems.

All delphinids have elongated, spindle-shaped bodies designed for rapid swimming. Their acoustic communication systems seem to be associated with highly developed social systems, and most are gregarious to varying degrees. They are highly intelligent, and adapt easily to captivity. This has led to extensive attempts to communicate with them, and their ability to perform for the public has led to a greater appreciation of their abilities.

Most of these animals dive no deeper than a couple of hundred meters and they tend to surface every few minutes to breath. With so many closely related species, niche separation by feeding depth, habitat, and food species is necessary and allows them to co-exist. Some species may school together, but feed at different depths. Small species tend to feed on a variety of small fishes and squids. Larger species are more catholic in their food habits, and killer whales, at the top of the food chain, eat seals, other cetaceans, diving birds, large fish, and sharks.

Females breed every 2–4 years, and the gestation period is about one year in smaller species and up to 16 months in the larger. Calves begin taking solid food at about 4–6 months, but may continue nursing for up to 2 years. Sexual maturity is reached at 4–8 years in females and somewhat later in males.

References
Minasian et al., 1984; Rice, 1984

North American Genera
Steno
Tursiops
Stenella
Delphinus
Lagenodelphis
Lagenorhynchus
Grampus
Feresa
Pseudorca
Globicephala
Orcinus
Lissodelphis

Rough-toothed dolphin | *Steno bredanensis*

Rough-toothed dolphins occur worldwide in warm temperate to tropical seas, occupying deep, offshore (pelagic) waters. Usually they are found in areas where the surface water temperature is at least 25° C. However, stranded animals have been found on beaches as far north as Washington State on the west coast and Virginia on the east coast. The distribution is inferred from stranded animals rather than known from at-sea observations.

The rough-toothed dolphin most closely resembles the more familiar bottlenose dolphin, *Tursiops truncatus.* However, it differs in having a distinctively-shaped, dark, cape-like color pattern on its back and in lacking the transverse groove which, in most long-beaked dolphins, separates the forehead from the beak. The head of *S. bredanensis* tapers smoothly from the area of the blowhole (on top of the head) to the end of the long beak, producing a rather cone-shaped profile. This dolphin has large, slightly protruding eyes, probably an adaptation for its deep-diving habits. *Steno* is robust in shape, with a thick girth and relatively large appendages—dorsal fin, flippers, and flukes. Adult males have a ventral keel, or post-anal hump, formed of dense connective tissue.

Adult coloration is highly variable. Overall coloration ranges from dark gray to purplish black, with yellowish white or pink blotches on the sides. Older animals, especially, often have white scratches and scars on their bodies, the result of aggressive interactions with conspecifics or attacks from the cookie-cutter shark, *Isistius brasiliensis,* and large squids. The ventral surface has a variable amount of white which, in older individuals, may extend onto the sides. There is no clear demarcation between dorsal and ventral coloration. The lips and lower jaw are also often white. Juveniles generally have a more muted color pattern, lacking contrasting spots or patches.

As is true for most species of pelagic dolphins, the habits of rough-toothed dolphins are little known. They occur in groups of 50 or more, but more often in schools of between 10 and 20. They appear to be relatively deep divers and display less inter-

est in bow-riding than most dolphin species. They have been observed skimming along the surface, swimming rapidly with the rostrum continually near the surface and the dorsal fin exposed, for rather prolonged periods. *Steno* is often found in the company of other species of small cetaceans.

Some individuals have been maintained in captivity for many years and have proven highly trainable. One female rough-toothed dolphin bred successfully with a bottlenose dolphin, producing an apparently healthy hybrid that lived in captivity for five years.

What little is known of the life history of rough-toothed dolphins in the wild comes primarily from studies off Japan. The breeding season is unknown. The length of newborns is probably around 1 m. Growth is most rapid in the first five years of life, with physical maturity attained by about the sixteenth year. Sexual maturation occurs in females at about ten years of age, when they are between 2.1–2.2 m in total length, and at about 14 years in males, when their average total length is 2.25 m. Maximum lifespan is estimated to be about 32 years.
M. W. Newcomer

Steno bredanensis

Size
Total length: 2–2.65 m (males); 2–2.55 m (females)
Weight: 90–155 kg

Identification
Distinguished from other long-beaked oceanic dolphins by the lack of a distinct crease separating the beak (rostrum) from the forehead and by the presence of vertical rugosities (wrinkles) on the otherwise smooth, conical teeth.

Other Common Names
Rough-toothed porpoise; steno

Status
Uncommon

References
Ferrero et al., 1994; Leatherwood and Reeves, 1983; Miyazaki and Perrin, 1994

Bottlenose dolphin | *Tursiops truncatus*

Whether or not *Tursiops* should be divided into subspecies is a matter of debate. The variation seen in *Tursiops* specimens has not been satisfactorily explained and suggests specific or subspecific variation. To date 24 nominal species of *Tursiops* have been described and several populations have been distinguished.

These populations differ in size. Coastal North Atlantic specimens have a modal length of 2.5–2.6 m and a maximum length of about 2.8 m. The offshore Atlantic population has a modal length of 2.9 m and a maximum reported length of 3.9 m; the maximum recorded weight for a western Atlantic offshore *Tursiops* is 494 kg for a sexually mature male that measured 2.79 m in length. Gulf of Mexico coastal animals are smaller, with a modal length of 2.4 m and a maximum length of 2.6 m. The Gulf of Mexico offshore animals have a reported maximum length of 3.8 m. Three populations have been recognized in the North Pacific: Northern Temperate Offshore, South California and Mexico Coastal, and Eastern Tropical Pacific Offshore. These have not been differentiated by size. The largest reported individual from the Pacific coast of the United States was a 3.4 m specimen from California.

Tursiops truncatus generally has a short, wide beak and a wide head and body. The flippers are relatively longer than those of most dolphins. The dorsal fin is situated midlength of the body and is moderately tall and curved (sickle-shaped). The flukes are moderate in size and generally have a deep notch. The pigmentation is shades of gray through brown. The body is marked by an indistinct cape that runs from the apex of the melon to the caudal peduncle. The sides are paler gray than the back, grading to white on the belly. Subtle eye-to-flipper and "bridle" marks occur on the head. Spots may occur in some populations.

In the Atlantic, *Tursiops* occurs coastally from Cape Hatteras, North Carolina to Panama, including the Caribbean islands. In the summer coastal *Tursiops* occur as far north as New Jersey. The offshore population follows the Gulf Stream. Nothing is known of the differentiation of the offshore population in the Gulf of Mexico. The Pacific coastal population extends from Panama to southern California.

The Atlantic coastal population of *Tursiops* feeds mainly on fish of the genera *Cynoscion* (sea trout), *Micropogonias* (croak-

ers), and *Leiostomus* (spot). The offshore population feeds on deep-water fish and squid. The coastal Pacific population feeds to a large extent on fish of the families Batrachoididae (midshipmen), Sciaenidae (drums), and Embiotocidae (flying fish).

Females of the mid-Atlantic coastal population reach sexual maturity at a mean length of 2.34 m and a mean age of 11 years. The data for males are less clear, but they seem to reach sexual maturity at an age of about 10 years. Mean length and weight at birth for this population are 1.17 m and 20 kg. Calving occurs through most of the year, with a peak in spring. This agrees very well with data from the Florida coastal population. Bottlenose dolphins are 0.9 to 1.30 m in total length at birth.

These dolphins are extremely gregarious, occurring in groups of up to several hundred animals. Coastal animals are frequently seen swimming just off the surf line. They normally enter bays and rivers and some populations are resident in those waters. Studies of *Tursiops* movements have identified resident groups with well-defined ranges and migratory groups that come into an area for only a brief time. Bottlenose dolphins are extremely fond of bow-riding boats and frequently put on an admirable display of acrobatics. *J. G. Mead*

Tursiops truncatus

Size
Different populations vary in size.
Maximum length: 2.6 m (Gulf of Mexico coastal population) to 3.4 m (coastal Pacific specimen)
Weight: about 200 kg (average, adult coastal animals)

Identification
Tursiops can be difficult to identify because of the lack of pronounced external diagnostic characters. It has a relatively short, broad snout, but this character varies from population to population. Its flippers are relatively longer (mean 17 percent, range 13–20 percent of total length) than those of any other dolphin with the exception of *Steno* (mean 19 percent, range 16–21 percent). *Tursiops* is easily distinguished from that genus by the definite border between the melon and the rostrum, which is not present in *Steno*. *Tursiops* has 20–26 teeth on each side of the upper jaw and 18–24 on each side of the lower jaw.

Recent Synonyms
Tursiops aduncus

Tursiops gephyreus
Tursiops gilli
Tursiops nuaana

Other Common Names
Gill's bottlenose dolphin, grand souffleur, oudre, souffleur, tursion (French)

Status
CITES—Appendix II

References
Mead and Potter 1990

Pantropical spotted dolphin | *Stenella attenuata*

Pantropical spotted dolphins inhabit tropical waters around the world. They are abundant off Mexico and Central America in the Pacific and occur sporadically as far north as New England in the Atlantic. In the western Atlantic and Caribbean they are primarily a high-seas pelagic species, found in deep water, usually far from land. In the eastern Pacific, a small form inhabits the high seas and a larger form the onshore waters of Mexico and Central America.

Systematic relationships among the small dolphins have not been well worked out. The genus *Stenella* may contain species that are more closely related to species in other genera (e.g., *Tursiops* or *Delphinus)* than they are to each other.

Female pantropical spotted dolphins mature sexually at about 9–11 years; males mature sexually at about 12–15 years. Nothing is known of the breeding system. Schools captured in purse seines are often formed of distinct subgroups containing cow-calf pairs, adult males, or juveniles.

The female bears a single calf after a gestation of about 11.5 months. Calves are unspotted at birth and begin to become spotted at about the time of weaning, when they are a year or two old, depending on the population. First, scattered small

Stenella attenuata

dark spots appear on the white underside of the calf. As the dark spots enlarge and begin to merge, paler spots begin to appear dorsolaterally. By adulthood, the ventral dark spots have merged and faded, so that the underside appears gray.

The diet may vary with population. In the offshore eastern tropical Pacific, it consists mainly of small epipelagic fishes, such as flying fishes and halfbeaks, and epipelagic squids. The reason for the dolphin's association with yellowfin tuna is unknown, but it may relate to some aspect of foraging efficiency or thermal ecology.

Predators include large sharks, the false killer whale, and probably the killer whale and the pygmy killer whale. Parasitism may be a major cause of natural mortality.

In the eastern tropical Pacific, pantropical spotted dolphins are pursued by purse-seine fishermen hunting the yellowfin tuna that swim with the dolphin school. These schools may also contain spinner dolphins *(Stenella longirostris)*. Once encircled with the net, many dolphins become entangled in the webbing and suffocate. The practice of fishing "on dolphins" has led to the deaths of millions of spotted and spinner dolphins since the early 1960s. Where this type of fishing occurs, spotted dolphins usually flee from ships, but in other regions, they commonly ride the bow wave. In very recent years, an international program of technological research and assistance to improve dolphin-rescue equipment and techniques has reduced the fishery kill to a few thousand a year, which will probably ensure that the populations survive.

Pantropical dolphins have been kept in captivity, but they are not as easily trainable or as hardy as other dolphins more commonly exhibited. *W. F. Perrin*

Size

Total length: 1.6–2.6 m (males); 1.7–2.4 m (females

Heaviest specimen: 119 kg (2.6 m male from Bay of Panama)

Identification

Distinguished from other small long-beaked dolphins by spots (in adults), high cape over eye, flipper stripe to cape, and dorsoventral division in coloration of tailstock. There are 35–48 teeth in each row.

Recent Synonyms

Stenella graffmani

Other Common Names

Spotter, spotted porpoise, delfin manchado

Status

Insufficiently Known (IUCN); common in some regions, but Northeastern stock in eastern tropical Pacific designated "Depleted" by U.S. government

Subspecies

Stenella attenuata attenuata, offshore tropical waters

Stenella attenuata graffmani, coastal waters of eastern tropical Pacific

References

Jefferson et al., 1994; Perrin and Hohn, 1994

Clymene dolphin | *Stenella clymene*

The Clymene dolphin, named after an ancient Greek heroine, was described from a skull in the 19th century. Its external appearance was unknown until the 1970s, when specimens stranded in Texas and New Jersey. Externally it resembles the spinner dolphin, *Stenella longirostris,* and less so, the common dolphin, *Delphinus delphis.* Its skull closely resembles that of the striped dolphin, *Stenella coeruleoalba.* It wasn't until complete specimens became available for study that the various skulls and sometimes misidentified sightings that had accumulated over the years could be sorted out.

The Clymene dolphin is found in tropical and semitropical waters of the Atlantic Ocean. In the western Atlantic, records extend from New Jersey to southern Brazil, including the Gulf of Mexico and the Caribbean. The single record from New Jersey is likely an extralimital one, as the Clymene dolphin is clearly a tropical animal; the normal range probably does not extend north of Cape Hatteras, North Carolina.

This striking small dolphin has a three-part color pattern of dark gray above, paler gray on the sides, and white below. It often has a distinctive "moustache mark" on the beak. Quite often it may also have one or more circular or star-shaped white scars about 6–8 cm in diameter; these are healed bites of the "cookie cutter" shark, *Icistius.* The flippers and dorsal fin are on the average smaller than in the spinner dolphin.

Almost nothing is known about the life history of this dolphin. Sexual maturity is reached when it is about 1.8 m in

Stenella clymene

length. One school that stranded in Louisiana consisted almost entirely of adult males; this may reflect a breeding system in which there is school segregation by age and sex. Schools typically consist of fewer than 50 individuals. Clymene dolphins have been seen in the company of spinner dolphins and common dolphins.

The little information available on stomach contents indicates that Clymene dolphins feed mainly on small mesopelagic fishes and squids at considerable depth, although some of the fishes may migrate toward the surface at night and be eaten there. The dolphin has been seen only in deep water (250–5,000 m or deeper); this may reflect its feeding habits.

The Clymene dolphin "spins" like the spinner dolphin, leaping high out of the water and rotating several times on its longitudinal axis before re-entering the water with a splash. The reason for its spinning behavior is not known.

As with other small dolphins, predators probably include sharks and the larger carnivorous toothed whales such as the killer whale, the false killer whale, and the pygmy killer whale.
W. F. Perrin

Size
Sexual dimorphism has not been documented
Total length: 1.8–2.0 m
Weight: 45–85 kg (lower end was for a stranded and possibly ill animal)

Identification
Distinguished from the very similar spinner dolphin, *Stenella longirostris*, by relatively shorter beak, lower approach of dorsal cape toward ventral white field, and triangular flipper stripe (as opposed to stripe with parallel sides). There are 38–49 teeth in each row.

Other Common Names
Short-snouted spinner dolphin, delfin de yelmo

Status
Insufficiently Known (IUCN), but relatively common in some regions

References
Jefferson et al., 1994; Perrin and Mead, 1994

Striped dolphin | *Stenella coeruleoalba*

These boldly patterned oceanic dolphins are most often encountered in the warm-temperate to tropical waters of the world's oceans and seas, where they feed on a wide range of shrimp, fish, and squid. On the Atlantic coast of North America, *Stenella coeruleoalba* can be found in the Gulf of Mexico, the Caribbean Sea, and in the ocean off the coast of the southeastern United States. Because this species is normally associated with the warm northward-flowing Gulf Stream, a few individuals have managed to wander as far as Nova Scotia, although sightings that far north are rare. On the Pacific coast, the range of striped dolphins extends from southern California well into South American waters. Here they are more pelagic than in the western Atlantic and can be found much farther offshore, at times associating with large schools of tuna.

In the eastern tropical Pacific, striped dolphins are shy, typically wary of boats, and can be difficult to approach. Here, they do not bow-ride and are more likely to flee approaching vessels. However, bow-riding has been reported off northern California and in the Atlantic. When porpoising, they tend to make long, flat leaps. Among their many acrobatic behaviors, they are best known for "roto-tailing." In this aerial display, the dolphin makes a high, arcing jump and violently and rapidly rotates its tail several times before reentering the water. Roto-tailing is extremely common in *Stenella coeruleoalba*.

Stocky and robust, the striped dolphin is the largest species of the five-member genus *Stenella*. It is also the most strikingly

Stenella coeruleoalba

pigmented and is easy to recognize when seen in full view. Its common name arises from the presence of a series of dark lateral stripes that originate at the eye. The main stripe extends the length of the body, to the anus. Usually there is a secondary stripe that begins immediately behind the eye and may appear nearly fused with the main stripe right behind the eye. Near the flipper it splits off ventrally, fading out at the all-white belly. Another eye-to-flipper stripe may be single or double. Depending on viewing conditions, these stripes may look dark blue, black, or even brownish. The flank above the main stripe ranges from light to dark gray. A swath of this flank pigment into the dark bluish-grey or black dorsal cape forms a bold shoulder blaze, a diagnostic character of striped dolphins. The color pattern gives the striped dolphin its specific name, *coeruleoalba,* which means "blue-white."

A gregarious animal, *Stenella coeruleoalba* can be seen in schools numbering up to several hundred animals, although school sizes of less than 200 are more common. According to data collected from the western Pacific, schools can be classified according to age and breeding status as juvenile, adult (breeding and nonbreeding), and mixed. Sexual maturity is reached between 7 and 15 years of age, with females typically maturing slightly earlier than males. Mature animals join to form adult breeding schools, and breeding takes place seasonally. After breeding, the males may leave, thus transforming the school into a nonbreeding one. After the pregnant females give birth in the summer and winter, it becomes a mixed

school. The calves stay with their mothers until they are weaned a year or two later, at which time they leave to join juvenile schools. Maximum longevity is estimated to be 57.5 years. *F. I. Archer, II*

Size

Males are slightly (5–7 cm) but not noticeably
 longer than females.
Total length: 1.8–2.5 (2.1) m
Estimated weight: 110–156 kg

Identification

Stenella coeruleoalba can be identified by the presence of a black or blue lateral eye-to-anus stripe and a pale to dark gray spinal blaze that intrudes into the dark dorsal cape. In North American waters, striped dolphins are most likely to be confused with the common dolphin *Delphinus delphis,* the spinner dolphin *Stenella longirostris,* or the Clymene dolphin

Stenella clymene, all of which have ranges overlapping that of *Stenella coeruleoalba.* The common dolphin can be distinguished from the striped dolphin by its lateral "criss-cross" or "hourglass" color pattern. Both spinner and Clymene dolphins can be distinguished by the simple tricolored pattern on their flanks. The bold eye-to-anus stripe and shoulder blaze of the striped dolphin is absent in all of these animals.

Recent Synonyms

Stenella euphrosyne
Stenella styx

Other Common Names

Streaker, blue-white dolphin

Status

Abundant

References

Leatherwood and Reeves, 1983; Leatherwood
 et al., 1982; Ridgway and Harrison, 1994

Atlantic spotted dolphin | *Stenella frontalis*

The Atlantic spotted dolphin is found only in the tropical and warm-temperate Atlantic. A large, heavily spotted form (formerly called *S. plagiodon)* inhabits coastal waters from the Carolinas south to southern Brazil in the Atlantic, the Caribbean, and the Gulf of Mexico. It is usually found within 250–350 km of the coast, inside or near the 100-fathom curve. A smaller and

more lightly spotted form occurs in the Gulf Stream off New England and east at least as far as the Azores.

As in the pantropical spotted dolphin, *S. attenuata,* calves are unspotted at birth and begin to acquire spots at about the time of weaning. However, in this species the ventral dark spots do not fuse and fade in adults; the adult has a white belly with

Stenella frontalis

ventral dark spots and the dorsal pale spots may be very small (a few mm across) and few in number, or may even be absent.

The Atlantic spotted dolphin is more robust in form than the pantropical spotted dolphin; although the size range is similar, adult *S. frontalis* of similar length weigh 10–30 kg more. The flukes, flippers, and dorsal fin are also proportionately larger.

Very little is known about the life history of this dolphin. The average length at birth is between 0.88 and 1.2 m. Six large-type females from the East Coast and the Gulf of Mexico measured 1.8–2.1 m in length; three others, which measured 1.8–1.9 m, were immature. The testes of four adult males weighed 502–1,210 g. In the large coastal form, schools typically consist of fewer than 50 animals and most often of 1–15, and age and sex segregation by school or sub-school has been observed.

The Atlantic spotted dolphin is known to feed on a wide variety of prey including small herring-like fishes, jacks, large squid, halfbeaks at the surface, mesopelagic fishes and squids, and bottom invertebrates. The feeding habits may not be as catholic as they seem; different populations may feed in different ways and may specialize on different prey.

Atlantic spotted dolphins have been kept in captivity, but not very successfully; some refuse to eat, and most die within a year. Keeping two or more individuals together and heating the tank water in fall and winter improves the chances of survival. *W. F. Perrin*

dark spots. In some individuals the pale spots on the back are so dense that the underlying color pattern is nearly obscured and the animal looks white at a distance. In the small, more pelagic form in the Gulf Stream off New England, both the

Size

Sexual dimorphism has not yet been documented

Total length: 1.7–2.3 m, with great geographical variation

Maximum weight: 143 kg

Identification

Distinguished from the pantropical spotted dolphin, *Stenella attenuata,* by shoulder blaze pointing toward base of dorsal fin, flipper stripe to eye or just below, no high dorsal cape over eye, and no dorsoventral division of coloration on tail stock. There are 30–42 teeth in each row.

Recent Synomyms

Stenella dubia

Stenella pernettyi

Stenella plagiodon

Other Common Names

Gulf Stream spotted dolphin, bridled dolphin, spotted porpoise, delfin moteado del Atlántico

Status

Insufficiently Known (IUCN), but *S. frontalis* is the most common offshore species in the Gulf of Mexico and off the southeastern United States. It may also be common off the coast of West Africa.

References

Jefferson et al., 1994; Perrin et al., 1994a

Spinner dolphin | *Stenella longirostris*

The spinner dolphin is a delightful animal, named for its unique acrobatic displays. For unknown reasons, it leaps high out of the water and rotates several times on its longitudinal axis, re-entering the water with a huge splash and a large smack that can be heard far away underwater. Typically the dolphin makes several such spinning leaps in succession. Suggested functions for these acrobatics include dislodging external parasites or remoras (commensal fish), communication with other spinners at the far side of the school, or satisfying sheer exuberance. We don't know why they do it, but it's great fun to watch, and it allows us to detect and identify spinner schools at a great distance. Reports of its aerial spinning behavior date back to 1769.

The spinner occurs in tropical waters around the world. It inhabits the waters of southern Mexico and Central America on the Pacific side of North America, and is found along the Atlantic coast from Florida to Central America, including in the Gulf of Mexico and the Caribbean. It exhibits very great geographical variation in color pattern and body size and shape; in the past, different populations were thought to be different species. The most prevalent color pattern consists of a dark gray back, pale gray sides, and a white belly; spinner dolphins in all regions except the eastern tropical Pacific exhibit this pattern. In the two subspecies occurring there, *S. l. orientalis* and *S. l. centroamericana,* the dorsal dark gray becomes paler on the side, obscuring the lateral field and most of the belly, leaving pale patches near the flippers and in the genital region. In adult males of these subspecies, the dorsal fin is canted forward and there is a large post-anal hump; the function of these adaptations is unknown. In some large males, the dorsal fin appears as if it were put on backwards. *S. l. orientalis* is also shorter than most other spinners. *S. l. centroamericana* is longer, due mainly to a proportionately very long beak. Spin-

Stenella longirostris

ners in insular Southeast Asian waters (as yet not described as a subspecies) do not differ in coloration, but they are very small; an adult male can be as short as 1.4 m and weigh as little as 22 kg. Just to the east, in the Philippines, spinners are as large as in most parts of the tropics.

The life of the spinner dolphin in the wild is better known than that of any other dolphin. Gestation lasts about 10.5 months, and the calf is about 0.77 m long at birth. Nursing lasts one to two years, making the female reproductive cycle about three years long. Females in the eastern tropical Pacific mature sexually at about 1.6–1.7 m, at 4–7 years of age. Males mature at about 7–10 years, at about 1.6–1.8 m.

Years of study in Hawaii have shown that schools of spinners there come into shallow bays in the morning and go into a quiescent, semi-active state to rest. This is presumably for protection from predators. At dusk they leave the bays to forage in deeper waters. During the night the dolphins disperse greatly. The schools that come back to the bays in the morning may vary greatly in make-up from those that left the evening before, suggesting that all the dolphins around an island (and possibly between islands) are a super-school composed of constantly shifting subunits, probably made up of extended family groups. Spinner dolphins that inhabit the high seas, as in the eastern tropical Pacific, may use spotted dolphin schools as surrogate bays for protection during resting periods; although the two species occur together, they appear to feed at different times of the day. The spinners feed primarily on small mesopelagic prey, and the spotted dolphin specializes more in surface-living forms.

In the eastern tropical Pacific, spinner dolphin schools often associate tightly with schools of pantropical spotted dolphins (*Stenella attenuata*) and yellowfin tuna. This makes both dolphin species vulnerable to suffocation in tuna nets. One population, *S. l. orientalis*, has been reduced to a quarter or less of its original size by the tuna fishery since the early 1960s. Very recently, however, fishery kills have been greatly reduced and the subspecies seems assured of survival. *W. F. Perrin*

Size
Slight sexual dimorphism
Total length: 1.3–2.4 m (averages from 1.4 to 2.0 m, depending on region)
Weight: 22–75 kg, depending on region

Identification
Stenella longirostris can be distinguished from other small long-beaked dolphins by its three-part color pattern. Its back is dark gray, the sides are light gray, and the underside is white (except in *S. l. orientalis* and *S. l. centroamericana*). The dorsal fin is not quite triangular, and the flipper stripe extends to the eye. *Stenella longirostris* has a longer beak than *Stenella cly-* mene. The lower margin of the cape forms a parallel line with the upper margin of the ventral coloration, and the sides of the flippers are parallel. There are 42–62 teeth in each row.

Recent Synonyms
Stenella microps
Stenella roseiventris

Other Common Names
Spinner porpoise, long-snouted spinner dolphin, delfin tornillon

Status
Insufficiently known (IUCN) but very common in most tropical waters. However, *S. l. orientalis* has been designated "Depleted" by the U.S. government.

Subspecies
Stenella longirostris centroamericana, coastal waters of Central America
Stenella longirostris longirostris, high-seas tropical waters of the world
Stenella longirostris orientalis, eastern tropical Pacific

References
Mammalian Species 599; Norris et al., 1994; Perrin and Gilpatrick, 1994

Long-beaked saddleback dolphin | *Delphinus capensis*

Delphinus capensis is restricted to nearshore tropical to temperate waters of some oceans. In the eastern North Pacific, this species is recorded from central California south to Peru, including the Gulf of California. In the Atlantic, records are available from coastal Venezuela south to the La Plata region of Argentina.

This dolphin's coloration consists of a crisscross pattern, with a relatively darker thoracic patch than the patch of *D. delphis.* The patch does not contrast as sharply with the dark gray back as in *D. delphis.* The flipper-to-anus stripe is weakly to strongly formed. The flipper stripe angles towards the corner of the mouth and may fuse with the lip patch at the corner of the gape, one-third of the way anterior along the gape, or may closely parallel the gape. The flipper stripe narrows moderately anterior to the eye. The eye patch does not contrast strongly with the adjacent thoracic patch, and the white of the abdomen rarely extends above the flipper stripe to below the eye. The flippers and dorsal fin may be a slightly paler color in some adults. Animals from southern Africa may have relatively longer beaks and an overall larger body size than animals from the eastern North Pacific.

Schools for both forms can range in size from fewer than 10 to several thousand individuals. An average group size of 183.8 is reported for the long-beaked saddleback dolphin in the waters off California.

Differences in feeding habits between the two species of saddleback dolphins have not yet been characterized. Feeding occurs primarily at night on the fish and squid of the deep scattering layer. The stomachs of two long-beaked individuals contained almost equal amounts of northern anchovies and Pacific hake. Based on this very small sample, the short-beaked saddleback dolphin may feed more extensively on squid than the long-beaked species.

Gestation is estimated at 10–11 months. Calves are usually born in the spring and summer and are less than a meter (39 inches) long at birth. *J. E. Heyning*

Delphinus capensis

Size
Males average 5 percent larger than females.
Total length: 2–2.54 m (males); 1.93–2.22 m (females)
Weight: 135 kg (maximum)

Identification
The overall pigmentation pattern is more muted than that of *Delphinus delphis,* and *D. capensis* is also slightly more slender than *D. delphis,* with a flatter melon that inserts onto the beak at a more gradual angle when viewed in profile.

Recent Synonyms
Delphinus delphis

Other Common Names
Common dolphin

Status
Common in nearshore waters; CITES Appendix II, which includes species that may become threatened with extinction unless trade in them is strictly controlled, and nonthreatened species that must be regulated in order to control threatened species

References
Evans, 1994; Heyning and Perrin, 1994

Short-beaked saddleback dolphin | *Delphinus delphis*

Short-beaked saddleback dolphins are found in temperate and tropical waters of all major oceans and some seas. In the North Pacific, *D. delphis* has been found from British Columbia south to Chile, and as far from the coast as 135° west longitude. Records from the western North Atlantic range from at least Florida to Newfoundland.

Coloration consists of the basic criss-cross pattern, with a relatively pale gray to medium golden-yellow thoracic patch, which contrasts sharply with the very dark gray to black back. The flipper-to-anus stripe is weakly formed or absent in most animals. One or more accessory stripes may be present on the abdomen; these are more common on animals from the North Atlantic. The flipper stripe narrows distinctly in front of the eye. There is always a wide, lightly pigmented region between the flipper stripe and the eye patch, which is black. Pale gray to white patches are found on the dorsal fin and flippers of many adults.

Schools can range in size from fewer than 10 to several thousand individuals. An average group size of 97.9 has been reported for the short-beaked saddleback dolphin in schools off the California coast.

Differences in feeding habits between the two species of saddleback dolphins have not yet been well characterized. When the stomach contents of 10 short-beaked saddleback dolphins from southern California were analyzed, they were found to contain primarily squid of the family Gonatidae and *Loligo opalescens,* followed by Pacific hake *(Merluccius productus)* and northern anchovies *(Engaulis mordax).*

Gestation is estimated at 10–11 months. Calves are usually born in the spring and summer months and are less than one meter long (39 inches) at birth. *J. E. Heyning*

Size
Males average 5 percent larger than females.
Total length: 1.72–2.23 m (males); 1.64–2.15 m (females)
Weight: 110 kg (maximum)

Identification
Distinguished from *Delphinus capensis* by the flipper stripe, which does not angle towards the corner of the gape: it fuses with the lip patch one-third to one-half of the gape length anterior to the corner of the mouth. The short-beaked saddleback dolphin is relatively heavier and deeper-bodied anteriorly than the long-beaked saddleback dolphin, with a more rounded melon that inserts onto the beak at a sharp angle when viewed in profile. The flippers and dorsal fin are larger than in *D. capensis.*

Other Common Names
Common dolphin

Status
Common in nearshore and offshore waters; CITES Appendix II, which includes species that may become threatened with extinction unless trade in them is strictly controlled, and non-threatened species that must be regulated in order to control threatened species

References
Evans, 1994; Heyning and Perrin, 1994

Delphinus delphis

Fraser's dolphin | *Lagenodelphis hosei*

This dolphin was unknown to science until 1956, when it was described from a skeleton collected in Borneo in the last century. Its external appearance remained unknown until several specimens were collected in the early 1970s. *L. hosei* is now known from many tropical areas around the world, although its natural history is for the most part still obscure. It probably went unnoticed for so long, despite its distinctive short beak and striking color pattern, because it usually flees from ships rather than riding the bow wave. At a distance it can easily be confused with the striped dolphin, *Stenella coeruleoalba,* because both have a lateral stripe.

In North American waters, Fraser's dolphin ranges from southern Mexico to Central America on the Pacific side and from the Gulf of Mexico to the Caribbean on the Atlantic side. It is most common in hot equatorial water. Its distribution is well known only in the eastern tropical Pacific, where it has been involved peripherally in the "tuna/dolphin problem" of incidental mortality in the purse-seine fishery for yellowfin tuna. This species is taken incidentally in many fisheries around the world in the tropics; it may be particularly vulnerable because of its high-speed swimming and deep-diving habits. In the eastern Pacific it is found only on the high seas, but in the Philippines it may be encountered in relatively shallow water close to shore (perhaps because of the propinquity of very deep water slightly offshore).

Very little is known of the life history of this species. Length at birth is about one meter. Sexual maturation occurs at about 7–8 years in males and females. Judging from large testis size (1–2 kg in adults), breeding may be promiscuous or polyandrous. Most schools consist of 100–1,000 individuals, but smaller groups may be seen. It is not known whether there is segregation by age or sex. Fraser's dolphins often school with other small odontocetes, notably melon-headed whales, *Peponocephala electra,* in the eastern Pacific.

Fraser's dolphins feed on small mesopelagic fishes, squids, and shrimps in the eastern Pacific. Most of the fishes consumed do not regularly swim to the surface; the dolphins apparently feed very deep.

Its high-strung nature makes this dolphin unsuitable for captivity; to date all captive animals have died within a few weeks. *W. F. Perrin*

Lagenodelphis hosei

Size
Sexual dimorphism has not been documented but is probably slight.
Total length: 2.3–2.7 m (males); 2.1–2.6 m (females)
Weight: 164–209 kg

Identification
Fraser's dolphin is distinguished from other pelagic tropical dolphins by its very short beak (30–60 mm), relatively small dorsal fin and flippers, broad black stripe down side (in adults), and pinkish belly (particularly in juveniles). There are 34–44 teeth in each row.

Other Common Names
Sarawak dolphin, short-snouted whitebelly porpoise, delfin de Fraser

Status
Insufficiently Known (IUCN), but common in some equatorial waters and in Southeast Asia

References
Mammalian Species 470; Perrin et al., 1994b

Atlantic white-sided dolphin | *Lagenorhynchus acutus*

The Atlantic white-sided dolphin is found only in the North Atlantic Ocean. The species was described from a skull in the Brooke's Museum, London, by J. E. Gray in 1828. The type locality was later determined to be near the Faroe Islands.

This dolphin is restricted to the cold-temperate portions of the North Atlantic, principally on the continental shelf and slope. Along the east coast of North America, Atlantic white-sided dolphins regularly occur offshore south of Cape Cod, Massachusetts. The northern limit of these dolphins in the western and central North Atlantic is not well known; however, they have been observed in the Davis Strait off west Greenland. The species is well known around Iceland, the Faroe Islands, and the British Isles, but it rarely enters the Baltic Sea. The southernmost records in the eastern Atlantic are from France.

The color pattern of these dolphins is complex. The dorsal surface, upper sides, flukes, and flippers are dark gray to black. The ventral and lower sides are white. A long gray area is found from in front of the eyes to the base of the flukes, and a white patch occurs between the gray and black areas along the middle of the sides. A narrow band on the sides of the tail stock is a brownish-yellow color.

Lagenorhynchus acutus

Female Atlantic white-sided dolphins are estimated to become sexually mature when they are between 2–2.2 m long, at 6–8 years of age. Gestation is estimated at 11 months. Calves are born in the summer and are about 1.1–1.2 m long at birth. They nurse for about 18 months. The calving interval is 2–3 years. Males probably reach sexual maturity at a length of 2.3–2.4 m, at about 8 or 9 years of age. The maximum reported age is 27 years for females and 22 years for males.

Most of what we know about the biology of this species comes from the examination of carcasses in mass strandings.

One hundred or more dolphins are sometimes involved in these strandings. Between 1968 and 1993, 348 Atlantic white-sided dolphins are known to have stranded along the New England coast. Typical school size is 50 to 60, but large herds, numbering in the high hundreds, can occur.

In the western North Atlantic, groups of these dolphins are often associated with, and probably feed with, fin whales, humpback whales, and pilot whales. The food items most commonly consumed by Atlantic white-sided dolphins off New England and Newfoundland are smelt, silver hake, and short-finned squid. Sand lances are also a major prey species.

The offshore population of Atlantic white-sided dolphins from Cape Hatteras, North Carolina, north to Nova Scotia is about 30,000 animals. The total population size throughout the range is unknown. Small numbers of these dolphins are hunted off Greenland and the Faroe Islands. Incidental catches are taken in various fisheries in the western North Atlantic, including the Atlantic drift gillnet fishery, the New England multispecies sink gillnet fishery, and the New England groundfish multispecies trawl fishery.

This species has rarely been held in captivity. Most of those held have been individuals rescued alive from mass strandings.

R. L. Brownell, Jr.

Size

Males are slightly larger than females.
Total length: 2.3–2.8 m (males); 1.9–2.4 m (females)
Weight: 180–230 kg

Identification

Like other members of the genus, these dolphins are stocky, with short, thick snouts. They are similar in appearance to white-beaked dolphins, but can be distinguished from all other east coast dolphins by their complex coloration. The lateral color is a mixture of black, gray, white, and brownish-yellow (or "mustard") patches. There are 30–40 teeth in each tooth row.

Other Common Names

Dauphin a flancs blancs de l'Atlantique, delfin de flancos blancos

Status

Insufficiently Known (IUCN), but very common throughout most of its range

References

Gaskin, 1992a; Reeves et al., 1996a

White-beaked dolphin | *Lagenorhynchus albirostris*

The white-beaked dolphin is endemic to the North Atlantic. A skeleton of a dolphin collected from Great Yarmouth, England, was described by Gray in 1846 as a new species, *Delphinus albirostris*. Later the same year, Gray established the genus *Lagenorhynchus* with *L. albirostris* as the type species for the genus.

Like the Atlantic white-sided dolphin, the white-beaked dolphin is found only in the North Atlantic and is restricted to the cold-temperate portions of that ocean. White-beaked dolphins are the more northerly distributed of the two species. They occur from off Cape Cod, New England, and the Gulf of Maine northward to southern Greenland and Iceland. In the eastern Atlantic, the dolphins range from the Barents Sea southward, occur all around the British Isles, into the Baltic Sea, off the coast of France, and are occasionally seen off Portugal. A few animals have been reported from the western Mediterranean.

These dolphins are mostly dark gray to black, but the color pattern is highly variable. The beak is usually white, often mottled with pale gray or with grayish or blackish spots. A pale gray area with an indistinct border originates on the up-

Lagenorhynchus albirostris

per flank between the dark dorsal and lateral fields. The sides are mostly pale gray. The ventral surface is mainly white.

Little is known about the reproductive biology of this species. The smallest sexually mature male that has been measured was 2.51 m in length, and the largest sexually immature male was 2.57 m. The smallest sexually mature female was 1.74 m long, and the largest sexually immature female was 2.49 m. The mean size of mature females is probably around 2.3–2.4 m. The length at birth is between 1.1 and 1.2 m. The length of the lactation period and the age at sexual maturity are unknown.

The little we know about the biology of these dolphins comes from animals that stranded, were entrapped in ice, or were taken incidental to fishing operations. White-beaked dolphins do not strand in large groups like Atlantic white-sided dolphins. Due to their coastal distribution, however, white-beaked dolphins are regularly entrapped in ice along the coasts of Newfoundland in years with heavy pack ice. Predation by killer whales almost certainly occurs, but it has not yet been documented.

Group size ranges from a few individuals to schools of 500. Limited data suggest that some schools are segregated by age and sex. White-beaked dolphins, like many other species of dolphins, frequently ride the bow wave or wake of vessels, and can be very acrobatic at the surface of the water. White-beaked dolphins are sometimes found in association with fin and humpback whales. In the Irish Sea, they are found with bottlenose dolphins and common dolphins.

The principal food items of white-beaked dolphins are clupeids (e.g., herring) and gadids (e.g., Atlantic cod, haddock, whiting, poor-cod, and bib). In addition, other fishes, squid, octopus, and benthic crustaceans are prey for these dolphins. Atlantic cod otoliths (ear bones) and bones represented 90 percent of the remains found in the stomachs of 20 dolphins examined from off Newfoundland.

An aerial survey off eastern Newfoundland and southeastern Labrador estimated the white-beaked population there at 5,500 animals. The occurrence of this species off the northeastern United States is seasonal; an aerial survey program off Cape Cod produced a population estimate of only about 600 dolphins. White-beaked dolphins are hunted opportunistically in various parts of their range. During the early 1980s an estimated 366 white-beaked dolphins were taken annually by fishermen along the Labrador coast. This species is also taken incidentally in fisheries in various parts of its range, but this fishery-related mortality is poorly documented.

A small number of white-beaked dolphins have been kept in captivity. These captives have come from seine net operations off Iceland, were rescued ice-entrapped animals from Newfoundland, or were stranded animals found in Europe. *R. L. Brownell, Jr.*

Size

Males are slightly larger than females.

Total length: 2.5–3.1 m (males); 1.8–2.4 m (females)

Weight: 354 kg (largest recorded male); 306 kg (largest recorded female)

Identification

Like other members of the genus, these dolphins are stocky, with short, thick snouts. They are similar to Atlantic white-beaked dolphins, but are much more robust and have a less complex color pattern. White-beaked dolphins are mostly black to dark gray, with an area of pale gray on the upper flank centered below the anterior insertion of the dorsal fin. There are 22–28 teeth in each toothrow and the first few teeth are usually concealed within the gums.

Other Common Names

delfin de pico blanco (Spanish). In Canada, the name "jumper" is used for both white-beaked and Atlantic white-sided dolphins.

Status

Insufficiently Known (IUCN), but very common throughout much of its range

References

Katona et al., 1983; Reeves et al., 1996b

Pacific white-sided dolphin | *Lagenorhynchus obliquidens*

Pacific white-sided dolphins are well known for their aerial displays, which include a variety of leaps, especially in the coastal waters off southern California. This species was described in 1865, based on three specimens that had been collected off San Francisco, California. The first live individuals were collected in 1954 off southern California, and various aquaria have displayed them since that time throughout the Unites States and Japan. Most of our scientific knowledge of this species has been published only in the past 40 years.

The Pacific white-sided dolphin is found only in the North Pacific Ocean. In the western Pacific, it occurs from the South China Sea northward throughout Japanese waters, around the Kuril Islands, Russia, and extends north to the Commander Islands. In the eastern Pacific, the species is found from the southern Gulf of California, Mexico, along the west coast of North America north to the Gulf of Alaska, and as far west as Amchitka in the Aleutian Islands. Across the Pacific these dolphins are generally found in a relatively narrow area between 38° and 47° N.

These dolphins have a white belly and are dark gray to black on the side and back. A black line separates the white ventral surface from darker lateral areas. The dark coloration of the upper body is interrupted by a pale gray lateral swath extending from below the dorsal fin onto the facial region. Gray "suspender stripes" begin above the eye on each side and run high on the back, widening behind the dorsal fin to form a lateral blaze. Dolphins from the Sea of Japan and southern Baja California, Mexico, are larger and heavier than those occurring elsewhere.

Females of this species from the central North Pacific become sexually mature at about 1.7–1.8 m, at 10–11 years of age.

Gestation is estimated to last about 10 months, and the calf is about 1 m long at birth. Males mature at about 1.7–1.8 m, at an age of 10–19 years.

Pacific white-sided dolphins are considered to be gregarious, and are generally seen in groups of tens to sometimes thousands of animals. Off the west coast of North America, groups of fewer than one hundred are the most common. In southern California waters, the dolphins are most abundant between November and April.

In the eastern North Pacific, these dolphins feed primarily on epipelagic fishes and cephalopods. The prey species most commonly consumed are northern anchovy, Pacific hake, Pacific saury, rock fish, horse mackerel, and market squid. Pacific white-sided dolphins are frequently observed in mixed-species aggregations of cetaceans and pinnipeds. One of the most unique associations is very large groups of Pacific white-sided dolphins with northern right whale dolphins *(Lissodelphis borealis)*. The reason for this close association is not known, but it may be food related.

Pacific white-sided dolphins were among the most commonly caught cetaceans in the Japanese and Korean squid high seas driftnet fisheries before a United Nations moratorium on high seas driftnet fisheries went into effect in 1993. Today, smaller numbers of the dolphins are still taken incidental to various fisheries in coastal waters throughout their range. The estimated number of Pacific white-sided dolphins in the North Pacific is between about 900,000 and 1,000,000. In the continental shelf and slope waters off California, the population is estimated at about 120,000 animals. *R. L. Brownell, Jr.*

Lagenorhynchus obliquidens

Size
Males are slightly larger than females.
Total length: 1.7–2.5 m
Weight: 75<n>200 kg (depending on region)

Identification
Pacific white-sided dolphins are stocky, with short, thick snouts. They are distinguishable from other west coast dolphins by their shape and coloration. Their three-part color pattern consists of a large, pale gray thoracic patch, a white belly with a black border, and a dark gray back and sides. There are 24–35 (mean, 30) teeth in each row.

Recent Synonyms
Lagenorhynchus ognevi

Other Common Names
Pacific white-striped dolphin, delfin de costados blancos del Pacifico, kama-iruka

Status
Insufficiently Known (IUCN), but very common throughout most of its range

References
Brownell et al., 1996; Walker et al., 1986

Risso's dolphin | *Grampus griseus*

Risso's dolphins, commonly referred to as grampus, are generally found in deep tropical and warm temperate waters worldwide. These dolphins typically occur in waters deeper than 180 m and appear in coastal waters only where the continental shelf is relatively close to shore. Sightings in cooler northern waters usually occur only during the summer months. The preference for deep water habitats makes study of this species a difficult task. Much of what is known about these oceanic animals is based on information obtained from stranded specimens, animals harvested in drive fisheries, seasonal studies of nearshore groups, and from occasional sightings at sea. At best, this provides a sketchy picture of grampus distribution since only a few scattered sightings define the boundaries of its range.

Preliminary photographic studies of grampus near Monterey Bay, California, suggest that they live in somewhat stable subgroups within larger herds. Grampus are very social. Though sometimes found alone or in small groups of fewer than 12 individuals, at times they are found in groups ranging from a few hundred to thousands. Hundreds of these dolphins will sometimes swim and surface in synchrony, shoulder-to-shoulder in a "chorus line." Segregation by age and sex typically occurs in the larger schools (of more than 60 animals), where discrete groups of adult animals, juveniles, and females with calves are obvious.

Grampus attain sexual maturity at lengths of 2.6–2.8 m. Calving season appears to vary from region to region. In the North Atlantic, records suggest that calving occurs in the sum-

mer; off the coast of central California, births are believed to occur in winter.

Newborn calves are about 1.2–1.5 m long. They are blue-gray with a white, anchor-shaped patch between their pectoral fins that stays with them for life. Unlike adults, calves are not scarred. As they grow, their bodies darken to a brownish-gray. As they continue to age, their skin lightens, becoming white along the head, flanks, and abdomen. The dorsal fin, flukes, and tips of the flippers remain dark. Throughout the aging process, grampus accumulate the body scars characteristic of their species.

The battered appearance of grampus skin is believed to be partially the result of the highly gregarious and social nature of this species. Interactions among individuals can be extremely physical, with animals often slapping, splashing, and leaping on one another. This "aggressive" behavior has also been observed during interactions between grampus and other marine mammals. Pacific white-sided dolphins *(Lagenorhynchus obliquidens)* and northern right whale dolphins *(Lissodelphis borealis)* have participated in chases, synchronous swimming, and group "rubbing" sessions with grampus. Grampus are extremely energetic during these interactions, often leaping clear of the water (breaching), swimming rapidly along the surface (porpoising), and making high-speed turns. All of these species have been observed at one time or another "bow-riding" on the waves created by larger migrating cetaceans, such as gray whales *(Eschrichtius robustus)* and humpback whales *(Megaptera novaeangliae).*

The appearance of large groups of grampus in an area may be in response to abundant food sources. Studies of stomach contents have shown squid to be their exclusive prey. Many cetaceans that specialize in squid predation have evolved to have a reduced number of teeth, especially in the upper jaw. Grampus usually have no teeth in the upper jaw and fewer than seven pairs of large, conical teeth in the lower jaw. Some of the scarring seen on grampus may be the result of scratches from squid beaks and circular marks from tentacles.

Grampus mortality has been documented in squid purse-seine and drift-gillnet fisheries. However, the number of animals killed annually during interactions with fishing operations is unknown. No reliable population estimate exists for the species as a whole, though the population off the Washington-Oregon-California coastline is estimated to number more than 32,000 animals. The population located along the east coast of North America, between Nova Scotia and Cape Hatteras, North Carolina, is estimated at 16,800 animals. *K. E. W. Shelden*

Grampus griseus

Size
No significant sexual dimorphism
Total length: 2.8–3.8 m
Weight: 400–600 (500) kg

Identification
The bodies of adult Risso's dolphins are heavily scarred; in addition to the natural process of graying with age, some may appear almost uniformly white. Other features include a large, blunt head lacking a beak and a tall,

slightly curved dorsal fin. Unique to these dolphins is a sharp groove that creases the melon (forehead); this indentation is visible only when viewing the animal head-on.

Recent Synonyms
Grampidelphis griseus

Other Common Names
Grampus, gray grampus, white-headed grampus

Status
Unknown, although thought to be relatively abundant in lower latitudes

References
Ellis, 1989; Kruse et al., 1999; Leatherwood et al., 1982; Martin, 1990

Pygmy killer whale | *Feresa attenuata*

The pygmy killer whale, along with a few other small cetaceans like Fraser's dolphin *(Lagenodelphis hosei)*, has an unusual scientific history. In 1827, J. E. Gray published the first description, based on a single skull with an unknown type locality. Gray published the description of a second pygmy killer whale skull in 1874 with a type locality given as "South Seas" (= South Pacific?). The pygmy killer whale then disappeared from the scientific literature until 1954, when M. Yamada described a "strange dolphin" collected in 1952 from Taiji, Japan. This strange dolphin proved to be *Feresa,* and Yamada's paper provided the first description of the complete skeleton and external appearance of the animal. Yamada was hampered because the specimen was in pieces when he acquired it. More than 10 years passed before the species was seen again—also in southern Japan. In 1963 Masaharu Nishiwaki and his colleagues examined 14 individuals collected at Sagami Bay, Izu Peninsula, and provided the first extensive descriptions of external and internal morphology for the species. Since 1963 the pygmy killer whale has been found around the world in temperate and tropical waters. In North America the species is primarily known from strandings on the Atlantic and Gulf coasts and, more recently, from sightings in the Gulf of Mexico.

These little black whales with white lips are poorly known in terms of their distribution, abundance, and biology. In the southeastern United States they have been known to strand individually or in small groups (3–7 individuals). Most of the stranded animals have been sexually mature. Based on the examination of ovaries and testes, sexual maturity seems to occur at a body length of about 2 m. Sexually mature males have unusually large testes for a small cetacean. Total testes weight averaged 1,463 g and 1.3 percent of total body weight for five males. This is similar to the situation in male pygmy sperm

Feresa attenuata

whales *(Kogia breviceps)* and suggests a similar reproductive strategy.

Breeding and calving seasons are not known, but most authors assume that calves are born in summer. Gestation is assumed to be about one year, and length at birth has been estimated at about 0.8 m. Pygmy killer whales have been sighted in the wild swimming alone and have been seen in herds numbering up to (rarely) several hundred. Ross and Leatherwood report that 16 herds sighted in the eastern tropical Pacific by U.S. tuna boat observers had an average size of about 25 ani-

mals. A few stranded pygmy killer whales have been held in marine zoological parks and oceanaria for a few days and some individuals have been reported to be aggressive. In the eastern tropical Pacific, pygmy killer whales chase and sometimes eat other small dolphins. Otherwise, food habits are poorly known, but the diet includes cephalopods and fish.

Pygmy killer whales have been taken in fisheries (both directly and indirectly) in various parts of the world, including the eastern tropical Pacific, Japan, Sri Lanka, and St. Vincent, Lesser Antilles. *D. K. Odell*

Size
Males may be somewhat longer than females.
Total length: about 2–2.59 m
Weight can be estimated from length: a 2.25 m long animal weighs about 140 kg

Identification
Feresa attenuata is small and black, with a relatively large dorsal fin and without a distinct beak. The lips are white and the flanks are grayish. There is a variable white patch in the anal-genital region (flanks) that often extends both anteriorly and posteriorly. At a distance,

Feresa is not easily distinguished from the melon-headed whale, *Peponocephala electra;* close-up, *Feresa* has a more rounded melon and more rounded flipper tips than does *Peponocephala,* and the latter typically lacks the white patches on the flanks. The two species are easily distinguished by tooth counts: 8–13 per row in *Feresa* and 20–25 per row in *Peponocephala.*

Other Common Names
Petty det (St. Vincent, Lesser Antilles), orca pigméo (portions of Latin America)

Status
Unknown

References
Klinowska, 1991; Leatherwood and Reeves, 1983; Odell and Asper, 1986; Ross and Leatherwood, 1994

False killer whale | *Pseudorca crassidens*

False killer whales are the second-largest members of the dolphin family. They are found in tropical and temperate waters around the world. This species is mainly known from mass strandings throughout its range. It is one of several species of delphinids that some fishermen on both coasts of North America call blackfish.

Along the west coast of North America, false killer whales are mostly found from southern Baja California, Mexico, southward. Along the east coast they are common from

Florida southward, and are not commonly found to the north except in the Gulf Stream. Migrations have not been reported, but northern records off North America appear to be correlated with seasonal ocean-warming events.

These dolphins are dark gray to black in color, with a paler gray patch on the underside between the flippers and lower ventral surface. The dark coloration is paler on the head.

Off Japan, females mature at body lengths of 3.4 to 3.8 m, at ages from 8 to 11 years. Longevity is estimated at about 60

Pseudorca crassidens

mass stranding known involved 835 individuals. The sex ratio of animals that have stranded, and of those that have been caught in fisheries, is about equal.

False killer whales commonly co-occur with at least ten other species of cetaceans. They feed primarily on a variety of fishes and squids, including bonito, mahimahi, yellowtail tuna, perch, and various species of open ocean squid. Food sharing between indivduals has been reported in the wild. In some regions these animals have acquired a reputation for stealing fish from the lines of commercial and sport fishermen.

No estimates of abundance are available for the false killer whale along the west coast of North America. In the northern Gulf of Mexico, the average estimated abundance was about 400 whales, based on sighting surveys during 1991–1994. No estimates of abundance are available for the greater Caribbean Sea or off the east coast of the United States. Some false killer whales are taken in Caribbean small cetacean fisheries and used for human consumption. They are also sometimes taken incidental to gillnet and longline fishing operations throughout their range. No human-caused fishing mortality is known from U.S. waters, but false killer whales are taken in the eastern tropical Pacific tuna purse seine fishery.

This species is not commonly kept in captivity, but specimens have been held in aquariums in the United States, Japan, and the Netherlands. A small number of hybrids between male false killer whales and female bottlenose dolphins have been born in Japanese and U.S. institutions. One of the female hybrids gave birth to a live calf, sired by a male bottlenose dolphin. *R. L. Brownell, Jr.*

years, based on the assumption that growth layer lines in the teeth are deposited annually. Length of gestation is estimated at just over 15 months. The average birth interval is approximately 7 years, and the mean size at birth is estimated at 1.75 m.

False killer whales are most often sighted in groups of fewer than ten to the low hundreds of animals. They are among the most common species involved in mass strandings. The largest

Size
Males are larger than females.
Total length: 3.7–6 m (males); 3.3–5.1 m (females)
Weight: 1,360 kg (maximum)

Identification
This large delphinid can be distinguished from the other members of its family by its distinctive sickle-shaped flipper. The anterior border of the flipper has a broad hump near the center and the posterior border is slightly concave near the tip. The dolphin's overall color is dark gray or black. The dorsal fin is falcate (sickle-shaped). The beak extends in a smooth line from the head, with no demarcation. There are 7–12 teeth in each toothrow.

Other Common Names
Faux-orque (French), orca falsa (Spanish), blackfish

Status
Insufficiently Known (IUCN), but very common throughout much of its range

References
Odell and McClune, 1996

Short-finned pilot whale | *Globicephala macrorhynchus*

Short-finned pilot whales occur in tropical to temperate waters from the outer edges of the continental shelf seaward, sometimes becoming coastal. They occur in the Atlantic from New Jersey southward to Venezuela, including the Gulf of Mexico. They have been sighted in Delaware Bay. Off New Jersey, both long-finned and short-finned pilot whales can be sighted. The two species are virtually indistinguishable from each other at sea. In the Pacific, short-finned pilot whales range from the Gulf of Alaska south to Guatemala.

Short-finned pilot whales are very gregarious and cohesive, with an average of 25 whales per school. Sightings of several hundred have been reported. Schools are composed of one or more adult males, adult females of all ages and reproductive status, and immature animals of both sexes. The schools may be made up of matrilineal kinship groups. Because there are more reproductive females than mature males in a school, it is thought that these whales are polygynous. Short-finned pilot whales travel at a speed of about 8 kilometers per hour (4 knots).

Schools of whales in tropical latitudes are known to join together to form large herds. Interestingly, they often line up in the same direction, bobbing up and down to breathe. The whales are probably resting and this behavior is known as logging.

Short-finned pilot whales are often sighted with short-beaked saddleback dolphins *(Delphinus delphis)* in the Atlantic and bottlenosed and whitesided dolphins *(Tursiops truncatus* and *Lagenorynchus obliquidens)* in the Pacific, presumably feeding on squid and fish. Juvenile short-finned pilot whales may actually learn additional or alternative feeding strategies from these dolphins rather than from their peers. An adult whale can consume upwards of 45 kg (100 lbs) of food per day.

Females reach sexual maturity at 8 years of age and males at about 13 years. Approximate life spans are 45 years for males and 55 years for females. Gestation lasts approximately 15–16 months, and typically one calf is born every three years. Calves are approximately 1.4 m (4.5 feet) long and weigh about 60 kg (132 lb) at birth. In her lifetime a female will produce 4–5 calves. A female can lactate at least eleven years after ovulation has ceased.

Mass strandings are a common occurrence, especially in the Atlantic, where whales usually strand on the coasts of the Carolinas, Florida, and Gulf of Mexico. For no apparent reason, entire schools come up onto a beach and die. Strandings in the Pacific are uncommon, but there are limited records, mostly of individual whales stranding in British Columbia. Because their massive weight is unsupported when they are on land, death can come from internal injuries, or whales can drown if their blowholes are covered with water before they can refloat themselves. Unfortunately, whales pushed back into the water often restrand elsewhere on the coastline. *A. Abend*

Globicephala macrorhynchus

Size

Males are larger than females.

Total length: 5.5 m (average), 7 m (maximum) (males); 4.25 m (average), 5 m (maximum) (females)

Weight: up to 3,000 kg (3.3 tons) (males); up to 1,500 kg (1.6 tons) (females)

Identification

This is a medium-sized black whale with an anchor-shaped gray patch; the anchor blades are above the flippers. A light gray saddle may appear behind the dorsal fin. The dorsal fin is placed far forward and is broad-based, thick, and very curved (sickle-shaped). The head is bulbous; in older males it is somewhat flattened and may protrude and overhang the mouth. The sickle-shaped pectoral flippers are about one-sixth the length of the body, and can be used to distinguish this species from the long-finned pilot whale, *Globicephala melas*. The flippers of *G. melas* are approximately one-fifth body length and have a recognizable elbow.

Recent Synonyms

Globicephala scammoni
Globicephala sieboldii

Other Common Names

Blackfish, pothead, Pacific pilot whale, shortfin pilot whale

Status

Common

References

Baird and Stacey, 1993; Boschung et al., 1983; Marsh and Kasuya, 1991; Watson, 1981

Long-finned pilot whale | *Globicephala melas*

Long-finned pilot whales inhabit cool temperate latitudes of the North Atlantic. They can be encountered anywhere on the continental shelf and slope from Cape Hatteras north to Baffin Bay. They are particularly common in shelf-edge and slope waters. An estimated 62,000 pilot whales were in the total population that was intensively exploited in drive hunts at Newfoundland between 1952 and 1968. This population was incompletely surveyed from aircraft in 1980, resulting in an estimate of 7,000–20,000 in Newfoundland waters. Aerial surveys of the shelf region between Cape Hatteras and Nova Scotia in 1978–1982 produced an estimate of about 11,000 pilot whales, but this may have included some short-finned pilot whales *(G. macrorhynchus):* there is some overlap in the distribution of the two species along the eastern United States, approximately between latitudes 35° N and 38–39° N. Shipboard surveys in the late 1980s yielded an estimate of 778,000 long-finned pilot whales in the northeastern Atlantic (from Greenland eastward). The North Atlantic population is separate from the population(s) of *G. melas* in the Southern Ocean.

The seasonal movements of long-finned pilot whales parallel those of their prey, which off eastern North America consist mainly of short-finned squid *(Illex illecebrosus)* and Atlantic mackerel *(Scomber scombrus)*. The whales move inshore in summer and autumn, following feeding squid, and offshore in winter and spring, following the squid to their spawning grounds. At the Faroe Islands, northwest of the British Isles, where large samples of pilot whales have been studied, ommastrephid and gonatid squids are the principal prey.

Globicephala melas has a bulbous head with only the hint of a "beak." The prominent dorsal fin is broad-based and sickle-shaped; it can be either pointed or rounded at the peak. The long flippers are also sickle-shaped. The overall coloration of adult long-finned pilot whales is black, but the color pattern

Globicephala melas

can be somewhat complex. A "saddle" of paler pigmentation may be present immediately behind the dorsal fin, and a narrow, elongated, paler "blaze" is sometimes evident behind the eye. These markings can be present or absent, muted or bold; there is much individual variation. A broad white or pale gray patch is present on the throat, and a pale stripe along the ventral midline widens in the ano-genital region.

Calves are much paler than adults. Their average length at birth is about 1.75–1.8 m and they weigh about 75 kg. Young pilot whales grow rapidly. Males usually become sexually mature at about 14 years of age, but their growth does not slow appreciably until they reach a length of 5.5 m and a weight of 1,700 kg, at about 20 years of age. Female growth does not slow until a length of 4.25 m and a weight of 1,000 kg are attained at an age of about 13 years; they are sexually mature at about 8 years.

Females normally give birth about every five years. The interbirth interval involves a gestation period of about a year, and several years of lactation and "resting." A female normally nurses her calf for at least 3 years, and it is not uncommon for a female to become pregnant before weaning her previous calf. In the population studied off Newfoundland, mating peaked during April and May, and most calves were born between July and September. Female pilot whales tend to live longer than males. Maximal ages are nearly 50 years for males and 60 years for females.

Pilot whales are gregarious, typically occurring in groups (pods) of 10 to 15 individuals. Such pods are usually associated with other, similar pods, forming loose aggregations of several hundred animals. Mass mortality due to stranding on shore is characteristic of pilot whale populations. The mechanisms that provoke mass strandings are not well understood. Efforts to rescue the whales by towing or driving them away from shore usually fail, as they soon return to the beach.

The cohesiveness of pilot whale pods and their tendency to approach particular stretches of coastline have facilitated "drive" hunting. In many parts of the North Atlantic, whalers have used boats to herd the whales into shallow water where they could easily be killed in large numbers with knives and lances. Such whaling continues, mainly at the Faroe Islands, and on a much smaller scale in Greenland. By-catches of long-finned pilot whales occur in various fisheries off eastern North America. For example, nearly 400 individuals are known to have been killed in an intensive mackerel trawl fishery centered along the outer continental shelf between Long Island, New York, and the Chesapeake Bay (Maryland and Virginia) from 1977 to 1991. *R. R. Reeves*

Size
Males are larger than females.
Total length: 6.25 m (males); 5.12 m (females)
Weight: 2,320 kg (males); 1,320 kg (females)

Identification
Although pilot whales are relatively easy to distinguish from other cetaceans, it is usually almost impossible to separate the two species of pilot whale from each other at sea. The flipper length:total body length ratio is larger for long-finned than for short-finned pilot whales. Also, long-finned pilot whales generally have a few more teeth and a more elongated rostrum than most short-finned specimens.

Recent Synonyms
Globicephala melaena

Other Common Names
Pothead (Newfoundland), blackfish (Caribbean), caa'ing whale (obsolete; mainly British), grindhval (Faroe Islands)

Status
Abundant and widespread

Subspecies
It has been assumed that the long-finned pilot whales in the North Atlantic are geographically isolated from those that occur in the circumpolar waters of the Southern Ocean, and the two populations may have slight differences in coloration. The name *Globicephala melas melaena* (= *melas*) has been applied to the northern population and *Globicephala melas edwardi* to the southern.

References
Bernard and Reilly, 1999; Donovan et al., 1993; Sergeant, 1962

Killer whale | *Orcinus orca*

Orcinus orca is the world's most widely distributed mammal, found in all oceans from the Arctic pack ice to the Antarctic pack ice. Although they are found in tropical waters and the open sea, killer whales are most abundant in nearshore waters and at high latitudes. They sometimes enter small bays and river mouths.

Coloration is black dorsally and white ventrally, with a white flank patch above the urogenital region and an oval white patch behind the eye. The bottom of the flukes is white or light gray. A gray or white saddle is present posterior to the dorsal fin. Individual and geographical variations in the pigmentation pattern have been noted. In adult males, the dorsal fin is straight and 1.0 to 1.8 m tall; the female's dorsal fin is shorter than 0.7 m and sickle-shaped. The head of the killer whale is rounded, with a slight beak. The flippers, which are egg-shaped, may attain 20 percent of the body length in males and 11 to 13 percent of the body length in females. Fluke width is about one-fifth of the body length for both sexes.

Killer whales usually occur in small pods of fewer than 10 individuals, although single whales, usually adult males, do occur. Matrilineal groups consisting of whales from 2–3 generations are the basic unit of social organization. Pod membership is typically stable, but cases of individuals and matrilineal groups switching pods are known. Nonreproductive adult fe-

males and males have been observed to care for and teach hunting techniques to the older calves of females with young calves. Behaviors such as breaching, spyhopping, flipper slapping, and lobtailing are common. The longest dive recorded was 17 minutes and the maximum depth of dive was 260 m. Swimming speeds usually are 6 to 10 km per hour.

Pods along the Pacific Northwest coast have been categorized as "resident" or "transient." Resident whales mainly eat fish and transient whales usually pursue marine mammal prey, although exceptions occur. Resident and transient whales do not intermingle socially, and preliminary mtDNA results suggest that these forms are genetically distinct. Resident whales have shorter dive times, more predictable travel routes, and larger pod size than transient whales.

Most killer whale sounds are in the range of 4 to 5 kHz. Clicks are believed to be used in echolocation and screams are assumed to be for communication. Different dialects have been documented from different pods. The smallest object discriminated by echolocation was a 10 mm plastic ring. Visual acuity is apparently well developed.

Diet varies regionally and among pods. Killer whales are known to prey upon fish, marine mammals, birds, and cephalopods. Orcas may travel 125–170 km per day while foraging. Most food items are swallowed whole, but pieces of flesh may be torn from larger prey. When attacking large whales, killer whales approach from several angles and drown their prey. Killer whales are known to kill seals and sea lions by hitting the prey with their flukes or ramming them. Killer whales often hunt cooperatively, may briefly strand themselves

Orcinus orca

to capture pinnipeds, and have been observed to hit ice floes from underneath to knock pinnipeds or penguins into the water. When they are chasing fish, killer whales may hunt individually or may circle a school of fish while one or two individuals break rank and swim through the school to feed.

Mating and calving appear to be nonseasonal. In the northeastern Pacific, most births occur between October and

March. The length of males at sexual maturity ranges from 5.2 to 6.2 m, with an average testis mass of 10,000 g. Females attain sexual maturity when they are between 4.6 and 5.4 m long, and first give birth at approximately 15 years of age. Gestation is estimated at 17 months, and the average calving interval is 5.3 years. Northeast Pacific calves average 2.4 m in length at birth, and remain dependent on their mothers for at least 2 years. Longevity may be 35 to 70 years. Killer whales have no significant predators other than humans. *J. E. Heyning*

Size
Males are larger than females in body size, flipper size, and dorsal fin height.
Total length: up to 9.0 m (males); up to 7.7 m (females)
Maximum weight: 5,568 kg (males); 3,810 kg (females)

Identification
The largest dolphins, killer whales are easily identified by their large size and distinctive black-and-white color pattern. They are black dorsally, the underside is white, and there are white patches on the flank above the urogenital region and behind the eye. The bottom of the flukes is white or pale gray. A gray or white saddle is present posterior to the dorsal fin.

Other Common Names
Orca

Status
Worldwide, locally common to rare; listed CITES appendix II

References
Mammalian Species 304; Dahlheim and Heyning, 1999; Hoyt, 1990

Northern right whale dolphin | *Lissodelphis borealis*

This lithe dolphin is endemic to, and ranges widely throughout, the temperate North Pacific, occurring from off the British Columbia coast south to the waters off northern Baja California. It is most common in deep continental shelf or offshore waters and is seen close to shore where submarine canyons or other features bring deep water near the coast. There appear to be inshore and southern shifts in its distribution during the cold-water months of October to June. It is among the most abundant of the oceanic dolphins that inhabit the temperate zone of the North Pacific.

Northern right whale dolphins are gregarious, forming herds of several hundred to thousands of individuals. They are often found in association with other marine mammals, especially the Pacific white-sided dolphin, *Lagenorhynchus obliquidens,* with which they appear to share a similar range and diet. They prey primarily on species of deepwater fish—especially those in the family Myctophidae—and squid, and they may dive deeper than 200 m in search of food.

During surface-swimming, right whale dolphins may be very undemonstrative, barely breaking the surface, or more energetic, performing low-angle leaps while swimming rapidly. They also occasionally belly-flop, fluke-slap, and side-slap. They are rapid swimmers, recorded at speeds as high as 34 km per hour. Depending on their predilection, they may ride the pressure (bow) wave of a ship.

The body of *Lissodelphis borealis* is very slender and tapers steadily to the base of the tail. The pectoral flippers and flukes are diminutive, and there is no hint of a dorsal fin or ridge.

L. borealis is the only North Pacific delphinid lacking this character. There is a tiny beak, separated from the forehead by a distinct transverse crease.

The body is mostly black, with a well-demarcated white ventral band originating in the region of the throat and extending to the mid-fluke notch. This band widens in the area of the thorax, filling the space between the flippers, and continues toward the tail as a narrow band. The head is all black

Lissodelphis borealis

except for a small white spot behind the tip of the lower jaw. On the dorsal surface, the outer two-thirds of each fluke is gray. On the ventral surface, the same area is white.

What little is known of reproduction in northern right whale dolphins derives from studies of specimens taken in the central North Pacific. Breeding, which has not been described in the literature, presumably occurs during the summer months. After a gestation period of about twelve months, the female gives birth to a single young that is approximately 1 m in length. Like most newborn delphinids, its color pattern is muted compared with that of the adult. The neonate may possess a row of vestigial hairs along either side of the rostrum. Full adult coloration is attained by the end of the first year. The duration of nursing is unknown.

Both sexes attain sexual maturity at an age of about 10 years. Males attain greater maximum lengths and weights than females, and their length at sexual maturity is greater (about 2.15 m as contrasted with about 2 m for females). Although northern right whale dolphins may live several decades, maximum life spans are not known. *M. W. Newcomer*

Size

Total length: 2–3.1 m (males); 2–2.6 m (females)
Heaviest recorded weight: 113 kg

Identification

This dolphin is mostly jet-black and is distinguished by its slender body and complete lack of a dorsal fin.

Other Common Names

Northern right whale porpoise

Status

Fairly common

References

Mammalian Species 425; Ferrero and Walker, 1993; Jefferson et al., 1994

Family Monodontidae

Narwhals and belugas are the only members of this family. Although they look very different, they are united by a variety of anatomical features that suggest a common ancestor. They are medium-sized, with belugas slightly larger at about 5 m. Maximum weight is about 900 kg for females and 1,600 kg for males in both species. Belugas are pure white as adults and narwhals are mottled black and white.

Both species are gregarious inhabitants of Arctic waters containing pack ice. Belugas tend to feed on benthic and midwater organisms and may penetrate far inland in larger rivers. Narwhals tend to be more pelagic and feed on a variety of open sea fishes, squids, shrimps, and molluscs.

The narwhal has long been an interesting oddity to humans because of its single, long tusk, usually limited to the male. In medieval times, it was thought to decorate the mythical beast we know as the unicorn. Although we have figured out which animal the tusk really belongs to, we still have no real idea of its use. It doesn't seem very useful for foraging, fighting, or ice-breaking, and why only the left tooth usually breaks through the gum and continues to grow with a sinestral spiral remains a mystery.

Belugas are also popular animals. Their attractive all-white coloration and tendency to occupy in-shore areas and rivers make them accessible to land-locked humans. They vocalize readily and frequently, emitting a variety of squeaks and chirps as they travel in groups. They are quite stocky, with a heavy blubber layer necessary to withstand the Arctic waters that form their home.

Narwhals remain in the Arctic all year, but belugas migrate southwards to the Maritime Provinces and to areas of similar latitudes in the North Pacific. Belugas have been extensively studied in Siberia as well as in North America.

References

Kleinenberg et al., 1964; Minasian et al., 1984; Rice, 1984

North American Genera

Delphinapterus
Monodon

Beluga │ *Delphinapterus leucas*

To the uninitiated, a group of swimming beluga seen from water level resembles whitecaps more than whales. As they charge through the cold, often ice-infested waters they inhabit, beluga roll at the surface and blow in a turbulent upwelling before disappearing completely. This activity is accompanied by a variety of chirps and whistles that are sometimes audible to humans. Old-time sailors who could hear these whale sounds through the sides of their wooden sailing ships called the beluga the "sea canary."

Beluga have a circumpolar distribution and are found in the Bering Sea, through the Canadian Arctic, in Hudson Bay, around Greenland, and north of Russia and Siberia. A small stock in the St. Lawrence River estuary is a remnant of a population that once numbered in the thousands.

Beluga are characterized by their fondness for warm-water estuaries in the summer. Throughout their range, they enter certain river mouths with great regularity, year after year, often in the face of severe human disturbance. It was thought that beluga entered the shallow, warm, fresh water to calve in an environment that is more benign than the Arctic Ocean, but

Delphinapterus leucas

vidals. The details of pod structure are unknown, but it is speculated, based on other mammals, that the basic unit of a pod is a female with daughters and granddaughters, mixed with younger sons and males from other pods.

Breeding occurs in winter, when the various summer stocks of beluga may be together. For example, whales from Hudson Bay and southeast Baffin Island may all winter together in Hudson Strait and Davis Strait. It is not known if beluga from the different groups interbreed or indeed if beluga are polygamous or monogamous. Gestation lasts about a year, and calves are born in the spring. Newborn beluga are approximately 1.5 m long and weigh about 100 kg. Calves are dark gray or brown and become paler gray to white as they mature. They nurse for two years on milk that is approximately 27 percent fat, and may stay with the mother longer. Adult females produce a calf every three years on average. As adults, beluga size depends somewhat on where they are found. Adult average length for females ranges from 3.3 m in Hudson Bay to approximately 4 m at southeast Baffin Island and in west Greenland (Baffin Bay). Males are bigger than females. Average male length ranges from 3.5–3.9 m in Hudson Bay to 4.5–4.8 m at southeast Baffin Island and in west Greenland.

Beluga have several adaptations allowing them to live in Arctic waters. They have no dorsal fin to be battered on the ice, and they are well insulated by a thick layer of blubber. Their gregarious behavior may help them exploit patchy food resources and detect predators such as polar bears (Ursus maritimus) and killer whales (Orcinus orca). However, it also predisposes them to episodic mass mortality if they are trapped by ice. Beluga are widely hunted for aboriginal subsistence and are a major tourist attraction in some areas. *R. E. A. Stewart*

males are also found in the estuaries and calves are also seen offshore. The current hypothesis is that beluga enter estuaries to molt. The warmer water allows increased skin temperature, accelerating the molt, and the lower salinity may make the process less irritating. It is after the molt, when the new skin of adults is shiny and white, that beluga are most striking in appearance.

Beluga occur in groups most of the year, not just when they are in estuaries. They are social animals and spend most of their time in pods ranging from a few to several hundred individuals.

Size
Total length: 3.5–4.85 m (males); 3.3–4 m (females)
Weight: 800–1,500 kg (males); 540–790 kg (females)

Identification
The adult beluga can be distinguished from the other common whale in its range, the narwhal (Monodon monoceros), by its white color and full dentition. Neonates are dark brown, gray-brown, or blue-gray compared to the slate gray color of newborn narwhals.

Recent Synonyms
Beluga angustata
Delphinapterus dorofeevi
Delphinapterus freimani

Other Common Names
White whale, belukha, sea canary (archaic)

Status
The presumed stocks in North America, named for their summering areas, are: Alaska: Bristol Bay: 1,000–1,500, stable; Norton Sound/Yukon River: 1,000–2,000, stable; Kotzebue Sound: no data; Northeast Chukchi Sea: 2,500–3,000, stable; Canada: Beaufort Sea: more than 20,000, abundant; Baffin Bay (high Arctic): 16,000–18,000, vulnerable; western Hudson Bay: more than 25,000, no status assigned; eastern Hudson Bay: more than 2,000, threatened; northern Hudson Bay: more than 700, no status assigned; southern Hudson Bay: more than 2,000, no status assigned; James Bay: more than 2,000, no status assigned; Ungava Bay: probably many fewer than 500, endangered; southeast Baffin Island: plus or minus 500, endangered; St. Lawrence: plus or minus 500, endangered.

No conservation status is assigned if the stock has not been reviewed or if it is thought to be abundant and of no immediate conservation concern. The estimate for Baffin Bay beluga is 10 years old and the stock is thought to be in decline. Stock definition and status are under constant revision, and these designations may change in the future. All but the St. Lawrence River stock support aboriginal subsistence harvests.

References
Mammalian Species 336; Born et al., 1994; Brodie, 1989; Smith et al., 1990

Narwhal | *Monodon monoceros*

Narwhals inhabit Arctic marine waters, where they live in close association with pack ice. They are much more abundant in the Western than in the Eastern Hemisphere. Narwhals show a marked preference for deep water and differ, in this respect, from belugas. All narwhal populations are migratory, moving between summering areas in deep sounds and fjords and wintering areas in dense offshore pack ice. Such movements are influenced by the formation and break-up of coastal fast ice.

Narwhals are deep divers (probably to depths of more than 1,000 m) and forage on bottom-dwelling organisms such as halibut, but their diet is diverse and includes pelagic fish, squid, and crustaceans (mainly shrimp). Satellite-linked radio telemetry, begun on narwhals in the early 1990s, has shown that they regularly dive to depths of 250 m and remain submerged for 11–15 minutes while on their inshore summering grounds. During autumn, in offshore waters, they often dive deeper than 500 m and stay below the surface for periods of up to about 20 minutes.

The most distinctive characteristic of the species is the long, straight, spiraled tusk of adult males. The tusk is an upper-jaw tooth that apparently begins to erupt through the lip at two or three years of age. It probably continues to grow throughout the animal's life, although many tusks are cracked or broken. Large tusks can be 3 m long (including the portion embedded in the skull) and weigh more than 10 kg. The tusk is usually the left member of a parallel pair of teeth; the right tooth remains concealed in the maxillary bone. A small percentage of males are twin-tusked, and females occasionally bear a tusk. All narwhals lack teeth inside the mouth. Their prey is probably captured by suction, and is swallowed whole. The primary function of the adult male's tusk probably relates in some way to male-male competition, judging from the scars on the melon and the incidence of tusk breakage.

The narwhal has a rounded head with no dolphin-like "beak." It also lacks the dorsal fin typical of most cetaceans. Body coloration changes with age. The birth color is pale gray; the pelage becomes darker gray or almost black in the yearling phase. White spotting begins on the belly and eventually spreads onto the sides. Adult narwhals are white ventrally, black dorsally, and mottled on the sides. Old males can become mainly white, with some dark spotting on the back, head, flippers, and tail flukes.

Study of the narwhal has been hindered by the lack of a reliable technique of age determination. However, both sexes certainly take several years to reach maturity. Most births occur in summer (July and August) after a gestation period of about 15 months. The calf remains with its mother and is nursed for at least one year. The interbirth interval is a minimum of two years and probably averages three. Narwhals can live for 25 years or more, and maximal longevity may be around 50 years.

In addition to being hunted for their edible skin, meat, and tusk ivory, narwhals experience predation from killer whales (regularly in summer) and polar bears (occasionally). Some

Monodon monoceros

mortality also results from winter ice entrapment. Narwhals are supremely adapted for survival in very severe ice conditions, as evidenced by their presence in small cracks in close pack ice. Nevertheless, their access to open water can some- times be blocked by wind-driven or fast-forming ice. If such entrapment occurs in early or mid-winter, the animals are in danger of suffocation, starvation, or easy predation (by humans or bears). *R. R. Reeves*

Size
Males are larger than females.
Total length (average, at physical maturity, not including the tusk): 4.76 m (males); 4.06 m (females)
Weight: 1,580 kg (males); 960 kg (females)

Identification
Monodon monoceros can be distinguished from *Delphinapterus leucas,* the only monodontid that shares its range, by the dark coloration on the back and sides and by the tusk of maturing and adult male narwhals.

Status
Seasonally common (migratory) in specific areas of the eastern Canadian Arctic and Greenland

References
Mammalian Species 127; Born et al., 1994; Hay and Mansfield, 1989; Martin et al., 1994

Family Phocoenidae

The porpoise family, with 4 genera and 6 species, includes 2 genera with 2 species in North America. The common names porpoise and dolphin are often used interchangeably, leading to considerable confusion and lending support to the argument for relying on scientific names. However, the confusion can be lessened if porpoise is reserved for phocoenids and dolphin is used for the smaller members of the family Delphinidae. As with other such groups, there are a variety of anatomical features separating the two families.

In our area, Dall's porpoises are limited to the Pacific coast, but harbor porpoises are found off both coasts. Harbor porpoises are near-shore animals, leading to problems for them: they become entangled in fishing nets and feel the effects of increasing pollution of coastal waters. Dall's porpoises spend more time offshore in deeper waters, and are much more likely to be seen running in front of ships. They are among the fastest of cetaceans.

Harbor porpoises are small (2 m, 100 kg), stocky animals with blunt heads and triangular dorsal fins. They feed primarily on small schooling fishes like herring and whiting, as well as on squid and crustaceans. They rarely stay under for more than 3 or 4 minutes at a time, and frequently breathe every 15 seconds or so. They become sexually mature at 3 or 4 years, and females breed every other year. A 75 cm, 6–10 kg calf is born, usually in May or June, after a gestation period of just under a year. They are social animals: group size may range from pairs up to 100. There is an annual seasonal migration between northern waters in summer and more southerly ones in winter.

Dall's porpoises are chunky animals with small heads and relatively small flukes and flippers. They are the largest phocoenids, ranging up to 2 m and 200 kg, and the color pattern is a striking black and white. Fast and playful, they frequently ride the bow waves of ships at sea. They reach sexual maturity a bit later in life than harbor porpoises, and the calves are slightly larger. They normally forage in small groups of about a dozen animals, and they also move seasonally between warmer and colder waters.

References
Minasian et al., 1984; Rice, 1984

North American Genera
Phocoena
Phocoenoides

Harbor porpoise | *Phocoena phocoena*

The harbor porpoise is confined to the Northern Hemisphere, with a nearly circumpolar distribution in temperate and subarctic latitudes. Although it is most often observed in relatively shallow (less than 100 m) coastal waters, it also occurs over offshore banks and around isolated landmasses such as Iceland. In the western North Atlantic it ranges south to the Carolinas and occasionally strays to Florida. In the North Pacific the harbor porpoise occurs from Alaska to about the latitude of Los Angeles, California.

The distribution and seasonal movements of the harbor porpoise are closely tied to those of the pelagic schooling fish that comprise the bulk of its diet, such as herring, mackerel, capelin, and alewife. Harbor porpoises will also take bottom fish and small squid, which brings them into contact with bottom gillnets and leads to many fatal entanglements. Studies of this species in the Bay of Fundy show that some occur there throughout the winter, even in February when the water temperature is 1° C. Most of the population inhabits the lower Bay from late June to early October, when the water is 8° to 15° C. More northerly populations, such as those of Labrador and the Aleutian Islands, are adapted to a lower and narrower range of temperatures.

The harbor porpoise's age at sexual maturity differs by region. This may reflect different exploitation histories. In general, both sexes mature at 3–5 years of age and the life span is at least 13 years under ideal conditions. Unfortunately, animals more than about 8 years of age are rare in modern samples. The reproductive cycle is fairly well known in the Bay of Fundy and in the Gulf of Maine. Mating usually occurs in July and August. In Fundy the peak of births is in May. Females can become pregnant again in the late summer of the same year. Lactation lasts about 9 months, but nursing probably tapers off

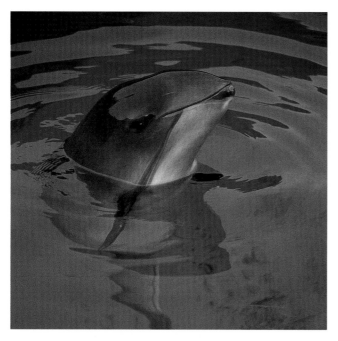

Phocoena phocoena

after about 4–5 months, because solid food has been found mixed with milk in the stomachs of net-killed calves in late summer.

Other than feeding aggregations, there is little visible evidence of sophisticated social structure in this species. However, groups often surface more or less in synchrony over a wide area and converge on concentrations of prey from a distance.

Active communication may occur between groups, although passive listening could explain much of what is observed.

The true porpoises (Phocoenidae) are a rather old group of small toothed whales, represented by six living species. The earliest fossils found to date are from the late Miocene and are all from the margins of the Pacific. *D. E. Gaskin*

Size
Females are 10–20 percent larger than males.
Total length: 1.45–1.85 (1.6) m
Weight: 45–90 kg (50)

Identification
The harbor porpoise is distinguished from Dall's porpoise, *Phocoenoides dalli,* in North Pacific waters by having gray flank shading, in contrast to the sharply defined black and white patches on the flanks of *P. dalli.* In the North Pacific, the harbor porpoise overlaps with *Lagenorhynchus obliquidens,* and in the North Atlantic with *L. acutus* and *L. albirostris.* The harbor porpoise is much smaller than these dolphins, and has a small, triangular fin in contrast to the large, distinctive, falcate fin of *Lagenorhynchus.*

Recent Synonyms
The name *Phocoena p. vomerina* has been applied to the North Pacific population. Recent genetic studies indicate significant isolation from east and west Atlantic stocks. Subspecific designation *(relicta)* for the isolated Black Sea harbor porpoise is not justified on genetic grounds.

Other Common Names
Common porpoise, puffing pig (eastern Canada and northern New England)

Status
Considered vulnerable or threatened in many parts of its range because large numbers are taken each year in gillnets in coastal waters of the North Atlantic and North Pacific

Subspecies
Phocoena phocoena phocoena, North Atlantic
Phocoena phocoena vomerina, North Pacific

References
Mammalian Species 42; Gaskin, 1992b

Dall's porpoise | *Phocoenoides dalli*

High speed, erratic movements, and a spray of water at surfacing are characteristic of Dall's porpoises. No other small cetacean is as fast and unpredictable in its movements. Dall's porpoises change direction quickly and disappear suddenly, often reappearing with their quick telltale sprays some minutes later. They also slow roll, exposing the back in an arching movement. The animals sometimes perform a series of about four slow rolls, followed by a longer, apparently deeper dive lasting several minutes. At other times they surface quickly, exposing just the dorsal fin, which is hard to see against the dark northern Pacific waters. Dall's porpoises are frequently attracted to boats, riding the bow, side, and stern waves for extended periods. They are therefore well known to boaters, but they are frequently mistaken for baby killer whales because of the black and white color pattern, since killer whales are much better known. Females with small calves typically avoid vessels.

Dall's porpoise is endemic to the North Pacific, occurring in temperate and subarctic waters cooler than 17° C, although there have been sightings in waters at temperatures of up to 22° C. This species occurs across the North Pacific and in the Bering Sea, Sea of Japan, and Okhotsk Sea. Its range extends to 62° north latitude, but there have been occasional more northerly sightings. The southern limits vary with season and water temperature, but are about 35° N in the western Pacific and 32° N in the east, with occasional sightings to 28° N. Seasonal inshore-offshore movements have been noted in some areas. In the eastern Pacific, there are north-south movements related to seasonal warming. Although the animals may occur in coastal areas, they are generally an oceanic species.

Dall's porpoise is a relatively small cetacean, characterized by a robust body with small head, flippers, and tail flukes. The color pattern in adults is a striking black and white. The truei-color morph is confined to the western North Pacific, occurring mainly off the eastern coast of Japan. Mixed schools of the two color types are common in the area of geographic overlap.

Unlike most cetaceans, Dall's porpoise breeds annually, producing one calf in June or July. Breeding occurs about a month later, in July–August. The exact timing of calving and breeding varies geographically. Females are lactating while pregnant with their next calf. The length of the gestation period is about 10–11 months. The time of weaning is poorly known; some solid food has been found in stomachs of a few 3–4 month old calves. Calves may remain with the mothers until the next calf is born. Newborns are large (0.95–1 m) in comparison with the size of the mothers (1.7–2 m). Growth is very rapid for the first year or so, then slows as the animals begin to mature sexually. Sexual maturity in females can be attained as early as two years, and females typically reproduce for the first time when

Phocoenoides dalli

they are 3–4 years old. Males are mature at about 4–5 years of age. Dall's porpoises are relatively short lived, with most individuals living less than 10 years. The maximum recorded age is 22 years.

There is some segregation of age classes and sexes, at least during the summer calving and breeding season. Mature females move into certain geographic areas to calve. Mature males occur in low numbers in these areas and are mainly found farther south, with juveniles and females without calves, during this time period. Schools studied in August–September in the southern areas of the western North Pacific were composed predominately of males. They included all mature males, mixtures of immature and mature males, and all immature males. About one-third of the schools in this area included females, most of which were immature, the mature females being farther north in the calving/breeding areas. School size is small, 2–12 animals. Larger groups (of up to several thousand) are composed of smaller groups scattered over a wide area.

In the high seas, prey consists of deep water species—mesopelagic fish (lanternfish) and squid; occasionally euphausids and decapods have been found when stomach contents were analyzed. In more coastal areas, small pelagic schooling fish (herring, anchovy, hake, and juvenile rockfish) and squid are eaten. Average prey size is about 6–9 cm, although larger (up to 48 cm), slender prey such as *Paralepis atlantica* can be eaten. There is some evidence that feeding is mainly nocturnal, possibly because prey migrate to the surface at night. The teeth of Dall's porpoise are very small (about the size of a grain of rice) and curved (spatulate). Between the teeth are "gum teeth," or dermal ridges, of unknown function. Prey is swallowed whole.

Killer whales and sharks have been reported as predators, and Dall's porpoises are heavily parasitized in the lungs, nasal passages, liver, pancreas, and in the blubber and muscles of the urogenital area. The level and species of parasite infestation varies geographically and can be used in differentiating populations.

Based on genetic studies, parasite species and infestation levels, and reproductive data, porpoises in the Bering Sea have been shown to be a separate population from those in the western North Pacific. Disjunct distribution of calving areas indicates several additional separate populations across the North Pacific Ocean.

Dall's porpoise is abundant throughout most of its range. However, estimates are not available for all populations, and those that exist may be inaccurate because the animals tend to approach survey boats, biasing the estimates. Population estimates for the dalli-type are: in the western and central North Pacific, 741,000 animals; Bering Sea, 220,000; off Japan, 226,000; for the truei-type, 217,000; California, Oregon, Washington, 116,000. Populations off the east coast of Japan and in the Sea of Japan are harvested by hand-held harpoon for food. In the 1980s, levels of catch increased, peaking in 1989 at 40,000 porpoises annually. This level of catch was considered too high to be sustained. Government regulations were implemented to reduce the catch, and in 1991 the level had dropped to 18,000. Populations in the Bering Sea and across most of the North Pacific were incidentally caught in high seas driftnet fisheries from 1952 until 1992, when a moratorium on high seas driftnet fishing was implemented. Although the catch was high in some areas, populations were not reduced below the Optimal Sustainable Level as defined under the U.S. Marine Mammal Protection Act. *L. L. Jones*

Size

Males are somewhat longer and heavier than females.
Total length: up to 2.2 mm (males); up to 2.1 m (females)
Weight: up to 210 kg (males)

Identification

Dall's porpoise is easily identified by its striking black and white color pattern, small triangular dorsal fin, and disproportionately small head, flippers, and tail fluke. Adult males have a pronounced dorsal hump anterior to the dorsal fin, a deeply keeled caudal peduncle, and canting of the dorsal fin. A black trident pattern is present in the genital area of females. Two color morphs occur. In the dalli-type, the body is black, with both lateral and ventral white patches; a ventral white patch extends to the midline from area of the dorsal fin to the genital area. In the truei-type, the white lateral patch extends anterior of the dorsal fin to the area of the pectoral fins. Intergrades between these two color morphs and rarer all-black or very pale (gray or white) individuals occur. Black flecking can be present in the white areas. Newborn and juvenile animals are gray with an off-white flank patch. At sexual maturity, the colors brighten to black and white and the trailing edges of the dorsal fin and flukes become white.

Status

Abundant throughout most of the range

Subspecies

None. *P. dalli truei* was named but has not been confirmed and the designation is not widely used.

References

Mammalian Species 319; Kasuya, 1978; Kasuya and Jones, 1984; Morejohn, 1979

Family Physeteridae

Both genera and all three species of physeterids occur in North American waters. Known to occur here since at least mid-Miocene times, sperm whales have changed little during that time. They have specialized to take advantage of the deeper, darker parts of the ocean floors, diving to depths of up to 3 kilometers beneath the surface of the sea. This habit, of course, renders them among the more difficult animals to study.

The size range is great, from 2 m and 400 kg in the smaller *Kogia* to 18 m and over 50,000 kg in male *Physeter*. The head is short and blunt in *Kogia*, but enormously elongated in *Physeter*. The dorsal fin is low in both genera, falcate in *Kogia* and thick and rounded in *Physeter*. Flippers are pointed and narrow in *Kogia*, rounded and broad in *Physeter*. *Kogia* tends to be darker dorsally and lighter ventrally, but *Physeter* is a more uniform gray, occasionally with lighter blotches on the venter.

Sperm whales produce a series of intense and powerful, monotonic clicking sounds that must function as echolocation or communication sounds. The unusual spermaceti organ, which can be 5 m long and weigh several thousand kg, is an oil-filled chamber that might be used as a resonating chamber to produce the loud clicks. These animals have the largest brains of any organism known, suggesting that they are using their sophisticated echolocation system to integrate information about the inky depths they inhabit.

Sperm whales may stay submerged for up to 80 minutes at a single deep dive, and they forage on large squids, including giant squids, as well as large sharks, skates, and fishes. They were favorite targets of early whalers, and frequently proved to be capable of defending themselves with powerful jaws and flailing flukes that could wreak havoc on both whaling boats and their human inhabitants. Although they are mainly restricted to deep water, they do occasionally come ashore in mass strandings that remain poorly understood.

References
Minasian et al., 1984; Rice, 1984

North American Genera
Physeter
Kogia

Sperm whale | *Physeter macrocephalus*

Sperm whales are found throughout the world's deep oceans up to the edges of the polar pack ice, although only males venture into the higher latitudes. They can be found in the North Pacific, including the Bering Sea, the Gulf of Alaska, and the Gulf of California, and in the North Atlantic, including deep areas of the Caribbean Sea, the Gulf of Mexico, and Davis Strait. The distribution of the whales along the eastern coast follows the edge of the continental shelf, where there is an abundance of squid, the preferred food of sperm whales.

Sperm whales associate in two types of groups: breeding schools and bachelor schools. The former consist of females of all ages as well as immature and pubertal (up to age 21) males. The average group size is 20–40 whales, but these groups may be as small as four individuals or as large as 150. Females are thought to be born into a group and remain in it throughout their lives. Each breeding school is accompanied by at least one large, socially mature male (there may be as many as five such males) during the breeding season. The breeding season is quite long, extending from January through August with a peak in March through June. Bachelor schools contain up to 50 older pubertal males and sexually mature males. Usually, each school is composed of individuals of about the same size and age. Unlike the breeding schools, membership in the bachelor schools is thought to be transient. The largest males are often solitary and are rarely seen in groups of more than six individuals unless they are accompanying a breeding school during the breeding season.

Females attain sexual maturity at 7–13 years of age and come into estrus every 3–5 years thereafter. They bear a single calf once every 3–6 years after a gestation period of 14–15 months. Calves nurse for two years or longer before weaning. Occasional reports of twins and even one of triplets are known, but there is no evidence that calves of multiple births survive.

Males begin puberty at age 7–11 years, but do not become fully sexually mature for another ten years, when they are 18–21 years old. It was long thought they did not actually mate

Physeter macrocephalus

until age 25–28. However, there is now debate over whether young males, who remain in the breeding schools year-round, may in fact breed more than the seasonally present older males. Based on tooth layer counts as age determinants, sperm whales can live at least 60–70 years.

Sperm whales are at the upper level of the food chain in the pelagic ecosystem. They feed almost exclusively on cephalopods (squid and octopi), consuming 3.0–3.5 percent of their body weight in food per day. Fish, sharks, skates, and rays have occasionally been reported as prey items as well. Despite the formidable array of teeth lining their lower jaws, sperm whales are suction feeders; they suck their prey into their mouths and swallow them whole. There are many reports of otherwise healthy whales with deformed jaws, indicating that the anterior portion of the jaw and its teeth are not necessary in acquiring food.

Several varieties of parasites exploit sperm whales at some point in their life cycles. Various species of worms (cestodes and nematodes) are found in the whales' blubber, stomach, intestines, and even the placenta. In some cases, whales are an intermediate stage with sharks hosting the adult parasite. The skin is also home to various ectoparasites such as diatoms, crustaceans, and fishes on either a temporary or permanent basis. None of these parasites appear to have significant effects on the morbidity or mortality of their hosts.

Widely known for their incredible diving abilities, sperm whales have been recorded diving as long as 60–90 minutes. One record of five whales reports a dive length of 138 minutes. Yankee whalers reported great diving depths of sperm whales based on the amount of line that ran out once their quarry was struck. The first modern documentation of deep diving came from incidents of whales being entangled in deep sea cables. One such entanglement occured at a depth of 1,135 m. More recently, diving depths have been recorded at 1,827 m using active sonar tracking and 2,250 m using passive acoustic tracking. Despite these impressive feats, most dives do not exceed 30 minutes and are much shallower, seldom reaching depths greater than 500 meters. Sperm whale muscle is extremely high in myoglobin content, giving the meat a dark, almost black, color. It is thought this is related to the high oxygen requirement of diving.

Whalers once hunted sperm whales extensively for their oil and spermaceti. Spermaceti is found in a wax-filled organ located in the large head, which is fully one quarter to one third or more of the total body length of the whale. The function of the spermaceti organ is not clearly understood, although several ideas have been put forth. These include its use as an acoustical lens, a buoyancy organ, or as a facilitator in evacuation of the lungs and absorption of excess nitrogen during diving. Industrial uses for spermaceti involved cosmetics, soap, smokeless candles, and machine oil. The whale's rich blubber layer was rendered for lamp oil and other industrial oils. A substance known as ambergris was also obtained by whalers. Ambergris is formed around the undigestible squid beaks in the lower intestine of sperm whales and is used by the perfume industry as a fixative agent.

The North Pacific and North Atlantic pre-exploitation populations are estimated to have been 1,260,000 and 330,000 animals, respectively. Today, populations are estimated at 930,000 for the North Pacific and 190,000 for the North Atlantic. With the cessation of pelagic whaling in 1979 and the enactment of a moratorium on virtually all commercial whaling in 1986, it is hoped sperm whale stocks will recover.
C. W. Potter and B. Birchler

Size

Total length: 11.0–18.3 m (males); 8.3–12.5 m (females)

Weight: 11,000–57,000 kg (males); 6,800–24,000 kg (females)

Identification

Sperm whales are distinguished by the large, barrel shaped head and the single blowhole located forward and left of center. Each side of the lower jaw has 17–29 mandibular teeth.

When the mouth is closed, these fit into shallow sockets in the upper palate. Up to 10 pairs of maxillary teeth may be present in the upper jaw, but these are quite small and seldom erupt from the gums.

Recent Synonyms

Physeter catodon

Other Common Names

Cachalot

Status

Endangered

References

Ellis, 1980; Evans, 1987; Leatherwood and Reeves, 1983; Rice, 1989

Pygmy sperm whale | *Kogia breviceps*

The similarity of the pygmy sperm whale to the dwarf sperm whale makes reliable identification at sea difficult at best. Pygmy sperm whales are usually seen in small groups of one to six animals. Cosmopolitan in distribution, they are found worldwide except for the higher latitudes. They are believed to inhabit the deeper waters beyond the continental shelf, feeding primarily on cephalopods and supplementing these with benthic fish and crustaceans.

Females become sexually mature at lengths of 2.7 to 2.8 m. Males are slightly longer at sexual maturity, at lengths of 2.7 to 3 m. The gestation period lasts nine to eleven months. Calves are approximately 1.2 m long at birth and nurse for about one year before being weaned. Pregnant, lactating females with calves have been found, suggesting some females may bear calves in successive years.

Knowledge of this whale's behavior at sea is limited because there have been so few documented sightings. The pygmy sperm whale's blow is not conspicuous. While resting, the whale remains still at the surface, its head just above the water and its tail hanging down. If surprised while resting, a whale may exhibit behavior referred to as "inking," in which it defecates a cloud of reddish-brown feces and, with the aid of this screen, dives out of sight.

Like its giant cousin, the sperm whale, the pygmy sperm

whale has a spermaceti organ, but because of its small size and cryptic behavior, it was not hunted commercially by Yankee whalers. Pygmy sperm whales have been taken incidentally in other fisheries and are occasionally taken with hand harpoons off southern Japan, Sri Lanka, and Indonesia. Pollution takes its toll: plastic bags are routinely found in the stomachs of stranded individuals. The whales may ingest the bags because they are texturally or visually similar to squid. The plastic becomes impacted in the stomach and intestine and can result in death.

Strandings of the animal are fairly common in the southeastern United States. However, because the overall number of whales spotted at sea as well as taken incidentally in commercial fisheries is low, the pygmy sperm whale is considered uncommon. Since little is known about this species aside from strandings, estimating population levels is difficult. Like all marine mammals, it is protected by the Marine Mammal Protection Act. *C. W. Potter and B. Birchler*

Kogia breviceps

Size

Total length: 2.7–3.4 m
Weight: 318–408 kg

Identification

Kogia breviceps is shark-like in appearance, with a pigmentation pattern behind the eye reminiscent of a gill slit. The body is robust; the dorsum is dark bluish-gray, blending into dull white or pink on the ventral surface; the lower jaw is under-slung. There are ten to sixteen pairs of sharp, needle-like teeth in the lower jaw; the upper jaw is toothless. The dorsal fin is small, falcate (sickle-shaped), and located on the posterior third of the body. Often confused with the dwarf sperm whale, the pygmy sperm whale's larger body size, small dorsal fin, and tooth count distinguish it.

Status

Uncommon

References

Caldwell and Caldwell, 1989; Ellis, 1980; Evans, 1987; Leatherwood and Reeves, 1983

Dwarf sperm whale | *Kogia simus*

The dwarf sperm whale was not distinguished from its close relative, the pygmy sperm whale, until 1966, making it difficult to describe its worldwide range with accuracy. It is seldom seen at sea and rarely positively identified. Stranding records as well as the occasional sighting at sea have shown it to have a cosmopolitan distribution. Like the pygmy, it avoids the higher latitudes and appears to be more tropical-temperate than the pygmy. It is thought that *K. simus* lives on or near the edge of the continental shelf, in contrast to *K. breviceps,* which is found in deep oceanic waters. Squid comprise the majority of the whale's diet, although benthic fish and crustaceans are also commonly found when stomach contents are analyzed. Dwarf sperm whales are known to dive to depths of at least 300 meters.

Due to the lack of documented sightings, dwarf sperm whale behavior remains a mystery. Like the pygmy sperm whale, its blow is very inconspicuous. "Inking," a form of defense behavior in which the whale excretes a cloud of feces and uses this as a screen while it dives out of sight, has been observed.

Dwarf sperm whales are found in very small groups, rarely of more than ten individuals. Like the sperm whale, *Physter macrocephalus, K. simus* is found in several types of groups: adult females with calves, adult males and females without calves, and immature animals.

Extremely limited data are available to evaluate the sexual maturity of these whales; evidence from a few specimens indicates that both males and females become sexually mature at approximately 2.1 to 2.2 m. Calving occurs over a prolonged period of five to six months or more and newborns measure slightly less than 1 m. Pregnant females accompanied by nursing calves have been sighted, which suggest that young may be borne in successive years.

Commercial harvest of dwarf sperm whales is rare, although they are found in fish markets in Sri Lanka, form an aboriginal industry in Indonesia, and are harpooned in Japan as well as in a pilot whale fishery in the Lesser Antilles. Plastic bags are routinely being found in the stomachs of stranded individuals and are thought to be a cause of mortality in this species.

In the United States, stranded dwarf sperm whales are found most frequently along southeastern coasts. They are found less frequently than pygmy sperm whales, and are probably less common. Nothing is known, however, of the total size of their population. *B. Birchler and C. W. Potter*

Kogia simus

Size
Total length: 2.1–2.7 m
Weight: 136–272 kg

Identification
The dwarf sperm whale is smaller than, but very similar in appearance to, the pygmy sperm whale *(K. breviceps)*. Both are shark-like, with a distinct gill slit pigmentation behind the eye and robust, dark bluish-gray upperparts that blend into a dull white or pink ventral surface; the lower jaw is under-slung. *K. simus* has seven to twelve pairs of sharp, needle-like teeth in the lower jaw; one to two pairs of unerupted teeth have been found in the upper jaw. The dorsal fin is relatively large, tall, and falcate (sickle-shaped), similar to that of a bottlenose dolphin, and is positioned near the center of the back. The larger size of the dorsal fin, its forward position, and the tooth count distinguish the dwarf sperm whale from the larger pygmy sperm whale.

Recent Synonyms
Kogia breviceps

Status
Uncommon

References
Mammalian Species 239; Caldwell and Caldwell, 1989; Ellis, 1980; Evans, 1987; Leatherwood and Reeves, 1983

Family Ziphiidae

Beaked whales are divided into 6 genera and 19 species worldwide, with 4 genera and 11 species represented in North America. Like most other cetaceans, they date from Miocene ancestors. They remain among the most poorly known marine mammals, at least partially owing to their proclivity for deep, offshore waters. Most of the few specimens that have been collected have come from strandings. One new species was described as recently as 1991.

Ziphiids are medium-sized whales, ranging in length from about 4–12 m and weighing up to about 11,000 kg. Most have relatively long and slender bodies with pronounced, narrow snouts. The dorsal fin tends to be displaced posteriorly, and is usually small and falcate. Flippers are small and pointed, and colors tend towards bluish-gray or brown, with occasional white ventral blotches. Curiously, many have only a single pair of teeth in the tip of the lower jaw, but there is considerable variation. Recent work has suggested that these whales use their teeth primarily for intraspecific fighting rather than for feeding.

Beaked whales likely feed at great depths on small and medium-sized squids and some fishes. Morphological studies on the reduced dentition, throat grooves, and tongue musculature suggest that beaked whales may be using suction to capture prey. They routinely dive for 15–45 minutes, and may stay down for up to 2 hours. They tend to occur in small pods of 3–20 individuals. Some species migrate seasonally between warmer and colder waters, probably in response to shifting food supplies.

Little is known about reproductive patterns in these relatively shy creatures. They likely become sexually mature at 8–12 years of age. Calves are born every other year, after gestation periods of 12–18 months. Lactation probably lasts for about a year.

References

Heyning and Mead, 1996; Reyes et al., 1991; Rice, 1984

North American Genera

Berardius
Ziphius
Hyperoodon
Mesoplodon

Baird's beaked whale | *Berardius bairdii*

Berardius bairdii is the longest member of the beaked whale family. Viewed from above, the rostrum and cranium are strongly reminiscent of the neck and body of a bottle. The genus is characterized by the presence of four teeth on the lower jaw. The two larger, anterior teeth are exposed in front of the rostrum and are often visible at sea. Both sexes are heavily scarred by the teeth of congeners. *Berardius* has a pair of throat grooves and normally does not have a notch in the flukes. The dorsal fin and flippers are relatively small. The pigmentation of immature animals is slate gray both dorsally and ventrally. Mature animals become darker gray or black and show numerous tooth scars. There are typically white or cloudy patches in the pigmentation ventrally, usually around the genital area, umbilicus, and throat.

Berardius bairdii is distributed in the east from the Sea of Japan, central coast of Japan, east coast of Kamchatka, the southern Bering Sea, Aleutian Islands, and the Gulf of Alaska

to the Gulf of California. It occupies the central North Pacific north of the Hawaiian Islands. There is evidence from Japan that *Berardius* is divided into several populations, some of which are more migratory than others. Virtually nothing is known of the abundance of this species because surveys have been done on only a portion of its known range.

This whale eats deepwater demersal species such as squid, skates, rattails, rockfish, and octopus as well as more pelagic species such as mackerel, sardines, and saury.

Females attain sexual maturity at the age of 8–10 years, when they are at least 10 m in length. Males are also sexually mature at 8–10 years of age, and at a minimum length of 9.5 m. The gestation length is 17 months, and calving peaks in the Japanese population in March and April. The mean length of calves at birth is 4.5 m. The maximum reported age of females is 39 years, and of males, 71 years.

Baird's beaked whales normally travel in schools of up to 50 animals or more. They dive for up to an hour, feeding at depths of at least 2,000 meters. They are not particularly fast swimmers. Their blow is low and bushy. Occasionally animals will breach, slap their flippers, and spyhop. They seldom raise their flukes while diving. *J. G. Mead*

Berardius bairdii

Size
Females are slightly larger than males.
Maximum length: 11.9 m (males); 12.8 m (females)
Weight: 6,800 kg (8.50 m male); 14,200 kg (10.81 m female, the heaviest recorded); 8,200 kg (8.20 m female)

Identification
Berardius bairdii is the largest of the beaked whales and can be distinguished by its length, by its long, narrow rostrum, by the pair of teeth that erupt in both sexes on the lower jaw anterior to the rostrum, by the presence of throat grooves, and by the lack of a fluke notch. Heavy scarring is evident in old individuals.

Other Common Names
Far-eastern bottlenose whale, giant bottlenose whale, northern four-toothed whale

Status
CITES Appendix II: more information is required before a determination of its status can be made

References
Balcomb 1989; Kasuya, 1977; Mead, 1984; Omura et al., 1955

Cuvier's beaked whale | *Ziphius cavirostris*

Cuvier's beaked whale is found in the deep waters of all oceans except polar waters, and in most seas. The body shape resembles that of other beaked whales, with a robust, cigar-shaped body, but with a short, indistinct beak. The dorsal fin is relatively small and is positioned about two-thirds of the body length posterior to the snout. The flippers are narrow and small and the flukes are relatively large, with no medial notch. There is one pair of throat grooves, which converge anteriorly. Coloration varies from dark brown to slate gray. Mature males have one pair of small, pointed teeth, which erupt from the tip of the lower jaw. The heads and backs of adult males become almost white with age. Linear white scars resulting from in-

traspecific fights are common in adult males, and oval scars are common in both sexes.

Pod size usually ranges from one to seven animals. This species seems to avoids boats, making observations at sea difficult. It is believed to be a deep-diving species. Cuvier's beaked whales feed primarily on deep-water squids. They are also known to consume fish and some decopod crustaceans.

Testis weights from adult males range from 370 to 4,200 grams. Calves average 2.7 m at birth. There is no known calving season. *J. E. Heyning*

Ziphius cavirostris

Size
Total length: 5.1–6.9 m
Weight: 2,500 kg

Identification
This species can be distinguished from other beaked whales by its large size, robust body, and poorly-defined beak.

Other Common Names
Goose-beaked whale

Status
Unknown; CITES Appendix II (more information is needed before its status can be determined)

References
Heyning, 1989a, 1989b

Northern bottlenose whale | *Hyperoodon ampullatus*

The northern bottlenose whale, *Hyperoodon ampullatus,* is widely distributed in the North Atlantic. It occurs as far north as the edge of the ice in the summer. Local concentrations of bottlenose whales in the summertime off Spitsbergen, Norway, in Iceland, and off Labrador may represent separate stocks. In the wintertime the bottlenose occurs south to Africa.

In the western Atlantic there are two main centers of distribution. In the winter, the whales are distributed on the continental shelf and farther offshore from New York to Grand Bank, Newfoundland. In the summertime *H. ampullatus* migrates north into the Davis Strait as far north as Baffin Island (63° N).

H. ampullatus is among the deepest diving whales and seems to avoid shallow waters. Most have been caught at depths of more than 1,000 m (3,300 ft.). Dives as long as 2 hours have been reported. Many of the reported "strandings" were lost or strayed but apparently healthy animals that swam into fjords, rivers, or streams.

In the Arctic Ocean, the bottlenose whale stays mainly near the boundaries between cold polar currents and warmer Atlantic currents. The migration north to the Arctic in early spring is a feeding migration, and the migration south to warmer areas is a breeding migration. Geographical segregation of males and females may occur. Fully-grown males are generally found closer to the ice than females and younger males.

Squid have been reported to be the main or only food item. In addition to squid the following animals have been recorded in the stomachs of bottlenose whales from Labrador: Greenland halibut *(Reinhardtius hippoglossoides),* redfish *(Sebastes),* rabbit-fish *(Chimaera monstrosa),* piked dog fish *(Squalus acanthias),* ling *(Molva molva),* and skate *(Raja).* One animal from Labrador also had deep-sea prawns *(Pandalus)* in the stomach

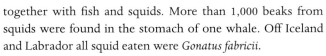

Hyperoodon ampullatus

together with fish and squids. More than 1,000 beaks from squids were found in the stomach of one whale. Off Iceland and Labrador all squid eaten were *Gonatus fabricii*.

In the North Atlantic, bottlenose whales occur in herds of 2–4 animals, but groups of up to 20 animals have been seen. Solitary animals are often old bulls. Groups of two and three animals seem to consist of individuals of the same sex and the same or nearly the same age. Schools of several hundred animals are observed migrating north in the spring. Mother and calf usually appear alone, but sometimes two females with their calves form a group. A group of animals will usually stay with an injured companion while it is alive. If a calf approaches a ship, the mother will swim between the ship and the calf and try to push the calf away.

Female bottlenose whales become sexually mature at a body length of 6.7–7 m (22–23 feet), when they are between 8

and 14 years of age, (usually at about 9 years). Males become sexually mature at a body length of 7.3–7.6 m (23–25 feet), at the age of 7–9 years. Mating and birth occur mainly in April. The gestation period is 12 months. The female gives birth to one calf, which is about 3 m (10 feet) long. It is difficult to determine the average duration of lactation, but from a year-old calf with both milk and squid in the stomach, we assume a suckling time of about one year. Examination of the ovaries indicates that the northern bottlenose whale gives birth every second year. Both mating and birth take place in warmer water.

The teeth of bottlenose whales consist of enamel, dentine, and cementum. Both cementum and dentine are formed annually, but dentine layers are most easily counted. Growth curves based on dentine layers indicates that males grow until they are about 20 years old, females up to about 15 years. Growth rates for males and females are equal until the whales are about 6 years old and have attained a length of about 7 m. From then on males grow faster than females. The lifespan of the northern bottlenose is at least 37 years. *I. Christensen*

Size

Males are larger than females.
Total length: 9–9.45 m (males); 8.0–8.5 m (females)
Weight: 10,000 kg (males); 7,500 kg (females)

Identification

Hyperoodon ampullatus is the only species of bottlenose whale that occurs in the North Atlantic. It can be distinguished from the other beaked whales in the family Ziphiidae by larger size and a long, tube-like snout that is distinct from the melon. In adult males the forehead is

very steep; in females and young animals, it slopes gently upward from the beak. The dorsal fin, located two-thirds of the way along the back, reaches about 30 cm (1 ft) in height. *H. ampullatus* is dark gray, with a pair of forward-pointing grooves on the throat. Older males become pale gray to white on the head and around the neck. In older bulls, two conical teeth erupt at the tip of the lower jaw.

Recent Synonyms

Hyperoodon rostratus

Other Common Names

Beaked whale, bottlenose whale

Status

Number and size of stocks unknown; protected by International Whaling Commission (IWC) since 1976

Subspecies

There is an unidentified ziphiid in the North Pacific that may be a *Hyperoodon*.

References

Benjaminsen and Christensen, 1979

Sowerby's beaked whale | *Mesoplodon bidens*

This species is known from cold temperate waters of the North Atlantic. The center of its distribution seems to be in the North Sea. *M. bidens* has been taken in Newfoundland, but a report of a specimen of *M. bidens* from the Madeira Islands is probably erroneous. Records occur more commonly from the eastern than from the western North Atlantic and most are from the coasts of the British Isles. The northernmost record is from Faeo Island, Norway, and the southernmost record is from Port Saint Joe, Florida. No records from the former Soviet Union are known to western scientists. Records from Sweden and Denmark are confined to the open Atlantic or to the shores of the Skagerrak and Kattegat. It is unlikely that any whale of the family Ziphiidae habitually dwells in the shallow Baltic Sea.

There has been a minor controversy over the presence of this species in the Mediterranean. Most reports of its presence there seem to be erroneous, but recent work has shown that at least one report is probably *M. bidens*.

Five strandings have been recorded from the western North Atlantic. The farthest north record is from Double Mer, Labrador. There are two records from the island of Newfoundland and two records from Nantucket Island, Massachusetts. The most recent record is from Port Saint Joe, Florida. This is not only the first record from the Gulf of Mexico but the southernmost record of this species.

There does not seem to be any seasonality in the European stranding records. The only country for which enough records exist to make a seasonal analysis valid is the United Kingdom (41 records). Strandings have been reported in every month except February, with a tendency towards a broad peak in the summer (July–September).

The teeth of adult males are distinctive and can be used to identify the species. They project about 20 or 30 mm above the gum and are located a third of the way back on the jaw (or about 300 mm from the tip of the jaw). The teeth are about 100 mm long, 40 mm wide and 15 mm thick. The alveolus (tooth-socket) is strongly slanted, so the teeth erupt in a dorso-anterior direction. Rows of vestigial teeth sometimes occur in both the upper and lower jaws.

No data are available about this whale's food habits, repro-

Mesoplodon bidens

ductive behavior, or other aspects of its lifestyle. The reported mean length of calves at birth is 2.4 m.

Vocalizations have only been observed in stranded animals. It is probable that the cow-like vocalizations of these animals in periods of stress gave rise to the name of "cowfish," which is used in New Zealand. The nematode *Crassicauda* has been reported in the kidneys and the barnacle *Conchoderma* attached to the teeth. *J. G. Mead*

Size
Maximum length: 5.5 m (males); 5.05 m (females)
Weight: no data available

Identification
Sowerby's beaked whales have bluish-gray or slate-colored backs. The sides are paler and the belly is white, and there are grayish or whitish streaks and spots scattered irregularly on the sides. This species is distinguished at sea by its

relatively long rostrum. The identification of females and juveniles is extremely difficult. Adult males can reliably be identified by the shape and position of their teeth.

Recent Synonyms
Mesoplodon dalei
Mesoplodon micropterus
Mesoplodon sowerbiensis
Mesoplodon sowerbyi

Other Common Names
North Sea beaked whale, dauphin de Dale, dauphin de Havre (French)

Status
CITES—Appendix II

References
Mead, 1984, 1989

Hubbs's beaked whale | *Mesoplodon carlhubbsi*

Hubbs first identified the type specimen of this whale as *Mesoplodon bowdoini*. The relationship of *M. carlhubbsi* to *M. bowdoini* is still unclear. It has been demonstrated that *M. carlhubbsi* is not related to *M. stejnegeri*.

In adult males the body is dark gray to black except for two white patches on the head. One patch covers the tip of the rostrum and lower jaw back to the posterior border of the teeth, and the other is a roughly circular pattern about 300 mm in diameter centered around the blowhole. In females and juveniles the dorsal surface of the body is medium gray, the sides are paler gray, and the belly is white. The anterior half of the rostrum and lower jaws are paler in color than the rest of the head. In both sexes the ventral surface of the flukes is paler than the dorsal surface and bears concentric striations radiating anteriorly from the position of the terminal caudal vertebrae. There is a faint patch of paler pigmentation on the dorsal surface of the flipper in both sexes. In females the area of the body wall just behind the flipper (the "flipper pocket") is pigmented darker than the surrounding body.

There are 35 records of this species from the temperate waters of the North Pacific, mostly from California. The distribution seems to be correlated with the deep subarctic current system. Its principal distribution appears to lie a bit to the south of the distribution of *M. stejnegeri*. The northernmost record in the eastern North Pacific is from Prince Rupert, British Columbia, and the southernmost record is southwest of San Clemente Island, California. The records from the western North Pacific all center about the Japanese whaling town of Ayukawa.

Analysis of the stomach contents of five individuals that stranded in California provide evidence of this whale's food habits. Beaks of the pelagic squids *Gonatus, Onychoteuthis, Octopoteuthis, Histioteuthis* and *Mastigoteuthis* were found in the stomachs. In addition, otoliths (small, calcareous particles from the ears) of the deepwater fish *Chauliodus, Lampanictis, Poromitra, Icicthys, Melamphaes,* and an unidentified melamphiid were identified. All of the fish except *Chauliodus* and possibly *Icicthys* could have been introduced secondarily either from squid stomachs or *Chauliodus* stomachs.

Mesoplodon carlhubbsi

The calving season is estimated to be in mid-summer in North American populations. The longest recorded fetus measured 0.9 m, and the shortest calf was 2.47 m long. The mean length at birth is 2.5 m. The ovaries of a sexually mature female weighed 13.2 g, and the mean testis weight of sexually mature males is 250 g.

One researcher who studied the scars of adult males concluded that they were inflicted by intraspecific conflicts, primarily between adult males, and that they had been inflicted with the mouth closed. This researcher hypothesized that the very dense structure of the rostrum reinforces it for fighting; the specific gravity of a section of the bone of an adult male's rostrum has the highest reported density of any mammalian tissue. The same study concluded that there was no evidence of interspecific aggression. *J. G. Mead*

Size

Length: 5.32 m (maximum, male and female)
Weight: Only one animal has been weighed: a
  5.32 m female weighed 1,432 kg.

Identification

The identification of *Mesoplodon* females and juveniles is extremely difficult. Adult males can reliably be identified by the shape and position of their teeth. This species was, for many years, confused with *Mesoplodon stejnegeri*. The males

of both species have large, flat, blade-like teeth that erupt in similar places on the mandible. The teeth of *M. carlhubbsi* are approximately 120 mm long and 60 mm wide. The teeth of *M. stejnegeri* tend to be slightly larger (140 mm by 70 mm), but they are difficult to differentiate. The shape of the crown of the teeth is more semicircular in *M. carlhubbsi* as opposed to square in *M. stejnegeri,* and the gum line extends dorsally 30 or 40 mm above the alveolus (tooth-socket) on the tooth in *M. carlhubbsi,*

so that the projecting teeth are partially sheathed by gum tissue. In *M. stejnegeri* the gum line is confluent with the alveolus.

Other Common Names

Arch-beaked whale

Status

CITES—Appendix II

References

Mead, 1984, 1989

Blainville's beaked whale | *Mesoplodon densirostris*

Mesoplodon densirostris occurs throughout the world in waters that range from tropical to warm temperate. It has the widest distribution of all *Mesoplodon* species. Sixteen sightings of this whale have been reported in the Hawaiian Islands, in water ranging from 700 to 1,000 meters deep. These sightings were made on the slopes of the islands, where there were water depths of up to 5,000 meters nearby. In the western North Atlantic this species is known from the Caribbean, the Gulf of Mexico, and the Bahamas.

There are 16 records of this species from the Atlantic coast of the United States and two records from Canada, both from the province of Nova Scotia. The Canadian records probably represent strays from the Gulf Stream waters.

In the eastern North Atlantic, records of *M. densirostris* are few. There are no records from the British Isles, one from Portugal, one from the Mediterranean coast of Spain, and one from the Madeira Islands. The type specimen may have come from France.

The few records of this species from the North Pacific include three specimens from Midway Island, two from Taiwan, one from Japanese waters, and two from California. Pods of 3 to 7 individuals have been reported off the Hawaiian Islands, principally off the Waianae Coast of Oahu.

This species is reported from all of the southern oceans. In the Indian Ocean there is one report from Australia, two from Mauritius, two from the Seychelles, and 14 from South Africa. There is one record from the Atlantic coast of South Africa and two records from the Pacific coasts of Australia.

Twenty-one fish otoliths (small, calcerous ear particles) representing two species were found in the stomach of an adult female *M. densirostris* in South Africa. Trace quantities of squid beaks were collected from three other *M. densirostris;* no fish remains were found in those stomachs.

Ten published weights range from 60 kg for a 1.9 m calf to 1,033 kg for a 4.56 m female, with a mean of 511 kg. The testis of an immature male weighed 27 g, and a minimum ovarian weight of 12 g at sexual maturity has been reported. The mean ovarian weight at sexual maturity is 14 g and the maximum ovarian weight of a nonpregnant female was 25 g. The minimum age of females at sexual maturity is 9 years. The longest reported fetus measured 1.9 m, and the shortest calf was 2.61 m long.

The vocalizations of a stranded juvenile male sounded like "whistles" or "chirps," but when they were recorded and analyzed, some of them were definitely pulsed.

An adult female *M. densirostris* that stranded in North Carolina had well-healed tooth scars inflicted by either *Orcinus* or *Pseudorca*. The scars did not penetrate the blubber and there was no evidence of serious injury.

Mesoplodon densirostris

Two vaginal fibromas were described in a stranded specimen of *M. densirostris*. This appears to be the only record of such growths in the genus. There have been three reports of what appeared to be the stalked barnacle *Conchoderma* attached to the teeth of adult males, and *Xenobalanus* and an unidentified balanoid barnacle were reported to be deeply embedded on the flank of a specimen of *M. densirostris* from South Africa.

This species has been the subject of studies of organochlorine pesticide accumulations on both sides of the Atlantic. Moderate amounts of such residues were reported from specimens from U.S. coastal waters. In Spain, this species had lower concentrations of pesticide residues than did other cetaceans from the same area. *J. G. Mead*

Size

Length: 4.73 m (maximum, male); 4.71 m (maximum, female)
Weight: 1,033 kg (4.56 m female)

Identification

Adult males can reliably be identified by the shape and position of their teeth, but identification of *Mesoplodon* females and juveniles is extremely difficult. Juveniles and adult females appear to be medium gray dorsally and white on the ventral surface of the body, with no outstanding pigmentation details. All the males that have been described or photographed were dark gray both dorsally and ventrally. The rostrum tends to have a flat surface midway along its dorsal border, which sometimes is diagnostic. The curve of the line of the mouth in side view is greater than in other species of *Mesoplodon*. This is a reflection of the shape of the lower jaw, which has a pronounced step to accommodate the relatively enormous teeth in adult males. The teeth are about 120 mm high, 80 mm wide, and 30 mm thick. It is the increased thickness that contributes to their bulk.

Recent Synonyms

Ziphius sechellensis

Other Common Names

Atlantic beaked whale, dense beaked whale

Status

CITES—Appendix II

References

Mead, 1984, 1989

Gervais's beaked whale | *Mesoplodon europaeus*

Gervais's beaked whale is the commonest species of *Mesoplodon* to be found stranded along the Atlantic coast of the United States, there presently being 50 confirmed and 4 unconfirmed records of it. The northernmost record is from New York.

This species inhabits the tropical to warm temperate waters of the Atlantic. The holotype of this species was found floating in the English Channel around 1840; hence the specific name *europaeus*. Since that time there has been only one other record of it from the eastern North Atlantic.

Aside from strandings on the west coast of Florida, this whale does not seem to be particularly common in the Gulf of Mexico, there being only three records of it, two from Texas and one from the Gulf coast of Cuba. A stranding was reported on the Caribbean coast of Cuba, four strandings were reported on the island of Jamaica, and a skull and some vertebrae were found on the island of Trinidad. In 1980 there were three reports of this species from the South Atlantic island of Ascension.

Little is known about this whale's food habits. Trace quantities of squid beaks were collected from the stomachs of three *M. europaeus*. No fish remains were found in those stomachs.

The information available about reproduction includes a reported minimum ovarian weight at sexual maturity of 12 g and a mean ovarian weight at sexual maturity of 18 g; the maximum recorded ovarian weight of a nonpregnant female was 19 g. The maximum known testis weight at sexual maturity is 160 g. Other statistics include: longest fetus: 2.18 m; shortest calf: 1.96 m; mean length at birth: 2.1 m; mean length of females at sexual maturity: 4.5 m. There are 6 published weights for this species, ranging from 49 kg for a 1.62 m calf to 1,178 kg for a 3.71 m female.

Cyamids were represented by numerous individuals of *Isocyamus* on a healing wound on the flank of an adult male *M. europaeus* that stranded in North Carolina. *Conchoderma* has been found attached to the teeth of males of this species from North Carolina. *J. G. Mead*

Mesoplodon europaeus

Size

Length: 4.56 m (maximum, males); 5.2 m (maximum, females)

Weight: 1,178 kg (3.71 m female)

Identification

Specimens of this whale are dark gray dorsally and medium gray ventrally. In juveniles the belly is white. Some adult females have a patch of white about 150 mm in diameter that extends from just in front of the genital slit to just posterior to the anus. The males that have been examined did not have this patch. Identifying *Mesoplodon* females and juveniles is extremely difficult, and females and juveniles of *M. europaeus* and *M. mirus* are virtually impossible to differentiate externally. Adult males can reliably be identified by the shape and position of their teeth. In *M. europaeus* the teeth are 60 or 70 mm high, 50 or 60 mm wide, and 10 mm thick, and are located in the front of the mouth about 100 mm from the tip of the lower jaw. In *M. mirus* the teeth are conical, about 10 mm in diameter and 30 mm long, and are located at the tip of the lower jaw.

Recent Synonyms

Mesoplodon gervaisi

Other Common Names

Gulf Stream beaked whale, Antillean beaked whale, European beaked whale

Status

CITES—Appendix II

References

Mead 1984, 1989

Ginkgo-toothed beaked whale | *Mesoplodon ginkgodens*

This species is known from warm temperate to tropical waters, primarily from the North Pacific, although it occurs in the South Pacific and Indian oceans. It is a relatively little known species, there being only 13 records. Two of these are from the eastern North Pacific, five are from Japan, where individuals were taken in small scale harpoon fisheries, three are from Taiwan, and there is one record each from Ceylon, Indonesia, and the Chatham Islands.

No data are available about its behavior or food habits, and the only reproductive information is the testis weight of a sexually mature male, 140 g. *J. G. Mead*

Mesoplodon ginkgodens

Size

Maximum reported length: 4.77 m (male); 4.9 m (female)

Weight: no data available

Identification

Adult males are darkly pigmented over the entire body. There is some indication of a faint pale patch on the anterior half of the rostrum and lower jaw, and males also show a pattern of white spots 30–40 mm in diameter whose distribution is centered on the rear third of the belly. These may be parasite scars rather than normal pigmentation. Adult males appear to lack linear scars. The only photographs of females show a body that is medium gray above and pale gray below. The identification of *Mesoplodon* females and juveniles is extremely difficult. Adult males can reliably be identified by the shape and position of their teeth, which in *M. ginkgodens* are broad and flat, about 100–120 mm in both dimensions and 20 mm in thickness. The teeth are located about 200 mm posterior to the tip of the mandible.

Recent Synonyms

Mesoplodon hotuala

Status

CITES—Appendix II

References

Mead, 1984, 1989

Hector's beaked whale | *Mesoplodon hectori*

Prior to 1981 *M. hectori* was thought to be a Southern Hemisphere species, but four strandings occurred in California over a 4.5 year period, too many to be dismissed as strays. This species is known from the South Atlantic coasts of Argentina and the Falkland Islands, and there are two specimens from the Indian Ocean coast of South Africa. Fifteen stranded *M. hectori* have been reported from the South Pacific. There are reports from Australia, Chile, and New Zealand, but this whale has yet to be recorded from the Indian Ocean coast of Australia, suggesting that it frequents more southerly, colder waters than *M. grayi* (which has not been reported from the United States or Canada).

Two lower beaks of *Octopoteuthis* and a fragment of an unidentified invertebrate were reported from the stomach of an adult *M. hectori* stranded in California, providing the only information on the food habits of this species.

Data on reproduction are equally scant. The testis weight of an immature male was 1.6 g, and of a mature male, 116 g. The shortest calf on record measured 2.1 m.

The stalked barnacle *Conchoderma* was found attached to the teeth of *M. hectori* from California. *J. G. Mead*

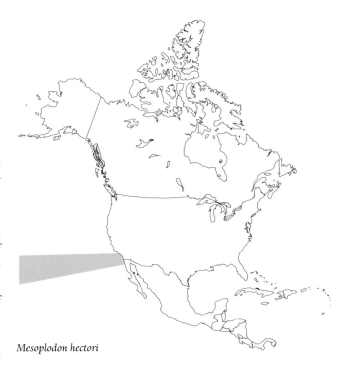

Mesoplodon hectori

Size
Length: 4.3 m (longest reported male); 4.43 mm (longest female)
Weight: no data available

Identification
Identification of *Mesoplodon* females and juveniles is extremely difficult, but adult males can reliably be distinguished from other *Mesoplodon* by the shape and position of their teeth. In *M. hectori* they are triangular and are located 20 mm from the tip of the mandible. Each tooth is about 70 mm long, 50 mm wide, and 10 mm thick. In external appearance, an adult male was described as dark dorsally and pale ventrally. The ventral surface of the head was pale. The ground color of the ventral surface of the flukes was white, with dark lines radiating out from the tailstock. The skin around the umbilical scar was white.

Recent Synonyms
Mesoplodon knoxi

Other Common Names
New Zealand beaked whale

Status
CITES—Appendix II

References
Mead, 1984, 1989

True's beaked whale | *Mesoplodon mirus*

Northern Hemisphere specimens of *M. mirus* have medium gray backs and pale gray ventral surfaces. One male had a paler area on the ventral surface that extended from between the flippers forward along the back, to above the eye, then turned ventrally, passing behind the angle of the mouth; it ended on the throat near the throat grooves. This pattern of pigmentation was not present in an adult female. Both the male and female had a dark area 50–100 mm in diameter around the eye and an area of white pigmentation 100–150 mm in diameter that extended from the anus to the midpoint of the genital slit. In Southern Hemisphere specimens there is a white area extending from the anterior insertion of the dorsal fin back to the anterior edge of the flukes. This patch runs posteroventrally to connect with its counterpart on the other side.

In the North Atlantic, this species inhabits temperate waters. Although there is considerable overlap, it appears to prefer slightly colder waters than *M. europaeus*. From the few Southern Hemisphere records it appears that the species is distributed in the warm temperate waters of the Indian Ocean and strandings of it may be expected in the South Pacific.

There are 16 records of True's beaked whale from the coast of North America and 6 from Europe. The northernmost record in the western North Atlantic is from Saint Ann's Bay, Nova Scotia, and the southernmost is from San Salvador Island, Bahamas. This whale has not been reported from the Gulf of Mexico. In the eastern North Atlantic it is found from the Hebrides Islands, Scotland, to Bidart, France. Since the discovery in 1959 of a specimen of *M. mirus* on the Indian Ocean coast of South Africa there have been 5 additional strandings reported on that coast. Two strandings occurred in Australia.

Two upper and four lower beaks of the inshore squid, *Loligo reynaudi,* were found in the stomach of an adult female from South Africa. Trace quantities of squid beaks have been collected from one United States stranding. No fish remains were found in those stomachs.

The shortest calf discovered measured 2.33 m and weighed 136 kg. Testis weights range from 7 g for an immature male to a maximum of 170 g; minimum, mean, and maximum mature (nonpregnant) ovarian weights are 11 g, 15 g, and 49 g, respectively.

The small pseudo-stalked barnacle, *Xenobalanus,* which commonly occurs on the appendages of cetaceans, was found on the flukes of two adults, one from New Jersey and one from Maryland, and was also reported to be attached to the flukes of two *M. mirus* from South Africa. *J. G. Mead*

Mesoplodon mirus

Size
Length: 5.33 mm (longest male); 5.1 m (longest female)
Weight: 1,394 kg (a 5.1 m female)

Identification
Females and juveniles of all species of *Mesoplodon* are extremely difficult to distinguish, and in *M. mirus* and *M. europaeus,* they are virtually impossible to differentiate externally. Adult males can reliably be identified by the shape and position of their teeth. In *M. mirus* the teeth are conical, about 10 mm in diameter and 30 mm long, and are located at the tip of the lower jaw, whereas in *M. europaeus* they are 60 or 70 mm high, 50 or 60 mm wide, and 10 mm thick, and are located in the anterior part of the mouth, about 100 mm from the tip of the lower jaw.

Status
CITES—Appendix II

Subspecies
None at present, but a Southern Hemisphere population of this species will probably be found to differ at the subspecific level.

References
Mead, 1984, 1989; Ross 1984

Stejneger's beaked whale | *Mesoplodon stejnegeri*

Stejneger's beaked whale is distributed throughout the cold temperate and subarctic waters of the North Pacific. Although sometimes known as the Bering Sea beaked whale, it is more likely that this species frequents the Aleutian Basin and the Aleutian Trench rather than the shallow waters of the northern or eastern Bering Sea. A series of sightings in the central Aleutian Islands was reported in 1985 by researchers surveying northern sea lions. The whales were seen in water that ranged in depth from 730 to 1,560 meters; the water depth in the adjacent Aleutian Basin reaches 3,500 meters. The sightings were of groups of 5–15 individuals, and the groups were composed of both small and large animals traveling in unison. This suggests a social structure similar to that observed in other species of odontocetes.

There are a total of 48 records of this species, of which 31 are from Alaskan waters. On the eastern side of the North Pacific, this whale's distribution ranges from Saint Paul Island to southern California. In the west it ranges from the Commander Islands to Japan. Its center of distribution seems to be the Aleutian Islands, where it has been known to strand in small groups, and there are records of sightings from the central Aleutians.

Information on the food habits of Stejneger's beaked whale is sparse. Trace quantities of squid beaks were collected from two *M. stejnegeri*. No fish remains were found in those stomachs.

Information on reproduction is equally scant. Immature ovarian weight is reported to be 2.6 g; the minimum mature ovarian weight is reported as 12 g. There are no reported fetuses or calves. *J. G. Mead*

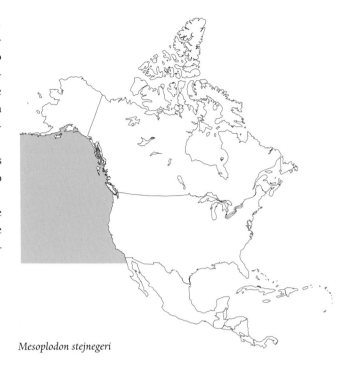

Mesoplodon stejnegeri

Size
Length: 5.25 m (longest reported female and male)
Weight: no data available

Identification
As far as is known, adults of both sexes have uniformly gray to black pigmentation. Identification of *Mesoplodon* females and juveniles is extremely difficult. Adult males can reliably be identified by the shape and position of their teeth.

Other Common Names
Bering Sea beaked whale, sabre-toothed beaked whale

Status
CITES—Appendix II

References
Mammalian Species 250; Mead, 1984, 1989

Order Sirenia

With only 2 families, 3 genera, and 5 species, Sirenia is a small order of mammals. In fact, one genus and species, Steller's sea cow, *Hydrodamalus gigas,* has gone extinct within recent times. Surviving sirenians, the dugongs and manatees, are large, sluggish marine animals that superficially resemble an intermediate form between cetaceans and walruses. However, they are probably more closely related to elephants and hyraxes than to other marine mammals.

References
Wilson and Reeder, 1993

West Indian manatee *(Trichechus manatus)*

Family Trichechidae

There are three species of manatees, in a single genus. Only one species occurs in North America. Manatees are large, slow-moving inhabitants of coastal rivers and estuaries along the East Coast as far north as the Chesapeake Bay. Adults get up to 3.5 m long and may weigh 1,000 kg. Inoffensive plant feeders, their only conflict with humans stems from their vulnerability to boat propellers, which causes serious wounds on many animals.

Manatees tend to be solitary creatures, although they do form larger aggregations in some warm-water lagoons in Florida during the winter. Human-induced changes in their habitats include an increase of warm-water industrial effluent in some areas, which may attract these animals due to their low tolerance for cold water. When they do congregate, they interact with each other through a variety of rubbing and nuzzling.

Although active animals surface to breathe every couple of minutes, they are capable of remaining submerged for almost half an hour when resting. They feed on a variety of submerged vegetation, both vascular plants and algae. In addition, they occasionally take overhanging vegetation from the shore. Captive animals eat up to 30 kg of plant material per day.

Breeding seems to occur throughout the year, and a single calf is born after a gestation period of about a year. The young remain with their mother for a year or two, limiting cows to one young every 2 or 3 years. They adapt readily to captivity, but do not breed well therein.

Fossils are known from the Miocene in South America and from the Pliocene in North America.

References
Rathbun, 1984; Wilson, 1993c

North American Genera
Trichechus

West Indian manatee | *Trichechus manatus*

The West Indian manatee exhibits many unusual features because it is adapted to life as a fully aquatic herbivore, a relatively unique mode of life among mammals. Manatees have also become symbolic of coastal conservation issues, are of concern for fear of extinction, and have become endearing to many because of their benign life style, odd appearance, and propensity for becoming tame in areas where they are not hunted. Some free-ranging manatees become so accustomed to people that they actually solicit human contact for petting, scratching and feeding.

Adaptations for aquatic herbivory in manatees include large body size, large and dextrous forelimbs (for manipulating food, bottom-walking, and sculling), and large prehensile lips studded with bristles. The teeth are molariform and continually progress forward. Worn teeth drop out of the anterior row and new teeth erupt throughout life, an unusual adaptation to an abrasive diet that has evolved only in manatees and certain marsupials. The lungs are long and unilobular, lying above a horizontally oriented diaphragm. Manatees are hindgut digesters, with a long large intestine and a cecum. The metabolic rate is unusually low for a mammal of its size, and manatees rapidly lose body heat to the surrounding water. This precludes their occurrence outside of warm tropical and subtropical regions of North America. In northern Florida and Georgia, some manatees make long (more than 500 km) seasonal migrations southward to avoid cool winter temperatures, whereas others make local movements to sources of constant warm water such as industrial effluents and natural groundwater discharges. Large aggregations of 300 or more animals can be found at some of these sites in winter.

Typical habitats are shallow coastal areas, estuaries, lagoons, and large rivers. A wide variety of aquatic plants are eaten, including non-indigenous floating and submerged species such as water hyacinth and hydrilla, as well as native rooted seagrasses in marine areas and true grasses along banks of rivers and estuaries. Manatees lack daily activity rhythms and feeding may take place at any time of day or night, except where hunting pressures or cold temperatures restrict their active periods. Seasonal movements of manatees may also occur in tropical regions in response to wet and dry season changes, but this is poorly documented. Small aggregations of up to 40 animals have been observed at freshwater springs in tropical marine areas, and manatees are frequently observed drinking at freshwater sources in otherwise marine habitats throughout their range.

Male and female manatees are indistinguishable except for the position of the external genital opening, which is rarely seen from the surface. Mating herds form around estrous females, and involve up to 20 or more males. These males escort the female for periods of about 1–3 weeks, with frequent jostling and forceful contact among individuals. Females apparently mate with more than one male, and give birth to a

Trichechus manatus

single calf after a gestation of about a year. The neonate is 1–1.5 m in length. Twins occur occasionally, an otherwise exceptionally rare event among marine mammals. Mothers and calves communicate with faint but audible squeaks and grunts, and calves typically remain very close to the female or within audible range until weaning occurs. Age at weaning varies from one to two years. Sexual maturity can be attained at ages as young as three or four years in both sexes. Longevity may exceed 60 years. There is no obvious social organization beyond mother-calf pairs, and home ranges of individual animals of all ages and both sexes show considerable overlap.

Manatees have no regular predators, but in many areas disturbing numbers are killed by humans. In Florida this is often the result of accidental encounters with speeding boats, whereas outside of the United States illegal hunting and incidental entanglement in fishing nets are leading causes of death. Coupled with substantial losses of habitat to coastal development and declines in water quality, the long-term future of this species may be precarious. However, manatees do not require wilderness or specialized habitat conditions, and populations and individuals will respond favorably to management actions and can live in fairly close contact with people. Increasing interest in manatee conservation throughout the range may lead to reduced pressures on the species and a more optimistic outlook for its future. *T. J. O'Shea*

Size
Females are larger than males.
Total length: 2.75–3.5 m
Weight: 500–1,650 kg

Identification
No other sirenian overlaps in range with *Trichechus manatus*. The West Indian manatee can be distinguished from other marine mammals in the region by its large spatulate tail, slow movements, large prehensile lips, and elongate forelimbs. It is dark gray, but the color can vary due to patches of algae and encrusting barnacles covering the dorsum.

Recent Synonyms
Manatus köllikeri

Other Common Names
Caribbean manatee, sea cow, manati, vaca marina

Status
Uncommon, endangered

Subspecies
Trichechus manatus latirostris, Florida and nearby areas of the United States
Trichechus manatus manatus, Greater Antilles, Gulf and Caribbean coasts of Mexico, Caribbean coasts and rivers of Belize, Guatemala, Honduras, Nicaragua, Costa Rica, and Panama

References
Mammalian Species 93; O'Shea, 1994

Order Artiodactyla

Artiodactyls, or even-toed ungulates, consist of 220 species in 81 genera worldwide. In North America, there are 12 species in 10 genera. Even-toed ungulates are found worldwide on all major land masses except Australia and Antarctica. The pigs and warthogs (Suidae), peccaries (Tayassuidae), and hippopotamuses (Hippopotamidae) are separated from the rest of the order by common morphological characteristics, including the absence of a ruminant stomach. Hippopotamuses (2 genera, 4 species) are found only in Africa and prefer areas with permanent water and adjacent marsh or grasslands. Pigs (5 genera, 16 species) inhabit primarily shrub-covered or forested areas, and none are native to North America. Peccaries (3 genera and 3 species) are restricted to the New World; they are found in arid scrub, woodland, and rain forest, often near water holes or streams. They are agile runners, gregarious, and may use group defense against predators.

Most species of the Order Artiodactyla, including the camels (Camelidae), chevrotains (Tragulidae), giraffes (Giraffidae), musk deer (Moschidae), deer (Cervidae), pronghorns (Antilocapridae), cows, sheep, goats, and antelope (Bovidae), are ruminants. Representatives of this order, including caribou in North America, are noteworthy for their long seasonal migrations in search of water and food.

Deer (16 genera, 43 species) are almost worldwide in distribution and occur in a variety of habitats from forests to deserts and tundra. Most species typically feed by grazing or browsing. The pronghorn *(Antilocapra americana),* which is closely related to deer, is the only species in the family Antilocapridae and is endemic to the grasslands and deserts of North America.

Bovidae (45 genera, 137 species) is the largest and most diverse family of the Artiodactyla. Most bovid genera are native to the Old World; the fauna of East Africa is particularly diverse. Nonbranching, but elaborately curved or spiraled horns may be present in both sexes.

References

Geist, 1971; Grubb, 1993; Sowls, 1984;
    Wemmer, 1987

White-tailed deer *(Odocoileus virginianus)*

Family Tayassuidae

Peccaries are classified into 3 genera, each with only a single species. All are found in South America; only the collared peccary makes it into North America. They are limited to the deserts of the southwestern United States, where they are also commonly known by the Spanish name, javelina.

They inhabit grasslands, desert scrub communities, and arid woodlands, where they are active mainly during the day, but occasionally forage at night as well. They are omnivorous, but feed heavily on fruits, seeds, roots, and tubers that they root out with tusks and feet. In some areas, they are quite fond of cacti, feeding both on fruits and on the fleshy pads of some kinds.

These are highly social animals, forming herds of 15–50 individuals that are subdivided into family groups. Females normally outnumber males in these groups. They are also territorial, marking their areas with dung piles and with secretions from well-developed rump glands. They also have facial glands, which are used between members of the group, presumably to reinforce recognition of herd mates.

They produce various grunting, snorting, and clicking vocalizations that also serve for group communication. Predators include pumas and jaguars, and the herd normally disperses rapidly in the presence of a potential predator.

References

Sowls, 1984

North American Genera

Pecari

Collared peccary | *Pecari tajacu*

Collared peccaries are found in a wide range of habitats from Argentina north to Texas, New Mexico, and Arizona. Populations in the northern extremes of their range are subjected to periods of snow and very cold weather and probably undergo periodic extinction and re-population.

Perhaps because of the poor insulating properties of their pelage, the activity patterns of collared peccaries are closely related to temperature. During hotter times of the year, when temperatures reach 30° C, groups of peccaries seek shade during the daytime and tend to be much more active during the cooler evenings and nights. During winter, when it is colder, peccary herds rest for only a brief period during the day and seek warmth during the cold nights by lying together in tight pods.

Peccaries are intensely social animals, and partly as a result of year-round group living have evolved a complex vocal and behavioral repertoire. They are capable of at least 15 distinctive aggressive, submissive, and alarm calls. Behaviorally, 31 distinct, graded, or linked behavior patterns have been docu-

mented. The most common behavior pattern observed is reciprocal grooming, where two or more animals stand head to tail and each rubs its head against the dorsal scent gland of another. More than 40 percent of all recorded behavioral interactions involve reciprocal grooming.

Collared peccaries exhibit a territorial breeding system. Group defense by all adult members of the herd is the norm. Linear dominance hierarchies are established under an alpha male; subordinate positions can be held by either males or females, depending largely upon size. There is high reproductive variance among males: dominant males are more likely to breed than subordinate ones. Most reproductively receptive females are bred. Although territorial groups are generally stable, feeding subgroups form and remain apart from the main group up to two weeks at a time. Feeding subgroups appear to be the nucleus for new territorial group formation.

Peccaries in the United States breed primarily from late November to mid-January. The alpha male does not herd females but will tend a female in estrus until he breeds her. Subgroups

Pecari tajacu

tend to coalesce during the breeding season. Twins are commonly observed.

Peccaries are generalist herbivores and in the drier parts of their range consume large amounts of cactus, particularly *Opuntia* species. Cacti are not highly nutritious and peccaries depend upon seasonal forbs, nut, and fruit crops for nutrition. Successful reproduction is probably closely related to the seasonal availability of protein-rich food sources. *J. A. Bissonette*

Size
No significant sexual dimorphism
Total length: 0.85–1.02 m in North America
Length of tail: vestigial, 30–50 mm
Weight: 15–25 kg, depending largely upon nutrition

Identification
Peccaries are pale gray to brown to almost black, with a distinctive salt and pepper effect caused by the white and dark banding of the individual bristles. Occasionally reddish individuals are seen. A paler collar, for which the animals are named, extends around the neck to the shoulders and is variable in shade, pattern, and size. They can be distinguished from suids (pigs) by both internal and external characteristics. Peccaries have three toes on each hind foot, their upper and lower canine teeth are relatively short and straight, they have a complex stomach, and they have no gall bladder. Suids have four toes, longer, curved canine teeth, a simple stomach, and a gall bladder. Peccaries have a scent gland located on the dorsal midline approximately 200–250 mm anterior to the tail. Four pairs of mammae are present; only the two posterior pairs appear to be functional.

Recent Synonyms
Dicotyles tajacu
Tayassu tajacu
The generic designation for the collared peccary remains controversial although the generic distinction between collared and white-lipped peccaries is commonly accepted. Both *Tayassu* and *Dicotyles* have been used as the generic name for collared peccaries, but both should be restricted to white-lipped peccaries according to the most recent taxonomic revisions.

Other Common Names
Javelina; many other local names in Central and South America

Status
Common in southern and western Texas, extreme south-central and southwestern New Mexico, in central, southeastern and southern Arizona, and in Mexico, Central America, and South America

Subspecies
Pecari tajacu angulatus, central, southern, and western Texas south into Tamaulipas, Nuevo Leon, eastern two-thirds of Coahuila, and south into central San Luis Potosi
Pecari tajacu bangsi, southern half of Panama south into South America

Pecari tajacu crassus, Vera Cruz, northern Oaxaca, Mexico
Pecari tajacu crusnigrum, northern Panama north through Costa Rica and Nicaragua, into southern Honduras
Pecari tajacu humeralis, western Oaxaca, north through western Guerrero, southern Michoacan to Colimi
Pecari tajacu nanus, island of Cozumel
Pecari tajacu nelsoni, Quintana Roo south to Belize, southern and central Guatemala, and central and southern Chaipas
Pecari tajacu nigrescens, most of Honduras except far eastern portions along border with Nicaragua, south to San Salvador, and eastern Guatemala
Pecari tajacu sonoriensis, central and southern Arizona, southwestern New Mexico south into Sonora, Sinaloa, Nayarit, and Jallisco, western third of Chihuahua, and Durango
Pecari tajacu yucatanensis, Yucatan, Campeche, Tabasco, western Quintana Roo, northwestern Belize, northern Guatemala, and northern Chiapas
Additional subspecies in South America

References
Mammalian Species 293; Bissonette, 1982

Family Cervidae

There are 43 species in 16 genera of cervids worldwide. The North American forms are restricted to 5 species in 4 genera. Deer are quite adaptable, and have occupied a variety of habitats. Most are forest animals, but they also occur in grasslands and in desert scrub habitats in the southwestern United States.

Deer tend to be gregarious, and frequently occur in herds of a few individuals ranging up to dozens. During migrations, caribou may form dense herds of thousands of individuals. Moose, on the other hand, are much more solitary. Social systems are probably mainly related to food availability and patchiness, with gregarious forms occupying large areas of available forage where there are definite anti-predator benefits to staying with the herd.

Most species are more active in the early morning and late evening, but there is a great deal of variation in activity peri-ods, with nocturnal and diurnal action equally likely in some cases. All are herbivorous, with some species specializing as grazers (grass-eaters) and others as browsers, eating the leaves and twigs of shrubs or trees. Caribou frequently scrape through snow to get at lichens underneath.

In most species, the active period of reproductive activity, known as the rut, occurs in the autumn. At this time, males herd females together in small harems and fight with each other for mating rights. Gestation lasts through the winter, and females give birth in the spring, when forage begins to green up. The calves are quite vulnerable for the first few weeks, and the female leaves her one or two young hidden in the grass while she forages nearby. During this time, the herds may disperse widely, with individuals becoming much more solitary.

References
Wemmer, 1987

North American Genera
Cervus
Odocoileus
Alces
Rangifer

Elk | *Cervus elaphus*

Most elk populations in the United States live on federally-managed lands, including national forests, national parks, and several wildlife refuges, among them the Charles M. Russell National Wildlife Refuge and the National Elk Refuge. Substantial populations also occur on large ranches, Native American reservations, and other public and private lands. Populations have been introduced into Michigan and Pennsylvania and have expanded in Nevada and California in recent years. In Canada, elk have increased their range into northern British Columbia since 1950 and occupy crown lands in Alberta, British Columbia, and Manitoba. Elk populations are an important part of the fauna in Canada's mountain parks, Jasper, Yoho, Kootenay, and Banff. Approximately 20,000 Manitoba elk occupy the aspen parklands of Manitoba, Saskatchewan, extreme east-central Alberta, and recently the Pembina Gorge area of North Dakota. This species presently occupies more habitat than at any time in this century, and populations are higher now as well, numbering around 782,500. The populations in Elk Island National Park and Riding Mountain National Park have been extensively investigated. In Alberta and the western United States, an industry centered around ranching elk has proliferated in recent years.

Perhaps the most spectacular improvement in elk populations is in California, where one population of Tule elk in the Owens Valley that consisted of approximately 600 individuals has now grown to more than 2,500 elk in 22 different populations. Habitat acquisition and reintroduction are the major reasons for the increase. The Tule elk, *C. e. nannodes,* the smallest

Cervus elaphus

of the four extant subspecies, is adapted to the hot, arid conditions of the California habitat.

Elk usually breed in late September or early October. Yearlings of both sexes are typically capable of breeding, although sexual maturity may be delayed when nutritional levels are inadequate. The gestation period is approximately 240 days, with parturition around the first of June. Typically one calf is produced each year; twinning is rare. Birth weights of newborn calves are approximately 14 (9–20) kg. Mean life expectancies vary according to harvest intensity, but elk can live beyond 20 years of age. Sex ratios typically favor females at adulthood, but are near equality at birth. Elk are gregarious animals, with herds of more than 200 occurring in open habitats. In more heavily forested habitats, group sizes are typically smaller.

Natural changes in habitat (such as fires) have largely benefitted elk. On the other hand, some high-quality winter habitats, which are composed of shrubby vegetation that developed following large fires earlier in the century, are now growing into conifer stands. Some conifers, such as Douglas fir, are palatable and highly digestible for elk, and even pole-size stands can provide needed cover during severe winters and from the sport hunter. However, as conifers begin to dominate the winter ranges and associated spring habitats and shade out other species, habitat quality may deteriorate, and eventually elk populations will respond negatively. Such long-term changes are not easily dealt with on short-term planning horizons.

The management of livestock on western public lands is receiving increasing attention. Livestock management that accommodates the elk's needs can be readily accomplished by providing ungrazed pastures within grazing allotments and by manipulating livestock grazing so that regrowing plants retain their palatability for elk. Modifying livestock grazing practices can provide more forage for elk, but the losses in woody plants may reduce the quality of the habitat for deer.

The future of elk populations in North America seems secure. Demand for hunting for food and recreation and the value of herds as tourist attractions should ensure the success of substantial populations. Improving habitat conditions on arid portions of the range, in conjunction with improvements in livestock management, will generally benefit elk. More effectively integrated management of forested habitats will help to retain elk populations in managed forests. The fire management policies that are now in force for the major wilderness areas and national parks should also benefit elk, which evolved with a natural fire regime in many regions. *J. M. Peek*

Size
Males are significantly larger than females. One subspecies, *C. e. nelsoni,* is smaller than the other three.

Total length: 2.06–2.62 (2.39) m (males); 1.98–2.48 (2.23) m (females)

Length of tail: 110–170 (130) mm (males); 80–190 (120) mm (females)

Weight: 178–497 (331) kg (males); 171–292 (241) kg (females)

Identification
Elk are distinguished from mule deer by larger size and darker coloration, yellowish rump patch, and antler configuration, which consists of one main beam with 1 to typically 6 points (sometimes more). They are distinguished from moose by paler coloration, deer-like antler configuration, and the presence of the rump patch.

Recent Synonyms
Cervus canadensis

Other Common Names
Wapiti

Status
Common across western states and provinces, especially in mountainous terrain

Subspecies
Cervus elaphus manitobensis, (Manitoba elk), Manitoba, Saskatchewan, extreme east-central Alberta, and the Pembina Gorge area of North Dakota

Cervus elaphus nannodes (Tule elk), 22 populations in California

Cervus elaphus nelsoni (Rocky Mountain elk), east of the Cascades in Oregon, Washington, and British Columbia; well distributed in Alberta, Arizona, Colorado, Idaho, Montana, New Mexico, Utah, and Wyoming; local distributions in southeast Alaska, Kansas, Nebraska, Nevada, North Dakota, Michigan, Minnesota, Oklahoma, Ontario, Pennsylvania, Texas, and Yukon

Cervus elaphus roosevelti (Roosevelt's elk), Oregon and Washington west of the crest of the Cascade Range, northwestern California, Vancouver Island, British Columbia, and Afognak and Raspberry islands, Alaska

References
Nowak, 1991; Peek, 1982

Mule deer | *Odocoileus hemionus*

The mule deer is the common deer of western mountains, forests, deserts, and brushlands. Size varies from large in the interior (the largest are found in the northern Rocky Mountains) to small along the Pacific coast. The winter coat of interior subspecies is pale brown or tan, and the animals have a large white rump patch and small tail with a black tip. Coastal subspecies are darker and grayer, with a smaller white rump patch completely covered by a large black tail; hence the common name black-tail. All races tend to be a rusty red in the new summer coat. In all localities, males are typically darker than females, particularly around the head, and they are about 20 percent larger. Only the males bear antlers, and finer specimens are sought by hunters of this popular game species.

The mule deer's distribution overlaps with that of the white-tailed deer in the northern Rocky Mountains; at the mouth of the Columbia River; in the southwest in Texas, New Mexico, and Arizona; and in Mexico. The two species are usually separated ecologically, with white-tailed deer in the moister habitat and mule deer in the drier habitat. In the northern ranges, white-tailed deer are found in the river bottoms and mule deer in the drier uplands, whereas in the southwest, mule deer are in the low deserts and white-tailed deer are on mesic mountaintops. Major predators on mule deer are wolves *(Canis lupus),* mountain lions *(Puma concolor),* which are deer specialists, coyotes *(Canis latrans),* and bobcats *(Lynx rufus).* The latter two primarily take fawns.

Odocoileus hemionus

Mule deer prefer mixed habitat with forested cover for protection from heat, cold, and wind, and open areas for feeding. Deer are usually active morning and evening, and periodically through the night. They usually bed in heavy cover during the

daytime, although they often show some daytime activity in the winter. They are herbivores, feeding on a wide range of plant species. The best foods are those that are growing rapidly, because new growth has high nutrient content and low fiber and secondary compounds. Acorns are a particularly rich and favored food in areas where oak trees are present. They are especially valuable when the deer are putting on fat in fall. Human activities such as logging and setting fires, which create secondary successional areas, usually benefit mule deer by creating suitable habitat. An exception is in coastal areas of British Columbia and southeastern Alaska where old-growth forests at low elevation are important as winter range.

Breeding occurs usually in October and November, and one or two fawns are born in early summer after a gestation period of about seven months. Sexual maturity is usually reached at yearling age and the first offspring, usually a singleton, is produced when the female is about 2.5 years old. Twinning is common among older females. Males compete for females during the rut and establish linear hierarchies. Large, old, dominant males guard estrous females (called a tending bond) and account for most breeding. Males do not contribute to rearing the offspring. Antlers are cast annually following the rut, and each successive set is larger until senescence. Growing antlers are nourished by the covering velvet, which dries up and is rubbed off by the deer's thrashing his antlers on trees and brush when antler growth is completed. Fawns weigh about 3.5 kg, have spotted coats, and remain hidden for the first week of life. The mother returns to nurse the fawn periodically until it is strong enough to follow at heel. Fawns are weaned and lose the spotted coat at about 4 months of age.

In mountainous areas, mule deer usually are migratory, spending the warmer months at higher elevations. Here they eat the succulent new growth of grasses and forbs (broad-leaved plants) and the new twigs of trees and shrubs. As summer progresses and the herbaceous plants mature and dry, the diet shifts more towards woody browse. With the first storms of winter, the deer are driven down to foothill areas, where most of their diet is composed of browse from shrubs. Winter ranges are often limited, and in years of severe snowfall, dieoffs are common. With spring snowmelt, migratory deer follow the new plant growth up the mountains, often remaining in favorable sites for several weeks before proceeding to their final destinations.

Populations in milder climates usually are not migratory. Females occupy home ranges of about 2.5 square km and males 5 square km. Migratory individuals have separate summer and winter home ranges connected by a migration pathway. Males usually disperse from the maternal home range and establish their own home ranges when they are yearlings. Females usu-ally establish home ranges near their mother's range. Both sexes form small social groups, seldom of more than three individuals, except during the winter when feeding aggregations form in larger open areas. *D. R. McCullough*

Size
Total length: 1.26–1.68 m (males); 1.25–1.56 m (females)
Length of tail: 130–220 mm (males); 120–210 mm (females)
Weight: 40–120 kg (males); 30–80 kg (females)

Identification
The mule deer is distinguished from the white-tailed deer by dichotomously branching antlers in the male, smaller and less erectile tail, larger ears, and longer (longer than 5 cm vs shorter than 3 cm) metatarsal gland, which is brown in mule deer and whitish in white-tailed deer. When alarmed, mule deer stot (four feet hitting the ground at each bound), whereas white-tailed deer spring from hind to front feet.

Other Common Names
Burro deer, black-tailed deer, Columbian black-tail, Sitka deer

Status
Mostly common and widespread in suitable habitat; the subspecies *O. h. cerrosensis,* from Cedros Island, Baja, Mexico, is rare.

Subspecies
Odocoileus hemionus californicus (California mule deer), southern Sierra and south coastal California
Odocoileus hemionus cerrosensis (Cedros Island mule deer), Cedros Island, Baja, Mexico
Odocoileus hemionus columbianus (black-tailed deer), Pacific coast from central California to British Columbia

Odocoileus hemionus crooki (desert mule deer), southwestern U.S. and north-central Mexico
Odocoileus hemionus fuliginatus (southern mule deer), coastal southern California and northern Baja, Mexico
Odocoileus hemionus hemionus (Rocky Mountain mule deer), Rocky Mountain cordillera and Great Basin
Odocoileus hemionus peninsulae (peninsula mule deer), southern Baja, Mexico
Odocoileus hemionus sheldoni (Tiburon Island mule deer), Tiburon Island, Mexico
Odocoileus hemionus sitkensis (Sitka deer), southeastern Alaska

References
Mammalian Species 219; Wallmo, 1981

White-tailed deer | *Odocoileus virginianus*

The white-tailed deer is one of the most widely distributed and familiar of our native North American mammals. It ranges from southern Canada throughout most of the United States (except the desert regions of Utah, Nevada, and California) as far south as northern South America. Throughout its range it exhibits considerable variation in size. Adult males in northern populations stand over 1 m at the shoulder and weigh upwards of 137 kg. Those in the southern United States average about 0.9 m and 50 to 100 kg. South American populations average about 0.8 m and 30 to 55 kg. The endangered Key deer in the Lower Florida Keys is the smallest subspecies, with males standing only about 0.6 m at the shoulder and weighing about 36 kg. On average females are about 20 percent smaller than males.

Prior to European settlement an estimated 23–40 million whitetails occupied a range similar to that of today, and were the principal source of meat for Native Americans. The hide was widely used for clothing, thread, and string; the bones for weapons, utensils, tools, and jewelry; the intestines and stomach for storage containers; and the teeth served as gaming de-vices and pendants. Even the hooves were used: they were boiled to make glue. Massive commercial and food exploitation by European settlers resulted in the whitetail's near extinction. As early as the late 1600s and early 1700s some of the colonies instituted conservation measures regulating take and hunting seasons. To little avail: whitetail populations had decreased to about 300,000–500,000 by the late 1800s. Subsequently, harvest regulations, intense management, reintroductions, and environmental changes have resulted in an increase in numbers, and today in the United States alone there are estimated to be about 15,000,000 whitetails. The average harvest is now about 2,000,000 per year. With some level of protection from over-exploitation whitetails seem to thrive, and habitat changes associated with humans have allowed them to expand their range. However, as a result of massive reintroduction and restocking programs, most existing populations do not represent original stock and the distinction of most subspecies, particularly in the southeastern United States, is uncertain.

Whitetails occupy diverse habitats from north-temperate to tropical and from semi-arid to rainforest. They prefer forest

edges and open woodlands in proximity to brushland, old-fields, and agricultural areas. Forest cutting and clearing creates the openings, edge, and brush habitat they favor. Density is related to the amount and quality of habitat, and intensely managed wildlife areas may support upwards of 80 deer per square km, although 20–30 or fewer individuals per square km is more typical. In some areas deer may make short fall migrations to areas where more winter food is available. In the north, where winter snows are deep, whitetails may congregate in sheltered areas known as "deer yards" to conserve energy and reduce predation.

Whitetails allocate much of their time to feeding and can select the most nutritious forage that is seasonally available. They are browsers, feeding on leaves, twigs and shoots of herbaceous vegetation, acorns and other mast, berries, seeds, mushrooms, and lichens. They also graze on grasses and herbs and, when they can, feed heavily on agricultural row crops such as corn and soybeans. They are wily and cautious, bound away at the slightest danger, and are excellent runners (capable of speeds of upwards of 60 km per hour) and swimmers. In flight, individuals raise or "flag" their tails, exposing the white underside and rump as a danger signal. They tend to be most active around dawn and dusk, spending much of the day and night bedded down in areas that provide cover.

Whitetails form several kinds of family groups. Matriarchal groups include a doe, her female fawns, and their offspring; fraternal groups consist of adult and subadult males; and mixed feeding groups are composed of both males and females. Although not territorial, whitetails occupy well-defined home ranges, which vary in size from 60 to 500 hectares. In many areas these tend to be long and narrow, which permits optimal exploitation of the patchy environments in which they live. Fawns undertake the smallest movements; yearlings move farther and more frequently than other age groups. Males move farther and occupy larger home ranges than females. Social rank is usually dependent upon size and age. Male and female dominance hierarchies are maintained through complex, stereotyped behavior and threat displays, which include stares, head raising or lowering, and chasing, accompanied by kicking or slapping with the foreleg. These reduce aggressive interactions; subordinate individuals learn to avoid or not intrude upon more dominant individuals. Whitetails also make a number of distinct vocal and nonvocal sounds that are associated with interspecific and intraspecific interactions, including bawls, snorts, wheezes, grunts, bleats, sniffs, and foot stomps.

Males form bachelor groups in the winter after the antlers are shed. These groups are stable until the new antlers sprout, but disband some time after the velvet is lost. The rutting season begins in the fall and lasts for several months. Males frequently spar with each other, apparently to establish dominance hierarchies prior to the breeding period. Sparring usually ceases before actual breeding. About 4 to 6 weeks after the onset of sparring, buck groups break up and mature males begin to pursue and court individual does. At this time the tolerance of bucks to each other decreases. Aggressive displays usually settle the issue of dominance, and actual fights between equally large and dominant bucks are rare. Fights, which are intense antler-shoving and neck twisting bouts, rarely last more than 30 seconds before the loser is driven back, after which the victor has an opportunity to tend the female and copulate with her if she is ready to stand.

During the rut males establish visual and olfactory signposts. These include "rubs" (stems of saplings rubbed with the forehead and antlers leaving scent from skin glands) and "scrapes" (a broken twig or branch above a cleared and pawed depression on the ground upon which the male usually urinates). Other behavioral cues include urine marking, in which the male urinates on a gland on his lower leg (the tarsal gland), producing a very strong odor that may be used to intimidate other bucks. Whitetails have other scent-producing glands that function in communication. These include interdigital glands between the toes, tarsal and metatarsal glands on the hind legs, preorbital glands just below the eye, and forehead glands.

Females come into estrus in autumn. Although many are capable of reproducing in their first year, most do so in their second year. Their breeding activity is influenced by the presence of rutting males and their physical condition. Females are receptive for about 24 hours, but if not inseminated they will come into heat several times at 21 to 30-day intervals. Gestation lasts about 200 days. Females usually give birth to one fawn their first year and two, or rarely three, in following years. Weight at birth is between 2 and 5 kg. The number of

Odocoileus virginianus

day, population management is clearly necessary and has focused on managed sport harvest. Nonhunting sources of mortality are high and include vehicular collisions (44 percent), malnutrition (43 percent), predation (5 percent), parasites and disease (4 percent), and fence entanglement (3 percent).

Whitetails molt twice a year. The red-brown to bright tan summer coat acquired in May and June is replaced in autumn by the gray-brown winter coat. Adults have a white band of hair around their nose and eyes and a black labial spot on the sides of their mandibles. The undersides, including tail, insides of legs, belly, and chin, are white. Antlers (not horns) occur in males and are true bony outgrowths of the skull. Male fawns have "buttons" or unbranched "spikes" their first year. Well-formed antlers with 8, 10, or even 12 points generally occur only in mature males. Antler growth begins in March and continues through August or September. At first the antlers are covered with a hairy "velvet," which later is sloughed or rubbed off. By late December or January, the antlers are shed. The size and shape of a buck's antlers reflect its age, nutrition, and heredity. Dominant males shed the velvet earlier and retain their antlers longer. Only rarely do females have antlers, probably formed in response to unusually high testosterone levels.

Whitetails closely resemble mule deer *(O. hemionus)* both in morphology and behavior. The two species occur together in many areas of the northwestern and southwestern United States and in the Rocky Mountains, where whitetails are expanding their range westward. Where they do occur together, they tend to be ecologically segregated. In the Rockies whitetails occur in riparian zones along river bottoms, and mule deer occur in the uplands and montane areas. In the southwest and in northern Mexico, however, whitetails occur in pine/oak montane forests, and mule deer occur in open, arid areas at lower elevations. Hybridization is known to occur both in captivity and in the wild. In captive breeding some viable offspring result, but the majority are sterile. *J. Laerm*

fawns, their size, and their chance of survival are related to the mother's nutritional level. Neonates nurse immediately and are able to stand in a few hours. The mother leaves them hidden in vegetation for the first month and they are nursed 3 or 4 times a day. Fawns usually double their birth weight in two weeks and triple it in a month. They begin to graze within a few weeks, are functional ruminants by 8 weeks, and are weaned in 8 to 10 weeks. Young females may follow their mother for two years, but males typically leave after a year. Fawns are born with a spotted coat that is lost in their first autumnal molt. Maximum longevity is about 20 years, but few survive 10, and in many areas average life expectancy is 2 to 3 years.

Historically, humans (both Native Americans and European settlers), wolves, and mountain lions were the principle predators, with bobcats, bears, and coyotes incidental predators. To-

Size

Males are about 20 percent larger than females. The species is geographically highly variable; northern populations are larger.
Total length: 0.85–2.4 m (males)
Length of tail: 100–365 mm (males)
Weight: 22–137 kg (males)

Identification

Whitetails can be distinguished from mule deer *(O. hemionus)* by several features. In whitetails the main beam of the antlers grows forward, the antlers are not dichotomously (equally) forked, and the tines rise vertically from the main beam. In mule deer the antlers

grow upward and are dichotomously (equally) forked. The whitetail's tail is brown above, white below, and fringed in white on the sides. The tail of the mule deer is black or black and white above and is always tipped with black. Whitetails also have shorter ears (about 50 percent the length of the head) than mule deer (about 66 percent).

Recent Synonyms

Dama virginiana

Other Common Names

Deer, whitetail; each of the subspecies has a common name

Status

Common, widespread; the Florida Key deer, *O. v. clavium,* and the Columbian white-tailed deer, *O. v. leucurus,* are listed as endangered.

Subspecies

In addition to the subspecies listed, 21 others occur south of the U.S.–Mexico border.
Odocoileus virginianus borealis (northern woodland white-tailed deer), eastern Canada and northeastern United States
Odocoileus virginianus carminis (Carmen Mountains white-tailed deer), Coahuila and Chihuahua, Mexico, and southwestern Texas

Odocoileus virginianus clavium (Key deer), Big Pine Key, Florida

Odocoileus virginianus couesi (Coues white-tailed deer), Chihuahua, Durango, Sinaloa, Sonora, and Jalisco, Mexico, and Arizona and New Mexico

Odocoileus virginianus dacotensis (Dakota white-tailed deer), northern Great Plains of the United States and Canada

Odocoileus virginianus hiltonensis (Hilton Head Island white-tailed deer), Hilton Head Island, South Carolina

Odocoileus virginianus leucurus (Columbian white-tailed deer), coastal Washington and Oregon

Odocoileus virginianus macrourus (Kansas white-tailed deer), central Great Plains and south-central United States

Odocoileus virginianus mcilhenny (Avery Island white-tailed deer), coastal Louisiana and Texas

Odocoileus virginianus nigribarbis (Blackbeard Island white-tailed deer), Sapelo Island, Georgia

Odocoileus virginianus ochrourus (northwest white-tailed deer), Rocky Mountains of the northwestern United States and western Canada

Odocoileus virginianus osceola (Florida coastal white-tailed deer), Gulf coasts of Florida, Alabama, and Mississippi

Odocoileus virginianus seminolus (Florida white-tailed deer), Peninsular Florida and southeastern Georgia

Odocoileus virginianus taurinsulae (Bulls Island white-tailed deer), Bulls Island, South Carolina

Odocoileus virginianus texanus (Texas white-tailed deer), southern Great Plains, Texas, New Mexico

Odocoileus virginianus venatorius (Hunting Island white-tailed deer), Hunting Island, South Carolina

Odocoileus virginianus virginianus (Virginia white-tailed deer), southeastern United States

References

Mammalian Species 388; Gerlach et al., 1994; Hall, 1984

Moose | *Alces alces*

The largest member of the deer family, the moose is one of the largest land mammals in North America. Only the largest bears and bison outweigh it. Males of this species display the largest antlers of any living mammal in the world. Only one species of moose is recognized throughout the Northern Hemisphere, and its distribution includes most regions of boreal forest north of latitude 45° N.

From its origins in Europe and Asia in Pleistocene times, moose spread to North America across the Bering Land Bridge less than 100,000 years ago. They moved south and east across North America only within the last 10,000 years, as giant ice sheets retreated to the northeast. The large size of the moose has made it especially important ecologically, as prey for wolves and bears, as a source of food for prehistoric and modern humans, and as a modifier of the forested ecosystems it inhabits. Renowned as a quarry of hunters, some 90,000 moose are harvested each year in North America, where the total moose population is estimated to be 0.8–1.2 million animals.

Aside from large palmate antlers, shed and regrown annually, moose are distinguished by an elongated head ending in a large cartilaginous nose and flexible upper lip, and a hanging dewlap of skin near the throat. The function of this "bell" is unknown. The moose has virtually no tail, although it could probably use one to ward off hordes of summertime insects.

Mature moose are dimorphic: males are larger than females. Moose in Alaska and the Yukon Territory are larger than those in southern ranges, and tundra moose have larger antlers than those in forested areas. An excellent sense of hearing is assisted by huge ears that can each be rotated 180 degrees. The moose

Alces alces

uses its keen sense of smell to locate food below snow, but its vision seems best developed for detecting moving objects. A moose will often stand immobile for many minutes staring at a suspicious intruder in its field of vision.

With very long legs and a thick coat made of hollow, insulating 15–25 cm-long hairs, moose are well adapted to survive cold, snowy winters. They routinely exist in areas with a snow

cover of 60–70 cm, but crusted snow makes movement difficult and increases their vulnerability to hunting wolves. With such a large body, a stomach producing heat via fermentation, and an inability to perspire, moose are limited to cool regions where temperatures do not exceed 27° C for long periods. They eliminate heat through evaporative cooling during respiration; above a temperature of 5° C their respiration rate is directly correlated with ambient temperature. Moose may also cool themselves in ponds and lakes and, near the southern limit of their range, shade is imperative even in winter.

The moose is a ruminant, with a four-chambered stomach adapted to a diet of woody plants, high in lignin. Its common name is adapted from a native Algonquian term, "moos," referring to its habit of eating trees. Most of a moose's active time is spent filling a large stomach that, when full, may weigh more than 65 kg. Its food consumption is prodigious, up to 20 kg per day of selected plants—leaves of trees and shrubs along with aquatic plants in summer, woody twigs of deciduous and coniferous plants in winter. Willows and aspen are among the most nutritious foods. Coniferous trees such as balsam fir are eaten only in winter, a time of food scarcity. Optimum forage is often produced after fire or similar forest disturbance, and moose populations often increase in response to improved nu-

trition. A moose typically occupies a small home range of 5–10 square kilometers or less, but long movements or even annual migrations may occur between seasonal ranges.

Moose usually mate in late September or early October, and eight months later they have a synchronous birth period in late May and early June. Newborn moose weigh 11–16 kg and gain an average of one kg in body mass each day through their first summer, while they are nursing. Cows usually give birth to single young, often every year, but twins are not uncommon when nutrition is favorable.

Calves remain with their mother throughout their first year, dependent on her defense from predators and learning firsthand where to find the best forage and most favorable habitats. Calf mortality is usually high—wolves and bears may claim half the calves born annually. Cows aggressively defend their young by lashing out with sharp hooves, and moose may escape from predators in water. Cow moose forcibly evict their previous offspring before bearing new calves. Outcast young bulls are very likely to explore at this age, and consequently they suffer greater mortality. Four to five years of growth are required for full physical and social maturity. At that age males sport their largest antlers and females reach their reproductive prime.

From about 5 to 12 years of age moose are in their reproductive prime, but as the processing of several tons of food per year begins to wear down their great molars, their foraging efficiency declines. Vulnerability to wolf predation increases after eight years of age, when arthritis, periodontal disease, and other senescence factors become prominent. For moose older than calves, annual nonhunting mortality is often 10–15 percent. For bulls, the rigors of rutting behavior and the physiological stress of growing a large set of antlers each year are quite significant, and large bulls may succumb after just two or three successful breeding seasons. Few bull moose survive more than 15 years, and the maximum recorded age for a cow moose is 22 years.

Moose are known for their individualistic behavior, and are rarely gregarious unless they are in mating harems in tundra or alpine habitats. Throughout their extensive North American range these large herbivores exist at low density, usually about 0.4 moose per square kilometer. Moose density is often limited by the combined actions of three great predators—humans, wolves, and bears (both brown and black). When only one of these predator species is present, as on the island of Newfoundland (humans) and Isle Royale National Park, Michigan (wolves), moose may increase to 2–3 animals per square kilometer. Rarely, in winter ranges, local aggregations of moose may reach a density of 20 per square kilometer, and then the effect of their browsing is pronounced. Although moose are remarkably free of infectious diseases, several parasites contribute to moose mortality. "Moose disease," a neurological disorder caused by a brainworm endemic to white-tailed deer, can prove fatal in regions of eastern North America where moose and deer coexist. Another parasite of deer and elk, the winter tick, plagues moose in all parts of North America but Alaska. An individual moose may harbor tens of thousands of ticks in winter, and the combined effects of loss of blood and irritation can cause mortality in late winter.

Moose have increased their range in New York and New England, and have flourished following introduction into Colorado and upper Michigan. *R. O. Peterson*

Size
Males are larger than females.
Total length: 2.5–3.2 (3.055) m (males); 2.4–3.1 (3.015) m (females)
Length of tail: 80–120 (100) mm
Weight: 360–600 (430) kg (males); 270–400 (350) kg (females)

Identification
Alces alces is light brown to almost black in color, with a long head, long ears, and a large nose. Males have palmate antlers.

Other Common Names
Known as "elk" in Scandinavia

Status
Common within geographic range

Subspecies
Alces alces americana, east of Great Lakes
Alces alces andersoni, Great Lakes through Canada to British Columbia
Alces alces gigas, Alaska and Yukon Territory, Canada

Alces alces shirasi, Colorado, Montana, and Wyoming

References
Mammalian Species 154; Franzmann, 1978; Franzmann and Schwartz, 1998

Caribou | *Rangifer tarandus*

Among the deer family, caribou are the best adapted to live in harsh environments with low productivity. Caribou form large migratory herds at the tree line, the core of the species range. Farther south, mountain ridges, bogs, and the boreal forest represent habitat where they can make their living. The caribou range shrank along with colonization of North America because logging, agriculture, and hunting negatively affect this species. Caribou numbers exceed 2,000,000 throughout the continent, although many populations in the southern part of the range cope poorly with predators and human activities.

Like other deer, caribou eat mostly leaves of shrubs and grass-like plants in the summer, but their huge consumption of lichens in winter is unique. Migratory caribou travel to the tundra in spring, where females deliver their calves on traditional calving grounds. On the open tundra, females can more easily detect predators and protect their neonates. Later in the

season, when the calves become more mobile, caribou form large groups and wander in the tundra and the forest in search of forage to rebuild their body reserves before the breeding season. They commonly enter the boreal forest in winter, where they feed on the rich carpet of lichens. However, they have to dig in snow to reach their food. The energy costs of this activity increase with snow depth. Feeding craters are then valuable, and animals compete for them: this is probably one important reason female caribou have antlers, a weapon to impose dominance. Caribou exhibit physical traits that make them well adapted to walking: migratory animals cover more than 5,000 km per year. Movements of forest dwelling and mountain caribou are not so extensive, but their feeding habits do not vary much. In some places, arboreal lichens replace terrestrial ones.

Caribou shed their antlers every year: males lose them earlier than females. Females often keep their old antlers until parturition in early June, when growth of the new ones is already advanced in males. Old antlers are whitish; new ones, covered with velvet, are black. Molting follows the antler cycle and begins later in pregnant females. The molt is completed in July, when the coat is dark brown. Progressively, the coat color be-

Rangifer tarandus

comes whitish and yellowish in autumn, particular on the belly and the sides, so that the animals are well camouflaged when snow arrives.

The breeding season lasts a few weeks in late October and early November. Males stop feeding to court females and to fight each other. They lose much of their body reserves in this effort to leave descendants. Gestation lasts seven months, so that calves are born from late May to mid-June. Unlike *Rangifer tarandus* in Eurasia (the reindeer), caribou rarely have twins. Females nurse their fawns until winter, but calves depend largely on forage after 45 days of age. Female body reserves reach an annual low after the first month of lactation. Calves can follow their mothers a few hours after birth. On good range, females give birth to their first calf when they are two years old and reproduce every year thereafter. They attain puberty later on poor ranges, and must often skip reproducing in some years to replenish their body reserves. Caribou reach senescence by 10–12 years of age. *M. Crête*

Size

Size varies widely among subspecies.

Total length: 1.6–2.1 (1.8) m (males); 1.37–1.86 (1.66) m (females)

Length of tail: 0.11–0.22 (0.16) m (males); 0.10–0.20 (0.15) m (females)

Weight: 81–153 (110) kg (males); 63–94 (81) kg (females)

Identification

Caribou are distinguished from moose by smaller size, paler coat, and shorter nose. The white-tailed deer *(Odocoileus virginianus)* is smaller, darker, often flags its long white tail, and does not bear palmate antlers. *Rangifer* is the only genus in the deer family in which both males and females bear antlers.

Other Common Names

Reindeer (Europe)

Status

Abundant in the core of species range; endangered as *R. t. caribou*

Subspecies

Rangifer tarandus caribou, eastern North America

Rangifer tarandus granti, Alaska, Yukon

Rangifer tarandus groenlandicus, mainland in the Northwest Territories; Baffin Island

Rangifer tarandus pearyi, Arctic islands

References

Banfield, 1961, 1974; Bergerud, 1978

Family Antilocapridae

The pronghorn is the only member of this family, and it is a North American endemic. It is the only surviving member of a group that included several genera and about a dozen species in the Pleistocene of North America. An open country denizen, the pronghorn is renowned for its speed and endurance.

With stocky bodies, long legs, and short, black horns that curl slightly backward in both sexes, pronghorns are distinctive looking animals. The horns are shed annually, and quickly re-grow each year. The horns of males have a forward-projecting "prong" that gives them the name. Pronghorns have large eyes that project out from the side of the head, giving them an exceptionally wide field of view in their open habitats.

Pronghorns graze and browse on a variety of vegetation. They take advantage of new growth of grasses in the spring, and shift their diets seasonally, depending on food availability and quality. Nutrition probably plays an important role in the reproductive cycle as well, with twins frequently produced in areas where food quality and quantity is high. The rut occurs in the fall, but males may defend territories even outside of the rutting period. Females give birth in late spring, and the fawns hide in the vegetation for a couple of weeks, until they are strong enough to keep up with the herd.

References
Van Wormer, 1969

North American Genera
Antilocapra

Pronghorn | *Antilocapra americana*

Pronghorns use flat or rolling, expansive areas at elevations from sea level to 3,350 m, but greatest densities are at 1,200–1,800 m. They are adapted to hot deserts or alpine plateaus, but snow depths exceeding 30 cm create foraging problems. They do best in habitats that average 30–38 cm of precipitation per year. These animals do not hide: they remain in the open, relying on their speed and keen eyesight, which has been compared to that of a human using 8x binoculars, for protection. Pronghorns lack dewclaws, an adaptation for fast running in open country. They have been clocked at speeds up to 72 km per hour. A highly developed sense of curiosity prompts them to investigate anything unusual in their habitat.

The common name is derived from the branching or "pronged" horns of bucks. These are true horns, composed of keratinized epithelial cells and a great deal of embedded hair, forming a black outer sheath over a bony core. Both sexes have horns; those of mature bucks average 330–410 mm in length. Those of does usually are 20–125 mm long and lack prongs. About one-third of does do not have horn sheaths even though small nipple-like cores can be felt under the skin. The outer sheaths of bucks' horns are shed annually, usually in Novem-

with heavy eyelashes that act as sun shades. The pelage is molted once a year during early summer. In late summer, the hair of the pronghorn is smooth and flexible, but as winter approaches, it lengthens and each hair, filled with many air cells, becomes a thick, spongy insulator.

Although twin births are the rule, three to seven ova are fertilized and begin embryonic development. Intrauterine mortality usually reduces the number of embryos to two within 6 weeks. Pronghorns have a long gestation period for their size—about 250 days. Females usually breed for the first time at 16 months of age, and first produce fawns at two years of age. Occasionally, females as young as 4–6 months old breed, and are slightly more than a year old when they give birth. On good range, older does produce twins about 98 percent of the time, but fewer first births involve twins. Newborn fawns are more drab in color than their parents and generally weigh 3–4 kg. They begin walking less than an hour after birth and can outrun a person when they are several days old. The greater portion of their first two weeks of life is spent hidden. They rise only to nurse.

The breeding season is short, beginning in September in northern areas and peaking at the end of that month. Some southern populations breed from June through August. In some populations, bucks defend a territory and hold a harem on it during the rut; in others, bucks defend a harem without a territory.

Pronghorns feed on a wide variety of plants. Studies have shown that forbs and shrubs are the principal foods and grass is consumed in quantity only during "green-up." Many plants that are poisonous to livestock are relished.

These animals generally do not jump fences, but they can pass under or through most barbed-wire fences. Woven wire topped with barbed wire and highway right-of-way fences form serious barricades. These curtail the movements of some herds and, during severe winters or droughts, can contribute to extensive mortality. Populations increase and decrease rapidly or move long distances, 300 km or more, in response to weather conditions. Translocations create new ranges, and pronghorn-proof fences along highways, and other human influences, eliminate others. Thus, ranges are in a constant state of flux, and pronghorn range maps are at best approximations. In general, populations in Mexico are decreasing and those in Canada and the United States are static.

More than 90 percent of all pronghorn belong to the subspecies *A. a. americana*. In Canada, these pronghorn were formerly found on the prairie steppes from the Red River and other areas of southwestern Manitoba westward to the Rocky Mountains and as far north as the present city of Edmonton, Alberta. To the east, in what is now Saskatchewan, they were seasonally found as far as 50° north latitude. In the United States, *A. a. americana* ranged from western Minnesota, west-

ber. The horns of does are shed, but not at a specific time of year.

The body is cinnamon to tan with black and white markings on the head and neck. A black line outlining the edge of the lower jaw below the ear distinguishes the male at all ages. In both sexes, the belly and lower sides are creamy white. The short tail is surrounded by a large, white rump patch. Hairs of the rump patch can be erected at will and apparently serve as a visual signal to other animals in the vicinity. Rump glands release a pungent odor when the rump patch is erected. A mane, which can be erected, is present along the back of the neck. The eyes are large (36 mm in diameter), black, and lustrous,

Antilocapra americana

ern Iowa, northwestern Missouri, Oklahoma, and Kansas westward to eastern Montana, southern Idaho, Oregon, and California. They were found as far south as southern Texas, central New Mexico, central Arizona, and the Colorado Desert of southern California. Those of Oregon, northern California, and parts of Nevada were, until recently, considered *A. a. oregona.*

A. a. sonoriensis formerly roamed southwestern Arizona and extreme southeastern California, as well as northwestern Sonora and northeastern Baja California. As of 1998, the U.S. population ranged along the Mexican border in western Arizona, mostly on public lands. These included the Cabeza

Prieta National Wildlife Refuge, Barry Goldwater Air Force Range, and Organ Pipe Cactus National Monument.

A. a. mexicana formerly ranged from southeastern Arizona and southwestern New Mexico eastward to the Jornada and Tularosa desert valleys and regions west of the Organ Mountains, and southward through extreme western Texas, Chihuahua, and Coahuila to northeastern Durango, Mexico. Pronghorn from Marathon Basin, Texas, are considered *mexicana,* but the rest of western Texas and southern New Mexico apparently is a natural intergrade zone between *americana* and *mexicana. B. W. O'Gara*

Size

Total length: 1.344–1.453 m (males);
    1.283–1.486 m (females)
Length of tail: 104–145 mm (males); 106–130
    mm (females)
Weight: 42–59 kg (males); 41–50 kg (females)

Identification

Pronghorns resemble Old World gazelles except for the prongs on the horns of males, the erectile mane, and white neck bands.

Recent Synonyms

Antilocapra anteflexa
Antilope (Dicranocerus) furcifer

Other Common Names

Antelope, pronghorn antelope, berrendo (Mexico)

Status

Common in suitable habitat; more than a million in western Canada, Mexico, and United States; numbers fluctuate with severity of winters and droughts

Subspecies

Antilocapra americana americana, grasslands and shrub steppes of western United States and Canada

Antilocapra americana mexicana, Marathon Basin, Texas, and north-central Mexico
Antilocapra americana peninsularis, Baja California
Antilocapra americana sonoriensis, northwestern Sonora, Mexico, and extreme southern Arizona

References

Mammalian Species 90; Yoakum and O'Gara, in press

FAMILY ANTILOCAPRIDAE 341

Family Bovidae

With 137 species in 45 genera, bovids are the largest group of artiodactyls. North America has 5 species in 4 genera. This is a varied group, ranging from the bison through muskoxen to mountain goats and mountain sheep.

Habitats used by this group range from open grasslands and tundra to the steepest mountain slopes and peaks. Bison, which are commonly associated with the Great Plains, were also common in forested regions over a much larger part of North America at one time. The slaughter of the great herds of bison is one of the one of the most common conservation disaster tales of North America. Fortunately they were not driven to extinction, and herds remain today in protected areas and in captivity.

Muskoxen are restricted to the Arctic region, and are highly adapted to such cold climates. Mountain goats and mountain sheep occupy western mountains, where they feed on a variety of grasses, forbs, mosses, lichens, and woody plants.

In most species of bovids, and in all North American species, both sexes bear horns. However, the males frequently have much larger and more massive horns than do the females. The horns are used in combat between males, and they are composed of a bony core attached directly to the skull, and a horny outer sheath.

Bovids are ruminants, which means they swallow large quantities of food, and then regurgitate it and rechew it at their leisure. This is known as chewing their cud, and helps to thoroughly break down the vegetative matter for digestion. Rumination may also allow rapid foraging followed by more leisurely digestion in a safer environment.

Bovids have played a major role in the evolution and development of human populations. Domestic cattle and sheep were derived from wild bovid ancestors, and most of the wild species have been hunted extensively for food and hides throughout human history.

References
Geist, 1975; Gray, 1987; Reynolds et al., 1982

North American Genera
Bison
Oreamnos
Ovibos
Ovis

American bison | *Bison bison*

Once numbering in the tens of millions, bison were brought to the brink of extinction in the 19th century, primarily through commercial hide hunting from 1871–1882. W. T. Hornaday counted only 541 plains bison in an 1887 census. Conservation efforts began in the 1880s and by 1910, herds had been re-established in Oklahoma and Montana.

Bison are gregarious grazers and reach highest densities on mixed grass and short grass prairies. Mixed groups in the Wichita Mountains in Oklahoma average 100 individuals in summer and 16 in winter. Rut occurs in July and August, during which dominant bulls "tend" individual cows until allowed to mate. Gestation averages 285 days, after which a single calf is born. Sexual maturity is usually attained at 2 years. Fecundity rates appear to increase with latitude, from 67 percent of cows 3 years and older in Oklahoma to 88 percent in Montana.

The species *B. bison,* of Holocene origin, apparently descended from *B. antiquus* about 5,000 years ago. A few authorities have suggested that it is conspecific with the European wisent, *B. bonasus,* but most taxonomists regard it as distinct. Less clear is the validity of the subspecies *athabascae.* Recent evidence that environmental influences may explain pelage differences between plains and wood bison, and comparisons of mitochondrial DNA, suggest that subspecific distinction may not be justified. This reassessment has important conservation implications because the presumed subspecies *athabascae* is listed as endangered.

Another taxonomic controversy concerns generic placement. Linnaeus classified American bison as *Bos bison,* and the species has long been known to be interfertile with *Bos taurus* (domestic cattle). Although most authorities still favor *Bison,* several recent reviews have advocated placing American bison in the genus *Bos.*

Bison share several infectious diseases with cattle, including brucellosis *(Brucella abortus),* anthrax *(Bacillus anthracis),* and bovine tuberculosis *(Mycobacterium).* These and Texas tick fever *(Babesia bigemina)* may have contributed to the rapid de-

Bison bison

cline of free-living bison in the 1870s and 1880s. There is controversy about what threat, if any, bison pose as sources for brucellosis infection in cattle. Recent studies suggest that the bacteria affect bison differently from cattle, and that transmission from bison to cattle is unlikely under most field conditions. *J. H. Shaw*

Size
Males are larger than females.
Total length: 3.05–3.8 m (males); 2.1–3.2 m (females)
Length of tail: 430–900 mm
Weight: 460–907 kg (males); 360–544 kg (females)

Identification
The bison is the largest land mammal native to the Western Hemisphere. Its dark, distinctive pelage is shaggiest on the head and shoulders, particularly in summer. The body is narrow for its height, with heavier forequarters than hindquarters and a distinctive hump at the shoulder. The short, dark, upwardly-curled horns are more massive in males.

Recent Synonyms
Bos bison

Other Common Names
American buffalo

Status
Nearly extinct late in 19th century; recovered to nearly 150,000 by 1995, with nearly 135,000 privately-owned. Nearly all herds in the United States are confined by fences. Status is secure for *B. b. bison; B. b. athabascae* is listed as endangered, Appendix I, IUCN.

Subspecies
Bison bison athabascae, wood bison, western Canada north of approximately 55° N. latitude
Bison bison bison, plains bison, most of North America south of approximately 55° N. latitude

References
Mammalian Species 266; Nowak, 1991; Reynolds et al., 1982

Mountain goat | *Oreamnos americanus*

The mountain goat belongs to a group of hoofed animals called rupicaprines, which literally means "rock-goats." The mountain goat is the only rupicaprine in North America, but there are a number of species inhabiting the mountains of Eurasia, of which the European chamois is probably the mountain goat's closest relative. Both of these species occur in high mountains, living at or above timberline, and often close to glaciers. The native range of the mountain goat is the northern Rocky Mountains, the Cascade Mountains, the Coast Range from central Idaho and Washington northward to southeastern Alaska, and the mountains of the central Yukon and Northwest Territories. However, it has been successfully introduced into a number of geographically isolated mountain ranges in Montana, Wyoming, and Colorado, and into the Black Hills of South Dakota, the Olympic Peninsula of Washington State, and several North Pacific coastal islands, including Kodiak Island in Alaska. The central and southern Rocky Mountain portion of this range, now established by introductions, was inhabited by the mountain goat at the end of the last Ice Age, but the species became extinct there, probably because of a warm, arid period that occurred about 5,000 years ago. When more suitable alpine climate returned, mountain goats were unable to recolonize these areas across intervening lowland valleys with unsuitable habitat without human assistance.

Suitable habitat for a mountain goat is open country with steep rocky cliffs, talus slopes, and meadows in which to forage. This unique combination of habitat requirements is met, in more southerly latitudes, only in the high alpine and subalpine zones of mountains. Farther north, as the general climate becomes cooler, these zones extend farther down the mountains, until at the extreme northern end of the mountain goat's range, they are found at quite low elevations. Various studies have shown that mountain goats spend about three-quarters of their time on cliff faces, where they are relatively safe from predators. Although at a distance such cliffs may appear to be barren, in fact there is quite a lot of vegetation growing in small pockets and even on rock cliffs on which the mountain goats can forage. Most of the rest of their time is spent in meadows or alpine fellfields adjacent to the steeper cliffs. The ground inhabited by mountain goats is astonishingly steep; several studies have shown that about three-fifths of a mountain goat population regularly occupies slopes steeper

Oreamnos americanus

than 50 degrees, and about ten percent of the time they may be found on slopes that rise at an astonishing 60 degrees or more.

Because they inhabit northern mountains, mountain goats in most places undergo a regular seasonal migration, occupying higher elevations in the summer and moving to somewhat lower elevations in the winter. This movement occurs in part because of the accumulation of snow and ice on the high peaks as winter progresses, but other factors may be involved as well. Even in winter, most goat populations stay at or above timberline. Here the steep terrain is an advantage, because winds sweeping over the treeless landscape can blow the ground free of snow. The steeper the slope, the more snow is blown away, and otherwise-hidden forage that the goats depend upon in winter is exposed. Mountain goats only rarely move down into the upper edge of the montane forest, for here the snow accumulates in deep drifts, which seriously impedes their movement and creates an environment essentially without winter forage.

A different pattern is seen, however, in mountain goats inhabiting the Pacific Coast ranges. These coast ranges, especially on the ocean side, are a region of very deep snowfall. Moreover, because of the proximity of the mountains to the ocean, the winter climate is much warmer than it is in the interior mountains. Mountain goats here spend much more of their time at lower elevations, often well within the dense coniferous forest that borders the northwest Pacific Coast. The higher elevations of these mountains regularly accumulate a snowpack too deep for the goats to move about in. Even at lower, less snowy elevations, however, they usually limit themselves to steep broken slopes and small outcrops. Their population densities in this habitat appear to be considerably lower than they are in more typical alpine habitats in the interior.

The ability of mountain goats to live in such steep, rocky landscapes is, of course, dependent upon their climbing ability. This in turn is based upon their extremely powerful forelimbs, which provide the required traction to move uphill, or braking to move safely downhill, and upon their specialized feet and hooves. The hooves of all four feet are almost pincer-like, and can be spread out to serve as brakes or pinched together to help the goat secure a better hold on a knob or ridge of rock. In addition, the bottom of the hoof is covered with a rough-textured foot pad that provides much more traction than the hoof of a typical ungulate. This natural "traction pad" enables mountain goats to traverse slippery rocks, or ice, and to find footholds on narrow ledges and in cracks. The goats can move about with great agility and can reach places that no potential predator could follow.

These predators include mountain lions, grizzly bears, and occasionally, wolverines. In addition, golden eagles have been reported to carry off newborn kids, but they are probably not often a serious threat. Lynx and coyotes may take an occasional mountain goat caught in an open meadow.

The annual cycle for mountain goats begins when snow-melt starts in spring. Then the goats, sometimes in small groups, begin gradually to drift upslope. Males and barren females usually migrate first, followed by females accompanied by kids and yearlings. Daily movements may range from a few hundred yards to a mile or more. Once on their summer range, the goats are not gregarious and go about singly and in pairs, females accompanied by young. Males are usually seen alone.

Young are born in late May or early June. Single births are most common, although twins are not rare. A newborn kid weighs 2.7–3.2 kg. The female usually gives birth on a steep cliff; fortunately the kids are precocial and are able to follow their mothers soon after they are born. After the young are a few days old, the goats spend more and more time on vegetated slopes, especially if small herds have formed.

Adult males begin to molt in June and usually shed their winter hair by the middle of July. Females and yearlings molt about a month later. The kid sticks close to its mother throughout the summer, nursing regularly. Lactation comes to an end in early fall, although the kid remains with its mother until a new one is born. Most breeding activity occurs in November and the first half of December, although some indi-

viduals continue in rut until early January. During this time the migration to the winter range may have begun; it is usually triggered by the first heavy snowfall of the winter.

In most mountain goat populations there are fewer young than adults, because mortality in kids and yearlings is rather high compared to that of adults. Particularly high kid and yearling mortality may occur during severe winters, but once mountain goats reach adulthood, they have relatively low mortality rates. Maximum age attained may be nearly 20 years, but most adults do not live past 10 years. Mountain goats become sexually mature at three years of age, and most females first become pregnant at that age. However, adult males usually do not participate successfully in the rut until they are a year or two older. This is because mountain goats do not form the gregarious herds typical of other montane ungulates such as sheep; their social life is instead organized hierarchically. Aggressive behavior between goats is common. Threat behavior includes displaying the sharp horns by tipping the head forward, a rush threat, and a lateral display in which two animals stand head-to-flank. They often circle, facing in opposite directions, during these maneuvers, and the horns may be thrust upward. The skin along their sides and flanks is particularly thick, and this "dermal shield" serves to mitigate serious damage in most cases. Occasionally, however, fatal injuries are inflicted. Outside of the breeding season, although adult males employ various threat behaviors, particularly lateral displays, to establish dominance among themselves, they often behave in a subordinate manner to females and even to juveniles. In other situations, however, males appear to dominate females, and this may relate to competition between the sexes for food resources. During the rut a dominant male will tend one or more females for long periods of time, and mark vegetation with special horn glands. Males also dig rutting pits into which they urinate and then paw the soil onto their coats. Particularly before and during the rut, males wander widely; females tend to remain in a stable home range. Yearling goats may move particularly long distances after their mothers have borne a new kid and chased them away; they will then establish a stable home range elsewhere in the vicinity and associate with other individuals in the population. *R. S. Hoffmann*

Size
Total length: 1.245–1.787 (1.537) m (males);
   1.346–1.549 (1.417) m (females)
Length of tail: 84–203 (102) mm (males);
   89–140 (108) mm (females)
Weight: 46.2–136.0 (61.7) kg (males); 45.8–83.9
   (57.2) kg (females)

Identification
The all-white pelage and short, black, recurved horns are diagnostic of this species. The only other montane ungulate that is all white in color is Dall's sheep, but its horns are pale amber and much longer: only in females and yearling males are they as short as those of the mountain goat.

Recent Synonyms
Oreamnos montanus

Other Common Names
Rocky Mountain goat

Status
Mountain goats primarily inhabit remote montane areas that are difficult for humans to reach. As a result, their populations have been less affected by human activities than those of any other large ruminant in North America.

Subspecies
Oreamnos americanus americanus, Coast and
   Cascade ranges from central British Colum-
bia to central Oregon
Oreamnos americanus columbiae, southern
   Yukon and southwestern Mackenzie south
   to central British Columbia
Oreamnos americanus kennedyi, south-central
   Alaska from Cook Inlet south to the Copper
   River
Oreamnos americanus missoulae, Rocky Moun-
   tains from southwestern Alberta and south-
   eastern British Columbia south to central
   Idaho and Montana

References
Mammalian Species 63; Chadwick, 1983;
   Von Elsner-Schack, 1986

Muskox | *Ovibos moschatus*

Muskoxen live in Arctic regions that have low precipitation, long, cold winters (8–10 months), and short, cool summers. Most muskoxen in North America live on the Arctic islands of northern Canada. Smaller populations occur primarily in tundra areas of the northern Canadian mainland, including the Ungava Peninsula of Quebec through an introduction. In northern and western Alaska populations were successfully reestablished after being extirpated in the late 1800s. Muskoxen also occur in northeastern and northern Greenland and have been introduced to western Greenland and in Russia to the Taimyr Peninsula and Northern Sakar Wrangell Island. They feed primarily on sedges, grasses, and willows. Their distribution is probably limited by snow depth, which affects the availability of winter forage.

Muskoxen are social ungulates. Females and subadults live year-round in mixed-sex groups that are usually larger in winter than in summer. Many adult males are solitary in summer, but most live in bull groups or mixed-sex groups in winter. Energetically conservative and generally sedentary, mixed-sex groups often move only short distances throughout the year. Adult males usually move more than adult females.

Muskoxen are polygynous, with a harem mating system in which one adult male breeds with several females. During the breeding season (rut) in August and September, a dominant male keeps other adult males away from his harem with aggressive displays, vocalizations, and scent marking. Efforts to establish dominance culminate in spectacular clashes in which two males, swinging their heads from side to side, back up for several meters, then gallop toward each other at speeds up to 50 km per hour and hit heads with tremendous force. Their bosses, massive helmets of horn, provide head protection during these dominance fights for females. Most calves are born in late April and May after a gestation of about 34 weeks. Calves are precocial and weigh 10–14 kg at birth. A single calf is produced; twins are extremely rare.

The principal predators of muskoxen are wolves (*Canis lupus*) and brown bears (*Ursus arctos*). Muskoxen use a unique group defense when threatened or disturbed. In response to the pres-

Ovibos moschatus

ence of a predator or other danger, they often run together into a tight circle or crescent-shaped formation, with their vulnerable rumps and flanks backed against one another and their formidable horns facing outward. Individuals in the group may dart forward to hook the approaching predator with their horns. When disturbed, muskoxen also sometimes stampede, galloping close together in a tight group.

In spite of adaptations to Arctic conditions, muskoxen can be affected by severe weather, particularly when deep or crusted snow or ground-fast ice (from freezing rain or temporary thaws) restricts forage availability. Such conditions have decreased calf production, survival rates, and local populations. Less is known about the effects of disease and parasites, although evidence of exposure to diseases such as contagious ecthyma and parainfluenza, and intestinal parasites and lungworms have been reported in wild muskoxen. Disease caused by *Yersinis pseudotuberculosis* bacteria has killed muskoxen in Canada.

The muskox vanished from Europe at the end of the Pleistocene and from northern Siberia more than 2,000 years ago. Vulnerable to over-exploitation by humans, it disappeared from Alaska and was on the edge of extinction in areas of Canada at the turn of the century. Protective legislation in Canada and the successful re-establishment of populations of muskox in Alaska reversed the downward trend. Increasing in numbers and expanding into areas of former habitation, the muskox persists as a unique component of the Arctic ecosystem. *P. E. Reynolds, R. T. Bowyer, and D. R. Klein*

Size

Males are larger than females.
Total Length: 2.086–2.645 m (males); 1.93–2.44 m (females)
Length of Tail: 70–120 mm (males); 60–120 mm (females)
Weight: 186–410 kg (650 kg in captivity) (males); 160–191 kg (235 kg in captivity) (females)

Identification

The muskox is a short, stocky ungulate (hoofed mammal) with a dark brown coat of long, coarse hair that hangs almost to the ground and, in winter, a thick layer of fine wool (quivit) beneath its heavy outer pelage. The muzzle, lower legs, and a patch in the middle of the back (saddle) are white. The thick coat and a prominent shoulder hump, similar to that of the American bison, give the

muskox a massive appearance, but the animal is relatively small, with a shoulder height of 1,217 to 1,521 mm. Both sexes have permanent horns, which begin as a rounded prominence (boss) on the forehead, curve down and outward along the side of the head, and turn upward to end in sharp tips.

Recent Synonyms

Bos moschatus

Other Common Names

Oomingmak

Status

Near extinction at the end of the 19th century because of human exploitation; now protected in Canada and populations re-established in Alaska

Subspecies

Ovibos moschatus moschatus, Arctic coastal Alaska eastward to Keewatin and the Hudson Bay coast of Manitoba
Ovibos moschatus niphoecus, northeastern Keewatin
Ovibos moschatus wardi, Greenland, Ellesmere Island, and Arctic Ocean islands of Northwest Territories

References

Mammalian Species 302

Bighorn sheep | *Ovis canadensis*

Considered by many a symbol of mountain wilderness, bighorn sheep are distributed throughout most mountainous areas of western North America, from northern Mexico to central British Columbia. Bighorns prefer open, treeless habitat, where they avoid predation by running to cliffs or very steep terrain. The availability of suitable "escape" terrain near foraging sites limits their local distribution. In winter, northern populations require foraging areas near escape terrain that is kept free of snow by steep slopes, mild temperatures, or wind. For desert populations, the availability of water appears to limit local distribution. Because of their specific habitat requirements, bighorn sheep exist in discrete populations, isolated to varying degrees from other populations. Populations usually include 50–150 sheep and rarely number more than 200 individuals. In much of their range, particularly in deserts, bighorn sheep occupy small islands of suitable habitat surrounded by large tracts of unsuitable habitat (flat deserts or forested areas), which they may at times traverse but do not use on a sustained basis.

Many bighorn sheep populations are migratory, with distinct winter and summer ranges. In some populations, seasonal migration involves simply moving a few hundred meters along a mountainside. Other populations use traditional routes to move 10–20 km between different ranges. Males have more complex and varied seasonal migrations than females, and a male may move as much as 50–60 km between parts of his yearly range. The reasons for long-distance movements include avoiding deep snow or predators and searching for high-quality forage, salt licks, water, or mates.

Bighorn sheep are mostly grazers and eat a wide variety of grasses and forbs. Their diet varies greatly with season, habitat, and geographic region. In desert populations, cacti are sometimes used as food and as a source of water. Browse can be an important part of the diet, particularly in spring and early summer. Natural salt licks are a major attraction, particularly in May–June. Highway salt and salt blocks placed for cattle attract sheep year-round.

Bighorns are very gregarious, and are usually found in groups of five to eighty individuals, with larger groups possible in some of the largest populations. The sexes live in separate groups for most of the year outside the rut, and often use different habitats. Females, lambs, and young males form nursery groups. Between the ages of one and four years, males gradually abandon nursery groups and join bachelor male groups. Male groups break up when males join females for the rut. The reasons for sexual segregation are not well understood, but probably involve differences in food requirememnts and predation risk. Females and lambs are more vulnerable than males to some predators.

Ovis canadensis

Although females from different populations may have overlapping seasonal ranges, it is extremely rare for females born in one population to emigrate permanently to another population. Male dispersal is also rare, but during the rut some males will leave their natal population to rut within another population. Within their natal population, however, adult sheep do not appear to associate preferentially with their relatives, unlike in some other ungulate species. During the rut, dominant males attempt to sequentially defend and mate with individual estrous females. Younger, subordinate males sometimes move in as a group to separate the estrous female from the dominant male and quickly mate with her. Several males commonly mate with one female during her estrus. A dominant male will often try to isolate an estrous female from competing males, usually by leading her to the periphery of the range or to a cliff site where he can block the only access to her. Although dominant males secure most of the matings, some lambs are fathered by subordinate rams. Dominance among males is dependent mostly upon age and body size, and is usually established through ritualized displays, front-leg kicks, and horn clashes. When two closely-matched males engage in a dominance contest they can fight for hours, rearing up on their hinds legs a few meters apart and clashing head-on. Although the massive curled horns and pneumatic structure of the skull absorb much of the impact, injuries and even death can result from these fights. Much less ritualized clashing occurs during the rut: males in pursuit of estrous females will hit each other on any part of the body.

Gestation lasts about 175 days. Individual ewes leave the group and seek precipitous terrain in areas with low densities of predators to give birth. The lamb can follow its mother within a day and ewes form groups within a few days of parturition. A single lamb is produced in almost all cases: twin births may be as rare as one in 500. In northern populations, the rut is highly synchronized, with most copulations taking place over a 12–15 day period in late November and early December. Most lambs are born in late May. In these populations, late-born lambs can suffer high mortality. In southern populations, the rut is more prolonged, and in some desert populations, breeding and births may occur in almost any month. Females may produce their first lamb at two years of age under favorable conditions, but in many populations, the majority of females first lamb at 3 years of age. Lambs weigh about 4 kg at birth; male lambs are heavier than females. Lactation lasts about 4–5 months, with a very slow and gradual weaning process. Lambs weigh 25–35 kg at weaning. Sexual dimorphism in weight increases from about 10 percent in lambs and yearlings to 70 percent in adults.

Females can live up to 19 years and males to 14 years, but even in the absence of hunting, few females survive beyond 15 years and very few males live past 12 years. Mortality of lambs is generally high and variable (20–80 percent) from year to year. Yearling mortality tends to vary between 5 and 30 percent. Sheep aged 2–6 years have low mortality (about 5 percent for females and 10 percent for males) in most years, but disease outbreaks can result in extremely high mortality,

over 80 percent in some cases. Mortality increases for sheep aged 7 years and older, especially for males.

Bighorn rams are hunted in most populations outside protected areas. Limited female hunts are allowed for some populations of the subspecies *canadensis*. Hunting mortality is usually less than 5 percent a year but can account for more than 60 percent of the mortality among males older than 4 years. Poaching is a problem in some populations because of the very high trophy value placed on the horns of mature males.

Other than hunting and poaching, major sources of death are predation and disease. Predators include wolves *(Canis lupus)*, coyotes *(Canis latrans)*, and cougars *(Puma concolor)*. Golden eagles *(Aquila chrysaetos)* take a few very young lambs. The importance of predation as a source of mortality can vary greatly between populations and from year to year. Diseases such as mange and pneumonia cause massive die-offs of bighorn sheep populations. Die-offs caused by pneumonia are sometimes followed by several years of very high lamb mortality, which appear to be linked to lingering effects of the disease, and which retards population recovery.

Bighorn sheep are hosts for numerous parasites. In many northern populations, all individuals are infected with nematode lungworms *(Protostrongylus stilesi* and *P. rushi)*. The normal life cycle of the lungworm involves a terrestrial snail as an intermediate host, but the fetus can be infected through the placenta before birth. The effects of lungworm on bighorn sheep are not well understood. In the past, lungworms were thought to be a cause of pneumonia, but pneumonia is rare and is mostly limited to populations south of 51°N. It appears that pneumonia is mostly a bacterial disease and that most sheep do not suffer any deleterious consequences from lung-worm infection. In some bighorn populations, however, heavy prenatal infections have been linked with high mortality of young lambs. Lungworms probably co-evolved with bighorn sheep; the pathogens that cause pneumonia were likely introduced to North America by European domestic livestock. Bighorn sheep are very vulnerable to diseases transmitted by domestic livestock, and are incompatible with domestic sheep. Some desert populations also appear threatened by introduced exotic ungulates.

Many populations in the United States, particularly of the desert subspecies, were extirpated during the last century, but reintroduction efforts have repopulated many ranges where there is suitable habitat. However, several historic ranges are no longer suitable for reintroduction because of habitat degradation. Reintroduction might be possible in parts of Mexico. In general, reintroductions of the desert subspecies have been less successful than for northern subspecies. Bighorn sheep, possibly of a subspecies different from *Ovis canadensis canadensis*, were formerly found in steep river valleys as far east as the Dakotas. Bighorns of the *canadensis* subspecies have been introduced in some of the eastern ranges. *M. Festa-Bianchet*

Size
Males are larger than females; body and horn size vary considerably among subspecies and populations. These measurements are for the largest subspecies, *O. c. canadensis,* for individuals seven years of age and older.

Total length: 1.6–1.9 m (males); 1.55–1.7 m (females)

Length of tail: 80–120 mm (males); 70–120 mm (females)

Weight: 75–105 kg in May, 95–135 kg in October (males); 48–64 kg in May, 65–85 kg in October (females)

Identification
Bighorn sheep and Dall's sheep *(Ovis dalli)* do not overlap in range. Bighorns are brown with a white rump patch; Dall's sheep are either white or dark gray. Female bighorns are sometimes confused with mountain goats *(Oreamnos americanus)* during the spring molt, but mountain goats are white with sharp black horns, and molting female bighorns are cream-colored with brown, blunt horns. Among yearlings the horns of males are almost twice as long as those of females; the horns of adult males are about four times longer than those of females.

Other Common Names
Mountain sheep (a term used for all wild sheep). Different subspecies are referred to as Rocky Mountain bighorn, California bighorn, and desert bighorn.

Status
Reintroduced and common in much of its former range in the United States. Locally rare and declining, especially some desert populations. Common in most of its historic range in Canada. Extirpated in most of its range in Mexico.

Subspecies
Ovis canadensis californiana, scattered populations east of the Rocky Mountains from central California to central British Columbia

Ovis canadensis canadensis, Rocky Mountains from Colorado to about 55° N in eastern British Columbia

Ovis canadensis mexicana, western Sonora; extinct in much of its former range in Sonora and Chihuahua

Ovis canadensis nelsoni, desert habitat from central Baja California to southwestern Colorado; scattered populations to eastern Texas

Ovis canadensis weemsi, extreme southern Baja California

References
Mammalian Species 230; Geist, 1971; Wishart, 1978

Dall's sheep | *Ovis dalli*

Dall's sheep are gregarious ungulates (hoofed mammals). These large herbivores inhabit extremely rugged mountains with subalpine grasses and low shrubs, on which they feed. These sheep typically migrate between summer and wind-swept winter ranges. Adult males and females seldom occur together outside rut (the mating season).

Dall's sheep are polygynous. Large, dominant males fight for possession of estrous females and do most of the mating. Dall's sheep do not have territories or hold harems, but males court, defend, and copulate with individual females, and then move on in search of additional mates. Fights between males are impressive encounters in which the edges of their massive horns are slammed together forcefully. The impact can be heard kilometers away. Rutting activities peak in November and December and then wane as the sheep become more solitary.

Lambs are born at secluded sites among precipitous cliffs in early to mid-May. Most females give birth to a single lamb; twinning is rare. The gestation period is 171 days, and births are highly synchronized. The lambs weigh 3–4 kg at birth, and

Ovis dalli

are able to follow their mothers over rough terrain within 24 hours. They are weaned by 3–5 months of age and may weigh 30 kg by 9 months. The horns continue to grow throughout life and sheep, especially males, can be aged from the annual rings of growth on these structures. Some older males may wear down (broom) the tips of their horns.

Dall's sheep are preyed upon by wolves *(Canus lupus)*, coyotes *(C. latrans)*, grizzly bears *(Ursus arctos)*, black bears *(U. americanus)*, wolverines *(Gulo gulo)*, and lynx *(Lynx canadensis);* golden eagles *(Aquila chrysaetos)* prey on lambs. The steep, rugged terrain in which the sheep live reduces their vulnerability to predators, but some sheep die from accidental falls and avalanches. Deep snow, low quality of forage, and high population density all have been associated with mortality

in this species. The ability of lambs to gain sufficient body mass over the summer to overcome harsh winter conditions is a critical factor in their survival. Only mature males are hunted, and current levels of harvest have little effect on most sheep populations.

Dall's sheep harbor a number of disease-causing organisms, including lungworms *(Protostrongylus)*, but these parasites have not been associated with the large-scale die-offs reported for *O. canadensis.*

Unlike other populations of wild sheep in North America, Dall's sheep still inhabit pristine, undisturbed environments. Human disturbance, development, and subsequent loss of habitat are not yet pressing problems for these unique mountain ungulates. *R. T. Bowyer and D. M. Leslie, Jr.*

Size
Males are much heavier than females.
Total length: 1.3–1.78 m (males); 1.324–1.62 m (females)
Length of tail: 70–115 mm (males); 70–90 mm (females)
Weight: 73–110 kg (males); 46–50 kg (females)

Identification
Ovis dalli is distinguished from *O. canadensis,* its only North American congener, by smaller body size and smaller, more widely flaring horns. *O. dalli* occurs farther north than *O. canadensis,* although their distributions converge in British Columbia. The subspecies of *O. dalli* differ in color: *O. d. dalli* and *O. d. kenainesis* have white pelage, and *O. d. stonei* has silver to grayish-black pelage with a white muzzle, leg trimmings, and rump patch.

Recent Synonyms
Ovis cowani
Ovis fannini
Ovis montana

Other Common Names
Stone's sheep, Fannin's sheep

Status
Locally abundant in dry, mountainous terrain at high latitudes

Subspecies
Ovis dalli dalli, most of Alaska and Yukon; extreme western Mackenzie; extreme northwestern British Columbia
Ovis dalli kenainesis, Kenai Peninsula of Alaska
Ovis dalli stonei, south-central Yukon and north-central British Columbia

References
Mammalian Species 393

Order Rodentia

Rodentia is the largest order of mammals, comprising 28 living families and more than 2,000 species. This worldwide group is also diverse ecologically, with aquatic or semiaquatic, fossorial, terrestrial, and arboreal representatives.

Muridae is the largest family of mammals (281 genera, 1,326 species) and includes the mice, rats, hamsters, voles, lemmings, and gerbils. These rodents are most diverse in the tropical and subtropical areas of the New and Old Worlds. Additionally, murids exhibit a wide range of food habits, and diets may include plant material, invertebrates, and small vertebrates.

The Sciuridae (50 genera, 273 species) includes the squirrels, chipmunks, marmots, and prairie dogs. Sciurids tolerate a wide range of environmental conditions and are found from the Arctic to the tropics and in arid as well as humid areas. The Sciuridae includes terrestrial (e.g., chipmunks), arboreal (e.g., tree and flying squirrels), and semifossorial (e.g., ground squirrels, marmots, and prairie dogs) species. They are usually herbivorous, but occasionally eat insects and small vertebrates.

The jerboas and jumping mice (Dipodidae) are also widespread in distribution, with most species occurring in the Old World. This family includes 52 species that inhabit arid deserts, semideserts, and steppes. The jerboas are most numerous in the Palearctic region (45 species), and the North American representatives of this family are limited to the 2 genera and 3 species in the subfamily Zapodinae. They are also proficient burrowers and may attempt to regulate environmental conditions within the burrow by periodically plugging the entrance hole. Their diet is dominated by seeds, other plant parts, and insects.

The semiaquatic beavers (Castoridae), two of the largest species of rodents, occur throughout the Northern Hemisphere, with one species in the Old World and the other in North America. They feed on the leaves, twigs, roots, and bark of trees, often storing logs under water for a winter food supply.

Although the Nearctic rodent fauna is dominated by murids and sciurids, Geomyidae (pocket gophers, 35 species) and Heteromyidae (pocket mice, kangaroo mice and kangaroo rats, 59 species) are also important. Pocket gophers (Geomyidae) are fossorial and solitary animals that occur in localized or isolated areas

North American porcupine *(Erethizon dorsatum)*

with soil suitable for digging. Their tunnel systems may be extensive and are marked by closed mounds of dirt.

Pocket mice, kangaroo mice, and kangaroo rats (Heteromyidae) inhabit a range of environments from arid deserts to humid tropical forests. They generally rest in their burrows during the day, often plugging the entrance to create a more favorable burrow environment. The heteromyid diet is dominated by seeds and vegetation, but may also include insects and other invertebrates.

The mammal fauna of the Nearctic includes two large-sized rodents—the beaver (described above) and the North American porcupine, *Erethizon dorsatum* (Erethizontidae)—and the medium-sized mountain beaver, *Aplodontia rufa* (Aplodontidae). Unlike its Neotropical relatives, the North American porcupine is mostly terrestrial, but frequently climbs trees seeking food or shelter. Porcupines are active throughout the year and eat leaves, twigs, seeds, nuts, berries, roots, and bark. The mountain beaver is smaller than both the beaver and porcupine, and is endemic to North America. This rodent occurs from southwestern British Columbia to northern California and inhabits forests and other densely vegetated areas. It burrows and constructs tunnel systems with multiple openings, often connecting nesting and feeding areas. Mountain beavers eat plant matter, but take twigs and bark when green forage is not available.

References
Mammalian Species 120; Hoffmann et al., 1993;
Holden 1993a; Musser and Carleton, 1993;
Nowak 1991; Patton 1993a, 1993b; Wilson
1993b, 1993c

Family Aplodontidae

The single species of mountain beaver is limited in distribution to coastal forests of northwestern North America. The name is a misnomer, as mountain beavers are neither particularly montane, nor are they aquatic like true beavers. Nocturnal and secretive, the mountain beaver spends most of its time underground in burrows and interconnected nesting and feeding chambers. They are solitary by nature, although other animals may also use their burrow systems. Their underground lifestyle allows these non-hibernating animals to store adequate food.

Mountain beavers are strictly vegetarians, and take a variety of plant foods. They harvest mainly herbaceous vegetation, including ferns, but are also capable of climbing trees in search of food if necessary. This habit has made the mountain beaver *Aplodontia non grata* in tree plantations, where the animals may cause damage by nipping branches. They deposit feces in designated chambers in the burrow system, and practice coprophagy, or reingestion of the fecal pellets, in order to maximize the nutritional intake from harvested food items.

This family is considered primitive in the evolution of rodent groups. Individuals reach sexual maturity in their second year, somewhat later than many other rodents. Mating occurs early in the year, and the young are born in the spring in a single litter. The gestation period is about a month, and usually only 2 or 3 young compose a litter. Lactation lasts for a couple of months, and the young remain in the natal burrow throughout the summer.

During dispersal in the fall, they are particularly vulnerable to predators such as raptors and coyotes. Because they are vulnerable to predation as long as they remain aboveground, they tend not to disperse over long distances. If they survive the first year, they may live up to six years, exceptionally long for rodents.

Reference
Alderton, 1996

North American Genera
Aplodontia

Mountain beaver │ *Aplodontia rufa*

Rather undistinguished-looking outwardly, somewhat resembling a giant pocket gopher, the mountain beaver is nonetheless very interesting biologically. The only species in its family, it is considered the most primitive living rodent, with an ancestry that goes back into the first half of the Tertiary Period, when modern mammals first evolved. It has no close living relatives and is found only in the Pacific Northwest, from southern British Columbia to northern California. The mountain beaver's skull is distinctive: it is flattened and almost triangular, with high cheek teeth that are conical except for a ridge along one side. Its diet is strictly limited to plants, and includes several species that other vertebrates find toxic, or at least unpalatable, such as rhododendron, bracken fern, devil's club, and stinging nettle. One mystery surrounding the mountain beaver is the origin of its common name, since the species is more often found in lowland than montane forests and is neither genetically nor behaviorally a close ally of the true beaver (*Castor canadensis*).

The mountain beaver prefers to live in moist forests and for-

est openings, especially where the understory is dense with sword fern and brambly thickets of salmonberry, blackberry, and thimbleberry. These plants are used not only as food but also to conceal the numerous entrances to extensive burrow systems. Many a hiker has seen a 15-cm (6-inch) diameter burrow opening under a tree root or clump of sword fern, or has unwittingly stepped right through the top of a shallow tunnel —without ever seeing the primarily nocturnal and fossorial mountain beaver.

The mountain beaver builds an underground nest of fern fronds, grass, and fine twigs, in which a litter of 2 to 4 young is born between February and May, following a month's gestation period. Almost naked and blind at birth, young mountain beavers develop very slowly, probably weaning in the nest at 6 to 8 weeks of age, but not reaching maturity until their second year.

Though capable of swimming and climbing, the mountain beaver rarely ventures far from its burrow entrance. As its small eyes and ears but strong set of sensory whiskers would indicate, it sees and hears poorly but has keen tactile and olfactory senses. It does not hibernate, but may stay underground in winter, especially where temperatures are low and snowfall high. In the fall some vegetation is harvested and dried, probably both for nest material and winter caches, but the caches are nowhere near the complete larder that pikas (*Ochotona princeps* and *O. collaris*) put by. In winter there is a diet shift from deciduous leaves to evergreen salal and Oregon grape, plus the bark of evergreen and deciduous trees. Damage to evergreen seedlings in reforestation projects, as well as to cultivated berries and gardens, can make the mountain beaver an unwelcome neighbor.

Aplodontia rufa

Many other animals make themselves at home in *Aplodontia* burrows, and fur-bearing predators rely on this species as a staple food resource. Native Americans are said to have eaten mountain beaver, but 19th-century naturalists who sampled it reported the meat to be tough, dark and strong—not even fit for dogs. Its skins were used by Northwest Coast tribes for robes and blankets. Naturalist Stanley Jewett reported sales of skins in Oregon for 10–20 cents apiece in the early 20th century. Today these skins (and skeletons) may be most useful as specimens for natural history collections. *E. Kritzman*

Size
Total length: 238–470 (354) mm
Length of tail: 19–55 (37) mm
Weight: 806–1,325 (1,065) g

Identification
The mountain beaver is dark brown with a whitish spot below each ear. It has a short, furred tail, small eyes and ears, and long vibrissae and claws.

Other Common Names
Sewellel, boomer

Status
Common, limited

Subspecies
Aplodontia rufa californica, Sierra Nevada Mountains, California and southwestern corner of Nevada
Aplodontia rufa humboldtiana, coastal northern California
Aplodontia rufa nigra, Point Arena, California
Aplodontia rufa pacifica, western Oregon, extreme northwestern California

Aplodontia rufa phaea, vicinity of Point Reyes, California
Aplodontia rufa rainieri, Cascade Mountains from southern British Columbia to the Columbia River
Aplodontia rufa rufa, southwestern British Columbia, western Washington, Cascade Mountains in Oregon and California

References
Mammalian Species 431; Bailey, 1936; Ingles, 1965

Family Sciuridae

With 50 genera and 273 species worldwide, squirrels are an important group of rodents. North America boasts 66 species in 8 genera. The family includes chipmunks, marmots, ground squirrels, prairie dogs, and flying squirrels in addition to tree squirrels. With the exception of flying squirrels, sciurids tend to be diurnal and among the more visible of rodents. Size variation is considerable in this group, ranging from tiny chipmunks to heavy-bodied marmots in North America.

"Flying squirrel" is a good example of an imprecise common name, as technically *Glaucomys* glides rather than flies. The habit undoubtedly developed as an extension of long-distance leaping from branch to branch and tree to tree in ancestral squirrels. Flying squirrels tend to glide downwards from a higher vantage point in one tree to a lower one in another, but they are able to use their well-developed gliding membranes to bank and turn and even rise a bit just before landing. They tend to rely on preexisting tree holes for nesting sites, although occasionally they take advantage of man-made structures and build their nests in attics. They are active year-round, although less so in the winter when they rely more on stored food.

Tree squirrels are perhaps the most obvious rodents in the world due to their diurnal habits and the ability of some species to adapt readily to suburban environments. They are strongly vegetarian, feeding on a variety of nuts, fruits, bark, buds, and even leaves in some cases. True tree squirrels in the genus *Sciurus* reach maximum diversity in the New World. Most are arboreal, although they may readily descend to the ground in search of food. Stong incisors allow them to gnaw open even the toughest of nuts, and they also bury acorns and other nuts underground for later retrieval during times of food shortage. They do not hibernate, but build sturdy nests in tree hollows or in the upper branches of trees.

Chipmunks are small, scansorial squirrels that have adapted to forest understory and montane habitats. Marmots, prairie dogs and ground squirrels are the most terrestrial members of the family. Several species of this latter group are almost fossorial, forming large colonies with underground burrow systems. However, all forage on the surface of the ground, and most are diurnal.

References
Hoffmann et al., 1993

North American Genera
Tamias
Marmota
Ammospermophilus
Spermophilus
Cynomys
Sciurus
Tamiasciurus
Glaucomys

Alpine chipmunk | *Tamias alpinus*

The alpine chipmunk occurs in the Sierra Nevada of California in the Hudsonian, Arctic-alpine, and Canadian life zones. It ranges higher in elevation (from about 2,300 to 3,900 m) than any other Sierra Nevada chipmunk species. It shows a trend toward breeding later at higher elevations. No active nests have been found, but the alpine chipmunk probably makes dens among rocks or in the ground. Litters consist of four or five young, born in July; active young have been observed by the end of July. By October, young-of-the-year reach adult size and are ready for hibernation.

Tamias alpinus occurs in rock-bordered alpine meadows and on talus slopes near timberline of the highest peaks of the Sierra Nevada. It occupies large rock slides bordered by lodgepole pine. Alpine chipmunks scamper with great agility through the jumbled rocks of boulder fields; few other species of chipmunks have such capability.

The alpine chipmunk's diet consists mostly of seeds from small alpine plants and sedges. They also consume fungi and many kinds of forbs and grasses. Plants collected by alpine chipmunks include blue blossom *(Ceanothus),* bitter cherry

Tamias alpinus

(Prunus emarginata), currant *(Ribes),* and huckleberry *(Vaccinium).* Pussypaws *(Spraguea umellata)* is a favorite food. *Tamias alpinus* gathers seeds by pulling grass stalks down to reach the heads and then stuffing its cheekpouches; there may be hundreds of seeds in the cheekpouches at any one time. Occasionally, the chipmunks may be predators of the eggs and young of the rosy finch *(Leucosticte arctua).*

The alpine chipmunk is the most common mammal near timberline and shares this habitat with the pika, yellow-bellied marmot, bighorn sheep, and ermine. Boulder fields offer good protection from predation. No predators have been described for the alpine chipmunk, and predation must be low, as evidenced by this chipmunk's diurnal behavior. Often one can watch these chipmunks chase each other at great speeds around trees and over the boulder fields. At the same time they have a clear view of potential aerial or terrestrial predators from their timberline vistas. Their call is a thin, high-pitched, repeated "sweet, sweet, sweet . . ." They also utter escape chatters, barks, and other calls.

Despite their cold and snowy habitat, alpine chipmunks can be seen running across the snow in fall. They are active until mid-October and re-emerge from hibernation in June. A likely competitor, the lodgepole chipmunk *(Tamias speciosus),* occurs over much of the alpine chipmunk's range and may restrict it to the higher elevations. *W. L. Gannon*

Size

Total length: 166–184 (174) mm (males); 169–181 (177) mm (females)
Length of tail: 63–81 (71) mm (males); 63–76 (72) mm (females)
Weight: 27.5–45.5 g

Identification

In the Yosemite region of the Sierra Nevada of California, the alpine chipmunk is the palest-colored species of chipmunk. In the same area it is also the smallest, except for the least chipmunk *(Tamias minimus).* Compared to other chipmunks, the alpine chipmunk has a shorter, bushier, and broader tail, which is frosted above and black at the tip. The underfur of the body is bright orange rather than dull yellow. Throughout its range, regardless of season, the alpine chipmunk is a small, pale chipmunk, orange (never yellowish) on its belly, with a tail that is brownish-grayish-black overlain with clay color. It has a strong preference for high-elevation boulder fields.

Recent Synonyms

Eutamias alpinus

Other Common Names

Mountain chipmunk

Status

Common, limited geographically

References

Mammalian Species 461; Grinnell and Storer, 1924

Yellow-pine chipmunk | *Tamias amoenus*

Tamias amoenus is widely distributed from Mammoth Pass in the Sierra Nevada Mountains of central California, northern Nevada, and Utah, northward throughout the western United States and, in Canada, the southern half of British Columbia and the Rocky Mountains of western Alberta. It is usually found in chaparral areas at the borders of meadows and rocky outcrops and near open forests of yellow pine or juniper. It is found over a wide range of elevations in Transition and Canadian Life Zones, from about 950 m to timberline at about 2,800 m. Each subspecies occupies a rather narrow band of this elevational range. Nearly half of the subspecies are restricted to small geographic areas.

Most of the slight differences among the subspecies are indistinguishable in individual animals. Obvious intergradation occurs in several subspecies at contiguous locations and it is difficult to identify individuals unless a series of animals is available for comparison. The races differ in color of the sides of the body, ranging from pinkish-cinnamon or cinnamon-buff to brownish or tawny shades. The crown of the head is black or grayish-black, mixed with cinnamon; the rump and thighs vary from grayish-cinnamon to grayish-buff; the hind feet from pale- pinkish-cinnamon to buff or brownish. The ears are brownish-black, margined on the back with buffy shades. Five dark longitudinal stripes on the body are separated by four unequal pale stripes. On each side of the head are three dark stripes, which are black or brownish-black mixed with tawny or cinnamon shades, separated by two pale stripes, which vary from creamy white through gray, mixed with tawny or cinnamon color.

Shrubs, grasses, and nearby cone-bearing trees produce the seeds that are favored for food. A variety of bulbs, flowers, fruits, fungi, plant buds, and even birds' eggs, insects, and small animals are eaten. Yellow-pine chipmunks tend to forage in open, sunny areas where trees and bushes are widely spaced and where half-rotten stumps, logs, or rocks are adjacent to their food plants.

Winter food, carried in internal cheek pouches, is stored in the nest chamber, which is underground or in a rock crevice. One underground nest was described as being 1.5 m beneath the surface and reached by a tunnel about 3 m long. One food store that was examined weighed 190 g and contained about 68,000 food items. Tree nests, made of dry grass, located up to 18 m above the ground, are also sometimes used. Most mammals that hibernate store fat in preparation for their period of dormancy, but in most chipmunks hibernation is intermittent, with frequent brief periods of activity during the winter, when the stored food is eaten. Energy is conserved by various depths of torpor and inactivity during the winter.

Tamias amoenus

Breeding occurs soon after emergence from four or five months of winter dormancy, usually in late April, and an average of four young are born after a 28-day gestation period. The young emerge from the nest in early July and are nursed and cared for by the mother until August. At birth the young have loose, translucent skin, with no hair except the vibrissae; the toes are webbed and end in tiny, white claws. At ten days of age hair growth has extended to the tail, shoulders, and flanks, and the adult pattern of head and body stripes is apparent. By 20 days the fur is sleek, standing partially erect; the toes are separated, and the hind legs can make spasmodic thrusts. On about day 22 the external ears open; the eyelids open at about day 27, when the fur is fully developed, with brighter color and even more prominent markings than are found on adults. On emergence from the den the young are curious and fearless—easy prey for the hawk, weasel, bobcat, or coyote looking for a meal. Survival is often as low as 30 percent, with winter dormancy the only period of relative safety from predation. *D. A. Sutton*

Size
Females are slightly larger than males.
Total length: 186–238 (211) mm
Length of tail: 72–109 (92) mm
Weight: 36–50 g

Identification
Tamias amoenus is larger than *T. alpinus* and *T. minimus,* and smaller than all other associated chipmunks; its reddish color resembles that of *T. speciosus,* with which it has been confused; it is less gray than *T. minimus* and *T. senex.*

Recent Synonyms
Eutamias amoenus
Tamias quadrivittatus amoenus

Status
Common in northwestern states and southwestern Canada

Subspecies
Tamias amoenus affinis (Columbian chipmunk), central Washington, southwestern British Columbia
Tamias amoenus albiventris (white-bellied chipmunk), northeastern Oregon, southeastern Washington
Tamias amoenus amoenus (Klamath chipmunk), northeastern California, eastern Oregon, southern Idaho
Tamias amoenus canicaudus (gray-tailed chipmunk), eastern Washington, northern Idaho
Tamias amoenus caurinus (Olympic chipmunk), Olympic Peninsula of Washington
Tamias amoenus celeris (Humboldt chipmunk), Humboldt County, Nevada
Tamias amoenus cratericus (Lava Beds chipmunk), Butte County, Idaho
Tamias amoenus felix (tawny chipmunk), western Oregon, western Washington, and southwestern British Columbia

Tamias amoenus ludibundus (Hollister's chipmunk), east-central British Columbia, west-central Alberta
Tamias amoenus luteiventris (buff-bellied chipmunk), western Wyoming, western Montana, southeastern British Columbia, southwestern Alberta
Tamias amoenus monoensis (Mono chipmunk), east-central California
Tamias amoenus ochraceus (ochraceous chipmunk), northwestern California
Tamias amoenus septentrionalis (Ootsa Lake chipmunk), west-central British Columbia
Tamias amoenus vallicola (Bitterroot Valley chipmunk), west-central Montana

References
Mammalian Species 390; Howell, 1929

Gray-footed chipmunk | *Tamias canipes*

Tamias canipes occurs in the Gallinas, Sacramento, Jicarilla, Capitan, White, and Guadalupe mountains of New Mexico, and in the Sierra Diablo and Guadalupe mountains in Texas. Its elevational range is about 1,600–3,600 meters. Fossils are known from Culberson County, Texas.

Gray-footed chipmunks are most active shortly after sunrise, at which time they do most of their feeding. They are found on rocky slopes where brush and timber offer shade and cover and cliffs afford runways, perches, and safe retreats. They are skillful at climbing rocks, cliffs, trees, and bushes. These chipmunks are shy; in thick brush and forests they are more often heard than seen. Their light "chipper" often is heard from bushes, and they may utter a slow, repeated, low "chuck-chuck-chuck" from a log, rock, or low branch of a tree. The call always ceases as soon as danger is suspected. When alarmed, they usually run to the ground and enter a burrow or disappear among rocks, brush, or crevices; occasionally they take to the trees. From these refuges, they soon reappear, care-

fully peer about, and return to gathering food. They either hibernate or remain in their dens feeding on their winter stores during cold weather; in late autumn they show no indication of becoming extremely fat as do other mammals that hibernate.

This species is a small, grayish chipmunk. The upperparts are marked with four whitish and five brownish stripes. The nape and shoulders usually have a wash of gray. The population of gray-footed chipmunks on a lava field in south-central New Mexico is darker than the population in the nearby Sacramento Mountains. The lava-dwelling population has more black hairs, but the total difference in color is not great. There is considerable geographic variation; those from the Sacramento Mountains are much larger and darker than those from the Guadalupe, Capitan, and Gallinas mountains.

One litter of about four young is produced each year, between mid-May and August. There is little time for August-born young to develop and gather winter stores of food before the weather turns cold.

Tamias canipes is primarily a forest-dwelling chipmunk, although some descend to lower life zones such as the lava field near Carrizozo, New Mexico. Its favorite haunts are downed logs at the edge of clearings. It also occurs in dense stands of timber and on brushy hillsides, particularly where crevices in rocks offer retreats. Except for deer mice, this chipmunk is the most common mammal in the Guadalupe Mountains, Texas, but in other parts of its range it is uncommon. In south-central New Mexico, *T. canipes* occurs in a variety of habitats. It ranges upward from pinyon-juniper to spruce-fir communities, but is most numerous in ponderosa pine and Douglas fir communities. In the Guadalupe Mountains, it inhabits coniferous forests. It also is found in small numbers below 2,100 meters elevation, where it is associated with rocky outcroppings.

Nests often are constructed in cavities of downed timber. One nest was found underground among roots of a decaying stump. Gray-footed chipmunks feed to some extent on seeds of spruces and firs, but acorns seem to form their principal food supply in late summer and autumn. Acorns are gathered and stored from the time they begin to ripen until they are all gone or buried by snow. Scattered acorn shells are the most

Tamias canipes

common mark of feeding grounds, and cheek pouches often contain one large or several small acorns. Sunflower, Douglas fir, and other seeds also are gathered and eaten or stored, as are currants, gooseberries, mushrooms, green vegetation, and insects. On a lava field in south-central New Mexico, the cheek pouches of one chipmunk were full of juniper berries. Mammals occurring in the same habitat include cottontails, rock squirrels, Texas antelope squirrels, pocket gophers, rock pocket mice, cactus mice, pinyon mice, white-throated, Mexican, and southern plains woodrats, porcupines, skunks, ringtails, bobcats, mountain lions, black bears, coyotes, gray foxes, elk, and mule deer. Two protozoan parasites have been reported, but no other parasites are known.   *T. L. Best*

Size
Males are slightly smaller than females.
Total length: 210–264 (237) mm
Length of tail: 91–115 (101) mm
Weight: 65–75 g

Identification
Tamias canipes is distinguished from all other chipmunks by the gray dorsal surfaces of the hind feet. Compared with *T. cinereicollis*, *T. canipes* has dorsal stripes that are mixed blackish and rusty; the centers are solid black

in *T. cinereicollis*. Compared with *T. quadrivittatus*, *T. canipes* has broader eye stripes, darker and grayer head, and shoulders with a grayish wash; the shoulder region is yellowish-orange in *T. quadrivittatus*.

Recent Synonyms
Eutamias canipes

Status
Common

Subspecies
Tamias canipes canipes, south-central New Mexico and western Texas
Tamias canipes sacramentoensis, south-central New Mexico

References
Mammalian Species 411; Bailey, 1931; Findley et al., 1975

Gray-collared chipmunk | *Tamias cinereicollis*

The gray-collared chipmunk is found only in montane coniferous forest at elevations of 1,950–3,440 meters. It is most common at 2,100–3,300 meters. Its range includes the mountain and plateau region of central Arizona, from the Bill Williams and San Francisco mountains southward across the Mogollon Plateau to the White Mountains and Prieto Plateau, and into the Black, Datil, Elk, Magdalena, Mimbres, Mogollon, San Francisco, and San Mateo mountains of New Mexico. Fossil remains have been found in Luna County, New Mexico (possibly late Wisconsinan in age). A jaw fragment was recovered from late Pleistocene deposits in Culberson County, Texas, but that specimen may be *T. canipes.*

This active chipmunk is a good climber. It will climb even the tallest trees to gather food, and often takes to the trees for protection, hiding in dense foliage. Its favorite haunts are log piles near clearings, near the edges of burned forests, or in dense pine, spruce, or fir forests. Generally it is shy, and when alarmed it commonly disappears among the logs or trees. When not alarmed, the gray-collared chipmunk may sit on a stump or log and slowly wave its tail from side to side as it makes a low "chuck-chuck-chuck" or sharp "chipper" call. The alarm call is a shrill, rapid "chipper."

Tamias cinereicollis stores acorns in large quantities in the ground or in hollow logs. It may hibernate from late November to mid-March, or not at all. This chipmunk does not become noticeably fat in autumn, but it does gather food for winter. Although its tracks can be abundant on snow in the mountains, probably during the coldest part of winter it remains in its den, either sleeping or feeding on stored food.

The gray-collared chipmunk has five black or brown dorsal stripes; the outermost pair may be difficult to discern. There are two whitish and three brown facial stripes, and the forehead is brown and washed with pale gray. The cheeks, neck, shoulders, anterior part of back, and rump are also gray. Summer pelage (May–July) is softer, fuller, and brighter than autumn pelage. In the fall and winter, the tints of gray, black, and white are not as pure and the sides are tinged with pale yellowish-brown, sometimes blending with the color of the back.

One litter of four to six (average is five) young is produced each year. The gestation period is about 30 days. Young usually are born in early June. They are aboveground by late July, but lactating females may occur into August. Young begin eating solid foods at 36–40 days and stop nursing at 41–45 days. The color of half-grown young in August and September is similar to that of adults, but the pelage is thinner and more silky. By September and October, the young are almost fully grown.

The gray-collared chipmunk occupies ponderosa pine and spruce-fir forests, and occurs up to timberline in the San Fran-

cisco Mountains, Arizona. This chipmunk is most common where Douglas fir and pine overlap. Of all the chipmunks in New Mexico, it is least likely to occur below the ponderosa pine forest, and usually occupies forests at higher elevations, but it may occasionally be common in oak and juniper habitat. In a second-growth pine forest, densities ranged from about 5 per hectare in May to 13 per hectare in August, when young-of-the-year were present.

Nests are placed under logs, stumps, and roots, or in hollows in trees. Woodpecker holes are often used as nest sites. One nest made of grass and weed fibers was in a crevice on the underside of a downed log; another, in a woodpecker hole in a large ponderosa pine, contained a mother and six young.

T. cinereicollis eats seeds of small plants, acorns of Gambel's oak, currants, gooseberries, shadblow berries, tubers, and starchy roots. It feeds heavily upon legumes in the summer. It also consumes green vegetation, mushrooms and other fungi, seeds of Douglas fir, ponderosa pine, pinyon pine, and insects.

Tamias cinereicollis sometimes occurs in the same geographic area as *T. dorsalis* and *T. minimus*. In Arizona, *T. cinereicollis* only occurs with *T. dorsalis* in a few places on the Mogollon Plateau and in the White Mountains; *T. cinereicollis* is usually found higher in the forest and in less rocky situations. In New Mexico, *T. cinereicollis* also occupies only the higher forests, with *T. dorsalis* occupying the lower zones. In the White Mountains of Arizona, *T. cinereicollis* occurs more often in spruce-fir and mixed-conifer forest than does *T. minimus*, which uses pine and mixed-conifer forest. Mammals occurring in the same habitat as the gray-collared chipmunk include shrews, cottontails, golden-mantled ground squirrels, tassel-eared and red squirrels, pocket gophers, Mexican woodrats, jumping mice, voles, elk, and mule deer. No parasites are known. *T. L. Best*

Tamias cinereicollis

Size
Males are slightly smaller than females.
Total length: 208–242 (224) mm
Length of tail: 90–109 (99) mm
Weight: 55–70 g

Identification
The gray-collared chipmunk is pale grayish in color on the cheeks, shoulders, and anterior part of the back. Prominent areas of gray in these three regions are unique to the species. Compared with *T. dorsalis*, which occupies lower elevations on mountains where gray-collared chipmunks occur, *T. cinereicollis* has conspicuous dorsal stripes. Compared with *T. minimus*, *T. cinereicollis* is larger and has gray on the neck, shoulders, and anterior back.

Recent Synonyms
Eutamias cinereicollis

Other Common Names
Ash-colored chipmunk

Status
Common

Subspecies
Tamias cinereicollis cinereicollis, east-central Arizona and western New Mexico
Tamias cinereicollis cinereus, west-central New Mexico

References
Mammalian Species 436; Bailey, 1931; Hoffmeister, 1986

Cliff chipmunk | *Tamias dorsalis*

These handsome gray chipmunks occur in open woodlands and forests of the Great Basin, from the border of Idaho south through the mountains of Arizona and western New Mexico to the Sierra Madre Occidental of Chihuahua and Sonora, Mexico. One isolated population lives on the Gulf of California and two others live about 800 kilometers east in the mountains of Coahuila. *Tamias dorsalis* is found from near sea-level up to 3,700 meters.

Cliff chipmunks almost always are found near large rocks, boulders, or cliffs, over which they run with skill. In or under the rocks and cliffs are refuges and places for nests and stores of food. Strangely, these chipmunks are extremely shy in many localities, but easy to approach in others.

The overall color of the upperparts of cliff chipmunks is smoke gray. There is a dark brown stripe down the middle of the back, but the other dorsal stripes usually are faint. Each side of the face, however, has five contrasting stripes, three of brown and two of white. The ears are pale smoke gray or grayish-white. Behind each ear is a prominent creamy white patch. The sides are cinnamon or brownish and the underparts

The breeding season of *Tamias dorsalis* is longer than that of any other western chipmunk. Mating occurs as early as March and as late as fall. One estrous female was the center of attention of 14 males in early June. Young are born after a gestation of about a month. Very small chipmunks, not long out of their dens, have been seen in late September and late November in New Mexico. As far as is known, individual females have only one litter a year. Three observed litters had 5, 5, and 6 young, respectively. Embryo counts go as high as 8.

Like other chipmunks, cliff chipmunks eat a great variety of seeds and fruits of grasses, forbs, shrubs, and trees. In Utah they have eaten insects, frogs, salamanders, snakes, birds, and eggs. Cheek pouches are very handy for quickly gathering seeds and, especially in the fall, for transporting them to storage. In Arizona, females disappear, presumably to hibernate, from late December until late April. Males can be seen throughout the winter, but are less active then.

Cliff chipmunks favor woodlands of scattered juniper (*Juniperus*) and pinyon pine (*Pinus monophylla*), but also do well in higher montane forests of ponderosa pine (*Pseudotsuga menziesii*) and spruce (*Picea*). In Coahuila, these chipmunks are common in oak (*Quercus*) groves with scattered madrone (*Arbutus*) and other trees. On the coast of Sonora, organpipe cactus (*Lamairocereus thurberi*), saguaro (*Carnegia gigantea*), and ocotillo (*Fouquieria diguetii*) supply food and cover for cliff chipmunks. In Utah and Nevada, their habitats include sagebrush (*Artemesia tridentata*), four-winged saltbrush (*Atriplex canescens*), chokecherry (*Prunus*), wild rose (*Rosa*), and cliffrose (*Cowania mexicana*).

Fossils of *Tamias dorsalis* from a cave in Utah and one in Nevada are about 2,300 and 8,000 years old.

When it occurs on the same mountain as *Tamias umbrinus, T. cinereicollis,* or *T. quadrivittatus* in the United States, or *T. durangae* in Mexico, the cliff chipmunk usually is at the bottom and the other species is in higher, denser, or cooler forests. However, on a mountain without one of these competitors, *T. dorsalis* will range all the way to the top. Golden-mantled ground squirrels and Sierra Madre mantled squirrels are sympatric with *T. dorsalis,* as is the larger rock squirrel. Tree squirrels associated with this chipmunk are the red squirrel, Abert's squirrel, and the Arizona gray squirrel in the United States, and the Nayarit squirrel in Mexico. *H. E. Broadbooks*

Tamias dorsalis

are creamy white. The beautiful bushy tail is edged with grayish-white or buff above, and underneath is brownish-orange or cinnamon. The winter pelage is similar, but the colors are brighter and a little deeper. In a spring and summer molt, the worn winter coat is replaced by a new summer pelage from front to rear. In the fall molt of September and October, which moves in the opposite direction, the summer fur is shed as a new winter pelage appears.

Size
Females are larger than males.
Total length: 204–226 (217) mm (males);
    212–235 (222) mm (females)
Length of tail: 82–100 (92) mm (males); 89–105
    (95) mm (females)
Weight: 54.5–63.8 (59.5) g (males); 58.8–66.7
    (62.9) g (females)

Identification
The cliff chipmunk is distinguished by the gray color and by the indistinctness of the stripes on the back.

Recent Synonyms
Eutamias dorsalis

Other Common Names
Gray chipmunk, gray-backed chipmunk, Gila striped squirrel, pallid chipmunk, chichimoke, and chichimuka

Status
Common, but often very shy

Subspecies

Tamias dorsalis carminis, northern and central Coahuila, Mexico

Tamias dorsalis dorsalis, Grand Canyon, Arizona, and northwestern New Mexico to northwestern Durango, Mexico

Tamias dorsalis grinnelli, central and eastern Nevada

Tamias dorsalis nidoensis, central Chihuahua, Mexico

Tamias dorsalis sonoriensis, Gulf of California coast near Guaymas, Sonora, Mexico

Tamias dorsalis utahensis, Utah and edges of bordering states

References

Mammalian Species 399; Hoffmeister, 1986

Merriam's chipmunk | *Tamias merriami*

Merriam's chipmunk is primarily found below the timberline of the California mountains it inhabits, typically at elevations of 2,300 to at least 2,500 meters. Its distribution is determined more by vegetation, habitat, and exposure than elevation. This chipmunk may be seen in late summer from early to mid-morning and from mid-afternoon to evening scampering about in search of seeds and nuts. When it travels through brush or trees it frequently jumps from limb to limb, maintaining balance with its plume-like tail while airborne. Its molting pattern, gestation period, and reproduction have not been well studied, but are probably similar to that of most other species of chipmunks. *T. merriami* nests in burrows in the ground, under rocks, in fallen logs, and may occasionally use holes higher up in trees.

In the San Bernardino Mountains of California its typical habitat consists of Jeffrey pine, Coulter pine, and oak, with an understory of manzanita, wild rose, and other plants typical of somewhat moist, higher elevations.

Where its range overlaps with *Tamias obscurus,* the two species closely resemble each other. The color of the pelage of *T. obscurus* is less like that of *T. merriami* where their ranges do not overlap, suggesting either that some hybridization has occurred or that the similarity has developed under the same environmental pressures in the areas of overlap. The two species are distinguishable using bacular (genital bone) morphology.

Merriam's chipmunk produces chip calls from elevated positions. Perched on top of a rock or stump, it calls vigorously for extended periods of time. The chip call is species-specific, with considerable geographic variation evident, and often includes a "terminal pulse," a burst of sound that follows the chip within milliseconds. This is distinctive of the species in parts of its range and is audible to the trained human ear. *D. J. Blankenship*

Tamias merriami

Size
No significant sexual dimorphism
Total length: 240–255 (247) mm
Length of tail: 100–115 (108) mm
Weight: 70–80 (75) g

Identification
Merriam's chipmunk typically sports a relatively long, bushy tail that is more than three-fourths the length of head and body, which, together with its larger body, distinguishes it from most species of chipmunks that share its range. The summer coat color is grayish with distinct dark dorsal stripes. These are all about the same width and are usually gray or brown, not red. The cheeks are grayish. *T. townsendii* differs in having brownish cheeks; *T. quadrimaculatus* differs in having brighter stripes. *T. speciosus* (in the San Bernardino Mountains) has distinct white stripes; those of *T. merriami* are grayish-white. Merriam's chipmunk is difficult to distinguish from *T. obscurus* where their ranges overlap, except by using bacular (genital bone) morphology.

Recent Synonyms
Eutamias merriami

Status
Common within its range

Subspecies
Tamias merriami kernensis, Kern County, California
Tamias merriami merriami, San Bernardino County, California
Tamias merriami pricei, San Mateo County, California

References
Mammalian Species 476; Blankenship and Brand, 1987; Brand, 1976; Merriam, 1897

Least chipmunk | *Tamias minimus*

The least chipmunk is the smallest and most wide-ranging North American chipmunk, occurring from western Quebec to the Yukon (northern Michigan to central Washington, but absent from the Great Plains) and southward to southern New Mexico. It is the only species of western chipmunk that occurs with the eastern chipmunk (in the upper midwest and adjacent areas in Canada). Here it is easily distinguished from the eastern chipmunk by its much smaller size, longer and bushier tail, and lack of a reddish rump and evenly-spaced alternating black-and-white stripes. The least chipmunk has 22 teeth to the eastern chipmunk's 20.

The subspecies of the least chipmunk are highly variable in coloration and even in size. Many look as different from each other as they do from other species. The five darker dorsal stripes can range from black to brown to tawny to pale reddish. The flanks and head range from dark grayish-brown to pale reddish-brown. The underside of the tail may be yellowish, reddish, or brown. Usually the lateral pair of darker stripes is prominent and wide, which would distinguish the least chipmunk from such species as the cliff chipmunk *(T. dorsalis)* or the Uinta chipmunk *(T. umbrinus)*. In the least chipmunk, the brightness or contrast between dark and pale stripes and flanks is intermediate between that of the cliff clipmunk (very dull) and the Colorado chipmunk *(T. quadrivittatus;* very bright). However, the pelage of a freshly-molted animal is usually noticeably brighter. Not knowing whether or not a chipmunk has molted can make the task of species identification difficult, but the least chipmunk is still relatively easy to distinguish among the 20 or so species of western chipmunks.

The least chipmunk occurs with the following other species of western chipmunks: *Tamias amoenus, T. dorsalis, T. quadrivit-* *tatus, T. ruficaudus, T. rufus, T. senex, T. speciosus, T. panamintinus, T. quadrimaculatus,* and *T. umbrinus.* Although it is most abundant in montane coniferous forest, the least chipmunk may also be found in aspen groves and is less confined to actual forest habitat than is any other species of chipmunk, being found in meadows, dry scrublands, and even sagebrush desert. In many areas of the Rocky Mountains, it is the only chipmunk to venture into the alpine tundra. The least chipmunk is more tolerant of heat and solar radiation than the other, larger species, and is less reliant on rocky slopes than the species with which it shares its range. In the Sierra Nevada it is limited to

Tamias minimus

the lower foothills, probably by aggressive interactions with the yellow-pine chipmunk *(T. amoenus)*. However, in the central Rocky Mountains, the least chipmunk occupies virtually all habitats from 1,525 meters to 3,660 meters elevation, a range unmatched by any other chipmunk and one that rivals that of the ubiquitous deer mouse *(Peromyscus maniculatus)*.

Like all chipmunks, the least chipmunk is primarily a seed-eater and is somewhat reliant on mast crops, especially conifer seeds. It is opportunistic, however, and also eats flowers, buds, leaves, and occasionally even insects, birds' eggs, and carrion. Mushrooms and other fungi are also very important foods. The least chipmunk makes greater use of seeds of grasses and nonwoody herbaceous plants (e.g., members of the sunflower family) than other chipmunks do. Its range of ecological habit may let it coexist with other chipmunk species by avoiding direct competition for food. Although some tree-nesting has been reported, it is found significantly less often in trees than are its congeners. It is often behaviorally subordinate to larger chipmunk species, and although solitary and territorial, like other chipmunks, it is more often seen in close proximity to conspecifics.

Like all of the ground-dwelling sciurids, least chipmunks are diurnal, not becoming active until dawn and retreating to their burrows at dusk. They scamper about on logs and rocks and occasionally in trees and shrubs, but they also traverse grassy, open areas to a greater degree than most other chipmunks (but less so than most ground squirrels). They express territory

ownership, alarm at danger, and even mate advertisement by a rich variety of vocalizations, delivered in synchrony with a particular positioning and pattern of movement of the body and usually from an exposed promontory such as a rock or a tree branch. Proper alignment of the conspicuous stripes is no doubt important to the chipmunk in communicating its message, and rhythmic movement of the tail usually accompanies a vocalization bout. The most common type of vocalization is called the chip, which is often delivered *ad nauseum*. Adults also have chipper and chuck calls and a very bird-like trill. Squeals are usually reserved to the young, although adult chipmunks in the hand will often squeal.

Least chipmunks are semifossorial; that is, they spend a portion of their lives in subterranean burrows and rock crevices. They not only escape danger, sleep, and raise their young to weaning in these burrows, but they also spend the winter in specially dug and provisioned hibernacula. Depending on latitude and elevation, least chipmunks begin hibernating in September through November and end in February through April. Hibernation is not as deep as in ground squirrels, and they do not accumulate as much body fat in preparation; rather, chipmunks cache a substantial quantity of seeds in their hibernacula and arouse periodically during winter to feed. By slowing their metabolism and heart rate for half the year, chipmunks are able to live longer than nonhibernating mammals of similar body size. A few individuals have been known to live as long as six or seven years.

Males emerge from their burrows in spring fully prepared to mate, usually a week or two in advance of the females. The trigger for this arousal and for the regrowth of the gonads—begun while the chipmunk is still in deep torpor—involves an internal biological clock, which is reset each year by photoperiod (relative length of day and night) and perhaps by climatic factors. Females are receptive to breeding for only a few days in spring, typically in April or May. At low elevations or in southerly latitudes, a few chipmunks may breed a second time during late summer. After a gestation period of 28–30 days, altricial (blind and helpless) young are born underground. Litter sizes range from 3 to 8, with 4 or 5 being most common. Weaned young first appear aboveground from mid-June to early August, when they are about 25 days old and three-fourths grown. Three litters observed on the day of emergence in northern Colorado all consisted of four young. The young do not breed until their first spring, but only about 30 percent of them can be expected to survive their first winter. After breeding, the chipmunk replaces its worn, relatively dull pelage from back to front. In females that have raised a litter, this molt is delayed until later in summer, after the energetic demands of lactation have ceased.

Least chipmunks are parasitized by a variety of fleas, ticks, and mites (externally) and by nematodes (internally). They may carry spotted or Colorado tick fever or even bubonic plague (transmitted by fleas). Curiously, although the bot or warble fly larvae that infest deer mice can heavily infest Uinta and Colorado chipmunks in Colorado, these parasites are virtually unknown in least chipmunks living in the same areas. Contrary to popular belief, chipmunks do not carry rabies. Consequently, least chipmunks are of little threat to human health or economies.

Least chipmunks may be preyed upon by forest raptors such as goshawks or Cooper's hawks, and by weasels, snakes, bobcats, martens, and foxes. Being strictly diurnal, they escape predation by owls and avoid competition with many other small herbivorous but nocturnal rodents. Because they scatter-hoard small quantities of seeds and other foods over a wide area, least chipmunks may be important dispersal agents for many species of trees, shrubs, herbaceous plants, and fungi. Their home ranges of one to six hectares are surprisingly large for such small animals. This is probably due to the scattered distribution of their food supply. In fact, least chipmunk home ranges are significantly larger in drier, less productive habitats than in moist, dense forest.

Chipmunks are known as "central place foragers" because they repeatedly return to the site of an underground nest, hibernaculum, or larder-hoard with cheek-pouches stuffed full of seeds from visits to various producing plants throughout their home range. Portions of their home ranges, especially in the vicinity of nests, are defended against other members of their species (except mates) and usually against members of other chipmunk species; some overlap with other chipmunks is usually allowed in peripheral areas of their home ranges. There is some indication that a male may help defend the territory of the female whose young he sired and may even help raise the young by maintaining the nest or bringing them food. Short-term bonds between adult males and their offspring have been observed after weaning and emergence from the natal burrow. Other than that, least chipmunks are strictly solitary, in spite of the impression one gains from visiting the "peanut populations" in the national parks of the American West. There, some individual chipmunks converge daily on the rich bounty of human-provided fodder from territories as far as two miles away and exhibit behavior completely at odds with their normally shy nature. *B. J. Bergstrom*

Size
Females are larger than males in some
    populations.
Total length: 185–216 (200.7) mm
Length of tail: 78–113 (90.1) mm
Weight: 32–50 (43.6) g

Identification
T. minimus is distinguished from all other chipmunks that share its range by at least slightly smaller size and usually a relatively longer tail and relatively shorter muzzle; it has a broad, brownish lateral stripe, and usually moves in a more animated way, with its tail held vertically; it flicks its tail up and down and only rarely sways it from side to side.

Recent Synonyms
Eutamias minimus

Status
Common, most widespread of western North American chipmunks

Subspecies
Tamias minimus atristriatus, Sacramento Mountains, Otero County, south-central New Mexico
Tamias minimus borealis, Ontario north of 50° N; Manitoba except for northern third and extreme southeastern corner; extreme northeastern North Dakota; north-central Montana (Big Snowy and Bear Paw ranges); Saskatchewan except extreme south and northeast; Alberta except extreme south; northeastern British Columbia; extreme southwestern Northwest Territory; extreme southeastern Yukon

Tamias minimus cacodemus, badlands of southwestern South Dakota
Tamias minimus caniceps, south-central Yukon; north-central British Columbia; west slope of Selwyn Mountains in Northwest Territory
Tamias minimus caryi, northeastern San Luis Valley (mostly in Alamosa County), Colorado
Tamias minimus confinis, Bighorn Mountains of north-central Wyoming and south-central Montana
Tamias minimus consobrinus, Absaroka Range of south-central Montana through Wind River Range of Wyoming; eastern Idaho; Wasatch Range of northern Utah and Uinta Mountains of northeastern Utah and southwestern Wyoming southwest to southwestern Utah, east to Park Range in northwestern Colorado; disjunct population in Kaibab Plateau, Arizona

Tamias minimus grisescens, central to south-central Washington

Tamias minimus hudsonius, extreme northern Ontario; northern third of Manitoba; northeastern Saskatchewan

Tamias minimus minimus, south-central Wyoming to extreme northwestern Colorado

Tamias minimus neglectus, central Wisconsin to northern Minnesota to Upper Peninsula of Michigan; southeastern corner of Manitoba; southern half of Ontario (north of Lake Huron)

Tamias minimus operarius, Laramie Mountains of Wyoming south through Front Range of Colorado to north-central New Mexico, west to west-central and southwestern Colorado and to east-central and southeastern Utah; extreme northeastern Arizona and northwestern New Mexico; disjunct populations in east-central Arizona and central New Mexico

Tamias minimus oreocetes, Rocky Mountains of southern Alberta through Glacier National Park, Montana

Tamias minimus pallidus, eastern and north-central Wyoming, eastern and central Montana; northwestern South Dakota; northwestern Nebraska; western North Dakota

Tamias minimus pictus, central and southern Idaho south through Great Salt Lake desert and northwestern Utah

Tamias minimus scrutator, south-central Washington through eastern Oregon, southwestern Idaho, south through Sierra Nevada of California and Nevada, and east across northern two-thirds of Nevada to extreme western Utah

Tamias minimus selkirki, single site in Selkirk Mountains of southeastern British Columbia

Tamias minimus silvaticus, southwestern to south-central South Dakota and extreme northwestern Wyoming

References

Armstrong, 1972; Bergstrom and Hoffmann, 1991; Durrant, 1952

California chipmunk | *Tamias obscurus*

California chipmunks are found in the mountains of Baja California, Mexico, and in the San Bernardino and San Jacinto mountains of California. Several subspecies have been described, only one of which, *Tamias obscurus davisi,* is found in the United States. This chipmunk is found from elevations of 1,700 meters in the lower, arid regions of its distribution to 2,500 meters in the higher regions of its range in the San Bernardino mountains, where it overlaps with *Tamias merriami.*

During late summer *Tamias obscurus* is very active from early to mid-morning and from mid- to late afternoon, especially when pinyon nuts are available. Then these chipmunks can be seen readily as they scurry about with their pouches bulging with nuts.

The California chipmunk is indistinctly colored throughout much of its range, and is generally gray or dusky in appearance. The primary exception is in the areas where its range overlaps with *Tamias merriami.* There its appearance is often brighter than in the more arid areas of its range. These chipmunks molt twice a year, in May through June or July and again in September through October. Prior to a molt, the coat is duller and grayer than the newly-acquired pelage after the molt has been completed. The gestation period and reproduction of this species has not been well studied but is probably typical of most other species of chipmunks.

In the San Bernardino Mountains of California, the typical habitat occupied by this species is pinyon pine *(Pinus monophylla)* and juniper *(Juniperus californicus),* with some scrub oak *(Quercus chrysolepsis)* and yucca *(Yucca brevifolia),* cactus *(Opun-*

tia), rabbitbrush *(Chrysothamnus viscidiflorus),* and sage *(Artemesia tridentata)* in the understory. The vegetation is generally sparse in these areas, but rocks are abundant and cracks in the rocks and burrows beneath them serve both as nests and food storage sites. Pinyon pine nuts are the primary food during the late summer months, and chipmunks may be found during the daytime climbing the pines in search of nuts. Investigation of a chipmunk's cheek pouches often reveals a surprising number of nuts, in their shells.

In areas where *Tamias obscurus* overlaps with *Tamias merriami* (for example in Holcomb Valley, in San Bernardino County), the typical habitat of *T. obscurus* includes pinyon pine and Jeffrey pine *(Pinus jeffreyi),* with an understory of manzanita *(Arctostaphylos glauca).* This habitat is less arid than is typical for *T. obscurus.*

This chipmunk's vocalization is a distinct chip call, which it produces while standing upright with its nose pointed to the sky, tail twitching vigorously with each burst of sound. The vocalizations are so sharp that they resemble a bark. They can be heard for a considerable distance, considering the size of the animal, and may be used in courtship. Even though the call varies with location, and intraspecific differences may be as great as the differences between different species, the call is generally unique to the species. *D. J. Blankenship*

Tamias obscurus

Size
No significant sexual dimorphism
Total length: 200–250 (229) mm
Length of tail: 70–120 (95) mm
Weight: 60–84 (69) g

Identification
The California chipmunk is gray to dusky brown with black or reddish stripes on the back and sides. The white stripes are more distinct on the face; on the body they are mixed with gray and often appear as a single lateral grayish-white stripe. The dark dorsal stripe that runs from head to rump is usually mixed with gray on the neck and shoulders and is most distinct on the back. This chipmunk has a relatively short tail edged with gray and sometimes reddish fur. The body appears somewhat stocky, in part due to the shorter tail.

Throughout most of its range north of Mexico, *Tamias obscurus* is not easily distinguished from *T. merriami.* In areas of sympatry the two chipmunks closely resemble each other. However, in the drier habitats occupied by *T. obscurus* alone, it is paler than *T. merriami,* the pelage is more gray and less yellowish, the reddish dorsal stripes are less distinct, and it has a slightly shorter tail. In areas of sympatry *T. obscurus* is brighter, with a slightly longer tail. *Tamias obscurus* is distinct from other chipmunks throughout its range in its bacular morphology. The baculum (genital bone) is distinctly broader and more robust in the distal end than that of *T. merriami.*

Recent Synonyms
Eutamias obscurus

Status
Common within its range

Subspecies
Tamias obscurus davisi, San Bernardino County, California
Tamias obscurus meriodionalis, Aguaje de San Esteban, Baja California, Mexico
Tamias obscurus obscurus, Sierra San Pedro Martír, Baja California, Mexico

References
Mammalian Species 472; Blankenship and Brand, 1987; Callahan, 1977

Yellow-cheeked chipmunk | *Tamias ochrogenys*

Yellow-cheeked chipmunks are in a group of relatively large chipmunks that thrive in the dark, moist, and grand redwood forests. They are also common in human-altered coastal madrone and Douglas fir second-growth forests of northwestern California. Their range extends along the seacoast in a narrow belt from the south side of the Eel River in Humboldt County, California, eastward no more than 40 km from the Pacific Coast, and southward to about 3 km north of Bodega and Freestone in Sonoma County, California. Where the humid coastal forests of northern California become patchy, the yellow-cheeked chipmunk's distribution also becomes discontinuous. The presence of other vegetation, such as coniferous woods with a brushy understory, may limit the distribution of this species. The elevational range of *T. ochrogenys* is from sea level to 1,280 m.

In fall, the yellow-cheeked chipmunk begins to acquire its winter pelage, which is long, silky, dense, and dull-colored. The fall molt begins at the rump and moves towards the head. The spring molt starts with the head and moves towards the tail. Males become sexually active in late March and remain so into July. Females are receptive reproductively from mid-March into the summer months; three to four young are a typical litter size. The genital bones (baculum and baubellum) of chipmunks, including those of the yellow-cheeked chipmunk, are distinctive and therefore useful taxonomically. The baculum of the male of this species most closely resembles that of Townsend's chipmunk from Washington, but differs in being longer at the tip and thicker along the shaft.

As determined by examining the cheek pouches, fungi are eaten in late winter and early spring. From observations in June and July, chipmunks also gather grass seeds, but like all chipmunks, yellow-cheeked chipmunks take a wide variety of foods. Food items and the months (or season) in which they were taken include: western raspberry *(Rubus leucodermis)* in fall; buckthorn *(Rhamnus)* and blue blossom *(Ceanothus)* in September, October, January, and March; wax myrtle *(Myrica californica)* in September; California huckleberry *(Vaccinium ovatum)* in September; poison oak *(Toxicodendron diversilobum)* in September; bull thistle *(Cirsium)* in September; Scotch broom *(Cytisus scoparius)* in November; oak acorn *(Lithospermum or Quercus)* in September, January, March, and April. Unidentified insect wing fragments have been found in stomachs.

Although no information is available on predators specific to this chipmunk, common carnivores take chipmunks: weasels

Tamias ochrogenys

and hawks are particularly efficient. The incidence of parasitism is low in this species although stomach nematodes *(Spirura)* and botfly larva *(Cuterebra)* have been found, as have lice and fleas.

More often heard than seen, yellow-cheeked chipmunks direct a unique call at intruders. They "would be lost [in the forest] but for their shrill, whistling chipper, or chuck chuck chuck [call]," mammalogist Vernon Bailey wrote in 1936. Its distinct, low-frequency, two-syllable "chip" is unlike that of any other species. *W. L. Gannon*

Females are slightly larger than males.
Total length: 233–297 (261) mm
Length of tail: 97–130 (110) mm
Weight: 60–116.2 (89.3) g (males); 78.0–117.5
 (94.1) g (females)

Identification

The yellow-cheeked chipmunk is small, dark, and long-tailed, with prominent alternating dark and pale longitudinal stripes on the face and back. The center stripe on the back is the longest, widest, and most conspicuous. On the face, a dark stripe through the eye and paler ones above and below the eye are most prominent. There is a large patch of white on the back of the ears. In autumn, adult pelage is dark tawny olive to blue-gray. *T. ochrogenys* can be distinguished from other Townsend-type chipmunks, the only other chipmunks in northwestern California, by its less bushy tail, the darker color of its back, a more distinctly marked dorsal stripe, greater length of head and body, and a two-syllable "chip" call of lower frequency than that of other species.

Recent Synonyms

Eutamias ochrogenys

Other Common Names

Redwood chipmunk

Status

Common, limited geographically

References

Mammalian Species 445; Bailey, 1936; Gannon and Lawlor, 1989; Levenson and Hoffmann, 1984

Palmer's chipmunk | *Tamias palmeri*

Palmer's chipmunks live only in the Spring Mountains of southwestern Nevada. These mountains, also known as the Charleston Mountains, lie just west of Las Vegas and are surrounded by desert, limiting the animal's range and preventing contact between it and its nearest relative, *Tamias umbrinus*. *Tamias palmeri* is found from elevations of 2,100 meters to the timberline (3,600 m). In Clark Canyon it is most abundant between 2,400 and 2,550 meters; above 2,250 meters, it is the most common mammal in the canyon.

Like most members of the squirrel family, *Tamias palmeri* is diurnal. While foraging on rock cliffs and canyon floors, it stays close to fallen logs and rock piles that afford shelter. It usually dens on or near the ground, although nests have been observed in trees. When the animals live near humans they can become fairly tame, but young raised in captivity never become accustomed to handling.

Palmer's chipmunk has three dark stripes (instead of the more usual five) and four paler ones on its back and sides. In summer pelage, the dark stripes are a satiny dark brown shaded with black. The two paler stripes in the center of the back are pale smoke-gray; the outer pair and the underparts are creamy white. Shades of cinnamon color the sides of the nose, top of the head, and thighs; the underside of the tail is pale yellowish-tan bordered with shiny dark fur. In winter, when the animal can be seen scampering across the snow on bright, milder-than-usual days, its colors are more muted: its upperparts are grayer and the stripes are somewhat less distinct. Palmer's chipmunk molts twice a year, shedding its winter coat in May, June, or July and its summer coat in August, September, or October. In spring the molt progresses from head to tail; in autumn, the pattern is reversed.

Tamias palmeri usually breeds in late April or May. After a gestation period of about 33 days, the female gives birth, usually to 3 or 4 young. The neonates are pink and hairless except for tiny incipient whiskers on the sides of the nose. The hair grows rapidly: before the chipmunks are two weeks old, their stripes have started to become apparent, and by the end of the fourth week, the hair is sleek and smooth. The ears, which are folded tightly against the side of the head at birth, stand up in two or three days. Littermates begin to appear outside the nest

Tamias palmeri

at about five weeks and sit on their haunches like adults to eat solid food a week later. Seeds, fruits, fleshy fungi, green vegetation, and insects constitute the adult's diet.

In Clark Canyon *Tamias palmeri's* range extends into the bristlecone pine community. At lower elevations it lives in white fir-Ponderosa pine, single-leaf pinyon-Utah juniper, and mountain mahogany-manzanita communities. Shrubs in the understory include Utah serviceberry, currant, and elderberry. No fossils of Palmer's chipmunk have been found.

A slightly smaller chipmunk, *Tamias panamintinus,* also inhabits the Spring Mountains. Their ranges overlap, but Palmer's chipmunk—named for the leader of an expedition that discovered the species in 1897—generally prefers somewhat higher elevations. Other rodents in the Spring Mountains include golden-mantled and antelope ground squirrels, the silky pocket mouse, three species of wood rats, one species of harvest mouse, and three species of white-footed mice. *S. Ruff*

Size
No significant sexual dimorphism
Total length: 210–223 (220) mm
Length of tail: 86.5–101.0 (94.6) mm
Weight: 50.0–69.4 g

Identification
T. palmeri can be distinguished from *Tamias panamintinus,* the only chipmunk that shares its range, by slightly larger size, grayer shoulders, and more solidly black and white stripes.

Recent Synonyms
Eutamias palmeri

Other Common Names
Mount Charleston chipmunk

Status
Common, limited

References
Mammalian Species 443; Hall, 1946

Panamint chipmunk | *Tamias panamintinus*

The small, handsome, Panamint chipmunk lives in the desert ranges at the western edge of the arid Great Basin in the southwestern United States. This species takes its name from the Panamint Mountains, where it was first collected by members of the U.S. Biological Survey on their Death Valley Expedition in the 1890s. It lives at relatively high elevations, 1,500 to 2,600 meters, in the mountains along the southern border of California and Nevada. Its distribution includes the eastern slope of the Sierras, the Grapevine, White, Panamint, and Inyo mountains of California, and the Spring (or Charleston) Mountains in Nevada.

The Panamint chipmunk is restricted to the pinyon pine and juniper forests of these mountains. This is a dry belt that covers the tops of the smaller mountains and, on higher mountains, lies just below the belts of sagebrush and boreal coniferous forest. At the lower edge of the pinyon-juniper zone, Panamint chipmunks live beside desert forms such as antelope ground squirrels, collared lizards, and spotted toads.

The Panamint chipmunk is better adapted than most species of chipmunk to living in a hot and dry climate; most other species live in cooler, higher zones. In the White and Inyo mountains, the Panamint chipmunk overlaps with the Uinta chipmunk, *Tamias umbrinus,* at 2,300 to 2,600 meters. In the Sierra Nevadas the alpine chipmunk, *T. alpinus,* occupies higher mountain crests, above 2,700 meters. And on Charleston Peak in the Spring Mountains, the only place Palmer's chipmunk is found, the two species overlap, but the Panamint chipmunk is most abundant at 2,200 meters, whereas Palmer's chipmunk is more common above 2,400 meters.

Like all chipmunks, the Panamint chipmunk is active during the day, darting about on the rocks and cliff ledges. It cannot easily burrow, for the soil in its habitat is thin and rocky, and there are few fallen trees in which it can hide. Instead it runs between rocks and takes cover in fissures of the granite cliffs.

The Panamint chipmunk is smaller than most other chipmunks, and it looks grayer. It has gray fur on the top of its head and on its rump and thighs. Its stripes, however, are bright. It has three dark brown stripes on its back, and between them are pale stripes, the upper creamy white and the lower grayish white. The lower dark stripes on the sides of its back and on its face, below its eye, are indistinct. The colors vary with the season. In the spring this chipmunk acquires a brightly colored new coat, which appears first on its head and shoulders and then grows back towards the tail. At the end of summer the longer, duller, and somewhat yellowish winter pelage comes in. By the end of winter, when the fur becomes worn, the stripes may be almost obliterated. Another distinctive character of the Panamint chipmunk is its flattened braincase, which gives a squarish look to the back of the skull.

One subspecies of Panamint chipmunk is known only from mountaintops of the Kingston Range in California. This habitat is completely surrounded by desert that is too hot and dry even for Panamint chipmunks, so the subspecies is restricted to these mountains. Here it is isolated from the other subspecies and cannot interbreed with it. As a consequence, the two subspecies have become somewhat different in appearance. The Kingston Range subspecies is smaller and darker than the other, more widespread, subspecies.

Tamias panamintinus hibernates occasionally, but it is often seen aboveground on mild days in the winter. When it is ac-

Tamias panamintinus

tive, like most chipmunks, it is very, very active. It runs about in a nervous manner, and it cannot easily be picked up. Even those few that have been born in captivity have not become used to being handled.

Panamint chipmunks mate in early and mid-April and give birth in May and June. The period of pregnancy is 36 days or more. There may be three to six young in a litter, but more often four or five. The newborns are very small, weighing only 4 g. The mother stays in the nest with them until they are weaned five weeks later.

Panamint chipmunks are hairless and pink at birth, with skin so thin it is translucent. They have no teeth, their eyes and ear canals are closed, and even their ear flaps are sealed down. In the middle of the first week their ear flaps stand up, by the end of the second week their hair comes in and stripes can be seen, and at four weeks they have sleek, smooth fur. In the second week they start to crawl and their first teeth erupt. When they are a month old their ear canals and eyes open, and they can see and hear. They first come out of their nest about the time they are weaned, at five weeks of age. At this time they are very jumpy when they see quick movements. By the next week they are calmer and more mature, and they eat solid food—then sit back on their haunches and clean their faces.
B. H. Blake

Size
No significant sexual dimorphism
Total length: 198–220 (206) mm

Length of tail: 85–102 (92) mm
Weight: 50–52 g

Identification
This species is distinguished from other chipmunks in its range by its paler color and gray-

ish, somewhat flattened head. It is larger than *T. alpinus* and *T. mininus* and smaller than *T. umbrinus, T. speciosus,* and *T. palmeri;* it is more reddish than *T. minimus;* its facial stripes are paler and the stripes on its back less contrasting than in *T. amoenus, T. umbrinus, T. speciosus,* and *T. palmeri.*

Recent Synonyms
Eutamias panamintinus

Status
Common, limited

Subspecies
Tamias panamintinus acrus, Kingston Range, southeastern California
Tamias panamintinus panamintinus, southeastern California and southwestern Nevada

References
Mammalian Species 468; Hirshfield and Bradley, 1977; Howell, 1929; Johnson, 1943

Long-eared chipmunk | *Tamias quadrimaculatus*

Tamias quadrimaculatus, brightly colored and the longest-eared of all the chipmunks, lives only in the central and northern Sierra Nevada Mountains of California and a small bit of Nevada on the eastern side of Lake Tahoe. From Lake Almanor in the north to Bass Lake near the southern border of Yosemite National Park, it is found from about 970 meters elevation up to 2,290 meters.

Up and around by sunrise, long-eared chipmunks forage on the ground or in bushes, using logs as highways and brush piles and large rocks as lookouts and feeding perches. In the fall they climb conifers for seeds in their cones, and in summer, for a time, they nest in trees.

The sides of this striking chipmunk are a bright reddish-brown, and patterns are conspicuous. On the back are five dark and four pale stripes. The inner pale stripes are grayish-white and the outer creamy white. The dark stripes are variable but usually reddish. On the face, pale and dark stripes contrast strongly. The dark stripe along the lower jaw expands into a broad black spot below the ear. The back of the ear is two-toned, the dark in front sharply set off from the whitish posterior half. Behind each ear is a large oval patch of white. The rump and thighs are grayish. The tail is edged with white, and the underside is reddish-brown. The winter pelage is duller than the summer. There are two molts each year. In the first, beginning in spring, bright new hair replaces a worn winter coat. In a fall molt in September and October the summer pelage is shed as new winter hair appears. Progress is from front to rear in the spring molt, but the reverse in the fall.

Mating in late April and May is followed by a one-month gestation and the birth of the young, probably in a burrow un-derground, in May, June, or July. Later the family moves to a hollow in a tree or tall stump. Two tree-nesting families, consisting of a mother and five young, have been observed. Only one litter is born each year. These chipmunks disappear around mid-November to hibernate for the winter, probably in a ground den, and are not seen again until late March. Just before hibernating they rapidly accumulate fat, gaining as much as 20 percent in weight. In all seasons they dig up underground fungi and eat a variety of seeds, fruits, and flowers of such

Tamias quadrimaculatus

plants as gooseberries and manzanitas. Winged termites, pupae of butterflies, and other insects also are eaten by these opportunists.

Tamias quadrimaculatus thrives in chaparral and forests of middle elevations in the Sierras. At both ends of its range this chipmunk has been found in open and logged forests of yellow pine *(Pinus ponderosa)*, sugar pine *(P. lambertiana)*, white fir *(Abies concolor)*, Douglas fir *(Pseudotsuga menziesii)*, incense cedar *(Libocedrus decurrens)*, and black oak *(Quercus kelloggii)*. Shrubs in its habitat are manzanita *(Arctostaphylos patula)*, deerbrush *(Ceanothus)*, and gooseberry *(Ribes)*. Underground fungi are *Boletus* and *Clitocybe*.

Tamias quadrimaculatus shares parts of its range with four other chipmunk species. The less distinctly striped *T. amoenus* overlaps at lower elevations on the western side of Yosemite National Park. Much smaller and shorter-eared, *T. amoenus* ranges as far south as Lake Tahoe. Two other chipmunks, both

reaching higher elevations and covering most of the long-eared chipmunk's range, are *T. speciosus,* which is smaller and has shorter ears and tail, and *T. senex,* the chipmunk most closely resembling *T. quadrimaculatus* in size and color. Compared to *T. quadrimaculatus,* the ears of an average *T. senex* are slightly shorter and less tapered and the whitish ear patches are not quite as large or as sharply defined. However, sometimes the similarity is so great as to defy positive field identification, and only the genital bones, the baculum of the male and the baubellum of the female, clearly identify the species. Other diurnal neighbors of long-eared chipmunks are the striped and chipmunk-like, but larger, golden-mantled ground squirrel, the grayish and much larger California ground squirrel, the dark brown Douglas's squirrel, and the nocturnal northern flying squirrel.

No fossils of *T. quadrimaculatus* are known. *H. E. Broadbooks*

Size
Females are larger than males.
Total length: 230–239 (233) mm (males);
   230–245 (239) mm (females)
Length of tail: 85–100 (91) mm (males); 90–101
   (94) mm (females)
Weight: 74.1–89.0 (78.1) g (males); 81.0–105.0
   (91.9) g (females)

Identification
Tamias quadrimaculatus is distinguished from other chipmunks by exceptionally long, slender ears and by the unusually large and conspicuous white patch behind the base of each ear.

Recent Synonyms
Eutamias quadrimaculatus

Other Common Names
Sacramento chipmunk, four-banded chipmunk

Status
Common, limited

References
Mammalian Species 469; Hall, 1946; Holdenried, 1940

Colorado chipmunk | *Tamias quadrivittatus*

The Colorado chipmunk is found in mountainous terrain across New Mexico and Colorado and in the northeastern corner of Arizona; it is also known to occur in extreme western Oklahoma. It is most common on rocky slopes in ponderosa pine forest or woodland (often with Rocky Mountain juniper or pinyon pine), although it may also occupy drier, shrubbier slopes at lower elevations. It ventures into moister fir and spruce forests at higher elevations in the southern part of its range. Where it is most common, it is closely associated with a small-rodent community that includes the northern rock mouse *(Peromyscus nasutus)*, the rock squirrel *(Spermophilus variegatus)*, and the Mexican woodrat *(Neotoma mexicana)*. However, it also shares habitat with the least chipmunk *(Tamias minimus)*, the red squirrel *(Tamiasciurus hudsonicus)*, Abert's squirrel *(Sciurus aberti)*, the golden-mantled ground squirrel *(Spermophilus lateralis)*, the bushy-tailed woodrat *(Neotoma cinerea)*, the deer mouse *(Peromyscus maniculatus)*, and the long-tailed vole *(Microtus longicaudus)*.

The geographic ranges of many species of western chipmunks adjoin each other but do not overlap. This is called parapatry. The Colorado chipmunk is parapatric with the gray-collared chipmunk *(Tamias cinereicollis)* of southern New Mexico and the Hopi chipmunk *(T. rufus)* of eastern Utah, western Colorado, and northeastern Arizona. The Colorado chipmunk is also parapatric with the Uinta chipmunk *(T. umbrinus)*, which is not a close relative, in northern Colorado. It may be that in each case, the parapatric species are so similar in their ecologies that competition between them prevents them from living in the same place. Chipmunks are solitary and territorial. They avoid other members of their own species, and this avoidance may be extended from interindividual interactions to interspecies interactions.

In the Front Range of Colorado, in and east of Rocky Mountain National Park, the Colorado chipmunk has the greatest predilection for rocky slopes and is more exclusively associated with ponderosa pine than are Uinta or least chipmunks. In this area, the Colorado chipmunk occurs only in the fooothills, up to 2,135 meters elevation, and the Uinta chipmunk is found from 2,135 m up to treeline at more than 3,355 m. The least chipmunk is found at all elevations where forests occur, at lower elevations in shrubland, and in alpine tundra at 3,660 m. The least chipmunk is different enough in its food habits and habitat preference that it can overlap with both other chipmunks, whereas the Uinta and Colorado chipmunks are ecologically very similar. The Uinta chipmunk is quite aggressive, especially toward the Colorado chipmunk, and may actively prevent it from occurring at the higher elevations. In a study area near 2,135 m, it was found that territories of Colorado chipmunks sometimes overlapped with those of least chipmunks but never with those of Uinta chipmunks. A parasitic bot fly that is found only below 2,288 m in the Front Range may help make the lower foothills safe for the Colorado chipmunk; infestations of bot fly larvae apparently affect the Uinta chipmunk more than the Colorado chipmunk, and may cause the Uinta chipmunk to avoid this area. In northern New Mexico, where the only other chipmunk is the least chipmunk, the Colorado chipmunk ranges into spruce-fir forests as high as 3,660 m. Clearly, its niche is potentially very broad where it is not forced to interact with a very similar species.

The Colorado chipmunk is a granivore, relying partly on mast crops such as pines, Douglas fir, and spruce. It also eats seeds of juniper *(Juniperus scopulorum)*; seeds and fruits of shrubs such as currant *(Ribes)*, ninebark *(Physocarpus monogynus)*, chokecherry *(Prunus virginiana)*, serviceberry *(Amelanchier alnifolia)*, snowberry *(Symphoricarpos)*, mountain mahogany *(Cercocarpus montanus)*, and others; occasionally seeds of grasses and composites; and, when available, a variety of fungi. When seeds and fungi are scarce, it will even consume insects, birds' eggs, and carrion. It generally nests in burrows under rocks, but it spends a significant amount of time in trees. It may occasionally nest in trees, but this has not been documented.

The reproduction, activity cycles, foraging behavior, hibernation, parasites, predators, and vocalizations of *T. quadrivittatus* are quite similar to those of *T. minimus*. Because of its southerly distribution into a more temperate climate and longer growing season, hibernation may be less consistent and shorter in the Colorado chipmunk than in many other western chipmunks, and females are more likely to raise a second litter annually. Colorado chipmunks may become somewhat inactive during the hottest parts of summer, when they may spend more time in their burrows to avoid heat and water stress.

When vocalizing, Colorado chipmunks sway their tails from side to side, whereas least chipmunks flick theirs up and down. The "pulse rate" of their chipping is slower than that of the least chipmunk. When a Colorado chipmunk is curious about (or perhaps threatened by) a human intruder, it faces the intruder and remains motionless except for the slow swaying of its tail. After a few seconds or minutes, it may dart off, sometimes to initiate a bout of chipping from a promontory, sometimes to disappear. When live-trapped Colorado chipmunks are handled by the nape of the neck, they are much more likely to squeal (a juvenile vocalization) than are least chipmunks, and if held for a few minutes, they typically go limp as if in a trance. This trance-like state lasts as long as several minutes after release. *B. J. Bergstrom*

Tamias quadrivittatus

Size

Females are slightly larger than males.
Total length: 212–245 (225.7) mm
Length of tail: 80–118 (95.5) mm
Weight: 54–80 (61.5) g

Identification

The Colorado chipmunk is distinguished from other chipmunks that share its range by its brighter pelage, with dark stripes blacker and pale stripes whiter than other chipmunks, and by its pattern of grayish forehead and orangish shoulders and flanks. It is as large as or larger than other chipmunks sharing its range. Compared to the least chipmunk, with which it is most likely to co-occur, the Colorado chip-

munk is larger, with a relatively longer muzzle and a relatively shorter tail, which it sways from side to side (instead of flicking it vertically). It is less animated in its movements and holds its tail horizontally when running. The Colorado chipmunk's dark stripes are blacker, especially the lateral pair, and its forehead is paler and grayer, as opposed to darker brown. In contrast to the Hopi chipmunk, it has much brighter stripes and a grayer head. Compared to the gray-collared chipmunk, it has brighter stripes and orange, rather than gray, shoulders. Compared to the Uinta chipmunk, the Colorado chipmunk has brighter, more orange flanks, more red on the underside of the tail, brighter stripes that extend all the way down

the rump to the base of the tail, and a paler, grayer head with larger, whiter patches behind the ears.

Recent Synonyms

Eutamias quadrivittatus

Status

Restricted to southern and central Rocky Mountains; fairly common and widespread in south but restricted to lowest montane elevations in northern part of range

References

Armstrong, 1972; Bergstrom and Hoffmann, 1991; Findley, 1987; Hoffmeister, 1986

Red-tailed chipmunk | *Tamias ruficaudus*

The red-tailed chipmunk is restricted to southeastern British Columbia, southwestern Alberta, northeastern Washington, northern Idaho, and western Montana. It occurs at elevations of 720–2,400 meters. No fossils are known.

This colorful chipmunk is diurnal. On sunny mornings, it often comes out into clearings and onto fallen trees. It sandbathes to groom its fur; the body is rolled from side to side in the sand and the animal may even move forward while half-buried in the sand. In late September, when the weather be-

comes quite cold, there is a noticeable decrease in the number of chipmunks. During cold days from mid-November to late March, it stays in its burrow and rarely is seen outside. Males become active earlier in spring than females.

In spring, the red-tailed chipmunk forages mostly on the forest floor, moving through ground vegetation nibbling seedlings, leaves, and flowers, and often stopping to search among leaves and litter. It may forage a distance of 45–60 meters within 3–4 minutes. It hoards food. Manipulation of food

Tamias ruficaudus

is probably to position it so that the lower incisors can gnaw off pieces while the food item is held against the upper incisors. Much foraging is in trees, and it has nest holes in living or standing-dead trees.

A mother and her young usually leave tree nests in the morning and come back at night; they usually visit the tree nest only once in late morning for nursing. The mother leaves the tree nest well before sunrise, but the young wait until the sun warms the nest. The young descend quietly and without delay, and feed or explore near the nest tree. The mother steadily calls during this time. Vocalizations include scolding notes that may run together and produce a trill.

This species is a large, dark-colored chipmunk. The general tone of the back is deep brownish-orange, the five dark stripes are black to brown, and the four pale ones are grayish to creamy white. The underparts of the body are creamy white and washed with pale pinkish-brown. The underside of the tail is brilliant reddish, bordered with black and pale pinkish-orange. The top of the head is brownish-orange sprinkled with grayish white.

The breeding season is from late April to late May, but may be as late as August for some females. Following a gestation period of about 31 days, one litter of four to six young (average is five) usually is born in late May or June. At lower elevations in Montana, parturition occurs from 29 May through 15 June, lactation from 10 June until 25 July, and the first young appear out of the nest on about 11 July, compared with 7–25 June, 14 June–29 July, and 21 July, respectively, at higher elevations. Young are 39–45 days of age at first emergence from the nest.

Although there is considerable turnover in population, some individuals may live 6–7 years; one lived 8 years in the wild.

Tamias ruficaudus inhabits dense coniferous forests and is most abundant in forest openings or edges, where shrubby undergrowth is abundant. It occurs in forests of western hemlock, western red cedar, Douglas fir, and Englemann spruce. The red-tailed chipmunk may be the most plentiful and widely distributed chipmunk in northern Idaho. It is abundant higher in the mountains, and is a common resident of the Englemann spruce-alpine fir association. The habitat is sharply seasonal; there is snow on the ground for six months. Snowmelt begins in late March or April, depending on exposure and elevation. The population is low following hibernation (May) and reaches maximum size in August. After the peak in August, the active population declines rapidly as adults enter hibernation. By October, the aboveground population is composed almost entirely of young-of-the-year. *T. ruficaudus* usually makes daily movements of 90–150 meters, although some individuals may move 180–270 meters.

The usual nesting site is in crevices in large boulders or under old log piles. Some young use tree dens until they disperse and establish an individual home range; they then dig a burrow in which to build a nest and store seeds for winter. The red-tailed chipmunk eats seeds of fir trees, honeysuckles, lo-custs, cranberries, and knotweed; fruits and seeds of nine-bark, wild rose, ponderosa pine, snow brush, Douglas fir, service-berry, buckbrush, grass, huckleberry, mountain maple, and bull thistle; and leaves and flowers of dandelion, currant, glacier lily, oyster plant, willow herb, and tarweed. This chipmunk occupies the same habitat as shrews, snowshoe hares, Columbian ground squirrels, red and northern flying squirrels, deer mice, bushy-tailed woodrats, voles, porcupines, short-tailed and long-tailed weasels, striped skunks, coyotes, black bears, elk, moose, mule deer, and white-tailed deer. The only ectoparasite known from *T. ruficaudus* is the flea *Ceratophyllus ciliatus*. No internal parasites are known. *T. L. Best*

Size
Males are slightly smaller than females.
Total length: 223–248 (235) mm
Length of tail: 101–121 (110) mm
Weight: 53–59 (57) g (males); 54–62 (58) g (females)

Identification
Tamias ruficaudus may occur with *T. amoenus* and *T. minimus*. Compared with *T. amoenus*, *T. ruficaudus* is larger, the tail is longer, and the head is more yellowish. Compared with *T. minimus*, *T. ruficaudus* is larger and the tail is reddish.

Recent Synonyms
Eutamias ruficaudus

Other Common Names
Rufous-tailed chipmunk, Coeur d'Alene chipmunk

Status
Common

Subspecies
Tamias ruficaudus ruficaudus, southern British Columbia and Alberta, Canada, western Montana, and east-central Idaho

Tamias ruficaudus simulans, southern British Columbia, Canada, northeastern Washington, northern Idaho, and northwestern Montana

References
Mammalian Species 452; Beg, 1971; Lockner, 1972

Hopi chipmunk | *Tamias rufus*

The Hopi chipmunk is a denizen of the buttes and canyonlands of eastern Utah, northern Arizona, western Colorado, and possibly northwestern New Mexico. It inhabits woodlands of pinyon *(Pinus edulis)* and juniper *(Juniperus osteosperma),* reaching its greatest abundance in the rocky rubble at the foot of slopes. Rock outcrops surrounded by brush at the lower edge of the yellow pine zone are especially favored sites. Individuals have been recorded at elevations from 1,375 to 2,900 m, but most records of occurrence fall between 1,680 and 2,150 m. In Colorado, its eastern range limit coincides with the woodland-forest ecotone on the slopes of the southern Rocky Mountains. Its western range limits in central Utah remain poorly documented.

Tamias rufus is related to the larger, chestnut-colored Colorado chipmunk *(T. quadrivittatus),* and may represent a small reddish form of that stock that became adapted to life in the canyonlands. The geographic ranges of the two species abut in western Colorado and northern Arizona. Although the two were long thought to interbreed, and were hence treated as races of the same species, detailed studies show that these species do not hybridize.

Like most of its relatives, the Hopi chipmunk nests in rock crevices or in piles of broken rock. The availability of nest sites may be a factor limiting chipmunk distribution and abundance—their hands and claws are relatively weak, better suited to harvesting and manipulating food than to excavating burrows. Their quickness and agility in crossing sheer rock faces and climbing overhangs is nothing short of remarkable.

T. rufus also resembles other chipmunks in consuming a tremendously variable diet. From summer on, diets may include seeds of Indian rice grass *(Oryzopsis hymenoides),* fruits and seeds of juniper, cliff rose *(Cowania mexicana),* squawberry *(Rhus trilobata),* and mountain mahogany *(Cercocarpus intricatus),* and seeds and nuts of Russian thistle *(Salsola kali),* pinyon pine, and Gambel and waxy-leaf oaks *(Quercus gambelii* and *Q. undulata).* As a rule, chipmunks do not consume the stems or leaves of plants, but will opportunistically eat flowers, insects, fungi, and shoots. From March through October, average diet composition is about 60 percent seeds, 32 percent flowers, and 7 percent insects. Chipmunks collect food either from the ground surface or, more typically, by deftly climbing in the crowns of bushes and shrubs. They usually do not consume food on the spot but use their capacious cheek pouches to carry it to an observation post for consumption or to the burrow for caching.

At Canyonlands National Park, Hopi chipmunks use the same habitat types as pinyon mice *(Peromyscus truei)*, canyon mice *(P. crinitus)*, and desert woodrats *(Neotoma lepida)*; all of these species typically prefer rough, broken terrain. Chipmunks show lower overlap with white-tailed antelope ground squirrels *(Ammospermophilus leucurus)*, Ord's kangaroo rats *(Dipodomys ordii)*, northern grasshopper mice *(Onychomys leucogaster)*, and plains pocket mice *(Perognathus flavescens)*, which prefer the flats and better-developed soils. *Tamias rufus* depends on regular access to free water, which may influence its choice of microhabitat, activity periods, and diet.

Activity periods of *T. rufus* are closely tied to ambient temperatures. In early spring and late fall, the chipmunks are active from shortly after sunrise to just before sunset. In midsummer, they remain in their burrows during midday heat. Like other western chipmunks, Hopi chipmunks do not hibernate, but rely on caches of stored food, which are consumed between short periods of torpor. They sometimes leave their burrows in midwinter, and can even be seen cavorting on snow-pack, but only when it is sunny and the air is still.

In Utah, mating occurs in late February and March, and litters averaging five young are born in the first two weeks of April after a 30–33 day gestation period. At birth, young weigh an average of 2.8 g. They grow at a steady rate of about 0.5 g per day until day 90. In captive-reared litters, the ear pinna unfolded at 2 to 3 days, the auditory meatus opened at 28 to 29 days, and the eyes opened at 29 to 33 days. Lower incisors

Tamias rufus

erupted at 10 to 12 days, upper incisors at 20 to 22 days, and cheekteeth in 34 to 37 days. In nature, litters first appear aboveground in early May. Weaning is gradual and is complete at six or seven weeks. By mid-June, mothers and their young can be seen basking in early morning sunlight, the young half- to three-quarters grown. Young leave their natal burrow the first summer and do not breed during their first year. Only a single spring breeding season is known.

Hopi chipmunks share the wariness common to most open-country chipmunks. It is possible to get two or three times closer to some other forest-dwelling species before they flee than to *T. rufus*. In parks they become bolder and better accustomed to humans, but nevertheless, even Hopi chipmunks born in captivity cannot be tamed; their grace and uncommon beauty can only be appreciated in the canyonlands. *B. D. Patterson*

Size
Females average slightly larger than males.
Total length: 197–221 (211) mm
Length of tail: 81–95 (87) mm
Weight: 52 g (spring) to 62 g (fall)

Identification
Tamias rufus can be distinguished from *Tamias minimus* and *T. quadrivittatus*, which border and in places overlap its range, by its dorsal stripes being tawny, not mixed with dark brown or black; its outer pair of pale stripes are white and the inner pair grizzled; the crown is pale buffy gray; and the baculum is short but robust. Body size is larger than in *T. minimus*, somewhat smaller than in *T. quadrivittatus*. The

underside of the tail is reddish, not yellowish, and the tail is carried almost horizontally when the animal is running, not vertically as in *T. minimus*.

Recent Synonyms
Eutamias quadrivittatus hopiensis
Eutamias quadrivitattus rufus
Eutamias rufus

Status
Common, limited

References
Armstrong, 1982; Patterson, 1984; Wadsworth, 1972

Allen's chipmunk | *Tamias senex*

Allen's chipmunks are among the largest representatives of these small squirrels in the far western United States. *Tamias senex* is distributed from the Sierras of Yosemite National Park north through the California Sierras and the Cascades of southern Oregon. In northern California it is found from the Pacific coast between the Eel and Klamath rivers in the west to the Warner Mountains in the northeastern corner of the state. Specimens from the humid, coastal redwood forests are characterized by larger size and much darker color than those from the relatively arid inland forests.

Original classifications confused coastal *T. senex* with *T. ochrogenys* and coastal representatives of *T. siskiyou,* and inland *T. senex* was confused with *T. quadrimaculatus.* External and cranial measurements of these animals are so similar that they will not differentiate individual animals, and are significant only when used for comparing a series of specimens. Unique genital bones, the male baculum and the female baubellum, were eventually used as an additional means of differentiating these four species and to show that chipmunks are readily distinguished from all other squirrels. These bones are remarkably uniform and unique for each species. It is unfortunate that they can be examined only after an animal has been sacrificed.

T. senex is primarily arboreal, occupying mature forests and foraging on the log-strewn forest floor and adjacent chaparral. Fruits of forest trees and shrubs, as well as ground-level herbs, grasses, fungi, and occasional insects make up its foods. Nests are located among logs or brush and in hollow trees. In inland areas the dominant trees include ponderosa pine, Jeffrey pine, sugar pine, black oak, Douglas fir, white fir, red fir, incense cedar, and mountain hemlock. Common shrubs include buckbrush, manzanita, blackberry, and chinquapin. Along the Pacific coast, the chipmunks inhabit a humid redwood belt less than 40 km wide that ranges from sea level to about 150 m elevation. Here the dominant tree is the coast redwood, with some Douglas fir, tanbark oak, western hemlock, and madrone interspersed. Common shrubs include salal, salmonberry, and western azalea.

There are two molts annually, with long, silky, dense, dull-colored winter pelage acquired in the autumn and short, coarse, brightly colored summer fur acquired after the spring breeding activity. A single annual reproductive cycle is initiated with mating upon emergence from hibernation, in late April at higher elevations and a bit earlier at lower elevations. After an estimated 28-day gestation period, an average of four young are born in late May or early June. They are nursed by the mother until early August.

The general color of inland specimens is orangish tinged with pale gray. The chipmunk's sides are clay color to tawny; they are darker and, along with the upperparts, more orangish in summer. The rump and thighs are dark smoke- to mouse-gray; the top of the head is pinkish-cinnamon to reddish with grayish-white; the underparts are creamy white. The dark

stripes on the face are pale yellowish-brown to brownish-gray, with a blackish patch behind the eye. Five dark stripes on the body are brownish-black. The median stripe is darkest, and all the dark stripes are sharply defined. There are grayish-white stripes, tinged with buff, on the face; on the body the median pale stripes are grayish-white to cinnamon, with the lateral pair paler anteriorly and more brownish posteriorly. The ears are brownish-black, with white or grayish-white patches and grayish-white borders on the back. The hind feet are clay color to pale yellowish-tawny. The top of the tail is brownish-black to pale gray, and below it is brown to pale yellowish-tawny, bordered with brownish-black and edged with gray.

In the coastal redwood forests this animal is a dark olive color. In contrast to the inland Allen's chipmunk, in the summer it is a bit more tawny and the pale stripes are whiter, the sides are dark tawny, and the rump and thighs are brownish. The top of the head is dark tawny and the underparts are pinkish-buff or cinnamon. The dark stripes do not have a blackish patch behind the eye, scarcely reach the rump, and the outer pair are indistinct. The pale body stripes are more cinnamon; the outer pair are pale yellowish-tawny and obscure posteriorly. The ears are brownish-gray, with posterior pale gray patches, and are margined posteriorly with pale gray.

Coastal animals molt in August and September to a dark tawny-olive pelage; the pale body stripes become grayish washed with cinnamon. These colors fade and become less tawny, but after the spring molt in June the colors are brighter

Tamias senex

tawny, the median pair of pale body stripes are whitish, like the outer pair, and the underparts are cinnamon buff.

Inland animals have relatively deep hibernation periods, but on the Pacific coast, where the climate is much milder, there is little or no deep hibernation, only reduced activity during inclement weather. *D. A. Sutton*

Size
Females are larger than males and coastal
 specimens are larger than those from inland.
Total length: 223–281 (248) mm
Length of tail: 94–122 (104) mm
Weight: 90–120 g

Identification
Tamias senex is a large chipmunk. Coastal specimens resemble *T. ochrogenys* and coastal

T. siskiyou, and can only be distinguished by skeletal features. Inland specimens are grayer than but similar to *T. quadrimaculatus* and inland *T. siskiyou*.

Recent Synonyms
Eutamias quadrimaculatus senex
Eutamias senex
Eutamias townsendii senex.

Other Common Names
Large mountain chipmunk, shadow chipmunk

Status
Common, restricted

References
Mammalian Species 502; Sutton and Nadler, 1974

Siskiyou chipmunk | *Tamias siskiyou*

The Siskiyou cshipmunk *(Tamias siskiyou)* is a large chipmunk that, like other Townsend chipmunk species, thrives in moist coniferous forests and second-growth forests usually dominated by Douglas fir. It was first elevated to species status in 1974 by Sutton and Nadler because, although it is very close in

appearance to other Townsend chipmunks, it is distinctive in some characters of the skull and unique in the shape of the genital bone and the form of its vocalizations. Compared with other Townsend chipmunk species, the winter pelage is darker than that of *T. senex* but more grayish (less brownish) than in

Tamias siskiyou

T. ochrogenys. The top of the head is brownish-gray sprinkled with pinkish-cinnamon and grayish-white. The median dorsal stripes are black. The outer pair of dorsal stripes is black overlaid with pale yellowish-brown. The general tone of the upperparts in summer pelage is more brownish than in the winter pelage. In summer pelage, the outer pair of pale dorsal stripes is clear grayish-white; the inner pair is much clouded with cinnamon. The sides are pale yellowish-tawny.

Tamias siskiyou ranges north of the Klamath River in northwestern California to the Rogue River in southwestern Oregon, and from the Pacific coast inland to Deschutes County, central Oregon. Dominant tree species associated with this chipmunk include Sitka spruce, incense cedar, and white and red fir. Siskiyou chipmunks are active in and around downed logs on the forest floor and ceanothus bushes *(Ceanothus cordulatus)* and forest-edge habitat near clearings.

Fungi, insects, berries, and seeds from shrubs and conifers are common foods for Siskiyou chipmunks. In the vicinity of the Siskiyou Mountains, these chipmunks are commonly observed at 1,000–1,200 m elevation and are most abundant in pine forests near the summits of ridges. They are also found in open, rocky, and chaparral-covered habitats. In September, they were found climbing in bushes of bitter cherry *(Prunus emarginata)* and gathering their red fruit. The next month (October), they were observed in the same area feeding more on acorns and pine nuts, to the point that their cheek pouches were greatly extended.

The genital bones (bacula and baubella) of *Tamias siskiyou* are the most distinctive of the Townsend chipmunks; the tip of the baculum is longer than the shaft, with a small, distinct keel. The call is also distinctive: it is an intense, one-syllable call that starts at a low pitch, rises, and then falls again. It has been described as an inverted chevron-shaped call, and it extends over the broad range of frequencies from 300 kHz to over 1,600 kHz and back to about 400 kHz. Calls are evenly spaced and delivered in a regular sequence.

Little other information is available about the natural history of the Siskiyou chipmunk. The only reproductive information is that one litter of 4–6 young is born in June.

Although no information is available on predators of *T. siskiyou,* several parasites have been noted. A botfly larva *(Cuterebra)* was found in the scrotal area of several male Siskiyou chipmunks and a flea *(Monopsyllus ciliatus protinus)* was reported on chipmunks from Port Orford and Chetco River, Oregon. The flea hosts were likely *Tamias siskiyou* from the Chetco River and *Tamias townsendii townsendii* from Port Orford. *W. L. Gannon*

Size

Total length: 250–268 mm
Length of tail: 98–117 mm
Weight: 65.0–85.0 g

Identification

Although similar in appearance to other *townsendii*-group chipmunks (*T. ochrogenys,* *T. senex,* and *T. townsendii*), the Siskiyou chipmunk is large and dull-colored. The outer lateral stripes on the dorsum are grayish or brownish and paler than the inner stripes. *Tamias amoenus,* the only sympatric chipmunk, is much smaller, reddish on the sides of the body, and its lateral dorsal stripes are white. All chipmunk species in the Townsend group are very similar and can be differentiated with certainty only by examining the genital bones or hearing the vocalizations.

Recent Synonyms

Eutamias siskiyou

Eutamias townsendii siskiyou

Status

Not known, presumed common locally

References

Bailey, 1936; Gannon and Lawlor, 1989; Howell, 1929; Jameson and Peeters, 1988; Levenson and Hoffmann, 1984; Sutton, 1987

Sonoma chipmunk | *Tamias sonomae*

Tamias sonomae occurs in California north of San Francisco Bay at elevations from near sea level to 1,800 meters. No fossils are known.

The Sonoma chipmunk has a shy, retiring nature. When foraging, it usually climbs through the smaller branches of bushes, but individuals often seek elevated positions such as stumps, lower limbs of pine and oak trees, and rock outcroppings, where they rest, watch intruders, and eat food gathered elsewhere. Sonoma chipmunks call from trees, bushes, the ground, and under bushes. In reaction to alarm calls, *T. sonomae* moves rapidly in a direct path to the center of the tree or bush in which it is foraging, or directly to the nearest log, tree, or bush from open ground, where it becomes still and attentive. This alarm-response behavior makes the chipmunk's movements visible to predators for the briefest possible time. Alarm calls are emitted more often by females than males in all age groups. Adult females spend more of their active time giving alarms after the juveniles emerge from the nest than they do earlier in the spring and summer.

Chipmunks from low elevations may breed more than 5 months earlier in the spring than individuals from high elevations. Males travel extensively during the breeding season (December–June). They enter the home range of a female in estrus to breed, and then move on, vying with other, similarly-attracted males over a wide area. One litter of three to five (average is four) young is born each year. Females alone raise the litter; they stay with the young and suckle them, at least at night, for about 3 weeks after the young emerge from the nest. Weaned young remain together for some weeks after the mother no longer associates with them.

Juvenile females tend to stay near where they were born; males disperse. This produces mother-daughter groups along with less-closely-related males. When juveniles first emerge

from the nest, the number of males and females is equal, but the sex ratio favors females among older juveniles by late autumn, and the following spring, first-year females outnumber first-year males. By autumn, first-year adults have a 1:1 sex ratio, suggesting high reproduction-related mortality among females during their initial breeding attempt. Among older adults, females show higher survivorship than males, especially at 3–5 years of age. Because of their nomadism and conflict during the reproductive period, adult males are exposed to more danger and suffer greater mortality than adult females, which maintain a limited home range.

The Sonoma chipmunk occurs in chaparral and open areas in redwood forests and the lower and drier forests of ponderosa pine. It requires habitat with trees, shrubs, logs, standing dead trees, and litter. Habitat includes chaparral, small brushy clearings in forests, and streamside thickets. *T. sonomae* is found in association with black oak, ponderosa pine, digger pine, Douglas fir, white fir, redwood, sticky laurel, incense cedar, madrone, manzanita, and serviceberry. One tree nest was in a 55-meter Douglas fir; it measured 45 by 25 centimeters, was made of dry grass, and was 15 meters from the ground. Although out in the open on a limb 2.5 meters from the trunk, the nest was beneath a dense growth of small branches and dry dead twigs.

In northwestern California, the Siskiyou chipmunk, *T. siskiyou*, occurs in fir forest that may surround habitat of *T. sonomae*. *T. siskiyou* is active among downed logs on the forest floor, but ranges into bushes of whitethorn at the edge of the forest where it meets *T. sonomae*. *T. sonomae* occurs in valley areas in the Salmon Mountains; here, *T. siskiyou* occurs at higher elevations than *T. sonomae* (about 1,800 meters). On the west slope of this range, at 990 meters elevation, both species occur together. *T. sonomae* also occurs in the same habitat as shrews, moles, cottontails, California ground squirrels, north-

Tamias sonomae

ern flying squirrels, Douglas's squirrels, California gray squirrels, voles, deer and pinyon mice, bushy-tailed woodrats, elk, and mule deer. Predators include red-tailed hawks. The only parasites reported are lice. *T. L. Best*

Size

No significant sexual dimorphism
Total length: 220–264 (245) mm
Length of tail: 100–126 (112) mm
Weight: 63–77 g

Identification

Within its geographic range, *T. sonomae* meets *T. amoenus*, *T. ochrogenys*, *T. senex*, and *T. siskiyou*. From *T. amoenus*, *T. sonomae* can be distinguished by its larger size, white-edged tail, and deep-reddish coloration. From *T.*

ochrogenys, *T. senex*, and *T. siskiyou*, *T. sonomae* differs as follows: body paler; legs, tail, and ears longer; tail broader and more bushy; cheeks in winter are gray instead of brown; ears in summer pelage are sparsely furred and unicolored instead of well furred and bicolored; central reddish area on underside of tail paler rather than darker anteriorly.

Recent Synonyms

Eutamias sonomae
Eutamias townsendii alleni

Status

Common

Subspecies

Tamias sonomae alleni, near San Francisco Bay, California
Tamias sonomae sonomae, northwestern California

References

Mammalian Species 444; S. F. Smith, 1978

Lodgepole chipmunk | *Tamias speciosus*

Tamias speciosus is a brightly colored chipmunk that inhabits the entire length of the high Sierras in California and Nevada To the south it lives on the summits of isolated San Bernardino and San Jacinto mountains just north and east of Los Angeles. It occurs from elevations of about 1,580 m to the timberline, at about 3,350 m.

Lodgepole chipmunks are found in open conifer forests, and more than other chipmunks, regularly climb trees to hide or

escape danger. But most of the time they forage on the ground, run along logs, and climb onto large rocks. In the summer, families of young nest with their mother in woodpecker holes in stumps and trees as high as 23 m. In campgrounds they are tame.

The colors of the lodgepole chipmunk are lively. The sides are bright reddish-brown, and strongly contrasting dark and pale stripes mark the face and back. Especially conspicuous are

Tamias speciosus

the broad outer white stripes on the body; the outer dark stripes are faint or missing. The top of the head and rump are grayish. The bushy tail has buffy edges and is cinnamon underneath, except for a black tip. The backs of the ears are two-toned, dark in front and grayish-white behind. The winter pelage differs from the summer in being paler and more grayish, with browner dark stripes. In the spring molt, which begins first in males and young and occurs later in breeding females, the worn hair is shed and replaced by a new summer coat. A molt line often shows a progression from front to back over the body. All of the summer pelage falls out and new winter hair grows in during a second molt in the autumn.

Mating probably occurs in late May, because young are born at the end of June and early in July. Gestation, known in other chipmunks, probably lasts a month. The number of young in the single annual litter, inferred from embryo counts, averages 4.2. In Yosemite National Park the woods are alive with young in July.

Seeds and fungi are favorite foods in every season. Filling out a varied diet are flowers, fruits, insects, and other arthropods. Lodgepole chipmunks quickly add a little fat just before hibernation around the end of October, and probably, like other chipmunks, store seeds in the burrow in which they spend the winter. They reappear aboveground about the middle of April.

Lodgepole chipmunks are never far from open forests (with associated chaparral) of red fir *(Abies magnifica),* ponderosa pine *(Pinus ponderosa),* Jeffrey pine *(P. jeffreyi),* and at timberline, whitebark pine *(P. albicaulis)* and lodgepole pine *(P. contorta).* Trees provide not only refuge and nest holes in dead snags and stumps, but also food, as do shrubs like manzanita *(Arctostaphylos)* and deerbrush *(Ceanothus).*

No fossils have been found.

Three other chipmunks are seen with *T. speciosus* in the Sierras. *T. amoenus* is very similar but slightly smaller and shorter-eared, with more distinct outer dark stripes. *T. quadrimaculatus* is larger and has longer, slimmer ears. *T. senex* is the largest of all, and also has longer ears and tail than *T. speciosus.* Other small diurnal mammal neighbors in the high Sierras are the golden-mantled, Belding's, and California ground squirrels, yellow-bellied marmot, snowshoe hare, and pika. The range of the lodgepole chipmunk and that of the lodgepole pine match closely in California, but the chipmunk is not dependent on the tree. The name, *Tamias speciosus,* means beautiful storer.

H. E. Broadbooks

Size
Females are larger than males in most localities.
Total length: 200–222 (210.5) mm (males);
　197–229 (214.2) mm (females)
Length of tail: 79–100 (85.9) mm (males);
　67–102 (87.9) mm (females)

Weight: 50.6–60.8 (56.8) g (males); 55.2–69.5
　(633.1) g (females)

Identification
This chipmunk can be distinguished by the conspicuous, pure white outer stripes on its back; these are usually broader than the relatively narrrow inner pale stripes and contrast sharply with the dark stripes. The underside of the tail has a long (13 to 20 mm) black tip.

Recent Synonyms
Eutamias speciosus

Other Common Names
Tahoe chipmunk, Sequoia chipmunk, Mt. Pinos chipmunk, San Bernardino chipmunk

Status
Common

Subspecies
Tamias speciosus callipeplus, Mt. Pinos, Ventura County, California
Tamias speciosus frater, northern and central Sierra Nevadas (including east shore of Lake Tahoe in Nevada) south to Huntington Lake, Fresno County, California
Tamias speciosus sequoiensis, southern Sierra Nevadas in California

Tamias speciosus speciosus, summits of isolated Piute, San Bernardino, and San Jacinto mountains in southern California

References
Mammalian Species 478; Grinnell and Storer, 1924; Ingles, 1965; Johnson, 1943

Eastern chipmunk | *Tamias striatus*

Eastern chipmunks occur in all deciduous forest associations and in hardwood stands within the boreal forests of the northern part of their range. Common to most areas where they are found are rocks, stumps, or fallen timber, which provide perching sites and cover for burrow entrances. These chipmunks commonly occur on well-drained slopes, and do not construct burrows in flood plains or in low, swampy areas. Within cities, they may inhabit wooded cemeteries, golf courses, and parks. In the suburbs, they are found along rock fences and in gardens. Their diurnal activity and chipping vocalizations make eastern chipmunks conspicuous members of the mammalian fauna.

Burrows of this species vary from short, dead-end tunnels for quick escapes to extensive systems with numerous entrances and chambers. Tree cavities are occasionally used. Some chambers of the burrow system are used to store food, mostly nuts and small seeds. Fruits, flowers, young leaves, roots, fungi, and some animal matter are also eaten. Individuals utilize food items in relation to their shifting availability. A core area around the burrow system is defended against other chipmunks, although home ranges of neighboring individuals broadly overlap. The size of the home range varies with the availability of food and water, and with reproductive condition. Agonistic behavior among neighbors includes threats, chases, and fighting, accompanied by considerable vocalization and tail-waving. Shifting of burrow systems is more characteristic of males than females, and more characteristic of young than adults. Juveniles typically establish their own burrow systems near their birthplaces. Wooded and rocky fencerows are important corridors for movements. Live trapping and genetic studies have shown that approximately 50 percent of the population each season consists of young recruits and emigrants. The average life expectancy in natural populations is slightly over one year.

There are two peaks of daily activity, with a midday slump. This slump is most pronounced on hot summer days, but ac-

tivity also diminishes on relatively cold, windy, or rainy days. Notable solitary behaviors of chipmunks include foraging, underground food-hoarding, perching, and vocalization. Chipping is usually done when in an alert posture, while perching. The function of this behavior has not been determined but may serve to advertise a territory. A burrow entrance for quick escape is usually located near the perch site. Aboveground activity peaks during the fall, when individuals spend much time foraging for nuts and other seeds. These items are transported in internal cheek pouches to the burrow system. Recent behavioral studies have shown that a chipmunk will forage at greater distances from its burrow only if the food items obtained have high nutritional value. Loads tend to be larger when brought back from some distance. The length of collecting bouts and the number of seeds collected also varies with the density of seeds and the presence of predators.

Food hoards in burrows are necessary for underground winter survival. Chipmunks do not accumulate fat like ground squirrels. Individuals do go into torpor during the winter, but rarely for more than several days at a time. In between bouts of

Tamias striatus

torpor, they utilize their food cache. They may appear aboveground during the winter on sunny, mild days.

Males emerge from winter burrows with testes enlarged and scrotal, and cluster near the burrow system of a female on her day of estrus. Two breeding periods may occur during the season, the timing of which varies with latitude. A female may produce litters in both periods, and some females born in the spring may produce a litter in late summer. Gestation lasts for one month, and the usual litter size is four or five. The young nurse for six weeks, and first appear aboveground shortly before lactation ends. They acquire a new pelage shortly after emergence, and reach adult size at five to seven months of age. Adult males molt shortly after breeding, in early spring, and adult females molt after the first litter has dispersed. A second molt occurs in adults in the central and southern part of the range. *L. S. Ellis*

Size

No significant sexual dimorphism
Total length: 215–285 (255) mm
Length of tail: 80–115 (95) mm
Weight: 80–150 (130) g

Identification

Tamias striatus can be distinguished from other members of its family by its pattern of dorsal and facial stripes and by having four upper cheekteeth. The color of its back varies from orange through red to brown, often mixed with gray. A dark brown stripe extends from the back of the head to the rump. Two paler, wider stripes, which can vary from grayish to reddish-orange to brownish, occur on either side of the dark dorsal stripe. On the sides, two narrow dark brown stripes enclose a slightly wider yellowish-white stripe. Pale stripes border the eyes.

Status

Common throughout most of its range

Subspecies

Tamias striatus griseus, western Ontario and southern Manitoba south through Minnesota and Wisconsin to northern Missouri and Illinois

Tamias striatus lysteri, eastern Ontario, Quebec, and Maritime Provinces south through New England to northwestern South Carolina, and west through most of Ohio, northern Indiana, and Michigan

Tamias striatus pipilans, central Mississippi and Alabama south into Louisiana and Florida

Tamias striatus striatus, central Illinois and Indiana south through Kentucky and Tennessee to northern Mississippi, Alabama, Georgia, and South Carolina

Tamias striatus venustus, central and southern Missouri, eastern Oklahoma, and Arkansas

References

Mammalian Species 168; Giraldeau et al., 1994; Elliott, 1978; Henisch and Henisch, 1970

Townsend's chipmunk | *Tamias townsendii*

The first specimen of *Tamias townsendii townsendii* was collected at the mouth of the Columbia River in Oregon by John K. Townsend in 1834 or 1835. In his notes he stated: "This pretty little fellow, so much resembling our common *striatus* (the eastern chipmunk), is quite common. It lives in holes in the ground; running over your foot as you traverse the woods.

It frequently perches itself upon a log or stump, and keeps up a continual clucking, which is usually answered by another at some distance, for a considerable time." The species was named in Townsend's honor by J. Bachman in 1839. The original description also included three present species, *Tamias ochrogenys, T. senex,* and *T. siskiyou. Tamias townsendii cooperi*

was first collected on Klikitat Pass in the Cascade Mountains of Washington in July, 1853 by J. G. Cooper and was described and named for him by S. F. Baird in 1855.

Townsend's chipmunks have two pale stripes separated and bounded by three dark stripes on each side of the head and five dark body stripes separated by four pale stripes. The upper pale stripe on the head extends forward from behind and above the eye to the nose, and the lower pale stripe extends from beneath the eye to behind the ear, becoming part of a white patch behind the ear. The pale body stripes fade out both anteriorly and posteriorly, becoming more or less obscured by tawny or grayish shades.

The body of coastal *T. t. townsendii* is dark brownish or olivaceous, in contrast to the paler, reddish or somewhat orange-shaded inland *T. t. cooperi*. Winter color resembles that of summer, but is somewhat darker, with the pale stripes more buffy white. An autumn molt in August produces an olivaceous body color, with a tawny shade in the pale stripes, fading in the spring molt to a more tawny body and white stripes that are tinged with cinnamon.

The elevational range of *T. t. townsendii* is from sea level to about 1,800 m in the western Cascade Range. The inland subspecies, *T. t. cooperi*, occurs from about 350 m elevation in the west to 2,000 m in the Cascade Range. Intergradation between the two subspecies is apparently common along their border, with individual animals showing intermediate characters, making it impossible to assign them with confidence to either subspecies.

Reproduction is concentrated in late spring and early summer, following intermittent hibernation. This is the time when climate and food availability are most satisfactory. The first young emerge from the den in early July, when the average litter of four has almost twice the body mass of the mother, who continues to nurse them until early August. The young animals mature rapidly and each individual is able to collect its own food store and prepare a nest in time for winter.

Foods include seeds of grasses, pine nuts, and a variety of fruits from huckleberry *(Vaccinium)*, wild strawberry *(Fragaria)*, bunchberry *(Cornus)*, and wild rose *(Rosa)*. Townsend's chipmunk eats several kinds of fungus and one animal was observed eating tree bark. Fruits are favored, in contrast to *T. amoenus*, which favors seeds. Only when snow is on the ground would food be a factor limiting distribution.

Nest site availability may influence home ranges of female *T. t. cooperi*, suggesting exclusive home range use by each individual. Talus slopes with loose rocks appear to be preferred. *T. amoenus* is usually found in open areas with scattered shrubs.

Some sorting out of breeding and nonbreeding individuals into typical habitat groups appears to occur. In one study the breeding adult animals were concentrated in riparian habitats and juveniles were more common in uplands. Townsend's chipmunks are most abundant in clearcut logged areas where there are many decaying logs, evergreen herbs, shrubs, and trees, few deciduous herbs and trees, and many kinds of fungus and lichen. In one clearcut plot where the slash had been burned, almost 70 percent of the chipmunk food consisted of fungi and lichens, and about 12 percent was made up of insects and other invertebrates.

Tamias townsendii

Individuals of the coastal subspecies have been described as quiet and gentle. They tend to keep to the shadows, out of sight, often unnoticed but for their birdlike calls. This is quite different from the quick, nervous actions of the inland subspecies, as well as most other western chipmunks. When escape is necessary, however, the coastal chipmunks are expert at climbing trees and skillful at hiding in dense vegetation, hollow logs, and in their warm nests, which are usually underground and where an abundant store of nuts and seeds provides for all the comforts of chipmunk life. *D. A. Sutton*

Size

Females are significantly larger than males. The subspecies *T. t. townsendii* is slightly larger than *T. t. cooperi*.
Total length: 230–280 (255) mm
Length of tail: 95–120 (110) mm
Weight: 90–118 g

Identification

No other chipmunk occurs in the coastal area occupied by *Tamias townsendii townsendii*. *Tamias townsendii cooperi* is larger than *Tamias amoenus* and *Tamias minimus,* which may be found with it in the Cascade Range.

Recent Synonyms

Eutamias townsendii
Tamias cooperi
Tamias hindei (typographical error for *hindsii)*

Status

Common within its range

Subspecies

Tamias townsendii cooperi, Cascade Range from southern Oregon to southern British Columbia
Tamias townsendii townsendii, Pacific coast from southwestern Oregon to southwestern British Columbia

References

Levenson and Hoffmann, 1984; Sutton, 1987; Sutton and Nadler, 1974

Uinta chipmunk | *Tamias umbrinus*

The geographic distribution of the Uinta chipmunk consists of six or seven disjunct (widely separated) populations occurring in parts of California, Nevada, Arizona, Utah, Idaho, Wyoming, Montana, and Colorado, centered around the mountain ranges of the Great Basin in Utah. During the last glacial phase of the late Pleistocene Epoch (25,000 to 10,000 years ago), this region was much cooler and moister, allowing the boreal forest to grow down to much lower elevations. Forest or woodland covered nearly the entire region, and coniferous-forest-dwelling mammals such as the Uinta chipmunk occurred over much wider areas. In the warmer and drier time that followed, the boreal forest shrank to higher elevations, and these communities found themselves isolated on various mountaintops, separated by desert. Prolonged isolation of such populations from one another results in genetic divergence and may eventually lead to their evolution into separate species.

In some parts of its range, the Uinta chipmunk may be sympatric with the least chipmunk *(Tamias minimus),* the yellow-pine chipmunk *(T. amoenus),* and the cliff chipmunk *(T. dorsalis).* There is generally some ecological distinction between two chipmunk species that are sympatric. For example, least chipmunks (in Colorado) and cliff chipmunks (in Utah) forage in open habitats, with little or no canopy cover, to a greater degree than Uinta chipmunks, and the latter spend more time foraging in trees. Some studies have found that Uinta chip-

munks more aggressively defend territories than other chipmunks, and that their aggression is targeted at all chipmunks. This may explain why the range of the Uinta chipmunk is parapatric with (i.e., abuts but does not overlap) that of the ecologically similar Colorado chipmunk *(T. quadrivittatus)* in Colorado. Here the Uinta chipmunk is found from 2,135 m elevation in the montane forest to treeline at 3,447 m, whereas the Colorado chipmunk occurs only at or below 2,135 m. Aggressive exclusion by the Uinta chipmunk may keep the Colorado chipmunk from occurring at higher elevations, but what keeps the Uinta chipmunk from inhabiting the lower elevations as well? The answer may be a parasitic bot fly that affects the Uinta chipmunk more negatively and occurs more abundantly in the lower-elevation habitats where the Colorado chipmunk lives. The Uinta chipmunk may also be parapatric with the Panamint chipmunk *(T. panamintinus)* along the eastern slope of the Sierra Nevada.

The Uinta chipmunk is associated with a small-rodent community composed of the least chipmunk, occasionally another chipmunk species, the golden-mantled ground squirrel *(Spermophilus lateralis)*, Abert's squirrel *(Sciurus aberti)*, the red squirrel *(Tamiasciurus hudsonicus)*, the bushy-tailed woodrat *(Neotoma cinerea)*, the deer mouse *(Peromyscus maniculatus)*, the red-backed vole *(Clethrionomys gapperi)*, the long-tailed vole *(Microtus longicaudus)*, and occasionally tree or heather voles *(Arborimus longicaudus or Phenacomys intermedius)*. The Uinta chipmunk is most closely associated with ponderosa pine *(Pinus ponderosa)* forests and woodlands of the montane life zone. These may include a substantial proportion of Douglas fir *(Pseudotsuga menziesii)* or juniper *(Juniperus)*. Uinta chipmunks may also occupy drier, more open habitats, especially pinyon pine *(Pinus edulis)*-juniper woodlands. At higher elevations, they may occupy subalpine spruce-fir *(Picea-Abies)* forests, or woodlands of limber pine *(P. flexilis)*, bristlecone pine *(P. aristata or P. longaeva)*, or whitebark pine *(P. albicaulis)*. They may be found in, but are not common in, stands of lodgepole pine *(P. contorta)*.

The reproduction and ecology of the Uinta chipmunk are quite similar to that of the least chipmunk, including activity cycles, foraging behavior, hibernation, parasites, predators, and vocalizations. The Uinta chipmunk is primarily a seed-eater, specializing on coniferous trees and a wide variety of shrubs, including juniper *(J. scopulorum)*, cliffbush *(Jamesia americana)*, maple *(Acer glabrum)*, and chokecherry *(Prunus virginiana)*. In addition to seeds, it occasionally eats buds, pollen, and fruits. It responds to mast crops such as ponderosa pine or Douglas fir by having better reproduction during good

Tamias umbrinus

cone-production years. A surprisingly large part of its diet consists of fungi: when a chipmunk is digging, it is not necessarily burying or uncovering seeds, but may be foraging for mushrooms and other hypogeous (belowground) fungi. Uinta chipmunks may also consume insects, especially the more digestible larvae. Very occasionally they eat birds' eggs and carrion. Seeds form the lion's share of their hibernacular caches, which sustain them through the long winter. Chipmunks do not hibernate as deeply as ground squirrels; they live on stored food rather than stored fat.

Of the three species of chipmunks inhabiting the Front Range of Colorado, the Uinta chipmunk spends the greatest proportion of its time in trees; in fact, some individuals are quite tree-squirrel-like in their food habits and arboreality. Uinta chipmunks of both sexes often sleep and nest in trees. Females have been observed raising litters in tree cavities and may take over abandoned birds' nests, often adding roofs to them. Most often, however, they spend the night in a burrow, usually under rocks, which is also where they cache seeds and stay during their winter torpor. *B. J. Bergstrom*

Size

Females are slightly larger than males.
Total length: 210–240 (224.6) mm
Length of tail: 84–119 (98.1) mm
Weight: 51–74 (59.3) g

Identification

The Uinta chipmunk is difficult to distinguish by sight from other chipmunks that share its range. It is medium-sized, with moderately-distinct dorsal stripes and generally a warm brownish pelage on the flanks, shoulders, and head, and is more likely to be seen in trees than other chipmunks sharing its range. The Uinta chipmunk can be distinguished only with difficulty from other chipmunks occupying its range. It is larger than the least and yellow-pine chipmunks and, compared to the former, tends to hold its tail horizontally rather than vertically when running and is less "animated." The Uinta chipmunk is generally a dark brownish color with moderately distinct striping; it is not markedly washed with gray, yellow, or red; its lateral pair of stripes is narrow and sometimes nearly obscured. It is easily distinguished from the cliff chipmunk, which is usually dull gray and whose stripes are nearly obscured. Compared to the Colorado chipmunk, its stripes are less distinct and do not extend all the way to the base of the tail, it is not as washed with gray on the head and flanks, its base coloration is medium brown, not reddish-brown, and the lateral stripe is not as distinctly black. However, a freshly-molted Uinta chipmunk in mid-summer may appear nearly as bright as a Colorado chipmunk. Compared to the Panamint chipmunk of eastern California, *T. umbrinus* is brown rather than reddish-gray.

Recent Synonyms
Eutamias quadrivittatus
Eutamias umbrinus

Status
Tamias umbrinus occurs in 6 or 7 distinct geographic areas in the mountainous west; it is a commonly-seen rodent in several national parks of the Great Basin and central to northern Rocky Mountains, usually at elevations above 1,830 meters.

Subspecies
Tamias umbrinus adsitus, southern Wasatch Range to Zion National Park, in Utah, and Kaibab Plateau in north-central Arizona
Tamias umbrinus fremonti, north-central and northwestern Wyoming to extreme eastern Idaho, and Absaroka Range of southern Montana
Tamias umbrinus inyoensis, extreme northwestern Utah across central and east-central Nevada to southern Sierra Nevada of California

Tamias umbrinus montanus, Snowy Range of south-central Wyoming; Rocky Mountain ranges of north-central Colorado west through the White River Valley into extreme eastern Utah
Tamias umbrinus nevadensis, Sheep Mountains, Clark County, southern Nevada
Tamias umbrinus sedulus, Henry Mountains, Garfield County, southern Utah
Tamias umbrinus umbrinus, northern Wasatch Range of Utah into extreme southeastern Idaho; Uinta Mountains of northeastern Utah and southwestern Wyoming

References
Armstrong, 1972; Bergstrom and Hoffmann, 1991; Clark and Stromberg, 1987; Hoffmeister, 1986

Alaska marmot | *Marmota broweri*

The Alaska or Brooks Range marmot has one of the most northerly distributions of any marmot in the world. Only the unrelated black-capped marmot of eastern Siberia ranges as far north; both inhabit areas underlain by permanently frozen soil. For many years, however, *M. broweri* was not recognized as a distinct species. Instead it was considered to be a subspecies of the North American hoary marmot, which occurs in the northern Rocky Mountains and Cascades.

The Alaska marmot occurs throughout the Brooks Range and its foothills, wherever there are boulder fields and talus slopes, particularly along the north slopes of the range. A few published records are coastal, but these are probably animals that were collected inland and then brought to the coast. Like many montane species of marmots, the Alaska marmot is dependent upon the right combination of rocks and vegetation. It is strictly herbivorous, spending much of its time grazing on the tundra vegetation adjacent to its dens. Because the vegetation of the Arctic tundra is relatively low in quality, the marmot must eat great amounts in order to maintain itself. The contents of the digestive tract of an animal that has been feeding for some time may make up as much as a third of its total weight. Because they require large quantities of their low-grade foods, marmots choose den sites close to productive foraging areas. Consequently, they indirectly compete with caribou, Dall's sheep, grizzly bears, and small rodents such as the northern red-backed vole, all of which depend on the same forage plants.

Dens are usually located in extensive fields of boulders, in rock-slides, and in talus, so long as the rocks are big enough that the spaces between them can admit the bulky body of the marmot. Alaska marmots also den in rock outcroppings containing fissures that allow them to dig dens into the underlying soil. Den entrances are securely protected by large boulders or rock ledges that discourage or prevent grizzly bears from digging the marmots from their dens. Grizzlies are prodigious diggers, and are among the most serious predators of Alaska marmots. The den is the focal point of marmot life; one or more observation points on tops of adjacent rocks are associated with each den entrance, and the marmot, before beginning to feed, carefully scrutinizes the foraging area and the sky above it for evidence of predators such as bears, golden eagles, and wolves. Arctic mosquitoes, which can become extremely abundant and active on quiet, warm days in summer, also influence the behavior and movements of Alaska marmots. During such weather, the marmots frequently remain underground, not emerging until the wind rises. Cool, cloudy, breezy days provide relief from the mosquitoes. Grizzly bears, wolverines, and wolves are a danger to adult marmots, and eagles are perhaps the principal predators on juveniles. The Alaska marmot has a characteristic warning call, which it employs when an eagle is seen overhead or a large carnivore is seen nearby.

Alaska marmots seem to associate in family groups, and a male may occupy a burrow adjacent to that of a female and

her young. There is some indication that summer burrows are at lower elevations and are associated with prime foraging sites, whereas winter burrows, in which the marmots must spend the greater part of the year in hibernation, may sometimes be at higher elevations in less productive areas. The Siberian black-capped marmot's winter burrows are particularly long (113 m) and penetrate deep into the ground below the layer of permafrost. In both species, all colony residents may hibernate together. Hibernation usually begins in September, after the first autumn snow storms have occurred, and the marmots emerge in June when the melting of the snow begins to expose the ground and reveal food plants. However, these seasonal dates are not well established.

Breeding activities may be initiated either within the burrow or, less often, after the adults emerge. Young animals spend a month or so in the burrow acquiring a dense, soft, and woolly juvenile pelage before they appear aboveground. During their first summer of life, juveniles exhibit three distinct pelages, the second and third of which are produced by coarser hairs growing out between the previous generation of hairs. The third juvenile pelage is essentially similar to that of the adult. Adults appear to molt once a year, in late summer or early fall, prior to hibernation. Like all marmots, the Alaska marmot produces only one litter a year. Litter size has not been adequately documented, but is probably similar to that of the black-capped marmot, which averages six young (3–11). This is an unusually large litter for marmots. Several years are probably required before Alaska marmots are sexually mature.

Nothing is known concerning the size of home ranges, seasonal movements, or population density of Alaska marmots. They appear to be very scattered in their distribution, primarily because suitable habitat is also scattered. Longevity is also unknown, but they may be rather long-lived rodents.
R. S. Hoffmann

Marmota broweri

Size

Total length: 582–652 (605) mm (males);
539–599 (579) mm (females)
Length of tail: 152–181 (163) mm (males);
133–164 (154) mm (females)
Weight: 3–4 (3.63) kg (males); 2.5–3.5 (3.18)
kg (females)

Identification

The only marmot to occur in the Brooks Range of northern Alaska, *M. broweri* is characterized by a relatively short tail and by the solid black dorsal surface of its head and nose.

Recent Synonyms

Marmota caligata broweri
Marmota marmota broweri

Other Common Names

Brooks Range marmot

Status

Widely scattered throughout the Brooks Range; population densities usually low; hunted by Inuits and Indians, but not intensively. This marmot is probably secure at present.

References

Bee and Hall, 1956; Hoffmann et al., 1979; Rausch and Rausch, 1971

Hoary marmot | *Marmota caligata*

The hoary marmot is an alpine-montane occupant, except in northern Alaska, where it occurs down to sea level. It lives in treeless montane meadows where there are rocky outcrops and talus in which to build burrows and where abundant sedges, grasses, and forbs provide food. In areas where the yellow-bellied marmot and hoary marmot are sympatric, the hoary marmot occupies alpine and subalpine meadows and the yellow-bellied marmot occupies lower-elevation montane meadows.

Hibernation occurs from September to May. Mating takes place immediately following emergence from hibernation in the spring. The young appear aboveground in late July, about 10 weeks after copulation. Sexual maturity is attained at 3 years and females have young every other year thereafter. Two to four young per litter is normal.

Marmota caligata

A wide variety of montane meadow plants are eaten, and preferences change over the summer. Leaves of sedges and grasses are eaten in spring. The flower heads of alpine forbs are readily eaten in summer. Hoary marmots are more gregarious and social than are woodchucks and yellow-bellied marmots. Feeding groups of 5 to 8 individuals from different families are seen. Social groups often consist of one adult male, two or more adult females, two-year-olds, yearlings, and young. Family members engage in frequent nose-to-cheek greetings and grooming. Dispersal does not take place until the third summer of life.

In late summer, hoary marmots accumulate fat reserves that amount to 20 percent of the total body weight; they use the fat during hibernation. Predators include martens, coyotes, and eagles. *G. E. Svendsen*

Size
Males are larger than females.
Total length: 625–850 mm
Length of tail: 170–250 mm
Weight: 5–6 kg

Identification
M. caligata is distinguished from *Marmota flaviventris* by larger size and by gray and white (rather than brown) fur.

Status
Common throughout its range in the mountains of North America

Subspecies
Marmota caligata caligata, Alaska and western Yukon Territories
Marmota caligata cascadensis, southern British Columbia and Washington
Marmota caligata nivaria, Idaho and Montana
Marmota caligata okanagana, eastern British Columbia

Marmota caligata oxytona, British Columbia and southern Yukon Territories
Marmota caligata raceyi, west-central British Columbia
Marmota caligata sheldoni, Montague Island, Alaska
Marmota caligata vigilis, Glacier Bay, Alaska

References
Barash, 1989

Yellow-bellied marmot | *Marmota flaviventris*

The yellow-bellied marmot, sometimes called the rockchuck, is found farther south than any other species of marmot in North America save for the eastern woodchuck. However, a few thousand years ago the yellow-bellied marmot occurred even farther south. Its range extended into northern Mexico, and these marmots occupied many mountain ranges in southern Nevada, eastern California, Arizona, New Mexico, and western Texas where they no longer occur. The conventional explanation for the marmot's disappearance from the southernmost part of its range is that it retreated northward after the last glacial period, as its more southern outpost became hotter and drier. However, this explanation has recently been challenged; marmot populations on the "sky islands" in the American southwest, like other island populations, may have been particularly vulnerable to human predation and habitat modification during the period of rapid climatic change at the end of the Ice Age, and this may have been a major contributing factor to its demise in the southwest.

Within its present-day range, populations are often isolated from one another on adjacent mountain ranges because the marmot does not find suitable habitat in valleys. The name rockchuck conveys this species' dependence on suitable rocky habitat in which to make dens. Yellow-bellied marmots typically inhabit meadows adjacent to talus slopes or rock outcrops over a wide range of elevations, where the rocks protect their dens from digging predators and provide observation posts from which to watch for potential danger. Marmots occur in this general habitat throughout the central and south-central Rocky Mountains, with an outlying population in the Black Hills of the western Great Plains. This species also occurs in the Cascade and Sierra Nevada ranges, and in the isolated mountain ranges dotting the northern and central Great Basin and Columbia-Snake River Plateau. In this latter area, it occupies relatively warm, arid regions at low to mid-elevations, so

long as suitable rocks and vegetation can be found together. However, throughout most of its range it occupies the montane forest, subalpine, and alpine zones of mountains.

The elevation that a population of yellow-bellied marmots inhabits significantly affects its life cycle. Populations at lower elevations, particularly in semi-arid regions where winter snowfall is less, emerge from hibernation earlier in the spring than do populations occurring at higher elevations, where there is usually a deep winter snow pack. The marmots emerge from hibernation in late winter and early spring with a long, full pelage that shows little signs of wear from their winter sleep. Upon emergence they begin to feed, although they continue to rely upon their body fat until vegetation becomes more abundant with the advance of spring. Breeding behavior is concentrated in the first several weeks after emergence, and litters first appear aboveground after a gestation period of about a month, earlier at low elevations and later at higher ones. There is only one litter per year throughout the range of this species, and its size ranges from 3–8 with an overall average of 4.3–4.8. Adult females produce slightly larger litters than do subadults and there are probably annual and geographic variations in litter size as well, but this has not been documented. Within a population, both breeding males and nonbreeding individuals of both sexes begin their single annual molt after the spring's breeding activities have been completed. Breeding females delay onset of the molt until their young are close to being weaned, usually in July and August.

Most yellow-bellied marmots live in small colonies consisting of a single adult male, one to several breeding females, both adult and subadult, and the young offspring of these females. However, some live singly, usually in submarginal habitat. These single individuals may be dispersing young; young males usually disperse as yearlings (in their second year of life). Young females may stay longer in their natal colonies than males do, and fewer of them disperse as far. Populations at high elevations often disperse later than those at lower elevations. This is probably related to the shorter growing season at high elevations: with less time to feed and raise young, and to accumulate fat for winter hibernation, females in this severe environment usually produce litters only every other year, allowing the young to remain with their mothers for a longer period.

During the active period of the year, marmots usually emerge from their burrows soon after sunrise. A short time may be spent sunning and grooming in front of the den, but foraging soon begins, peaking in mid-morning, followed by another interval of sunning and grooming, and often a return to the burrow if the day is particularly sunny and warm. A second foraging period usually occurs in the afternoon and by sundown most animals have returned to the den for the night. This general pattern is variable, depending upon weather, and varies geographically with climatic zones. Selected foraging areas have greater food abundance, except that the marmots avoid areas of tall vegetation, probably because it impedes their ability to spot predators.

Behavior between individuals in a colony is generally amicable, although a dominance hierarchy is well established,

Marmota flaviventris

with the adult male dominant over females, and adult females over subadults and young. The adult male of a colony guards the colony's territory, particularly against the intrusion of other adult males or dispersing yearlings. Females may also take part in territorial defense on occasion.

Marmot population density in a particular region is strongly correlated with the availability of suitable habitat, particularly areas of foraging and den sites. Territories are about one-half hectare in size, but vary according to local habitat conditions. Where extensive rock slides or boulder fields are closely interspersed with areas of rich vegetation at intermediate elevations, population densities are greatest. Densities become progressively lower both downslope into hotter, more arid environments and upslope into less productive, more severe alpine environments. Marmot density may also be influenced by the presence or absence of large grazing ungulates such as deer, elk, or mountain sheep. If such grazers are absent, productivity of the plants utilized by marmots may be reduced by the dominance of perennial grasses. Moderate grazing may reduce grass competition and permit better growth of the herbaceous plants that marmots favor. On the other hand, heavy grazing may reduce the supply of food available to marmots, which may be particularly critical during the late summer and early fall, when they are accumulating fat prior to the onset of hibernation.

Timing of entrance into hibernation varies depending upon environmental factors and the age and sex of the marmot. A productive growing season permits marmots to achieve readiness for hibernation sooner. Adult males and nonbreeding females, having fewer metabolic demands, have more time to forage than do females who are caring for young and producing milk for unweaned offspring. As a consequence, they may enter hibernation sooner than breeding females, who must achieve their fat storage after the young have been weaned. Juveniles devote a great deal of energy to growth during their first summer of life. Newborns weigh only about 30–35 grams, and are born hairless and blind. They remain in the burrow for about a month and are nearly weaned and have nearly doubled their weight when they emerge. Juveniles grow faster at higher elevations, apparently to compensate for the shorter summer season, but they are typically among the last to hibernate. The young usually hibernate with their mother during their first winter, but adult males usually hibernate alone.

Hibernation is probably the time of greatest mortality for marmots of all ages. The animals remain in their underground dens throughout the period of hibernation, surviving on accumulated fat. Over the winter they may lose up to half of their body weight, and it is critical that they obtain a certain threshold weight by the time they enter hibernation. The earlier the young are weaned, the more time they and their mothers will have to achieve this threshold; an early-arriving spring enhances their chance of surviving. The timing of the onset of winter and spring are critical to survival, and therefore to marmot population densities.

Yellow-bellied marmots are relatively immune to attacks by predators during the hibernation period. However, during the active summer season a number of carnivores may prey on them, including wolves, coyotes, badgers, bobcats, and martens, as well as the larger hawks and owls. The golden eagle is probably the primary avian predator; yellow-bellied marmots are a principal prey item for the eagles in most parts of their range. Even so, predation appears to be a minor source of mortality, particularly for marmots living in colonies; it is probably of greater significance in peripheral populations. *R. S. Hoffmann*

Size
Total length: 490–700 (618) mm (males); 470–670 (574) mm (females)
Length of tail: 149–220 (180) mm (males); 126–220 (165) mm (females)
Weight: 2.95–5.22 kg (males); 1.59–3.97 kg (females)

Identification
This species is distinguished from the closely related hoary marmot by its smaller size, conspicuous buffy to yellowish sides of its neck, yellow to russet belly, and a large oval pad on the inner rear sole of the hind foot.

Recent Synonyms
Marmota flaviventer

Other Common Names
Rockchuck

Status
Widely distributed and often common, but populations are often separated by areas of unsuitable habitat, particularly in the southern part of the range. Such small, isolated populations are vulnerable.

Subspecies
Marmota flaviventris dacota, Black Hills of eastern Wyoming and western South Dakota
Marmota flaviventris engelhardti, south-central Utah
Marmota flaviventris flaviventris, Cascade and Sierra Nevada ranges from northern Oregon south to the central Sierra Nevada, California
Marmota flaviventris fortirostris, White Mountains, southeastern California
Marmota flaviventris luteola, south-central Rocky Mountains from southern Wyoming south to extreme north-central New Mexico
Marmota flaviventris nosophora, extreme southern Alberta south through central and western Montana, central and eastern Idaho, and north-central Wyoming to northeastern Utah
Marmota flaviventris notioros, Wet and Greenhorn mountains, Colorado
Marmota flaviventris obscura, central Colorado to northeastern New Mexico
Marmota flaviventris parvula, central Nevada
Marmota flaviventris sierrae, southern Sierra Nevada, California

References
Mammalian Species 135; Armitage et al., 1990; Carey, 1985; Van Vuren and Armitage, 1991

Woodchuck | *Marmota monax*

The woodchuck is a semifossorial occupant of forest borders, favoring the edge of brushy woodland, especially along fields, roads, and streams. Burrows are constructed beneath rocks, stumps, building foundations, or other supportive structures. Woodchucks use burrows to spend the night, to escape from predators and inclement conditions, to raise young, and to hibernate over winter. They are diurnal vegetarians, and will feed at almost any time during the daylight hours, but are most active early in the morning and again in the late afternoon before the sun goes down.

Woodchucks are not gregarious. Seldom will more than one adult occupy a burrow. They breed at one year of age. Mating

Marmota monax

occurs in March and April and gestation is about 30 days. A single litter per year is produced, which may contain from two to seven young. Young are born naked, blind, and helpless. They are weaned at six weeks and begin to wander from the natal burrow and live by themselves shortly after that.

The general color of *M. monax* is dark grayish to brown. The tip of the hair shaft is pale buff, giving a grizzled appearance to the pelage. The feet are blackish-brown; the underparts are reddish-brown. There is one molt annually. The body is short and thickset. The head is broad and the ears are short, thick, and rounded. The tail is well-furred, moderately bushy, and short. The legs are short and strong, with four well-developed toes that bear strong, curved claws. The skull is broad and flat and the rostrum large and massive. The incisors are heavy, pale yellow to ivory, with faint grooves running the length of the tooth.

Woodchucks eat a variety of green vegetation including dandelion, chickweed, sorrel, clover, alfalfa, beans, peas, grains,

and grasses. They may also eat the bark and buds of trees and shrubs in spring. Huge fat reserves are accumulated during the summer and early fall, then the fat is used during the winter-long hibernation. The woodchuck is a true hibernator. It curls into a ball with its head between its forelegs, its nose resting on its lower abdomen, and its hind parts and tail wrapped over its head. Its body temperature drops from 32° C (90° F) to near the ambient temperature of the hibernaculum, its heartbeat drops from 75 per minute to around 4 per minute, and it appears lifeless. *G. E. Svendsen*

Size
Males average 3 percent heavier than females.
Total length: 415–675 mm
Length of tail: 100–150 mm
Weight: 3–4 kg

Identification
Marmota monax is distinguished from *Marmota flaviventris* by smaller size, by the reddish-brown pelage on its chest lacking a yellow wash, and by the fur on its head lacking white.

Other Common Names
Ground hog, whistle-pig

Status
Common throughout its range

Subspecies
Marmota monax bunkeri, eastern Nebraska to eastern Oklahoma
Marmota monax canadensis, most of Canada, northern Great Lakes region
Marmota monax ignava, northern Quebec and Labrador
Marmota monax johnsoni, Gaspé Peninsula, Quebec
Marmota monax monax, eastern United States south of Great Lakes

Marmota monax ochracea, Yukon Territories and Alaska
Marmota monax petrensis, British Columbia south to northern Idaho
Marmota monax preblorum, Maine, New Hampshire, and Massachusetts
Marmota monax rufescens, central Great Lakes region

References
Mammalian Species 591; Barash, 1989

Olympic marmot | *Marmota olympus*

The Olympic marmot is restricted to the Olympic Peninsula of Washington, where it is limited to alpine and subalpine habitat at elevations between 1,700 to 2,000 meters. Its preferred habitat is montane slope with abundant rock talus and lush meadows. Burrows are constructed beneath rocks. Daily activity aboveground begins shortly after sunrise, when the marmots emerge from their burrows and begin feeding. By mid-morning, they feed less and sun more. They retreat to their burrows in the middle of the day and emerge again in late afternoon to feed before retiring to their burrows before dark.

Preferred foods in spring, after emergence from hibernation in May and June, are grasses and sedges. The marmots' diet changes to include a wide variety of flowering plants that grow in the moist alpine meadows as summer progresses. By September, Olympic marmots are fat and lethargic, they spend more and more time in their burrows, and soon enter eight months of hibernation.

Social groups of Olympic marmots typically include one adult male and one or more adult females, two-year-olds, yearlings, and young. *Marmota olympus* is one of the more social species of marmots. Individuals from different families may congregate at feeding sites and family members spend considerable time grooming one another. They use a nose-to-cheek greeting when two individuals meet. Females produce young every other year and young disperse as two-year-olds. Mating occurs shortly after emergence from hibernation; gestation is about 30 days. Young are born helpless and remain in the burrow until they are about six weeks old, when they begin daily activity outside the burrow. They are weaned during a three-week period between mid-July and early August.

Mortality is high for young-of-the-year during hibernation, and for dispersing two-year-olds. Smaller marmots are more likely to die than are larger individuals. Predators include coyotes, martens, and eagles. *G. E. Svendsen*

Marmota olympus

Size
Males are larger than females.
Total length: 680–785 mm
Length of tail: 195–252 mm
Weight: 5–7 kg

Identification
The Olympic marmot resembles the hoary marmot, except its color is brownish drab mixed with white rather than black and white.

Status
Restricted to the Olympic Peninsula of Washington

References
Barash, 1989; Lee and Funderburg, 1982

Vancouver marmot | *Marmota vancouverensis*

Confined to Vancouver Island, British Columbia, *Marmota vancouverensis* has the most restricted range of any North American marmot. Most of the known colonies occur in a small area (80 square kilometers) in the mountains of southeastern Vancouver Island, where it lives in alpine and subalpine communities at about 1,000–1,460 meters elevation. Steep south-facing slopes where the snow disappears in early spring provide the ideal habitat. Deep soil for burrowing and an abundance of large rocks and boulders for look-outs are also important habitat requirements. This species also occupies disturbed habitats and a number of colonies are located in recently logged areas adjacent to alpine meadows.

The Vancouver marmot lives in small colonies consisting of adults and their associated young. Underground burrows are used for dens and much of the animal's aboveground activity occurs close to the burrow. In summer, *M. vancouverensis* is most active in the mornings and evenings and the hot midday is usually spent in the burrow. Most of the time aboveground is spent either feeding or resting on look-out sites near the den. When alarmed by intruders or predators, Vancouver marmots emit a piercing, high-pitched whistle.

In early spring, grasses and sedges are important foods; forbs, particularly lupine *(Lupinus latifolius)*, asters *(Aster)*, peavine *(Lathyrus nevadensis)*, meadowrue *(Thalictrum occidentale)*, cow-parsnip *(Heracleum lanatum)*, and paintbrush *(Castilla)* are eaten in summer. Predators include the golden eagle, wolf, and cougar.

Despite its mild maritime climate, high elevations on Vancouver Island receive heavy snowfall in winter, and the Vancouver marmot spends 7 to 8 months in hibernation. Aboveground activity steadily declines from late August through September, and by early October most marmots have entered hibernation. *M. vancouverensis* emerges from hibernation in late April or early May, when there is still snow on the ground.

Marmota vancouverensis

Fur color is quite variable, depending on the stage of the molt, which begins in July. In early summer, adults tend to be mottled in appearance, with patches of old faded fur and new dark fur. However, by late summer, just before entering hibernation, most Vancouver marmots are an attractive uniform dark brown or black with striking white markings on the nose, forehead, chin, and undersides. Some individuals may not complete the molt before hibernation, retaining patches of old fur until the next summer. Young-of-the-year have a dark, woolly coat.

Mating occurs in May within a few weeks after hibernation has ended. The gestation period is about one month. Females usually have three young, although the litter size can range from 2 to 5. Because their first month is spent underground in the burrow, little is known about the growth and development of the young. Young-of-the-year first appear outside the burrow in late June or July. Females reach sexual maturity by 3 or 4 years of age.

Because it has a localized distribution and a small population, estimated at 100 to 200, the Vancouver marmot has been listed by various governmental agencies as endangered. It is the only endangered mammal endemic to Canada. Bones recovered from 700- to 2,700-year-old archeological sites, histor-

ical museum specimens, and observational records suggest that *M. vancouverensis* was more widespread on Vancouver Island in the past. Long-term environmental changes, prehistoric hunting, and recent forestry operations could have impacted populations. Nevertheless, no obvious threats have been identified and reasons for the range decline are unknown. A recently approved national recovery plan recommends restoring this species by captive breeding and introductions.
D. Nagorsen

Size
Males are larger than females.
Total length: 580–750 (668) mm
Length of tail: 162–300 (200) mm
Weight: 3.0–6.5 kg

Identification
Unlike other marmots, the Vancouver marmot has brown to nearly black fur, with white markings on the face, chest, and belly. No other marmot occurs within its range.

Other Common Names
Vancouver Island marmot

Status
Endangered

References
Mammalian Species 270; Banfield, 1974; Bryant and Janz, 1996; Martell and Milko, 1986

Harris's antelope squirrel | *Ammospermophilus harrisii*

Harris's antelope squirrel occurs below 1,350 meters elevation in the southwestern United States and northwestern Mexico. No fossils of *A. harrisii* are known.

This diurnal species is active even in the hottest part of the day. It does not hibernate, and is active every month of the year. Harris's antelope squirrels are vigorous runners. They scurry about the desert floor, stopping frequently to dig, and shallow holes in the soil are clear signs of their presence. At times, these antelope squirrels sit atop bristle-spined cholla cactus to view the surrounding area. How they negotiate the climb over the thorns is a mystery, for the soft pads of their feet never contain spines, nor are there scars to indicate former difficulties. They commonly sit erect on their hind feet. When disturbed, *A. harrisii* runs with its tail straight up in the air, uttering chipperings as it hurries to nearby shrubbery to enter a burrow. Before escaping, it often stops, calls, and stamps with its forepaws. As in other *Ammospermophilus,* the calls are long, high-pitched trills.

Size is medium for the genus, the tail is medium to short, and the ears are small. Each foot has five toes. The back is pale brown to blackish, and there is one whitish stripe along each side of the body. Color around the eye, throat, chin, inner surface of the legs, and the whole underside of the body is whitish, with a few black hairs interspersed. A line of whitish-yellow on the flanks distinctly separates the color of the back and sides from that of the undersurface. The hairs are short and somewhat coarse, but lie smoothly, giving the animal a glossy appearance. Geographic variation is primarily in size rather than in color.

Harris's antelope squirrels breed in December or January and usually produce one litter of five to nine young per year. The gestation period is about 30 days. Females prepare a round nest that is often completely covered with nest material, leaving only one opening. Newborn antelope squirrels are naked, with pink, rather transparent skin. Their eyes and ears are closed. They cannot crawl, but they can right themselves when placed on their backs. Their mass at birth averages 3.6 grams

Ammospermophilus harrisii

(range, 3.0–4.1). At three weeks, their claws are well developed, but the young still cannot walk without falling over. They are very vocal even at this age and frequently utter a half-muffled trill, especially when they are disturbed. At 3–4 weeks, the ears open and the young are fully covered with short hairs, resembling adults. Young first emerge from their burrows at 4–5 weeks of age, when the eyes have just opened. At seven weeks, they are weaned. Males may reach sexual maturity during their first year, but females do not come into breeding condition until the spring following their birth.

Harris's antelope squirrel occupies a variety of desert habitats. It is the most conspicuous small diurnal mammal of the desert plains from Tucson, Arizona, to the Colorado River, but it has a spotty distribution. Its burrows are usually under a desert shrub such as palo verde, mesquite, or creosotebush, but sometimes they are in the open. Other habitats include open areas in plains, valleys, canyons, and river bottoms.

A. harrisii is omnivorous. Its food is mainly the fruit and seeds of cactus, but numerous other seeds and green plants are eaten as well. Its forepaws, face, intestinal tract, and muscles are sometimes stained from the juices of cactus fruits, and the squirrels can suffer pricks from the small, sharp spines on the fruits. *A. harrisii* also feeds on seeds of the screw-pod mesquite,

shelling the beans and then carrying them in its cheek pouches to storage in the burrow. The capacity of the cheek pouches is considerable; one contained 44 mesquite beans. Stored food enables the squirrels to stay below ground during the coldest weather.

Harris's antelope squirrels are never found abundantly; they occur singly, here and there. Individuals have an average range of movement of 274 meters. In southeastern Arizona, density ranges from 0.08 to 0.36 per hectare, with greatest densities in late spring to late summer (0.24–0.36 per hectare) and lowest densities in autumn to early spring (0.08–0.24 per hectare).

Ammospermophilus harrisii is widely sympatric with the round-tailed ground squirrel, *Spermophilus tereticaudus.* These species often are found only a few meters apart in south-central Arizona, and have often been observed entering the same kangaroo rat dens. Other associated mammals include desert shrews, desert cottontails, antelope and black-tailed jackrabbits, pocket gophers, desert, Ord's, Merriam's, and banner-tailed kangaroo rats, several species of pocket mice, deer mice, cactus mice, grasshopper mice, desert and white-throated woodrats, badgers, coyotes, gray and kit foxes, bobcats, mule deer, and bighorn sheep. Parasites include nematodes, lice, ticks, and fleas. *T. L. Best*

Size
No significant sexual dimorphism
Total length: 216–267 (238) mm
Length of tail: 67–92 (79) mm
Weight: 122 g

Identification
Harris's antelope squirrel differs from other similar-sized ground squirrels by its grayish dorsum and tail and by the presence of one white stripe along each side of the body from shoulder to rump. It is distinguished from other members of the genus by the mixed black and white undersurface of the tail; other *Ammospermophilus* have a white undersurface of the tail.

Recent Synonyms
Spermophilus harrisii

Other Common Names
Harris's spermophile, marmot squirrel, gray-tailed antelope squirrel, Yuma antelope ground squirrel

Status
Common

Subspecies
Ammospermophilus harrisii harrisii, western and southern Arizona, western New Mexico, and north-central Sonora, Mexico
Ammospermophilus harrisii saxicolus, southwestern Arizona and northwestern Sonora, Mexico

References
Mammalian Species 366; Neal, 1965a, 1965b

Texas antelope squirrel | *Ammospermophilus interpres*

The Texas antelope squirrel occupies the Chihuahuan Plateau of Mexico, western Texas, and south-central New Mexico. The species is restricted to rocky habitats on and around desert mountain ranges. In Trans-Pecos Texas, it occurs at elevations of 540–1,830 meters, but is most common between 1,050 and 1,650 meters. Remains of *A. interpres* have been recovered from prehistoric cave deposits in Coahuila, Mexico, and Val Verde County, Texas.

Fidgety, nervous, and seldom still for long, Texas antelope squirrels are nimble-footed and can run with surprising speed. Their peculiar habit of carrying the tail arched forward over the back, exposing to view the contrasting-colored undersurface, is a readily usable field characteristic of this genus. The nervous flickering of the tail when the animals are excited and the mellow, rolling, trill-like calls further help to identify them. *A. interpres* often sits on prominent boulders and on tops of junipers or large shrubs. It usually is seen running from bush to bush, sitting on a point of rock, or running over the rocks with its short, bushy tail curled tight over its rump. Its activities are restricted to daylight hours, with most activity occurring during the hottest parts of the day. It probably does not hibernate.

Ammospermophilus interpres has one white stripe bordered with blackish on each side of the body, no distinct head stripes, and hairs on the underside of the tail that are white medially. The back is gray. The shoulders, hips, and outer surface of its legs are yellowish-brown. The underside is white. The third of the tail nearest the body is the same color as the back; the rest is grayish-black. The tail is white beneath, with two black bands and a whitish border.

Breeding begins in February. One litter of 5 to 14 young is reared each year, but a second litter may be reared by some females. The young remain in the nest until they are about 25 percent of adult size, at which time they venture aboveground and begin eating solid foods. In May, half-grown young may be out of their burrows getting their own food, including various seeds and fruits, and climbing catclaw and mesquite bushes to secure ripening pods, which often are found scattered in abundance about their burrows.

The Texas antelope squirrel is found in habitats with creosote-bush, tarbush, lechuguilla, and sotol, and in desert, grassland, and woodland habitats. It does not occur far away from boulders and areas with junipers and large shrubs. It is most common on hard-surface gravelly washes or rocky slopes, and is less common or absent on level, sandy terrain. Canyons, bare cliffs, and rocks seem to be factors determining the range of the Texas antelope squirrel.

It usually lives in burrows, but crevices in and between rocks may serve as den sites. It makes use of abandoned burrows of other rodents and there usually is no mound of earth to mark

Ammospermophilus interpres

the entrance. It burrows under the edge of boulders or around the base of bushes or cacti. One burrow was 9 centimeters in diameter, 3 meters in length, and access was by three openings. Midway in the tunnel was the nest chamber, which measured 135 by 18 by 10 centimeters. The nest was composed of rabbit fur, shredded bark, feathers, dry grasses, and bits of cotton.

The diet consists of a variety of seeds, berries, and insects, including the seeds, fruit, and fleshy parts of many species of cactus. The beans of mesquite and various other legumes are gathered for food, as are the seeds of creosote-bush, sotol, yucca, juniper, salt grass, ripe fruits of cactus, and other seed-bearing plants. In spring and early summer, considerable green vegetation is eaten. One Texas antelope squirrel had eaten so much cactus fruit that its muscles were tinted throughout with the purple color of the fruit. Internal cheek pouches are used to carry food.

In western Texas, *A. interpres* occurs in the same habitat as rock squirrels, pocket gophers, Nelson's pocket mice, cactus mice, pinyon mice, deer mice, white-throated and Mexican woodrats, yellow-nosed cotton rats, eastern and desert cottontails, ring-tails, and mule deer. On the lava beds of southern New Mexico, it occurs with rock squirrels, gray-footed chipmunks, rock pocket mice, deer mice, spotted skunks, coyotes, and bobcats. In Mexico, *A. interpres* is an important food source for predators, including humans, because it is numerous and easy to capture.

The caecum of one Texas antelope squirrel contained numerous nematodes of the family *Oxyuridae*, but no other parasites are known. *T. L. Best*

Size
No significant sexual dimorphism
Total length: 220–235 (226) mm
Length of tail: 68–84 (74) mm
Weight: 99–122 (110) g

Identification
The Texas antelope squirrel is medium-sized and has the longest tail and hind limbs in the genus. Compared to *A. leucurus, A. interpres* is smaller, darker, and two distinct black bands are visible on the undersurface of the tail; *A. leucurus* has a single band. Compared to *A. harrisii,* which is similar in dorsal coloration, *A. interpres* can be distinguished by the white on the medial undersurface of the tail; the undersurface of the tail of *A. harrisii* is gray.

Recent Synonyms
Tamias interpres

Other Common Names
Trader spermophile

Status
Common

References
Mammalian Species 365; Bailey, 1931

White-tailed antelope squirrel │ *Ammospermophilus leucurus*

Antelope squirrels are conspicuous rodents throughout North American deserts. The white-tailed antelope squirrel is the most widespread species, found from the Colorado Plateau and Great Basin to the Mojave Desert and Baja California peninsula. A colony on Isla San Marcos in the Sea of Cortez may be a recent introduction or a remnant of the last glacial period, when a landbridge connected the island to the mainland.

Unlike other ground squirrels, prairie dogs, and chipmunks, antelope squirrels are active throughout the year, and seem to be in constant motion. They are remarkably adapted to the desert heat and aridity, with a tolerance for both high body temperatures and dehydration. They have efficient kidneys, and their behavior permits activity even during the hottest summer days in the desert. They are avid and adept climbers and often issue a high trilling call, particularly in response to hawks or other predators, from perches atop junipers *(Juniperus),* Joshua trees *(Yucca brevifolia),* or saguaro *(Carnegia gigantea).* They are easily observed as they bounce along at a run, the tail, with its white underside, curled over the back. Usually they stop, tail twitching over the back, before entering their shallow burrows (often abandoned kangaroo rat burrows).

White-tailed antelope squirrels are generally pale brown on

top and white beneath, with two white stripes extending from the shoulder to the hip. Subspecies range from grayish to brown to cinnamon, and the winter pelage is generally longer, softer, and darker than the short, bristly summer pelage. Antelope squirrels get their name from the white bottom of the broadly haired tail, displayed as conspicuously as the white rear of a fleeing pronghorn antelope as the squirrel runs away.

White-tailed antelope squirrels are omnivorous, feeding on green vegetation and seeds of various shrubs, yucca, and cacti, but also catching and eating insects and even small rodents. Seeds of yuccas *(Yucca)* and chollas *(Opuntia)* are particular favorites.

These antelope squirrels breed from February to June, regardless of environmental conditions. Litter sizes range from 5 to 14, depending on the availability of green vegetation. Young weighing about 3 g each are born after a gestation period of one month, develop slowly relative to other ground squirrels, and are weaned after two months. Young first appear aboveground one or two weeks before weaning. Instead of territories, white-tailed antelope squirrels form stable, linear dominance heirarchies. During winter, several antelope squirrels may share a burrow, huddling together to keep warm.

Within their wide range of desert habitats, white-tailed antelope ground squirrels prefer shrubby areas with sandy to rocky soil. They occur from the lowest valley floors to the juniper belt, and from the low elevation, warm desert of the Baja California Peninsula to the high, cold deserts of the Great Basin and Colorado Plateau. Other common rodents in the same habitat are pocket mice *(Perognathus* and *Chaetodipus)*, kangaroo rats *(Dipodomys)*, woodrats *(Neotoma)*, and white-footed mice *(Peromyscus)*.

Although similar in external appearance to other ground squirrels, antelope squirrels diverged from the other ground squirrels, marmots, and prairie dogs fairly early, perhaps 15 to 20 million years ago. Antelope squirrels first appear in the fossil record during the late Miocene, about 10 million years ago. All fossil records of the genus, as well as all living species, are found only in the North American deserts. A closely related species, *Ammospermophilus insularis,* is restricted to Isla Espiritu

Ammospermophilus leucurus

Santo in the southern Sea of Cortez. Harris's antelope squirrel *(A. harrisi)* occupies the Sonoran Desert of Arizona, southwestern New Mexico, and Sonora, Mexico. Nelson's antelope squirrel *(A. nelsoni)* occurs only in the San Joaquin Valley of California. The most distantly related species, the Texas antelope squirrel *(A. interpres)* lives in the Chihuahuan Desert from New Mexico and Texas south to Durango, Mexico. The long association of antelope squirrels with the developing regional deserts has made the genus useful in studying relationships among the regions. The white-tailed antelope squirrel, centrally located and spanning the greatest range of desert regions, is of particular interest in this regard. *D. J. Hafner*

Size

No significant sexual dimorphism
Total length: 188–239 (211) mm
Length of tail: 42–87 (58) mm
Weight: 96–117 (105) g

Identification

Ammospermophilus leucurus is distinguished from sympatric ground squirrels (of about the same size), larger rock squirrels and prairie dogs, and smaller chipmunks by the unique combination of distinctive white stripes on the sides, white undersurface of the broadly haired tail, and lack of facial stripes. From a distance, white-tailed antelope squirrels can be distinguished by their agile, long-legged, bouncing run and their erect and twitching tail held over the back. The white-tailed antelope squirrel is not sympatric with any other antelope squirrel.

Other Common Names

White-tailed antelope ground squirrel; white-tailed ground squirrel; antelope chipmunk

Status

Relatively common and widespread

Subspecies

Ammospermophilus leucurus canfieldae, central Baja California, Mexico
Ammospermophilus leucurus cinnamomeus, northeastern Arizona, southeastern Utah, southwestern Colorado
Ammospermophilus leucurus escalante, southwestern Utah and nothwestern Arizona
Ammospermophilus leucurus extimus, Baja California Sur, Mexico

Ammospermophilus leucurus leucurus, western Utah, southwestern Idaho, southeastern Oregon, Nevada, southern California, northwestern Arizona, and northeastern Baja California
Ammospermophilus leucurus notom, northeastern Utah
Ammospermophilus leucurus peninsulae, northern Baja California
Ammospermophilus leucurus pennipes, eastern Utah, western Colorado, northwestern New Mexico
Ammospermophilus leucurus tersus, northwestern Arizona

References

Mammalian Species 368

Nelson's antelope squirrel | *Ammospermophilus nelsoni*

Nelson's antelope squirrel occurs in the San Joaquin Valley of California, and on the slopes and ridgetops in the foothills along the western edge of the valley, in the Cuyama and Panoche valleys, and on the Carrizo and Elkhorn plains. The elevational range is about 50–1,100 meters. Post-Pleistocene fossils resembling *A. nelsoni* have been found near McKittrick, Kern County, California.

These antelope squirrels are active early or late in the day and are not early risers, rarely being found aboveground until well after sun-up. During cold periods, mid-day is used for aboveground activities, and during warm periods the early morning and late afternoon hours are used. The squirrels are cautious about coming out of their burrows; they never come out hastily. When they move, their actions are abrupt, as though they have suddenly decided what to do. Their quiet calls are short trills, more noticeable to human observers by the associated convulsive movement of the body than by the sound itself. When foraging, they move close to the ground, often stopping in the shelter of a bush or pausing in the open to search quietly, with body extended, for food. They show great agility in climbing and catch grasshoppers by leaping with the insect until both come down at the same place at the same time. Often they stretch out to their full length and roll over and wallow in the fine powdery dust along the washes. They are social.

The ears are short and broad, the tail is 25–33 percent of the total length, and the legs are relatively long. There is a whitish stripe on each side reaching from behind the shoulder to the rump. The underparts, feet, and eyelids are whitish. The upperparts are dull yellowish-brown, as are the outer surfaces of the legs. Geographic variation is primarily in color and size. Populations in the southern San Joaquin Valley are smaller and less yellowish, with a gradual increase in size to the largest, more yellow northern populations.

The breeding period is late winter through early spring; gestation is 26 days. Six to 11 young (average is nine) usually are born in March and are first seen aboveground about the first week in April. This is the only breeding season, and it coincides with the one period of the year when green vegetation is present. Neonates weigh about 5 grams, average 58 millimeters long, and are hairless, quite active, and able to make mewing sounds. At about 30 days, when the eyes open, the young are well furred and begin to appear aboveground. Weaning may be started or completed before the young come aboveground. During weaning, the female forages alone and leaves any young that approach her. She keeps contact by occasional visits or by using the calls by which family groups communicate. She does not allow the young to nurse even though they nuzzle her from time to time. Change from juvenile to adult pelage

Ammospermophilus nelsoni

begins about the time the young become independent, and usually by mid-May the adult summer coat is present. After the first year, it is difficult to tell age groups apart. The usual life span is less than a year, but some individuals live 5–6 years.

Nelson's antelope squirrels usually inhabit open, rolling land and gentle slopes with shrubs. During the breeding season, burrows most often used by adult females and their young are under shrubs such as ephedra or saltbush. *A. nelsoni* seldom excavates burrows: it utilizes burrows dug by kangaroo rats. The burrows are somewhat complicated, with two or three passageways converging at a depth of 30 centimeters or more. The entrances are 4–20 centimeters in diameter.

Nelson's antelope squirrels are omnivorous and consume vegetable and animal food of many types, including rodents, lizards, and their own kind (probably as carrion). The cheek pouches of one squirrel contained 744 seeds, but these squirrels do not store food in their burrows. Insects make up about 90 percent of the diet from mid-April to December. Seeds usually comprise about 10 percent of the diet, except from March to May and in December and January, when they may reach 20 percent of the diet. Both green vegetation and insects are selected more often than seeds, possibly due to their water content.

Six or eight individuals constitute a colony of average size. However, antelope squirrels are not distributed evenly over their geographic range. There may be more than 10 per hectare in some areas, but generally the density is lower than one per hectare. The home range of both sexes is about 4.4 hectares, with areas of concentration within this range. Only 50 percent or less of the home range is covered each day. *A. nelsoni* occurs in the same habitat as cottontails, black-tailed jackrabbits, pocket gophers, Heermann's, Fresno, and giant kangaroo rats, pocket mice, deer mice, woodrats, long-tailed weasels, badgers, bobcats, coyotes, and kit foxes. Predators include red-tailed hawks, great-horned owls, barn owls, prairie falcons, badgers, coyotes, and kit foxes. Parasites include cestodes, nematodes, acanthocephalans, ticks, and fleas.

Human activity is the greatest threat to *A. nelsoni*. Because of intense agricultural development of the San Joaquin Valley, its habitat has been subjected to extreme destruction. *T. L. Best*

Size
Males are slightly larger than females.
Total length: 234–267 (249) mm (males);
 230–256 (238) mm (females)
Length of tail: 66–78 (73) mm (males); 67–78
 (72) mm (females)
Weight: 142–179 (155) g

Identification
Ammospermophilus nelsoni is the only species of its genus present in the San Joaquin and adjacent valleys, California. The whitish stripes on the sides and the tail carried forward over the back are conspicuous features. When the animal is running, the tail is displayed so that at a distance it looks like a bit of thistledown blowing along the ground.

Recent Synonyms
Spermophilus nelsoni

Other Common Names
San Joaquin antelope squirrel, Nelson's
 spermophile, antelope chipmunk

Status
Uncommon

References
Mammalian Species 367; Grinnell and Dixon, 1918

Uinta ground squirrel | *Spermophilus armatus*

Uinta ground squirrels were named for the Uinta Mountains of Utah and Wyoming, where the first specimens were collected in 1858. These ground squirrels occur in the valleys, foothills, and montane meadows of the Rocky Mountains of eastern Idaho, southern Montana, western Wyoming, and north-central Utah, where they inhabit sagebrush, grassy meadows, pastures, and sometimes cultivated fields and lawns.

These squirrels are perhaps best recognized in the field by their rather uniform brownish or grayish coloration and grayish undertail. The head and neck are always gray, but the back can vary from grayish to sayal brown to cinnamon buff. Some individuals have faint cinnamon coloration in the nose and legs.

Like other western ground squirrels, *S. armatus* is diurnal. It emerges from hibernation in early spring, usually in late March or early April. The dates of emergence vary with elevation and with the timing of the arrival of spring weather. The adult males emerge first, followed by the adult females and yearlings. Mating occurs underground in the female's burrow within two to four days of emergence, and the females become aggressive and establish territories soon after. The males are non-territorial. The young are born after a gestation period of 23 days and appear aboveground at 22 days of age. Average litter size is 5.4 pups; females bear only one litter per year. After weaning the litter, the females abandon their territories to their pups, but return to the nest burrow at night. During the summer drought, the green grasses and forbs that the squirrels feed upon dry out and lose nutritional value. The squirrels then consume large quantities of seeds to store fat in preparation for hibernation. Adult males enter hibernation by mid-July, followed by adult females, yearlings, and the last pups by early September. Individual squirrels are active aboveground for only about three months per year.

Juvenile females tend to settle near the maternal nests, whereas juvenile males tend to disperse farther from their natal burrow. Yearling females breed, but have smaller litters (4.6 vs. 6.0) than adults. Yearling males may breed successfully if they gain extra weight during their first year, emerge from hibernation with scrotal testes while sexually receptive females are available, and if there are few adult males with whom to compete that year.

Spermophilus armatus

The maximum life span is about seven years, but few squirrels live beyond four years of age. Mortality is highest among males, and the sex ratio becomes progressively biased in favor of females. After the breeding season the males become subordinate to the territorial females, and become rather secretive and difficult to see. Females and young prefer open habitats, possibly because it is easier to detect predators there. They produce six different calls (chirp, churr, squeal, squawk, teeth-clatter, and growl), which are used in intimidating other squirrels or in response to predators. Predators include badgers *(Taxidea taxus),* which may account for up to 28 percent of mortality, weasels *(Mustela),* and birds of prey. Population densities of 82 squirrels per hectare have been recorded. *E. Yensen*

Size
Males are slightly larger than females.
Total length: 270–320 (290) mm
Length of tail: 43–81 (65) mm
Weight: 250–600 g (varies seasonally)

Identification
S. armatus is speckled gray to brown above and grayish-white to buffy below; the head, neck, and underside of tail are grayish; the ears are large and prominent; and the hind foot is longer than 35 mm. *S. beldingi,* which occurs to the west of the Uinta's range, is more brownish on the back, has a brownish rather than gray head and neck, and the underside of its tail is brick red. *S. elegans* is much buffier, and the underside of its tail is also buffy. *S. mollis* is much smaller and has tiny ears and a short, round tail.

Recent Synonyms
Citellus armatus

Status
Locally abundant, but spotty within the limited range

References
Balph, 1984

California ground squirrel | *Spermophilus beecheyi*

The California ground squirrel's range encompasses extreme south-central Washington and western Oregon, most of California, and much of northwestern Baja California. It also inhabits western Nevada north and west of Reno, where the high desert meets the Sierra Nevada Mountains. However, *S. beecheyi* occupies only part of this vast geographic area. It is found in successional habitat such as roadsides, farmlands, chaparral, and open grassy areas, but is absent from vast tracts, including the climax forests of redwood and fir and much of the pine belt. Common on the coast and in the lower valleys, it is most abundant in the rolling agricultural lands of the valleys and foothills of the west, thriving on well-drained, semi-arid lands where the winters are mild. However, stable populations are known to exist as high as 2,200 m in the central Sierra Nevada Mountains of California.

A strictly ground-dwelling species (although quite capable of climbing trees and other structures) the California ground squirrel is commonly found in stubble fields, along fencerows in grazed pasturelands, or, at high elevations, along forest breaks and meadow edges, always where the soil is well drained and view-obstructing cover is controlled. The burrow entrance, when not located under a rock outcropping or tree stump, is commonly marked by a raised entrance mound of dirt, which diverts water and acts as an observation platform. Members of a colony may share a common burrow network, but they tend to avoid one another and each may have its own entrance to the interconnecting burrow system.

S. beecheyi is an opportunistic forager whose diet consists of a wide range of forbs, grasses, seeds, berries, young leaves of shrubs, and a variety of insects. Like other squirrels, *S. beecheyi* will eat carrion and has been known to prey on birds' nests, devouring both eggs and young. It has also been observed to prey on the eggs of grunion, a beach-spawning fish of California. Colonies of California ground squirrels are common in heavily populated areas, including rural parks, where their diets may be supplemented with garbage and food handouts.

The introduction of agriculture, especially the planting of cereal crops, has had a profound effect on the abundance of *S. beecheyi,* as grains are preferred food items. Abundant food, coupled with the common agricultural practice of weed control, which keeps the vegetation low along field edges, results in optimum ground squirrel habitat. In agricultural areas, ground squirrel populations have been observed to greatly increase after the sowing of grains and then decrease when crops are rotated or the field is allowed to lie fallow.

The California ground squirrel is large; pre-estivation adults weigh nearly a kilogram. The dorsal pelage is essentially brown, with buff flecking that is heaviest around the rump and flanks. A grayish mantle runs across the shoulders and neck. The mantle forms a triangular dorsal patch that ranges from jet black in one subspecies *(S. b. douglasii)* to barely visible in others. The belly is a pale gray and the tail, which is bushier than that of most other ground squirrel species, is darkish gray above and somewhat paler below.

The annual cycle of *S. beecheyi* is tied to climatic variation. The timing of breeding varies widely throughout its range, occurring earliest in the warmer, drier, southern end of its distribution. The squirrel may breed as early as January there and as late as late April in the north or at higher elevations. Breeding is usually limited to a few weeks, and only one litter is produced each year. Gestation lasts about thirty days. The young are born altricial, but development and growth rates are rapid, with weaning occurring in less than a month. Litter size varies

Spermophilus beecheyi

according to the mean temperature of the region. In central Oregon, where the freeze-free period averages about 195 days, litters average 5.5 young, whereas in southern California, which averages 325 freeze-free days, litters average 8.4 young. This increased litter size in southern populations may be a response to the lengthier period of aboveground activity and the correspondingly greater exposure to predation.

Adult *S. beecheyi* are often active only a few months of the year. Males may enter estivation in early summer and remain underground until the following spring. Adult females follow as soon as they complete lactation, usually in late summer or early fall. Therefore, the aboveground fall and winter populations are composed almost entirely of young squirrels. For adults, the seasonal cycle of fat deposition is vital to survival, and the squirrels devote much of their aboveground time to feeding. An adult male may gain as much as 120 g per week on a diet of barley and carrots.

S. beecheyi is one of several sciurids that are dominant secondary vectors of bubonic plague. As host to the flea *Diamanus montanus,* which is a primary vector of the disease, these squirrels are potent sources of human infection. *R. E. Cole and G. J. North*

Size
Males are usually somewhat larger than females.
Total length: 357–500 mm
Length of tail: 145–227 mm
Weight: 350–885 g

Identification
A gray mantle and absence of stripes distinguish *Spermophilus beecheyi* from all other ground squirrels in its range.

Recent Synonyms
Citellus beecheyi

Other Common Names
Beechey ground squirrel

Status
Common to abundant; widespread in the western United States

Subspecies
Spermophilus beecheyi beecheyi, western California, south from San Francisco Bay and the Sacramento/San Joaquin Rivers to about 25 miles north of San Diego, and east to the western San Joaquin Valley
Spermophilus beecheyi douglasii, northern California, western Oregon, and south-central Washington, east to the Great Basin, and south to the Sacramento River
Spermophilus beecheyi fisheri, Sacramento and San Joaquin valleys
Spermophilus beecheyi nesioticus, Santa Catalina Island

Spermophilus beecheyi nudipes, chaparral habitats of southwestern California and into northwestern Baja California
Spermophilus beecheyi parvulus, creosotebush habitat of the Mohave and San Bernardino deserts of south-central California
Spermophilus beecheyi rupinarum, restricted to a small area of suitable habitat in north-central Baja California surrounded by desert
Spermophilus beecheyi sierrae, montane and upper montane forests of the central Sierra Nevada Mountains of California, west probably to the blue oak zone of the Sierra foothills and east to the Great Basin Desert

References
Jameson and Peeters, 1988; Linsdale, 1946; Tomich, 1964, 1982

Belding's ground squirrel | *Spermophilus beldingi*

Though unassuming in appearance, Belding's ground squirrel is a squirrel of contrasts. Individuals invariably have pleasant dispositions and relate well to humans, winning for themselves a place in the hearts of many campers. However, the squirrels are colonial, and their large colonies can pose a threat to pastures and grain and alfalfa farming. Their tameness and colonial habits have made them a particularly attractive subject for scientific inquiry. The species is noted for its altruistic behavior towards kin (nepotism), for the brutality of male combat, and for cannibalism. The majority of this squirrel's life is spent in hibernation, with all foraging, growth, and reproduction restricted to a frantic three-month period each year.

Belding's ground squirrel is medium-sized and relatively stocky. The basic coat color is grayish, with a faint pink wash. A broad brown band begins on the shoulders, extends along the back, and contrasts only slightly with the color of the sides. There are no distinct spots or stripes. The pelage is paler on the ventral surfaces. The tail is moderately furred, slightly bushy, and is distinctively reddish, tipped with black. White edges may be noted around the tail, and the eyes are highlighted by a narrow white ring.

Populations of Belding's ground squirrels can be found at

elevations ranging from 550 to 3,650 m, though it is generally considered to be a high-elevation species. They are common in the central Sierra Nevada Mountains, particularly on the eastern slopes, and occur northward through east-central Oregon in the Cascade Range and eastward to parts of southwestern Idaho and northern Nevada. They require succulent vegetation and are rarely found far from water. Colonies are common in alpine meadows, and the squirrels are also easily observed along roadsides and in cultivated fields where vegetation is short and the soil is loose enough for burrowing. The burrow opening is about 5 cm in diameter, and is often indicated by a slight mound, somewhat asymmetrically placed around the sloping tunnel.

Like most herbivores, Belding's ground squirrels feed selectively. Grass blades are often pulled up one at a time, and the tender base is eaten first. Younger leaves and flowers are selected from a wide variety of low-growing annuals and herbaceous perennials. Grass seeds and the seed pods of lupine and iris are eaten as well, particularly later in summer as herbs dry out. Assorted arthropods and carrion are eaten opportunistically. Despite the presence of cheek pouches, these squirrels do not store food in burrows. Occasionally, an individual will be

observed collecting huge mouthfuls of dry grass, but this is used solely to line the underground nest. Trash and scraps of cloth may also be collected for nest lining.

Every Belding's ground squirrel hibernates for 8–9 months each year. Age and sex cohorts stagger their entry into and emergence from hibernation, so that some members of the population are likely to be aboveground over a 4–5 month period. At lower elevations, the squirrels begin to emerge from hibernation in mid-March; they may not be seen until mid-May at some high-elevation sites. Emergence may begin when snow is still present, and on average, occurs about one week before green vegetation is available. As this species is not known to store food for use during hibernation, spring and summer offer the only opportunity the squirrels have to deposit sufficient body fat for hibernation and for their week of activity in early spring before new vegetation appears. Adult males are the first to enter hibernation, as early as late June at lower elevations, followed by adult females, yearling females, yearling males, and finally the young born that summer.

As with many of the hibernating ground squirrels, it is difficult to give a single weight that characterizes this species. In early spring, males are heavier than females. During the 2–3 week mating season, the males lose weight and the females gain. During gestation, the female's weight continues to increase, and as the mating period comes to an end, the males too begin to gain weight. Generally it is only during gestation that female mass exceeds the mass of the typical male. Female mass drops after giving birth and continues a modest decline during lactation. When the young are weaned, the females gain weight rapidly. All reproducing females show this pattern. Yearling males do not generally participate in mating activity, and their mass increases throughout the summer. Adult males emerge from hibernation at around 225–300 g, lose weight during the mating period, then rapidly gain, to enter hibernation weighing nearly 400 g. Yearling males emerge at around 150–175 g and reach 375–400 g before hibernating. Their body length continues to increase into their second year. Adult females emerge from hibernation at around 200 g. After the young are weaned, they reach a pre-hibernation weight of about 350 g. Yearling females emerge weighing around 150–175 g and typically enter hibernation weighing 325–350 g. Yearling females attain their adult length during this first year. Juveniles are not sexually dimorphic to any noticeable degree, and all enter hibernation at approximately 250 g. Weights vary with elevation and ambient conditions: animals at higher elevations are often substantially lighter. If the hibernation period is extended due to heavy snowfall, or if little food is available upon emergence, the animals can be very lean in the early spring.

In spring, a hiker in the Sierra Nevada will often hear a Belding's ground squirrel long before one is seen. To the squirrel, the hiker is a potential source of danger deserving of an alarm call. The typical alarm call is a "trill," a series of 5–8 short whistles given in quick succession. The trill call is repeated for as long as the threat exists. If you look in the direction of a trill, you are likely to see a Belding's ground squirrel standing on its toes on a mound or a rock, balancing itself with its tail. This unique posture is called a "picket-pin." On closer inspection you might see numerous squirrels "picketing," all keeping an eye on the potential threat. Only a few of them (usually adult females) will be giving alarm calls. Alarm calling can be dangerous if it attracts a predator's attention. The trill alarm call is associated with a modest level of danger, a threat that the squirrels want to keep an eye on but that they have a good chance of escaping. A whistle alarm call (one brief note) warns of extreme danger, such as a raptor, which can descend upon a squirrel very quickly. A whistle call results in a mad dash for the nearest cover. The Belding's predators are numerous, and include Cooper's hawks, golden eagles, goshawks, peregrine falcons, prairie falcons, badgers, bobcats, coyotes, foxes, martens, and weasels. Badgers and coyotes are known to dig up hibernating squirrels.

The alarm calling behavior of Belding's ground squirrels has attracted the attention of behavioral scientists. The squirrels that give calls are most likely to be adult females, from 4 to 7 years of age. They expose themselves to the risk of predation because they are surrounded by their own offspring and their sisters, so the benefit to their relatives outweighs the risk to themselves, a textbook example of kin-selected altruism. As juveniles, females take up residence within a few meters of their mothers, whereas males disperse hundreds of meters or more to other colonies where they are not very closely related to any other individual. A mother ground squirrel is very protective of her litter when unrelated females or males are in the area, as these individuals may enter her den and kill her offspring. Their discriminating behavior towards relatives has led to extensive studies on how these squirrels learn to recognize relatives. A process called "phenotype matching" is used, in which an individual is nicer to squirrels that look like itself or the ones it was raised with. Sisters can recognize each other even though they were separated before weaning. Social play near burrows may be how juveniles learn about kin.

Adult males emerge from hibernation approximately 1–2 weeks before females. Females enter estrus within a week of their emergence. Males follow females around until they come into estrus, which lasts only 1–5 hours on a single afternoon. Competition among the males for access to the females is fierce. All breeding males acquire battle scars, including severe upper body lacerations and broken bones, and some are killed. Most females mate with more than one male (2–3 on average). In part, this is because males interfere with the copulations of other males. The first male to mate is responsible for fathering more than 50 percent of the litter. Typically, the largest males are the more successful ones. Some males are never able to mate. After mating, males play no role in raising the young and are chased away by females. Nearly all adult females breed. At higher elevations, little more than half of the yearling females breed, but this proportion appears to increase at lower elevations. Gestation lasts from 23–25 days. The typical litter size varies with the mother's age, from 3–4 young for yearling females to an average litter size of 6–8 for females aged 2–5 years. Beyond that, the average litter size drops again to 3–4. The young are born hairless, sightless, with the ear canals

Spermophilus beldingi

closed, and weighing only 7 g. They are weaned after 25–28 days, at which time they begin to appear aboveground. Juveniles may remain with their mother for up to 2 weeks after weaning. At this point the juvenile males begin to disperse and the females dig their own burrows.

In some populations, 50–60 percent of all adult males and 30 percent of females that emerge in spring disappear before the end of summer. The adult sex ratio is male-biased, but in yearlings, before males start to reproduce, the sex ratio is about even. Females live for an average of 4–6 years, but males typically survive for only 3–4 years. Few males live longer than 6 years; some females live longer than 11 years. The difference in longevity is due to the mortality associated with dispersal and breeding in adult males. *G. Bachman*

Size
Males are slightly larger and heavier than females. Weight varies dramatically with time of year.
Total length: 270–315 (300) mm (males); 265–295 (290) mm (females)
Length of tail: 60–75 mm
Weight: 300–450 (360) g (males); 230–400 (300) g (females)

Identification
The basic coat color is gray, with a faint pink wash. There are no spots or stripes, but there is a broad brown band running down the back, which fades into the gray of the sides. The tail is relatively short, slightly bushy, distinctively reddish underneath, and tipped with black. *S. armatus,* which occurs to the east of *S. beldingi,* lacks the pinkish wash and has a gray head, neck, and underside of the tail.

Recent Synonyms
Citellus beldingi

Other Common Names
Oregon ground squirrel

Status
Locally abundant (abundant in suitable habitat, which is itself relatively common)

Subspecies
Spermophilus beldingi beldingi, eastern to northeastern California
Spermophilus beldingi creber, northeastern to central Nevada and southwestern Idaho
Spermophilus beldingi oregonus, northern California and central to southeastern Oregon

References
Mammalian Species 221; Sherman and Morton, 1979

Idaho ground squirrel | *Spermophilus brunneus*

This rare ground squirrel is the only endemic mammal species in Idaho. *Spermophilus brunneus brunneus* is known historically from 36 mountain meadows surrounded by forests of ponderosa pine *(Pinus ponderosa)* and Douglas-fir *(Pseudotsuga mensiesii)* at 1,150–1,550 m elevation. It currently occupies 24 sites in less than 500 hectares of habitat in an area of about 40 by 100 km. *S. b. brunneus* is limited to small, drier meadows with pockets of deeper soils too small, shallow, or unproductive to be inhabited by *S. columbianus*. Nest and hibernation burrows of *S. b. brunneus* are built in well-drained soils more than 1 m deep. As a result of fire suppression, the meadows it inhabits have been invaded by conifers in recent years, decreasing the habitat and isolating populations that now differ substantially from each other genetically. Most populations number fewer than 50 animals, and in 1998 there were less than 500 *S. b. brunneus* individuals.

S. b. endemicus is probably more numerous. It occurs in the low rolling foothills north of the Payette river at 670–975 m elevation and is distributed patchily over an area of 70 x 30 km. The habitat of *S. b. endemicus* was originally covered with sagebrush *(Artemisia tridentata)* and native bunchgrasses. These rangelands have been converted by intensive wildfires to annual grasslands of introduced cheatgrass *(Bromus tectorum)* and medusahead *(Taeniatherum caput-medusae)*. The effects of this change in food and cover on the animals are not known.

Like other ground squirrels, *Spermophilus brunneus* is diurnal. Idaho ground squirrels feed on grasses and a large variety of green forbs, and are especially fond of fresh shoots, bulbs, and flowers. Prior to hibernation they consume large numbers of seeds. Occasionally they eat insects. there are no known fossils of the Idaho ground squirrel.

These ground squirrels sometimes remain motionless in response to aerial predators, and their dorsal coloration corresponds to the predominant soil color in the range of each subspecies. *S. b. brunneus* is reddish-gray and occurs on reddish soils derived from basalt lava. *S. b. endemicus* is grayish-brown and occurs on light-colored soils derived from lake sediments. Molt occurs in May or June, and is diffuse, without a "molt line."

The two subspecies are distinct morphologically and probably represent distinct species.

Spermophilus brunneus

S. b. endemicus has not been studied in detail. In *S. b. brunneus*, adults emerge from hibernation in late March or early April. Females emerge a few days after the males and are sexually receptive for a few hours on the day they emerge from hibernation. They mate below ground, each male guarding his mate from rival males until she is no longer receptive. Some females mate with more than one male; heavier males displace lighter males, mate with the female, and the last/longest-guarding male sires most of the pups. guarding males are heavily preyed upon by prairie falcons and goshawks. There is one litter of 2–10 (average 5–6) pups per year. females dig nest burrows and provide all parental care; males do not live near their mates or care for the young. females give alarm calls to warn young of mammalian and avian predators (badgers, weasels, goshawks, red-tailed hawks, northern harriers, and prairie falcons). The active season lasts 4–5 months, and individual squirrels spend about 8–9 months of the year in aestivation and hibernation. Mortality is highest during hibernation; 75–90 percent of juveniles and 40–60 percent of adults do not survive.   *E. Yensen and P. Sherman*

Size

Males are about 2.5 percent larger than females.
Total length: 209–258 (233) mm
Length of tail: 39–62 (54) mm
Weight: 120–290 g (varies seasonally)

Identification

Spermophilus brunneus can be distinguished from *S. mollis* by the pale spots on its back, russet-colored legs, nose, and undertail, off-white eye ring, and much larger ear pinnae. *S. columbianus*, the other ground squirrel in its range, is about twice the length and three times the mass of S. brunneus, has a reddish throat and face and a much longer, whitish bushy tail that ripples behind as it runs.

No other ground squirrels have the following combination of characteristics: small size (total length less than 260 mm, tail shorter than 65 mm, hind foot shorter than 39 mm), medium-sized ears (13–18 mm), distinct spots on the back, russet colored legs, nose, and undertail, grayish-white underparts, and off-white eye ring.

Recent Synomyms
Citellus brunneus
Citellus townsendii brunneus

Other Common Names
Idaho spotted ground squirrel

Status
Very rare and local; threatened

Subspecies
Spermophilus brunneus brunneus, Adams and Valley counties, Idaho
Spermophilus brunneus endemicus, Gem, Payette, and Washington counties, Idaho

References
Mammalian Species 560; Gavin et al., 1999; Sherman, 1989; Yensen, 1991

Merriam's ground squirrel | *Spermophilus canus*

Merriam's ground squirrel includes populations with 46 chromosomes that formerly were regarded as conspecific with Townsend's ground squirrel. The subspecies *canus* is widespread throughout most of eastern Oregon, whereas *vigilis* has a limited distribution within a portion of the Snake River drainage along the Oregon–Idaho border.

There is little published information on the ecology of *Spermophilus canus.* In most respects, its habits resemble those of the Piute ground squirrel *(S. mollis).* The species occurs in habitats dominated by big sagebrush *(Artemisia tridentata),* western juniper *(Juniperus occidentalis),* and greasewood *(Sarcobatus vermiculatus),* in grasslands and pastures, and in or near agricultural land where the squirrels may damage crops. Remains of this species have been found in regurgitated pellets of barn owls *(Tyto alba)* and great horned owls *(Bubo virginianus).*

The Merriam's ground squirrel has a very brief annual period of aboveground activity. In Oregon, adults emerge from hibernation around early March and the single litter is born in late April or early May. After fattening on a diet of grasses and forbs, the animals become dormant by early August. *E. A. Rickart*

Spermophilus canus

Size
Measurements for *S. c. canus; S. c. vigilis* is about 12 percent longer than *S. c. canus.*
Total length: 190–217 (201) mm
Length of tail: 37–42 (39) mm
Weight: no weights have been published

Identification
Indistinguishable externally from *S. mollis* and *S. townsendii.* All three species are relatively small in size and have short ears and unmarked pelage.

Recent Synonyms
C. mollis (part)
Citellus townsendii (part)
Spermophilus townsendii (part)

Other Common Names
Townsend's ground squirrel (part), Malheur Valley ground squirrel *(S. c. vigilis),* sage squirrel, sage rat

Status
Common (subspecies *vigilis* has limited distribution)

Subspecies
Spermophilus canus canus, eastern Oregon and extreme northwestern Nevada
Spermophilus canus vigilis, west of Snake River in extreme west-central Idaho and extreme eastern Oregon

References
Mammalian Species 268; Bailey, 1936; Verts and Carraway, 1998

Columbian ground squirrel | *Spermophilus columbianus*

Living in colonies, Columbian ground squirrels prosper in such varied habitats as alpine meadows, south-facing mountain slopes, wheatfields, and agricultural bottomlands. In agricultural and grazing systems, *Spermophilus columbianus* densities can attain levels that make the animals destructive pests. In more natural settings, these ground squirrels are an important food item for a number of carnivores, including coyotes, badgers, and mountain lions.

Adult Columbian ground squirrels are active for about 90–100 days each year. During this period they mate, have

young, and put on enough body fat to survive a period of hibernation that lasts for about 70 percent of the year. Breeding starts shortly after females emerge from hibernation in the early spring (males emerge before females) and continues for about three weeks. The time of breeding varies with elevation, with greater variability noted at higher elevations. Females usually breed when they are two years of age, males at age three. Most mating takes place in underground burrows.

If mating is successful, a litter of 3–5 pinkish, hairless, blind, and toothless young will be born a month later. Young are kept underground and nursed for about 30 days. During the nursing period the young squirrels grow rapidly, but full adult size is not attained until the second summer of life, when the squirrels are yearlings.

Male and female Columbian ground squirrels exhibit territoriality and dominance. Adult males have overlapping home ranges, but within each individual male's home range is a core area or territory that he will defend, and in which he exhibits dominance over other males. The resource he is defending is the right to breed with females within his territory. Adult females establish home ranges near nest burrows, and will actively defend part of the range as a territory. The establishment of territories by adult females probably helps defend juveniles from other adult squirrels, especially during the time between birth and emergence aboveground.

Once the young emerge from underground, they must gain weight and avoid predators. In addition to predators on the ground, squirrels (especially juveniles) must be ever alert for the presence of golden eagles and red-tailed hawks. Columbian ground squirrels communicate by giving a number of calls (chirps, churrs, teeth clicking, growls, and squeals), each type of call conveying a particular meaning. Aerial predators elicit a multiple series of loud, rapid chirping calls; terrestrial predators generate fewer, more widely spaced calls.

Adults and juveniles that accumulate the most body fat during the summer have the best chance of surviving the long period of hibernation. Throughout their range of distribution, Columbian ground squirrels are mainly herbivores, eating a variety of flowers, seeds, bulbs, and fruits; on occasion they will eat insects and even consume meat (including others of their own species).

Columbian ground squirrels undertake two types of movements: excursions, which are temporary absences from the home range, and dispersal movements. Excursions are commonly undertaken by yearling females; yearling males are more likely to disperse. A greater proportion of yearlings disappears during the active season than do squirrels of any other age group. The loss results from dispersal movements, with more males leaving an area than females. Adult squirrels behave aggressively toward yearlings, particularly yearling males. Yearling females, on the other hand, may remain close to the area in which they were born—and in many cases will inherit the nest burrows of their mothers when they breed.

A number of behaviors are associated with maintaining the colony. Greeting behavior, referred to as "kissing," which involves sniffing and touching the side of the mouth, occurs frequently among members of the same social group and seems to solidify social bonds. During the breeding season and after the young have been born, adult male and female squirrels engage in chases that can result in serious fighting. Young Columbian ground squirrels spend considerable time playing together; their play appears to foster group socialization. Scent-marking behavior can involve mouth-cheek rubbing, in which glands at the edge of the mouth are rubbed against the ground, and twist-marking, a forward spiral movement during which glands on the side of the head and back are rubbed on the ground. Scent-marking is usually demonstrated by dominant males. The development of marking behavior is significant for young squirrels: among littermates, the one who marks most frequently becomes dominant.

The summer burrow is often used for hibernation. Hibernation dens are dome-shaped and are frequently lined with finely shredded grass; a drain keeps water from entering the nest. Within the nest the sleeping animal lies curled up in a ball, the head parallel with the bottom of the nest. The hibernation den of adult males often has a cache of food in it. The food generally is used in spring, when the males, emerging ear-

Spermophilus columbianus

lier than females, often find the ground snow-covered and food scarce. When they are ready for hibernation, the squirrels close their dens with an earthen plug.

In addition to occasionally being agricultural pests, Columbian ground squirrels are hosts of the tick that carries Rocky Mountain spotted fever, and may also be natural reservoirs for the Powassan or St. Louis encephalitis virus. *C. L. Elliott*

Size

No significant sexual dimorphism
Total length: 325–410 mm
Length of tail: 80–116 mm
Weight: 340–812 g

Identification

S. columbianus is grayish mixed with black above, with indistinct buff spotting. The front of the face, front legs, and belly are reddish-brown; the front feet are buff. The bushy tail is mostly reddish, but edged with white and with

some black hairs above, especially at the base and tip. Richardson's, Townsend's, and Washington ground squirrels tend to be smaller, and none has reddish-brown forelegs and feet; the Idaho ground squirrel is much smaller and has a white chin.

Recent Synonyms

Citellus columbianus

Status

Common, limited

Subspecies

Spermophilus columbianus columbianus, southern British Columbia, eastern Washington, central and northern Idaho, western Montana
Spermophilus columbianus ruficaudus, northeastern Oregon

References

Mammalian Species 372; Whitaker, 1980

Wyoming ground squirrel | *Spermophilus elegans*

Although ground squirrels are widely distributed throughout North America, *Spermophilus elegans* exists only in three isolated, subspecific populations. Its distribution is determined both by habitat availability and by competition with other spe-

cies. This very active species occupies mountain meadows from 1,500 meters elevation to talus slopes above the timberline in northwestern Colorado, southern Wyoming, extreme western Nebraska, and extreme northeastern Utah. In south-

treat to its extensive but solitary burrow system. Toward the end of the active season, in July, and prior to hibernation in late July to early September, time spent feeding decreases.

The timing of emergence from hibernation and the subsequent timing of breeding varies with snow depth, climatic conditions, and latitude. Males usually emerge from hibernation in late March or April, one to two weeks before females emerge, and mating occurs within five days after the females emerge. Gestation is estimated at 22–23 days, and there is only one litter of approximately six young born per female per season.

Neonates are blind and virtually helpless, with reddish, hairless skin. Small vibrissae are present on the snout. At five days the young have gray-pigmented skin on their backs and sides, but body hair does not appear until day six. It emerges first on the snout and cheeks. By day 24 the eyes are open and by day 28 young squirrels have the hair coloration of adults. Weaning occurs at 28–42 days, but the young confine their activity to the burrow entrance until they are 42–49 days old, when they begin to follow their mother.

During the breeding season males aggresively defend territories, but when breeding is over, they become passive and spend most of their time feeding to put on weight for hibernation. During gestation and lactation, the females become territorial, but they only agressively defend their burrow entrances, not open spaces like the males do. Male offspring disperse from the natal area, but female young often remain in or near their mother's range throughout their lives. Females and their young form a somewhat cohesive group, but they are not sociable and do not intermingle with groups or individuals from other litters. *H. D. Smith*

Spermophilus elegans

western Montana and contiguous areas of Idaho it is limited by *S. armatus* to valley bottoms and foothills covered with sage and grass. It also lives in brushy and grassy areas of north-central Nevada.

This colonial dwelling but asocial ground squirrel is completely diurnal. Although active aboveground throughout the day, it exhibits bimodal activity patterns. The squirrels are most active in mid-morning and early evening. They spend about 39 percent of their active time feeding and 36 percent watching for danger. Inclement weather causes *S. elegans* to re-

Size

No significant sexual dimorphism
Total length: 253–307 mm
Length of tail: 59–79 mm
Weight: 286–411 g

Identification

Spermophilus elegans generally has pale, drab upperparts flecked with pale pinkish-buff, clay-colored, or pinkish-cinnamon markings; it is difficult to distinguish *S. elegans* from other ground squirrels, particularly from *S. richardsoni* in areas where their ranges overlap. Where these species are sympatric, *S. elegans* can be identified by a shorter hind foot (less than 43 mm), a total length less than 275 mm, and a darker, paler-edged tail. Where it is sympatric with *S. beldingi, S. elegans* can be distinguished by its longer tail, which has a buff, not reddish, underside. Where it is sympatric with *S. townsendii, S. elegans* can be identified by cinnamon rather than white underparts. In sympatry with *S. armatus, S. elegans* can be distinguished by the buff, not gray, underside of its tail.

Recent Synonyms

Citellus elegans

Status

Common, restricted

Subspecies

Spermophilus elegans aureus, southwestern Montana and contiguous areas of Idaho
Spermophilus elegans elegans, north-central and northeastern Colorado, southern Wyoming, extreme western Nebraska, and extreme northeastern Utah
Spermophilus elegans nevadensis, north-central Nevada

References

Mammalian Species 214; Hall, 1946; Nowak, 1991

Franklin's ground squirrel | *Spermophilus franklinii*

This ground squirrel, named after the Arctic explorer Sir John Franklin, is found throughout the north-central states from Indiana to the Dakotas, and in a narrow band of aspen parkland across the Canadian prairies to central Alberta. Although diurnal like other ground squirrels, Franklin's ground squirrels are less commonly seen because they inhabit a variety of closed habitats, including tall grass in disturbed areas, shrubland, and woodland edges. In campgrounds and picnic areas individuals can become tame and may be seen in mowed areas adjacent to their preferred habitat. But much of the time one is aware of their presence from hearing their loud whistles of alarm, or a musical "trill" that is similar to, but more full-throated than, the trill given by thirteen-lined ground squirrels. Throughout their range Franklin's are distributed sporadically, usually in small colonies but occasionally in larger concentrations adjacent to marshland. Numbers in local sites fluctuate markedly and local populations may die out, leaving an area squirrel-less for a year or two before it is recolonized.

S. franklinii has a gray head with a prominent white eye-ring. Below the nape and on the shoulders the pelage grades into a brown color with indistinct buff and black barring, giving a slightly mottled appearance. The chest and belly are buffy-white to gray. The tail, which has longer hair than that of most ground squirrels, is gray like the head, often with white-tipped hairs that give it a pale border. The bushy tail, the generally gray coloration, and its occurrence in wooded areas can cause an observer to confuse Franklin's ground squirrel with the eastern gray squirrel *(Sciurus carolinensis)*.

Like other north-temperate ground squirrels, Franklin's are seasonal hibernators, spending 7–8.5 months in underground hibernacula in periodic bouts of torpor. Emergence in spring is from mid-April to early May, varying with local climatic conditions. Males usually precede females by a few days to two weeks. Breeding begins soon after the females emerge and extends over about two weeks. The single litter a female produces each year is born after an estimated gestation period of 26–28 days. Litter size ranges from 2 to 13; usually 7–9 juveniles emerge from the natal burrow about 30 days after birth. Juveniles grow rapidly and are nearly the size of adults when they hibernate, in late August to early October. By that time adults have already entered hibernation, the males as early as late July, most females by mid- to late August. When adults begin hibernation their weight is 50–100 percent greater than when they emerged the previous spring. This accumulated body fat is largely used up during the long winter. Survival through the winter is a chancy prospect in most populations; usually fewer than half of the animals present in late summer emerge the following spring.

Although most species of ground squirrel incorporate animal protein in their diets opportunistically, Franklin's have a deserved reputation for exceptional carnivory—so much so that baits such as sardines and bacon have been used in live-trapping studies. Insects are a common component of their diets, as is true for thirteen-lined ground squirrels, but Franklin's are also known to eat mice, toads, small birds, and even young snowshoe hares. In marsh habitats they take their toll on ducks' eggs. At Delta Marsh in Manitoba they accounted for a quarter of the almost 100 nests identified as suffering predation. To break an egg, the squirrel curls its body around the egg and bites through the shell while the egg is pressed against the hind feet and legs. The bulk of the diet, however, consists of green vegetation, fruits, and seeds.

Franklin's ground squirrels are probably relatively asocial compared to other ground squirrels, but little is known of their social life. They live in groups and the home ranges of both males and females overlap extensively. It seems likely that mating is promiscuous, as in other ground squirrels, and that juvenile females are more philopatric than their dispersing male

Spermophilus franklinii

brethren. In 1929 the naturalist Ernest Thompson Seton wrote of this species ". . . less is known of its life history than of that of any of its kinsmen." Some 65 years later that statement still holds. *J. O. Murie*

Size
Males are slightly larger than females.
Total length: 355–410 (371) mm
Length of tail: 120–158 (136) mm
Weight: 370–500 (450) g (males in spring);
    340–425 (380) g (females in spring); 570–950
    (700) g (males in late summer); 500–760
    (500) g (females in late summer)

Identification
This ground squrrel can be distinguished from others in its range by larger size, gray head and

neck, and a long, gray, bushy tail. It is smaller than the eastern gray squirrel, *Sciurus carolinensis,* and has a shorter, less bushy tail, more mottled dorsal pelage, and shorter ears.

Recent Synonyms
Citellus franklinii

Other Common Names
Gray gopher, gray ground squirrel, bush gopher, whistling squirrel

Status
Sparsely distributed throughout range, but can be locally abundant

References
Iverson and Turner, 1972; Murie, 1973; Sowls, 1948

Golden-mantled ground squirrel | *Spermophilus lateralis*

The golden-mantled ground squirrel is a familiar resident of open woodlands, brushy forest-edge habitats, dry margins of mountain meadows, and rocky slopes in mountainous parts of the western United States and Canada, from Colorado westward to California, Oregon, and Washington, and from British Columbia and Alberta south to Arizona and New Mexico. The

animals are quick to invade sunny, disturbed areas, including avalanche tracks, landslides, and logged or burned sites, where weedy pioneer plants provide an abundant food supply. Elevational range is from about 1,200 m in northern California to over 3,900 m in Colorado.

Golden-mantled ground squirrels are nearly omnivorous,

eating fungi; leaves, stems, flowers, fruit, and seeds of herbs; most fleshy fruits; seeds of conifers and grasses; insects (in all stages: eggs, larvae, pupae, adults); eggs and nestling birds; small mammals; and carrion. Too frequently they become pests in established camps and campgrounds, where individuals can become brazen beggars. Food is eaten where it is found or is carried—in capacious cheek pouches—to the burrow for storage.

Golden-mantled ground squirrels generally are solitary and the concentrations of individuals seen at artificial food supplies are only informally structured by individual interactions. Aboveground activity includes dust-bathing as well as foraging. The animals use rock shelters or burrow actively beneath boulders, stumps, or logs. Their burrows can be distinguished from those of pocket gophers (Geomyidae) because ground squirrels leave little or no earth to mark the entrance of the burrow and the entrance remains open, not plugged with soil. Burrows are about 10 cm in diameter and may be nearly a meter deep and two meters long. The nest chamber is in a side burrow or at the end of the tunnel and may be lined with grasses, shredded vegetation, or rubbish. There is no separate latrine chamber, but food is stored in a separate chamber.

These squirrels are deep hibernators (and are frequent subjects of laboratory studies of hibernation). Entry into hibernation is based on endogenous physiological changes, and occurs in the laboratory at room temperature. In August and September, there is a three-fold increase in body fat, especially deposited between the shoulders, in mesenteries, and around the kidneys. This fat fuels the animals until emergence in March or April, with body mass dropping about 0.2 percent per day. Entering hibernation from late August to early November (de-

pending on elevation and latitude), the animals curl into tight balls, exposing minimal radiative surface. Individuals in low-elevation populations arouse occasionally and come aboveground.

Males emerge from hibernation in breeding condition. Females come into estrus about two weeks later. Gestation takes about four weeks, and a single litter averaging five (range, 2–8) altricial young is produced each year, usually in July. Development is rapid, as the young must fatten for hibernation. The single annual molt occurs after the reproductive season, earlier for males than females. Females often molt over an extended period, while lactating, and are readily distinguishable by their ragged appearance.

Golden-mantled ground squirrels frequently are associated with various species of chipmunks, which they often resemble not only in appearance but in foraging habits and daily and annual cycles. Relationships with other ground squirrels are not well studied, but there appears to be rather strong habitat segregation from open-habitat ground squirrels (such as the Wyoming ground squirrel, *Spermophilus elegans*) with which they are broadly sympatric.

Predators include coyotes, badgers, long-tailed weasels, bobcats, and diurnal raptorial birds, including red-tailed hawks and goshawks. Ectoparasites include fleas and ticks; endoparasites include nematodes and protists. Hibernation stress may be a frequent cause of mortality. Infection with the flea-borne plague bacterium *(Yersinia pestis)* is not uncommon, and that fact coupled with their strong tolerance for humans has made golden-mantled ground squirrels a focus for studies of plague in some western national parks. D. M. Armstrong

Spermophilus lateralis

Size

Females may be slightly larger or slightly smaller than males, depending on location. Northern animals are somewhat larger than those in the south.

Total length: 245–295 (275) mm

Length of tail 70–120 (95) mm

Weight: 175 g (spring) to more than 350 g (fall)

Identification

S. lateralis can be distinguished from other *Spermophilus* by a white lateral stripe bordered on either side by a black stripe, and by the presence of a yellowish-buff to rusty reddish-brown "mantle" on the shoulders and head. It is sometimes mistaken for a large chipmunk *(Tamias)*, but can be distinguished easily because the lateral stripes do not continue onto the cheeks. Antelope ground squirrels *(Ammospermophilus)* also have lateral stripes but are reddish rather than buffy to brownish in general color and have a distinctive white tail that is generally carried vertically. Also, they are desert-dwellers and do not overlap golden-mantled ground squirrels in habitat.

The Sierra Madre golden-mantled ground squirrel *(Spermophilus madrensis)* of the Sierra Madre Occidental of Chihuahua and Durango and the Cascade golden-mantled ground squirrel *(Spermophilus saturatus)* of British Columbia and Washington are closely related but are also allopatric.

Recent Synonyms

Callospermophilus lateralis

Citellus lateralis

Status

Common in suitable habitat

Subspecies

Spermophilus lateralis arizonensis, Mogollon Rim, Coconino Plateau, Arizona

Spermophilus lateralis bernardinensis, San Bernardino Mountains, California

Spermophilus lateralis castanurus, southeastern Idaho, west-central Wyoming, north-central Utah

Spermophilus lateralis certus, Spring (Charleston) Mountains, Nevada

Spermophilus lateralis chrysodeirus, Sierra-Cascade ranges, California and Oregon

Spermophilus lateralis cinerascens, Yellowstone region of Montana, Idaho, and Wyoming

Spermophilus lateralis connectens, Blue Mountains, Oregon, Washington, adjacent Idaho

Spermophilus lateralis lateralis, southern Rocky Mountains, Wyoming, Colorado, and New Mexico; Wasatch Mountains, Utah; Kaibab Plateau, Arizona

Spermophilus lateralis mitratus, Coast Ranges, northern California and southern Oregon

Spermophilus lateralis tescorum, northern Rocky Mountains, British Columbia, Alberta, Montana, and Idaho

Spermophilus lateralis trepidus, Great Basin of Nevada, southern Idaho, and eastern Oregon

Spermophilus lateralis trinitatis, Trinity Mountains and vicinity, California

Spermophilus lateralis wortmani, Red Desert, southwestern Wyoming, adjacent Colorado

References

Mammalian Species 440; Armstrong, 1987; McKeever, 1964

Mexican ground squirrel | *Spermophilus mexicanus*

Mexican ground squirrels are diurnal and mostly occur in grassy habitats, but they can also commonly be found in short grasses associated with brushy plant species or in arid regions. Their range is the southern Great Plains and Chihuahuan desert of North America from southeastern New Mexico through western Texas and southward into northeastern Mexico. An adjunct portion of the range occurs in central Mexico.

The species has adapted well to human activity and is a common inhabitant of roadsides, cemeteries, and golf courses. Although they prefer sandy soils in which to establish elaborate burrow systems, Mexican ground squirrels can occur in soils with higher clay or gravel content. Their burrow openings are round, enter the ground at only slightly obtuse angles, and are rarely plugged near the surface opening. Several entrances to a single burrow system are not uncommon. In the northern parts of their range, Mexican ground squirrels hibernate from September to March.

Mexican ground squirrels are social and occur in colonies of from a few to several individuals. Like thirteen-lined ground squirrels, they assume an erect position when alarmed, and in-

Spermophilus mexicanus

dividuals avoid tall grasses that prevent clear viewing of the surrounding area. An alarm call may be uttered at the approach of danger. One litter of four to six offspring is produced in March or April after a gestation time of 28 days.

Mexican ground squirrels are omnivores, feeding on the seeds of a variety of grasses and forbs, green plant material, and larval and adult insects. Cheek pouches are used to carry food and nesting materials to burrows. Hoarding of seeds in food chambers has been noted. These ground squirrels are known to drink free-standing water. *E. G. Zimmerman*

Size
Males are larger than females.
Total length: 280–380 mm
Length of tail: 110–166 mm
Weight: 137–330 g

Identification
Mexican ground squirrels are medium-sized for the genus. Their upperparts have nine rows of white spots on a brown or buffy-brown background. The underparts are whitish or buff. The tail is about one-third the length of the body and is moderately bushy. The ears are short and rounded. Well-developed cheek pouches are present. Mexican ground squirrels are distinguishable from the closely related thirteen-lined ground squirrel *(Spermophilus tridecemlineatus)* by their paler coloration and larger body size.

Recent Synonyms
Citellus mexicanus

Other Common Names
Gopher, picket pen

Status
Common, albeit sporadic, in grassy habitats with suitable soils

Subspecies
Spermophilus mexicanus mexicanus, a narrow band of central Mexico from southern Zacatecas, eastern half of Jalisco, Guanajuato, Queretaro, Hidalgo, Mexico, Tlaxcala, and Puebla
Spermophilus mexicanus parvidens, southeastern New Mexico, western Texas, eastern Coahuila, Nuevo Leon, and Tamaulipas

References
Dalquest and Horner, 1984; Davis and Schmidly, 1994

Mohave ground squirrel | *Spermophilus mohavensis*

Mohave ground squirrels are rarely seen because of their patchy, scattered distribution and their tendency to remain underground for more than half of the year. This long period of torpor allows them to avoid summer drought and winter cold and to take advantage of green vegetation, which is available only in spring and early summer. Within their 20,000-square-kilometer corner of the Mojave Desert, they occur in a wide variety of habitats.

Spermophilus mohavensis is active throughout the day, even when air temperature exceeds 43° C and soil temperature exceeds 66° C. During the hottest midday hours, it forages mostly in the shade of low bushes, and will retreat to the shade or to its burrows to cool off after it has been active in direct sunlight. Burrows are located on the boundary of the home range, along sandy washes or underneath bushes; the home burrow is closed each evening with a soil plug. *Spermophilus mohavensis* is rather docile and can be approached easily in the wild. When alarmed, it rarely runs long distances, but instead retreats down a nearby burrow or simply crouches low, its pelage color blending in with the sandy background.

The Mohave ground squirrel is pale brown with tinges of pinkish-cinnamon on its feet and forehead. The creamy white underside of the short, broadly haired tail is displayed as it runs slowly from bush to bush, carrying its tail over the back in the manner of the antelope ground squirrel. Unlike the latter, which has a more conspicuous white underside of the tail, *Spermophilus mohavensis* does not twitch its tail. The winter pelage is molted in May; timing of the fall molt is not known.

Spermophilus mohavensis becomes extremely fat before entering estivation in midsummer, adding 100–200 g of body

Spermophilus mohavensis

mass. Squirrels that retire underground weighing 165–300 g emerge at 70–80 g. Males emerge in February, up to two weeks before females, and set up territories. Emerging females stay with the males for several days, then depart to establish home ranges and nest burrows. After a gestation period of 30 days, 4–9 fetal-like young, weighing about 5 g each, are born. They are weaned in 32 days. During drought years, when plant growth is severely reduced, *Spermophilus mohavensis* may respond by failing to reproduce rather than risk delay in accumulating fat prior to estivation. Thus, prolonged years of drought may result in the extinction of local populations as adults die from old age and predation and are not replaced.

Spermophilus mohavensis prefers relatively level areas of sandy or mixed sand and gravel soil with rather sparse growth of shrubs, but is found from creosotebush *(Larrea divaricata)* and saltbush *(Atriplex)* communities at 610 m elevation to Joshua tree *(Yucca brevifolia)* and blackbrush *(Coleogyne ramosissima)* habitats up to 1,800 m elevation. Although omnivorous, *Spermophilus mohavensis* specializes in diet at different times of the spring and early summer, perhaps due to the changing water content in plants or because of arthropod availability. Seeds of the Joshua tree are a favorite and preferred, but not limiting, food. *Spermophilus mohavensis* will defend a Joshua tree from

conspecifics and against the subordinate antelope ground squirrel. Other common rodents in the same habitat are several species of pocket mice *(Chaetodipus* and *Perognathus),* four species of kangaroo rats *(Dipodomys),* deer mice *(Peromyscus maniculatus),* cactus mice *(P. eremicus),* grasshopper mice *(Onychomys),* and desert woodrats *(Neotoma lepida).*

The current species-contact boundary between *Spermophilus mohavensis* and its close relative, *Spermophilus tereticaudus,* is remarkably coincident with a network of rivers and lakes that existed in the region during cool, wet periods of the Pleistocene, most recently about 10,000 years ago. The two species may have differentiated on either side of this pluvial network. Fossils that may represent *Spermophilus mohavensis* have been found in late Quaternary deposits in the Mojave Desert, but their assignment to subgenus, and particularly to species, is tentative. The two species, well differentiated genetically and morphologically, now meet along a broad front of about 240 km and overlap no more than about 30 km. There is some evidence that *Spermophilus tereticaudus* may be displacing *Spermophilus mohavensis* from parts of its range, which is also subject to increasing developmental pressures from the populous and rapidly expanding Los Angeles metropolitan area.
D. J. Hafner

Size

No significant sexual dimorphism
Total length: 210–230 (223) mm
Length of tail: 57–72 (66) mm
Weight: 70–300 g (depending on time of year)

Identification

S. mohavensis can be distinguished from the antelope ground squirrel *(Ammospermophilus leucurus)* by lack of distinctive white stripes on the sides. *Spermophilus beecheyi* is larger (total

length, 357–500 mm), with a longer tail and variegated upperparts. *Spermophilus tereticaudus,* a close relative, is smaller and has a longer, less broadly haired tail that lacks a white undersurface.

Other Common Names
Mohave Desert spermophile, Mohave Desert
   ground squirrel

Status
Small, scattered populations (may be locally
abundant in early summer) within a limited
segment of the Mojave Desert

References
Mammalian Species 509; Booth, 1968; Jameson
   and Peeters, 1988

Piute ground squirrel | *Spermophilus mollis*

The Piute ground squirrel includes populations that formerly were considered conspecific with Townsend's ground squirrel. In fact, most of the literature on "Townsend's ground squirrel" actually refers to this species. *Spermophilus mollis* is widely distributed throughout the Great Basin and in adjacent regions along the Snake River in southern Idaho. A disjunct population in south-central Washington is provisionally included within this species (as *S. m. nancyae*). Late Pleistocene and early Holocene fossils have been found within the present distributional range.

Spermophilus mollis is characterized by small size, very short ears, and short, harsh pelage unmarked by stripes or spots. The color is a uniform pale gray above and creamy white below, with a general wash of pinkish-buff. The face, thighs, and tail are tinged with cinnamon color. Worn pelage is brownish and sometimes slightly dappled. Piute ground squirrels are indistinguishable externally from *S. townsendii* and *S. canus,* but the three species have differing chromosome numbers: the karyotypes are 2n=38 (*S. mollis*), 2n=36 (*S. townsendii*), and 2n=46 (*S. canus*).

Piute ground squirrels occur in desert communities dominated by sagebrush (*Artemisia*), shadscale (*Atriplex*), greasewood (*Sarcobatus*), or non-native annuals. They occur also in or near agricultural lands, where they occasionally cause considerable crop damage. Under favorable conditions they form dense colonies of more than 30 adults per hectare. They do not, however, display the complex social behavior seen in some other squirrels.

Like other ground squirrels, *Spermophilus mollis* is semifossorial and strictly diurnal. It is most active during early morning and late afternoon, generally remaining underground during midday. Physiological adaptations for coping with the extreme heat and dryness of the late active season include a low resting metabolic rate, tolerance of high temperatures, and efficient kidneys for water conservation.

Activity is strongly seasonal, being restricted to a four to five month period from late winter to early summer that coincides with the primary plant growing season. Animals remain underground for the balance of the year, spending most of this time in deep physiological torpor with minimal metabolic activity. Because it encompasses both summer and winter tem-

perature extremes, the period of inactivity represents a merging of estivation and hibernation.

Piute ground squirrels break hibernation in late winter. Adult males appear aboveground in late January or early February, and breeding occurs two to three weeks later when the females emerge. The timing of emergence and breeding varies geographically and from year to year as a function of local climate and weather patterns, but individuals within a population are highly synchronous.

Females are reproductively mature as yearlings, whereas males in some populations do not mature until their second year. As with other ground squirrels, a single litter is produced annually. Litter size as measured by embryo counts is large, with mean values ranging from 5.9 to 9.0 among yearlings and from 7.0 to 10.8 among older females. Perhaps because of this high fecundity, postnatal growth is slow relative to other species. At birth the young are unpigmented and hairless, and weigh between 2.8 and 5.2 g. The eyes open at about 20 days of age and the first solid food is taken at 26 days. It is then that the young first emerge from natal burrows (generally in late March or early April). Juveniles are weaned by 34 days and reach 50 percent of the average lean adult weight (about 70 g) at about 42 days.

The adult diet consists of leaves, succulent stems, and the flowering parts and seeds of grasses, forbs, and shrubs. Roots, bulbs, insects, and carrion also are eaten. Food items are not cached; energy to be used during the dormant period is stored as body fat. A shift in diet from green vegetation to seeds toward the end of the active season helps promote seasonal fattening and results in a more than two-fold increase in body weight.

Animals enter estivation during late spring and early summer, before the onset of seasonal drought. Adult males generally start to fatten about six weeks after they emerge from hibernation, whereas the fattening of adult females is delayed by two to three weeks, until after the young are weaned. Adult males become dormant first, followed by adult females, juvenile females, and juvenile males. The inactive season usually lasts about nine months for adults. Due to predation and starvation, there is only about a 30 percent survival rate through this period. Poor food availability can either lengthen or shorten the active season, or may cause a separate brief period of activity during autumn.

Important predators of the Piute ground squirrel include badgers (which are a major source of mortality during the inactive season), coyotes, long-tailed weasels, prairie falcons, rough-legged hawks, red-tailed hawks, ferruginous hawks,

Spermophilus mollis

Swainson's hawks, and ravens. *S. mollis* is the primary food resource for regional breeding populations of several predatory birds. As its common name implies, it was formerly an important food item for the Piute and other indigenous peoples of the region. *E. A. Rickart*

Size

Figures are for *S. m. mollis; S. m. artemesiae* is about 12 percent shorter than *S. m. mollis* and *S. m. idahoensis* is about 16 percent longer.

Total length: 201–233 (213) mm

Length of tail: 44–61 (52) mm

Weight during mating period: 107–205 (154) g (males); 82–164 (121) g (females)

Identification

The Piute ground squirrel can be distinguished from most other *Spermophilus* by its relatively small size, very short ears, and plain (unmarked) pelage. It is similar to *S. washingtoni,* but lacks conspicuous dorsal spots, and is indistinguishable externally from *S. townsendii* and *S. canus.*

Recent Synonyms

Citellus idahoensis

Citellus mollis

Citellus townsendii (part)

Spermophilus townsendii (part)

Other Common Names

Townsend's ground squirrel (part), sagebrush or least Idaho ground squirrel (for *S. m. artemesiae),* Snake Valley or Payette ground squirrel (for *S. m. idahoensis)*

Status

Common, although the subspecies *artemesiae, idahoensis,* and *nancyae* have limited distributions

Subspecies

Spermophilus mollis artemesiae, central Idaho on the Snake River plain north of the Snake River

Spermophilus mollis idahoensis, west-central Idaho northeast of the Snake River

Spermophilus mollis mollis, most of Nevada except for the extreme south and northwest, and portions of extreme northeastern California, extreme southeastern Oregon, southern Idaho south of the Snake River, and western Utah

Spermophilus mollis nancyae, south-central Washington north of the Yakima River and west of the Columbia River

References

Mammalian Species 268; Alcorn, 1940; Davis, 1939

Arctic ground squirrel | *Spermophilus parryii*

No North American ground squirrel except the aptly named Arctic ground squirrel, *Spermophilus parryii,* is confronted with the harshness of the far northern latitudes. The unique survival strategies of this large ground squirrel focus on the extremes of a long winter, short growing season, permafrost, strong winds, low temperatures, poor drainage, and limited cover, all part of the Arctic environment. Arctic summers are very short, and during this brief five-month interval the entire regenerative cycle of this species must take place.

Hibernation is not an unusual physiological state for a ground squirrel, but this species must of necessity remain dormant for seven months of the year, longer than the dormancies observed in other, closely related species. Animals begin to emerge from their hibernacular chambers about mid-April. Males emerge first and quickly establish territories that they defend against intruders. Females select the natal burrow systems they will use to raise their young without enticement from males, and become part of the breeding harem of the male dominating that territory. They do not engage in the defense of the male territory. Breeding begins almost immediately upon emergence, which means that gonadal development is triggered during hibernation.

All females are pregnant by the middle of May. An average litter of six to eight young is born in late May or early June, following a gestation period of 25 days. Six weeks later, in early July, young animals begin to emerge from the nest, timidly at first, extending the distance away from the burrow entrance daily. The adult female cares for her offspring for a week or two following their appearance aboveground, after which they begin to fend for themselves. Growth of the young ground squirrels is very rapid. Within a month after emergence, they are 80 percent the size of adults. By the middle of September they have attained adult size and weight and are ready to enter hibernation.

Ground squirrels must forage actively to attain a prehibernation weight of 600 to 700 grams. In spite of the long daylight hours of the Arctic summer, the animals respond to a diurnal rhythm and are underground for at least seven hours of "night." Food includes berries, seeds, and leaves of various Arctic plant species, including species in the genera *Arbutus, Vaccinium, Polygonum,* and *Astragalus.* Although primarily vegetarians, the squirrels will at times feed on dead birds, insect larvae, beetles, and dead of their own species. They are camp beggars and will eagerly take items of high fat content. One addicted visitor, an adult male, made daily visits to glean coffee grounds from a campsite. He made several trips to fill his cheek pouches when coffee grounds were especially bountiful. He did not return the following year.

Burrows are constructed in areas of good drainage where the permafrost is a meter or more below the surface, enabling animals to tunnel deeply. Much of the Arctic ground squirrel's range includes tundra, where traditional burrow systems are excavated on alluvial terraces, high banks above streams, and low ridges. In forested areas, this species is found in open meadows or above the tree line.

Two distinct populations seem to be present within inhabited areas. Breeding colonies made up of male-dominated territories are found in ideal habitat and less densely populated refugee populations are found in marginal areas that are only periodically suitable for ground squirrel habitation.

Six distinct earthwork structures can be described for this

species. These include boundary pits, duck holes, single burrows, double burrows, refugee burrows, and hibernacula. Boundary pits and duck holes are relatively simple structures. Boundary pits are shallow depressions, ten to twenty centimeters deep, excavated by the dominant male at the site of successful encounters with rivals. A duck hole consists of a simple tunnel with one to four openings a meter or more apart. It is used as a quick escape from predators and is not permanently occupied. Refugee burrows are newly excavated, are found in less than ideal habitat, and are subject to floods and extensive predation pressure. Single and double burrows are similar, complex structures. The double burrow is actually two unconnected single systems that are so close together that the surface mounds have merged. Tunnels are generally multilevel, usually no more than one meter beneath the surface, and all include side tunnels, several openings to the surface, and one or more nest chambers. Extensive systems involve twenty meters or more of tunnel. Only double burrows are used by breeding females as natal systems to rear their young.

Hibernacula appear to be reworked portions of existing burrow systems. A hibernaculum most often has a hidden entrance, without a visible excavation mound. Excavated soil is used to plug the tunnel that would otherwise connect this earthwork to the existing burrow system. The hibernacular chamber is lined with dry sedges and grasses that are "woven" with the feet and nose into a dense, compact, hollow ball. Pieces of fur, lichen, and leaves may also be incorporated into this nest, which is about 46 cm (18 inches) in diameter. Animals have been observed transporting grasses by mouth from distances of more than 100 meters from the hibernaculum. Seed caches of *Polygonum, Vaccinium,* and *Astragalus* weighing more than 2 kg have been found in these subterranean locations. There is no indication that these stores are utilized extensively during periods of arousal from hibernation. Instead, they are probably used to meet post-emergent energy demands for pregnancy, lactation, and territorial defense, before enough new vegetation has appeared in the spring to meet the animals' needs. Field studies indicate that although post-emergent weights are lower than pre-emergent weights, the lowest body weights occur in mid-May, supporting this interpretation.

Arctic ground squirrel colonies are not as highly ordered as are some rodent social systems. Vocalization is, however, an important element of survival from potential predator attack. A shrill whistle alerts other squirrels to an aerial predator in the vicinity, and a sharp "cheek-chick" alarm call signals the presence of terrestrial danger. The Inuit name for the ground squirrel, sik-sik, is derived from this latter call. Primary terrestrial predators include the grizzly, red fox, arctic fox, wolf, and wolverine. The ermine, although not a serious threat to an adult ground squirrel, may prey upon the young prior to and

Spermophilus parryii

shortly after they emerge from the nest. The gyrfalcon, rough-legged hawk, golden eagle, long-tailed jaeger, snowy owl, and glaucous gull are principal aerial predators.

Arctic ground squirrels are born naked. Body hair begins to appear on the second day, and by the tenth day the young are completely haired. As the young animals mature, their pelage begins to show signs of wear, spotting becomes less conspicuous, and there are indications of a partial molt. By early August, a winter pelage has replaced the thinned, partly molted hair. Subadults overwinter in this pelage. Adults experience two molts during the active period, a June/July spring molt and an August/September fall molt. The spring molt begins anteriorly, appearing first around the nose and muzzle. Distinct molt lines follow the hair replacement sequence, which proceeds in a somewhat erratic manner posteriorly. Spring fur tends to be reddish-brown over all and abundantly covered with white flecks on the back. The underparts are a tawny to grayish-white. The fall molt proceeds rapidly from posterior to anterior. Hair replacement results in a grayish winter pelage, although the distinctive cinnamon-brown color of the head and the dorsal flecking remain. Molt lines are not evident in the fall molt. Curiously, some animals seem to retain the gray winter pelage all year long; either they skip the spring molt or the sequence of the first molt is more compressed than usual.

The number of conflicts between individuals increases as fall approaches and territories are newly established. Defended areas are frequently contested early in August, but by the end of the month challenges are usually not successful. The area defended circumscribes the hibernaculum by a radius of about 15 meters. Unsuccessful combatants are forced to seek habitat of lesser quality and likely will not survive the winter. Populations are greatly reduced by early to mid-September as females begin to enter hibernation. Adult males remain active until the end of that month or early October. The last to enter hiberna-

tion are the young-of-the-year. Animals are rarely found aboveground later than the middle of October. The aboveground interlude for this robust ground squirrel, a brief 138 days for females and 168 days for males, concludes as the last animal enters hibernation. Many will not survive the winter. *F. A. Iwen*

Size
Males tend to be slightly larger than females.
Total length: 332–495 mm
Length of tail: 77–153 mm
Weight: 530–816 g (Prehibernation weights are higher.)

Identification
S. parryii is distinguished from other northern ground squirrels by its reddish-brown upper surface, abundantly flecked with whitish spots. The cinnamon or tawny-colored head and smaller size further differentiate it from the hoary marmot, *Marmota caligata,* with which it is sometimes associated.

Recent Synonyms
Spermophilus undulatus

Other Common Names
Barrow ground squirrel, sik-sik or sik-rik (Inuit)

Status
Locally abundant, colonial

Subspecies
Spermophilus parryii ablusus, Alaska Peninsula north to Seward Peninsula, south to Anchorage, and eastward to Mt. McKinley National Park; introduced on three Aleutian Islands, Unalaska, Umnak, and Kavalga
Spermophilus parryii kennicottii, Point Hope eastward along Arctic slope to Parry Peninsula (MacKenzie District), south to Ogilvie and Wernecke mountains (MacKenzie District)
Spermophilus parryii kodiacensis, known only from Kodiak Island, Alaska
Spermophilus parryii lyratus, St. Lawrence Island, Bering Sea, Alaska
Spermophilus parryii nebulicola, Shumagin Islands, Alaska
Spermophilus parryii osgoodi, south of Brooks Range in the vicinity of Fort Yukon and Circle, Alaska

Spermophilus parryii parryii, along the Arctic coast of the Northwest Territories from Franklin Bay (MacKenzie District) east to the Melville Peninsula (Keewatin District), south to the Seal River (west shore of Hudson Bay), west to Thompson Landing (north shore Great Slave Lake), northwest to the Mackenzie River, and north
Spermophilus parryii plesius, from Tanana Hills (Alaska) east to MacKenzie Mountains west of Fort Norman (MacKenzie District), south to Fort Liard (MacKenzie District) and south to the head of the Klappan River, British Columbia, then northwest to the Chitina River Glacier, Alaska

References
Butterworth, 1958; Carl, 1971; MacClintock, 1970; Melchior, 1971

Richardson's ground squirrel | *Spermophilus richardsonii*

Agricultural practices on the short-grass prairies of Canada and the northern U.S. have placed humans in conflict with this energetic ground-dwelling squirrel. Its burrowing activities and its willingness to substitute cereal grains and forage crops for the native grasses destroyed by cultivation give Richardson's ground squirrel an ill-deserved reputation as a pest. When not harassed by humans, it becomes accustomed to people and makes an entertaining guest in picnic grounds and parks. Because it comes aboveground to forage during daylight hours, is of medium size, and has a shrill alarm call, Richardson's ground squirrel is one of the most recognized rodents of the prairies, where it is commonly known as the prairie gopher.

Richardson's ground squirrel is an obligate hibernator, and spends a substantial amount of its lifetime sequestered underground in a hibernaculum. The active season lasts for 7–8 months, from March to September, but each individual squirrel is aboveground for only a portion of this time. The first ani-

mals to appear in spring are males, followed about 2 weeks later by females. Females usually mate on their third day out of hibernation, then give birth underground 23 days later. The young first come aboveground when they are 28–30 days old, and juveniles rapidly make the transition from milk to a diet of leaves and seeds. Adults fatten in May and are ready to hibernate in June, by which time fat accounts for 20–30 percent of body weight. Adult females usually enter hibernation a week or two after adult males, so the active season for both sexes is about 110 days. By July, the only animals still seen aboveground are the young-of-the-year, now grown to about 80 percent of adult size. Juvenile females enter hibernation in August, whereas juvenile males remain active for another month or more and complete growth to full adult size.

The mating season, which lasts 2–3 weeks between mid-March and early April, is a period of intense male–male competition characterized by long chases and vigorous fights. All males sustain severe injuries and use up their fat reserves; many do not survive to the end of the mating season. Each female is receptive to males for only 3 hours on one afternoon of one day a year, but she usually mates with two or three males in this brief period. As soon as she is impregnated, the female becomes aggressive to all males, including her mates. By mid-pregnancy, each female prepares her own nest chamber where the litter will be born and reared in isolation. Litter size is generally 6 to 8 and the sex ratio is 1:1. Young males, however, experience greater mortality than young females in their first year of life, so the sex ratio among adults is typically three to five females per male.

Females commonly live for 2 to 4 years and very occasionally survive to 6 years old. Males rarely survive for more than 2 years. Richardson's ground squirrels live in matrilineally structured societies. Females remain in close proximity to their female kin throughout their lives, are more amicable to kin than non-kin, and sometimes sleep with female kin even as adults (except when pregnant and lactating). Males generally disperse when they are 9–12 weeks old and may disperse again each mating season, so they rarely reside near kin of either sex.

Each animal hibernates in isolation, but female kin may select separate chambers within the same burrow system. The hibernaculum is filled with dry grass, which serves as an insulative nest, and within which the animal curls up into a tight ball. Females do not store food in the hibernaculum, whereas most males store seeds under the nest material. These seed caches, which may be as massive as 1 kg, enable males to replenish their fat reserves at the end of the hibernation season before they face the demands of the mating season. As with other hibernating squirrels, hibernation consists of a series of torpor bouts interrupted by brief periods during which the ani-

Spermophilus richardsonii

mal rewarms to normal mammalian body temperature. The duration of torpor bouts is longest in December and January, when animals remain continuously in torpor for 22–25 days at a body temperature near 0° C.

The chief predators of Richardson's ground squirrels are badgers, long-tailed weasels, and Swainson's hawks, but the squirrels are also food items for foxes, coyotes, rattlesnakes, ferruginous hawks, prairie falcons, eagles, and owls. As with several other species of ground-dwelling squirrels, Richardson's ground squirrels give at least two types of alarm calls. One call (a short chirp of descending sound frequency) is given in response to aerial predators such as hawks, whereas the other (a long high-pitched whistle) is given in response to terrestrial predators such as weasels. The response of the listening squirrels also differs; listeners to the aerial call run quickly for cover but listeners to the terrestrial call stand up on their hind legs and scan the horizon. Because this response is ineffective when the "predator" is a vehicle on the highway, many ground squirrels are killed on roads. When in hibernation, Richardson's ground squirrels are safe from all predators except badgers, which use their excavating skills to dig down 50–100 cm to the hibernaculum. *G. R. Michener*

Size

Total length: 283–337 (307) mm (23 males); 264–318 (291) mm (316 females)

Length of tail: 65–88 (75) mm (23 males); 55–82 (70) mm (316 females)

Weight: 440–745 (611) g (35 males, pre-hibernation); 290–500 (388) g (249 males, post-hibernation); 330–590 (452) g (116 females, pre-hibernation); 120–290 (214) g

(368 yearling females, post-hibernation); 175–360 (267) g (170 older females, post-hibernation)

Identification
This ground squirrel is distinguished from *Spermophilus tridecemlineatus* by larger size and lack of pronounced spotted dorsal pelage, and from *Spermophilus columbianus* by smaller size and lack of pronounced tawny pelage on nose.

It can be distinguished from *Spermophilus elegans* on the basis of geographic range, but is not reliably distinguishable on the basis of pelage color.

Recent Synonyms
Citellus richardsonii

Other Common Names
Prairie gopher, flickertail

Status
Common on unbroken prairie and overgrazed pasture

References
Mammalian Species 243; Michener, 1998; Michener and Locklear, 1990

Cascade golden-mantled ground squirrel | *Spermophilus saturatus*

The Cascade golden-mantled ground squirrel is a resident of the Cascade Mountains in Washington State and southern British Columbia. It is most common on the east side of the range, being found only occasionally on the western side. It inhabits krumholtz and talus in alpine habitat, forests, and meadows, and sagebrush *(Artemesia tridentata)* near stands of yellow pine *(Pinus ponderosa)*. It is separated in range from its close relative *Spermophilus lateralis* by the Columbia River, which runs between the states of Oregon and Washington. These two species are so similar that some biologists classify *S. saturatus* as a subspecies of *S. lateralis*. No fossil record of *Spermophilus saturatus* is known.

Like all other ground squirrels, *Spermophilus saturatus* is active during the day. It forages on the ground on a wide range of leaves, fruits, flowers, and underground fungi, depending on availability. It dens almost exclusively underground, and only rarely climbs trees in search of food.

The Cascade golden-mantled ground squirrel has a stocky body and relatively long hair. The tops and sides of its head and shoulders have a poorly defined russet mantle. Its eyes are surrounded by a pinkish-buff ring and its ears are tawny. Its back is dark gray-brown with a white stripe on each side that runs from shoulder to hip. These stripes are bordered above and below by poorly defined black stripes. Its tail, feet, and belly are buff colored. It molts once a year, in June or July.

S. saturatus breeds in early to late April, depending on the elevation and amount of winter snowfall. After a gestation period of 28 days, the female gives birth to up to five young. The neonates are quite undeveloped at birth, but during the first five weeks that the mother nurses them they open their eyes, grow fur, and develop the ability to stand on their four feet and to control their body temperatures. Usually only about three young survive to emergence; those that do appear aboveground for the first time about 36 days after birth. Over the next week they add solid adult food to their diet as their mother weans them. Juvenile males and females usually dis-

perse from where they were born and establish their own home ranges elsewhere.

During the late summer and fall, *S. saturatus* of all ages and sexes begin to fatten in order to get ready for winter. During this time, squirrels can increase their weight by more than 50 percent and noticeably increase in girth. Each squirrel separately prepares an underground den, packed with dry grass, in which it spends fall through early spring. This time of hibernation includes very important changes in their physiology. For most of the time, their metabolic rate drops to only about five percent of what it is during the summer and their body temperature drops to only a few degrees above freezing. This allows them to live for up to eight months on just their body fat; these squirrels almost never store any food in their dens for winter feeding. They arouse from torpor at intervals of several days to two weeks throughout the winter.

The Cascade golden-mantled ground squirrel shares its range with several other rodents, most notably yellow pine and Townsend's chipmunks, Douglas's squirrel, the deer mouse, the southern red-backed vole, and the Pacific jumping mouse. S. C. Trombulak

Spermophilus saturatus

Size
No significant sexual dimorphism
Total length: 286–315 (302) mm
Length of tail: 92–118 (108) mm
Weight: 300 g (at fall immergence); 200 g (at spring emergence)

Identification
This species can be distinguished from *Spermophilus lateralis,* the only other ground squirrel with a russet-colored head and black and white stripes on the body, by a larger body size and a range exclusively north of the Columbia River.

Recent Synonyms
Callospermophilus saturatus

Status
Common

References
Mammalian Species 322; Ingles, 1965; Trombulak, 1987

Spotted ground squirrel | *Spermophilus spilosoma*

The spotted ground squirrel is found throughout much of the arid and semi-arid regions of the southwestern United States and Mexico. It occurs in desert scrubland and grasslands from central Mexico through western Texas, New Mexico, Arizona, and southern Utah in the west, and through the Oklahoma panhandle, eastern Colorado, western Kansas and Nebraska, the southeastern corner of Wyoming, and the southwestern corner of South Dakota in the east. It shares some parts of this range with other, closely-related ground squirrels, including the thirteen-lined ground squirrel *(S. tridecemlineatus)* in Nebraska. Spotted ground squirrels prefer dry, deep, sandy soils with sparse vegetation. Populations are not very large, with densities averaging 2–7 squirrels per hectare (5–17 per acre).

Spotted ground squirrels feed primarily on green grasses, forbs, and seeds. Insect larvae, insects, and even other small vertebrates such as lizards and kangaroo rats are also eaten. Principal predators of spotted ground squirrels include most larger snakes and hawks.

In the northern parts of its range the spotted ground squirrel hibernates. It is not known if spotted squirrels in the south hibernate for as long, or at all. The young from the previous year are the first in a population to emerge from hibernation in spring. Males begin to emerge in early April and are followed about two weeks later by the females. Breeding occurs when the females are emerging from hibernation, and the young are born about 28 days later. Litter size ranges from five to eight.

The young emerge from their natal nest when they are about three to four weeks old, weighing about 40–50 g. They are completely independent of their mothers in about three to four more weeks.

Adult males are active for only about 115–135 days and begin to re-enter hibernation as early as July. Adult females are active for about 10 days later than are males and begin hibernation in mid-September. Young-of-the-year remain active latest in the year, but most will have entered hibernation by October. Like all ground-dwelling squirrels in North America, the spotted ground squirrel is active only during daylight hours. This diurnal activity pattern makes it one of the few small mammals easily observed in the wild. During hot weather spotted ground squirrels may be active only for a short period early in the morning and again late in the afternoon. *P. J. Young*

Spermophilus spilosoma

Size

Total length: 185–253 mm
Length of tail: 55–92 mm
Weight: 100–200 g (adult weights vary over
    geographic range)

Identification

One of the smallest North American ground squirrels, the spotted ground squirrel can be distinguished from other ground squirrels in its geographic range by lack of a bushy tail, the presence or absence and the pattern of dorsal spots, and the color of the ventral surface. *Spermophilus spilosoma* has irregularly-spaced dorsal spots that are paler than the rest of the pelage (although indistinct in some populations) and white underparts. *S. tridecemlineatus* has longitudinal rows of pale spots between dark stripes, *S. mexicanus* has longitudinal rows of spots without any dark stripes, and *S. perotensis,* which does not occur north of Mexico, has buff-colored underparts and may or may not have buff-colored dorsal spots.

Other Common Names
Gopher

Status
Common in some areas, but occurs in low-density populations

Subspecies
Spermophilus spilosoma altiplanensis, Chihuahua, Mexico

Spermophilus spilosoma ammophilus, northern Chihuahua, Mexico
Spermophilus spilosoma annectens, southern Texas and the Rio Grande River valley
Spermophilus spilosoma bavicorensis, Chihuahua, Mexico
Spermophilus spilosoma cabrerai, central Mexico
Spermophilus spilosoma canescens, south-central Mexico
Spermophilus spilosoma cryptospilotus, four corners area of Arizona, Utah, Colorado, and New Mexico
Spermophilus spilosoma marginatus, western Texas, New Mexico, southeastern Colorado, southwestern Kansas, and the panhandle of Oklahoma

Spermophilus spilosoma obsoletus, northeastern Colorado, northwestern Kansas, western Nebraska, and southeastern Wyoming
Spermophilus spilosoma pallescens, central Mexico
Spermophilus spilosoma pratensis, northern Arizona
Spermophilus spilosoma spilosoma, central Mexico

References
Mammalian Species 101; Findley et al., 1975; Hoffmeister, 1986

Round-tailed ground squirrel | *Spermophilus tereticaudus*

Spermophilus tereticaudus is characterized by rather plain pelage, without stripes or spots. Two color phases occur: cinnamon and drab. The upperparts are drab or cinnamon; the sides of the head are washed with white or gray. The underparts are white, except the underside of the tail, which is buff or cinnamon. These squirrels molt twice a year, exchanging the silkier winter coat in March, April, or May for a shorter, coarser summer coat that is shed in August or September.

Round-tailed ground squirrels live in the Sonoran and Mojave deserts of the southwestern United States. They occur from 70 m below sea level in Death Valley to nearly 1,200 m above sea level. An 8,100-year-old fossil was found in a packrat midden in Arizona.

Round-tailed ground squirrels occur primarily in sandy, relatively flat desert. They may occupy plains, sand dunes, wash edges, or slopes, but generally avoid rocky hills. They commonly inhabit communities dominated by mesquite *(Prosopis juliflora)* and creosotebush *(Larrea tridentata).* Other perennials in areas occupied by these squirrels include cholla *(Opuntia),* barrel cactus *(Ferocactus),* hackberry *(Celtis),* saltbush *(Atriplex),* cottonwood *(Populus),* desert willow *(Chilopsis),* palo verde *(Cercidium),* and bursage *(Ambrosia).* Burrows are dug in loose soil, often near the bases of shrubs or along washes, and usually have very little soil built up around the entrance.

Like other ground squirrels, *Spermophilus tereticaudus* is diurnal. This heat-tolerant species can remain active when air temperatures exceed 45° C, although it seeks the shade of

Spermophilus tereticaudus

shrubs during the hottest hours. In contrast to the constant body temperatures of most other mammals, the body temperature of *S. tereticaudus* can increase considerably when it is active on the surface at air temperatures above 30° C. Round-tailed ground squirrels are active nearly year-round in some locations, but in other areas remain mostly in their burrows between September and January. They do not hibernate, but may enter torpor.

Round-tailed ground squirrels forage on the ground and in shrubs and small trees. They are agile climbers. They are semi-colonial, and burrows are shared in the winter. In other seasons, they are occupied by a single squirrel (or a mother and her litter), and territorial behavior is exhibited. Round-tailed ground squirrels tend to be shy and quickly seek the shelter of their burrows when alarmed. From the burrow entrance, they emit high-pitched whistles or peeps.

Round-tailed ground squirrels breed from late February to April, and a litter of 1–12 (average 6) young is born after a gestation period of 25 to 35 days. The hairless neonates weigh 2.7–4.7 g. Although their eyes and ears are closed, they utter high-pitched squeaks. By 3 weeks, the skin is pigmented and covered with hair. The eyes open at 25–27 days, when the young squirrels begin running about. Weaning occurs at about 5 weeks, and they become sexually mature at 10–11 months.

The diet of *Spermophilus tereticaudus* consists mainly of seeds, leaves, and buds. Mesquite leaves and pods, creosote-bush fruits, grasses, and annual plants are frequently eaten. Ground squirrels also consume insects in the spring and fall and may occasionally eat live or dead lizards, birds, or mammals. Predators of round-tailed ground squirrels include coyotes, badgers, ravens, hawks, falcons, and snakes. *K. A. Ernest*

Size
No significant sexual dimorphism
Total length: 202–278 mm
Tail length: 60–112 mm
Weight: 110–170 g

Identification
This ground squirrel is distinguished from other ground squirrels and antelope squirrels that overlap its range by the lack of markings (stripes or spots) on its pelage and by its long, slender tail.

Recent Synonyms
Citellus tereticaudus

Other Common Names
Roundtail ground squirrel

Status
Relatively common

Subspecies
Spermophilus tereticaudus apricus, northern Baja California, Mexico

Spermophilus tereticaudus chlorus, southern California
Spermophilus tereticaudus neglectus, southern and western Arizona, western Sonora, Mexico
Spermophilus tereticaudus tereticaudus, northern Baja California (Mexico), southeastern California, and southern Nevada

References
Mammalian Species 274; Dunford, 1977; Hoffmeister, 1986

Townsend's ground squirrel | *Spermophilus townsendii*

For many years the name *Spermophilus townsendii* was applied to a group of morphologically and ecologically similar ground squirrels with a broad distribution throughout the high desert country of the western United States. Chromosomal and biochemical studies of these squirrels have revealed three distinct subgroups that do not appear to intergrade. These are now recognized as separate species. As now defined, Townsend's ground squirrel includes only those populations that have 36 chromosomes. It is restricted to a region north of the Columbia River and south of the Yakima River in south-central Washington.

There is little published information on the ecology of this species. It occurs principally in habitat dominated by sagebrush *(Artemisia)*, but is found also on agricultural land, where it is considered a pest. The diet includes green vegetation and seeds

of a wide variety of plants, as well as insects. The principal predator is the badger, which is particularly adept at excavating squirrels from their underground burrows during the hibernation period.

Animals emerge from hibernation during late January or early February and mating occurs shortly thereafter. Litter size is large; embryo counts for 52 females ranged from 4 to 16 (average 8.6). Young are born in early March and emerge from natal burrows in late March or early April. After accumulating sufficient energy in the form of body fat, they enter estivation in late May (adult males) through June (juveniles). *E. A. Rickart*

Spermophilus townsendii

Size
Total length: 200–232 (212) mm
Length of tail: 39–54 (46) mm
Mean weight during mating period: 174 g
    (males); 125 g (females)

Identification
Indistinguishable externally from *S. mollis* and *S. canus*. All three species are relatively small with short ears and plain (unmarked) pelage. The parapatric species *S. washingtoni* is similar in size but has speckled dorsal pelage. No sympatric species closely resembles *S. townsendii*.

Recent Synonyms
Citellus townsendii
Spermophilus mollis yakimensis

Other Common Names
Sage squirrel, sage rat

Status
Limited distribution

Subspecies
None. Formerly included taxa are now recognized as two separate species, *S. mollis* and *S. canus*.

References
Mammalian Species 268; Scheffer, 1941

Thirteen-lined ground squirrel | *Spermophilus tridecemlineatus*

The thirteen-lined ground squirrel is most often seen standing upright on a roadside or mowed area such as a cemetery, golf course, or lawn. If startled it will run into its nesting burrow or a short "escape burrow." Often it will remain just inside the entrance and give its warning call. The original habitat of these squirrels was probably short-grass prairie, especially open sandy areas with clumps of low grass. This species has adapted well to man's habit of mowing grass and is probably much more abundant than it originally was.

This squirrel's warning call is a relatively soft, trilled whistle, which may be heard fairly often if one observes these squirrels over extended periods. Although many squirrels may inhabit a small area, they are among the least social of their genus.

However, they do have a "greeting" in which noses and lips touch. Scent-marking occurs in many ground squirrels, including this species. The animal uses its oral glands to mark objects by rubbing the sides of the mouth and cheeks rapidly back and forth over them.

Burrows vary in size depending on the type of burrow, type of soil, and age of the animal. The nesting burrows of mature adults may be up to 30 cm (12 inches) deep and 6–7 m (20 feet) long, but those of younger animals are much smaller. Within the burrow, a nest of plant material is built in a side chamber. Burrows are plugged from the inside at night. Escape burrows are short and are scattered throughout the home range of the squirrel.

In September and October, these squirrels put on a great amount of fat, often doubling their spring weight. Soon they are in their hibernating burrow, not to come aboveground until spring. Like many other hibernators, they awaken periodically during the winter, although reasons for their awakening are not well understood. The timing of entrance into and emergence from hibernation varies with elevation and latitude, but emergence generally occurs in late March or early April. The accumulation of fat and entrance into hibernation are governed by day length, and emergence time is apparently determined by an internal cycle. Body temperatures go from about 37° C in the active state to about 3° C during hibernation, heartbeats from over 200 to not more than 5 per minute, and the breathing rate from about 50 to about 4 breaths per minute. These changes help conserve energy during a time when the animals are not feeding. Weight loss may be up to half of an individual's pre-hibernation weight.

Ground squirrels are diurnal. They emerge from their burrows in the morning as the bright sun begins to warm the day, and may be active throughout the day. They emerge on cloudy days, but bad weather will keep them in their burrows, where they feed on stored food.

Thirteen-lined ground squirrels are omnivorous. They feed heavily on seeds of grasses and herbs, but also eat many caterpillers, grasshoppers, beetles, and grubs. Often they eat only

Spermophilus tridecemlineatus

the internal organs of larger insects. Birds, birds' eggs, snakes, and lizards are occasionally eaten. Quantities of seeds are stored in the burrow, probably to be used in early spring and during bad weather in the summer.

Males emerge from hibernation before females. Mating occurs shortly after the females emerge, usually in April or early May. Neither males nor females defend territories; males simply seek out the females. Mating takes place aboveground and is obvious. Females may mate with more than one male, usually with the largest ones. The male plays no further role in the reproductive process. Gestation is 27 or 28 days. Usually only one litter is produced per year, although a few second litters were born to large females in Texas. Litters of 6 to 13 young (average, 8 or 9) are produced. The young become independent at about 6 weeks and attain adult weight at about 11 weeks.

Home ranges of males may be as large as five hectares, but those of females are much smaller. Many predators, including badgers, foxes, weasels, bull snakes, and hawks, feed on ground squirrels. *J. O. Whitaker, Jr.*

Size
No significant sexual dimorphism
Total length: 170–310 (250) mm
Length of tail: 60–132 (82) mm
Weight: 110–140 g in June, nearly twice that in fall prior to hibernation

Identification
This species is unique in having a pattern of 13 alternating pale and dark stripes running the length of its dorsum. In the dark stripes are a series of small white square spots. The tail is mixed brown and white, similar in color to the back.

Recent Synonyms
Citellus tridecemlineatus
Spermophilus badius
Spermophilus hoodii

Other Common Names
Gopher, striped ground squirrel, striped gopher, thirteen-lined gopher, striped spermophile

Status
Often abundant

Subspecies
Spermophilus tridecemlineatus alleni, northwestern Wyoming
Spermophilus tridecemlineatus arenicola, eastern New Mexico, northwestern Texas, western Oklahoma, western Kansas, and southwestern Colorado
Spermophilus tridecemlineatus blanca, south-central Colorado
Spermophilus tridecemlineatus hollisteri, central New Mexico
Spermophilus tridecemlineatus monticola, west-central New Mexico and east-central Arizona

Spermophilus tridecemlineatus olivaceous, west-central South Dakota and northeastern Wyoming
Spermophilus tridecemlineatus pallidus, northern Great Plains
Spermophilus tridecemlineatus parvus, south-central Wyoming, northeastern Utah, and northwestern Colorado
Spermophilus tridecemlineatus texensis, central Texas, much of Oklahoma, southeastern Kansas, and southwestern Missouri
Spermophilus tridecemlineatus tridecemlineatus, central United States and south-central Canada

References
Mammalian Species 103; Johnson, 1928; Joy, 1984; McCarley, 1966; Whitaker, 1972

Rock squirrel | *Spermophilus variegatus*

Spermophilus variegatus displays considerable variation in coloration and pattern within and among subspecies, as might be suggested by its specific epithet. *Variegatus,* however, refers to the dappled or wavy pattern of black, white, and buff pelage that so characterizes this squirrel. In addition to possessing this characteristic dappled pelage, rock squirrels exhibit varying degrees and patterns of black pelage across the head, shoulders, and back. Even the venter can vary tremendously, ranging from buffy or grayish-white to a reddish-buff. Adults molt once a year, between the end of May and mid-summer, depending on elevation. The duration of the molt is five or six weeks.

As might be expected, given its common name, the rock squirrel is most commonly found in and among rocky canyons, cliffs, and hillsides, and only infrequently is it seen in trees. Nevertheless, on first appearance this ground squirrel resembles a tree squirrel of the genus *Sciurus* in size and in proportions. Both have bushy tails, although the tail of *S. variegatus* is neither as long nor as bushy as a tree squirrel's. However, like all ground squirrels, it differs from arboreal squirrels morphologically in having the fourth digit longer than the third or middle digit of the forefoot.

The rock squirrel has an extensive geographical range, extending from northern Utah southward into the Mexican state of Puebla and from central Texas westward into California and to the island of Tiburon in the Gulf of California. Elevationally, the rock squirrel has been found from sea level to 2,900 m.

Although nests have been found in trees on rare occasions, rock squirrels typically den in burrows, which are commonly located under rocks and trees and adjacent to prominent features that offer good vantage points from which to stand look-

out. It is common for burrows to be used over successive years, although there is evidence to indicate that rock squirrels might move from one den to another, especially if disturbed, during the course of a year. Abandoned burrows are often inhabited by burrowing owls and other animals.

As is common among ground squirrels, the rock squirrel tends to be colonial. Within a colony there are a dominant male and a number of subordinant males. During the breeding season, which lasts about one month (March) in Utah and 1.5 months (March and April) in Texas, juveniles and females have free movement within the colony, but the dominant male drives off other males in breeding condition. The immediate burrow area is defended by the female against all other adults.

Rock squirrels have one or two litters per year, depending on the length of the winter, which in turn depends on latitude and elevation. Litters consist of one to seven (typically four) hairless offspring. The young are born blind, unpigmented, and with their ears closed. Their forelegs provide a slow crawling locomotion. After three days the skin has begun to develop some pigmentation; by the seventh day the neonate is fully active and has hair other than the vibrissae with which it was born. By the tenth day locomotion is provided by all four legs. At about 2.5 weeks the offspring are fully haired and are much more coordinated, and by about 8 weeks they emerge from the burrow while the female stands watch.

Food habits of the rock squirrel tend towards buds, nuts,

Spermophilus variegatus

fruits, and seeds such as pinyon, wild lupine, acorns, juniper berries, grapes, and corn. It is in pursuit of these foods that rock squirrels are sometimes seen in trees. *Spermophilus variegatus* also feeds on grasshoppers, beetles, earthworms, and even young turkeys. On one occasion a rock squirrel was observed killing and eating a kangaroo rat, and on another occasion a rock squirrel was seen catching a robin. Although the rock squirrel is largely a vegetarian, it will eat meat if the opportunity arises.

The fossil record of *S. variegatus* is fairly extensive. It is known from the late Pleistocene and the early Holocene in Arizona, and from the late Pleistocene in California, New Mexico, Texas, and Wyoming. Based on the fossil record, the range of the rock squirrel was greater during the Pleistocene than it is today, extending westward to a point just north of present-day Los Angeles and north of its northern Colorado range into the middle of eastern Wyoming. *D. F. Schmidt*

Size

Males are generally larger than females.
    Subspecies exhibit considerable variation in
    size and weight.
Total length: 466–503 mm
Length of tail: 189–233 mm
Weight: 450–875 g

Identification

Spermophilus variegatus is the largest ground squirrel within its extensive range. It can be distinguished from *Spermophilus annulatus* and *S. adocetus* in Mexico because the sides of its head are grayish or mixed black and white, whereas those of *S. annulatus* and *S. adocetus* are tawny or buff. Both *S. beecheyi* and *S. atricapillus,* which occur outside of the range of *S. variegatus,* are smaller than *S. variegatus* and have whitish shoulders and neck.

Recent Synonyms

Sciurus buccatus
Sciurus grammurus
Sciurus macrourus
Sciurus variegatus

Status

Common, limited

Subspecies

Spermophilus variegatus buckleyi, central Texas to the Rio Grande

Spermophilus variegatus couchii, Coahuila northwest into Chihuahua, south into northern San Luis Potosi, and into western Tamaulipas

Spermophilus variegatus grammurus, northern Colorado to central Chihuahua, most of Sonora, and from west-central Texas to southeastern California

Spermophilus variegatus robustus, east-central Nevada

Spermophilus variegatus rupestris, eastern Sonora and central Chihuahua to central Nayarit and central Zacatecas

Spermophilus variegatus tularosae, south-central New Mexico

Spermophilus variegatus utah, northern Utah to northwestern Arizona and southern Nevada

Spermophilus variegatus variegatus, central Nayarit and northern San Luis Potosi to southernmost Puebla

References

Mammalian Species 272; Hoffmeister, 1986

Washington ground squirrel | *Spermophilus washingtoni*

The Washington ground squirrel occurs in the low elevation Columbia Basin of southeastern Washington and northeastern Oregon. The native vegetation of this region is a shrub-steppe of perennial bunchgrasses *(Agropyron, Poa, Festuca),* with varying amounts of big sagebrush *(Artemesia tridentata)* and forbs. The squirrel's range is limited by the Blue and Ochoco mountains to the south, the Columbia River on the west and north, and higher elevations and coniferous forests to the east. There are late Holocene fossils from eastern Washington that probably belong to this species.

Spermophilus washingtoni is most abundant in areas with deep, well-drained sandy soils or softer soils with less clay. This species also prefers areas with abundant grass. In good habitat, densities can reach 250 per hectare.

Like other ground squirrels, *Spermophilus washingtoni* is diurnal. It feeds on a large variety of grasses, green forbs, roots, bulbs, flowers, seeds, seed pods, and insects. Badgers may be its most important predators.

Washington ground squirrels have brownish-gray backs with distinct grayish-white spots 3–4 mm wide, rather than the diffuse speckling found in "unspotted" ground squirrels. The underparts are grayish-white and this color extends up on the side of the body almost to the shoulders to form a line on the side, a characteristic shared with Townsend's ground squirrels. The underside of the tail, nose, and lower legs are pinkish-

Spermophilus washingtoni

cinnamon. The ear pinnae are very small. The only other ground squirrels in their range, *S. columbianus* and *S. beldingi,* are much larger and unspotted and have larger ears and longer tails. The Columbian ground squirrel has a reddish throat and underparts, and the tail of Belding's ground squirrel is brick-red below. Washington ground squirrels molt in May or June; the molt is diffuse, without a "molt line."

Adults emerge from hibernation in late January or early February and mate soon after. There is one litter per year of 5–11 (average 8) pups in late February or early March. The pups are weaned and appear aboveground in late March. The active season lasts about 5 months, and individual squirrels spend as much as 8 months of the year in aestivation and hibernation. Burrows are similar to those of *S. townsendii.*

Vast areas of the Columbia Basin have been converted to agriculture by the use of center-pivot sprinkler irrigation systems, and little of the Washington ground squirrel's habitat remains in its former range. *S. washingtoni* disappeared from 35 of 179 known sites during the 1980s alone, and fewer than 80 populations remain. Unfortunately, most of these are small and hence extinction-prone. Further, these populations are isolated from each other, and once the squirrels disappear from a site, reestablishment cannot occur by natural dispersal. Other threats include poisoning and shooting for target practice. *E. Yensen*

Size
Males are slightly larger than females.
Total length: 185–245 mm
Length of tail: 32–65 mm
Weight: 120–300 g (varies seasonally)

Identification
Spermophilus washingtoni is generally similar to *Spermophilus townsendii* (small size, very reduced ear pinnae), but with well-defined spots on the back. It differs from *S. brunneus* in having smaller ear pinnae and less reddish coloration in the legs, nose, and tail. *S. columbianus* is much larger, has larger ears, a reddish throat, rusty legs, nose, and venter, and a longer, bushier tail.

Recent Synomyms
Citellus townsendii
Citellus washingtoni

Status
Rare and local; classified as Threatened (IUCN)

References
Mammalian Species 371; Betts, 1990

Gunnison's prairie dog | *Cynomys gunnisoni*

Gunnison's prairie dog is the smallest and least specialized of the prairie dogs, being quite ground squirrel-like in its appearance and behavior. The highly-specialized and colonial black-tailed and Mexican prairie dogs, and also the white-tailed and Utah prairie dogs, may have evolved independently from a common *C. gunnisoni* ancestor. Although it is generally accepted that prairie dogs have evolved from ground squirrels in North America, there has been much disagreement concerning their closest ground squirrel relatives. It has recently been suggested that the group of long-tailed ground squirrels that includes the Arctic ground squirrel, Richardson's ground squirrel, and their relatives may have been the ancestral stock from which prairie dogs evolved, but recent studies of DNA indicate that they are most closely related to the desert ground squirrels.

The distribution of Gunnison's prairie dog is now limited to montane valleys and high plateaus in the southern Rocky Mountains, centering around the "Four Corners" region where Arizona, Colorado, New Mexico, and Utah meet; the species is restricted to those four states. Its populations in this region of high physical relief are fragmented, with significant gaps between known colonies. This precarious situation has

been further exacerbated by campaigns that have been waged for many years against all prairie dogs as agricultural pests, and also because, like other prairie dogs, they are susceptible to plague.

The seasonal cycle of Gunnison's prairie dog resembles that of the other species. Females bear a single litter each year whose size ranges from 1 to 7, but is most commonly 3 or 4 in the southern part of the range and 4 or 5 in the northern. Fewer yearling females have litters than do adults (two or more years old), and yearlings have smaller litters on average. Litters are born from early April to late May, again depending upon latitude and elevation, after a gestation period of about a month; the young then spend another month in the burrow, where they grow to a weight of about 100 grams before emergence. This size at emergence is similar to that of other prairie dogs. Females continue to nurse the pups for a short time after they have emerged. After the young are weaned, the female may remain at the natal burrow with them or may leave them and move to another part of the colony.

Gunnison's prairie dog colonies are generally smaller than those of other species, often consisting of fewer than 50 to 100 individuals. Within the colony, social organization apparently can be either simple or complex, perhaps depending upon the size of the colony and the nature of the habitat it occupies. Unlike the habitats of the highly social black-tailed prairie dog, habitats of Gunnison's prairie dogs are highly variable both topographically and vegetationally, and visual contact between individuals in the colony is sometimes (or even often) obstructed. However, unlike black-tails, Gunnison's prairie dogs do not cut down tall vegetation in order to maintain an open, unobstructed view in the colony. In this respect, they resemble colonies of social ground squirrels rather than of black-tailed prairie dogs.

Within a colony, individuals are organized into clans that usually consist of an adult male, several adult or yearling females, and their young. In addition, peripheral animals occur who are not integrated into any clan. Within the area occupied by a clan there is much overlap of individual home ranges (the size of which varies from about 300 to nearly 1,500 square meters) and no territorial aggression is seen between members of a clan. Athough clan boundaries are not distinct, there is much less overlap between home ranges of different clans, although this appears to depend upon population density and habitat structure. Territorial defense between members of different clans often occurs, and in dense populations there is more overlap and more antagonism. In a typical small colony with low density (12 per hectare), there was less antagonism between members of different clans, and common feeding areas existed between clan boundaries, whereas in a high-density population (60 per hectare), overlap between clans occurred, with high frequency of territorial defense in which all age and sex groups took part. Such high-density populations in open

Cynomys gunnisoni

habitat are more similar to black-tailed prairie dogs not only in space use, but also in behavior and social structure.

Another consequence of high density and/or habitat productivity is seen in reproduction. In two adjacent colonies studied, the more productive site had significantly larger litters. Females reached sexual maturity more rapidly, and young females dispersed at an earlier age than they did in the less favorable habitat, where most yearling females did not breed and remained in their natal clan.

Gunnison's prairie dogs, like other species, are primarily herbivores. Their principle aboveground activity is foraging; in early spring upon emerging from hibernation they feed primarily on vegetative plant parts of both herbs and grasses, as well as on leaves and new growth of such shrubs as big sage and rabbitbrush. As the season progresses, and green vegetation becomes drier, they turn to the reproductive portions of plants, such as flowers and then seeds. Only occasionally is an insect captured and consumed. They are strictly diurnal foragers, never appearing before sunrise and usually going back into their burrows no later than an hour before sunset. During hot summer weather, surface activity decreases during midday, and they may remain inactive during heavy rain or snowfall. Entrances to burrows are marked by the mound of subsoil accumulated at the entrance as a result of digging activities, but this species makes no attempt to modify the mound as does the black-tailed prairie dog. Their burrows may also be shallower than those of black-tails. The majority of burrow entrances do not have well-developed mounds around them. Burrows abandoned by prairie dogs may be utilized by ground squirrels living in the same area.

Hibernation has long been assumed to occur in Gunnison's prairie dogs, but until recently there had been no detailed evidence concerning this physiological response. It has now been established that Gunnison's and white-tailed prairie dogs hibernate, entering a torpid state identical to that seen in hibernating ground squirrels and marmots. Gunnison's prairie dogs remain active late into the fall before entering into hibernation in October or November. White-tailed prairie dogs, particularly adults, become torpid much earlier in the fall. Spring emergence from hibernation in Gunnison's prairie dogs occurs in March or April; the timing probably varies from year to year, and is likely influenced by the depth of the winter snow pack.

Climatic factors may be an important determiner of over-winter mortality; the early onset of snow cover may inhibit the attainment of adequate fat reserves, and if coupled with a late snow melt the following spring, may lead to starvation.

The burrow system provides refuge from most predators. These include badgers, coyotes, long-tailed weasels, and formerly, black-footed ferrets, which are now all but extinct. In addition, a number of hawks regularly prey on the species, the most common being the red-tailed hawk. Gunnison's prairie dog seems exceptionally vulnerable to plague, which has been known to eliminate entire colonies. *R. S. Hoffmann*

Size

Total length: 317–390 (335) mm (males); 309–338 (325) mm (females)
Length of tail: 40–60 (51) mm (males); 46–61 (54) mm (females)
Weight: 460–1,300 (816) g (males); 465–750 (644) g (females)

Identification

Gunnison's prairie dog is the only prairie dog species within its range, but it comes into contact with the white-tailed prairie dog in west-central Colorado. The terminal half of the tail of *C. gunnisoni* is gray dorsally, bordered by white, whereas the tail tip of *C. leucurus* is all white.

Other Common Names

Zuni prairie dog

Status

This prairie dog is the target of control campaigns that have exterminated it in some localities. In addition, it is subject to mass die-offs caused by the plague bacillus *(Yersinia pestis),* which is transmitted by fleas. Its populations are thus vulnerable, although it remains abundant in some areas.

Subspecies

Cynomys gunnisoni gunnisoni, south-central Colorado and north-central New Mexico
Cynomys gunnisoni zuniensis, southeastern Utah, southwestern Colorado, northwestern New Mexico, and northeastern Arizona

References

Mammalian Species 25; Fitzgerald and Lechleitner, 1974; Pizzimenti, 1976; Rayor, 1988

White-tailed prairie dog | *Cynomys leucurus*

The white-tailed prairie dog is somewhat larger than the closely related Utah prairie dog and very similar to it. It is, however, much more widely distributed than that relict species. It occurs from the central plains of eastern Wyoming through inter-mountain valleys of the central Rocky Mountains and to the eastern edge of the Great Basin. The ancestral white-tailed prairie dog occupied the northern and central Great Plains during the latter part of the Ice Age. It probably gave rise to the Utah prairie dog quite recently, after earlier splitting off from the line leading to the least-specialized Gunnison's prairie dog. These three species are closely related to each other, and less closely related to the black-tailed prairie dog group. The entire genus may itself be a recently-evolved group; new studies suggest that its closest relatives may be a North American lineage of true ground squirrels.

Like the Utah prairie dog, the white-tailed prairie dog forms colonies consisting of a variable number of family groups.

Young pups and their mothers occupy burrow systems together. The young are born in late April or early May after a gestation period of about 30 days, and emerge aboveground in late May or early June. About 10 days after emergence, the pups are no longer confined to their birth burrows but may intermingle with pups of other litters. Adult males seem to live apart from these family groups and do not interact with them. The males defend individual territories throughout the year, and only allow females to enter during the breeding season in late March to early April. These male territories are within larger home ranges, not all parts of which are defended; females may defend their natal burrow within their home ranges. The home ranges of adult males are about one hectare in size, whereas females have home ranges about twice as large. There are seasonal changes in home range use, but no differential pattern of use by time of day, age, or sex.

There are two principal periods of movement in this species.

Cynomys leucurus

The first, in early spring, when both adult males and females move about, is associated with the breeding season. The second, in mid- to late summer, is the time when juvenile dispersal predominates. After three or four weeks aboveground, many pups begin to leave their natal home ranges. This juvenile dispersal is mostly seen among male pups at first, and they tend to move farther, often occupying the periphery of the colony or going beyond it. Young females may stay within the natal burrow and hibernate there, but some also disperse. Juvenile home ranges vary in size from about 0.3 to 2.3 hectares, but the ranges of males and females are the same average size (1.1 to 1.2 hectares). Dispersal of the young coincides not only with peak density in the colony, but also with the cessation of annual plant growth and the drying out of the vegetation. However, dispersal occurs after the young prairie dogs are no longer dependent upon lush green vegetation and the colony has switched its diet from leafy green plants to seeds and roots. About mid-July, many adult animals begin to disappear underground, and may become torpid during this period when heat and water stress is greatest and green vegetation is no longer available. Adult males tend to disappear first, followed by adult females, and by late August all adults are inactive. Some juveniles begin to hibernate in late August but others remain active until late October or even early November; male and female juveniles tend not to differ in their schedule. They do not reappear on the surface until late February–early April, depending upon spring weather conditions.

During the active season, mortality from predation may be high. Predators known to capture white-tailed prairie dogs include badgers, coyotes, bobcats, long-tailed weasels, red foxes, and, perhaps most important in the past, the black-footed ferret. Golden eagles, and probably large hawks such as the ferruginous hawk and prairie falcon, are significant predators. Plague is also a major source of mortality among prairie dogs, including this species.

Population densities may fluctuate drastically from year to year in individual colonies and throughout larger portions of the species range. For example, one colony studied over a period of three years fluctuated from a high of 67 animals to a low of 11 in a period of a little more than one year. Average density is about 3.2 per hectare, with a range of 0.72–6.2.

Like other prairie dogs, white-tailed prairie dogs have long been persecuted as "pests." This has led to drastic declines in their populations throughout most of their range and to their extirpation in many parts of their original distribution. *R. S. Hoffmann*

Size

Total length: 352–390 (366.6) mm (males);
   322–375 (348.8) mm (females)
Length of tail: 40–70 (54.9) mm (males); 46–60
   (52.3) mm (females)
Weight: 850–1,675 (1,239) g (males); 705–1,050
   (868) g (females)

Identification

The white-tailed prairie dog's range meets
that of Gunnison's prairie dog in west-central
Colorado; it is larger than the latter, with an
all-white tail tip, whereas *C. gunnisoni* has a tail
tip fringed with white around a darker gray
center. On the northern edge of its range, the
white-tail meets the black-tailed prairie dog in
southwestern Montana and across Wyoming.
Where both species occur, the "black-tail" is
easily distinguished by its black tail tip.

Status

This species has been severely reduced by so-
called "pest control" throughout its range.
Colonies of considerable size still exist, but
they are scattered, often widely, and the species
is threatened in many parts of its range.

References

Mammalian Species 7; Bakko and Nahorniak,
   1986; Clark, 1977; Hoogland, 1981

Black-tailed prairie dog │ *Cynomys ludovicianus*

The black-tailed prairie dog exhibits the most complex social
behavior of all prairie dogs, although the behavior of this
highly colonial rodent has antecedents in other members of
the genus. Black-tailed prairie dogs appear to share these social
attributes with the closely-related but less-known Mexican
prairie dog *(Cynomys mexicanus)*.

In contrast to their cousins, the white-tailed prairie dogs,
black-tails live in short to mid-grass prairies throughout the
Great Plains from Saskatchewan and Alberta on the north,
southward to extreme north-central Mexico and southwestern
Texas. Both species occur in a narrow strip running diagonally
from northwestern to southeastern Wyoming, but here they
are separated by elevation. The white-tailed prairie dogs live
higher in the mountains, occupying meadows with a more diverse grass and herb cover than the habitat occupied by the
black-tails of the plains. Across the Great Plains, black-tailed
prairie dogs formerly lived in very large colonies commonly referred to as "towns." Early explorers describe such prairie dog
towns as extending for miles and containing tens of thousands
of individuals. The largest aggregation ever recorded was a
town in Texas of nearly 65,000 square kilometers (25,000
square miles), estimated to contain 400 million individuals.

Such incredible aggregations are a thing of the past, but
black-tailed prairie dogs still live in much larger colonies than
is typical of white-tailed and Gunnison's prairie dogs. Colonies
as a whole are subdivided by topographical or vegetational features into semi-discrete units that have been termed "wards."
Within each ward are social units called "coteries," equivalent
to the clans or harems of other prairie dogs. Each coterie consists of one or more adult males, several adult and subadult females, and juveniles of both sexes. As in other species of prairie
dogs, these are extended family groups whose members coop-
erate to defend their territory against members of other coteries. The average size of a coterie is usually less than 0.5 hectare,

and defines the home range for each member of the coterie.
Territorial defense is not seen within a coterie, and coteries
normally do not overlap, in contrast to the situation observed
in dense populations of Gunnison's prairie dog. The borders of
the coterie are vigorously defended against all prairie dogs
from other coteries. Within a ward, densities can vary from
fewer than 10 to more than 30 adults and yearlings per hectare,
not counting juveniles. This is much higher than is normally
seen in white-tailed prairie dogs, although these densities may
be achieved under certain circumstances in the Gunnison's
prairie dog.

In contrast to other prairie dogs, black-tails do not breed until they are at least two years old; moreover, they breed earlier,
in February and March, and the young do not emerge from

their natal burrows until May or June. The usual litter size is 3 to 4 young, so that the black-tail exhibits both smaller litter size and more prolonged development in the burrow than is seen in other prairie dogs. The burrow itself is typically longer and deeper than that of other prairie dogs and has a more complex entrance-mound structure. The mound is not simply composed of the dirt scattered from burrow excavation. Instead, it is augmented and shaped into "crater" and "dome" mounds. The former is a relatively high, conical structure with a crater in the middle leading into the burrow, whereas the latter is lower and broader. Mounds of each sort, connected by main burrows, are arranged symmetrically around a vertical axis in each burrow system, and serve to induce windflow through the complex burrow, regardless of changes in wind direction. Air enters dome mounds and exits at crater mounds. The mounds also provide the resident prairie dogs with vantage points from which to observe the colony, and individuals vocalize and perform display activities on the mounds. These behaviors contribute to the complex social interactions of the coterie and ward to which it belongs.

All prairie dogs have a fundamental series of vocalizations, which include a repetitious bark and a "chuckle" that are considered alarm calls; snarls, growls, and tooth chatters conveying threat; screaming to indicate distress, and distinctive "contact" calls that appear to enhance group cohesion. Interestingly, although most of the alarm and threat vocalizations are similar among the various species, the contact call differs. It is described as a "raspy chatter" in Gunnison's prairie dog, a "laughing bark" in the white-tail and a "we-oo" for the black-tail. The first two species sit upright or crouch on the mound, or even

Cynomys ludovicianus

move through the colony, emitting this vocalization, but the two-syllable contact call of the black-tailed prairie dog is accompanied by a distinctive performance. The first syllable is given as the animal throws its head up and back, stands on its hind limbs with its back arched, and extends its forelegs out and up, so that the whole posture reminds one of a cheerleader on tip-toes. This position is held briefly and the second syllable of the call is given as the animal relaxes and comes down on all four feet. The whole performance takes less than a second. Sometimes, however, the vocalization is given from within the burrow, where the posturing cannot occur.

Another behavioral proclivity of the black-tailed prairie dog that is not seen in other species is the clipping of tall plants that grow within the ward. This is not usually a feeding activity, as the material thus clipped is not consumed, but it results in an unobstructed view for the resident prairie dogs across their portion of the colony. Clipping the tall plants presumably enables the prairie dogs to detect potential predators at a greater distance. Since black-tailed prairie dogs live in such large, dense colonies (in contrast to the looser, lower-density colonies of white-tails and most Gunnison's prairie dogs), their colonies are almost certainly more conspicuous to predators. When a predator is visually detected, members of the ward respond by emitting alarm calls. Not all the individuals aboveground necessarily give calls; some remain silent. The proportion of animals giving calls may be related to the number that were "alert" on their mounds, and therefore likely to detect the predator's approach; there is some evidence that in dense colonies, the proportion of individuals in alert posture is less than in colonies with lower densities. There is also some evidence that alarm calls differ subtly in response to terrestrial or to aerial predators. The principal predators of black-tailed prairie dogs are badgers and coyotes. In the past, black-footed ferrets and gray wolves also preyed on them. Raptors that prey on prairie dogs include golden eagles, prairie falcons, and large hawks such as ferrugineous and red-tailed hawks.

Black-tailed and Mexican prairie dogs do not hibernate. Black-tails are periodically active all winter, even in the northern parts of their range, where snow cover may be continuous for long periods. Although surface activity is only intermittent during winter, on relatively warm, sunny days, black-tailed prairie dogs emerge from their burrows and are active on the snow. By February and March, black-tails begin breeding, and their young are born earlier in the year than the young of other species, although they do not emerge from the burrow until about the same time that the young of other species do. Females continue to nurse their young for a few days after they emerge, but the young soon make the transition to solid food. At the time of emergence, young weigh on the order of 110–170 grams, and after two and one-half months they have attained a weight of about 570 grams.

Black-tailed prairie dogs, like other prairie dogs, are completely diurnal, and spend most of their aboveground time in foraging. In the early spring, as soon as plant growth begins, prairie dogs selectively forage on the young shoots of grasses. This dependence on growing grass continues, but several uncommon herbs also are eaten later in the spring when they become available. As summer approaches, plant growth rates decline, and more grass seeds are available. These then become a more important part of the diet. By fall most plants are dormant, but a few herbs remain succulent and are selected by the prairie dogs. As winter approaches and seeds become scarce, stems and roots are more frequently eaten, and later in winter roots become a principle source of forage, the prairie dogs digging pits to obtain them.

During cold weather, when food is scarce and other species of prairie dogs resort to hibernation, black-tails may remain in their burrows for long periods without access to either food or water. They appear to be able to survive because physiological adaptations permit them to control their metabolism even though water-deprived and starving. Although it has not been directly observed, it is probable that black-tailed prairie dogs in their burrows in winter for long periods behave like black bears in their winter sleep, with only slightly depressed temperature but with a reduced breathing rate and concomitant lowered oxygen consumption.

The dark side of the black-tailed prairie dog's adaptation to a life of high population density and frequent social interaction is infanticide, which is a major source of juvenile mortality in the species. It accounts for total or partial loss of nearly half of all litters born, and the most common killers are females with young, who attack the offspring of close genetic relatives. This situation, as far as is known at present, is unique among mammals other than primates. Another potential risk in such high-density social groups is that of extreme inbreeding. Black-tailed prairie dogs have evolved several behavioral safeguards: young males leave their natal coterie before reaching breeding age; adult males leave their coterie before their daughters reach breeding age, or if they have not, the daughter's estrus is suppressed; and finally, a female in estrus avoids mating with any father, son, or brother present in her coterie. *R. S. Hoffmann*

Size
Total length: 358–429 (387.8) mm (males); 340–400 mm (371.2) (females)
Length of tail: 70–95 (82.2) mm (males); 60–95 (76.1) mm (females)
Weight: 575–1,490 (907) g (males); 765–1,030 (863) g (females)

Identification
The only species that the black-tailed prairie dog might be confused with is its white-tailed cousin. Both occur in central Wyoming, but they are easily distinguished by the colors of their respective tail tips.

Status
This species was once distributed more or less continuously across the Great Plains of North America, from Alberta and Saskatchewan south to extreme north-central Mexico, and from eastern Nebraska west to the Rocky Mountains. Over much of this area, prairie dogs have been exterminated by intensive agriculture and poisoning efforts; remaining colonies are small, scattered, and vulnerable to further human pressure.

Subspecies
Cynomys ludovicianus arizonensis, central New Mexico south to southeastern Arizona, southwestern Texas, and adjacent Mexico
Cynomys ludovicianus ludovicianus, Great Plains from extreme southern Saskatchewan south to eastern New Mexico and the Texas panhandle

References
Mammalian Species 535; Chesser, 1983; Hoogland, 1982; Hoogland and Folts, 1982; King, 1955

Utah prairie dog | *Cynomys parvidens*

This endangered species of prairie dog is restricted to the southwestern quarter of the state of Utah; hence its common name. For a prairie dog, it is small, often smaller than Gunnison's prairie dog. The Utah prairie dog has never been widespread, but it was locally abundant until early in the 20th century, when control programs initiated by federal, state, and local authorities resulted in widespread persecution in the mistaken notion that prairie dogs seriously damaged rangeland and competed with livestock for forage. The range of this prairie dog has declined by about 90 percent during the past century and it now occurs in only a few places. At the present time it persists, but it remains rare and local and in danger of extinction. This species may have been more widespread in the Great Basin during the end of the last Ice Age, when moister conditions prevailed there, but the fossil record is virtually nonexistent.

Like all prairie dogs, Utah prairie dogs are colonial and diurnal, and feed primarily on herbs and grasses. Their colonies contain numerous burrows. The opening to each burrow is marked by a mound of scattered earth resulting from burrow excavation. Some burrow systems may interconnect. Small mounds at single-entrance burrows are most common, but older systems may have large mounds and many entrances. Excavation of the burrow systems of a captive colony revealed that nest chambers used in the active season were relatively close to the surface, whereas hibernating animals were found in deeper chambers (100–200 cm below the surface), the burrows to which were plugged with earth. Only one individual was found in each hibernaculum.

Population densities in colonies vary greatly, from 0.4 to 12 per hectare, and appear to be controlled by habitat conditions. Young are raised in burrows located in the center of the colony, and after they emerge, remain close to their natal burrows for a week or two until they are weaned in mid- to late June. Thereafter, both juveniles and adults spend increasing amounts of time in the moister, peripheral area of the colony, especially to forage. Areas of more productive vegetation support denser populations, but these prairie dogs do not inhabit areas where vegetation is tall enough to obstruct their view.

Breeding has not been observed, and may occur in the burrows. A single litter of three to six young is born each spring. The gestation period is probably similar to that of the white-tailed prairie dog, as is the molt pattern. The closest relative of the Utah prairie dog is probably the white-tailed prairie dog, whose range closely approaches that of the Utah prairie dog from the northeast. It is likely that the Utah prairie dog represents a species that has recently diverged from the ancestral white-tailed prairie dog, probably as a result of changes in climate and vegetation during the cycles of the last Ice Ages. *R. S. Hoffmann*

Cynomys parvidens

Size
Sexual dimorphism is apparently slight, but data are scarce.
Total length: 299–370 (341.0) mm (males); 290–368 (319.7) mm (females)
Length of tail: 49–62 (53.8) mm (males); 47–56 (51.7) mm (females)
Weight: 460–1,250 (636) g (males); 410–790 (516) g (females)

Identification
This small prairie dog is restricted to southern Utah, east of the range of Gunnison's and west of the range of the white-tailed prairie dog. It is characterized by an all-white tail tip, as in *C. leucurus,* but its dorsal color is brighter and is reddish to rich cinnamon, rather than buffy to grayish.

Status
This species has suffered severe persecution within its restricted distribution, and it is now exterminated in more than 90 percent of its former range. It is classified as endangered under federal law.

References
Mammalian Species 52; Crocker-Bedford et al., 1977; Egoscue and Frank, 1984; Pizzimenti, 1975

Abert's squirrel | *Sciurus aberti*

Abert's squirrels live chiefly in forests of ponderosa pine *(Pinus ponderosa)* in the southwestern United States and in western Mexico as far south as Durango. In Mexico the habitat may include other species of long-needled pines. The squirrels may also occur below the pines, in pinyon woodland, and above the pines in mixed coniferous forest, but ponderosa forests are the heartland of the species. Ponderosa seeds, buds, and cambium of twigs form an essential part of the diet, and most nesting and shelter-seeking take place in the pines as well. Especially when other foods are scarce the squirrels clip the terminal twigs, mostly from the higher crowns of selected trees called feeding or target trees, strip off the outer bark, and consume the cambial layer. Accumulations of barked twigs under the trees are readily recognizable and serve to indicate the presence of the squirrels. Feeding trees can usually be recognized by the sparse appearance of the foliage. Feeding by Abert's squirrels reduces growth, male and female cone production, and seed quality of the pines. In laboratory tests laboratory-reared squirrels feed preferentially upon twigs from feeding trees, rather than from trees not fed upon by squirrels in the wild. The basis for this discrimination by the squirrels seems to be the chemical content of the individual trees: target trees are significantly lower in xylem oleoresin flow rate, and in beta-pinene and beta-phellandrine, iron, and mercury, and are higher in carbohydrates and sodium than nontarget trees. At least some of these characteristics are genetically determined. Feeding by the squirrels exerts selective pressure on the trees, which have evolved to avoid squirrel predation by developing secondary chemical defenses. Elaboration of these chemicals carries an energetic cost, however. Where no squirrels occur in a pine forest, target trees grow faster than nontarget trees. The squirrels even seem to prefer the target trees for nesting purposes.

In summer Abert's squirrels may feed heavily upon truffles and false truffles, fungi that grow beneath the surface of the ground. The feces of the squirrels carry large numbers of fungal spores, which are thus disseminated about the forest. Upon germination, the fungi form a symbiotic relationship with the roots of the pines that enhances nutrient uptake by the trees, and benefits the fungi as well. Indeed, the well-being of the pines may depend upon the presence of the fungi. Thus the question, "Are the squirrels friends or enemies of the pines?" is not easily answered. Seasonally other foods are eaten. At lower elevations pinyons are utilized, and other conifers may be used as well.

Adult Abert's squirrels occupy home ranges of 4 to 10 hectares. Home ranges are larger in summer than in winter, and those of females in summer are about two hectares larger than those of males. Populations are known to fluctuate

Sciurus aberti

markedly, reported densities ranging from 2 to 82 per square kilometer.

By mid-March males are in mating condition, with descended testes. Females in estrus are pursued by groups of males, led by a dominant male who may copulate first and most often. Subordinate males obtain copulations as well, and there is some evidence that females may solicit their attention while rebuffing dominant males. Females build nests in pon-derosas, or occasionally in other trees, and two to four young are born after a gestation of 40 to 46 days. Young are blind and naked at birth, are weaned by 10 weeks of age, and are probably independent at 15 or 16 weeks.

There is a well marked spring molt which is usually completed by July. The autumn molt is less obvious, and includes growth of additonal hairs to produce the thick winter pelage. The conspicuous ear tufts are grown by October. *J. S. Findley*

Size
No significant sexual dimorphism
Total length: 463–584 mm
Length of tail: 195–280 mm
Weight: 540–971 g; mean of 34 individuals 620 g

Identification
Sciurus aberti is a large, bushy-tailed, grayish tree squirrel with long ears bearing elongated tufts of hairs in winter. The back is chiefly gray, usually with a rusty or brownish mid-dorsal stripe; the ventral surface is usually white, but may be gray or black. The tail is gray above and white below, or almost all white in the Kaibab Plateau subspecies. The colors of the upper- and underparts are usually separated by a well-marked black lateral line. *S. aberti* may occur with other tree squirrels and can be distnguished from them as follows: from the Arizona gray squirrel *(Sciurus arizonensis)* by much larger ears that are tufted in winter, by white underside of tail, and by black lateral stripes; from the red squirrel *(Tamiasciurus hudsonicus)* by larger size, longer, winter-tufted ears, and white underside of tail; from the fox squirrel *(Sciurus niger)* by larger, winter-tufted ears, white underside of tail, and by the lack of any orangish coloration laterally, ventrally, or in the tail; and from the Nayarit squirrel *(Sciurus nayaritensis)* by larger, winter-tufted ears, black lateral line, and white underside of tail. *S. aberti* can be distinguished from the rock squirrel *(Spermophilus variegatus),* which occurs through much of the range of Abert's squirrel and is sometimes seen in trees, by larger size, longer, winter-tufted ears, white underside of tail, and lack of gray and black mottling on back.

Recent Synonyms
None. The subspecies *S. a. kaibabensis* was formerly regarded as a distinct species, *Sciurus kaibabensis.*

Other Common Names
Tassle-eared squirrel

Status
Rare to common

Subspecies
Sciurus aberti aberti, mountains of central Arizona and southwestern New Mexico

Sciurus aberti barberi, Sierra Madre Occidental of west-central Chihuahua
Sciurus aberti chuscensis, Chuska Mountains of northwestern New Mexico and northeastern Arizona
Sciurus aberti durangi, Sierra Madre Occidental of southwestern Durango
Sciurus aberti ferreus, foothills and lower mountains of the eastern slope of the Rocky Mountains in Colorado and adjacent Wyoming
Sciurus aberti kaibabensis, Kaibab Plateau of northern Arizona
Sciurus aberti mimus, mountains of north-central New Mexico and the San Juan Mountains of Colorado
Sciurus aberti navajo, tableland adjacent to the western slope of the Abajo Mountains, San Juan County, Utah
Sciurus aberti phaeurus, Sierra Madre Occidental of southwestern Chihuahua and northwestern Durango

References
Mammalian Species 80; Allred et al., 1994; Hoffmeister, 1986; Snyder, 1992, 1993

Arizona gray squirrel | *Sciurus arizonensis*

As its name implies, *Sciurus arizonensis* is primarily an Arizona squirrel. Its center of distribution is the western and southern slopes of the central Arizona high country (below the Mogollon Rim). It also occurs on several isolated mountain ranges (but not all) farther south in Arizona and in northern Sonora, Mexico, and at a few localities in western New Mexico. It has been suggested that *Sciurus arizonensis* may actually be a fox squirrel, and that it and the Mexican fox squirrel *(Sciurus nayaritensis)* are both subspecies of *Sciurus niger.*

The Arizona gray squirrel is associated with the dense, mature, mixed broadleaf communities of riparian deciduous forests in canyon bottoms and along streamsides. The upper limits of distribution of this species are usually the elevations at which the oak-pine woodlands blend into pine forests. In places where the riparian forest canopy is diverse and dense—and contains large evergreen oaks (like *Quercus emoryi*) and Arizona walnut *(Juglans major)*—the squirrel's lower limits can extend downward in elevation into chaparral and even desert grasslands.

Arizona gray squirrels greatly favor walnuts (the juice of which often stains their paws, faces, and undersides a brownish-orange) whenever they are available, but they also eat acorns, juniper berries, fungi, tree flowers and buds, and pine seeds (harvested from cones).

Sciurus arizonensis

Except where these attractive squirrels are regularly fed and are accustomed to observation by people, or when they are actively foraging for food on the ground, they are rarely seen. In part this is because the Arizona gray squirrel is nowhere common, but it is also the result of its quiet, secretive nature. When in a tree, the squirrel's typical response to disturbance is to sit or lie quietly on a limb and outwait an impatient human intruder. When surprised on the ground, its usual tactic is to run to the nearest tree, climb up at least partway, and then travel from one tree to another until disappearing in the top of one that is suitably tall or dense.

Birth of young apparently occurs most often in June, but in every month from January through June some females are pregnant. Average litter size is three (range 2–4), but one study showed that this number had dropped to 1.5 young per female by fall–winter. Apparently not all females breed every year, and none has more than one litter per year. *R. Davis and R. Sidner*

Size
No significant sexual dimorphism
Total length: 455–574 mm
Length of tail: 200–310 mm
Weight: 527–884 (655) g

Identification
As with all tree squirrels, the tail is bushy and about the same length as the head and body.

This species is distinguished from other tree squirrels within its range by its large size, white underparts, salt and peppered steel-gray back and sides (mottled with brown or rusty-yellow), lack of ear tufts, and by its lack of a black lateral line separating the dorsal and ventral pelage.

Status
Uncommon, limited

References
Mammalian Species 496; Brown, 1984;
    Hoffmeister, 1986

Eastern gray squirrel | *Sciurus carolinensis*

Eastern gray squirrels hardly need description because they are the most commonly seen native mammal east of the Mississippi River, where they are loved by many and hated by others. The natural home of this species is forests of hardwoods or mixed hardwoods and evergreens. The larger the trees, the better the habitat, because such trees have larger cavities and produce more squirrel food than do smaller trees. Leaf nests the size of bushel baskets are often built as extra sleeping quarters, especially when a shortage of tree dens occurs. Squirrels are abundant, active during daylight, and good to eat. They are

of such hybrids exist. In the northern portions of their range black (melanistic) forms are common. Black forms (captured in northern states) have been released in Washington, D.C., where they are thriving and moving out into the suburbs. White (albino) gray squirrels are extremely rare in the wild but in a few towns, such as Olney, Illinois, they have become abundant by enforcement of laws giving them protection.

Gray squirrels eat a variety of foods, taking advantage of whatever is available. In addition to acorns and other nuts they consume flowers, many kinds of seeds, flower and leaf buds, the cambium layer of tree bark, and fungi in many forms. They eat mushrooms (including some that are deadly to humans), dig shallow holes to get small fungal truffle-like objects, and eat the bark of dead trees for the fungal mycelia within. Birds' eggs and nestlings, insects, insect eggs, and even carrion may be eaten when the opportunity occurs. Their love of sunflower seeds brings them into conflict with people who feed birds.

Gray squirrels begin their mating activities about the time of the winter solstice and continue through January and February. Following a 40-day gestation period, young are born during February and March. Another lesser mating period occurs during June and July with resulting births occurring between late July and mid-September. Occasionally births occur at other times of the year. The mother-to-be selects a secure and dry tree den, which she lines with leaves and bark fibers. Here she gives birth to one to six blind and hairless young, usually two or three. She raises the young by herself and drives off all other squirrels that approach her nest. Within a few days hair begins to appear on the young and after five weeks their eyes open. At eight or nine weeks they are weaned and shortly thereafter are abandoned by their mother.

Every September, those squirrels born during the previous winter, plus a few adults, strike out in all directions to find permanent residences of their own. This phenomenon is referred to as the fall reshuffle. When an abundance of squirrels coincides with a poor fall nut crop, more squirrels than usual will be moving about more actively than usual, looking for future home sites. On rare occasions, when an unusually large population of squirrels coincides with a drastic failure of the fall nut crop, the spectacular sight of so many squirrels moving about may give the false impression that a mass of squirrels is moving in one direction. This phenomenon is incorrectly called a migration, when it actually is nothing more than a big fall reshuffle.

Both fox and gray squirrel abundance varies greatly from year to year, but is always highest in late August and September. At this time they are also most visible while scurrying about burying acorns and other nuts. These nuts are buried individually, slightly below the surface of the ground, close to where they have fallen, to be dug up and eaten later during the

therefore much sought after by hunters during fall hunting seasons. Squirrels thrive in cities where tree-lined streets and wooded parks provide good habitats. Here gardeners, home-owners, and people who feed birds often find them a nuisance.

Gray squirrels appear gray above and on their flanks and white below. The gray portion often has a red-brown cast, which when especially pronounced can give the impression that the animal is a gray-fox squirrel hybrid. No valid records

Sciurus carolinensis

winter. Over the course of winter squirrel numbers decline, sometimes drastically, depending mostly on the availability of food, the severity of the winter, and parasites, especially mange mites. These may cause a squirrel to lose much of its hair and may also cause severe secondary infections, which in combination with cold winters and food shortages can be fatal. Predators such as foxes, bobcats, hawks, and black rat snakes take a few squirrels, but their impact seems not to affect overall abundance.

That portion of a forest where a gray squirrel spends its lifetime (its home range) is generally no more than one or two hectares (three or four acres) and frequently overlaps the home ranges of other squirrels. Here each animal becomes intimately acquainted with its environs and learns the best places to hide from enemies. At night and during bad weather, as many as seven or eight squirrels may occupy a communal den, where they groom each other and conserve heat during cold winter nights.

The average life span of gray squirrels is eleven to twelve months. In other words, half of all squirrels alive on New Year's Day will die before the next year begins. Averages, however, are deceptive and because squirrels become wiser with age, some individuals will live longer and a few have been known to pass the ten year mark in the wild.

Eastern gray squirrels have been released in California, Oregon, Washington, British Columbia, South Africa, Great Britain, Italy, and Australia. Only the Australian immigrants disappeared; the other colonies are doing fine. *V. Flyger*

Size
No significant sexual dimorphism
Total length: 383–525 (473) mm
Length of tail: 150–243 (193) mm
Weight: 338–750 (520) g

Identification
Sciurus carolinensis can be distinguished from *Sciurus niger,* the only other member of its genus sharing its range, by smaller size.

Other Common Names
Cat squirrel, migratory squirrel

Status
Common to abundant

Subspecies
Sciurus carolinensis carolinensis, southern states west to eastern Texas, Oklahoma, and Kansas, north to southern Iowa, Illinois, Indiana, and Ohio; southern Virginia
Sciurus carolinensis extimus, south Florida
Sciurus carolinensis fuliginosus, southern Louisiana and southernmost Mississippi
Sciurus carolinensis hypophaeus, southern Minnesota, eastern North Dakota, and southernmost Manitoba

Sciurus carolinensis matecumbei, Florida Keys
Sciurus carolinensis pennsylvanicus, northern states, southern Ontario and Quebec, Virginia and West Virginia, and south in the Appalachian Mountains to eastern Tennessee and western North Carolina

References
Mammalian Species 480; Barkalow and Shorten, 1973; Flyger and Gates, 1982; Gurnell, 1987; Shorten, 1954

Western gray squirrel | *Sciurus griseus*

The largest native tree squirrel in the Pacific West, the western gray squirrel is found at mid-elevations from north-central Washington through west-central Oregon to inland and coastal southern California. The distribution of this squirrel is closely associated with the distribution of oak-conifer woodlands in this region. The historic expansion of *Sciurus griseus* into north-central Washington, which is beyond the range of oak, is believed to be a response to the planting of walnut trees by early settlers. The recent distribution of *Sciurus griseus* has been greatly reduced and fragmented due to increasing residential development and other habitat loss as well as competition with introduced sciurid species.

Although *Sciurus griseus* is diurnal, its wary and secretive behavior can make it difficult to see. Unlike some other members of the squirrel family, this species is intolerant of human presence. Especially active in the early morning, this squirrel prefers to travel through the trees, although it is not as agile as some other tree squirrels. Western gray squirrels consume pine cones while in the trees, but most foraging occurs on the ground. Hypogeous fungi, acorns, pine nuts, maple seeds, aspen catkins, and green vegetation are included in the diet. In the fall, acorns are stored in many small holes in the ground (scatter hoarding) to be found again later, presumably by scent. During winter and early spring when the sap is running, these squirrels feed on the cambium layer of trees. This feeding behavior is more common when populations are high and there is increased competition for food.

Sciurus griseus uses nests year-round for shelter. The squirrels nest in cavities or build round stick nests called dreys. Dreys are often used for rearing young, whereas cavities are used for sleeping. Squirrels might use different nests during the course of the day and several squirrels may use the same nest at different times. Except for nests with young, nests usually harbor only one squirrel at a time.

Sciurus griseus

The western gray squirrel has a long, bushy, blackish-gray tail that is edged in white. The dorsal pelage is silver-gray and that of the ventral surface of the body is white. A patch behind the ears is a pale reddish-brown.

Sciurus griseus typically produces one litter a year; however, there is considerable variation in the timing of reproduction of individual females. Two peaks of reproductive activity occur, one in spring and one in summer, but the breeding season extends from December through July. During the breeding season, there is much chasing, with more than one male often associated with a given female. After a gestation period of approximately 44 days, 2 to 5 young are born. May is the earliest that young have been observed to leave the nest.

Individual western gray squirrels can live 8–10 years in the wild. Potential predators of this squirrel include raptors (e.g., red-tailed hawks, great-horned owls, goshawks, golden eagles), carnivores (e.g., bobcats, coyotes, cougars, martens, domestic dogs and cats), and humans. *Sciurus griseus* appears particularly susceptible to being killed by automobiles. Epizootic outbreaks of scabies have been reported in the past and some re-searchers suggest that disease is responsible for cyclic population fluctuations.

Individual western gray squirrels occupy home ranges that vary from 0.12–6.5 hectares. Smaller, and often overlapping, home ranges have been reported where food is plentiful. Radio tracking has revealed that these squirrels expand their home ranges in the late summer, apparently in search of particular food resources. Although the squirrels require mast-producing trees and forests of larger trees with sufficient canopy cover for arboreal travel, the mix of conifer and oak trees varies within the range of this species. In Washington, *Sciurus griseus* inhabits three different vegetation types: white oak–Douglas fir woodlands in the Puget Sound area, white oak–ponderosa pine forests in the Columbia River Gorge, and the grand fir––Douglas fir zone in north-central Washington. In California, the squirrel's habitat ranges from the valley oaks low in the Sacramento Valley to the red-fir forest in Fresno County.

Other tree squirrels found in the range of *Sciurus griseus* include the native Douglas's squirrel *(Tamiasciurus douglasii)*, the northern flying squirrel *(Glaucomys sabrinus)*, and the introduced eastern gray and fox squirrels. Although there might be limited competition between the first two species and the western gray squirrel for food resources and tree-hole nesting sites, Douglas's squirrel is found more often at higher elevations, where it is closely associated with coniferous trees. The introduced tree squirrels are often more aggressive, are more tolerant of humans, and, when food is plentiful, have the ability to produce two litters per season and increase their numbers rapidly. Therefore, in certain habitats, such as riparian areas, these introduced tree squirrels can replace the native western gray squirrel. The California ground squirrel *(Spermophilus beecheyi)* is also more aggressive than the western gray squirrel. In California and Oregon, where the two species naturally co-occur, competition for food has been observed,

along with population declines of the western gray squirrel and increases of the California ground squirrel. Recent expansion of the California ground squirrel in southern Washington has resulted in a decrease of western gray squirrel populations.

M. A. O'Connell

Size
No significant sexual dimorphism
Total length: 510–770 (623) mm
Length of tail: 240–380 (315) mm
Weight: 500–950 (793) g

Identification
The western gray squirrel can be distinguished from *Sciurus carolinensis* and *Sciurus niger,* which have been introduced into its range, and from *Spermophilus beecheyi,* by its large ears, counter-shaded pelage of silver gray on the dorsal surface and pure white on the ventral surface, and by the pepper-gray aspect of the long, plume-like tail.

Recent Synonyms
Sciurus fosser
Sciurus heermanni
Sciurus leporinus

Other Common Names
Columbian gray squirrel, silver gray squirrel

Status
Threatened species in Washington State; sensitive species in Oregon

Subspecies
Sciurus griseus anthonyi, southern California
Sciurus griseus griseus, central California north into central Washington
Sciurus griseus nigripes, coastal California from San Francisco south to San Simeon

References
Mammalian Species 474; Maser et al., 1981; Washington, 1993

Mexican fox squirrel | *Sciurus nayaritensis*

The Mexican fox squirrel inhabits mixed pine-oak forests in the Chiricahua Mountains of Arizona and the Sierra Madre Occidental, Mexico, southward as far as southern Jalisco. In the Chiricahua Mountains it occurs at 1,560–2,700 meters elevation, but usually is found at about 1,650–1,950 meters. No fossils are known.

This beautiful tree squirrel is a forager; it does not cache food, and it does not regularly bury nuts. Depending upon its feeding habits and time of year, it may be secretive or readily observed. It may be especially difficult to locate early in the summer, when females are pregnant and nursing young. The Mexican fox squirrel also can be shy and hard to find in winter, when forests are bare and open. It frequently spends time on the ground.

Young-of-the-year often lose their hold on the trunks of trees and fall to the ground. This clumsiness in climbing also is a noticeable characteristic of adults. They often slip and slide on tree trunks or branches. When danger is perceived, the squirrel's usual defense is to remain motionless. Usually the Mexican fox squirrel is silent, except for chucking and barking alarm calls. When it is vocalizing, it invariably is in a tree. Alarm barks vary among individuals, but generally are more raspy and gruff than the "quirk" calls of tassel-eared squirrels, and may be followed by a whirring screech or scream.

This is a large tree squirrel. The tail is bushy, the ears are

Sciurus nayaritensis

thinly haired, the pelage is thick and soft, and the underfur is long. It is vividly colored; the upperparts are brownish with reddish or yellow-orange, and the underparts are reddish or yellow-orange. This color extends onto the sides, legs, and feet.

Young are born in spring and summer. The one litter produced each year usually contains two or three young. A young was observed on 13 July, and on 16 August a female had enlarged mammary glands and probably was still nursing. Nothing is known about developmental stages of young, but they probably are similar to those of other tree squirrels.

The Mexican fox squirrel inhabits partially open Apache pine-oak forest, and is most abundant in the thick growth of canyon bottoms. Apparently it avoids the oak-covered slopes, except possibly when acorns are numerous. The lower canyons are not its exclusive range, however; it has been seen in large oaks at 2,250 meters elevation, in Douglas fir at 2,580 meters, and, in some seasons, at the upper limit of evergreen oaks at 2,400 meters. *S. nayaritensis* is not numerous, but there is some fluctuation in numbers from year to year. It nests in oaks and pines, either in leaf nests out on the branches or in hollows and holes in the trunks.

Food items include the seeds of pines and Douglas fir, acorns, and walnuts. Roots, bulbs, and buds apparently supply food when acorns or other tree seeds are not available. Other mammals occurring in the same habitat include rock squirrels, pocket gophers, woodrats, deer mice, bobcats, mountain lions, skunks, raccoons, gray foxes, coyotes, mule deer, and white-tailed deer. Ectoparasites include lice and fleas, but no endoparasites are known.

In the Chiricahua Mountains, this squirrel is mostly restricted to the recreational areas of the mountains, which attract a great number of people. It is conspicuous, and even after considerable association with humans, it has not learned wariness. Now legally protected, the Mexican fox squirrel once suffered from the depredations of irresponsible humans.
T. L. Best

Size
Males are slightly smaller than females.
Total length: 495–613 (554) mm
Length of tail: 237–298 (270) mm
Weight: 684 g (males); 707 g (females)

Identification
No other tree squirrels occur with *S. nayaritensis* in the United States, but *S. arizonensis* and *S. aberti* occur elsewhere in Arizona. In contrast to *S. aberti*, *S. nayaritensis* never has ear tufts. Compared with *S. arizonensis*, the underparts of *S. nayaritensis* are orangeish rather than whitish, the upperparts are reddish rather than mostly gray with some brown, and the tail is bordered with tan or yellow rather than white.

Recent Synonyms
Sciurus alstoni

Other Common Names
Nayarit squirrel, Apache squirrel, Chiricahua Mountain squirrel, Apache fox squirrel, Chiricahua Nayarit squirrel

Status
Uncommon; *S. n. chiricahuae* is listed as a category two species by the Fish and Wildlife Service of the United States Department of the Interior. This category is for taxa that may become listed as endangered or threatened.

Subspecies
Sciurus nayaritensis apache, Sierra Madre Occidental of northern Mexico
Sciurus nayaritensis chiricahuae, Chiricahua Mountains, Arizona
Sciurus nayaritensis nayaritensis, Sierra Madre Occidental of west-central Mexico

References
Mammalian Species 492; Hoffmeister, 1986

Eastern fox squirrel | *Sciurus niger*

Eastern fox squirrels, so called because their striking tails are suggestive of foxtails, are twice the size of gray squirrels *(S. carolinensis)*. Compared to the latter their coat colors vary greatly, depending on locality, from uniform pale gray to black with white feet. Many appear reddish (rufous) or yellowish; others have black heads and feet. Belly fur is always a paler shade. The ranges of the two species overlap and both species often occur in the same wooded area. The larger size of fox squirrels and the difference in color is usually sufficient to recognize them from a distance.

The habits of eastern fox squirrels and eastern gray squirrels are alike in many ways. They eat the same foods, occur over much of the same range, and often occupy the same woodland. They also share the same parasites, nest in tree hollows, have the same breeding habits and seasons, utter similar sounds, and wave their tails about in a like manner when excited. Fox squirrels spend more time foraging and running about on the ground than than do the grays and may be encountered in fields as far as 183 meters (200 yards) or more from any trees. In contrast, only a demented gray squirrel would stray so far from the security of trees. Fox squirrels prefer running across the ground from tree to tree, whereas gray squirrels generally travel between trees by jumping from branch to branch. Fox squirrels are more easygoing than the grays, getting up later in the morning and turning in earlier toward evening. The home range of an individual fox squirrel may exceed 20 hectares (50 acres), which is more than ten times that of gray squirrels.

Eastern fox squirrels never reach the abundance levels attained by gray squirrels. They are savanna animals, prefering open, park-like habitats where trees are scattered and the understory is open, rather than dense forests. Such habitat has declined in the easternmost states and expanded in the Midwest. As a result, fox squirrels have been increasing and spreading in the Midwest, but declining over most of their former range. Remaining eastern colonies are often confined to small and continually shrinking localities.

Both eastern fox and gray squirrels are unusual in rarely having either tapeworms or roundworms in their gut. This is because the acorns they eat contain large amounts of tannins, which are deadly poisons to most animals, including worms. Captive squirrels on diets of other foods may harbor such parasitic worms. Both species are plagued by fleas, lice, bot flies, and a variety of mites.

Eastern fox squirrels accumulate porphyrin compounds in their teeth and bones. In humans, this results in porphyria, the

Sciurus niger

disease thought to have afflicted George III of England (and depicted in the movie *The Madness of King George.*) However, in fox squirrels this condition seems not to be pathogenic. The accumulation of porphyrin in the squirrels' tissues gives their bones a pink cast, and when their bones and teeth are exposed to ultraviolet light, they fluoresce brilliant red, a condition found in no other healthy mammal. Curiously, although eastern gray squirrels eat the same foods, and the ranges of the two species overlap, they do not evidence this condition.

Fox squirrels have been released in California, Oregon, Washington, and Colorado, and are doing well. They have become city-dwellers in midwestern states and in some of the western states where they were turned loose.

Like gray squirrels, eastern fox squirrels can be affectionate and interesting pets. Both live to a ripe old age of fifteen years or more in captivity. The more placid nature of fox squirrels makes them easier to handle than gray squirrels.

Fox squirrels are important game animals in the Midwest and portions of the East. Two of the subspecies, *S. n. cinereus* and *S. n. avicennia,* are considered endangered and are not hunted. *V. Flyger*

Size
No significant sexual dimorphism
Total length: 454–698 (595) mm
Length of tail: 200–330 (263) mm
Weight: 696–1,233 (800) g

Identification
The eastern fox squirrel can be distinguished from all other mammals by the pink cast of its bones. At a distance it can be distinguished from the gray squirrel by its larger size, and often more colorful pelage.

Recent Synonyms
Macroxus neglectus
Sciurus cinereus

Other Common Names
Fox squirrel, cat squirrel, stump-eared squirrel

Status
Common in some regions, but some sub-species threatened or endangered locally

Subspecies
Sciurus niger avicennia, southern tip of Florida
Sciurus niger bachmani, Alabama and Mississippi
Sciurus niger cinereus, Eastern Shore of Maryland
Sciurus niger limitis, central Texas
Sciurus niger ludovicianus, western Louisiana, eastern Texas, and southwestern Arkansas
Sciurus niger niger, southernmost Virginia to Florida Panhandle

Sciurus niger rufiventer, Oklahoma north to Canadian border, east to western New York, Pennsylvania, and West Virginia, and south to Tennessee and northern Arkansas
Sciurus niger shermani, peninsular Florida
Sciurus niger subauratus, along the Mississippi River from its mouth almost to the southern border of Tennessee
Sciurus niger vulpinus, southern Pennsylvania, eastern West Virginia, and northern Virginia

References
Mammalian Species 479; Allen, 1943; Flyger and Gates, 1982; Gurnell, 1987

Douglas's squirrel | *Tamiasciurus douglasii*

These energetic little squirrels are highly active in trees and on the ground throughout all seasons. They are primarily found in the coniferous forests of the far West from sea level to mountains. In its limited western distribution, *T. douglasii* is the counterpart of its relative, *T. hudsonicus,* which is widespread in temperate forests in North America. Where these species overlap, they may interbreed. A third species, *T. mearnsi,* is known only from a very limited area in Baja California about 350 miles from the southernmost record for *T. douglasii.*

Douglas's squirrel is active only during daylight hours and, except for breeding, rearing young, or confrontational encounters with other squirrels, is solitary. It lives primarily in coniferous forests, including forest edges where salal and rhododendrons form the mid-canopy in areas of greater light filtration. This squirrel also ventures into habitats where deciduous hardwoods are interspersed with conifers. It spends a great deal of time and energy cutting and storing green cones for use as winter food. Each squirrel builds several nests, mostly on limbs of trees and in tree hollows, but also underground for use in harsh weather. The latter type is typically near or in a cone midden. Nests are constructed of bark and twigs and the lichens and mosses that grow on them. The squirrels have a repertoire of calls from a low "chirr" to a sharp staccato "cough."

Douglas's squirrel has a distinct chestnut-brown band along the middle of the back that blends to a reddish- or brownish-gray on the side. A short blackish stripe on each side separates this fur from the gray to orange underparts. Short orange hairs form a ring around each dark eye, and tufts of blackish hairs tip the small ears. The tops of the feet are the color of the belly, and sometimes one or more white patches occur on the chest and throat area. The wide, somewhat flattened, bushy tail is similar in color to the back, except that the last third is blackish. In winter, the squirrel becomes grayer all over, the blackish side stripes fade, and the ear tufts are more prominent. The spring molt begins in May and June, and the autumn molt occurs from late August to early October.

Tamiasciurus douglasii generally breeds from March to June, and occasionally again in August to October. The gestation period is about 38 or 39 days, and litter size is generally 4 to 6, with up to 8 young recorded. Litter size appears to be correlated with the size of the cone crop available at the time of rearing and launching the young. The correlation may even be established prior to the litter's being conceived. The female has eight teats, and she rears the young alone. Born blind and hairless, the young reside in the nest for 8 weeks or so. In the week or two before they are weaned, when they are about two-thirds the size of adults, they venture forth for several hours at a time. Mother and young usually remain together through the end of the year. Yearlings may become reproductively active the following spring, but usually breed for the first time in their second year. Douglas's squirrels eat both the seeds and shoots of conifers. They also eat nuts, fruits, forest fungi, and even birds' eggs and nestlings.

Douglas's squirrel can be most readily confused with the

Tamiasciurus douglasii

red squirrel *(Tamiasciurus hudsonicus)* in the limited areas where the two species overlap. Other rodents of similar size with bushy tails in the range of Douglas's squirrel are readily distinguishable and include the yellow-pine chipmunk, Townsend's chipmunk, the Sonoma chipmunk, Merriam's chipmunk, the long-eared chipmunk, the lodgepole chipmunk, Belding's ground squirrel, the golden-mantled ground squirrel, the northern flying squirrel, and the bushy-tailed woodrat.

J. M. Taylor

Size
No significant sexual dimorphism
Total length: 270–348 mm
Length of tail: 102–156 mm
Weight: 141–312 g

Identification
Douglas's squirrel can be distinguished from *Tamiasciurus hudsonicus,* its closest relative in the region, by gray to orange underparts, and from three other tree squirrels that share parts of its range *(Sciurus griseus* and two introduced species, *S. carolinensis* and *S. niger)* by its much smaller size and reddish- to brownish-gray

back marked by a chestnut-brown band along the middle of the back.

Other Common Names
Chickaree, spruce squirrel

Status
Common, although declining in urban areas where the introduced *Sciurus niger* occurs

Subspecies
Tamiasciurus douglasii albolimbatus, interior Oregon and California
Tamiasciurus douglasii douglasii, coastal Wash-

ington, Oregon (except southern coast), and coastal British Columbia near the U.S.–Canadian border
Tamiasciurus douglasii mollipilosus, coastal California and southern Oregon, subcoastal along Cascade Range and eastward to interior in northern Oregon and Washington, becoming coastal again in southern British Columbia

References
Maser et al., 1981; Nowak, 1991; Verts and Carraway, 1998

Red squirrel | *Tamiasciurus hudsonicus*

The red squirrel has one of the widest distributions of any North American squirrel. It can be found in coniferous forests from the Atlantic to the Pacific Coast, and from the most northern forests of Alaska to isolated mountain ranges of southern Arizona and New Mexico. Although most common in the coniferous forests of Canada, Alaska, and the Rocky Mountains, red squirrels also occupy mixed coniferous and deciduous forests as far south in the United States as South Carolina in the East and Illinois in the Midwest.

The onset of the breeding season of red squirrels coincides with the spring thaw; breeding is later during years of heavy or late snowfall. The breeding season may start as early as mid-January to late-February, and extends into late September in some parts of the range. Breeding is a noisy affair. Courtship includes chases that may involve several males and females running through the branches chattering and making a distinctive "buzz" call reminiscent of cicadas. Females are receptive to males for only one day each breeding season, and will chase away all intruders at other times. Gestation lasts 33–35 days and the young are born blind and helpless. The young emerge from their nest at about 40 days of age and are completely weaned and independent in seven to eight weeks. Throughout most of its range the red squirrel has only one litter per year, but in the southeastern and southwestern parts of its range some females apparently have two litters in some years. The average litter size ranges from two to five, though litters of seven or eight are not uncommon in some areas. Litter size varies from one geographic region to another and from year to year.

Red squirrels are very vocal small mammals. Their characteristic bark and chatter (rattle) call are familiar to most anyone who has spent time in a coniferous forest. The chatter is a territorial call and is the first line of defense in protecting their stored food supply. It announces to other red squirrels and potential competitors that a territory is occupied. The bark call is apparently an expression of aggression, and is used against most intruders, including humans. A highly aggravated red squirrel may bark continuously for more than an hour. Other vocalizations include growls, squeaks, and screeches.

The primary food source of the red squirrel is conifer seeds. Conifer cones are collected from the trees just before the cones mature, and stored in one or more central locations where they are easily guarded. The scales of the cones are stripped away as the seeds are eaten, forming large piles of debris known as middens. These midden piles are then used as storage areas for more cones, providing a moist, cool environment that prevents the cones from opening and shedding their seeds. A choice midden site may be occupied by one squirrel after an-

Tamiasciurus hudsonicus

other for decades and can become quite large in size. Red squirrels feed on a wide variety of other foods including insects, birds' eggs, small vertebrates, and mushrooms. Mushrooms, including several species that are toxic to people, are eaten fresh or are hung in the branches of trees, dried, and then stored in caches to be eaten later.

Red squirrels use cavities in trees for nests, but also construct exposed spherical "ball" nests from lichen, grass, and twigs, and may even use underground nests in burrows at times.

Although they are usually found in lesser abundance, in good habitat the density of red squirrels can be quite high, as many as 7–8 per hectare (17–20 per acre). Red squirrels are an important fur resource, accounting for a major portion of the income of some trappers. Red squirrels adapt easily to the presence of people and can be nuisances when they make nests in the attics of homes and cabins. In some areas they may harvest up to two-thirds of the conifer cone crop, and may inhibit the natural regeneration of some conifer species. They also cause damage to some trees by clipping off branches to collect cones or buds for food. However, red squirrels also benefit the coniferous forest by spreading the spores of hypogeous (be-lowground) fungi such as truffles and false truffles, which are symbiotic with different species of conifers and provide valuable minerals to the trees.

One subspecies of red squirrel, the Mt. Graham red squirrel (*T. h. grahamensis*) is a federally listed endangered species. This subspecies occurs on only one small, isolated mountain range in southeastern Arizona, where past logging has greatly reduced the amount of available habitat. The squirrel was thought to have been extinct in the 1950s, but several sightings occurred in the 1970s. Since its being listed as endangered in 1988, the size of the population has been as low as 150 individuals. In recent years the subspecies appears to be recovering, but plans for the development of an astrophysical observatory and more campgrounds are a potential threat to its survival.
P. J. Young

Size
Total length: 280–350 mm
Length of tail: 95–150 mm
Weight: 140–250 g

Identification
The red squirrel's coat color varies by season and geographic region, but almost always has a red tint. Typically the back is rusty olive brown, the head and legs are grayer, and the ventral surface is white. In summer adults have a prominent black stripe along the side between the dark back and white belly. In winter the colors are brighter, the stripe is less distinct, and the feet and ventral surface become more grayish. There is a prominent white eye ring. The red squirrel does not overlap in range much with the closely related Douglas's squirrel (*Tamiasciurus douglasii*), except in logged areas of the Pacific Northwest. The two species can be distinguished by the color of the eye ring and belly, which are orange in Douglas's squirrel. The third species in this genus, *Tamiasciurus mearnsii*, is found only in the San Pedro Martír Mountains of Baja California Norte, Mexico, more than 600 km (373 miles) from either of its sibling species.

Other Common Names
Pine squirrel, chickaree, barking squirrel, mountain boomer, boomer

Status
Common throughout most of its range; one subspecies, *T. h. grahamensis*, is endangered

Subspecies
Tamiasciurus hudsonicus abieticola, mountain areas of North and South Carolina, Tennessee, Virginia, and West Virginia
Tamiasciurus hudsonicus baileyi, central Wyoming and central Montana
Tamiasciurus hudsonicus columbiensis, northern Rocky Mountains
Tamiasciurus hudsonicus dakotensis, western South Dakota, eastern Wyoming and Montana
Tamiasciurus hudsonicus dixiensis, southwestern Utah
Tamiasciurus hudsonicus fremonti, Colorado and southeastern Utah
Tamiasciurus hudsonicus grahamensis, Pinaleño Mountains of southeastern Arizona
Tamiasciurus hudsonicus gymnicus, Vermont, New Hampshire, Maine, Nova Scotia, and New Brunswick
Tamiasciurus hudsonicus hudsonicus, Ontario and Manitoba
Tamiasciurus hudsonicus kenaiensis, southern coast of Alaska and Kenai Peninsula
Tamiasciurus hudsonicus lanuginosus, central coast of British Columbia
Tamiasciurus hudsonicus laurentianus, southeastern Quebec
Tamiasciurus hudsonicus loquax, northeastern United States from Indiana and Michigan to New Jersey, New York, and Rhode Island; north into southern Ontario and Quebec
Tamiasciurus hudsonicus lychnuchus, Sacramento Mountains, New Mexico
Tamiasciurus hudsonicus minnesota, Illinois, Iowa, Wisconsin, and Minnesota
Tamiasciurus hudsonicus mogollonensis, northern and central New Mexico, westward through the Mogollon Plateau in Arizona
Tamiasciurus hudsonicus pallescens, north-central North Dakota, southeastern Manitoba, and southeastern Saskatchewan
Tamiasciurus hudsonicus petulans, northern panhandle of Alaska and southwestern Yukon
Tamiasciurus hudsonicus picatus, southern panhandle of Alaska and northern coast of British Columbia
Tamiasciurus hudsonicus preblei, Saskatchewan, Alberta, Yukon, and most of Alaska south of the Arctic treeline
Tamiasciurus hudsonicus regalis, Upper Peninsula of Michigan and islands in Lake Superior
Tamiasciurus hudsonicus richardsoni, western Montana, central Idaho, and eastern Oregon
Tamiasciurus hudsonicus streatori, northern Idaho, eastern and northern Washington, and southern British Columbia
Tamiasciurus hudsonicus ungavensis, central and northern Quebec, Labrador
Tamiasciurus hudsonicus ventorum, western Wyoming, southeastern Idaho, and northern Utah

References
Mammalian Species 586; MacClintock, 1970; Obbard, 1987

Northern flying squirrel | *Glaucomys sabrinus*

With its large, dark eyes and lustrous, dense, soft coat, the northern flying squirrel is surely one of the continent's most beautiful mammals. They occur widely in the northern part of North America and in scattered mountainous regions well into the south and southwest. They are most often associated with fairly dense conifer forest, but they also live in mixed conifer-deciduous forest, and occasionally in pure stands of deciduous hardwood trees. They often seem to be most abundant near surface water, in the form of swamps or streams, perhaps because the mushrooms and other fungi that form a large part of their diet are most abundant there. They also feed on seeds, nuts, fruit, insects and other invertebrates, birds' eggs, and on the flesh of small birds and mammals. They do not hibernate, and have been seen to be active at temperatures as low as –24° C.

Both species of *Glaucomys* are almost entirely nocturnal, with activity peaks several hours long shortly after sunset and just before dawn. They forage both in tree-tops and on the ground, but are best known for their ability to glide between trees. The gliding membrane, which stretches between fore and hind limbs, gives them aerodynamics remarkably like a hang-glider's, and allows northern flying squirrels to glide as far as 90 m (although 20 m is more common). They typically make their nests inside hollow trees, but sometimes in mats of moss, inside "witch's brooms" (dense clusters of branches in conifers), or in accumulated heaps of twigs, dried grass, and lichens.

Northern flying squirrels vary in dorsal color from a pale cinnamon brown to dark ashy brown, with underparts that are usually creamy white, washed at the base with gray. They (and all flying squirrels) have a cartilaginous rod several cm long that extends out from the side of the wrist, which is used for steering while gliding. Their broad tails are flattened horizontally and are usually darker near the tip than at the base. They often have pale patches of fur at the base of the ears.

Northern flying squirrels typically produce two to four young per litter, but occasionally as many as six; the gestation period is 37 to 42 days. They typically have one litter per year, born in the late spring, but some may have a second litter in the summer. Newborns weigh only 5 to 6 g and are virtually hairless, but already the gliding membrane is present. Their teeth begin to erupt on about day 26, and the eyes open on day 32. They begin to explore outside the nest by day 40, can take solid food at that time, and are weaned at about 60 days. Young often remain with their mother for several more months, probably often staying with her through their first winter. Longevity is typically three or four years. Home range sizes range from 0.8 hectares to several square kilometers, and densities from less than 1 to more than 10 per hectare.

Habitats utilized by northern flying squirrels vary widely. In

Glaucomys sabrinus

the southern Appalachians they occur in spruce-fir and mixed hemlock forest from 1,000 m to 1,800 m. In New York, forest of mixed beech, sugar maple, red oak, birch, hemlock, and white pine forms optimal habitat. In the Great Lakes region, they occur in similar habitat, but also in cedar swamps and spruce-fir forest. In Utah, they are often in Engelmann spruce and in mixed white fir and cottonwood at elevations from 2,400 to 3,100 m. In the Pacific Northwest, they are most abundant in mature rain forest composed of cedar, fir, hemlock, and spruce. In Alaska, they occur in taiga forest of white spruce, paper birch, and quaking aspen.

Given their broad geographic range, it is not surprising that northern flying squirrels become prey to many predators. Owls, hawks, weasels, martens, lynx, foxes, wolves, trout, and many others are all documented predators. Northern flying squirrels form one of the primary prey species for the northern spotted owl *(Strix occidentalis);* a pair of the owls may eat as many as 500 flying squirrels annually. Because they serve as food to this endangered species, and because they play a crucial role in dispersing the spores of symbiotic fungi that help forest trees absorb nutrients, northern flying squirrels are sometimes referred to as a "keystone species" in the Pacific Northwest. Several subspecies that live in isolated patches of high-elevation forest in the southern Appalachian Mountains are recognized as being endangered, because they exist in small, isolated populations that are being further reduced by logging. *L. R. Heaney*

Size
No significant sexual dimorphism
Total length: 275–342 mm
Length of tail: 126–153 mm
Weight: 75–140 g

Identification
Distinguished from the southern flying squirrel *(Glaucomys volans)* by its larger size, longer fur, tail that darkens toward the tip, and ventral hair that is gray at the base (rather than nearly white). All other squirrels lack the gliding membrane that extends between the fore and hind limbs.

Status
Several subspecies in the southern Appalachian Mountains are endangered

Subspecies
Glaucomys sabrinus alpinus, northern and eastern British Columbia
Glaucomys sabrinus bangsi, central Idaho, western Montana, and the Black Hills (western South Dakota and northeastern Wyoming)
Glaucomys sabrinus californicus, high peaks in southern California

Glaucomys sabrinus canescens, northwestern Minnesota, eastern North Dakota, and south-central Manitoba
Glaucomys sabrinus coloratus, mountains of western North Carolina and eastern Tennessee
Glaucomys sabrinus columbiensis, south-central British Columbia and adjacent Washington
Glaucomys sabrinus flaviventris, north-central California
Glaucomys sabrinus fuliginosus, southwestern Oregon to southwestern British Columbia
Glaucomys sabrinus fuscus, high mountains in east-central West Virginia
Glaucomys sabrinus goodwini, northern New Brunswick and adjacent Quebec
Glaucomys sabrinus gouldi, Nova Scotia
Glaucomys sabrinus griseifrons, Prince of Wales Island, Alaska
Glaucomys sabrinus klamathensis, south-central Oregon
Glaucomys sabrinus lascivus, Sierra Nevada of California
Glaucomys sabrinus latipes, northern Idaho and adjacent parts of Washington, Montana, British Columbia, and Alberta
Glaucomys sabrinus lucifugus, mountains of central and northern Utah

Glaucomys sabrinus macrotis, New England, southern Ontario, northern Michigan, and northern Wisconsin
Glaucomys sabrinus makkovikensis, northeastern Newfoundland and adjacent Quebec
Glaucomys sabrinus murinauralis, mountains of southwestern Utah
Glaucomys sabrinus oregonensis, coastal Oregon, Washington, and southwestern British Columbia
Glaucomys sabrinus reductus, west-central British Columbia
Glaucomys sabrinus sabrinus, from western Newfoundland through Quebec and northern Ontario to northwest portion of Northwest Territory
Glaucomys sabrinus stephensi, northwestern California
Glaucomys sabrinus yukonensis, central and southern Yukon and southern and central Alaska
Glaucomys sabrinus zaphaeus, central and northern British Columbia

References
Mammalian Species 229; Jackson, 1961; Weigl, 1978

Southern flying squirrel | *Glaucomys volans*

Flying squirrels are capable only of gliding, not of true flight. The squirrel's major adaptation for gliding is the patagium, a loose flap of skin along the sides of the body attached to the front and hind legs. When the animal launches itself, the legs are extended laterally, stretching the patagium to produce a broad gliding surface. The patagium is supported at the wrist by a scimitar-shaped cartilage, and muscles within the patagium strengthen its edge and control the shape of its airfoil. The broad, flat tail serves as a stabilizer and rudder and may also provide added lift. The shape of the flying squirrel's "wing" and the aerodynamic principles involved in its function are analogous to a hang glider's. Most glides range from about 6 to 18 meters, although glides up to 91 meters have been observed.

The southern flying squirrel and its larger relative, the northern flying squirrel, are the only nocturnal members of the squirrel family in North America. When active at night, they often reveal their presence by their distinctive high-pitched squeaks. Flying squirrels have large, black eyes, and their pelage differs from that of other squirrels in being extremely fine, dense, and silky. The southern flying squirrel is a

soft shade of brown, grayish brown, or tawny on the upperparts and creamy white, sometimes tinged with yellow or buff, on the underparts. The sides of the face are gray, often with a buffy wash, and the edge of the patagium is blackish.

The southern flying squirrel is a woodland dweller. Although primarily associated with hardwoods, especially oaks and hickories, it inhabits coniferous and mixed conifer-hardwood forests of diverse types ranging from swamps to dry scrub. Flying squirrels can also be common in wooded urban parks and residential areas. In the United States and Canada, southern flying squirrels are typically found at low elevations, whereas the Mexican and Central American populations are primarily associated with pine-oak woodland and cloud forest habitats at higher elevations, usually between 1,200 and 3,000 meters.

A natural cavity or old woodpecker hole in a live or dead tree is the typical nest site, but flying squirrels also construct outside nests in trees or masses of hanging vines or Spanish moss. These nests typically have an outer shell of coarser leaf fragments and sticks and an inner lining of finer material such as shredded inner bark or palmetto fibers. Flying squirrels sometimes construct their nests on an old birds' nests or modify gray squirrel or fox squirrel nests for their use. They also readily occupy bird houses or nest boxes, and sometimes build their nests in attics of houses, in outbuildings, or in cabins. There is evidence that they may occasionally nest at ground level or even underground.

Flying squirrels forage for food in trees and on the ground. They consume a wide variety of plant materials including fruits, nuts, seeds, bark, buds, flowers, sap, fungi, and lichens. They appear to be more carnivorous than many other squir-

rels, eating insects and other invertebrates, birds, eggs and nestlings, mice, and carrion. In the fall, they are active in hoarding acorns or other kinds of nuts. The nuts are typically cached in crevices or cavities in tree trunks, but may be stored in nest boxes or buildings.

Throughout their range in the eastern United States, southern flying squirrels nest communally during the colder months. The largest aggregation on record was 50 individuals found in a tree hollow in Illinois, but the number usually averages between three and eight. The primary function of huddling is assumed to be heat conservation in winter. However, the level of communal nesting is as great near the southern boundary of the range in Florida as it is near the northern boundary in Massachusetts and Michigan, which suggests that the behavior may have some social as well as physiological function.

Most flying squirrels probably breed for the first time when they are about a year old. The breeding season varies with latitude, occurring from spring to fall in the north and from late summer to winter in the south. At any given locality, there are usually two peaks of breeding, reflecting the difference in the timing of the first breeding of earlier- and later-born females of the previous year. Some older females produce two litters during the breeding season. The gestation period is 40 days. The average litter size is 3, ranging from 1 to 6. At birth, the young weigh about 4 g and are blind and hairless, except for vibrissae and short hairs on the chin and snout, and they are uncoordinated in their movements. The ears, which are folded over and sealed at birth, become erect between 2 and 6 days of age, and by 7 days hair is visible over most of the body. The eyes open between the 24th and 30th day of age, and weaning occurs at 5 to 7 weeks, by which time the young weigh about 43 g and resemble miniature adults. When they are about 12 weeks of age, the young begin a molt from the juvenile to the first adult pelage. At this age they are usually still associated with their mother and may stay with her until she has another litter. Families frequently remain together over winter.

The maximum age of flying squirrels in the wild is about 5 or 6 years, but captives have lived up to 10 years. Flying squirrels are host to more than 20 kinds of ectoparasites and internal parasites. Although rarely a direct cause of death, parasites may be a contributory cause when an animal is stressed by starvation. Accidents, including drowning, striking objects while gliding, being run over by vehicles, and even getting caught by the patagium on a barbed wire fence, account for some deaths. However, predation is probably the primary mortality factor in flying squirrel populations. Known or suspected predators include hawks and owls, house cats, bobcats, weasels, raccoons, and snakes. An unusual case of predation on the species was the discovery of a flying squirrel in the stomach of a trout.

The southern flying squirrel is of some interest from a public health standpoint. It has been shown to be a reservoir of epidemic typhus in several southern states and has been the source of some human cases of the disease.

Although in general southern flying squirrels are probably not serious competitors with other species in the woodland community, under some circumstances they may adversely affect the endangered red-cockaded woodpecker *(Picoides borealis)* in southeastern pineland habitats by usurping its nest cavities. The southern flying squirrel also has been implicated as a cause of declining populations of the northern flying squirrel in the southern Appalachians because it carries a parasitic roundworm, *Strongyloides robustus,* which has no apparent effect on the southern flying squirrel but is injurious to the northern species. In this region, the northern flying squirrel exists in isolated populations restricted to higher elevations. The southern flying squirrel is more widely distributed at lower elevations, but it has been able to invade the habitats of the northern flying squirrel, and this range expansion has been accompanied by an increased incidence of the parasite in the northern flying squirrel. *J. N. Layne*

Glaucomys volans

Size
Total length: 198–255 (231) mm
Length of tail: 81–120 (101) mm
Weight: 46–85 (70) g

Identification
Distinguished from the northern flying squirrel *(Glaucomys sabrinus),* the only other member of the genus, by its smaller size (total length less than 260 mm) and in having the hairs on the underparts white to the base rather than gray at the base.

Other Common Names
Eastern flying squirrel

Status
Common

Subspecies
Glaucomys volans chontali, District of Yautepec, Oaxaca, Mexico
Glaucomys volans goldmani, highlands of Chiapas, Mexico
Glaucomys volans herreranus, higher elevations in parts of Tamaulipas, San Luis Potosi, Veracruz, Oaxaca, Queretaro, and Michoacan, Mexico
Glaucomys volans madrensis, Sierra Madre Occidentale, Chihuahua, Mexico
Glaucomys volans oaxacensis, higher elevations in parts of Guerrero and Oaxaca, Mexico
Glaucomys volans querceti, southeastern Georgia and peninsular Florida
Glaucomys volans saturatus, southeastern United States except southeast Georgia and peninsular Florida

Glaucomys volans texensis, western Louisiana and eastern Texas
Glaucomys volans underwoodi, highlands of central Guatemala and Honduras
Glaucomys volans volans, eastern North America from southern Quebec, Nova Scotia, and northern Michigan west to western Minnesota, eastern Nebraska, and Kansas, and south to southern Missouri, Tennessee, and North Carolina

References
Mammalian Species 78; Muul, 1968; Wells-Gosling, 1985

Family Geomyidae

This family of 5 genera and 35 species is limited to North and Central America. Pocket gophers are named for the fur-lined cheek pouches, or pockets, that they use for food storage and transport. They are inhabitants of open country, where they dig extensive underground burrow systems, and are rarely seen aboveground. The family is one whose evolutionary history has been difficult to unravel, and systematic mammalogists are still working diligently to establish species limits and to analyze geographic variation among myriad local populations that often differ morphologically from site to site.

Geomyids have thick, tapering bodies and short legs that are well adapted to their fossorial lifestyle. The feet bear strong claws that are used in combination with sturdy incisors to bore a series of tunnels beneath the surface of the soil. The mouth can be closed even while the incisors remain protruding, allowing the animals to dig their way along without getting a mouthful of dirt. They can also close off their tiny eyes and ears to avoid contamination.

Foraging on roots and tubers is done from the underground tunnels, but some species will venture aboveground at night to harvest grasses as well. They can be pests in agricultural areas, not only because of their direct competition for plant resources, but because of their mounds and burrows, which are sometimes viewed as a threat to domestic livestock. Gopher control programs are widespread in areas where they come into conflict with humans.

References
Anderson and Jones, 1984; Patton, 1993a

North American Genera
Thomomys
Geomys
Pappogeomys (Cratogeomys)

Botta's pocket gopher | *Thomomys bottae*

Botta's pocket gopher has an extremely broad geographic range, from southern Oregon to the tip of the Baja California peninsula on the west coast, eastward through the central Great Basin to the southern Rocky Mountains, southward throughout the interior deserts and desert mountain ranges of the Southwest, and into the lowlands of the northern Mexican states of Sonora, Sinaloa, Chihuahua, Coahuila, and Nuevo Leon. Across this broad range, the species may be found in virtually any patch of friable soil, from rich and deep valley bottoms to shallow and rocky montane slopes and desert outwash areas. It ranges in elevation from below sea level in Death Valley National Park to above timberline in the Sierra Nevada, Rocky Mountains, and in isolated desert ranges. Consequently, Botta's pocket gopher can be found associated with an extremely wide range of local vegetation types, from desert scrub to coniferous forests. However, as with other pocket gophers, it is a resident of open habitats (meadows, along stream sides, and so forth) where soils are sufficiently deep to maintain permanent burrow systems.

Given its broad geographic and ecologic range, it is not surprising that Botta's pocket gopher is one of the world's most variable small mammals in general aspects of body size and coloration, a fact exemplified by the large number of subspecies described. Most populations average small to moderate in body size, but some (particularly those in agricultural fields) become quite large. This variation in size has an effect on the degree of sexual dimorphism that is exhibited within populations. Males always average somewhat larger than females, but the degree of dimorphism increases with an increase in male body size, because growth continues in males throughout life but truncates in females with their first pregnancy. Individuals inhabiting deep and friable soils tend to be larger than those occurring in shallow and harder soils. Body size is often seen to vary with elevation, but the size variation probably relates to elevational variation in soil depth.

Individuals range in dorsal color from dark blackish-brown through various shades of reddish and yellowish browns, pale grays and yellows, to nearly white. Ventral coloration usually mirrors that of the back, but patches of white on the throat, chest, and/or abdomen are not uncommon. The general coloration of a given population is closely tied to the color of the soil that is inhabited—animals in dark and humic soils are

Thomomys bottae

dark, and those in the pale sands of the deserts are pale gray or near-white. Melanistic or albonic individuals may be common, particularly in smaller and more isolated populations.

The great degree of differentiation observed among populations (of this and other species of pocket gophers) results only in part from the broad range occupied. Pocket gophers live in small, local populations. Both sexes dig burrow systems, which they occupy as individually defended and mutually exclusive territories. Male burrows tend to be longer and have more branches than those of females, so each male system may contact the systems of several females. Typically all adult females in a population reproduce during the season, but relatively few males do. Competition between males for reproductive access to females is apparently high, as some males do not breed at all and others sire litters from several adjacent females. As a consequence, the sex ratio of adult populations is typically skewed strongly in favor of females. This skew in sex ratio is particularly dramatic in populations where male body size is largest, and thus where the degree of sexual dimorphism is greatest.

Litter size varies greatly geographically, but is usually at a modal number of 4 to 5, with a maximum size of 10 pups per pregnancy. However, litter size can vary significantly between local populations that live in habitat of differing quality. Females in alfalfa fields in the California deserts have litters averaging more than six pups, and females in adjacent desert scrub average only about four pups per litter. The gestation period is short, about 19 to 21 days; the young are altricial at birth, with no hair and with the eyes closed. However, growth is rapid, and young are expelled from their mother's burrow by about 35 days of age. Dispersal is largely aboveground, during the

dark of the night, and young females have a greater chance of finding a place to settle and construct a burrow than do young males, particularly in dense populations. When the breeding season is three or more months long, females can and do breed in the season of their birth, but males apparently do not reach reproductive maturity until the following year. Consequently, adult female body size becomes limited by their ascendancy into reproductive activity and males continue to grow for a more prolonged period.

The breeding season itself varies extensively in its timing, typically in relation to the availability of local resources. For example, breeding occurs from January through April at low elevations in central and coastal California, following the onset of the winter rainy season and flush growth of green vegetation. This is a period adequate for a maximum of two litters by a given female. At high elevation in the Sierra Nevada, however, breeding does not occur until after snow melt in the late spring, again coinciding with the spurt of green plant growth. The growing season at high elevations can probably accommodate only a single litter per female per season. However, there can be considerable plasticity in the breeding season length for a given female. In irrigated alfalfa fields in the California deserts, the breeding season lasts from January or February through November (the time of actual irrigation), whereas adjacent desert populations breed only during the January/February–April period. The desert female will produce one litter per season, but the female in the alfalfa field can potentially produce 5 or 6 litters. The length of the breeding season, the precocious breeding of juvenile females, the average litter size, and the eventual degree of adult sexual dimorphism all result from variations in general habitat quality among populations.

Juveniles of both sexes are forced from their mother's burrow following weaning. Their dispersal distance is generally limited, with maximum distances of less than one kilometer and average distances of less than 400 meters recorded. However, locations where populations have been extirpated are typically recolonized quickly, particularly in areas where gophers are generally common, suggesting that dispersal is a major means of colony formation. Mature gophers occasionally relocate, but this is rare; usually an adult remains in its territory until death. Population density ranges from fewer than five adults per hectare in remote desert regions to a maximum of some 80 adults per hectare in irrigated alfalfa fields.

Maximum longevity is less than 3 years for females and typically less than 2 years for males; somewhat more than 50 percent of any given population may completely turn over each year. Only about 15 to 20 percent of the young born each season survive to breed in the following one. Young are frequently taken by predators during their dispersal, and both young and adults are taken as they push excavated dirt from the entrance to their burrows. Common predators are raptors and owls, a variety of snakes, and mammalian carnivores, especially weasels, badgers, bobcats, and coyotes.

Botta's pocket gopher is still considered a major agricultural pest through most of its range, but this species is also an extremely important positive agent in soil aeration and production.

Botta's pocket gopher has high potential for gene flow among local populations in areas where the animals are relatively uniformly distributed, and low potential where local populations are limited to small patches of suitable habitat otherwise surrounded by inhospitable lands. The degree of differentiation between, and thus evolutionary potential of, these two extreme population types has been considered of importance in explaining the very high level of diversity recognized for Botta's pocket gopher, and other gophers as well. *J. L. Patton*

Size
Males are somewhat larger than females.
Total length: 170–280 mm (males); 150–240 mm (females)
Length of tail: 62–92 mm (males); 55–73 mm (females)
Weight: 110–250 g (males); 80–160 g (females)

Identification
A small to large-bodied species that varies markedly in color throughout its range, Botta's pocket gopher typically has small, rounded ears with only a small subauricular black patch (markedly evident only in pale-colored desert populations) and usually two pairs of pectoral and two of inguinal mammae (total number of nipples eight).

Recent Synonyms
None. Botta's pocket gopher is known to hybridize limitedly with the southern pocket gopher *(Thomomys umbrinus)* in the Patagonia Mountains of southern Arizona and with Townsend's pocket gopher *(Thomomys townsendii)* around the edges of Honey Lake Valley in northeastern California. As a consequence, some authors have considered all three species to represent a single one.

Other Common Names
Valley pocket gopher

Status
This species is locally abundant throughout its range, although some populations in the western deserts are small and probably ephemeral. Botta's pocket gopher is very common in agricultural lands, and is often considered a commercially important pest.

Subspecies
194 subspecies have been formally recognized in the literature. However, a great many of these clearly only identify local variants and probably do not warrant formal taxonomic recognition. Indeed, appropriate reviews of geographic variation that are necessary to document the validity of particular subspecies have only been completed for populations of Botta's pocket gophers in the states of Arizona and California. In both cases, the number of subspecies recognized was greatly reduced relative to the original number identified.

References
Grinnell, 1927; Howard and Childs, 1959; Patton and Smith, 1990

Camas pocket gopher | *Thomomys bulbivorus*

Camas pocket gophers live only in the Willamette Valley and adjacent drainages of tributaries of the Willamette River in northwestern Oregon. They are quite common in agricultural and pastoral lands where, like nearly all pocket gophers living in similar circumstances, they are considered agricultural pests. They build complex tunnel systems that sometimes exceed 240 meters in total length, with several main tunnels parallel to the surface of the ground and branches that slope to the surface. The surface tunnels are typically plugged with dirt, and a large surface mound of dirt identifies the presence of the

Thomomys bulbivorus

animal. Nearly all activity is confined to the below-ground tunnel systems, although the presence of gopher remains in owl pellets indicates that individuals are sometimes aboveground. They may be exposed when they are pushing dirt from their burrows; juveniles may be preyed upon when they are dispersing from their natal burrows.

All pocket gophers are renowned for being intolerant of conspecifics. The Camas pocket gopher is typically solitary. Each individual occupies its own, self-dug burrow system. Interconnections between burrows are plugged except during the breeding season, when males apparently enter the burrow systems of females for mating.

The breeding season extends through the late spring and early summer (April through early July). Females usually give birth to four young per pregnancy, but litter sizes can range up to 8 or 9. The breeding season is sufficiently short to suggest that a female produces only one litter each year. Young are weaned by about 6 weeks of age, and sexual maturity presumably is attained by the breeding season following birth (that is, at about one year of age).

Camas pocket gophers cut and store for food the roots of many forbs, herbs, and grasses, as well as the roots of fruit and nut trees and root crops, such as carrots and potatoes. They also eat aboveground plant parts. Their penchant for crop plants has contributed to their being considered a major pest in agricultural areas, and they are subjected to a variety of methods of control, including poisoning and trapping. *J. L. Patton*

Size

Males are larger than females in most measurements and in weight.
Total length: 300 mm (males); 270 mm (females)
Length of tail: about 85 mm
Weight: 457 g (males); 344 g (females)

Identification

This species is considerably larger than any other pocket gopher of the genus *Thomomys,* especially in comparison with the other species in central and western Oregon. The color of the back is a dull sooty brown. The ears and nose are blackish; the ventral areas are typically dark grayish-brown, often with an irregular-shaped white patch on the throat. The tips of the upper incisors angle distinctly forward in front of the mouth, rather than pointing downwards, giving the animal a bucktoothed appearance.

Other Common Names

Camas rat

Status

Common, local

References

Mammalian Species 273; Wight, 1922

Wyoming pocket gopher | *Thomomys clusius*

The Wyoming pocket gopher is limited in distribution to southeastern Sweetwater County and southwestern Carbon County in south-central Wyoming, in the vicinity of Bridger's Pass. It is an upland species, preferring the drier ridge tops, and is often associated with loose, gravelly soils and greasewood habitats.

No specific studies have been made on reproduction, behavior, or diet of the Wyoming pocket gopher, but the general life history features of this species are probably similar to that of nearby populations of the northern pocket gopher. It lives in self-dug burrows, which are usually plugged with dirt and evident by surface mounds. Only one individual has been caught in a given burrow system, suggesting a solitary lifestyle. The roots and shoots of forbs and grasses probably are the main food. *J. L. Patton*

Thomomys clusius

Size
No significant sexual dimorphism
Total length: 161–184 mm
Length of tail: 50–70 mm
Weight: 44–72 g

Identification
The very small size of this pocket gopher, combined with its pale yellow color, lack of dark-colored patches behind and below the ears, and fringe of white hair on the ears, distinguish it from races of the northern pocket gopher, *Thomomys talpoides*, which may be found close by or may even be sympatric. The Wyoming pocket gopher is most similar morphologically, especially in size, to the pygmy pocket gopher, *Thomomys idahoensis pygmaeus*, which occurs in southwestern Wyoming. It has a chromosome complement (2n=44) that is distinctly different from any described for populations of either *Thomomys talpoides* or *T. idahoensis*.

Recent Synonyms
None. Previously considered as a subspecies of the northern pocket gopher, *Thomomys talpoides*.

Status
Known from only about 50 specimens from a limited area, but may be abundant within its range.

References
Clark and Stromberg, 1987; Thaeler and Hinesley, 1979

Idaho pocket gopher | *Thomomys idahoensis*

The Idaho pocket gopher occurs from central Idaho through southern and western Montana, and in a separate area in southwestern Wyoming and closely adjacent areas of southeastern Idaho and northeastern Utah. Within this range, it is found in rather shallow and stony soils, with sympatric and larger northern pocket gophers *(Thomomys talpoides)* preferring deeper soils that are more free of rocks and stones. These two species are sympatric near Fort Bridger in south-central Wyoming, an unusual occurrence for pocket gophers. Usually only one species is found in a given geographic area.

There are few data on the life history of this species. Like all pocket gophers, this species lives in self-dug burrows, with each system apparently occupied by only a single individual, suggesting a solitary existence. No information is available on breeding season, litter size, or other reproductive features, although the species probably breeds in the spring following snow melt. Similarly, no information is available on longevity or specific diet. However, pocket gophers generally live less than two years, and their food typically consists of both below-ground and aboveground plant parts, primarily forbs and grasses. *T. idahoensis* is active all year, storing excavated soil in snow tunnels during the winter. The soil settles to the ground and remains after snowmelt as evidence of winter activity. *J. L. Patton*

Thomomys idahoensis

Size
Females are slightly smaller than males.
Total length: 167–203 mm
Length of tail: 40–70 mm
Weight: 46–88 g

Identification
The Idaho pocket gopher is distinguishable from nearby or sympatric populations of the northern pocket gopher, *Thomomys talpoides,* and Townsend's pocket gopher, *Thomomys townsendii,* by its very small size and pale, yellowish (Idaho and Montana populations) to dark brown (Wyoming populations), uniformly-colored dorsum, its lack of dark ear patches, and its lack of contrasting gray-colored cheeks. It has a different chromosomal complement (2n=56 or 58) from other pocket gophers within its general range.

Recent Synonyms
None. Both recognized subspecies were previously considered races of the northern pocket gopher, *Thomomys talpoides.*

Other Common Names
Pygmy pocket gopher for the subspecies *T. i. pygmaeus*

Status
Locally common, although its range is restricted

Subspecies
Thomomys idahoensis confinus, western Montana
Thomomys idahoensis idahoensis, extreme eastern Idaho and adjacent Montana
Thomomys idahoensis pygmaeus, southwestern Wyoming and adjacent parts of southwestern Idaho and northern Utah

References
Clark and Stromberg, 1987; Davis, 1939; Thaeler, 1972

Western pocket gopher | *Thomomys mazama*

The western pocket gopher is limited in distribution to west of the Cascade Mountains from northern California north through western Oregon and western Washington to the southern end of Puget Sound and the Olympic Peninsula. Here it inhabits the deep, humic, volcanic soils of alpine meadows and small glacial prairies. It is a medium-sized species, similar in size to the mountain pocket gopher and northern pocket gopher, which occur in close proximity.

No specific studies have been made on reproduction, behavior, or diet of the western pocket gopher, but its general life history features are probably similar to that of nearby populations of the northern pocket gopher. It lives in self-dug burrows, which are usually plugged with dirt and evident by surface mounds. Only one individual has been caught in a given burrow system, suggesting a solitary lifestyle. The roots and shoots of forbs and grasses probably are the main food. *J. L. Patton*

Thomomys mazama

Size

Males are slightly larger than females.
Total length: 191–233 mm
Length of tail: 53–78 mm
Weight: 75–125 g

Identification

This is a pale to dark reddish-brown pocket gopher with gray underparts tipped with buff, long ears (but somewhat shorter than those of the mountain pocket gopher), and a subauricular black patch of fur 5 to 6 times the area of the ear. This species is very similar to some populations of the northern pocket gopher, but can be distinguished by the very long baculum (penis bone) in males (22 to 31 mm versus 12 to 17 mm). Some individuals are completely melanistic.

Recent Synonyms

None. Some subspecies were previously referred to either the northern pocket gopher, *Thomomys talpoides,* or to the mountain pocket gopher, *Thomomys monticola.*

Other Common Names

Mazama pocket gopher

Status

Populations in Washington state, particularly those around the southern margins of Puget Sound in the vicinity of Tacoma, are very small, fragmented, and considered endangered.

Subspecies

Thomomys mazama couchi, vicinity of Shelton, Mason County, Washington
Thomomys mazama glacialis, Roy Prairie, Pierce County, Washington state
Thomomys mazama helleri, mouth of the Rouge River, Curry County, Oregon
Thomomys mazama hesperus, coastal ranges of northwestern Oregon
Thomomys mazama louiei, Cathlamet Tree Farm, Wahkiakum County, Washington
Thomomys mazama mazama, Cascade Range from central Oregon through northern California

Thomomys mazama melanops, Olympic Mountains, Clallam County, Washington
Thomomys mazama nasicus, Deschutes River region, central Oregon
Thomomys mazama niger, central coast of Oregon
Thomomys mazama oregonus, northern and northwestern edge of Williamette Valley, Oregon
Thomomys mazama premaxillaris, Yolla Bolly Mountains, Tehama County, California
Thomomys mazama pugetensis, vicinity of Olympia, Thurston County, Washington
Thomomys mazama tacomensis, vicinity of Tacoma, Pierce County, Washington (presumably extinct)
Thomomys mazama tumuli, north of Tenino, Thurston County, Washington
Thomomys mazama yelmensis, Yelm Prairie and vicinity, Thurston County, Washington

References

Johnson and Benson, 1960

Mountain pocket gopher | *Thomomys monticola*

The mountain pocket gopher is limited in distribution to the central Sierra Nevada Mountains of California and western Nevada, from the high country of Yosemite National Park north through the southern Cascade Range to Mount Shasta in north-central California, and on South Yolla Bolly Mountain in northwestern California. It can be found in montane meadows, pastures, and rocky slopes in pine, fir, spruce, and hemlock forests above 1,545 m (5,000 feet) in elevation.

As is true of other pocket gophers, the mountain pocket gopher is solitary, with each individual maintaining its own, self-dug burrow system. Burrow home ranges are not interconnected with those of other individuals. The maximum size of the burrow system is 187 square meters (2,016 square feet), with a single linear dimension of 37 meters (120 feet). One or more nest chambers are in the center. A tunnel system radiates from this area, connecting deeper runs from below-surface feeding burrows. The mountain pocket gopher is active all year. It burrows in the snow pack during winter, both to feed on the surface of the ground and to use snow tunnels as a depository for excavated earth. Food is frequently cached in special chambers within the burrow system. Besides the roots, bulbs, and corms that grow below the ground surface, which are eaten throughout the year, the stems of grasses obtained from burrows under the snow provide most of the winter food. Leaves and bark of shrubs are also eaten in winter. The period of greatest vulnerability to individuals is probably late spring, when the snow melts, exposing the winter nests and the snow burrows built on water-soaked ground.

Population density ranges typically from 10 to 30 adults per hectare, depending upon the year, season, and locality. There are more females than males in the adult population. Breeding commences in the late spring and extends throughout the summer months, but an individual female probably does not produce more than one litter each season. Young-of-the-year are found only in the months of August and September. The typical litter size is 3 to 4 young. Both males and females become reproductively mature the spring following their birth. Young pocket gophers disperse from their natal burrows following weaning, but usually establish a territory in the general area of their birth. Local populations of mountain pocket gophers are relatively isolated and largely limited to separate montane meadows and stream-side connections, although some movement of individuals of both sexes may occur between nearby meadows.

Average longevity is less than three years, and population turnover is complete about every four to five years. Potential or actual predators include striped skunks, coyotes, weasels, goshawks, red-tailed hawks, spotted owls, and horned owls. Pocket gophers have a pronounced effect on their environ-

Thomomys monticola

ment, although the mountain pocket gopher's restriction to the higher montane meadows means that it is not an agricultural pest, unlike most other pocket gophers. Mountain pocket gophers are important agents in soil production and turnover; an average of about 4.2 metric tons of earth is brought to the surface by their excavations each month during the snow-free season in Sierra Nevada meadows. This excavation provides aeration and mixture of soils, as well as fresh sites for plant colonization and growth. *J. L. Patton*

Size

Males are only slightly larger, on average, than
    females.
Total length: 190–227 mm
Length of tail: 55–95 mm
Weight: 75–105 g

Identification

A uniformly brown animal, the mountain
pocket gopher has conspicuously large and
pointed, rather than rounded, ears in comparison to the nearby northern pocket gopher
(Thomomys talpoides), Mazama pocket gopher
(Thomomys mazama), or Botta's pocket gopher
(Thomomys bottae), and it has a large, black
postauricular patch that is about three times
the area of the ear.

Recent Synonyms

Thomomys pinetorum

Other Common Names

Sierra Nevada pocket gopher

Status

Locally abundant

References

Ingles, 1952

Northern pocket gopher | *Thomomys talpoides*

The northern pocket gopher, like most other pocket gophers,
is seldom seen, although the telltale earthworks it produces
are obvious in a variety of landscapes. This species has the
greatest range of any pocket gopher in North America and it
occurs in the greatest variety of habitats. Although it occurs
over an elevational range of 915 to more than 3,750 m (3,000 to
more than 12,300 feet), it is most common between 1,220 and
2,745 m (4,000 and 9,000 feet). It occupies a variety of open
vegetation types ranging from sagebrush steppe, mountain
meadows, and tundra to agricultural fields, valley grasslands,
and even people's yards. The northern pocket gopher prefers
deep, well-developed, and well drained soils, but is found even
in rocky soils or areas with compacted clays. It occurs in open
areas within forests or in forests where the trees are widely
scattered, but it needs locations with sufficient food plants
with belowground parts to meet its energetic needs. Therefore, closed canopy situations, with their sparse groundcover,
are avoided.

Most northern pocket gophers are brown or grayish-brown
to yellow-brown in color and have relatively short, soft fur that
is not as glossy as that of some of their relatives. They exhibit a
complicated spring molt: the fur is replaced from the nose toward the rear in such a way that the pelage appears to have
waves or bands across the body. A second molt in the fall is not
nearly as conspicuous, and may commence before the spring
molt is finished.

Northern pocket gophers are active throughout the year.
They do not hibernate, but may observe one or two brief periods of inactivity in the summer and mid-winter. Breeding occurs in spring, predominantly from March through April in
most localities, or later at the highest elevations. Parturition,
following a gestation of 18–20 days, is generally between mid-
May and mid-June, but can be as late as July. Young (yearling)
females produce offspring later than older females. The young
are altricial and weigh about 3 g (always less than 7 g). They

are deposited in a nest that is a part of the burrow system and
is lined with fur or soft vegetation. When a female first gives
birth, her pubic bones become permanently separated by the
enzyme relaxin, allowing easy birth through the narrow birth
canal. Litters usually number from 4 to 7. The young are
weaned at about 40 days and grow to adult size in 3 to 6
months. They breed in the spring following their birth. Only
one litter is produced each year. Individuals can live up to 5 or
6 years under ideal conditions; however, it is much more likely
that they will persist for about 18–24 months, and that there
will be complete population replacement over about a 5-year
period. Sex ratios are close to 1:1.

The northern pocket gopher's food consists of herbs and
forbs, as well as some grasses. Woody material is generally
avoided. Surprisingly, prickly pear is commonly consumed at
some sites. In addition to the many bulbs, corms, roots, and
rhizomes harvested during the tunneling process, some aboveground plant parts are taken, especially from those species
close to a burrow opening. Many plant parts are stored in side
passages of the tunnel system. When stored food spoils, it is
covered with soil. Grasses, important to many small mammals,
are generally of seasonal significance to northern pocket go-

phers and seem to be of low preference if other plant material is available. However, at some localities, e.g., along the Front Range of Colorado, 50 percent of the diet may consist of grasses. The diet changes dramatically from season to season, based on plant nutrient content and availability. Many agricultural crops are favored. I have watched northern pocket gophers near Logan, Utah, stuff their pouches so full of alfalfa that they dragged on the ground.

Pocket gophers have good olfaction, but their hearing and especially their eyesight are poor. Important to their underground existence are their sensitive vibrissae, wrist bristles, and the tips of their tails, which are used when they back up in their burrows, a common occurrence.

Few pocket gopher species co-occur, and those that overlap in range generally are separated ecologically. Body size often differs in those few instances where species co-occur. In several places where *T. talpoides* overlaps with *Geomys*, *Thomomys* is relegated to poor soils that are stony or compacted. True sympatry is indeed rare.

Except during the breeding season, the northern pocket gopher is solitary, territorial, and intolerant. When northern pocket gophers encounter one another, the negative interaction begins with a chattering of the teeth and progresses from there until one drives the other away. Only during the breeding season is more than one individual found in the same burrow system. Because they can reach densities of up to 20 per hectare (52 per acre), the proximity of their burrow systems sometimes falsely signals sociality.

Pocket gophers are preyed upon by a variety of animals, especially those that are good at digging, such as badgers. They are known to be eaten by great horned owls, some hawks, foxes, bobcats, weasels, skunks, and occasionally by snakes and other vertebrate predators. Young, recently weaned animals weighing about 40–45 g are especially vulnerable because they often disperse over the ground surface. Individuals often have significant loads of both internal and external parasites and at least some of the chewing lice, e.g., *Thomomydoecus*, cospeciate with their hosts. In addition to animal-caused mortality, abiotic factors such as cold and burrow flooding and lack of food are significant agents of mortality.

Pocket gophers dig elaborate burrow systems that are as small as possible in diameter given the body size of the occupant. Digging is accomplished with both feet and teeth, although *Thomomys*, as a genus, is considered a tooth digger compared to *Geomys*, and has larger jaw muscles and smaller leg muscles than *Geomys*. Feeding and digging cause tooth wear, and the incisors of pocket gophers grow rapidly, up to 3.65 cm per year. The upper incisors grow less than the lower incisors. The prodigious digging activity of this pocket gopher is alluded to in its species name. *Talpoides* is derived from the Latin word *talpinus*—molelike.

Thomomys talpoides

As they dig, pocket gophers decrease the soil density, thus increasing the soil volume. This expanded soil is brought to the surface and bulldozed out in somewhat fan-shaped mounds that radiate from the burrow opening. During the winter, gophers burrow through snow and will backfill these burrows with excavated soil. When spring arrives, the linear casts of soil are deposited on the ground surface. Between the casts and the mounds, up to 40 percent of the ground in certain sites may be covered by soils disturbed by gophers in any one year. In extreme situations it has been estimated that populations of northern pocket gophers may move 5 to 38 tons of soil per acre per year.

Burrow systems may extend for up to 150 m (500 feet). They are often bi-layered, with the bottom layer as deep as 2 m (6 feet) below the ground and the upper layer 20–45 cm (6–18 inches) below the surface. The lower layer contains food storage and nest sites; the upper is for foraging and storage of feces. Generally the entire burrow system is closed. Holes are plugged with soil except on some sunny days when the pocket gophers "aerate" their burrows by leaving the openings exposed.

Among the more interesting influences of northern pocket gophers is the connection between their digging activities and mima mounds, landscape features of the grasslands of western and midwestern North America. Mima mounds are circular mounds up to 2 m high and generally 20–50 m in diameter. They may number up to 100 per hectare and are most likely caused by the digging activities of pocket gophers over long periods of time. Generally each of these mounds is occupied by a single pocket gopher, but the large ones, covering 200 square meters, may be inhabited by as many as six individuals.

The prodigious digging abilities of pocket gophers and their consumption of a variety of plants can be beneficial or damaging, depending on where their activities take place. On rangelands, where they may turn over 3.6–7 tons of soil per year per acre, their activity is usually valuable, because they are mixing rich organic material from the surface with the subsoil, which speeds up the soil-forming process. This alters the physical, chemical, and biotic characteristics of the soil, often resulting in an increased number of plant species, in higher densities, on gopher-manipulated soils as compared to adjacent areas. These activities can initiate, direct, or retard the process of succession. Northern pocket gophers have had all three effects on Mount St. Helens, Washington, where in many microsites they survived a cataclysmic volcanic eruption.

On many agricultural lands, pocket gopher activities are deemed undesirable. In Canada, it has been estimated that at an average population density, pocket gophers consume about 245 kg of plant material per hectare per year (1,460 pounds per acre). This magnitude of consumption in a field, a tree nursery, or a recent reforestation site can be extremely damaging. In addition, where there is local irrigation, the tunnels of pocket gophers may re-route irrigation water, causing flooding, and their mounds can dull the blades of farm implements. In one unusual incident, pocket gophers dug into sites where radioactive waste material had been stored and brought some of these materials to the surface. The site had been carefully manicured and planted to stabilize the soil surface, thus providing good soil and food that attracted the gophers like a magnet. If underground cables cross an area where pocket gophers dwell, the animals may gnaw through the outer sheath of the cables and cause significant damage.

To alleviate these nuisance activities, people have tried a wide variety of control measures. In yards or other very small areas, a variety of traps have been used to decrease population levels. Various techniques for placing poisoned grain in artificial burrow systems that would eventually be intersected by the normal burrowing activities of the gophers are used where law permits. One of the more innovative control efforts of recent years is to apply the scents of predatory mammals to vegetation as a deterrent. Using feces, urine, and scent gland secretions in this way seems to decrease the amount of plant damage in some areas.

The northern pocket gopher has been a conspicuous element of the western landscape since the Pliocene. Its genetic and nongenetic plasticity has served it well, and it will probably continue to play both useful and destructive roles in western ecosystems. *J. A. MacMahon*

Size

Females tend to be slightly shorter and lighter than males (often by about 10 percent). Weight varies with latitude and elevation.
Total length: 165–260 mm
Length of tail: 40–75 mm
Weight: 60–160 g

Identification

The genus *Thomomys* is distinguished from other geomyid genera by the presence of upper incisors with smooth anterior surfaces. *Thomomys talpoides* is differentiated from other *Thomomys* mainly by a skull character, the absence of a sphenoidal fissure, and by having ears less than 6.9 mm long.

Status

Common and widespread

Subspecies

More than 55 recognized, several of which may warrant species rank. They include:
Thomomys talpoides aequalidens, southeastern corner of Washington and possibly adjacent Idaho
Thomomys talpoides agrestis, south-central Colorado

Thomomys talpoides andersoni, small area of southeastern Alberta
Thomomys talpoides attenuatus, southeastern quarter of Wyoming, extending just into Colorado
Thomomys talpoides bridgeri, southeastern corner of Idaho, extending east and south into western Wyoming and possibly into northern Utah
Thomomys talpoides bullatus, eastern half of Montana, extending into extreme western North Dakota, south into western and central Colorado, and north into Saskatchewan
Thomomys talpoides caryi, very small area of north-central Wyoming, possibly extending north into south-central Montana
Thomomys talpoides cheyennensis, small area of extreme southeastern Wyoming extending into adjacent west-central Nebraska
Thomomys talpoides cognatus, very small area of extreme southeastern British Columbia and possibly adjacent Alberta and northern Montana
Thomomys talpoides columbianus, extreme south-central Washington and adjacent Oregon along Columbia River

Thomomys talpoides confinis, very small area of extreme western Montana and possibly adjacent Idaho
Thomomys talpoides devexus, east-central Washington
Thomomys talpoides douglasii, western Washington and possibly adjacent northwestern Oregon along the Columbia River
Thomomys talpoides durranti, extreme west-central Colorado extending into Utah, and a disjunct area in southeastern Utah
Thomomys talpoides falcifer, central Nevada
Thomomys talpoides fisheri, northeastern California extending into extreme western Nevada in the Reno-Virginia City area
Thomomys talpoides fossor, southwestern Colorado extending into northern New Mexico, and extreme eastern Utah, with a disjunct area straddling the Arizona–New Mexico border
Thomomys talpoides fuscus, central Idaho and northwest into north-central Washington and southern British Columbia
Thomomys talpoides gracilis, northeastern Nevada and adjacent Utah, and southwest into central Nevada
Thomomys talpoides immunis, south-central Washington

Thomomys talpoides incensus, south-central British Columbia, possibly extending into northern Washington

Thomomys talpoides kaibabensis, north-central Arizona

Thomomys talpoides kelloggi, small area of south-central Montana

Thomomys talpoides levis, south-central Utah, extending southwest into Arizona

Thomomys talpoides limosus, extreme south-central Washington on the Oregon border

Thomomys talpoides loringi, south-central Alberta

Thomomys talpoides macrotis, small area of north-central Colorado (Douglas County)

Thomomys talpoides medius, southeastern British Columbia, possibly extending into northeastern Washington and northwestern Idaho

Thomomys talpoides meritus, northwestern Colorado and adjacent Wyoming

Thomomys talpoides monoensis, extreme southwestern central Nevada and adjacent eastern California

Thomomys talpoides moorei, central Utah

Thomomys talpoides nebulosus, small area of extreme western South Dakota and eastern Wyoming

Thomomys talpoides ocius, extreme northwestern Colorado, eastern Utah, and southwestern Wyoming

Thomomys talpoides oquirrhensis, north-central Utah (Oquirrh Mountains near Salt Lake City)

Thomomys talpoides parowanensis, mountains of southwestern Utah

Thomomys talpoides pierreicolus, western South Dakota and adjacent Montana, extreme eastern Wyoming, and northwestern Nebraska

Thomomys talpoides pryori, south-central Montana (Pryor Mountains)

Thomomys talpoides quadratus, eastern half of Oregon and southeast into southern Idaho, northwestern Nevada, and northeastern California

Thomomys talpoides ravus, northeastern Utah and possibly adjacent Wyoming

Thomomys talpoides relicinus, south-central Idaho (Minidoka County)

Thomomys talpoides retrorsus, east-central Colorado (along Platte-Arkansas rivers divide)

Thomomys talpoides rostralis, central Colorado and north along Front Range into Wyoming

Thomomys talpoides rufescens, central South Dakota, most of North Dakota, eastern Saskatchewan and western Manitoba, eastern Minnesota, and possibly western Montana

Thomomys talpoides saturatus, northern Idaho, adjacent western Montana, and southeastern British Columbia

Thomomys talpoides segregatus, southeastern British Columbia (near Wynndel)

Thomomys talpoides shawi, south-central Washington (Mt. Rainier)

Thomomys talpoides talpoides, north-central Montana, north into Alberta, and east into Saskatchewan and Manitoba

Thomomys talpoides taylori, Valencia County in northwestern New Mexico

Thomomys talpoides tenellus, northwestern Wyoming, north into Montana and possibly into adjacent Idaho (Yellowstone area)

Thomomys talpoides trivialis, central Montana

Thomomys talpoides uinta, northeastern Utah

Thomomys talpoides wallowa, northeastern Oregon and adjacent Washington

Thomomys talpoides wasatchensis, northeastern Utah and possibly adjacent Idaho (along Wasatch Front)

Thomomys talpoides whitmani, small area of southeastern Washington (Walla Walla County)

Thomomys talpoides yakimensis, small area of south-central Washington

References

Andersen and MacMahon, 1981; Chase et al., 1982; Huntly and Inouye, 1988; Teipner et al., 1983

Townsend's pocket gopher | *Thomomys townsendii*

Thomomys townsendii has a typical pocket gopher lifestyle, living underground in tunnels it digs with the long claws on each powerful front limb and with its incisors. The lips close behind the front teeth, so the animal can dig with the incisors without getting dirt in its mouth. Because pocket gophers make their homes underground, soil type greatly influences where they live. Townsend's pocket gophers inhabit areas with deep, relatively moist soils in the northern Great Basin. These soils occur in Pleistocene lake beds and along the river valleys of several drainage systems, including the Humboldt River drainage of Nevada, Honey Lake Valley in California, the Malheur Basin in southeastern Oregon, and the Snake River Valley in Idaho. Although the species is currently distributed in disjunct patches, fossils of this gopher from Pleistocene deposits show that it once occurred over a broader area.

As a general rule, only one kind of pocket gopher occurs in any particular area. Apparently the underground niche cannot be shared by more than one species. In the northern Great

Basin, nearby populations of *Thomomys bottae* tend to occur in more desert-like habitats, and species in the *Thomomys talpoides* group occur at higher elevations. Individuals of both *Thomomys townsendii* and *Thomomys talpoides* have been found in

the same field in the Reese River valley west of Austin, Nevada. No indication of hybridization between the two forms has been reported in this area. Contact occurs between *Thomomys townsendii* and neighboring species of pocket gophers in Honey Lake Valley in California. On the west side of the valley, *T. townsendii* is in contact with a northern California representative of *Thomomys bottae,* a widespread species. On the east side of the valley, *T. townsendii* is in contact with a Great Basin form of *Thomomys bottae.* In a very small area in these contact zones both types occur in the same fields. A limited number of hybrid individuals are found in each contact area. Genetic studies of the western contact zone have shown that the female parent of each of the hybrids was a *T. bottae* and the male parent was a *T. townsendii.* The large *T. townsendii* males, which weigh nearly three times as much as the female *T. bottae,* are too big to fit into the relatively small burrows of the female *T. bottae.* Therefore, it appears that the female controls matings, perhaps searching out the largest male in the neighborhood with which to mate.

The color of the fur in *Thomomys townsendii* varies across its range from pale grayish tan to cinnamon to very dark brown. Occasional animals are melanistic (all black) or albino (all white). The nose is sooty black, gray, or dark brown. Most animals also have a black spot behind each ear. Usually the tops of the feet and tail are white, and there is a white chin patch. In some areas a white blaze on the top of the head is fairly common.

Thomomys townsendii breeds in the spring. A study in the Malheur Basin in Oregon showed that females had at least two litters a year in quick succession, so that pregnant females were also nursing young. Pregnant females have been found throughout the range of the species from February through

Thomomys townsendii

June. A female may have from three to seven young, but four or five is the most common litter size.

Thomomys townsendii occurs in areas with shadscale and sagebrush vegetation types. Like other pocket gophers, *Thomomys townsendii* depends primarily on the underground roots and stems of grasses and herbs for its food supply. Fur-lined cheek pouches open to the outside at the sides of the mouth. The animal uses its front feet to shove pieces of vegetation into the cheek pouches to carry to underground storage areas for later consumption. *M. F. Smith*

Size
Total length: 232–315 (278) mm (males); 226–287 (260) mm (females)
Length of tail: 60–99 (82) mm (males); 58–92 (78) mm (females)
Weight: 201–417 (295) g (males); 122–308 (233) g (females)

Identification
Townsend's can be distinguished from other pocket gophers in the northern Great Basin by its larger size. Furthermore, *Thomomys townsendii* lives in a restricted geographic region, in relatively deep, moist soils of river valleys and Pleistocene lake beds, whereas other pocket gophers in the area occur in desert or in montane habitats.

Recent Synonyms
Geomys townsendii
Thomomys nevadensis
Thomomys relictus

Status
Common; restricted geographic distribution

Subspecies
Thomomys townsendii nevadensis, Humboldt and Quinn river drainage systems in Nevada and southeastern Oregon, and Honey Lake Valley in California
Thomomys townsendii townsendii, Snake River drainage in Idaho and southeastern Oregon

References
Davis, 1937; Patton and Smith, 1994; Rogers, 1991a, 1991b

Southern pocket gopher | *Thomomys umbrinus*

Very few studies have been accomplished on the southern pocket gopher, especially compared to the vast amount of information available on Botta's and northern pocket gophers. Most populations of southern pocket gophers occur in the relatively inaccessible higher elevations of the Sierra Madre Occidental, the western part of the Central Plateau, and the volcanic peaks of the Transverse Volcanic Belt of western and central Mexico. Populations are known from five mountain ranges in the southwestern United States, four in Arizona (Pajarito, Santa Rita, Patagonia, and Huachuca mountains) and one in New Mexico (Animas Mountains), and from the semitropical western Mexican coast, from central Sinaloa through Nayarit. Based on a combination of chromosomal and biochemical character differences, there are apparently five distinct geographic population groups distributed across this area. Across its range, local populations of southern pocket gorphers may differ in color and in body size nearly as much as do populations of Botta's pocket gopher. Pale color and very small size are attributes of the xeric-adapted populations in the lowlands of the Central Plateau of Mexico; dark, rich reddish-brown to blackish-brown, larger-bodied animals are found in the deeper, more humic soils of montane meadows in the Sierra Madre Occidental and from the isolated volcanoes of central Mexico. The population from the shores of Lago Patzcuaro in the state of Michoacan, Mexico, is black. This pocket gopher ranges in habitat from low-lying desert grassland and scrublands through the oak and pine-oak woodlands of intermediate elevations, to grassy meadows within higher elevation pine and fir forests. Southern pocket gophers have increased in some areas due to an expansion of farming in former grasslands and because of irrigation of some sectors of the deserts.

The population biology of this species is, where known, essentially the same as that for the more common Botta's pocket gopher. Individuals of both sexes live in self-dug, exclusive-use burrow systems, and surface mounds of fresh earth provide clear evidence of their presence in an area. Populations typically contain a larger number of adult females than adult males, and males are usually larger in size than females, with the degree of difference increasing as the average size of males

Thomomys umbrinus

increases. The breeding season varies greatly throughout the species' range. Separate winter and summer peaks were noted in populations from the Mexican state of Coahuila, but animals in southern Arizona bred only during the late winter and early spring. It is likely that populations in the higher elevations breed only following snow melt. Litter size averages about 4 to 5 pups, with a maximum of around 8 to 10. Longevity is probably less than 2 or 3 years, and most young probably are taken by predators before they reach reproductive maturity. Common predators include hawks and owls, snakes, weasels, badgers, bobcats, and coyotes. Southern pocket gophers are vegetarians, like all pocket gophers, and relish both below-ground and aboveground plant parts, primarily of forbs. Individuals are active year-round, constructing burrows under snow at high elevations during the winter months. Tunnel excavation and mound-building can occur any time, day or night, suggesting that there is no typical pattern of daily activity rhythm. *J. L. Patton*

Size

Males are, on average, larger than females; size varies among populations.
Total length: 210–250 mm (males); 180–230 mm (females)
Length of tail: 65–80 mm (males); 55–70 mm (females)
Weight: 110–175 g (males); 80–120 g (females)

Identification

The southern pocket gopher is the only species of its genus throughout most of its range in Mexico. *Pappogeomys* or *Zygogeomys,* both of which are considerably larger, may be sympatric. *Pappogeomys* has much enlarged foreclaws and *Zygogeomys* has a soft, distinctly silky pelage and totally grayish-black coloration. In the north of its range, the southern pocket gophers meets *Thomomys bottae,* and the two are not always easy to distinguish. Typically, the southern pocket gopher is smaller in body size, has a darkened, bluish-hued mid-dorsal stripe, and only three pairs of mammae (1 pectoral and 2 inguinal). This species also typically occupies higher elevation habitats (oak woodland

and pine forests) than Botta's pocket gopher, which is more common in deeper valley soils.

Recent Synonyms

None. However, the southern pocket gopher hybridizes limitedly with Botta's pocket gopher in the Patagonia Mountains of southern Arizona. As a result, some authors have considered these species to be the same.

Status

Locally abundant and common, although many populations are probably small and may be ephemeral. The population from the top of the Animas Mountains in extreme southwestern New Mexico is considered as endangered by the New Mexico Department of Fish and Game, primarily because of its isolated geographic range and presumably small overall population size.

Subspecies

Many of these subspecies are in need of re-evaluation. Only two, *T. u. emotus* and *T. u. intermedius,* occur north of Mexico.

Thomomys umbrinus albigularis, mountains of Hidalgo

Thomomys umbrinus arriagensis, Arriaga Plain of southwestern San Luis Potosi and southern Zacatecas

Thomomys umbrinus atrodorsalis, mountains near the city of San Luis Potosi

Thomomys umbrinus atrovarius, lowlands of southern Sinaloa and northern Nayarit

Thomomys umbrinus camargensis, vicinity of Camargo, southern Chihuahua

Thomomys umbrinus chihuahuae, Sierra Madre of southern Chihuahua and eastern Sonora

Thomomys umbrinus crassidens, mountains of west-central Zacatecas

Thomomys umbrinus durangi, foothills of south-central Durango

Thomomys umbrinus emotus, Animas Mountains of southwestern New Mexico

Thomomys umbrinus evexus, extreme north-central Durango

Thomomys umbrinus eximus, mountains of southeastern Sonora and northeastern Sinaloa

Thomomys umbrinus extimus, coastal plain of southwestern Nayarit,

Thomomys umbrinus goldmani, Mexican Plateau in states of Coahuila, Chihuahua, and Zacatecas

Thomomys umbrinus intermedius, mountains of southern Arizona

Thomomys umbrinus juntae, mountains and plains of central Chihuahua

Thomomys umbrinus madrensis, Sierra Madre of northern Chihuahua and northeastern Sonora

Thomomys umbrinus martinensis, vicinity of San Martin Texmelucan, Puebla

Thomomys umbrinus musculus, mountains of eastern Sinaloa, western Durango, and northern Nayarit

Thomomys umbrinus nelsoni, south-central Chihuahua

Thomomys umbrinus newmani, Plano Salado of extreme western San Luis Potosi

Thomomys umbrinus orizabae, slopes of Mount Orizaba, Puebla

Thomomys umbrinus parviceps, vicinity of Chacala, northwestern Durango

Thomomys umbrinus peregrinus, mountains in state of Mexico and Federal District

Thomomys umbrinus potosinus, lowlands in vicinity of city of San Luis Potosi

Thomomys umbrinus pullus, vicinity of Lago Patzcuaro, Michoacan

Thomomys umbrinus sheldoni, Sierra Madre of southern Durango, Nayarit, and Zacatecas

Thomomys umbrinus sonoriensis, Rio Yaqui basin of northeastern Sonora

Thomomys umbrinus supernus, mountains northeast of Guanajuato City

Thomomys umbrinus tolucae, slopes of Volcan de Toluca, Mexico

Thomomys umbrinus umbrinus, mountains of eastern Puebla and western Veracruz

Thomomys umbrinus vulcanius, slopes of Mount Popocatepetl, Mexico State

Thomomys umbrinus zacatecae, mountains of southern Zacatecas, northern Jalisco, and Aguascalientes

References

Anderson, 1972; Hafner et al., 1987

Desert pocket gopher | *Geomys arenarius*

The desert pocket gopher has a soft, short, drab-brown pelage that is usually somewhat paler to whitish on the ventral surfaces. Its muscular front legs and torso give it a thick-set body that is obviously adapted for living underground. Massive claws on the front feet aid in digging. External, fur-lined cheek pouches allow the pocket gopher to carry large amounts of vegetation back to the burrow system during its brief excursions to the surface of the ground. The small eyes and reduced ears are ideal for traveling through subterranean tunnel systems. The desert pocket gopher's short, stout tail is useful as a guide when the animal has to move backward rapidly through a tunnel.

A larger pocket gopher species, *Pappogeomys castanops,* occurs within the range of *Geomys arenarius* in the Tularosa Basin and possibly elsewhere, and a smaller species, *Thomomys bottae,*

is known to occur at least in the western part of the desert pocket gopher's range.

The desert pocket gopher inhabits sandy or disturbed soils of the upper Rio Grande Valley in south-central New Mexico, extreme western Texas, and northern Chihuahua (Mexico). Its need for friable soils serves as an effective barrier to expanding its range: rocky mesas and harsher desert surround much of its range. This species is typically found in sandy soils bordering river drainages as well as in the sand dunes of the Tularosa Basin in New Mexico.

Like other pocket gophers, *Geomys arenarius* is fossorial, spending most of its life below the surface of the ground. It occasionally surfaces briefly to forage for vegetation or to disperse a short distance, but it returns to its subterranean envi-

Geomys arenarius

ronment, leaving a distinctive mound of dirt to effectively close the hole that it used. By plugging the burrow system the pocket gopher maintains suitable climatic conditions inside, as well as keeping predators and other unwanted organisms on the outside. A single burrow system may have as many as 20 to 30 mounds and be more than 25 meters in length. The burrow system consists of a deep primary burrow as well as shallow secondary burrows that are used for feeding and surfacing.

Because individuals are solitary throughout their lives, only one pocket gopher normally occupies a burrow system. Individuals make aggressive movements and noises and attempt to bite other pocket gophers or organisms that try to enter the burrow system. Although individuals are rarely seen aboveground, the species can be active at any time of the day or night.

Only during brief breeding periods and when they are raising young will more than one individual share a burrow system. The breeding season lasts throughout the warmer parts of the year, and females can have as many as two litters per year, each litter consisting of four to six young.

Although the desert pocket gopher is effectively isolated by soil type, it can be very common in localized habitats. Because of this, the species is often regarded as a pest in agricultural areas where crops and irrigation canals may be damaged. Alfalfa crops are commonly affected by *Geomys arenarius*. In areas where it is a pest, control measures usually involve trapping and/or poisoning.

Because pocket gophers have rather nasty dispositions and generally do poorly in captivity, they do not make good pets. Holding the tail is the safest way to handle an individual, but handling is not recommended. *S. L. Williams*

Size
Males are larger than females.
Total length: 218–302 (254) mm
Length of tail: 52–106 (83) mm
Weight: 165–254 g

Identification
Pocket gophers in the genera *Geomys* and *Pappogeomys* have a large central groove on the upper incisor. *Geomys* also has another, smaller, groove along the inner margin of the incisor. This dental character separates *Geomys* *arenarius* from *Pappogeomys castanops* and *Thomomys bottae,* the other pocket gophers in its range. Species of *Geomys* can be distinguished from each other only by cranial or genetic characters.

Other Common Names
Rio Grande pocket gopher (local), Tularosa pocket gopher (local), sand pocket gopher

Status
Common, restricted

Subspecies
Geomys arenarius arenarius, south-central New Mexico, western Texas, and northern Chihuahua, Mexico
Geomys arenarius brevirostris, Tularosa Basin, south-central New Mexico

References
Mammalian Species 36; Davis and Schmidly, 1994; Findley et al., 1975; Schmidly, 1977; Williams and Genoways, 1978

Attwater's pocket gopher | *Geomys attwateri*

As with all members of this fossorial family, Attwater's pocket gopher has a cylindrical body that is heaviest anteriorly, and the mostly-naked tail is short and thick. The body is covered with short, fine hair, which is pale brown to black and usually paler on the belly. Fur-lined, external cheek pouches are present. The eyes are small and the ears are rudimentary but fully functional. Long, curved claws on the front feet are used for digging, as are the large incisors, which protrude outside the closed mouth.

Attwater's pocket gopher is found only in Texas. It occurs from the Brazos River in the south-central portion of eastern Texas south along the west bank of the Brazos River to the Gulf of Mexico, then southwest along the coast beyond Rockport, and northwestward to Atascosa County. Major rivers in Texas mark the ranges of neighboring species of pocket gophers, although the range of Attwater's pocket gopher broadly overlaps that of *G. personatus* in several counties in southern Texas. Within its range, *G. attwateri* is limited to sandy or sandy-loam soils that permit cost-effective burrowing.

Attwater's pocket gopher has distinct summer and winter pelages, but pelage from two successive molts may be present at one time, giving the appearance of continuous molt. A spring molt to summer pelage begins about March and ends in early July, and the autumn molt to winter pelage begins in early October and continues until the spring molt begins. Molting begins on the head and proceeds posteriorly, advancing more quickly dorsally. Two molt lines become apparent as one molt ceases near the rump and the next molt begins on the head.

Three age classes are recognized, and criteria determining them (body mass, evidence of sexual maturity, and pelage) differ between males and females. Regardless of sex, the pelage of juveniles is gray. Adult pelage usually is brownish and corresponds to soil color. Subadults of either sex may have a mixture of juvenile and adult pelage.

Capture of young, reproductively active individuals and multiple captures of individuals from one burrow system have been used to determine the breeding season of Attwater's pocket gopher. Some reproductively active males may be found in any month, so the occurrence of reproductively active females (open vagina, obviously pregnant) better defines the breeding season as October through June. Mean litter size ranges from 2.0 to 2.6 young and females may have more than one litter per reproductive season. After they are weaned, young may be sealed off in a section of the maternal burrow and left to fend for themselves or they may be forced aboveground to disperse. It would be difficult to investigate the former; however, evidence exists in the literature to support the latter.

Geomys attwateri

Within its range, Attwater's pocket gopher is only found in friable soils typically dominated by grasses. *G. attwateri* is found in coastal prairie, which is dominated by perennial bunchgrasses and seasonally occurring forbs, and in south-central Texas it occurs in habitat dominated by annual plants. Not surprisingly, its diet is largely composed of the most commonly available species of grasses. However, there is some selection, particularly by reproducing females, presumably of more nutritious perennial dicot species. Both belowground and aboveground plant parts are eaten in roughly equal proportions.

The burrow systems of Attwater's pocket gopher are complex and dynamic. As with most other pocket gophers, the system consists primarily of shallow feeding tunnels and includes at least one deep spiral tunnel that leads to a nest. Nests may be found a meter or more below the surface. Unlike other pocket gophers, which have linear, branching burrows, Attwater's pocket gopher has burrows that include multiple loops or convolutions. These convoluted systems may be a method of sequestering resources in an area of low primary productivity, or may be the result of social interactions.

Attwater's pocket gopher is an abundant rodent, ranging in density from 11.4 to 43.7 per hectare. A solitary, aggressive species, its density may be regulated by intraspecific interaction mediated by resource availability, a hypothesis that is supported by some ecological and behavioral studies. The average

Pocket gophers are generally considered pests because they weaken soil with their burrows, invade gardens and consume vegetables, and deposit mounds of soil on the ground. A considerable amount of time and effort goes toward trapping and poisoning them. Investigators report that these pocket gophers move between 56,940 and 69,946 liters of soil per hectare per year from belowground to the surface, which can have a great impact. However, ecological studies reveal a more balanced perspective. Mounds produced by *G. attwateri* do not persist longer than several months. Although some vegetation is killed as a result of being buried, perennial species often survive and annual species may germinate on these disturbed sites, and there is increased biomass of vegetation immediately around the mound. Finally, the presence of Attwater's pocket gopher has been shown to influence competitive interactions between grass and dicot species. These findings are not surprising in light of the co-evolution of the grassland habitat and an abundant inhabitant such as Attwater's pocket gopher. *L. R. Williams*

length of life for *G. attwateri* is about 12.5 months, but some individuals live as long as 2.5 years. It is likely that the security of an established burrow system greatly reduces predation while permitting the pocket gophers to tunnel and forage.

Size

Males are significantly heavier than females.
Total length: 192–235 (216.5) mm
Length of tail: 51–70 (62.5) mm
Weight: 163 g (males); 131 g (females)

Identification

Attwater's pocket gopher occurs with three other pocket gophers, Baird's pocket gopher *(G. breviceps)* and the plains pocket gopher *(G. bursarius)* in eastern and southeastern Texas, and the Texas pocket gopher *(G. personatus)* farther south in the Coastal Bend of Texas. Attwater's pocket gopher is intermediate in size, but the four species are difficult to distinguish except by using cytological and biochemical characteristics.

Status

Common, abundant

References

Mammalian Species 382; Cameron et al., 1988; Gregory et al., 1987; Schmidly, 1983; Williams and Cameron, 1986a, 1986b

Baird's pocket gopher | *Geomys breviceps*

As is typical of pocket gophers, *G. breviceps* is found only in friable soils (sandy loams, or generally sandy soils) in which burrowing is easy.

Most of what is known of the ecology of *G. breviceps* has been learned from studies of *G. b. sagittalis* in the vicinity of College Station, Texas. Reproductive activity, as indicated by the presence of pregnant and post-partum females, begins in January or February and continues through September. The position of the testes is not a reliable indicator of sexual activity of male pocket gophers; length of testes is reliable, but requires sacrifice of males.

Increases in the percentage of sexually immature females in September and October and again in December and January suggests that females have two litters per reproductive season. Estimates of the average number of litters per season in a population of *G. breviceps* range from 1.31 to 1.70, based on num-

bers of pregnant females and autopsies of post-partum females, respectively. Litter size is estimated to average about 2.6, with a range of 1 to 4. The onset of maturity is documented only for females. Reabsorption of the pubic symphasis occurs when females weigh more than 90 g and ovarian development begins. Regardless of age, the sex ratio favors males in this species.

Burrows average 6 cm in diameter and are found at depths ranging from 10 to 68 cm. Burrow systems are described as complex. They range in total length from 55 to 180 m and rarely extend into clay subsoils. Most pocket gophers have nests deep within the burrow system, and the nests of *G. breviceps* are commonly found as deep as 30 cm underground. However, during wetter months, *G. breviceps* uses aboveground mounds as nesting and living quarters to avoid temporary floods. In common with other pocket gophers, the nest consists of dried vegetation. *G. breviceps* is believed to spend

Geomys breviceps

virtually all its time in the burrow system. It is considered solitary and aggressive toward other individuals and is thought to be primarily nocturnal.

The diet is composed of a variety of roots, stems, and leaves representative of the plants within the vicinity of the nest. Food is obtained during the excavation of lateral tunnels, which may radiate from the mound, and is transported in the fur-lined cheek pouches to the mound, where it is generally stored. Food stores recovered from caches in disturbed prairie and fallow farmland or fields contained at least 15 plant species, including Bermuda grass *(Cynodon dactylon)*, nut-grass bulbs *(Cyperus esculentus)*, crow-poison bulbs *(Nothoscordium bivalve)*, bur-clover *(Medicago denticulata)*, Johnson grass *(Sorghum halepense)*, mullein *(Verbascum thapsus)*, plantain *(Plantago occidentalis)*, and bull-nettle roots *(Cnidoscolus texanus)*. Cellulose-digesting bacteria occur in the caecum and large intestine of *G. breviceps*. The animals also reingest fecal pellets, a common trait of herbivorous rodents.

The population density of *G. breviceps* in a prairie habitat in the vicinity of College Station, Texas, was estimated to be 0.55 individuals per hectare, which is low for pocket gophers. In spite of that low density, *G. breviceps* may transport soil to the surface at a rate of 132.5 kg per hectare per year in tall-grass prairie habitat and 2,606 kg per hectare per year in grassland

containing post oak trees *(Quercus stellata)* and yaupon *(Ilex vomitoria)*. Loss of vegetation as a result of mound building has been estimated to be 0.2% per hectare in tall-grass prairie and 3.44% per hectare in grassland. Therefore, *G. breviceps* has a substantial impact on its habitat.

G. breviceps occurs in areas of high biological diversity. Its isolated pockets of habitat are surrounded by a variety of other habitat types, which support many potential predators of the Louisiana pocket gopher. Those predators include king snakes *(Lampropeltis getulus)*, great-horned owls *(Bubo virginianus)*, red-tailed hawks *(Buteo jamaicensis)*, long-tailed weasels *(Mustela frenata)*, and striped skunks *(Mephitis mephitis)*.

In contrast to the limited recent ecological investigation of this species, a considerable amount of genetic work has been conducted, focusing on differentiation of neighboring species and evolutionary relationships. *L. R. Williams*

Size

Total length: 192–222 (208) mm
Length of tail: 54–67 (61.4) mm
Weight: 78–150 (100) g

Identification

Baird's pocket gopher is found in southeastern Oklahoma, southwestern Arkansas, western Louisiana, and eastern Texas. Two other species of pocket gophers, *G. attwateri,* and *G. bursarius,* also occur in the region, and the three are not easily distinguished except by cytological and biochemical characteristics and some

skull characteristics. Knowledge of each species' distribution is helpful for proper identification in the field.

Recent Synonyms

Geomys bursarius breviceps

Other Common Names

Louisiana pocket gopher

Status

Common; distribution fragmented

Subspecies

Geomys breviceps breviceps, near Mer Rouge, Morehouse Parish, Louisiana
Geomys breviceps sagittalis, eastern bank of the Brazos River in central and southeastern Texas, eastward into western Louisiana and from there north into western Arkansas and eastern Oklahoma

References

Mammalian Species 383; Bohlin and Zimmerman, 1982; Burton and Bickham, 1989; Cothran and Zimmerman, 1985; Schmidly, 1983

Plains pocket gopher | *Geomys bursarius*

Plains pocket gophers usually inhabit deep sandy or loamy soils, in which they spend most of their lives in underground burrow systems. This species travels on the surface only to feed on green vegetation. However, as evidenced by the frequent occurrence of skeletal parts of pocket gophers in owl pellets, such excursions may be common.

The species is a common, albeit sporadic, inhabitant of grassy habitats of the Great Plains of North America from southern Manitoba, eastern North Dakota, Minnesota, and western Wisconsin south through Iowa, portions of Missouri, Illinois, and Indiana, and southward from southern South Dakota to north-central Texas. Eastern Wyoming, Colorado, and New Mexico are also within its range. Until recently, populations of this wide-spread pocket gopher were considered to be a single but morphologically variable species. However, studies utilizing chromosomal, biochemical, and molecular markers have revealed five distinct species, formerly recognized as subspecies of one wide-ranging species. Those species that have been separated include *Geomys attwateri*, *G. breviceps*, *G. texensis,* and *G. knoxjonesi.* On morphological grounds, some investigators consider certain populations in portions of Kansas, Oklahoma, and Texas to be members of another species, *G. lutescens.* However, verification of this arrangement has not been presented.

The species has adapted well to human activity and is a common inhabitant of roadsides, cemeteries, golf courses, lawns, and cultivated fields. Sandy soils resulting from road construction or floodplains of waterways provide suitable avenues for dispersal. The burrow systems of the plains pocket gopher may be extensive, with several plugged, vertical tunnels leading to the surface, where excavated soil is thrown out in conspicuous mounds. Pocket gophers are considered a nuisance species in many areas as a result of the mounds of soil they throw out from their excavations, and poisoning and trapping programs are common in these areas.

Plains pocket gophers are solitary, rarely coming in contact with one another except to mate. One or two litters of one to eight offspring are produced from March through August. Food consists primarily of underground roots and tubers, although green vegetation is sometimes consumed. *E. G. Zimmerman*

Geomys bursarius

Size

Males are larger than females.
Total length: 225–325 mm
Length of tail: 60–121 mm
Weight: 120–250 g

Identification

Plains pocket gophers are medium-sized rodents. Throughout their range, body size is correlated with the texture of the soils in which the gophers live. Their upperparts vary in color from light brown to chocolate brown to black; pelage color is highly correlated with soil color. The underparts are grayish to buff.

The tail is about one-fourth the length of the body and is sparsely haired. The eyes are much reduced, and the external ears are rudimentary. Well-developed, fur-lined cheek pouches are present. The forelimbs are equipped with long, curved claws for digging, the thumb is missing, and the hind limbs are much reduced in size.

Other Common Names
Salamander, tuza

Status
Common in suitable habitat

Subspecies
Geomys bursarius bursarius, southern Manitoba, eastern North and South Dakota, and northwestern Wisconsin
Geomys bursarius halli, southwestern Nebraska
Geomys bursarius illinoiensis, narrow, crescent-shaped band running northeast through Illinois into northwestern Indiana

Geomys bursarius industrius, south-central Kansas
Geomys bursarius jugossicularis, southwestern Kansas, southeastern Colorado, and southward through the Oklahoma panhandle to northeastern New Mexico and northwestern Texas
Geomys bursarius lutescens, southern South Dakota, southward through the western two-thirds of Nebraska, northeastern Colorado, and northwestern Kansas
Geomys bursarius major, western half of Oklahoma southward through the Texas panhandle and north-central Texas

Geomys bursarius majusculus, Iowa, eastern third of Nebraska and Kansas, northern Missouri
Geomys bursarius missouriensis, southeastern Missouri, isolated populations in northern Arkansas
Geomys bursarius wisconsinensis, western third of Wisconsin

References
Block and Zimmerman, 1991; Davis and Schmidly, 1994

Jones's pocket gopher | *Geomys knoxjonesi*

Jones's pocket gopher is restricted to regions of western Texas and eastern New Mexico with deep, sandy soil. Throughout its arid range, its habitat is characterized by the presence of aeolian (wind-deposited) soils, indicating that it may be a specialist in reference to soil composition. Alternatively, it may be that *G. knoxjonesi* has been displaced by *G. bursarius* from the harder, more endurate soils surrounding this region. *G. knoxjonesi* typically occurs in native yucca-grassland communities, although it has adapted well to grassy roadsides, pastures, and lawns. Pocket gophers are fossorial, spending their entire lives underground, so little is known about their nesting habits. However, burrows are generally designed with a central nest site connected to a multitude of feeding burrows. Typically, the presence of pocket gophers is documented by the small mounds of dirt (often refered to as mima mounds in the early literature) that are deposited on the surface when the animals excavate new burrows.

Pocket gophers can readily be distinguished from other species of mammals because of their fur-lined external cheek pouches, short tails, reduced external ears, and the greatly enlarged claws on their front feet. Within the genus *Geomys,* it is difficult if not impossible to distinguish among the different species without genetic or geographic data. The color pattern—pale buffy brown on the back, grading to paler sides and white on the ventor—sometimes can be used to distinguish *G. knoxjonesi* from *G. attwateri, G. breviceps, G. pinetis,* and *G. tropicalis* (a Mexican species), which are generally darker. It is extremely difficult to distinguish *G. knoxjonesi* from *G. personatus* based on pelage color, and *G. arenarius* is essentially identical in color and size. *G. bursarius* usually cannot be distinguished from *G. knoxjonsei* without genetic data. For a number of years,

these two taxa were considered to be conspecifics. Only after intensive genetic studies (starch-gel analysis of proteins, DNA markers, and chromosomes) of a hybrid zone between the two taxa were they recognized as distinct species.

The ranges of two other genera of pocket gophers *(Thomomys* and *Pappogeomys)* approach that of *G. knoxjonesi* in eastern New Mexico and western Texas, and *P. castanops* is known to be sympatric with *G. knoxjonesi* at two localities. However these genera are easily distinguishable based on the number of grooves on the upper incisors. *Pappogeomys* has a single groove on each upper incisor, *Geomys* has two, and *Thomomys* has no grooves.

Geomys knoxjonesi breeds in the fall of the year. Most young are born in the spring and early summer. The gestation period is unknown, but probably approaches 23 days, as is typical for most species of rodents. If so, this indicates delayed implantation or sperm storage by females following the fall breeding season. Generally only one litter is raised per year, with two to four young (average two) being produced per litter. The young are born hairless and blind and require maternal care for the first few weeks. Growth and development are similar to that observed for other rodent species, with young being weaned at approximately three to four weeks of age. As is true of other species of *Geomys*, *G. knoxjonesi* is extremely territorial. Males and females only come into contact during the mating season and aggressively defend their territory (burrow system) the remainder of the year. *Geomys knoxjonesi* appears to feed on a variety of tubers, roots, and stems. These include yucca, sunflowers, and grasses.

Many arid-adapted species of rodents occur in the region occupied by *G. knoxjonesi,* including kangaroo rats, pocket mice, harvest mice, deer mice, grasshopper mice, and ground squirrels. Except for *P. castanops,* these species are all terrestrial rather than fossorial. *R. D. Bradley and R. J. Baker*

Geomys knoxjonesi

Size

Significant sexual dimorphism
Total length: 203–282 (236) mm
Length of tail: 57–104 (81) mm
Weight: 160–185g

Identification

Geomys knoxjonesi is small in size for the genus. Its tail is shorter than the head and body, but proportionately long compared to that of other species of pocket gopher. It is pale in coloration, with buffy-brown upperparts; the sides and ventor are paler to white, and the feet are white. *Geomys knoxjonesi* does not occur with other species of *Geomys* except *G. bursarius,* with which it has a narrow contact zone in eastern New Mexico. These two species generally cannot be distinguished without genetic data. Although *Geomys knoxjonesi* is sympatric with the yellow-faced pocket gopher *(Pappogeomys castanops)* in at least two localities in eastern New Mexico and western Texas, it is readily distinguishable by its smaller size, paler coloration, and smoother pelage.

Recent Synonyms

Geomys bursarius knoxjonesi

Status

Common

References

Baker, Davis, Bradley, Hamilton, and Van Den Bussche, 1989; Baker and Genoways, 1975; Bradley, Davis, and Baker, 1991; Bradley, Davis, Lockwood, Bickham, and Baker, 1991; Davis and Schmidly, 1994; Findley, Harris, Wilson, and Jones, 1975

Texas pocket gopher | *Geomys personatus*

The Texas pocket gopher has a soft, short, drab-brown pelage that is usually somewhat paler to whitish on the ventral surfaces. The muscular front legs and torso give it a thick-set body. This animal is obviously adapted for life underground, with small eyes and and reduced ears that are ideal for traveling through subterranean tunnel systems. It has massive front claws for digging, and its fur-lined, external cheek pouches allow the pocket gopher to move quantities of vegetation through the burrow system. It has a short, stout tail that is useful as a guide for rapidly backing through the tunnels when necessary.

Other species of pocket gophers may be found in the vicinity of the Texas pocket gopher, including *Pappogeomys castanops* and one or more other species of *Geomys.* However, the other pocket gophers tend to inhabit soils that would not be selected by *G. personatus.*

The Texas pocket gopher inhabits deep, sandy soils in the lower Rio Grande Valley, south Texas, and northern Tamaulipas (Mexico). Much of the distribution of this species can be explained by the presence of sandy soil that was deposited by river drainages or exists as inland remnants of previous sandy coastlines. This preference for sandy soils serves as an effective barrier to the pocket gopher's expanding its range, because much of soil of the surrounding terrain has more silt, clay, or gravel. As a result, it is not uncommon for populations to be effectively isolated from one another. One result is considerable size variation in the species. The largest individuals are found in southern populations at or near the current coastal beaches. The smallest individuals are found in isolated northern populations that are confined to small pockets of compacted sandy soil inland from the coast.

As a fossorial rodent, *Geomys personatus* forages on root systems and is capable of pulling entire plants through the soil into its burrow system. Individuals may surface briefly to forage for vegetation or to disperse short distances. However, they always return to the subterranean environment, closing the hole they used with a distinctive mound of dirt. By keeping the burrow system plugged, a suitable internal climate is maintained and the burrow system is protected from intruders. The mounds left by the pocket gopher indicate the extent of the burrow system, which may exceed 30 meters in length in coastal populations.

Like other pocket gophers, the Texas pocket gopher lives by itself in a burrow system and will fight aggressively to keep all intruders out of the burrow. Because surveillance and maintenance of the burrow system is a continuous activity, the Texas pocket gopher can be active at any time during the day or night. However, the solitary, fossorial life-style of the pocket gopher means that it is rarely seen aboveground.

Geomys personatus

It is only during breeding and raising of young that more than one individual will share a burrow system. *Geomys personatus* probably has a prolonged breeding season throughout the cooler parts of the year. Pregnant females have been reported in most winter and spring months. Females may have one or two litters per year, each consisting of two to four young.

The Texas pocket gopher feeds on the roots of grasses and on the roots, stems, and leaves of herbaceous plants. The species can be a problem in orchards, lawns, or where burrowing activity contributes to the erosion or collapse of paved roads on sandy substrates.

Because pocket gophers are aggressive and will attempt to bite when threatened, the safest way of handling one is to hold it by the tail. However, handling pocket gophers is not recommended, and they generally do poorly in captivity. *S. L. Williams*

Size
Significant sexual dimorphism
Total length: 216–360 (270) mm
Length of tail: 62–125 (86) mm
Weight: 165–400 g

Identification
Other species of pocket gophers that live in the vicinity of *G. personatus* include *Pappogeomys castanops* and various other members of the genus *Geomys.* A small groove along the inner margin of the incisor of *Geomys* is the most distinctive feature separating that genus from

Pappogeomys. Cranial or genetic differences are the best methods of distinguishing among species of *Geomys.*

Other Common Names
South Texas pocket gopher, Carrizo Springs pocket gopher (local), Del Rio pocket gopher (local), Nueces pocket gopher (local), Padre Island pocket gopher (local), Rio Grande pocket gopher (local), seaside pocket gopher (local)

Status
Common, restricted (status of northern subspecies questionable)

Subspecies
Geomys personatus davisi, north side of the Rio Grande in Webb and Zapata counties, Texas
Geomys personatus fallax, north and northwest of Nueces Bay along the lower Nueces River, Texas
Geomys personatus fuscus, north side of the Rio Grande in Kinney and Val Verde counties, Texas

Geomys personatus maritimus, coastal mainland Texas between Baffin Bay and Flour Bluff

Geomys personatus megapotamus, sandy soils of southern Texas and northeastern Tamaulipas, Mexico

Geomys personatus personatus, Mustang and Padre islands, Texas

Geomys personatus streckeri, sandy soils of Dimmit and Zavala counties, Texas

References

Mammalian Species 170; Davis, 1940; Davis and Schmidly, 1994; Wilkins and Swearingen, 1990; Williams and Genoways, 1981

Southeastern pocket gopher | *Geomys pinetis*

In this account the pocket gophers occurring in the southeastern United States are treated as a single species *(Geomys pinetis)*. However, when populations become isolated because they cannot disperse, it is possible for local populations to develop unique morphological features. Such differences resulted in the recognition of a great number of species and subspecies of *Geomys* in the southeastern United States. Some isolated populations (for example, *G. colonus, G. p. cumberlandius,* and *G. fontanelus)* maintain unique cranial features and/or coloration, thus raising controversy about their taxonomic status. Unfortunately, some of these isolated populations may no longer exist, making it impossible to confirm their taxonomic status with today's sophisticated methods of genetic analyses.

The southeastern pocket gopher has a soft, short, cinnamon-colored to dark brown dorsal pelage; the fur is usually somewhat buff or tan on the ventral surfaces. Muscular front legs and torso give this pocket gopher a thick-set body that is obviously adapted for a fossorial way of life. It has massive claws on its front feet for digging. Its external, fur-lined cheek pouches are particularly beneficial in allowing the pocket gopher to carry great amounts of vegetation back to the burrow system after its brief excursions to the surface of the ground. Small eyes and reduced ears are ideal for traveling through subterranean tunnel systems. Its short, stout tail facilitates moving backward through the tunnels when it has to do this.

The southeastern pocket gopher inhabits deep, sandy soils that are often associated with the long-leaf pine forest of the coastal plains of Florida (north of Lake Okeechobee), and in the southern halves of Alabama and Georgia. Open water, shallow water tables, and compact soils serve as effective barriers to the distribution of this species.

Like other pocket gophers, *Geomys pinetis* spends most of its life below the surface of the ground and is rarely seen aboveground. It occasionally surfaces briefly to forage for vegetation or disperse short distances, but soon returns to its subterranean environment, leaving a distinctive mound of dirt securely closing the hole that it used. A series of such characteristic mounds indicates the extensiveness of the burrow system,

which often exceeds 25 meters in length. The mounding activity of the southeastern pocket gopher may be the basis for one familiar local name, "salamander," a derivation of "sandy mounder." The term "gopher" is locally applied to the native gopher tortoise, *Gopherus polyphemus.*

Burrow systems usually consist of a deep primary burrow and shallow secondary burrows that are used for foraging and surfacing. Typically a single burrow system will be occupied by only one individual. The southeastern pocket gopher will aggressively defend its burrow system against other pocket gophers as well as against other organisms. Surveillance and maintenance of the burrow system is a continuous job, and the southeastern pocket gopher can be active at any time during the day or night.

Only when they are breeding and raising young will more than one individual share a burrow system. Although males are reproductively active throughout the year, the females have breeding peaks during February–March and July–August. A female can have one or two litters a year. Litters usually include one to three young. In about a month the young are old enough to support themselves, and they disperse to make their own burrow systems. Young females reach sexual maturity in about six months.

In areas where suitable soils exist the southeastern pocket gopher can be locally common and can be a pest of lawns and orchards. The pocket gopher feeds on root systems as well as the stems and leaves of some herbaceous plants. Control measures usually involve trapping or poisoning.

Like all pocket gophers, *Geomys pinetis* is aggressive, and handling is not recommended. To avoid being bitten, the safest way of handling an individual is to hold it by the tail. Generally, pocket gophers do poorly in captivity. *S. L. Williams*

Geomys pinetis

Size
Significant sexual dimorphism
Total length: 215–324 (260) mm
Length of tail: 57–120 (85) mm
Weight: 135–208 g

Identification
Pocket gophers in the genera *Geomys* and *Pappogeomys* have a large central groove on the upper incisor. *Geomys* also has another, smaller, groove along the inner margin of the incisor. This dental character is diagnostic of *Geomys;* species of *Geomys* can be distinguished from each other only by cranial or genetic characters.

Recent Synonyms
Geomys colonus
Geomys fontanelus
Geomys pinetis austrinus
Geomys pinetis floridanus
Geomys pinetis goffi
Geomys pinetis mobilensis

Other Common Names
Sandy mounder, salamander, colonial pocket gopher (local), Cumberland Island pocket gopher (local), Sherman's pocket gopher (local)

Status
Varies geographically; restricted

Subspecies
Geomys pinetis cumberlandius, Cumberland Island, Georgia
Geomys pinetis pinetis, southern Alabama and Georgia and all but the southern third of Florida

References
Mammalian Species 86; Golley, 1962; Wilkins, 1984, 1987; Williams and Genoways, 1980

Llano pocket gopher | *Geomys texensis*

The Llano pocket gopher is distributed in south-central Texas. *G. t. texensis* has been collected from the northern portion of the range in Gillespie, Kimble, Llano, Mason, McCulloch, and San Saba counties. *G. t. bakeri* has been taken in the southern portion of the range along the Sabinal and Frio rivers in Uvalde and Zavala counties, and in soils along Seco and Parker creeks, tributaries of the Frio River in Medina County. No specimens have been collected in Kerr and Bandera counties, which connect the ranges of the two subspecies, but *G. texensis* probably exists there. This distribution is bordered by that of *G. attwateri* to the east and *G. personatus* to the south.

The small size of this species is especially evident in measurements of body length, skull length, nasal length, and skull breadth. The pelage is russet brown on the dorsum, grading to a paler color along the sides. The pelage is paler in gophers collected in more sandy, paler surface soil in Uvalde and Zavala counties than in those from Medina County, where the soil is darker and loamy. The basal portions of the hairs are gray. A dark dorsal stripe extends from the head to the rump. The ventral surface is white, with gray at the base of the hairs. The tail is sparsely haired and consists of a mixture of brown and white hairs. The feet are white. The subadult

Geomys texensis

pelage is tawny brown, whereas the adult pelage is a darker, richer brown.

G. texensis bakeri is smaller in body and cranial measurements than *G. t. texensis*. *G. t. texensis* occurs in sandy-loam soils in the central basin region of the Edwards Plateau, where soils are porous and well drained, whereas *G. t. bakeri* inhabits loamy sand that is denser and less friable. *G. t. bakeri* is smaller and has cranial changes that alter the skull shape. *G. texensis* was probably isolated in central Texas approximately 9,000 years ago as warmer and drier conditions during the late Wisconsin to Holocene periods accelerated erosion. Fossils from central Texas indicate that distribution of geomyids on the Edwards Plateau was more extensive in the past.

As with other pocket gophers in Texas, *G. texensis* lives alone in underground burrow systems. The animals rarely come to the surface except to expel soil from digging. The average burrow size matches the size of the gopher; burrows are located about 50 cm below the surface. *G. t. texensis* is found in live oak-mesquite-ashe juniper habitats in the northern portion of the range, whereas *G. t. bakeri* is found in mesquite-blackbrush-desert hackberry habitats in the southern portion of the range. Both subspecies are found in deep brown loamy sands or grav-

elly sandy loams, in well-drained soil with loam as deep as 2 m. *G. texensis* is isolated from other species of *Geomys* in central Texas by intervening shallow, stony to gravelly, clayey soils.

Little is known about the population demography, reproduction, food habits, or behavior of this species, although it presumably is similar to other species of pocket gophers in the area. Like these other pocket gophers, *G. texensis* probably feeds on a variety of grasses and forbs, ingesting both underground and aboveground parts. Breeding by pocket gophers in this area of Texas occurs during spring and early summer. *G. t. texensis* collected in mid-March showed signs of reproductive activity, pregnancy, lactation, and contained embryos. One litter containing 2–3 offspring is produced each year; young are born blind, naked, and helpless. *G. N. Cameron*

Size
No significant sexual dimorphism in one subspecies *(bakeri)*, but males are larger than females in the other *(texensis)*
Total length: 185–272 mm
Length of tail: 51–80 mm
Weight: 125–212 g (males); 105–165 g (females)

Identification
The Llano pocket gopher is smaller than nearby *Geomys attwateri, G. bursarius,* and *G. personatus,* particularly in cranial measurements. External measurements of *G. attwateri* are comparable to *G. t. bakeri,* but the skull

of *G. attwateri* is longer and wider, and the animal has a paler, buffy-tan pelage and a uniform, nonglossy appearance. Populations of *G. attwateri* in the eastern part of southern Texas have pelage color similar to that of *G. t. bakeri.*

Recent Synonyms
Geomys bursarius texensis

Status
Locally abundant but narrowly distributed geographically, with occurrence in only a few counties in central and south-central Texas

Subspecies
Geomys texensis bakeri, Medina, Uvalde, and Zavala counties, Texas
Geomys texensis texensis, Gillespie, Kimble, Llano, Mason, McCulloch, and San Saba counties, Texas

References
Bock and Zimmerman, 1991; Davis and Schmidly, 1994; Smolen et al., 1993

Yellow-faced pocket gopher | *Pappogeomys castanops*

In the United States, the yellow-faced pocket gopher ranges from the Arkansas River drainage in southeastern Colorado and western Kansas southward through the Oklahoma Panhandle, western Texas, and eastern New Mexico to the Rio Grande. It also occurs in Cameron County, Texas, in the lower Rio Grande Valley. In Mexico, the species occurs south of the Rio Grande in eastern Chihuahua and northeastern Durango, across southern Coahuila and northern Zacatecas, in parts of Nuevo Leon, and in extreme northern Tamaulipas. Two chromosomal races, which may represent separate species, occur in Mexico.

Within this range, the species usually inhabits deep sandy or silty soils that are relatively free from rocks. However, where *Geomys* is present, the yellow-faced pocket gopher is restricted to denser, shallower, sometimes rocky soils. In southeastern Colorado, the yellow-faced pocket gopher seems to be able to displace *Thomomys bottae* into the rockier, shallower soils; it has replaced *T. bottae* in several places in Trans-Pecos Texas in recent years, apparently because it can tolerate drier conditions. The yellow-faced pocket gopher is found in mesquite and cactus communities in the western parts of its range, and in pastures of native short grasses in the high plains to the east. Like other pocket gophers, this species is considered an agricultural pest: it does extensive damage in orchards, gardens, potato patches, and other croplands. It feeds on fleshy, tuberous roots of desert shrubs and on the roots and leaves of low-growing forbs.

The burrow system is long, averaging 76 meters in western Texas, with numerous shorter tunnels leading away from a central, main horizontal shaft, and with distinct levels. A shallower, more extensive network is used for foraging, and a deep level contains the nest and food storage chambers. Tunnel depths range to more than 1.3 meters. Plugs and mounds embedded with dry grass and feces are characteristic of their burrows. There is apparently only one nest per burrow system, with a single entrance, a feature common to *Geomys* burrow systems but unlike the multiple-nest burrows of *Thomomys*.

Pappogeomys castanops

As with other pocket gophers, the burrow system of the yellow-faced pocket gopher is occupied normally by but a single individual. However, during the breeding season both sexes can be found in a single burrow, and young stay with females until they are weaned and disperse. Individual home ranges are typically large, so that local densities of adults seldom exceed 10 animals per hectare. In western Texas, females breed from January until October, with an apparent peak in March and April. A single female can produce as many as three litters in one season, and females born early in the season become sexually mature within the reproductive season of their birth. Litter sizes average two or three, with a range from one to five. Females live for an average of just over one year, males somewhat less. The distribution of burrow systems within a local population is clumped, with the burrows of adult females in the center, surrounded by those of adult males and subadults of both sexes. The home ranges of adult females vary little in position over time, but those of adult males and subadults are considerably more labile. Dispersing young usually secure a home range burrow system rather close to their natal one, although long-distance moves may occur. The sex ratio of local populations can vary from approximately equal numbers of males and females to more than two females for every male.

This species is known from many late Pleistocene fossil deposits from the south-central United States and adjacent Mexico. None of the fossils are apparently older than about 15,000 years before the present. *J. L. Patton*

Size

Males are typically substantially heavier than females and larger in all average measurements.

Total length: 220–315 mm

Length of tail: 60–95 mm

Weight: 385–410 g (males); 225–290 g (females)

Identification

A moderate to large pocket gopher, although one of the smallest species in its genus, the yellow-faced pocket gopher is pale yellowish-buff to dark reddish-brown on the upperparts, with a mixture of dark-tipped hairs on the back and top of the head; the underparts are whitish to bright orangish. All hairs are grayish at the base, usually with slightly darker hues on the back. The eyes are relatively large compared to those of *Geomys* or *Thomomys*. The outer surface of the upper incisor has one median groove, slightly displaced inwardly, distinguishing this genus from *Geomys* (two grooves) and *Thomomys* (no grooves).

Recent Synonyms

The subgenus *Cratogeomys* is considered by some authors as a genus separate from *Pappogeomys*.

Geomys clarkii

Pseudostoma castanops

Status

Locally common throughout its range in the United States and north-central Mexico

Subspecies

Pappogeomys castanops angusticeps, vicinity of Eagle Pass, Maverick County, Texas

Pappogeomys castanops bullatus, Rio Grande Valley and foothills in Coahuila and Nuevo Leon, Mexico

Pappogeomys castanops castanops, southeastern Colorado and southwestern Kansas along the Arkansas River

Pappogeomys castanops clarkii, southern Trans-Pecos Texas south to the Rio Grande and across the river into Chihuahua and Coahuila, Mexico

Pappogeomys castanops consitus, eastern Chihuahua, Mexico

Pappogeomys castanops dalquesti, west-central Texas north of the Edwards Plateau and south of the Llano Estacado

Pappogeomys castanops elibatus, high mountains of southeastern Coahuila

Pappogeomys castanops excelsus, Bolsón de Mapimí of southwestern Coahuila and northwestern Durango, Mexico

Pappogeomys castanops goldmani, eastern Durango, southwestern Coahuila, and central Zacatecas, Mexico

Pappogeomys castanops hirtus, vicinity of Albuquerque, Bernalillo County, New Mexico

Pappogeomys castanops jucundus, upper drainage of Rio Salado, east-central Coahuila, Mexico

Pappogeomys castanops lacrimalis, Pecos River Valley from central New Mexico to western Texas

Pappogeomys castanops parviceps, Tularosa Basin of southwestern New Mexico and western Texas

Pappogeomys castanops perexiguus, western Coahuila and adjacent Chihuahua, Mexico

Pappogeomys castanops peridoneus, eastern San Luis Potosí, Mexico

Pappogeomys castanops perplanus, high plains of the Panhandle and Llano Estacado of western Oklahoma, eastern New Mexico, and western Texas

Pappogeomys castanops planifrons, southwestern Tamaulipas and adjacent Nuevo León, Mexico

Pappogeomys castanops sorididulus, central Coahuila, Mexico

Pappogeomys castanops subnubilus, southeastern Coahuila, western Nuevo León, northern San Luis Potosí, and northeastern Zacatecas, Mexico

Pappogeomys castanops subsimus, southeastern Coahuila, Mexico

Pappogeomys castanops surculus, eastern Durango and northern Zacatecas, Mexico

Pappogeomys castanops tamaulipensis, lower reaches of the Rio Grande in the vicinity of Brownsville, Texas, and adjacent Tamaulipas, Mexico

Pappogeomys castanops ustulatus, northeastern Coahuila and northern Nuevo León, Mexico

References

Mammalian Species 338; Hollander, 1990

Family Heteromyidae

The 6 genera and 59 species of heteromyid rodents are limited to the New World, and most are found in North America. Pocket mice, kangaroo mice, and kangaroo rats inhabit a range of environments from arid deserts to humid tropical forests. They generally rest in their burrows during the day, often plugging the entrance to create a more favorable burrow environment. The heteromyid diet is dominated by seeds and vegetation, but may also include insects and other invertebrates.

These mice are similar to geomyids in having external, fur-lined cheek pouches that can be used to store and transport seeds. When captured in a live trap, these animals frequently have their cheek pouches stuffed full of seeds, and occasionally, of whatever was used to bait the trap. All are nocturnal, and most are adapted to arid or semi-arid habitats. Kangaroo rats and mice are strongly bipedal, with their body form modified to accommodate enlarged hindquarters. Pocket mice are more traditionally mouse-shaped, and as with pocket gophers, the pocket refers to the external cheek pouches.

Many species are extremely well adapted to desert environments and capable of existing with little or no free water intake. Seeds make up an important part of the diet of most species, although other kinds of vegetation, and even occasional insects are also taken. Kangaroo rats are aptly named, both for their appearance and for their ability to make prodigious leaps of up to 2 m at a single bound. Mammalogists sometimes capture them by running them down on foot after spotting them crossing a desert road at night. The rats' agility and leaping ability makes this a lively exercise, with the rodent frequently the winner.

Breeding is highly dependent on food availability. In good years with abundant food supplies, females may have 2 or 3 litters in succession, yielding 5–7 young per litter. In poor years, the number of litters and litter size may be reduced. Most individuals live about a year, but a few make it for much more than that. These animals adapt easily to captivity, particularly if sandy soil is available for dusting and grooming their coats.

References
Genoways and Brown, 1993; Nowak, 1991; Patton, 1993b

North American Genera
Perognathus
Chaetodipus
Microdipodops
Dipodomys
Liomys

White-eared pocket mouse | *Perognathus alticola*

White-eared pocket mice are the rarest of the silky pocket mice *(Perognathus)*, occurring as isolated, relictual populations at a few scattered localities in the Transverse and San Bernardino ranges fringing the western Mojave Desert, California. The subspecies *P. a. alticola* was first collected in 1893, and was last found in 1934 in a highly urbanized area of the San Bernardino Mountains near Little Bear Lake. Fewer than 40 specimens are known. Most individuals were captured on the dry floor of open pine forest among bracken ferns. Localities ranged from about 1,646 to 1,768 m above sea level.

The Tehachapi pocket mouse *(P. a. inexpectatus)* was first captured in 1926, and additional specimens have been taken oc-

casionally since then. In the 1970s and 1980s it was collected at four distinct sites. Most individuals have been taken in open grassland and upland arid shrub communities at elevations from about 1,067 to 1,829 meters. *P. a. inexpectatus* has 54 chromosomes, which are very similar in structure to those of populations of the Great Basin pocket mouse, *P. parvus.* There are some structural differences, suggesting that the two subspecies of *P. alticola* may be separate species. There are no known fossils of either subspecies.

Little is known about the life history of white-eared pocket mice other than that they are nocturnal. They are probably similar in habits to their close relative, *P. parvus,* most populations of which hibernate in winter, eat a variety of seeds, green vegetation, and insects, and do not need access to green vegetation or water to maintain a positive water balance. Captive individuals of *P. a. inexpectatus* ate green vegetables and seeds.
D. F. Williams

Perognathus alticola

Size
Males have been reported to be larger than females.
Total length: 130–183 (155.2) mm
Length of tail: 70–97 (78.9) mm
Weight: 16–24 g

Identification
Of the species of silky pocket mice sharing its geographic range, *Perognathus alticola* is distinguished from *P. inornatus inexpectatus* and *P. longimembris* by its lobed antitragus (part of the external ear), and longer, darker hairs (crest) on the distal portion of the tail. From *Chaetodipus californicus, P. alticola* can be distinguished by the absence of both whitish and blackish spine-like hairs projecting from the fur on the back and sides, and by a shorter and less crested tail.

Recent Synonyms
Perognathus alticolus, although incorrect, is in wide use.

Other Common Names
Tehachapi pocket mouse

Status
Extremely rare within limited, relictual habitats; *P. a. alticola* was last collected in 1934 and may be extinct.

Subspecies
Perognathus alticola alticola, San Bernardino Mountains around Little Bear Valley and Strawberry Peak, San Bernardino County, California
Perognathus alticola inexpectatus, Transverse Ranges from Techachapi Pass to near Mt. Pinos in Kern, Ventura, and Los Angeles counties, California

References
Mammalian Species 463; Stephens, 1906; Williams et al., 1993

Arizona pocket mouse | *Perognathus amplus*

As its common name implies, the Arizona pocket mouse is widely distributed in Arizona, but it also occurs in northwestern Mexico. Within its range, this glossy little mouse is most abundant in flat habitats with scattered small shrubs or bunchgrasses and fine-textured, firm soils. Populations in different geographic regions are similar in measurements of length and weight but vary considerably in fur color; the darkest individuals occur on black volcanic soils.

Like other heteromyid rodents, Arizona pocket mice are solitary creatures that spend the day in undergound burrows, emerging only at night. They forage preferentially in small openings between small shrubs, but will venture into large open areas when the moon is dark and when Merriam's kangaroo rat, a competitor that uses large open spaces, is absent. In the wild, Arizona pocket mice eat almost exclusively seeds of forbs or woody plants, although in captivity they avidly con-

Perognathus amplus

sume lettuce and mealworms along with millet, a preferred seed. In the wild they harvest seeds tirelessly from low-growing plants or from the soil, transporting the seeds in external fur-lined cheek pouches to a storage area in the burrow that they defend vigorously against intruders. Judging from the behavior of individuals in captivity, Arizona pocket mice manage their seed stores carefully, moving them around frequently within the burrow. Not all parts of the burrow system are equally humid, so this movement may optimize the free water content of seeds or reduce their spoilage.

When temperatures cool in autumn, Arizona pocket mice retreat to their burrows, remaining inactive aboveground until temperatures warm again in the spring. While in the burrow, their body temperatures cool and their metabolic rate slows, an energy-saving strategy that may account for a lifespan—up to 10 years in captivity—that is extraordinary for such a diminutive mammal. This torpor is not true hibernation, however, because individuals arouse from time to time to eat stored seeds.

Males emerge from winter inactivity before females do in anticipation of the spring breeding season. During this season, the mice emit a distinctive odor reminiscent of stale movie theatre popcorn, perhaps as a chemical signal of sexual competence. By late April most females have emerged and become pregnant with litters of 1–7 young. Juveniles appear in May and June, and populations reach peak density in late summer. The size of this population peak fluctuates considerably from year to year, depending on the amount of precipitation the previous winter and therefore, presumably, the availability of seeds. This correlation with precipitation suggests that food is what limits populations of the Arizona pocket mouse, either because it limits the number of young that females can produce, or because it determines survival probability, or both. *M. V. Price*

Size

No significant sexual dimorphism
Total length: 135–173 (153) mm
Length of tail: 75–88 (83) mm
Weight: 9.2–14.0 (11.3) g

Identification

This is a small pocket mouse, lacking stiff hairs on the rump. It has orangish-tan upperparts sprinkled with black to varying degrees, and white or pale tan underparts. The tail is longer than the head and body, slightly darker on top, and lacks a terminal tuft. *Perognathus amplus* can be distinguished from *P. flavus* and *P. parvus* by having a tail longer than the head and body; and from *P. longimembris* by generally larger size and a longer tail, although in some areas these two species are difficult to separate. No other small silky pocket mice share the range of *P. amplus*.

Status

Common

Subspecies

Perognathus amplus amplus, central to south-western Arizona and northwestern Sonora, Mexico

Perognathus amplus cineris, north-central Arizona

Perognathus amplus pergracilis, northwestern Arizona

Perognathus amplus taylori, south-central Arizona and northwestern Sonora, Mexico

References

Hoffmeister, 1986; Price, 1978; Price et al., 1984; Reichman and Price, 1993

Olive-backed pocket mouse | *Perognathus fasciatus*

Perognathus fasciatus is an especially beautiful animal, with its olive-colored back and yellowish lateral stripe constrasting with a pure white belly. The olive-backed pocket mouse is a resident of grassland, shrub-steppe, and desert scrub habitats of the northern Great Plains and adjacent intermountain basins to the west. It is the only species of pocket mouse east of the Rocky Mountains to extend its range far north into Canada. Over most of its range, it is the only species of silky-haired pocket mouse residing in its preferred semi-arid bunch-grass and desert scrub habitats. However, it can be found with its closest relative, *Perognathus flavescens,* and the smaller, more distantly-related *Perognathus flavus,* in narrow zones of overlap, generally along the north-south aridity gradient that marks the transition from mixed-grass to tallgrass prairies from North Dakota southward into western Nebraska, and along the eastern slope of the Rocky Mountains into southern Colorado.

Few details are available on the natural history of the olive-backed pocket mouse, but most of what is known suggests little variation from patterns common to other species of silky-haired pocket mice. Although they appear to be active at night year-round, olive-backed pocket mice enter burrows, plug the entrances, and become torpid in their grass-lined nests for short periods of time during cold weather. They appear to be solitary. They may have two periods of reproductive activity between April and August, giving birth after a gestation period of about one month to a litter of three to six altricial young. A predilection for sandy or sandy-loam soils may be explained by their need to sand-bathe to remove excess oils from their fur and to clean their cheek pouches. Olive-backed pocket mice are opportunistic seed-eaters, stuffing their fur-lined cheek pouches with almost any available seed that is small enough to

Perognathus fasciatus

be efficiently gleaned and returned to special storage chambers in underground burrows.

Silky-haired pocket mice are notoriously conservative in their external morphologies (most species look pretty much alike). Thus, the closest relatives of the olive-backed pocket mouse remained unclear until chromosome and DNA data became available. Based on similarities in chromosome numbers and shapes and in mitochondrial DNA variation, the closest relative of *Perognathus fasciatus* has been identified as *Perognathus flavescens. B. R. Riddle*

Size
No significant sexual dimorphism
Total length: 125–142 (134.7) mm
Length of tail: 57–68 (61.7) mm
Weight: 8–14 g.

Identification
Perognathus fasciatus is most similar to *Perognathus flavescens,* but can be distinguished by its olivaceous dorsum. It is significantly larger than *Perognathus flavus* and smaller than *Perognathus parvus.*

Recent Synonyms
Perognathus flavescens olivaceogriseus

Status
Widespread but generally not abundant

Subspecies
Perognathus fasciatus callistus, arid basins in southwestern Wyoming, northwestern Colorado, and northeastern Utah

Perognathus fasciatus fasciatus, northern Great Plains and adjacent open country in Wyoming and Montana

References
Mammalian Species 303; Clark and Stromberg, 1987; Jones et al., 1983; Riddle, 1995; Williams and Genoways, 1979; Williams et al., 1993

Plains pocket mouse | *Perognathus flavescens*

Sand dunes and stabilized sand soils are habitat for the diminutive plains pocket mouse. Shy and nocturnal, their tiny tracks, found early in the morning before being erased by wind, are usually the only clue to their presence, yet they frequently can be seen at night by observers traversing dunes and sandy spots along arroyos with a lantern. Their activity appears to be suppressed by full moonlight, and they are inactive on the surface during the coldest months. In the Southwest, they have periods of torpor, but some individuals may appear on the surface during any month. In the Great Plains, they generally are absent from the surface between November and early March.

Burrows with tiny openings are dug in the friable sands, usually under the protection of a shrub or other plant or in the sandy bank of a dry stream bed. The opening to the burrow usually is only 2–3 centimeters in diameter and is kept closed when the occupant is in residence. From within the burrow, the mouse pushes and pats a plug of soil firmly into the tunnel's entrance. It may place an additional plug farther into the tunnel. Burrows are simple, extending from about 5 cm to 2.5 meters, reaching a depth of 50 centimeters, and usually having only one opening. There are enlarged areas along the burrow's length where seeds are cached and the animal rests, but tunnel branches and elaborate chambers have not been found. The mouse makes caches (of 70–560 grams) of seeds in enlarged areas of the tunnel.

Females are pregnant between about April and August, depending on climate, and have two to seven young, with modes of four or five. Gestation is about 25–26 days. Most females probably have only one litter, though under favorable conditions two or three litters are possible. Females born early in the season often breed when they are about 10–12 weeks old. Determination of age based on tooth wear indicates that individuals rarely live more than 1–2 years in the wild, though a male I captured as an adult lived for more than five years in captivity.

Seeds and insects are the main food, though plains pocket mice also eat some green herbaceous vegetation. Fruits or seeds of a variety of grasses, sedges, forbs, and woody plants have been found in the cheek pouches or in caches. Included are the fruits of pinyon pine *(Pinus edulis),* Utah juniper *(Juniperus osteosperma),* and oak *(Quercus),* but the mice mostly eat the smaller, more abundant seeds of herbaceous plants. Arthropods may comprise more than 50 percent of the diet in times of their abundance or seed scarcity. Ants have been found in caches, cheek pouches, and stomachs. Seeds of corn (maize) form a large portion of the diet in some areas of the Great Plains, where plains pocket mice may live next to or within corn fields. These mice are agile climbers and often climb the stems of sedges and other plants to gather food.

Perognathus flavescens

Due to the extreme patchiness of their habitat in the mountain states, local variation is extreme, though highly predictable, based on environmental variables, especially rainfall and soil color. The color of their fur varies locally more than do structural features. Nearly black mice live on the black volcanic sands near Flagstaff, Arizona, and nearly white mice live on the white gypsum dunes of the Tularosa Basin, New Mexico. *D. F. Williams*

Size

No consistent, significant sexual dimorphism, but extensive geographic variation in size and proportions

Total length: 117–155 (132.3) mm
Length of tail: 50–89 (68.3) mm
Weight: 7–16 (10.1) g

Identification

Of the species of silky pocket mice sharing its geographic range, *Perognathus flavescens* is distinguished from *P. flavus* and *P. merriami* by larger size, smaller buffy patch behind its ear, and relatively longer tail. Compared to *P. fasciatus* (Great Plains populations), *P. flavescens* is smaller, with a narrower, buffy lateral line and without an olivaceous hue to the upper surfaces. *P. flavescens* has a relatively and absolutely shorter, less crested tail with a shorter tuft of hairs at its end than *P. longimembris*, *P. amplus*, and *P. parvus*, which are marginally sympatric on the western periphery of its range.

Recent Synonyms

Perognathus apache

Other Common Names

Apache pocket mouse

Status

Rare to common on sandy soils; habitat patchy and widely separated in some areas

Subspecies

Perognathus flavescens apache, northeastern Arizona and southeastern Utah
Perognathus flavescens caryi, western Colorado, eastern Utah, and northwestern New Mexico
Perognathus flavescens cockrumi, Great Plains from central Kansas to west-central Oklahoma
Perognathus flavescens copei, southern Great Plains of western Oklahoma, western Texas, and eastern New Mexico
Perognathus flavescens flavescens, west-central Great Plains from North Dakota to southwestern Kansas and eastern Colorado
Perognathus flavescens melanotis, south-central New Mexico to northern Chihuahua, western Texas, and southeastern Arizona
Perognathus flavescens perniger, northeastern Great Plains
Perognathus flavescens relictus, San Luis Valley, south-central Colorado

References

Armstrong, 1982; Reed and Choate, 1986a, 1986b; Williams, 1978

Silky pocket mouse | *Perognathus flavus*

As the name indicates, the silky pocket mouse is one of the soft-furred species of *Perognathus*. Like all members of this genus, the silky pocket mouse has a pair of fur-lined cheek pouches that open externally near the mouth. The mouse uses these pouches like shopping bags; that is, it collects seeds or nest materials and carries them in the pouches until it can deposit them in the burrow. The species is, on average, the smallest member of the genus and is among the smallest of rodents in North America. Probably because of its size and secretive habits, the life history of the silky pocket mouse is poorly known.

The species occupies the semidesert grasslands of the central and southern Great Plains and the Mexican Plateau. Silky pocket mice exhibit specializations common to many rodents that occupy arid or semiarid regions. They reduce water losses by restricting their activities to cool and humid nights, and they obtain water from their food. They construct complex burrows, and seal them with a plug of dirt during the daylight hours to maintain the humidity within the tunnels. Burrows are often located under the edges of rocks, in crevices, among the roots of shrubs or cacti, or under the cover of a bush.

Silky pocket mice are yellowish- or reddish-brown on the back and sides and white on the underside. A distinct buff-colored patch of fur (postauricular patch) is located behind each ear. In some parts of the range, the sides of the mouse are

paler in color than the back, giving the appearance of a pale yellowish stripe on the lower sides. In the northern parts of the range, some individuals may have a pronounced wash of blackish hairs interspersed among the yellowish-buff of the back.

This species prefers areas with thin, low grasses and a minimum of bare soil. In eastern Wyoming, it is found on loamy or moistened claylike soils occupied by such grasses as grama *(Bouteloua)* and needlegrass *(Stipa).* However, silky pocket mice in western Texas inhabit desert erosion pavement soils that contain at least 50 percent rocks. The mice typically forage by sifting through the sand with their forepaws for small seeds, and they occasionally climb grass stalks to harvest ripening seeds. In New Mexico, seeds of Russian thistle *(Salsola kali),* pigweed *(Chenopodium),* and fescue grasses *(Festuca)* were the most common seeds found in cheek pouches. Cheek pouches sometimes contain leaf, flower, and stem parts, indicating that vegetative matter is eaten, but *P. flavus* probably does not feed on insects as do other pocket mice. Seeds are carried back to the burrow in the cheek pouches and stored in caches within the burrow system. The storage of food may permit silky pocket mice to remain active all year long, even on cold winter nights. In suitable habitats, densities as high as 370 per hectare are known, but 60 per hectare is more normal. The home range, estimated to be 0.2–0.6 hectares, shifts with available resources and may change every few months.

Pocket mice generally do not breed in captivity. Consequently, details of reproduction for the silky pocket mouse are based on meager records of field observation and are incomplete. Females normally produce one litter each spring, but may bear a second litter in years when sufficient food is available. Two litters may be produced annually by mice in the southern parts of the species' range. Embryos have been found from March through October, which implies that breeding may begin in late February. The gestation period is about 28 days and two to six are born in a litter. When they emerge from the burrow and begin foraging on their own, the juvenile mice are dull gray in color and noticeably thin. In late summer a molt occurs: the gray hair is replaced with a black-tipped yellow pelage, signaling the attainment of adulthood. There-

Perognathus flavus

after, silky pocket mice undergo one molt annually, during the summer.

The ranges of two other soft-haired pocket mice, *Perognathus flavescens* and *P. fasciatus,* overlap with *P. flavus* in the southwestern United States. Both of these species generally prefer habitats that are sandier and shrubbier. In recent years, *Perognathus merriami* was considered a subspecies of *P. flavus.* The two species are similar in appearance and can be distinguished only by biochemical analysis. The ranges of the two species overlap in western Texas and eastern New Mexico and there is no known habitat separation of the two in the overlap zone. *B. R. Chapman and S. S. Chapman*

Size
No significant sexual dimorphism
Total length: 100–130 (113) mm
Length of tail: 44–60 (50) mm
Weight: 5–10 g

Identification
Perognathus flavus can reliably be distinguished from *P. merriami,* a closely-related species, only by protein electrophoresis. *P. flavescens* and *P. fasciatus,* which share the western portion of the range of *P. flavus,* are slightly larger, have longer tails, and have less distinct, or indistinct, buffy spots behind the ears, and *P. fasciatus* has a dark olive-brown dorsum.

Other Common Names
Baird's pocket mouse

Status
Locally common

Subspecies
Perognathus flavus bimaculatus, northwestern Arizona
Perognathus flavus bunkeri, eastern Colorado, western Kansas, western Oklahoma
Perognathus flavus flavus, southeastern Arizona, southern and eastern New Mexico, northern Texas Panhandle, extreme western Texas, western Chihuahua, north-central Durango
Perognathus flavus fuliginosus, north-central Arizona
Perognathus flavus fuscus, west-central Chihuahua
Perognathus flavus goodpasteri, east-central Arizona
Perognathus flavus hopiensis, northeastern Arizona, southeastern Utah, southwestern Colorado, northwestern New Mexico

Perognathus flavus medius, Zacatecas, western San Luis Potosi, southeastern Durango
Perognathus flavus mexicanus, western Veracruz, Puebla, Queretaro, southern Hidalgo
Perognathus flavus pallescens, western Coahuila, southeastern Chihuahua, east-central Durango
Perognathus flavus parviceps, western Jalisco
Perognathus flavus piperi, eastern Wyoming, western Nebraska, northeastern corner of Colorado
Perognathus flavus sanluisi, south-central Colorado
Perognathus flavus sonoriensis, central Gulf of California coast in Sonora

References
Mammalian Species 471; Forbes, 1962, 1964; Jones et al., 1985

San Joaquin pocket mouse | *Perognathus inornatus*

The San Joaquin pocket mouse inhabits west-central California from the upper Sacramento Valley in Tehama County southward through the San Joaquin and Salinas valleys and contiguous areas to the Mojave Desert in Los Angeles, Kern, and extreme western San Bernardino counties. It is also found in the Tehachapi Mountains and in the foothills of the western Sierra Nevadas below about 600 meters. The only fossils that may be of *P. inornatus* are from a Pleistocene deposit at McKittrick, Kern County, California.

Perognathus inornatus is a medium-sized pocket mouse with a tail that averages longer than the length of its head and body. The ears are small. The posterior third of the sole of the hind foot is haired, the pelage is soft, and the vibrissae are rather short. The upperparts are yellowish to pinkish overlaid with blackish hairs; the extent of overlay determines the overall tone in the various subspecies. The lateral line is moderately well marked, the underparts are white, and the tail is faintly bicolored. The pelage of young-of-the-year is grayish and soft. Subspecies differ in the number of chromosomes, in color and body size, in the relative length of the tail, and in characters of the skull.

This small pocket mouse is nocturnal. It spends the day underground in a simple burrow, foraging at night on the surface of the ground. It is not skilled at climbing in vegetation. It hibernates in autumn, winter, and spring.

Sandbathing serves as a means of grooming the pelage. When sandbathing, the San Joaquin pocket mouse digs rapidly in the substrate with its forepaws, then lowers its cheek to the sand, extends its body, and slides forward on its side. It may then rub the same side again or rub the opposite side or belly. This pocket mouse tends to concentrate its sandbathing at one location, and the sandbathing spots of one animal affect the behavior of others. Sandbathing may have originated from a movement pattern for spreading scent; scent-marking consists of depressing the anal-genital area against the substrate and walking forward.

The San Joaquin pocket mouse breeds from March to July. At least two litters of four to six young are produced each year. The estrous cycle is 5–6 days long. During estrus, females are involved in chasing, fighting, sandbathing, scent-marking, digging, naso-anal contact, and grooming.

Vocalizations include growls, squeals, and low grunts. Tooth-chattering and foot-drumming are used in communication, but drumming is rare and the sound is barely audible to the human ear. Tooth-chattering, done by rapidly bringing the incisors together, usually occurs in conjunction with aggressive behavior.

This species inhabits arid annual grassland, savanna, and desert scrub associations, with sandy washes, fine-textured soils, and grassy or weedy ground, and sites with sage, filaree, oats, and brome grass. At the northern extreme of its range it occurs on a rocky slope in chamise and buck brush chaparral at an elevation of 420 meters. Green vegetation is available for only a few weeks in winter and early spring; dry brome grass is present for the remainder of the year. *P. inornatus* is a granivore and subsists mainly on minute seeds of grasses, shrubs, and forbs. Insects do not form a large part of its diet, but it will eat soft-bodied insects such as cutworms.

The burrows are conspicuous in the short grass. Like other pocket mice, it digs small burrows (2–3 centimeters in diameter), usually in sandy soil near the bases of bushes. Occupied burrows are plugged with earth during the daytime. It routinely builds a nest within the burrow and will inhabit burrows of Heermann's kangaroo rats.

Perognathus inornatus

Density is quite variable among localities and from year to year. The number of *P. inornatus* may be lower on areas grazed by cattle, but in an alkali-sink community in Fresno County, California, density was 7.3 per hectare on a grazed site and 5.0 per hectare on ungrazed sites. Its average home range was 148 square meters on sites grazed by cattle and 258 square meters on ungrazed sites. The sex ratio varied from 2.5 males to 1 female on sites grazed by cattle to 3:1 on ungrazed sites.

Mammals occurring in the same habitat include black-tailed jackrabbits, desert cottontails, California ground squirrels, San Joaquin, Heermann's, and giant kangaroo rats, San Joaquin antelope squirrels, grasshopper mice, badgers, coyotes, and kit foxes. Predators include barn owls, coyotes, badgers, and kit foxes. The only ectoparasite known is the mite *Ischyropoda armatus*.

Much of the San Joaquin Valley has undergone extensive agricultural development. Most of the habitat originally occupied by this species has been destroyed. *T. L. Best*

Size
Males are slightly larger than females.
Total length: 149 mm (males); 147 mm (females)
Length of tail: 76 mm (males); 75 mm (females)
Weight: 7–12 g

Identification
Perognathus inornatus may be sympatric with *P. alticolus* and *P. parvus*. It differs from both in some characters of the skull and is, on average, smaller than both (length of hind foot usually is less than 21 mm compared with more than 21 mm).

Status
Uncommon

Subspecies
Perognathus inornatus inornatus, eastern San Joaquin and adjacent valleys, California

Perognathus inornatus neglectus, western and southern San Joaquin and adjacent valleys, California

Perognathus inornatus psammophilus, west-central California

References
Mammalian Species 450; Eisenberg, 1963

Little pocket mouse | *Perognathus longimembris*

Little pocket mice are common throughout arid regions of western North America, ranging predominantly from southern Oregon through most of Nevada, southern California, and into northern Baja California. These tiny rodents are noted for their economical use of energy and water, and as a consequence are capable of inhabiting some of the driest and most unproductive regions of the continent. They are most abundant in the Colorado, Mojave, and Great Basin deserts, but populations also thrive in open grassland, shrub-steppe, and coastal sage habitats.

Pocket mice are so named because they have fur-lined cheek pouches external to their mouths, which they use primarily to transport food during their nocturnal foraging trips. *Perognathus longimembris* eats the vegetation of annual plants and some insects during the brief intervals when these foods are available following periodic rains, but the bulk of its diet consists of small seeds. Seeds are hoarded in burrow systems and guarded jealously by these solitary mice, because large caches are needed to survive the many months of dormancy during which the animals remain continuously underground. Little pocket mice are always the smallest members of guilds of

Perognathus longimembris

graniverous rodents who compete for the seed resources in their arid habitats.

Little pocket mice can subsist indefinitely on the water created as a byproduct of their metabolism. They do not need to have a succulent diet or drink because their evaporative, fecal, and urinary water losses are so low. Kidney anatomy suggests that these mice are capable of producing urine that is among the most concentrated of any mammal's. Consequently, they can be kept in captivity with little or no maintenance whatsoever.

Breeding is initiated in the spring soon after the mice emerge from dormancy, and the young are born 25 days later. The average litter consists of 3.3 young that collectively weigh at birth about half as much as the mother. The babies are weaned after 14–18 days and reach sexual maturity when they are 6 weeks old. Reproductive output and population size vary greatly from year to year in response to changes in the productivity of the environment. The mice may not breed in drought years when few annual plants germinate, but adults may have multiple litters and youngsters born in the first litter may breed later that summer during years when food is abundant.

After reproductive obligations are completed and a seed cache has been accumulated, the mice retire to their burrows and remain underground until the next spring. This dormant period may last as long as 9 months in some adults, but can be much shorter for youngsters born late in the summer. Little pocket mice are physiological hibernators in that they reduce their body temperature, and hence their metabolic rate, during periodic episodes of torpor, and thus they can survive long dormant seasons with limited seed stores. The frequency at which the mice warm up changes throughout the dormant season and at any point in time is a function of temperature. The longest bouts of torpor last 5 days at 8° C.

In contrast to the start of dormancy, the date that surface activity is resumed in the spring is remarkably constant from year to year. *Perognathus longimembris* selects the warmest available environment (below about 30° C) at all times. In the summer, soil temperature is highest near the surface and the mice rest during the day in shallow burrows, but in the winter the gradient is reversed and the mice build their winter nests in the deepest parts of their burrow systems. Spring emergence occurs when the soil temperature becomes warmer above than below, and it has been suggested that the lack of a deep gradient allows the mice to move upward and experience very warm surface soils that could trigger emergence. Males may be more sensitive to these thermal cues because they emerge about 1–2 weeks before females. *A. R. French*

Size
No significant sexual dimorphism.
Total length: 110–151 (131) mm
Length of tail: 56–86 (73) mm
Weight: 6.5–10.5 g

Identification
The coloration of this mouse varies from gray to reddish-brown to cream dorsally, with paler buff or white hairs on the undersurface. *P. longimembris* is the smallest pocket mouse in its range. It can be most easily distinguished from immature *P. inornatus* by its relatively long tail, which is 1.1–1.3 times longer than the head and body, and from *P. amplus* by a hind foot length of 19.5 mm or less.

Status
Common

Subspecies
Perognathus longimembris aestivus, north-central Baja California
Perognathus longimembris arizonesis, extreme southwestern and south-central Utah, northwestern and north-central Arizona, and southeastern Nevada
Perognathus longimembris bangsi, eastern boundary of the Colorado Desert in southern California
Perognathus longimembris bombycinus, lower Colorado River Valley of California, Arizona, and Mexico, extending southward along the northeastern coast of Baja California

Perognathus longimembris brevinasus, arid regions just east of the mountains that form the Los Angeles Basin of southern California
Perognathus longimembris gulosus, western margin of the Pleistocene Lake Bonneville in eastern Nevada and western Utah
Perognathus longimembris internationalis, extreme south-central California and north-central Baja California
Perognathus longimembris kinoensis, adjacent to Kino Bay in Sonora, Mexico
Perognathus longimembris longimembris, Mojave Desert and Owens Valley of California
Perognathus longimembris nevadensis, Great Basin Desert from southeast Oregon into north-central Nevada

Perognathus longimembris pacificus, coastal plains of southern California

Perognathus longimembris panamintinus, Great Basin Desert of western Nevada and southeastern California

Perognathus longimembris pimensis, south-central Arizona

Perognathus longimembris salinensis, Saline Valley, Inyo County, California

Perognathus longimembris tularensis, upper Kern River Valley, Tulare County, California

Perognathus longimembris venustus, San Agustin, north-central Baja California

References

Genoways and Brown, 1993

Merriam's pocket mouse | *Perognathus merriami*

Merriam's pocket mice occur in southwestern Oklahoma, western and southern Texas, extreme eastern New Mexico, and adjacent areas of Mexico to the south (including the northern parts of the states of Tamaulipas, Nuevo Leon, Coahuila, and Chihuahua). They occur from sea level to 1,830 m (6,000 ft.), and in southwestern Texas appear limited mainly by lack of suitable habitat at higher elevations.

Merriam's pocket mice are common in short-grass prairie, desert scrub, and open, arid brushland. They are more limited by form and height than exact type of vegetation and are most common in areas with short, sparse ground cover that is less than about 15 cm (6 inches) high, as opposed to tall, dense ground-level vegetation. For example, they often are abundant in grazed or over-grazed pastures and grasslands. They also occur on a wide variety of soil types from stony or gravelly soils to hard-packed soils (caliche) to deep sand. Fossil remains of this species dating to the Pleistocene have been recovered from several caves and other deposits in Texas and eastern New Mexico.

The silky hair of *Perognathus merriami* is yellowish-orange with a slight blackish tinge. The amount of black and overall tone varies with location, subspecies, and time of year. The color is fairly uniform from sides to mid-back, and these mice seldom develop an inconspicuous dark line on the back as is sometimes seen in *Perognathus flavus*. The underside is white or pale buff, and the pale belly, feet, and legs are clearly demarcated from the darker sides. There is a small white spot under the ears, which are small and bounded on the top and back by a distinct creamy-buff patch. This patch usually is smaller in Merriam's than in silky pocket mice. There also is a pale ring around each eye and a dark, transverse stripe just behind the nose. The tail is darker above than below but not sharply bicolored. Like most countershaded mice, they appear uniformly dark gray when viewed from above at night. Adults replace their pelage once a year, in late July or August, and the molt proceeds in an even pattern from head to tail.

Like all pocket mice, Merriam's are nocturnal foragers, although on occasion they may be active outside their burrows during the day. Most of the day is spent sleeping, digging, or maintaining their home burrow system. They are most common in areas where the vegetation is intermediate in density and height: less than 30–60 cm (1–2 feet) high, dense enough

Perognathus merriami

to provide cover and sufficient seeds, but not so high or dense as to impede their movements. They construct narrow, elaborate burrow systems as deep as 60 cm underground, usually starting at the base of a clump of vegetation. In these burrows they often make separate nest, food, and toilet chambers. In addition to the home burrow system, they also dig "escape hatches," shallow refuge burrows concealed under rocks or logs. The tiny, oblong silhouettes of the mice are common sights on roads and roadsides through short-grass prairies, brushlands, and scrub deserts in western and southern Texas. *P. merriami* is easily captured by hand. Typically, one of these previously stationary silhouettes will scoot for the roadside and then stop at the edge of the vegetation: when approached closely, the mouse will suddenly jump erratically like a grasshopper to try to avoid capture. Merriam's pocket mice are readily tamed after a short time in captivity and are sometimes used in educational displays, where they are maintained in ant-farm-like enclosures with sufficient space between the panes for burrowing, yet narrow enough to expose the burrow system. These displays should be kept out of direct, glaring light, the sandy soil must be wetted every few days, and seeds must be added on a regular basis.

Seeds, especially of grasses and forbs, constitute the bulk of the diet in adults, although some green vegetation and insects may be taken. Seeds are cached along the walls of the nest chamber or in a separate chamber for food storage. *P. merriami* seldom drinks water, obtaining most of the water it needs from the food it eats. The mice can survive for years in captivity without drinking free water.

P. merriami may breed in all seasons except winter (December to March in Texas). Females may have two or more litters of three to six young per year. The gestation period is unknown but is probably similar to the 26 days or more estimated for *Perognathus flavus*. As in other pocket mice, the young are born naked except for a few tactile hairs on the snout, with their eyes and ears closed. Post-natal development

has not been described but again is probably similar to silky pocket mice, in which the incisors erupt on day 5, the ears open on day 14, and the eyes open on day 15. The first pelage is soft and silky and lacks the black-tipped hairs found in adults. Molt to a second, darker subadult pelage occurs sometime before or during weaning. Young leave the burrow near the time of weaning, which probably occurs two to four weeks after birth. They can live to more than four years of age in captivity but life span in the wild seldom exceeds two years and most individuals live one year or less.

No habitat or behavioral differences have been noted where *P. merriami* occurs with *P. flavus* in western Texas and adjacent New Mexico. In Coahuila, Mexico, *P. merriami* lives on alluvial soils along arroyos dominated by mesquite, whereas *P. flavus* is confined to arid flats dominated by lechuguilla (*Agave lechuguilla*) and creosote-bush (*Larrea tridentata*). Where Merriam's occurs near the plains pocket mouse in the panhandle region of Texas and Oklahoma, *P. merriami* uses more clay-based soils, rather than the deep sandy soils or dunes occupied by *P. flavescens.*

The taxonomic history of *Perognathus merriami* is complex. It was treated as a separate species from *Perognathus flavus* until Daniel F. Williams and Don E. Wilson, in separate studies, suggested that the two were conspecific. Electrophoretic results in subsequent genetic studies by the author and others strongly suggest that two species are involved. *P. merriami* and *P. flavus* appear to maintain their genetic identities in their area of overlap in Texas and New Mexico, although no absolute genetic differences were found between the two. Given the lack of fixed differences and the apparent hybridization at some locales, further study of these species, employing rapidly evolving genetic markers such as mitochondrial and/or satellite DNA, would be illuminating.

Perognathus merriami was named in honor of Dr. C. Hart Merriam, Chief of the U.S. Biological Survey from 1885 to 1910. *M. D. Engstrom*

Size

No significant sexual dimorphism
Total length: 95–121 (112) mm
Length of tail: 42–61 (54) mm
Weight: 5–9 (8) g

Identification

This tiny pocket mouse is very similar to the silky pocket mouse, *Perognathus flavus*, with which it co-occurs in western Texas and eastern New Mexico, and no single external characteristic will separate all *P. merriami* from all *P. flavus*. Where the two species occur together they may occasionally hybridize, further complicating identification. Merriam's pocket

mouse is distinguished from the silky pocket mouse in having a relatively longer tail; shorter, slightly coarser pelage; paler coloration on the mid-back with a yellowish rather than pinkish cast; and smaller buffy spots behind the ears. In the northern part of its range in Texas and Oklahoma, *P. merriami* also occurs near the plains pocket mouse, *Perognathus flavescens*. Although similar in size and color, Merriam's differs from the plains pocket mouse in being slightly smaller, with a shorter tail and hind foot. The two can easily be distinguished by characteristics of the skull.

Recent Synonyms

Perognathus flavus merriami

Status

Common, localized

Subspecies

Perognathus merriami gilvus, western portion of range
Perognathus merriami merriami, eastern portion of range

References

Mammalian Species 473; Baker, 1956; Davis and Schmidly, 1994

Great Basin pocket mouse | *Perognathus parvus*

The Great Basin pocket mouse occupies almost the entire Great Basin region of western North America. Its range extends from south-central British Columbia southward through central and western Washington and Oregon, southern Idaho, east-central California, virtually the entire state of Nevada, northwestern Arizona, and most of Utah west of the Green and Colorado rivers, except for the Uinta and Wasatch mountains.

The Great Basin pocket mouse is found in arid and semiarid habitats. Its presence is strongly associated with sandy habitats where sagebrush is a dominant plant. It occupies steppe and arid open shrub and woodland habitats. In mountainous regions, *P. parvus* occurs in desert and dry grassland habitats but is excluded from dense forests.

Like other desert heteromyids, *P. parvus* can exist on a diet of dry seeds, obtaining its water as a byproduct of metabolizing carbohydrates. Nevertheless, Great Basin pocket mice will consume succulent vegetation and insects. The key to their surviving on a diet of seeds, with no free water, is that the seeds are cached underground, where the humidity is higher than on the surface, and where they absorb water. The pocket mouse's water conservation adaptations include production of very concentrated urine (up to 22 percent electrolytes, compared to about 6 percent in humans) and dry feces. *Perognathus parvus* and other smaller heteromyids can maintain a positive water balance at higher ambient temperatures than larger species of desert rodents. As a consequence, they can feed earlier in the evening, when temperatures are warmer, and thereby may reduce competition with larger rodents.

Great Basin pocket mice, along with other members of the genus *Perognathus,* commonly enter torpor for various durations in all seasons. Torpor is most frequent between November and March, when they may spend 90 percent of their time in this state. Entering torpor results in a substantial savings in energy. It has been estimated that hibernation (winter torpor) reduces the demand for food from a normal 300 g of seeds to only 50 g over a five-month period.

Reproductive activity begins early in spring (April). The length of the breeding season varies from year to year, ending as early as July or as late as October. At the northern limits of distribution in British Columbia, the length of the breeding season is reduced. One to three litters of 2–8 young are produced annually. Mean litter size is approximately five young. The number of litters produced annually is strongly related to precipitation and the production of seeds by winter annuals. Drought years may result in a cessation of breeding. Estimates of gestation length range from 21–28 days, which is slightly longer than in many similar-sized rodents. *G. L. Kirkland, Jr.*

Perognathus parvus

Size

Variable throughout the range, but males are slightly larger than females.

Total length: 160–181 (174) mm (males); 160–190 (172) mm (females)

Length of tail: 85–97 (91) mm (males); 85–90 (88) mm (females)

Weight: 21.5–31.0 (25.4) g (males);16.5–28.5 (20.5) g (females)

Identification

The Great Basin pocket mouse is the largest member of the genus *Perognathus*. Like other members of the genus, it is distinguished by its soft pelage, absence of spine or bristles, and somewhat hairy soles on the hind feet. External features that distinguish *P. parvus* from other sympatric pocket mice include hind feet longer than 20 mm, hairs of the inside of ears buffy (not white or yellow), antitragus of ear lobed, tail dark above and only slightly crested or tufted, and presence of olivaceous lateral line. Like other members of the family Heteromyidae, the Great Basin pocket mouse has fur-lined external cheek pouches.

Recent Synonyms

Perognathus laingi

Perognathus xanthonotus

Status

Common

Subspecies

Perognathus parvus bullatus, Colorado Plateau region of east-central Utah in Emery and Wayne counties

Perognathus parvus clarus, southwestern Montana and southward through eastern Idaho, southwestern Wyoming, and into northern Utah

Perognathus parvus columbianus, the Columbia Plateau region of east-central Washington

Perognathus parvus idahoensis, south-central Idaho

Perognathus parvus laingi, south-central British Columbia

Perognathus parvus lordi, north-central and eastern Washington with extensions northward into southern British Columbia

Perognathus parvus mollipilosus, the Modoc Plateau and adjacent areas of northeastern California and south-central Oregon

Perognathus parvus olivaceous, most of Nevada, adjacent east-central California, and the Great Basin region of Utah, with an extension eastward around the southern end of the Wasatch Mountains and northward into the Duchesne and Uintah basins of northeastern Utah

Perognathus parvus parvus, southeastern Washington, central and southeastern Oregon, eastward into southwestern Idaho, and southward into extreme northwestern Nevada

Perognathus parvus trumbullensis, southwestern Utah and adjacent northwestern Arizona

Perognathus parvus xanthonotus, limited to the eastern desert slopes of the Tehachapi Mountains, Kern County, California

Perognathus parvus yakimensis, south-central Washington

References

Mammalian Species 318; Genoways and Brown, 1993

Bailey's pocket mouse | *Chaetodipus baileyi*

The geographic range of Bailey's pocket mouse, more or less coincident with the Sonoran desert, extends from western mainland Mexico and Baja California to southern California, Arizona, and New Mexico. Within its range this large, drab spiny pocket mouse is most abundant in close association with large shrubs or small trees on the pebbly soils that mark transitions from sandy flats to rocky slopes. There is relatively little geographical variation in size or pelage color, although variation does exist in chromosome numbers, and within populations, older individuals can be much larger than young ones.

In many respects Bailey's pocket mouse is similar to other desert-dwelling heteromyid rodents. It is solitary, nocturnal, lives in burrows, eats mostly seeds that it stores avidly against lean times, and does not need to drink water. Breeding is controlled by rainfall. In the Sonoran desert there are often two reproductive periods, one in spring following winter rains and another in early autumn following summer monsoons. Males become reproductively competent earlier in the spring than do females, and they optimistically remain so after females have lost interest in the fall. Population sizes respond to seed avail-

Chaetodipus baileyi

ability, growing in years of good rains and shrinking during droughts. The animals are active all year round.

Like many other pocket mice, *C. baileyi* forages most often in the shelter of perennial plants and modifies its behavior in response to the risk of predation from owls. In the presence of owls, individuals make furtive, short trips into risky open areas between shrubs, especially when the moon is bright. They are noticeably more leisurely when they forage under shrubs or when there is no moon. These precautions are taken despite an impressive ability to hear approaching owls and to escape capture with last-split-second evasive leaps in 90 percent of cases. Individuals never shed their caution in captivity, remaining nervous and rattling the tail truculently when approached.

Bailey's pocket mouse is unique among Sonoran desert rodents in its ability to consume seeds of the dominant shrub jojoba *(Simmondsia chinensis),* which contain chemical compounds toxic to most mammals. It also is unusually slow in harvesting seeds from sand, especially in comparison with kangaroo rats. Perhaps this robust mouse is successful in grubbing

a living from tough, pebbly desert soils by virtue of its muscular shoulders, short forelimbs, blunt-clawed forefeet, and suspicious nature. *M. V. Price*

Size
Males are significantly larger than females.
Total length: 206–240 (211) mm (males);
176–228 (201) mm (females)
Length of tail: 76–140 (114) mm (males);
86–125 (109) mm (females)
Weight: 28.2 g (males); 24.5 g (females)

Identification
C. baileyi is a large pocket mouse with grayish, harsh fur on the back and rump washed to varying degrees with yellow. Its rump lacks spines. The underparts are whitish and the tail is long, buff or gray above, whitish below, and strongly crested. Most other Sonoran desert *Chaetodipus* are smaller in size, have hind feet shorter than about 25 mm (adult *C. baileyi* generally have hind feet at least 25 mm long), and some also have rump spines, which are lacking in *C. baileyi.* In the eastern portions of its range, *C. baileyi* can be distinguished from *C. hispidus* by its long, crested tail and lack of a conspicuous yellow lateral line. Male *C. baileyi* also are unusual in having a straight baculum that lacks a terminal hook or knob.

Recent Synonyms
Perognathus baileyi

Status
Common

Subspecies
Chaetodipus baileyi baileyi, southeastern Arizona to Sonora, Mexico
Chaetodipus baileyi domensis, southwestern Arizona to western Sonora, Mexico
Chaetodipus baileyi extimus, southern Baja California, Mexico
Chaetodipus baileyi fornicatus, Monserrate Island, Gulf of California, Mexico
Chaetodipus baileyi hueyi, southern California to northern Baja California, Mexico
Chaetodipus baileyi insularis, Tiburon Island, Gulf of California, Mexico
Chaetodipus baileyi mesidios, central Baja California, Mexico
Chaetodipus baileyi rudinoris, northern Baja California, Mexico

References
Mammalian Species 297; Hoffmeister, 1986; Longland and Price, 1991; Morgan and Price, 1992; Price, 1993

California pocket mouse | *Chaetodipus californicus*

Surprisingly, though they live in patches of habitat distributed through some of the most densely populated areas of California, relatively little is known about the life history of California pocket mice. Fossils of this species from the Rancho La Brea tar pits date from about 30,000 to 15,000 years ago. Today, California pocket mice are rare to uncommon in arid grassland and desert and coastal scrub communities and common in lowland and montane chaparral below about 1,200 and 1,900 meters elevation in west-central and southern California. They prefer dense patches of chaparral with only small openings,

though the edges between shrubs and open areas with sparse herbaceous plants show high use. Periodic fires are a component of these communities. Most California pocket mice may be killed by a hot fire, but individuals move in from outside the burn area and establish residence within a year of the burn.

The basic gait of California pocket mice is quadrupedal, but they climb with agility into shrubs and small trees to forage. Seeds, insects, and a small amount of green leaves make up their diet. Like most other pocket mice, California pocket mice gather food, consisting mostly of seeds, in their external, fur-lined cheek pouches, and cache it in chambers in their burrows. They do not drink water, deriving all they need from their food. When food is scarce, California pocket mice become torpid for 10–14 or more hours during the day. These episodes of diurnal torpor can occur at any time of the year. Surface activity is reduced or absent during cold and wet weather, which might indicate extended periods of torpor.

Populations fluctuate in response to drought and periodic fire. Both events reduce population size, but numbers can increase to previous densities within a year or two when conditions are favorable. Females have a mode of 4–5 young after a 25-day gestation. Young are weaned in about 3 weeks and females may first conceive when they are about 3 months old. Adult size is attained at about 3 months of age. Most other aspects of this mouse's population biology are unknown.

When it arouses from its daytime sleep, the mouse usually first washes itself in a slow, methodical manner. Mice also frequently wash when exploring or if confronted with something new in their environment, but in a swift, perfunctory manner that involves wiping only the head and nose with the forepaws. Sand or dust bathing also occurs frequently. This behavior may be an important grooming activity, and it also has social significance. Odorous secretions from specialized glands on the tail near its base are deposited during dust bathing, and some dust baths are located at peripheral points in an individual's home range. Sounds produced include tooth chattering in aggressive situations, a scratchy, low-pitched growl given when an animal or its nest is threatened, and a squeal of higher pitch when attacked or injured. *D. F. Williams*

Chaetodipus californicus

Size

No significant sexual dimorphism
Total length: 190–235 (216.1) mm
Length of tail: 103–143 (124.7) mm
Weight: 18–29 (23) g

Identification

Of the species of hispid-haired pocket mice (*Chaetodipus*) with whitish, spine-like stiff hairs on their rumps that share its geographic range, *C. californicus* is distinguished from *C. spinatus*

and *C. fallax* by its longer ear (greater than 9–10 mm), larger size, and relatively longer tail. *C. arenarius*, *C. penicillatus*, and *C. formosus* lack rump spines.

Status

Common

Subspecies

Chaetodipus californicus bensoni, Diablo and Temblor ranges westward to Salinas Valley, west-central California

Chaetodipus californicus bernardinus, slopes of San Gabriel and San Bernardino mountains, southwestern California

Chaetodipus californicus californicus, San Francisco Peninsula and hills on east side of San Francisco Bay, California

Chaetodipus californicus dispar, coastal terrace and hills from San Luis Obispo southward to Santa Monica, California

Chaetodipus californicus femoralis, coastal terrace and hills from San Diego County, California, southward in Baja California to the Sierra San Pedro Mártir

Chaetodipus californicus marinensis, coastal slopes from the Salinas Valley west and south from Monterey Bay to Morro Bay, California

Chaetodipus californicus mesopolius, slopes of Sierra San Pedro Mártir, Baja California

Chaetodipus californicus ochrus, transverse ranges and southeastern and western slopes of the Sierra Nevada, California

References

Eisenberg, 1963; Eisenberg and Isaac, 1963; Tucker, 1966; Williams et al., 1993

San Diego pocket mouse | *Chaetodipus fallax*

The San Diego pocket mouse is a medium-sized member of the genus *Chaetodipus,* which includes approximately 15 additional species ranging in weight from about 15 to 50 g. *C. fallax* is found in desert and coastal environments in southern California and northern Baja California, Mexico. The various subspecies occupy habitats that vary from sparse, low, desert shrublands to dense, high, coastal sage scrub vegetation. They tend to concentrate their activities around shrubs, as do other species of desert pocket mice. *C. fallax* is also often found in rocky habitats. It occurs from sea level to at least 1,400 m in mountain ranges of the Mojave and Colorado deserts.

Chaetodipus fallax has a broad region of yellowish to orangish hair on its sides that contrasts with its dark brown back. Like many species in the genus, it has a number of stiff, bristly hairs or spines in the rump region. *C. fallax* is most similar in appearance to *C. californicus,* with which it overlaps in both geographical range and habitat. However, *C. fallax* has slightly smaller ears (usually shorter than 9 mm) than *C. californicus* (usually longer than 9 mm).

Chaetodipus fallax is a member of the family Heteromyidae, which is restricted to the New World and is represented by numerous species in the southwestern deserts. Most heteromyid rodents, including *C. fallax,* have diets composed largely of seeds, but insects and plant foliage are also consumed. All heteromyids have a pair of fur-lined pouches located in the cheek region near the mouth, which are used for carrying large quantities of seeds during foraging. The fur lining of these cheek pouches prevents seeds being carried by the animals from coming into direct contact with skin and absorbing body water. This water-conserving adaptation is essential for *C. fallax,* which can survive, without drinking free water, on just the water in its food and the water that is produced as a byproduct of metabolism. *C. fallax* has been shown to prefer those seed types that yield the most metabolic water when consumed.

Like other heteromyid rodents, *C. fallax* is nocturnal and seeks shelter in burrows during daylight. Burrow systems can be quite elaborate, consisting of a network of tunnels and chambers. Usually one or two chambers are used as dens for

Chaetodipus fallax

sleeping; the remaining chambers are used for hoarding seeds. Individuals also store seeds in shallow surface holes, although this method of seed hoarding is thought to be more prevalent among kangaroo rats, which are also heteromyids. Another important difference between these groups of desert rodents is that many pocket mice undergo a period of winter dormancy, whereas kangaroo rats do not. The pocket mouse's dormancy period in the warm southern deserts tends to be brief (perhaps 1 to 2 months).

Although some reproduction occurs throughout the year, *Chaetodipus fallax* breeds mainly during spring. Because of their solitary, aggressive nature, heteromyids are very difficult to breed in captivity, and little specific information exists on the breeding of *C. fallax*. However, based on data available for closely related species and from *C. fallax* females captured while pregnant, the litter size probably ranges between 2 and 6. Young become sexually mature at 5 to 6 months of age. Females can produce 1 to 3 litters per year. Typical longevity in nature is only 4 to 6 months, but it is not unusual for some individuals to survive 1 to 2 years, and San Diego pocket mice often live 5 to 6 years in captivity. A high rate of predation by their primary predators—owls, snakes, and mammalian carnivores—lowers average longevity, one of the penalties these animals pay for living in habitats that are relatively devoid of protective vegetation cover. All desert heteromyid rodents have overcome this challenge to some degree, and are more adept at evading predators than other nocturnal rodents of the North American deserts. However, quadrupedal pocket mice such as *C. fallax* exhibit less spectacular evolutionary specializations for avoiding predation than their bipedal relatives, the kangaroo rats, and are consequently more vulnerable to predators. *W. S. Longland*

Size

No significant sexual dimorphism
Total length: 176–200 mm
Length of tail: 88–118 mm
Weight: 17–22 g

Identification

Distinguished from *Chaetodipus californicus*, with which it shares the northwestern portion of its range, by its smaller ears. Distinguished from *Chaetodipus spinatus*, with which it shares much of its range, by less pronounced spiny bristles on its rump, lack of bristles in the flank region, and a broader, more prominent region of yellowish to orangish hair on its sides. Other co-occurring pocket mice lack distinct spiny bristles in the rump region.

Recent Synonyms

Perognathus fallax

Status

Common, widespread

Subspecies

Chaetodipus fallax anthonyi, Isla Cedros, Pacific Ocean, Baja California, Mexico
Chaetodipus fallax fallax, southeastern California and northwestern Baja California, Mexico

Chaetodipus fallax inopinus, coastal west-central Baja California, Mexico
Chaetodipus fallax majusculus, coastal northwestern Baja California, Mexico
Chaetodipus fallax pallidus, south-central California
Chaetodipus fallax xerotrophicus, northern to north-central Baja California, Mexico, east of the ranges of *C. f. inopinus* and *C. f. majusculus*, inland from the coast

References

Williams et al., 1993

Long-tailed pocket mouse | *Chaetodipus formosus*

The long-tailed pocket mouse occurs in dry regions of western North America, including parts of Nevada, Utah, Arizona, California, and the Baja Peninsula. Most of its range lies within the Great Basin and Mojave and Colorado deserts. Almost everywhere throughout its range, this mouse lives in habitats containing rocks. Long-tailed pocket mice have been captured in lava beds, on pebbly soils of desert scrublands, on gravelly surfaces of dry stream beds, and among large boulders on hillsides and in shallow arroyos. There are only a few places where they inhabit rockless situations, and these include sandy areas along creek beds and beneath patches of mesquite (*Prosopis juliflora*).

Plant communities most often associated with long-tailed pocket mice include those containing mixtures of creosote (*Larrea tridentata*) and burro bushes (*Ambrosia dumosa*) and ones dominated by shadscale (*Atriplex confertifolia*) and various types of sagebrush (*Artemisia*). These mice also are found among desert thorn (*Lycium*), blackbrush (*Coleogyne ramosissima*), catclaw (*Acacia*), desert tea (*Ephedra*), tetradymia (*Tetradymia*), and various species of yuccas (*Yucca*) and cacti (*Opuntia* and *Echinocereus*). Population densities have been estimated as high as 30 mice per hectare in certain habitats. Home ranges tend to be circular, averaging 5,500 square meters.

Similar to other pocket mice, *Chaetodipus formosus* is nocturnal and lives in underground, self-constructed burrows. Sometimes its presence can be detected by small piles of soil at the base of rocks. Long-tailed pocket mice become inactive on cold nights and only occasionally appear aboveground during the winter months. They probably enter torpor during this pe-

Chaetodipus formosus

rio. In contrast, much time is spent outside their burrows during the warmer months, although activity also drops in midsummer during years of low food availability.

Long-tailed pocket mice are primarily vegetarians and only occasionally eat animal material. In the Mojave Desert, for example, their food consists of 45 percent seeds, 40 percent flowers and leaves, 6 percent fruits, 5 percent stems and unknown items, and 4 percent arthropods. Of 36 plants identified in their stomachs, seeds of grasses and various parts of the small annual *Thelypodium lasiophyllum* appear to be the most important components of their diet. These semifossorial mice occasionally climb into branches of low shrubs to forage for food, and they are known to carry seeds, fruits, and sepals in their external fur-lined cheek pouches.

The breeding season of *Chaetodipus formosus* begins sometime in spring and can continue into summer. Weaned young have been captured in traps as early as May and as late as November. Females normally produce one litter annually, and based on embryo counts, bear two to seven young per pregnancy. Reproductive output in this pocket mouse is closely tied to vegetative growth during the breeding season. Under favorable conditions, a doubling in population size is considered a

successful reproductive season for this species. In exceptionally good growing seasons, populations have been reported to increase fivefold. In these instances, about 70 percent of the females become pregnant during the breeding season, litter sizes average nearly six, and young born early in the season are able to breed by late summer.

For many years, all species of pocket mice were classified as belonging to the genus *Perognathus,* which was divided into two subgenera *(Perognathus* and *Chaetodipus).* Traditionally, long-tailed pocket mice were placed with the former subgenus. In 1981, biochemical analysis showed that the long-tailed pocket mouse belonged to the subgenus *Chaetodipus.* This subgenus has now been given generic status. *K. N. Geluso*

Size
No significant sexual dimorphism
Total length: 172–211 mm
Length of tail: 86–125 mm
Weight: 17–25 g

Identification
Chaetodipus formosus is a medium-sized pocket mouse with soft pelage and no stiff, bristly hairs on its rump. The tail is long, with a distal crest and a conspicuous terminal tuft. *C. baileyi* is larger in body size and has longer hind feet; *C. arenarius,* a Mexican species, is smaller in body size and has shorter ears; and *C. penicillatus* also has noticeably shorter ears.

Recent Synonyms
Perognathus formosus

Status
Common

Subspecies
Chaetodipus formosus cinerascens, Baja California from San Felipe southward to near El Mármol
Chaetodipus formosus formosus, south-central and southwestern Utah, and north-central and northwestern Arizona
Chaetodipus formosus incolatus, western Utah and northeastern Nevada

Chaetodipus formosus infolatus, Baja California from near El Mármol southward to near Santa Rosalia
Chaetodipus formosus melanurus, northwestern Nevada and extreme northeastern California
Chaetodipus formosus mesembrinus, Colorado Desert of southeastern California and northeastern Baja California
Chaetodipus formosus mohavensis, Mojave Desert of southeastern California and southern Nevada, and parts of western Nevada

References
Durrant, 1952; Genoways and Brown, 1993; Hoffmeister, 1986

Hispid pocket mouse | *Chaetodipus hispidus*

Hispid pocket mice occur in a variety of habitats but are almost always associated with grasses. The species is reported to occur on pinyon-juniper mesas, short and mixed grass plains, mesquite grasslands, tall grass prairies, and oak uplands. It is also common in desert or mixed grasslands associated with prickly pear cactus or mesquite in the southwestern United States and Mexico. Although they prefer sandy soils in which to establish elaborate burrow systems, they will live in soils with higher clay content. The openings of their burrows may be plugged during the day. These pocket mice decrease their activities in winter in northern parts of their range, and they may estivate during hotter times of the year.

Hispid pocket mice are solitary, and become social only during the breeding season. One or two litters of four to seven offspring are produced in northern parts of the range. Breeding is noted to occur throughout the year in southern parts of the range. Little is known about gestation or development of young. Nesting chambers are about 50 mm in diameter and are reportedly lined with grasses.

These pocket mice are primarily granivores, feeding on the seeds of a variety of grasses and those of other plants such as mesquite, yucca, and cactus. They ingest some green vegetation and are known to include insects in their diet in early spring. Hispid pocket mice are not known to drink free-standing water. Cheek pouches are used to transport food and nesting materials to burrows. Hoarding of seeds in food chambers has been noted. *E. G. Zimmerman*

Chaetodipus hispidus

Size
Sexual dimorphism is not evident.
Total length: 198–223 mm
Length of tail: 90–113 mm
Weight: 30–47 g

Identification
Hispid pocket mice are distinguished by their medium size, the presence of cheek pouches, and a tail that is only slightly shorter than the body. The pelage is distinctly coarse, as their common name "hispid" implies. The upper-parts are olive buff and are separated from the white underparts by a distinct ocraceous (yellow-orange) stripe. They are less likely to move by leaping or hopping than are some members of the family, and their hind feet are not unusually large for mice of their size; they have five toes. The auditory bullae of the skull are large, although not extensively inflated. The upper incisors have a distinct groove. Where its range overlaps with those of other pocket mice, the hispid pocket mouse can be distinguished by its larger, robust body, the prevalent lateral body stripe, and a bicolored tail lacking a terminal tuft.

Recent Synonyms
Perognathus hispidus

Status
Common in grassy habitats within its range

Subspecies
Chaetodipus hispidus hispidus, eastern two-thirds of Texas, southward throughout most of

Tamaulipas, and northern Coahuila and Nuevo Leon

Chaetodipus hispidus paradoxus, southern North Dakota south through eastern Wyoming, and Colorado and the western two-thirds of South Dakota, and Nebraska; western Kansas, Oklahoma, and Texas; eastern and southern New Mexico; southeastern Arizona southward into central Chihuahua

Chaetodipus hispidus spilotus, southeastern Nebraska and southward through eastern Kansas and Oklahoma

Chaetodipus hispidus zacatacae, southern Coahuila south through eastern Zacatecas, most of San Luis Potosi, northeastern Jalisco, Hidalgo, and Tlaxcala

References
Mammalian Species 320; Caire et al., 1989; Dalquest and Horner, 1984

Rock pocket mouse | *Chaetopidus intermedius*

Rock pocket mice occur in rocky habitats from south-central Utah to western Sonora, Chihuahua, and Trans-Pecos, Texas. Only rarely is *Chaetodipus intermedius* associated with silty or sandy soils. These mice are active at night and are associated with rocky gulches, canyons, or boulders. Their burrows are small and inconspicuous and are usually located near or under rocks. Rock pocket mice feed on a variety of seeds; their diet varies according to availability. Breeding starts in February or March and continues into July. Litter size ranges from three to six. Juveniles have been observed in the months of April through August.

These mice can alter their basal metabolic rates according to season. They exhibit higher rates in the winter and lower basal rates in the summer. *Chaetodipus intermedius* undergoes torpor during colder periods, but can remain active as long as two hours at temperatures below freezing.

Rock pocket mice are medium-sized, relatively long-tailed mice with comparatively harsh fur with weak "spines" on the rump. The soles of the hind feet are naked to the heels. The tail is longer than the head and body and distinctly tufted at the tip. The fur is a drab grayish brown on the back with a pale orange-brown line on the sides and white underneath. *D. S. Rogers*

Chaetodipus intermedius

Size
Some sexual dimorphism
Total length: 157–188 (172) mm
Length of tail: 84–112 (96) mm
Weight: 10.5–19.9 g

Identification
Chaetodipus intermedius is usually confused with either *C. penicillatus* or *C. nelsoni.* The rock pocket mouse and *C. penicillatus* overlap broadly; all three species co-occur only in Trans-Pecos, Texas. *C. penicillatus* differs from the rock pocket mouse by the absence of rump spines, and by having a larger hind foot and a broader nose. The rock pocket mouse is

smaller than *C. nelsoni,* has fewer rump spines, and has whitish soles of the hind feet (the soles of the hind feet are black in *C. nelsoni*).

Recent Synonyms
Perognathus intermedius

Other Common Names
Intermediate pocket mouse

Status
Common

Subspecies
Chaetodipus intermedius ater, central New Mexico
Chaetodipus intermedius beardi, south-central New Mexico
Chaetodipus intermedius crinitus, south-central Utah, north-central and northwestern Arizona

Chaetodipus intermedius intermedius, western Arizona, southern and central New Mexico, northern and central Chihuahua

Chaetodipus intermedius lithophilus, northwestern Sonora

Chaetodipus intermedius minimus, Turner's Island, Gulf of California, Sonora

Chaetodipus intermedius phasma, western Arizona, northwestern Sonora

Chaetodipus intermedius rupestris, south-central New Mexico

Chaetodipus intermedius umbrosus, central Arizona

References

Anderson, 1972; Davis and Schmidly, 1994; Genoways and Brown, 1993; Schmidly, 1977

Nelson's pocket mouse | *Chaetodipus nelsoni*

This spiny pocket mouse occurs in the Chihuahuan Desert of the Mexican Plateau (from the states of Zacatecas, Durango, and San Luis Potosi northward to Chihuahua, Coahuila, Nuevo Leon, and Tamaulipas) and in adjacent areas in western Texas and extreme southern New Mexico. Nelson's pocket mouse shows a strong preference for rocky places in Chihuahuan desert shrub vegetation. It prefers rocky soils on slopes where cactus, creosote, sotol, and lechuguilla provide scattered cover and is seldom taken on sandy or other fine soils.

Mating begins in February and continues throughout July, with peaks of pregnancy in females in March, May, and July. The gestation period is about one month and the young leave the nest when they are about four weeks of age. The number of embryos per litter averages 3.2, with extremes of two and four. The annual population turnover is about 86 per-cent; that is, only 14 of each 100 individuals survive more than one year.

Unlike some other species of pocket mice, which hibernate during the colder winter months, *C. nelsoni* is active throughout the year. It feeds entirely on the seeds of various desert shrubs and grasses.

C. nelsoni is commonly trapped in association with kangaroo rats *(Dipodomys),* deer mice *(Peromyscus),* and woodrats *(Neotoma),* as well as other pocket mice *(Perognathus). D. J. Schmidly*

Chaetodipus nelsoni

Size

No significant sexual dimorphism
Total length: 182–193 mm
Length of tail: 104–117 mm
Weight: 14–18 g

Identification

This drab gray, medium-sized pocket mouse has a harsh pelage and a distinctly tufted tail that is longer than the head and body. It is distinguished from *C. intermedius* and *C. penicillatus,* two closely related and morphologically similar species, in having numerous elongate, black-tipped spiny hairs on the rump that over-reach the normal guard hairs.

Recent Synonyms

Perognathus nelsoni

Status
Locally abundant when habitat is suitable

Subspecies
Chaetodipus nelsoni canescens, Chihuahuan Desert region of northern Mexico and adjacent parts of the United States
Chaetodipus nelsoni nelsoni, Chihuahuan Desert region of the Mesa Central in Mexico

References
Mammalian Species 484; Anderson, 1972; Davis and Schmidly, 1994; Genoways and Jones, 1973; Williams et al., 1993

Desert pocket mouse | *Chaetodipus penicillatus*

The desert pocket mouse occupies one of the largest geographical ranges of the coarse-furred pocket mice, being a common inhabitant of warm deserts throughout the United States and Mexico. This mild-mannered nocturnal burrower is found in association with sandy soils on creosote-scrub flats or in washes bordered by small desert trees such as mesquite or palo verde. Rocky soils are avoided. Mice from different geographical areas vary somewhat in size or in pelage color, with paler forms occurring in the west.

Desert pocket mice emerge from their burrows at dusk to search for seeds, usually under the shelter of shrub canopies. They prefer to collect seeds from light organic litter, and they select seeds that are large relative to the texture of the substrate. Mesquite and palo verde seeds are a staple food by virtue of their large size and abundance in shrub microhabitats. Harvested seeds are crammed into fur-lined cheek pouches and carried away to the burrow, where they are carefully sorted, stored, and defended against thieves.

Dry seeds comprise most of the diet, although insect larvae and some green material are eaten occasionally. Desert pocket mice are even stingier water-misers than the famous kangaroo rats. Whereas these pocket mice do not deign to eat lettuce in captivity, kangaroo rats devour their daily ration and beg for more.

Most reproduction occurs in spring or late summer after rains have stimulated production of a new seed crop. Females become reproductive soon after emerging in about March from a brief period of winter inactivity and can produce several litters of 2–4 young. Gestation spans 3–4 weeks, and the young are weaned after another 3 weeks. When conditions are good, spring-born young breed during late summer of their first year, and populations increase rapidly, reaching peak densities in the fall. The onset of winter inactivity varies from year to year. In years of exceptional summer rainfall, reproduction continues through the summer and the mice wait until fall to amass their winter seed caches. They continue to work until they have collected enough seed to last the winter, and then they disappear underground.

Desert pocket mice have a clever strategy for minimizing the amount of food they have to store—they save energy during winter by turning down their body's thermostat and

Chaetodipus penicillatus

entering a quiescent state called torpor. They also use torpor as a temporary energy-saving strategy during other seasons. On cold mornings, one often finds sleepy, uncoordinated pocket mice in one's live-traps. After riding briefly in a breast-pocket (another good reason to call them "pocket mice"), the animals warm up, utter an occasional squeaky complaint, and upon release wobble somewhat unsteadily home to their caches. *M. V. Price*

Size

In some subspecies males are larger than females.

Total length: 155–185 (170) mm
Length of tail: 83–110 (93) mm
Weight: 13–20 (16) g

Identification

C. pencillatus is medium-sized, lacks spine-like hairs on the rump, and has a yellowish-brown to yellowish-gray upper pelage and whiteish underparts; the tail is long, strongly crested, white below and dusky above and on the tuft. This species is distinguished from other spine-less *Chaetodipus* by size, pelage color, or (in males) by baculum shape. *C. baileyi* is larger and grayer, and males have a straight baculum; *C. hispidus* is larger, with a distinct yellow lateral line, poorly haired tail, and trifid baculum

tip; *C. formosus* has a more heavily haired and crested tail. Two Mexican species, *C. arenarius* and *C. pernix,* are smaller, and the latter has a distinct buffy lateral stripe.

Recent Synonyms

Perognathus penicillatus

Other Common Names

Sonoran Desert pocket mouse

Status

Common

Subspecies

Chaetodipus penicillatus angustirostris, southern California to northeastern Baja California, Mexico
Chaetodipus pencillatus atrodorsalis, central Mexico

Chaetodipus penicillatus eremicus, north-central Mexico to southern New Mexico and southwestern Texas (considered a separate species by some)
Chaetodipus penicillatus penicillatus, west-central Arizona
Chaetodipus penicillatus pricei, southern Arizona to northwestern Mexico
Chaetodipus penicillatus seri, Tiburón Island, Gulf of California, Mexico
Chaetodipus penicillatus sobrinus, southeastern Nevada, northwestern Arizona
Chaetodipus penicillatus stephensi, eastern Mojave Desert, California

References

French, 1993; Price and Podolsky, 1989; Reynolds and Haskell, 1949; Williams et al., 1993

Spiny pocket mouse | *Chaetodipus spinatus*

Most of the geographic range of the spiny pocket mouse is in Baja California, along the eastern half of that peninsula; in the southern third of the peninsula the mouse occurs from coast to coast. It is also found on many islands in the Gulf of California and on a few islands off the southern Pacific coastline of the peninsula. In the United States, it is found in extreme south-central and southeastern California. The eastern limit of its distribution in southern California occurs at upland sites adjacent to and west of the Colorado River, which forms the border between California and Arizona. The western limit of the range of a closely related species, the rock pocket mouse *(C. intermedius),* is east of the river. The spiny pocket mouse usually inhabits rough desert landscapes of boulders, washes, rocky slopes, coarse soil, and sparse vegetation characteristic of the lower Sonoran life zone. Its habitats are identical to those of the rock pocket mouse east of the river, yet nowhere do the two species occur together. The spiny pocket mouse occurs at elevations up to 900 m in the Turtle Mountains in southeastern California.

The upper pelage of the spiny pocket mouse is drab brown and shaggy. The hairs are dark gray near their base, pale tan in the middle, and black at the tips. The lateral line, when present, is faint. The underparts are buffy white. The ears are small and dusky, and there is a small white spot at the base of each ear. The tail is brown above and whitish below, with a distinct crest near the tip. Spines, the character giving the species its common name, are located mostly on the rump, but scattered spines may be found as far forward as the shoulder region. The spines, which are modified hairs, are not as stiff as those of porcupines.

Little is known about the natural history of the spiny pocket mouse despite its wide range and the many reports of its occurrence. It is nocturnal, thereby escaping the intense heat and aridity of the desert during the day. Its diet probably consists of seeds and it may eat green vegetation following the brief periods of rain. As in most species of the family Heteromyidae occurring in desert habitats, water is probably derived from its food, because water is scarce in its habitat much of the time.

Chaetodipus spinatus

One report suggested that the spiny pocket mouse becomes dormant during cold periods. The only record of reproduction detailed the occurrence of four embryos in one specimen. Nothing is known about growth, development, physiological function, and behavior; information about ecology is anecdotal.

Other species of rodents reported from the spiny pocket mouse's habitat in southern California include the white-tailed antelope squirrel *(Ammospermophilus leucurus)*, the canyon mouse *(Peromyscus crinitus)*, the desert woodrat *(Neotoma lepida)*, a deer mouse *(Peromyscus maniculatlus)*, and three other members of the genus *Chaetodipus*, Bailey's pocket mouse *(C. baileyi)*, the San Diego pocket mouse *(C. fallax)*, and the long-tailed pocket mouse *(C. formosus)*. There is no fossil record of this species. *J. A. Lackey*

Size
No significant sexual dimorphism
Total length: 164–225 (198) mm
Length of tail: 89–128 (114) mm
Weight: 13–18 g

Identification
Where it occurs in the United States, the spiny pocket mouse can be distinguished from all pocket mice in the genus *Perognathus* (the "silky" pocket mice), and from *Chaetodipus formosus, C. hispidis, C. baileyi,* and *C. penicillatus,* by its pronounced rump spines. Lack of a well-marked lateral line distinguishes the spiny pocket mouse from *C. intermedius, C. fallax,* and *C. californicus.*

Status
Most populations are probably secure because the species inhabits areas of little agrcultural value, and on islands it prefers rocky desert slopes.

Subspecies
Chaetodipus spinatus broccus, Baja California Sur mainland, Mexico

Chaetodipus spinatus bryanti, Baja California Sur, San Jose Island, Gulf of California, Mexico

Chaetodipus spinatus evermanni, Baja California Norte, Meija Island, Gulf of California, Mexico

Chaetodipus spinatus guardiae, Baja California Norte, Angel de la Guarda Island, Gulf of California, Mexico

Chaetodipus spinatus lambi, Baja California Sur, Espiritu Santo Island, Gulf of California, Mexico

Chaetodipus spinatus latijugularis, Baja California Sur, San Francisco Island, Gulf of California, Mexico

Chaetodipus spinatus lorenzi, Baja California Norte, North and South San Lorenzo islands, Gulf of California, Mexico

Chaetodipus spinatus magdalenae, Baja California Sur, Magdalena Island, Pacific Ocean, Mexico

Chaetodipus spinatus marcosensis, Baja California Sur, San Marcos Island, Gulf of California, Mexico

Chaetodipus spinatus margaritae, Baja California Sur, Margarita Island, Pacific Ocean, Mexico

Chaetodipus spinatus occultus, Baja California Sur, Carmen Island, Gulf of California, Mexico

Chaetodipus spinatus oribates, Baja California Norte, mainland, Mexico

Chaetodipus spinatus peninsulae, Baja California Sur, mainland, Mexico

Chaetodipus spinatus prietae, Baja California Norte, mainland, Mexico

Chaetodipus spinatus pullus, Baja California Sur, Coronado Island, Gulf of California, Mexico

Chaetodipus spinatus rufescens, extreme southern California

Chaetodipus spinatus seorsus, Baja California Sur, Danzante Island, Gulf of California, Mexico

Chaetodipus spinatus spinatus, extreme southeastern California and northeastern Baja California Norte, Mexico

References
Mammalian Species 385; Genoways and Brown, 1993; Grinnell, 1914; Huey, 1964

Dark kangaroo mouse | *Microdipodops megacephalus*

The dark kangaroo mouse is restricted to the Great Basin Desert. Its distribution is centered in Nevada, with populations extending into the adjoining states of California, Oregon, and Utah. Like the pale kangaroo mouse, *Microdipodops pallidus*, it inhabits stabilized dunes and other sandy soils; where the two overlap, the dark kangaroo mouse occurs on fine gravelly soils. Its preferred habitat, characterized as Upper Sonoran life zone, is primarily valley bottoms and alluvial fans dominated by big sagebrush *(Artemesia tridentata)*, rabbitbrush *(Chrysothamnus)*, and horsebrush *(Tetradymia)*.

Although the bodies of kangaroo mice appear identical to those of kangaroo rats, the tail differs in being shorter and in lacking a well-developed crest of hair at the tip. Both kangaroo mice, *Microdipodops megacephalus* and *M. pallidus,* have a fat de-

Microdipodops megacephalus

posit in the middle of the tail, which is unique in North American small mammals and is similar to fat deposits in the tails of small desert mammals in Africa and Australia. This fat deposit increases in size from spring to fall, reaching its greatest size prior to the animal's entry into hibernation. Individuals with the largest fat deposit tend to survive to the following year, suggesting an overall better body condition.

The dark kangaroo mouse usually emerges from hibernation in March and reenters hibernation by November. Aboveground activity is greatest during the first two hours after sunset, with only periodic forays the remainder of the night. Like other bipedal rodents, *M. megacephalus* forages in the open where shrub canopy cover is sparse. Consequently, moonlight inhibits aboveground activity. Although primarily granivorous, the dark kangaroo mouse eats a wide variety of insects. When feeding on seeds, it seeks out clumps of seeds instead of harvesting individual seeds. As with other heteromyid species,

these animals do not drink water. They conserve water by restricting their activity to night, when it is cooler, and by producing concentrated urine and dry feces; they gain water from foodstuffs.

The dark kangaroo mouse can be aggressive to others of its species. However, it appears that other, co-existing species are behaviorally dominant. This includes the little pocket mouse, which is only half the size of a kangaroo mouse. Kangaroo mice readily enter live traps baited with seeds from March through April, but after that, when little pocket mice emerge from hibernation, kangaroo mice are rarely captured. When little pocket mice reenter hibernation at the end of August, kangaroo mice again enter traps and are commonly encountered through the autumn.

Pregnant individuals have been found from April through September. Litter size varies from two to seven, with a mean of 3.9. It is probable that multiple litters are produced, particularly in favorable years. Dark kangaroo mice have been kept in captivity for up to 5.5 years.

Microdipodops megacephalus lives in highly diverse small mammal communities. Common coexisting rodents include Merriam's, Ord's, and Panamint kangaroo rats, and little pocket mice, deer mice, western harvest mice, and grasshopper mice. *M. J. O'Farrell*

Size
No significant sexual dimorphism
Total length: 138–177 (160) mm

Length of tail: 67–103 (86) mm
Weight: 10.0–16.9 (13.1) g

Identification
This kanagroo mouse is distinguished by brownish, blackish, or grayish dorsal pelage.

The dorsal surface of the tail is darker than the body and has a black tip; the hind foot is 25 mm or shorter.

Status
Common

Subspecies
Microdipodops megacephalus albiventer, Desert Valley, Lincoln County, Nevada

Microdipodops megacephalus ambiguus, Smoke Creek and Black Rock deserts and the lower part of the Humboldt River Valley in Nevada and extreme eastern Lassen County, California

Microdipodops megacephalus atrirelictus, southwestern Owyhee County, Idaho

Microdipodops megacephalus californicus, inter-montane valleys of eastern Plumas County, California, and southern Washoe and Ormsby counties, Nevada

Microdipodops megacephalus leucotis, valley floors of the Bonneville Basin in south-central Tooele County, Utah

Microdipodops megacephalus medius, southwestern Pershing County, Nevada

Microdipodops megacephalus megacephalus, central and northeastern Nevada, from northern Elko County to northern Nye and Lincoln counties, and from western Lander County eastward to near the Utah border

Microdipodops megacephalus nasutus, Fletcher, Mineral County, Nevada

Microdipodops megacephalus nexus, Humboldt and Lander counties, Nevada

Microdipodops megacephalus oregonus, southeastern Oregon, Modoc and Lassen counties, California, and Washoe and Humboldt counties, Nevada

Microdipodops megacephalus paululus, Pine, White, and Snake valleys in west-central Utah

Microdipodops megacephalus polionotus, Mono Lake Basin and the head of Owens Valley, Mono County, California

Microdipodops megacephalus sabulonis, south-central Nevada

References
Mammalian Species 46; Genoways and Brown, 1993; Hall, 1946; Harris, 1987

Pale kangaroo mouse | *Microdipodops pallidus*

The pale kangaroo mouse is a Nevada species, with only a single, small population occurring in eastern California. The distribution in Nevada is restricted to the west-central portion of the state. The only other species of kangaroo mouse, *Microdipodops megacephalus,* has a wider distribution, and overlaps portions of the range of *M. pallidus.* The pale kangaroo mouse is restricted to valley bottoms containing stabilized dunes with fine, wind-blown sand. Elevations range from 1,188 to 1,737 meters, and always appear to be in the zone below that dominated by big sagebrush *(Artemisia tridentata).* Preferred habitat is characterized as Upper Sonoran life zone, which is dominated by saltbush *(Atriplex)* and greasewood *(Sarcobatus vermiculatus).*

Morphologically, kangaroo mice resemble miniature kangaroo rats: the skull contains a greatly inflated auditory apparatus and the hind legs are enlarged, allowing bipedal, hopping locomotion. However, the tail is relatively short and lacks the well-developed crest of hair characteristic of kangaroo rats. Also, the tail contains a fat deposit in the middle, which may be of value in balance and is also a potential energy store.

Pale kangaroo mice live in a high, cold desert and use hibernation to maintain body weight and conserve stored seeds during periods of food shortage. *M. pallidus* is primarily granivorous, eating Indian rice grass *(Achnatherum hymenoides)* and a variety of forbs. The summer diet is supplemented with insects, including beetles, centipedes, and moth pupae.

Aboveground movement is characterized by a burst of activity just after sunset, with occasional forays through the remainder of the night. As with other bipedal rodents, foraging is concentrated in open areas away from shrub canopy. *M. pallidus* appears to be relatively nonaggressive compared with other heteromyid rodents, and probably avoids surface encounters with other individuals by rapidly hopping away. Belowground, the burrow system appears to be short and simple. Apparently nest chambers are not regularly used.

Microdipodops pallidus

Pregnant individuals have been found from March into September. Litter size varies from two to six with an average of 3.9. As with other heteromyids, it is suspected that multiple litters and larger litter sizes occur during years with high vegetation productivity.

Pale kangaroo mice live in a rich small mammal community. Common coexisting rodents include Merriam's, Ord's, and desert kangaroo rats, the little pocket mouse, the deer mouse, and the western harvest mouse. *M. J. O'Farrell*

Size
No significant sexual dimorphism
Total length: 150–173 (160) mm
Length of tail: 74–99 (87) mm
Weight: 10.3–16.8 (13.5) g

Identification
M. pallidus is distinguished by its pale pinkish-cinnamon dorsal coloration; the dorsal surface of the tail is the same color as the body and lacks a dark tip; the hind foot is 25 mm or more in length.

Other Common Names
Pallid kangaroo mouse

Status
Common

Subspecies
Microdipodops pallidus ammophilus, Railroad Valley, Nye County, Nevada
Microdipodops pallidus pallidus, southwestern Nevada, Pershing County, through Fish Lake Valley to Oasis, and in the Deep Spring Valley, Inyo County, California
Microdipodops pallidus purus, Emigran and Desert valleys, Lincoln County, Nevada
Microdipodops pallidus restrictus, Soda Spring Valley, Mineral County, Nevada
Microdipodops pallidus ruficollaris, valleys of western Nye County, eastward to western Lincoln County, Nevada

References
Mammalian Species 47; Genoways and Brown, 1993; Hall, 1946

Agile kangaroo rat | *Dipodomys agilis*

The agile kangaroo rat primarily occurs in woodland and chaparral communities in west-central California; its range extends southward to the foothills of the San Gabriel and San Bernardino mountains along the northern side of the Los Angeles Basin. It occupies elevations of 500–2,250 meters. Fossils that may be of this species are known from Newport Bay Mesa and Rancho La Brea in southern California.

Occasionally, the agile kangaroo rat may be active during daylight hours, but usually it is active outside its burrow only at night. Like other species of kangaroo rats, it is solitary most of the year. It can harvest a large quantity of seeds: one 58-gram individual moved about 300 grams of sunflower seeds in one night. The capacity of its cheek pouches is about 30 of these seeds. These kangaroo rats are excellent swimmers; their large hind feet give them considerable agility in the water. The gait is a series of short hops; if hurried, agile kangaroo rats move rapidly on all four feet. They can make sharp turns to avoid predators.

Dipodomys agilis is intermediate in size for the genus. The hind feet are elongated and well adapted for hopping. Each hind foot has five toes. The front feet are small and are impor-

tant in manipulation of food and in construction of burrows. The tail is 1.55 times the length of head and body and is bicolored, with a blackish crest and tuft. The kanagroo rat's upperparts are dark reddish-brown. External, fur-lined cheek pouches—one on each side of the mouth—are used to carry food from where it is found to storage places in or near the burrow. Along the anterior part of the back, there is a specialized glandular area in the skin. The function of the gland is unknown, but may be related to scent production.

The breeding season is March to July, but some litters may be born in autumn. One litter of two to four young (average is 2.5) is born each year. The young sometimes make squeaking sounds, but adults rarely vocalize. The young's pelage is darker than that of adults, and the hairs on its tail are not elongated into a crest.

In most of its range in California, *D. agilis* is most often found in open chaparral and coastal sage-scrub communities. In the San Gabriel Mountains, it is most abundant in level tracts of coastal sage. Except for the San Diego pocket mouse, it is the most abundant mammal in this habitat. *D. agilis's* limited power of digging restricts it to areas of loose soils, and as a

Dipodomys agilis

result, its burrows often are located in sandy areas within the chaparral community. Large colonies occur locally on sandy soils adjacent to large washes. These kangaroo rats are absent in heavy chaparral where a layer of plant debris covers the ground, such as on the north slopes, which are covered with scrub oak and lilac.

Agile kangaroo rats often burrow within and at the edges of arroyos. The entrances of burrows may be closed in the daytime. One burrow was oval in cross section and about 5 cm in diameter. The entrance sloped gently downward and the main burrow was about 20 cm below the surface for about 2.5 meters, then about 0.5 meter below for 2 meters, where it terminated in another entrance that was under a small perennial plant. This terminal entrance was nearly perpendicular for 15–18 cm. There were six branches to the burrow, varying from a few cm to 1 meter in length, each terminating in a chamber of greater diameter than the burrow. A nest made of the hulls of grass seeds was in one chamber. The other chambers were used to store acorns, grass seeds, and parts of flowers. Most of these storage chambers were closed with earth; they contained 26–149 acorns. The open chamber was only partially full.

Foods consumed by the agile kangaroo rat include seeds of forbs, grasses, and shrubs. *D. agilis* stores seeds of laurel-sumac and chamise, and will eat some insects. Scrub oak acorns and juniper tree berries have been found in cheek pouches. One immature individual had its cheek pouches stuffed with about 550 seeds of bromegrass.

In southern California, populations of 5 to 15 per hectare occur in pinyon-juniper habitat from mid-September to mid-March, but populations may range in size from 6 to 232 per hectare. During peak populations, most individuals are juveniles.

Species occurring in the same area as the agile kangaroo rat include cottontails, black-tailed jackrabbits, California ground squirrels, pocket gophers, California pocket mice, Merriam's and Stephen's kangaroo rats, dusky-footed woodrats, California mice, bobcats, gray foxes, coyotes, and mule deer. Predators include Pacific rattlesnakes, great-horned owls, bobcats, foxes, and coyotes. The coyote probably is one of the major predators; remains of *D. agilis* are often found in coyote feces, and coyotes excavate many burrow systems in colonies of these kangaroo rats. Parasites include protozoans, mites, ticks, and fleas. *T. L. Best*

Size
Males are slightly larger than females.
Total length: 285–320 (302) mm (males);
    277–305 (295) mm (females)
Length of tail: 170–195 (181) mm (males);
    170–192 (178) mm (females)
Weight: 66–79 (72) g (males); 63–78 (66) g
    (females)

Identification
The large body size and large ears of *D. agilis* distinguish it from all sympatric species. Compared with *D. simulans, D. agilis* is larger in most characters of the body and skull, the ears and hind feet are longer, and it has two more chromosomes than *D. simulans*. Compared with *D. stephensi, D. agilis* has much larger ears

and usually occupies less open habitats. Compared with *D. merriami,* which has four toes on each hind foot, *D. agilis* has five toes on each hind foot.

Recent Synonyms
Dipodomys wagneri
Perodipus perplexus

Other Common Names
Pacific kangaroo rat, nimble kangaroo rat

Status
Common

Subspecies
Dipodomys agilis agilis, coastal southern
    California
Dipodomys agilis perplexus, coastal and south-
    central California

References
Genoways and Brown, 1993

California kangaroo rat | *Dipodomys californicus*

This species is found in northern California (north of Suisun Bay) and south-central Oregon, chiefly from east of the humid coastal areas to the foothills of the Cascade and Sierra Nevada mountains. It generally occupies chaparral and other shrub communities, but appears to be restricted to places where open areas are available. *Dipodomys californicus* is so similar in parts of its range to Heermann's kangaroo rat that it was shown to be distinct only in 1976.

These rodents evidently require well-drained soils throughout the winter, and often make burrows at the bases of shrubs and near old stumps. Where soils are unsuitable for burrowing, they often make their homes under large boulders. They are also known to use burrows of ground squirrels *(Spermophilus)*.

Wet weather is thought to be a principal cause of population decimation during severe winters, but in spite of their sensitivity to climatic moisture, these animals may be active on rainy nights or on snow in temperatures as low as –11 °C. After heavy rains they may be seen pushing mud out of their burrows.

Seeds and berries of manzanita, seeds of buckbrush, rabbitbrush, lupines, bur-clover, and wild oats, and some small tubers have been found in the cheek pouches of this species. Green vegetation is eaten in the summer, perhaps after seed stores laid away the preceding year are depleted. This animal does not prepare large caches, but rather deposits stores here and there in the soil, a cheekful at a time.

Breeding occurs primarily from February through September, with the greatest activity in February, March, and April, and this species evidently is capable of producing more than one litter per year. Litters usually number about three in the spring, and about two in other seasons. *D. A. Kelt*

Dipodomys californicus

Size
Males are slightly larger than females.
Total length: 260–340 mm (307.3, males; 304.8, females)
Length of tail: 152–217 mm (187.9, males; 184.3, females)
Weight: 60–85 g

Identification
Dipodomys californicus is a medium-large kangaroo rat with a relatively broad face and dark color. The tail has broad dark dorsal and ventral stripes and a distinct white tuft. With rare exceptions this species has four toes on the hindfoot.

Status
Uncertain; no subspecies are threatened or endangered.

Subspecies
Dipodomys californicus californicus, north of the Sacramento-San Joaquin estuary system, on

the western side of the Sacramento Valley and in the coastal range, north to southern Oregon, and east of the Cascade Range on the Modoc Plateau between California and Nevada

Dipodomys californicus eximius, vicinity of Marysville Buttes, Sutter County, California

Dipodomys californicus saxatilis, foothills on the eastern edge of the Sacramento Valley, from roughly the South Fork of the American River north to Battle Creek, Tehama County, California

References

Mammalian Species 324; Best, 1993; Grinnell, 1922; Williams et al., 1993

Gulf Coast kangaroo rat | *Dipodomys compactus*

Gulf Coast kangaroo rats that occur on the barrier islands of Texas and Tamaulipas, Mexico, exhibit two distinct color phases, a grayish-cream phase that is paler than that of any other species of kangaroo rat and an orangish-yellow (pale ochraceous-buff) phase. The dorsal pelage of specimens from the Texas mainland is reddish-yellow (yellowish, ochraceous-buff) and is slightly darker then the orangish-yellow phase from the islands. In all three color phases the predominant shade covers the entire back and is purest on the sides and flanks. The upperparts are lightly washed with black. The ears, underside of the feet, and dorsal and ventral tail stripes are similar to the dorsal color. The cheeks are white.

There are no known fossils. Based on features of the teeth and skull, *D. compactus* is regarded as the most primitive living species of kangaroo rat. The Gulf Coast kangaroo rat is considered to be primarily granivorous (seed eating); however, an individual of this taxon that was kept in captivity ate insects

Dipodomys compactus

when they were placed in its cage. It would appear that this species reproduces in the summer. Two placental scars have been reported from these animals in July and two small embryos in August. Another specimen had scrotal testes in July. Under laboratory conditions, *D. compactus* is strongly nocturnal.

Dipodomys compactus inhabits sparsely vegetated areas with sandy soils throughout its range. On the barrier islands it is sometimes found on level soil, but is usually confined to dune areas and is always on the side away from prevailing winds. The island subspecies has been reported in association with various plants including sea-oats *(Uniola),* bluestem *(Andropogon),* shoregrass *(Monanthochloe),* croton *(Croton),* sunflowers *(Helianthus),* and fimbry *(Fimbristylis).* Gulf Coast kangaroo rats from the Texas mainland inhabit areas of loose, deep sand that have scattered vegetation, such as open mesquite savanna. In addition to sites where such conditions occur naturally, these kangaroo rats occupy areas that have been cleared of native brush by farmers and ranchers and firebreaks that have been plowed along roadsides. Vegetation found in such areas has included three-awn *(Aristida)*, grama *(Bouteloua)*, windmill grass *(Chloris)*, bluestem, prickly pear *(Opuntia)*, and mesquite *(Prosopis)*. Gulf Coast kangaroo rats from both the islands and the mainland occur with the spotted ground squirrel *(Spermophilus spilosoma)*, gophers *(Geomys)*, Merriam's pocket mouse *(Perognathus merriami)*, the northern grasshopper mouse *(Onychomys leucogaster)*, the hispid cotton rat *(Sigmodon hispidus)*, the southern plains woodrat *(Neotoma micropus)*, and the badger *(Taxidea taxus)*. *D. compactus* from the mainland is also associated with the hispid pocket mouse *(Chaetodipus hispidus)* and the white-footed mouse *(Peromyscus leucopus)*.

Dipodomys compactus shares approximately half of its range on the mainland of south Texas with Ord's kangaroo rat. In areas where they occur together, these taxa use slightly different types of habitat. Ord's kangaroo rat occurs primarily on undisturbed brushland that has hard-packed soil and thick vegetation. The Gulf Coast kangaroo rat generally occupies sites in which the soil is softer and the vegetation is lower and more open.

In the last two decades there has been extensive residential, recreational, and commercial development of some portions of the habitat of *D. compactus* on the barrier islands of Texas. This has undoubtedly affected the animals, but they are probably still abundant in most of the undeveloped portions of these islands. In the late 1800s and early 1900s *D. compactus* was abundant in yellow-sand prairie on the mainland of southeastern Texas, and a kangaroo rat that may have been this species was common in the sandy, black-oak region south of the Medina River in Bexar County. Portions of the south Texas mainland have undergone considerable habitat modification due to ranching and farming activities. Kangaroo rats have probably been excluded from the most-altered sites, such as tracts converted to intensive agriculture, but are probably fairly common in other, less extensively modified areas. *G. D. Baumgardner*

Size

Males are slightly larger than females in external measurements, but smaller in most cranial ones.

Total length: 203–255 (228.1) mm (males); 210–266 (227.6) mm (females)

Length of tail: 104–135 (119.3) mm (males); 105–132 (119.4) mm (females)

Weight: 46–60 (53) g (males); 44–46 (45) g (females)

Identification

D. compactus is a medium-size kangaroo rat with five toes on each hind foot. The only kangaroo rat of similar size that occurs near it is Ord's kangaroo rat *(D. ordii)*. Compared to *D. ordii*, the tail of *D. compactus* is shorter, the stripe on the underside of the tail is paler in color and more broken in appearance, the hair on the tip of the tail is less frilled out, and the pelage is shorter and courser. The dorsal fur of *D. compactus* from the mainland of south Texas has a reddish-yellow cast whereas the hair of *D. ordii* tends toward brownish hues. On the barrier islands of Texas and Tamaulipas, Mexico, distinct grayish-cream and orangish-yellow color phases occur in *D. compactus*.

Recent Synonyms

Dipodops sennetti

Status

Abundant to rare, depending on habitat

Subspecies

Dipodomys compactus compactus, Mustang and Padre islands of Texas and the barrier islands of Tamaulipas, Mexico

Dipodomys compactus sennetti, eastern two-thirds of the south Texas mainland

References

Mammalian Species 369

Desert kangaroo rat | *Dipodomys deserti*

The desert kangaroo rat occupies the most arid regions of southwestern North America. It inhabits all of the dunes within its geographic and elevational range. Elevations where it occurs range from –60 meters in Death Valley, California, to 1,710 meters in Huntoon Valley, Nevada. There is no fossil record of this species, but *D. deserti* probably originated in the early Pleistocene in the southwestern United States, most probably in southeastern California and the lower Colorado Desert.

Although desert kangaroo rats are nocturnal, they often are out of their burrows in daytime. They kick sand out of the burrow during the day, plug entrances to the burrow, open up others, and dig new tunnels. No burrow has more than one occupant at a time, except when a female has young. *D. deserti* is extremely solitary and drives away animals that invade its territory.

Desert kangaroo rats frequently traverse open areas at high speeds in their search for large clumps of seeds. The cruising radius in one night may reach hundreds of meters. They also dust bathe in the sand; this activity helps keep their fur clean.

Footdrumming and tooth-chattering are used in communication; desert kangaroo rats drum more than any other species of kangaroo rat. They begin to drum, or stamp their hind feet, as early as 30 days after birth, and communicate this way throughout their lives. They also may squeal, grunt, or give purring growls. Young have soft, squeaking voices and cry like newborn puppies. Desert kangaroo rats are excellent swimmers. Like other kangaroo rats, they do not hibernate.

Dipodomys deserti, like all *Dipodomys,* has externally opening, fur-lined cheek pouches that are used to transport seeds. There are four toes on each hind foot and the feet are covered with relatively long hairs. The upperparts of the body are pale brown to grayish, depending on the subspecies, and the underparts are white. The tail is more than half the total length, is crested with long hairs, and the tip is white. The fur of juveniles is similar in color to that of adults, but is shorter and less dense. Geographic variation among populations is not great. This may be because *D. deserti* inhabits almost uniform terrain (loose sandy soil) and because there are no geographic barriers within the range.

Gestation is 29–32 days. One or two litters are born each year. Females sit on their hind legs during parturition and close their eyes slightly during the abdominal contractions. Young are born head first; the female assists delivery by pulling at the fetal membranes. She continually kicks sand onto the neonates, perhaps to dry them. At birth, newborn desert kangaroo rats are about 52 millimeters long; they are naked, pink, and have transparent skin. While nursing, the mother stands on her hind legs; the young rest on their backs, extending their feet into the air and gently kicking her underside as they nurse.

After the eyes of juveniles are fully open, they nurse less each day. Males exhibit paternal behavior and may be gentler with the young than the mother is.

The desert kangaroo rat is well adapted to life in the hottest, driest deserts. It is closely restricted to areas where accumulations of wind-driven sand have reached considerable depths. Mounds used as sites for burrows are sometimes in open spaces, but are usually under vegetation. Burrows are not found in areas of rapidly shifting dunes. The surface above the burrow is a lumpy, uneven area that can measure 3–9 meters across. Numerous entrances, which may be plugged with dirt, slope down from the surface to a labyrinth of passages that wind to a depth of up to 1.2 meters. The underground network includes a number of storerooms and a roughly spherical nest chamber that is filled with dry grasses and other plant material. Desert kangaroo rats feed on a variety of plants, including dried plants from the previous year, leaves of sage, and seeds of creosotebush. They drink water when it is available, but can survive long periods on a dry diet.

Population density is typically about 0.2–1.4 per hectare, but abundance varies considerably at the same locality throughout the year. Desert kangaroo rats occur in the same habitat as Arizona, long-tailed, and desert pocket mice, kangaroo mice, and Merriam's, Ord's, chisel-toothed, and Panamint kangaroo rats. Occasionally they share burrows with the round-tailed ground squirrel and the desert cottontail. Predators include snakes, hawks, owls, bobcats, spotted skunks, coyotes, and foxes. Parasites include a variety of helminths, mites, ticks, lice, and fleas.
T. L. Best

Dipodomys deserti

Size

Males are larger than females.

Total length: 342 mm (males); 331 mm (females)

Length of tail: 201 mm (males); 195 mm (females)

Weight: 91–148 g (males); 83–141 g (females)

Identification

Dipodomys deserti is one of the largest kangaroo rats. Characters of the skull distinguish it from all other *Dipodomys:* the mastoid bones have at most an inconspicuous spicule between them, and the skull is the flattest in the genus. The only other large kangaroo rat to share the range of *D. deserti* is *D. spectabilis*. Where their ranges approach each other in south-central Arizona, *D. deserti* differs from *D. spectabilis* in the maxillary bridge of the orbit, which is broader in *D. spectabilis*.

Status

Common

Subspecies

Dipodomys deserti aquilus, northwestern Nevada and northeastern California

Dipodomys deserti arizonae, south-central Arizona and northern Sonora, Mexico

Dipodomys deserti deserti, southern Nevada, southeastern California, southwestern Arizona, and northwestern Mexico

Dipodomys deserti sonoriensis, western Sonora, Mexico

References

Mammalian Species 339; Hoffmeister, 1986

Texas kangaroo rat | *Dipodomys elator*

The Texas kangaroo rat inhabits only a few counties of north-central Texas. *Dipodomys elator* was reported historically from nine counties in north-central Texas and one county in southwestern Oklahoma. Now, because of changing land-use patterns and other factors, the species is probably extinct in Oklahoma and occurs in substantial populations only in three Texas counties.

Dipodomys elator is nocturnal and prefers moonless or cloudy nights for its activities. It is mostly likely to be glimpsed bounding across a road in front of an automobile on a dark night. It is active throughout the year, but few are seen when the weather is wet. This absence may be due to a lack of opportunity for dust-bathing, which helps *D. elator* to remove oils from its pelage. It is generally asocial and lives singly in burrows or in mother-sibling groups.

The tail of *D. elator* is relatively thick and long, with dark stripes above and below and white stripes on the side that end in a white tuft. The kangaroo rat's belly is white, and its back is a buffy color interspersed with black. The nose and eye rings are black; white thigh patches are present and meet at the base of the tail. The hind feet of the Texas kangaroo rat are large and the front feet are small. The ears are relatively short and rounded, with white patches. External cheek pouches are present. Adults molt once annually. Pelage replacement begins on the nose and between the shoulders and proceeds in all directions from these centers. The fur on the belly and flanks is replaced last. The silky, sometimes sparse, juvenile pelage is replaced in two juvenile molts, one in late summer and another early in the spring.

Little is known about reproduction of the Texas kangaroo rat. Females may give birth to two to four young between mid-

spring and early fall. Young kangaroo rats mature rapidly: pregnant subadult females and juvenile males with enlarged testes have been recorded in July and September. This species has an extended breeding period, but most births probably occur in late spring and summer.

The Texas kangaroo rat is found in clay and clay-loam soils, usually in areas of sparse vegetation. The first specimens of *D. elator* were captured around burrows excavated at the bases of mesquite trees, but disturbed areas along fence rows, pasture roads, brush piles, and eroded areas are also utilized as burrowing sites. Burrows have also been observed around livestock corrals, barns, grain storage facilities, and other man-made structures. The burrows are constructed in slightly elevated areas and contain at least six interwoven tunnels with multiple outside entrances. The tunnels average about 45 cm in depth and are 5–12.5 cm in diameter. Burrows contain a nest chamber and food storage tunnels.

Dipodomys elator has been observed foraging in dense stands of grasses, usually in areas adjacent to mesquite pasture land with short grass cover. The adult diet consists of a variety of seeds from both wild and cultivated plants, cut stems and pieces of grass, leaves and fruits of selected forbs, and a few insects.

Other mammals often found associated with the Texas kangaroo rat include Virginia opossums, least shrews, two species of rabbits, thirteen-lined ground squirrels, plains pocket gophers, two species of pocket mice, plains harvest mice, two species of deer mice, hispid cotton rats, southern plains woodrats, house mice, coyotes, badgers, striped skunks, and armadillos. Known predators of *D. elator* include barn owls, coyotes, bobcats, and domestic cats.

No fossils of *D. elator* have been discovered. *J. R. Goetze and C. Jones*

Dipodomys elator

Size
Males are significantly larger than females in most cranial measurements.
Total length: 260–345 (302.5) mm
Length of tail: 161–205 (183) mm
Weight:: 65–90 g

Identification
Distinguished from *Dipodomys ordii,* the only species of kangaroo rat that shares its range, by the presence of a terminal white tuft on its tail, as opposed to a dark tail tuft on *D. ordii.* The Texas kangaroo rat is larger than Ord's kangaroo rat and the two species are ecologically separated throughout their ranges.

Other Common Names
Loring's kangaroo rat

Status
Uncommon, limited. Listed as Category Two by the U.S. Fish and Wildlife Service (more information is needed to determine its status) and as threatened by the Texas Department of Parks and Wildlife.

References
Mammalian Species 232; Genoways and Brown, 1993; Stangl et al., 1992

Big-eared kangaroo rat | *Dipodomys elephantinus*

The big-eared kangaroo rat occurs only in the southern part of the Gabilan Range, in San Benito and Monterey counties, California, from the vicinity of the Pinnacles to near Hernandez. No fossils of *D. elephantinus* are known.

Like other kangaroo rats, big-eared kangaroo rats have small forefeet and enlarged hind feet. The tail is long, crested, about 1.5 times the length of the head and body, and the ventral stripe on the distal half of the tail is narrower than the lateral white stripes. The upperparts are cinnamon, the ears are mostly brownish, and the underparts are white.

Young are born during the spring and summer months. The gestation period is about 30 days and litter size is about two. Young are born pink and helpless, but develop rapidly. Juveniles are grayer than adults, especially on the back.

Big-eared kangaroo rats occur on chaparral-covered slopes, where they forage at night. Food items are gathered with the forefeet and eaten or placed into the external fur-lined cheek pouches. Locomotion primarily is accomplished by hopping on the hind feet. In much of its range, this species occurs only under dense vegetation, but it occupies open habitats near Hernandez. Its occurrence in open habitats appears to coincide with the absence of other species of kangaroo rats. Where

Dipodomys elephantinus

D. elephantinus occurs with *D. heermanni,* the former occupies densely vegetated habitat and the latter occupies the more open habitat.

Other mammals occurring in the same habitat include cottontails, California pocket mice, California mice, woodrats, coyotes, foxes, and mule deer. Predators include owls, coyotes, and foxes. Parasites include protozoans, chiggers, and ticks.

The International Union for Conservation of Nature and Natural Resources has listed the big-eared kangaroo rat as a rare species, because its habitat is at risk from repeated brush fires and increasing human use. *T. L. Best*

Size

Males are slightly larger than females.

Total length: 310–336 (326) mm (males); 305–330 (323) mm (females)

Length of tail: 197 mm (males); 193 mm (females)

Weight: 79–91 (85) g

Identification

Dipodomys elephantinus is moderately dark in color, has the longest ears of any kangaroo rat (19 millimeters), and is one of the largest kangaroo rats in California; only desert and giant kangaroo rats, which occur in southern and eastern California, are larger. *D. heermanni* and *D. venustus* occur in the same area as *D. elephantinus.* From *D. heermanni, D. elephantinus* differs in larger size, larger ears, and darker coloration. *D. elephantinus* is paler and less conspicuously marked than *D. venustus.*

Other Common Names

Elephant-eared kangaroo rat

Status

Rare

References

Mammalian Species 255; Grinnell, 1922

Heermann's kangaroo rat | *Dipodomys heermanni*

Heermann's kangaroo rat is distributed across a wide range of habitats in California, from Lower and Upper Sonoran life zones to the Transition zone, and from the foothills of the Sierra Nevada and Tehachapi mountains to the Coastal zone near Berkeley, Morro Bay, and Pt. Concepción. Some authors have speculated that the comparatively broad habitat tolerances of this species may be correlated with relatively high levels of genetic variation.

Although a proficient burrower, this species frequently uses tunnels excavated by ground squirrels *(Spermophilus).* The extent of burrowing depends to some degree on the structure of the soil; in areas with fine, deep soils, burrows may exceed 10 m in length, are 15 to 50 cm beneath the surface, and possess numerous loops and side branches. Where soils are sandier and looser, burrows are correspondingly shorter and simpler. Burrow entrances are of two types. Main entrances are usually

Dipodomys heermanni

situated beneath bushes or boulders, and descend gradually. Other, narrower tunnels rise almost vertically to the surface. The animals first appear at night at the entrances of these vertical tunnels, before exiting via the main entrances. Dust bathing is important to all kangaroo rats, and most burrows of *D. heermanni* have at least one place nearby for this activity. They generally bathe after foraging.

Like most kangaroo rats, this species is solitary, but it evidently is not strongly territorial. Home ranges vary in size, and local populations fluctuate yearly, usually between 2 and about 30 animals per hectare. The animals spend up to 23 hours per day within their burrows, but exit soon after dark for a foraging bout that lasts about 40 minutes. They often return to their burrows for about 4 hours, and then return to the surface for foraging bouts of varying lengths.

Seeds are the most nutritionally important part of the diet of these animals, although green vegetation is important as well, especially in winter and spring. Most seeds are carried to the burrow, but succulent vegetation is eaten outside the burrow. A large percentage of the plant species growing near the burrow is utilized. Unlike some species of kangaroo rat, *D. heermanni* is not capable of surviving without free water. The animals apparently meet their daily water requirement with water in their food or from dew.

In captivity, the estrous cycle lasts about 14–17 days in this species. In the wild, breeding takes place from February to October, peaking in April. Litter sizes average 2 to 3 young, which weigh 3.4 to 3.9 grams. Fine hairs begin to appear on the third day, and the eyes open about day 14. Weaning begins by about day 17, and by day 40 the young are digging small pits with their forefeet. By two months they dig tunnels to 15–20 cm long. Adult weight is obtained by 10 to 16 weeks, and adult pelage by 17 to 20 weeks. *D. A. Kelt*

Size

Males are slightly larger than females.
Total length: 250–313 mm (300.4 mm, males; 295.1 mm, females)
Length of tail: 160–200 mm (178.8 mm, males; 175.6 mm, females)
Weight: 70–80 g

Identification

This is a medium-large kangaroo rat with a relatively broad face. Its ear pinnae and auditory bullae are of moderate size. It has five, rather than four, toes on the hind foot. *D. heermanni* may occur with four other kangaroo rats. It can be distinguished from *D. venustus* and *D. elephantinus* by its smaller ears (about

12–15 mm versus 15–18 mm); additionally, *D. elephantinus* is much larger than *D. heermanni*. *D. ingens*, the giant kangaroo rat, is also much larger, usually weighing 120–180 g, and is readily distinguished from *D. heermanni* on body size alone. The fourth sympatric species, *D. nitratoides*, is smaller than *D. heermanni* and has only four toes on the hind foot. Two other species deserve comment: *D. californicus*, which occurs north of *D. heermanni*, has four hind toes. *D. agilis* occus south of *D. heermanni* and has a narrower face, somewhat smaller hind feet, and larger ears than *D. heermanni*.

Other Common Names

Morro Bay kangaroo rat, Tulare kangaroo rat

Status

One subspecies, the Morro Bay kangaroo rat, *Dipodomys heermanni morroensis,* is listed as endangered by the U.S. government, the state of California, and the International Union for Conservation of Nature and Natural Resources.

Subspecies

Dipodomys heermanni arenae, coastal ranges in San Louis Obispo and Santa Barbara counties, California, from near Oceano south to the Santa Inez River

Dipodomys heermanni berkeleyensis, hills and valleys east of San Francisco Bay, in Alameda and Contra Costa counties, California

Dipodomys heermanni dixoni, grassland and savanna habitat on the eastern edge of the San Joaquin Valley, in Merced and Stanislaus counties, California

Dipodomys heermanni goldmani, from the Coast near Monterey Bay northeast to San Jose, Santa Clara County, and south in the Salinas Valley to near Soledad, Monterey County, California

Dipodomys heermanni heermani, grassland and savanna communities in the northeastern San Joaquin Valley, from Amador County south to Mariposa County, California.

Dipodomys heermanni jolonensis, Lower Sonoran life zone in the Salinas Valley from near Peachtree and San Lucas, Monterey County, south to at least Creston, San Luis Obispo County, California

Dipodomys heermanni morroensis, sandy soils along Morro Bay, San Luis Obispo County, California

Dipodomys heermanni swarthi, southwestern margin of the San Joaquin Valley, Kern County, west to the Carrizo Plain, San Louis Obispo County and the upper Cuyama Valley, Santa Barbara County, California

Dipodomys heermanni tularensis, floor of the San Joaquin Valley from near Tracy, San Joaquin County, south and southwest to the foothills of the Tehachapi and Temblor ranges, Kern County, California

References

Mammalian Species 323; Best, 1993; Grinnell, 1922; Tappe, 1941; Williams et al., 1993

Giant kangaroo rat | *Dipodomys ingens*

Giant kangaroo rats are curious, bold, and assertive inhabitants of the most arid southwestern edge of central California's San Joaquin Valley and adjacent valleys and plateaus of the Inner Coastal ranges. They are found from elevations of about 90 to 885 meters, though today most extant habitat lies at elevations above 200 meters. Few colonies are located above 760 meters. Giant kangaroo rats mainly inhabit sandy-loam soils located on level and gently sloping ground vegetated with annual grasses and forbs and widely scattered desert shrubs. Extant habitat has been fragmented, mostly by irrigated croplands, into six major geographic units, which in turn have been broken into dozens of smaller colonies by agricultural and petroleum development. Fossil giant kangaroo rats are known from late Pleistocene (38,000 years before present) brea deposits in an area they still inhabit.

Though they often emerge from their burrows in the twilight hours around sunset, and less frequently in the daytime, giant kangaroo rats are mainly active at night. Except when harvesting seeds at the end of the growing season of herbaceous plants, they are out of their burrows for only about 15 minutes per night during a 1.8-hour period starting near sunset.

Giant kangaroo rats are inveterate diggers, frequently remodeling their burrows, closing old entrances and creating new ones. They live solitary lives within their shallow burrows, which average less than 30 centimeters in depth and have branching side tunnels that typically do not reconnect. Besides an enlarged chamber for nesting, which may or may not contain nesting material such as plant fibers and animal hairs, there are several enlarged chambers where seeds are stored. There may be up to 24 of these larders in an individual's burrow, some empty or containing seed hulls and others each containing 1–9 liters of seeds, mostly peppergrass *(Lepidium),* filaree *(Erodium cicutarium),* Arabian grass *(Schismus arabicus),* and brome grasses *(Bromus).* As herbaceous plants ripen, giant kangaroo rats cut the seed heads and place them either in shallow, thimble-shaped pits arranged in a honeycomb pattern and covered with dirt after they are filled or in densely compacted piles on the surface. Surface piles are sometimes enormous for such a small animal. In one study, a stack was found that measured 1.2 by 1.8 meters and was 10 centimeters deep; in another, stacks averaged 29 liters, and ranged from about 2.5 to 53.2 liters. The stacked seedheads cure in the sun for about 4–6 weeks before being moved to larders in the burrows. Besides seeds, giant kangaroo rats eat small amounts of green foliage such as leaves of clover *(Trifolium depauperatum)* and filaree, and insects.

Long-term occupancy of a site by giant kangaroo rats results in a mounded topography, with burrow systems located on mounds a few to several centimeters above the intervening ground. The mound is the center of the individual's territory, which is tiny compared to those of most kangaroo rats and other small mammals, averaging about 0.04 hectares. These precincts of individual kangaroo rats support lusher, greener vegetation that is richer in nitrogen than are the herbaceous plants on surrounding ground. The plants on precincts are 3–5 times more productive than the surrounding plants, and the species composition differs, consisting mostly of plants with larger seeds favored by the kangaroo rats. Following harvest of the seed heads, and after the annual vegetation dies, the kangaroo rat clears the plant litter from its precinct, creating a barren landscape that contrasts with surrounding, vegetated ground.

The occupant of a precinct and its granaries vigorously defends them against all intruders. A giant kangaroo rat produces long, rapid drumming sounds by striking its huge hind feet alternately on the ground while standing on its hind feet. Presumably, this is one aspect of their territoriality. Drumming in the burrows and on the surface is greatest in late spring and summer during and after seed harvest. During the day, interloping birds and antelope squirrels *(Ammospermophilus nelsoni)* bent on stealing from the surface caches are aggressively chased from the precinct. The giant kangaroo rat emerges from its burrow through a vertical shaft, and, with its boldly black-and-white-striped tail held stiffly curved upward, runs at top speed at the intruder. At the boundary of its territory it reverses direction, and dives down the shaft at full speed, its long, upward-projecting tail being the last to disappear.

The better habitats for giant kangaroo rats are shared with few or no other small nocturnal mammals. The San Joaquin antelope squirrel is the only other common mammal. During the day, these ground squirrels enter giant kangaroo rat burrows, usually reappearing shortly. Presumably they are using the shallow portions of tunnels not plugged at the surface to shelter from heat and predators. Occasionally, the occupant of a burrow emerges and chases off the antelope squirrel.

Giant kangaroo rats have major impacts on their communities. They increase and enrich plant productivity. They are the base of the food chain for most predatory vertebrates. Their burrows provide shelter for the endangered blunt-nosed leopard lizard *(Gambelia sila)*, the threatened antelope squirrel, and other animals, and create favorable microhabitats for two endangered plants, *Lembertia congdoni* and *Caulanthus californicus.* When shrubs such as saltbushes *(Atriplex)* and snakeweed

Dipodomys ingens

(Gutierrezia) sprout during rare, heavy, late-spring rains, giant kangaroo rats gnaw through the stems, eventually eradicating most or all shrubs on their precincts and surrounding ground.

Most females enter estrus in the cool, wet winter in central California, in mid or late December or January. When population density is high and most precincts are occupied, adult females may have only a single litter of from 1–4 young. Under these circumstances, young-of-the-year do not breed. During years of drought and low or no seed production, females breed only once or not at all. During years with a prolonged wet season or where population density is low and there are many vacant precincts, adult females may have 2–3 litters and young-of-the-year females may begin breeding when they are about 12–13 weeks old. The gestation period is about 32 days. The young appear on the surface when they weigh about 50–70 or more grams and are presumably about 6.5 to 8.5 weeks old. Severe drought results in population decline, mainly by reduction or cessation of reproduction, whereas torrential rainfall over several days results in great, rapid population decline, presumably by drowning, death from wetting and hypothermia, and other factors related to too much moisture. *D. F. Williams*

Size
Total length: 312–347 (333.2) mm (males);
 323–348 (328.9) mm (females)
Length of tail: 157–197 (185.5) mm (males);
 179–194 (182.9) mm (females)
Weight: 93–180 (138) g (males); 101–195 (132) g
 (females)

Identification
Of the species of kangaroo rats sharing its geographic range, *D. ingens* is distinguished from *Dipodomys heermanni* by longer hind feet, a wider head, and greater mass; *D. nitratoides* is much smaller in all characters and has four instead of five toes on the hind feet.

Status
Endangered, United States and California

References
Mammalian Species 377; Braun, 1985; Grinnell, 1932; Williams, 1992

Merriam's kangaroo rat | *Dipodomys merriami*

Merriam's kangaroo rat uses a broader range of habitats than some other species of *Dipodomys*. It can be found in habitats that consist of sandy soils, clays, gravel, or rocks. Where *D. merriami* occurs with other species of kangaroo rats that prefer sand, it usually inhabits the harder, rockier substrates. The burrows of *D. merriami* usually are simple in structure and consist of rather shallow systems with openings near the bases of shrubs. Like other kangaroo rats, *D. merriami* is active at night and uses its burrows as a daytime refuge and for rearing young. Merriam's kangaroo rat possesses a number of morphological, physiological, and behavioral adaptations to conserve water loss, and it can survive without drinking water. This species is not social. Adults are solitary except for mating and during the time females raise young. Breeding occurs from February through May. Litter size ranges from one to four. Both sexes have been observed to mate with more than one partner.

Merriam's kangaroo rat is relatively small, four-toed, relatively slender footed, and usually buff-colored. Its tail is much longer than the head and body, ending with a dusky to dark tuft at the tip. The body has dorsal and ventral dusky stripes, and the underparts are white. *D. S. Rogers*

Dipodomys merriami

Size
Males are larger than females.
Total length: 195–282 (247) mm
Length of tail: 120–182 (146) mm
Weight: 33.2–53.1 g

Identification
D. merriami is distinguished from some species of *Dipodomys* by the presence of only four toes. With the exception of *D. nitritoides,* Merriam's kangaroo rat can be distinguished from other four-toed species by their relatively larger size and white-tufted tails. Merriam's kangaroo rat does not co-occur with *D. nitritoides,* but it is generally larger in size and possesses a longer and wider rostrum.

Status
Common

Subspecies
Dipodomys merriami ambiguus, western New Mexico, western Texas, southern and eastern Chihuahua, northeastern Durango, southern Coahuila, and central Nuevo Leon
Dipodomys merriami annulus, central Baja California
Dipodomys merriami arenivagus, south-central California and northern Baja California
Dipodomys merriami atronasus, central Durango, southeastern Coahuila, southeastern Aguascalientes, southwestern San Luis Potosi, southwestern Tamaulipas
Dipodomys merriami brunensis, south-central Baja California
Dipodomys merriami collinus, south-central California
Dipodomys merriami frenatus, southwestern Utah and northwestern Arizona

Dipodomys merriami insularis, San Jose Island, Baja California
Dipodomys merriami margaritae, Santa Margarita Island, Baja California
Dipodomys merriami mayensis, southern Sonora and northern Sinaloa
Dipodomys merriami melanurus, southern Baja California
Dipodomys merriami merriami, western and southern Nevada, eastern and southern California, southeastern Utah, western and southern Arizona, western and central Sonora
Dipodomys merriami mitchelli, Tiburon Island, Sonora
Dipodomys merriami olivaceus, southeastern Arizona, northeastern Sonora, northwestern Chihuahua, southwestern New Mexico

Dipodomys merriami parvus, southern California
Dipodomys merriami quintinensis, northern
Baja California

Dipodomys merriami trinidadensis, southern
California and northern Baja California
Dipodomys merriami vulcani, northwestern
Arizona

References
Anderson, 1972; Davis and Schmidly, 1994;
Genoways and Brown, 1993; Schmidly, 1977

Chisel-toothed kangaroo rat | *Dipodomys microps*

Like other kangaroo rats, the chisel-toothed kangaroo rat is adapted to desert regions of southwestern North America. It is one of the few mammals that can subsist on the salty leaves of the desert shadscale or saltbush, *Atriplex confertifolia.* This kangaroo rat is distinctive in its ability to use its specially flattened lower incisors to peel the salty epidermal skin from each saltbush leaf and thereby gain access to the nutrient-rich, water-filled layers of cells underneath. The diet of *Dipodomys microps* is unusual among kangaroo rats in its higher proportion of leaves to seeds. The high water content of the diet permits the chisel-toothed kangaroo rat to spend less energy on water conservation and more energy on reproduction. Because it can eat perennial shrubs, it is able to reproduce when climatic factors prevent the growth of annual herbs on which other kangaroo rats depend. In addition, coprophagy—the ingestion of feces—allows these kangaroo rats to assimilate up to 90 percent of the food they eat. However, when leaves are not available, seeds form a predominant part of the diet, physiological mechanisms for water conservation (such as urine concentra-

tion) are increased, and reproduction is more similar to other kangaroo rats.

These attractive, moustached animals have the large eyes, fur-lined cheek pouches, large hind feet, long, tufted, bicolored tail, and white racing stripe along the flank typical of all kangaroo rats. The long hind limbs resemble those of Australian kangaroos and allow the animal to jump quickly away from predators such as foxes, coyotes, owls, and snakes. These kangaroo rats can attain maximum speeds of 21 km per hour. The tail tuft probably increases the maneuverability and balance of the animals during jumps, and the long facial whiskers, which maintain contact with the ground even while the animal is in midair, probably aid in orientation during jumping. Unlike other kangaroo rats, this acrobat often climbs into and around shrubbery to gather foliage.

Chisel-toothed kangaroo rats are common, nocturnal inhabitants of the arid Great Basin between the Sierra and the Rocky mountains in the western United States. The 13 subspecies range from southern Idaho and Oregon through Nevada and western Utah to northern Arizona and southeastern California. This basin, which was formed from the prehistoric Lake Bonneville, has bestowed upon *D. microps* another of its common names, the Great Basin kangaroo rat. Diversification and speciation of this kangaroo rat were probably influenced by the recession and filling of the Pleistocene lake. Even today, *D. microps* can move quickly into territory previously underwater once the land is colonized by shrubs.

Dipodomys microps is most abundant in desert valleys dominated by saltbush, as well as in upland desert areas with blackbush *(Coleogyne ramosissima),* and is less common in communities with an understory of perennial grasses. Individual home ranges vary from 4 to 5 hectares and are larger for males. Density varies from 0.2 to 34 animals per hectare and depends on habitat and time of year. Although a few animals live on sand dunes, the Great Basin kangaroo rat prefers rocky slopes or gravelly substrates to facilitate digging its underground burrows. The vegetation used to line the nest chamber often weighs as much as, or more than, the animal itself, especially in winter.

Burrow entrances may be scattered or clumped into mounds and are located near the base of shrubs, where the soil is loose. The mounds often are 30 to 60 cm high and may be 2–4 m in

Dipodomys microps

diameter, with several openings. The tunnels themselves are about 6 to 8 cm wide and can reach 175 cm below the surface, although most extend about 30 cm below ground. The deepest tunnels often lead to winter nest chambers. Leaves and seeds are commonly cached within burrows. These storage areas are sometimes pilfered by grasshopper mice and other kangaroo rats. Although a burrow system may have up to 18 side branches and multiple nest or food-caching chambers, only one adult animal occupies it.

Underground, *D. microps* is active all year and around the clock. Aboveground, the chisel-toothed kangaroo rat is also active year-round, but terrestrial activities, such as sandbathing, social interactions, foraging, and caching, usually occur only in the first few hours after sunset and are not influenced by moonlight.

Kangaroo rats use auditory communication in the form of foot drumming, which vibrates messages through the soil. Olfactory information from secretions from glands on the back of the animal may be present at commonly used sandbathing sites.

Females can produce more than one litter of up to 4 young each year under exceptionally good environmental conditions, but usually they give birth to only one litter of two young 31 to 32 days after mating. Each blind and naked neonate weighs about 4 g and is weaned within 21 to 28 days of birth, when it weighs about 21 g. The appearance of young aboveground often coincides with a peak in the new growth and water content of the kangaroo rat's preferred food, saltbush. Females can reproduce in the year of their birth, but males do not. Estrus occurs at 12-day intervals and pregnant females can be found from February to June in some parts of the range. However, males produce sperm from October to June. During nonreproductive periods, the female's clitoris may enlarge and resemble a phallus, making identification of the sexes difficult. *V. Hayssen*

Size
Males are 2–8 percent larger than females.
Total length: 245–295 (270) mm
Length of tail: 135–175 (158) mm
Weight: 40–70 (55) g

Identification
Chisel-shaped lower incisors distinguish *D. microps* from all other kangaroo rats. *D. microps* shares its range with two other five-toed kangaroo rats, *D. panamintinus* and *D. ordii*. *D. microps* has a hind foot shorter than 44 mm in the part of its range shared with *D. panamintinus* (length of hind foot: 42–48 mm). *D. microps* differs from *D. ordii* in having a more prominent face-mask, darker tail-stripes, and a metallic gray pelage.

Other Common Names
Great Basin kangaroo rat, small-faced kangaroo rat, Inyo pocket rat

Status
Common

Subspecies
Dipodomys microps alfredi, Gunnison Island, Great Salt Lake, Utah
Dipodomys microps aquilonius, northwestern Nevada
Dipodomys microps bonnevillei, northwestern Utah, northeastern Nevada

Dipodomys microps celsus (*D. m. woodburyi* is a synonym), northwestern Arizona, southwestern Utah
Dipodomys microps centralis, eastern and central Nevada
Dipodomys microps idahoensis, southwestern Idaho
Dipodomys microps leucotis, north-central Arizona
Dipodomys microps levipe, southeastern California
Dipodomys microps microps, southeastern California
Dipodomys microps occidentalis, western and southern Nevada
Dipodomys microps preblei, southeastern Oregon, northwestern Nevada
Dipodomys microps russeolus, Dolphin Island, Great Salt Lake, Utah
Dipodomys microps subtenuis, Carrington Island, Great Salt Lake, Utah, northwestern Utah

References
Mammalian Species 389

Fresno kangaroo rat | *Dipodomys nitratoides*

Dipodomys nitratoides occurs at elevations of about 50–800 meters in the San Joaquin and adjacent valleys of California. Its range has been greatly reduced by destruction of its natural habitat.

The Fresno kangaroo rat is nocturnal, does not hibernate, and is solitary except during estrus. When two or more individuals are placed together, fighting ensues. They stand on their hind feet, sniff, leap, and attempt to kick and bite each other. Responses between males and females change cyclically as the female passes through estrus. Nonvocal communication includes tooth-chattering and foot-drumming. Vocalizations include growls, squeals, and low grunts.

Although kangaroo rats are good swimmers, *D. nitratoides* is notably averse to getting wet. When Fresno kangaroo rats get wet, they immediately rub and roll in a dusty place to dry themselves. The tail is groomed by rapidly running it through the front paws as they are held against the mouth.

The Fresno kangaroo rat is one of the smallest members of the genus. The upperparts are yellowish-brown and the underparts are white. There is little difference in pelage shade between juveniles and adults, but there is a difference in the texture of the coat; the pelage of juveniles is finer than that of adults. Adults molt throughout the year, but most molt from July through October. The new coat can be distinguished by its darker color. The Fresno kangaroo rat is adapted for bipedal locomotion; the tail, which helps it balance, is 1.48 times the length of the head and body.

The breeding season primarily is from December to August. The gestation period is 32 days, average litter size is 2.3 (usu-

Dipodomys nitratoides

ally two), and average mass at birth is 4.0 g. On the day preceding the birth of a litter, the female generally is quite active. Both nest building and food caching are carried on to great lengths. These activities remain intense for 1–2 days after parturition. In caring for the young, the female crouches over them, keeping her back arched to prevent crushing them. This allows the young to nurse while they are kept warm. The mother retrieves young that have wandered out of the nest by picking them up by a fold of skin with her incisors. The young are well developed at birth, except for the teeth. Lower incisors appear at 4 days and upper incisors appear at 7 days. Adult mass is attained in 2.5–3 months. Eyes open at 10–11 days, ears open at 8–9 days, and pelage is complete when the young are 6–10 days old. There is active grooming among siblings at 14 days, the weaning period is 21–24 days, and young first leave the burrow at about 14–18 days.

Generally, *D. nitratoides* inhabits arid, often strongly alkaline, plains sparsely clothed with grass and in places saltbush. Typical vegetation includes grasses and herbs, with Mormon tea in the Panoche Valley being replaced in the San Joaquin Valley by more xerophylic shrubs.

Burrows usually are at the base of some low bush, and runways, worn in the grass, often lead from a burrow to neighboring clumps of vegetation. Burrow entrances are 6–8 centimeters in diameter and occur in a variety of soil conditions. The area occupied by a burrow system varies from about 2 by 2 meters to 3.5 by 3.5 meters. Surface openings are either slanting or vertical and vary in number. Openings in use may show no newly excavated soil for long periods of time. When digging, *D. nitratoides* stands firmly on its hind legs, which are spread well apart, and scratches rapidly with the front feet. The soil is pushed back under the body and then sent flying backwards with several strong kicks of the hind legs. As the burrow becomes deeper, the soil accumulates and gets in the way. When this happens, the animal turns around, comes out of the opening, and pushes the soil a little with the front feet. Then it turns and starts down the burrow, kicking backward to scatter soil away from the opening. Each trip moves the soil farther away and in a different direction, resulting in a more or less fan-shaped distribution of loose soil around the burrow opening.

The Fresno kangaroo rat is a granivore. It feeds on seeds of annuals and shrubs such as saltbush. In the spring, early rains cause the growth of grasses and herbs that form a food source. The dampness of the soil may influence the locus and amount of food caching: Fresno kangaroo rats store food in small pit caches made in the walls of the burrow system, where seeds can be kept dry enough to keep them from sprouting or molding.

Mammals occurring in the same habitat as *D. nitratoides* include desert cottontails, black-tailed jackrabbits, California ground squirrels, San Joaquin antelope squirrels, pocket gophers, giant kangaroo rats, California pocket mice, San Joaquin pocket mice, southern grasshopper mice, deer mice, and western harvest mice. Predators include rattlesnakes, barn owls, bobcats, badgers, long-tailed weasels, coyotes, and kit foxes. Ectoparasites include chiggers, ticks, and fleas. Internal parasites include protozoans and cestodes.

Much of the habitat of *D. nitratoides* has been destroyed by farming activities. This species is not able to maintain its burrow systems and live in areas under irrigation and cultivation.
T. L. Best

Size
Males are slightly larger than females.
Total length: 215–253 (240) mm (males);
   211–250 (235) mm (females)
Length of tail: 141 mm (males); 137 mm
   (females)
Weight: 44 (40–53) g

Identification
Several other species of kangaroo rats occur within or near the range of *D. nitratoides*. *D. merriami* is not sympatric, but is similar morphologically. Its white lateral tail stripes are always broader than the dark dorsal one,

and the dark ventral tail stripe is narrower or almost lacking, whereas in *D. nitratoides* the dark dorsal and ventral tail stripes are broader than the white lateral tail stripes. *D. ingens*, *D. panamintinus*, *D. heermanni*, and *D. microps* have five toes on the hind foot instead of four as in *D. nitratoides*; they also are much larger.

Other Common Names
San Joaquin kangaroo rat

Status
Endangered

Subspecies
Dipodomys nitratoides brevinasus, western San
   Joaquin and adjacent valleys, California
Dipodomys nitratoides exilis, northeastern San
   Joaquin and adjacent valleys, California
Dipodomys nitratoides nitratoides, eastern and
   southeastern San Joaquin and adjacent
   valleys, California

References
Mammalian Species 381; Culbertson, 1946

Ord's kangaroo rat | *Dipodomys ordii*

Ord's kangaroo rat occurs from southern Alberta and Saskatchewan to southern Hidalgo, Mexico, and from central Oregon and eastern California to central Kansas and Oklahoma. Fossils have been recorded from Colorado, Idaho, Kansas, New Mexico, South Dakota, and Texas.

Dipodomys ordii is nocturnal and active all year. Males generally are more abundant and active than females. Activity increases under cloud cover, particularly in winter, decreases during inclement weather, on clear nights, or under moonlight, and ceases when temperatures are below −11° C or when snow cover is greater than 40 percent. In moonlight, there is a shift in use of microhabitat from more open areas to areas with greater cover. Occasionally, this species is active out of the burrow during the daylight hours. Intraspecific aggression is rare, but during confrontations, a tooth-chattering sound is emitted; the loser retreats making faint chuckling noises and squeaky snorts.

This is a medium-sized, relatively short-tailed, five-toed species with disproportionately long hind legs and feet, an adaptation for hopping. The front feet are used to manipulate food and for burrowing. The dorsal pelage is brownish, reddish, or blackish, depending on the subspecies, and the entire ventral surface is white. Grooming the pelage to remove excess body oil and parasites is accomplished by sliding and rolling in sand

and dust. The underparts and sides are dusted by sliding over the sand, propelled by strong thrusts of the hind legs. The feet and tail receive careful grooming. *D. ordii* drinks by scooping water into the mouth with the forefeet, and it is an excellent swimmer.

The timing of reproduction varies among populations, from one or two distinct breeding seasons to some reproductive activity throughout the year. Overall, the length of the breeding season is about 7 months of the year. Most males are capable of reproduction all year; the reproductive cycle, timing, and length of the breeding season is regulated by the female's cycle, which is strongly affected by the environment. The onset of reproductive activity is correlated with rainfall and the appearance of green vegetation, and may be related to energetic costs of gestation and care of offspring. Gestation is 28–32 days, and litter size is one to six (average is 3.5). There may be two litters a year. In captivity, the maximum number of litters per year was five, the maximum number of young per year was 20, the maximum number of litters per lifetime was nine, and the maximum number of young per lifetime was 38. Sexual maturity is reached at about 83 days. The usual lifespan is about one year, but in captivity, this species can live more than 7 years.

Ord's kangaroo rat responds to vocalizations made by newborns that are in the frequency range corresponding to that used by adults in detection and avoidance of predators. Vocalizations by newborns become variable and infrequent at 14 days of age, which coincides with a marked increase in physical activity, thermoregulatory ability, and solid food intake. When born prematurely or ill, neonates cannot vocalize and are ignored or eaten by the mother.

Dipodomys ordii lives in a variety of vegetation types, but all habitats are associated with fine-textured, sandy soils. Major habitat types include semi-arid grasslands, mixed-grasslands, and scrublands (including pinon-juniper woodlands). Dominant plants of these habitats may include junipers, sage brush, saltbush, broomweed, grasses, yuccas, and mesquites. Ord's kangaroo rat is primarily a seed-eater. Throughout its range a wide variety of food is consumed; the most common are seeds of grasses and forbs, followed by green vegetation, other vegetative material, and occasionally animal material (e.g., beetles and other arthropods).

The size of a home range is generally 0.43–1.36 hectares. Depending upon locality and suitability of habitat, population density may be 10–50 kangaroo rats per hectare. Density is correlated with rainfall and primary plant productivity.

In New Mexico, Ord's kangaroo rat is sympatric with Merriam's kangaroo rat and the silky pocket mouse. Ord's kangaroo rats occur in the grass habitat, Merriam's kangaroo rats occupy stands of creosotebush, and silky pocket mice are found

Dipodomys ordii

in both habitats. In Nevada, spatial overlap between Ord's and chisel-toothed kangaroo rats occurs only in summer, between Ord's and Panamint kangaroo rats in winter, spring, and summer, and between Ord's and Merriam's kangaroo rats in all seasons.

Depending upon locality, species associated with Ord's kangaroo rat may include cottontails, jackrabbits, chipmunks, ground squirrels, antelope squirrels, pocket gophers, kangaroo rats, kangaroo mice, pocket mice, grasshopper mice, deer mice, white-footed mice, pinyon mice, cactus mice, pygmy mice, woodrats, harvest mice, cotton rats, voles, deer, and pronghorns. Predators include barn, great-horned, long-eared, and burrowing owls, badgers, long-tailed weasels, kit and red foxes, and coyotes. Endoparasites include protozoans, cestodes, and nematodes. Ectoparasites include chiggers, mites, ticks, lice, and fleas. *T. L. Best*

Size
Males are slightly larger than females.
Total length: 210–365 (243) mm (males);
    208–360 (242) mm (females)
Length of tail: 129 mm (males); 127 mm
    (females)
Weight: 52 g

Identification
The range of *D. ordii* overlaps with that of several other species of kangaroo rats. Compared with *D. microps*, *D. ordii* has lower incisors that are awl-shaped instead of chisel-shaped. Where

sympatric with *D. panamintinus,* the length of the hind foot of *D. ordii* is more than 44 millimeters; the foot of *D. panamintinus* is shorter. *D. ordii* has a longer, bushier, and slightly more crested tail than *D. compactus,* and its pelage is longer, silkier, and has a brownish hue, rather than the orange cast of *D. compactus.* All additional *Dipodomys* that are sympatric with *D. ordii* have four toes on each hind foot instead of five.

Status
Common

Subspecies
Dipodomys ordii attenuatus, western Texas
Dipodomys ordii celeripes, northwestern Utah
    and northeastern Nevada
Dipodomys ordii chapmani, west-central Arizona
Dipodomys ordii cinderensis, southwestern Utah
    and east-central Nevada
Dipodomys ordii cineraceus, northern Utah
Dipodomys ordii columbianus, southern Washington, western Oregon, southern Idaho, northeastern California, and northern Nevada
Dipodomys ordii cupidineus, southwestern Utah
    and northwestern Arizona

Dipodomys ordii durranti, southern Texas and northeastern Mexico

Dipodomys ordii evexus, central Colorado

Dipodomys ordii extractus, northern Chihuahua, Mexico

Dipodomys ordii fetosus, east-central Nevada and west-central Utah

Dipodomys ordii fremonti, south-central Utah

Dipodomys ordii idoneus, north-central Mexico

Dipodomys ordii inaquosus, north-central Nevada

Dipodomys ordii longipes, southeastern Utah, southwestern Colorado, northeastern Arizona, and northwestern New Mexico

Dipodomys ordii luteolus, central Great Plains

Dipodomys ordii marshalli, north-central Utah

Dipodomys ordii medius, eastern New Mexico and western Texas

Dipodomys ordii monoensis, western Nevada and eastern California

Dipodomys ordii montanus, south-central Colorado and north-central New Mexico

Dipodomys ordii nexilis, east-central Utah and west-central Colorado

Dipodomys ordii obscurus, southern Chihuahua, northwestern Coahuila, and northern Durango, Mexico

Dipodomys ordii oklahomae, central Oklahoma

Dipodomys ordii ordii, southeastern Arizona, southern New Mexico, western Texas, and north-central Mexico

Dipodomys ordii pallidus, west-central Utah

Dipodomys ordii palmeri, southern Mexico

Dipodomys ordii panguitchensis, south-central Utah

Dipodomys ordii parvabullatus, Tamaulipas, Mexico

Dipodomys ordii priscus, southwestern Wyoming, northeastern Utah, and northwestern Colorado

Dipodomys ordii pullus, central Chihuahua, Mexico

Dipodomys ordii richardsoni, southeastern Colorado, western Kansas, northeastern New Mexico, northern Texas, and western Oklahoma

Dipodomys ordii sanrafaeli, east-central Utah, west-central Colorado

Dipodomys ordii terrosus, northern Great Plains, south-central Canada

Dipodomys ordii uintensis, northeastern Utah

Dipodomys ordii utahensis, north-central Utah

References

Mammalian Species 353; Garner, 1974

Panamint kangaroo rat | *Dipodomys panamintinus*

Dipodomys panamintinus occurs at elevations from about 1,100 to 2,700 meters in eastern California and western Nevada. No fossils are known.

The Panamint kangaroo rat is a nocturnal, seed-eating rodent that lives on metabolic water. It is active throughout the year, except when there is more than 40 percent snow cover, but its tracks have been found in the snow. Each night, the periods of greatest activity are about 2 hours after sunset and about 6–9 hours after sunset; it is inactive, or its activity level is low, toward sunrise.

This species is solitary except during estrus. Fights occur when two or more animals are closely confined. Fighting is not continuous, but consists of brief, vigorous skirmishes interrupted by periods of withdrawal. The results of aggressive behavior often are fatal. Responses between males and females change cyclically as the female passes through estrus. Males are more involved in sandbathing, digging, and kicking sand on the days preceding or following estrus than on the actual day of estrus. Nonvocal communication includes tooth-chattering and foot-drumming. Vocalizations include low-pitched growls.

Dipodomys panamintinus

When moving slowly, *D. pamintinus* travels by quadrupedal hopping, bipedal hopping, or bipedal walking. When moving rapidly, it uses bipedal hopping; the length of the hop is about the length of the body. When it is frightened, the hopping becomes modified into a series of erratic bipedal leaps. *D. panamintinus* employs sudden and unpredictable alterations in the direction of movement when it is attempting to escape predators, not because of loss of balance and control, but because of its remarkable ability to maintain equilibrium at all times. Panamint kangaroo rats rarely climb vegetation, and they are excellent swimmers. Their large hind feet give them considerable agility in the water.

In early winter, the external, fur-lined cheek pouches often contain many green shoots of grass and only a few seeds, but during drier months, seeds are gathered more often. When foraging, each food item is handled with the forepaws. All han-

dling of objects is done beneath the head, well out of view of the dorsally-positioned eyes. Neither visual nor olfactory cues appear to be of major importance in distinguishing between food or nonfood objects. No objects, including those located directly beneath the nose, are rejected prior to being touched or manipulated. Seeds are hulled prior to being placed into cheek pouches, resulting in a 40 percent more efficient use of the pouches. About nine seeds can be pouched per second.

The Panamint kangaroo rat is medium-sized for the genus. Each of the large hind feet has five toes. The tail is heavily crested and is 1.4 times the length of the head and body. The upperparts are pale brownish and underparts are white. Facial crescents and the end of the nose are blackish, as are the eyelids and the anterior part of the ears; the posterior part of the ears is whitish. The tail has a ventral stripe that may extend to the end of the vertebrae. There is one molt per year, which usually occurs in June or July.

The peak of the breeding season is February or March. The gestation period is 29–30 days, litter size is 3–4, and mass of newborns is 4.5 grams. The young are born in a nest. They are fully furred at 10–14 days of age, their ears open at 12–14 days,

and their eyes open at 17–18 days. The toes are separate at birth, but the cheek pouches are only slight indentations on the lower side of the jaw. They rapidly indent to become functional in about 2–3 weeks. Active grooming begins at 24 days, weaning begins at 27–29 days, the young leave the burrow at 28 days, and sexual activity begins at 24–56 days. Juveniles molt from March through October. Young in juvenile pelage look like adults, but are paler and have shorter hair at the end of the tail.

Panamint kangaroo rats occur in areas where Joshua trees, juniper trees, creosotebushes, yuccas, cacti, and catclaws are common and widely scattered. The soil occupied may be coarse sand, gravelly desert flats, alkaline, or the surface may be impregnated with salts and have a crust. These kangaroo rats avoid cliffs and areas with desert pavement. They occupy holes in small mounds of sand that have accumulated around clumps of brush. One animal may occupy a burrow that has 12 or more tunnels, the mouths of which are connected on the surface by well-defined runways.

There is great variability in size of home range throughout the year; the average is 0.43 hectares. Peaks in size of home range are in February (1.2 hectares) and July (1.0 hectares). Home ranges usually are elliptical in shape, and there is no difference between sexes in size of home ranges. However, in some parts of the range, males may occupy home ranges that have significantly more pinyon pines than do the home ranges occupied by females.

Other mammals associated with Panamint kangaroo rats include white-tailed antelope squirrels, Mohave ground squirrels, pocket mice, kangaroo mice, chisel-toothed, Ord's, and Merriam's kangaroo rats, deer mice, grasshopper mice, harvest mice, and desert woodrats. Internal parasites include protozoans, nematodes, and cestodes. Ectoparasites include chiggers, ticks, and fleas. *T. L. Best*

Size
Males are slightly larger than females.
Total length: 292 mm (males); 288 mm (females)
Length of tail: 172 mm (males); 170 mm (females)
Weight: 72 g

Identification
Several other species of kangaroo rats occur within or near the range of *D. panamintinus.* Compared with *D. merriami,* which has four toes on each hind foot, *D. panamintinus* is larger and has five toes on each hind foot. *D. microps* has flattened incisors that are wider than those of *D. panamintinus. D. ordii* is smaller, its tail is 110–130 percent of the length

of head and body (compared with 140–150 percent for *D. panamintinus*), the white stripe on the tail is as wide as or wider than the ventral dark tail stripe, and the ventral tail stripe never reaches the end of the vertebrae.

Recent Synonyms
Perodipus leucogenys
Perodipus mohavensis
Perodipus panamintinus

Other Common Names
Mojave kangaroo rat

Status
Common

Subspecies
Dipodomys panamintinus argusensis, Argus Mountains, California
Dipodomys panamintinus caudatus, southern Nevada and eastern California
Dipodomys panamintinus leucogenys, western Nevada and eastern California
Dipodomys panamintinus mohavensis, south-central California
Dipodomys panamintinus panamintinus, Panamint Mountains, California

References
Mammalian Species 354; Hall, 1946

Dulzura kangaroo rat | *Dipodomys simulans*

This is the most common kangaroo rat of southern and coastal California. It occupies coastal chaparral and grassland communities from the Los Angeles Basin and San Jacinto Mountains of southern California southward through the mountains and plains of northern Baja California to near Magdalena Bay in southern Baja California, Mexico. It occupies elevations from sea level to more than 2,250 meters. Fossils that may be of this species are known from Newport Bay Mesa and Rancho La Brea in southern California.

The Dulzura kangaroo rat is nocturnal, with a peak of activity near dusk and a second prior to dawn. Occasionally it may also be active during daylight hours. Considerable time is spent grooming, presumably to enhance temperature regulation and reduce the number of ectoparasites. This kangaroo rat is an excellent swimmer. Its large hind feet give it considerable agility in the water. Its gait is a series of short hops, and if hurried it moves rapidly on all four feet. It is quite agile and can make sharp turns to avoid predators.

Dipodomys simulans is intermediate in size for the genus. The hind feet are elongated and well adapted for hopping. The front feet are small and are important in manipulation of food and burrowing. The long tail is bicolored, with a blackish crest and tuft, and there are five toes on each hind foot. The upperparts vary from pale grayish-brown to dark reddish-brown, depending on where in its range it occurs. An external fur-lined cheek pouch is located on each side of the mouth. These cheek pouches are used to carry food from where it is gathered to where it is stored in, or near, the burrow. Along the anterior part of the back, there is a specialized glandular area in the skin; the function of the gland is unknown, but may be related to scent production.

These kangaroo rats generally are larger in the southern part of their geographic range than in the north. In the southern populations, males have longer tails and more fused vertebrae in the pelvic girdle, and females have wider nasal bones, longer forearms, and shorter hind feet.

Breeding may occur during any month of the year, but peaks occur in winter and spring. One litter of two to four young (average is 2.5) is born each year. The young may make squeaking sounds, but adults rarely vocalize. Maternal behavior includes nursing, grooming, and other forms of general maintenance of the young.

The Dulzura kangaroo rat primarily eats seeds, but may eat green vegetation and insects during some months of the year. Its diet varies from season to season, depending upon what seeds and other foods are available. Like most other species of kangaroo rats, Dulzura kangaroo rats probably spend only a few hours outside their burrow each night. Once food items are located, they may be eaten immediately or placed into the cheek pouches and taken back to the burrow. The entrances of burrows often are closed in the daytime.

These kangaroo rats usually occur on gravely or sandy soils on slopes, washes, and open chaparral areas. In some areas, they are restricted to coarse sand in the dry washes; they burrow within and at the edges of these washes. Burrows have an average of three, 6-cm high openings. The average burrow depth is 32 cm; on average, a burrow has seven side branches and two food caches. The longest burrow measured was 276 cm. The size of burrows is correlated with body size in males. The most complex burrows are in the northern part of the Dulzura kangaroo rat's range, where the generally smaller kangaroo rats occur. This region has the lowest temperatures throughout the year and the greatest winter-spring precipitation. Wider, less complex burrows are found in southern Baja California, where larger individuals occur and where there is greatest summer-autumn precipitation and the warmest July and annual mean temperatures. The tendency to build less complex burrows may be related to the difficulty of digging the burrow: the warmer temperatures and greater summer–autumn precipitation may make the soil difficult to excavate, resulting in the construction of longer tunnels but fewer of them. The soil can be excavated more easily in the moister, cooler, northern regions, and perhaps also the denser vegetation there provides more food for storage, necessitating more tunnels.

Populations are relatively stable throughout the year, but are largest in winter and spring. Maximum densities are 45 per

Dipodomys simulans

hectare. Average life span is about 10 months, but Dulzura kangaroo rats may live more than 6 years in captivity.

Species occurring in the same habitat as *D. simulans* include cottontails, black-tailed jackrabbits, California ground squirrels, pocket gophers, California pocket mice, Merriam's and Stephens's kangaroo rats, dusky-footed woodrats, California mice, bobcats, gray foxes, coyotes, and mule deer. Predators include owls, bobcats, foxes, and coyotes. Parasites include protozoans, mites, ticks, and fleas. *T. L. Best*

Size
Males are slightly larger than females.
Total length: 277–302 (284) mm (males);
273–291 (282) mm (females)
Length of tail: 163–181 (170) mm (males);
160–180 (168) mm (females)
Weight: 58–70 (59) g (males); 55–67 (56) g (females)

Identification
The large ears of *D. simulans* distinguish it from all sympatric species except *D. agilis,* which has larger ears. Compared with *D. agilis, D. simulans* is smaller in most characters of the body and skull, the ears and hind feet are shorter, and it has two fewer chromosomes. Compared with *D. merriami,* which has four toes on each hind foot, *D. simulans* has five toes on each hind foot and is larger. Compared with *D. stephensi,* the only other five-toed kangaroo rat that occurs in its range in the United States,

D. simulans has much larger ears.

Recent Synonyms
Dipodomys antiquarius
Dipodomys paralius

Perodipus cabezonae
Perodipus streatori

Other Common Names
San Borja kangaroo rat, Santa Catarina kangaroo rat, Cabezon kangaroo rat

Status
Common

Subspecies
Dipodomys simulans peninsularis, central and southern Baja California, Mexico
Dipodomys simulans simulans, southwestern California and northwestern Baja California, Mexico

References
Genoways and Brown, 1993

Banner-tailed kangaroo rat | *Dipodomys spectabilis*

The banner-tailed kangaroo rat occurs from northeastern Arizona southward to Aguascalientes and San Luis Potosi, Mexico, and from southern Arizona eastward into western Texas. Fossil remains have been found in cave deposits in Arizona, New Mexico, Texas, and Coahuila, Mexico.

Banner-tailed kangaroo rats are active all year, they are nocturnal, they do not hibernate or aestivate, and when the weather is rainy, wet, or cold, they remain in their burrows. Activities are confined to small areas near the large earthen mounds that contain their complex burrow systems. Usually only one individual occupies a burrow system. *D. spectabilis* has good swimming ability, and it sandbathes to scent-mark its territory and to clean its pelage. These kangaroo rats advertise their territories by footdrumming on their earthen mounds, and they use footdrumming as a long-distance warning signal; chasing is used as a closer-distance threat. Usually gentle and timid, these kangaroo rats will fight furiously to defend their burrow mound from invasion by other banner-tailed kangaroo rats.

Banner-tailed kangaroo rats are adapted to locomotion by hopping, with hind legs and feet that are much larger and

longer than the forelegs. Like other kangaroo rats, they have external fur-lined cheek pouches they use for gathering seeds. The tail is long, covered with short hairs on the half nearest the body, and there are long hairs toward the tip. At the end of the tail is a conspicuous white tip that waves in the air as the animal moves; it is the basis for the name of this colorful species.

The body is yellowish-brown above and white underneath in adults, but young are grayish on the back.

Dipodomys spectabilis reproduces year-round, except perhaps in October and November. Onset and termination of reproduction are earlier in northern populations than in southern populations. From one to three litters per year are born after a gestation period of 22–27 days. Neonates weigh about 8 grams and are toothless, hairless, and wrinkled. The eyes and ears are closed, and they show the color pattern of adults in shades of pink. They are weaned at 20–25 days of age. Young males grow faster in mass than young females; age at maturity is 300 days.

Banner-tailed kangaroo rats live in desert grasslands with scattered shrubs such as creosotebushes and mesquites. The mounds of earth that contain the burrow are conspicuous features of the landscape. They ordinarily are constructed in open locations, sometimes in the centers of cleared areas as large as 10 meters in diameter, but many are built under the protection of shrubs. These low, rounded mounds rise to varying heights above the surface of the surrounding soil; usually they are circular and average 4 meters in diameter and 30 centimeters in height. There are three to 12 openings in each mound, each 10–15 centimeters in diameter. Radiating in various directions from some of the openings are well-used runways, some extending 30–50 meters or more to neighboring burrows. In addition to providing protection from the elements and predators, the mounds often contain large caches of grass seeds and other seeds. Deep within the mound, temperature varies less than 5° C year-round.

Although there may be as many as three mounds per hectare, only about two-thirds of the mounds in an area will have evidence of recent activity by kangaroo rats. Of those that appear to be inhabited, 40–95 percent have kangaroo rats inside. It may take months or years for these elaborate mounds to be constructed, but they soon collapse when not maintained. Each new mound begins as a small satellite burrow near an existing mound, which is enlarged into a small raised mound and then into a full-sized mound.

Mounds constructed by banner-tailed kangaroo rats are an important part of the desert-grassland ecosystem. In addition

Dipodomys spectabilis

to meeting the requirements of the kangaroo rat, the mounds also serve as home to a variety of animals including grasshoppers, locusts, crickets, cockroaches, scorpions, black widow spiders, centipedes, amphibians, rattlesnakes, bullsnakes, kingsnakes, many species of lizards, pocket mice, and other small mammals.

Other mammals that occur in the same habitat include antelope and black-tailed jackrabbits, desert and eastern cottontails, round-tailed and spotted ground squirrels, Harris's antelope squirrels, pocket gophers, pocket mice, Ord's and Merriam's kangaroo rats, grasshopper mice, white-footed mice, white-throated and southern plains woodrats, and pronghorns. Predators include coyotes, badgers, long-tailed weasels, kit foxes, great horned owls, and barn owls. Banner-tailed kangaroo rats are resistant to infection by plague. Internal parasites include protozoans and cestodes, and external parasites include a variety of mites, ticks, and fleas. *T. L. Best*

Size
Males are slightly larger than females.
Total length: 315–349 (342) mm (males);
310–345 (338) mm (females)
Length of tail: 185–208 (199) mm (males);
180–205 (196) mm (females)
Weight: 100–132 (126) g (males); 98–130 (120) g (females)

Identification
The banner-tailed kangaroo rat is one of the largest and most spectacularly colored of the

kangaroo rats. The only large species of *Dipodomys* in the United States with which *D. spectabilis* may be sympatric, or is likely to be confused, is *D. deserti*. The ranges of these species approach each other in southern Arizona. *D. spectabilis* can be distinguished by the darker and sharply contrasting dorsal and ventral stripes of the tail, darker body color, and mastoid bones that do not meet behind the parietals of the skull.

Status
Common

Subspecies
Dipodomys spectabilis baileyi, central and eastern New Mexico, western Texas
Dipodomys spectabilis clarencei, northwestern New Mexico, northeastern Arizona
Dipodomys spectabilis cratodon, central Mexico
Dipodomys spectabilis intermedius, Sonora, Mexico

Dipodomys spectabilis perblandus, southern Arizona, northern Sonora, Mexico

Dipodomys spectabilis spectabilis, southwestern New Mexico, southeastern Arizona, northern Mexico
Dipodomys spectabilis zygomaticus, southern Chihuahua, Mexico

References
Mammalian Species 311; Monson and Kessler, 1940

Stephens's kangaroo rat | *Dipodomys stephensi*

This colorful kangaroo rat inhabits level or gently sloping topography at elevations of 85–850 meters in portions of western Riverside, southern San Bernardino, and northern San Diego counties, California. Extensive loss of habitat has left only isolated populations; it is one of several species in the genus *Dipodomys* threatened with extinction in California as a result of agricultural and urban development. Pleistocene fossils similar to *D. stephensi* are known from Orange County, California.

Stephens's kangaroo rat is a nocturnal, burrowing rodent that eats seeds of annual forbs. It may spend only about an hour outside its burrow each night. It is solitary, and will fight furiously when placed with other members of the species. Other adult kangaroo rats are tolerated only for brief periods during the mating season.

Dipodomys stephensi has an external, fur-lined cheek pouch on either side of the mouth. Its tail is 1.5 times the length of the head and body, bicolored, and crested. The hind feet are long and adapted for hopping, and the front feet are small and specialized for gathering and manipulating food and for burrowing. *D. stephensi* is capable of surviving without free water for short periods of time, because it can acquire water from its food and can conserve water, but body mass drops significantly during long periods without water.

Breeding occurs from late spring to mid-summer. In years with greater than average rainfall, females may produce two

Dipodomys stephensi

litters, and females born early in the year may mature and produce their first litters by the end of the summer. When there is little rainfall, reproduction may be suspended and survivorship may be low. Females build elaborate nests during the week before parturition and produce an average of 2.7 young per litter. The neonates are naked, pink, and have facial vibrissae that are 5 mm long. A gray pigmentation develops on the dorsal surfaces of the head, body, and tail by 2–3 days of age. By 9–10 days of age, the pelage is dark brown on the dorsal and lateral surfaces of the body, the young start to crawl out and around the nest, and begin scratching behind the ear with the hind foot. When disturbed, the young make rapid, high-pitched squeaking sounds. Their ears open in 10–11 days and their eyes open in 14 days. Young reach about 90 percent of adult size in 2 months. Molt to adult pelage begins at an age of 3 months.

Stephens's kangaroo rat inhabits sparsely-vegetated annual grassland and coastal sage-scrub communities. Each site occupied by one of these kangaroo rats consists of a well-developed network of trails connecting burrow openings. Most surface activity appears to be restricted to runways, areas around burrow entrances, and sandbathing sites. Burrows are up to 45 centimeters in depth (usually 21–23 cm) in gravelly and sandy soils, or these kangaroo rats may use abandoned burrows of pocket gophers and California ground squirrels. The subterranean network of tunnels mirrors the surface network of trails and provides ready access to all portions of an individual's range, providing protection, especially from aerial predators such as owls.

Monthly population densities can vary from 7 to 52 individuals per hectare, but average 20–36 individuals per hectare throughout the year. Peaks in numbers of *D. stephensi* occur in late spring and early summer, following peaks in reproductive activity in spring. Late summer, autumn, and winter are typically periods of declining or low density. Reproductive activity and change in density are closely associated with seasonal patterns of precipitation. Home ranges vary from 420 to 1,600 square meters and are generally about 570–970 square meters.

Deer mice are the most common mammals found in association with Stephens's kangaroo rats. San Diego pocket mice, agile and Dulzura kangaroo rats, and desert woodrats, may also occupy the same habitat. Predators include snakes, barn owls, long-eared owls, foxes, coyotes, and domestic dogs and cats. The only parasites reported from this species are chiggers.
T. L. Best

Size
No significant sexual dimorphism
Total length: 280–300 (284) mm (males);
    277–295 (282) mm (females)
Length of tail: 165–180 (172) mm (males);
    164–175 (172) mm (females)
Weight: 45–73 (62) g

Identification
Compared with *D. merriami,* which has four toes on each hind foot, *D. stephensi* has five toes on each hind foot and is larger. Compared with *D. agilis* and *D. simulans,* the only other five-toed kangaroo rats that occur in its range, *D. stephensi* has much smaller ears and usually occupies more open habitats.

Recent Synonyms
Dipodomys cascus
Perodipus stephensi

Other Common Names
Bonsall relict kangaroo rat

Status
Endangered

References
Mammalian Species 73; Burke et al., 1991

Narrow-faced kangaroo rat | *Dipodomys venustus*

The narrow-faced kangaroo rat occurs along the coast of central California at elevations from sea level to 1,770 meters. No fossils are known.

Dipodomys venustus is a medium-sized, dark-colored kangaroo rat with five toes on each hind foot. Its black nose merges into a black band at the base of the whiskers. The top of the head, back, sides, and thigh patches are yellowish brown. The ears are large and nearly black, with pale spots at the base and at the top of the fold. The ankles, sides of the heel, sole, and tail stripes are nearly black. The underside of the body is white. The tail is 159 percent of the length of the head and body.

The narrow-faced kangaroo rat lives in maritime areas where the annual rainfall is about 75 centimeters and temperatures are moderate. The precipitation is seasonal (82 percent occurs from November through March), but the dryness of the long summer and autumn is tempered by frequent fogs and proximity to the ocean, giving *D. venustus* a relatively mild, moist habitat. The narrow-faced kangaroo rat inhabits slopes

clothed with chaparral or a mixture of chaparral and oaks or digger pine. It usually locates its burrows on sandy, well-drained, and deep soils, often on abandoned agricultural land.

A burrow consists of a main runway, a few blind side branches, a nest, and food caches. One burrow was 2.4 meters long with a 1.4-meter side branch, five food caches, and a nest. Burrows at least 2 years old are no more complex than those only months old. Often, both main burrow openings and one or both of the auxiliary burrow openings are under weeds or shrubs. Each animal apparently has several supplementary burrows not too closely associated with the main one, which partially offsets the lack of protection offered by such a simple main burrow system. The supplementary burrows are simple, often unbranched runways without nests, caches, or sidepockets. On the surface, the two burrow types can be distinguished because usually the main burrow openings are plugged, while the subsidiary burrow openings always are open. When disturbed in the main burrow, the kangaroo rat will break out through a side branch that ends near the surface and go directly to another opening. Burrows are 5–50 centimeters below the ground surface, and during the rainy period, they are damp because the rain soaks into the ground to a depth of 1.5 meters. Burrows are absent from orchards and cultivated areas: even light harrowing completely destroys them.

The nest cavity usually is lower than the rest of the burrow and filled with seed coats of annual plants. It often contains live insects such as crickets and dung beetles. One or two litters of two to four young per litter are produced each year. A nest found on 31 May contained one young that was too small to run; it squirmed and made a suckling noise.

Although some green material is used as food, the diet is made up almost entirely of seeds of annuals, as determined by cheekpouch contents and underground and surface caches. One or two underground caches, containing up to 3,145 cubic centimeters of seeds, were found in each burrow examined in December. Surface caches generally are 10 centimeters deep

Dipodomys venustus

and about 5 centimeters in diameter, and are usually are grouped more or less fanwise about the mouth of the burrow, but can also be found singly at some distance from any burrow. Except for a little debris, only mature seeds or seed husks have been found in the caches. Caching occurs during the summer and autumn when seeds ripen and fall. Some seeds are carried as far as 50 meters from the source.

Potential predators include coyotes, bobcats, and house cats. Internal parasites include protozoans and cestodes. Ectoparasites include chiggers, mites, ticks, and fleas. *T. L. Best*

Size

Males are slightly larger than females.
Total length: 295–332 (318) mm (males);
    293–330 (314) mm (females)
Length of tail: 180–203 (193) mm (males);
    175–200 (191) mm (females)
Weight: 70–97 (83) g (males); 68–96 (82) g
    (females)

Identification

Compared with *D. agilis*, *D. venustus* has darker pelage, bolder facial markings, much larger ears, a much longer tail, and a proportionally longer rostrum. Compared with *D. elephantinus*, *D. venustus* is smaller and darker, especially on the head; the cheeks have less white, the ears are blacker, and the facial marking is bolder.

The dark ventral tail stripe is wider, rather than narrower, than the lateral white stripe at midlength on the tail. *Dipodomys venustus* is darker and has much larger ears than *D. heermanni*.

Recent Synonyms

Dipodomys sanctiluciae
Perodipus venustus

Other Common Names

Santa Cruz kangaroo rat

Status

Uncommon

Subspecies

Dipodomys venustus sanctiluciae, coastal mountains from the southern end of Monterey Bay southward to the Santa Lucia Mountains east of Morro Bay, and east to the Salinas Valley
Dipodomys venustus venustus, disjunct populations in the Santa Cruz Mountains and adjacent areas west of the Santa Clara Valley, the Diablo Range in Santa Clara, Stanislaus, Merced, San Benito, and Fresno counties, and the northern end of the Gabilan Range in Monterey and San Benito counties

References

Mammalian Species 403; Hawbecker, 1940

Mexican spiny pocket mouse | *Liomys irroratus*

The only location in the United States where the Mexican spiny pocket mouse occurs is a seven-county area just north of the Rio Grande in the extreme south of Texas. There it lives in dense brushy areas along ridges that once formed the old banks of the Rio Grande, or in the few remnants of subtropical palm forest near there. South of the Rio Grande, *Liomys irroratus* occurs throughout much of central Mexico from sea level along the Gulf coast to nearly 3,000 meters in elevation in the Mexican state of Oaxaca. It lives in a variety of brushy and rocky areas in Mexico but most are semiarid habitats. In many places where it occurs it is one of the most common rodents.

Like other pocket mice, this species forages for seeds and stores them in the fur-lined cheek pouches that give this group of rodents the common name of pocket mice. What little we know of their food habits comes from identifying cheek pouch contents or finding caches of seeds in burrows. In southern Texas, their food includes seeds of hackberry, mesquite, and other shrubs. These mice are nocturnal, staying in burrows during the day. The entrance to the burrow is often covered with leaves or other vegetation, or with a small mound of soil.

Mexican spiny pocket mice are grayish-brown with white underparts. Most have a buffy stripe between the dark upperparts and the white underside. The fur on the back has a harsh appearance caused by the mix of stiff spiny hairs and soft slender hairs. The specific name, *irroratus,* is from the Latin word meaning "sprinkled with dew," probably referring to the color pattern on the back. Juveniles are gray and the pelage consists of predominately long, soft hairs. All members of the genus *Liomys* also share a unique, spoon-shaped claw on the hind foot thought to be used in grooming. These mice only molt once a year, usually in April or May, but as early as February and as late as September.

Liomys irroratus

Liomys irroratus breeds throughout the year, but the peak reproductive period appears to be during the fall or winter. The number of young varies from two to eight, with an average litter size of four. Other rodents occurring with Mexican spiny pocket mice in Texas include Merriam's pocket mouse, the hispid pocket mouse, the northern grasshopper mouse, the cotton rat, and one species of woodrat. Fossil material of *Liomys irroratus* has been recovered from caves in Nuevo Leon and Tamaulipas, Mexico, from late Pleistocene and sub-Recent deposits. *R. C. Dowler*

Size
Total length: 216–262 (238) mm (males);
   207–251 (226) mm (females)
Length of tail: 106–138 (120) mm (males);
   102–131 (113) mm (females)
Weight: 40–60 g (males); 35–50 g (females)

Identification
This species is distinguished from the other pocket mice *(Chaetodipus hispidus* and *Perognathus merriami)* in southernmost Texas by upper incisors that lack grooves, darker color with a more spiny appearance to the fur, and hind feet with some hair on the sole.

Status
Common, limited

Subspecies
Liomys irroratus texensis, southernmost Texas and south into Mexico
Six other subspecies, *L. i. alleni, L. i. bulleri, L. i. guerrerensis, L. i. irroratus, L. i. jaliscensis,* and *L. i. torridus,* are all restricted to Mexico.

References
Mammalian Species 82; Genoways, 1973

Family Castoridae

With only two species worldwide, and only a single species in North America, this is a small family. However, in terms of bulk, beavers are second only to capybaras in size, among rodents. They weigh up to 30 kg, and their size is matched by their economic importance and impact upon early exploration and settling of North America by European immigrants.

Beavers are highly adapted for an aquatic existence, but are also capable of ranging far afield in search of forage. They are robust animals with a distinctively flattened tail that is used as a warning device when slapped against the water and also serves as a rudder while the animal swims. Their eyes and nostrils are adapted for extensive underwater forays.

Beavers are among the few animals capable of altering their environment, much as humans do. They use their powerful jaw muscles and strong incisors to gnaw down saplings and small trees (occasionally large trees as well), which they then weave into complicated dams that increase the surface area and depth of water in the surrounding area. They also construct lodges from the same material, and provide underwater entrances that allow them to easily escape danger.

The fur of the beaver was so highly prized in the last century that it played a major role in encouraging the exploration of western North America. Records kept by the men trapping beaver, as well as the extensive data produced by fur companies such as the Pacific Fur Company and the Hudson Bay Company, are unique. Beaver were trapped on the North American continent for trade beginning in the 17th century, and after the Lewis and Clark expedition in 1804, trapping became a major factor in western exploration. Major fur-trading companies soon developed to provide trappers with supplies and to move the furs to overseas markets. John Jacob Astor's Pacific Fur Company developed trading posts throughout the West and even included a California office to supply the China trade. Mountain men, as the beaver trappers became known, form a colorful and important part of the history of North America—and the settlers who moved West during the latter half of the 19th century were able to do so because of the explorations of men lured by a rodent.

The dams and lodges constructed by beavers inspired awe and curiosity in early naturalists. Lewis H. Morgan was arguably the first American ethologist, and his study *The American Beaver and His Works* stands as a milestone.

References
Morgan, 1868; Wilson and Eisenberg, 1990

North American Genera
Castor

American beaver | *Castor canadensis*

Beavers occur in lakes, ponds, and streams throughout North America, except in southern Florida, the deserts of the southwestern United States and Mexico, and the Arctic tundra. They were a major stimulus for exploration of the continent by Europeans seeking new supplies of fur, and by 1900 many beaver populations had been eliminated or markedly reduced. With regulation of trapping and translocation programs conducted by game management agencies in this century, beavers have become re-established throughout their original range and in some new areas not formerly occupied. Beavers are now abundant and are even considered pests in some environments.

Before seeing beavers themselves, a person walking along a stream may notice unmistakable signs of their presence: water backed up behind a dam made of sticks and mud, a dome-shaped lodge in the middle of a pond made of the same materials, trees cut at an angle or in a conical shape near the base, logs with bark stripped off strewn over the ground. Perhaps no other mammals except humans modify their environment as much as beavers do; their reputation as builders is well deserved, although experiments have shown that less foresight is involved in the construction work of beavers than the casual observer might assume. The curious naturalist must also keep in mind that beavers may be present in an area without leaving much physical evidence—they may live in burrows with under-

water entrances in the banks of streams or lakes, instead of lodges as described above; during summer, or all year in certain environments, they may cut few trees but eat mostly herbaceous vegetation. Conversely, dams, lodges, and felled trees may be prominent in a site recently abandoned by beavers, although dams usually start leaking if they aren't being maintained by the animals and the stumps of felled trees lose their freshly-gnawed look relatively quickly.

A bit of patience is required to see the animals responsible for these remarkable habitat modifications. The best time to see beavers is usually in the early evening, starting an hour or two before dark. A person watching from the bank of an active beaver pond will probably first see a dark brown, streamlined animal swimming gracefully in the water. If a large, flat, paddle-shaped tail is visible, the observer can be confident that he or she is watching a beaver. If the tail is hidden underwater, it is possible to confuse a beaver with a muskrat; although the latter is much smaller than an adult beaver, size is difficult to judge under these viewing conditions. The beaver may dive and swim underwater for several meters before surfacing or entering a lodge or bank burrow. If it resurfaces, it may be lo-

cated by searching for the triangular wake it makes as it swims. If it enters a lodge or burrow, it may remain there for minutes to hours before appearing again.

A close-up view of a beaver reveals several adaptations for its semi-aquatic life style and its use of trees for food and construction materials. Webbing between the digits of the hind feet aids in swimming, whereas the clawed digits of the forefeet are used in surprisingly precise manipulations of food. The claws of the second digits of the hind feet are split like a comb and are used in grooming. Fur-lined lips that close behind the incisors enable beavers to carry branches underwater without taking water into the lungs. The outer surfaces of the large, ever-growing incisors are covered by an orange layer of enamel, harder than the enamel of most mammals' teeth because iron is substituted for some of the calcium. As the softer, inner, dentine layer of the incisors wears down faster than the enamel, a chisel-shaped cutting edge is formed.

Beavers use these specialized teeth for felling trees, one of their most familiar habits. This yields not only construction materials but also an important source of food, especially for the winter when animals in northern latitudes may be confined under ice for several months. Beavers eat the inner bark and leaves of many different species of both evergreen and deciduous trees and shrubs, although aspen and willow are preferred when available. In the fall, they collect branches in a food cache, usually placed in the water close to a lodge or bank burrow. When their pond freezes over, the upper part of the cache may be visible above the ice, but is unavailable to the beavers. They swim under the ice from the lodge to the cache, harvest branches not frozen in, and carry them back to a platform inside the lodge, but above water level, for consumption.

In summer months beavers may rely mainly on terrestrial and aquatic herbaceous vegetation, so relatively little tree cutting is observed. In some areas, the fleshy roots, rhizomes, and runners of aquatic plants may be an important source of winter food. A few studies have demonstrated increased use of pine and other conifers for food in spring, but the reasons for this are unknown. Like other mammalian herbivores, beavers rely on symbiotic microorganisms for partial digestion of cellulose. In the case of beavers, fermentation of the fibrous tissue of plants occurs in the caecum, a large chamber located at the junction of the small and large intestine. Beavers make use of the products of microbial action in the caecum by producing soft, green fecal material which they reingest, a behavior known as coprophagy. Another kind of feces, which is not reingested, is usually excreted in the water. These feces are quite different in appearance—like balls of sawdust.

Beavers are fairly unique among mammals in that they are usually monogamous. They may mate for life, but this occurs infrequently because members of a pair typically are of different ages. Usually when a breeding adult dies, it is replaced by a younger, dispersing beaver from another colony. This age difference seems to be common, so most beavers that attain breeding status have more than one mate in a lifetime, with the average pair bond lasting 2 to 3 years. Beaver polygyny is rare, but has been reported. Its occurrence may depend on population density and resources, but little is currently known. A typical beaver colony is composed of the breeding pair with one to two litters of young born in different years. The number of individuals per colony is highly variable but averages about six beavers.

Young beavers, called kits, are born in late April through June, depending on latitude. Winter food is important for reproduction, especially to northern beavers, because breeding (January and February) and gestation (approximately 106 days) occur during the winter. Ice covers their aquatic habitat for almost the entire breeding-to-birthing interval, making the food they have stored for this time period critical to survival and reproduction. Hence, winter food quality is correlated with greater fecundity. With adequate food, beaver litters average three to four kits, but litter sizes from one to six or seven have

been recorded, and adult females may not reproduce successfully every year.

Once kits reach six months of age, mortality is low until they leave their natal colony. Both age of dispersal and of sexual maturity are variable. Sexual maturity may occur early (1.5 years old) or late (2.5 years old or older) depending on colony composition and potential to breed elsewhere. Breeding opportunities depend in part on population density, but dispersal may not. Territory quality and opportunities to breed on the natal territory have yet to be fully evaluated as factors affecting dispersal. If dispersal is delayed, a third age class of young may be present in the colony, which inflates colony size above the usual six.

Beavers in the wild that are protected from trapping may live to be 20 years of age, but they typically live 10 to 15 years. Many predators kill and eat beavers, but only the wolf, where it occurs, exerts significant predation pressure. Bears prey opportunistically on beavers, but only under special circumstances do they regularly prey on them. Other than natural predators, humans are the main cause of beaver mortality. Due to their ease of capture and the obvious sign they leave, beavers are the species most exploited by many fur trappers throughout North America. In locations with regular trapping, most beavers do not live past three to four years of age.

Beavers have several adaptations in addition to stored food for surviving long, harsh winters in northern environments. The interiors of their lodges are generally warmer and show less extreme fluctuations in temperature than the external environment. The walls of the lodge provide insulation, and huddling by the family members occupying a lodge may also help in temperature regulation. Beavers store some fat, in the tail and elsewhere, and they conserve energy by being less active and having slightly reduced body temperatures in winter. Because they live under ice in winter and may have no cue to the daily cycle of light and darkness occurring outside the lodge, they may show circadian cycles of activity with periods of 26 to

Castor canadensis

28 hours. In some cases, all occupants of one lodge exhibit the same cycle, but this kind of social coordination of their activity cycles doesn't always happen.

In recent years, students of beaver behavior have focused on the effects of tree size and distance from water on the animals' selection of trees for cutting. As distance increases, beavers become more choosy, preferring trees of intermediate sizes. This may reflect the fact that intermediate-sized trees yield a higher rate of return of energy or nutrients than either smaller or larger trees of the same species, or it may be related to increased predation risk at greater distances from water. Selection of woody species is related to energy content and bulk of bark and leaves. Another important influence on tree selection is concentration of toxic natural plant compounds in bark. For example, beavers discriminate among individual aspen trees that differ in concentration of a particular toxic compound. Recent experiments suggest that beavers use smell to distinguish more preferred from less preferred tree species. They also may strip small patches of bark from standing trees, a kind of sampling behavior.

Little is known about other aspects of beaver behavior, possibly because beavers are secretive and nocturnal and their interactions with each other occur at such a low rate. What work has been done reveals few behavioral differences between males and females. Males may be slightly more attentive to trespassing beavers from other colonies, and females more involved with rearing young. Beaver families typically occupy territories containing one or a few ponds. They mark the boundaries of these territories with scent mounds—piles of mud on which they deposit secretions from two specialized types of glands located near the anus. The mounds may become quite large as various members of a family add to them, and as many as 25 mounds may occur in a small area at one end of a pond. Recent research has shown that various compounds contained in secretions deposited on these mounds serve different functions, including individual and sibling recognition as well as territoriality.

The beaver's tail serves many functions. When the beaver swims, the tail moves from side to side and up and down, acting like a rudder. The tail also acts as a fifth leg, bracing the beaver against falling over backwards as it walks up the lodge on its hind legs with an armload of mud to pile on top. This is a sight to behold. Finally, and most notably, beavers use their tails in warning other beavers of potential danger. Because beavers are nocturnal and have relatively poor vision, visual communication is difficult, and olfactory communication is not suited to rapid transmission. To warn colony members of approaching danger, a beaver vigorously slaps the water with its tail, producing a loud, startling noise. Colony members on land instantly know danger is near and may retreat to the safety of water. This is basically the same as yelling, and the beavers can discriminate among slappers. This discrimination is interesting because some beavers choose to ignore the tail-slaps of certain colony mates, typically ignoring the young beavers.

Because of their wide distribution, potential to reach high population densities, and extensive modifications of freshwater environments by cutting trees and building dams, beavers are keystone animals in many areas, influencing many different aspects of communities in which they occur. They affect hydrology, nutrient cycling, and invertebrate populations in streams. The water temperature increases where beavers are present, which may be beneficial or detrimental for fish spawning, depending on whether colder than optimal temperatures prevailed prior to beaver activity, as in montane streams. By opening up forests and creating ponds and marshes with standing dead trees, beavers create a mosaic of habitat patches suitable for various species of birds, mammals, and other animals that would be rare or absent in closed forests with fast-flowing streams running through them. When beavers abandon a pond after exhausting the food supply, a successional process begins that eventually leads to a beaver meadow, which may ultimately be reclaimed by forest. Some researchers have argued that beavers were responsible for much pristine meadow habitat in North America.

The rapid recovery and reestablishment of beaver populations since 1900, leading to the currently large population, has caused concern among wildlife managers. Road flooding, bottomland timber loss, and ornamental tree cutting have put beavers on the nuisance list. Often a great fervor to remove them has resulted, which in some cases is called for but in others overlooks their benefits to the stability and diversity of aquatic ecosystems. In other places their benefits are recognized: beavers are being introduced on degraded western streams to aid in erosion control and regeneration of riparian habitats.

Clearly the most obvious short-term solution to a problem beaver is to remove it, whether by killing it or by live-trapping and translocation. Live-trapping may not solve the problem, for beavers often return. Longer-term solutions can involve habitat modification to make sites less attractive to beaver settlement, or living with the beavers but draining their ponds from time to time. Valuable trees can be protected with screening or by using chemicals that beavers avoid. Applying beaver scent (commercially-manufactured castoreum) near trees or in an area can prevent cutting or colonization. *S. H. Jenkins and D. W. Smith*

Size
No significant sexual dimorphism
Total length: 1,000–1,200 mm
Length of tail: 230–325 mm
Weight: 16–30 kg

Identification
The beaver is the largest North American rodent and the only North American mammal with a broad, flat, scaly tail. Its hind feet are webbed and its pelage consists of long, brown, often shiny guard hairs with grayish underfur.

Other Common Names
Canadian beaver, North American beaver

Status
Abundant, widespread

Subspecies
Twenty-four subspecies have been described, but their status is uncertain because of widespread transplantation.

References
Mammalian Species 120; Hill, 1982; Novak, 1987

Family Muridae

Muridae is the largest family of mammals (281 genera, 1,326 species), and includes the mice, rats, hamsters, voles, lemmings, and gerbils. These rodents, making up about a quarter of all of the known species of mammals, are most diverse in the tropical and subtropical areas of the New and Old Worlds, and murids are the only rodents native to Australia. They are divided into 15 subfamilies, only 2 of which, Arvicolinae and Sigmodontinae, are found in North America.

These are all relatively small animals, ranging from tiny harvest mice and pygmy mice up to muskrats. They have radiated to fill almost all available terrestrial habitats, and some have even become arboreal or aquatic. Food habits vary widely throughout the group, and diets may include a variety of vegetation types, invertebrates, and small vertebrates.

Arvicoline rodents (voles, lemmings, and muskrats) form a strictly Northern Hemisphere group, with a sizeable radiation in North America. They tend to be small burrowers, and frequently use runways through grassy areas that can easily be found by predators, including humans. They undergo frequent, sometimes cyclic, oscillations in population density. In some areas, local populations of voles or lemmings may occasional become so dense as to be readily apparent to humans.

The life span of these animals is short, but they have rapid reproductive rates to accomodate this turnover. They reach reproductive maturity at an early age, and females typically have large litters. The resultant high numbers of offspring provide prey for a variety of aerial and terrestrial predators.

Lemmings are the most northern in their distribution, and have adapted to the vagaries of Arctic climates and tundra ecosystems. Dense coats of fur that protect them from the cold, and they take advantage of high vegetative production in the short Arctic summers to forage night and day.

References
Elton, 1942; Musser and Carleton, 1993; Tamarin, 1985

North American Genera
Oryzomys
Reithrodontomys
Peromyscus
Podomys
Ochrotomys
Baiomys
Onychomys
Sigmodon
Neotoma
Clethrionomys
Phenacomys
Arborimus
Microtus
Neofiber
Lemmiscus
Ondatra
Lemmus
Synaptomys
Dicrostonyx

Coues's rice rat | *Oryzomys couesi*

Oryzomys couesi aquaticus is found in suitable habitat in southernmost Texas, particularly in Cameron and Hildago counties, and across the border in Tamaulipas, Mexico. Its range apparently abuts that of *O. palustris texensis,* which is found from Willacy County, Texas, northeastward to the Mississippi River Valley.

Most abundant in cattail-bulrush marshes, Coues's rice rat is found in association with smaller numbers of white-footed mice and hispid cotton rats. In the brushlands around the marshes, *Peromyscus leucopus* and *Sigmodon hispidus* become numerically dominant.

Coues's rice rat is a brownish, long-tailed rat. It is substantially different in color from its only congener in the United States, the grayish *Oryzomys palustris texensis.* The dorsum and sides of *Oryzomus couesi* are dark and pale brown, respectively, and the midventrum is a still paler brown. It is also significantly larger and heavier than *O. palustris texensis,* but the two are similar morphologically: both have long, slender tails, smallish ears, and soft, water-repellent fur. Chromosomal studies indicate that the two species have similar diploid numbers (2n-56), but that their sex chromosomes differ.

Coues's rice rat likely is as highly aquatic, nocturnal, and carnivorous as the marsh rice rat, *O. palustris.* Its slightly larger size may contribute to the significantly longer distances traveled by males; larger animals typically move farther, regardless of sex. Adults increase mean body weight significantly during the nonbreeding (winter) months, but the sex ratios do not differ from unity throughout the year.

A good climber, Coues's rice rat builds its nests about one meter above the water in tall cattails or small trees near the water's edge. Cattail nests are made solely of cattail leaves, whereas tree nests are composed of leaves, twigs, and small vines. All nests are globular, with finely shredded leaves woven tightly together in the interior and loosely woven whole leaves on the outside. Larger individuals build larger nests. During periods of flooding of the cattail marshes, Coues's rice rat migrates to nearby trees, returning to its preferred habitat shortly after the return of normal water levels.

In Mexico, the breeding season of Coues's rice rat likely resembles that of *O. palustris,* which breeds from March to October in most locations but may breed throughout mild winters. However, the presence of juveniles in Texas in November (but not from April to June) suggests that *O. couesi aquaticus* may have a somewhat different pattern. The gestation period probably is about 25 days and litters likely average near five, based on values from *Oryzomys palustris.*

In southernmost Texas, resaca habitat (marshes surrounding oxbow lakes) is shrinking because these areas are being converted to farmland. Resacas bordered by bulrushes and cattails are almost entirely confined to Cameron-Hildago counties, and in total provide habitat for only a few thousand Coues's rice rats. Because of its restricted distribution and its low numbers, Coues's rice rat is presumably one of the rarest rodents in the United States. *R. K. Rose*

Oryzomys couesi

Size
Males are slightly larger than females.
Total Length: 390–410 mm
Length of tail: 130–140 mm
Weight: 67–71 g

Identification
This rice rat is distinguished from *Peromyscus,* which are shorter-tailed, smaller, and usually reddish brown, by its brownish dorsum and sides and paler brown venter. Marsh rice rats *(Oryzomys palustris)* are smaller and predominantly gray rather than brown. Cotton rats

(Sigmodon), which are also sympatric, have yellow-tipped brown fur and blackish feet. Rice rats differ from introduced rats in the genus *Rattus* by smaller size, slenderer tails, more delicate appearance, and much smaller feet.

Other Common Names
Resaca rice rat

Status
Seemingly rare in the US, where they perhaps are restricted to resaca (oxbow lake marsh) habitat.

Subspecies
Oryzomys couesi aquaticus, Texas-Tamaulipas borderlands
Up to 24 other subspecies occur from Mexico southward into Central America.

References
Benson and Gehlbach, 1979

Marsh rice rat │ *Oryzomys palustris*

Oryzomys palustris is distributed from coastal Texas northward to southeastern Kansas and southern Missouri and Illinois, and eastward to southern New Jersey, except that it does not occur in the Appalachian Mountains. Although found at locations up to 950 m elevation, it is most abundant in coastal marshes. In tidal marshes of the Gulf and Atlantic coasts, the marsh rice rat is probably the most common mammal, although the hispid cotton rat or the meadow vole may rival its numbers in the drier sections of these marshes.

A medium-sized, long-tailed rat, *O. palustris* is grayish-brown with a darker mid-dorsal stripe. The bicolored tail is

long and slender, and the feet and belly are whitish. The ears are relatively small. The soft fur is water repellent, trapping air when these highly aquatic rodents are swimming. Marsh rice rats can swim 10 m or more underwater during a dive. They seek water for safety from predators and probably to feed as well. Individuals are known to have swum across water barriers at least 300 m wide. *O. palustris* is probably a good colonizer of islands lying close to mainland marshes.

A highly carnivorous rodent, second in North America only to grasshopper mice *(Onychomys), O. palustris* consumes carrion, crabs, clams, snails, insects, fish, baby turtles or birds, and

Oryzomys palustris

even birds' eggs. Sometimes it eats plant material. This rat is opportunistic in its diet, taking carrion when it is available, hunting as a true predator at other times, and eating plant tissue when necessary. Highly scansorial, marsh rice rats readily climb tall marsh grasses or shrubs, and often place their softball-sized nursery nests in them. During storm tides they often seek refuge in these nests or cling to branches in taller vegetation. They also nest in the masses of flotsam atop wrack lines in tidal marshes, and have been known to appropriate nests from marsh wrens, round-tailed rats, or muskrats, the latter being larger but equally aquatic rodents.

The breeding season of the marsh rice rat varies. It is seasonal from March to October in most locations but continuous throughout the year in others. Sometimes reproduction is delayed until May, suggesting that local conditions may regulate reproduction more than in most small mammals. After a gestation period of about 25 days, a litter averaging about five is born nearly naked, blind, and helpless. Each neonate weighs

about 3.5 g at birth, but growth is rapid and by early in their second week of life the eyes are open and solid food is being consumed. Young are weaned before 20 days, when their weights range from 18 to 27 g. Maturity is attained by 60 days, when animals raised in the lab weighed 40 to 60 g. In some locations or years, females may reach puberty by six weeks of age.

Active all year and mostly nocturnal, marsh rice rats likely alter their behaviors greatly in response to winter conditions. Because they are small, they lose heat rapidly, particularly when wading or swimming in cold Atlantic Coast tidal marshes during the winter months. They build shallow burrows in the intertidal zone, which they apparently use as temporary refuges while foraging in this food-rich strip. They readily swim to live traps placed on floats. Because marsh rice rats are active mostly at night, owls, particularly barn owls, are their main predators, although northern harriers, water snakes, and a few medium-sized mammalian predators also eat them. *R. K. Rose and R. D. Dueser*

Size

Total length: 193–262 (226) mm (males); 191–253 (217) mm (females)
Length of tail: 93–121 (106) mm (males); 85–116 (102) mm (females)
Weight: 46–80 (56) g (males); 40–60 (48) g (females)

Identification

Marsh rice rats can be distinguished from *Peromyscus,* which are reddish-browns, by a brownish-gray back, browner sides, whitish belly and feet, and by smaller size, and from rats in the genus *Rattus* by smaller size, more delicate appearance, and much smaller feet.

Recent Synonyms

Oryzomys argentatus (= O. p. natator)

Other Common Names

Rice rat

Status

Abundant

Subspecies

Oryzomys palustris natator, peninsular Florida
Oryzomys palustris palustris, southeastern United States

References

Mammalian Species 176; Humphrey and Setzer, 1989; Negus et al., 1961

Fulvous harvest mouse | *Reithrodontomys fulvescens*

The distribution of the fulvous harvest mouse is centered in Mexico and extends southward to Honduras, Guatemala, and El Salvador, and northward to Arizona, southwestern and central Texas, central Oklahoma, southeastern Kansas, southern Missouri, Arkansas, and western Mississippi. Recent range extensions into extreme southern New Mexico, western Texas, western Oklahoma, and northern Missouri have been reported.

The upperparts of the pelage vary from a reddish-yellow buff to tawny to pinkish-cinnamon or salmon, mixed medially with blackish to blackish-brown hairs that sometimes form a darker band down the midline from nose to tail. The underparts vary from white to grayish-white to gray, often tinged with buff or pale pinkish-cinnamon. The tail is brown to dark brown above and grayish-white to soiled white below. The feet are grayish-white to buffy-white and the ears are varying shades of brown, often with a tawny or reddish-yellow tinge on the inner surface.

The juvenile pelage is dark and dull and is composed of long guard hairs and shorter cover hairs. The subadult pelage is coarser, with more intense buffy tones and distinctive dorsal bands. The adult pelage is brightest, with buffy tones more dominant. Molts begin from two centers, the venter and forehead. The molt from the venter proceeds dorsally and then anteriorally to meet the posteriorly expanding molt from the forehead. One or two molts occur annually.

Breeding is bimodal, with a lull in summer. Litter size ranges from 2 to 4. Details of the estrous cycle, including the length of gestation, are little studied. Young are born blind and hairless, weighing about 1 g. Hair appears at 3–4 days of age on the ventral surface and at 11 days on the dorsal surface. The eyes open at 9–12 days. When the mice are weaned at about 13–16 days, they weigh 3.0–3.5 g and exhibit climbing behavior.

Fulvous harvest mice occur in grassy fields containing shrubs. Mesquite-grassland, grassland, pine-grass ecotones, and grass-brush habitats are commonly inhabited. Rocky outcrops and cactus are utilized frequently. In southern and eastern Texas, populations exhibit bimodal patterns of density, with peaks during summer and winter. Population density varies from 6–30 per hectare. Individuals may live for a year, but seldom live longer than 14 months. Some studies report a 1:1 sex ratio, but others report a ratio of 2:1, skewed toward males. Such a skewed ratio could reflect decreased trappability of females; however, similar skewed sex ratios have been found in laboratory-born litters.

The diet of *R. fulvescens* is dominated by invertebrates during spring and summer and seeds in fall and winter. Occasionally herbs and grasses are eaten. In coastal Texas invertebrates are a dominant component of the diet in all seasons because of their nearly continuous availablity in this subtropical environment.

Little is known of interspecific interactions involving *R. fulvescens*. On the Texas coastal prairie there is little evidence of such interactions with other rodents. Similarly, sympatric populations of *R. fulvescens* and *R. montanus* in Oklahoma showed no evidence of competition. In both areas, however, habitat segregation was observed. Owls and hawks commonly feed on fulvous harvest mice.

Reithrodontomys fulvescens is strictly nocturnal, with activity concentrated between sunset and midnight. Under laboratory conditions, fulvous harvest mice remain in the nest during periods when the lights are on, leave the nest for long periods when it is dark, and then, after this activity, make brief excursions from the nest until the lights are turned on again. During winter photoperiod and temperature conditions, activity is more evenly spaced during the day. The fulvous harvest mouse is an adept climber, routinely captured in vegetation more than a meter above the ground. It constructs baseball-size nests of grasses and sedges in vegetation off the ground. Such nests often are observed to contain a pair of mice. Evidence from trapping suggests that male and female pairs may travel together, indicating a spatial association of the sexes and suggesting that pair-bonding may exist in this species. Nests often have one or two entrances, which are plugged when the nest is occupied; nests built during the winter have thicker walls and more shredded grass than nests built during warmer seasons.

G. N. Cameron

Reithrodontomys fulvescens

Size

Males may weigh more than females.
Total length: 134–189 mm
Length of tail: 73–116 mm
Weight: 6.5–25 g

Identification

Three species of *Reithrodontomys* occur in eastern Texas: *fulvescens, montanus,* and *humulis.*
R. *fulvescens* differs from R. *montanus* in that
the latter is more grayish-brown and has a distinctly bicolored tail that is usually less than
half the total length of the mouse. R. *humulis* is
smaller than R. *fulvescens,* has duller coloration,
and its tail is always shorter than 70 mm instead
of considerably longer. The tail of an adult fulvous harvest mouse is usually longer than 80
mm, and this species has a bright, fulvous
(reddish-brown or tawny-reddish) color on its
sides; the upperparts are golden brown, sometimes with black interspersed on the back.

Status

Common, widespread

Subspecies

Reithrodontomys fulvescens amoenus, Oaxaca,
Mexico

Reithrodontomys fulvescens aurantius, Missouri,
eastern Texas, Oklahoma, Arkansas,
Louisiana, and Mississippi

Reithrodontomys fulvescens canus, southeastern
New Mexico, western Texas, and Coahuila,
Durango, and Chihuahua, Mexico

Reithrodontomys fulvescens chiapensis, Chiapas,
Mexico, and Guatamala, Honduras, and
El Salvador

Reithrodontomys fulvescens difficilis, Veracruz,
Mexico

Reithrodontomys fulvescens fulvescens, Arizona
and Sonora, Mexico

Reithrodontomys fulvescens griseoflavus, Durango,
Tamaulipas, Michoacan, Jalisco, Zacatecas,
San Luis Potosi, and Guanajuato, Mexico

Reithrodontomys fulvescens helvolus, Oaxaca,
Mexico

Reithrodontomys fulvescens infernatis, Oaxaca,
Mexico

Reithrodontomys fulvescens intermedius, southern
Texas and Coahuila, Nuevo Leon, and
Tamaulipas, Mexico

Reithrodontomys fulvescens laceyi, central and
northern Texas

Reithrodontomys fulvescens meridionalis,
Nicaragua

Reithrodontomys fulvescens mustelinus,
Michoacan, Guerrero, and Oaxaca, Mexico

Reithrodontomys fulvescens nelsoni, Jalisco and
Colima, Mexico

Reithrodontomys fulvescens tenuis, Sonora,
Chihuahua, Durango, Nayarit, and Sinaloa,
Mexico

Reithrodontomys fulvescens toltecus, Hidalgo, Distrito Federal, Queretaro, and Michoacan,
Mexico

Reithrodontomys fulvescens tropicalis, Veracruz,
Tamaulipas, Hidalgo, Queretaro, and San
Luis Potosi, Mexico

References

Mammalian Species 174; Caire et al., 1989;
Davis and Schmidly, 1994; Jones et al., 1985;
Matson and Baker, 1986; Schmidly 1983

Eastern harvest mouse | *Reithrodontomys humulis*

Reithrodontomys humulis occurs from Maryland and Virginia,
southern Ohio, and Kentucky south to Florida and west to
central Oklahoma and the Gulf coast of Alabama, Mississippi,
Louisiana, and eastern Texas.

The eastern harvest mouse has been recorded from waste
fields of matted grass and broom sedge, grassy or weedy areas,
tangled patches of briar, roadside ditches, brackish meadows,
and wet bottomlands. Meadows, marshlands, and weed-covered
banks of irrigation ditches seem to offer optimum habitat conditions. These harvest mice are seldom found in forested areas.
They feed on the multitude of little seeds, choice green sprouts,
and small insects that are abundant throughout their range.

Eastern harvest mice typically construct nests of shredded
grass and plant fiber, which they place in tangled herbage.
These nests serve the mice throughout the year, for they do
not hibernate. Although breeding may occur throughout the
year, most births take place between late spring and late fall.
The young number from two to seven (the average is about
four) per litter.

This species has been trapped in association with shrews,
deer mice, voles, and house mice. *D. J. Schmidly*

Reithrodontomys humulis

Size

No significant sexual dimorphism
Total length: 107–128 mm
Length of tail: 45–60 mm
Weight: 10–15 g

Identification

R. humulis is a small brown mouse with a deep longitudinal groove near the middle of the upper incisors. Within its range, *R. humulis* is easily distinguished from other harvest mice by the length of its tail, which is considerably shorter than the head and body, by the dark mid-dorsum of its upperparts, and by special features of the skull and teeth.

Recent Synonyms

Mus humulis
Reithrodontomys merriami

Status

Common

Subspecies

Reithrodontomys humulis humulis, southeastern United States east of the Mississippi River
Reithrodontomys humulis merriami, eastern Texas, Oklahoma, and western Arkansas and Louisiana west of the Mississippi River
Reithrodontomys humulis virginianus, Maryland and Virginia

References

Mammalian Species 565; Caire et al., 1989; Choate et al., 1994; Davis and Schmidly, 1994

Western harvest mouse | *Reithrodontomys megalotis*

This widespread mouse is most abundant in relatively open, mesic habitats dominated by herbaceous vegetation and dense litter, such as prairies, meadows, overgrown pastures, stream valleys, and estuarine marshes. It has wide ecological tolerances, however, and also occupies deserts and sand dunes, riparian shrublands, grassy and weedy clearings in pine/oak forests, abandoned fields, fence rows, ditch banks, and highway rights-of-way. It ranges elevationally from 77 m below sea level at Death Valley, California, to 4,000 m on the Popocatepetl and Orizaba volcanoes in central Mexico. This adaptable mouse has profited from human agricultural practices and become widespread in the central Great Plains, the Midwest, and southern Canada.

The western harvest mouse's nests are composed of plant material, with an outer layer of coarsely-woven grasses and fibrous plant matter and an inner lining of softer plant "down." Nests are usually located on the surface of the ground under bushes, fallen logs, or matted grasses and weeds, but sometimes they are built in burrows or suspended in vegetation slightly above the ground. They are spherical in shape, about 75 mm in diameter, and typically have a single opening near the base. Damage to nests is repaired immediately. Each mouse might use several nests for different occasions; an old nest can serve as a latrine.

The diet of this opportunistic mouse consists of a variety of seeds, insects, and herbs—seemingly whatever is available at the time. Leaves and stems of woody vegetation are avoided, but this agile creature will climb shrubs to eat flowers and seeds. Ground- and shrub-dwelling insects such as beetles and

weevils are consumed throughout the year. Moth larvae are favored in the spring. Western harvest mice do not cache food, but they accumulate reserves of body fat during the autumn and winter months. These mice prefer to drink fresh water but probably drink brackish water in estuarine habitats. Although they do not hibernate, western harvest mice become torpid when exposed to cold ambient temperatures, osmotic stress, or water deprivation.

In the more seasonal northern parts of its range, the western harvest mouse is reproductively active from early spring to late autumn, save for a midsummer depression. In the less seasonal southern parts of its range, however, it reproduces throughout the year. Females have a high biotic potential—they reach sexual maturity as early as 4 weeks of age, they are polyestrous, and they have a short gestation period (23 to 25 days) followed by a post-partum estrus. One to 9 fetuses have been noted but litters typically have 3 to 7 young (5). Newborn pups are pink, hairless (except for vibrissae), and there is a slight male bias in the sex ratio. At birth each pup weighs about 1.5 g, with the combined litter weight generally exceeding half that of the female. The eyes and ears open, the juvenile pelage emerges, and the incisors erupt by day 11 or 12. Young begin to eat solid food at about 2 weeks of age and are weaned at 3 to 4 weeks of age. Females kept in optimal captive conditions have been known to give birth to 14 litters totaling 58 young over a 12-month period. Senility begins at about 45 weeks of age and is accompanied by reduced litter size in females. Few individuals reach the age of 12 months.

This attractive mouse has two maturational molts during its

lifetime. The juvenile pelage is relatively short, sparse, and grayish brown. It is replaced at about the time the young leave the nest by the subadult pelage, which is longer, thicker, and brighter than that of juveniles but duller than that of adults. The subadult pelage is replaced by the adult pelage at about the time that individuals reach sexual maturity. Adult mice have two characteristic pelages. The relatively short, sparse summer pelage is brownish above and on the sides, with a poorly defined mid-dorsal stripe, and grayish below, sometimes with a darker spot on the chest. The winter pelage is longer, thicker, and paler overall, and the tail is more distinctly bicolored. The spring molt progresses posteriorly from the top of the head, shoulders, and throat, whereas the autumnal molt is more irregular. Pelage replacement is delayed in pregnant or lactating females.

The western harvest mouse has a relatively large surface-area-to-volume ratio, but several behavioral adaptations serve to minimize energy loss. Mice are extremely tolerant of one another, they are nonterritorial, and they are nocturnal to the point of being less active on bright moonlit nights, especially in habitats with scant ground cover. They spend the day in a nest, frequently huddled in a ball with other western harvest mice; in captivity they even huddle with house mice and deer mice. Communal living favors parasitism, however, and the western harvest mouse is host to many parasites, including protozoans, spiny-headed worms, tapeworms, roundworms, fleas, chiggers, mites, and a louse; it is also a vector for a unique strain of

hantavirus. Predators include owls, hawks, jays, snakes, canids, mustelids, felids, and scorpions.

This prolific mouse has well-pronounced fluctuations in abundance, reaching densities of up to 60 mice per hectare in late summer when ground cover is densest. Circular to elliptical home ranges average about half the size of a football field.

Reithrodontomys megalotis

Western harvest mice use runways constructed by voles and cotton rats, but they do not contribute to runway maintenance; they seldom use tunnels dug by pocket gophers. Displaced mice successfully "home" from distances up to 300 m away.

Recent detailed chromosomal analyses indicate that *Reithrodontomys megalotis* likely consists of two or more sibling species. Mice from the Great Plains *(R. m. dychei)*, the Southwest *(R. m. megalotis),* and California *(R. m. longicaudus)* compose one species that has a diploid number of 42, with up to 4 supernumerary chromosomes. Mice in the Sierra Madre Oriental *(R. m. saturatus),* the interior highlands of Guanajuato and Queretaro *(R. m. amoles),* and the Sierra Madre Occidental *(R. m. zacatecae)* have diploid numbers of 40, 48, and 50, respectively. Protein electrophoresis has confirmed the distinctiveness of *R. m. zacatecae* as compared to *R. m. dychei, R. m. megalotis, R. m. longicaudus,* and *R. m. limicola.* Also, *R. m. zacatecae* and *R. m. saturatus* coexist in central and western Michoacan with no evidence of interbreeding. A critical reappraisal of the southern forms is warrranted. *W. D. Webster*

Size

No significant sexual dimorphism, but there is pronounced geographic variation.
Total length: 118–170 (140) mm
Length of tail: 50–96 (70) mm
Weight: 8–15 g

Identification

The following group of characteristics identifies *Reithrodontomys megalotis,* which is easily confused with other species of harvest mice: pelage bristly and relatively short; ears buffy to reddish-brown and comparatively small; tail about as long as head and body and distinctly bicolored, with relatively long hairs that tend to obscure the scales; feet whitish.

Other Common Names

Long-tailed harvest mouse, desert harvest mouse, dusky harvest mouse

Status

Common to abundant

Subspecies

Reithrodontomys megalotis alticolus, highlands of Oaxaca and Guerrero; possibly Chiapas

Reithrodontomys megalotis amoles, Guanajuato and Queretaro

Reithrodontomys megalotis arizonensis, higher elevations in the Chiricahua Mountains of Arizona

Reithrodontomys megalotis aztecus, Four Corners region (where Utah, Colorado, Arizona, and New Mexico meet) eastward to southwestern Kansas and the panhandles of Oklahoma and Texas

Reithrodontomys megalotis catalinae, Santa Catalina and San Clemente islands, California

Reithrodontomys megalotis distichlis, Monterey County, California

Reithrodontomys megalotis dychei, Great Plains region from southeastern Alberta eastward and southward to western Indiana, northeastern Arkansas, and northeastern Colorado (includes *R. m. pectoralis* of southwestern Wisconsin).

Reithrodontomys megalotis hooperi, western Tamaulipas

Reithrodontomys megalotis limicola, Ventura, Los Angeles, and Orange counties, California

Reithrodontomys megalotis longicaudus, southwestern Oregon southward to northwestern Baja California del Norte

Reithrodontomys megalotis megalotis, intermontane basins and plateaus from south-central British Columbia southward to Guanajuato, and from eastern California eastward to western Texas

Reithrodontomys megalotis peninsulae, central Baja California del Norte

Reithrodontomys megalotis ravus, Tooele County, Utah

Reithrodontomys megalotis santacruzae, Santa Cruz Island, California

Reithrodontomys megalotis saturatus, Sierra Madre Oriental from Nuevo Leon southward to Veracruz and Puebla, and thence westward in Sierra Volcanica Transversal to Michoacan and Jalisco

Reithrodontomys megalotis zacatecae, Sierra Madre Occidental from western Chihuahua southward to Michoacan (see comments below)

References

Mammalian Species 167; Hooper, 1952; Jones et al., 1983

Plains harvest mouse | *Reithrodontomys montanus*

The diminutive plains harvest mouse is a denizen of grassy habitats The name *montanus,* referring to mountains, was given to this species because it was first discovered in a mountainous area of Colorado in 1855. This name is somewhat misleading as the species was later found to inhabit grassy areas through much of the Great Plains far from any mountains. It occurs from southwestern South Dakota and southeastern Montana south through eastern Wyoming, Colorado, and New Mexico, all of Nebraska and Kansas, and most of Oklahoma and Texas. In the southwestern part of its range it occurs in extreme southern Arizona and parts of the Mexican states of Sonora, Chihuahua, and Durango. The locations where it lives range in elevation from about 80 meters in east-central Texas to over 1,900 meters in Durango, Mexico.

The plains harvest mouse is small, with a diffuse, dark stripe down the middle of its back. The remainder of the fur on the back is grayish-brown and the underside is white. The tail, which is shorter than the length of the body, has a distinct bicolored appearance, with a sharp dark line above and paler color below. To the untrained eye, these mice may be confused with small deer mice *(Peromyscus),* but a tiny groove on the upper incisors of all harvest mice readily distinguishes them. The name *Reithrodontomys,* meaning "groove toothed mouse" refers to this characteristic.

Reithrodontomys montanus lives in open grassy areas, including hay fields, cultivated fields of wheat and sorghum, undisturbed mixed prairie, and grazed grasslands. In the central part of their range, plains harvest mice reach their highest densities in short grass associations, where three-awn *(Aristida fenderiana)* and bristlegrass *(Setaria)* are common. Taller grasses, such as big bluestem *(Andropogon gerardii)* and little bluestem *(Schizachyrium scoparium)* also support populations, but usually in lower numbers. In other parts of its range, *Reithrodontomys montanus* is found in different grass associations, but shorter species of grasses seem to be preferred over tall grasses. Population densities average from about 2 to 7 mice per hectare. Home ranges of individual mice can be as low as 0.04 hectares but average about 0.2 hectares.

Plains harvest mice breed throughout the year in much of their range, but in the northern areas reproduction may be limited during the coldest months. Their nests are made of grasses shaped into a ball, with an opening at one end. They are suspended just off the ground in grasses or may be located on the ground. The gestation period is about 21 days and the neonates, born naked and blind, weigh about one gram. After 6 days the young are covered with hair and by day 8 their eyes are open. They are weaned at about 2 weeks and have reached adult size by the age of 5 weeks. Sexual maturity is reached at about two months of age. The number of young in a litter averages about four, but may number as few as one and as many as nine.

Reithrodontomys montanus

The plains harvest mouse is found in association with many other rodents, including pocket mice, deer mice, grasshopper mice, cotton rats, and woodrats. It is often the least abundant species in a rodent community. Foods of this harvest mouse include seeds and flower heads of weeds and grasses, cactus fruits, and insects such as grasshoppers. Fossil material of *Reithrodontomys montanus* has been recovered from at least ten faunas, all Pleistocene in age and from areas that are near or within its modern range. *R. C. Dowler*

Size
No significant sexual dimorphism
Total length: 54–146 (116) mm
Length of tail: 20–69 (54) mm
Weight: 6–13 g

Identification
Reithrodontomys montanus has grooved upper incisors, which distinguishes it from species of *Peromyscus.* Compared to other harvest mice in its range, *Reithrodontomys montanus* is larger than *R. humulis,* paler in color, and has paler ears. Its distinctly bicolored tail is usually shorter than head and body length; the tail of *R. megalotis,* which is also bicolored, is usually about the same length as the head and body length, and that of *R. fulvescens* is much longer.

Status
Common

Subspecies
Reithrodontomys montanus albescens, western Kansas and eastern Colorado north to southeastern North Dakota

Reithrodontomys montanus griseus, eastern New Mexico, most of north-central Texas, Oklahoma, eastern Kansas, and southeastern Nebraska

Reithrodontomys montanus montanus, southeastern Arizona, south-central New Mexico north just into Colorado, western Texas, and part of the Mexican states of Chihuahua, Durango, and Sonora

References
Mammalian Species 257

Salt marsh harvest mouse | *Reithrodontomys raviventris*

These docile harvest mice are found only in the tidal and diked salt marshes bordering the series of bays known as the San Francisco Bay. They differ from the much more active western harvest mouse, *R. megalotis,* which inhabits the adjacent grasslands, in tail characteristics, behavior, and various genetic characters. Studies of its chromosomes and other genetic traits indicate a closer relationship to the geographically much more distant *R. montanus.* The salt marsh harvest mice of the southern end of the South San Francisco Bay often have red bellies and the shortest tail lengths; a gradual north-to-south change is evident in both of these characters.

The principal habitat of these cover-dependent mice is the dense cover offered by pickleweed *(Salicornia virginica),* which characterizes the middle zone of tidal marshes. Salt marsh harvest mice disappear from marshes in which the upper zone, the band of peripheral halophytes, has been destroyed, primarily because there is no escape cover during high tides. They are good swimmers but are removed by predators when they are forced into the open for extended periods of time.

Recent circumstantial evidence indicates that these mice have two and sometimes three litters per year in the wild. Their population numbers, however, typically are not large because so much of their original habitat has been destroyed or modified. Formerly continuous populations are now broken into disjunct and often widely separated smaller populations.

Much of their former habitat has been converted into salt ponds or filled to become industrial parks, housing tracts, or garbage dumps. Most of the remaining tidal marshes are interrupted, narrow strips lining outboard dikes and lack most of their upper zones of vegetation. This situation is especially common within the range of the southern subspecies, *R. r. raviventris.* Many of the southernmost tidal marshes have been freshened by the outflows of sewage plants and have become brackish in nature, undergone vegetative changes, and lost most of their mice.

Diked marshes have become refugia for salt marsh harvest mice in many parts of their range; however, these marshes are being compressed both by development and by changes in tide levels. Many diked marshes are too dry, too small, or lack appropriate corridors for movement between subunits. All marshes are close to developed lands, especially those in the South San Francisco Bay. Mice are preyed upon not only by native owls and skunks but also by introduced rats, cats, and red foxes.

The impact of random genetic drift on the smaller populations is not known. Genetic studies that will help us understand the variability within and the potential for survival of these populations are underway. *H. S. Shellhammer*

Reithrodontomys raviventris

Size

Total length: 118–175 mm
Length of tail: 56–95 mm
Weight: 7.6–14.5 g.

Identification

Reithrodontomys raviventris can be distinguished from *R. megalotis* by its narrower, more pointed, more unicolored tail and its more docile behavior.

Status

Endangered under both federal and state laws

Subspecies

Reithrodontomys raviventris halicoetes, marshes of upper Marin Peninsula, San Pablo and Suisun bays, and the northern Contra Costa County coast, California

Reithrodontomys raviventris raviventris, marshes of South San Francisco Bay, Alameda County, and the lower Marin Peninsula, California

References

Mammalian Species 169; Fisler, 1965; Shellhammer, 1989

Texas mouse │ *Peromyscus attwateri*

Peromyscus attwateri has a partially branching and somewhat discontinuous distribution in Missouri, Kansas, Arkansas, Oklahoma, and Texas because of the close restriction of these mice to rocky situations.

Texas mice have been recorded in cedar glade, juniper-grass, oak-juniper, oak, and ravine forest plant associations. These mice are known to breed in fall, winter, and spring. The number of young per litter varies from one to six and averages about four. Texas mice feed on seeds, berries, green plants, and insects.

The Texas mouse has been trapped in association with *P. pectoralis, P. boylii, P. maniculatus,* and *P. leucopus.* Other species of mammals that often occur with this mouse include eastern woodrats, harvest mice, shrews, and squirrels. *D. J. Schmidly*

Peromyscus attwateri

Size

No significant sexual dimorphism
Total length: 187–218 mm
Length of tail: 96–112 mm
Weight: 25–35 g

Identification

P. attwateri is medium in size for the genus, with a tail that is about as long as the head and body, large hind feet (24–27 mm in adults), ankles that are usually dark or dusky, and ears that are medium in size compared to those of other deer mice. Within its range, *P. attwateri* is easily confused with *P. pectoralis* and *P. boylii.* Male Texas mice can best be distinguished from male white-ankled mice *(P. pectoralis)* by the shape of the baculum, the tip of which is short and rounded in *P. attwateri.* Texas mice differ from brush mice *(P. boylii)* in having larger hind feet (greater than 24 mm in adult *attwateri* compared to less than 23 mm in adult *boylii)* and in minute details of the lower molar teeth.

Recent Synonyms

Peromyscus boylii cansensis
Peromyscus boylii laceyi

Common Names

Attwater's mouse

Status

Common

References

Mammalian Species 48; Carleton, 1989; Choate et al., Dalquest and Horner, 1984; Davis and Schmidly, 1994

Brush mouse | *Peromyscus boylii*

The brush mouse occupies mountainous regions from northern California and Nevada to central Mexico. Throughout this area, it is restricted to rock outcroppings and brushy or forested areas at elevations greater than 2,000 meters. The range of *Peromyscus boylii* includes a broad climatic zone (desert to montane forest), but rock ledges, boulders, brush piles, and fallen trees are a crucial component of its habitat, offering shelter, concealment, and denning sites. Although the brush mouse has been reported to be an adept climber and may occasionally nest in tree cavities, its nests generally are constructed in rock crevices or under boulders or fallen trees.

The brush mouse is medium in size compared to other members of the genus *Peromyscus*. Its tail is equal to or longer than the head and body; its length differentiates *P. boylii* from *P. crinitus, P. leucopus,* and *P. maniculatus,* all of which are generally smaller in size overall. The tail of *P. boylii* is bicolored (white underneath and dark gray above) and is tufted at the end. The mouse's back is a medium brown. The sides are a paler brown, grading to white or cream on the underparts. A broad, bright orange lateral line extends from the cheek to the hindquarters and can help distinguish this mouse from other

species of *Peromyscus*. The ankles are dusky gray, in contrast to the white ankles of *P. pectoralis*, the species it most closely resembles. The ears and hind feet of *Peromyscus boylii* are similar in size and are useful characteristics in distinguishing the brush mouse from *Peromyscus truei* and *Peromyscus difficilis*, both of which have larger ears, and *Peromyscus attwateri*, which has a much larger hind foot. Several closely related species occur in Mexico, including *Peromyscus beatae, P. levipes, P. simulus, P. spicilegus,* and *P. aztecus*. These species were formerly classified as subspecies of *Peromyscus boylii,* but recent chromosome and biochemical data suggest that they represent distinct species. These species are extremely difficult to distinguish from each other.

Peromyscus boylii breeds throughout most of the year, although most young are born in the spring and early summer. The gestation period is about 23 days. Several litters are commonly produced per year, generally of two to five young (average three). The young are born hairless and blind. Growth and development are similar to that observed for other *Peromyscus* species; the young are weaned at three to four weeks of age. *P. boylii* appears to feed on a variety of nuts, fruits, and seeds, including acorns, pine nuts, fir seeds, hackberries, juniper berries, cactus fruits, and many different grass seeds.

Several other species of *Peromyscus* inhabit the same geographical range as that of the brush mouse, including *P. attwateri, difficilis, leucopus, maniculatus, pectoralis,* and *truei*. Other species of small mammals that often occur with the brush mouse include harvest mice, woodrats, cotton rats, shrews, tree squirrels, and chipmunks. *R. D. Bradley and D. J. Schmidly*

Peromyscus boylii

Size
No significant sexual dimorphism
Total length: 175–210 (194) mm
Length of tail: 89–115 (104) mm
Weight: 22–36 g

Identification
P. boylii is medium in size. Its tail is well haired, tufted at the end, and is longer than the head and body. A broad pale-yellowish-orange pectoral patch extends to the hindquarters. *P. boylii*

is sympatric with several other species of *Peromyscus* and is difficult to distinguish; however, *P. boylii* is smaller than most other species except *P. crinitus, P. leucopus,* and *P. maniculatus,* and can be distinguished by its longer tail (in relation to head and body length). Additional characteristics include smaller ears than either *P. truei* or *P. difficilis;* a smaller hind foot than *P. attwateri;* paler color than two Mexican species, *P. levipes* and *P. beatae;* and darker ankles than *P. pectoralis.*

Status

Common

Subspecies

Peromyscus boylii boylii, northern California and extreme western Nevada

Peromyscus boylii glasselli, restricted to San Pedro Nolasco Island, Gulf of California, Sonora

Peromyscus boylii rowleyi, southwestern United States from California to Colorado and

Texas, south along the Mexican Plateau (central Mexico) to Hidalgo

Peromyscus boylii utahensis, central Utah

References

Carleton, 1989; Davis and Schmidly, 1994; Schmidly et al., 1988

California mouse | *Peromyscus californicus*

Peromyscus californicus is restricted to California south of San Francisco Bay (38°N), occurring southward along the coastal ranges to San Quintin, Baja California Norte. California mice also occupy lower elevations of the western slopes of the southern Sierra Nevada Mountains from northwestern Mariposa County southward to Kern County. The elevational range is from sea level to 2,440 m.

The California mouse is active throughout the night, with bursts of activity near dusk and dawn. These mice are highly arboreal. Adults are fairly sedentary and nest under fallen logs or other debris, in trees, or in the dens of the dusky-footed woodrat *(Neotoma fuscipes)*. Nests are globular and composed of dry grasses, weeds, and sticks and lined with fine grasses. Compared to most *Peromyscus,* California mice are rather slow

Peromyscus californicus

and passive and are not likely to bite when handled. They have long, dense, fine fur that is effective against cold but ineffective in shedding water. Two molts occur per year, in early summer and late autumn.

California mice live from 9 to 18 months. Populations are typified by low but stable densities, with peaks in breeding from November to May, coinciding with the rainy season. In contrast to most mammals, *P. californicus* is exclusively monogamous; individuals reside in small, semi-permanent family groups. Males and females form long-term pair bonds and males show extensive care of young. Breeding occurs throughout the year, with females producing several litters. Following a gestation period of about 30–33 days, from 1 to 3 altricial young are born. Lactation is prolonged and the presence of the male increases survival of offspring. Young are weaned at about 5 weeks of age. Unlike most mammals, females disperse greater distances from the natal area than do males.

The food of California mice includes seeds, fruits, grasses, forbs, fungi, and arthropods. Seeds of California laurel *(Umbellularia californica)* are a staple in the diet in the northwestern region of its distribution. Habitat selection and distributional limits of the California mouse may be set by availability of adequate water and specific food and shelter needs.

California mice are abundant in chaparral and oak woodland near Berkeley, moist laurel and redwood forests of the Santa Cruz Mountains, coastal sage scrub in southern California, and brush-covered slopes in Baja California Norte. Fossils are known from a late Quaternary site in Kern County and a late Pleistocene site in Contra Costa County. *J. F. Merritt*

Size
No significant sexual dimorphism
Total length: 220–285 mm
Length of tail: 117–156 mm
Weight: 33.2–54.4 g

Identification
The California mouse is easily distinguished from all other *Peromyscus* by its large size—it is the largest species of *Peromyscus* in North America. The fur is long and lax, yellowish-brown or gray with a blackish-brown back and grayish belly. The tail is longer than the head and body and is not sharply bicolored.

Status
Common

Subspecies
Peromyscus californicus californicus, California from San Francisco Bay south to the Santa Monica Mountains and east to the Sierra Nevada foothills
Peromyscus californicus insignis, San Gabriel Mountains south into Baja California, Mexico

References
Mammalian Species 85; Gubernick, 1988; Gubernick and Nordby, 1993; Gubernick et al., 1993; Ribble, 1991

Canyon mouse | *Peromyscus crinitus*

Canyon mice occur in arid shrublands and grasslands, especially in the canyonlands and "slickrock" deserts of the West. Often their habitat is almost devoid of vegetation, consisting of colluvial talus, desert pavement, bare canyon walls, or rocky mesas and buttes. Bare rock—vertical or horizontal—seems to be the common denominator of suitable habitat. Plant associations differ widely and include stands of blackbrush, creosote-bush, pygmy conifers, agave, saltbush, bunchgrasses, and sagebrush. With their predilection for rocky habitats, canyon mice sometimes are the only terrestrial mammals living atop isolated buttes and mesas.

These animals are omnivorous over the course of the year, seemingly emphasizing insects and some green vegetation during the growing season and seeds and fruits in cooler months. Canyon mice meet their need for water from their diet. They are active year-round, although torpor can be induced by food deprivation (and concomitant water shortage) in the laboratory and probably occurs in the wild.

Canyon mice are almost exclusively nocturnal, moving with remarkable agility through their complex habitats and negotiating vertical or even overhanging walls with apparent ease. They sandbathe, and if fine sand or soil is not available their lax pelage becomes matted and oily. Inactive periods are passed in a nest of shredded plant fibers, usually located in a natural crevice among the rocks.

Canyon mice are polyestrous and exhibit spontaneous ovulation. Breeding occurs in the warmer months, with reports of reproductive activity from March to November. Gestation ranges from 24 to 31 days, depending on whether or not the female is lactating. Litter size ranges from one to five (average about three) young. The young are altricial (although in common with some other desert-dwelling species, they are relatively less so than many other species of *Peromyscus*). Development is rapid, as birth weight is doubled in the first week, the eyes open during week three, and at four weeks the young are weaned. Reproductive maturity occurs at 10 weeks of age.

Several other rodents share broad habitats with canyon mice, and removal experiments suggest that competition may occur with other granivores (such as the San Diego pocket mouse, *Chaetodipus fallax*) as well as with the desert woodrat (*Neotoma lepida*), which is folivorous. Habitat segregation is typical between canyon mice and sympatric species of *Peromyscus*, with canyon mice frequently occurring in the most desolate, rocky terrain, and other, larger-bodied species (such as the cactus mouse, *P. eremicus*, pinyon mouse, *P. truei*, or brush mouse, *P. boylii*) occupying shrublands, woodlands, or oak brush, respectively; the similar-sized deer mouse (*P. maniculatus*) occupies disturbed, early successional sites.

Doubtless most carnivorous vertebrates able to capture canyon mice take a toll, although predator-pressure on them may be less than on some other small rodents because of their inaccessible and generally inhospitable habitat. Reported endoparasites include flatworms and roundworms, and ectoparasites include fleas, mites, ticks, lice, and botfly larvae (warbles).
D. M. Armstrong

Peromyscus crinitus

Size
Females average slightly larger than males over the range of the species, but sexual dimorphism has not been shown to be statistically or biologically significant.
Total length: 162–191 (175) mm
Length of tail: 79–118 (92) mm
Weight: 13–23 (17) g

Identification
The canyon mouse is a small to medium-sized *Peromyscus* with relatively long ears (as long as or longer than the hind foot) and a tail as long as the head and body or longer. The tail is thinly haired, with a distinct "pencil" of hairs at the tip. The dorsal pelage is distinctly long and soft, varying in color from brown to pale buff; the venter is white, sometimes with a buffy pectoral or anal patch.

Status
Often abundant in suitable (very restricted) habitat

Subspecies
Peromyscus crinitus auripectus, Colorado Plateau, south and east of Green and Colorado rivers
Peromyscus crinitus crinitus, northern Great Basin of Oregon, Idaho, northeastern California, northwestern Nevada
Peromyscus crinitus delgadilli, Sierra del Pinacate, Sonora
Peromyscus crinitus disparalis, southwestern Arizona and adjacent northwestern Sonora
Peromyscus crinitus doutii, Colorado Plateau, north and west of Green and Colorado rivers
Peromyscus crinitus pallidissimus, island in Gonzaga Bay, Baja California Norte
Peromyscus crinitus pergracilis, Great Basin of western Utah and eastern Nevada
Peromyscus crinitus stephensi, southeastern California, adjacent Baja California Norte, southern Nevada, southwestern Utah

References
Mammalian Species 287; Armstrong, 1982; Egoscue, 1964

Cactus mouse | *Peromyscus eremicus*

The cactus mouse occurs from southern Nevada to Baja California, east to western Texas, and south to San Luis Potosi, Mexico. It is also known from several islands in the Gulf of California. It prefers low desert areas and rocky foothills, slopes, and plains with scattered vegetation and sandy soils. It typically lives in a burrow, but can be found in piles of debris, chaparral, clumps of cactus, or in rock crevices. The cactus mouse is nocturnal. Food items include seeds, insects, and green vegetation. It may enter a daily torpor and aestivate during the hot, dry months of summer.

Litter size ranges from one to four and as many as three to four litters may occur in a year. The gestation period is about

20–25 days. Young cactus mice weigh about 2.2 g at birth, their ears unfold after the first day, and the eyes open in 11–15 days. Juveniles probably begin to molt at about five weeks of age. The average life span is probably one year. *W. Caire*

Peromyscus eremicus

Size

Considerable variation exists among subspecies, and the extent of sexual dimorphism varies across the range of the species. Females are usually larger than males. No sexual dimorphism is reported for specimens from Arizona.

Total length: 169–218 mm
Length of tail: 92–117 mm
Weight: 18–40 g (usually about 24 g in males and 27 g in females)

Identification

The cactus mouse is medium sized, with a tail that is usually markedly longer than the head and body. Its pelage is long and soft to silky. The body is pale gray washed with reddish-brown above and whitish on the underparts. Dark to melanistic populations can be found on lava flows. The sides and top of the head are grayish, and the lateral line is pale yellowish-buff. The bicolored tail is finely ringed, thinly haired, and lacks a prominent tuft on the tip. The ears are relatively large, thin, and barely covered with fine hairs. The soles of the hind feet are naked to the heel.

Cactus mice are found with three other species of the subgenus *Haplomylomys*: *P. californicus, P. eva,* and *P. merriami.* (The other members of this subgenus, *P. caniceps, dickeyi, guardia, interparietalis, pembertoni,* and *pseudocrinitus,* are restricted to islands in the Gulf of California.) There is great geographic variation, and usually a combination of diagnostic characters is needed to separate *P. eremicus* from the three sympatric forms listed above. In general, *P. californicus* is usually larger and differs in having a well-haired tail, dark brown upperparts, and in lacking the pale yellowish-buff lateral line; *P. eva,* which occurs in Mexico, has a longer tail, longer skull, and its pelage is shorter and appears more finely textured; and *P. merriami* is generally larger in size both externally and cranially, is darker in color, and often has a cinnamon-colored pectoral patch. Members of the subgenus *Haplomylomys,* including *P. eremicus,* have less complex molar teeth than members of other subgenera within the genus *Peromyscus.*

Status

Common in suitable habitat

Subspecies

Additional study is needed to clarify the status of many of the following subspecies:

Peromyscus eremicus alcorni, Chihuahua, Mexico
Peromyscus eremicus anthonyi, Arizona and New Mexico, Chihuahua and Sonora, Mexico
Peromyscus eremicus avius, Ceralvo Island, Gulf of California
Peromyscus eremicus cedrosensis, Cedros Island, Gulf of California
Peromyscus eremicus cinereus, San Jose Island, Gulf of California
Peromyscus eremicus eremicus, Arizona, California, Nevada, New Mexico, and Texas; Baja California, Chihuahua, Coahuila, Durango, and Sonora, Mexico
Peromyscus eremicus fraterculus, California and Baja California, Mexico
Peromyscus eremicus insulicola, Espiritu Santo Island, Gulf of California
Peromyscus eremicus papagensis, Arizona and Sonora, Mexico
Peromyscus eremicus phaeurus, Coahuila, Durango, Nueva Leon, San Luis Potosi, and Zacatecas, Mexico
Peromyscus eremicus polypolius, Margarita Island, Gulf of California
Peromyscus eremicus pullus, Arizona
Peromyscus eremicus sinaloensis, Sonora, Chihuahua, Durango, and Sinaloa, Mexico
Peromyscus eremicus tiburonensis, Tiburon Island, Gulf of California

References

Mammalian Species 118; Carleton, 1989; Hoffmeister, 1986

Cotton mouse | *Peromyscus gossypinus*

Because they sometimes inhabit buildings, cotton mice are well known to residents of the southern United States. Three of the six currently recognized subspecies occupy most of the species' range *(P. g. gossypinus, P. g. megacephalus, P. g. palmarius)*, two are known only from the localities in Florida where they were originally described *(P. g. allapaticola* and *P. g. restrictus)*, and one is restricted to extreme southern Florida *(P. g. telmaphilus)*.

A medium-sized rodent with large ears and eyes, the cotton mouse is dark golden-brown above and has white underparts and feet. The middorsal area is dusky. The tail is sparsely haired and dark on the upper surface but fades to white underneath. The soles of the feet have prominent ridges, a feature contributing to climbing ability. Cotton mice look very similar to white-footed mice. Their ability to hybridize in captivity (although rarely if at all in nature) reflects their close relationship and suggests that these "sister species" have only recently diverged.

Cotton mice prefer to live in somewhat wet habitats, especially bottomland hardwood forests, hammocks, and swamps. They may also be found in drier situations such as upland forests, old fields, palmetto thickets, pine flatwoods, and beach dunes, and are even known to occur along rocky bluffs and in caves. Cotton mouse talents include the ability to climb, swim, and dive, decided advantages in their sometimes wet habitats. Nesting sites are found in logs, stumps, brush piles, palmettos, and in moss on floating logs. In some areas, elevated nests are preferred: this mouse has been found in an abandoned gray squirrel nest that was 6 meters from the ground in a live oak tree. Like other *Peromyscus,* they are strongly nocturnal and do

Peromyscus gossypinus

not hibernate. They are, however, known to enter torpor during summer heat.

In the southern parts of the range breeding occurs throughout the year, but with a decline in activity during the summer and a peak in late autumn and early winter. Litter size is usually 3–4 and the young are born after a 23-day gestation period. Newborn young are pink and hairless, except for stiff hairs on the snout. Their eyes are closed and the ears are folded over and sealed to the sides of the head. Fine hairs appear on the dorsum by day 5 and, by day 10, cotton mice are fully covered by gray pelage. The ears are unfolded by 5 days and most individuals have their eyes open by 2 weeks of age. Weaning occurs by about 4 weeks of age, when the young are about 85 percent of adult size. Molting of the gray pelage begins at about 5 weeks, with the brown adult pelage appearing first along the side of the body and progressing to the back, head, and tail.

Density estimates as high as 97 per hectare have been reported in a wet lowland forest, but drier areas more typically support up to eight mice per hectare. Home ranges 0.5–1 hectare in area are usual. Like most small mammals that serve as food for species higher on the food chain, the life span is short: individuals have an average longevity of 4–5 months. Cotton mice are omnivorous and probably eat whatever is available, although animal foods appear to dominate. These mice exhibit considerable homing ability, probably the result of random wandering until a familiar area is encountered. *A. V. Linzey*

Size
Total length: 142–206 mm
Length of tail: 55–97 mm
Weight: 17–46 g

Identification
Several other species of *Peromyscus* have ranges that overlap or adjoin that of the cotton mouse. Co-occurring races of the oldfield mouse *(Peromyscus polionotus)* and deer mouse *(Peromyscus maniculatus)* have markedly smaller body sizes. The greatest difficulty arises in distinguishing this species from the white-footed mouse *(Peromyscus leucopus)*. Although the cotton mouse is generally larger than its close relative, size is a dependable identifier only if individuals are known to be the same age.

Status
Common in most parts of the range, but one Florida subspecies *(Peromyscus gossypinus allapaticola)* is listed as endangered by the United States government, and others are very restricted in distribution.

Subspecies
Peromyscus gossypinus allapaticola, Key Largo, Florida
Peromyscus gossypinus gossypinus, coastal areas of southeastern United States (except peninsular Florida) west to southwestern Louisiana
Peromyscus gossypinus megacephalus, south-central United States north to southern Illinois and east to eastern Tennessee
Peromyscus gossypinus palmarius, central peninsular Florida

Peromyscus gossypinus restrictus, small region on west coast of peninsular Florida
Peromyscus gossypinus telmaphilus, extreme southern mainland Florida
An additional subspecies listed in many references, *P. g. anastasae* (found on Anastasia Island, Florida, and Cumberland Island, Georgia, but now extinct in the former location), is no longer considered to be subspecifically distinct from the adjoining mainland populations, *P. g. palmarius* and *P. g. gossypinus*.

References
Mammalian Species 70; Hamilton and Whitaker, 1979

Osgood's mouse | *Peromyscus gratus*

A study published in 1984 concluded that Osgood's mouse is genetically different enough from the pinyon mouse *(Peromyscus truei)* to be considered a separate species. Although the distributions of these two species generally do not overlap, they have been found together in southwestern New Mexico. *Peromyscus gratus* is distributed in mountainous areas from the Mogollon Plateau in New Mexico southward through the Sierra Madre Occidental and Sierra Madre Oriental into southern Mexico.

Osgood's mouse occurs in some of the most diverse habitats of any rodent associated with mountains. Although it may prefer foothills where juniper, pinyon, oak, or other shrubby vegetation occurs, the species has been reported from elevations of 1,829–3,110 m in open valleys, cultivated land, grassland, yucca-mesquite, humid sub-tropical forest, and cool coniferous forest on mountain-tops. Regardless of the vegetation, Osgood's mouse is usually associated with rocky areas. This mouse can climb expertly and makes its home in fissures and crevices in rocks. Although this species may occur in a variety of habitats, *P. gratus* is usually not as common as other rodents in any given habitat type.

Osgood's mice are attractive, medium-sized mice with large ears. The back is brownish to brownish-black and the underparts and hind feet are whitish. The tail, which is brownish on top and whitish underneath, is long and covered with short hairs, except at the tip, where longer hairs grow. Local habitat can influence the pelage coloration. Because of the affinity Osgood's mouse has for rocks, lava flows make particularly attractive homes for this species, and in such areas, *Peromyscus gratus* may be dark in color. This helps camouflage the mice as

they travel among the black lava rocks. *Peromyscus gratus erasmus* is a darkly colored subspecies found only in the vicinity of the Guadiana lava field in the Sierra Madre Occidental.

Although *Peromyscus gratus* may reproduce year-round, most reproductive activity occurs during spring and summer. Following about 26 days of gestation, usually three, but occasionally up to six, babies are born. Like the young of most *Peromyscus,* juvenile Osgood's mice are gray. *J. K. Frey*

Peromyscus gratus

Size
No significant sexual dimorphism
Total length: 171–231 (199) mm
Length of tail: 76–124 (106) mm
Weight: 19–32.8 (26.9) g

Identification
Peromyscus gratus is larger than *Peromyscus truei*, its tail is longer rather than shorter than the head and body, and its ears are shorter rather than longer than the hind feet. *P. gratus* is smaller than *Peromyscus difficilis* and has a shorter tail and hind feet. It is difficult to distinguish *P. gratus* from *Peromyscus nasutus*; it is slightly larger and has a slightly longer tail and slightly shorter hind feet and ears.

Recent Synonyms
Peromyscus truei (part)

Other Common Names
Pinyon mouse (formerly, when it was known as *P. truei*)

Status
Unknown

Subspecies
Peromyscus gratus erasmus, Guadiana lava field near Durango, Durango
Peromyscus gratus gentilis, in the west from the Mogollon Plateau of New Mexico south through the Sierra Madre Occidental to northern Jalisco, in the east from southeastern Coahuila down the Sierra Madre Oriental to southern San Luis Potosi and northwestern Guanajuato
Peromyscus gratus gratus, eastern Hidalgo west to northern Jalisco and western Michoacan
Peromyscus gratus zapotecae, southern Puebla and Oaxaca

References
Mammalian Species 161; Baker and Greer, 1962; Ceballos-G. and Galindo-L., 1984; Janecek, 1990

Northwestern deer mouse | *Peromyscus keeni*

Peromyscus keeni is now considered the predominant deer mouse of most of the Pacific Northwest. The taxonomy of deer mice from this region has been complicated by extensive insular endemism. Historically two or three closely related species *(Peromyscus maniculatus, P. sitkensis,* and *P. oreas)* have been recognized. These taxa were considered to include a large number of subspecies, many of which were restricted to one or a few small islands. From the Olympic Peninsula of Washington north to southern Alaska, and west of the Cascade and Coastal mountain ranges, *P. maniculatus* was long thought to be the predominant deer mouse of the Pacific Northwest, inhabiting the entire mainland and most of the coastal islands. *Peromyscus sitkensis* was originally described as occurring on Baranof and Chicagof islands in the Alexander Archipelago of Alaska and on Prevost (= Kunghit) Island in the Queen Charlotte Islands of British Columbia, Canada. Subsequent studies either suggested broader distributions of *P. sitkensis* or questioned its specific validity. Despite considerable data supporting the specific status of *P. oreas* in the Cascade Mountains of Washington and the southern Coastal Mountains of British Columbia, this taxon long remained a subspecies of *P. maniculatus.*

A recent series of studies, combining genetic analyses (of chromosomes, protein genes, and mitochondrial DNA) and examination of morphologic variation, have now resolved much of the confusion surrounding the taxonomy and distribution of deer mice in the Pacific Northwest. These studies

culminated in the recognition of *P. keeni. Peromyscus keeni* includes (and taxonomically subsumes) all of what was formerly recognized as *P. sitkensis* and *P. oreas* and apparently includes all of the previously recognized subspecies of *P. maniculatus* from west of the Coastal Mountains north of about 50° N latitude, making it the predominant deer mouse in this region. At lower elevations in the southern portion of its range, the northwestern deer mouse frequently co-occurs with *P. maniculatus.* Curiously, the northwestern deer mouse is absent from southeastern Vancouver Island.

The habitat of *P. keeni* can be generally characterized as rainy and mild. In the Pacific Northwest *P. maniculatus* appears to be restricted to lower elevations; *P. keeni* occupies habitats ranging from western coastal lowlands to high-elevation sub-alpine forests. At lower elevations, northwestern deer mice often associate with edge vegetation, along logging roads, or around the periphery of small islands. They appear to avoid closed-canopy forested habitats. Throughout their range, these deer mice are fond of buildings and are frequent pests in rural areas, especially during winter.

Compared to most other deer mice, northwestern deer mice tend to be large, with long tails, generally darker coloration, and denser fur. Information about the ecology and life history of northwestern deer mice is scant. Breeding seems to occur from late April through early July and litters typically consist of 4–7 pups. Observations of unusual jumping ability are common and several authors contend that northwestern deer mice are more arboreal than are *P. maniculatus.* I. F. Greenbaum

Peromyscus keeni

Size

Total length: 181–236 (210) mm
Length of tail: 92–114 (109) mm
Weight: 10–30 g

Identification

Peromyscus keeni differs from *Peromyscus maniculatus,* the only other deer mouse in its range, by being significantly larger and having a longer tail (typically longer than 100 mm). *P. keeni* is also distinct from Pacific Northwest populations of *P. maniculatus* in the arrangement of its chromosomes.

Recent Synonyms

Populations from various portions of the range have previously been referred to *P. maniculatus, P. sitkensis,* or *P. oreas.*

Other Common Names

"White-footed mouse" and "deer mouse" have been applied to *Peromyscus maniculatus,* "Sitka deer mouse" to *P. sitkensis,* and "Cascade" or "Columbian deer mouse" to *P. oreas.* No common name has previously been applied to *P. keeni.* "Northwestern deer mouse" is adopted here.

Status

Common

Subspecies

Peromyscus keeni algidus, northernmost coastal British Columbia, Canada

Peromyscus keeni hylaeus, northern coastal British Columbia, Canada

Peromyscus keeni interdictus, all except southeastern Vancouver Island, British Columbia, Canada

Peromyscus keeni isolatus, select islands off northeastern Vancouver Island, British Columbia, Canada

Peromyscus keeni keeni, Graham and Moresby islands, British Columbia, Canada

Peromyscus keeni macrorhinus, central and southern coastal British Columbia, Canada

Peromyscus keeni ocaenicus, Forrester Island, Alaska

Peromyscus keeni oreas, Washington State from the western face of the Cascade Mountains and north of the Columbia River

Peromyscus keeni prevostensis, several of the small Queen Charlotte Islands, British Columbia, Canada

Peromyscus keeni sitkensis, several of the islands in the Alexander Archipelago, Alaska

References

Allard et al., 1987; Calhoun and Greenbaum, 1991; Gunn and Greenbaum, 1988; Hogan et al., 1993, 1997; Sheppe, 1961

White-footed mouse | *Peromyscus leucopus*

The geographic range of the white-footed mouse extends from the Atlantic coast to Montana in the northwest, Arizona in the southwest, and as far south as southern Mexico. In Canada it is found in extreme southern Saskatchewan, Ontario, Quebec, and Nova Scotia. It does not occur on the coastal plains of North Carolina, South Carolina, Georgia, and Alabama, nor anywhere in Florida.

Within its range the white-footed mouse is found in many habitats, but especially in warm dry forests at low to mid-elevations; it is less common at high elevations and in cool, moist coniferous forests. The white-footed mouse usually is the most abundant rodent in the mixed (deciduous and coniferous) forests in eastern states, and it may be similarly abundant in hedgerows bordering agricultural areas, where it often forages well out into brushy fields and croplands at night. In the western parts of its range it is more restricted in distribution, usually occurring in wooded areas along watercourses and in valleys and ravines. Its habitat in southwestern states includes semi-desert vegetation, strikingly different from plant communities found in its habitats in the Northeast. In southern Mexico it is most abundant in agricultural and highly disturbed habitats, and rarely is found in forests. A seemingly constant feature of its habitat is some form of canopy, if only of shrubs, woody debris such as fallen trees, or crop plants. In terms of variety of habitats occupied, the white-footed mouse is one of the most broadly-adapted species in the genus *Peromyscus*.

The diet of *P. leucopus* is as diverse as the habitats it occupies, and may vary seasonally and geographically. Major components of its diet are insects, seeds, including various nuts, green vegetation, and fruits; in a study in New York, insects were the most commonly occurring food item.

Longevity in the white-footed mouse can reach several years in captivity, but under natural conditions there is an almost complete replacement of a population each year. Surprisingly, white-footed mice suffer relatively little mortality during the winter in the Northeast, but high mortality (as evidenced by the disappearance of marked individuals) occurs in the spring and early summer—perhaps as a consequence of increased predation pressure at that time.

White-footed mice are territorial (defend specific areas), at least during the breeding season. The territories of individuals of opposite sex overlap more than do territories of mice of the same sex. The size of home ranges (areas used during normal daily activities) vary depending on many factors, such as population density, age, season, and habitat characteristics; a typical home range in this species is 0.1 hectares, but may be much larger. White-footed mice are good climbers, and the home range includes a significant vertical component.

The nests of *P. leucopus* may be built inside logs, in standing trees, or in buildings. The mice may cap an abandoned bird's nest, thereby forming a spherical nest. Nest materials consist of such items as grass, hair, feathers, milkweed floss, shredded bark, and moss.

The white-footed mouse is nocturnal, but occasionally is diurnal during the winter. Food-hoarding has been described as considerable in some studies, but as minimal in others. Season, geographic location, and other factors may affect this behavior. Torpor, a condition resembling hibernation, often occurs in white-footed mice during winter in the colder parts of their range. Torpor includes a drop in body temperature from the normal 35° C to as low as 17° C, and in the rate of breathing from 700 breaths per minute in active mice to as few as 60 in torpid mice. There is a low turnover rate of water in this species, likely a substantial advantage in the parts of its range where water is scarce. White-footed mice are excellent swimmers, as indicated by frequent dispersal to islands in lakes, and confirmed by laboratory studies.

The white-footed mouse is a frequent host of the botfly, *Cuterebra fontinella (=angustifrons)*. The larval botfly resides be-

Peromyscus leucopus

neath the skin of the mouse and may reach 20 mm in length. There may be up to 4 or 5 larvae per host, which probably has a substantial effect on locomotion and possibly on the energy of the mouse. The botfly larvae often are located near or in the scrotum, leading some researchers to hypothesize an effect on reproduction.

The breeding season of *P. leucopus* extends from March to October in northern populations. In more southerly latitudes the breeding season is longer; in southern Mexico these mice breed throughout the year. In the north, reproductive activity peaks in spring and fall. There are usually 4–6 young per litter in the north, somewhat fewer in the southern United States, but 4–6 in southern Mexico. Older and larger females usually have larger litters than do young, first-time mothers. A female may give birth to several litters per year. The young are born after a gestation period of at least 22 days, but the gestation period is longer when the mother is nursing a previous litter. In a laboratory population derived from animals from Michigan,

the eyes opened at an average age of 12.3 days, the ear opening appeared at 10.4 days, the incisors erupted through the gums at 4.6 days, and the ear pinnae became upright at 2.5 days. The average age at sexual maturity in northern female mice occurred at 44 days, and at 38 days in mice from southern Mexico. The first pelage of the white-footed mouse is gray, and is replaced at about 40 days of age by a dull brown coat; subsequent pelages of older mice are more glossy, and may be bright reddish in northern populations.

Because of their abundance, white-footed mice play a significant role in the ecology of their communities. They are taken by a wide variety of predators, including weasels and other carnivores, owls, snakes, and others. They are not an important consumer of crops, and thus are not a detrimental species in agricultural areas. In some parts of its range the white-footed mouse is an important host of a tick that transmits Lyme disease. *J. A. Lackey*

Size (in the United States)
Total length: 150–205 mm
Length of tail: 65–95 mm
Weight: 15–25 g

Identification
Geographic and individual variation and overlap with the ranges of many similar species make identification of the white-footed mouse challenging. Compared with the "long-tailed" forms of the deer mouse (*Peromyscus maniculatus*), the adult white-footed mouse has a shorter tail, less than about 45 percent of total length, which is sparsely haired rather than distinctly hairy, and indistinctly bicolored rather than sharply bicolored (dark above, white below); the tuft of hairs at the tip of the tail is less than about 5 mm long, rather than longer. The ears are not more than 18 mm long from the notch, rather than 18 mm or longer. Compared with the "short-tailed" forms of *P. maniculatus*, color differences are largely as noted for the long-tailed forms. In size, the white-footed mouse averages larger in most respects than the "short-tailed" forms, with tail length usually more than 70 mm and ear length usually more than 16 mm; both measures usually are less in the short-tailed forms of *P. maniculatus*. In the southeastern states, the white-footed mouse may be confused with the cotton mouse, *P. gossypinus*, which has a hind foot usually longer than 22 mm (22 mm or less in the white-footed mouse). The oldfield mouse (*P. polionotus*) occurring in southeastern states is smaller than the white-footed mouse, with a

total length of 110–153 mm, a tail length of 40–60 mm, and a hind foot 15–19 mm long, and its pelage varies from pale cinnamon to almost white, compared with brown or reddish-brown in the white-footed mouse. Also occurring in the southeastern states, the golden mouse (*Ochrotomys nuttalli*) is similar in size to the white-footed mouse, but has a bright golden-cinnamon pelage. In southern states, the white-footed mouse can be distinguished from the brush mouse, *P. boylii*, white-ankled mouse, *P. pectoralis*, pinyon mouse, *P. truei*, rock mouse, *P. difficilis*, northern rock mouse, *P. nasutus*, and Texas mouse, *P. attwateri*, by tail length, which is less than head and body length in the white-footed mouse but equal to or greater than head and body length in the other species. In addition, the pinyon mouse has ears up to 27 mm in length; the white-ankled mouse has white ankles and pale gray pelage, and the brush mouse has dusky ankles. The sexes of *P. leucopus* are identical in appearance.

Other Common Names
Wood mouse, deer mouse

Status
Some subspecies with small distributions in the United States (e.g., *P. l. ammodytes* or *P. l. easti*) may be vulnerable; the status of Mexican populations is unknown.

Subspecies
Peromyscus leucopus affinis, southern Oaxaca and southern Veracruz, Mexico

Peromyscus leucopus ammodytes, Monomoy Island, Massachusetts

Peromyscus leucopus aridulus, Saskatchewan to Kansas

Peromyscus leucopus arizonae, southeastern Arizona to Durango, Mexico

Peromyscus leucopus castaneus, Yucatan and Campeche, Mexico

Peromyscus leucopus caudatus, southern half of Nova Scotia

Peromyscus leucopus cozumelae, Cozumel Island (off the Yucatan Peninsula), Mexico

Peromyscus leucopus easti, eastern Virginia

Peromyscus leucopus fusus, eastern Massachusetts

Peromyscus leucopus incensus, Veracruz, Oaxaca, and Pueblo, Mexico

Peromyscus leucopus lachiguiriensis, southern Oaxaca, Mexico

Peromyscus leucopus leucopus, Oklahoma to Virginia and south to the Gulf of Mexico

Peromyscus leucopus mesomelas, San Luis Potosi and Veracruz, Mexico

Peromyscus leucopus noveboracensis, North Dakota to Maine; south to Oklahoma and North Carolina

Peromyscus leucopus ochraceus, central Arizona

Peromyscus leucopus texanus, Texas and northeastern Mexico

Peromyscus leucopus tornillo, southeastern Colorado, western Kansas, western Oklahoma, northern Texas, and New Mexico

References
Mammalian Species 247; Baker, 1983; Lackey, 1978

Deer mouse | *Peromyscus maniculatus*

The oldest fossils certain to be *Peromyscus* are from early Pliocene deposits in the western United States, and the genus did not become common until the late Pleistocene. The species *P. maniculatus* evolved in the late Pleistocene.

Among the dozens of living species of *Peromyscus,* the close relatives of *P. maniculatus* form the *P. maniculatus* group. These siblings of the deer mouse are *P. melanotis,* the black-eared mouse from central Mexico; *P. keeni,* the northwestern deer mouse, from southeastern Alaska, southwestern British Columbia (including the Queen Charlotte Islands), and western Washington; *P. polionotus,* the oldfield or beach mouse, which occurs in the southeastern United States; *P. sejugis,* the Santa Cruz Island mouse, from the Gulf of California; and *P. slevini,* Slevin's mouse, from the Gulf of California.

The deer mouse is more variable morphologically and more widespread geographically and ecologically than any other species of North American mouse, so it is not surprising that it has differentiated into many subspecies. Currently 57 are recognized. With so many subspecies, all based on morphological variations, particularly pelage coloration, body size, tail length, and ear size, it is impractical to try to describe the deer mouse in other than general terms. What *all* deer mice have in common are 16 teeth (one incisor and three molars in each jaw); large, black, bulging eyes; relatively large, naked ears; moderate (for a mouse) size; fine, smooth-lying fur; a well-haired, sharply bicolored (blackish above, white below) tail, tipped with a tuft of short, stiff, hairs something like a watercolor brush (penicillate), and white feet. Most deer mice have snow-white underparts with blackish hair bases. The color of dorsal pelage varies with age and locality. Juveniles are gray, subadults yellowish-brown, and adults are some shade of yellow-, orange-, or reddish-brown, mixed with black or gray. There is a single annual molt, usually in late summer or early fall in the northern part of the range.

The subspecies of deer mice segregate into two broad categories, long-tailed, large-eared forest inhabitants and short-tailed, small-eared open country forms. Darker, richer colors characterize the pelage of subspecies of humid regions, and paler, drabber colors prevail in arid conditions. This taxonomic matrix is especially complex in some areas where forest and open country forms occur together or are separated only by habitat and yet do not interbreed. They act like species, but ac-

tually they are the overlapping ends of rings or chains of intergrading subspecies.

The deer mouse is the most widespread North American rodent. It is found in almost every habitat from the Arctic coast of Labrador to the rain forests of southeastern Alaska, from cabins on the tundra beyond the edge of the taiga in Canada, through temperate and boreal forests, to timber line in the mountains, in cliffs and rock slides, in swamps and bogs, across prairies, deserts, and scrublands, and into the subtropics in Mexico.

This mouse feeds on whatever seeds, nuts, berries, and fruit are available in any of the many habitats in which it lives. In moist humus-rich soil it digs for the subterranean fruiting bodies of the fungus *Endogone*. It is also an opportunist, taking insects and other animal matter, and feasting on whatever foods it finds in and around houses. The deer mouse is a great hoarder, using for its caches containers such as hollow logs, woodpecker holes and other tree cavities, birds' nests, burrows in the ground, shoes, teapots, and excavations in mattresses. Shelters of some of these sorts serve also as nests for the mouse.

The deer mouse is crepuscular and nocturnal, rarely, unless disturbed, leaving its nest during daylight hours. Woodland forms are scansorial, at home on the ground but also climbing tree trunks easily and moving about with agility among limbs and vines in the forest and on joists and rafters, on shelving, and in walls in houses. Deer mice tunnel through snow and also run about on the surface of snow to forage.

Peromyscus maniculatus

Depending on the setting, the home ranges of deer mice vary from a few hundred square meters to a hectare or more. Males usually have larger home ranges than do females. In winter as many as a dozen deer mice may huddle together in a bird box, tree hole, or other secure nest to conserve warmth. Females often are territorial during the breeding season. Males may stay briefly with females after mating, but usually they are solitary except in cold weather.

Gestation is 21–27 days, or longer when the female is lactating. There is a post-partum estrus. Litter size is 1–8, usually 3–5 (there are six mammae). There are 2–4 litters per year, on average; possibly more in warmer climates. Deer mice may breed year-round or breeding may be seasonally correlated with temperature or rainfall. Young are born with eyes and ears sealed, and naked except for vibrissae. They begin to breed when they are 5–7 weeks old. Longevity is seldom more than one year in nature; 4–8 years in captivity.

Population abundance varies in 3–5 year fluctuations, sometimes correlated with abundance of food. In late summer there may be as many as 15 or more individuals per acre. Because of its abundance and immense range, the deer mouse is one of North America's most important small mammal prey species. It is a primary prey of owls, weasels, and foxes, and is often taken by coyotes and bobcats.

Because of its wide distribution and great morphological variation, reflected in its many subspecies, the deer mouse has a very high degree of genetic, chromosomal, and biochemical variability. It breeds readily, is easily handled, and can be maintained without difficulty in captivity. These factors combine to make it supreme among North American mammals as a laboratory subject for studies of genetics and evolution, as well as for a wide variety of biomedical and physiological investigations. It is an excellent subject for field studies on populations and on behavioral and evolutionary ecology.

The deer mouse is highly significant epidemiologically. In nature it is the primary host of the very virulent hantavirus that causes HPS (Hantaviral Pulmonary Syndrome), a serious disease of humans found most often in the western United States, especially in the Southwest. In the same area it also is a host of plague. In the eastern United States, deer mice, white-footed mice, and white-tailed deer are major hosts in Lyme disease. (The mice are hosts to the larval stage of the tick that carries the bacterium.)

In rural areas in the north and northwest, woodland varieties of the deer mouse are unwelcome pests in houses, but they are easily controlled by trapping. On the other hand, some find them welcome, attractive, tame, and conspicuous visitors in woodland campgrounds. *C. O. Handley, Jr.*

Size

Total length: 120–225 mm
Length of tail: 50–125 mm
Weight: 10–30 g

Identification

Within the range of the deer mouse, a number of similar species can be distinguished from it as follows: the white-footed mouse *(P. leucopus)* has an indistinctly bicolored tail that is shorter than head and body length and lacks a stiff-haired tip. The northwestern deer mouse *(P. keeni)* has a longer tail and longer foot than sympatric deer mice. Brush and white-ankled mice *(P. boylii* and *P. pectoralis)* have longer tails than sympatric deer mice. The black-eared mouse *(P. melanotis),* a Mexican species, has white-edged, black ears, a dark, richly-colored dorsal pelage, and a tail averaging longer than that of sympatric deer mice. These species often are difficult to distinguish from the deer mouse.

Other mice are more easily distinguished. The California mouse *(P. californicus)* is large (total length 225 mm or more, weight 40 g or more). Cactus and mesquite mice *(P. eremicus* and *P. merriami)* have very pale coloration and long, thinly haired, indistinctly bicolored tails. The canyon mouse *(P. crinitus)* has pale coloration, a long tail, and long, very soft pelage. Pinyon and rock mice *(P. truei* and *P. difficilis)* have very large ears (18–26 mm). The plateau mouse *(P. melanophrys),* a Mexican species, is very large (235 mm or more in length). The golden mouse *(Ochrotomys nuttalli)* has uniformly orange upperparts and cream-colored underparts, without sharp demarcation. Grasshopper mice *(Onychomys)* have stout bodies (up to 40 g) and short, white-tipped tails.

Other Common Names

Wood mouse, woodland deer mouse, prairie deer mouse

Status

One of the most abundant mammals of North America

Subspecies

Hall (1981) listed 66 subspecies; recent studies have shifted 9 of these to *P. keeni.*

References

King, 1968; Osgood, 1909

Mesquite mouse | *Peromyscus merriami*

The mesquite mouse occurs in *bosques*—dense thickets of mesquite, often mixed with cholla, prickly pear, palo-verde, vines, and grasses. Ground cover in its habitat tends to be dense and the substrate typically has a litter of dead vegetation. Mesquite mice are strictly nocturnal, foraging mostly on the ground for seeds, small fruits, and insects. Elevations of capture range from sea level to about 1,160 m along the Arizona-Sonora border.

There has been some uncertainty over the years as to the validity of this species. Named in 1907, *Peromyscus merriami* was deemed indistinguishable from the cactus mouse in 1909. *Peromyscus merriami* was resurrected as a valid species in 1952, and *Peromyscus goldmani* was recognized as a subspecies. Since that time the specific distinctiveness and integrity of the mesquite mouse has been confirmed by a number of studies using both traditional and biosystematic characters.

Mesquite mice appear to breed throughout the year, probably with less activity during the hot summer months and most actively in late winter and early spring. Embryo counts average about 2.6 (range 2 to 4).

Typical mammalian associates include the Arizona cotton rat *(Sigmodon arizonae),* the white-throated woodrat *(Neotoma albigula),* Merriam's kangaroo rat *(Dipodomys merriami),* the desert pocket mouse *(Chaetodipus penicillatus),* and Harris's antelope squirrel *(Ammospermophilus harrisii).* The mesquite mouse has been taken together with the cactus mouse at a number of localities, but there appears to be rather strong and consistent habitat segregation. The mesquite mouse typically occupies densely vegetated valley floors and the riparian zone of desert washes, whereas the cactus mouse occurs in adjacent rockier, upland situations.

"Merriam's mouse" was used as the common name for decades, but it has been argued recently that "mesquite

Peromyscus merriami

mouse" is not only descriptive of the species' distinctive habitat, but is less likely to be equivocal, given the number of other rodents named for pioneer American mammalogist C. Hart Merriam.

Peromyscus merriami is thought to be ancestral to the larger-bodied, relatively shorter-tailed *Peromyscus pembertoni*, a poorly known species restricted to Isla San Pedro Nolasco in the Sea of Cortez off the coast of Sonora. *D. M. Armstrong*

Size
Sexual dimorphism appears to be insignificant.
Total length: 185–225 (202) mm
Length of tail: 95–120 (107) mm
Weight: 20–30 g

Identification
The mesquite mouse is a small- to medium-sized *Peromyscus* with a nearly naked tail that is longer than head and body, relatively small ears without white rims, and two pairs of mammae. It can be distinguished from the closely related cactus mouse, *P. eremicus,* by generally larger size, both externally and cranially (especially longer hind foot and maxillary toothrow and greater mastoidal breadth, the mastoid processes projecting beyond the braincase),

and a longer, thinner-shafted baculum that is slightly curved ventrally (rather than dorsally) and has a spatulate base. The mesquite mouse is generally darker in dorsal color than the cactus mouse, has a creamy (rather than white) venter, and frequently has a cinnamon-colored pectoral patch. Their karyotypes are virtually indistinguishable, but the two species are slightly but consistently distinctive in their protein biochemistry. The canyon mouse, *P. crinitus,* is similar to the mesquite mouse in size, but has a more densely haired tail with a prominently tufted tip.

Other Common Names
Merriam's mouse

Status
Common in suitable habitat, which is, however, localized and fragmented. The animals occur in coastal Sonora but not on islands in the Sea of Cortez.

Subspecies
Peromyscus merriami goldmani, extreme southern Sonora southward to central Sinaloa
Peromyscus merriami merriami, south-central Arizona southward to extreme southern Sonora

References
Hoffmeister, 1986; Hoffmeister and Diersing, 1973; Lawlor, 1971

Northern rock mouse | *Peromyscus nasutus*

The northern rock mouse, one of the more uncommon species of *Peromyscus* found in the Rocky Mountain foothills, lives in and among rocky outcrops and in boulder-strewn regions within the pinyon-juniper-oak woodlands zone. Its range is centered in New Mexico, with extensions reaching north into Colorado along the Sangre de Cristo Mountains and southeast into Texas and northern Mexico where appropriate montane habitat is available. The species is limited to the west along the mountains dividing Arizona and New Mexico, and to the northwest along the Mogollon Plateau into Utah. The range map for this species can be very misleading: the northern rock mouse is actually distributed in many disjunct populations and only where there is suitable habitat. Occasionally, it is found among lava flows such as the Carrizozo Malpais in central New Mexico, far from its typical mountain habitats. These populations may represent relics isolated from a time when continuous habitats were present in the Southwest.

Peromyscus nasutus is a fairly large, gray-brown mouse with a long, hairy, prehensile tail and large ears. It is semi-arboreal and a very good climber, using its long tail for balance and as a prop when climbing. Its hearing range has been reported to be up to 100 kHz, which is within the ultrasonic range used by some bats. Based on this information, it is thought that these mice might make and perceive ultrasonic squeaks and chirps

and use them to navigate through their rocky and often dark terrain. In montane habitats its coloration is best described as dusky brown; it has a pale underbelly and a corresponding bicolored tail. Color variations have been reported, most notably an almost melanistic phase in some locations, such as in the lava flows near Carrizozo.

The northern rock mouse is found primarily in pinyon-juniper-oak woodlands, and acorns are reported as a favorite

Peromyscus nasutus

food. Other components of this mouse's diet include pinyon pine nuts, juniper berries, various grasses and other plant materials, and being opportunistic, an occasional insect or mushroom. Due to their scarcity and the difficulty in identifying them, little is known concerning their home ranges, movements, or social behavior. There are reports of four to six young, with young being born from mid-spring through early fall, depending on locality.

The classification of this species has seen numerous changes and reversals since it was first described in 1891. It closely resembles *Peromyscus difficilis* found in the mountain ranges of eastern and western central Mexico. Several hundred miles of desert scrub habitat separate these two species and, although they may be closely related, they represent genetically distinct species. The northern rock mouse possesses an added pair of bi-armed chromosomes (AN=3D58) compared to *P. difficilis* in Mexico (AN=3D56); in addition, there are allozyme and mtDNA differences. The fossil record indicates the presence of the northern rock mouse in Bexar County, in central Texas, from the Wisconsin glacial epoch. *J. V. Planz*

Size

Sexual dimorphism has not been reported for this species.
Total length: 194–198 (195) mm
Length of tail: 98–102 (99) mm
Weight: 24–32 g

Identification

Peromyscus nasutus, a large-eared, long-tailed member of the genus, is easily confused with *P. truei, P. gratus,* or *P. boylii,* which often share its range. The northern rock mouse is distinguished primarily by its long, fur-covered tail, dusky coloration, and large, petal-like ears.

Recent Synonyms

Peromyscus difficilis nasutus

Other Common Names

Colorado cliff mouse, juniper mouse

Status

Rare, limited to specific habitat

References

Bailey, 1931; DeWalt et al., 1993; Hoffmeister and de la Torre, 1961; King, 1968; Kirkland and Layne, 1989; Zimmerman et al., 1978

White-ankled mouse | *Peromyscus pectoralis*

The white-ankled mouse inhabits the Central Plateau and the Sierra Madre Oriental of Mexico and the adjacent areas of western and central Texas, as well as extreme southern New Mexico and Oklahoma. This species shows a decided preference for rocky situations, whether in the arid mountains of central Mexico and west Texas, the humid slopes of the Sierra Madre Oriental in northeastern Mexico, or the oak and juniper covered rocky outcrops and ravines of the Texas Hill Country.

P. pectoralis occurs in a variety of vegetational associations, including oak-juniper, catclaw, gramma-bluestem, cedar-oak, and pine-oak. In the mountainous regions of Mexico and western Texas where *pectoralis* and *boylii* occur sympatrically, *pectoralis* occupies the arid and semiarid brush-covered foothills at

lower elevations and *boylii* is more common in the pine-oak associations of higher elevations. *P. pectoralis* and *P. attwateri* both occur in central Texas, where *pectoralis* specializes in areas of rock ledges and leaf litter and *attwateri* in areas of open, grassy cover with scattered rocks.

P. pectoralis breeds throughout most of the year. The average litter size is three, but ranges from two to five. The gestation period is about 23 days and growth and development is similar to that of related species. These mice feed on a variety of seeds, including juniper berries, acorns, and hackberries, as well as insects.

Several other species of *Peromyscus* inhabit the same geographic range as that of the white-ankled mouse, including *attwateri, nasutus, truei, boylii, maniculatus, leucopus, hooperi,* and *eremicus.* Other species that often occur with the white-ankled mouse include harvest mice, woodrats, cotton rats, shrews, and squirrels. *D. J. Schmidly*

Peromyscus pectoralis

Size

No significant sexual dimorphism
Total length: 185–219 mm
Length of tail: 92–117 mm
Weight: 24–39 g

Identification

P. pectoralis is medium in size, with a tail that is equal to or decidedly longer than the head and body, an ear that is shorter in length than the hind foot, ankles that are usually white, and a tail that is hairy and coarsely ringed. Over much of its range *P. pectoralis* is sympatric with *P. boylii* and *P. attwateri.* The best single diag-

nostic feature to distinguish *pectoralis* from *boylii* and *attwateri* is the baculum of males; the baculum of *pectoralis* has a long, pointed, cartilaginous tip, whereas in *boylii* and *attwateri* the cartilaginous tip is short and rounded.

Recent Synonyms

Peromycus attwateri pectoralis

Other Common Names

Encinal mouse

Status

Common

Subspecies

Peromyscus pectoralis collinus, eastern slopes of the Sierra Madre Oriental in Nuevo Leon, Tamaulipas, and San Luis Potosi
Peromyscus pectoralis laceianus, northern part of the Mexican Plateau and adjacent parts of Texas
Peromyscus pectoralis pectoralis, southern part of the Mexican Plateau

References

Mammalian Species 49; Carleton, 1989; Dalquest and Horner, 1984; Davis and Schmidly, 1994

Oldfield mouse | *Peromyscus polionotus*

This small member of the deer mouse group lives in areas of loamy or sandy soils over much of the southeastern United States. Its range extends north to southernmost North Carolina and Tennessee and west into northeastern Mississippi. Soils that are poorly drained or those with an underlying hardpan appear to restrict its distribution. The species has a somewhat disjunct but locally common distribution. Eight forms inhabiting coastal beaches of Alabama and Florida are collectively known as beach mice.

As is common with deer mice, *Peromyscus polionotus* is primarily nocturnal. Activity is highest on moonless or cloudy

nights. These mice typically inhabit burrows that have an entrance about 2.5 centimeters in diameter, a tunnel leading to a nest chamber 0.3 to 0.9 meters deep, and an escape tunnel that leads from the back of the nest chamber to within about 2.5 centimeters of the surface. Often there is a mound of soil around the entrance, and burrows frequently are plugged with subsoil during occupancy. The mice also use surface holes leading to tunnels made by moles.

Oldfield mice show considerable variation in pelage color, with locally distinct forms in the 16 described subspecies. The upperparts of inland forms are fawn-colored or brownish-gray, slightly darker along the midline. Underparts are white with hairs pigmented at the base (inland forms), or completely unpigmented (some beach forms). Inland forms have a dark dorsal tail-stripe; the stripe is reduced or lacking in beach forms. Beach forms also show larger areas of unpigmented hair on the head and a smaller area of pigmentation on the back. Coat color is genetically controlled and it has been postulated that the reduced pigmentation of beach forms is an adaptation to the pale color of beach sands, providing protection against predation.

Oldfield mice typically inhabit the early successional stages of abandoned or disturbed fields and other open sandy habitats. Common annual and biennial plants of these habitats include crab grass *(Digitaria sanguinalis),* scratch daisy *(Croptilon divaricatum),* horseweed *(Conyza canadensis),* and camphor weed *(Heterotheca subaxillaris).* Invasion of these habitats by broomsedge *(Andropogon)* usually reduces their suitability for oldfield mice. Beach mice occupy grass-covered beach dunes

and the scrub areas immediately landward. Common dune plants include sea-oats *(Uniola paniculata),* beach grass *(Panicum amarum),* and bluestem *(Schizachyrium maritimus).* Scrub plants along the Gulf Coast include live and laurel oaks *(Quercus virginiana* and *Q. myrtifolia),* dwarfed specimens of magnolia *(Magnolia grandiflora),* and on the Atlantic Coast, palmetto *(Serona repens),* sea grape *(Coccoloba uvifera),* and wax myrtle *(Myrica cerifera).*

Peromyscus polionotus breeds throughout the year; however, breeding is considerably reduced in summer. Trapping and genetic evidence indicate that the species is monogamous, with pairs remaining together for extended periods. Gestation lasts about 24 days (about 28 if conception is postpartum) and females may breed following parturition. Most litters consist of three to four young. They are born with whiskers around the nose, but are otherwise pink, hairless, and quite helpless at birth. The eyes open at about 13–14 days, and young are weaned at 20–25 days. Captures of young weighing 6–7 grams indicate aboveground activity by young soon after weaning. This species feeds primarily on seeds of grasses and herbs; arthropods are eaten when available. Seeds have been found in the nest chambers, indicating at least some hoarding of food.

Three larger species of mice, the white-footed mouse *(P. leucopus),* the cotton mouse *(P. gossypinus),* and the Florida mouse *(Podomys floridanus)* inhabit the southeastern United States and have overlapping ranges with *P. polionotus.* White-footed and cotton mice usually occupy moister, more wooded habitats than does the oldfield mouse. However, they may be captured at the same site on occasion. The Florida mouse inhabits dry habitats such as pine forests, coastal scrub, and hammocks. It can be distinguished from the oldfield mouse by the bright orange-buff color of its shoulders, the presence of only five tubercles on the soles of its hind feet *(P. polionotus* usually has 6), and by its larger size. The eastern harvest mouse *(Reithrodontomys fulvescens)* is about the same size as the oldfield mouse. However, it has grooved upper incisors and its belly fur is dusky rather than white. Several fossils of *Peromyscus polionotus* have been located; it probably arose in the late-Pleistocene.

N. R. Holler

Peromyscus polionotus

Size
Females are slightly larger than males; there is some variation among subspecies.
Total length: 110–150 (135) mm
Length of tail: 40–60 (54) mm
Weight: 10–15 (13) g

Identification
The oldfield mouse is distinguished from other *Peromyscus* by smaller size, a fawn-colored dorsum with hair that is slate-gray at the base, white underparts, and a bicolored tail; its skull is smaller than in neighboring subspecies of *P. maniculatus* or *P. gossypinus.*

Recent Synonyms
Hesperomys niveiventris
Mus polionotus
Peromyscus leucocephalus
Peromyscus phasma

Peromyscus subgriseus arenarius
Peromyscus subgriseus baliolus
Sitomys nieventris subgriseus

Other Common Names
Beach mouse

Status
Locally abundant; classified as Endangered under the federal Endangered Species Act as

P. p. allophrys, P. p. ammobates, P. p. phasma, P. p. trissyllepsis; and as Threatened as P. p. niveiventris. Probably extinct as P. p. decoloratus.

Subspecies

Peromyscus polionotus albifrons, western Florida panhandle

Peromyscus polionotus allophrys, Gulf coastal Florida

Peromyscus polionotus ammobates, coastal Alabama

Peromyscus polionotus colemani, northern Alabama, Georgia, and South Carolina

Peromyscus polionotus decoloratus, north Atlantic coastal Florida

Peromyscus polionotus griseobracatus, western Florida panhandle

Peromyscus polionotus leucocephalus, Gulf coastal Florida

Peromyscus polionotus lucubrans, south-central South Carolina.

Peromyscus polionotus niveiventris, south Atlantic coastal Florida

Peromyscus polionotus peninsularis, Gulf coastal Florida

Peromyscus polionotus phasma, north Atlantic coastal Florida

Peromyscus polionotus polionotus, southern Alabama and Georgia

Peromyscus polionotus rhoadsi, central peninsular Florida

Peromyscus polionotus subgriseus, northern peninsular Florida

Peromyscus polionotus sumneri, eastern Florida panhandle

Peromyscus polionotus trissyllepsis, Gulf coastal Alabama and Florida

References

Bowen, 1968; Golley, 1962; Humphrey, 1992

Pinyon mouse | *Peromyscus truei*

Pinyon mice are common inhabitants of arid and semiarid regions of western North America. Their range extends from the panhandle of north-central Texas west to the Pacific Coast. They reach their northern distributional limit in central Oregon and extend as far south as southern Mexico. These mice are found at elevations from near sea level to higher than 2,300 meters.

Peromyscus truei

Like other species of *Peromyscus,* pinyon mice are nocturnal. All important activities such as feeding, reproduction, and dispersal take place during the dark hours. *P. truei* sleeps intermittently during the day. It does not hibernate, but in conditions of severe water stress it appears to enter a state of diurnal torpor.

Peromyscus truei is a mouse of medium size, with relatively long ears. When measured from the notch, the length of the ears (usually more than 22 mm) is equal to or greater than the length of the hind feet in most populations. The mouse's color varies from pale yellowish-brown to dark grayish-brown above; the underparts and feet are white. Its fur is relatively long and silky. The tail has a dark dorsal stripe and is tipped with long hairs. In mice found west of the Sierra Nevada, in Mexico, and in the central Texas Panhandle, the tail is longer than the body. Individuals from the remainder of the range have tails shorter than the body. The juvenile pelage of this mouse is gray. A postjuvenile pelage precedes the adult pelage, and an additional molt may occur between the juvenile and postjuvenile molts in this species. After the full adult pelage is acquired, a seasonal molt occurs in the fall, and a second seasonal molt may take place in the spring.

Reproduction is known to occur from mid-February to mid-November. The average gestation period is approximately 26 days. However, when females who have recently given birth and are still lactating become gravid, gestation may last up to 40 days. Usually there are three to six pinyon mice in a litter. They are born hairless, with their ears folded closed; each weighs about 2.3 grams. Their eyes open and ears unfold at 16 to 21 days; hair is acquired by about day 11 to 14. Nursing persists for 3 to 4 weeks. The postjuvenile molt is evident by week seven and completed by week 10 or 11.

Peromyscus truei is linked ecologically with pinyon pine and juniper, and is found most often on rocky slopes associated with these plant species. It is not, however, restricted to pinyon-juniper situations. Pinyon mice have been recorded in association with yellow pine *(Pinus ponderosa)*, bristle-cone pine *(Pinus aristata)*, redwood *(Sequoia sempervirens)*, Douglas fir *(Pseudotsuga menziesii)*, riparian live oak *(Quercus)*, chaparral, eucalyptus *(Eucalyptus)*, Joshua tree *(Yucca brevifolia)*, desert scrub, and scrub oak *(Quercus)* habitats. The diet of adults consists of juniper *(Juniperus)* seeds and berries, acorn mast, other vegetation, and invertebrates. *F. D. Yancey, II and C. Jones*

Size
No significant sexual dimorphism
Total length: 171–231 (195) mm
Length of tail: 76–123 (98) mm
Weight: 15–50 g

Identification
Peromyscus truei is distinguished by the presence of large ears that, when measured from the notch, usually are equal to or slightly longer than the hind feet. Several other species of *Peromyscus* have geographic distributions that overlap that of *Peromyscus truei*, and some occur in the same habitats. Of these species, pinyon mice most often are confused with brush mice *(Peromyscus boylii)*, northern rock mice *(Peromyscus nasutus)*, Texas mice *(Peromyscus attwateri)*, and California mice *(Peromyscus californicus)*. Pinyon mice are distinguished from brush mice, northern rock mice, and Texas mice by the size of the ears; all except pinyon mice have ears shorter than their hind feet. *P.truei* is smaller than *P. californicus* and has shorter hind feet.

Other Common Names
Big-eared cliff mouse, piñon mouse, Palo Duro mouse *(Peromyscus truei comanche)*

Status
Common, limited; Threatened *(Peromyscus truei comanche* only)

Subspecies
Peromyscus truei chlorus, southern California
Peromyscus truei comanche, panhandle of northwestern Texas

Peromyscus truei dyselius, west-central California
Peromyscus truei gilberti, central, north-central, and west-central California; southwestern Oregon
Peromyscus truei lagunae, southern tip of Baja California
Peromyscus truei martirensis, southern California and northern Baja California
Peromyscus truei montipinoris, south-central California
Peromyscus truei nevadensis, eastern Nevada and western Utah
Peromyscus truei preblei, central Oregon
Peromyscus truei sequoiensis, northwestern California and southwestern Oregon
Peromyscus truei truei, eastern California, Nevada, eastern and southern Utah, southwestern Wyoming, Arizona, Colorado, New Mexico, far western Oklahoma, and extreme northwestern Texas

References
Mammalian Species 161; Eisenberg, 1968; Hoffmeister, 1951; Millar, 1989

Florida mouse | *Podomys floridanus*

Although Florida evokes images of coastal marshes and tree-lined waterways, the sandy uplands in the central and coastal parts of the state are hot, dry, and (before human interference) subject to frequent fires. Some of the flora and fauna of these xeric uplands have a surprising affinity with plants and animals from the southwestern United States and from Central America. Along with prickly pear cactus *(Opuntia)* and pocket gophers *(Geomys pinetis)*, the Florida mouse occurs primarily in the longleaf pine sandhills, slash pine-turkey oak sandhills, and sand pine scrub of central and coastal Florida. Although it resembles the cotton mice *(Peromyscus gossypinus)* and oldfield mice *(Peromyscus polionotus)* that also occur in the state, studies of the parasites, genetics, morphology, and copulatory behavior of *Podomys* suggest a closer relationship to mice from Mexico and Guatemala.

A distinctive feature of the Florida mouse is its close association with tortoise burrows. Burrows of the gopher tortoise *(Gopherus polyphemus)* are conspicuous structures in Florida sandhills and scrub. "Gophers" are unique among tortoises in their construction of particularly deep, long burrows: they average about 1.8 m in depth and 4.5 m in length. More than 360 species of invertebrates and vertebrates are known to use these burrows, and *Podomys* relies extensively on them. Most Florida mice consistently use one or two burrows, constructing small tunnels off the sides of the main burrow. Compared to other species of the family Muridae, *Podomys* appears well-adapted to

Podomys floridanus

its life underground. It is a less active climber; it is an active digger, using its forepaws rather than its hindlimbs to dig and throw sand backwards; and its nests are relatively small, flat structures.

Compared to *Peromyscus* of similar size, *Podomys* has larger newborns, smaller litters, and slower development. Litters are born in nests of shredded vegetation built in the side passages of tortoise burrows. Under favorable conditions, Florida mice reproduce throughout the year. After a gestation of about 23 days, the female gives birth to 1 to 5 young (average litter size is 3). Newborns weigh 2–3 g and are nursed almost continuously for 2 weeks. The gray juvenile pelage has developed by 14 days of age, the eyes open at approximately 16 days, and the young are weaned between 3 and 4 weeks. Both sexes apparently disperse. Adult females have non-overlapping home ranges that are significantly smaller than the home ranges of males.

Florida mice emerge at night to feed on insects, seeds, pawpaws, and other plant materials. Acorns of several oak species appear to be a particularly important food. The mice pick up food in the paws or mouth and crouch on their haunches to eat. Small acorns often are split in half; larger acorns are opened at the hilum (the basal scar underneath the "cap"). Florida mice are preyed upon by bobcats *(Felis rufus)* and presumably by snakes, raptors, foxes, and raccoons.

Florida mice, gopher tortoises, and the plant communities in which they reside are threatened by widespread habitat destruction and conversion. *C. A. Jones*

Size
No significant sexual dimorphism
Total length: 178–220 (194.7) mm
Length of tail: 80–101 (87.7) mm
Weight: 27.0–47.0 (35.5) g

Identification
Podomys floridanus can be distinguished from the species of *Peromyscus* that live in Florida by its larger size, relatively larger ears (at least 16 mm) and hind feet (at least 24 mm), and by the bright orange color on the cheeks, shoulders, and lower sides.

Recent Synonyms
Peromyscus floridanus

Other Common Names
Florida deer mouse, gopher mouse

Status
Known only from dry habitats in Florida; Species of Special Concern (Florida Game and Fresh Water Fish Commission, 1990); Threatened (Florida Committee on Rare and Endangered Plants and Animals, 1978); under review for listing by the National Biological Survey

References
Mammalian Species 427; Jones, 1993; Layne, 1992

Golden mouse | *Ochrotomys nuttalli*

Often described as attractive, cute, and relatively docile, the golden mouse does not wander far from its natural surroundings and is less known to nonbiologists than many of its relatives. It is especially common in densely forested lowlands and floodplain communities, but it is known from other habitats as well, including upland pine forests. Populations are often localized and most abundant in habitats with dense undergrowth, which often includes honeysuckle, greenbrier, or

other vines. The golden mouse's thermoregulatory abilities and affinity for water generally resemble those of *Peromyscus* that live in mesic habitats.

A semi-arboreal species with a semi-prehensile tail, the golden mouse uses elevated components of its habitat for nest sites, feeding platforms, and havens from predators and periodic flooding. Its nest has a single opening. The outside of the nest is constructed of coarse materials that may include whole leaves and vines. The inner nesting chamber is walled with finely shredded materials. Rarely placed on the ground, most often nests are located 1.5 to 4.5 m above the ground, usually in vines or shrubs. Nests may also be located in trees, sometimes in Spanish moss, which may be incorporated into the nest. Golden mice sometimes remodel abandoned birds' nests into homes of their own.

The golden mouse sometimes consumes invertebrates, but its main fare is seeds, nuts and berries. In a Kentucky study 23 kinds of seeds were found on feeding platforms. Sumac *(Rhus),* cherry *(Prunus),* dogwood *(Cornus),* blackberry *(Rubus),* and greenbrier *(Smilax)* seeds are all consumed. *Ochrotomys* has relatively large cheek pouches for transporting food items to the nest or to a feeding platform, where it consumes its food away from predators in a physiologically favorable microclimate.

The reproductive season varies somewhat in different parts of this mouse's range, a reflection of climatic differences. At relatively high elevations in eastern Tennessee the golden mouse breeds from mid-March through early October, with peaks in late spring and early autumn; in South Carolina there is limited activity most of the year, with a small peak in spring and a large peak in late summer and fall. In Texas it breeds all year, but with little reproduction in hot summer months.

The golden mouse may produce several litters annually. Mean litter size ranges from about 2.4 to 3.0, with litter sizes at northern latitudes somewhat larger than in the south. The gestation period is 25 to 30 days. Newborn golden mice are reddish and nearly hairless, their eyes and ears are sealed, and their digits are not separated. They can cling to a finger and can right themselves when turned over. When they are a day old they can take a few wobbly steps. By day seven the dorsum is covered with reddish-brown fur and the youngster is readily identifiable as a golden mouse. The ears open at about 10 days and the eyes at 13 days. Golden mice are weaned by 21 days of age. Adult size is gained at 8–10 weeks, but there is some evidence that golden mice grow throughout life. When frightened the young either remain motionless or climb the nearest available object, confirming their semi-arboreal nature and the importance of above-ground cover. *J. F. Pagels*

Ochrotomys nuttalli

Size
Males are slightly larger than females.
Total length: 140–190 (165) mm
Length of tail: 67–97 (80) mm
Weight: 18–27 g

Identification
The golden mouse closely resembles members of the genus *Peromyscus,* but it can be distinguished from *Peromyscus* and other mice within its range by its coloration. Its dorsal pelage is burnished to golden, the feet are creamy, and the underparts are creamy and washed with pale yellow; the degree of brightness varies among and within subspecies. The pelage is extremely soft and dense and individual hairs are fine.

Recent Synonyms
Peromyscus nuttalli

Status
Common

Subspecies
Ochrotomys nuttalli aureolus, westerns portions of Virginia and the Carolinas, northern Georgia and northern Mississippi, and most of Tennessee, Kentucky, and West Virginia

Ochrotomys nuttalli flammeus, western Arkansas and nearby Oklahoma
Ochrotomys nuttalli floridanus, northern to south-central Florida
Ochrotomys nuttalli lisae, most of Mississippi River Valley from south-central Louisiana to southern Missouri and Illinois
Ochrotomys nuttalli nuttalli, most of Piedmont and Coastal Plain of the southeastern United States except Florida

References
Mammalian Species 75; Knuth and Barrett, 1984; Linzey and Linzey, 1967

Northern pygmy mouse | *Baiomys taylori*

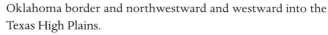

The range of the northern pygmy mouse extends northward from central Mexico in three projections. One projection follows the western coast of Mexico to southern Sonora. A middle projection extends northwest through Durango and Chihuahua, reaching its northern limit in southeastern Arizona. The eastern projection extends northward into northern Texas, and then eastward along the Texas coast to the Louisiana border. Recent range extensions are reported toward the Oklahoma border and northwestward and westward into the Texas High Plains.

The pelage of adult northern pygmy mice varies from reddish brown thorough gray to almost black above, and white to creamy buff or gray below. The tail is covered with short hairs; its color differs among subspecies and may be uniformly gray or paler ventrally. Juvenile mice are uniformly gray above and paler below. A postjuvenile molt begins at 38–46 days and ends at 60–74 days. The first evidence of this molt is the presence of bright brownish hairs on the head. Adults molt during all months of the year, but an annual molt occurs during the rainy season. This molt begins anteriorly and proceeds posteriorly over the back.

Baiomys taylori enters torpor at ambient temperatures near 20° C (when body temperature is 23–25° C). If an individual's body temperature drops below 22° C, arousal is difficult without an external source of heat. The length of torpor is variable and is influenced by the amount of food and water available before entrance into torpor and by ambient temperature. *B. taylori* stores brown fat between the shoulder blades, which is used as an energy source during torpor. During arousal from torpor, vacuoles reappear in the brown fat tissue, the mouse's heart rate increases to 800 beats per minute, its respiratory rate increases to 200 breaths per minute, and its metabolic rate increases 5–7 times above basal.

Northern pygmy mice occur in a variety of habitats including coastal prairie, midgrass prairie, mixed-grass prairie, mixed-desert shrub, prickly pear-short grass communities, post oak savannah, pine-oak forest, and oak-hickory associations. This species has not been taken above 2,438 meters and occupies drier habitats than *B. musculus.* Population density ranges from 2–84 per hectare, and is lowest during summer

Baiomys taylori

of cotton rats increases, northern pygmy mice are more frequently captured in marginal habitats, indicating negative interspecific interactions between these rodents. In the laboratory, *B. taylori* was significantly more aggressive when paired with harvest mice (*Reithrodontomys fulvescens*) than with cotton rats. In the absence of cover, *S. hispidus* kills *B. taylori* in laboratory situations. When cover is added, the species avoid each other. There is less evidence of competition between *B. taylori* and other sympatric rodents, such as *R. fulvescens, Peromyscus leucopus, Oryzomys palustris, Mus musculus, Cryptotis parva*, or *Neotoma micropus*. Where they are sympatric, *B. taylori* occupies highlands, whereas *B. musculus* occupies mesic lowland; in addition, the crepuscular activity pattern of *B. taylori* and the diurnal habitats of *B. musculus* lead to temporal separation.

Snakes, including rattlesnakes, cottonmouths, and coachwhips, and owls (barn owls and great-horned owls) prey on northern pygmy mice.

Breeding is year-round in the northern pygmy mouse, with peaks in late fall and early spring. *B. taylori* is polyestrous. Gestation lasts 20–23 days, the average mass of neonates is 1.0–1.2 g, and litter size averages 2.5 (range 1–5). Both post-partum estrus and delayed implantation are reported. Neonates are naked, with erupted incisors. Their eyes open at 12–15 days and skull sutures close at 50 days. The young are weaned at 17–24 days. Growth is rapid for the first 35 days. Adult size is attained at 50 days of age, and the average age at sexual maturity is 61.5 days for females and 70–80 days for males.

Male parents help care for young by grooming them and returning them to the nest. Nests are usually found under fallen logs or prostrate cactus pads, or within thick clumps of grass. They are usually a ball formed of finely shredded grass, corn silk, or cactus fibers, and may be maintained by more than one individual. A central cavity may contain fur and have one or two exits. Several runways lead from the nest. Some authors report that *B. taylori* constructs burrow systems. *G. N. Cameron*

and highest during autumn and winter. Dense ground cover is an integral component of optimal habitat and any disturbance to this cover (e.g., fire or cattle grazing) degrades the habitat for *B. taylori*. Highest densities occur in areas of dense ground cover, particularly in prickly pear-short grass communities. The northern pygmy mouse's median life span is 23 weeks, with a maximum recorded life span of 170 weeks for laboratory-reared animals.

These mice eat the stems and fruit of prickly pear cactus, grass seeds, grass leaves, mesquite beans, and granjeno berries. Animal material (e.g., insects, terrestrial snails, small snakes) is taken in captivity and is presumed to be included in natural diets.

Habitat segregation occurs between northern pygmy mice and the hispid cotton rat *(Sigmodon hispidus)*. When the density

Size
No significant sexual dimorphism
Total length: 87–123 mm
Length of tail: 34–53 mm
Weight: 6–9.5 g

Identification
Baiomys taylori is the smallest North American rodent. It is distinguished from *Baiomys musculus*, the other, larger member of the genus, which occurs from Mexico south to Nicaragua, by hind feet that are shorter than 16 mm and a shorter and narrower skull. In addition, the rostrum of *B. taylori* is deflected more abruptly rather than gradually curving toward the tip of the nasal bones, the molars of *B. taylori* have

higher crowns than those of *B. musculus*, and the teeth are less complicated.

Status
Not common, restricted

Subspecies
Baiomys taylori allex, Nayarit, Jaliasco, Michoacan, and Colima, Mexico
Baiomys taylori analogus, San Luis Potosi, Hidalgo, Veracruz, Distrito Federal, Jalisco, Guanajuato, Queretaro, and Michoacan, Mexico
Baiomys taylori ater, southeastern Arizona, southwestern New Mexico, and Durango, Mexico

Baiomys taylori canutus, Sonora, Nayarit, and Sinaloa, Mexico
Baiomys taylori fuliginatus, San Luis Potosi, Mexico
Baiomys taylori paulus, Chihuahua, Zacatecas, and Durango, Mexico
Baiomys taylori subater, eastern Texas
Baiomys taylori taylori, eastern, central, and southern Texas; Veracruz, San Luis Potosi, Tamaulipas, and Nuevo Leon, Mexico

References
Mammalian Species 285; Caire, 1989; Davis and Schmidly, 1994; Matson and Baker, 1986; Schmidly, 1983

Mearns's grasshopper mouse | *Onychomys arenicola*

Onychomys arenicola was considered to be conspecific with *O. torridus* until 1979, when a study of chromosome morphology revealed diagnostic differences between populations in the Chihuahuan Desert and those to the west of the Continental Divide near the southern border of New Mexico and Arizona. Additional studies of protein and mitochondrial DNA variation have confirmed the distinction between *O. arenicola* and *O. torridus,* and further revealed that *O. arenicola* is more closely related to *O. leucogaster* than to *O. torridus.* Because *O. arenicola* has been considered a distinct species for less than two decades, some of the earlier literature on *O. torridus* actually refers to *O. arenicola.* To know which species was studied, it is necessary to check specimen locality information.

Much of what is known about the adaptations of grasshopper mice for a predatory lifestyle is similar across the three extant species, and is described in the species accounts for *O. leucogaster* and *O. torridus.* Mearns's grasshopper mouse's physiological adaptations to xeric habitats are probably similar to those described for *O. torridus.* B. R. Riddle

Onychomys arenicola

Size

No significant sexual dimorphism
Total length: 121–158 (138.7) mm
Length of tail: 35–56 (47.5) mm
Weight: 20–35 g

Identification

Onychomys arenicola is distinguishable from *Onychomys leucogaster* by relatively longer tail (equal to or longer than half the head-body length) and generally smaller overall body size.

It is more difficult to distinguish from *Onychomys torridus,* which has similar body size and tail to head-body proportions. All three species are diagnosable with chromosome morphology and mitochondrial DNA characters.

Recent Synonyms

Onychomys torridus canus
Onychomys torridus surrufus
Onychomys torridus torridus (part)

Other Common Names

Southern grasshopper mouse, Chihuahuan grasshopper mouse

Status

Abundant

References

Mammalian Species 59; Riddle, 1995; Riddle and Honeycutt, 1990; Sullivan et al., 1986

Northern grasshopper mouse | *Onychomys leucogaster*

With their well-deserved reputation as voracious little insectivores and carnivores, grasshopper mice have attracted the attention of many biologists. Northern grasshopper mice are the most robust and large-bodied of the three extant species of

grasshopper mice, but all are morphologically and behaviorally suited to a life of hunting and handling formidable prey. Grasshopper mice are probably descended from essentially seed-eating ancestors, and even now, seeds form a small por-

Onychomys leucogaster

tion of their diets. Yet, a convincing case can be made for viewing these animals as being well-adapted to a predatory existence analogous in many ways to large mammalian carnivores. Morphologically, northern grasshopper mice have unusually long fingers and claws *(Onychomys* means "clawed mouse") that provide great dexterity in such tasks as grasping and manipulating large grasshoppers, crickets, or beetles. Molar teeth are high-cusped and provide large surfaces for shearing animal matter, and enlarged surface areas for muscle attachment on the lower jaw and skull indicate increases in biting and chewing strength.

If large home ranges, actively maintained territories, complex courtship, tight social bonds, and the capacity to communicate over large distances sound more like attributes of a coyote or wolf than of a mouse, then grasshopper mice could be viewed as mouse-analogs of their carnivore relatives because they possess all of these behavioral traits. Fundamental to the complex social system of grasshopper mice is their characteristic "howling" vocalization. The howl is a loud (about 12 kHz) and pure-tone sound that lasts about a second and is audible to the human ear. This vocalization contains a wealth of information about the identity, size, sex, and location of each adult grasshopper mouse in a population. Because the howls of grasshopper mice travel far through the dry air of their arid and semiarid habitats, it is an ideal form of communication among these wandering and distantly-spaced little predators. Within home ranges as large as three hectares, territories are maintained through marking with a distinctive scent produced by anal glands.

As might be expected in a territorial predator, northern grasshopper mice are highly aggressive toward possible intruders of the same sex. A subordinate animal caught in the wrong place is likely to be aggressively pursued and when caught, killed by the dominant animal with a bite through the neck at the base of the skull. The same attack behavior is used by grasshopper mice against other rodents, including much bigger animals such as kangaroo rats. Nevertheless, most of their diet consists of invertebrates rather than other small mammals.

The courtship and copulatory behavior of northern grasshopper mice is one of the most complex known in rodents, and involves a sophisticated sequence of circling, sniffing, grooming, and finally, mounting, at which time the male and female remain in a copulatory lock for up to a minute. Just as highly developed is the female–pup bond, where a mother takes great care to defend and groom her pups, naked and blind at birth, until their eyes are opened at about two weeks of age. The father maintains a more active role than most rodents do in defending and raising the pups, which may reflect the need of the young to be taught the sophisticated behaviors required for a life of pursuing and capturing prey.

Northern grasshopper mice are widespread throughout western North American grassland and shrub steppes. Recent analyses of mitochondrial DNA and protein variation and fossils have provided information on the pattern and timing of speciation in the genus *Onychomys. Onychomys leucogaster* appears more closely related to *Onychomys arenicola* than to *Onychomys torridus,* which diverged from the former two species about three million years ago. All three species are inhabitants of semiarid and arid habitats and remain active throughout the year. Northern grasshopper mice are commonly found in association with kangaroo rats, pocket mice, and prairie dogs. They commonly occupy abandoned burrows of these other rodents, but also construct a variety of burrows that function as nests, food caches, or defecation chambers. *B. R. Riddle*

Size
No significant sexual dimorphism
Total length: 119–190 mm
Length of tail: 29–62 mm
Weight: 26–49 g

Identification
This species is generally distinguishable from *Onychomys torridus* and *Onychomys arenicola* by tail less than one-half head-body length, larger size, and stocky appearance. However, geographic variation is pronounced, and these diagnostic traits don't always hold. For example, northern grasshopper mice from the Great Basin and Columbia Plateau are similar in body size to *Onychomys torridus* (although distinguishable by short tail and stocky appearance); and populations from the Gulf Coastal Plain of Texas and Mexico have tails greater than one-half head-body length, but are distinguishable from geographically adjacent *Onychomys arenicola* by larger overall body size.

Status
Abundant

Subspecies
Onychomys leucogaster albescens, trans-Pecos Texas and northern Chihuahua
Onychomys leucogaster arcticeps, central and southern Great Plains
Onychomys leucogaster brevicaudus, central and northern Nevada, southern Idaho, and eastern Utah
Onychomys leucogaster durranti, northeastern Oregon and eastern Washington
Onychomys leucogaster fuliginosus, northwestern Arizona south of the Colorado and Little Colorado rivers
Onychomys leucogaster leucogaster, tallgrass prairie in eastern North Dakota and South Dakota, western Wisconsin, southern Manitoba
Onychomys leucogaster longipes, Gulf Coastal plain of Texas and northeastern Mexico

Onychomys leucogaster melanophrys, west and north of Colorado River in Utah and Arizona
Onychomys leucogaster missouriensis, Alberta and Saskatchewan south through Montana and western North and South Dakota into intermountain basins in Wyoming
Onychomys leucogaster pallescens, east of Colorado River to Rio Grande Valley in north-central New Mexico
Onychomys leucogaster ruidosae, central and southwestern New Mexico into southeastern Arizona

References
Mammalian Species 87; Carleton and Eshelman, 1979; Engstrom and Choate, 1979; Hafner and Hafner, 1979; Riddle, 1995; Riddle and Choate, 1986; Riddle and Honeycutt, 1990; Riddle et al., 1993; Van Cura and Hoffmeister, 1966

Southern grasshopper mouse | *Onychomys torridus*

Like its cousin, the northern grasshopper mouse, *Onychomys torridus* is a highly efficient predator. This is the grasshopper mouse of warm desert scrub habitats throughout the Sonoran and Mojave deserts (interestingly, absent from the southern

Onychomys torridus

Baja Peninsular desert), Sinaloan thorn scrub to the south, and California chaparral to the west.

The adaptations of grasshopper mice for a predatory lifestyle are described in the species account for *O. leucogaster.* The southern grasshopper mouse is perhaps more likely than its larger northern relative to demonstrate a peculiar behavior when it captures a scorpion: it immobilizes the venomous tail before killing the scorpion with bites to the head. It deals with large beetles that secrete defensive substances from the tip of the abdomen by jamming the beetle's abdomen into the ground prior to striking a death-blow to the head. An examination of the gastric morphology of *O. torridus* revealed a stomach architecture specialized for breaking down hard arthropod exoskeletons.

Both *O. torridus* and *O. arenicola* are denizens of warm, extremely arid desert scrub habitats. Neither species has the long evolutionary history of physiological adaptation to xeric deserts that several other common associates (e.g., *Dipodomys, Chaetodipus,* and *Perognathus*) have had. Nevertheless, grasshopper mice are probably capable of obtaining enough water from the bodies of arthropods and other small mammals to survive without a supply of drinking water. *B. R. Riddle*

Size
No significant sexual dimorphism
Total length: 130–160 (143.9) mm
Length of tail: 40–62 (50.7) mm
Weight: 20–40 g

Identification
This grasshopper mouse is distinguishable from *Onychomys leucogaster* by relatively longer tail (equal to or longer than half the head-body length) and generally smaller overall body size. It is more difficult to distinguish from *Onychomys arenicola,* which has similar body size and tail to head-body proportions. All three species are diagnosable with chromosome morphology and mitochondrial DNA characters.

Other Common Names
Scorpion mouse

Status
Abundant

Subspecies
Onychomys torridus clarus, Owens Valley, California
Onychomys torridus knoxjonesi, northern Sinaloa
Onychomys torridus longicaudus, west-central and southern Nevada west into California and east into Arizona and southwestern Utah
Onychomys torridus macrotis, northwestern Baja California

Onychomys torridus pulcher, southeastern California
Onychomys torridus ramona, southwestern California
Onychomys torridus torridus, west-central and southern Arizona into adjacent New Mexico and central and northern Sonora
Onychomys torridus tularensis, San Joaquin Valley, California
Onychomys torridus yakiensis, southern Sonora

References
Mammalian Species 59; Carleton and Eshelman, 1979; Hafner and Hafner, 1979; Hollander and Willig, 1992; Riddle, 1995; Riddle and Honeycutt, 1990; Sullivan et al., 1986; Van Cura and Hoffmeister, 1966

Arizona cotton rat | *Sigmodon arizonae*

Until it was discovered that hispid cotton rats had more than twice as many chromosomes as do Arizona cotton rats, these two types of cotton rats were thought to be members of the same species.

Members of the genus *Sigmodon* are at least vaguely vole-like in general appearance and also in their grass eating–runway constructing way of making a living. However, with their larger body size and scaly tails, Arizona cotton rats look much more like salt-and-pepper-colored rats than voles.

As with all cotton rats, the affinity for grass greatly influences their distribution. In the United States, Arizona cotton rats occur in southeastern and central Arizona, but only in grassy sites around ponds, along drainages, in riparian situations, along irrigated agricultural fields, and most any place there are grasses and weeds or brush (even in some quite arid, desert situations). The isolated population in extreme western Arizona, near Parker, occurs in grassy patches along the Colorado River.

The distribution of Arizona cotton rats extends southward into Mexico, from the western foothills of the Sierra Madre

Sigmodon arizonae

eastward to the Gulf Coast, through Sonora and Sinoaloa to Nayarit; but, as in the United States, only where the necessary grassy habitat is available.

When conditions are optimal, such as just after the summer rains in most years, local populations can increase greatly in number. At such times, these diurnal vole-like rats are easily seen as they run along their grass-lined runways in search of food.

Little is known of the life history of the Arizona cotton rat as a species distinct from the hispid cotton rat. However, what is known for the hispid cotton rat should apply reasonably well to its sibling species. Except for the most arid portion of the summer, it probably breeds throughout the entire year. Litter size likely ranges from about 2 to 10, and females can probably have more than one litter a year; gestation should be about 27 days, and weaning probably occurs after 15 to 25 days. The young are precocial (fully developed at birth) and they run around looking and acting like miniature adults within a few hours after birth. *R. Davis and P. J. Young*

Size
Total length: 200–349 mm
Length of tail: 85–156 mm (usually 110 mm or more)
Weight: 125–211 (172) g

Identification
Arizona cotton rats can be distinguished from yellow-nosed and tawny-bellied cotton rats by larger size (their hind feet usually measure 34 mm or longer), and by the lack of an orangish-brown belly and orangish eye and nose rings. They are most similar to hispid cotton rats, which are smaller (hind feet usually 30–32 mm) and, with one exception, occur to the east of the distribution of Arizona cotton rats.

Recent Synonyms
Sigmodon hispidis (before 1970)

Status
Two subspecies are probably extinct; the status of the others is unknown

Subspecies
Sigmodon arizonae arizonae, one locality in central Arizona (probably now extinct)
Sigmodon arizonae cienegae, central and southeastern Arizona to northern Sonora, Mexico
Sigmodon arizonae plenus, along Colorado River
Sigmodon arizonae jacksoni, one locality in central Arizona (probably now extinct)
Sigmodon arizonae major, southern Sonora and south through Sinaloa, Mexico

References
Hoffmeister, 1986; Zimmerman, 1970

Tawny-bellied cotton rat | *Sigmodon fulviventer*

The tawny-bellied cotton rat is found in a variety of grass and grass-shrub habitats from New Mexico and southeastern Arizona southward along the Sierra Madre Occidental to the Mexican states of Jalisco and northern Michoacan. Where it is found in association with other species of cotton rats (*Sigmodon hispidus, S. leucotis,* and *S. ochrognathus),* it appears to be the dominant species.

Sigmodon fulviventer is the largest of the cotton rats, with captive animals reaching well over 200 g. The back is "pepper and salt" in color and the underparts are washed with buff. The tail is dark and usually is covered with just enought hairs to hide the scales. *Sigmodon hispidus* has a more sparsely-haired tail.

Gestation is about 35 days and litters usually number 4 or 6. Young are raised in nests woven out of grasses; these can often be found by following a runway system. The young leave the nest when they are about one week old and begin to breed when they are about 6 weeks old. *K. A. Shump, Jr.*

Sigmodon fulviventer

Size
No significant sexual dimorphism
Total Length: 223–270 (246) mm
Tail length: 94–109 (102) mm
Weight 200–222 g

Identification
S. fulviventer is distinguished from other cotton rats by its large size and by its coloration: the back is "pepper and salt" and the belly is tawny. It has a more heavily haired tail than *S. hispidus*, with smaller tail scales.

Other Common Names
Yellow-bellied cotton rat

Status
Common, limited

Subspecies
Sigmodon fulviventer fulviventer, Jalisco, Mexico
Sigmodon fulviventer goldmani, New Mexico
Sigmodon fulviventer melanotis, north Michoacan, Mexico
Sigmodon fulviventer minimus, New Mexico and southeastern Arizona into northern Mexico

References
Mammalian Species 94; Baker, 1969; Peterson, 1973

Hispid cotton rat | *Sigmodon hispidus*

The hispid cotton rat is distributed from northern South America through most of Central America and Mexico and into the southeastern and south-central United States. In the United States, *S. hispidus* extends from Florida north to Virginia, west to Kansas and Nebraska, and southwest to southern New Mexico and southeastern Arizona. An isolated population occurs from near Yuma, Arizona, into western Mexico, southern Arizona, and southeastern California along the Colorado River and in the Imperial Valley. Recent range extensions northward into central Virginia, Kentucky, northern Missouri, southern Nebraska, and northern New Mexico have been documented. In addition, western expansion of the range

Sigmodon hispidus

into western Colorado and from the Colorado River drainage into the Imperial Valley of California have been noted.

The pelage of the hispid cotton rat is grizzled, with blackish or dark brownish hairs interspersed with buffy or grayish hairs. Its sides are only slightly paler, and the underparts are pale to dark grayish, sometimes faintly washed with buff. Coat color may vary with soil color. The pelage is uniform throughout the life of the animal, although several molts occur. The juvenile pelage is complete a week after birth and is characterized by short hairs that are somewhat darker than the adult pelage. A rapid molt to subadult pelage begins ventrally and ends dorsally at 5–6 weeks of age. Molt to adult pelage follows immediately and is complete when the rat is about 3 months old. The tail, which is important in temperature regulation, is dark and coarsely ringed. Animals from northern latitudes store significantly more fat than animals from southern latitudes.

Sigmodon hispidus is most common in habitats dominated by grasses, primarily little bluestem and bushy beardgrass, with mixed forbs, including goldenrod and ragweed. Old fields and agricultural crops such as cotton or corn are suitable habitats. Grass height and density are important components of habitat; vegetative cover is important for protection from avian predators. Populations of hispid cotton rats fluctuate seasonally, with peak densities of 14–70 per hectare in late summer-early fall and minimum densities of less than 1–25 per hectare during winter in northern areas; fluctuations at southern latitudes show a second decline in abundance during summer. As its range expanded northward, *S. hispidus* competitively excluded *Microtus ochrogaster;* other evidence suggests that hispid cotton rats excluded pygmy mice *(Baiomys taylori)* to marginal habitats in south Texas. In Mexico, *S. fulviventer* is competitively dominant to *S. hispidus.*

Agnostic behavior is important in social organization, with rank determined largely by body mass. The social rank of hispid cotton rats affects movement, with subordinate individuals suppressed by dominant individuals. Such behavioral interactions appear to be mediated by urinary and fecal pheromones. Social rank also affects susceptibility to predators. Because of differences in activity, subordinate individuals tend to be taken by avian predators and dominant individuals by mammalian predators.

Hispid cotton rats are most active at dawn and dusk, although they can be captured at all hours of the day. Cotton rats swim by using the hind feet for propulsion. Their fur is not as water repellent as that of the more aquatic rice rat *(Oryzomys palustris),* but narrow bodies of water do not form significant barriers. In northern portions of their distribution, hispid cotton rats build surface and burrow nests from woven grass that range from cup-shaped to hollow-ball-shaped. In northern latitudes nests are woven more tightly to increase their ability to insulate. In southern latitudes, the rats normally do not build nests. Hispid cotton rats will climb in aboveground vegetation. Cotton rats exhibit homing when displaced from 300 to 1,500 m, with relative success decreasing with distance displaced.

Hispid cotton rats eat both grasses and forbs, with the bulk of the diet composed of the former. They can select available food items and combine them into a nutritious diet. In southern latitudes, insects are eaten during some seasons.

Reproduction peaks in spring and autumn at southern latitudes, and some reproduction occurs year-round. A single, autumn peak is seen in northern latitudes. Litter size ranges from 1–15, with significant variation latitudinally; litter size is 7–9 in Kansas, 3–4 in Texas, and 2–3 in Central America. Gestation is approximately 27 days, with lactation lasting an additional 12 days. Neonates are covered by a fine coat of pale-colored hair, are well-developed, and weigh an average of 7 g. Their eyes open 18–36 hours after birth. Growth is rapid, averaging 1–2 g per day. Body growth is divided into three periods: from 1 to 40 days, length increases rapidly; from 41 to 100 days, the increase is moderate; and from 101 days onward, there is little growth. Most skull dimensions reach minimum adult size during the first 100 days of life. A combination of body length, molting stage, fusion of cartilage, skull measurements, and eye-lens weight can be used to determine the age of cotton rats accurately up to 6 months (body mass is reliable as an aging criterion only until 70 days of age). Males are sexually mature by one month of age, and females mature by 30–40 days. *G. N. Cameron*

Size
Males are typically larger than females.
Total length: 224–365 mm
Length of tail: 81–166 mm
Weight: 110–225 g (males); 100–200 g (females)

Identification
S. hispidis can be distinguished from *S. fulviventer* and *S. ochrognathus* by its large tail scales (0.75 mm rather than 0.5 mm wide), its sparsely haired, rather than heavily haired, tail, and its long and narrow, instead of short and broad, skull. *S. hispidus* is separated from *S. arizonae* by cranial characters that are not readily visible externally.

Status
Common, widespread

Subspecies
Sigmodon hispidus alfredi, southeastern Colorado
Sigmodon hispidus baileyi, Durango, Mexico
Sigmodon hispidus berlandieri, eastern and southern New Mexico, western and southern Texas, central and eastern Mexico south to Distrito Federal
Sigmodon hispidus borucae, Costa Rica and western Panama
Sigmodon hispidus chiriquensis, Costa Rica and Panama
Sigmodon hispidus confinis, eastern Arizona
Sigmodon hispidus eremicus, southeastern California, southwestern Arizona, Baja California, and Sonora, Mexico
Sigmodon hispidus exsputus, Florida Keys
Sigmodon hispidus floridanus, Florida

Sigmodon hispidus furvus, Honduras
Sigmodon hispidus griseus, El Salvador, Honduras, and Nicaragua
Sigmodon hispidus hispidus, Missouri, Tennessee, Kentucky, Louisiana, Mississippi, Alabama, Florida, Georgia, North Carolina, and South Carolina
Sigmodon hispidus inexoratus, Jalisco, Mexico
Sigmodon hispidus insulicola, Captiva Island, Florida
Sigmodon hispidus komareki, Alabama, Georgia, Tennessee, South Carolina, and North Carolina
Sigmodon hispidus littoralis, Florida
Sigmodon hispidus microdon, Yucatan, Campeche, and Quitana Roo, Mexico
Sigmodon hispidus obvelatus, Morelos, Puebla, and Oaxaca, Mexico

Sigmodon hispidus saturatus, Tabasco, Chiapas, Veracruz, and Oaxaca, Mexico, Guatamala, Belize

Sigmodon hispidus solus, island off Matamoros, Tamaulipas, Mexico

Sigmodon hispidus spadicipygus, southern tip of Florida

Sigmodon hispidus texianus, Nebraska, Kansas, Oklahoma, Iowa, Missouri, Arkansas, and Texas

Sigmodon hispidus toltecus, Tamaulipas, Oaxaca, San Luis Potosi, and Veracruz, Mexico

Sigmodon hispidus tonalensis, Chiapas, Mexico

Sigmodon hispidus virginianus, Virginia

Sigmodon hispidus zanjonensis, Honduras and Guatemala

References

Mammalian Species 158; Caire et al., 1989; Cameron and McClure, 1988; Davis and Schmidly, 1994; Jones et al., 1985; Matson and Baker, 1986; Schmidly, 1983

Yellow-nosed cotton rat | *Sigmodon ochrognathus*

All members of the genus *Sigmodon* are similar to voles in both appearance and habits: they are fuzzy balls of fur, with short ears and tails, they eat grass and make runways, and they are often active during the day. But among the cotton rats, because of its small size, and because it typically occurs in grassy patches in montane situations, the yellow-nosed cotton rat is especially vole-like.

In the United States and northern Mexico, the distribution of the yellow-nosed cotton rat is rather limited; it is found only on isolated "sky island" mountains of northern Sonora, southeastern Arizona, extreme southwestern New Mexico, and in the Trans-Pecos region of southwestern Texas. Farther south in Mexico, however, its range extends southward along the eastern slope of the Sierra Madre Mountains all the way to central Durango.

On the isolated mountains where it occurs, the yellow-nosed cotton rat is found at all elevations from the foothills to the tops; it inhabits grassy slopes in oak-pine woodlands as well as montane meadows within ponderosa pine and Douglas fir forests. Its nests are sometimes constructed on the surface of the ground, in thickets of grass, or under clumps of vegetation. Underground nests are also used, and access to these is often provided through pocket gopher burrows.

Reproduction apparently can occur throughout most of the year (except, at least in Arizona, during the most arid portions of the summer) and females as young as 45 days of age sometimes breed. Gestation lasts about 34 days. There are two to six young in a litter, and these young (rather than being naked, blind, and helpless like those of most other mice and rats) are amazingly precocial at birth; within a few hours, a new-born yellow-nosed cotton rat looks and acts like a miniature adult. Weaning occurs by 15 days or earlier, but the young cotton rat may begin eating vegetation when it is as young as 8 days. Green vegetation, including grass, is the major component of a cotton rat's diet, but prickly pear fruit is reported to be a popular item when and where it occurs.

In the Rincon Mountains just east of Tucson, Arizona, there are several dry, grassy meadows within the forests at the high-

Sigmodon ochrognathus

est elevations. Meadows like these, if they were farther north in Arizona, would be expected to contain voles. However, voles are absent, and probably have been since the Pleistocene, but these meadows are occupied now by the vole-like yellow-nosed cotton rat.

The yellow-nosed cotton rat (like several other species of southern mammals, including other *Sigmodon* species) has expanded its range northward in the past 100 years. Its northward expansion was documented by plotting the year of first capture at localities of increasing latitude: the farther north the locality, the later the initial capture record. Surprisingly, this expansion has sometimes occurred across gaps of habitat that seem quite unsuitable. Fossil evidence suggests that this recent northward surge may be one of several that this species has made at intervals throughout the Holocene. *R. Davis and R. Sidner*

Size
No significant sexual dimorphism
Total length: 132–264 mm (139 mm in
    Durango, 222 mm in AZ, 259 mm in TX)
Length of tail: 80–114 mm (96 mm in AZ,
    114 mm in TX)
Weight: 51–106 g (78 g in AZ)

Identification
This is the only *Sigmodon* species with the following combination of traits: hind foot length of 30 mm or less, underparts silvery or whitish, color inside the pinna of ear the same as the dorsum, and orangish eye rings and nose (usually in marked contrast with the brownish base color of the sides and dorsum).

Status
Uncommon, limited

References
Mammalian Species 97; Hoffmeister, 1986

White-throated woodrat | *Neotoma albigula*

White-throated woodrats occur over much of the southwestern United States and central and western Mexico, from sea level to as high as 2,500 m. Their range overlaps the ranges of several other species of woodrats, including *Neotoma micropus, N. lepida, N. stephensi, N. goldmani,* and *N. mexicana,* and abuts the range of *N. floridana* on the east and *N. fuscipes* on the west.

The white-throated woodrat has a soft, short pelage that is brownish above with interspersed black hairs. The throat hairs and hairs of the pectoral region are white to the base. The tail, which is rather long-haired, is brownish or dusky above, whitish below, and distinctly bicolored. The ears are long. In areas where black lava is the substrate, melanistic forms appear, although they have white patches on the inguinal region, inside the hind limbs, and on the thoracic-jugular area. There is probably only one annual molt in this species.

Neotoma albigula breeds throughout the year in Arizona and in the more southern portions of its range, although the breeding period varies geographically. Gestation is about 38 days and litter size varies from 2–3; young weigh 10.9 g at birth. Lactation occurs for 20–25 days after birth, although young may begin eating cactus at about the time their eyes open (by 17 days of age). Attainment of sexual maturity has been reported from about 3 months after birth to as long as 300 days.

White-throated woodrats feed primarily, but not exclusively, on cactus, particularly prickly pear *(Opuntia).* They are also known to consume parts of juniper trees *(Juniperus),* various parts of mesquite *(Prosopis),* soapweed *(Yucca glauca),* yucca blades, grass, catclaw *(Acacia),* and cholla cacti *(Opuntia).* Since the dens of this woodrat are frequently constructed of various types of cacti and woody vegetation of mesquite, juniper, and other shrubs, the animals can eat their dens during periods of food shortage. Woodrats are capable of obtaining water from cacti, and may not need free water. Their consumption of cacti, which contain various toxins, suggests that physiological adaptations have evolved that permit the close association of these rodents with this source of food and water. Woodrats are eaten by a variety of predators, including badgers, coyotes, foxes, bobcats, humans, owls, hawks, snakes, and gila monsters.

Fossils of the *N. floridana* group (including *N. micropus,* a species closely related to *N. albigula)* from the late Illinoian period, which are about 500,000 years old, are known from the Great Plains; equally old fossils of *N. albigula* are known from New Mexico. Fossilized and ancient woodrat dens have become a major tool in understanding the distribution of prehistoric vegetation, and contribute to our understanding of ancient climates; they are thus useful in studies of global climatic change.

Neotoma albigula is generally found in arid regions across a variety of habitats. It may be found on rocky mountainsides, in arid scrublands and cactus flats, on forested hillsides supporting pinyon-juniper, or in a variety of desert areas, including those with a lava substrate. Populations in New Mexico have been reported as stable in size throughout the year, maintaining a density of one per hectare, but densities as high as 12.7 per hectare have been reported in Arizona. Woodrat density may be related to the number of suitable nest sites, the presence or absence of competing species of woodrats, or other factors, such as food availability. Since *N. albigula* overlaps a large number of species of woodrats, and abuts the ranges of two others, numerous interspecific interactions have been reported, with *N. albigula* seeming to competitively exclude (possibly through aggression) several species in areas of sympatry. In southeastern Colorado, *N. albigula* may hybridize with *N. micropus.*

White-throated woodrats are primarily nocturnal, although they may be active during daylight hours. Generally this species constructs elaborate dens (up to 2 m in diameter and 60 cm in height) of cactus pads and branches (prickly pear, cholla), as well as woody vegetation of trees and shrubs. A nest chamber measuring 15–25 cm in diameter is placed above the ground near the center of the lodge. The thorny dens offer shelter from predators and from the high temperatures that characterize much of the geographic range of this species. Foraging occurs away from the den and a series of well-defined runways radiates from each woodrat house. Dens are utilized for shelter by a number of other vertebrate and invertebrate species, including shrews *(Notiosorex, Sorex)*, opossums *(Didelphis)*, skunks *(Mephitis)*, rabbits *(Sylvilagus)*, rodents *(Peromyscus, Microtus)*, lizards *(Coleonyx, Callisaurus, Uta)*, and a variety of arthropods and insects. Some white-throated woodrats do not construct dens, but nest in rock crevices or in burrows under boulders.

White-throated woodrats have been known to carry all sorts of items to their dens, including empty rifle shells, bottle caps, and bones. This behavior gave them the common name packrat, and led to a number of legends of their exchanging gold nuggets for worthless trinkets left for them by gold miners. Although these tales are apocryphal, one mechanism for studying the home ranges of this species is to scatter numbered sticks throughout an area, then open a den to see which sticks were carried there by the woodrat. *M. A. Mares*

Neotoma albigula

Size
Total length: 282–400 (328) mm
Length of tail: 76–185 (152) mm
Weight: 224 g (mean for males); 188 g (mean for females); weight varies from 135 to 283 g, for sexes combined

Identification
The white-throated woodrat can be distinguished from other species of *Neotoma* by the brown dorsal pelage, the throat and pectoral regions with hairs white to the base, and the bicolored tail (brownish or dusky above, whitish below).

Other Common Names
Packrat

Status
Common

Subspecies
Neotoma albigula albigula, Arizona, New Mexico, western Texas, Chihuahua, Sonora
Neotoma albigula brevicauda, southeastern Utah, southwestern Colorado
Neotoma albigula durangae, Chihuahua, Coahuila, Durango
Neotoma albigula laplataensis, northern Arizona, northwestern New Mexico, southwestern Colorado, southeastern Utah
Neotoma albigula latifrons, Michoacán
Neotoma albigula leucodon, Durango, Jalisco, Zacatecas
Neotoma albigula mearnsi, southwestern Arizona
Neotoma albigula melanura, Chihuahua, Sonora
Neotoma albigula melas, south-central New Mexico
Neotoma albigula robusta, western Texas
Neotoma albigula seri, Sonora (Tiburón Island)
Neotoma albigula sheldoni, Sonora
Neotoma albigula subsolana, Coahuila, Nuevo León
Neotoma albigula venusta, southeastern California, westernmost Arizona, northwestern Sonora, northeastern Baja California
Neotoma albigula warreni, southeastern Colorado, western Oklahoma Panhandle, northeastern New Mexico, northern Texas Panhandle

References
Mammalian Species 310; Hoffmeister, 1986

Bushy-tailed woodrat | *Neotoma cinerea*

Bushy-tailed woodrats are found from the Northwest Territories to northeastern Arizona, and from coastal northwestern California to central North Dakota. These handsome rodents are marked by a bushy, squirrel-like tail that is about 75 percent as long as the body, and by large, thinly haired, almost translucent ears; they are whitish to buff beneath, pale gray to brownish-black above.

Nocturnal and active year-round, bushy-tailed woodrats usually den in caves, crevices in cliffs, and narrow openings among jumbles of large boulders. They will also den in abandoned buildings and mine tunnels, the human-made equivalents of their natural den sites. They bring a diverse assortment of objects to these sites—primarily sticks and bones, but also any other item that attracts their attention. The reputation these animals have as industrious thieves is deserved: a watch, sock, or toothbrush that has disappeared overnight can often be found in the nearest active packrat den.

Bushy-tailed woodrats are mediocre house builders. Most frequently, they simply deposit what they have collected into crevices or between boulders, thus protecting their dens from predators and the weather. Within their dens, they construct cup-shaped, and at times roofed, nests, relying largely on fibrous plant material for building material.

The insulation provided by den and nest is critically important, since no other species of woodrat gets as far north (65° N) or as high (4,342 m on White Mountain Peak, California). On the other hand, high-elevation populations of bushy-tailed woodrats are unable to tolerate elevated temperatures, and succumb to them far sooner than most other mammals.

Neotoma cinerea

These animals have some obvious morphological adaptations to cold temperatures, including the bushy tail and relatively thick fur. They are also among the largest of all woodrats. Since larger animals have lower surface area-to-mass ratios than do smaller animals of the same shape, larger woodrats are better protected against the cold than smaller ones. Not surprisingly, the largest bushy-tailed woodrats are those from the farthest north and from the highest elevations.

Bushy-tailed woodrats eat only plant foods, preferring foliage to woody parts. Compared to the desert woodrat *(Neotoma lepida)* and the white-throated woodrat *(N. albigula)*, bushy-tailed woodrats are less picky about ingesting plant material with a high fiber content. Perhaps this is why the first upper molars of this species are more complex than the corresponding teeth of desert and white-throated woodrats: the complexity of that tooth provides more enamel surface area for the grinding of fibrous material.

Bushy-tailed woodrats wander short distances (usually 100 m or less) from their dens to collect and retrieve foodstuffs. Back at the den site, they leave it out to dry, and then move it to a storage area. This they will do whenever food is available, but they pick up the pace in late summer and autumn, laying in substantial stores for the winter.

Except during the breeding season, or when females are raising young, bushy-tailed woodrats are found one to a den. They are highly territorial, males excluding other males, but not females, from their territory. Both males and females have a gland on the chest that exudes a brownish, musky-smelling material that is used as a territorial marker; this gland is far better developed in the males. Both sexes also mark their territories with musky-scented urine. Packrat urine contains a high

proportion of calcium compounds. When the organic material washes out, the insoluble calcium compounds may be left behind, creating distinctive white streaks on the rocks of arid areas. These are readily distinguished from the white streaks left by birds, since they tend to run along rock ridges, and bird streaks tend to be smeared over the rocks.

Bushy-tailed woodrats are born between March and August, and begin breeding the following year. After a gestation period of about 30 days, females give birth to between 2 and 4 young. A female may produce 2 or 3 litters in a season. The young are weaned when they are about four weeks old, and many disperse to new territories by the time they are four months old.

The extinction of local populations of bushy-tailed woodrats is apparently a fairly common event, with much of the mortality occurring during the winter months. Long-tailed weasels, martens, coyotes, bobcats, and a variety of raptors are known to prey on these rodents.

A good deal of what a bushy-tailed (or other) woodrat collects simply accumulates near its den, producing often-substantial middens. Woodrats often urinate and defecate on these middens. If the midden is in the open, the urine is just washed away. But if the midden is in a sheltered spot in an arid area—in a desert cave, for instance—the urine will crystallize and become almost rock-hard. As long as the midden remains dry, it can last for tens of thousands of years. Indeed, many woodrat middens are so old that they are beyond the 40,000-year range of radiocarbon dating. Since the ancient middens contain plant materials gathered nearby, they also contain a de-tailed record of the vegetation that surrounded the site at the time the midden grew. During the past two decades, analyses of these middens have revolutionized our understanding of the environmental history of the arid west. *D. K. Grayson*

Size
Total length: 310–470 (379) mm (males); 273–410 (356) mm (females)
Length of tail: 129–223 (165) mm (males); 120–193 (155) mm (females)
Weight: 181–585 (337) g (males); 166–370 (275) g (females)

Identification
This species can be distinguished from all other woodrats by its large size and bushy, almost squirrel-like tail.

Other Common Names
Bushy-tailed packrat

Status
Common

Subspecies
Neotoma cinerea acraia, western Utah to eastern California
Neotoma cinerea alticola, eastern Oregon and adjacent Idaho, Nevada, and California
Neotoma cinerea arizonae, western Colorado, eastern Utah, northern Arizona, northeastern New Mexico
Neotoma cinerea cinerea, Montana and adjacent states and provinces
Neotoma cinerea cinnamomea, southwestern Wyoming, northwestern Colorado
Neotoma cinerea drummondii, eastern British Columbia and adjacent provinces
Neotoma cinerea fusca, western Oregon
Neotoma cinerea lucida, southern Nevada and adjacent California
Neotoma cinerea macrodon, eastern Utah

Neotoma cinerea occidentalis, western Oregon, Washington, northern Idaho, northwestern Montana, western British Columbia, southern Yukon, and adjacent Northwest Territories
Neotoma cinerea orolestes, northern New Mexico to eastern Wyoming
Neotoma cinerea pulla, northwestern California and adjacent Oregon
Neotoma cinerea rupicola, western Nebraska, western South Dakota, southwestern North Dakota

References
Mammalian Species 564; Betancourt et al., 1990; Escherich, 1981; Finley, 1958

Arizona woodrat | *Neotoma devia*

The Arizona woodrat, one of the smallest woodrats, lives in both low desert and desert mountains in western and northern Arizona. Its range is bordered by the Colorado River in the west and the Grand Canyon in the north, but neither the river nor the canyon is a complete barrier to this animal's travels. Its distribution within Arizona is usually restricted to habitats surrounding major tributaries of the Colorado River, such as the Little Colorado in the northeast and Gila River to the southwest.

Like most woodrats, *Neotoma devia* is a midden-builder, which gives rise to one of its common names, packrat, but the dens of *Neotoma devia* are skimpy compared to those of other woodrats. The dens are typically located at the bases of cliffs and rock outcroppings, where the woodrats fill horizontal or diagonal fissures in the rocks with cholla cactus and other favorite foods such as wolfberry, creosote-bush, and mesquite. Mormon tea is a preferred food, and the woodrats carry it considerable distances from where it is growing to their den sites during their nocturnal forays.

Over most of its range, the Arizona woodrat is sympatric with the widespread white-throated woodrat, *Neotoma al-*

bigula. Because of its much smaller size, *Neotoma devia* seems unable to compete for choice den sites and thus consistently occupies more marginal locations. This competition may be a factor limiting population numbers of *Neotoma devia* in areas where the white-throated woodrat is abundant.

The Arizona woodrat is typically a pale golden to buffy color on its back and sides, with a white underbelly. The fur is fairly long and soft. A patch of dark gray fur in the throat region distinguishes this species from most of its cogeners. Stephen's woodrat *(Neotoma stephensi)* also has this characteristic, and can be found with *Neotoma devia* in the far northeastern part of its range, but Stephen's woodrat has a somewhat bushy tail and its belly fur is orange, which makes distinguishing the two species easy. The ears of the desert woodrats set them apart from other members of the genus. *Neotoma devia* has large, petal-like ears, often 30 mm or more in length, which look proportionately large compared to the ears of the white-throated woodrat.

The mean litter size of *Neotoma devia* is approximately 2.1 and the gestation period is 36 days. Two young are typical and they weigh about 10 grams at birth. The eyes open in 11 to 13 days and the young are weaned at about 21 days. Females mature between 2 and 3 months of age. Young can be born throughout the year. *Neotoma devia* undergoes three molts during its development, starting with a slate gray juvenile pelage. This is followed by a bicolored gray side and brown back pattern. Adult coloration appears about 10 months after birth. Thereafter, the animals undergo an annual molt, usually in mid-summer.

The ecological histories of southwestern plant biotas have been elucidated through the study of materials collected in woodrat middens, but little paleontological work has been reported on the woodrats themselves. Desert woodrat fossils

Neotoma devia

have been reported from the late Pleistocene and early Holocene in locations in southwestern Texas and Chihuahua, Mexico, but which species they most closely resemble has not been determined. *J. V. Planz*

Size
Males are larger than females.
Total length: 262–308 (290) mm (males); 262–298 (283) mm (females)
Length of tail: 111–149 (131) mm (males); 117–136 (128) mm (females)
Weight: 96.7–132.3 g

Identification
Neotoma devia can be distinguished from *Neotoma albigula,* which shares much of its

range, by its generally smaller size, paler coloring, and dark-colored fur in the throat region. It is more difficult to distinguish this species from its closest relative, *Neotoma lepida,* which is slightly larger and has darker pelage. The two species are significantly different chromosomally and based on mtDNA data.

Recent Synonyms
Neotoma lepida auripila
Neotoma lepida devia

Other Common Names
Arizona desert woodrat, Arizona packrat, western Arizona woodrat

Status
Common, limited to specific habitat

References
Betancourt et al., 1990; Harris, 1984; Hoffmeister, 1986

Eastern woodrat | *Neotoma floridana*

The eastern woodrat, a medium-sized rodent, is found over a broad geographic area from southern Florida to northwestern Nebraska. Eastern woodrats are sharply bicolored. Adults have a dorsal surface of medium brown with black guard hairs and juveniles are a slate gray color. The ventral surface of both adults and juveniles is white from chest to tail tip.

Over most of their range, woodrats occur in wooded areas, particularly where there is a dense understory. In grasslands,

woodrats can be found in hedgerows and rocky outcrops. However, an opportunistic woodrat will readily inhabit an abandoned building or a discarded automobile.

Woodrat dens are constructed of sticks and are often built around a large rock or fallen log. They are occupied by only one individual at a time, with the exception of females with litters of young, but are occupied by a succession of individuals over time. Because each new occupant adds sticks to the den,

very old dens can grow to heights of five feet, though dens of two to three feet in height are more common. Dens protect woodrats from adverse weather and some predators. Predators of the eastern woodrat include great horned owls, coyotes, and skunks. However, their major and most dangerous predators are snakes and weasels, which can pursue the woodrat into its den.

In addition to protection, woodrat dens also provide residents with space for a nest chamber and a storage site. It is the habit of collecting and storing both food and nonfood items that has earned the eastern woodrat its other common name of packrat. Beginning in early fall, woodrats collect and store fruits, seeds, and leaves to serve as food during the winter. Although the cache does not serve as the sole source of the winter diet, caches taken from some dens have yielded as much as a bushel of plant material. Woodrats also store nonfood items such as pieces of shiny metal and other objects discarded by humans. The reason they store inedible objects is unclear, but perhaps it is to examine novel objects in the relative safety of the den rather than outside, where a predator is more likely to take advantage of the woodrat's curiosity.

Eastern woodrats are quite solitary and will only tolerate the presence of other individuals during the breeding season. The length of the breeding season varies geographically. In Kansas and Oklahoma breeding occurs from early spring to fall, but in Florida and Georgia reproduction can occur throughout the year. Females born in early spring have been known to breed in the late summer of the same year, but males are thought not to attain sexual maturity until they are a year old.

Young are born with their eyes and ears closed and with

Neotoma floridana

only a sparse coat of hair. As soon as it is born, each neonate attaches to one of its mother's four teats, and rarely lets go until it is three to four weeks old. When females are threatened they will exit the den and scamper up a nearby tree with each youngster holding tenaciously to a teat.

Young woodrats develop rapidly. Weaning occurs at about four weeks, and juveniles disperse at about three months of age. In order to survive, a newly independent individual must find a vacant den, establish residency, and build a store of food that will last through the approaching winter. *D. Post*

Size

Total length: 305–450 (320) mm (males);
   300–399 (369) mm (females)
Length of tail: 130–180 (160) mm (males);
   130–172 (157) mm (females)
Weight: 220–384 (299) g (males); 174–260 (216)
   g (females)

Identification

Neotoma floridana is very similar externally to
Neotoma magister, but the skull characters of the
two species differ: *N. floridana* has a bifurcated
anterior palatal spine. It is a paler shade of gray
than *N. micropus,* and is larger than *N. albigula*
and *N. mexicana. N. cinerea* has larger ears and a
bushy tail.

Other Common Names

Packrat

Status

Common

Subspecies

Neotoma floridana attwateri, central and eastern
   Oklahoma and Kansas, the southwestern
   quarter of Missouri, and the northwestern
   quarter of Arkansas
Neotoma floridana baileyi, restricted to a small
   portion of north-central Nebraska
Neotoma floridana campestris, northwestern
   Kansas, east-central Colorado, and a small
   portion of southwestern Nebraska
Neotoma floridana floridana, southern Georgia,
   southern South Carolina, and northern
   Florida
Neotoma floridana haematoreia, a small portion
   of northeastern Georgia, the northwestern
   third of South Carolina, all but a small portion of northwestern North Carolina, and
   the southeastern third of Virginia
Neotoma floridana illinoensis, all but the southern quarter of Mississippi, all of Alabama,
   all of Arkansas except the northeastern
   quarter, the northern half of Louisiana, the
   eastern third of Tennessee, and a small
   portion of southeast Missouri
Neotoma floridana rubida, a small portion of
   southeastern Texas, the southern half of
   Lousiana, and the southern quarter of
   Mississippi
Neotoma floridana smalli, Key West, Florida

References

Mammalian Species 139; Hayes and Richmond,
   1993; Rainey, 1956

Dusky-footed woodrat | *Neotoma fuscipes*

Dusky-footed woodrats occur in a narrow band from the Columbia River south through the interior valley of Oregon,
thence along the Pacific coast and through the interior valleys
and wooded foothills of California into northern Baja California. From the California–Oregon border, the range extends
south and eastward along the Cascade Range into the northern counties of California. Dusky-footed woodrats occur in
coastal plain, transition, and Sonoran life zones with high tree
cover and dense understory vegetation. This species is a habitat specialist in scrub and woodland communities of dense
chaparral, sclerophyll woodland, riparian woodland, mixed deciduous forest with dense understory, and in the northern portion of the range, mixed coniferous forests. Both grazing and
shrub removal greatly reduce populations of this woodrat.

Neotoma fuscipes may co-occur with two related species,
Neotoma cinerea and *Neotoma lepida. Neotoma cinerea* is a higher-
elevation form, preferring talus slope habitats; there may be
some limited sympatry in the northern portion of the range of
N. fuscipes. Neotoma lepida occurs in sage scrub, chaparral, and
desert, and may occasionally be sympatric in the southeastern
portion of the distribution of *N. fuscipes.*

Neotoma fuscipes

The dusky-footed woodrat occurs with a number of other small mammals. It is most commonly associated with *Peromyscus truei, P. maniculatus,* and *P. californicus,* which use similar habitats and sometimes share the large stick houses built by *N. fuscipes.*

Dusky-footed woodrats are nocturnal and are generally solitary and territorial. They move easily over the substrate and spend substantial time feeding in the overstory vegetation. They build elaborate stick houses that are often more than a meter in diameter and a meter high and contain several cache, nest, and resting chambers. A latrine may be located within the structure but is more frequently adjacent to the house. Individuals may have as many as three houses (mean 1.8) and move periodically from house to house. Houses are used by a succession of individuals over a long period of time, and other small rodents, reptiles, and insects use the structures as homes. Houses can be on the ground, in the canopy, on rocky slopes, or in abandoned structures. Seven to 37 houses per hectare have been recorded.

Population density varies by habitat type, with greatest numbers in closed-canopy woodlands (35 per hectare) and lowest in open habitats (5 per hectare). Home range size differs by sex: the ranges of males are 15 percent greater than those of females. These woodrats attain sexual maturity at 6 months of age. The breeding season extends from February to September. Gestation is 33 days and females generally produce one litter of 2–4 young per year. Young at birth are reddish to gray in color and hairless. They are mobile before their eyes open. They are weaned at 21 days of age, and remain with the mother for a short period post-weaning. Subadult females frequently disperse to nearby unoccupied houses; subadult males disperse over much greater distances.

Also known as packrats or trade rats, dusky-footed woodrats frequently pick up items they encounter while foraging and drop whatever they were carrying at the time. Hundreds of man-made items have been described from woodrat houses. Two behaviors are particularly notable: when disturbed the animals foot-stomp or tail-rattle, and they mark objects and trails in their habitat with urine and with ventral glandular secretions that leave a dark stain.

Fossils from the last interglacial period of the Pleistocene have been found in the central range of the current distribution of the species. *J. A. Cranford*

Size
No significant sexual dimorphism
Total length: 335–468 (404) mm
Length of tail: 158–241 (199) mm
Weight: 205–360 g

Identification
Neotoma fuscipes can be distinguished from sympatric or parapatric species by its grayish-brown dorsum, pale or white venter, the sooty-colored pelage on the top of the hind feet, and its faintly bicolored tail. *Neotoma cinerea* has a bushy tail, and *Neotoma lepida* has belly hairs that are slate colored at the base and an overall gray body washed with reddish-brown or tawny-reddish. The hairs at the throat of *Neotoma albigula* are white to the base.

Recent Synonyms
Neotoma splendens

Other Common Names
Packrat, trade rat

Status
Common within its range

Subspecies
Neotoma fuscipes annestens, San Francisco Bay south to Strawberry Canyon
Neotoma fuscipes bullatior, California, from San Miguel southwest along the Carrizo Plains to McKittrick
Neotoma fuscipes fuscipes, northeastern California southwest to San Francisco Bay
Neotoma fuscipes luciana, coastal California from Monterrey Bay to Morro Bay
Neotoma fuscipes macrotis, extreme nothern Baja California northward along coast to Morro Bay
Neotoma fuscipes marirensis, northern Baja California
Neotoma fuscipes monochroura, Oregon Cascade Mountains and south in coastal California to San Francisco Bay
Neotoma fuscipes perplexa, California Coast Range from Pacheco Pass south to Coalinga
Neotoma fuscipes riparia, San Joaquin Valley, California
Neotoma fuscipes simplex, southern Sierra Nevada of California
Neotoma fuscipes streatori, north-central California

References
Mammalian Species 386; Ingles, 1965; Linsdale and Tevis, 1951

Desert woodrat | *Neotoma lepida*

The common name of this largely nocturnal rat is misleading. Although it does occur in desert scrublands of California, Nevada, southeastern Oregon, southwestern Idaho, western Utah, western Arizona, northwestern Sonora, and Baja California, it also occurs in large numbers in coastal sage scrub habitats in semiarid southern California, right down to the Pacific shoreline. Although it lives chiefly in semiarid and arid habitats where seasonal and prolonged drought is customary

and surface water uncommon, this woodrat has very high water requirements. Its water needs are met by a vegetarian diet that includes succulent leafy material; during drier periods extensive use is made of the most succulent groups of plants, especially of cacti of the genus *Opuntia,* and of the fleshy leaves of *Yucca* species. Desert woodrats commonly select *Opuntia* and *Yucca* plants in which to establish their stick nests. If not within clumps of these plants, woodrats often construct their nests in crevices in rocky outcrops where succulent plant material is available nearby as a combined food and water source.

The nest of the desert woodrat appears to be a haphazard array of twigs, leaves, spines, and other debris. Indeed, the name packrat derives from its common practice of carting off nearly anything within its reach and strength, including scraps of metal, plastic, and bone, and even mammalogists' traps! These are all stacked on its nest. This seemingly poorly designed pile, with its abundant plant spines, provides a daytime retreat for protection from predators and essential insulation from solar radiation as well as a more humid microclimate to reduce water loss.

To meet its vegetarian diet, the desert woodrat appears to select nearly any leafy material within foraging range of its one or more nest sites. What it does not eat is deposited on or within the nest, contributing to nest construction. Thus the nest itself represents an excellent sample of the plants that grow within the home range of the nest owner during the time of nest occupation. In addition, woodrats habitually urinate and defecate on or within a portion of the nest. These metabolic waste materials form a resinous concretion that en-

Neotoma lepida

velops some of the plant materials of the nest, resulting in a remarkable, long-lasting state of preservation. This has provided paleoclimatologists a wealth of information about past plant distributions and climates over the last 40,000 years in southwestern North America. In nests sheltered from the weather in rocky caves and crevices, scientists are able to identify species of plants that have been protected and preserved for millennia; this, together with radiocarbon dating, provides information on plant communities in the area of the nest, and the approximate dates that these communities existed. From this information, reasonable inferences on the prevailing climates can be made, enabling a reconstruction of past climates at least through the last pluvial (glacial) period.

Desert woodrats that live in wetter settings nearer to the coast are larger than those living in the drier interior. For example, the mean body weight of a combined male-female sample from a semiarid coastal sage scrub habitat near Claremont, California, was 145.9 g; that of a sample from an arid creosote-bush scrub habitat near Joshua Tree, California, was 125.5 g. Population weights correlate positively with levels of primary plant productivity across this distributional gradient, suggesting that natural selection is driving body size in the species. Larger animals occur where resources are more abundant, and smaller individuals occur in sparser habitats. The reasons for, and advantages of, these size differences remain to be thoroughly investigated.

Wherever the desert woodrat occurs, it co-occurs with several other rodent species. Among the nocturnally active species the woodrat is nearly always the largest. This large size, together with a rather aggressive nature, seems to place it at the top of a size-related dominance hierarchy, ensuring it first choice of space and desired resources such as succulent plant material. This behavioral attribute, together with high fecundity during favorable seasons and years, and an ability to subsist on a wide variety of plant material, ensures a high level of success for the species. Indeed, it must be considered one of the most successful of rodents throughout its distribution, including the harshest deserts in North America. *R. E. MacMillen*

Size
Males are larger than females.
Total length: 225–383 mm
Length of tail: 95–188 mm
Weight: 130–160 g

Identification
The tail of *N. lepida* is markedly bicolored, and the throat hairs are gray to the base rather than white. This woodrat can be distinguished from *Neotoma fuscipes*, with which it is sympatric in southern and central California, by being smaller, paler gray-brown on the dorsum, and having immaculately white rather than gray-black feet.

Other Common Names
Desert packrat

Status
Common in arid and semiarid scrublands of southwestern North America

Subspecies
Neotoma lepida abbreviata, San Francisco Island, Gulf of California, Baja California, Mexico

Neotoma lepida arenacea, La Paz and Cabo San Lucas, Baja California, Mexico

Neotoma lepida aridicola, El Barril, near San Francisquito Bay, Gulf of California, Baja California, Mexico

Neotoma lepida aureotunicata, Punta Peñascosa, Sonora, Mexico

Neotoma lepida auripila, Cabeza Prieta National Wildlife Refuge, southeastern Yuma County and western Prima County, Arizona

Neotoma lepida bensoni, Sierra Pinacate, northwestern Sonora, Mexico

Neotoma lepida californica, west-central California east and south of San Francisco Bay

Neotoma lepida devia, west-central Arizona

Neotoma lepida egressa, Pacific coast of Baja California from San Telmo south to El Rosario

Neotoma lepida felipensis, northeastern Baja California between the Gulf of California and Sierra San Pedro Martir

Neotoma lepida flava, extreme southwestern Yuma County, Arizona

Neotoma lepida gilva, south-central California and north-central Baja California, Mexico, to Gulf of California

Neotoma lepida grinnelli, extreme southeastern Nevada and southeastern California, along the Colorado River

Neotoma lepida harteri, south-central Maricopa County and west-central Pima County, Arizona

Neotoma lepida insularis, Angel de la Guarda Island, Gulf of California, Baja California, Mexico

Neotoma lepida intermedia, coastal southwestern California and northwestern Baja Califonia, Mexico; discontinuously near Porterville, California

Neotoma lepida latirostra, Danzante Island, Gulf of California, Baja California, Mexico

Neotoma lepida lepida, western Utah, Nevada except in extreme northwest, southeastern California, and extreme northeastern Baja California, Mexico

Neotoma lepida marcosensis, San Marcos Island, Gulf of California, Baja California, Mexico

Neotoma lepida marshalli, Carrington and Stansbury islands, Great Salt Lake, Utah

Neotoma lepida molagrandis, central Baja California, Mexico, from Pacific Ocean to Gulf of California

Neotoma lepida montrabilis, extreme southwestern Utah and northwestern Arizona

Neotoma lepida nevadensis, southeastern Oregon, northwestern Nevada, and extreme northeastern California

Neotoma lepida notia, southern portion of Sierra de la Laguna, Baja California, Mexico

Neotoma lepida nudicauda, Carmen Island, Gulf of California, Baja California, Mexico

Neotoma lepida perpallida, San José Island, Gulf of California, Baja California, Mexico

Neotoma lepida petricola, coastal central California between Monterey Bay and Morro Bay

Neotoma lepida pretiosa, southern Baja California from Pacific Ocean (including Santa Margarita and Magdalena islands) to Gulf of California, Mexico

Neotoma lepida ravida, south-central Baja California, Mexico, from central highlands to Gulf of California, and along Gulf from Santa Rosalia to Loreto

Neotoma lepida sanrafaeli, central and eastern Utah and northwestern Colorado

Neotoma lepida vicina, Espiritu Santo Island, Gulf of California, Baja California, Mexico

References
Betancourt et al., 1990; MacMillen, 1964

Allegheny woodrat | *Neotoma magister*

Allegheny woodrats currently range from Pennsylvania and New Jersey south to the Tennessee River, roughly following the spine of the Appalachian Mountains. They are typically found along cliff faces, in rocky, talus slopes, in caves, or in buildings.

Unlike many other species of woodrats, the Allegheny woodrat generally does not build a large house from sticks. More typically, it constructs a cup-like nest of twigs, shredded bark, or grass in the crevices of boulders or in a cliff, on a ledge inside a cave, or in an abandoned building. The nest site is often "barricaded" with piles of sticks or other items that may provide an element of protection.

Allegheny woodrats build middens consisting of piles of sticks, leaves, fungi, the dung of other animals, trash, and novel items from their environment. Some of these piles seem to serve as food storage, but the function (if any) of many middens is not clear. *Neotoma magister* regularly uses latrine sites, and large accumulations of feces often provide evidence of its presence.

The Allegheny woodrat has large black eyes, large ears, soft fur, and a hairy tail. Adults are gray to cinnamon-brown with a white or gray belly. The pelage is generally darker during the winter months. The tail is usually bicolored. Adults sometimes have brown stains on the belly that are caused by excretions from the ventral gland. Staining is often particularly pronounced in males during the summer months. Juveniles tend to be grayer than adults.

Breeding usually takes place between March and September. After a gestation of about 35 days, Allegheny woodrats have one to four offspring in a litter, averaging about two. The number of litters that an individual produces in a year seems to depend on weather and food availability. During favorable years, females can give birth to up to four litters.

This nocturnal species feeds on a wide variety of plant material, including nuts, seeds, fruits, leaves, and fungi. When alarmed or angered, Allegheny woodrats thump their rear feet.

Allegheny woodrat populations apparently were isolated from other woodrats during the Pleistocene. They were probably restricted to the southern Appalachians during the last glaciation, and rapidly colonized the northern states as the glaciers retreated during the past 10,000 years.

In recent years, Allegheny woodrat populations have declined precipitously in several areas. The species has been extirpated from New York and several populations have become extinct in New Jersey, Pennsylvania, Ohio, Maryland, and Indiana. The species is listed as threatened or endangered in several states. Several theories have been proposed to explain the

Neotoma magister

decline, including harsh winter conditions, decreased food supplies resulting from defoliation by gypsy moths, and infestations by parasites. Recent studies suggest that the raccoon roundworm *(Baylisacaris procyonis)* is an important factor in its decline in some areas.

Until recently, *Neotoma magister* was classified as a subspecies of *N. floridana.* J. P. Hayes

Size

Total length:368–465 (414) mm (males);
   352–446 (409) mm (females)
Length of tail: 147–215 (185) mm (males);
   142–210 (185) mm (females)
Weight: 228–485 (360) g (males); 230–456
   (338) g (females)

Identification

No other woodrats occur within its range. *Neotoma magister* can only be distinguished reliably from *N. floridana* by features of the skull,
although *N. magister* is often somewhat larger and may have a hairier tail. *Neotoma* can be distinguished from *Rattus* by its hairy, generally bicolored tail, fine and silky hair, and longer vibrissae.

Recent Synonyms

Neotoma floridana magister

Other Common Names

Allegheny cliff rat

Status

Declining in some areas, particularly in the northern portions of the range, with several local extinctions reported. Listed as threatened or endangered by several states.

References

Hayes and Harrison, 1992; Hayes and
   Richmond, 1993; Poole, 1940

Mexican woodrat | *Neotoma mexicana*

The Mexican woodrat occurs from northern Colorado south through western and central Mexico and into Guatemala and Honduras. Although predominantly montane, its elevational range is from 15 m in Nayarit, Mexico, to 4,025 m on Tajumulco Volcano in Guatemala. Throughout its range it lives in rock outcrops or on rocky slopes and cliffs. In Mexico and in the United States, Mexican woodrats are found in pinyon-juniper woodland, scrub oak, ponderosa pine, and mixed deciduous-coniferous forest. In Mexico they also occur in tropical thorn forest and scrub and in boreal forest. Fossil remains of *Neotoma mexicana* have been found in Pleistocene deposits in Arizona, New Mexico, Texas, and Mexico.

Woodrats are commonly called trade rats or packrats because of their habit of collecting and accumulating things, and Mexican woodrats are no exception, although they have the weakest collecting instinct of the genus. They sometimes build the houses typical of most woodrats, but more often construct their nests in well-protected areas like rock crevices, tree cavities, or abandoned buildings. Rock crevices and tree cavities containing nests are stuffed with sticks, cactus joints, and other items collected by the inhabitant.

Mexican woodrats eat a wide variety of plant material, including green foliage, seeds, and berries. They sometimes store large amounts of food such as dried cuttings of foliage or large seeds like acorns. Although they often occur in arid environments, they do not have special physiological adaptations for such climates. Like other woodrats they are nocturnal. Mexican woodrats are common prey of owls, foxes, coyotes, bobcats, weasels, and rattlesnakes.

Neotoma mexicana is a medium sized, grayish-brown woodrat with white underparts. The tail is black or dusky above and grayish to whitish below. At the northern limits of its range, *Neotoma mexicana* breeds from March through May, producing

Neotoma mexicana

two litters per year. Farther south the breeding season can be much longer. The gestation period is about 33 days and the litter size is from 1 to 4. The pups are weaned at 4 to 6 weeks of age. Females born early in the year are capable of breeding and bearing young later in the same year. Sexual maturation in males proceeds more slowly. The young usually experience three molts during the first year.

Mexican woodrats, like other *Neotoma,* are aggressive toward each other and tend to be solitary. Each active nest is occupied by one adult male or an adult female and her young. If a nursing female is startled in her nest, she may drag her young, firmly attached to her nipples, with her if she leaves the nest. Because Mexican woodrats are principally montane, the distribution is often disjunct, with adjacent populations isolated on the tops of mountains. Often two or more species of woodrats with different elevational distributions occur in such areas. When more than one species is present in an area, their ranges rarely overlap, apparently the result of interspecific aggression. *J. E. Cornely*

Size
Total length: 290–417 mm
Length of tail: 105–206 mm
Weight: 151–253 g

Identification
Neotoma mexicana is medium in size for genus, its throat hairs are usually gray at the base, and its tail is not bushy.

Other Common Names
Trade rat, packrat

Status
Common

Subspecies
Neotoma mexicana atrata, southern New Mexico
Neotoma mexicana bullata, southern Arizona
Neotoma mexicana chamula, southeastern Mexico and Guatemala
Neotoma mexicana distincta, eastern Mexico
Neotoma mexicana eremita, west-central Mexico

Neotoma mexicana fallax, Colorado
Neotoma mexicana ferruginea, Guatemala and Honduras
Neotoma mexicana griseoventer, east-central Mexico
Neotoma mexicana inopinata, Arizona, Colorado, New Mexico, and Utah
Neotoma mexicana inornata, northern Mexico

Neotoma mexicana isthmica, southeastern Mexico and Guatemala
Neotoma mexicana mexicana, Arizona, New Mexico, Texas, and northern Mexico
Neotoma mexicana navus, central Mexico
Neotoma mexicana ochracea, central Mexico
Neotoma mexicana parvidens, southern Mexico
Neotoma mexicana picta, southern Mexico
Neotoma mexicana pinetorum, Arizona and New Mexico
Neotoma mexicana scopulorum, Colorado, New Mexico, and Oklahoma
Neotoma mexicana sinaloae, western Mexico
Neotoma mexicana solitaria, Guatemala and Honduras
Neotoma mexicana tenuicauda, western and central Mexico
Neotoma mexicana torquata, central Mexico
Neotoma mexicana tropicalis, southeastern Mexico
Neotoma mexicana vulcani, Guatemala

References
Mammalian Species 262

Southern plains woodrat | *Neotoma micropus*

Southern plains woodrats inhabit the southern Great Plains of the United States and Mexico. The eastern portion of this woodrat's range abuts that of the eastern woodrat, *Neotoma floridana*. *N. micropus* and the white-throated woodrat, *N. albigula,* have overlapping distributions over much of their ranges.

The southern plains woodrat has dense, soft, pale to dark gray fur; buffy or black hairs are sometimes present along the back. The belly is also gray, except for the throat and chest regions, which are white. The tail is blackish-gray above and whitish or pale gray on the underside. First year individuals usually have two and frequently three molts. Adults have one annual molt, usually acquiring their winter coat between June and October, but no later than November.

Neotoma micropus usually breeds in early spring and produces one litter per year; in parts of the range (especially southern populations), it may have a more continuous breeding season, producing two or more litters per year. The peaks usually occur in early spring and late fall. The breeding season may coincide with changes in vegetation. The gestation period lasts from 30 to 39 days. Litter sizes are usually of two or three. Neonates are covered with pale gray hair except on the venter and the limbs, which are naked. The skin is dark gray or black; the venter and limbs are pink to red. The ears, which are either folded or erect at birth, are fully erect within two days. The eyes are open at the end of the second week, and by then the hair is well developed. Weaning occurs 30 days after birth, and dispersal at six months. Individuals attain adult size by nine months, and may live as long as 27 months in the wild.

Southern plains woodrats eat many different kinds of vegetation, including leaves, berries, roots, nuts, seeds, acorns, prickly pear pads and fruits, beans and pods of mesquite, joints and spiny fruits of tree cactus, and leaf blades, fruit capsules, and seeds of yucca. Hawks, owls, roadrunners, raccoons, foxes, coyotes, bobcats, and snakes are the primary predators of *Neotoma micropus.*

Fossils of *Neotoma micropus* are known from Pleistocene deposits throughout Kansas, Texas, New Mexico, Chihuahua, and Tamaulipas.

Neotoma micropus inhabits a wide variety of habitats, including rocky hillsides and shrubby grasslands. In general, these areas are characterized by grasses, creosotebush, mesquite, and cactus. Populations of these woodrats may reach high levels and then crash; crashes are due to changes in habitat (for example, elimination of cactus due to excessive rainfall). The eastern range limit of *Neotoma micropus* abuts the western range limit of *Neotoma floridana*. Although hybridization has been documented, *N. micropus* prefers grassland-cactus habitats and *N. floridana* prefers mesic woodland habitats. The ranges of the southern plains woodrat and the white-throated woodrat overlap greatly. Hybridization has also been reported between these two species, although habitat separation is generally maintained. In areas of sympatry, *N. micropus* prefers flat, semi-arid plains of grassland-cactus habitats, and *N. albigula* prefers rocky areas or canyons in association with junipers and yucca.

Like most rodents, woodrats are active between dusk and midnight. When disturbed, individuals thump or drum their hindfeet. This behavior may be a means of communicating territorial ownership. Southern plains woodrats usually occupy a single den during their lifetime. These dens are built under mesquite, acacia, yucca, and cactus, or atop kangaroo rat burrows, in sand dunes, under ledges or rock outcrops, or in the sides of gullies; prickly pear cactus patches are preferred. Dens, which may reach 29 cm in height and 84 cm in diameter, are constructed of sticks, cactus, and manure. They usually have three twig- and cactus-lined entrances, but five are not uncommon. A large chamber is located in the center of the den, sur-

Neotoma micropus

rounded by several smaller chambers that serve for food storage and for a nest. A series of trails or runways connects dens to feeding areas and other dens.

Southern plains woodrats are usually found in association with least shrews, eastern cottontails, jackrabbits, armadillos, kangaroo rats, cotton rats, grasshopper mice, ground squirrels, harvest mice, white-footed mice, pocket mice, and pygmy mice. *J. K. Braun*

Size

Males are slightly larger and heavier than females.

Total length: 334–411 (370) mm (males); 310–382 (356) mm (females)

Length of tail: 131–175 (153) mm (males); 130–165 (147) mm females

Weight: 210–317 g (males); 180–274 g (females)

Identification

N. micropus can be distinguished from other species of *Neotoma* with adjacent or overlapping ranges by gray coloration, throat and chest hairs that are white basally, and bicolored tail.

Other Common Names

Hoary woodrat, Baird woodrat, black woodrat, plains woodrat, gray woodrat, rata de campo

Status

Common

Subspecies

Neotoma micropus canescens, New Mexico, west Texas, and the Oklahoma Panhandle

Neotoma micropus leucophaea, south-central New Mexico

Neotoma micropus littoralis, southeastern Tamaulipas

Neotoma micropus micropus, central Oklahoma and Texas, eastern Coahuila, Nuevo Leon, Tamaulipas, and southeastern San Luis Potosi

Neotoma micropus planiceps, southeastern San Luis Potosi

References

Mammalian Species 330

Stephen's woodrat | *Neotoma stephensi*

Stephen's woodrat ranges from western New Mexico west through central and western Arizona and northward to southern Utah. It is sympatric with the desert woodrat *(N. lepida)*, the white-throated woodrat *(N. albigula)*, and the Mexican woodrat *(N. mexicana).*

Neotoma stephensi's nest sites usually are found near or at the base of junipers *(Juniperus)*, which are the main source of food, water, and shelter for this species. Although juniper occurs throughout the majority of its range, Stephen's woodrat also has been found in association with yellow pines *(Pinus ponderosa)*, cacti *(Opuntia)*, and agave *(Agave).* Other elements of its habitat include rock piles, walls, and crevices.

The red tree vole *(Phenacomys longicaudus)* and Stephen's woodrat are the only known conifer leaf specialists among North American mammals. Both of these mammals apparently are unaffected by tannins and terepenoids, chemical compounds produced by conifers that inhibit digestion in most mammals. It has been suggested that Stephen's woodrats forage selectively, choosing juniper sprigs that have low concentrations of these compounds.

Pelage color varies among populations of Stephen's woodrats. In areas where the substrate is dark, the pelage may be correspondingly dark. In general, the dorsum is a yellowish to grayish buff and the venter is creamy in color. *N. s. stephensi* is markedly darker than *N. s. relicta;* its throat hairs are gray at the base and its tail is nearly black. *N. s. relicta* has an overall pale, buffy color, throat hairs that are white to the base, and its tail has fewer black hairs than does the tail of *N. s. stephensi.*

The breeding season for *N. stephensi* extends from February through July. Females are sexually mature around nine months of age and can produce up to five litters per year. Typically, a single young is born following a gestation period of 31 days; on rare occasions, twins are born. In comparison to other species of woodrats, the young develop slowly and are weaned late.

Neotoma stephensi

Two weeks after birth, the eyes are open and the young may begin to feed on juniper. Weaning occurs at 35 days of age and foraging outside the den begins at approximately 42 days of age.

Deposits from the Grand Canyon indicate the presence of *N. stephensi* during the late Pleistocene. Based on midden examination, this species has been associated with juniper for some 15,000 years. Other woodrats, such as the Mexican woodrat, and mice, including the pinyon mouse *(Peromyscus truei)*, the brush mouse *(P. boylii)*, and the cactus mouse *(P. eremicus)* occur in the same rocky habitat as Stephen's woodrat. *A. M. Wallace and C. Jones*

Size

Males are significantly larger than females.
Total length: 274–312 (293) mm
Length of tail: 115–149 (132) mm
Weight: 117–180 g (males)

Identification

Neotoma stephensi is a small to medium-sized woodrat that often is confused with *N. lepida* (desert woodrat) and *N. albigula* (white-throated woodrat). The presence of a semi-bushy tail and an overall dusky-gray coloration are distinguishing features of this mammal.

Recent Synonyms

Neotoma lepida stephensi

Status

Restricted range

Subspecies

Neotoma stephensi relicta, southern Utah, northern Arizona, and northwestern New Mexico

Neotoma stephensi stephensi, central Arizona and west-central New Mexico

References

Mammalian Species 328; Hoffmeister, 1986; Hoffmeister and de la Torre, 1960; Vaughn, 1982

Western red-backed vole | *Clethrionomys californicus*

Western red-backed voles live in a variety of forest habitats in western Oregon and northern California, from the Columbia River south to about 100 km north of San Francisco Bay, and from the Pacific Ocean east to the summit of the Cascade Range. In the Coast Range of Oregon, *Clethrionomys californicus* occurs in immature and mature conifer forests, in plant communities that include lodgepole pine *(Pinus contorta),* Douglas fir *(Pseudotsuga menziesii),* western hemlock *(Tsuga heterophylla),* Sitka spruce *(Picea sitchensis),* western red cedar *(Thuja plicata),* big-leaf maple *(Acer macrophyllum),* rhododendron *(Rhododendron macrophyllum),* salal *(Gaultheria shallon),* and salmonberry *(Rubus spectabilis).* On the west slope of the Cascade Mountains of Oregon, *C. californicus* occurs in Douglas fir forests that include conifers such as western hemlock, western red cedar, silver fir *(Abies amabilis),* and grand fir *(Abies grandis),* and understory vegetation such as Oregon mountain grape *(Berberis nervosa),* salal, vine maple *(Acer circinatum),* wild blackberry *(Rubus macropetalus),* huckleberry *(Vaccinium parvifolium),* rhododendron, and sword fern *(Polystichum munitum).* Farther east in the Cascade Mountains of Oregon, the overstory also may contain white fir *(Abies concolor)* and ponderosa pine *(Pinus ponderosa).* In California, during years of abundance, western red-backed voles reportedly occur in brushlands of manzanita *(Arctostaphylos)* and silk-tassel *(Garrya).* No fossils of western red-backed voles have been found.

Western red-backed voles build nests underground in burrows, under logs, or under old leaves, and forage mostly under the surface of the forest floor where the temperature is more

stable than that of the aboveground environment. In the Cascade Mountains *Clethrionomys californicus* is mainly nocturnal, whereas in the Coast Range it is active at any time. Population densities are greatest in dark, dense forests with little or no undergrowth. Western red-backed voles are found more frequently in upland regions than in riparian areas, and more frequently in old-growth forest that is at least 200 years old than in mature stands that are about 100 years old. Habitats used by *C. californicus* typically have a canopy cover of western hemlock or other conifer, many decaying logs, abundant lichen, and relatively few deciduous trees. *C. californicus* uses large, sound logs with large overhang areas as travel routes and perhaps as cover to avoid predators; soft, decaying logs may be used for foraging, nesting, or internal travel routes.

In Oregon, the diet of western red-backed voles consists largely of fungus and lichens. Hypogeous (underground) fungi generally are not available in summer, but continue to occur in stomach contents of *C. californicus,* suggesting that the voles cache supplies. They may help to disseminate spores of hypogeous fungi and bacteria that contribute significantly to certain forest ecosystems. *C. californicus* eats conifer seeds when they fall and occasionally eats insect larvae. The diet of western red-backed voles is related to their habitat; individuals found at higher elevation are in habitats subjected to more drastic climatic changes, so their diet is more variable than that of individuals at lower elevations. At higher elevations, where temperatures cool earlier in the year, the fungal fruiting season is abbreviated; these voles eat more lichen than those that live at lower elevations.

Clethrionomys californicus has a chestnut brown to reddish brown dorsal stripe grading to dark gray or buffy gray on the sides and belly. The tail is long and indistinctly bicolored, dusky above and whitish below. Juveniles are darker and have a less distinct median stripe on the back. *C. c. californicus* is darker than the other two subspecies and the red stripe on the back is largely obscured by black hair; *C. c. mazama* is paler, and

Clethrionomys californicus

C. c. obscurus is intermediate. The pelage is long and soft in winter and short and coarse in summer.

Clethrionomys californicus on the west slope of the Cascade Mountains in northern Oregon breeds from February to November. At lower elevations west of the Cascade Mountains, the voles breed throughout the year. After a gestation period of about 18 days, the female gives birth to 1–7 hairless young. Females breed soon after giving birth and have 3 or 4 litters per year.

Other small mammals that live in the forest with western red-backed voles include five other species of voles, five species of shrews, the coast and shrew moles, one species of jumping mouse, one species of deer mouse, two species of wood rats, four species of chipmunks, Douglas's and western gray tree squirrels, the northern flying squirrel, the golden-mantled ground squirrel, the mountain beaver, and one species of pocket gopher. *Clethrionomys californicus* is preyed upon by bobcats, coyotes, martens, ermines, long-tailed weasels, spotted skunks, feral domestic cats, saw-whet owls, and northern spotted owls. *L. F. Alexander*

Size
No significant sexual dimorphism
Total length: 121–165 mm
Length of tail: 34–56 mm
Weight: 15.0–40.0 g

Identification
Clethrionomys californicus can be distinguished from sympatric vole-like mammals in the genera *Phenacomys* and *Microtus* by dental characters and by a distinct, reddish stipe down the back that is not present in *Microtus* or *Phenacomys*.

Recent Synonyms
Clethrionomys occidentalis
Evotomys californicus
Evotomys mazama
Evotomys obscurus

Other Common Names
California red-backed vole

Status
Common

Subspecies
Clethrionomys californicus californicus, coastal western Oregon and northwestern California

Clethrionomys californicus mazama, Cascade Range of Oregon and California
Clethrionomys californicus obscurus, western Cascade Range of Oregon and Siskiyou Mountains of southwestern Oregon and northern California

References
Mammalian Species 406; Doyle, 1990; Maser et al., 1981

Southern red-backed vole | *Clethrionomys gapperi*

Southern red-backed voles reside in forests of the Hudsonian and Canadian life zones. In the west, they occur in the Rocky Mountains south to southwestern Arizona and New Mexico. Their southern limit in the Northwest is marked by the Columbia River. Their range extends northward in British Columbia and transcontinentally through Canada, where they meet *Clethrionomys rutilus* in the northwest. In the east, *Clethrionomys gapperi* occurs in the Appalachian Mountains south into northern Georgia. A third southward extension from Canada occurs into northern Michigan and onto the northern Great Plains.

Southern red-backed voles are active year-round, with daily peaks at dusk and during the hours of darkness. Like other voles, they do not hibernate or undergo torpidity. During winter, voles usually forage under the snow, and their home range in the subnivean environment is larger than the home range during the snow-free season. Nests of red-backed voles are simple and globular, 75–100 mm in diameter, and lined with grass, stems, dead leaves, and moss. As a rule, nests are not located in trees. Instead, voles use natural cavities, abandoned holes, and the nests of other small mammals. *Clethrionomys gapperi* is semifossorial, traveling in natural runways along and beneath logs, rocks, and roots of trees. Unlike grassland-dwelling voles, *C. gapperi* does not construct elaborate runways; instead, it commonly uses the burrow systems of other forest-dwelling small mammals such as short-tailed shrews.

The southern red-backed vole is brilliantly colored and can be distinguished easily by a broad, reddish band running from its forehead to its rump. The nose, sides of the head, and body are gray, often with a yellowish cast. Belly colors range from silvery white to pale yellowish, and the tail is bicolored—dark brown above and whitish below. Young voles are gray until the postjuvenile molt, which begins at one month of age. The first seasonal molt occurs in autumn and voles attain winter pelage by November. Summer pelage is attained by mid-May.

Clethrionomys gapperi is a prolific breeder, but unlike meadow voles, does not undergo cyclic population explosions. Red-backed voles do not breed during winter. They commence breeding in late March and continue through November. After a gestation period of 17–19 days, the female gives

birth to 4 to 5 young. Two or three litters are produced annually. Neonates are blind, toothless, hairless, pink, and weigh about 1.9 g. Weaning begins at day 12, at which time the eyes are open and the body is covered with short hair. Weanlings weigh about 12 g and begin to eat solid food at about 14 days of age. By three months of age, young voles reach sexual maturity.

These voles are omnivorous, opportunistic feeders, taking advantage of whatever the forest has to offer, including nuts, seeds, berries, mosses, lichens, ferns, fungi, plants, and arthropods. Unlike most species of *Peromyscus,* red-backed voles consume few insects. During summer and autumn, various subterranean fungi are a staple in their diet. Winter foods include seeds, roots, bark, and miscellaneous plants.

Southern red-backed voles inhabit chiefly mesic habitats in coniferous, deciduous, and mixed forests with abundant litter of stumps, rotting logs, and exposed roots. *C. gapperi* occupies a wide range of habitats in Canada, including muskegs, sedge marshes, mesic prairies, tundra and shrub habitats, and bogs of spruce and fir. In the western United States habitats include forests of ponderosa pine, red and white cedar, hemlock, Douglas fir, Engelmann spruce-subalpine fir, and aspen, as well as grassy meadows, willow-grass-sedge, and krumholz. In the Midwest, the voles live in coniferous forests (pine, cedar, spruce, balsam fir, hemlock, and tamarack), deciduous forests

Clethrionomys gapperi

(maple, basswood, oak, aspen, birch), mixed forests, and thick brush. Suitable habitats in eastern North America include forests, cut-over woodlots, forest-edge communities, marsh-grass, old fields, and sedge and chelone communities. Southern red-backed voles are less able to colonize early post-burn communities than many other small mammals seem to be.

Clethrionomys gapperi is known from the Irvingtonian (Late Kansan) age to Early Recent in various regions of North America. It may have existed in the refugium south of the ice sheet during Pleistocene glaciation and expanded north since that time, coming in contact with *Clethrionomys rutilus* at the edge of the Canadian Arctic tundra.

Other small mammals often found in the same areas as southern red-backed voles include *Peromyscus maniculatus, Zapus princeps, Phenacomys intermedius, Sorex cinereus,* and *Sorex vagrans* in western North America, and *Peromyscus maniculatus, Peromyscus leucopus, Napaeozapus insignis, Blarina brevicauda, Sorex cinereus,* and *Sorex fumeus* in eastern North America. *Clethrionomys* is Greek for "kind of dor-mouse"; *gapperi* refers to Gapper, a zoologist. *J. F. Merritt*

Size
No significant sexual dimorphism
Total length: 116–172 mm
Length of tail: 30–50 mm
Weight: 6–42 g

Identification
Distinguished from *Clethrionomys rutilus* in the northwestern part of its range by possessing a brighter red back and grayer sides; the tail is thinner, with sparser and less bristly hairs. Species of *Clethrionomys* are difficult to distinguish morphologically; no single character is sufficient to distinguish *Clethrionomys gapperi* from other species of *Clethrionomys*.

Recent Synonyms
Clethriomomys gapperi rufescens
Clethrionomys gapperi uintaensis
Evotomys fuscodorsalis
Evotomys pygmaeus

Other Common Names
Red-backed vole, Gapper's red-backed mouse, boreal red-backed vole, red-backed mouse

Status
Common

Subspecies
Clethrionomys gapperi arizonensis, White Mountains and Blue Range of eastern Arizona
Clethrionomys gapperi athabascae, northeastern British Columbia, Alberta, central to northern Saskatchewan, eastern Manitoba, and southern Northwest Territories to Great Slave Lake
Clethrionomys gapperi brevicaudus, northeastern Wyoming to Black Hills region of western South Dakota

Clethrionomys gapperi carolinensis, Appalachian Mountains from northern Georgia north through eastern Tennessee, western North Carolina, western Virginia, and West Virginia
Clethrionomys gapperi cascadensis, central Washington to southern British Columbia
Clethrionomys gapperi caurinus, northward in British Columbia along coast and on some coastal islands
Clethrionomys gapperi galei, Rocky Mountains of central and northern Colorado, Wyoming, and Montana, from Uinta Mountains of north-central Utah to extreme southwestern Alberta
Clethrionomys gapperi gapperi, Appalachian Mountains from Virginia north to New Jersey, New York, Connecticut, and Massachusetts, west to Michigan, Wisconsin, and Minnesota, and from southern Quebec west through southern Ontario to southeastern Manitoba
Clethrionomys gapperi gaspeanus, southern Quebec and northern New Brunswick
Clethrionomys gapperi gauti, northern New Mexico to southern Colorado south of the Gunnison and Arkansas rivers
Clethrionomys gapperi hudsonius, western half of Quebec west through Ontario to the eastern half of Manitoba
Clethrionomys gapperi idahoensis, eastern Oregon and Washington through Idaho and western Wyoming, north to Flathead Lake region of Montana
Clethrionomys gapperi limitis, southwestern New Mexico
Clethrionomys gapperi loringi, extreme northeastern corner of South Dakota, North Dakota north and east of the Missouri River; isolated population in the Killdeer Mountains of central North Dakota

Clethrionomys gapperi maurus, corner of southeastern Kentucky and southwestern Virginia
Clethrionomys gapperi nivarius, northwestern Washington
Clethrionomys gapperi occidentalis, northwestern Washington north to southwestern British Columbia
Clethrionomys gapperi ochraceus, New York north and east and along Atlantic coast to Maine, New Brunswick, Prince Edward Island, and southeastern Quebec
Clethrionomys gapperi pallescens, Nova Scotia
Clethrionomys gapperi paludicola, region of Pymatuning Reservoir, northwestern Pennsylvania
Clethrionomys gapperi phaeus, northwestern British Columbia and southern tip of Alaska
Clethrionomys gapperi proteus, eastern Quebec and Labrador
Clethrionomys gapperi rhoadsii, southern New York and New Jersey
Clethrionomys gapperi rupicola, crest of Kittatinny Mountains of eastern Pennsylvania
Clethrionomys gapperi saturatus, northwestern Idaho, northwestern Montana, eastern Washington, and north through the center of British Columbia
Clethrionomys gapperi soleus, southern Alaska
Clethrionomys gapperi stikinensis, southeastern Alaska and northwestern British Columbia
Clethrionomys gapperi ungava, northern Quebec
Clethrionomys gapperi wrangeli, Wrangell and Revillagigedo islands of coastal southwestern Alaska

References
Mammalian Species 146; Merritt and Merritt, l978; Merritt and Zegers, 1991

Northern red-backed vole | *Clethrionomys rutilus*

The beautiful northern red-backed vole is sometimes called the "house mouse of the North" because of its tendency to enter human habitations and because it occurs at more northerly latitudes than the real house mouse *(Mus musculus)*. In North America its distribution is restricted to the northwestern portion of the continent, but it also occurs across northern Eurasia. It has broader habitat preferences in North America, where it uses both dry tundra and the northern boreal forest; only the latter, also called taiga, is used by the species in Eurasia. The southern limit of its range in North America is conterminous with the northern limit of a close relative, *Clethrionomys gapperi,* which suggests that a strong negative interaction (competition) may occur between these two species. Such competitive interactions have been documented between red-backed voles and other species of *Clethrionomys* in northern Europe, and the red-backed vole usually gets the worst of such encounters.

Characteristics of the red-backed vole vary with the habitat it uses. In taiga, it prefers to eat tree seeds, berries, mushrooms, lichens, leaves, and even some insects. In tundra, where tree seeds do not occur and fungi and fruit are less abundant, its diet is strongly dominated by leaves. Tundra inhabitants tend to be larger and have brighter red pelage than taiga animals, and litter sizes also tend to be larger in tundra. The lower tundra vegetation provides less cover and the shallower, denser snow pack there provides less insulation against the cold winter air. Thus, the differences in characteristics of red-backed voles living in tundra and taiga may represent adaptations to regional conditions.

The normal breeding season in this mouse follows the local growing season, from April-June to September; the length depends on the time of snow melt, and is shorter at more northern latitudes. Winter breeding occurs infrequently. Mean litter size varies from 6 to 8 depending on season and location. Young mature rapidly and can breed during the year of their birth, although those born late in the summer do not breed until the following year. Young animals stop growing and overwinter at subadult size, and mature animals lose weight before entering the winter. This species remains active all winter, and survival though the winter may be enhanced by smaller size because less food is then required for maintenance.

Though the appearance of the two sexes is similar, their behavior is not. Like other species of *Clethrionomys,* breeding females maintain nonoverlapping territories. Breeding males have larger home ranges that overlap those of several females and other males, which suggests a promiscuous mating system in which females care for the young alone. The size of a female's territory can vary from more than 0.5 hectare in poor habitat to less than 0.1 hectare in favorable habitat. Territories tend to be smaller when competing species are present.

Population densities vary from less than one to more than 60 per hectare in different years. North America populations are noncyclic; that is, they do not seem to reach peak densities at regular intervals, as do some northern European populations. At snow melt the population consists entirely of breeding overwintered animals, but in 6 to 8 weeks the first cohort of young joins the breeding population. By the end of summer nearly all the overwintered animals have died. Sex ratios remain equal except in late summer; because overwintered males tend to die before females, by late summer most of the remaining overwintered animals are female. Perhaps because of the poorer insulative quality of the snow, populations in tundra suffer greater winter mortality and generally enter the breeding season at lower densities than populations in taiga. However, higher rates of population growth during the breeding season, in part because of larger litter size, often allow densities in tundra to match those in taiga by the end of summer.

G. O. Batzli

Clethrionomys rutilus

Size

Total length: 127–161 (145) mm
Length of tail: 30–48 (40) mm
Weight: 23–40 (30) g

Identification

This vole is distinguished from *Clethrionomys gapperi*, which occurs on the southern edge of its range, by a thicker, shorter tail and brighter reddish color on its back.

Other Common Names

Northern red-backed mouse, red-backed vole, tundra redback vole

Status

Common

Subspecies

Clethrionomys rutilus albiventer, St. Lawrence Island, Alaska
Clethrionomys rutilus dawsoni, northern mainland Canada west of Hudson Bay and most of Alaska
Clethrionomys rutilus glacialis, Glacier Bay area of Alaska
Clethrionomys rutilus insularis, offshore islands, Prince William Sound, Alaska
Clethrionomys rutilus orca, mainland and inshore islands, Prince William Sound, Alaska

Clethrionomys rutilus platycephalus, near MacKenzie River delta, Northwest Territories, Canada
Clethrionomys rutilus washburni, north-central mainland of Northwest Territories, Canada
Clethrionomys rutilus watsoni, Cape Yakataga, Alaska

References

Bee and Hall, 1956; Manning, 1956; Martell and Fuller, 1979; Whitney, 1976

Western heather vole | *Phenacomys intermedius*

Phenacomys intermedius is worthy of its generic appellation, which means "deceiver mouse," because in external appearance it may be mistaken for the montane vole, *Microtus montanus,* or for young meadow voles *(Microtus pennsylvanicus).* The color of the pelage varies across the range of this species. The back is speckled gray to brownish. The underside and feet are a paler whitish to silver gray. The fur is long and silky in adults. The tail is less than 50 mm long, thin, sparsely haired, and bicolored—dark gray above and white below. Stiff orange hairs in the ears help to distinguish it from other voles.

Although there is overlap in their general distributions, the western heather vole is much less common and more sparsely distributed than species of *Microtus.* The western heather vole is an occupant of mountainous regions and typically occurs at higher elevations (1,400–3,690 m) near or above timberline. It has been found at elevations as low as 755 m in Washington and Oregon, probably as a result of forest clear-cutting at higher elevations. The western heather vole's range extends from northwestern British Columbia and southwestern Alberta south along the Cascade and Rocky mountains into Washington, Oregon, northern California, Montana, Idaho, Wyoming, Colorado, Utah, and northern New Mexico. One subspecies occurs in the Sierra Nevada Mountains of northeastern California and neighboring Nevada.

Phenacomys intermedius is terrestrial and occurs in a variety of boreal habitats, including open coniferous forest, riparian areas, forest edge, and moist alpine and subalpine meadows. These voles are also associated with krumholtz (low lying, wind-blown bushes). Most habitats have a shrub understory, often of various heaths including blueberry, bearberry, and sheep laurel. The western heather vole is herbivorous and feeds on the barks of heaths and willows during the winter.

Seeds and foliage are utilized when seasonally available. Food may be cached in piles outside the entrances of burrows. In summer, a short underground burrow system leads to a nest made of grass, leaves, and moss; nests are often located under rocks, stumps, or logs. Winter nests are built on the ground, next to a bush, rock, or stump. The nests are constructed of leaves, grass, and twigs, are lined with various grasses, and are protected against snow with lichens.

Breeding takes place from May through August. During this time, adults are solitary except when they come together to mate. Males are aggressive towards other males during the

Phenacomys intermedius

mating season, and females defend their nesting territories against other voles. Aggression subsides during the winter and family groups may huddle together in communal nests.

Females have up to three litters per year and provide the only parental care for the young. Two to nine young are produced after a minimum gestation of 19 days. Females that have overwintered have larger litters (4.4 young) on average than do young-of-the-year (3.6). The young weigh about 1.9 g at birth. Rates of development vary somewhat geographically. The eyes open at 15 to 16 days after birth, and by 18 days of age, the young begin eating solid food. Males and females become sexually mature in four to six weeks. Males may weigh as little as 15 g when mature. Individuals born late in the breeding season mature the following year. The few estimates of population density suggest that numbers of *Phenacomys intermedius* are usually very low compared to species of *Microtus* (e.g., less than 4.3 per hectare in Alberta).

The biology of the western heather vole is poorly known and may remain so. Spotty distribution, low population numbers, and the reluctance of western heather voles to enter traps make studying this species difficult. Moreover, when captured in live-traps, western heather voles have a high rate of mortality. Survival in the laboratory environment is also poor.

J. G. Hallett

Size
No significant sexual dimorphism
Total length: 122–155 (138) mm
Length of tail: 26–41 (33.6) mm
Weight: less than 30–40 g

Identification
Phenacomys intermedius is similar externally to the montane vole *(Microtus montanus)* and to immature meadow voles *(M. pennsylvanicus)*. It can be distinguished by the enamel pattern of the lower molars: the re-entrant angles extend more than halfway across the molars and are deeper than the external angles.

Status
Uncommon

Subspecies
Phenacomys intermedius celsus, western Nevada and northeastern California
Phenacomys intermedius intermedius, British Columbia, Washington, Oregon, Idaho, Montana, Wyoming, Colorado, Utah, and New Mexico

Phenacomys intermedius laingi, British Columbia
Phenacomys intermedius levis, British Columbia, Alberta, and Montana
Phenacomys intermedius oramontis, southern British Columbia and western Washington and Oregon

References
Mammalian Species 305; Innes and Millar, 1982

Eastern heather vole | *Phenacomys ungava*

Phenacomys ungava occurs throughout much of Canada, from northwestern Yukon taiga down the eastern edge of the Rocky Mountains to the east coast of Labrador. Although the species is widely distributed across boreal North America, it is very sparse where it is detected. In the eastern part of its range, it is generally found in relatively dry open coniferous forest with an understory of heaths; it is less often found in shrubby vegetation at forest edge or in wet meadows. In the northwestern part of its range, *Phenacomys ungava* can be found in deciduous shrubby habitat such as willow thickets, poplars, or birch-meadows, in deciduous or coniferous riparian habitat, or in a variety of forest types. The common denominator appears to be a requirement for low cover, presumably for protection from predation.

Behaviorally, *Phenacomys ungava* tends to be solitary, aggregating only during the breeding season, and in the winter huddling communally in nests. Females raise their young in solitude. The species is extremely docile, and in captivity is very easy to handle (although it is difficult to keep for any length of time as captives often refuse to eat). It is occasionally seen in the wild, and does not seem to be very wary of predators, which include owls, hawks, martens, and weasels.

The diet of *Phenacomys ungava* is highly variable and dependent on season and local resources. The species is herbivorous, eating bark of shrubs, berries, leaves, seeds, lichens, or fungus, or any combination of the above. Eastern heather voles often cache food, collecting it in piles at burrow entrances. Density of the species is often correlated with the abundance of locally preferred foods, such as sheep laurel. Individuals are most active in the evening through the early night, and this appears to be the time when food caches are accumulated, presumably to be eaten at leisure during the daylight hours. Although some researchers have suggested that the caches are stored through winter, *Phenacomys ungava* does not hibernate.

Individual voles build underground nests, each with several tunnels leading to entrances obscured by vegetation. A latrine area is usually found at the surface; the main nest is usually un-

Phenacomys ungava

usually high number of trapped specimens suggests a "population explosion."

The breeding season of *Phenacomy ungava* extends from May to August, but might be shorter at higher elevations. After a three-week gestation period, litters of two to eight (average number is five) altricial young are born. The young are weaned after approximately three weeks, but do not reach adult weight until they are 100 days old. Females are capable of breeding at four to six weeks of age, but these young females produce smaller litters (average of four) relative to the litter size of adult females (average of six). Up to three litters may be produced in one season. Males do not breed until they have overwintered. The life expectancy of *P. ungava* has been extrapolated from toothwear to be a maximum of four years.

In studying fossils (primarily teeth) of arvicoline rodents, paleontologists have found it difficult to assign individuals to species; they have never distinguished *Phenacomys ungava* from *P. intermedius*. The genus is thought to have originated in Asia three or four million years ago, and the *P. intermedius* group to be less than 400,000 years old. Fossils have been found south of its current range at many localities from Maryland and Virginia in the east to Nevada in the west.

Both *Phenacomys ungava* and *P. intermedius* possess 56 chromosomes; the two karyotypes differ only in that *P. intermedius* possesses a pair of bi-armed chromosomes that in *P. ungava* are single-armed. Some mammalogists have suggested that the two species intergrade along the eastern slope of the Canadian Rockies; however, this has not been quantified. Until such time, the two species are considered to be distinct. *S. B. George*

der a rock, shrub, log, root, or stump. Although the species is considered to be sparse in distribution, it is not clear whether this is due to actual low numbers or because these voles are hard to trap—more *P. ungava* remains are found in marten feces and owl pellets than would be expected based on densities calculated from trapping data. *Phenacomys ungava* does not experience the extreme, relatively regular population cycles noted in other arvicoline species, but from time to time an un-

Size
No significant sexual dimorphism has been noted
Total length: 122–155 mm (138)
Length of tail: 26–41 mm (33)
Weight: 25–40 g

Identification
This vole is best distinguished from other voles in its range by its teeth—the inside angles of the molars are much deeper than the outside angles. Variable in color, the fur is usually grizzled brown with a yellowish wash. The tail is short, and the ears are hardly visible above the fur. The eartips, nose, and rump of *Phenacomys*

ungava are usually more tawny or yellowish than those of other voles.

Recent Synonyms
Phenacomys intermedius

Other Common Names
Ungava vole

Status
Uncommon, but widely distributed

Subspecies
Phenacomys ungava crassus, Labrador
Phenacomys ungava mackenzii, southern Yukon

and Northwest Territories, south along eastern slope of the Rocky Mountains, across northern plains provinces to Hudson Bay
Phenacomys ungava soperi, southeastern Alberta east to southwestern Manitoba
Phenacomys ungava ungava, eastern Manitoba, northeastern Minnesota, Ontario, and Quebec

References
Mammalian Species 305; Banfield, 1974; Peterson, 1966

White-footed vole │ *Arborimus albipes*

White-footed voles are found only on the Pacific coast of North America, from the Columbia River south to Humboldt Bay, California. There is one fossil specimen from the Snake Range of Nevada, dated to about 13,000 years before present. Few Recent specimens have been collected and little is known of this mammal's habits. Most individuals have been found associated with riparian alder/small stream habitat. The diet of white-footed voles is limited to plant material, including both roots and a variety of green herbaceous plants.

Arborimus albipes is nocturnal. Its small eyes and the structure of its claws suggest that it may be a burrower, unlike its nearest relatives, *A. longicaudus* and *A. pomo,* which are arboreal. Virtually no information on the behavior of white-footed voles exists. The fur is long, soft, and a warm brown color; the belly is gray or gray washed with pale brown. The long, thinly haired tail is black on top and white below. The feet are usually white on top (hence the common name of the species), and the ears, which are usually hidden by the fur, are hairless. Young are produced year-round, and litter size varies from two to four. Nothing is known about the length of gestation, age at weaning, or development of the young. *S. B. George*

Arborimus albipes

Size
Sexual dimorphism unknown, but in a closely related species, *A. pomo,* females are significantly larger than males.
Total length: 149–182 mm
Length of tail: 57–75 mm
Weight: 17–28.5 g

Identification
This species is distinguished from other *Arborimus* by its warm brown color (other species are reddish-brown) and from other voles by the long, distinctly bicolored tail, the naked ears, and the white feet (no other vole possesses this combination, although some other species may possess one or two of these characteristics).

Recent Synonyms
Phenacomys albipes

Status
Rare and limited to a small range; may be common within a highly restricted habitat type

References
Mammalian Species 494 *(Phenacomys albipes);* Maser et al., 1981

Red tree vole │ *Arborimus longicaudus*

The secretive, nocturnal red tree vole is one of least studied and most specialized voles in North America. It is found only along the coast and in the Western Cascades of Oregon, where it spends most of its life in the tops of tall conifers, eating needles of Douglas fir *(Pseudotsuga menziesii)* and, occasionally, other conifers. The voles clip small twigs and bring the twigs and needles back to their nests. They lick the needles to obtain water from dew, rain, and condensation from fog. Home ranges are thought to be small—one or more trees. Dispersal ability, and the ability to colonize new habitats, seems limited. Early mammalogists reported that red tree voles occupied only areas of extensive forest. Recent studies have shown them to be most abundant in old-growth forests; they are undergoing declines due to logging. Red tree voles are rare in sapling, pole, and

managed sawtimber stands, and young stands may serve as barriers to their dispersal.

Red tree voles build nests wherever there is a suitable foundation and a readily accessible food supply. Only one adult occupies each nest. Whorls of branches provide support in young trees; the large branches of old-growth trees can support the large nests needed for maternal nests or nurseries. Nests are constructed of resin ducts (leftovers from eaten needles), lichen, feces, conifer needles, and fine twigs. They are sometimes built in cavities and hollows in trees or under the moss covering large branches of old trees. Nests range from 2 to 50 m above the ground and may be in trees of any size. Even in old growth, however, voles select the largest available trees for nesting and most commonly build their nests in the lower third of the live crown. Several nests may be built in large trees. The voles are not at all alarmed by living so high in trees; when threatened, some will launch themselves from branches and free-fall as far as 18 m, land, and race for cover.

Red tree voles breed throughout the year, but their litters, of one to four young, are usually born between February and September. Gestation is 28 days but may be extended to 48 days in lactating females. Nursing may be extended and the development of the young is slow. This low reproductive potential may be interpreted as an adaptation to the difficulty of converting conifer needles into energy for metabolism. These adaptations to a restricted diet are only adaptive in a relatively stable environment, such as old growth.

Old-growth trees provide stability, whereas in growing trees, the voles have to relocate their nests. Needles are concentrated on fewer (but larger) trees in old growth, providing

Arborimus longicaudus

maximum food availability. The tall, multilayered canopies of old growth have high humidity and fog interception, providing the voles with water. Large branches provide solid support for nests, protection from storms, and facilitate travel among trees—all contributing to the formation of colonies of red tree voles. Old growth, however, is also the preferred habitat of the northern spotted owl *(Strix occidentalis),* the primary predator of the red tree vole. *A. B. Carey*

Size

Females are slightly larger than males.

Total length: 158–206 (males, 172; females, 184) mm

Length of tail: 60–94 (males, 70; females, 77) mm

Weight: 25–47 g

Identification

The pelage of this vole is thick, relatively long, and soft. Northern Oregon coastal populations are slightly larger, with brownish-red backs. The central and southern Oregon subspecies is brighter brown to orangish-red. The undersides are pale gray and, in southern populations, sometimes washed with reddish-orange. The tail is long, hairy, and black to brown. The eyes are small and the ears are pale and hairless. The California congener, *Arborimus pomo*, is similar in size and color to *A. longicaudus longicaudus*, but its chromosome count in different, and their ranges do not overlap.

Recent Synonyms

Phenacomys longicaudus

Other Common Names

Reddish tree mouse

Status

Uncertain; rarely seen; geographically limited to western Oregon

Subspecies

Arborimus longicaudus longicaudus, central and southern Oregon

Arborimus longicaudus silvicola, coastal northern Oregon

References

Mammalian Species 532; Carey, 1991; Johnson and George, 1991; Maser et al., 1981

Sonoma tree vole | *Arborimus pomo*

The Sonoma tree vole is distributed from extreme northwestern California along the humid coastal forest belt south through Sonoma County. It is found commonly in sites at the edges of forests or adjacent to gulches, meadows, or fields. It may occur more often in deep forest than is recognized: because these voles build their nests so high in trees, it is difficult to find them in deep forest. In fact, many records of *Arborimus pomo* are of voles captured after the trees in which they nested had been cut down.

This vole has reddish fur that is gray at the base; many hairs are slightly tipped with black. The belly is white (again, with a gray base to the hairs). The skin of the tail is black and is covered with reddish fur. Older adults have a grizzled appearance from a sprinkling of pale hairs across their backs.

Sonoma tree voles subsist entirely on the needles and young bark of a few coniferous species. They prefer Douglas fir needles to grand fir, and efficiently strip and eat only the outer part of the needle, discarding the center vascular bundle. Only needles from young, terminal twigs are taken, and a fresh supply is collected daily and stored on top of the nest. Sonoma tree voles are nocturnal. Although they may be active in the nest, eating during the day, they leave the nest only at night. Enormous quantities of needles are consumed—on average about 2,400 needles daily for an adult—yielding a correspondingly enormous quantity of refuse and excretions. Red tree voles drink far less water per day than other microtine rodents, possibly because of the high water content of their diet. Little urine is voided, and the nests remain clean and odor-free.

Arborimus pomo nests are constructed haphazardly of the uneaten conifer needle refuse and twigs. The main chamber is usually at the top of the mass of needles, and in larger nests, there is a smaller, secondary chamber that is used for excre-

Arborimus pomo

tion. Runways in and out of the nests appear to be randomly located; there is usually an escape hatch in an inconspicuous place. Nests are found most commonly in Douglas fir, grand fir, or Sitka spruce trees. None have been found in redwoods, unless the redwood has branches intertwined with a food tree (e.g., Douglas fir). Nests tend to be at least 10 m (30 feet) above the ground [and can be more than 30 m (100 feet) from the ground]. Nests of adult females with or without young tend to be larger (at least 30 cm in diameter by 25 cm in depth, and up to 1 m in diameter by 65 cm in depth). The nests of males and subadult females are separate and much smaller. Nests of males sometimes have been found on the ground, and males have often been caught on the ground.

Although occasionally a subadult (probably related) individual will share a nest with an adult, *A. pomo* is usually solitary. A large tree often has more than one nest, however. Sonoma tree voles are excellent climbers and are extremely active, moving long distances to gather the amount of food necessary for survival. Owls and Stellar's jays are common predators; jays will systematically destroy nests in search of young voles.

Young are produced year-round, and litter size is very small (often only one or two). Subadult females, presumably from earlier litters, are sometimes found in nests with adult females and their unweaned young. Offspring are highly altricial and grow more slowly than most microtines, not leaving the nest at all until they are a month of age.

Until recently, *Arborimus pomo* and *A. longicaudus* were considered to be conspecific. However, chromosomally, they are distinct (*A. pomo:* 2N=40 or 42; *A. longicaudus:* 2N=48 or 52), and the former species tends to be smaller than the latter. A fossil dating to 6,000 years before present from Nye County, Nevada, has been identified as *A. longicaudus,* but no attempt has been made to re-determine its specific affinity since *A. pomo* was described. *S. B. George*

Size
Females are significantly larger than males.
Total length: 158–176 (166) mm (males); 170–187 (182) mm (females)
Length of tail: 60–72 (67) mm (males); 66–83 (73) mm (females)
Weight: 25–47 g

Identification
The Sonoma tree vole is distinguished from other microtine rodents in its range by bright reddish fur, a long, blackish, rather hairy tail, and long toes; it is distinguished from *Arborimus longicaudus* by slightly brighter color, slightly smaller size, and by karyotype.

Recent Synonyms
Arborimus longicaudus

Other Common Names
California red tree vole, pomo vole

Status
Locally common

References
Mammalian Species 593; Howell, 1926; Johnson and George, 1991

Insular vole | *Microtus abbreviatus*

The insular vole occurs on two of the three islands in the St. Matthew Islands group in the Bering Sea. Its colonies are found most commonly in the moist lowlands and on the lower slopes of the islands, up to about 245 meters elevation.

Insular voles, like many of their relatives, are active diurnally. In areas of high vole populations, their high-pitched, musical alarm calls can frequently be heard when they are disturbed. Voles live in burrows that are often dug near rocky outcroppings and near small streams. The burrow systems may be extensive, with several openings to the surface, and each system may be occupied by closely related individuals. Burrows run about 10 to 20 cm below the surface of the ground. Dried roots and grass have been found in nest chambers. Other chambers, which can be as large as 50 by 26 cm, may be used for storage of foods such as grasses, willows, and herbacious annual flowers.

Microtus abbreviatus is found most commonly in the vegetation of the moist, relatively well drained lowlands and lower slopes of the mountains or in the rye grass *(Elymus arenarius)* of the beach ridges. Insular voles feed on tufted hairgrass *(Deschampsia caespitosa),* arctic dock *(Rumex arcticus),* round-leaf willow *(Salix ovalifolia),* and roseroot *(Sedum rosea).*

The annual breeding period probably extends from late May to mid-August. The gestation period is 21 days. In captivity, an average of 2.5 young were born; wild-caught females had an average of six embryos. The young are well furred at six days of age, eyes open on the eleventh day, and they are fully weaned by the fifteenth. Insular voles molt from juvenile to subadult pelage at one month and then into adult pelage at about three and a half months. Adult voles are brownish dorsally, have pale yellowish sides, rump, tips of the ears, and face, and a buffy-colored belly. *Microtus abbreviatus* is a fairly docile species when handled and seldom attempts to bite.

Voles are well known for their tremendous population fluctuations. Numbers of *M. abbreviatus* may fluctuate widely; however, because of the inaccessibilty of these islands there are only scattered observations of this species since 1885. Predators include the arctic fox, the only other terrestrial mammal that occurs on the islands (polar bears are known to visit), long-tailed jaegers *(Sterocorarius longicaudus),* and snowy owls *(Nyctea scandiaca). J. A. Cook and D. R. Klein*

Microtus abbreviatus

Size
No significant sexual dimorphism
Total length: 136–176 (145) mm
Length of tail: 25–32 (25.3) mm
Weight: 45–79 g

Identification
This large, short-tailed vole closely resembles *Microtus gregalis* of the eastern Palearctic and *M. miurus* of Alaska. *Microtus abbreviatus* is distinguished from these closely related forms by skull and chromosomal characters.

Recent Synonyms
Microtus fisheri

Other Common Names
St. Matthew Island vole

Status
Limited; numbers fluctuate widely; last high in 1993

Subspecies
Microtus abbreviatus fisheri, St. Matthew Island in the Bering Sea
Microtus abbreviatus abbreviatus, Hall Island in the Bering Sea

References
Klein, 1959; Rausch and Rausch, 1968

Beach vole | *Microtus breweri*

The beach vole is a recent offshoot of the meadow vole *(Microtus pennsylvanicus),* the most prolific mammal on earth and the North American vole with the largest geographic range. However, the beach vole, found only on Muskeget Island, Massachusetts, a tiny, sandy island off the coast of Nantucket Island and Cape Cod, has evolved toward lower fecundity. Compared to the meadow vole, the beach vole has a smaller litter size (average 3.5 compared with 4.5 for the meadow vole), greater body weight (average 54 versus 45 grams for the meadow vole), and longer life span (13.1 weeks versus 8.8 weeks for the meadow vole). In addition, the beach vole seems to provide better parental care and is less aggressive.

The beach vole evolved within the last 3,000 years, the time that Muskeget Island has been isolated from Nantucket Island and Cape Cod. This isolation took place during glacial melt, which raised the sea level and formed islands from this morainal area at the southern edge of recent glaciation. The island has a white-footed mouse *(Peromyscus leucopus)* population and occasional breeding populations of marsh hawks *(Circus cyaneus)* and short-eared owls *(Asio flammeus)*. There are no other mammals and no other resident avian predators on the island.

As on many other islands, evolution has led to changes. The beach vole has often been considered a subspecies of the meadow vole, because they have similar chromosomes (46 with a fundamental number of 50 and similar G bands) and other general vole-like similarities. They are both robust voles, with relatively short tails and compressed muzzles. However, the beach vole is paler and more grizzled looking, perhaps an adaptation to the sandy substrate on which it lives. In addition, many individuals have a distinctive white blaze. The blaze is usually found on the forehead, but may occur on the chin or throat. It varies from a single white guard hair to a mixture of white guard hairs and underfur. It is believed to be a non-selected remnant of founders that were introduced on the island in 1893 from a nearby islet that has since disappeared. In 1988, a detailed statistical analysis of skull and tooth characteristics clearly identified the beach vole as a distinct species. There is no fossil record of the beach vole.

Even with reduced fecundity as compared with the meadow vole, the beach vole is very prolific. The breeding season runs from April to October, with occasional winter breeding. There is a three week gestation period and a two week nursing period until weaning. Females can mate immediately after giving birth. Once a female begins to breed, she can produce a litter averaging 3.5 pups every three weeks or so.

The beach vole population on Muskeget Island is unique because it shows no cyclic tendencies. In many other vole species studied there are population density cycles of two to five years that involve changes in density from several to several hundred voles per hectare. What triggers these cycles is unknown and is cause for much research. Current explanations range from predation to genetic changes in behavior of the voles.

Beach voles living in a favorable habitat consisting of an almost pure stand of beach grass *(Ammophila breviligulata)* showed almost no annual changes of density; in fact, one sub-population had the flattest density curve of any vole population studied. In a poorer habitat that consisted mainly of beach grass interspersed with poison ivy *(Toxicodendron radicans)*, there were pronounced annual cycles. Density declined as the

Microtus breweri

habitat degenerated during the winter. Even so, the beach vole population remained at densities that would be considered relatively high compared to the meadow vole populations in nearby eastern Massachusetts (about 75–80 per 0.8-hectare grid).

The comparison of vole population processes on Muskeget with cyclical mainland meadow vole populations has resulted in a dispersal-related model of population regulation. Because the dispersal of island populations is limited, and the population does not cycle, dispersal might be a factor in the mainland species that do cycle. The island population is an excellent control for studying the causes of cycles in mainland populations.

Beach grass is not only the major food of beach voles, but also makes up the major component of their habitat. The voles make tunnels in the grass; they live both above and below ground, using aboveground nests and underground burrows as well as nests in the sandy soil. Beach voles can be active throughout a 24-hour period; their activity is related to season, weather, and habitat. When active, they procure food, search for mates, and mark their territories with urine and feces.

Female beach voles are territorial, occupying areas of about 200 square meters. Their territories are about three times larger than those of mainland females. Males, on the other hand, seem to range freely, overlapping many ranges of females. Male beach voles have territories about 50 percent larger than their mainland counterparts. The males seem to patrol their ranges looking for receptive females with which to mate. Beach voles appear to be solitary in the breeding season and communal in the winter nonbreeding season. Their social system is very similar to that of the mainland progenitor species, the meadow vole.

The beach vole is the only mammalian species endemic to the state of Massachusetts. Much of its ecology and population biology can be explained by evolution in isolation. Although not quite in the class of Darwin's finches on the Galapagos Islands, the beach vole on Muskeget Island is valuable for studying evolutionary and demographic processes in voles and in other organisms as well. *R. H. Tamarin*

Size
No significant sexual dimorphism
Total length: 165–215 (187) mm
Length of tail: 35–60 (50.3) mm
Weight: 45.1–62.9 g

Identification
Microtus breweri is restricted to Muskeget Island, Massachusetts, where it is the only vole present. It is distinguished from *Microtus pennsylvanicus,* the mainland progenitor species, by larger size, a longer and narrower skull, coarser and paler fur, and a reduced number of closed triangles on the posterior upper molar.

Recent Synonyms
Microtus pennsylvanicus breweri

Other Common Names
Beach mouse, beach meadow mouse

Status
Microtus breweri is limited to Muskeget Island, a one-square-mile sandy island located off the western coast of Nantucket Island, Massachusetts. Depending on season and year, total numbers of the species fluctuate between 2,000 and 25,000 voles.

References
Mammalian Species 45; Moyer et al., 1988; Wetherbee et al., 1972; Zwicker, 1989

California vole | *Microtus californicus*

The California vole occurs from southwestern Oregon through central and western California, with disjunct subspecies in northern Baja California, the Mojave Desert, and the White Mountain/Panamint ranges. It is primarily a low elevation species inhabiting grasslands and wet meadows, but can also be found in coastal wetlands and open oak savannah with good ground cover. Like other voles, it is herbivorous and most of the diet consists of grasses, sedges, and forbs. During the summer dry season it survives on seeds and fleshy roots, but cannot reproduce without succulent green vegetation in the diet. When harvesting seedheads from tall grasses, California voles reach up and clip grass stems to bring the fresh seed heads within reach. This results in a neat stack of clipped stalks about the length of a vole body.

California voles are semifossorial, constructing complex networks of surface runways as well as extensive underground burrow systems. Vole presence can be assessed by examining these runways for fresh vegetation clippings and fecal pellets. Nests of fine shredded grasses are constructed in small chambers in the burrow system, usually only a few centimeters below the surface, and sometimes under logs or boards. California voles are active throughout the year; there is no hibernation and no food storage. Individual voles have short bursts

of activity every few hours, but the greatest overall amount of daily activity occurs around dawn and dusk. This crepuscular pattern of activity is most pronounced in the summer when the days are hot and dry.

Reproduction may occur throughout the year in some coastal populations, where green vegetation persists and temperatures are moderate all summer. However, much of the California vole's range has a Mediterranean-type climate with hot, dry summers and cool, wet winters. Here, reproductive activity starts soon after the first rain each fall and ceases when the vegetation drys out in early summer. Litter size ranges from 1 to 11, with a mean of 4.7. There is a post-partum estrus, and successful females may produce as many as 4 or 5 litters in a season. After a 22-day gestation period, pups are born. Altricial, and weighing about 2.5 g at birth, they mature quickly and are weaned at just over two weeks of age. Females can begin breeding at about three weeks of age (occasionally at weaning), but males mature more slowly, taking a leisurely five to six weeks (occasionally 25 days). California voles born early in the season can mature and reproduce in the winter or spring of their birth, but voles born late in the season usually do not mature until the next reproductive season. As with many arvicoline rodents, sexual maturation can be suppressed on the natal home range by the presence of the mother, and pheromones produced by unfamiliar males can cause females in early pregnancy to abort their litters. Estrus is stimulated by the presence of a male, and ovulation is induced by copulation.

California voles are sexually dimorphic, with males about 6 percent longer and 11 percent heavier than females. They are very aggressive intrasexually during the breeding season, but nonreproductive individuals and individuals of the opposite sex are generally tolerated. Home ranges are small, about 80 square meters for females and 125 square meters for males, and vary seasonally and with density. Males are territorial toward other males, but their home ranges extensively overlap those of females. Reproductive females tend to be intrasexually territorial as well, but may sometimes be found in small groups. These clusters of mothers and daughters appear to be formed as density increases. Aggression and territorial behavior are generally relaxed during the nonbreeding season.

Local abundance of voles is notoriously variable. Some coastal populations of California voles appear to maintain fairly stable densities of around 200 per hectare, with an annual

Microtus californicus

cycle of abundance. Populations in more strongly seasonal habitats usually show the dramatic two- to five-year cycles for which voles are famous. Peak densities of 1,000 voles per hectare have been reported, although a typical peak may be closer to 450 per hectare. During population lows, California voles may be virtually absent or restricted to a few patches of optimal habitat such as perennial bunchgrasses. A variety of predators consume voles, including many snakes, mammals such as foxes, coyotes, feral cats, and weasels, and birds such as hawks and owls. Even wading birds like herons and egrets can be seen stalking voles in grassy meadows. A successful vole will live for about a year, but the mean life span is often only a few months. *E. J. Heske and W. Z. Lidicker, Jr.*

Size
Size varies considerably over the range of the species. A large sample of adults from central and northern California had the following dimensions:
Total length: 139–207 (172) mm
Length of tail: 38–68 (51) mm
Weight: 33–81 (52) g (males); 30–68 (47) g (nonpregnant females)
Several subspecies in the southern part of the range are significantly larger; males can reach a total length of 217 mm and a weight of 108.5 g

Identification
M. californicus is a medium-sized vole with an aggressive temperament. The tail is of moderate length and the belly fur is pale with gray at the base. In the northern and eastern parts of its range, *M. californicus* occurs at lower elevations than *M. montanus;* it has a shorter and less obviously bicolored tail than *M. longicaudus.* In the northwest, *M. oregoni* is much smaller and has only five (instead of six) plantar tubercles (toe pads). *M. townsendii,* although slightly larger, is best distinguished using cranial and dental characters.

Other Common Names
California meadow mouse

Status
Common, but local abundance may vary greatly from year to year. Generally local and rare in the southern parts of its range.

Subspecies
Microtus californicus aequivocatus, coastal Baja California del Norte from San José to San Telmo
Microtus californicus aestuarinus, Central Valley of California, extending to Petaluma on the north side of the Sacramento River Delta
Microtus californicus californicus, coastal ranges of central California from the Sacramento River Delta south to the Morro Bay area
Microtus californicus constrictus, California coast from Cape Mendocino north to Eureka
Microtus californicus eximius, southwestern Oregon south into northern California along the coast ranges, reaching the coast in the vicinity of Mendocino, and then south to the Marin headland

Microtus californicus grinnelli, western slopes of the Sierra Juárez, Baja California del Norte (probably extinct)

Microtus californicus halophilus, eastern shore of Monterey Bay, California

Microtus californicus huperuthrus, Sierra San Pedro Mártir, Baja California del Norte (probably extinct)

Microtus californicus kernensis, Tehechapi Mountains and southernmost San Joaquin Valley, California

Microtus californicus mariposae, western slopes of the Sierra Nevada, north into Placer County and south to the Tehachapis

Microtus californicus mohavensis, Mojave River Valley in the vicinity of Victorville (Mojave Desert)

Microtus californicus paludicola, saltmarshes of South San Francisco Bay from El Cerrito on the east side to Redwood City on the west; generally synonymized with *M. c. californicus*

Microtus californicus sanctidiegi, southern coastal California except for the Los Angeles Basin, extending north to the Pismo Beach area and south to the mouth of the Tijuana Rver; introduced on San Clemente Island

Microtus californicus sanpabloensis, saltmarshes around the mouth of San Pablo Creek, Contra Costa County, California

Microtus californicus scirpensis, alkaline marshes along the Amaragosa River near Shoshone, Inyo County, California

Microtus californicus stephensi, Los Angeles Basin

Microtus californicus vallicola, Owens Valley and adjacent foothills, from Benton south to Olancha

References

Jameson and Peeters, 1988; Lidicker, 1973, 1980; Lidicker and Ostfeld, 1991

Gray-tailed vole | *Microtus canicaudus*

The gray-tailed vole is similar in appearance and habits to the montane vole *(Microtus montanus)* of eastern Oregon, from which it recently diverged. Although these two species can hybridize in the laboratory, offspring are often deformed and survival is low. The two species were once contiguous but are no longer in contact with one another.

The current distribution of gray-tailed voles is limited to the lower elevation grasslands of the Willamette Valley of western Oregon, with a small range extending into southern Washington. These voles have adapted well to the agricultural fields in the Willamette Valley, which are mostly planted in small grains or are permanent pastures of legumes and grasses. Gray-tailed voles also occur along railroad and highway rights-of-way and on recently cleared lands, but they do not extend into forests. Hawks and owls frequently perch on power poles or dead trees adjacent to grassland areas in the valley, where they feed extensively on these voles. Other predators include weasels, foxes, feral cats, skunks, great blue herons, and snakes.

Population densities are known to fluctuate markedly, but the periodicity and cause of these fluctuations are unknown. In fenced enclosure experiments, populations increased from 12 to more than 100 animals in three months. The latter density is comparable to about 600 individuals per hectare.

Breeding occurs primarily from March through November, with a slight decline during the hot, dry periods of mid-July and August. Some breeding occurs during mild winters. An average of 4–5 young are born after a 21 day gestation period. Development is rapid, and recently weaned females can breed

Microtus canicaudus

at 18 days of age. Littermates and related individuals exhibit some kin recognition and tend to avoid breeding with siblings or parents.

Gray-tailed voles construct intricate and extensive underground burrow systems, which are occupied by one or more males, females, and juveniles. The mating system appears to be polygynous or promiscuous, with males occupying home ranges that overlap each other and those of several females. In the laboratory, males provide paternal care, which is unusual for microtine rodents. During winter, when rains typically flood much of their habitat, gray-tailed voles are sometimes forced onto small, dry island habitats, although they are excellent swimmers and continue to use runways and burrows that are submerged. As many as 20 to 30 voles have been observed clinging to a fence post at the edge of a flooded field. Predation by great blue herons, hawks, and other predators is very high during winter.

Gray-tailed voles are frequently used as laboratory animals. They have been used to investigate restrictions in dietary selenium and vitamin E in native plant species and to ascertain the feasibility of enhancing the nutritional quality of residues of ryegrass for animal feed. Gray-tailed voles were also used in a series of laboratory and field studies to validate testing procedures for conducting an ecological risk assessment of the effects of insecticides on mammals. Because members of the genus *Microtus* are ubiquitous, they make excellent models with which to test the effects of environmental stresses on wild species. *J. O. Wolff*

Size
Males are slightly larger than females.
Total length: 140–168 (150) mm
Length of tail: 32–45 (38) mm
Weight: 35–55 g

Identification
Distinguished from Townsend's vole *(Microtus townsendii)* by a shorter tail that is gray beneath and brownish above, and by yellowish-gray or brown fur compared to the dark, almost blackish fur of Townsend's vole. Distinguished from the Oregon vole *(Microtus oregoni)* by its more robust body and larger eyes.

Recent Synonyms
Microtus montanus canicaudus

Status
Common within its range

References
Mammalian Species 267; Wolff et al., 1994

Rock vole | *Microtus chrotorrhinus*

The common name rock vole aptly describes the habitat of *Microtus chrotorrhinus*. Rocks and boulders are conspicuous features of its habitat throughout its range. Water, either in the form of surface or subsurface streams, is another key habitat component. Originally considered to be a species restricted the Canadian Life Zone (boreal coniferous forests), rock vole populations also occupy Transition Zone (mixed deciduous-coniferous) forests in New York, West Virginia, Cape Breton Island (Nova Scotia), and Minnesota.

Although rock voles have been taken in a variety of habitats, the optimal habitat for this species appears to be pristine northern hardwoods and mixed deciduous-coniferous forests characterized by accumulations of rock. Rock voles live among mossy rocks and boulders in forests that are carpeted with dense herbaceous vegetation. Ground cover plants at such sites include bunchberry *(Cornus canadensis)*, bluebead lily *(Clintonia borealis)*, Canada mayflower *(Maianthemum canadense)*, false miterwort *(Tiarella cordifolia)*, wood sorrel *(Oxalis montana)*, false Solomon's seal *(Smilacina)*, Labrador tea *(Ledum groenlandicum)*, goldenrods *(Solidago)*, mosses, and ferns. The exten-

Microtus chrotorrhinus

sive use by rock voles of bunchberry as a food suggests that this plant may be a good indicator of the vole's potential presence. Rock voles cut herbaceous vegetation and pull the cuttings down into the subterranean galleries where they apparently spend much of their time; cut vegetation can reveal the presence of *M. chrotorrhinus.* In West Virginia and presumably elsewhere in the southern Appalachians, the presence of rock vole populations is revealed by accumulations of freshly cut vegetation cached under flat rocks at the edges of streams.

The rock vole appears to be less fecund than other microtine rodents. Litter size generally averages between three and four throughout the range. Exceptions include a reported mean of 2.9 from West Virginia and a mean of 5.3 from Quetico Provincial Park, Ontario. In the morphologically similar meadow vole, mean litter size is usually between four and six young. Litter size in the smaller but ecologically associated southern red-backed vole, *Clethrionomys gapperi,* is generally 4–5 young. The gestation period in rock voles is 19–21 days, which is typical for many small rodents. Rock voles also exhibit post-partum estrus, in which females mate within 24 hours of giving birth. This enhances reproductive output by allowing females to gestate a second litter while they are nursing the first. Reproductively active rock voles have been collected from early spring (March) until late fall (October). *G. L. Kirkland, Jr.*

Size

No significant sexual dimorphism
Total length: 140–185 mm
Length of tail: 42–64 mm
Weight: 30–48 g

Identification

Microtus chrotorrhinus is a medium-sized vole with a yellowish-orange or pale yellowish wash on the snout. Some individuals also have a dull pale yellowish wash on the rump. The only other North American vole with a yellowish-orange wash on the face is the yellow-cheeked vole *(Microtus xanthognathus),* whose range lies to the northwest of the rock vole's. The meadow vole *(M. pennsylvanicus),* which is sympatric with *M. chrotorrhinus,* is approxi-

mately the same size but has darker brown pelage, lacks the yellowish wash on the face and rump, and is a grassland species seldom taken in the deep forest habitats preferred by the rock vole. The two species occasionally are taken together in alpine tundra habitats and on recent clearcuts.

Other Common Names

Yellow-nosed vole

Status

Uncommon to rare

Subspecies

Microtus chrotorrhinus carolinensis, southern Appalachian Mountains of West Virginia, Virginia, North Carolina, and Tennessee

Microtus chrotorrhinus chrotorrhinus, across eastern Canada from the Atlantic coast of Quebec and the Maritime provinces (including an apparently disjunct population on Cape Breton Island) westward to southwestern Ontario and adjacent northern Minnesota, and northern New England, the mountains of eastern New York, and northeastern Pennsylvania

Microtus chrotorrhinus ravus, coastal regions of southeastern Labrador and adjacent northeasternmost Quebec

References

Mammalian Species 180

Long-tailed vole | *Microtus longicaudus*

Long-tailed voles occur throughout most of the western United States and Canada, extending as far north as southeastern Alaska. Populations in the southern parts of the range are usually isolated and restricted to mountaintop habitats. This island-like distribution in the mountains of New Mexico, Ari-

zona, and California is the result of the change in climate and habitat that followed the Pleistocene glaciation. During the Pleistocene the climate was cooler and wetter throughout this southwestern region, and long-tailed voles were more broadly distributed. However, the warmer and dryer climatic pattern

that followed could not support long-tailed voles, and now they can only be found in cooler, moister habitats near the peaks of mountain ranges such as the Henry Mountains in Utah, the San Bernardino Mountains in California, and the Sacramento, Mimbres, and Graham mountains in Arizona and New Mexico.

The breeding season extends from May through October. Very little is known about their gestation, development, growth, and reproductive behavior, since these voles are not abundant and have not been the focus of intensive study. The average litter size is five pups, but ranges from two to eight. The pups are born with eyes and ears closed, and measure only 24 mm from head to rump. Neonates produce ultrasonic sounds when they are disturbed or stressed, and these calls attract attention from the parents. Long-tailed voles have an average lifespan of less than one year, and each female only produces about two litters in her lifetime. This low reproductive output is in part the reason for low population densities in the natural environment. Density is also related to the quality of the herbaceous and shrub cover: the more cover, the higher the density. Some populations have been observed to reach higher densities during good growing seasons. Populations in California varied from 5 to 16 animals per hectare, and a population in New Mexico varied from 20 to 120 voles per hectare. The latter very high density is unusual.

Long-tailed voles are found in a wide variety of habitats, including coniferous and hardwood forests, brushy thickets, forest-meadow ecotones, along rivers and streams, and in sagebrush. They are frequently found in areas that have had disturbances such as fire, clear-cutting, or surface mining.

The diet of long-tailed voles is varied. They consume fruits, seeds, fungi, bark, and leaves. Fruits and seeds make up a large

Microtus longicaudus

part of the diet, followed by the leaves and stems of herbaceous plants and grasses. In the winter months the diet of necessity shifts to include less desirable foods such as the leaves of sagebrush, bark, and roots.

Long-tailed voles do not construct or maintain runway systems as do other species of voles. Their home ranges are larger than those of many other voles, and some individuals regularly move 50–60 m in daily foraging.

Barn owls, great-horned owls, long-eared owls, short-eared owls, and prairie falcons probably eat long-tailed voles. However, what we know of the food habits of such birds is based on analyses of the food pellets they regurgitate after digestion, and the remains of skulls of long-tailed voles are extremely difficult to distinguish from skulls of montane voles *(Microtus montanus)*. Montane voles are far more abundant, so it is likely that the remains found in many pellets are this species. Mammals, including martens, long-tailed weasels, and ermines, also eat these voles.

The scientific name, *Microtus longicaudus,* is descriptive. *Microtus* is derived from the Greek words *mikros* (small, little) and *-otus* (ear), and refers to the small ears. *Longicaudus* is derived from the Latin words *longus* (long) and *-cauda* (tail), and describes the noticeably long tail. *M. J. Smolen*

Size

Males are very slightly larger than females.
Total length: 155–202 mm
Length of tail: 49–81 mm
Weight: 36.0–59.0 g

Identification

Microtus longicaudus is a small, thick-bodied vole characterized by a long, bicolored tail. Other voles that occur sympatrically have shorter tails. Of these voles, only *M. californicus,*

M. pennsylvanicus, and *M. townsendi* have head and body to tail or tail to hindfoot proportions that approximate those of *M. longicaudus.* These species can reliably be distinguished from *Microtus longicaudus* only by examining the skull.

Status
Common, limited

Subspecies
Microtus longicaudus abditus, northwestern coastal Oregon
Microtus longicaudus alticola, eastern Utah and northern Arizona
Microtus longicaudus angusticeps, southwestern coastal Oregon and northwestern coastal California
Microtus longicaudus baileyi, northern Arizona
Microtus longicaudus bernardinus, southern California

Microtus longicaudus coronarius, Coronation, Warren, and Forrester islands, Alaska
Microtus longicaudus halli, northeastern Oregon and southeastern Washington
Microtus longicaudus incanus, central Utah
Microtus longicaudus latus, Nevada and western Utah
Microtus longicaudus leucophaeus, southeastern Arizona
Microtus longicaudus littoralis, southeastern Alaska and northwestern British Columbia
Microtus longicaudus longicaudus, northeastern California, Nevada, Oregon, Washington, Idaho, Montana, Wyoming, eastern Utah,

Colorado, New Mexico, and eastern Arizona
Microtus longicaudus macrurus, western Washington and southwestern British Columbia
Microtus longicaudus sierrae, California and western Nevada
Microtus longicaudus vellerosus, Alberta, central and eastern British Columbia, Yukon, and eastern Alaska

References
Mammalian Species 271; Hoffmeister, 1986; Ingles, 1965

Singing vole | *Microtus miurus*

The singing vole has many unique and interesting morphological and life history features. It occurs in the northwesternmost reaches of the continent, where it inhabits well-drained tundra as well as subalpine and alpine zones. Relatively little is known about it because of its remote distribution. Its closest relative, the insular vole, *M. abbreviatus,* is known only from Hall and St. Matthews islands in the Bering Strait.

Singing voles construct their burrow systems in well-drained soil or under rocks, and are often associated with willows. On the North Slope of Alaska they can reach densities of 50 per hectare. Voles from the northern part of the range are somewhat larger than those from the south. Sexual dimorphism is slight, with females reported to be very slightly smaller in a variety of measurements. Based on lightest weights at sexual maturity and data from a captive colony, Youngman suggested that males may mature sexually earlier than females. Nevertheless, both sexes often breed in the summer of their birth. Singing voles usually reproduce in late spring and summer, although a few pregnancies may occur at any time of the year. Litter size has been reported to be 4 to 12 (the average size litter is 8.4 for adults and 6.5 for subadults), with postpartum estrus occurring in captivity. The gestation period is 21 days. Males have enlarged flank glands when they are reproductively active. The weight of neonates averages 2.3 g. Adults rarely survive a second winter.

Numerous predators are known to take singing voles, including grizzly bears, wolves, wolverines, red foxes, and weasels. Long-tailed jaegers *(Stercorarius longicaudus)* are often seen cruising above mountain slopes, hunting voles. Vole densities fluctuate strongly, with declines associated with reduced body mass and poor reproduction. At Toolik Lake, Alaska, densities varied from 5 to 50 per hectare over a four-year period, and five years of data suggest that multi-annual cycles may occur at Umiat. Stomach content analysis and feeding trials have established that singing voles feed primarily on shrubs, forbs, and horsetails. Preferred species on the North Slope include bistorta *(Polygonum bistorta),* cottongrass *(Eriophorum angustifolium),* common horsetail *(Equisetum arvense),* coltsfoot *(Petasites frigidus),* willows *(Salix glauca* and *S. reticulata),* and bearberry *(Arctostaphylos rubra).*

Singing voles may be semicolonial, and seem to have a promiscuous mating system. Males' home ranges average 1,250 square meters and those of females average only 450 square meters. The ranges of adults of both sexes usually over-

lap the ranges of several members of the opposite sex. Ranges of same-sex individuals overlap to a much lesser extent. Curiously, males show stronger territorial behavior in early summer and females in late summer. Activity on the surface occurs both day and night. In captivity there is a peak in wheel-running around midnight. Compared to other vole species, *M. miurus* has an unusually gentle disposition.

Especially in late summer, singing voles often sit in exposed places and make a metallic, churring sound. This "singing" has been interpreted as a warning signal because it occurs when juveniles are present and is associated with the presence of potential predators in the vicinity. If true, *M. miurus* is similar in this behavior to ground squirrels *(Spermophilus)*, pikas *(Ochotona)*, and taiga voles *(M. xanthognathus)*. Because of their consistent association with the construction of haypiles in late summer, another explanation is that these calls represent territorial defense.

The behavior for which these voles are most noted is the construction of haypiles. In this way, too, they resemble pikas. Haypiles are constructed toward the end of summer, mostly by juveniles. One study (Bee and Hall, 1956) of 13 individuals claimed that each vole built its own pile, usually taking several weeks to complete the task. It seems more plausible, however, that an individual may construct more than one pile, and cooperative construction by siblings has been postulated. Haypiles provide high quality food during the long winter, and vary in size from less than one liter to 30 liters. The hay is placed off the ground at the base of a shrub or on a well-drained slope. Sometimes unpalatable species of plants are layered with palatable ones, seemingly to provide better curing conditions. A large variety of plant species have been found in haypiles, but a common type consists of willow *(Salix)* shoots harvested from

Microtus miurus

as high on the stalk as 1.5 meters. Other frequently collected genera are horsetails and scouring rushes *(Equisetum)*, fireweeds and willow-herbs *(Epilobium)*, sweet coltsfoot *(Petasites)*, Jacob's ladder *(Polemonium)*, mountain avens *(Dryas)*, licorice-root *(Hedysarum)*, lupine *(Lupinus)*, and aster *(Aster)*. Murie described underground stores of roots, rhizomes, and renewal buds in the Alaskan Range that he attributed to singing voles. We think it likely that these were made by *M. oeconomus*. It has been suggested that singing voles over-winter in family groups, although this has not been substantiated. *W. Z. Lidicker, Jr., and G. O. Batzli*

Size
Total length: 125–163 (147) mm (males); 126–168 (148) mm (females)
Length of tail: 20–36 (25) mm (males); 23–32 (26) mm (females)
Weight: 22.5–60 (39) g (males); 28–52 (38) g (females)

Identification
Microtus miurus is a smallish, short-tailed vole, usually quite buffy in color on the flanks and venter, and with rather enlarged claws. Other *Microtus* species with overlapping distributions have moderate to long tails, white or gray venters, and smaller claws.

Recent Synonyms
Briefly (1960s) considered to be conspecific with *M. gregalis* of Siberia

Other Common Names
Alaska haymouse, Alaska vole, Toklat vole

Status
Moderately abundant, but densities vary significantly from year to year

Subspecies
Microtus miurus cantator, southwesternmost Yukon Territory and adjacent British Columbia (St. Elias Mountains), and westward into adjacent Alaska to the north slopes of

the Wrangel and Chugach mountains
Microtus miurus miurus, Kenai Peninsula north to the Anchorage area
Microtus miurus muriei, Seward Peninsula across northern Alaska, most of Yukon, and a short distance into the Northwest Territories
Microtus miurus oreas, Alaskan Range and westward across southern Alaska
Two other forms, *andersoni* and *paneaki,* are of doubtful validity and generally are synonymized with *murei.*

References
Batzli and Henttonen, 1990, 1993; Bee and Hall, 1956; Murie, 1961; Youngman, 1975

Mogollon vole | *Microtus mogollonensis*

The Mogollon vole has recently been recognized as a species distinct from the Mexican vole *(Microtus mexicanus)*. *Microtus mogollonensis* occurs throughout most of the higher forested mountains of the southwestern United States. Its close relative, the Mexican vole, occurs in mountainous areas of Mexico. As elevations increase in the southwestern deserts, the climate becomes increasingly cooler and wetter, creating conditions favorable to the growth of evergreen trees. Mogollon voles are usually associated with these coniferous forests, occurring in "islands" of mountain-top forest habitat surrounded by a "sea" of inhospitable lower-elevation desert. Some of these mountain-top populations have been isolated from other populations since the end of the last ice age (about 20,000 years ago). Because of this isolation, Mogollon voles from each mountain range tend to differ slightly from voles on other mountains.

Microtus mogollonensis is usually associated with grassy meadows in coniferous forest, but may occasionally be found in other habitats, particularly in the northern portion of its range. Like most other voles, it utilizes grass for food and cover. However, unlike most other rodents, which eat grass seeds, voles eat the green vegetative portion (leaves and stems). Most mammals do not eat the vegetative portion of grass because it is low in nutritional value, extremely fibrous, and may contain a high concentration of silica (a hard, glassy mineral). Voles have many special adaptations of the teeth, jaw musculature, and digestive tract that allow them to utilize this food resource. For example, they have large molars with spe-

cialized grinding surfaces, which grow continuously through life. These adaptations prevent the tough grass from wearing the molars down to the gum, and allow the grass to be finely ground, aiding its digestion.

The presence of this species may easily be detected by the runways it constructs. These are small dirt paths about 35 mm wide on which the voles travel. Mogollon voles keep their runways free of debris and clip any vegetation that grows on them. In tall, dense grass, the runways may become tunnel-like, with a grass roof. The runways form a complex network linking underground burrow entrances and feeding areas. Like other voles, Mogollon voles may be active and may be seen darting down their runways at any time. Recent vole activity may be detected by the presence of fresh, usually bright green fecal pellets in "toilet areas" along the runways and small piles of freshly cut clippings of green grass in feeding areas. Other small mammals, particularly shrews *(Sorex)* and deer mice *(Peromyscus)*, may also utilize the vole's runways for moving about.

Microtus mogollonensis has one of the lowest reproductive potentials of any North American vole. Although pregnant females may have up to six embryos, they average only about 2.4 embryos. This small number is not surprising in light of the fact that *M. mogollonensis* has only two pairs of mammary glands rather than four pairs as found in most other voles. Limited data suggest that most reproduction occurs during the warmer, wetter months and that unlike many other species of *Microtus,* reproduction may cease during the winter.

Of the vole species occurring in the Southwest, Mogollon voles are best adapted for dry conditions. They occur in some of the driest habitats of any species of vole in North America. In areas where *M. mogollonensis* occurs with other species of vole, competition usually results in the Mogollon vole being excluded from the wetter, grassier areas. Factors that affect grass growth such as livestock grazing, drought, and stream

Microtus mogollonensis

and wetland degradation have resulted in serious threats to many populations of Mogollon vole.

M. mogollonensis has relatively fewer species of worms parasitizing its digestive tract than other voles, which may be due to the relatively dry habitats it uses. Many kinds of parasites require moist habitats during certain parts of their life cycle. However, an alternative interpretation is that some species of parasites have become extinct due to small population sizes in the isolated mountain-top habitat. *J. K. Frey*

Size
No significant sexual dimorphism
Total length: 123–144 (134) mm
Length of tail: 25–34 (28) mm
Weight: 18–42 (28) g

Identification
Within its range, *Microtus mogollonensis* can be distinguished from *Microtus longicaudus* and *M. pennsylvanicus* by shorter tail; from *M. longicaudus, M. pennsylvanicus* and *M. montanus* by tannish rather than whitish belly and underside of tail, and brownish rather than blackish upperside of tail; from these species and from *M. ochrogaster* by four rather than six or eight mammae.

Recent Synonyms
Microtus mexicanus (part)

Other Common Names
Formerly known as Mexican vole

Status
Federal and state (Arizona) endangered *(M. m. hualpaiensis),* Federal Category 2: more information about its status is needed before a determination can be made *(M. m. navaho).*

Subspecies
Microtus mogollonensis guadalupensis, Guadalupe Mountains, Texas
Microtus mogollonensis hualpaiensis, northwestern Arizona south of the Colorado River

Microtus mogollonensis mogollonensis, southeastern Colorado, New Mexico, east-central Arizona
Microtus mogollonensis navaho, southwestern Colorado, Navajo Mountain, Utah, northeastern and north-central Arizona south of the Colorado River

References
Conley, 1976; Frey and LaRue, 1993; Frey and Moore, 1990; Frey and Patrick, 1995; Hoffmeister, 1986

Montane vole | *Microtus montanus*

The montane vole is one of the most common, widespread, and ecologically important small mammals of the intermontane west. As its name implies, it is found primarily in the mountains, and its elevational distribution extends above timberline. In the southern part of its range it tends to occur at higher elevations. It is found in a variety of habitats including dense woods, wet meadows, and stream sides. However, it is most common in open mesic grassland and it is there that populations of this species reach their highest densities. One study reported 185 voles per hectare, but estimates in the great Klamath Basin irruption (popuation boom) of 1957–58 were 1,200–1,600 per hectare.

The great numbers of these rodents put them at the prey base for numerous species of owls, hawks, falcons, and mammalian predators, including coyote, weasels, and other furbearers. Experimental techniques used to control damage by *M. montanus* include the use of the scent of predators. The montane vole's great numbers and seeming periodicity of abundance have been of particular interest to ecologists because these patterns challenge our ideas of what regulates animal populations. Early workers thought populations had 3–4 year cycles of abundance. More recent research has identified some stable populations, and documented the dependence of the changes in abundance on the timing of the growing season and weather events.

Adult females are territorial among themselves, as are adult males. The species is presumed to be polygynous, because the male has a territory that encompasses those of several females. At about 15 days postpartum, the female abandons her young and nest and establishes another territory. At very high densities she has nowhere to go and stays with the young, which, in these extended maternal families, do not breed. All aspects of

the social structure observed in the field have been confirmed in laboratory experiments. The copulatory pattern of this species also correlates with a polygynous mating system. The montane vole has been used as a model polygynous species in comparison with the monogamous *M. ochrogaster*.

Litter size varies from one to ten pups. A classic laboratory study showed that the mean litter size of first litters in females that start breeding as subadults is 3.6, by the fifth litter the average is 4.9, and thereafter the average declines. Females first bred as adults averaged 4.2 pups in the first litter and 5.8 in the fifth litter, with a subsequent decline. Gestation is 21 days. Estrus follows immediately upon parturition; it can also be induced by the male.

In field populations with winter snow, most voles die in the season of their birth. Most of the voles that over-winter are those born late in the growing season. Winter breeding occurs, usually when the population is growing. In a study of individually marked voles followed through the winter, some adult females continued to breed under the snow, and young voles were even recruited into the breeding population. In many years, spring breeding is triggered by a naturally occurring plant compound (6-methoxybenzoxazolinone), and this allows the voles to respond to the availability of new grass.

During the main growing season, montane voles can be active at any time of day, but have peaks of activity in the morning and evening. Voles forage in and near runways in the grass, but brood nests are typically below the surface. Montane voles do not hibernate. They remain active beneath the snow in

Microtus montanus

their burrows and in the cozy space that forms among ice crystals at the surface of the ground.

Among the diseases carried by montane voles are tularemia and girardia. *Microtus montanus* has been used extensively in laboratories as an experimental model for the study of human disease, especially African trypanosomiasis.

Montane voles are known from the fossil record. *F. J. Jannett, Jr.*

Size

There is significant sexual dimorphism in some populations: males may be 38 percent heavier than females. At peak densities individuals are larger than at low densities.
Total length: 140–220 mm
Length of tail: 24–64 mm
Weight: 18–90 g

Identification

Individuals usually cannot be distinguished from other species with certainty except by examining dental and/or cranial characters. Most adult males have oily skin glands on their hips, whereas the males of most other sympatric voles do not have these glands. *M. montanus* differs from the long-tailed vole in having a shorter tail. Some pale-colored individuals closely resemble the western heather vole, and some darker brown individuals resemble the common meadow vole.

Recent Synonyms

Microtus canicaudus, found mostly in the Willamette Valley, was once recognized as a

subspecies of *M. montanus* but is now considered a distinct species because of chromosomal differences.

Other Common Names

Mountain vole

Status

Common and widespread, and in some localities a significant agricultural pest

Subspecies

Microtus montanus amosus, central Utah
Microtus montanus arizonensis, east-central Arizona and west-central New Mexico
Microtus montanus canescens, south-central British Columbia and central Washington
Microtus montanus codiensis, northwestern Wyoming
Microtus montanus dutcheri, south-central California
Microtus montanus fucosus, southern Nevada
Microtus montanus fusus, southwestern Colorado and adjacent parts of Utah and New Mexico

Microtus montanus micropus, northern Nevada and adjacent parts of Colorado, Idaho, and Oregon
Microtus montanus montanus, northeastern California and adjacent parts of Oregon and Nevada
Microtus montanus nanus, a broad band through Washington, Oregon, Idaho, Montana, Wyoming, Utah, and Colorado
Microtus montanus nevadensis, southern Nevada
Microtus montanus pratincola, west-central Montana
Microtus montanus rivularis, southwestern Utah
Microtus montanus undosus, west-central Nevada
Microtus montanus zygomaticus, north-central Wyoming

References

Anderson, 1959; Jannett, 1980; Negus and Pinter, 1965; Oregon State University Extension Service, 1959

Prairie vole | *Microtus ochrogaster*

The prairie vole is found throughout the prairie states of the United States and into the south-central provinces of Canada. The subspecies *M. o. ludovicianus*, apparently recently extinct, was found in the coastal prairies of eastern Texas and western Louisiana. *Microtus ochrogaster* builds well-defined runways on and below the ground, with holes 5 cm in diameter leading to the underground runways. The surface runways are well worn and are of bare, packed soil or are covered with a layer of grass clippings. The commonness of these runways in an area is a good index of population size.

Activity patterns apparently are based on four-hour cycles, with diurnal activity high in the winter, but low in summer when daytime temperatures are high. Other environmental factors, including cover density, food availability, and competitors, also seem to affect specific activity patterns.

This vole's pelage is typically grayish-brown; the hairs have black and brownish-yellow tips, giving the back a grizzled appearance. The sides are slightly paler; the belly is a neutral gray or is washed with whitish or pale cinnamon; the tail is strongly bicolored. In winter the dorsal fur is slightly darker and the belly fur is more buffy. Molting occurs any time during the year, typically requiring 3 weeks for completion. The first area to molt is the chest, followed by the legs and sides. Molting fronts typically meet on the back. Several color variations have been found in wild populations including black, albino, and yellow, as well as spotted.

Reproduction occurs throughout the year, with lowest levels of activity in December and January and highest levels from

Microtus ochrogaster

May to October. Specific peaks of activity seem to depend heavily on moisture availability. The reported sizes of field populations vary widely from a few dozen to several hundred animals per acre. Intervals between cyclic population peaks appear to vary from 2 to 4 years. During population highs *M. ochrogaster* may strongly impact its environment and may be a

major problem where people plant trees, because the voles eat the basal inner bark.

Monogamy apparently is the rule, and following a gestation of 21 days, the female gives birth to an average of four young. The neonates are pink and hairless, but brown fur appears by the second day. They are capable of crawling by day 5, eat solid food by day 12, are weaned when they are 2 to 3 weeks old, and start their molt about day 24. Nearly all growth is completed by two months.

Seeds, stems, and leaves of a wide variety of prairie plants comprise the majority of the prairie vole's diet, and insects are consumed when they are available. The natural habitat includes the numerous prairie types in its range as well as various upland agricultural habitats, fence rows, and fallow fields. Suitable cover for runways appears to be a major consideration, and timbered areas are avoided. Fossils are known from 14 states. Several have been found in the Southwest, outside the vole's present range.

Other small rodents found in the same habitat with prairie voles commonly include the cotton rat, two species of white-footed mice, the three species of microtine mice mentioned previously, two species of harvest mice, and not uncommonly the alien house mouse.

Prairie voles have been used in numerous behavioral, reproductive, and physiological studies for more than 30 years. *D. T. Stalling*

Size

No significant sexual dimorphism
Total length: 130–172 mm
Length of tail: 24–41 mm
Weight: 37–48 g

Identification

Three other species of rodents of similar size and appearance, *M. pennsylvanicus, M. pinetorum,* and *Synaptomys cooperi,* have ranges that overlap that of *M. ochrogaster.* It can be distinguished from *M. pennsylvanicus* by having a considerably shorter tail; only five plantar tubercles (toe pads), not six, on the hind foot; coarser body fur; and yellowish or rusty rather than silver-tipped belly fur. The other two species have tails about half the length of the tail of *M. ochrogaster,* and *M. pinetorum* has reddish instead of grizzled back fur. In *S. cooperi* the back fur is brownish mixed with black and silver, the belly fur is silvery, and the upper incisor teeth have lengthwise grooves, unlike the teeth of *M. ochrogaster.*

Recent Synonyms

Arvicola austerus
Arvicola cinnamonea
Arvicola haydenii
Hypudaeus ochrogaster
Microtus ludovicianus

Status

Common

Subspecies

Microtus ochrogaster haydenii, central Oklahoma and northeastern New Mexico to eastern Montana and southwestern North Dakota
Microtus ochrogaster ludovicianus, coastal prairies of southeastern Texas and southwestern Louisiana (probably extinct)
Microtus ochrogaster minor, central Wisconsin and eastern South Dakota to the central prairies of Alberta and the southeastern corner of Manitoba
Microtus ochrogaster ochrogaster, central Tennessee and north-central Arkansas to southeastern South Dakota and southern Michigan
Microtus ochrogaster ohionensis, southwestern Ohio, western Kentucky, and western West Virginia
Microtus ochrogaster similis, northeastern and central Wyoming and southeastern and central Montana
Microtus ochrogaster taylori, southwestern Kansas southward into the eastern Oklahoma Panhandle

References

Mammalian Species 355; Schwartz and Schwartz, 1981

Tundra vole | *Microtus oeconomus*

The tundra vole, widely distributed at northern latitudes in the Old World, is restricted to Alaska and northwestern Canada in North America. These voles probably reached the New World by way of the Bering land-bridge during the Pleistocene. *Microtus oeconomus* occurs on the northern slope of the Brooks Range in Alaska, giving it the northernmost distribution record for the genus in North America. Pleistocene fossil remains of the tundra vole were found in the Old Crow Basin, Yukon Territory.

Tundra voles are medium-sized for the genus, with short ears and a short tail. The upperparts of the body vary from dusky gray to rich buff, tawny, cinnamon brown, or rusty brown. In all color variations there is a mixture of black-tipped hairs. The sides are paler than the body and the underside is white, sometimes washed with dark buff. The tail is bicolored, pale dusky to black above and whitish to pale buff below.

As the common name implies, tundra voles inhabit moist meadow habitats in the Arctic tundra of North America. They are common around lakes, streams, and marshes. Only two other North American species of *Microtus* are found in the tundra. *Microtus miurus,* the singing vole, occurs in drier tundra habitats than the tundra vole and *Microtus pennsylvanicus* oc-

Microtus oeconomus

curs sporadically in the tundra. *Microtus oeconomus* also occupies meadows in the northern coniferous forest. Its summer food consists of clipped sedges *(Carex)* and grasses such as cottongrass *(Eriophorum angustifolium)*. Tundra voles store grass seeds and rhizomes of sedges and forbs in the autumn to provide food for the long Arctic winter. These caches are large enough that Inuit seek them out to supplement their own food supplies.

The breeding season lasts from May to September and females have 2 or 3 litters annually. The gestation period is 20 to 21 days and neonates weigh 3 g. On rare occasions winter breeding may occur. Females have eight mammae, and litters are relatively large, usually with 4 to 8 young per litter. There are two annual molts, one in the spring and one in the fall.

The tundra vole is active throughout the year, day and night. These voles dig shallow burrows in soil and vegetation above the permafrost. Nests are constructed of vegetation and lined with fine grasses and sedges. Tundra voles travel in well-developed runways, which are often located in frost cracks. In some areas burrows are dug into peat hillocks. Large quantities of peat may be brought to the surface by the voles. On barrier islands and beach areas in Alaska, runways are evident between burrows in sand dunes and vegetated areas.

Microtus oeconomus is an important prey for many northern predators including snowy and short-eared owls, rough-legged hawks, peregrine falcons, gyrfalcons, jaegers, gulls, shrikes, weasels, arctic foxes, and wolverines. *J. E. Cornely*

Size
Total length: 152–225 mm
Length of tail: 30–54 mm
Weight: 25–80 g

Identification
This is a medium-sized vole with a body 2.8 to 3.6 times as long as the tail; the tail is 1.8 to 2.4 times as long as the hind foot; and the anterior lower molar has only four closed triangles. The skull is broader and the body is significantly larger than in *Microtus miurus*, and slightly larger than in *Microtus pennsylvanicus;* both have second upper molars with 4 closed angular sections, but *M. pennsylvanicus* has a rounded posterior loop and *M. oeconomus* does not.

Other Common Names
Called "root vole" in the Old World

Subspecies
Microtus oeconomus amakensis, Amak Island, Bering Sea, Alaska
Microtus oeconomus elymocetes, Montague Island, Prince William Sound, Alaska
Microtus oeconomus innuitus, St. Lawrence Island, Bering Sea, Alaska
Microtus oeconomus macfarlani, Alaska, Yukon, and Northwest Territories, Canada

Microtus oeconomus operarius, western Alaska
Microtus oeconomus popofensis, Shumagin Islands, Alaska
Microtus oeconomus punakensis, Big Punak Island, Alaska
Microtus oeconomus sitkensis, southeastern Alaska
Microtus oeconomus unalascensis, Aleutian Islands, Alaska
Microtus oeconomus yakutatensis, southeastern Alaska, northwestern British Columbia

References
Lance and Cook, 1998; Tamarin, 1985

Creeping vole | *Microtus oregoni*

Creeping voles are restricted to the Pacific Northwest, where they occur from southern British Columbia to northern California and from sea level along the Pacific coast to higher elevations in the Coast and Cascade ranges of Oregon and Washington. These voles prefer grassy and herbaceous sites within moist coniferous forests and are found in all stages of forest succession including recent clearcuts. Creeping voles feed on a variety of forbs and grasses and up to 36 percent of the diet may consist of fungi.

Creeping voles are good burrowers and construct subterranean tunnels in moist forest soils. Nests are constructed underground or under rotting logs or root clumps. These voles spend a considerable amount of time under forest litter and are not as active aboveground as are most other voles and mice. Individual home ranges are estimated at 0.05 to 0.38 hectares for males and 0.04 to 0.23 hectares for females, depending on habitat.

The creeping vole's reproductive season normally extends from March to September, though some reproduction can occur earlier or later if weather conditions are favorable. Mean litter size is 3.4 (range 1–6) and the gestation period is 23–24 days. The young open their eyes when they are 12 days old and can be weaned when they are 15 days old. Females can start breeding when they are 23–24 days old, but most females probably are not successful breeders until they are 35–38 days old.

Population densities appear to be relatively low and stable in mature forest stands, usually with fewer than 15 individuals per hectare. However, densities can be much higher in favorable habitat. A density of 54 per hectare was recorded in a clearcut, and 138 per hectare were caught in an abandoned field surrounded by forest in British Columbia. Densities fluctuate considerably within and between years. These fluctuations appear to be in response to changes in habitat quality, and are not the

Microtus oregoni

typical 3–4 year multi-annual cycles observed in some other vole species.

Creeping voles have many predators, including bobcats, coyotes, ermines, and at least four species of owls and many other raptors. They also have several potential competitors, including Townsend's, gray-tailed, long-tailed, and red-backed voles, and deer mice. However, competition with these species appears to be minimized by different food habits and different use of microhabitat. Predation may be a factor in determining overall numbers and densities of creeping voles, but competition with other mice and voles does not appear to affect the distribution or habitat use of this species. *J. O. Wolff*

Size
Males are slightly larger than females.
Total length: 130–153 (140) mm
Length of tail: 30–41 mm
Weight: 17–20 g

Identification
The creeping vole's dorsal fur is short, dense, and sooty-gray to dark brown or almost black, with a mixture of yellowish hairs. The belly is a dusky gray to white. The eyes are small. The tail is short, almost black on top, and gray underneath. Creeping voles can be distinguished from other voles by their small size and tiny eyes.

Other Common Names
Oregon vole

Status
Uncommon to common; patchy distribution

Subspecies
Microtus oregoni adocetus, southernmost Oregon into northern California

Microtus oregoni bairdi, restricted to the vicinity of Klamath Falls, Oregon, near the Oregon–California border

Microtus oregoni oregoni, northern Washington into northern California and all along the Pacific coastline

Microtus oregoni serpens, northern Washington into southern British Columbia

References
Mammalian Species 233; Gashwiler, 1972

Meadow vole | *Microtus pennsylvanicus*

The meadow vole is the most prolific mammal on earth. This robust vole, with a relatively short tail and compressed muzzle, can breed about a month after birth. The breeding season through much of its range is from April to November, with occasional winter breeding. There is a 3-week gestation period and a 2-week nursing period until weaning. Females have a postpartum estrus, meaning that they can mate immediately after giving birth. Once a female begins to breed, she can produce a litter of three to ten pups every three weeks or so. One captive female on record produced 17 litters in one year.

The meadow vole is generally dull brown above with a gray belly. The animals molt as they go from juveniles to subadults and from subadults to adults. In addition, seasonal molts produce a thicker, finer winter pelage compared to a sparser, coarser summer coat. Immature voles are darker than adults.

Meadow vole population processes have been of great interest to biologists for more than 50 years because of the cycles of density that this and related species undergo. The cycles range from two to five years in duration and involve changes in density from several to several hundred voles per hectare. Although introductory biology and ecology textbooks give various explanations for these cycles, their underlying mechanisms are unknown and are the basis for much research. Current explanations for these cyclic changes in density range from predation to genetic changes in behavior of the voles.

The habitat of the meadow vole is grassy fields and meadows, preferably wetter rather than drier. The voles cannot survive and reproduce in other habitats, although they are occa-

sionally seen making short exploratory forays into forest floors and other habitats, or are seen in them during dispersal movements from one suitable habitat to another. Oldfield and meadow grasses provide both habitat and food. Meadow voles are primarily herbivores, eating most species of grasses, sedges, and herbaceous plants. They eat the leafy parts as well as the seeds. Meadow voles also occasionally eat insects and animal remains. The voles make tunnels in the grass about 3 cm in diameter, and live both above and below the ground, having aboveground nests and underground burrows and nests. Aboveground nests are especially visible after snowmelt in the spring, before they are covered by new growth of grass. Voles can be active throughout a 24-hour period; their activity is related to season, weather, and habitat quality. When active, they procure food, search for mates, maintain their burrow systems, and mark their territories with urine and feces.

Meadow voles have a social system in which females are territorial, occupying spaces averaging 70 square meters. Males, on the other hand, seem to range more freely, overlapping the ranges of many females. The males have ranges about three times larger than the territories of females, and seem to patrol their ranges looking for receptive females with which to mate. Meadow voles tend to be solitary in the breeding season and communal in the winter nonbreeding season.

In addition to being the most prolific mammal on earth, the meadow vole has one of the largest distributions of any small mammal, certainly the largest of any North American vole. At peak densities during population cycles, which may be synchronized over most of its range, the meadow vole is probably the most abundant mammal in North America. Because of this abundance and distribution, this vole has a major impact on human and nonhuman ecosystems. In nonhuman ecosystems, voles make up a major food resource for predators of all kinds, including hawks, owls, weasels, and foxes; nestlings are especially at risk of predation by the larger shrews and snakes. Throughout its range, the meadow vole is probably the main

Microtus pennsylvanicus

staple for its predators. Human ecosystems are especially vulnerable to vole damage during periods of high density and in winter. During winters when vole densities are high and food is scarce, voles do severe damage to orchards, especially apple orchards, where they girdle the trees below snow level. Many trees are killed in this way. In addition, meadow voles do damage to summer crops and to stored hay.

Meadow voles are very aggressive little animals. When cornered or captured, they often chatter at their captor, a behav-

ior in which the animals are actually sharpening their ever-growing incisors in preparation for biting.

Meadow voles share their ranges and habitats with other vole species, white footed and deer mice (*Peromyscus leucopus* and *P. maniculatus*), cotton rats (*Sigmodon hispidus*), and jumping mice (*Zapus hudsonius*), to name a few. The meadow vole is known from Pleistocene fossils from at least 10 states, from Florida to Kansas. *R. H. Tamarin*

Size
No significant sexual dimorphism
Total length: 140–195 (167) mm
Length of tail: 33–64 (42) mm
Weight: 33–65 g

Identification
Microtus pennsylvanicus is distinguished from other voles in its range by five closed triangles on the first lower molar, three transverse loops with no triangles on the third lower molar, four closed triangles with a posterior loop on the second upper molar, and three closed triangles on the third upper molar.

Other Common Names
Meadow mouse, field mouse

Status
Abundant

Subspecies
Microtus pennsylvanicus acadicus, Nova Scotia, Prince Edward Island
Microtus pennsylvanicus admiraltiae, Admiralty Island, southern Alaska
Microtus pennsylvanicus alcorni, southern Alaska, southwestern Yukon Territory
Microtus pennsylvanicus aphorodemus, western edge of Hudson Bay, Canada (southeastern Keewatin, Churchill, Manitoba)

Microtus pennsylvanicus chihuahuensis, Chihuahua, Mexico
Microtus pennsylvanicus copelandi, Grand Manan Island, New Brunswick, Canada
Microtus pennsylvanicus drummondii, central and western Canada, north and central North Dakota, northwestern Montana, northern Idaho
Microtus pennsylvanicus enixus, central Quebec, Laborador
Microtus pennsylvanicus finitus, southwestern Nebraska, northeastern Colorado
Microtus pennsylvanicus fontigenus, southern and eastern Quebec, eastern Ontario
Microtus pennsylvanicus funebris, northeastern Washington, southwestern British Columbia
Microtus pennsylvanicus insperatus, northeastern Wyoming, western North and South Dakota, eastern and north-central Montana, southeastern Alberta, and southwestern Saskatchewan
Microtus pennsylvanicus kincaidi, central Washington state
Microtus pennsylvanicus labradorius, northern Quebec
Microtus pennsylvanicus magdalenensis, Magdalen and Grosse islands, Quebec
Microtus pennsylvanicus microcephalus, southeastern British Columbia

Microtus pennsylvanicus modestus, northern and western New Mexico, southern and central Colorado
Microtus pennsylvanicus nigrans, southeastern Virginia, northeastern North Carolina
Microtus pennsylvanicus pennsylvanicus, northeastern, east-central, southeastern, and north-central United States, Quebec southeast of the St. Lawrence River, southeastern Ontario, New Brunswick
Microtus pennsylvanicus provectus, Block Island, Rhode Island
Microtus pennsylvanicus pullatus, southeastern and south-central Montana, southeastern and east-central Idaho, central and north-central Utah
Microtus pennsylvanicus rubidus, northwestern British Columbia, southeastern Alaska
Microtus pennsylvanicus shattucki, coastal islands of south-central Maine
Microtus pennsylvanicus tananaensis, central and eastern Alaska
Microtus pennsylvanicus terraenovae, Newfoundland
Microtus pennsylvanicus uligocola, northeastern Colorado

References
Mammalian Species 159; Tamarin, 1985

Woodland vole | *Microtus pinetorum*

The pelage of woodland voles varies with age and season. The young are born with a fuzzy fur that is replaced by a darkened subadult pelage by the time the vole is three weeks old. The chestnut-brown pelage follows shortly afterwards. There is a seasonal molt. The summer pelage begins to appear in May or June and November signals the start of the winter molt to a darker pelage. The progress of the molt can be seen as lines or waves of hair replacement on the body of the animal. Not all

woodland voles are chestnut colored: albino animals have been observed as well as individuals with yellower or tawnier tints.

Woodland voles occur throughout most of the eastern United States and extreme southern Ontario in Canada. Their range extends westward to eastern Texas, Oklahoma, Kansas, and Nebraska. The distribution of woodland voles was greatly affected by the Pleistocene glaciation. Climatic changes that occurred with the advancing ice masses changed some arid habitats to moister grasslands, allowing woodland voles to spread throughout wide areas in the southwest. Fossils of woodland voles dating from the late Pleistocene have been found in caves in Texas and northern Mexico in numbers that indicate that they were not uncommon. These remains are thought to be from the regurgitated pellets of carnivorous birds of prey that roosted in the caves during the Pleistocene. As the climate warmed after the retreat of the glaciers, the western range of the species receded, and now only small relictual populations can be found in the Edwards Plateau region of Texas.

The breeding season varies, extending from January through November for populations in the Northeast. Populations farther north have a shortened breeding season, and populations in the South can breed throughout the year. Females may have from one to four litters per year. Gestation ranges from 20 to 24 days. Litter sizes are low, varying from one to four, with two pups the average. Because each female has only four mammae, and the pups are tenacious feeders, there is intense competition among pups and litters of more than four usually do not survive. Woodland voles are born with their eyes and ears closed. They grow rapidly, are weaned 17 days after birth, and become sexually mature when they are about two months old. Young begin to appear in populations in the Northeast in late March.

Woodland voles occur in a wide variety of habitats. They are common throughout the beech-maple forests of the eastern and central states. Prime habitat frequently has a thick leaf layer or dense grassy patches. Their diet is primarily vegetation and consists of roots, fruits, corms, bulbs, and seeds. The choice of food item varies with the season, and the winter diet can include less desirable foods such as bark, roots, and acorns. Winter feeding on the bark and roots of trees is the main reason that woodland voles are considered pests in apple orchards. These voles also irritate farmers when they consume sweet and white potatoes, peanuts, nursery stocks, lily bulbs, and planted seeds.

The avian predators of woodland voles include barn owls (Tyto alba), long-eared owls (Asio otus), screech owls (Otus asio), short-eared owls (Asio flammeus), great-horned owls (Bubo virginianus), barred owls (Strix varia), red-tailed hawks (Buteo lineatus), broad-winged hawks (Bueto platypterus), and marsh hawks (Circus cyaneus). Pilot black snakes (Elaphe obsoleta), red foxes (Vulpes vulpes), gray foxes (Urocyon cinereoargenteus), and opossums (Didelphis virginiana) also prey on these voles.

Woodland voles construct subsurface runways and burrows and spend much of their time underground. Most burrows are from 5 to 10 cm below the surface. The nesting chambers are globular and have numerous exits. The nest is thickly lined with dried grasses, leaves, and roots. Numerous families of woodland voles share a burrow system and the young are frequently pooled into nursery colonies.

A number of other species of small mammals are commonly found with woodland voles. The hairy-tailed mole (Parascalops breweri) is an especially close associate, frequently sharing the same burrow systems. Jumping mice (Napaeozapus insignis), red-backed voles (Clethrionomys gapperi), white-footed mice (Peromyscus leucopus), deer mice (Peromyscus maniculatus), meadow voles (Microtus pennsylvanicus), prairie voles (Microtus ochrogaster), smoky shrews (Sorex fumeus), and short-tailed shrews (Blarina) are also found in habitats that have woodland voles.

The woodland vole's generic name, Microtus, is derived from the Greek words mikros (small, little) and -otus (ear), and refers to the small ears common to this genus. Pinetorum, derived from the Latin words pinetum (a pine woods) and -orium (belonging to a place of), describes the vole's habitat. M. J. Smolen

Microtus pinetorum

Size

No sexual dimorphism
Total length: 111–139 (121) mm
Length of tail: 12–29 (24) mm
Weight: 14–37 g

Identification

Woodland voles are adapted for a semi-fossorial life. They have reduced eyes and ears, and their foreclaws are large and ideal for digging. The body is cylindrical and slender and covered with smooth, silky fur. The tail is short

and facial vibrissae are well developed. This vole is chestnut-colored above and on the sides and a paler gray or silvery color below. The tail is bicolored, but unlike other voles, the colors grade gently and no sharp, distinct line is noticeable. This and the small size, chestnut-brown color, short tail, and small eyes distinguish this species from other voles that occur sympatrically. Both the meadow vole (*Microtus pennsylvanicus*) and prairie vole (*Microtus ochrogaster*) are larger and heavier, and both have a darker, coarser pelage. The red-backed vole (*Clethrionomys gapperi*) has coarser, brown to reddish dorsal fur, its eyes are noticeably large, and it has a long, scaly, coarsely-haired tail.

Recent Synonyms

Pitymys pinetorum

Other Common Names

Pine vole, pine mouse, mole mouse, potato mouse, mole pine mouse, bluegrass pine mouse

Status

Locally abundant, with higher densities in areas that are moist and have dense cover

Subspecies

Microtus pinetorum auricularis, eastern Texas, the Edwards Plateau of Texas, Louisiana, southeastern Arkansas, Mississippi, and western Tennessee and Kentucky

Microtus pinetorum carbonarius, eastern Tennessee and Kentucky

Microtus pinetorum nemoralis, northeastern Texas, eastern Oklahoma and Kansas,

southeastern Nebraska, Arkansas, Missouri, Iowa, southeastern Minnesota, and southwestern Wisconsin

Microtus pinetorum parvulus, southern Georgia and northern Florida

Microtus pinetorum pinetorum, southern Alabama, Georgia, South Carolina, North Carolina, and southern Virginia

Microtus pinetorum scalopsoides, Illinois, southern Wisconsin, Indiana, Michigan, Ohio, West Virginia, Pennsylvania, Virginia, Maryland, New Jersey, Delaware, New York, Connecticut, Rhode Island, Massachusetts, Vermont, New Hampshire, and southern Maine

Microtus pinetorum schmidti, west-central Wisconsin

References

Mammalian Species 147; Baker, 1991; Barbour and Davis, 1974; Hoffmeister, 1989; Lowery, 1974; Schmidly, 1983

Water vole | *Microtus richardsoni*

The water vole's range forms two disjunct bands. The westernmost portion of the range extends south through the Coast Mountains of western British Columbia and both the Blue and Cascade mountains of Washington and Oregon. The eastern and larger portion of the range extends southward through the Rocky Mountains of southeastern British Columbia and southwestern Alberta and into western Montana, western Wyoming, Idaho, and central Utah.

Water voles generally occur at elevations from 1,524 to 2,378 m in Canada and 914 to 3,201 m in the United States, although low-elevation records are known. Locally, the distribution of the water vole is discontinuous. It is found in subalpine and alpine meadows close to water, especially swift, clear spring-fed or glacial streams with gravel bottoms, and along the edges of high-elevation ponds. Large expanses of coniferous forest, mountain slopes, and valleys present seemingly insurmountable barriers to movement between occupied habitats. Its present habitat requirements suggest that *M. richardsoni* was an occupant of the tundra region bordering the Cordilleran glacial front. Its range presumably became limited during the post-Pleistocene period as the species followed the retreating tundra-like vegetation into high montane areas. Holocene and late Pleistocene fossils have been recovered in Montana, Wyoming, and Alberta.

The water vole's pelage is long. The upperparts are grayish-brown or dark reddish-brown, often darkened with black-tipped hairs. The underparts are grayish with a white or silvery-white wash. The tail is dusky above and grayish below. Both sexes have large flank glands, which are masses of lipid-secreting cells. These are clearly visible in captive-born young at 33 days of age and are apparent on field-captured young as small as 90 mm (head and body) and 19 g. The flank glands of both sexes and all age classes become enlarged during the breeding season. The hair covering the enlarged glands is greasy and matted. As the breeding season ends, the gland regresses, dries, and sloughs off, and new hair erupts on the flank.

The breeding season usually extends from early June through August, although it can begin in late May and continue into September. Ovulation appears to coincide closely with the appearance of the first green herbaceous vegetation as the snow melts. Births occur from June until late September. A minimum gestation period of 22 days has been observed in the laboratory.

Young of both sexes born early in the breeding season mature and reproduce in the breeding season of their birth. More than 25 percent of all young are reproductively active in their first year. However, overwintered adults are responsible for most reproduction. Average litter size increases with age and reproductive experience. Average litter size is 5–6 (range 2 to 10).

The young are born naked and blind, weigh about 5 g, and can vocalize. By the third day, sparse fur covers the body and the pinnae are free from the head. White fur begins to appear on the belly by day 4. The incisors erupt by day 6. Pups run and climb by day 10. Their eyes open two days later and they can run swiftly. Captive young swam voluntarily on day 17 and were weaned by day 21. They still nested together at 32 days, but nested singly by day 40. The testes of young males were descended by day 38, and the voles appeared to court by day 60.

Overwintering young grow beneath the winter snow and reach adult size by the spring melt. Usually they are the only voles seen aboveground at the time of the June snowmelt. Young-of-the-year first appear on the surface in the second or third week of July, and a second group of young emerges in August. Most water voles overwinter only once and die in their second fall or winter, although some individuals survive two winters.

Water voles swim and dive well. They are active 24 hours a day, with peak activity during periods of darkness. They live beneath snow for 7 to 8 months each year, excavating tunnels through the snow. These tunnels run along the soil surface but do not lead to the snow surface. No water vole activity was observed on the snow surface after 6 cm of snow covered the ground.

Surface runways (5 to 7 cm wide) pass through areas of herbaceous vegetation, willow, and moss. These runways parallel and criss-cross springs and streams, which are incorporated into the runway system. Submerged and water-level burrow entrances are found along stream banks. Vole activity is usually restricted to within 5 to 10 m of stream banks, but the animals move farther inland where springs drain boggy areas and join streams.

Water voles occupy subterranean nests year-round. Nests are sometimes found on top of the soil surface after the snow melts. These nests may have been used throughout the winter or may be used only during the snowmelt, when many subterranean spaces become flooded. Subterranean passages and nest chambers are excavated and re-excavated between June and late September. Tunnels, which are about 6 cm deep, are located immediately below the thick network of plant roots and mosses. Short runways branch to nest chambers, feeding areas, and stream edges. Numerous openings in stream banks and close to streams allow easy access to areas above and below the soil surface. Both interconnecting and blind tunnels serve as temporary shelters, retreats, and feeding shelters.

Well-worn surface runways and droppings, cut segments of vegetation, and mounds of recently excavated soil indicate the presence of water voles. Small groups of droppings are sometimes found along runway systems, on top of piles of freshly excavated soil, or at entrances to subterranean passages.

Summer nests are located in small rises in the soil surface or

Microtus richardsoni

beneath logs and stumps. A large dome nest (7 cm in diameter) fills each nest chamber and is occupied by a single individual. Nests are constructed of short segments of leaves and stems of grasses, sedges, and rushes.

Overwintered females maintain minimally overlapping or non-overlapping home areas. When population numbers are low, they may be scattered widely along streams. When population density is high, they cluster in streamside areas, but home-area overlap is minimal or nonexistent. Overwintered males traverse longer portions of streams and overlap the seasonal ranges of individuals of both sexes. When female density is low, males move extensively between female ranges. When population density is high, a male usually is found repeatedly in one area near a group of females. This suggests a polygamous mating system. Active defense via individual encounters and the deposition of feces, urine, and secretions from flank glands along runways and subterranean passes are probably involved in maintaining home areas.

Seeds of *Vaccinium*, bulbs of *Erythronium,* and conifer seeds are in the summer diet, along with small amounts of insect matter and willow buds. Water voles probably feed on subterranean parts of plants throughout the year, but surface digging for roots and rhizomes has not been observed. Winter foods may consist of dry aerial portions of herbaceous vegetation, plus preformed buds of perennials and roots, rhizomes, and corms. Winter foods include the roots of *Pedicularis,* willows (chiefly *Salix barrattiana),* *Erythronium gradiflorum, Arnica,* and *Antennaria,* and bear grass, *Xerophyllum tenax.* There is no evidence of food storage for winter.

Other small mammals found in water vole habitat include

water shrews, cinereus shrews, marsh shrews, montane shrews, and pygmy shrews. Long-tailed voles, montane voles, meadow voles, heather voles, and red-backed voles share the water vole's range, as do northern bog lemmings, meadow jumping mice, northern pocket gophers, yellow-pine chipmunks, and Columbian ground squirrels. The water vole is not known to be a major prey species, but it is taken by ermine, martens, and perhaps hawks. *D. R. Ludwig*

Size
Males are longer and heavier than females.
Total length: 234–274 (252) mm
Length of tail: 66–98 (83) mm
Weight: 72–150 g (males); 68–140 g (females)

Identification
Except for the muskrat, the water vole is the largest arvicoline rodent within its geographic range. Water voles can be distinguished from other voles by their large hind feet (at least 23 mm). Adults of both sexes have prominent flank glands during the breeding season.

Other Common Names
Richardson's water vole, Richardson('s) vole, Richardson's meadow vole, Richardson('s) meadow mouse, water rat, big-footed meadow mouse, giant water vole

Status
Uncommon, limited to alpine and subalpine areas along spring-fed streams

Subspecies
Microtus richardsoni arvicoloides, Coast Mountains of western British Columbia and the Blue and Cascade mountains of Washington and Oregon

Microtus richardsoni macropus, Rocky Mountains of western Washington and Oregon and Idaho, Montana, and Wyoming.
Microtus richardsoni myllodontus, Rocky Mountains of southeastern Idaho and northern Utah
Microtus richardsoni richardsoni, Rocky Mountains of British Columbia, Alberta, and northern edge of Washington, Idaho, and Montana

References
Mammalian Species 223; Banfield, 1974

Townsend's vole | *Microtus townsendii*

One of the largest voles in North America, Townsend's vole occurs from Triangle Island, British Columbia, south through Vancouver Island, British Columbia, western Washington and Oregon, and into northwestern California. These voles are found from sea level to about 1,830 m in the Olympic Mountains in Washington. There is no known fossil record of these rodents.

Townsend's vole is an inhabitant of wet meadows and marshes with dense grass and sedge cover, and appears to avoid forested areas and dense brush. During the wet winters of the Pacific Northwest they often live in areas that are shallowly flooded most of the winter. *Microtus townsendii* readily enters the water and is a good swimmer, even capable of crossing small streams. During wet periods the voles construct nests on or above the soil surface, often on low ridges or hummocks. They are active throughout the year and both day and night. Their runways are used by generation after generation, often being worn down 2.5 to 5 cm into the soil surface. The only time they may not use the runways is during the summer, when tall, dense vegetation provides complete concealment. A variety of grassland and marshland vegetation make up the Townsend's vole diet, including rushes *(Juncus),* bulrushes, horsetail *(Equisetum arvense),* clover *(Trifolium),* alfalfa *(Medicago sativa),* and numerous species of grasses. They sometimes cache bulbs or roots for later consumption.

The size and abundance of Townsend's voles make them a staple in the diet of numerous predators, including short-eared, great horned, snowy, and barn owls, northern harriers, rough-legged and red-tailed hawks, great blue herons, shrikes, raccoons, spotted and striped skunks, weasels, mink, coyotes, red and gray foxes, bobcats, feral cats, and snakes. In one Oregon location *Microtus townsendii* skulls made up more than 30 percent of the skulls found in barn owl pellets. In British Columbia avian predators removed an impressive 25 percent of a population of Townsend's voles in one week!

The length of the breeding season is influenced by population density. Breeding usually occurs from February to October, with reports of limited winter breeding (December to February) in a few populations. Gestation is 22 to 24 days and litter sizes usually range from 4 to 6. Young are weaned at 15 to 17 days of age. Survival rates of Townsend's voles are highest when population densities are increasing and lowest during decreases. Mortality is higher in postweanlings than in any other age class. Female survival is greater than that of males.

These large voles attain the highest average density of any North American *Microtus*. Densities as high as 800 voles per hectare have been recorded. Depending on the interactions of spacing behavior, predation, food availability, and habitat availability, populations of Townsend's voles undergo annual fluctuations, but multiannual cycles are uncommon. When densities are higher than 100 per hectare, Townsend's voles may competitively exclude other species of *Microtus* and deer mice *(Peromyscus)* from their habitat. Breeding adults of this species have well-developed hip glands and have been observed scent-marking with them. These glands are more prominent in males and regress during nonbreeding periods. *J. E. Cornely*

Microtus townsendii

Size
Total length: 169–225 mm
Length of tail: 48–70 mm
Weight: 47–83 g

Identification
Microtus townsendii is a large, dark-brownish vole with large ears that extend above the fur; tail is long, usually blackish or brownish; the feet are brownish or blackish, with brown claws. It is usually distinguishable from sympatric *Microtus,* which are less than 160 mm long, by total length alone.

Status
Abundant

Subspecies
Microtus townsendii cowani, Triangle Island, British Columbia
Microtus townsendii cummingi, Bowen Island and Texada Island, British Columbia
Microtus townsendii laingi, Vancouver Island, British Columbia
Microtus townsendii pugeti, Shaw, San Juan, and Cypress islands, San Juan County, Washington

Microtus townsendii tetramerus, Vancouver Island and adjacent islands, British Columbia
Microtus townsendii townsendii, southwestern British Columbia, western Washington, western Oregon, and northwestern California

References
Mammalian Species 325; Maser and Storm, 1970

Taiga vole │ *Microtus xanthognathus*

The taiga vole has a limited distribution, occurring from the western shores of Hudson Bay west through Manitoba and Alberta and north to central Alaska. Unlike most grass-dwelling voles, taiga voles inhabit fire-successional and riparian, boreal, sphagnum forest habitats near streams and other moist areas. The preferred habitat is often limited to less than 10 years, and consequently, populations are ephemeral, patchy, and unpredictable in distribution. The diet of taiga voles consists primarily of grasses, other monocots, and horsetail, with berries and selected dicots taken seasonally. Taiga voles are active day and

night and use both surface and underground runways. Aboveground runways are maintained and kept free of debris, apparently to provide for unobstructed movement when the animals travel and forage. Nests are approximately 15 cm in diameter, are constructed of dried grass, and are located along an underground burrow system 15–20 cm below the ground surface. Major predators of taiga voles are weasels, martens, foxes, and several species of hawks and owls.

Densities are highly variable and can reach 100 animals per hectare, but lower densities are more common. Animals born

during the summer overwinter, breed the following summer, and do not survive a second winter. Young-of-the-year maintain a body mass of about 30 g through the winter, until early May, and then gain mass rapidly, to weights of more than 100 g through June and July.

The social organization of taiga voles is polygynous, with the territories of males overlapping the home ranges of two or three females. Mating occurs from May through mid-July, and females bear two litters of 8–9 pups each. At the end of the breeding season, from August to September, groups of 5 to 10 individuals form and construct underground communal nests and food caches (middens). Rhizomes of horsetail and fireweed are cached, and a grass nest is constructed about 25–30 cm underground. The nesting area has up to seven entrance and escape routes; the only access to the food cache is through the nest area. Communal nesting provides warmth by huddling and perhaps affords increased vigilance in detection of predators. Taiga voles remain in these communal groups through seven snowy months, from October through April.

Taiga voles have several forms of communication. Scent glands located in the flanks of both males and females are used for individual recognition, territorial marking, and in other social interactions. During agonistic encounters or prior to marking a territory, a vole will scratch the gland with its hind foot to stimulate the flow of sebum, which is then rubbed on the walls of a tunnel or an object, or is displayed to an opponent. Males also scent-mark by dragging their perineal region on the ground or substrate. Piles of droppings are deposited along runways, at intersections of runways, and along the edges of territories as scent posts, presumably to deter intruders. Taiga voles also communicate by emitting a high-pitched squeak or whistle, which acts as an alarm call. The call is given when intruders approach within 10–20 m of an individual's territory.

Microtus xanthognathus

The high frequency of the call makes it difficult for a person to locate the position of the caller. After one vole gives a call, others often join in as a predator moves through the area.

Other rodents that may overlap the range of taiga voles include red-backed voles *(Clethrionomys rutilus or C. gapperi)*, tundra voles *(Microtus oeconomus)*, and lemmings. The food habits and microhabitats of these species differ considerably from those of taiga voles, so competition among them is unlikely. Taiga voles appear to fill a relatively narrow niche and possess a unique set of life history and behavioral features that set them apart from other, similar small mammals. *J. O. Wolff*

Size

Males are slightly larger than females.
Total length: 152–226 mm
Length of tail: 38–53 mm
Weight: 85–158 g

Identification

The taiga vole has small, dark, beadlike eyes, small ears, a short tail, grayish-brown fur, and a characteristic yellowish-orange nose. It can be distinguished from other *Microtus* by its large size and distinct yellow nose. The rock vole *(Microtus chrotorrhinus)* also has a yellow nose, but is smaller and is not sympatric. The brown lemming *(Lemmus sibiricus)* has a much shorter tail and lacks a yellow nose.

Other Common Names

Yellow-cheeked vole, chestnut-cheeked vole

Status

Uncommon, patchy, and ephemeral distribution within its range

References

Wolff, 1980; Wolff and Johnson, 1979; Wolff and Lidicker, 1980, 1981; Youngman, 1975

Sagebrush vole | *Lemmiscus curtatus*

Unlike most other voles, the relatively obscure, drab buff to ash-gray sagebrush vole usually lives in colonies in semibrushy canyons ranging in elevation from 305 to 3,700 meters. The vegetation is often dominated by sagebrush or rabbitbrush mixed with bunchgrass, on well-drained but sometimes rock-covered soils. Although sagebrush voles live in these semiarid habitats, instead of moist habitats like most other voles, they have not adaped to the diet of seeds and insects used by most desert-dwelling rodents. Instead, they are entirely vegetarian and eat almost anything green, including green seed heads and pods. They do not store food, but occasionally pull freshly cut food into burrows to prevent its drying out.

Lemmiscus curtatus usually occurs in colonies. Its burrows have eight to 30 entrances that tend to be located under cover. The burrows, often paved with sage and grass clippings, range from 80 to 460 mm deep and have numerous connecting passages. Some burrows contain nests, which are constructed primarily of leaves, stems, and sometimes seedheads of grass. Feathers and paper have also been found in nests. Nests may also be located under logs.

Lemmiscus curtatus

Surface runways are usually indistinct but are wider (60–80 mm) than those of other voles. They are usually located under cover, are not well kept, but have fewer fecal deposits in them than the runways of other voles. In winter, tunnels under and through the snow are used more often than surface runways on the snow.

Although crepuscular, *Lemmiscus curtatus* is essentially active 24 hours a day, year-round. Activity peaks from 2 to 3 hours before sunset until 2 or 3 hours after full dark and again in the morning from 1 to 2 hours before daylight until 1 to 2 hours after sunrise. Surface winds influence activity: sagebrush voles are only active aboveground when there is little or no detectable wind.

Sagebrush voles appear to breed year-round, but reproductive activity varies seasonally and geographically. Reproduction is often highest in spring and autumn and corresponds with growth of succulent green vegetation. Reduced reproductive activity occurs during summer dry periods and winter cold. Since the gestation period is a short 25 days and postpartum estrus occurs within 24 hours of parturition, a female can produce three or more litters a year. After parturition the female closes the nest entrances, leaves her litter of 2–13 neonates, and goes in search of a male, presumably aided by his scent.

Newborn sagebrush voles are blind and helpless, with pink, hairless skin. When they are 5 days old the young are fully haired and by day 7 are fully pigmented. The eyes open around day 11, and by day 21 the young are weaned and independent. Females are sexually mature by day 60 and males by day 75, but neither are fully grown until after day 90.

Populations of *Lemmiscus curtatus,* like those of other voles, fluctuate radically, often in a short period of time. Climatic variables that determine the amount of succulent vegetation secondarily control the population fluctuations. *H. D. Smith*

Size
No significant sexual dimorphism
Total length: 103–142 mm
Length of tail: 16–30 mm
Weight: 17–38 g

Identification
The sagebrush vole is distinguished from other North American rodents in the subfamily Arvicolinae by its pale buffy to ash-gray coloration, short tail (about the same length as the hind foot), large bullae, and the structure of its third molars.

Recent Synonyms
Lagurus curtatus

Status
Common, restricted

Subspecies
Lemmiscus curtatus curtatus, southwestern Nevada and contiguous areas of eastern California
Lemmiscus curtatus intermedius, south-central to northern Nevada, southeastern Oregon, southwestern Idaho, and western Utah
Lemmiscus curtatus levidensis, central to eastern Idaho, southern Montana, all but northeastern Wyoming, northwestern Colorado, and extreme northeastern Utah
Lemmiscus curtatus orbitus, central Utah
Lemmiscus curtatus palidus, central to eastern Montana, south-central Canada, North Dakota, and extreme northwestern South Dakota
Lemmiscus curtatus pauperrimus, central to eastern Oregon, south-central Washington, and perhaps the northeastern edge of California

References
Mammalian Species 124; Durrant, 1952; Hall, 1946; Nowak, 1991

Round-tailed muskrat | *Neofiber alleni*

This aquatic to semi-aquatic rodent lives in the freshwater marshes of peninsular Florida and south-central and southeastern Georgia. It can be particularly abundant at times in the shallow prairies, or marshes, of north-central Florida and in the Everglades-Okeechobee area, where densities of 40–48 animals per hectare (100–120 per acre) have been recorded. It prefers a water depth of 30–45 cm (12–18 inches). The species is rare to absent in swampy areas and along swift-flowing streams.

Round-tailed muskrats build spherical to somewhat dome-shaped houses 18 to 60 cm (7 to 24 inches) in diameter (an average of 30 cm) at the surface of the water. The house is tightly woven from emergent grasses and sedges, and sometimes

pickerel weed *(Pontederia),* smartweeds *(Polygonum),* and coontail *(Ceratophyllum)* are used. There are two underwater entrances, known as plunge holes. A house is constructed by bending stems over to form a platform, then bringing additional material onto the platform through the plunge holes and adding it from the inside. Typically one adult occupies each house, and houses may be used for three months or perhaps longer. The duration of use is greatly affected by water conditions. The animals also construct platforms about 10 by 15 cm (4 × 6 inches) in size at the surface of the water that are used for feeding and defecation. Plunge holes are usually present at each end.

Round-tailed muskrats resemble diminutive muskrats. They possess the typical vole body shape. Their underfur is dense, gray to brown on the back and grading to pale gray-brown or buff on the belly. The guard hairs are a glossy rich brown to black. The round tail is dull black and sparsely haired. These muskrats molt once each year. The molt can occur in any month but is usually in autumn. The adult molt is unpatterned, spreading from the rump, upper back, head, and legs.

In central Florida *Neofiber alleni* breeds year-round, but is most likely to breed in late autumn when emergent cover is best developed. The intensity of reproduction is affected by water levels, which in turn affect vegetative cover. The gestation period is 26–29 days and usually 2–3 young are born. Four to six litters are produced annually. Neonates are blind, nearly naked, and pink. Shiny gray to black hair soon appears, and by two weeks the pelage is long, dull, and lax. At three weeks of age the young eat adult fare. At 30 days they resemble small adults, and they are sexually mature at 90 to 100 days, when they weigh about 275 grams.

The stems of aquatic grasses are the main item in the diet,

Neofiber alleni

but round-tailed muskrats also eat stems, roots, and seeds of other emergents. The animals are nocturnal, with a peak of activity occurring shortly after dark. Predators include cottonmouth moccasins, red-shouldered hawks, northern harriers, barn owls, and bobcats.

The round-tailed muskrat is often considered a link between the small voles and the larger muskrat. It occupies an ecological niche closer to that of its larger relative, but when water levels are low the animals may burrow in the wet substrate, where they can survive for considerable periods. *D. E. Birkenholz*

Size
No significant sexual dimorphism
Total length: 285–381 (345) mm
Length of tail: 99–168 (133) mm
Weight: 190–350 (328) g

Identification
Neofiber alleni is much smaller than the muskrat *(Ondatra zibethicus),* which is not found in its range; it is at least twice the size of the cotton rat *(Sigmodon hispidus)* and the rice rat *(Oryzomys palustris),* which sometimes share drier parts of its habitat.

Other Common Names
Florida water rat, water rat

Status
Local, common to rare within range

Subspecies
Neofiber alleni alleni, northern to east-central Florida
Neofiber alleni appalachicolae, eastern panhandle of Florida
Neofiber alleni exoristus, extreme eastern Georgia

Neofiber alleni nigrescens, south-central Florida
Neofiber alleni struix, southern Florida (differences are slight and the utility of these forms has been questioned)

References
Mammalian Species 15; Birkenholz, 1963

Muskrat | *Ondatra zibethicus*

Muskrats are distributed throughout most of North America from Alaska to the southern United States. They are semi-aquatic and occur in both brackish and freshwater lakes, ponds, streams, rivers, and marshes. They are absent from parts of the southern United States where tidal fluctuation, periodic flooding, or drought limit distribution.

Muskrats generally are crepuscular and nocturnal, and feed on a wide variety of aquatic plants. The most important are cattails and bulrushes. Muskrats can remain submerged for as long as 15 minutes while feeding. Although primarily herbivorous, depending on season, habitat, and water levels, muskrats may consume animal material including fish, crustaceans, snails, and even young birds.

In marshes, muskrat houses or lodges are rounded hillocks about two meters in diameter and a meter high, constructed of cut vegetation. Tunnels extend from the dry interior nest area of the house to the surrounding marsh. Muskrats also construct dens along the banks of streams or dikes. Feeding platforms and well-used swimming channels throughout marshes also indicate the presence of muskrats. In good habitat, population densities of up to 40 individuals per hectare are normal, although density temporarily may reach 150 per hectare. When such abnormally high population densities occur, habitats can be destroyed for years because the muskrats "eat-out" the existing vegetation.

Most muskrats are dark brown, with the underside slightly paler in color. Long, coarse, glossy guardhairs cover the short,

Ondatra zibethicus

dense, silky underfur. The pelage traps a blanket of air that provides both insulation and buoyancy. The tail is about as long as the head and body and is essentially hairless. It is flattened laterally and is used as a rudder when the muskrat swims. The hind feet are larger than the forefeet and are partially webbed. Fringes of stiff hairs along the sides of the toes further enhance swimming ability. The common name refers to the animal's musky odor, which is especially evident during the breeding season. Paired ventral glands in the perianal region produce a yellowish substance that is secreted in the urine and feces, with which the muskrat marks houses, defecation posts, and other sites within a defended territory. The musk glands of males are much more active than those of females, and under favorable conditions deposited scent probably lasts for weeks.

Muskrats share their habitats with a variety of potential predators. Mink, raccoons, river otters, and coyotes are the most important mammalian predators. The barn owl *(Tyto alba),* barred owl *(Strix varia),* harrier *(Circus cyaneus),* alligator *(Alligator mississippiensis),* and cottonmouth snake *(Agkistrodon piscivorous)* also take muskrats, as do many other predators. Nonetheless, when habitat is sufficient populations flourish and may provide an important economic resource. Historically, muskrats have been very important in the fur trade. Millions of muskrat pelts enter the fur market each year. Because of their potential economic value, muskrats have been introduced in a number of other regions throughout the world, including Japan, parts of South America, and Europe, including Scandinavia and Russia.

Populations usually remain stable despite harvest pressure, predation, parasites, and disease because of the muskrat's high reproductive potential. Litter size averages 6 to 7 after a gestation period of only 25 to 30 days. Two or three litters are produced yearly in northern latitudes, and in southern areas mature females may have five or six litters per year. Neonates are blind and helpless, but grow rapidly. They are able to swim by 2 weeks of age and are weaned at 3 to 4 weeks, when they begin to feed independently. Young generally become sexually mature the spring following their birth, and are then forced to disperse. Although muskrats may live 10 years in captivity, average life span in the wild probably is about 3 years. *G. A. Feldhamer*

Size
Geographic variation is more significant than sexual dimorphism. Larger individuals occur in northern areas.
Total length: 410–620 mm
Length of tail: 180–295 mm
Weight: 680–1,800 g

Identification
The muskrat can be distinguished from the smaller round-tailed muskrat *(Neofiber alleni)* by a laterally flattened tail and partially webbed hind feet. The introduced nutria *(Myocastor coypus),* which occurs with the muskrat in the south, is larger and has a round tail.

Other Common Names
Mudcat, muskbeaver, musquash (North American Indian name)

Status

Widespread, common in suitable habitats

Subspecies
Ondatra zibethicus albus, central Canada
Ondatra zibethicus aquilonius, Labrador and Quebec
Ondatra zibethicus bernardi, southwestern United States
Ondatra zibethicus cinnamominus, Great Plains region
Ondatra zibethicus goldmani, southwestern United States
Ondatra zibethicus macrodon, mid-Atlantic coastal region
Ondatra zibethicus mergens, northwestern United States
Ondatra zibethicus obscurus, Newfoundland
Ondatra zibethicus occipitalis, coastal Oregon and Washington
Ondatra zibethicus osoyoosensis, Rocky Mountains
Ondatra zibethicus pallidus, southwestern United States
Ondatra zibethicus ripensis, southwestern United States
Ondatra zibethicus rivalicius, Gulf Coast region
Ondatra zibethicus spatulatus, northwestern Canada and Alaska
Ondatra zibethicus zalophus, southern Alaska
Ondatra zibethicus zibethicus, eastern United States and Canada

References
Mammalian Species 141; Errington, 1963; Perry, 1982

Brown lemming | *Lemmus sibiricus*

Brown lemmings live in the treeless regions of the north, either in arctic tundra north of the tree line or in subarctic alpine tundra above the tree line. Though they become extremely abundant every 3–4 years, and sometimes wander on top of the snow in late spring, they do not migrate *en masse* during periods of superabundance. Large-scale movements of that kind are restricted to the closely related Norwegian lemmings *(Lemmus lemmus),* which periodically abandon their overpopulated alpine habitats, move downslope in large numbers, and

sometimes drown while swimming across streams, lakes, or fjords. Such mass migrations, as they are called in the European literature, have led to the popular myth of mass suicide by lemmings.

Lemmings are relatively large, entirely herbivorous rodents with unusually short tails. Like others members of the subfamily Arvicolinae, they have stout bodies, small ears and eyes, and blunt muzzles. Breeding adults of this species are tawny brown to cinnamon on their backs and sides, with paler, more buffy colors underneath; a rusty-colored patch develops on the rump of older adults. The pelage of young animals tends to be darker than that of adults.

Female lemmings can breed immediately after giving birth (post-partum estrus) and can produce a new litter after a 3-week gestation period. Rapid production of successive litters, large litter size in summer (a mean of 8), ability to breed during some winters (mean litter sizes of 3 in mid-winter and 4–5 in early and late winter), and early sexual maturity (normally at 5–6 weeks of age, but as early as 3 weeks old in some summers) provide the reproductive potential needed for the dramatic increases in population density seen during some years. Reproduction does not occur during snow melt in the spring

(May through early June) nor during formation of the snow pack in the fall (September through early October).

Peak densities of brown lemmings, averaged over all habitat types in a local region of Arctic tundra, can reach 150–200 trappable animals per hectare. The peak is typically followed by 1–3 years of very poor survival and low densities (often less than one lemming per hectare), then a year of good survival and increasing densities, followed by another peak year (a pattern referred to as a population cycle). Brown lemmings reach their greatest abundance in low-lying, wet habitats that are dominated by swards of perennial monocots (sedges and grasses) and mosses. This relatively dense vegetation provides cover, food, and nesting materials.

Lemmings eat only live plant parts. Because the aboveground parts of perennial monocots die back in late summer, only frozen vegetables, 1–2 cm of basal leaf sheaths, and moss shoots are available as winter forage. As a result, up to half the diet of brown lemmings can consist of mosses during the winter, and they are one of only a few mammals to rely so heavily on such indigestible food (25 percent digestible). Because of the low digestibility of mosses and monocots and the high metabolic rates of lemmings, they must eat large amounts of food, and therefore spend a large part of each day foraging. This they do, night and day, for 1–2 hours at a time at roughly 3-hour intervals.

Most male lemmings have larger home ranges (2.5 hectares or less) than most females (1.5 hectares or less, often much less), and males tend to be more active (70 percent of the day) than females (60 percent of the day). Substantial overlap in home ranges of multiple individuals, and the fact that only females have been captured in nests with the young, suggest that breeding is promiscuous and that females alone rear the young. Males probably spend much time searching for mates. Both sexes use narrow, cleared runways (5 cm wide) as the major routes of travel between their nests, foraging areas, and mates.

During summer, lemmings build nests of dried plants in burrows under the moss layer; during winter the globular

Lemmus sibiricus

nests are larger (20–25 cm in diameter), lined with finely chopped vegetation, and placed in the base of the snow pack. Cold winter air temperatures create a temperature gradient in the snow pack. Warmer snow at the base evaporates and recrystalizes at higher, colder levels. This results in 5–10 cm of loose snow crystals at the bottom of the snow pack (the depth hoar layer) allowing lemmings easy access to their food supply. It may also make them more accessible to predators.

Several species of arctic predators (birds, including snowy owls and pomarine jaegers, and mammals, including least weasels and arctic foxes) rely upon lemmings as a main source of food and only breed successfully when lemming populations are relatively high. Weasels are probably the most effective predators of lemmings during winter, when they add insult to injury by lining lemming nests with the fur of their victims and using the nests as their own. *G. O. Batzli*

Size
Males are 5–10 percent larger than females.
Total length: 130–180 (150) mm
Length of tail (including hair at tip): 18–26 (21) mm
Weight: 45–130 (80) g

Identification
Lemmus sibiricus is the only brown-colored lemming in North America.

Recent Synonyms
Lemmus trimucronatus (may be correct species name)

Other Common Names
Siberian lemming (Eurasia)

Status
Common

Subspecies
Lemmus sibiricus alascensis, north-central coast of Alaska
Lemmus sibiricus harroldi, Nunivak Island, Alaska
Lemmus sibiricus helvolus, southern Yukon and northern British Columbia, Canada
Lemmus sibiricus minusculus, southwestern Alaska
Lemmus sibiricus nigripes, Pribilof Islands, Alaska
Lemmus sibiricus phaiocephalus, southwestern

Canadian archipelago, including Banks and Victoria islands
Lemmus sibiricus subarcticus, Brooks Range and foothills, northern Alaska
Lemmus sibiricus trimucronatus, northern Canadian mainland west of Hudson Bay, and southeastern Canadian archipelago, including King William, Prince of Wales, Southampton, and Baffin islands
Lemmus sibiricus yukonensis, central Alaska from Canada to the Bering Sea

References
Batzli et al., 1980; Bee and Hall, 1956; Stenseth and Ims, 1993

Northern bog lemming | *Synaptomys borealis*

Despite a large geographic range in North America, the northern bog lemming is infrequently encountered. It is especially rare from localities south of the U.S.–Canadian border, but even in northern latitudes its presence is unpredictable. This pattern of low abundance is particularly interesting because many other species in its taxonomic group, the microtine rodents, often reach very high densities in appropriate habitat. Just why the northern bog lemming occurs as such a minor component of small mammal communities is not understood, and the simple fact of its rarity will make explanations of this pattern difficult. One of the consequences of a large but patchy distribution is the possibility for populations in different localities to diverge morphologically. Several subspecies of the northern bog lemming are recognized, although many were described from very few individuals. *Synaptomys borealis* is a species in need of taxonomic reevaluation at the subspecific level.

The northern bog lemming shares the general body plan of many microtine rodents in having a stocky build, short legs and tail, inconspicuous ears, and a rather blunt nose. Its general coloration is grizzled gray to brown on the back and pale gray underneath. The fur has a coarse, ruffled appearance, and the tail is bicolored, brown above and whitish below. Northern bog lemmings share several additional features of their natural history with other microtine rodents. Breeding seasons extend from May to late August, with litter sizes ranging from 2 to 8, and probably averaging 4–5 young per litter. Females are capable of breeding a day after giving birth and are capable of having two or three litters per breeding season, so it appears that the potential for rapid reproduction is there.

Sedges and grasses constitute a large portion of the habitat of these lemmings and are their primary foods. Clippings of sedge and grass stems and leaves, along with parts of small leafy plants, can be found where the lemmings are active. The clippings are most readily seen scattered on the runways that the lemmings and other associated microtines cut through the vegetation, and occasionally they are found in accumulations like small haystacks. Fresh clippings may be seen inside burrow entrances as well. One can distinguish actively used from inactive runways by the presence of freshly clipped vegetation and fresh droppings. Northern bog lemmings often leave droppings repeatedly at a site, creating a scent "signpost" in the form of a small pile of droppings.

During the snow-free months northern bog lemmings are active both above and below ground. Foraging activities are largely confined to their runway systems, where vegetation is harvested and either consumed or removed to underground nests via the burrow systems they excavate. Predation from a

wide variety of avian and mammalian predators is highest in the snow-free period, so most activity occurs below ground at that time. In winter, however, losses to predators are considerably less (most perhaps due to weasel predation) and the lemmings construct globular nests of mosses, grasses, and sedges beneath the snow, at ground level. These winter nests and associated ground-surface runways, which are lined with clipped vegetation and earth, can be seen just after snow melt. Northern bog lemmings are active all winter long.

The northern bog lemming has a greater affinity for boreal habitats than its closest relative, the southern bog lemming.

Synaptomys borealis

During the last glacial period, when boreal conditions extended far to the south, northern bog lemmings inhabited regions as far south as Kansas and Tennessee. The present range of this lemming reflects the northward retreat of the boreal forest.

Northern bog lemmings have been found in varied habitats, with perhaps the greatest variation occurring along the southern boundary of their distribution. The most distinctive situation is that of *S. b. artemisiae,* a race that inhabits sagebrush slopes in southern British Columbia. More typically, lemmings are found where moisture levels are high and the growth of sedges and grasses or both is sufficient to provide cover and a reliable food supply. Such conditions are met in the Pacific Northwest in high-elevation sedge-grass meadows associated with pine or spruce forests, in a wide variety of habitats in New England, including spruce-fir forests; wet meadows, sphagnum bogs, and alpine tundra; and at northern latitudes in sphagnum bogs, riparian zones in mature spruce forests, subalpine meadows, various tundra communities, and in early successional grasslands associated with recently burned forests.

Small mammal species associated with the northern bog lemming vary from place to place within the lemming's large distributional range. The most commonly cited species found with the northern bog lemming is the meadow vole, *Microtus pennsylvanicus,* with which the lemming will share runway systems. In the Pacific Northwest lemmings have been found with vagrant shrews, deer mice, water voles, and southern red-backed voles. In more northerly latitudes they occur frequently with masked shrews, brown lemmings, tundra voles, and northern red-backed voles. In New England they have been caught with southern red-backed voles, masked shrews, deer mice, and meadow mice. *S. D. West*

Size
No significant sexual dimorphism
Total length: 110–140 mm
Length of tail: 17–27 mm
Weight: 27–35 g

Identification
Synaptomys borealis can be distinguished from other sympatric genera by a short tail (slightly longer than the hind foot) and longitudinally grooved upper incisors, and from the southern bog lemming, *S. cooperi,* by buff-colored hairs at the base of the ears, eight rather than six mammae, mandibular molars without triangles on the outer side, and by its palate, which ends in a sharply pointed, backward-projecting spine.

Other Common Names
Campagnol-lemming boréal

Status
Uncommon to rare, patchily distributed

Subspecies
Synaptomys borealis artemisiae, Okanogan Valley of British Columbia and Washington State
Synaptomys borealis borealis, northeastern British Columbia, northern Alberta, southwestern half of the Mackenzie district, northwestern Saskatchewan
Synaptomys borealis chapmani, southeastern British Columbia, northeastern Washington, northern Idaho, northwestern Montana, southwestern Alberta
Synaptomys borealis dalli, interior British Columbia, most of the Northwest Territories, Alaska south of the Brooks Range

Synaptomys borealis innuitus, northern Quebec
Synaptomys borealis medioximus, northeastern Quebec and Labrador
Synaptomys borealis smithi, northern Ontario, Manitoba, northeastern Saskatchewan
Synaptomys borealis sphagnicola, Gaspé Peninsula of Quebec, northeastern New Brunswick, Maine, northern New Hampshire
Synaptomys borealis truei, southeastern Alaska, coastal British Columbia, northwestern Washington mainland

References
Banfield, 1974; Clough and Albright, 1987

Southern bog lemming | *Synaptomys cooperi*

Southern bog lemmings are seldom seen despite a relatively wide distribution in the eastern United States and adjoining southeastern Canada. Four subspecies occupy restricted geographical ranges, two of which are isolated from the main distribution. In the southern portion of the range, this species is limited to higher elevations.

Southern bog lemmings are usually dark brown above and light gray on the underside. Although smaller in body size than other voles, they have a relatively large head, and facial hairs surrounding the snout can be erected to make the face appear larger than it really is. The pelage is molted seasonally, with replacement progressing from irregularly located areas of the body.

Like most small rodents, *Synaptomys cooperi* is most active after sunset and at dawn, with constant, lower levels of activity between these peaks. There is seasonal variation, with diurnal activity declining in summer. This species is active throughout the year. In grassy habitats, southern bog lemmings make runways, which they use in their nightly travels. Their presence can be detected by neatly clipped piles of grass cuttings and tell-tale green droppings. Where they live in high elevation moist forests, they do not make runways and are more difficult to locate. Individuals are docile and rarely attempt to bite when handled. However, they can be difficult to maintain in captivity.

Southern bog lemmings may breed throughout the year, although frequency of breeding in the eastern part of the range is very low between November and February. The young, usually numbering three, are born after a gestation period of 23–26 days. Neonates are mostly pink, but have pale gray pigmentation on the back. In addition to whiskers on the sides of the snout, they have a sprinkling of hairs on the head and back. At birth, their eyes are closed and their ears are folded down against the head. The ears unfold by the second day, but the eyes do not open until 10–12 days of age. The body is well furred by 7 days and the young look like smaller versions of adults by 2 weeks. Weaning is completed by 3 weeks, at which time they have nearly reached adult size. Adult pelage is attained by 5–6 weeks.

Despite their name, southern bog lemmings occur in a wide variety of habitats, including grasslands, mixed deciduous/coniferous woodlands, spruce-fir forests, and freshwater wetlands. Small patches of habitat, such as clearings within woodlands, may support small, very localized, populations. In the eastern portion of the range, the distribution of *Synaptomys cooperi* is influenced by interactions with the meadow vole *(Microtus pennsylvanicus);* the southern bog lemming is the poorer competitor for living space. The outcome of interactions with the prairie vole *(Microtus ochrogaster),* however, appears to depend upon which species has prior claim to habitat. Home ranges of individuals are quite small, ranging from 0.04 to 0.67 hectares. Food consists almost entirely of green vegetation, primarily grasses and sedges but also including mosses, fruit, fungi, bark, and roots.

Although southern bog lemmings may become locally abundant, they are considered to be uncommon in many parts of their range. Furthermore, they appear to occur at lower densities in the eastern portions of the range than in the midwestern United States. There is some evidence that in Kansas this species undergoes multiannual fluctuations in density, with reported peak densities ranging from 34–106 per hectare. *Synaptomys* is generally found in relatively small numbers at paleontological sites, suggesting that low densities may not be a recent phenomenon. The fossil record also indicates that southern bog lemmings once ranged much farther south than at present. Late Pleistocene remains of this species have been found in Mexico and Texas. Until approximately 11,000 years ago, the current range of *Synaptomys cooperi* was occupied by the northern bog lemming *(S. borealis).*   A. V. Linzey

Synaptomys cooperi

Size
No significant sexual dimorphism
Total length: 94–154 mm
Length of tail: 13–24 mm
Weight: 21.4–50 g

Identification
The southern bog lemming is distinguished from voles (*Microtus*) by its very short tail (slightly longer than hind foot) and broad upper incisors that have a longitudinal shallow groove along the front surface. *Synaptomys borealis,* with an overlapping range in northern Minnesota, New Hampshire, Maine, New Brunswick, and the Gaspé Peninsula (Quebec), is very similar, but has narrower lower incisors and eight nipples instead of six.

Other Common Names
Southern lemming mouse

Status
Uncommon to locally abundant

Subspecies
Synaptomys cooperi cooperi, northeastern United States and southeastern Canada
Synaptomys cooperi gossii, midwestern United States
Synaptomys cooperi helaletes, southeastern Virginia and northeastern North Carolina
Synaptomys cooperi kentucki, Kentucky
Synaptomys cooperi paludis, Meade County, Kansas
Synaptomys cooperi relictus, Dundy County, Nebraska
Synaptomys cooperi stonei, southern Appalachian Mountains north to coastal New Jersey

References
Mammalian Species 210; Hamilton and Whitaker, 1979

Collared lemmings | *Dicrostonyx*

Collared lemmings are found throughout the Arctic reaches of North America and Asia. They are the rodents most specialized for life in the Arctic tundra and are among the few that molt to a white coat in the winter. These rodents are active thoughout the year; they spend the winter mainly under the cover of snow.

The scientific name for the genus, *Dicrostonyx,* is derived from the Greek roots for forked (dicro) and claw (stonyx), referring to the unique double claw that develops on the forefeet in winter, caused by the enlargement and hardening of cornified pads under the third and fourth toes. These cornified pads fuse with the normal claw, and this structure becomes notched (or forked) after differential wear by digging in hard packed snow and ice. The common name "collared lemming" refers to the dark, often reddish, band of hair that occurs across the chest in individuals in many populations; "varying lemming" derives from the molt to a white coat in winter; and "hoofed lemming" refers to the unusual winter digging claws.

Collared lemmings are renowned for their remarkable fluctuations in population size. Populations commonly vary in density from fewer than one individual per hectare in low years to 50 individuals or more per hectare in peak populations. Local irruptions are tracked by predators, especially arctic foxes, weasels, several species of owls, and parasitic jaegers, for which collared lemmings are a primary food resource. Although the stuff of legend and cartoon panels, lemming mass migrations to the sea and collective suicides are mainly myth. Local populations of collared lemmings rise and fall for reasons other than the availability of food and the animals seldom migrate en masse.

The number of species of collared lemmings and their distribution have been the subject of considerable confusion over the past 100 years, and the classification of *Dicrostonyx* varies considerably among authors as a result. The number of species recognized in recent summaries has ranged from two (one wide-ranging species, *D. torquatus,* in both Asia and North America, and *D. hudsonius,* confined to the Ungava Peninsula of northern Quebec and Labrador), to nine species in North America alone. Much of this instability and controversy stems from the discovery of extraordinary variation in the numbers and conformation of chromosomes among many geographic populations of collared lemmings. Some of these distinctive chromosomal forms produce subfertile hybrids (offspring less fertile than their parents) in laboratory breeding experiments, a harbinger of distinct species. Based on these preliminary results, most of the known "chromosomal races" of *Dicrostonyx* have been recognized as separate species by some authors. Recent work, however, suggests that more of these distinctive populations are more interfertile than originally suspected and that many "chromosomal races" do not represent separate biological species.

In the following accounts we have followed the conservative application of species names for North American collared lemmings used by Jarrell and Fredga (1993), with one exception. Those authors recognized two North American species, *Dicrostonyx groenlandicus,* ranging over most of the Arctic, and *D. hudsonius.* We recognize a third species, *D. richardsoni,* from the western Hudson Bay region, which genetic and breeding data suggest is distinct (see the account of that species for further discussion). We warn the reader, however, that this is not the last word on this issue. The number of species from Alaska, in particular, is still in doubt. For example, the Aleutian island subspecies, *Dicrostonyx groenlandicus unalascensis,* is large, does not turn white or develop winter digging claws, and may not be totally interfertile with other Alaskan races: it might represent a separate species rather than a subspecies. Further studies are needed to document the diversity of collared lemmings and illuminate the evolutionary history of these fascinating animals. *M. D. Engstrom*

Other Common Names
Varying lemmings, hoofed lemmings

References
Banfield, 1974; Eger, 1995; Jarrell and Fredga, 1993; Mead and Mead, 1989; Nowak, 1991

Northern collared lemming | *Dicrostonyx groenlandicus*

Collared lemmings occur only on the Arctic tundra, with a distribution extending farther north than that of any other rodent. In summer, they occupy the high, dry, and rocky areas of the tundra, where they shelter in shallow underground burrows or under rocks. Nesting chambers are often lined with dry grasses, feathers, and muskox fur. The summer diet consists mostly of shrubs, herbs, and sedges. In the winter, collared lemmings may move to lower meadows where the blanket of snow is thicker and remains for a longer period of time. Winter nests typically are built on the tundra surface, under the snow, and sometimes even in the middle of snow-banks. Willow buds, leaves, twigs, and bark make up the majority of the winter diet. When winter lemming population density is high, willows may appear completely stripped in the spring.

On a seasonal basis, collared lemmings show remarkable physical changes, which presumably are adaptive for animals inhabiting an Arctic environment. These morphological changes are elicited by changes in day length, as the length and direction of photoperiod is used to predict future environmental conditions. Under the influence of decreasing day length in late summer and autumn, collared lemmings increase in body mass, molt to a white pelage, and develop bifid, or forked, "digging" claws. These changes are reversed (i.e., lemmings decrease in mass, molt to the summer pelage, and lose the bifid claws) in late winter and spring under the influence of increasing day length.

In spring and summer, collared lemmings are relatively small in size, weighing between 30 and 50 grams. The pelage varies from light grayish-buff to dark-gray, with aspects of buffy to reddish-brown above; the underparts are grayish-white. In the winter, the lemmings may weigh from 50 to 112 grams. The collared lemming is the only North American rodent that turns completely white in the winter. Guard hairs of the winter pelage can be twice as long, and the underfur twice as thick, as that of the summer pelage, changes that dramatically improve insulation. The digging claws that develop in the fall are unique to the genus *Dicrostonyx*. They form from the pads on the third and forth digits of the front paws, which grow into compressed, cornified tissue separated from the normal claw by a groove and a deep notch at the tips. These claws enable collared lemmings to dig through wind-packed snow and ice. The soles of the feet are well-furred at all times.

Dicrostonyx groenlandicus

The Inuit often regard collared lemmings in summer and winter pelage as different species. When the lemmings molted to the white winter pelage, at a time coincident with the first autumn snows, the Inuit called them *kilangmiutak,* which means "that which drops from the sky"; they use the white fur to trim garments and to make doll clothes.

Collared lemmings typically begin breeding under the snow in early March; the breeding season extends to early September. During snow-melt in June, they experience a breeding hiatus, presumably due to the diminished food supply and the flooding of the tundra at this time. Collared lemmings may reproduce in the winter, although this may depend upon a good snow pack. The average litter size in the field is four or five young, but can range from one to seven. The gestation period ranges from 19 to 21 days. In the wild, females have been observed to produce up to three litters in a breeding season. Females have eight mammae. Young weigh approximately 3.8 grams at birth, open their eyes around day 12, and wean and disperse at 15–20 days of age. Pups born in the late summer and fall show enlargement of the toe pads by day 15 and possess well-developed bifid claws shortly after weaning. Autumn and winter-born young develop the winter pelage as juveniles. Pups born in late spring do not show the development of the bifid claw or white pelage until autumn. *T. R. Nagy and B. A. Gower*

Size
Total length: 110–177 (145) mm
Length of tail: 10–20 (14) mm
Weight: 30–50 g (summer) 50–112 g (winter)

Identification
The soles of the feet are densely furred and the ears are entirely concealed in fur. In summer, the upper body is grayish-buff to dark gray, with buffy and reddish-brown aspects. In winter, the pelage is white and the lemming has enlarged, forked claws on digits three and four of the forepaws. For characteristics that distinguish *D. groenlandicus* from other North American collared lemmings, see the account for *D. richardsoni*.

Recent Synonyms
Dicrostonyx torquatus groenlandicus

Other Common Names
Northern varying lemming, northern hoofed lemming

Status
Common

Subspecies
Dicrostonyx groenlandicus clarus, Prince Patrick, Melville, and South Borden islands in the western High Arctic
Dicrostonyx groenlandicus exsul, St. Lawrence Island in the Bering Sea
Dicrostonyx groenlandicus groenlandicus, much of the eastern High Arctic from northern Greenland west to Bathhurst, Rignes, and Prince of Wales islands, south through the northern two-thirds of Baffin Island, and on the mainland, along the northwestern edge of Hudson Bay south to Chesterfield Inlet
Dicrostonyx groenlandicus kilangmiutak, on southwestern Arctic islands, including Victoria, Banks, and King William, and in tundra on the adjacent mainland south to the northern margin of Great Slave Lake and west to the Yukon-Alaska border
Dicrostonyx groenlandicus lentus, southern third of Baffin Island
Dicrostonyx groenlandicus nelsoni, Seward Peninsula and south to Kuskokwim Bay, south-central Alaska
Dicrostonyx groenlandicus nunatakensis, alpine tundra in the Ogilvie Mountains of north-central Yukon Territory
Dicrostonyx groenlandicus peninsulae, mainland Alaska Peninsula
Dicrostonyx groenlandicus rubricatus, North Slope and portions of the Brooks Range from the Canadian border west to Kotzebue Sound, Alaska
Dicrostonyx groenlandicus unalascensis, Unmak and Unalaska islands in the Aleutians

References
Banfield, 1974; Nagy et al., 1993; Nowak, 1991

Ungava collared lemming | *Dicrostonyx hudsonius*

Dicrostonyx hudsonius is found only in the northern half of the Ungava Peninsula of northern Quebec and Labrador and on the adjacent Belcher and King George islands, Northwest Territories, in eastern Hudson Bay. It is confined to tundra and occurs from sea level to nearly 1,000 meters elevation. This species is limited to the south by woodland and in all other directions by sea. The Ungava collared lemming (or its fossil progenitors, *D. simplicior* and *D. henseli)* appears to have been widely distributed over much of the Arctic reaches of North America and Asia during the mid- to late Pleistocene (about 800,000 to 50,000 years ago). During the height of the late-Pleistocene glaciations, however, this lineage appears to have survived only in suitable habitat southeast of the Wisconsinan

ice sheets. From its purchase there, these refugial populations in the northeastern United States and southeastern Canada likely recolonized the Ungava Peninsula, but the species was replaced in most other parts of its former range in North America by *D. groenlandicus.* Quaternary fossils of *D. hudsonius* have been reported from Pennsylvania, West Virginia, and Quebec.

Ungava collared lemmings occur in tundra habitats, old beach terraces, rocky hillsides, and alpine meadows above timber-line. In mosaic habitats of dwarf-wooded thickets and tundra near tree-line on the mainland, *D. hudsonius* is usually found in relatively dry lichen-heath tundra and rock ridges, although it has been observed using runways through thickets of willow and birch.

The Ungava collared lemming has a stocky body, blunt, stout head, proportionately short limbs and tail, and small eyes. Its small external ears are concealed in the fur. In winter, like most other species of *Dicrostonyx,* it molts to a white, highly insulative coat and develops bifurcated digging claws on the forefeet. In summer, adults are brownish-gray, usually with a dull reddish patch of hair around the ears, although occasional individuals have a darker reddish-brown coat similar to that of *D. richardsoni.* A pale yellowish-orange line on the sides of the body between the legs and the edge of the rump separates the back from the gray belly, and there is usually an indistinct reddish band or collar across the chest. Juveniles and subadults have fewer highlights than adults and are nearly uniform brownish-gray. As in most *Dicrostonyx,* the Ungava collared lemming has a thin black stripe that starts at the tip of the nose and continues down the back to the rump. This stripe is most pronounced in young animals and often is obscured in adults. *Dicrostonyx hudsonius* replaces its coat twice a year, molting to the shorter summer pelage in spring and to the white winter pelage in fall.

Little is known about the natural history of *D. hudsonius,* although it undoubtedly is very similar in habits to other collared lemmings (for a detailed description see the account of *D. richardsoni*). Ungava collared lemmings are taken by a variety of predators, including short-eared owls, snowy owls, rough-legged hawks, glaucous gulls, skuas, gyrfalcons, long-tailed jaegers, arctic foxes, weasels, and even wolves. Like other collared lemmings, *D. hudsonius* spends most of its time in burrows, moving between burrows, and feeding. In summer, the lemmings occupy relatively simple, shallow burrows less than a meter in length, which usually have one entrance. Individuals use more than one burrow within a home range to rest or escape from predators. Somewhere within the burrow there is usually a round, slightly flattened nest constructed of grasses, often with a pile of scat underneath. In winter, *D. hudsonius* tunnels in snow and constructs nests above the surface of the ground. Foxes are said to listen for the sound of collared lemmings digging to capture them in winter. The diet of the

Dicrostonyx hudsonius

Ungava collared lemming is probably similar to that of other *Dicrostonyx,* as its burrows have been noted in the vicinity of willow, blueberry, arctic avens, and other plants known to be preferred collared lemming foods. In winter it is known to eat sedges and willow bark.

Dicrostonyx hudsonius can breed throughout the year, although fall and winter breeding may not occur in all years and are most common in increase phases of population cycles. Litter size is unknown, although the mean of 3 to 4 reported for other collared lemmings probably applies: embryo counts averaging between 4 and 5 have been reported for pregnant females. Growth and development have not been described for this species, but are also probably similar to other *Dicrostonyx.* Winter-born individuals achieve larger body size (length and mass) than do those born in summer; large animals found in early spring are suggestive of successful winter reproduction and/or overwintering of individuals from the previous summer. As in other *Dicrostonyx,* population size can vary tremendously between years. Although periods of peak abundance are often asynchronous among localities, common peak years have been reported across islands in eastern Hudson Bay, where there is probably a very low rate of exchange of individuals. The unusual sex-determining system of other collared lemmings, in which some females have XY sex chromosomes (the usual complement of males in mammals) has not been reported for *D. hudsonius.*

Dicrostonyx hudsonius is sometimes placed in a separate subgenus (*Dicrostonyx*) from other collared lemmings (*Misothermus*). The name *hudsonius* derives from its proximity to Hudson Bay. *M. D. Engstrom*

Size

No significant sexual dimorphism
Total length: 125–166 (145) mm
Length of tail: 12–16 (14) mm
Weight: 35–85 (60) g

Identification

The Ungava collared lemming is geographically isolated from other species of *Dicrostonyx*. In summer, the following characteristics distinguish this species from superficially similar voles with which it shares portions of its range (for example, *Microtus pennsylvanicus, Synaptomys borealis, Clethrionomys gapperi,*

Phenacomys intermedius): very short, well-haired tail; small concealed ears; broad fore and hind feet that are well haired above and below; brownish-gray upperparts with a thin black stripe running down the back; gray belly, usually with a subdued reddish band across the chest; and relatively large body size. In winter, *Dicrostonyx hudsonius* is the only species of rodent on the Ungava Peninsula that molts to a white coat and develops bifurcated digging claws on the forefeet. For comparison of this species to other collared lemmings see the account of *D. richardsoni.*

Other Common Names

Labrador collared lemming, varying lemming, hoofed lemming

Status

Common, localized

References

Borowik and Engstrom, 1993; Krohne, 1982; Manning, 1976

Richardson's collared lemming | *Dicrostonyx richardsoni*

Richardson's collared lemming occurs only in extreme northeastern Manitoba and the corner of the Northwest Territories of Canada west of central Hudson Bay. It occurs in tundra near sea level and is limited to the south and west by woodland and to the north presumably by the presence of *D. groenlandicus.* No fossils have been assigned to *D. richardsoni,* although some deposits of collared lemmings from the eastern U.S. and Canada could include this species.

These lemmings occur in a variety of tundra habitats, but are most common in open, dry areas such as old raised sand beaches, dry parts of lichen-heath tundra, rock ridges and sand or gravel ridges. They avoid marshy habitats and wooded areas in all but periods of peak abundance. They also occur and dig burrows in a variety of soils from dry sand and gravel ridges to deep peat, clay, and even mud.

These lemmings are well adapted to Arctic conditions and in winter, like most other species of *Dicrostonyx,* molt to a white, highly insulative coat and develop bifurcated digging claws on the forefeet. Their body shape is typical both of animals living in extremely cold climates and those that burrow. They have stocky bodies, blunt, stout skulls, proportionately short limbs and tail, and small eyes. Their small external ears are concealed in the fur. The winter coat is about twice as long as the summer pelage and although it appears white, each hair is dark at the base. In winter, the long white hair and compact body lend the overall impression of an animated, slightly elongate powder puff. In summer, the upperparts vary in color among individuals and with age. In general, adults are reddish to grayish brown, often with a subdued "salt and pepper" appearance, because some of the buffy hairs are black-tipped and some are red-tipped. The sides of the body and cheeks are reddish-orange; sometimes there is a reddish-orange patch behind the ears, and there is usually a reddish band or collar

across the chest. The rest of the belly is reddish to buffy gray. Juveniles and subadults are less red and more uniformly gray-brown. As in most *Dicrostonyx,* Richardson's have a thin black stripe on the back from the tip of the nose to the base of the tail. This stripe is most pronounced in young animals and often is obscured in adults. The lemmings are well camouflaged in winter on snow and in summer against the mottled dull background of the tundra. Adults replace their pelage twice a year, once in spring and once in the fall. In spring, the molt begins on the head and progresses evenly towards the back and belly. In fall, the pattern is reversed, the molt starting on the belly and progressing towards the mid-back and head.

Richardson's collared lemmings are active 24 hours a day. In summer there is a slight lull between 12 p.m. and 6 a.m., when many of their principle predators (short-eared owls, snowy owls, arctic foxes, and weasels) are about. Rough-legged hawks and parasitic jaegers, which are diurnal, also take large numbers of lemmings. *D. richardsoni* is more active in summer than in winter, and most of its active time is spent feeding or moving between burrows. Levels of activity are similar between the sexes, but males make more longer-distance movements and have much larger home ranges than do females. In summer, the lemmings occupy relatively simple burrows that are less than 1 meter in length. These have one or two entrances. The animals use several burrows within their home ranges to rest or escape from predators. Females with young utilize 8–10 burrows or refuges in their home range, and males may have as many as 40. Burrows often are dug down to the level of the permafrost and thus are cool regardless of the outside temperature. Richardson's collared lemmings will use almost any object as a shelter, including boards, cardboard, metal lids, discarded oil barrels, and rocks. Collared lemmings have excellent vision and take refuge whenever they see a potential predator (such as a person) approaching; one of the best ways to see a lemming is to flip over a discarded board or other object lying on tundra. Pregnant females usually renovate one home burrow into a nest in which they raise their young. These maternal burrows are relatively elaborate in that they have more than one entrance and often have side chambers, one for a nest and another for a latrine area. The globular nests are constructed of grasses, lichens, and dead leaves. In winter the lemmings may initially occupy the same burrows as in summer, but will eventually abandon them for snow tunnels, where they build winter nests. These winter nests can be found scattered across the tundra surface in spring and are a sure sign of the presence of lemmings.

Richardson's collared lemmings eat a variety of vegetation, including the green parts of plants, berries, flowers, succulent roots, and occasionally bark of willow. In general they prefer herbs and shrubs over grasses or sedges and choose flowering shoots of herbs and leaves of shrubs when available. Some preferred foods include willow (*Salix*), arctic avens (*Dryas integrifolia*), blueberry (*Vaccinium uliginosum*), bearberry (*Arctostaphylos*), flowers of a variety of other herbs, and grasses. Collared lemmings will drink free water, although the young have to learn how to drink and swallow without choking.

Dicrostonyx richardsoni can breed throughout the year, although fall and winter breeding may not occur in all years and are most common during increase phases of population cycles. During population increases nearly all mature females are pregnant throughout the summer months: they enter estrus and mate usually within 24 hours after the birth of each litter. Litter size ranges from 1 to 8 with a mean of 3 to 4. In captivity, one pair produced 17 litters in quick succession, although this record of fecundity is probably seldom matched in the wild. The gestation period averages 20 to 21 days. In captivity both sexes participate in care of the young, but in the wild there is no evidence that males provide any assistance and adults are usually solitary. The young are born tiny, blind, and helpless, but grow and mature rapidly. They weigh only 4 grams, on average, at birth, but grow to about 50 grams within 60 days.

Dicrostonyx richardsoni

Newborns are naked except for short bristles on the face, and are dark on the back and pink underneath. At birth the teeth have not erupted and the eyes and ears are closed, although the young vocalize almost immediately, making shrill, high-pitched cries. The skin becomes progressively darker until the fourth day, when hairs appear on the head and neck; the pups are nearly covered in guard hairs by day 8 and the complete first coat is in place by day 15. The young begin to molt to a second, subadult pelage between days 26 to 30; it is completed 7 to 14 days later. The incisors erupt between days 4 and 5, the ears open between days 9 and 10 (functional on day 11), and the eyes open on day 12. Young born during the winter develop bifid foreclaws by day 25. Unlike most arvicoline rodents, winter-born individuals grow faster and achieve a larger body size (length and mass) than do those born in summer. Females leave the young between 16 to 22 days after birth, effectively weaning them, and move to a new home burrow within their home range, where they soon give birth to another litter. Males and females usually reach reproductive maturity at about 3 months of age; however, females can potentially breed at a very young age, perhaps as early as 25 to 30 days. In captivity, Richardson's collared lemmings can live to be more than 2 years old, but in the wild they seldom live beyond 7 months.

Adult *D. richardsoni* are usually solitary except for brief periods at mating. Females are territorial, occupy relatively small home ranges (0.06 to 0.56 hectares, smallest for lactating females) and raise litters in a burrow located at the periphery of their home range. Males are nonterritorial, polygynous, and occupy relatively large home ranges encompassing the home burrows of several females. Home ranges of males are smaller (0.2 to 0.6 hectares) at high population densities and may be more than 10 times as large at low densities. Males regularly visit all the females in their home range and are driven off, often violently, by all except females in estrus. Males spend most of their time feeding and searching for receptive females, and in this quest often move long distances in short periods, especially at low population densities: in one study, an industrious male moved over 3 kilometers in a 24 hour period on several occasions. Both males and females may practice infanticide, entering the home burrows and killing the offspring of other individuals. This phenomenon is probably most common at high population densities.

Collared lemmings are renowned for their fluctuations in population size. Over a 3-year period at Churchill, Manitoba, *D. richardsoni* varied in density from 25 adults per hectare in peak populations to approximately one individual per 15 hectares in a low year, a more than 300-fold decrease. Peak densities of over 40 individuals per hectare have been reported in other years. At Churchill, peaks usually occur every 3rd or 4th summer, followed by sharp declines during late fall and winter. Changes in abundance are localized and not coincident across localities. They do not appear to result from different weather conditions, food availability, or predator abundance, although high densities of predators may accentuate declines or perpetuate lows. Density-dependent differences in age structure, reproductive success, and rate of recruitment of young have been implicated as factors influencing cycles, including increases in rates of infanticide at high densities.

As is true of most *Dicrostonyx,* Richardson's collared lemmings have an unusual sex-determining mechanism. Some females are XY (the usual sex chromosome complement of males) and others have two X chromosomes (XX), as is typical of female mammals. Males are always XY, as expected. In the laboratory, this leads to an excess of female progeny. In the field, however, trapping records usually indicate a 50:50 ratio of males to females or even an excess of males. Whether these records of sex ratios in the wild are accurate or are the result of relatively greater mobility and trappability of males is unknown. Collared lemmings are the only group of North American mammals with this odd system of sex determination.

The taxonomic status of *D. richardsoni* is unsettled. In 1948, Thomas H. Manning demonstrated that Richardson's and the northern collared lemming approached one another very closely geographically in the western Hudson Bay region, near Baker Lake and Chesterfield Inlet, with no evidence of hybridization or intergradation. We have taken specimens of both genetic stocks at Baker Lake (although *D. groenlandicus* is by far the more common there). In 1983, Grace W. Scott and Kenneth C. Fisher found that accidental crossing of the two stocks led to the demise of their captive colony, leading them to suggest that hybrids between *D. groenlandicus* and *D. richardsoni* were sterile. Later (1993), we demonstrated that substantial genetic differences, including conformation of sex chromosomes, existed between the two species. Our subsequent studies have confirmed this pattern and suggest that *D. richardsoni, D. groenlandicus,* and *D. hudsonius* are about equally divergent from one another and represent the major evolutionary lineages of North American collared lemmings. Thus, in this account, we recognize Richardson's collared lemming as a distinct species. *Dicrostonyx richardsoni* presumably was named in honor of Sir John Richardson, the famed physician and naturalist who accompanied Sir John Franklin on two early Arctic expeditions and who described the Alaskan subspecies *D. groenlandicus rubricatus.* M. D. Engstrom

Size
No significant sexual dimorphism
Total length: 115–150 (130) mm
Length of tail: 9–15 (12) mm
Weight: 35–90 (55) g

Identification
Dicrostonyx richardsoni is similar to the other North American species of collared lemmings, *D. groenlandicus* and *D. hudsonius,* and can be distinguished from them mainly by differences in color of summer pelage, pattern of cusps on the molar teeth, and conformation of chromosomes. Richardson's collared lemming abuts the range of *D. groenlandicus* near the west-central margin of Hudson Bay, but is isolated from *D. hudsonius.* In summer, adult *D. richardsoni* are dark reddish-brown above, with buff on the sides and a subdued mix of reddish hairs on the face and back. In contrast, the summer pelage of *D. groenlandicus* is usually more steel gray, with a mix of contrasting red, orange, and white highlights on the sides, back, and behind the ears. The summer pelage of *D. hudsonius* is a more uniform brownish-gray, with a subdued pale buff band on the sides. The molar teeth of *D. hudsonius* are relatively simple. Those of *D. groenlandicus* are more complex, with a well-developed extra fold of enamel on the inner rear edge of the molars (easiest to see on the upper teeth). Individuals of *D. richardsoni* are variable in this characteristic, some displaying a small extra fold on one or more molars and others having a simple pattern reminiscent of *D. hudsonius.* This feature is seldom as well developed in *D. richardsoni* as it is in *D. groenlandicus,* however, and Richardson's is more similar to *D. hudsonius* in this regard. The three species also differ in the appearance and conformation of the sex chromosomes.

Recent Synonyms
Dicrostonyx groenlandicus richardsoni
Dicrostonyx torquatus richardsoni

Other Common Names
Richardson's varying lemming, Richardson's hoofed lemming

Status
Common, localized

References
Engstrom et al., 1993; Manning, 1948; Scott and Fisher, 1983; Stenseth and Ims, 1993

There are 15 genera and 51 species in this family worldwide, and only 2 genera and 4 species in North America. Most of the Old World species are desert-dwellers known as jerboas. The North American representatives all are small, long-tailed mice mainly restricted to montane or woodland habitats. Although they move about on all four legs, they are also capable of hopping up to 3 m at a single bound when alarmed. Frequently found in riparian areas, they are also adept in the water, and can dive and swim to escape predators.

Jumping mice eat a variety of vegetative material, and also take insects. Living in northern climates, they spend much of the winter in hibernation, and this requires considerable fat stores. They may feed heavily on insects when they first come out of hibernation in the spring, when insect populations are also burgeoning. Long winters in hibernation take a heavy toll on local populations, with only about a third of the individuals surviving through the winter.

These mice produce one or two litters per year in grassy nests that sometimes are placed in bushes or trees. The young must develop and gain weight rapidly in order to be ready to enter hibernation in the fall. Local populations vary considerably in density from year to year, depending on food availability.

References
Krutzsch, 1954; Wrigley, 1972

North American Genera
Napaeozapus
Zapus

Woodland jumping mouse | *Napaeozapus insignis*

The meadow jumping mouse, *Zapus hudsonius,* may enter woods, especially in the absence of *Napaeozapus,* but the woodland jumping mouse almost never occurs in open areas. The two species may occur together where herbaceous ground cover is abundant along a stream leading into woods. *Napaeozapus* is nocturnal. It is more colorful than *Zapus* and often takes long jumps, up to 4 meters (12 feet). It makes no runways, but may use those of other species.

Like *Zapus,* the woodland jumping mouse hibernates about half the year, putting on about seven or eight grams of fat prior to hibernation and losing it during hibernation.

Napaeozapus feeds heavily on *Endogone* and related genera of fungi, this food comprising about a third of its diet. Butterfly larvae, beetles, and fruit (especially blackberries) comprise smaller amounts of the diet. Seeds of *Impatiens* are particularly important, and the bright, turquoise-blue color of the plant's endosperms can sometimes be seen through the mouse's stomach wall.

The gestation period is thought to be about 29 days, very long considering that the gestation of *Zapus* is about 18 days. Litters of three to six young are produced in late June or early July. At birth the young weigh about 0.9 grams. Their eyes open at about the 26th day, and they are weaned at about one month. *J. O. Whitaker, Jr.*

Napaeozapus insignis

Size

No significant sexual dimorphism
Total length: 210–255 (233) mm
Length of tail: 126–158 (141) mm
Weight: 14–31 g

Identification

Like the meadow jumping mouse *(Zapus hudsonius),* the woodland jumping mouse has huge hind feet and a very long tail. It is redder in color than the yellowish meadow jumping mouse, and the tip of the tail is white. The small premolar is absent; there are only three molariform teeth on each side of the upper jaw.

Recent Synonyms

Napaeozapus algonquinensis
Napaeozapus gaspensis

Status

Relatively uncommon over much of its range

Subspecies

Napaeozapus insignis abietorum, much of Ontario and Quebec

Napaeozapus insignis frutectanus, Michigan to southeastern Manitoba
Napaeozapus insignis insignis, New York and southern Ontario to New Brunswick and the Gaspe Peninsula
Napaeozapus insignis roanensis, through the Appalachian Mountains
Napaeozapus insignis saguenayensis, northeastern Quebec through Newfoundland

References

Mammalian Species 14; Wrigley, 1972

Meadow jumping mouse | *Zapus hudsonius*

Grassy or weedy fields are the domain of the meadow jumping mouse. These animals also may occur in woods. They are especially abundant in stands of *Impatiens.* Where meadow and woodland jumping mice occur together, meadow jumping mice seldom enter the woods, although both may occur where thick vegetation is found along a creek or at the edge of a woods.

Jumping mice are primarily nocturnal. They use runways of other species such as *Microtus,* but make no runways of their own. When frightened, they usually skulk away under the grass or make off by a progression of short leaps. Maximum

jumps are about a meter, in contrast to the much longer leaps of the woodland jumping mouse.

Meadow jumping mice feed on a variety of seeds, fruits, invertebrates, and fungi. Invertebrates such as beetles and cutworms are heavily eaten in spring before seeds begin to ripen, and then a progression of seeds is eaten as plants mature over most of the active season. The mice obtain the heads of certain grasses such as timothy by reaching as high as they can, cutting the stalk off, pulling it down to the ground and then cutting again, until the rachis is reached. The rachis and glumes are eaten and the excess parts are dropped onto a pile of match-stick-

Zapus hudsonius

length pieces of stem. These foods are supplemented by fruits, especially strawberries and blackberries, as they become available. Also, subterranean fungi, *Endogone* and its relatives, are dug up and eaten, especially later in the season. Fungi form about 12 to 15 percent of the diet of meadow jumping mice. The mice apparently find it by smell.

Meadow jumping mice sleep about half of the year, entering hibernation in late September and October and emerging in late April or early May. To survive hibernation, an individual must accumulate about six grams of fat, which is the amount burned during hibernation.

Males emerge first from hibernation, and mating takes place soon after the females' emergence. A litter contains three to six young and is born after an 18-day gestation. There are three peaks of breeding, one in May or June, another in July, and the third in August or early September. Individuals breeding in July are probably young born late in the previous year. Apparently only a few of the individuals from late litters become large enough to accumulate enough fat to survive hibernation. The remainder perish. *J. O. Whitaker, Jr.*

Size

No significant sexual dimorphism
Total length: 180–234 (202) mm
Length of tail: 101–137 (118) mm
Weight: 12–30 g

Identification

The meadow jumping mouse is a small mouse with very large hind feet and a very long tail. It is distinguished from the woodland jumping mouse (*Napaeozapus insignis*) by its lack of a white tip on the tail, and by its having four molariform teeth, including the small anterior premolars. The upper incisors are heavily grooved. The other two species of meadow jumping mice are very similar, although slightly larger. They occur in western North America.

Recent Synonyms

Zapus australis
Zapus brevipes

Zapus hardyi
Zapus labradorius
Zapus luteus
Zapus microcephalus
Zapus ontarioensis
Zapus rafinesquei

Other Common Names

Hudson Bay jumping mouse, kangaroo mouse

Status

Common in proper habitat in much of its range

Subspecies

Zapus hudsonius acadicus, New York to Nova Scotia and New Brunswick
Zapus hudsonius alascensis, Alaska
Zapus hudsonius americanus, much of the eastern United States as far west as eastern Indiana
Zapus hudsonius campestris, Montana, Wyoming, and western South Dakota

Zapus hudsonius canadensis, Ontario and Quebec
Zapus hudsonius hudsonius, much of southern Canada
Zapus hudsonius intermedius, western Tennessee to North Dakota
Zapus hudsonius ladas, eastern Quebec and Newfoundland
Zapus hudsonius pallidus, Kansas, Nebraska, and Missouri
Zapus hudsonius preblei, southwestern Wyoming and north-central Colorado
Zapus hudsonius tenellus, southern British Columbia

References

Mammalian Species 11; Quimby, 1951; Whitaker, 1963

Western jumping mouse | *Zapus princeps*

Western jumping mice are distributed in the Rocky Mountains from the Yukon south into Arizona and New Mexico, westward through eastern Oregon, and through the Cascade and Sierra Nevada mountains of California. Their range extends eastward in the northern Great Plains to eastern North and South Dakota. They occur from high mountain meadows to riparian streamsides and marshes, and are commonly associated with streams and areas where moist soils support heavy vegetative communities rich in forbs, herbs, and grasses.

Zapus princeps commonly co-occurs with several other small mammals, especially *Peromyscus, Microtus,* and *Thomomys* species in meadow and streamside communities. In co-occurance with *Peromyscus maniculatus* in subalpine meadows, *Zapus princeps* excludes this species during its 90-day active season, but *Peromyscus* recolonizes the habitat after *Zapus* disappears into hibernation in the fall.

Population densities vary considerably by habitat type. Dry, low-elevation grass-dominated habitats have very low densities (3 per hectare). Sub-alpine meadow densities vary from 20–40 per hectare, with highest densities correlated with increased proportions of forbs rather than grasses. Home ranges vary with environmental quality from 0.19–0.61 hectares, and are linear along watercourses and habitat boundaries, but become elliptical away from natural margins. Males have home ranges larger than those of females only during the breeding season.

Reproduction is restricted to the short active season, and only one litter (range 2–8; mean 5) is produced, after an 18-day gestation period. The young nurse for 30 days and at weaning have only 45 days to reach hibernation mass. Juveniles are recognizable as a distinct age class following hibernation, and only then reach adult size. Although adults have very low mortality over winter, juvenile mortality exceeds 50 percent of those who entered hibernation.

Diets vary by season and resource availability. After emergence from hibernation, fungi, arthropods, and insects predominate, but as seeds become available they dominate in the diet. In the weeks preceding hibernation, forb and grass seeds comprise 90 percent of the diet and account for the fat deposited prior to hibernation. Western jumping mice gain .65 to 2.1 grams per day during this period, and by the onset of hibernation, an individual's body mass has increased from about 22 to 35 grams. Fat deposits are utilized during hibernation,

Zapus princeps

which averages 280 days, at a mean rate of 0.06 grams per day. Hibernacula are located at a mean depth of 59 cm. Each has a nest chamber 14 cm in diameter, and the average hibernaculum temperature is 4.6° C over the hibernation season.

Fossils of forms presumed to be ancestral to *Zapus princeps* are known from the Upper Pliocene into the Pleistocene of Kansas and Oklahoma. *J. A. Cranford*

Size
No significant sexual dimorphism
Total length: 216–247 (231) mm
Tail length: 129–148 (138) mm
Weight: 18–24 g (prior to hibernation,
    up to 35 g)

Identification
Zapus princeps often has a lateral line of pale yellowish-buff, and it has a more grizzled dorsal pelage than *Z. hudsonius.* It is also larger, its tail is less distinctly bicolored, and its ears have a border of whitish hairs. *Zapus trinotatus* is strongly tricolored: its dorsum is brown to cinnamon-brown, its sides are orange-brown and its ventrum is white. The closely related genus *Napeozapus* can be distinguished by its white tail tip (12–35 mm), which is lacking in all *Zapus* species.

Recent Synonyms
Zapus alleni
Zapus major
Zapus nevadensis

Status
Common within its range; densities are highly variable from year to year and by microhabitat type.

Subspecies
Zapus princeps chrysogenys, La Sal Mountains, Utah
Zapus princeps cinereus, south-central Idaho and northwestern Utah
Zapus princeps curtatus, northwestern Nevada
Zapus princeps idahoensis, southwestern Alberta, western Montana, central Wyoming, central Idaho, east-central Washington, and southeastern British Columbia
Zapus princeps kootenayensis, southwestern British Columbia, northern Idaho, and northeastern Washington
Zapus princeps luteus, mountains of central New Mexico and eastern Arizona
Zapus princeps minor, southeastern Alberta, southern Saskatchewan, southwestern Manitoba, North Dakota, northeastern South Dakota, and northeastern Montana
Zapus princeps oregonus, southeastern Washington, Oregon east of Cascade Mountains, southwestern Idaho, and northeastern Nevada
Zapus princeps pacificus, southwestern Oregon south through Sierra Nevada of California
Zapus princeps princeps, eastern Wyoming through Colorado to northern New Mexico
Zapus princeps saltator, Yukon, British Columbia, and southeastern Alaska
Zapus princeps utahensis, western Wyoming, central Utah, and southeastern Idaho

References
Cranford, 1978, 1983; Ingles, 1965; Jones et al., 1985; Krutzsch, 1954

Pacific jumping mouse | *Zapus trinotatus*

If you spot a small mammal bounding through tall grass in a mountain meadow full of yellow skunk cabbage along the northwestern coast of the United States, chances are it's a jumping mouse. Some biologists describe Pacific jumping mice as "nervous" and "high-strung." Their locomotion is erratic and evasive. They bound by pushing off with both hind feet and landing on both forefeet. Pacific jumping mice have long hind legs and hind feet similar to those of kangaroo rats *(Dipodomys)*. The tail apparently aids in balance when leaping: a mouse whose tail was accidentally severed turned somersaults when it attempted to leap and could not land properly.

Pacific jumping mice, like the woodland jumping mouse *(Napeozapus insignis)* and the other two species in the genus *Zapus,* are colorful. *Zapus trinotatus* has a distinct orange-yellow band on each side, the back is rusty to dark brown, and the belly is white with a yellowish wash. In adult mice the molt starts on the nose and between the shoulder blades and progresses from these areas down to the rump.

Zapus trinotatus occupies a geographic range that extends from the Frazer River in southwestern British Columbia southward along the humid coastal strip through western Washington, Oregon, and California to Point Reyes and Elk Valley, Marin County, California.

Males become sexually active in May or June and remain so through September. Females are receptive beginning in May. Usually one litter of four to eight pups is born each year, in July or August. Gestation is from 18 to 23 days. The pups are born hairless and weighing about 0.5 g; their eyes are closed and their ears are folded. The young become independent at about one month of age.

Pacific jumping mice are found chiefly in riparian and wet meadow habitats within redwood, fir, and spruce forests west

of the crest of the Cascade-Sierra Nevada Mountains. Near the coast, they inhabit alder-salmonberry *(Alnus-Rubus spectabilis),* riparian alder *(Alnus),* and wet meadow skunk cabbage *(Veratrum)* communities in redwood *(Sequoia sempervirens)* and Douglas fir *(Pseudotsuga menziesii)* forests. To a lesser extent, they are found in lodgepole pine-salal *(Pinus contorta-Gaultheria shallon),* Sitka spruce-salal *(Picea sitchensis),* headland prairie, and headland scrub communities. Nearer the Cascade-Sierra crest, Pacific jumping mice occur in dense forests, alpine meadows, and wet-grassy areas of the Olympic Peninsula and Cascade Mountains of Washington. In the central portion of its range, the Pacific jumping mouse is found in riparian-deciduous montane woodlands, wet meadows where the ground is peaty, and brushy successional stages of redwood, Douglas fir, and mixed coniferous forests. In the southern portion of the range, Pacific jumping mice are again found in the loose, humus-filled, dark-soil meadows of the redwood biome, in areas where rushes *(Juncus),* sedges *(Carex),* bracken fern *(Pteris aquilinia),* sword fern *(Polystichum munitum),* and other grasses and herbaceous plants occur. Pacific jumping mice become more numerous when rainfall exceeds 30 cm annually in an area, especially in riparian habitats.

Barn owls *(Tyto alba),* great-horned owls *(Bubo virginianus),* and other nocturnal and crepuscular raptors are predators of the Pacific jumping mouse. Other predators include bobcats, snakes, martens, minks, weasels, skunks, red and gray foxes, and coyotes.

Pacific jumping mice systematically cut sections of grass stalks to get at the seed-rich heads, leaving characteristically neat piles of stem cuttings. Grass seeds comprise more than 50 percent, and fungi make up about 10 percent, of their diet. They are adept at finding, selecting, and consuming fungi (mostly hypogeous Phycomycetes). Pacific jumping mice also eat fruit, insects, and even mollusks and small fish opportunistically.

Pacific jumping mice are associated with other mammals, in particular voles *(Microtus oregoni, M. longicaudus, M. richardsoni,* and *Clethrionomys californicus),* moles and shrews *(Scapanus orarius, Sorex vagrans,* and *S. trowbridgii),* deer mice *(Peromyscus maniculatus),* shrew-moles *(Neurotrichus gibbsii),* chipmunks *(Tamias townsendii, T. siskiyou,* and *T. senex),* and mountain beavers *(Aplodontia rufa).* Often, Pacific jumping mice can be found in the runways of shrew-moles and mountain beavers; the mice are not known to make their own runways or burrows. Parasites associated with Pacific jumping mice include coccidia, protozoans, fleas, mites (of several orders), and ticks.

Pacific jumping mice are crepuscular and nocturnal. When eating they seize food with the forepaws and sit on their haunches to nibble at it. They squeak and "drum" their tails when fighting. Escape behavior has been described as a sudden, nearly vertical leap of up to 180 cm followed by a dive into dense brush. They also may hop away in erratic bounds.

Zapus trinotatus

Although some of their nests have been found in trees, Pacific jumping mice prefer to nest and hibernate below ground level in abandoned burrows; nests have been found from 30 to 76 cm below the surface and as close as 10 cm to another nest. Some of these nests have interconnecting burrows, suggesting that the mice may hibernate in groups. The mice gain considerable fat during fall in preparation for hibernation. Hibernation can last as long as six months, but it may be shorter in duration depending on the ambient temperature. The mice become active again at environmental temperatures above –6° C. *W. L. Gannon*

Size

Total length: 211–250 mm
Length of tail: 112–155 mm
Weight: 20–30 g

Identification

Pacific jumping mice are small dipodid rodents clearly adapted for jumping, with hind legs and hind feet enlarged relative to small forefeet and a very long, sparsely haired tail. The upper incisors are grooved; the pelage is strikingly tricolored, with the back dark brown, sides orange-yellow, and underside white tinged with yellow. There is a distinct line of buffy hairs between the sides and the belly.

Other Common Names

Point Reyes jumping mouse, coast jumping mouse

Status

Limited geographically; abundant in some years, rare in others

Subspecies

Zapus trinotatus eureka, Sonoma County to the Klamath River in northern California
Zapus trinotatus montanus, central Oregon
Zapus trinotatus orarius, Marin County, California
Zapus trinotatus trinotatus, coastal areas of western Oregon, Washington, and British Columbia

References

Mammalian Species 315; Bailey, 1936; Krutzsch, 1954

Family Erethizontidae

This largely South American family has 4 genera and 12 species, but only one reaches northward into the United States. The North American porcupine is mainly restricted to wooded habitats, and is particularly fond of feeding on the cambium layer of coniferous trees in the west. Second only to the beaver in size among North American rodents, porcupines are made even more formidable by their outer covering of spines.

Porcupines are at home on the ground, climbing in trees and shrubs, and even swimming in the water, where their quills provide extra buoyancy. They den in burrows in the ground and in hollow trees, and sometimes in natural caves and hollows. They tend to be solitary, getting together only for breeding. After a lengthy gestation period for a rodent, a single young is produced. The young are precocial, and able to survive on their own after a couple of weeks, although normally the mother may nurse them for somewhat longer.

References
Costello, 1966; Woods, 1993

North American Genera
Erethizon

North American porcupine | *Erethizon dorsatum*

A slow-moving rodent with poor eyesight, the North American porcupine has a surprisingly broad distribution, from the conifer forests of eastern Canada and New England to the upper Great Plains and northward to Alaska. It occurs in a variety of habitats from heavy forest to open tundra, desert chaparral, and even rangelands. It is found from sea level to high mountain areas in the Rockies and Alaska. Porcupines are not good at dispersing overwater to islands, and are not found on Newfoundland, Anticosti Island, Prince Edward Island, Cape Breton Island, Grand Manon Island, and Campobello Island on the east coast, nor on Vancouver Island or the Queen Charlotte Islands off British Columbia. Extra-limital areas of distribution include the San Bernadino Mountains of southern California (one report, in 1906), northern Mexico, and the south bank of the Tennessee River in southern Tennessee.

Porcupines have very broad food habits. During the winter they feed almost exclusively on the bark, cambium, and phloem of trees, especially conifers such as the eastern hemlock, a favored food source in eastern North America. Other important food trees include the white pine *(Pinus strobus)*, balsam fir *(Abies balsamea)*, sugar maple *(Acer saccharum)*, red maple *(Acer rubrum)*, and beech *(Fagus grandifolia)*, in eastern North America. In the west, porcupines often feed on the western hemlock *(Tsuga heterophylla)*, Douglas fir *(Pseudotsuga menziesii)*, and ponderosa pine *(Pinus ponderosa)*. Lodgepole pine *(P. contorta)*, western white pine *(P. monticola)*, and spruce and fir trees are also eaten. One can often locate porcupines in winter by the presence of severely girdled, shiny white trunks and branches that starkly contrast with tree parts that have not been eaten. There are often piles of fecal pellets in the vicinity, since porcupines usually spend long periods of time in the same tree. Porcupines also consume many shrubs and canes. In the early spring, porcupines change their food habits dramatically, leaving the trees and feeding on the ground. They often feed on new, succulent stems of grasses, sedges, and wildflowers. During the late summer and fall they sometimes consume agricultural crops, especially corn. They also climb into oak trees to feed on acorns. Porcupines lose weight during the winter months and gain rapidly during the summer.

Porcupines can live at least ten years. They are usually solitary, except during the winter months in rocky areas, where they sometimes den communally. Females begin estrus at about one year of age, and males are sexually mature at two and a half years. Estrus normally occurs from September through November; in some areas, breeding may occur as late as January. Heat usually lasts 8–12 hours. Males search for females by olfaction, sniffing the bases of trees, rocks, and other parts of the habitat, and finally lure females to the ground. Courtship is very elaborate and vocal, sometimes including loud, shrill screeches. Even though porcupines are usually quite lethargic and sedentary, during the breeding season males can become very aggressive towards other males, and fights are not uncommon.

The gestation period is 204–215 days, unusually long for rodents in general, but not at all uncommon for porcupines and other rodents in the suborder Hystricognatha. Most births occur in late April and early May, when porcupines are very terrestrial and grasses and forbs are abundant. Almost always there is only one young, which weighs 400–530 grams at birth. Neonates are very precocial, being born with open eyes, erupted teeth, well-developed quills that harden within a few hours of birth, and a complex repertoire of defensive behav-

iors. Newborn porcupines back up towards intruders and raise their tails in a defensive posture. The young are capable of feeding on their own within a week, but usually stay close to their mothers until late summer or fall. Females communicate with their young throughout the summer by low grunts, moans, and whines, and by clicking their teeth. Porcupines seem to be especially sensitive and responsive to low-frequency sounds.

Porcupines do not throw their quills. When cornered, a porcupine erects its quills, lowers its head, and raises its tail. It often backs up towards its attacker and lashes out with its heavy, well-quilled tail, driving quills into the intruder's face and body. This "tail flailing" is apparently part of the common defensive repertoire of porcupines; juveniles often include this behavior in their patterns of "play." The vision of porcupines is extremely poor, but all indications are that they have well-developed senses of hearing and smell.

The population density of porcupines is variable. They appear to go through population cycles, which have been reported to peak every 12 to 20 years. Reported densities vary from 0.77 to 12 per square kilometer. In an Ontario study, densities ranged from 11.8 per square kilometer in 1962 to 0.8 per square kilometer in 1979, with a more or less steady decline in numbers over this 17-year period. Artificially high concentrations may occur in rocky areas that are used as winter denning sites, or near agricultural areas, especially alfalfa pastures in the spring or cornfields in the fall. In the west porcupines can also occur in higher than normal densities in riparian habitats. Home ranges vary by season. Winter ranges are restricted to small areas near den sites, or to forested areas where favored tree species grow. Home ranges are much larger in the spring and summer. One study reported a winter feeding area in New York of 5.4 hectares, but in the summer porcupines may range over an area of 13–14 hectares. During the summer, linear daily

Erethizon dorsatum

tors are coyotes, cougars, bobcats, gray wolves, and the great horned owl. The common raven has also been reported as a predator on porcupines.

Humans are also potential predators, since porcupines often damage buildings and signs, being especially attracted to the glue that bonds layers of plywood, and are notorious for gnawing vehicle tires. They also damage plastic tubes used to gather sap for maple syrup and power lines that carry electricity to ski areas, rural businesses, and farms. The forest industry has reported porcupine damage to seedlings and mature trees; the damage, which can be severe at times, is well-documented. Because of this, it was once common for states to offer a bounty on porcupines, but such widespread control practices are no longer common or warranted. Local control of problem individuals near sugarhouses or timber sites adjacent to denning areas is usually sufficient to reduce damage, and in the East, the management of hemlock trees (by harvesting mature hemlocks and not planting them near rocky areas or winter den sites) in areas where porcupines are a problem can significantly reduce the general damage by encouraging the animals to winter elsewhere.

Porcupines harbor mange mites *(Sarcoptes scabiei)*, lice *(Trichodectes setosus)*, ticks *(Ixodes* and *Dermacentor)*, tapeworms *(Monecocestus)*, and nematodes *(Wellcomia evaginata, Dipetalonema arbuta, Dirofilaria spinosa,* and *Molinema diacantha)*. In some individuals the parasite load can be very heavy. Few diseases have been reported. They do not carry many diseases or parasites that are a threat to humans, although they carry tularemia *(Francisella tularensis)*, and it has been reported that they can transmit the disease to humans via dogs. They also have been reported to carry tick fever via the tick *Dermacentor andersoni* (in Colorado). *C. A. Woods*

movements can be up to 129 meters, and over the course of a month porcupines often travel as far as 1,500 meters. They can shift their home range over distances as large as 8–10 km. They are most active at night, especially between 9 p.m. and 7 a.m., and it is not uncommon to find a porcupine beside a highway.

Because they are large and well quilled, porcupines have few natural enemies. The fisher *(Martes pennanti),* a well-documented predator, is very effective at killing porcupines without being damaged by quills. Fishers are rare in most of the porcupine's range, but they are so effective at controlling porcupines that they have been reintroduced into certain areas, including parts of Vermont, Montana, Michigan, and Wisconsin. Other preda-

Size
Males are heavier than females (but females apparently have longer tails).
Total length: 600–1,300 (772) mm
Length of tail: 175–250 (214) mm
Weight: 3.5–18 kg. Average in New York state: 6.1 kg (males); 5.1 kg (females); in Alberta, Canada: 9.1 kg (males); 8.9 kg (females)

Identification
The North American porcupine is the only mammal in the United States and Canada with quills, and does not overlap in distribution with any other species of porcupine. With its long quills, bulky size, and large head, it is distinct from all other rodents in its range. It can be distinguished from other New World porcupines as follows: from the Mexican porcupine, *Sphiggurus mexicanus,* which can occur as far north as San Luis Potosi in central Mexico, by

its well-developed hallux (opposable first toe). In other New World porcupines the hallux is absent or its function taken over by a broad movable pad. It is larger in mass and has a longer tail than the short-tailed porcupine, *Echinoprocta rufescens,* which is most similar in morphology. Prehensile-tailed porcupines *(Coendou* and *Sphiggurus)* have long, prehensile tails and are much paler in coloration.

Other Common Names
Porc-epic (eastern Canada), hedgehog, quillpig, quiller

Status
Common and widespread

Subspecies
Erethizon dorsatum bruneri, Great Plains east of the Rocky Mountains

Erethizon dorsatum couesi, western Texas, New Mexico, and central Arizona
Erethizon dorsatum dorsatum, Canada east of Yukon and British Columbia (except for Labrador and Newfoundland) and northeastern and north-central United States
Erethizon dorsatum epixanthum, central Washington south into California, Idaho, Nevada, Utah, western Colorado, Wyoming, and western Montana
Erethizon dorsatum myops, most of Alaska and the Yukon Territory
Erethizon dorsatum nigrescens, British Columbia and northern Washington State
Erethizon dorsatum picinum, Labrador

References
Mammalian Species 29; Dodge, 1982; Roze, 1989; Seton, 1953

Order Lagomorpha

There are 80 species in 13 genera of lagomorphs distributed throughout the world. In North America, we have 17 species in 4 genera. The lagomorphs are terrestrial animals native to most major land masses but absent from Australia as natives, and from southern South America, the West Indies, Madagascar, and many islands of the Ethiopian region. They are primarily grazers, but eat a wide variety of food items. When grasses and other forage are scarce, individuals may browse more, taking shrub stems and tree bark.

The 54 species of hares and rabbits (Leporidae), which are native to or have been introduced into most regions of the world, inhabit grasslands, shrublands, and forests as well as tundra and alpine habitats. They are most active at dusk or at night. Rabbits may rest in burrows or in surface nests, which are connected by obvious trails. Hares, in contrast, prefer rock crevices and caves; they run to escape predators. Rabbits are small, solitary to gregarious, and give birth to altricial young. Hares are generally larger, often solitary, and produce precocial young.

The pikas (Ochotonidae) of the Palearctic region and western North America (2 genera, 26 species) inhabit open plains, deserts, steppes, and forests. Many species are found in rock outcrops where they shelter in burrows under the rocks and forage nearby. Pikas are active throughout the day and may be seen sunning themselves on rocks or harvesting hay to provision a winter food supply. These animals do not hibernate during the long and severe winters, but use stored hay as food. Many of the Palearctic and Oriental lagomorphs are gregarious and live in colonies, but the North American species are highly territorial.

References
Chapman and Flux, 1990; Hoffmann, 1993

Black-tailed jackrabbit *(Lepus californicus)*

Family Ochotonidae

There are 26 species in 2 genera of pikas worldwide. Only two species in a single genus occur in North America. They occupy montane meadow and talus slope habitats in western North America.

With their stocky bodies and short legs, pikas resemble large, soft-furred rodents such as South American guinea pigs. They also resemble African hyraxes, but they are in fact not closely related to either rodents or hyraxes. Their closest relatives are rabbits and hares, which they also resemble—they look like junior bunnies.

Behaviorally, pikas have two characteristics that set them apart. They have distinctive whistling vocalizations that are used in courtship, and they spend long hours in harvesting herbs and grasses, which they form into hay piles on the talus slopes they inhabit, providing a food supply during the long winters.

Pikas are active throughout the day, from early morning through evening, especially during cloudy weather. They come out to sun themselves even on very cold days in winter. They do not hibernate, but use their stored food piles to help get them through the times of food shortages. However, they do not gather sufficient food to completely meet their needs, so some foraging must occur all winter long.

North American pikas have complex social systems and well-defined territories. Neighboring territories are usually occupied by members of the opposite sex. These territories are defended against all comers for most of the year. During the breeding season, males extend their territories to include an adjoining female. Subsequently, they retreat to their respective territorities to work on accumulating their haypiles.

References
Smith, 1978; Smith and Ivins, 1984

North American Genera
Ochotona

Collared pika | *Ochotona collaris*

Collared pikas occur in the mountainous regions of central and southern Alaska from west and northwest of Cook Inlet southeast almost to Skagway. There are unverified reports of their occurrence in the Brooks Range of the Alaskan Arctic. In Canada, they are found from the Yukon Arctic south to northwestern British Columbia, and west to near the MacKenzie River in the Northwest Territories. These mammals are usually found above timberline, but may reside at elevations down to near sea level.

Ochotona collaris is diurnal, spending most of the day foraging and gathering food for winter caches. A lesser part of the day may be spent sunning or basking on exposed rocks. Although they inhabit areas with long, harsh winters, these pikas do not hibernate. During the warmer months, they collect grasses, sedges, weeds, leaves, and other vegetation, as well as dried fecal material of other species. These materials are piled into haystacks that are used as food stores over the winter.

The collared pika is a small lagomorph with relatively short legs; the hind limbs are slightly longer than the forelimbs. Its ears are short and round and its tail is inconspicuous. The pelage is long, dense, and soft. The underparts are creamy white; the upperparts are drab, washed with gray or black. A grayish patch about the nape and shoulders forms an indistinct collar. There is a creamy-buff patch of fur above the facial gland on each side of the face.

Reproduction apparently occurs during late spring and summer. Females may produce two litters per year. Two to six helpless, blind, nearly naked young are born following a gestation period of approximately 30 days. The young reach adult size in 40 to 50 days, and females can breed at about one year of age. The diet of adults consists of vegetable matter; most plants common in an area are eaten. In addition, pikas are known to be copraphagic, a common practice among lagomorphs that allows assimilation of nutrients that otherwise would go unutilized.

Ochotona collaris is most abundant in areas of talus slope or broken rock. Its home range usually consists of a rocky area within which the pika seeks shelter and an adjacent meadow

Ochotona collaris

or other patch of vegetation where it forages and gathers. A considerable portion of each individual's home range comprises its territory, which, except during the breeding season, it defends against all other pikas. At the onset of the breeding season, males may expand their territory to include that of one or more females, which may assist in defense of the territory. Collared pikas are very vocal; both sexes emit loud, short, sharp calls. These sounds may function as alarms during territorial defense, as well as signals for sexual recognition during the breeding season.

Collared pikas are agile climbers with keen hearing and acute vision. Other small mammals found in association with them include hoary marmots *(Marmota caligata),* arctic ground squirrels *(Spermophilus parryii),* and northern red-backed voles *(Clethrionomys rutilus).* Their primary predator seems to be the ermine *(Mustela erminea),* but they also are consumed by martens *(Martes americana),* red foxes *(Vulpes vulpes),* and large birds of prey.

A single annual molt occurs in *O. collaris,* whereas *O. princeps,* the only other ochotonid that occurs in North America, molts twice a year. Although the ranges of the two species are separated by an 800-km hiatus that extends through British Columbia and Alberta, Canada, some authors consider these two taxa to be conspecific. *F. D. Yancey, II and C. Jones*

Size

No significant sexual dimorphism
Total length: 178–198 (189) mm
Tail inconspicuous
Weight: 117–145 (129) g

Identification

Ochotona collaris can be distinguished from *O. princeps,* the only other pika in North America, by the presence of an indistinct, grayish "collar," a gray patch on the nape and shoulders. Also, *O. collaris* has a creamy-buff patch of fur on the side of the face over the facial gland; it is rusty brown in *O. princeps.*

Other Common Names

Cony, rock cony, rock rabbit, mouse hare, whistling hare, little chief hare, piping hare

Status

Common, limited

References

Mammalian Species 281; Nowak, 1991

American pika | *Ochotona princeps*

The American pika is distributed discontinuously in mountainous areas throughout western North America. Near the southern limits of its distributional range, American pikas are generally found only at elevations higher than 2,500 meters, although populations occur at lower elevations toward the northern part of its range. Fossil remains dating back as long ago as a half-million years have been found throughout the intermontane region of western North America. At this cooler time the species was more widespread and found at lower elevations.

American pikas are nonhibernating, diurnal animals that occupy talus or piles of broken rock. Pikas are generalized herbivores, and during the summer they can be seen darting off of the talus to forage or gather hay from nearby meadows. The hay is carried back to the talus and stored by individuals to serve as a source of food over winter. The hay is not dried or cured on the talus before storage. Pikas, like most lagomorphs, produce two types of fecal droppings: a hard, brown, round pellet and a soft, black, shiny string of caecal material.

American pikas spend much of their time sitting still, facing upward on the top of sloping rocks, apparently surveying their territory. They are individually territorial, and male and female territories are similar in size. Most individuals live next-door to an animal of the opposite gender. Communication among pikas normally involves characteristic vocalizations and scent-marking. All American pikas give short calls, and normally these are uttered when they are about to leave their territory to forage, upon their return, or as an alarm call when they have sighted a predator. A long-call, actually a song, is performed by males during the breeding season and may have a mating function. Pikas of both genders scent-mark by rubbing a cheek gland on the rocks. The frequency of cheek-rubbing may be elevated during the breeding season or upon the colonization of a vacant territory. Most pika communication is used in many contexts, the most important of which appear to be individual recognition and the establishment and maintenance of territories.

Ochotona princeps

Females first breed as yearlings, and all females of breeding age initiate two sequential litters. Litter size is small (generally three young), and does not vary with female age, habitat productivity, or between first and second litters. Due to energetic constraints, most females are able to raise only one of their two litters to weaning. The timing of reproduction in *O. princeps* is highly seasonal, and first litters are normally conceived when snow still blankets the talus. Gestation lasts 30 days. Young first become independent approximately 30 days following birth and grow rapidly throughout the summer. The most important factor leading to the survival of juveniles is their ability to find and colonize a vacant territory. Because adult *O. princeps* are relatively long-lived (some living up to 6 years of age), vacant territories are not abundant, nor can the time or location of a territory's availability be predicted. Also, juveniles are subject to high rates of aggressive behavior by unfamiliar adults, so they tend to avoid interactions with adults. As a result, most young remain near their site of birth throughout the summer and colonize a nearby vacant territory should one become available.

Potential predators of American pikas include coyotes, martens, longtail weasels, and ermine. Of these, the smaller weasels are the most successful predators, as they can follow pikas into the crevices between the rocks where they live. *A. T. Smith*

Size

No significant sexual dimorphism
Total length: 162–216 mm
No visible tail
Weight: 121–176 g

Identification

This pika's overall body form is typical of all pikas: short-legged, apparently tailless, egg-shaped, and with moderately large, round ears. Its appearance is unlike that of any other small mammal within its range.

Other Common Names

Rocky Mountain pika, southern pika, rock rabbit, piping hare, hay-maker, mouse-hare, whistling hare, cony

Status

Common

Subspecies

Ochotona princeps albata, central California
Ochotona princeps barnesi, central Utah
Ochotona princeps brooksi, southern British Columbia
Ochotona princeps brunnescens, southern British Columbia, Washington, Oregon
Ochotona princeps cinnamomea, central Utah

Ochotona princeps clamosa, southeastern Idaho
Ochotona princeps cuppes, southeastern British Columbia, northeastern Washington, northern Idaho
Ochotona princeps fenisex, southern British Columbia, Washington
Ochotona princeps figginsi, Colorado, southern Wyoming
Ochotona princeps fumosa, central Oregon
Ochotona princeps fuscipes, southwestern Utah
Ochotona princeps goldmani, central Idaho
Ochotona princeps howelli, west-central Idaho
Ochotona princeps incana, southern Colorado, northern New Mexico
Ochotona princeps jewetti, northeastern Oregon
Ochotona princeps lasalensis, east-central Utah
Ochotona princeps lemhi, central Idaho
Ochotona princeps littoralis, southwestern British Columbia
Ochotona princeps lutenscens, southwestern Alberta
Ochotona princeps moorei, central Utah
Ochotona princeps muiri, central California, west-central Nevada
Ochotona princeps nevadensis, northeastern Nevada
Ochotona princeps nigrescens, southern Colorado, northern New Mexico

Ochotona princeps obscura, north-central Wyoming
Ochotona princeps princeps, southeastern British Columbia, southwestern Alberta, northern Idaho, western Montana
Ochotona princeps saturata, central British Columbia
Ochotona princeps saxatilis, Colorado, southern Wyoming
Ochotona princeps schisticeps, northeastern California, northwestern Nevada
Ochotona princeps septentrionalis, central British Columbia
Ochotona princeps sheltoni, east-central California, west-central Nevada
Ochotona princeps taylori, southern Oregon, northern California
Ochotona princeps tutelata, central Nevada
Ochotona princeps uinta, northern Utah
Ochotona princeps utahensis, south-central Utah
Ochotona princeps ventorum, south-central Montana, western Wyoming, east-central Idaho
Ochotona princeps wasatchensis, central Utah

References

Mammalian Species 352; A. T. Smith, 1978; Smith and Ivins, 1984

Family Leporidae

There are 15 genera and 54 species of rabbits and hares in the world. Fifteen species in three genera make up the North American complement. These animals are all well adapted for foraging in open habitats. They have large ears and well-developed senses of hearing to detect predators, and all are capable of instant flight and considerable speed to escape their enemies.

These animals occupy a wide variety of habitats, from arid southwestern deserts to snow-covered boreal forests. Most are nocturnal or crepuscular, and they have large eyes to increase visual acuity in dim light. All are strictly vegetarian, feeding on a variety of grasses and forbs.

There seems to be a correlation between latitude and litter size, in that northern forms frequently have larger litter sizes than do southern ones. This is correlated with a shorter gestation length in the north as well. Both adaptations take advantage of a short growing season, coupled with abundant food resources, to produce the maximum number of young in the shortest possible time.

Most species are solitary, although frequently individuals congregate on particularly productive feeding grounds. Vocalizations are limited to shrill alarm cries given when the animal is captured, although many use enlarged hind feet to drum on the ground as another means of giving an alarm signal.

With soft, pliable fur and enough meat on their bones to make a good meal, rabbits and hares have long been used by humans. Leporids can also be pests in agricultural areas, resulting in various attempts at control programs. Many species have been moved around and introduced into various areas, complicating the process of determining evolutionary relationships in some cases. These introduced populations often also result in the biggest pest problems.

References
Chapman and Flux, 1990

North American Genera
Brachylagus
Sylvilagus
Lepus

Pygmy rabbit | *Brachylagus idahoensis*

Pygmy rabbits are found in close association with tall, dense stands of big sagebrush *(Artemesia tridentata)* on plains, alluvial fans, riparian gullies, and in fenced right-of-ways along roads. Pgymy rabbits are dietary and habitat specialists, and this habitat type dictates their elevational as well as their spatial distribution. In the big sagebrush habitat type, the pygmy rabbit must be considered a keystone species for the following reasons: first, it does not flourish in habitats dominated by other vegetative species; second, it exhibits unique fossorial behavior, and its extensive burrow systems are utilized by invertebrates and other vertebrates within the habitat type; and third, it offers terrestrial and avian predators a dependable food supply.

The pygmy rabbit's range once included most of the Great Basin and adjacent appropriate habitat in the intermountain areas of the western United States, but many historic populations of pygmy rabbits have disappeared. Fire has had a devastating effect on mature stands of big sagebrush and thus on the pygmy rabbit. Massive rangeland improvement projects have replaced big sagebrush with exotic bunch grasses. Robust stands of big sagebrush have been, and continue to be, lost to

Brachylagus idahoensis

agriculture or metropolitan development. There has been some rather recent range expansion by the pygmy rabbit into northeastern and southeastern Utah and southwestern Wyoming, and an isolated population occurs in southeastern Washington.

Pygmy rabbits are most active at dawn and dusk, but can often be observed feeding at other times of the day, even within the upper canopy of sagebrush. In summer the rabbits often rest outside the burrow or retreat to its cool recesses. In winter, individuals are often observed sunning themselves in the late morning and early evening next to a burrow in the snow. When the snow is so deep that it covers the sagebrush, pygmy rabbits may construct extensive burrows within the snow pack that give them access to the sagebrush canopy. They may even cease to have a burrow entrance at the snow surface. Predators such as the coyote *(Canis latrans)* and red fox *(Vulpes vulpes)* attempt to capture pygmy rabbits by breaking into snow tunnels. Weasels *(Mustela)* readily enter their burrow systems at all times of the year and thus are important predators. This rabbit also serves as an important prey base for many species of diurnal and nocturnal birds of prey. When pygmys are disturbed by a potential predator, they emit an alarm call—a buzzing, one-to seven-syllable squeal—as they scurry for the den entrance or even from within the burrow.

Pygmy rabbits have one molt per year. The new pelage in autumn is very long, silky, and gray on the upper body and white, often tinged with buff, on the abdomen. By mid-winter the fur is worn, but still silver-gray. By spring and summer darker gray dominates. The small size and scurrying movements of pygmy rabbits often make observers think they are young cottontail rabbits.

Pregnant females have been observed from late February through late May. The gestation period has not been documented, but is probably 27 to 30 days. An average of six young are born per litter and a female may have as many as three litters per year. Young-of-the-year do not breed, but both sexes are fertile the next breeding season. The sex ratio at birth is 1:1. Juvenile mortality is highest in the first five weeks of life. Mortality of adults is highest in late winter and early spring, with a maximum estimated annual mortality of 88 percent. Although pygmy rabbits are unique among North American leporids in their construction of burrows, no nesting chambers have been found in the few burrows excavated. This leads to speculation that the female pygmy rabbit may make a nest similar to those used by cottontail rabbits *(Sylvilagus)*, a shallow hole at the ground surface that is lined with vegetation as well as hair plucked from her underside, give birth to altricial young in this nest, and crouch over the nest to nurse them.

The pygmy rabbit is sympatric with several other leporids, including the brush rabbit *(Sylvilagus bachmani)*, the mountain cottontail *(S. nuttallii)*, the desert cottontail *(S. audubonii)*, the snowshoe rabbit *(Lepus americanus)*, the white-tailed jackrabbit *(L. townsendii)*, and the black-tailed jackrabbit *(L. californicus)*. Pygmy rabbits have many of the same diseases and internal parasites as these cottontails and hares, but are not known to exhibit the population cycles documented for the other species. Pygmy rabbits may occur in densities of only 0.7 rabbits per hectare or in colonies of up to 45 per hectare. The fact that pygmy rabbits readily give alarm calls signifies a degree of socialization not known for other North American leporids. This social system has yet to be fully described.

Wild-caught pygmy rabbits have been known to live in captivity for longer than two years with only periodic access to big sagebrush as a food source. They are, however, considered fragile in captivity, and are subject to dramatic loss in body weight followed by unexplained death. Continued habitat fragmentation and loss signal extreme concern for the future of the pygmy rabbit. *J. T. Flinders*

Size

Females are often slightly larger than males.

Total length: 252–285 (275) mm (males); 230–305 (283) mm (females)

Length of tail: 15–20 (17) mm (males); 15–24 (18) mm (females)

Weight: 373–435 (411) g (males); 415–458 (432) g (females)

Identification

B. idahoensis is smaller than all other North American leporids. It can be distinguished from other cottontail rabbits sharing its range by its small, inconspicuous tail with buff, rather than white, underside; its very short, rounded ears, which are densely haired inside and out; its short hind legs and resultant scurrying, rather than leaping, gait; its one- to seven-syllable alarm call; its unique construction of simple to extensive burrow systems in soil and snow; and its probable obligate association with sagebrush *(Artemesia)*.

Recent Synonyms

Sylvilagus idahoensis

Status

Locally abundant, but most populations decreasing due to habitat fragmentation and destruction

References

Mammalian Species 125; Green and Flinders, 1980

Swamp rabbit | *Sylvilagus aquaticus*

The swamp rabbit is found in marshy lowlands along the Gulf Coast from South Carolina to Texas, and occurs north into Oklahoma, Kansas, Missouri, Illinois, Indiana, and Tennessee.

Unlike most cottontails, the swamp rabbit is territorial. The male is vocal in protecting his territory, and practices "chinning"—marking his territory with pheromones from a gland on his chin. The European rabbit *(Oryctolagus cuniculus)* scent-marks the same way. Swamp rabbit home ranges vary in size, but do not exceed about eight hectares (20 acres). Favored resting sites include the tops of brush-covered stumps and logs, the low crotches of trees, honeysuckle tangles, cane patches, and open, grassy places in floodplains.

This species eats a variety of plants, but prefers sedges,

grasses, and in some cases, tree seedlings. Most feeding activity occurs at dusk. The swamp rabbit appears to suffer little from predation. However, when chased by dogs, it is adept at eluding them, often taking to the water.

The breeding season of the swamp rabbit varies slightly throughout its range, but generally lasts from late January to August. In Texas and on the Gulf Coast, the species apparently breeds year-round. Its gestation period is about 37 days. The young (commonly three to a litter) are born virtually hairless, with their eyes tightly closed. Nests are constructed against or under fences, the bases of trees, brush and lumber piles, and abandoned buildings. The female nurses her young at dawn and dusk; nursing continues for a time after the young have left the nest. Orphan rabbits from other nests are often adopted.

J. A. Chapman

Sylvilagus aquaticus

Size

No significant sexual dimorphism
Total length: 452–552 (501) mm
Length of tail: 50–74 (59) mm
Weight: 1,646–2,668 g

Identification

The swamp rabbit is the largest North American cottontail. Its head and back are rusty brown to black; its throat, belly, and the underside of the tail are white. Its eyes are surrounded by prominent, cinnamon-colored rings. Two other rabbits, the eastern cottontail, *S. floridanus,* and the marsh rabbit, *S. palustris,*

also inhabit swamp rabbit habitat. Swamp rabbits are noticeably larger than these species, with smaller ears in relation to body size.

Other Common Names

Cane-cutter

Status

Common; range diminishing in the north

Subspecies

Sylvilagus aquaticus aquaticus, southern Indiana, Illinois, and Missouri, extreme southeastern Kansas, eastern Oklahoma and Louisiana,

Alabama, Mississippi, Texas to the coastal lowlands, and northern Georgia
Sylvilagus aquaticus littoralis, coastal lowlands from Aransas County, Texas, through Louisiana and Alabama to Mobile Bay, Mississippi

References

Mammalian Species 151; Chapman and Feldhamer, 1982; Chapman and Flux, 1990

Desert cottontail | *Sylvilagus audubonii*

The desert cottontail is typically found at lower elevations in the desert Southwest and arid intermountain West. It lives below sea level in Death Valley, but its range includes woodlands and grasslands to nearly 2,000 m. (6,000 ft.). Its ability to reduce heat load and water loss enables it to thrive in desert environments.

The desert cottontail is most active in the early morning and evening. Temperature, rainfall, and wind affect behavior; this rabbit prefers to travel and forage on still days, or at night when temperatures dip below 26° C (80° F). During hot days, the animal usually rests in a hide—a depression in the vegeta-

tion or ground—or in a burrow. Pellet piles on logs and tree stumps suggest that these places are used for lookout posts. When alarmed, a desert cottontail becomes motionless rather than running for cover.

Although the desert cottontail is not gregarious, occasionally several rabbits forage together. A rabbit's home range normally comprises about 4 hectares (10 acres), but can encompass half again that many, depending on the type and extent of cover. Population density may exceed 15 per hectare.

The desert cottontail is found in diverse habitats. Along rivers it is associated with riparian brush like willows, in up-

Sylvilagus audubonii

lands with pinyon-juniper stands, and in desert areas with sagebrush, rabbitbrush, and a variety of cacti. Habitat determines feeding sites. In heavy cover adjacent to grasslands, much foraging takes place under the shelter of bushes. When feeding in open areas, the desert cottontail is very cautious. It moves slowly, with front feet forward and neck stretched out, hopping only when it must to reach food.

The desert cottontail feeds on a variety of grasses, shrubs, and forbs. Seasonal availability of food plants seems to be the most important factor influencing its diet. Important food plants include Johnson grass *(Sorghum halepense),* sow thistle *(Sonchus),* honeysuckle *(Lonicera),* sedges *(Carex),* and blackberries *(Rubus).* This rabbit also relishes acorns.

The desert cottontail can breed year-round, but normally limits its sexual activity to eight months. Gestation is 28–30 days. Sexual maturity comes at an early age; some mating occurs in animals as young as three months! The young, commonly two to four in a litter, are altricial. They are nursed by the female in the form or nest until they can forage for themselves in two to three weeks. *J. A. Chapman*

Size
Females are about two percent larger than males.
Total length: 372–397 (385) mm
Length of tail: 45–60 (56) mm
Weight: 755–1,250 g

Identification
The desert cottontail is relatively large and long-legged. Its slender feet lack the long, dense pelage of many other members of the genus. The ears are long, pointed, and sparsely haired on the inner surface. The large ears are useful in distinguishing the desert cottontail from both the eastern cottontail *(S. floridanus)* and the mountain cottontail *(S. nuttallii).* The vibrissae (whiskers) are generally black. The tail is large, dark above, and white underneath.

Other Common Names
Audubon's cottontail

Status
Common, widely distributed throughout the Southwest and Plains states

Subspecies
Sylvilagus audubonii arizonae, southeastern California, southern Nevada, western Arizona, and western mainland Mexico south to about Quaymas
Sylvilagus audubonii audubonii, California, from a line between San Jose and Sonora north through the Sacramento Valley to about Redding
Sylvilagus audubonii baileyi, southeastern Montana, southwestern North Dakota, western South Dakota, Wyoming, except the extreme northwestern edge, western Nebraska, extreme northwestern and eastern Colorado, not including the central Rocky Mountains, extreme northeastern Utah, and northwestern Kansas
Sylvilagus audubonii cedrophilus, southwestern Colorado, except the central Rocky Mountains, northwestern and central New Mexico, southeastern Utah, and northwestern Arizona
Sylvilagus audubonii confinis, Baja California from about Camala south
Sylvilagus audubonii goldmani, southern mainland Mexico from about Navojoa south to about Mazatlan
Sylvilagus audubonii minor, southeastern Arizona, southwestern New Mexico, extreme southwestern Texas, and central Mexico as far south as Monterrey
Sylvilagus audubonii neomexicanus, southwestern Kansas, eastern New Mexico, and northwestern and central Texas from about Austin to the Apache Mountains
Sylvilagus audubonii parvulus, south-central Texas south to about Ciudad Madero on the coast of Mexico, then inland to about Las Herreras, then south to Mexico City
Sylvilagus audubonii sanctidiegi, extreme southwestern California from about Ventura south to about Colonet, Baja California
Sylvilagus audubonii vallicola, central California from about Mariposa south to Yermo and west and north along the coast to about San Jose

References
Mammalian Species 106; Chapman and Feldhamer, 1982; Chapman and Flux, 1990

Brush rabbit | *Sylvilagus bachmani*

The brush rabbit is restricted to the Pacific Coast of North America. It is found from the Columbia River in the north to the tip of Baja California in the south, from Pacific Ocean beaches east to the Cascade-Sierra Crest. It occurs at elevations from sea level to about 2,070 meters (3,000 ft.).

The brush rabbit lives in dense, brushy cover. It uses burrows, but does not dig its own. Runways and tunnels afford escape paths through thickets. When pursued by dogs or other predators, the brush rabbit climbs into shrubs or low trees to avoid being caught. The brush rabbit often thumps the ground with a hind foot when frightened. Thumping may last for several minutes. This animal squeals or cries, as other rabbits do, when frightened or in pain.

Grasses are the most important element in a brush rabbit's diet. Favored species include creeping eragrostis *(Eragrostis hypnoides),* spike rush *(Eleocharis palustris),* foxtail grass *(Hordeum murinum),* soft chess grass *(Bromis hordeaceus),* and oats *(Avena fatua).* The brush rabbit also likes to nibble on thistles and shrubs such as wild rose *(Rosa)* and blackberries *(Rubus).*

Wary and secretive, the brush rabbit typically scans its foraging area from just inside dense, brushy cover before venturing into the open. After entering a clearing, it may remain mo-

Sylvilagus bachmani

tionless for some time, watching for signs of danger. Though it avoids open areas when pursued, the brush rabbit likes to lie in the sun, especially on mornings following heavy rain or fog at night.

The brush rabbit is gregarious—at least when foraging. However, each individual maintains a personal space that ranges from about .30 m to about 7.32 m (1–24 feet), and if another rabbit enters that space, conflict ensues, often resulting in a chase.

In California, the brush rabbit's breeding season lasts from December through May. In Oregon, it breeds from February to August. During this time females produce three to four litters of about three young each. The nest is a cavity, approximately 7.6 by 15.2 cm (3 by 6 inches) lined with fur and small amounts of dried grass and covered with a "plug" of fur to conceal the young, which are fed only at night. The young rabbits are altricial, but leave the nest within two weeks. *J. A. Chapman*

Size
No significant sexual dimorphism
Total length: 303–369 (336) mm
Length of tail: 10–30 (20) mm
Weight: 511–917 g

Identification
The brush rabbit is a very small cottontail, unlikely to be confused with other cottontail species. Its legs and ears are short, its tail diminutive. The species is generally dark gray on the back and sides and pale gray on the belly and underside of the tail.

Status
Common

Subspecies
Sylvilagus bachmani bachmani, central California coast between the Salinas River and Morro

Sylvilagus bachmani cerrosensis, Cedros Island, Baja California, Mexico

Sylvilagus bachmani cinerascens, southwestern California from about Bakersfield to extreme northern Baja California

Sylvilagus bachmani exiguus, central Baja California from El Crucero north to about San Vincente

Sylvilagus bachmani howelli, Baja California from about the California–Mexico border south along the Sierra de Juarez Mountains to about San Vincente

Sylvilagus bachmani macrorhinus, San Mateo and Santa Cruz counties, California

Sylvilagus bachmani mariposae, foothills of the Sierra Nevada Mountains in central California from about Sacramento to Bakersfield

Sylvilagus bachmani peninsularis, southern Baja California from El Crucero south

Sylvilagus bachmani riparius, known only from the type locality near Vernalis, Stanislaus County, California

Sylvilagus bachmani rosaphagus, Baja California along the coastal plain between about Ensenada and Rosario, Mexico

Sylvilagus bachmani tehamae, from north of Klamath Falls, Oregon southward along the east side of the coast range to about Sacramento, California, and from about Redding, California, south along the Sierra Nevada range to about Placerville

Sylvilagus bachmani ubericolor, western Oregon and California between the Columbia River in the north to San Francisco Bay in the south, and east to the summit of the Cascade Sierra Nevada Mountains

Sylvilagus bachmani virgulti, central California coast range between Berkeley and Mariposa

References
Mammalian Species 34; Chapman and Feldhamer, 1982; Chapman and Flux, 1990

Eastern cottontail | *Sylvilagus floridanus*

The eastern cottontail has the widest distribution of any of the cottontails. It thrives in diverse habitats from southern Canada to northern South America. This cottontail is generally considered a mammal of farmland, field, and hedge. However, historically it also occurs in natural glades, woodlands, deserts, swamps, prairies, hardwood forests, rain forests, and boreal forests. It has been widely transplanted, and populations are now established in many parts of the United States that at one time had no eastern cottontails. The range of this species overlaps that of seven other cottontails and six species of hares. No other cottontail occurs sympatrically with so many other leporids.

No single habitat type can be classified as preferred cover for the eastern cottontail. Habitat preference varies from season to season, between regions, and with varying behavioral activities. In some areas, brush piles are favored as shelter and resting cover. In other areas, natural growing vegetation is used most often. Overgrown fields are especially good habitat for these cottontails.

Eastern cottontails normally have home ranges of 1–2 hectares. However, habitat quality and seasonal behavior influ-

Sylvilagus floridanus

ence home range size and movements. Eastern cottontails do not maintain territories, and except during the breeding season, home ranges overlap indiscriminately. Population densities for this species have been reported at more than 10 per hectare (four per acre).

Food habits of the eastern cottontail vary by season and distribution. Grasses and herbaceous vegetation comprise most of the diet in spring and summer; woody species such as brambles predominate during the fall and winter. Feeding activity generally peaks at sunrise and sunset.

The eastern cottontail escapes danger by flushing or slink- ing. The flush is a fast, zig-zag dash to cover. Slinking is movement low to the ground with the ears laid back. Adult social behaviors include animated courtship and vocal communication, as well as dominant-subordinate interactions among males. Eastern cottontails appear to establish hierarchies; fighting is rare.

The eastern cottontail is among the most fecund of the lagomorphs. Females may produce 35 young in seven litters annually. Gestation averages 30 days. The young, usually three to six per litter, are born in a nest of dried grasses and leaves lined with fur. *J. A. Chapman*

Size
Females are about 1 percent larger than males.
Total length: 395–477 (430) mm
Length of tail: 25–61 (45) mm
Weight: 801–1,533 g

Identification
The eastern cottontail is a large rabbit with long, dense, brownish to grayish fur on the upperparts and white fur on the underside of the body and tail. Because this species has the widest distribution of any cottontail, identifying features vary according to locality. Although it is generally easy to identify the eastern cottontail among other sympatric rabbits, New England and Appalachian cottontails can be hard to distinguish where the ranges of the three overlap. The eastern cottontail often has a distinct white spot on the forehead, and the other two species commonly have a black fringe on the front edge of their ears and a black spot between the ears. However, skull characteristics are the best way to separate the eastern cottontail from look-alikes.

Other Common Names
Florida cottontail

Status
Common; range expanding in some areas. The species has been widely introduced.

Subspecies
Sylvilagus floridanus alacer, southeastern Kansas, southern Missouri, eastern Oklahoma, Arkansas, Alabama, Louisiana except along the coast, and southeastern Texas
Sylvilagus floridanus ammophilus, Oak Lodge, east of Micco, Florida, known only from the type locality

Sylvilagus floridanus aztecus, southern Mexico between Mapastepec on the east and Colotepec on the west, north of the summit of the Sierra Madre
Sylvilagus floridanus chapmani, central Texas to southeastern Mexico, as far south as about Tampico on the east and San Luis Potosi on the west
Sylvilagus floridanus chiapensis, eastern Mexico along the northern Sierra Madre de Chiapas in Chiapas and southeastern Guatemala
Sylvilagus floridanus cognatus, central New Mexico
Sylvilagus floridanus connectens, eastern Mexico along the eastern foothills of the Sierra Madre Occidental east to the coast between Tampico and Alvarado
Sylvilagus floridanus costaricensis, western Costa Rica and extreme southern Nicaragua along the southern edge of Lake Nicaragua
Sylvilagus floridanus floridanus, peninsular Florida from about Ocala south
Sylvilagus floridanus hesperius, central Arizona from the Nevada border southeast through Flagstaff to about Phoenix
Sylvilagus floridanus hitchensi, known only from the type locality, Smith Island, Virginia
Sylvilagus floridanus holzneri, southeastern Arizona and extreme southwestern New Mexico through central Mexico to about Guadalajara
Sylvilagus floridanus hondurensis, El Salvador, eastern Honduras, and central Nicaragua
Sylvilagus floridanus llanensis, extreme southeastern Colorado, southwestern Nebraska, western Oklahoma, and north-central Texas
Sylvilagus floridanus mallurus, Massachusetts south and east along the Atlantic coast and along the Appalachian Mountains, into northern Florida and west to the Alabama-Mississippi border

Sylvilagus floridanus mearnsi, midwestern United States and the Great Lakes region of Canada, from Lake Erie to Montreal, south to western Virginia, west to northeastern Nebraska, and north to north-central Minnesota
Sylvilagus floridanus orizabae, central Mexico between Orizaba and Monterrey, west from Monterrey to about Torreon, then south to about Uruapan and east to Orizaba
Sylvilagus floridanus paulsoni, extreme southeastern Florida, near Homestead
Sylvilagus floridanus restrictur, southeastern Mexico along the Sierra Madre between Puerto Vallarta and Lazaro Cardenas
Sylvilagus floridanus robustus, the west side of the Sierra Madre Occidental from Saltillo, Mexico, north along the Guadalupe Mountains to the Texas-New Mexico border
Sylvilagus floridanus russatus, foothills and lowlands of the east side of the Sierra Madre Oriental near Veracruz, Mexico
Sylvilagus floridanus similis, southeastern Saskatchewan and southern Manitoba south through most of North and South Dakota, western and central Nebraska, extreme eastern Wyoming, southeastern Montana, northeastern Colorado, and northwestern Minnesota
Sylvilagus floridanus subcinctus, central Mexico in the area around and between Guadalajara, San Luis Potosi, and Mexico City
Sylvilagus floridanus yucatanicus, coastal plain of the Yucatan Peninsula from about Campeche to Rio Lagartos and inland to about Merida

References
Mammalian Species 136; Chapman and Feldhamer, 1982; Chapman and Flux, 1990

Mountain cottontail | *Sylvilagus nuttallii*

The mountain cottontail is found in the intermountain West from just above the Canadian border south to Arizona and New Mexico, and from the eastern slopes of the Rocky Mountains west to the Cascade-Sierra crest. It is generally associated with sagebrush, but may occur in timbered areas in the southern parts of its range.

This species inhabits wooded or brushy areas, commonly near rocky ravines. Riparian zones with abundant willows are also favored habitats. Where the mountain cottontail and desert cottontail *(S. audubonii)* occur sympatrically, the mountain cottontail frequents higher, rocky, sagebrush areas, and the desert cottontail inhabits adjacent desert valleys.

The mountain cottontail lives in burrows and rock crevices where vegetation is sparse, and in "forms" (above-ground nests) where cover is dense. Its most important food items are sagebrush, western juniper, and various grasses. In spring and summer, grass is preferred. The mountain cottontail feeds most actively at dawn and dusk, almost always in the shelter of brush or in clearings only a few meters from cover.

The mountain cottontail is more solitary than most other

Sylvilagus nuttallii

members of the genus—perhaps because of the expansive, relatively uniform habitat in which it is usually found. In patches of desirable habitat these rabbits will concentrate.

The female mountain cottontail builds a cuplike nest lined with fur and dried grass. Four to eight young are born after a 28–30 day gestation. When the young reach a weight of about 75 grams (5 oz), they leave the nest for brief periods. Females produce as many as five litters each year, for an average of 22 young per breeding female per year. *J. A. Chapman*

Size
Females are about 4 percent larger than males.
Total length: 338–390 (362) mm
Length of tail: 30–54 (48) mm
Weight: 628.5–871 g

Identification
The mountain cottontail is medium-sized for the genus. Its hind legs are long and its feet are covered with long, dense hair. Unlike *S. audobonii,* the ears are relatively short, rounded at the tip, and hairy on the inner surface. The whiskers are white or partly white, never black. The tail is large and grizzled, dark above and white on the underside.

Other Common Names
Nuttall's cottontail

Status
Common, but apparently declining in southwestern North Dakota

Subspecies
Sylvilagus nuttallii grangeri, southern Alberta and Saskatchewan north to Calgary and Saskatoon, and south through Montana, Wyoming, southern Idaho, central Nevada, most of Utah, north-central Arizona, and the northwestern corner of Colorado

Sylvilagus nuttallii nuttallii, eastern Washington, extreme south-central British Columbia, northwestern Idaho, eastern Oregon, northeastern California, and northwestern Nevada
Sylvilagus nuttallii pinetis, north-central Colorado, south and west to southeastern Utah and northeastern Arizona, and south to northern New Mexico

References
Mammalian Species 56; Chapman and Feldhamer, 1982; Chapman and Flux, 1990

Appalachian cottontail | *Sylvilagus obscurus*

The Appalachian cottontail is a newly described rabbit that was previously included with the New England cottontail group. The Appalachian cottontail occurs from the northern terminus of the Appalachian Mountains in Pennsylvania to the southern terminus in Alabama. It occurs almost exclusively in dense conifers and deciduous cover at high elevations. In the

Sylvilagus obscurus

southern Appalachians this species is associated with conifer/ heath habitat, especially mountain laurel and blueberry. Both are characteristic species of high elevation boreal forests.

The Appalachian cottontail also occurs in six- to seven-year-old clear-cut areas at high elevations. In Alabama, the southern limit of its range, it frequents mountain slopes and associated foothills. At the type locality in the Dolly Sods Scenic Area, West Virginia, this rabbit is found on a high, wind-swept plateau, where most of the vegetation has suffered mechanical damage from winterkill and strong, persistent winds. This area originally supported a climax forest of red spruce, but was denuded by logging and fires in the late 1800s. Currently its heath plains and bogs are covered with rhododendron, mountain laurel, blueberry, and other montane shrub vegetation.

The Appalachian cottontail eats a variety of grasses, ferns, forbs, and shrubs. In addition, it appears to be the only cottontail that feeds extensively on conifer needles.

The Appalachian cottontail exhibits both solitary and social behaviors. Rabbits groom and dust alone, but vocalize when among others of their kind, and there is some evidence that they establish hierarchies. The basic behavior patterns of this cottontail are similar to those of other rabbits and hares.

The breeding season of the Appalachian cottontail lasts from early March to early September. Like all cottontails it is a synchronous breeder. Gestation lasts about 28 days. Litter size is three to five and the average number of young produced annually is about 24 per female. *J. A. Chapman*

Size
Females are slightly larger than males.
Total length: 386–430 (408) mm
Length of tail: 22–65 (45) mm
Weight: 756–1,038 g

Identification
The Appalachian cottontail is a medium-size rabbit with fine, silky fur. Its upperparts are pinkish buff to reddish buff and the back is overlaid with a distinct black wash, giving a penciled effect. The belly is bright white to buffy white. The cheeks have a distinctive grizzled appearance, and the front edges of the short, rounded ears are covered with black hair. There is usually a distinct black spot between the ears, and there is never a white spot on the forehead. The Appalachian cottontail looks a great deal like the New England cottontail *(S. transitionalis)*, and is also similar in appearance to the eastern cottontail *(S. floridanus)*.

Recent Synonyms
Sylvilagus transitionalis

Status
Poorly known, limited

References
Chapman and Morgan, 1973; Chapman et al., 1977, 1992

Marsh rabbit | *Sylvilagus palustris*

Unlike other cottontails, the marsh rabbit is confined solely to marshy habitats. Its range extends from the Dismal Swamp of Virginia south through southern Georgia, into Florida, and west to Mobile Bay, Alabama. This rabbit does not occur above 152 meters (500 feet) elevation.

The marsh rabbit is most often found associated with brackish water, although it does occur around freshwater marshes. It is also found in raised "hummocks" in marshes featuring trees such as magnolia *(Magnolia grandiflora)*, tupelo *(Nyssa sylvatic)*, and sweet gum *(Liquidambar styraciflua)*, with shrubs like blackberry *(Rubus)*. More often, however, the marsh rabbit is found around cattails *(Typha)*. A key habitat component for this species is pooled water—plenty of it. The marsh rabbit and the swamp rabbit both like to swim, the marsh rabbit with an alternate paddling motion.

This species is most active at night. Although it feeds on a variety of plants, it prefers herbs such as centella *(Centella respanda)*, marsh pennywort *(Hydrocotyle)*, cattail, rush *(Juncus)*, and water hyacinths *(Eichhornia crassipes)*.

Sylvilagus palustris

Marsh rabbits breed year-round. The gestation period is believed to be 30–37 days. Their nests are usually constructed of soft grass and rabbit fur and placed among sedges along the water's edge. Litter size is small for cottontails, averaging only two to three. *J. A. Chapman*

Size
No significant sexual dimorphism
Total length: 425–440 (433) mm
Length of tail: 33–39 (36) mm
Weight: 1,200–2,200 g

Identification
The marsh rabbit is small, with a dark brown body and slender, petite feet that are red to buff in color. The tail is small, commonly with a white underside, and the ears are broad and short. The marsh rabbit is similar in color to the swamp rabbit *(S. aquaticus),* but they are easily distinguished by the marsh rabbit's smaller size, dark tail, and dainty feet. The belly of the marsh rabbit is reddish-brown and the back of the neck is a dark cinnamon color. The back, rump, upper tail and hind legs range from chestnut brown to a rusty red in color. The abdomen is white, with the rest of the belly varying from buff to brown.

Status
Common, except for the Florida Keys marsh rabbit, which is considered an endangered subspecies.

Subspecies
Sylvilagus palustris hefneri, confined to the type locality in Monroe Country on the Florida Keys
Sylvilagus palustris paludicola, peninsular Florida from about Gainesville south
Sylvilagus palustris palustris, coastal plain and lowlands east of the Appalachian Mountains from north Hampton County, Virginia, south through eastern North and South Carolina, Georgia, southern Mississippi, and northern Florida

References
Mammalian Species 153; Chapman and Feldhamer, 1982; Chapman and Flux, 1990

New England cottontail | *Sylvilagus transitionalis*

The New England cottontail is much more restricted in range than originally reported. The taxonomic separation of the Appalachian cottontail from the New England cottontail has greatly reduced the range of both species. The New England cottontail is restricted to parts of Maine, New Hampshire, Vermont, Massachusetts, Connecticut, Rhode Island, and New York as far west as the Hudson River.

This cottontail inhabits a variety of habitats within its range, but shows a preference for boreal environments characterized by eracacious plants such as mountain laurel *(Kalmia)* and

Sylvilagus transitionalis

blueberry *(Vaccinium),* with an overstory of conifers and hardwoods. There are, however, no individual plants or plant groups that define the habitat of this species within its range. Recent reports suggest that rabbit densities are declining and inhabited range shrinking. In fact, the type locality, Liberty Hill, New London, Connecticut, no longer has a population of New England cottontails.

The New England cottontail feeds on a wide variety of plants. In the summer it prefers grasses and clovers. During the winter primary food items are forbs and the twigs of shrubs. Home ranges of New England cottontails are relatively small—usually less than one hectare in size (2.5 acres). Males tend to have larger home ranges than females.

This cottontail is secretive, and rarely ventures into the open. Its behavioral patterns include solitary grooming and feeding, but distinctive social interactions occur during mating and the establishment of dominance within groups.

The breeding season of the New England cottontail lasts from March to September. The female builds a nest in a depression and lines it with grass and fur. Nests are commonly 10 cm (4 inches) deep, 12 cm (5 inches) wide, and covered with a cap or plug of nest material. Following a gestation period of 28 days, three to eight altricial young are born. Females nurse their young for about 16 days. *J. A. Chapman*

Size
Females are slightly larger than males.
Total length: 398–439 mm
Length of tail: 47–69 mm
Weight: 995–1,347 g

Identification
The New England cottontail is a medium-sized rabbit with a pinkish to tawny-reddish-buff back overlaid with a distinct black wash, giving the rabbit a penciled effect. The front edges of the short, rounded ears are rimmed with black hair. The New England cottontail is virtually identical in appearance to the Appalachian cottontail *(S. obscurus)* and similar in appearance to the eastern cottontail *(S. floridanus).* The latter species lacks the black penciled effect on the back and often has a white spot on the forehead.

Status
Limited

References
Mammalian Species 55; Chapman et al., 1992; Dalke, 1942

Antelope jackrabbit | *Lepus alleni*

Antelope jackrabbits inhabit the desert plains of southern Arizona southward into northern Nayarit, Mexico; a population is also present on Tiburon Island in the Gulf of California. This hare occurs at elevations from near sea level in Mexico to 1,500 meters in southern Arizona. Fossils resembling *L. alleni* are known from middle Pleistocene (Irvingtonian) deposits in Sumter County, Florida.

This colorful jackrabbit is nocturnal and crepuscular, and it rarely utters sounds. When browsing on mesquite *(Prosopis)* it rears up on its hind feet, its forefeet hang limp, and its ears flop

freely. Attempting to reach higher, it stands on its toes and places its forepaws on a branch to crop off leaves, bark, or buds. It does not have burrows, but it may have nests beneath the ground level with some hair as lining. It rests by day in places known as shelter forms, which may be made by backing up next to or under clumps of grass, weeds, or brush. These are often merely sitting places beside a cactus or mesquite that show no evidence of digging or scratching.

L. alleni may be the fastest member of the genus, with running speeds of up to 72 kilometers per hour. When it runs, a conspicuous white area is displayed on the rump. This white area appears to shift each time the jackrabbit turns, the white being kept toward the observer. This flash of white while running resembles that of the pronghorn antelope, giving the animal one of its common names.

Antelope jackrabbits have large, whitish ears that are nearly naked except for long fringes of white hair on the edges and tips. The large surface areas of the ears are probably significant sites of heat exchange with the environment, and may help cool the animal. The upperparts of the body are yellowish brown, strongly mixed with black. The sides, including the outer side of the limbs, hips, and rump, are white with fine black points on some of the hairs. The chin, throat, undersurface, inner sides of the forelegs, and tail are white.

The breeding season is from late December through September. The gestation period is about 6 weeks in length. The average number of young per litter is two (range, 1–5), and a female may have three or four litters per year. The young are precocial, as are all hares; that is, at birth the young are fully clothed with hair, their eyes are open, and they can hop. Newborns do not show the characteristic white rump. The mother may scatter her young at, or soon after, birth, and return at night to nurse them. The duration of parental care is short; the young hares become independent in a matter of days.

The antelope jackrabbit occurs in a variety of habitats. It appears to favor areas where grasses, mesquites, and catclaws *(Acacia)* abound, but it also occurs in desert habitats having little grass. *L. alleni* lives on dry valley slopes distant from water sources, and if water is available, it does not drink. The diet primarily consists of green grass, other green vegetation, and many species of cactus. Its food is highly succulent, with cactus increasingly consumed as drought conditions become more severe. Digestive powers are rapid and efficient. Food apparently traverses the digestive tract in about 12 hours. Antelope jackrabbits seek minerals by digging into and biting the soil.

The average size of a home range is 643 hectares and population density is often about 0.5 per hectare, but the hares may become so numerous at times that 12–15 can be seen at once. In recent years, the number of antelope jackrabbits has decreased significantly in areas of southern Arizona where Lehmann lovegrass *(Eragrostis lehmanniana)* has been intro-

Lepus alleni

duced and become established, replacing the native vegetation favored by the hares.

In much of southern Arizona, *L. alleni* and *L. californicus* occur in equal numbers. These species often are seen together, sometimes sitting under the same bush or running side by side. On grassy slopes at elevations of about 1,050 meters, *L. alleni* usually is several times as numerous as *L. californicus,* but in the mesquites along the valley bottoms and on the barren creosotebush desert, *L. californicus* usually is more numerous.

In southern Arizona, antelope jackrabbits occupy the same habitat as black-tailed jackrabbits, round-tailed ground squirrels, Harris's antelope squirrels, white-throated woodrats, Arizona, Bailey's, and desert pocket mice, Merriam's and banner-tailed kangaroo rats, southern grasshopper mice, desert cottontails, skunks, badgers, coyotes, peccaries, and mule deer. Predators include bobcats, coyotes, and golden eagles. Parasites include cestodes, nematodes, chiggers, fleas, and botflies. *T. L. Best*

Size
No significant sexual dimorphism
Total length: 553–670 (622) mm
Length of tail: 48–76 (58) mm
Weight: 2,700–5,900 (3,800) g

Identification
Compared with other species of hares in North America, the antelope jackrabbit is large; the ears are especially large. It can be distinguished from *Lepus californicus,* the only other hare that shares its range, in having ears that are white on the outside and without black tips, sides of body that are pale grayish rather than brownish, and longer ears on average.

Other Common Names
Allen's hare, Allen's jackrabbit, wandering jackrabbit, blanket jack, saddle jack, Mexican jackrabbit, burro jack, jackass rabbit

Status
Common

Subspecies
Lepus alleni alleni, south-central Arizona and most of Sonora, Mexico
Lepus alleni palitans, southern Sonora to northern Nayarit, Mexico
Lepus alleni tiburonensis, Tiburon Island, Gulf of California, Sonora, Mexico

References
Mammalian Species 424; Hoffmeister, 1986; Vorhies and Taylor, 1933

Snowshoe hare | *Lepus americanus*

The snowshoe hare occurs across most of Canada and the northeastern United States, throughout Alaska, and down through the Rocky Mountains into Utah and New Mexico. The species is found in a variety of habitat types, including alder swamps, aspen "bluffs," and hardwood forests in the southern part of its range, and mixed and evergreen forests in the north. This common resident of the boreal forest resides in dense thickets that have ample vegetative cover, and is usually observed around dawn or dusk.

Most leporids are nocturnal, and the snowshoe hare is no exception to this rule, crouching under sheltering logs and vegetation during daylight hours and emerging to search for food after sundown. It usually moves to and from feeding sites on well-travelled runways, and although forest openings are commonly visited while foraging, it never strays far from cover. It feeds on a variety of woody and succulent plants.

The snowshoe hare is active year-round and can produce two to five litters a year, beginning in March and ending in July or August. The gestation period ranges from 34 to 40 days. Litter sizes vary from 1 to 8 young, depending on time of year

Lepus americanus

and female nutritional status. Females do not excavate dens, but rather leave young unattended in sheltered areas and visit them daily. Snowshoe hares are born furred, with their eyes open, and their growth is rapid. They are fully weaned after a month, and can attain adult weight in 3–5 months. Although wild hares rarely become accustomed to humans, young that are raised in captivity can make good pets.

Over most of the species' range, snowshoe hare populations undergo large fluctuations in numbers. This phenomenon, known as the 10-year cycle, is characterized by a period of several years during which hare numbers increase, followed by a rapid population decline. The cycle is believed to be caused by an interaction between food shortages and an overabundance of predators, both avian and mammalian, that kill many hares during some winters. *L. americanus* populations in southern Canada and the United States do not usually undergo such dramatic fluctuations; instead they tend to vary less or remain stable from year to year.

In summer, *L. americanus* has a rusty brown back and head with a grayish belly and chin. The ears are black-tipped, and the nostrils and tail are white. Molting occurs in autumn, and the winter pelage is almost pure white except for the black-tipped ears and yellowish underpaws. The spring molt returns the hare to its summer coloration, although some subspecies (*L. a. oregonus* and *L. a. washingtonii*) retain their brown color throughout the year. The snowshoe hare's common name comes from its disproportionately large hind feet, which enable it to travel effectively in deep, soft snow during winter.

Lepus americanus is absent from the tundra area of northern Canada, where it is replaced by *Lepus articus*, a much larger, stouter, more thickly furred relative. Although their ranges sometimes overlap around treeline, the two species rarely occur in the same locale, snowshoe hares preferring to remain where forest cover is present. *D. Murray*

Size
Females are 10–40 percent larger than males.
Total length: 363–520 (450) mm
Length of tail: 25–57 (44.0) mm
Weight: 900–1,700 (1,300) g (males); 900–2,200 (1,500) g (females)

Identification
The snowshoe hare is a medium-sized hare with large ears and hind feet, dark brown with gray chin and belly in summer and white with black-tipped ears in winter.

Other Common Names
Snowshoe rabbit, varying hare

Status
Common, limited

Subspecies

Lepus americanus americanus, central Canada

Lepus americanus bairdii, northwestern United States

Lepus americanus cascadensis, southern British Columbia and Washington

Lepus americanus columbiensis, Rocky Mountains of Alberta and British Columbia

Lepus americanus dalli, northwestern Canada and Alaska

Lepus americanus klamathensis, south-central Oregon

Lepus americanus oregonus, eastern Oregon

Lepus americanus pallidus, west-central British Columbia.

Lepus americanus phaeonotus, western Great Lakes region

Lepus americanus pineus, Washington and Idaho

Lepus americanus seclusus, Wyoming

Lepus americanus struthopus, northeastern States, Maritime Provinces and Gaspe Peninsula; introduced in Newfoundland.

Lepus americanus tahoensis, Nevada and California

Lepus americanus virginianus, southern Quebec and Ontario, Massachusetts, Tennessee, North Carolina

Lepus americanus washingtoni, western Washington

References

Banfield, 1974

Arctic hare │ *Lepus arcticus*

The arctic hare primarily occurs at elevations from sea level to 900 meters. In Canada it is found north of the tree line, as far north as northern Ellesmere Island, Northwest Territories, and also on the rock-strewn plateaus and mountains of eastern Newfoundland. In Greenland it is common in most of the ice-free coastal region. It also occurs on tiny islands off Greenland that are accessible when ice is present, and frequently is found on ice 3–5 kilometers from land. Fossil remains have been found on Banks Island, Northwest Territories, in northern Greenland, and in Alaska.

This beautiful hare moves by a series of four-legged hops, each hop carrying it about 1.2 meters. When disturbed, it stands erect on its hind legs, forefeet tucked close to its body, and hops about until the source of danger is located. It can run up to 64 kilometers per hour, and can easily swim across small streams. Throughout winter, it makes trails, often on slopes that are exposed to strong winds that remove most of the snow from the sparse vegetation.

Lepus arcticus

Although usually solitary, arctic hares may form groups of 100–300 individuals. When resting, these hares usually sit near rocks, dozing or asleep, sheltered from wind, and if possible warmed by the sun. Often, two or more rest together. In winter, an arctic hare may protect itself from extreme cold by burrowing into snow, but typically it uses only a depression in the snow or the lee of a rock for shelter. Dens consist of a tunnel and a terminal chamber.

Arctic hares always face up a slope; to go lower on the slope, the hare runs down, then turns to face up-slope again. It paws away snow with the front feet only, digging in one place for awhile, then moving to another before exhausting the supply of lichens or willow twigs it has uncovered. If the snow is soft or thin, it reaches the food by scraping the snow with the nose or forelegs. When the snow has a hard crust, it stamps on the crust with the forelegs to make a hole; pieces of snow are then pushed aside with the nose. The sound made when an arctic hare beats or drums against the snow crust in search of food is similar to that of a distant drum roll.

The large feet are padded with a heavy brush of hair. The claws are well-adapted to digging through snow. Its highly modified incisors are used to feed on small, snow-covered Arctic plants. The arctic hare changes color with the seasons. Its winter pelage is long and soft. During the molt to summer pelage, it removes loose tufts of hair by rolling in the snow, often leaving loose tufts of hair scattered on the ground or clinging to vegetation. The upperparts are gray in summer in southern subspecies and white in the others. In winter, all arctic hares are white, except for the black tips of the ears.

Mating usually occurs in April and May. The gestation period is about 53 days. Young are born in a nest, which usually is placed in a well-sheltered place under or between rocks. The nest is lined with dry grass, moss, and fur from the mother. One litter of two to eight young (average is five) is born each year. During the first 2–3 days after the birth of the litter, the mother does not leave the young. When danger approaches, the young hares slink into hiding places among stones. Their gray color and habit of remaining motionless make them difficult to see. The young first leave the mother at an age of 2–3 weeks, about the time their coats turn white. Weaning occurs several weeks later, when the young are about 8–9 weeks old. Until then, the female nurses them at average intervals of 18–20 hours. The duration of each nursing bout is 1–4 minutes. When nursing, the female typically sits upright, with ears erect, eyes open, hind feet spread wide under her haunches, her front legs fully extended and her front feet rather far apart.

The arctic hare is widely distributed in tundra regions of northern Canada and Greenland. Conditions are more favorable for it farther north; its populations are larger there, it is larger in size, and its fur is much finer than in more southern populations. It is highly adapted to cold and barren habitat. Throughout most of the range, it spends the summer north of the tree limit, but in winter it may penetrate more than 160 kilometers into the timber belt. It may be rare for years in a locality, then suddenly become common.

Woody plants are the basic year-round food. The arctic hare eats mosses, lichens, berries, and buds, bark, roots, and young blooms of willows; other foods are mountain sorrel and various kinds of grasses. It displays great diversity in summer diet, but mainly feeds on willows and grasses. Willows are the main species consumed in all seasons and make up 95 percent of the winter diet.

The arctic hare may be an important competitor of muskoxen and caribou in the winter, when all three species feed on willows. Except during years when lemmings are scarce, there is no significant predation on adult hares; arctic hares can outrun gray wolves and arctic foxes. The agility of the arctic hare protects it so well that camouflage is of little importance during the short Arctic summer. However, young arctic hares often are hunted by red and arctic foxes, weasels, snowy owls, gyrfalcons, and rough-legged hawks. Parasites include protozoans, nematodes, lice, and an extraordinary number of fleas. *T. L. Best*

Size
No sexual dimorphism
Total length: 558–633 (606) mm
Length of tail: 45–100 (67) mm
Weight: 2,500–6,800 (4,400) g

Identification
Throughout most of its range, the arctic hare is the only species of hare present. Compared with *L. americanus,* which shares a portion of its range in Canada, the fur of *L. arcticus* is white all the way to the base. Compared with *L. timidus,* which occupies similar habitats in northern Europe and Asia, *L. arcticus* is paler and more grayish (less brownish) in summer pelage.

Recent Synonyms
Lepus glacialis

Other Common Names
Labrador hare, polar hare, Greenland hare, American arctic hare, Canadian arctic hare, alpine hare, oo-ka-lik, ka-choh, ukkulirk, ookalik, okollik

Status
Common

Subspecies
Lepus arcticus andersoni, north-central Canada
Lepus arcticus arcticus, northern Baffin Island and vicinity, Canada
Lepus arcticus bangsii, Labrador and Newfoundland, Canada
Lepus arcticus banksicola, Banks Island, Canada
Lepus arcticus groenlandicus, northern Greenland
Lepus arcticus hubbardi, Prince Patrick Island, Canada
Lepus arcticus labradorius, northeastern Canada
Lepus arcticus monstrabilis, northernmost Canada
Lepus arcticus porsildi, southern Greenland

References
Mammalian Species 457; Parker, 1977

Black-tailed jackrabbit | *Lepus californicus*

The black-tailed jackrabbit's historical range encompasses an area from the Pacific Ocean on the west to Arkansas and Missouri on the east. In the north it ranges from southern Washington to South Dakota and in the south it is found throughout Baja California and well into south-central Mexico. *Lepus californicus* has been introduced in a number of eastern states, including Massachusetts, Maryland, New Jersey, Virginia, and Florida, where it has successfully colonized. Although common over much of its range, the blacktail's densest populations are on the agricultural and range lands of the West, especially in semiarid to arid regions. However, healthy populations are known to inhabit very diverse habitats from sea level to elevations of 3,800 m.

This long-legged hare depends on speed and agility as its primary antipredation strategy, and can leap 6.1 m (20 feet) horizontally and almost 2 m (6 feet) vertically during its escape maneuvers. The mostly nocturnal *L. californicus* has no compelling need to stay close to dense cover, and commonly feeds in open pasture and rangelands or among commercial crops. During the day the jackrabbit will often seek shade, lying un-der a bush or other cover in a shallow scrape. The use of shallow soil depressions has been observed in very hot regions. Home ranges vary between 10 and 20 hectares, with those of females slightly larger than those of males.

Two adaptations allow the black-tailed jackrabbit to exploit the resources of some of the hottest and driest regions. It has extraordinary thermoregulation capabilities and an amazing ability to survive on limited supplies of suboptimum foods.

This hare can obtain most or all of its water from its food. In addition, it has a number of physiological mechanisms that reduce water loss, including the ability to increase its resting daytime body temperature, storing heat for nighttime dissipation, and the ability to reduce its metabolic rate to decrease evaporative water loss. It eliminates excess salt through its urine. By increasing blood flow to its long ears and by assuming a slightly splayed standing position, it maximizes the convective transfer of heat.

L. californicus utilizes a wide array of vegetative resources in its diet, reflecting the diversity of environments, some only minimally productive, that it is able to exploit. Under ideal

conditions, forbs, grasses, and in some places, a wide range of agricultural crops, make up the majority of its diet. However, the hare is able to maintain a thriving population even in such harsh environments as the shrublands of the Southwest, where plants such as the creosote-bush, unpalatable to most mammals, may make up a significant portion of its forage.

Not considered highly gregarious, blacktails often congregate in surprisingly large groups, usually near some preferred food source. Population densities of jackrabbits fluctuate dramatically, with peaks reached about every 6 to 10 years. The number of hares in peak populations also varies substantially. A density of 470 individuals per square kilometer is not unusual and as many as 1,500 per square kilometer have been observed. Given such population densities, and with its fondness for grasses and herbacious plants, the black-tailed jackrabbit can be a serious agricultural pest, damaging crops and competing with livestock. In the 1800s and early in this century, rabbit drives were a common form of pest control. In a single day, as many as five to six thousand jackrabbits were herded into pens and destroyed.

Jackrabbits are preyed upon extensively by the larger mammalian carnivores, especially coyotes. Eagles and certain larger hawks and owls also prey upon them. Hunters, who pursue them both for sport and for food, have been responsible for their introduction into areas outside their natural range.

The black-tailed jackrabbit matures at about one year of age, though it may reproduce at 7 to 8 months. The breeding season is relatively well synchronized. In the north it lasts about 128 days. In the central and western portion of its range, it may last as long as 240 days. In the south, breeding has been reported in all months of the year. Like other hares, it is an induced ovulator, with a gestation lasting approximately 43 days.

Lepus californicus

The female digs a shallow scrape that she may or may not line with fur or fine vegetation. Neonates are precocial: they are fully furred, with eyes open, and are able to run around within a few hours. Litter size is inversely proportional to the relative length of the breeding season, averaging 4.4 young in the north and 2.3 young in the south. Blacktails in the north produce a mean of 3.8 litters annually; in the south an average of 7.0 litters are raised each year. Across all latitudes, reproductive females produce a mean of approximately 14.2 young annually.

G. J. North and R. E. Marsh

Size
Total length: 465–630 mm
Length of tail: 50–112 mm
Weight: 1,300–3,300 g

Identification
Lepus californicus is a large, slender hare with long legs and ears. The tail has a black dorsal surface that may continue as a line onto the lower back. The upperparts may range from a brown to dark gray that blends well with background vegetation. The belly and the underside of the tail are usually a pale gray. The ears are edged and sometimes tipped with black. Unlike the white-tailed jackrabbit (*L. townsendii*), it molts only once annually and does not take on a white winter coat.

Other Common Names
California jackrabbit

Status
Common to abundant; widespread in western and central U.S.; limited in introduced areas

Subspecies
Lepus californicus altamirae, narrow strip about 200 miles long on the eastern seaboard of Tamaulipas, Mexico
Lepus californicus asellus, inland central Mexico, mostly in the state of San Luis Potosi and bordering states to the west
Lepus californicus bennettii, narrow strip along the southern coast of California and southward about 200 miles along the west coast of the Baja peninsula

Lepus californicus californicus, most of central and northern coastal California and northward along the coast into southern Oregon
Lepus californicus curti, one island in the Gulf of Mexico off the coast of Tamaulipas
Lepus californicus deserticola, throughout the Great Basin of the United States from southern Idaho southward, through much of Utah and Nevada, the eastern part of southern California, and the western half of Arizona, and extending a short distance into Mexico to the Gulf of California
Lepus californicus eremicus, southeastern quarter of Arizona and southward through the northern half of Sonora, Mexico
Lepus californicus festinus, a small inland area in the Queretaro region northeast of Mexico City

Lepus californicus magdalenae, Magdalena and Margarita islands off the west coast of Baja California Sur, Mexico

Lepus californicus martirensis, most of the northern two-thirds of the Baja Peninsula, Mexico

Lepus californicus melanotis, Nebraska, Kansas, and Oklahoma, and portions of the adjoining states, including most of northern Texas

Lepus californicus merriami, southeastern Texas and southward about 322 km (200 miles)

into the states of Coahuila, Nuevo Leon, and Tamaulipas, Mexico

Lepus californicus richardsonii, small inland area in south-central California

Lepus californicus sheldoni, Carmen Island, off the east coast of Baja California Sur in the Gulf of California

Lepus californicus texianus, New Mexico, western Texas, and southward into the states of Chihualina, Coahuila, Durango, and Zacatecas, Mexico

Lepus californicus wallawalla, eastern Oregon and into far northeastern California and the northwestern corner of Nevada

Lepus californicus xanti, extreme southern portion of the Baja Peninsula, Mexico

References

Chapman and Flux, 1990; Dunn et al., 1982; Hanselka et al., 1971; Hoagland, 1992; Jameson and Peeters, 1988; MacCracken and Hansen, 1984

White-sided jackrabbit | *Lepus callotis*

The white-sided jackrabbit inhabits grassy plains from southwestern New Mexico, near the Mexican border, through the southern half of the Mexican tableland. The range in the United States is restricted to about 120 square kilometers in southern Hidalgo County, New Mexico. A specimen that is about 7,000 years old from Burnet Cave, Eddy County, New Mexico, may be *L. callotis.* No other fossils are known.

The most conspicuous behavioral trait of *L. callotis* is its tendency to form male-female pairs. This pair bonding is most evident during the breeding season. Once the pair bond is established, the male defends the pair from intruding males. The breeding season lasts at least 18 weeks, extending from mid-April to mid-August, but pregnant individuals can be found from March to October. The average number of young per litter is two, with a range of one to four.

The white-sided jackrabbit constructs and uses resting places called shelter forms. Its shelter forms are slightly larger than those of *L. californicus,* averaging 37 by 18 by 6 centimeters. Dense stands of tobosagrass usually surround the shelter form, which is located in clumps of grass. *L. callotis* sometimes occupies underground shelters, although that is rare.

This jackrabbit's back is pale brownish-red mixed with black. The underside of the tail is white, its upper surface is black, and many of the hairs are tipped with white. The sides are white, and the rump and thighs are white and lined with a few black hairs. The underparts are white, with a trace of the darker color usually present in front of the thighs. The ears are scantily coated with short hairs and their concave surfaces are almost bare, with a dusky spot along the posterior border.

Lepus callotis is most active from 10 p.m. until 5 a.m., particularly on clear nights with bright moonlight. In New Mexico, white-sided jackrabbits are flushed only in tobosagrass, and appear to flee to other tabosagrass stands. When flushed and running, the jackrabbit flashes its white sides alternately. It also

sometimes leaps straight upward, extending the hind legs and flashing the white sides, when escaping.

Lepus callotis avoids hilly areas, instead selecting level topography with little cover of shrubs. In New Mexico, it is found at elevations of 1,525–1,620 meters in an area that averages 38 centimeters of precipitation annually. Here the desert-grassland community is dominated by blue grama, black grama, ring muhly, buffalo grass, wolftail, bottlebrush-grass, and squirreltail. The more common shrubs include soap-tree, yucca, and honey mesquite.

Density is greatest in habitats composed primarily of grasses. In the only intensive study of habitat selection by white-sided jackrabbits, this species was observed in grassland habitat 97.1 percent of the time, in grass-forb association 2.4 percent of the time, and in grass-shrub type 0.5 percent of the time. All the nongrassland habitat was adjacent to large expanses of grassland. More than 99 percent of its diet is grass. Average densitiy is about one jackrabbit per 32 hectares.

The white-sided jackrabbit has been reported as rare throughout its range, and has been proposed for listing as a threatened or endangered species. Livestock grazing may be one of the factors contributing to its decline and its apparent replacement by the highly adaptable *L. californicus*. Prospects for the survival of *L. callotis* in many parts of its range are poor. In areas where grassland is interspersed with scattered shrubs and forbs, *L. californicus* is more common than *L. callotis*. Only *L. californicus* is found where shrubs and forbs are the dominant vegetation. Overgrazing and deterioration of grassland seem to favor the occurrence of *L. californicus* more than *L. callotis*.

Other mammals occurring in the same habitat as *L. callotis* include shrews, cottontails, ground squirrels, prairie dogs, pocket gophers, pocket mice, kangaroo rats, deer mice, pygmy mice, white-throated woodrats, grasshopper mice, cotton rats, foxes, skunks, long-tailed weasels, coyotes, bobcats, deer, and pronghorns. Predators include coyotes, kit foxes, golden eagles, marsh hawks, red-tailed hawks, swainson's hawks, and great horned owls. White-sided jackrabbits also have been used as food by humans. *T. L. Best*

Lepus callotis

Size

Males are smaller than females.
Total length: 525–532 (529) mm (males);
    541–575 (558) mm (females)
Length of tail: 47–92 (71) mm
Weight: 1,500–2,200 (1,800) g (males);
    2,500–3,200 (2,900) g (females)

Identification

Compared with *L. californicus,* the only other hare that shares its range in the United States, *L. callotis* can be distinguished by its whitish rather than brownish-gray sides and white-tipped rather than black-tipped ears. The ears of *L. callotis* are generally shorter (average length, 118.2 mm; range, 102–136) than those of *L. californicus* (average length, 131.9 mm; range, 120–147).

Recent Synonyms

Lepus mexicanus
Lepus nigricaudatus

Other Common Names

Gaillard jackrabbit, beautiful-eared jackrabbit, snow sides

Status

Rare

Subspecies

Lepus callotis callotis, central Mexico
Lepus callotis gaillardi, southwestern New Mexico to Coahuila, Mexico

References

Mammalian Species 442; Bednarz and Cook, 1984; Dunn et al., 1982

Alaskan hare | *Lepus othus*

The Alaskan hare occurs in the Arctic tundra region of western and northwestern Alaska from sea level to more than 600 meters elevation. The range extends from the Selawik-Kotzebue area in the north to the Cold Bay area in the south, and includes all of the Seward Peninsula, most of the Alaska Peninsula, and most of the western coast of Alaska. Fossil remains have been found in two late Rancholabrean sites in Alaska, Canyon Creek and Porcupine River Cave. These sites are outside the current range of *L. othus,* and the remains from Canyon Creek may be of *L. arcticus*.

Lepus othus is one of the largest species of hares. The skull is massive and the upper incisors are strongly recurved. Its stout claws facilitate digging through hard-crusted snow to reach vegetation. In winter pelage, it is white except for the extreme tips of the ears, which are black. In May, it may still be in winter pelage near snow fields at higher elevations, where it can be observed loping over the tundra, pale underparts flashing and large hind feet conspicuous; tail flagging also occurs. In summer pelage (August), the nose, sides of the face, and top of the head are brownish-orange; the top of the head is darkest. The front half of the outer surface of the ears is similar in color to the head. The back half of the ears is white and the tips are brownish. The tail is white or gray.

Alaskan hares are solitary except during the April–May mating season, when groups of 20 or more may be seen. Conception occurs from mid-April to May, and the gestation period is about 46 days. Usually, one litter of 5 to 7 young (average is 6) is born per year. The young may be born in nest sites aboveground with no brush or in the thick shelter of willow or alder brush. Some nests are located in natural depressions in the moss and cotton sedges, and have no lining; in those nests, the backs of the young are well beneath the top of the surrounding tundra, but the young are continuously exposed to cold, wind, and rain.

The time of birth seems to coincide with the loss of snow cover in late May. The young are precocial, and this timing enhances their chance of survival, because the snow has melted, their brown pelage blends in with the color of the ground surface, food is abundant, and ambient temperatures are relatively high. On some young, a white center stripe about 10 millimeters long is present on the forehead. The pupils are dark and the iris is dark blue. The young begin drifting away from the mother a few weeks after birth.

Females show signs of nursing for 5–9 weeks after parturition. This prolonged nursing period helps maintain a rapid rate of growth. The estimated average growth rate for juveniles is 37.2 grams per day over a 102-day growth period, from a birth weight of 100 g to a minimum adult weight of 3,900 g. The hind foot attains 95 percent of the average adult size in 112 days, an average rate of growth of 2.6 millimeters per day. Rapid growth allows at least a minimum adult body mass to be reached during the short summer, thereby increasing the hare's chances of survival through its first winter.

Lepus othus inhabits tundra in the coastal regions of Alaska.

Lepus othus

It lives in dense alder thickets, and in summer, when the vegetation is leafed out, it is nearly impossible to see. It comes out of the thickets in the evenings to feed. During snow and rain *L. othus* makes no attempt to seek shelter. Near the Kashunuk River, it was found in all habitats from sedge flats and wet meadows to the upper slopes of the Askinuk Mountains. The two subspecies are associated with distinct habitat types, and each subspecies is composed of a complex of disjunct populations. *Lepus othus othus* prefers tundra or alluvial plain, whereas *L. o. poadromus* lives primarily in coastal lowland areas.

During April and May, the diet consists mainly of shrubs, especially woody willow tissue and crowberry leaves. In early spring, Alaskan hares may be seen feeding at the edge of melting snow patches, where crowberries from the previous summer are abundant. The hares seldom drink water.

Population density varies among localities and years. Pilots flying over the Alaska Peninsula report seeing many Alaskan hares during some years, but no hares in other years. Alaskan hares are particularly difficult to see in summer when their pelage is brown. Predators include golden eagles, rough-legged hawks, snowy owls, gyrfalcons, arctic foxes, red foxes, weasels, wolverines, gray wolves, and polar bears. When attacked by a snowy owl, the alaskan hare may strike at the owl with its forefeet when the bird swoops low. Between attacks it races toward the nearest patch of willows for shelter. Because the red fox is present throughout the year and probably capable of taking both adult and juvenile hares, it may be the most important predator. No ectoparasites are known; endoparasites include nematodes. *T. L. Best*

Size
Total length: 565–690 (597) mm
Length of tail: 65–104 (74) mm
Weight: 3,900–7,200 (4,800) g

Identification
The Alaskan hare can be distinguished from
L. arcticus and *L. timidus* on the basis of skull
characters, but these species are also separated
geographically. *L. othus* may occur with
L. americanus. Compared with *L. americanus,*
L. othus has longer ears, a tail that is always
white, and winter pelage that is white to the
base of the hairs.

Recent Synonyms
Lepus poadromus

Other Common Names
Alaska tundra hare, St. Michaels's hare, swift
hare, Alaska arctic hare, tundra hare, Alaska
Peninsula hare, ukalisukruk, ugalishugruk,
ushkanuk, okhotsk, oo-skon

Status
Uncommon

Subspecies
Lepus othus othus, northern and western Alaska
Lepus othus poadromus, southwestern Alaska

References
Mammalian Species 458; Walkinshaw, 1947

White-tailed jackrabbit | *Lepus townsendii*

The white-tailed jackrabbit is distributed in west-central North America from the prairies of southern Saskatchewan and Alberta to the Rocky Mountains of northern New Mexico, and from Lake Michigan in Wisconsin to east of the Cascade Mountains of Washington and the Sierra Nevada Mountains of California. *Lepus townsendii* has been increasing its range to the east and north as suitable open habitats have been created. However, a range reduction has occurred in the southeast as habitat alterations there favored the sympatric black-tailed jackrabbit. There are some introduced populations of white-tailed jackrabbits in Wisconsin. The white-tailed jackrabbit is found at elevations from 40 m to 4,300 m, which may be the widest range for any species of hare. Fossils are common from the early Holocene when the white-tailed jackrabbit was apparently more numerous than the black-tailed jackrabbit.

However, by the middle Holocene, with the beginning of the warming trend, the black-tailed jackrabbit seems to have become more prevalent.

White-tailed jackrabbits are primarily nocturnal animals and spend most of their time between sunset and sunrise feeding and grooming. They are among the least sociable hares, except during the breeding season when small groupings may be formed. Otherwise, they are essentially solitary animals, except for an occasional, temporary aggregation. The daylight hours are usually spent resting in forms (shallow depressions) dug near bushes or rocks. Nests for young are lined with dry leaves, grasses, and hair from the mother, but a nest is not always made. Where there is persistent snow cover, cavities with connecting tunnels may be dug into the snow .

The summer pelage of the white-tailed jackrabbit is yellow-

Lepus townsendii

ish to grayish-brown on the upperparts and white or pale gray on the underparts. The throat is darker. In the northern or mountainous parts of its range, there is a winter molt to a thick white pelage with tinges of buff. In southern localities or at lower elevations, there may be no color change or only a partial change. The molt to summer pelage begins around the eyes and rump and then spreads around the head, flanks, and back. The winter molt reverses the process. The tips of the ears are always black, and the tail remains white, with a buffy dorsal stripe present on some. The juvenile pelage is essentially a duller version of the adult pelage, with fewer and finer guard hairs, so that more underfur shows through.

Depending on elevation and latitude, breeding may begin in February and one to four litters may be produced per year. The litter size can range from 1 to 11 young, but 4 or 5 is most common. The gestation period can last from 30 to 43 days, with a postpartum estrus in many populations. Neonates are born fully haired, with their eyes open and incisors erupted. They weigh about 90 g at birth and have some mobility within half an hour. Young begin foraging at approximately 2 weeks of age, are fully weaned by 1 month, and are independent after about 2 months. The maximum longevity in the wild is about 8 years.

Lepus townsendii is herbivorous and feeds on succulent grasses and forbs when available. It resorts to shrubs during the drier winter. Young tend to feed on grasses. In sympatry, black-tailed jackrabbits seem less selective in the plant species they eat, which may give them a competitive advantage over the white-tailed jackrabbit. Open grassland is the preferred habitat of the white-tailed jackrabbit; sagebrush and meadowland are used less frequently. Where the distributions of the two species overlap, black-tailed jackrabbits tend to be found more often in sagebrush. In mountainous habitats, white-tailed jackrabbits predominate on the slopes and ridges and black-tailed jackrabbits are more common on the valley floors.
B. K. Lim

Size
Females usually slightly larger than males
Total length: 565–618 (589) mm (males); 575–655 (612) mm (females)
Length of tail: 72–102 (85) mm (males); 66–100 (85) mm (females)
Weight (winter): 2,600–4,300 (3,400) g (males); 2,500–4,300 (3,600) g (females)

Identification
Lepus townsendii is larger than *Lepus californicus* and has a white tail (occasionally with a dusky dorsal stripe); *Lepus californicus* has a black dorsal stripe on its tail.

Recent Synonyms
Lepus campestris

Other Common Names
Prairie hare

Status
Locally common

Subspecies
Lepus townsendii campanius, east of the Continental Divide
Lepus townsendii townsendii, west of the Continental Divide

References
Mammalian Species 288; Dunn et al., 1982

Appendix

Common and Scientific Names of Plants Cited

The editors have compiled this list of scientific names for many of the plant common names mentioned in the species accounts. However, all of the warnings about the lack of precision of common names apply to plants as well as to animals, and some errors may have crept in.

alder: *Alnus* species; red alder: *Alnus rubra*

alfalfa: *Medicago sativa*

Arabian grass (also called Mediterranean grass): *Schismus arabicus*

arctic avens: *Dryas integrifolia*

arctic dock: *Rumex arcticus*

aspen: *Populus tremuloides* or *P. grandidentata*

aster: *Aster* species

barrel cactus: *Ferocactus* species

basswood: *Tilia* species

beach grass: species in a number of genera are known as beach grasses

bearberry: *Arctostaphylos* species (bearberry is sometimes called manzanita on the West Coast)

bear grass: *Xerophyllum tenax*

beardgrass (bushy beardgrass): *Andropogon glomeratus*

beech: *Fagus* species; American beech: *Fagus grandifolia*

Bermuda grass: *Cynodon dactylon*

birch: *Betula* species; paper birch: *Betula papyrifera*

blackberry (and raspberry): *Rubus* species; Pacific or California blackberry: *Rubus ursinus*

blackbrush (also called blackbush): *Coleogyne ramosissima*

bluebead lily: *Clintonia borealis*

blueberry: *Vaccinium* species; bog bilberry, bog blueberry, or alpine blueberry: *Vaccinium uliginosum*

blue-blossom: *Ceanothus thyrsiflorus*

bluestem (also called big bluestem): *Andropogon gerardii;* little bluestem: *Schizachyrium scoparium;* seashore bluestem: *S. maritimus*

bottlebrush: *Elymus* species

bracken fern: *Pteridium aquilinum*

bristlegrass: *Setaria* species

brome-grass: *Bromus* species

broomsedge: *Andropogon virginicus*

buckbrush: *Ceanothus cuneatus* (in California); *Symphoricarpos orbiculatus* (Great Plains)

buckthorn: *Rhamnus* species

buffalo grass: *Buchloë dactyloides* (Great Plains); *Monroa squarrosa* (from California eastward to the Great Plains)

bull-nettle: *Cnidoscolus texanus*

bull thistle: *Cirsium vulgare*

bulrushes: *Scirpus* species

bunchberry: *Cornus canadensis*

bunchgrass: species of *Agropyron, Poa, Festuca,* and other genera are all known locally as bunchgrass

bur-clover: *Medicago polymorpha*

burro bush or burro-weed: in California, *Ambrosia dumosa;* plants in other genera are known as burro bush, burro-brush, or burro-weed elsewhere

bursage: *Ambrosia* species; annual bursage: *Ambrosia acanthicarpa;* perennial bursage: *A. tomentosa*

California laurel: *Umbellularia californica*

camphor-weed: *Heterotheca* species

Canada mayflower: *Maianthemum canadense*

cardon: *Pachycereus* species; Mexican cardon: *Pachycereus pringlei*

catclaw: species of *Acacia, Mimosa,* and other genera are known locally as catclaw

cattail: *Typha* species

ceanothus (also known as snowbush, snowbrush, or mountain whitethorn): *Ceanothus* species

centella: *Centella erecta*

century-plant: *Agave* species

chamise: *Adenostoma fasciculatum*

cheatgrass: *Bromus* species

cherry: *Prunus* species; bitter cherry: *Prunus emarginata*

chinquapin: *Castanea pumila*

cholla: *Opuntia* species

chokecherry: *Prunus virginiana*

cliffbush: *Jamesia americana*

cliffrose: *Purshia mexicana*

clover: *Trifolium* species

coontail: *Ceratophyllum* species

corn: *Zea mays*

cottongrass: *Eriophorum* species

cow-parsnip: *Heracleum lanatum*

crab grass: *Digitaria sanguinalis*

creosote or creosote-bush: *Larrea tridentata*

croton: *Croton* species

crowberry: *Empetrum* species

crow-poison (also called false garlic): *Nothoscordium bivalve*

currant: *Ribes* species; wax or squaw currant: *Ribes cereum*

cypress (bald cypress): *Taxodium distichum*

dandelion: *Taraxacum* species

dagame tree: *Calycophyllum candidissimum* (native from Mexico to Colombia and Venezuela and in Cuba; a cultivated ornamental elsewhere)

deerbrush: *Ceanothus integerrimus*

desert tea (also called Mormon-tea or Mexican-tea): *Ephedra* species

desert thorn: *Lycium* species

desert willow: *Chilopsis linearis*

devil's club: *Oplopanax horridus*

dogwood: *Cornus* species; Pacific (or mountain) dogwood: *Cornus nuttallii*

Douglas fir: *Pseudotsuga menziesii*

elderberry: *Sambucus* species; blue elderberry: *Sambucus mexicana*

ephedra: *Ephedra* species (*see also* desert tea and Mormon tea)

eragrostis (also known as lovegrass): *Eragrostis* species; creeping eragrostis: *Eragrostis hypnoides*; Lehmann lovegrass: *E. lehmanniana*

eucalyptus: *Eucalyptus* species

false miterwort: *Tiarella cordifolia*

false Solomon's seal: *Smilacina* species

fan palm: any species of several genera of palms with fan-like leaves

fescue grass or fescues: *Festuca* species

filaree: *Erodium cicutarium*

fir: *Abies* species (*see also* Douglas fir, which is in another genus); balsam fir: *A. balsamea*; grand fir: *A. grandis*; red fir: *A. magnifica*; silver fir (also called Pacific silver fir): *A. amabilis*; white fir: *A. concolor*

fireweed: *Epilobium* species; narrow-leaved fireweed: *Epilobium angustifolium*

fimbry: *Fimbristylis* species

foxtail: a number of species, especially in the genus *Alopecurus*, are known as foxtail grasses

glacier lily: *Erythronium grandiflorum*

goldenrod: *Solidago* species

gooseberry: *Ribes* species

grama: *Bouteloua* species; black grama: *Bouteloua eriopoda*; blue grama: *B. gracilis*

granjeno: *see* hackberry

grapes: *Vitis* species

greasewood: *Sarcobatus vermiculatus*; see also Nevada greasewood

greenbrier: *Smilax* species

hackberry: *Celtis* species; desert (or spiny) hackberry, also known as granjeno: *Celtis pallida*; net-leaf hackberry: *C. reticulata*

hazelnut: *Corylus* species

hemlock: *Tsuga* species; eastern hemlock: *Tsuga canadensis*; western hemlock: *T. heterophylla*

hickory: *Carya* species; bitternut hickory: *Carya cordiformis*; shagbark hickory: *C. ovata*

honeysuckle: *Lonicera* species; Japanese honeysuckle: *Lonicera japonica*

horsebrush: *Tetradymia* species

horsetail: *Equisetum* species; common horsetail: *Equisetum arvense*

horseweed: *Conyza canadensis*

huckleberry: *Gaylussacia* species; in some areas, *Vaccinium* species are called huckeberry: e.g., California huckleberry: *V. ovatum*; red huckleberry: *V. parvifolium*

hydrilla: *Hydrilla verticillata*

incense cedar: *Calocedrus decurrens*

Indian rice grass: *Achnatherum hymenoides*

iodine bush: *Allenrolfea occidentalis*

Johnson grass: *Sorghum halepense*

jojoba: *Simmondsia chinensis*

Joshua tree: *Yucca brevifolia*

juniper: *Juniperus* species; Ashe juniper (also called rock cedar or post cedar): *Juniperus ashei*; common juniper: *J. communis*; Rocky Mountain juniper: *J. scopulorum*; Utah juniper: *J. osteoperma*; western juniper: *J. occidentalis*

Labrador tea: *Ledum groenlandicum*

lechuguilla: *Agave lecheguilla*

Lehmann lovegrass: *Eragrostis lehmanniana*

lupine: *Lupinus* species

madrone: *Arbutus* species; Pacific madrone: *Arbutus menziesii*

magnolia: *Magnolia* species; southern magnolia: *Magnolia grandiflora*

manzanita (also known as bearberry): *Arctostaphylos* species

maple: *Acer* species; big-leaf maple: *Acer macrophyllum*; red maple: *A. rubrum* ; sugar maple: *A. saccharum*; vine maple: *A. circinatum*.

mastic tree (also called gumbo-limbo): *Bursera simaruba*

meadowrue: *Thalictrum* species

medusa-head grass: *Taeniatherum caput-medusae*

mesquite: *Prosopis* species; honey mesquite: *Prosopis glandulosa*

Mormon tea (also called Mexican tea or desert tea): *Ephedra* species

morning-glory: *Ipomoea* species

mountain laurel: *Kalmia latifolia*

mountain mahogany: *Cercocarpus* species

mountain sorrel: *Oxyria digyna*

mullein: *Verbascum* species

needlegrass: *Stipa* species

Nevada greasewood: *Glossopetalon spinescens*

ninebark: *Physocarpus* species

nut-grass (also known as nut-sedge): *Cyperus* species

oak: *Quercus* species (*see also* tan-bark oak and poison oak, which belong to other genera); black oak (California black oak): *Quercus kelloggii*; blue oak: *Q. douglasii*; Gambel's oak: *Q. gambelii*; live oak: *Q. virginiana*; laurel oak: *Q. myrtifolia*; maul oak or canyon live oak: *Q. chrysolepis*; post oak: *Q. stellata*; waxy-leaf or Rocky Mountain scrub oak: *Q. undulata*

oats: *Avena* species; wild oats: *Avena fatua*

ocotillo: *Fouquieria splendens*; Mexican ocotillo: *Fouquieria diguetii*

Oregon grape: *Berberis* species

organpipe cactus: *Stenocereus thurberi*

oyster plant: species in any of four genera (*Rhoeo, Scolymus, Scarzonera, Tragopogon*) are known as oyster plants

paintbrush: *Castilleja* species

palmetto: plants of several genera (*Chamaerops, Rhapidophyllum, Sabal*) are known as palmettos; saw palmetto: *Serenoa repens*

palo-verde: *Cercidium* species

peavine: *Lathyrus* species

pawpaw: *Asimina triloba*

pennywort: *Hydrocotyle* species; marsh pennywort: *Hydrocotyle americana*

peppergrass: *Lepidium* species

pickerel weed: *Pontederia* species

pickleweed: *Salicornia* species

pigweed: *Chenopodium* species; species of *Amaranthus* and other genera are also known as pigweed

pine: *Pinus* species; Coulter pine: *Pinus coulteri*; digger pine: *P. sabiniana*; eastern white pine: *P. strobus*; Great Basin or western bristlecone pine: *P. longaeva*; jack pine: *P. banksiana*; Jeffrey pine: *P. jeffreyi*; limber pine: *P. flexilis*; lodgepole pine: *P. contorta*; longleaf pine: *P. palustris*; pinyon pine: *P. edulis*; single-leaf pinyon pine: *P. monophylla*; ponderosa pine: *P. ponderosa*; Rocky Mountain bristlecone pine: *P. aristata*; sand pine: *P. clausa*; slash pine: *P. elliottii*; sugar pine: *P. lambertiana*; western white pine: *P. monticola*; whitebark pine: *P. albicaulis*; yellow pine: in the West, *P. ponderosa*; in the East, *P. palustris* and *P. echinata* are sometimes called yellow pine.

plantain: *Plantago* species

poison ivy: *Toxicodendron radicans*

poison oak (western poison oak): *Toxicodendron diversilobum*

prickly pear: *Opuntia* species

pulque: *Agave salmiana*

pussypaws: *Calyptridium* or *Cistanthe* species

rabbitbrush: *Chrysothamnus* species

ragweed: *Ambrosia* species

raspberry (and blackberry): *Rubus* species; western (or blackcap) raspberry: *Rubus leucodermis*

redwood: *Sequoia sempervirens*

rhododendron: *Rhododendron* species

ring muhly: *Muhlenbergia torreyi*

roseroot: *Sedum rosea*

royal palm: *Roystonea* species

rush: *Juncus* species

Russian thistle: *Salsola* species

ryegrass: various species of *Elymus* are called "wild rye"; *Lolium* species are also ryegrasses

sagebrush: *Artemisia* species; big sagebrush or big sage: *Artemisia tridentata*

saguaro: *Carnegiea gigantea*

salal: *Gaultheria shallon*

salmonberry: *Rubus spectabilis*

saltbush (or saltbrush): *Atriplex* species; four-winged saltbrush: *Atriplex canescens*; spiny saltbrush: *A. confertifolia*

salt grass: *Distichlis* species

saltwort: *Salicornia* species; perennial saltwort, leadgrass, or woody grasswort: *Salicornia virginica*

scratch daisy: *Croptilon divaricatum*

Scotch broom: *Cytisus scoparius*

scrub oak: *Quercus* species

sea grape: *Coccoloba uvifera*

sea-oats: *Uniola paniculata*

sedge: *Carex* species

serviceberry: *Amelanchier* species; Utah serviceberry: *Amelanchier utahensis*

shadblow: *Amelanchier arborea*

shadscale (also known as spiny saltbush): *Atriplex* species

sheep laurel: *Kalmia* species

shoregrass: *Monanthochloë littoralis*

silk-tassel (also called silk-tassel bush or silk-tassel tree): *Garrya* species

silk tree: *Ceiba* species

skunk cabbage: yellow or western skunk cabbage (west of the Great Plains): *Lysichiton americanum;* eastern or wet- meadow skunk cabbage: *Veratrum* species

smartweed: *Polygonum* species

snakeweed: *Gutierrezia* species

snowberry: *Symphoricarpos* species

snow brush or snowbush: *Ceanothus* species

soap-tree, soapweed, or soap-plant: *Yucca* species

soft chess: *Bromis hordeaceus*

sotol: *Dasylirion* species

sow thistle: *Sonchus* species

Spanish moss: *Tillandsia usneoides*

spike rush: *Eleocharis* species

spruce: *Picea* species; Engelmann spruce: *Picea engelmannii;* red spruce: *P. rubens;* Sitka spruce: *P. sitchensis*

squawberry: *Lycium* species or *Mitchella repens,* depending on region

squirreltail: *Elymus* species

stinging nettle: *Urtica* species

sumac: *Rhus* species

sunflower: *Helianthus* species

sweet gum: *Liquidambar styraciflua*

sword fern: *Polystichum* species

sycamore: *Platanus* species

tamarack: *Larix* species

tanbark oak: *Lithocarpus densiflorus*

tarbush: *Flourensia cernua*

tetradymia: *Tetradymia* species

thimbleberry: *Rubus* species

three-awn: *Aristida* species

tobosagrass: *Hilaria mutica*

toyon: *Heteromeles arbutifolia*

tufted hairgrass: *Deschampsia cespitosa*

tupelo: *Nyssa* species; black or upland tupelo, also known as black gum: *Nyssa sylvatica*

turkey oak: *Quercus* species

walnut: *Juglans* species; Arizona walnut: *Juglans major*

water hyacinth: *Eichhornia crassipes*

wax myrtle: *Myrica* species

western azalea: *Rhododendron occidentale*

western red cedar: *Thuja plicata*

wild rose: *Rosa* species

willow: *Salix* species (see also desert willow, which is in another genus); round-leaf willow: *Salix ovalifolia*

windmill grass: *Chloris* species

wolftail (grass): *Lycurus phleoides*

wood sorrel: *Oxalis* species

yaupon: *Ilex vomitoria*

yew: *Taxus* species; Pacific yew: *Taxus brevifolia*

Glossary

aestivate, aestivation: *see* estivate

alkali-sink: a sunken area of land where the soil is strongly impregnated with alkalis, which are destructive to vegetation

allopatric: living in different areas; species are allopatric when their ranges do not overlap

altricial: born in an underdeveloped and therefore dependent state; the opposite of precocial

amphipods: a family of small crustaceans sometimes known as "sand fleas," although they bear no relation to fleas

arroyo: a gully

arvicoline: refers to a subfamily of rodents, the Arvicolinae, which includes voles, lemmings, and muskrats

beak (cetacean): the elongated mouth of some dolphins

blastocyst: an early stage in development of an embryo, when the cells are not yet differentiated into organs

boreal: northern

brown fat: an unusual type of fat that is found almost exclusively in animals that hibernate

bulla: a bony compartment on the mastoid bone of the skull that surrounds the middle and inner ear

caecum, cecum: a blind branch of the alimentary canal, present in many mammals and best developed in certain herbivorous species

calcar: a cartilagenous calcaneum bone of the ankle; a *keeled calcar* (on a bat) is a ridgelike growth on the calcar that facilitates muscle attachment and helps support the interfemoral membrane

cape (on a whale): a distinctive color marking behind the head and across the shoulders

caudal peduncle: the "tail stock" of a cetacean, the portion of the animal from the dorsal fin down to the tail

chaparral: a thick, low, brushy vegetation type

CITES: Convention on International Trade in Endangered Species; Appendix I includes species threatened with extinction that are or may be affected by trade; Appendix II includes species that although not necessarily threatened with extinction may become so unless trade in them is strictly controlled, as well as nonthreatened species that must be subject to regulation in order to control threatened species; and Appendix III includes species that any party identifies as being subject to regulation within its jurisdiction for purposes of preventing or restricting exploitation, and for which it needs the cooperation of other parties in controlling trade

congeners: species that are members of the same genus

convergent evolution: the evolution of similar characteristics, as adaptations to similar ways of life, by species of quite different ancestry

copepods: a family of enormously abundant tiny crustaceans

coprophagy: ingestion of fecal matter

crepuscular: occurring in twilight; animals that are active around dawn and dusk are described as crepuscular (*see* diurnal and nocturnal)

cryptic: hidden

delayed development: after fertilization, the blastocyst implants in the uterine wall, but then ceases dividing, or divides only very slowly, for some period of time

delayed implantation: the fertilized ovum develops only to about an early blastocyst stage, and then is retained in a dormant state in the uterus, without implanting in the uterine wall, for a period of time

dimorphism: occurring in two forms; sexual dimorphism may refer to size or other differences between males and females

distal: toward the open or free end of a structure; opposite of proximal

diurnal: active during daylight hours (*see* nocturnal and crepuscular)

dorsal (dorsum): the upperparts of an animal

dorsal fin: fin on the back of certain cetaceans

echolocation: a system of high-frequency sounds and their echoes used by most bats and some insectivores and cetaceans to navigate and locate their prey

ectoparasites: parasites that live externally on the body of their hosts

electrophoresis: a biochemical laboratory technique used to study differences in protein structure in different species

endemic: native to, prevalent in, or restricted to a certain geographic area

endoparasites: parasites that live inside the body of their hosts

Eocene: an epoch of the Tertiary Period between the end of the Paleocene, about 54 million years ago, and the beginning of the Oligocene, about 30 million years ago

ericaceous: pertaining to plants in the family Ericaceae, which includes *Azalea, Rhododendron, Kalmia,* and other genera

estivate: to spend the summer in a dormant condition (*see* hibernate)

estrus: the period of time when a female is receptive to mating. A female in estrus is carrying an egg or eggs ready to be fertilized. The frequency with which females of a species come into estrus is referred to as the estrous cycle. Polyestrous animals come into season more than once a year; monoestrous species experience estrus just once annually. In some species, females come into estrus immediately after giving birth: this is known as post-partum estrus.

euphausiids: small, shrimplike zoöplankton commonly known as krill

falcate: curved (sickle-shaped)

fluke: tailfin of a whale

folivores, folivorous: animals that feed on leaves; leaf-eating

forbs: low-growing, herbaceous plants other than grasses

fossorial: dwelling underground

friable: easily crumbled

gape (of a cetacean): area of the mouth when opened during feeding; sometimes called "free gape."

glumes: in botany, the husk or scale-like bract on the axis of the spikelet in grains and grasses

granivores, granivorous: animals that eat seeds or grains; seed-eating

halophyte: a plant that grows in salt-impregnated soil

hammock (or hummock): a piece of elevated, rich land with hardwood trees growing on it

harem: a group of females controlled by a male for mating purposes

hallux: opposable first toe

headland (as in headland prairie or a headland scrub community): a strip of unplowed land near a fence

hibernate: to spend the winter in a dormant condition (see estivate)

Holarctic: the entire arctic, comprising the Nearctic (the arctic and north temperate parts of North America) and the Palearctic (Eurasia)

hypogeous fungi: underground fungi

induced estrus: estrus brought on by any external factor

inguinal: pertaining to, or located on, or near, the groin

interfemoral membrane, or uropatagium: membrane that stretches between the hind limbs of bats

karst: refers to areas with limestone caves

karyotype: the size, shape, and number of the set of chromosomes characteristic of a species or subspecies

keeled sternum: a breastbone that has a ridge along the center shaped like the keel of a ship

krumholtz: low-lying, wind-blown bushes

lacrimal shelf: a ridge of bone underneath the eye socket

lactational pregnancy: pregnancy that occurs while a female is still nursing earlier-born offspring

lappet: a fleshy membrane that hangs loosely, for example, in the ear of some bats

mast (crops): beechnuts, acorns, chestnuts, etc.

mastoid bones or bullae: see bulla

maxillary bridge: the bony area underneath the nose, joining the upper jaws

melon: the bulging forehead of a dolphin, caused by a fatty deposit

mesenteries: membranes around internal organs that attach them to the body wall or to other organs

mesic: wet or moist habitat

microtine: a name referring to a subgroup of rodents that includes the voles, lemmings, and muskrats; Arvicolinae is a newer name for this subfamily (see arvicoline), but "microtine" is still widely used

midden: a dunghill or refuse heap

Miocene: an epoch of the Tertiary Period between the end of the Oligocene, about 23 million years ago, and the beginning of the Pliocene, about 5 million years ago

molossid: refers to a family of bats, the Molossidae, or free-tailed bats

monoestrous: see estrus

morphology: the study of the form and structure of animals (or plants)

mysids: a family of crustaceans that are small enough to not be noticed by fishermen; some of them are known as opossum shrimp because of the way they carry their eggs around

Nearctic: designating the arctic and north temperate parts of North America

neonate: newborn

nictitating membrane: a transparent third eyelid

nocturnal: active at night (see diurnal and crlpuscular)

occipitals: large, strong bones at the base of the skull

Oligocene: an epoch of the Tertiary Period between the end of the Eocene, about 30 million years ago, and the beginning of the Miocene, about 23 million years ago

orbit: the bony cavity in which the eye sits

Palearctic: biogeographic region comprising Europe, Asia north of the Himalayas, and Africa north of the Sahara

parietals: bones that form part of the top and sides of the skull

pectoral: located on or near the chest

pelage: the hairy or furry covering of a mammal

pelagic: referring to the ocean surface or the open sea, as opposed to coastal waters

pheromones: odiferous chemical compounds produced by animals, frequently involved in courtship

phyllostomid: referring to a family of bats, the Phyllostomidae, or leaf-nosed bats

pinna: the external ear (plural: pinnae)

plantigrade: walking on the whole sole of the foot

plantar tubercles: nodules, or small bumps, on the underside of the toes or sole of the foot

Pleistocene: the geological period extending from about 1,000,000 years ago to about 10,000 years ago

polyandrous: a mating system in which females mate with more than one male

polyestrous: see estrus

polygamous: a mating system in which both sexes mate with more than one mate

polygynous: a mating system in which males mate with more than one female

post-auricular: behind the ear, on the shoulder

postpartum estrus: see estrus

precocial: born in a fully-developed state; the opposite of altricial

rachis (plant part): the straight stem in a kind of flower cluster

Recent (geology): designating the current era, from the close of the Pleistocene until the present

recent synonyms: other scientific names by which an organism has been known

resaca (oxbow lake marsh) habitat: marshy habitat formed in a regenerating oxbow lake

riparian: on, relating to, or near the banks of a river or stream

rorqual: a whale in the family Balaenopteridae; "rorqual" is of Scandinavian origin and probably meant "tube whale," referring to the long furrows in the throat, chest and sometimes the belly that allow the throat to expand enormously for feeding

rostrum: a snout, beak, or beaklike projection; the front, or facial, part of the skull

ruminant: an animal that swallows large quantities of food, and then regurgitates and rechews it; most artiodactyls are ruminants

rut, rutting season: periodic sexual excitement of the males of some species, such as artiodactyls

saggital crest: a bony structure running along the top of the braincase, which facilitates muscle attachment

saltatorial: moving by hopping or leaping

scansorial: climbing or able to climb

sclerophyll: refers to plants with tough leaves that are difficult for most animals to chew and digest

scrub: habitat with thick, shrubby growth

seral: referring to the series of plant communities that succeed one another before a stable, or climax, plant community, is reached

spermatogenesis: the production and development of sperm

sperm competition: the theory that in some species, competition in males occurs at the level of fertilization; in these species, the females copulate with multiple males and the males have very large testes in proportion to body size

spicule: a small, hard, pointed mass

spyhopping: the behavior in which a whale raises its head out of the water, supposedly for a look around

subfertile: less than fully fertile; subfertile offspring have a much reduced level of fertility relative to that of their parents, and produce fewer offspring than their parents did

sympatric: living in the same area

synchronous breeding: a breeding system in which all the members of a population tend to breed at the same time

taiga: the coniferous forests in far northern regions of Eurasia or North America

talus: a sloping pile of rock fragments at the base of a cliff

thorax: in mammals, the body cavity formed by the spine, ribs, and breastbone

torpor: a state of inactivity

tragus: a flap, sometimes movable, in the opening of the outer ear

tubercle: a hard bump or nodule on the skin or on a bone

tundra: a flat, boggy, treeless arctic region

type locality: the place where the original specimen that a species was described and named from was found

underparts: the whole underside of an animal from chin to tail (*see* venter)

unicuspid: a tooth with only a single cusp

uropatagium, or interfemoral membrane: membrane stretched between the hind limbs of bats

vector: an organism that carries disease

venter: the underside of the animal (opposite of dorsum), usually used to refer to the underside of the body (abdomen and thorax) (*see* underparts)

vespertilionid: refers to a family of bats, the Vespertilionidae

vestigial: a rudimentary organ that was more functional in an earlier stage of the animal's development

vibrissae: long, stiff hairs, which are called whiskers when they occur on the face, and which extend an animal's sense of touch

water column: used to describe a vertical transect through the ocean, providing reference to specific depths at which whales feed

xeric: dry habitat

xerophyllic: adapted to a dry environment

zygomatic arch: cheekbone

Two references that are not cited in individual accounts were used throughout the book. For taxonomy, the editors relied upon Wilson and Reeder, 1993. For the distribution of subspecies, the primary resource was Hall, 1981. *Mammalian Species* accounts are grouped together at the end of this bibliography and listed in numerical order.

Alcorn, J. R. 1940. Life history notes on the Piute ground squirrel. *Journal of Mammalogy*, 21:160–170.

Alderton, D. 1996. *Rodents of the world*. Facts on File, New York, 192 pp.

Alexander, L. F. 1996. A morphometric analysis of geographic variation within *Sorex monticolus* (Insectivora: Soricidae). *University of Kansas Publications, Museum of Natural History*, 88: 1–54.

Allard, M. W., S. J. Gunn, and I. F. Greenbaum. 1987. Mensural discrimination of chromosomally characterized *Peromyscus oreas* and *Peromyscus maniculatus. Journal of Mammalogy*, 68:402–406.

Allen, D. L. 1943. *Michigan fox squirrel management.* Michigan Department of Conservation. Lansing, 404 pp.

Allred, W. S., W.S. Gaud, and J. S. States. 1994. Effects of herbivory by Abert's squirrels on cone crops of ponderosa pine. *Journal of Mammalogy*, 75:700–703.

Andersen, D. C., and J. A. MacMahon. 1981. Population dynamics and bioenergetics of a fossorial herbivore, *Thomomys talpoides* (Rodentia: Geomyidae), in a spruce-fire sere. *Ecological Monographs*, 51:179–202.

Anderson, A. E. 1983. A critical review of literature on the puma. *Colorado Division of Wildlife Special Report*, 54:1–91.

Anderson, S. 1959. Distribution, variation, and relationships of the montane vole, *Microtus montanus. University of Kansas Publications, Museum of Natural History*, 9:415–511.

Anderson, S. 1972. Mammals of Chihuahua: Taxonomy and distribution. *Bulletin of the American Museum of Natural History*, 48:149–410.

Arita, H. T., and S. R. Humphrey. 1988 [1989]. Revisión taxonómica de los murciélagos magueyeros del género *Leptonycteris* (Chiroptera: Phyllostomidae). *Acta Zoológica Mexicana*, Nueva Serie, 29:1–60.

Arita, H. T., and D. E. Wilson. 1987. Long-nosed bats and agaves: The tequila connection. *Bats*, 5(4)3–5.

Armitage, K. B., J. C. Melcher, and J. M. Ward, Jr. 1990. Oxygen consumption and body temperature in yellow-bellied marmot populations from montane-mesic and lowland xeric environments. *Journal of Comparative Physiology. B. Biochemical, Systematic and Environmental Physiology*, 160:491–502.

Armstrong, D. M. 1972. Distribution of mammals in Colorado. *Monograph of the Museum of Natural History, The University of Kansas*, 3:1–415.

Armstrong, D. M. 1982. *Mammals of the canyon country: a handbook of mammals of the Canyonlands National Park and vicinity.* Canyonlands Natural History Association, Moab, Utah, 263 pp.

Armstrong, D. M. 1987. *Rocky Mountain mammals.* Colorado Associated University Press, Boulder, 223 pp.

Armstrong, D. M., B. H. Banta, and E. J. Pokropus. 1973. Altitudinal distribution of small mammals along a cross-sectional transect through the Arkansas River watershed, Colorado. *Southwestern Naturalist*, 17:315–326.

Bailey, V. 1931. Mammals of New Mexico. *North American Fauna*, 53:1–412.

Bailey, V. 1936. The mammals and life zones of Oregon. *North American Fauna*, 55:1–416.

Baird, R. W. and P. J. Stacey. 1993. Sightings, strandings and incidental catches of short-finned pilot whales, *Globicephala machroryhncus*, off the British Columbia coast. *Report of the International Whaling Commission*, Special Issue, 14:475–479

Baker, R. H. 1956. Mammals of Coahuila, Mexico. *University of Kansas Publications, Museum of Natural History*, 9:125–335.

Baker, R. H. 1969. Cotton rats of the *Sigmodon fulviventer* group. *Miscellaneous Publications, Museum of Natural History, University of Kansas*, 51:1–428.

Baker, R. H. 1983. *Michigan mammals.* Michigan State University Press, 624 pp.

Baker, R. H., and J. K. Greer. 1962. Mammals of the Mexican state of Durango. *Publications of the Museum, Michigan State University*, 2:1–154

Baker, R. J., S. K. Davis, R. D. Bradley, M. J. Hamilton, and R. A. Van Den Bussche. 1989. Ribosomal-DNA, mitochondrial-DNA, chromosomal, and allozymic studies on a contact zone in the pocket gopher, *Geomys. Evolution*, 43:63–75.

Baker, R. J., and H. H. Genoways. 1975. A new subspecies of *Geomys bursarius* (Mammalia: Geomyidae) from Texas and New Mexico. *Occasional Papers, The Museum, Texas Tech University*, 29:1–18.

Baker, R. J., T. Mollhagen, and G. Lopez. 1972. Notes on *Lasiurus ega. Journal of Mammalogy*, 52:849–852.

Baker, R. J., J. C. Patton, H. H. Genoways, and J. W. Bickham. 1988. Genic studies of *Lasiurus* (Chiroptera: Vespertilionidae). *Occasional Papers, The Museum, Texas Tech University*, 117:1–15.

Bakko, E. B., and J. Nahorniak. 1986. Torpor patterns in captive white-tailed prairie dogs *(Cynomys leucurus). Journal of Mammalogy*, 67:576–578.

Balph, D. F. 1984. Spatial and social behavior in a population of Uinta ground squirrels: interrelations with climate and annual cycle. Pp. 336–352, in *The biology of ground-dwelling squirrels* (J. O. Murie and G. R. Michener, eds.). University of Nebraska Press, Lincoln, 459 pp.

Banfield, A.W. F. 1961. A revision of the reindeer and caribou. *National Museum of Canada Bulletin,* 177:1–137.

Banfield, A.W. F. 1974. *The mammals of Canada.* The University of Toronto Press, Toronto, 438 pp.

Barash, D. P. 1989. *Marmots: Social behavior and ecology.* Stanford University Press, Stanford, California, 360 pp.

Barbour, R. W., and W. H. Davis. 1969. *Bats of America.* University Press of Kentucky, Lexington, 286 pp.

Barbour, R. W., and W. H. Davis. 1974. *Mammals of Kentucky.* University Press of Kentucky, Lexington, 322 pp.

Barkalow, F. S. Jr., and M. Shorten. 1973. *The world of the gray squirrel.* J. P. Lippincott, Philadelphia, 160 pp.

Batzli, G. O., and H. Henttonen. 1990. Demography and resource use by microtine rodents near Toolik Lake, Alaska, U.S.A. *Arctic and Alpine Research,* 22:51–64.

Batzli, G. O., and H. Henttonen. 1993. Home range and social organization of the singing vole *(Microtus miurus). Journal of Mammalogy,* 74:868–878.

Batzli, G. O., R. G. White, S. F. MacLean, Jr., F. A Pitelka, and B. D. Collier. 1980. The herbivore-based trophic system. Pp. 335–410, in *An Arctic ecosystem: the coastal tundra at Barrow, Alaska* (J. Brown et al., eds.). Dowden, Hutchinson and Ross, Stroudsburg, PA, 571 pp.

Bauer, E., and P. Bauer. 1996. *Bears: Behavior, ecology, and conservation.* Voyageur Press, Inc. Stillwater, MN, 159 pp.

Bednarz, J. C., and J. A. Cook. 1984. Distribution and numbers of the white-sided jackrabbit *(Lepus callotis gaillardi)* in New Mexico. *Southwestern Naturalist,* 29:358–360.

Bee, J. W., and E. R. Hall. 1956. Mammals of northern Alaska on the Arctic slope. *Miscellaneous Publications, Museum of Natural History, University of Kansas,* 8:1–309.

Beg, M. A. 1971. Reproductive cycle and reproduction in red-tailed chipmunk, *Eutamias ruficaudus. Pakistan Journal of Zoology,* 3:1–13.

Beier, P., D. Choate, and R. H. Barrett. 1995. Movement patterns of mountain lions during different behaviors. *Journal of Mammalogy,* 76:1056–1070.

Bekoff, M., ed. 1978. *Coyotes: Biology, behavior, and management.* Academic Press, New York, 384 pp.

Bekoff, M., and M. C. Wells. 1986. Social ecology and behavior of coyotes. *Advances in the Study of Behavior,* 16:251–338.

Bell, G. P. 1985. The sensory basis of prey location by the California leaf-nosed bat, *Macrotus californicus* (Chiroptera: Phyllostomatidae). *Behavioral Ecology and Sociobiology,* 16:343–347.

Bell, G. P., G. A. Bartholomew, and K.A. Nagy. l986. The role of energetics, water economy, foraging behavior, and geothermal refugia in the distribution of the bat, *Macrotus californicus. Journal of Comparative Physiology,* 156B:441–450.

Bell, G. P., and M. B. Fenton. 1986. Visual acuity, sensitivity and binocularity in a gleaning insectivorous bat, *Macrotus californicus* (Chiroptera: Phyllostomidae). *Animal Behaviour,* 34:409–414.

Bellwood, J. J. 1992. Florida mastiff bat, *Eumops glaucinus floridanus.* Pp. 216–223, in *Rare and endangered biota of Florida,* Volume I: *Mammals* (S. R. Humphrey, ed.). University Press of Florida, Gainesville, 392 pp.

Benjaminsen, T., and I. Christensen. 1979. The natural history of the bottlenose whale, *Hyperoodon ampullatus* (Forster). Pp. 143–164, in *Behaviour of Marine Animals,* Volume 3: *Cetaceans* (H. E. Winn and B. L. Olla, eds.). Plenum Press, New York, 438 pp.

Benson, D. L., and F. R. Gehlbach. 1979. Ecological and taxonomic notes on the rice rat *(Oryzomys couesi)* in Texas. *Journal of Mammalogy,* 60:225–228.

Bergerud, A. T. 1978. Caribou. Pp. 83–101, in *Big game of North America* (J. L. Schmidt and D. L Gilbert, eds.). Stackpole Books, Harrisburg, PA, 494 pp.

Bergstrom, B. J., and R. S. Hoffmann. 1991. Distribution and diagnosis of three species of chipmunks *(Tamias)* in the Front Range of Colorado. *Southwestern Naturalist,* 36:14–28.

Bernard, H., and Reilly, S. B. 1999. Pilot whales—*Globicephala,* Lesson 1828. Pp. 245–279, in *Handbook of marine mammals: The second book of dolphins and the porpoises* (S. H. Ridgway and R. Harrison, eds.). Academic Press, San Diego, vol. 6: 486 pp.

Best, P. B. 1977. Two allopatric forms of Bryde's whale off South Africa. *Report of the International Whaling Commission,* Special Issue, 1:10–38.

Best, T. L. 1988. Morphologic variation in the spotted bat *Euderma maculatum. American Midland Naturalist,* 119:244–252.

Best, T. L. 1993. Patterns of morphologic and morphometric variation in heteromyid rodents. Pp. 197–235, in *Biology of the Heteromyidae* (H. H. Genoways and J. H. Brown, eds.). Special Publication, American Society of Mammalogists, 10:1–719.

Betancourt, J. L., T. R. Van Devender, and P. S. Martin, eds. 1990. *Packrat middens: The last 40,000 years of biotic change.* University of Arizona Press, Tucson, 467 pp.

Betts, B. J. 1990. Geographic distribution and habitat preferences of Washington ground squirrels *(Spermophilus washingtoni). Northwestern Naturalist,* 71:27–37.

Birkenholz, D. 1963. A study of the life history and ecology of the round-tailed muskrat *Neofiber alleni* (True) in north-central Florida. *Ecological Monographs,* 33:255–280.

Bissonette, J. A. 1982. Collared peccary. Pp. 841–850, in *Wild mammals of North America* (J. A. Chapman and C. A. Feldhamer, eds.). Johns Hopkins University Press, Baltimore, MD, 1147 pp.

Black, H. L. 1974. A north temperate bat community: structure and prey populations. *Journal of Mammalogy,* 55:138–157.

Blankenship, D., and L. Brand. 1987. Geographic variation in vocalizations of California chipmunks *Tamias obscurus* and *T. merriami. Bulletin of the Southern California Academy of Science,* 86:126–135.

Block, S. B., and E. G. Zimmerman. 1991. Allozymic variation and systematics of plains pocket gophers *(Geomys)* of south-central Texas. *Southwestern Naturalist,* 36:29–36.

Bogan, M. A. 1974. Identification of *Myotis californicus* and *M. leibii* in southwestern North America. *Proceedings of the Biological Society of Washington,* 87:49–56.

Bogan, M. A. 1975. Geographic variation in *Myotis californicus* in the southwestern United States and Mexico. *Fish and Wildlife Service, Wildlife Research Report,* 3:1–31.

Bohlin, R. G., and E. G. Zimmerman. 1982. Genic differentiation of two chromosomal races of the *Geomys bursarius* complex. *Journal of Mammalogy,* 63:218–228.

Boness, D. J., W. D. Bowen, and O. T. Oftedal. 1988. Evidence of polygyny from spatial patterns of hooded seals *(Cystophora cristata). Canadian Journal of Zoology,* 66:703–706.

Boness, D. J., and H. J. James. 1979. Reproductive behavior of the grey seal *(Halichoerus grypus)* on Sable Island, Nova Scotia. *Journal of Zoology,* London, 188:477–500.

Booth, E. S. 1968. *Mammals of southern California.* University of California Press, Berkeley, 99 pp.

Born, E. W., R. Dietz, and R. R. Reeves, eds. 1994. Studies of white whales *(Delphinapterus leucas)* and narwhals *(Monodon monoceros)* in Greenland and adjacent waters. *Meddelelser om Grønland, Bioscience* 39, 259 pp.

Borowik, O. A., and M. D. Engstrom. 1993. Chromosomal evolution and biogeography of collared lemmings *(Dicrostonyx)* in the eastern and High Arctic of Canada. *Canadian Journal of Zoology,* 71:1481–1493.

Boschung, H. T., Jr., J. D. Williams, D. W. Gotshall, D. K. Caldwell, and M. C. Caldwell. 1983. *The Audubon Society field guide to North American fishes, whales, and dolphins.* Alfred A. Knopf, New York, 848 pp.

Bowen, W. D., O. T. Oftedal, and D. J. Boness. 1985. Birth to weaning in 4 days: remarkable growth in the hooded seal, *Cystophora cristata. Canadian Journal of Zoology,* 63:2841–2846.

Bowen, W. W. 1968. Variation and evolution of Gulf coast populations of beach mice, *Peromyscus polionotus. Bulletin of the Florida State Museum, Biological Sciences,* 12:1–91.

Bradley, R. D., S. K. Davis, and R. J. Baker. 1991. Genetic control of pre-mating-isolating behavior; Kaneshiro's hypothesis and asymmetrical sexual selection in pocket gophers. *Journal of Heredity,* 82:192–196.

Bradley, R. D., S. K. Davis, S. F. Lockwood, J. W. Bickham, and R. J. Baker. 1991. Hybrid breakdown and cellular DNA content in a contact zone between two species of pocket gophers *(Geomys). Journal of Mammalogy,* 72:697–705.

Braham, H. W., W. M. Marquette, T. W. Bray, and J. S. Leatherwood. 1980. The bowhead whale: whaling and biological research. *Marine Fisheries Review,* 42(9–10):1–96.

Brand, L. R. 1976. The vocal repertoire of chipmunks (genus *Eutamias)* in California. *Animal Behaviour,* 24:319–335.

Braun, S. E. 1985. Home range and activity patterns of the giant kangaroo rat, *Dipodomys ingens. Journal of Mammalogy,* 66:1–12.

Brigham, R. M., and M. B. Fenton. 1991. Convergence in foraging strategies by two morphologically and phylogenetically distinct nocturnal aerial insectivores. *Journal of Zoology,* London, 223:475–489.

Bright, W. 1993. *A coyote reader.* University of California Press, Berkeley, 220 pp.

Brodie, P. F. 1989. White whale—*Delphinapterus leucas.* Pp. 119–144, in *Handbook of marine mammals: River dolphins and the larger toothed whales* (S. H. Ridgway and R. Harrison, eds.). Academic Press, London, vol. 4: 442 pp.

Brown, D. E. 1984. *Arizona's tree squirrels.* Arizona Game & Fish Department, Phoenix, 114 pp.

Brown, J. 1974. A comparative study of the chromosomes of three species of shrews, *Sorex bendirii, Sorex trowbridgii,* and *Sorex vagrans. Wasmann Journal of Biology,* 32(2):303–326.

Brown, L. N. 1967. Ecological distribution of six species of shrews and comparison of sampling methods in the central Rocky Mountains. *Journal of Mammalogy,* 48:617–623.

Brownell, R. L. Jr., P. B. Best, and J. H. Prescott, eds. 1986. *Right whales: Past and present status.* Report of the International Whaling Commission, Special Issue, 10. 289 pp.

Brownell, R. L., Jr., W. A. Walker, and K. A. Forney. 1999. Pacific white-sided dolphin—*Lagenorhynchus obliquidens,* Gill 1865. Pp. 57–84, in *Handbook of marine mammals: The second book of dolphins and the porpoises* (S. H. Ridgway and R. Harrison, eds.). Academic Press, London, vol. 6: 486 pp.

Bryant, A. A., and D. W. Janz. 1996. Distribution and abundance of the Vancouver Island marmot *(Marmota vancouverensis). Canadian Journal of Zoology,* 74:667–677.

Buchler, E. R. 1976. The use of echolocation by the wandering shrew *(Sorex vagrans). Animal Behaviour,* 24:858–873.

Buckland, S. T., J. M. Breiwick, K. L. Cattanach, and J. L. Laake. 1993. Estimated population size of the California gray whale. *Marine Mammal Science,* 9(3):235–249.

Bueler, L. E. 1973. *Wild dogs of the world.* Stein and Day, New York.

Burke, R. L., J. Tasse, C. Badgley, S. R. Jones, N. Fishbein, S. Phillips, and M. E. Soule. 1991. Conservation of the Stephens' kangaroo rat *(Dipodomys stephensi):* planning for persistence. *Bulletin of the Southern California Academy of Sciences,* 90:10–40.

Burns, J. J. 1981. Bearded seal—*Erignathus barbatus.* Pp.145–170, in *Handbook of marine mammals: Seals* (S. H. Ridgway and R. Harrison, eds.). Academic Press, London, vol. 2: 359 pp.

Burns, J. J., J. J. Montague, and C. J. Cowles, eds. 1993. The bowhead whale. *Special Publication, The Society for Marine Mammalogy,* Lawrence, Kansas, 2:1–787.

Burt, W. H. 1934. The mammals of southern Nevada. *Transactions of the San Diego Society of Natural History,* 7:375–427.

Burton D. W., and J. W. Bickham. 1989. Heterochromatin variation and DNA content conservatism in *Geomys attwateri* and *G. breviceps* (Rodentia: Geomyidae). *Journal of Mammalogy,* 70:580–591.

Buskirk, S., A. Harestad, M. Raphael, and R. Powell, eds. 1994. *Martens, sables, and fishers: Biology and conservation.* Cornell University Press, Ithaca, New York, 496 pp.

Butterworth, B. B. 1958. Molt patterns in the Barrow ground squirrel. *Journal of Mammalogy,* 39:92–97.

Caire, W., J. D. Taylor, B. P. Glass, and M. A. Mares. 1989. *Mammals of Oklahoma.* University of Oklahoma Press, Norman, 567 pp.

Caldwell, D. K., and M. C. Caldwell. 1989. Pygmy sperm whale—*Kogia breviceps;* Dwarf sperm whale— *Kogia simus.* Pp. 235–260, in *Handbook of marine mammals: River dolphins and the larger toothed whales* (S. H. Ridgway and R. Harrison, eds.). Academic Press, London, vol. 4: 442 pp.

Calhoun, S. W., and I. F. Greenbaum. 1991. Evolutionary implications of genic variation among insular populations of *Peromyscus maniculatus* and *Peromyscus oreas. Journal of Mammalogy,* 72:248–262.

Callahan, J. R. 1977. Diagnosis of *Eutamias obscurus* (Rodentia: Sciuridae). *Journal of Mammalogy,* 58:188–201.

Cameron, G. N., and P. A. McClure. 1988. Geographic variation in life history traits of the hispid cotton rat *(Sigmodon hispidus).* Pp. 33–64, in *Evolution of life histories of mammals: theory and patterns* (M. Boyce, ed.) Yale University Press, New Haven, 373 pp.

Cameron, G. N., S. R. Spencer, B. D. Eshelman, L. R. Williams, and M. J. Gregory. 1988. Activity and burrow structure of Attwater's pocket gopher *(Geomys attwateri). Journal of Mammalogy,* 69:667–677.

Carey, A. B. 1991. *The biology of arboreal rodents in Douglas-fir forests.* USDA Forest Service, General Technical Report PNW-GTR-276, 47 pp.

Carey, H. V. 1985. The use of foraging areas by yellow-bellied marmots. *Oikos,* 44:273–279.

Carl, E. A. 1971. Population control in arctic ground squirrels. *Ecology,* 52(3):395–413.

Carleton, M. D. 1989. Systematics and Evolution. Pp. 7–141, in *Advances in the study of* Peromyscus *(Rodentia)* (G. L. Kirkland, Jr., and J. N. Layne, eds.). Texas Tech University Press, Lubbock, 367 pp.

Carleton, M. D., and R. E. Eshelman. 1979. A synopsis of fossil grasshopper mice, genus *Onychomys,* and their relationship to Recent species. *University of Michigan, Museum of Paleontology, Papers on Paleontology,* 21:1–63.

Carraway, L. N. 1990. A morphologic and morphometric analysis of the "*Sorex vagrans* species complex" in the Pacific coast region. *Special Publications, The Museum, Texas Tech University,* 32:1–76.

Catesby, M. 1748. *The natural history of Carolina, Florida, and the Bahamas.* B. White, London. 2 vols.

Ceballos-G., G., and C. Galindo-L. 1984. Mamíferos silvestres de la cuenca de México. *Publicación del Instituto de Ecología,* 12:1–299.

Chadwick, D. H. 1983. *A beast the color of winter.* Sierra Club Books, San Francisco, 208 pp.

Chapman, J. A., K. L. Cramer, N. J. Dippenaar, and T. J. Robinson. 1992. Systematics and biogeography of the New England cottontail, *Sylvilagus transitionalis* (Bangs, 1895),with the description of a new species from the Appalachian Mountains. *Proceedings of the Biological Society of Washington,* 105(4):841–866.

Chapman, J. A., and J. E. C. Flux. 1990. *Rabbits, hares and pikas.* I.U.C.N., Gland, Switzerland, 168 pp.

Chapman, J. A., A. L. Harmon, and D. E. Samuel. 1977. Reproductive and physiological cycles in the cottontail complex in western Maryland and nearby West Virginia. *Wildlife Monographs,* 56:1–73.

Chapman, J. A., and R. P. Morgan, II. 1973. Systematic status of the cottontail complex in western Maryland and nearby West Virginia. *Wildlife Monographs,* 36:1–54.

Chase, J. D., W. E. Howard, and J. T. Roseberry. 1982. Pocket gophers. Pp. 239–255, in *Wild mammals of North America* (J. A. Chapman and C. A. Feldhamer, eds.). Johns Hopkins University Press, Baltimore, MD, 1147 pp.

Chesser, R. K. 1983. Genetic variability within and among populations of the black-tailed prairie dog. *Evolution,* 37:320–331.

Choate, J. R., J. K. Jones, Jr., and C. Jones. 1994. *Handbook of mammals of the south-central states.* Louisiana State University, Baton Rouge, 304 pp.

Clapham, P. 1996. *Humpback whales.* Colin Baxter Press, Grantown-on-Spey, Scotland, 72 pp.

Clark, B. S., D. M. Leslie, Jr., and T. S. Carter. 1993. Foraging activity of adult female Ozark big-eared bats *(Plecotus townsendii ingens)* in summer. *Journal of Mammalogy,* 74(2):422–427.

Clark, T. W. 1977. Ecology and ethology of the white-tailed prairie dog *(Cynomys leucurus). Milwaukee Public Museum, Publications in Biology and Geology,* 3:1–97.

Clark, T. W., ed. 1986. *The black-footed ferret.* The Great Basin Naturalist Memoirs No. 8, Brigham Young University, Provo, Utah, 208 pp.

Clark, T. W. 1989. Conservation biology of the black-footed ferret, *Mustela nigripes. Wildlife Preservation Trust, Special Scientific Report,* Philadelphia, 3:1–175.

Clark, T. W., and M. R. Stromberg. 1987. *Mammals in Wyoming.* University of Kansas, Museum of Natural History, Lawrence, 314 pp.

Clough, G. C. 1963. Biology of the arctic shrew, *Sorex arcticus. American Midland Naturalist,* 69:69–81.

Clough, G. C., and J. J. Albright. 1987. Occurrence of the northern bog lemming, *Synaptomys borealis,* in the northeastern United States. *Canadian Field-Naturalist,* 101:611–613.

Cockrum, E. L., and A. L. Gardner. 1960. Underwood's mastiff bat in Arizona. *Journal of Mammalogy,* 41:510–511.

Cole, F. R, and D. E. Wilson. 1996. Mammalian diversity and natural history. Pp. 9–40, in *Measuring and monitoring biological diversity: Standard methods for mammals* (D. E. Wilson, F. R. Cole, J. D. Nichols, R. Rudran, and M. S. Foster, eds.). Smithsonian Institution Press, Washington, DC, 409 pp.

Conaway, C. H. 1952. Life history of the water shrew *(Sorex palustris navigator). American Midland Naturalist,* 48:219–248.

Conley, W. 1976. Competition between *Microtus:* a behavioral hypothesis. *Ecology,* 57:224–237.

Cope, J. B., and S. R. Humphrey. 1977. Spring and autumn swarming behavior in the Indiana bat, *Myotis sodalis. Journal of Mammalogy,* 58:93–95.

Costello, D. F. 1966. *The world of the porcupine.* Lippincott, Philadelphia, 157 pp.

Cothran, E. G., and E. G. Zimmerman. 1985. Electrophoretic analysis of the contact zone between *Geomys breviceps* and *Geomys bursarius. Journal of Mammalogy,* 66:489–497.

Cowan, I. McT., and C. J. Guiguet. 1956. *The mammals of British Columbia,* third edition. British Columbia Provincial Museum, Handbook, 11: 413 pp.

Cranford, J. A. 1978. Hibernation in the western jumping mouse *(Zapus princeps). Journal of Mammalogy,* 59:496–509.

Cranford, J. A. 1983. Ecological strategies of a small hibernator, the western jumping mouse *(Zapus princeps). Canadian Journal of Zoology,* 61:232–240.

Crawshaw, P. G., Jr., and H. B. Quigley. 1991. Jaguar spacing, activity and habitat use in a seasonally flooded environment in Brazil. *Journal of Zoology,* London, 223:357–370.

Crocker-Bedford, D. C., and J. J. Spillett. 1977. Home ranges of Utah prairie dogs. *Journal of Mammalogy,* 58:672–673.

Crooks, K. R., and D. Van Vuren. 1994. Conservation of the island spotted skunk and island fox in a recovering island ecosystem. Pp. 379–386, in *Proceedings of the Fourth California Islands Symposium: Update on the status of resources* (W. L. Halvorson and G. J. Maender, eds.). Santa Barbara Museum of Natural History, Santa Barbara, CA, 530 pp.

Crooks, K. R., and D. Van Vuren. 1995. Resource utilization by two insular endemic carnivores, the island fox and the island spotted skunk. *Oecologia,* 104:301–307.

Crooks, K. R., and D. Van Vuren. 1996. Spatial organization of the island fox *(Urocyon littoralis)* of Santa Cruz Island, California. *Journal of Mammalogy,* 77:801–806.

Culbertson, A. E. 1946. Observations on the natural history of the Fresno kangaroo rat. *Journal of Mammalogy,* 27:189–203.

Cummings, W. C. 1985. Right whales—*Eubalaena glacialis* and *Eubalaena australis.* Pp. 275–304, in *Handbook of marine mammals: The sirenians and baleen whales* (S. H. Ridgway and R. Harrison, eds.). Academic Press, London, vol. 3: 362 pp.

Dahlheim, M. E., and J. E. Heyning. 1999. Killer whale—*Orcinus orca* (Linnaeus, 1758). Pp. 281–322, in *Handbook of marine mammals: The second book of dolphins and the porpoises* (S. H. Ridgway and R. Harrison, eds.) Academic Press, London, vol. 6: 486 pp.

Dalke, P. D. 1942. The cottontail rabbits in Connecticut. *State Geological and Natural History Survey Bulletin,* Hartford, 65:1–97.

Dalquest, W. W. 1948. Mammals of Washington. *University of Kansas Publications, Museum of Natural History,* 2:1–444.

Dalquest, W. W., and N. V. Horner. 1984. *Mammals of north-central Texas.* Midwestern State University Press, Wichita Falls, Texas, 261 pp.

Dalquest, W. W., and D. R. Orcutt. 1942. The biology of the least shrew-mole, *Neurotrichus gibbsii minor. American Midland Naturalist,* 27:387–401.

Dalquest, W. W., and V. B. Scheffer. 1944. A new mole from Washington state. *Murrelet,* 25:27–28.

Davis, R. B., C. F. Herreid II, and H. L. Short. 1962. Mexican free-tailed bats in Texas. *Ecological Monographs,* 32:311–46.

Davis, W. B. 1937. Variations in Townsend pocket gophers. *Journal of Mammalogy,* 18:145–158.

Davis, W. B. 1939. *The Recent mammals of Idaho.* Caldwell, Idaho, The Caxton Printers, Ltd., 400 pp.

Davis, W. B. 1940. Distribution and variation of pocket gophers (genus *Geomys)* in the southwestern United States. *Bulletin of the Texas Agricultural Experiment Station,* 590:1–38.

Davis, W. B. 1941. The short-tailed shrews (*Cryptotis*) of Texas. *Journal of Mammalogy*, 22:411–418.

Davis, W. B., and L. Joeris. 1945. Notes on the life history of the little short-tailed shrew. *Journal of Mammalogy*, 26:136–138.

Davis, W. B., and D. J. Schmidly. 1994. *The Mammals of Texas.* Texas Parks and Wildlife, Nongame and Urban Program, University of Texas Press, Austin, 338 pp.

Decker, D. M. 1991. Systematics of the coatis, genus *Nasua* (Mammalia: Procyonidae). *Proceedings of the Biological Society of Washington*, 104(2):370–386.

DeWalt, T. S., E. G. Zimmerman, and J. V. Planz. 1993. Mitochondrial DNA phylogeny of the *boylii* and *truei* groups of the genus *Peromyscus*. *Journal of Mammalogy*, 74:352–362.

Diersing, V. A. 1980. Systematics and evolution of the pygmy shrews (subgenus *Microsorex*) of North America. *Journal of Mammalogy*, 61:76–101.

Diersing, V. A., and D. F. Hoffmeister. 1977. Revision of the shrew *Sorex merriami* and a description of a new species of the subgenus *Sorex*. *Journal of Mammalogy*, 58:321–333.

Dodge, W. E. 1982. Porcupine. Pp. 355–366, in *Wild mammals of North America* (J. A. Chapman and C. A. Feldhamer, eds.). Johns Hopkins University Press, Baltimore, MD, 1147 pp.

Domning, D. P. 1982. Evolution of manatees: a speculative history. *Journal of Paleontology*, 56:599–619.

Donovan, G. P., C. H. Lockyer, and A. R. Martin, eds. 1993. The biology of Northern Hemisphere pilot whales: a collection of papers. *Report of the International Whaling Commission*, Special Issue, Cambridge, UK, 14:1–479.

Doyle, A. T. 1990. Use of riparian and upland habitats by small mammals. *Journal of Mammalogy*, 71:14–23.

Dragoo, J. W., and R. L. Honeycutt. 1997. Systematics of mustelid-like carnivores. *Journal of Mammalogy*, 78:426–443.

Dunford, C. 1977. Social system of round-tailed ground squirrels. *Animal Behaviour*, 25:885–906.

Dunn, J. P., J. A. Chapman, and R. E. Marsh. 1982. Jackrabbits: *Lepus californicus* and allies. Pp. 124–145, in *Wild mammals of North America* (J. A. Chapman and C. A. Feldhamer, eds.). Johns Hopkins University Press, Baltimore, MD, 1147 pp.

Durrant, S. D. 1952. Mammals of Utah: Taxonomy and distribution. *Miscellaneous Publications, Museum of Natural History, University of Kansas*, 6:1–549.

Easterla, D. A. 1973. Ecology of the 18 species of Chiroptera at Big Bend National Park, Texas. *Northwest Missouri State University Studies*, 34(3):54–65.

Eger, J. L. 1977. Systematics of the genus *Eumops* (Chiroptera: Molossidae). *Royal Ontario Museum, Life Sciences, Contribution*, 110:1–69.

Eger, J. L. 1995. Morphometric variation in the Nearctic collared lemmings (*Dicrostonyx*), *Journal of Zoology*, London, 235:143–161.

Egoscue, H. J. 1964. Ecological notes and laboratory life history of the canyon mouse. *Journal of Mammalogy*, 45:387–396.

Egoscue, H. J., and E. S. Frank. 1984. Burrowing and denning habits of a captive colony of the Utah prairie dog. *Great Basin Naturalist*, 44:495–498.

Eisenberg, J. F. 1963. The behavior of heteromyid rodents. *University of California Publications in Zoology*, 69:1–100.

Eisenberg, J. F. 1968. Behavior patterns. Pp. 451–490, in *Biology of Peromyscus (Rodentia).* (J. A. King, ed.). Special Publication, American Society of Mammalogists, No. 2: 593 pp.

Eisenberg, J. F. 1989. *Mammals of the Neotropics. The northern Neotropics*, Vol. 1, *Panama, Columbia, Venezuela, Guyana, Suriname, French Guiana.* University of Chicago Press, Chicago, IL, 449 pp.

Eisenberg, J. F., and D. E. Isaac. 1963. The reproduction of heteromyid rodents in captivity. *Journal of Mammalogy*, 44:61–67.

Eisenberg, J. F., and D. E. Wilson. 1978. Relative brain size and feeding strategies in the Chiroptera. *Evolution* 32:740–751.

Elliott, L. 1978. Social behavior and foraging ecology of the eastern chipmunk (*Tamias striatus*) in the Adirondack Mountains. *Smithsonian Contributions to Zoology*, 265:1–107.

Ellis, R. 1980. *The book of whales.* Alfred A. Knopf, New York, 202 pp.

Ellis, R. 1989. *Dolphins and porpoises.* Alfred A. Knopf, Inc., New York, 270 pp.

Elton, C. 1942. *Voles, mice and lemmings.* Clarendon Press, Oxford. 496 pp.

Emmons, L. H. 1988. A field study of ocelots (*Felis pardalis*) in Peru. *Revue d'ecologie (Terre Vie)*, 43:133–157.

Engstrom, M. D., A. J. Baker, J. L. Eger, R. Boonstra, and R. J. Brooks. 1993. Chromosomal and mitochondrial DNA variation in four laboratory populations of collared lemmings (*Dicrostonyx*). *Canadian Journal of Zoology*, 71:42–48.

Engstrom, M. D., and J. R. Choate. 1979. Systematics of the northern grasshopper mouse (*Onychomys leucogaster*) on the central Great Plains. *Journal of Mammalogy*, 60:723–739.

Errington, P. L. 1963. *Muskrat populations.* Iowa State University Press, Ames, 665 pp.

Escherich, P. C. 1981. Social biology of the bushy-tailed woodrat. *University of California Publications in Zoology*, 110:1–132.

Evans, P. G. H. 1987. *The natural history of whales and dolphins.* Facts on File Publications, New York, 343 pp.

Evans, W. E. 1994. Common dolphin, white-bellied porpoise—*Delphinus delphis*. Pp. 191–224, in *Handbook of marine mammals: The first book of dolphins* (S. H. Ridgway and R. Harrison, eds.). Academic Press, London, vol. 5: 416 pp.

Fagerstone, K. A. 1987. Black-footed ferret, long-tailed weasel, short-tailed weasel, and least weasel. Pp. 548–573, in *Wild furbearer management and conservation in North America* (M. Novak, J. A. Baker, M. E. Obbard, and B. Malloch, eds.). Ontario Ministry of Resources, Toronto, 1150 pp.

Faure, P. A., and R. M. R. Barclay. 1994. Substrate-gleaning versus aerial-hawking: plasticity in the foraging and echolocation behaviour of the long-eared bat, *Myotis evotis*. *Journal of Comparative Physiology*, 174:651–660.

Faure, P. A., J. H. Fullard, and J. W. Dawson. 1993. The gleaning attacks of the northern long-eared bat, *Myotis septentrionalis*, are relatively inaudible to moths. *Journal of Experimental Biology*, 178:173–189.

Fay, F. H. 1981. Walrus—*Odobenus rosmarus*. Pp. 1–24, in *Handbook of marine mammals: The walrus, sea lions, fur seals and sea otter* (S. H. Ridgway and R. Harrison, eds.). Academic Press, London, vol. 1: 235 pp.

Feldhamer, G. A., R. Klann, A. Gerard, and A. C. Driskell. 1993. Habitat partitioning, body size, and timing of parturition in pygmy shrews and other shrews. *Journal of Mammalogy*, 74:403–411.

Fenton, M. B. 1983. *Just bats.* University of Toronto Press, Toronto, 165 pp.

Ferrero, R. C., J. Hodder, and J. Cesarone. 1994. Recent strandings of rough-toothed dolphins (*Steno bredanensis*) on the Oregon and Washington coasts. *Marine Mammal Science*, 10:114–116.

Ferrero, R. C., and W. A. Walker. 1993. Growth and reproduction of the northern right whale dolphin, *Lissodelphis borealis*, in the offshore waters of the North Pacific Ocean. *Canadian Journal of Zoology*, 71:2335–2344.

Findley, J. S. 1987. *The natural history of New Mexican mammals.* University of New Mexico Press, Albuquerque, 164 pp.

Findley, J. S., A. H. Harris, D. E. Wilson, and C. Jones. 1975. *Mammals of New Mexico.* University of New Mexico Press, Albuquerque, 360 pp.

Findley, J. S., and G. L. Traut. 1970. Geographic variation in *Pipistrellus hesperus*. *Journal of Mammalogy*, 51:741–765.

Finley, R. B. 1958. The wood rats of Colorado: distribution and ecology. *University of Kansas Publications, Museum of Natural History*, 10:213–552.

Fisler, G. F., 1965. Adaptations and speciation in harvest mice of the marshes of San Francisco Bay. *University of California Publications in Zoology*, 77:1–108.

Fitzgerald, J. P., and R. R. Lechleitner. 1974. Observations on the biology of Gunnison's prairie dog in central Colorado. *American Midland Naturalist*, 92:146–163.

Fleischer, L. A. 1987. Guadalupe fur seal, *Arctocephalus townsendi*. Pp. 43–48, in *Status, biology, and ecology of fur seals* (J. P. Croxall and R. L. Gentry, eds.). United States Department of Commerce, National Marine Fisheries Service, NOAA Technical Report, 51:1–212.

Flyger, V., and J. E. Gates. 1982. Fox and gray squirrels. Pp. 209–229, in *Wild mammals of North America* (J. A. Chapman and C. A. Feldhamer, eds.). Johns Hopkins University Press, Baltimore, MD, 1147 pp.

Forbes, R. B. 1962. Notes on food of silky pocket mice. *Journal of Mammalogy*, 43:278–279.

Forbes, R. B. 1964. Some aspects of the life history of the silky pocket mouse, *Perognathus flavus*. *American Midland Naturalist*, 72:438–443

Franzmann, A. W. 1978. Moose. Pp. 67–82, in *Big Game of North America* (J. L. Schmidt and D. L. Gilbert, eds.). Stackpole Books, Harrisburg, PA, 494 pp.

Franzmann, A. W., and C. C. Schwartz, eds. 1998. *Ecology and management of the North American moose*. Smithsonian Institution Press, Washington, DC, 733 pp.

Freeman, P. W. 1981. A multivariate study of the family Molossidae (Mammalia: Chiroptera): morphology, ecology, evolution. *Fieldiana, Zoology*, New Series, 7:1–173.

Freeman, P. W., and H. H. Genoways. 1998. Recent northern records of the nine-banded armadillo (Dasypodidae) in Nebraska. *Southwestern Naturalist*, 43:490–494.

French, A. R. 1993. Physiological ecology of the Heteromyidae: Economics of energy and water utilization. Pp. 509–538, in *Biology of the Heteromyidae* (H. H. Genoways and J. H. Brown, eds.). American Society of Mammmalogists Special Publication, No. 10: 719 pp.

French, T. W. 1980. Natural history of the southeastern shrew, *Sorex longirostris* Bachman. *American Midland Naturalist*, 104:13–31.

French, T. W. and G. L. Kirkland, Jr. 1983. Taxonomy of the Gaspé shrew, *Sorex gaspensis* and the rock shrew, *S. dispar*. *Canadian Field-Naturalist*, 97:75–78.

Frey, J. K., and C. T. LaRue. 1993. Notes on the distribution of the Mogollon vole *(Microtus mogollonensis)* in New Mexico and Arizona. *Southwestern Naturalist*, 38:176–178.

Frey, J. K., and D. W. Moore. 1990. Nongeographic morphologic variation in the Mexican vole *(Microtus mexicanus)*. *Transactions of the Kansas Academy of Science*, 93:97–109.

Frey, J. K., and M. J. Patrick. 1995. Gastrointestinal helminths from the endangered Hualapai vole, *Microtus mogollonensis hualpaiensis* (Rodentia: Cricetidae). *Journal of Parasitology*, 81:641–643.

Fritzell, E. K. 1987. Gray fox and island gray fox. Pp. 408–421, in *Wild furbearer management and conservation in North America* (M. Novak, J. A. Baker, M. E. Obbard, and B. Malloch, eds.). Ontario Ministry of Natural Resources, Toronto, 1150 pp.

Gambell, R. 1985. Sei whale—*Balaenoptera borealis*. Pp. 155–170, in *Handbook of marine mammals: The sirenians and baleen whales* (S. H. Ridgway and R. Harrison, eds.). Academic Press, London, vol. 3: 362 pp.

Gambell, R. 1985. Fin whale—*Balaenoptera physalus*. Pp. 171–192, in *Hand-*

book of marine mammals: The sirenians and baleen whales (S. H. Ridgway and R. Harrison, eds.). Academic Press, London, vol. 3: 362 pp.

Gannon, W. L., and T. E. Lawlor. 1989. Variation of the chip vocalization of three species of Townsend chipmunks (genus *Eutamias*). *Journal of Mammalogy*, 70:740–753.

Gardner, A. L. 1973. The systematics of the genus *Didelphis* (Marsupialia: Didelphidae) in North and Middle America. *Special Publications, The Museum, Texas Tech University*, 4:1–81.

Gardner, A. L. 1982. Virginia opossum. Pp. 3–36, in *Wild mammals of North America* (J. A. Chapman and C. A. Feldhamer, eds.). Johns Hopkins University Press, Baltimore, MD, 1147 pp.

Gardner, A. L. 1993a. Order Didelphimorphia. Pp. 15–23, in *Mammal species of the world: A taxonomic and geographic reference*, second edition (D. E. Wilson and D. M. Reeder, eds.). Smithsonian Institution Press, Washington, DC, 1207 pp.

Gardner, A. L. 1993b. Order Xenarthra. Pp. 63–68, in *Mammal species of the world: A taxonomic and geographic reference*, second edition. (D. E. Wilson and D. M. Reeder, eds.). Smithsonian Institution Press, Washington, DC, 1207 pp.

Garner, H. W. 1974. Population dynamics, reproduction, and activities of the kangaroo rat, *Dipodomys ordii*, in western Texas. *Graduate Studies, Texas Tech University*, 7:1–28.

Gashwiler, J. S. 1972. Life history notes on the Oregon vole, *Microtus oregoni*. *Journal of Mammalogy*, 53:558–569.

Gaskin, D. E. 1982. *The ecology of whales and dolphins*. Heinemann Educational Books Limited, London, 459 pp.

Gaskin, D. E. 1992a. Status of Atlantic white-sided dolphin, *Lagenorhynchus acutus*, in Canada. *Canadian Field-Naturalist*, 106:64–72.

Gaskin, D. E. 1992b. Status of the harbour porpoise, *Phocoena phocoena*, in Canada. *Canadian Field-Naturalist*, 106:36–54.

Gavin, T. A., P. W. Sherman, E. Yensen, and B. May. 1999. Population genetic structure of the northern Idaho ground squirrel *Spermophilus brunneus brunneus*. *Journal of Mammalogy*, 80:156–168.

Geffen, E., A. Mecure, D. J. Girman, D. W. MacDonald, and R. K. Wayne. 1992. Phylogenetic relationships of the fox-like canids. *Journal of Zoology* (London), 228:27–39.

Geist, V. 1971. *Mountain Sheep*. University of Chicago Press, 383 pp.

Geist, V. 1975. *Mountain sheep and man in the northern wilds*. Cornell University Press, Ithaca, NY, 248 pp.

Genoways, H. H. 1973. Systematics and evolutionary relationships of spiny pocket mice, genus *Liomys*. *Special Publications, The Museum, Texas Tech University*, 5:1–368.

Genoways, H. H. and J. H. Brown, eds. 1993. *Biology of the Heteromyidae*. Special Publication, American Society of Mammalogists, No. 10: 719 pp.

Genoways, H. H., and J. K. Jones, Jr. 1973. Notes on some mammals from Jalisco, Mexico. *Occasional Papers, The Museum, Texas Tech University*, 9:1–22.

Gentry, R. L. 1981. Northern fur Seal—*Callorhinus ursinus*. Pp. 143–160, in *Handbook of marine mammals: The walrus, sea lions, fur seals and sea otter* (S. H. Ridgway and R. Harrison, eds.). Academic Press, London, vol. 1: 235 pp.

Gentry, R. L., and G. L. Kooyman, eds. 1986. *Fur seals: Maternal strategies on land and at sea*. Princeton University Press, 291 pp.

George, S. B. 1988. Systematics, historical biogeography, and evolution of the genus *Sorex*. *Journal of Mammalogy*, 69:443–461.

George, S. B., H. H. Genoways, J. R. Choate, and R. J. Baker. 1982. Karyotypic relationships within the short-tailed shrews, genus *Blarina*. *Journal of Mammalogy*, 63:639–645.

George, S. B., and J. D. Smith. 1991. Inter- and intraspecific variation among coastal and island populations of *Sorex monticolus* and *Sorex vagrans.* Pp. 75–91, in *The biology of the Soricidae* (J. S. Findley and T. L. Yates, eds.). Special Publication No. 1, The Museum of Southwestern Biology, Albuquerque, 91 pp.

Gerlach, D., S. Atwater, and J. Schell, eds. 1994. *Deer.* Stackpole Books, Harrisburg, PA, 384 pp.

Giraldeau, L., D. C. Kramer, I. Deslandes, and H. Lair. 1994. The effect of competitors and distance on central place foraging eastern chip-munks, *Tamias striatus. Animal Behaviour,* 47:621–632.

Gittleman, J. L., ed. 1989. *Carnivore behavior, ecology, and evolution.* Cornell University Press, Ithaca, New York, 620 pp.

Glendenning, R. 1959. Biology and control of the coast mole, *Scapanus orarius orarius* True, in British Columbia. *Canadian Journal of Animal Science,* 39:34–44.

Godin, A. J. 1977. *Wild mammals of New England.* Johns Hopkins University Press, Baltimore, 304 pp.

Golley, F. B. 1962. *Mammals of Georgia: A study of their distribution and functional role in the ecosystem.* University of Georgia Press, Athens, 218 pp.

Gore, J. A. 1992. Gray bat, *Myotis grisescens.* Pp. 63–70, in *Rare and endan-gered biota of Florida,* Volume I: *Mammals* (S. R. Humphrey, ed.). University Press of Florida, Gainesville, 392 pp.

Gould, E., W. McShea, and T. Grand. 1993. Function of the star in the star-nosed mole, *Condylura cristata. Journal of Mammalogy,* 74:108–116.

Gray, D. R. 1987. *The muskoxen of Polar Bear Pass.* Fitzhenry and Whiteside, Markham, Ontario, 191 pp.

Green, J. S., and J. T. Flinders. 1980. Habitat and dietary relationships of the pygmy rabbit. *Journal of Range Management,* 33(2):136–142.

Greenhall, A. M., and U. Schmidt, eds. 1988. *Natural history of vampire bats.* CRC Press, Boca Raton, FL, 272 pp.

Gregory, M. J., G. N. Cameron, L. M. Combs, and L. R. Williams. 1987. Agonistic behavior in Attwater's pocket gopher, *Geomys attwateri. Southwestern Naturalist,* 32:143–146.

Grinnell, J. 1914. An account of the mammals and birds of the Lower Colorado Valley with especial reference to the distributional problems presented. *University of California Publications in Zoology,* 12:51–294.

Grinnell, J. 1922. A geographical study of the kangaroo rats of California. *University of California Publications in Zoology,* 24:1–125.

Grinnell, J. 1927. Geography and evolution in the pocket gophers of California. *Smithsonian Institution Annual Report, Publication* 2894:335–343.

Grinnell, J. 1932. Habitat relations of the giant kangaroo rat. *Journal of Mammalogy,* 13:305–320.

Grinnell, J., and J. Dixon. 1918. Natural history of the ground squirrels of California. *Monthly Bulletin of the State Commission of Horticulture* (California), 7:597–708.

Grinnell, J., J. S. Dixon, and J. M. Linsdale. 1937. *Fur-bearing mammals of California: their natural history, systematic status, and relations to man.* University of California Press, Berkeley, 2 vols. 769 pp.

Grinnell, J., and T. I. Storer. 1924. *Animal life in the Yosemite: an account of the mammals, birds, reptiles, and amphibians in a cross-section of the Sierra Nevada.* University of California Press, Berkeley, 752 pp.

Grubb, P. 1993. Order Artiodactyla. Pp. 377–414, in *Mammal species of the world: A taxonomic and geographic reference,* second edition (D. E. Wilson and D. M. Reeder, eds.). Smithsonian Institution Press, Washington, DC, 1207 pp.

Grzimek, B. (ed.) 1975. *Grzimek's animal life encyclopedia. Mammals III.* Van Nostrand Reinholt, NY 657 pp.

Gubernick, D. J. 1988. Reproduction in the California mouse, *Peromyscus californicus. Journal of Mammalogy,* 69:857–860.

Gubernick, D. J., and J. C. Nordby. 1993. Mechanisms of sexual fidelity in the monogamous California mouse, *Peromyscus californicus. Behavioral Ecology and Sociobiology,* 32:211–219.

Gubernick, D. J., S. L. Wright, and R. E. Brown. 1993. The significance of father's presence for offspring survival in the monogamous California mouse, *Peromyscus californicus. Animal Behaviour,* 46: 539–546.

Gunn, S. J., and I. F. Greenbaum. 1986. Systematic implications of karyo-typic and morphologic variation in mainland *Peromyscus* from the Pacific northwest. *Journal of Mammalogy,* 67:294–304.

Gurnell, John. 1987. *The natural history of squirrels.* Facts on File Publications, New York, 201 pp.

Hafner, M. S., and D. J. Hafner. 1979. Vocalizations of grasshopper mice (genus *Onychomys). Journal of Mammalogy,* 60:85–94.

Hafner, M. S., J. C. Hafner, J. L. Patton, and M. F. Smith. 1987. Macrogeographic patterns of genetic differentiation in the pocket gopher *Thomomys umbrinus. Systematic Zoology,* 36:18–34.

Haley, D., ed. 1986. *Marine mammals of the eastern North Pacific and Arctic waters.* Second Edition. Pacific Search Press, Seattle, WA, 295 pp.

Hall, E. R. 1946. *Mammals of Nevada.* University of California Press, Berkeley, 710 pp.

Hall, E. R. 1951. American weasels. *University of Kansas Publications, Museum of Natural History,* 4:1–466.

Hall, E. R. 1981. *The mammals of North America.* John Wiley and Sons, New York, 2 vols., 1271 pp.

Hall, E. R., and R. M. Gilmore. 1932. New mammals from St. Lawrence Island, Bering Sea, Alaska. *University of California Publications in Zoology,* 38:391–404.

Hall, E. R., and J. K. Jones, Jr. 1961. North American yellow bats, "*Dasypterus,*" and a list of the named kinds of the genus *Lasiurus* Gray. *University of Kansas Publications, Museum of Natural History,* 14:73–98.

Hall, J. S. 1962. A life history and taxonomic study of the Indiana bat, *Myotis sodalis.* Reading Public Museum and Art Gallery, Reading, PA, No. 12:1–68.

Hall, L. K. 1984. *White-tailed deer: ecology and management.* Stackpole Books, Harrisburg, PA. 870 pp.

Hamilton, W. J., Jr. 1940. The biology of the smoky shrew (*Sorex fumeus fumeus* Miller). *Zoologica,* 25:473–491.

Hamilton, W. J., Jr. 1944. The biology of the little short-tailed shrew, *Cryptotis parva. Journal of Mammalogy,* 25:1–7.

Hamilton, W. J., Jr., and J. O. Whitaker, Jr. 1979. *Mammals of the eastern United States.* Cornell University Press, Ithaca, New York, 346 pp.

Handley, C. O., Jr. 1959. A revision of the American bats of the genera *Euderma* and *Plecotus. Proceedings of the United States National Museum,* 110:95–246.

Handley, C. O., Jr. 1991. Mammals. Pp. 539–616, in *Virginia's endangered species: Proceedings of a symposium.* McDonald and Woodward, Blacksburg, Virginia, 672 pp.

Hanselka, C. W., J. M. Inglis, and H. G. Applegate. 1971. Reproduction in the blacktailed jackrabbit in southwestern Texas. *Southwestern Naturalist,* 16:214–217.

Hansen, K. 1992. *Cougar: the American lion.* Northland Press, Flagstaff, AZ, 129 pp.

Harris, A. H. 1984. *Neotoma* in the late Pleistocene of New Mexico and Chihuahua. *Contributions in Quaternary Vertebrate Paleontology, Special Publication, Carnegie Museum of Natural History,* 8:164–178.

Harris, J. H. 1987. Variation in the caudal fat deposit of *Microdipodops megacephalus. Journal of Mammalogy,* 68:58–63.

Hash, H. S. 1987. Wolverine. Pp. 575–585, in *Wild furbearer management and conservation in North America* (M. Novak, J. A. Baker, M. E. Obbard, and B. Malloch, eds.). Ontario Ministry of Natural Resources, Toronto, 1150 pp.

Hawbecker, A. C. 1940. The burrowing and feeding habits of *Dipodomys venustus. Journal of Mammalogy,* 21:388–396.

Hay, K. A., and Mansfield, A. W. 1989. Narwhal—*Monodon monoceros.* Pp.145–177, in *Handbook of marine mammals: River dolphins and the larger toothed whales* (S. H. Ridgway and R. Harrison, eds.). Academic Press, London, vol. 4: 442 pp.

Hayes, J. P., and R. G. Harrison. 1992. Variation in mitochondrial DNA and the biogeographic history of woodrats *(Neotoma)* of the eastern United States. *Systematic Biology,* 41:331–344.

Hayes, J. P., and M. E. Richmond. 1993. Clinal variation and morphology of woodrats *(Neotoma)* of the eastern United States. *Journal of Mammalogy,* 74:204–216.

Hayward, B. J., and S. P. Cross.1979. The natural history of *Pipistrellus hesperus* (Chiroptera: Vespertilionidae). *Western New Mexico University Office of Research,* No. 3:1–36.

Henisch, B., and H. Henisch. 1970. *Chipmunk portrait.* Carnation Press, State College, PA, 97 pp.

Herd, R. M., and M. B. Fenton. 1983. An electrophoretic, morphological, and ecological investigation of a putative hybrid zone between *Myotis lucifugus* and *Myotis yumanensis* (Chiroptera: Vespertilionidae). *Canadian Journal of Zoology,* 61:2029–2050.

Herly, R. H. 1979. Dietary habits of two nectar and pollen feeding bats in southern Arizona and northern Mexico. *Journal of the Arizona-Nevada Academy of Science,* 14:13–18.

Heyning, J. E. 1989a. Cuvier's beaked whale—*Ziphius cavirostris.* Pp. 289–308, in *Handbook of marine mammals: River dolphins and the larger toothed whales* (S. H. Ridgway and R. Harrison, eds.). Academic Press, London, vol. 4: 442 pp.

Heyning, J. E. 1989b. Comparative facial anatomy of beaked whales (Ziphiidae) and a systematic revision among the families of extant Odontoceti. *Natural History Museum of Los Angeles County, Contributions in Science,* 405:1–64.

Heyning, J. E., and J. G. Mead. 1996. Suction feeding in beaked whales: Morphological and observational evidence. *Natural History Museum of Los Angeles County, Contributions in Science,* 464:1–12.

Heyning, J. E., and W. F. Perrin. 1994. Evidence for two species of common dolphins (Genus *Delphinus)* from the eastern North Pacific. *Natural History Museum of Los Angeles County, Contributions in Science,* 442:1–35.

Hill, E. P. 1982. Beaver. Pp. 256–281, in *Wild mammals of North America* (J. A. Chapman and C. A. Feldhamer, eds.). Johns Hopkins University Press, Baltimore, MD, 1147 pp.

Hill, J. E., and J. D. Smith. 1984. *Bats: A natural history.* University of Texas Press, Austin, 243 pp.

Hirshfield, J. R., and W. G. Bradley. 1977. Growth and development of two species of chipmunks: *Eutamias panamintinus* and *E. palmeri. Journal of Mammalogy,* 58:44–52.

Hoagland, D. B. 1992. Feeding ecology of an insular population of the black-tailed jackrabbit *(Lepus californicus)* in the Gulf of California. *Southwestern Naturalist,* 32:280–286.

Hoffmann, R. S. 1993. Order Lagomorpha. Pp. 807–828, in *Mammal species of the world: A taxonomic and geographic reference,* second edition (D. E. Wilson and D. M. Reeder, eds.). Smithsonian Institution Press, Washington, DC, 1207 pp.

Hoffmann, R. S., C. G. Anderson, R. W. Thorington, Jr., and L. R. Heaney. 1993. Family Sciuridae. Pp. 419–466, in *Mammal species of the world: A taxonomic and geographic reference,* second edition (D. E. Wilson and D. M. Reeder, eds.). Smithsonian Institution Press, Washington, DC, 1207 pp.

Hoffmann, R. S., J. W. Koeppl, and C. F. Nadler. 1979. The relationship of the amphiberingian marmots (Mammalia: Sciuridae). *Occasional Papers of the Museum of Natural History, The University of Kansas,* 83:1–56.

Hoffmann, R. S., and R. S. Peterson. 1967. Systematics and zoogeography of *Sorex* in the Bering Strait area. *Systematic Zoology,* 16:127–136.

Hoffmeister, D. F. 1951. A taxonomic and evolutionary study of the piñon mouse, *Peromyscus truei. Illinois Biological Monographs,* 21:1–104.

Hoffmeister, D. F. 1986. *Mammals of Arizona.* University of Arizona Press, Tucson, 602 pp.

Hoffmeister, D. F. 1989. *Mammals of Illinois.* University of Illinois Press, Urbana, 348 pp.

Hoffmeister, D. F., and L. de la Torre. 1960. A revision of the woodrat *Neotoma stephensi. Journal of Mammalogy,* 41:476–491.

Hoffmeister, D. F., and L. de la Torre. 1961. Geographic variation in the mouse *Peromyscus difficilis. Journal of Mammalogy,* 42:1–13.

Hoffmeister, D. F., and V. E. Diersing. 1973. The taxonomic status of *Peromyscus merriami goldmani* Osgood, 1904. *Southwestern Naturalist,* 18:354–357.

Hoffmeister, D. F., and W. W. Goodpaster. 1962. Life history of the desert shrew *Notiosorex crawfordi. Southwestern Naturalist,* 7:236–252.

Hogan, K. M., S. K. Davis, and I. F. Greenbaum. 1997. Mitochondrial DNA analysis of the systematic relationships within the *Peromyscus maniculatus* species group. *Journal of Mammalogy,* 78:733–734.

Hogan, K. M., M. A. Hedin, H. S. Koh, S. K. Davis, and I. F. Greenbaum. 1993. Systematic and taxonomic implications of karyotypic, electrophoretic and mitochondrial-DNA variation in *Peromyscus* from the Pacific Northwest. *Journal of Mammalogy,* 74:819–831.

Holden, M. E. 1993. Family Dipodidae. Pp. 487–499, in *Mammal species of the world: A taxonomic and geographic reference,* second edition (D. E. Wilson and D. M. Reeder, eds.). Smithsonian Institution Press, Washington, DC, 1207 pp.

Holdenried, R. 1940. A population study of the long-eared chipmunk *(Eutamias quadrimaculatus)* in the central Sierra Nevada. *Journal of Mammalogy,* 21:405–411.

Hollander, R. R. 1990. Biosystematics of the yellow-faced pocket gopher, *Cratogeomys castanops* (Rodentia: Geomyidae) in the United States. *Special Publications, The Museum, Texas Tech University,* 33:1–62.

Hollander, R. R., and M. R. Willig. 1992. Description of a new subspecies of the southern grasshopper mouse, *Onychomys torridus,* from western Mexico. *Occasional Papers, The Museum, Texas Tech University,* 148:1–4.

Hoogland, J. L. 1981. The evolution of coloniality in white-tailed and black-tailed prairie dogs (Sciuridae: *Cynomys leucurus* and *C. ludovicianus). Ecology,* 62:252–272.

Hoogland, J. L. 1982. Prairie dogs avoid extreme inbreeding. *Science,* 215:1639–1641.

Hoogland, J. L., and D. W. Folts. 1982. Variance in male and female reproductive success in a harem-polygymous mammal, the black-tailed prairie dog (Sciuridae: *Cynomys ludovicianus). Behavioral Ecology and Sociobiology,* 11:155–163.

Hooper, E. T. 1952. A systematic review of the harvest mice (genus *Reithrodontomys)* of Latin America. *Miscellaneous Publications, Museum of Zoology, University of Michigan,* 77:1–255.

Hoover-Miller, A. A. 1994. Harbor seal *(Phoca vitulina)* biology and management in Alaska. *Marine Mammal Commission, Washington, DC, Contract Report,* T75134749.

Horwood, J., 1990. *Biology and exploitation of the minke whale.* CRC Press, Inc., Boca Raton, FL, 238 pp.

Howard, W. E., and H. E. Childs, Jr. 1959. Ecology of pocket gophers with emphasis on *Thomomys bottae mewa. Hilgardia,* 29:277–358.

Howard, W. E., and R. E. Marsh. 1982. Spotted and hog-nosed skunks. Pp. 664–673, in *Wild mammals of North America* (J. A. Chapman and C. A. Feldhamer, eds.). Johns Hopkins University Press, Baltimore, 1147 pp.

Howell, A. B. 1926. Voles of the genus *Phenacomys. North American Fauna,* 48:1–66.

Howell, A. H. 1929. Revision of the North American chipmunks. *North American Fauna,* 52:1–157.

Hoying, K. M., and T. H. Kunz. 1998. Variations in size at birth and postnatal growth in the eastern pipistrelle bat *Pipistrellus subflavus* (Chiroptera: Vespertilionidae). *Journal of Zoology,* London, 245:15–27.

Hoyt, E. 1990. *The whale called killer.* E. P. Dutton, New York, 291 pp.

Huey, L. M. 1964. The mammals of Baja California, Mexico. *Transactions of the San Diego Society of Natural History,* 13:85–168.

Humphrey, S. R., ed. 1992. *Rare and endangered biota of Florida,* Volume I: *Mammals.* University Press of Florida, Gainesville, 392 pp.

Humphrey, S. R., and T. H. Kunz. 1976. Ecology of a Pleistocene relict, the western big-eared bat *(Plecotus townsendii)* in the southern Great Plains. *Journal of Mammalogy,* 57:470–494.

Humphrey, S. R., A. R. Richter, and J. B. Cope. 1977. Summer habitat and ecology of the endangered Indiana bat, *Myotis sodalis. Journal of Mammalogy,* 58:334–346.

Humphrey, S. R., and H. W. Setzer. 1989. Geographic variation and taxonomic revision of the rice rats *(Oryzomys palustris* and *O. argentatus)* of the United States. *Journal of Mammalogy,* 70:557–570.

Huntly, N., and R. Inouye. 1988. Pocket gophers in ecosystems: patterns and mechanisms. *BioScience,* 38:786–793.

Hutterer, R. 1993. Order Insectivora. Pp. 69–130, in *Mammal species of the world: A taxonomic and geographic reference,* second edition (D. E. Wilson and D. M. Reeder, eds.). Smithsonian Institution Press, Washington, DC, 1207 pp.

Ingles, L. G. 1952. The ecology of the mountain pocket gopher, *Thomomys monticola. Ecology,* 33(1):87–95.

Ingles, L. G. 1965. *Mammals of the Pacific states: California, Oregon and Washington.* Stanford University Press, Palo Alto, CA, 506 pp.

Innes, D. L., and J. S. Millar. 1982. Life history notes on the heather vole, *Phenacomys intermedius levis,* in the Canadian Rocky Mountains. *Canadian Field-Naturalist,* 96:307–311.

International Union for the Conservation of Nature and Natural Resources. 1982. *IUCN mammal red data book.* IUCN Publications, Gland, Switzerland, 516 pp.

International Whaling Commission. 1977. *Report of the special meeting of the scientific committee on sei and bryde's whales, La Jolla, California, December 1974.* Special Issue, 1:1–9.

Iverson, S. J., W. D. Bowen, D. J. Boness, and O. T. Oftedal. 1993. The effect of maternal size and milk energy output on pup growth in grey seals *(Halichoerus grypus). Physiological Zoology,* 66:61–88.

Iverson, S. L., and B. N. Turner. 1972. Natural history of a Manitoba population of Franklin's ground squirrels. *Canadian Field-Naturalist,* 86:145–149.

Jackson, H. H. T. 1918. Two new shrews from Oregon. *Proceedings of the Biological Society of Washington,* 31:127–130.

Jackson, H. H. T. 1961. *Mammals of Wisconsin.* University of Wisconsin Press, Madison, 504 pp.

Jameson, E. W., Jr., and H. J. Peeters. 1988. *California mammals.* University of California Press, Berkeley, 403 pp.

Janecek, L. L. 1990. Genic variation in the *Peromyscus truei* group (Rodentia: Cricetidae). *Journal of Mammalogy,* 71:301–308.

Jannett, F. J., Jr. 1980. Social dynamics of the montane vole, *Microtus montanus,* as a paradigm. *Biologist,* 62:3–19.

Jarrell, G. H., and K. Fredga. 1993. How many kinds of lemmings? A taxonomic overview. Pp. 45–57, in *The biology of lemmings* (N. C. Stenseth and R. A. Ims, eds.). Linnean Society Symposium Series 15, Academic Press, London, 683 pp.

Jefferson, T. 1799. A memoir on the discovery of certain bones of a quadruped of the clawed kind in the western part of Virginia. *Transactions of the American Philosophical Society,* 4:246–260.

Jefferson, T. A., S. Leatherwood, and M. A. Webber. 1994. *Marine mammals of the world.* FAO, Rome, 320 pp.

Jefferson, T. A., M. W. Newcomer, S. Leatherwood, and K. Van Waerebeek. Right whale dolphins—*Lissodelphis borealis* and *Lissodelphis peronii.* Pp. 335–362, in *Handbook of marine mammals: The first book of dolphins* (S. H. Ridgway and R. Harrison, eds.). Academic Press, London, vol. 5: 416 pp.

Johnson, D. H. 1943. Systematic review of the chipmunks (genus *Eutamias)* of California. *University of California Publications in Zoology,* 48:63–148.

Johnson, G. E. 1928. Hibernation of the thirteen-lined ground squirrel *Citellus tridecemlineatus* (Mitchill). I. A comparison of the normal and hibernating states. *Journal of Experimental Zoology,* 50:15–30.

Johnson, M. L., and S. B. Benson. 1960. Relationships of the pocket gophers of the *Thomomys mazama- talpoides* complex in the Pacific Northwest. *Murrelet,* 41:17–22.

Johnson, M. L., and S. B. George. 1991. Species limits within the *Arborimus longicaudus* species- complex (Mammalia: Rodentia) with a description of a new species from California. *Natural History Museum of Los Angeles County, Contributions in Science,* 429:1–16.

Johnson, M. L. and T. L. Yates. 1980. A new Townsend's mole (Insectivora: Talpidae) from the state of Washington. *Occasional Papers, The Museum, Texas Tech University,* 63:1–6.

Jones, C., R. S. Hoffman, D. W. Rice, M. D. Engstrom, R. O. Bradley, D. J. Schmidly, C. A. Jones, and R. T. Baker. 1997. Revised checklist of North American mammals north of Mexico, 1997. *Occasional Papers, The Museum, Texas Tech University,* 173:1–19.

Jones, C. A. 1993. Observations regarding the diet of Florida mice, *Podomys floridanus* (Rodentia: Muridae). *Brimleyana,* 18:131–140.

Jones, C.A., S. R. Humphrey, T. M. Padgett, R. K. Rose, and J. F. Pagels. 1991. Geographic variation and taxonomy of the southeastern shrew *(Sorex longirostris). Journal of Mammalogy,* 72:263–272.

Jones, J. K., Jr., D. M. Armstrong, and J. R. Choate. 1985. *Guide to the mammals of the Plains States.* Universty of Nebraska Press, Lincoln, 371 pp.

Jones, J. K., Jr., D. M. Armstrong, R. S. Hoffmann, and C. Jones. 1983. *Mammals of the northern Great Plains.* University of Nebraska Press, Lincoln, 379 pp.

Jones, J. K., Jr., R. S. Hoffmann, D. W. Rice, C. Jones, R. J. Baker, and M. D. Engstrom. 1992. Revised checklist of North American mammals north of Mexico. *Occasional Papers, The Museum, Texas Tech University,* 146:1–23.

Jones, M. L., S. L. Swartz, and S. Leatherwood, eds. 1984. *The gray whale.* Academic Press, New York, 600 pp.

Jonkel, C. 1978. Black, brown (grizzly), and polar bears. Pp. 227–248, in *Big game of North America* (J. L. Schmidt and D. L. Gilbert, eds.). Stackpole Books, Harrisburg, PA, 494 pp.

Joy, J. E. 1984. Population differences in circannual cycles of thirteen-lined ground squirrels. Pp. 125–141, in *The biology of ground dwelling squirrels* (J. O. Murie and G. I. Michener, eds.). University Nebraska Press, Lincoln, 459 pp.

Junge, J. A., and R. S. Hoffmann. 1981. An annotated key to the long-tailed shrews (genus *Sorex*) of the United States and Canada, with notes on Middle American *Sorex*. *Occasional Papers of the Museum of Natural History, The University of Kansas*, 94:1–48.

Kalcounis, M. C., and R. M. Brigham. 1998. Secondary use of aspen cavities by tree-roosting big brown bats. *Journal of Wildlife Management*, 62:603–611.

Kasuya, T. 1978. The life history of Dall's porpoise with special reference to the stock off the Pacific coast of Japan. *Scientific Reports of the Whales Research Institute* (Tokyo), 30:1–63.

Kasuya, T., and L. L. Jones. 1984. Behavior and segregation of the Dall's porpoise in the northwestern North Pacific Ocean. *Scientific Reports of the Whales Research Institute* (Tokyo), 35:107–128.

Katona, S. K., V. Rough, and D. J. Richardson. 1983. *A field guide to the whales, porpoises and seals of the Gulf of Maine and eastern Canada: Cape Cod to Newfoundland,* third edition. Charles Scribner's Sons, New York, 255 pp.

Kaufmann, J. H. 1962. Ecology and the social behavior of the coati, *Nasua narica,* on Barro Colorado Island, Panama. *University of California Publications in Zoology,* 60:95–222.

Kaufmann, J. H. 1982. Raccoon and allies. Pp. 578–585, in *Wild mammals of North America* (J. A. Chapman and C. A. Feldhamer, eds.). Johns Hopkins University Press, Baltimore, 1147 pp.

Kelly, B. P. 1988a. Bearded seal, *Erignathus barbatus*. Pp 77–94, in *Selected marine mammals of Alaska: Species accounts with research and management recommendations* (J. W. Lentfer, ed.). Marine Mammal Commission, Washington, DC, 275 pp.

Kelly, B. P. 1988b. Ringed seal, *Phoca hispida*. Pp. 57–76, in *Selected marine mammals of Alaska: Species accounts with research and management recommendations* (J. W. Lentfer, ed.). Marine Mammal Commission, Washington, DC, 275 pp.

Kenyon, K. W. 1969. The sea otter in the eastern Pacific ocean. *North America Fauna,* 68:1–352.

King, J. A. 1955. Social behavior, social organization, and population dynamics in a black-tailed prairie dog town in the Black Hills of South Dakota. *Contributions from the Laboratory of Vertebrate Biology, University of Michigan,* 67:1–123.

King, J. A. 1968. *Biology of* Peromyscus (*Rodentia*). Special Publication, American Society of Mammalogists, vol. 2: 593 pp.

Kirkland, G. L., Jr., and J. S. Findley. 1996. First Holocene record for Preble's shrew *(Sorex preblei)* in New Mexico. *Southwestern Naturalist,* 41:320–322.

Kirkland, G. L., Jr., and J. N. Layne, eds. 1989. *Advances in the study of* Peromyscus (*Rodentia*). Texas Tech University Press, Lubbock, 367 pp.

Kirkland, G. L., Jr., R. R. Parmenter, and R. E. Skoog. 1997. A five-species assemblage of shrews from the sagebrush-steppe of Wyoming. *Journal of Mammalogy,* 78:83–89.

Kirkland, G. L., Jr., and H. M. Van Deusen. 1979. Shrews of the *Sorex dispar* group: *Sorex dispar* Batchelder and *Sorex gaspensis* Anthony and Goodwin. *American Museum Novitates,* 2675:1–21.

Klein, D. R. 1959. Saint Matthew Island reindeer range study. *U.S. Fish and Wildlife Service, Special Scientific Report, Wildlife,* 42:1–48.

Kleinenberg, S. E., A. V. Yablokov, B. M. Bel'kovich, and M. N. Tarasevich. 1964. *Beluga* (Delphinapterus leucas): *Investigation of the species.* Academy of Sciences of the USSR, Moscow, 376 pp (in translation).

Klinowska, M. 1991. *Dolphins, porpoises and whales of the world.* The IUCN Red Data Book. IUCN, Gland, Switzerland, 429 pp.

Knuth, B. A., and G. W. Barrett. 1984. A comparative study of resource partitioning between *Ochrotomys nuttalli* and *Peromyscus leucopus. Journal of Mammalogy,* 65:576–583.

Koford, C. B. 1983. *Felis wiedi* (tigrillo, caucel, margay). Pp. 471–472, in *Costa Rican Natural History* (D. H. Janzen, ed.). University of Chicago Press, 816 pp.

Koopman, K. F. 1993. Order Chiroptera. Pp. 137–241, in *Mammal species of the world: A taxonomic and geographic reference,* second edition (D. E. Wilson and D. M. Reeder, eds.). Smithsonian Institution Press, Washington, DC, 1207 pp.

Krohne, D. T. 1982. The karyotype of *Dicrostonyx hudsonius. Journal of Mammalogy,* 63:174–176.

Kruse, S., D. K. Caldwell, and M. C. Caldwell. 1999. Risso's dolphin (*Grampus griseus*) (G. Cuvier, 1812). Pp. 183–212, in *Handbook of marine mammals: The second book of dolphins and the porpoises* (S. H. Ridgway and R. Harrison, eds.). Academic Press, London, vol. 6: 486 pp.

Krutzsch, P. H. 1954. North American jumping mice (genus *Zapus*), *University of Kansas Publications, Museum of Natural History,* 7(4):349–472.

Kunz, T. H. 1973. Population studies of the cave bat (*Myotis velifer*): reproduction, growth, and development. *Occasional Papers of the Museum of Natural History, The University of Kansas,* 15:1–43.

Kunz, T. H. 1974. Feeding ecology of a temperate insectivorous bat (*Myotis velifer*). *Ecology,* 55:693–711.

Kunz, T. H., ed. 1982. *Ecology of Bats.* Plenum Press, New York, 425 pp.

Kurta, A., G. P. Bell, K. A. Nagy, and T. H. Kunz. 1989. Energetics of pregnancy and lactation in free-ranging little brown bats (*Myotis lucifugus*). *Physiological Zoology,* 62:804–818

Kurta, A., T. H. Kunz, and K. A. Nagy. 1990. Energetics and water flux of free-ranging big brown bats (*Eptesicus fuscus*) during pregnancy and lactation. *Journal of Mammalogy,* 71:59–65.

Laack, L., M. E. Ludlow, and M. E. Sunquist. 1987. Ecology and behavior of ocelots in Venezuela. *National Geographic Research,* 3(4):447–461.

Lackey, J. A. 1978. Reproduction, growth, and development in high-latitude and low-latitude populations of *Peromyscus leucopus* (Rodentia). *Journal of Mammalogy,* 59:69–83.

Lance, E. W., and J. A. Cook. 1998. Biogeography of tundra voles (*Microtus oeconomus*) of Beringia and the southern coast of Alaska. *Journal of Mammalogy,* 79:53–65.

Lavigne, D. M., and K. M. Kovacs. 1988. *Harps and hoods: Ice-breeding seals of the northwest Atlantic.* University of Waterloo Press, Waterloo, Ontario, Canada, 173 pp.

Lawlor, T. E. 1971. Distribution and relationships of six species of *Peromyscus* in Baja California and Sonora, Mexico. *Occasional Papers of the Museum of Zoology, University of Michigan,* 661:1–22.

Layne, J. N. 1992. Florida mouse. Pp. 250–264, in *Rare and endangered biota of Florida,* Volume I: *Mammals* (S. R. Humphrey, ed.). University Press of Florida, Gainesville, 392 pp.

Leatherwood, S., and R. R. Reeves. 1983. *The Sierra Club handbook of whales and dolphins.* Sierra Club Books, San Francisco, 302 pp.

Leatherwood, S., R. R. Reeves, W. F. Perrin, and W. E. Evans. 1982. *Whales, dolphins, and porpoises of the eastern North Pacific and adjacent Arctic waters: A guide to their identification.* United States National Marine Fisheries Service, NOAA Technical Report NMFS Circular 444, 245 pp.

Leatherwood, S., B. S. Stewart, and P.A. Folkens. 1987. *Cetaceans of the Channel Islands National Marine Sanctuary.* National Marine Sanctuary Program, National Marine Fisheries Service, Santa Barbara, CA, 66 pp.

Le Boeuf, B. J., and R. M. Lewis, eds. 1994. *Elephant seals: Population ecology, behavior, and physiology.* Unviersity of California Press, Berkeley, 414 pp.

Lee, D. S., and J. B. Funderburg. 1982. Marmots: *Marmota monax* and allies. Pp. 176–191, in *Wild mammals of North America* (J. A. Chapman and C. A. Feldhamer, eds.). Johns Hopkins University Press, Baltimore, 1147 pp.

Lentfer, J. W. 1988. *Selected marine mammals of Alaska: Species accounts with research and management recommendations.* United States Marine Mammal Commission, Washington, DC, 275 pp.

Leonard, M. L., and M. B. Fenton. 1984. Echolocation calls of *Euderma maculatum* (Vespertilionidae): Use in orientation and communication. *Journal of Mammalogy,* 65:122–126.

Levenson, H., and R. S. Hoffmann. 1984. Systematic relationships among taxa in the Townsend chipmunk group. *Southwestern Naturalist,* 29:157–168.

Lidicker, W. Z., Jr. 1973. Regulation of numbers in an island population of the California vole, a problem in community dynamics. *Ecological Monographs,* 43:271–302.

Lidicker, W. Z., Jr. 1980. The social biology of the California vole. *Biologist,* 62:46–55.

Lidicker, W. Z., Jr., and R. S. Ostfeld. 1991. Extra-large body size in California voles: Causes and fitness consequences. *Oikos,* 61:108–121.

Linscombe, G., N. Kinler, and R. J. Aulerich. 1982. Mink. Pp 629–643, in *Wild mammals of North America* (J. A. Chapman and C. A. Feldhamer, eds.). Johns Hopkins University Press, Baltimore, 1147 pp.

Linsdale, J. M. 1946. *The California ground squirrel: A record of observations made on the Hastings natural history reservation.* University of California Press, Berkeley, 475 pp.

Linsdale, J. M., and L.P. Tevis. 1951. *The dusky-footed wood rat: A record of observations made on the Hastings natural history reservation.* University of California Press, Berkeley, 664 pp.

Linzey, D. W., and A. V. Linzey. 1967. Growth and development of the golden mouse, *Ochrotomys nuttalli nuttalli. Journal of Mammalogy,* 48(3):445–458.

Lockner, F. R. 1972. Experimental study of food hoarding in the red-tailed chipmunk, *Eutamias ruficaudus. Zeitschrift fur Tierpsychologie,* 31:410–418.

Long, C. A. 1972a. Notes on habitat preference and reproduction in pigmy shrews, *Microsorex. Canadian Field-Naturalist,* 86:155–160.

Long, C. A. 1972b. Taxonomic revision of the mammalian genus *Microsorex* Coues. *Transactions of the Kansas Academy of Science,* 74:181–196.

Long, C. A. 1992. Status and economic importance of the North American badger, *Taxidea taxus* (Schreber). *Journal IUCN/SSC, Mustelid Specialist Group,* 7:4–7.

Long, C. A., and R. S. Hoffmann. 1992. *Sorex preblei* from the Black Canyon, first record for Colorado. *Southwestern Naturalist,* 37:318–319.

Long, C. A., and C. A. Killingley. 1983. *Badgers of the world.* Charles C. Thomas, Springfield, IL, 404 pp.

Longland, W. S., and M. V. Price. 1991. Direct observations of owls and heteromyid rodents: can predation risk explain microhabitat use? *Ecology,* 72:2261–2273.

Loughlin, T. R., A. S. Perlov, and V. A. Vladimirov. 1993. Range-wide survey and estimation of total number of Steller's sea lions in 1989. *Marine Mammal Science,* 8:220–239.

Lowery, G. H., Jr. 1974. *The mammals of Louisiana and its adjacent waters.* Louisiana State University Press, Baton Rouge, 565 pp.

MacClintock, D. 1970. *Squirrels of North America.* Van Nostrand Reinhold, New York, 184 pp.

MacCracken, J. G., and R. M. Hansen. 1984. Seasonal foods of blacktail jackrabbits and Nuttall cottontails in southwest Idaho. *Journal of Range Management,* 37:256–259.

Macdonald, D. 1984. *The encyclopedia of mammals.* Facts on File Publications, New York, 895 pp.

Macdonald, D. 1987. *Running with the fox.* Facts on File Publications, New York, 224 pp.

MacMillen, R. E. 1964. Population ecology, water relations, and social behavior of a southern California semidesert rodent fauna. *University of California Publications in Zoology,* 71:1–66.

Mammalian Species, a series published by the American Society of Mammalogists, is cited by number in each appropriate account. They are listed separately, in numerical order, at the end of this bibliography.

Manning, R. W. 1993. Systematics and evolutionary relationships of the long-eared myotis, *Myotis evotis* (Chiroptera: Vespertilionidae). *Special Publications, The Museum, Texas Tech University,* 37:1–58.

Manning, T. H. 1948. Notes on the country, birds and mammals west of Hudson Bay between Reindeer and Baker Lake. *Canadian Field-Naturalist,* 62:1–28.

Manning, T. H. 1956. The northern red-backed mouse, *Clethrionomys rutilus* (Pallas), in Canada. *National Museum of Canada Bulletin,* 144:1–67.

Manning, T. H. 1976. Birds and mammals of the Belcher, Sleeper, Ottawa and King George islands, Northwest Territories. *Canadian Wildlife Service, Occasional Paper,* 28:1–42.

Marsh, H., and T. Kasuya. 1991. An overview of the changes in the role of a female pilot whale with age. Pp. 281–285, in *Dolphin Societies* (Karen Pryor and Kenneth Norris, eds.). University of California Press, Berkeley, 397 pp.

Martell, A. M., and W. A. Fuller. 1979. Comparative demography of *Clethrionomys rutilus* in taiga and tundra in the low Arctic. *Canadian Journal of Zoology,* 57:2106–2120.

Martell, A. M., and R. J. Milko. 1986. Seasonal diets of Vancouver Island marmots. *Canadian Field- Naturalist,* 100:241–245.

Martín, A. R. 1990. *Whales and dolphins.* Salamander Books Ltd., London, 192 pp.

Martín, A. R., M. C. S. Kingsley, and M. A. Ramsay. 1994. Diving behaviour of narwhals *(Monodon monoceros)* on their summer grounds. *Canadian Journal of Zoology,* 72:118–125.

Martin, C. O., and D. J. Schmidly. 1982. Taxonomic review of the pallid bat, *Antrozous pallidus* (Le Conte). *Special Publications, The Museum, Texas Tech University,* 18:1–48.

Maser, C., B. R. Mate, J. F. Franklin, and C. T. Dyrness. 1981. *Natural history of Oregon coast mammals.* United States Department of Agriculture, Forest Service, General Technical Report, PNW-133, 496 pp.

Maser, C., and R. M. Storm. 1970. *A key to Microtinae of the Pacific Northwest.* OSE Book Stores, Corvallis, 162 pp.

Matson, J. O., and R. H. Baker. 1986. Mammals of Zacatacas. *Special Publications, The Museum, Texas Tech University* 24:1–88.

McCarley, H. 1966. Annual cycle, population dynamics, and adaptive behavior of *Citellus tridecemlineatus. Journal of Mammalogy,* 47:294–316

McCord, C. M., and J. E. Cardoza. 1982. Bobcat and lynx. Pp 728–766, in *Wild mammals of North America* (J. A. Chapman and C. A. Feldhamer, eds.). Johns Hopkins University Press, Baltimore, 1147 pp.

McCracken, G. F., and M. K. Gustin. 1991. Nursing behavior in Mexican free-tailed bat maternity colonies. *Ethology* 89:305–321.

McKeever, S. 1964. The biology of the golden-mantled ground squirrel, *Citellus lateralis. Ecological Monographs,* 34:383–401.

Mead, E. M., and J. I. Mead. 1989. Quaternary zoogeography of the Nearctic *Dicrostonyx* lemmings. *Boreas,* 18:323–332

Mead, J. G. 1977. Records of sei and Bryde's whales from the Atlantic coast of the United States, the Gulf of Mexico, and the Caribbean. *Report of the International Whaling Commission,* Special Issue, 1:113–116.

Mead, J. G. 1984. Survey of reproductive data for the beaked whales (Ziphiidae). Pp. 91–96, in *Reproduction in whales, dolphins, and porpoises* (W. F. Perrin, R. L. Brownell, and D. P. DeMaster, eds.). Report of the International Whaling Commission, Special Issue, vol. 6: 495 pp.

Mead, J. G. 1989. Beaked whales of the genus *Mesoplodon.* Pp. 349–430, in *Handbook of marine mammals: River dolphins and the larger toothed whales* (S. H. Ridgway and R. Harrison, eds.). Academic Press, London, vol. 4: 442 pp.

Mead, J. G., and R. L. Brownell, Jr. 1993. Order Cetacea. Pp. 349–364, in *Mammal species of the world: A taxonomic and geographic reference,* second edition (D. E. Wilson and D. M. Reeder, eds.). Smithsonian Institution Press, Washington, DC, 1207 pp.

Mech, L. D. 1981. *The wolf: the ecology and behavior of an endangered species.* University of Minnesota Press, Minneapolis, 384 pp.

Melchior, H. R. 1971. Characteristics of arctic ground squirrel calls. *Oecologia,* 7:14–190.

Mercure, A., K. Ralls, K. P. Koefeli, and R. K. Wayne. 1993. Genetic divisions among small canids: mitochondrial DNA differentiation of swift, kit, and arctic foxes. *Evolution,* 47(5):1313–1328.

Merriam, C. H. 1895. Synopsis of the American shrews of the genus *Sorex. North American Fauna,* 10:57–100.

Merriam, C. H. 1897. Notes on the chipmunks of the genus *Eutamias* occurring west of the east base of the Cascade-Sierra system, with descriptions of new forms. *Proceedings of the Biological Society of Washington,* 11:189–212.

Merriam, C. H. 1918. Review of the grizzly and big brown bears of North America. *North American Fauna,* 41:1–136.

Merritt, J. F., and J. M. Merritt. 1978. Population ecology and energy relationships of *Clethrionomys gapperi* in a Colorardo subalpine forest. *Journal of Mammalogy,* 59:576–598.

Merritt, J. F., and D. A. Zegers. 1991. Seasonal thermogenesis and body mass dynamics of *Clethrionomys gapperi. Canadian Journal of Zoology,* 69:2771–2777.

Messick, J. P. 1987. North American badger. Pp 584–597, in *Wild furbearer management and conservation in North America* (M. Novak, J. A. Baker, M. E. Obbard, and B. Malloch, eds.). Ontario Ministry of Natural Resources, Toronto, 1150 pp.

Messick, J. P., and M. G. Hornocker. 1981. Ecology of the badger in southwestern Idaho. *Wildlife Monographs,* 76:1–53.

Michener, G. R. 1998. Sexual differences in reproductive effort of Richardson's ground squirrels. *Journal of Mammalogy,* 79:1–19.

Michener, G. R., and L. Locklear. 1990. Differential costs of reproduction for male and female Richardson's ground squirrels. *Ecology,* 71: 855–868.

Millar, J. S. 1989. Reproduction and development. Pp. 169–232, in *Advances in the study of* Peromyscus *(Rodentia)* (G. L. Kirkland, Jr., and J. N. Layne, eds.). Texas Tech University Press, Lubbock, 367 pp.

Miller, B., R. Reading, and S. Forrest. 1996. *Prairie night: Black-footed ferrets and the recovery of endangered species.* Smithsonian Institution Press, Washington DC, 254 pp.

Minasian, S. M., K. C. Balcomb, III, and L. Foster. 1984. *The world's whales.* Smithsonian Institution Press, Washington, DC, 224 pp.

Miyazaki, N., and W. F. Perrin. 1994. Rough-toothed dolphin—*Steno bredanensis.* Pp. 1–21, in *Handbook of marine mammals: The first book of dolphins* (S. H. Ridgway and R. Harrison, eds.). Academic Press, London, vol. 5: 416 pp.

Mondolfi, E. 1986. Notes on the biology and status of the small wild cats in Venezuela. Pp. 125–146, in *Cats of the world: Biology, conservation, and management* (S. D. Miller and D. D. Everett, eds.). National Wildlife Federation, Washington, DC, 501 pp.

Monson, G., and W. Kessler. 1940. Life history notes on the banner-tailed kangaroo rat, Merriam's kangaroo rat, and the white-throated wood rat in Arizona and New Mexico. *Journal of Wildlife Management,* 4:37–43.

Montgomery, G. G., ed. 1985. *The evolution and ecology of armadillos, sloths, and vermilinguas.* Smithsonian Institution Press, Washington, DC, 451 pp.

Morales, J. C., and J. W. Bickham. 1995. Molecular systematics of the genus *Lasiurus* (Chiroptera: Vespertilionidae) based on restriction-site maps of the mitochondrial ribosomal genes. *Journal of Mammalogy,* 76:730–749.

Morejohn, G. V. 1979. The natural history of Dall's porpoise in the North Pacific Ocean. Pp. 45–83, in *Behavior of marine animals,* Volume 3: *Cetaceans* (H. E. Winn and B.L. Olla, eds.). Plenum Press, New York, 438 pp.

Morgan, L. H. 1868. *The American beaver and his works.* J. B. Lippincott, Philadelphia, 330 pp.

Morgan, K. R., and M. V. Price. 1992. Foraging in heteromyid rodents: the energy cost of scratch digging. *Ecology,* 73:2260–2272.

Moyer, C. A., G. H. Adler, and R. H. Tamarin. 1988. Systematics of New England *Microtus,* with emphasis on *Microtus breweri. Journal of Mammalogy,* 69:782–794.

Mugaas, J. N., and J. Seidensticker. 1993. Geographic variation of lean body mass and a model of its effect on the capacity of the raccoon to fatten and fast. *Bulletin of the Florida Museum of Natural History, Biological Sciences,* 36:85–107.

Mugaas, J. N., J. Seidensticker, and K. P. Mahlke-Johnson. 1993. Metabolic adaptation to climate and distribution of the raccoon *Procyon lotor* and other Procyonidae. *Smithsonian Contributions to Zoology,* 542:1–34.

Murie, A. 1961. The Alaska haymouse. Pp. 173–188, in *A naturalist in Alaska.* Devin-Adair, Old Greenwich, CT, 302 pp.

Murie, J. O. 1973. Population characteristics and phenology of a Franklin ground squirrel *(Spermophilus franklinii)* colony in Alberta, Canada. *American Midland Naturalist,* 90:334–340.

Murie, O. J. 1959. Fauna of the Aleutian Islands and Alaska Peninsula. *North American Fauna,* 61:1–364.

Musser, G. G., and M. D. Carleton. 1993. Family Muridae. Pp. 501–755, in *Mammal species of the world: A taxonomic and geographic reference,* second edition (D. E. Wilson and D. M. Reeder, eds.). Smithsonian Institution Press, Washington, DC, 1207 pp.

Muul, I. 1968. Behavioral and physiological influences on the distribution of the flying squirrel, *Glaucomys volans. Miscellaneous Publications of the Museum of Zoology, University of Michigan, Ann Arbor,* 134:1–66.

Nagorsen, D. W., and R. M. Brigham. 1993. *Bats of British Columbia.* Royal British Columbia Museum, University of British Columbia, Vancouver, 164 pp.

Nagy, T. R., B. A. Gower, and M. H. Stetson.1993. Development of collared lemmings, *Dicrostonyx groenlandicus,* is influenced by pre- and postweaning photoperiods. *Journal of Experimental Zoology,* 267:533–542.

National Marine Fisheries Service, NOAA. 1992. *Recovery plan for the Steller sea lion* (Eumetopias jubatus). Silver Spring, MD, 92 pp.

Navo, K. W., J. A. Gore, and G. T. Skiba. 1992. Observations on the spotted bat, *Euderma maculatum,* in northwestern Colorado. *Journal of Mammalogy,* 73:547–551.

Neal, B. J. 1965a. Growth and development of the round-tailed and Harris antelope ground squirrels. *American Midland Naturalist,* 73:479–489.

Neal, B. J. 1965b. Reproductive habits of round-tailed and Harris antelope ground squirrels. *Journal of Mammalogy,* 46:200–206.

Negus, N. C., and A. J. Pinter. 1965. Litter sizes of *Microtus montanus* in the laboratory. *Journal of Mammalogy,* 46:434–437.

Negus, N. C., E. Gould, and R. K. Chipman. 1961. Ecology of the rice rat, *Oryzomys palustris* (Harlan), on Breton Island, Gulf of Mexico, with a critique of the social stress theory. *Tulane Studies in Zoology,* 8(4):95–123.

Neilson, A. L., and M. B. Fenton. 1994. Responses of little brown myotis to exclusion and to bat houses. *Wildlife Society Bulletin,* 22:8–14.

Newcombe, C. L. 1930. An ecological study of the Allegheny cliff rat (*Neotoma pennsylvanica* Stone). *Journal of Mammalogy,* 11:204–211.

Norris, K. S., R. Würsig, R. S. Wells, and M. Würsig. 1994. *The Hawaiian spinner dolphin.* University California Press, Berkeley, 408 pp.

Novak, M. 1987. Beaver. Pp. 282–313, in *Wild furbearer management and conservation in North America* (M. Novak, J. A. Baker, M. E. Obbard, and B. Malloch, eds.). Ontario Ministry of Natural Resources, Toronto, 1150 pp.

Novak, M., J. A. Baker, M. E. Obbard, and B. Malloch, eds. 1987. *Wild furbearer management and conservation in North America.* Ontario Ministry of Natural Resources, Toronto, 1150 pp.

Nowak, R. M. 1979. North American Quaternary *Canis.* University of Kansas, Museum of Natural History, Monograph, 6:1–154.

Nowak, R. M., 1991. *Walker's mammals of the world.* Fifth Edition. Johns Hopkins University Press, Baltimore, Maryland. 2 vols: 1:1–642; 2:643–1629.

Nowak, R. M. In press. Another look at wolf taxonomy. In *Ecology and conservation of wolves in a changing world* (L. D. Carbyn, S. H. Fritts, and D. R. Seip, eds.). Canadian Circumpolar Institute, Edmonton, Alberta.

Obbard, M. E. 1987. Red squirrel. Pp. 264–281, in *Wild furbearer management and conservation in North America* (M. Novak, J. A. Baker, M. E. Obbard, and B. Malloch, eds.). Ontario Ministry of Natural Resources, Toronto, 1150 pp.

Odell, D. K., and E. D. Asper. 1986. *A review of pygmy killer whale,* Feresa attenuata, *strandings in the southeastern United States.* International Whaling Commission document SC/38/SM13, 5 pp.

Odell, D. K., and K. M. McClune. 1999. False killer whale—*Pseudorca crassidens* (Owen, 1846). Pp. 213–243, in *Handbook of marine mammals: The second book of dolphins and the porpoises* (S. H. Ridgway and R. Harrison, eds.). Academic Press, London, vol. 6: 486 pp.

O'Farrell, T. P. 1987. Kit fox. Pp. 423–31, 433–41, in *Wild furbearer management and conservation in North America* (M. Novak, J. A. Baker, M. E. Obbard, and B. Malloch, eds.). Ontario Ministry of Natural Resources, Toronto, 1150 pp.

Oftedal, O. T., D. J. Boness, and W. D. Bowen. 1988. The composition of hooded seal milk: An adaptation for postnatal fattening. *Canadian Journal of Zoology,* 66:318–322.

Olin, G. 1975. Mammals of the southwest deserts. *Southwest Parks and Monuments Association, Popular Series* 8:1–102.

Omura, H. 1966. Bryde's whale in the northwest Pacific, pp. 70–78, in *Whales, dolphins, and porpoises, Proceedings, International Symposium on Cetacean Research* (K. S. Norris, ed.). University of California Press, Berkeley, 789 pp.

O'Neal, G. T., J. T. Flinders, and W. P. Clary. 1987. Behavioral ecology of the Nevada kit fox (*Vulpes macrotis nevadensis*) on a managed desert rangeland. *Current Mammalogy,* 1:443–481.

Oregon State University Extension Service. 1959. *The Oregon meadow mouse irruption of 1957–1958.* Oregon State College, Corvallis, 88 pp.

Osgood, W. H. 1909. Revision of the mice of the American genus *Peromyscus. North American Fauna,* 28:1–285.

O'Shea, T. J. 1994. Manatees. *Scientific American,* July 1994.

Palmer, F. G. 1937. Geographic variation in the mole, *Scapanus latimanus. Journal of Mammalogy,* 18(3):280–314.

Paradiso, J. L., and A. M. Greenhall. 1967. Longevity records for American bats. *American Midland Naturalist,* 78:251–252.

Parker, G. R. 1977. Morphology, reproduction, diet, and behavior of the arctic hare (*Lepus arcticus monstrabilis*) on Axel Heiberg Island, Northwest Territories. *Canadian Field-Naturalist,* 91:8–18.

Patterson, B. D. 1984. Geographic variation and taxonomy of Colorado and Hopi chipmunks (genus *Eutamias*). *Journal of Mammalogy,* 65:442–456.

Pattie, D. L. 1969. Behaviour of captive marsh shrews. (*Sorex bendirii*). *Murrelet,* 50(3):27–32.

Patton, J. L. 1993a. Family Geomyidae. Pp. 469–476, in *Mammal species of the world: A taxonomic and geographic reference,* second edition (D. E. Wilson and D. M. Reeder, eds.). Smithsonian Institution Press, Washington, DC, 1207 pp.

Patton, J. L. 1993b. Family Heteromyidae. Pp. 477–486, in *Mammal species of the world: A taxonomic and geographic reference,* second edition (D. E. Wilson and D. M. Reeder, eds.). Smithsonian Institution Press, Washington, DC, 1207 pp.

Patton, J. L., and M. F. Smith. 1990. The evolutionary dynamics of the pocket gopher *Thomomys bottae,* with emphasis on California populations. *University of California Publications in Zoology,* 123:1–161.

Patton, J. L., and M. F. Smith. 1994. Paraphyly, polyphyly, and the nature of species boundaries in pocket gophers (genus *Thomomys*). *Systematic Biology,* 43:11–26.

Peek, J. M. 1982. Elk. Pp. 851–861, in *Wild mammals of North America* (J. A. Chapman and C. A. Feldhamer, eds.). Johns Hopkins University Press, Baltimore, 1147 pp.

Pelton, M. R. 1982. Black bear. Pp. 504–514, in *Wild mammals of North America* (J. A. Chapman and C. A. Feldhamer, eds.). Johns Hopkins University Press, Baltimore, 1147 pp.

Perrin, W. F., D. K. Caldwell and M. C. Caldwell. 1994a. Atlantic spotted dolphin—*Stenella frontalis.* Pp. 173–190, in *Handbook of marine mammals: The first book of dolphins* (S. H. Ridgway and R. Harrison, eds.). Academic Press, London, vol. 5: 416 pp.

Perrin, W. F., and J. W. Gilpatrick, Jr. 1994. Spinner dolphin—*Stenella longirostris.* Pp. 99–128, in *Handbook of marine mammals: The first book of dolphins* (S. H. Ridgway and R. Harrison, eds.). Academic Press, London, vol. 5: 416 pp.

Perrin, W. F., and A. A. Hohn. 1994. Pantropical spotted dolphin—*Stenella attenuata.* Pp. 71–98, in *Handbook of marine mammals: The first book of dolphins* (S. H. Ridgway and R. Harrison, eds.). Academic Press, London, vol. 5: 416 pp.

Perrin, W. F., S. Leatherwood, and A. Collet. 1994b. Fraser's dolphin—*Lagenodelphis hosei.* Pp. 225–240, in *Handbook of marine mammals: The first book of dolphins* (S. H. Ridgway and R. Harrison, eds.). Academic Press, London, vol. 5: 416 pp.

Perrin, W. F., and J. G. Mead. 1994. Clymene dolphin—*Stenella clymene.* Pp. 161–172, in *Handbook of marine mammals: The first book of dolphins* (S. H. Ridgway and R. Harrison, eds.). Academic Press, London, vol. 5: 416 pp.

Perry, H. R. 1982. Muskrats. Pp 282–325, in *Wild mammals of North America* (J. A. Chapman and C. A. Feldhamer, eds.). Johns Hopkins University Press, Baltimore, 1147 pp.

Petersen, M. K. 1973. Interactions between cotton rats *Sigmodon fulviventer* and *Sigmodon hispidus*. *American Midland Naturalist*, 90:319–333.

Petersen, M. K., 1979. Behavior of the margay. *Carnivore*, 2:69–76.

Peterson, R. L. 1966. *The mammals of eastern Canada*. Oxford University Press, Toronto, 465 pp.

Peterson, R. S., and G. A. Bartholomew. 1967. *The natural history and behavior of the California sea lion*. Special Publication No. 1, American Society of Mammalogists, 79 pp.

Phillips, M. K., and W. T. Parker. 1988. Red wolf recovery: A progress report. *Conservation Biology*, 2:139–141.

Pierson, E. D., W. E. Rainey, and D. M. Koontz. 1991. Bats and mines: Experimental mitigation for Townsend's big-eared bat at the McLaughlin Mine in California. Pp. 31–42, in *Proceedings V: Issues and technology in the management of impacted wildlife, April 8–10, 1991, Snowmass, CO* (R. D. Comer et al., eds.). Thorne Ecological Institute, Boulder, 223 pp.

Pizzimenti, J. J. 1975. Evolution of the prairie dog genus *Cynomys*. *Occasional Papers of the Museum of Natural History, The University of Kansas*, 39:1–76.

Pizzimenti, J. J. 1976. Genetic divergence and morphological convergence in the prairie dogs, *Cynomys gunnisoni* and *Cynomys leucurus*. I. Morphological and ecological analyses. II. Genetic analyses. *Evolution*, 30:345–366; 367–379.

Poole, E. L. 1940. A life history sketch of the Allegheny woodrat. *Journal of Mammalogy*, 21:249–270.

Powell, R. A. 1993. *The fisher: Life history, ecology, and behavior*. Second edition. University of Minnesota Press, Minneapolis, 237 pp.

Price, M. V. 1978. The role of microhabitat in structuring desert rodent communities. *Ecology*, 59:910–921.

Price, M. V. 1993. A functional-morphometric analysis of forelimbs in bipedal and quadrupedal heteromyid rodents. *Biological Journal of the Linnean Society*, 50:339–360.

Price, M. V., and R. H. Podolsky. 1989. Mechanisms of seed harvest by heteromyid rodents: Soil texture effects on harvest rate and seed size selection. *Oecologia* (Berlin), 81:267–273.

Price, M. V., N. M. Waser, and T. A. Bass. 1984. Effects of moonlight on microhabitat use by desert rodents. *Journal of Mammalogy*, 65:353–356.

Quakenbush, L. T. 1988. Spotted seal, *Phoca largha*. Pp 107–124, in *Selected marine mammals of Alaska: Species accounts with research and management recommendations* (J. W. Lentfer, ed.). Marine Mammal Commission, Washington, DC, 275 pp.

Quimby, D. C. 1951. The life history and ecology of the jumping mouse, *Zapus hudsonius*. *Ecological Monographs*, 21:61–95.

Rainey, D. G. 1956. Eastern woodrat, *Neotoma floridana*: Life history and ecology. *University of Kansas Publications, Museum of Natural History*, 8(10):535–646.

Rathbun, G. B. 1984. Sirenians. Pp. 537–547, in *Orders and families of recent mammals of the world* (S. Anderson and J. K. Jones, Jr., eds.). John Wiley and Sons, New York, 453 pp.

Rausch, R. L., and V. R. Rausch. 1968. On the biology and systematic position of *Microtus abbreviatus* Miller, a vole endemic to the St. Matthew Islands, Bering Sea. *Zeitschrift für Säugetierkunde*, 33:65–99.

Rausch, R. L., and V. R. Rausch. 1971. The somatic chromosomes of some North American marmots. *Mammalia*, 35:85–101.

Rayor, L. S. 1988. Social organization and space-use in Gunnison's prairie dog. *Behavioral Ecology and Sociobiology*, 22:69–78.

Reduker, D. W., T. L. Yates, and I. F. Greenbaum. 1983. Evolutionary

affinities among southwestern long-eared *Myotis* (Chiroptera: Vespertilionidae). *Journal of Mammalogy*, 64:666–677.

Reed, K. M., and J. R. Choate. 1986a. Geographic variation in the plains pocket mouse (*Perognathus flavescens*) on the Great Plains. *Texas Journal of Science*, 38:227–240.

Reed, K. M., and J. R. Choate. 1986b. Natural history of the Plains pocket mouse in agriculturally disturbed sandsage prairie. *Prairie Naturalist*, 18:79–90.

Reeves, R. R., B. S. Stewart, and S. Leatherwood. 1992. *The Sierra Club handbook of seals and sirenians*. Sierra Club Books, San Francisco, 359 pp.

Reeves, R. R., C. Smeenk, R. L. Brownell, Jr., and C. C. Kinze. 1999a. Atlantic white-sided dolphin—*Lagenorhynchus acutus* (Gray, 1828). Pp. 31–56, in *Handbook of marine mammals: The second book of dolphins and the porpoises* (S. H. Ridgway and R. Harrison, eds.). Academic Press, London, vol. 6: 486 pp.

Reeves, R. R., C. Smeenk, C. C. Kinze, R. L. Brownell, Jr., and J. Lien. 1999b. White-beaked dolphin—*Lagenorhynchus albirostris* (Gray, 1846). Pp. 1–30, in *Handbook of marine mammals: The second book of dolphins and the porpoises* (S. H. Ridgway and R. Harrison, eds.). Academic Press, London, vol. 6: 486 pp.

Reichman, O. J., and M. V. Price. 1993. Ecological aspects of heteromyid foraging. Pp. 539–574, in *Biology of the Heteromyidae* (H. H. Genoways and J. H. Brown, eds.). Special Publication, American Society of Mammalogists, No. 10: 719 pp.

Reijnders, P., et al.. 1993. *Seals, fur seals, sea lions and walrus*. IUCN, Cambridge, UK, 88 pp.

Renouf, D. (ed.). 1991. *Behaviour of pinnipeds*. Chapman and Hall, New York, 410 pp.

Reyes, J. C., J. G. Mead, and K. V. Waerebeek. 1991. A new species of beaked whale, *Mesoplodon peruvianus* sp. n. (Cetacea: Ziphiidae) from Peru. *Marine Mammal Science*, 7:1–24.

Reynolds, H. G., and H. S. Haskell. 1949. Life history notes on Price and Bailey pocket mice of southern Arizona. *Journal of Mammalogy*, 30:15–156.

Reynolds, H. W., R. D. Glaholt, and A. W. L. Hawley. 1982. Bison. Pp. 972–1007, in *Wild mammals of North America* (J. A. Chapman and C. A. Feldhamer, eds.). Johns Hopkins University Press, Baltimore, 1147 pp.

Ribble, D. A. 1991. The monogamous mating system of *Peromyscus californicus* as revealed by DNA fingerprinting. *Behavioral Ecology and Sociobiology*, 29:161–166.

Rice, D. W. 1977. Synopsis of biological data on the sei whale and Bryde's whale in the eastern North Pacific. *Report of the International Whaling Commission*, Special Issue, 1:92–97.

Rice, D. W. 1979. Bryde's whales in the equatorial eastern Pacific. *Report of the International Whaling Commission*, 29:321–324.

Rice, D. W. 1984. Cetaceans. Pp. 447–490, in *Orders and families of recent mammals of the world* (S. Anderson and J. K. Jones, Jr., eds.). John Wiley and Sons, New York, 453 pp.

Rice, D. W. 1989. Sperm whale—*Physeter macrocephalus*. Pp. 177–234, in *Handbook of marine mammals: River dolphins and the larger toothed whales* (S. H. Ridgway and R. Harrison, eds.). Academic Press, London, vol. 4: 442 pp.

Rice, D. W., and A. A. Wolman. 1971. Life history and ecology of the gray whale (*Eschrichtius robustus*). Special Publication, American Society of Mammalogists, No. 3: 142 pp.

Riddle, B. R. 1995. Molecular biogeography in the pocket mice (*Perognathus* and *Chaetodipus*) and grasshopper mice (*Onychomys*): the late Cenozoic development of a North American aridlands rodent guild. *Journal of Mammalogy*, 76:283–301.

Riddle, B. R., and J. R. Choate. 1986. Systematics and biogeography of *Onychomys leucogaster* in western North America. *Journal of Mammalogy*, 67:233–255.

Riddle, B. R., and R.L. Honeycutt. 1990. Historical biogeography in North American arid regions: an approach using mitochondrial-DNA phylogeny in grasshopper mice (genus *Onycomys*). *Evolution*, 44:1–15.

Riddle, B. R., R. L. Honeycutt, and P. L. Lee. 1993. Mitochondrial DNA phylogeography in northern grasshopper mice *(Onychomys leucogaster)*—the influence of Quaternary climatic oscillations on population dispersion and divergence. *Molecular Ecology*, 2:183–193.

Riedman, M. L. 1990. *The pinnipeds: Seals, sea lions, and walruses.* University of California Press, Berkeley, 439 pp.

Riedman, M. L., and J. A. Estes. 1991. The sea otter *(Enhydra lutris):* Behavior, ecology, and natural history. *United States Fish and Wildlife Service, Biological Report* 90(14):1–126.

Roemer, G. W., D. K. Garcelon, T. J. Coonan, and C. Schwemm. 1994. The use of capture-recapture methods for estimating, monitoring, and conserving island fox populations. Pp. 387–400, in *Proceedings of the Fourth California Island Symposium: Update on the status of resources* (W. L. Halvorson and G. J. Maender, eds.). Santa Barbara Museum of Natural History, Santa Barbara, CA, 530 pp.

Roest, A. I. 1991. Captive reproduction in Heerman's kangaroo rat, *Dipodomys heermanni. Zoo Biology*, 10:127–137.

Rogers, L. L. 1987. Effect of food supply and kinship on social behavior, movements, and population growth of black bears in northeastern Minnesota. *Wildlife Monographs*, 97:1–72.

Rogers, M. A. 1991. Evolutionary differentiation within the northern Great Basin pocket gopher, *Thomomys townsendii.* I. Morphological variation. II. Genetic variation and biogeographic considerations. *Great Basin Naturalist*, 51:109–126; 127–152.

Rosatte, R. C. 1987. Striped, spotted, hooded, and hog-nosed skunk. Pp. 598–613, in *Wild furbearer management and conservation in North America* (M. Novak, J. A. Baker, M. E. Obbard, and B. Malloch, eds.). Ontario Ministry of Natural Resources, Toronto, 1150 pp.

Ross, G. J. B. 1984. The smaller cetaceans of the south east coast of southern Africa. *Annals of the Cape Provincial Museums, Natural History*, 15(2):173–410.

Ross, G. J. B., and S. Leatherwood. 1994. Pygmy killer whale—*Feresa attenuata.* Pp. 387–404, in *Handbook of marine mammals: The first book of dolphins* (S. H. Ridgway and R. Harrison, eds.). Academic Press, London, vol. 5: 416 pp.

Roze, U. 1989. *The North American porcupine.* Smithsonian Institution Press, Washington, DC, 261 pp.

Rudd, R. L. 1955. Age, sex, and weight comparisons in three species of shrews. *Journal of Mammalogy*, 36: 323–339.

Samuel, D. E., and B. B. Nelson. 1982. Foxes. Pp. 475–490, in *Wild mammals of North America* (J. A. Chapman and C. A. Feldhamer, eds.). Johns Hopkins University Press, Baltimore, 1147 pp.

Sanderson, G. F. 1987. Raccoon. Pp. 486–499, in *Wild furbearer management and conservation in North America* (M. Novak, J. A. Baker, M. E. Obbard, and B. Malloch, eds.). Ontario Ministry of Natural Resources, Toronto, 1150 pp.

Scammon, C. M. [1874] 1968. *The marine mammals of the north-western coast of North America, described and illustrated: together with an account of the American whale-fishery.* Reprint, with an introduction by V. B. Scheffer. Dover Publications, New York, 319 pp.

Scheffer, T. H. 1941. Ground squirrel studies in the four-rivers country, Washington. *Journal of Mammalogy*, 22:270–279.

Scheffer, V. B. 1958. *Seals, sea lions, and walruses.* Stanford University Press, Stanford, CA, 179 pp.

Scheffer, V. B. 1991. *The year of the seal.* Lyons and Burford, New York, 205 pp.

Schmidly, D. J. 1977. *The mammals of trans-Pecos Texas.* Texas A & M University Press, College Station, 225 pp.

Schmidly, D. J. 1983. *Texas mammals east of the Balcones Fault Zone.* Texas A & M University Press, College Station, 400 pp.

Schmidly, D. J. 1984. The furbearers of Texas. *Texas Parks and Wildlife Department, Bulletin*, 111, 1–54.

Schmidly, D. J. 1991. *The bats of Texas.* Texas A & M University Press, College Station, 224 pp.

Schmidly, D. J., R. D. Bradley, and P. S. Cato. 1988. Morphometric differentiation and taxonomy of three chromosomally characterized groups of *Peromyscus boylii* from east-central Mexico. *Journal of Mammalogy*, 69:462–480.

Schwartz, C. W., and E. R. Schwartz. 1981. *The wild mammals of Missouri.* University of Missouri Press, Jefferson City, 356 pp.

Scott, G. W., and K. C. Fisher. 1983. Sterility of hybrids of two subspecies of the varying lemming *Dicrostonyx groenlandicus* bred in captivity. *Canadian Journal of Zoology*, 61:1182–1183.

Scott-Brown, J. M., S. Herrero, and J. Reynolds. 1987. Swift fox. Pp. 423–41, in *Wild furbearer management and conservation in North America* (M. Novak, J. A. Baker, M. E. Obbard, and B. Malloch, eds.). Ontario Ministry of Natural Resources, Toronto, 1150 pp.

Seal, U., E. T. Thorne, M. Bogan, and S. Anderson, eds. 1989. *Conservation biology and the black-footed ferret.* Yale University Press, New Haven, Connecticut, 302 pp.

Seidensticker, J., and S. Lumpkin, eds. 1991. *Great cats: Majestic creatures of the wild.* Rodale Press, Emmaus, PA, 240 pp.

Sergeant, D. E. 1962. The biology of the pilot or pothead whale *Globicephala melaena* (Traill) in Newfoundland waters. *Bulletin of the Fisheries Research Board of Canada*, 132:1–84.

Seton, E. T. 1953. Porcupines. Pp. 603–633, in *Lives of game animals.* Branford, Boston, 4 vols., 2:441–949.

Sheldon, K. E. W., and D. J. Rugh. 1995. The bowhead whale *(Balaena mysticetus):* Its historic and current status. *Marine Fisheries Review*, 57(3–4):1–20.

Shellhammer, H. S. 1989. Salt marsh harvest mice, urban development, and rising sea levels. *Conservation Biology*, 3:59–65.

Sheppe, W., Jr. 1961. Systematic and ecological relations of *Peromyscus oreas* and *P. maniculatus. Proceedings of the American Philosophical Society*, 105:421–446.

Sherman, P. W. 1989. Mate guarding as paternity insurance in Idaho ground squirrels. *Nature*, 338:418–420.

Sherman, P. W., and M. L. Morton. 1979. Four months of the ground squirrel. *Natural History Magazine*, 88(6):50–57.

Shorten, M. 1954. *Squirrels.* Collins, London, 212 pp.

Smith, A. T. 1978. Comparative demography of pikas *(Ochotona):* effect of spatial and temporal age-specific mortality. *Ecology*, 59:133–139.

Smith, A. T., and B. L. Ivins. 1984. Spatial relationships and social organization in adult pikas: a facultatively monogamous mammal. *Zeitschrift fur Tierpsychologie*, 66:289–308.

Smith, J. D. 1972. Systematics of the chiropteran family Mormoopidae. *Miscellaneous Publications, Museum of Natural History, University of Kansas*, 56:1–132.

Smith, S. F. 1978. Alarm calls, their origin and use in *Eutamias sonomae. Journal of Mammalogy*, 59:888–893.

Smith, T. G., D. J. St. Aubin, and J. R. Geraci. 1990. Advances in research on the beluga whale, *Delphinapterus leucas. Canadian Bulletin of Fisheries and Aquatic Sciences,* 224:1–206.

Smolen, M. J., R. M. Pitts, and J. W. Bickham. 1993. A new subspecies of pocket gopher *(Geomys)* from Texas (Mammalia: Rodentia: Geomyidae). *Proceedings of the Biological Society of Washington,* 106:5–23.

Snyder, M. A. 1992. Selective herbivory by Abert's squirrels mediated by chemical variability of ponderosa pine. *Ecology,* 73:1730–1741.

Snyder, M. A. 1993. Interactions between Abert's squirrel and ponderosa pine: the relationship between selective herbivory and host plant fitness. *American Naturalist,* 141:866–879.

Sowls, L. K. 1948. The Franklin ground squirrel, *Citellus franklinii* (Sabine), and its relationship to nesting ducks. *Journal of Mammalogy,* 29:113–137.

Sowls, L. K. 1984. *The peccaries.* The University of Arizona Press, Tucson, 251 pp.

Spencer, A.W., and D. Pettus. 1966. Habitat preferences of five sympatric species of long-tailed shrews. *Ecology,* 47:677–683.

Stains, H. J. 1984. Carnivores. Pp. 491–522, in *Orders and families of recent mammals of the world* (S. Anderson and J. K. Jones, Jr., eds.). John Wiley and Sons, New York, 453 pp.

Stangl, F. B., Jr., T. S. Schafer, J. R. Goetze, and W. Pinchak. 1992. Opportunistic use of modified and disturbed habitat by the Texas kangaroo rat *(Dipodomys elator). Texas Journal of Science,* 44:25–35.

Stenseth, N. C., and R. A. Ims, eds. 1993. *The biology of lemmings.* Linnean Society Symposium Series 15, Academic Press, London, 683 pp.

Stephens, F. 1906. *California mammals.* The West Coast Publishing Company, San Diego, 351 pp.

Stewart, B. S. 1997. Ontogeny of differential migration and sexual segregation in northern elephant seals. *Journal of Mammalogy,* 78:1101–1116.

Stewart, B. S., and R. L. DeLong. 1995. Double migrations of the northern elephant seal, *Mirounga angustirostris. Journal of Mammalogy,* 76:196–205.

Stewart, B. S., and S. Leatherwood. 1985. Minke whale—*Balaenoptera acutorostrata.* Pp. 91–136, in *Handbook of marine mammals: The sirenians and baleen whales* (S. H. Ridgway and R. Harrison, eds.). Academic Press, London, vol. 3: 362 pp.

Stewart, B. S., et al. 1994. History and present status of the northern elephant seal population. Pp. 29–48, in *Elephant seals: Population ecology, behavior and physiology* (B. J. Le Boeuf and R. M. Laws, eds.). University of California Press, Los Angeles, 414 pp.

Stirling, I. 1988. *Polar bears.* University of Michigan Press, Ann Arbor, 220 pp.

Storm, G. L., R. D. Andrews, R. L. Phillips, R. A. Bishop, D. B. Siniff, and J. R. Tester. 1976. Morphology, reproduction, dispersal, and mortality of midwestern red fox populations. *Wildlife Monographs,* 49:1–82.

Sullivan, R. M., D. J. Hafner, and T. L. Yates. 1986. Genetics of a contact zone between three chromosomal forms of the grasshopper mouse (genus *Onychomys*): a reassessment. *Journal of Mammalogy,* 67:640–659.

Sutton, D. A. 1987. Analysis of Pacific coast Townsend chipmunks (Rodentia: Sciuridae). *Southwestern Naturalist,* 32:371–376.

Sutton, D. A., and C. F. Nadler. 1974. Systematic revision of three Townsend chipmunks *(Eutamias townsendii). Southwestern Naturalist,* 19:199–211.

Svendsen, G. E. 1982. Weasels. Pp. 613–628 in *Wild mammals of North America* (J. A. Chapman and C. A. Feldhamer, eds.). Johns Hopkins University Press, Baltimore, 1147 pp.

Tamarin, R. H., ed. 1985. *Biology of New World* Microtus. Special Publication, American Society of Mammalogists, No. 8: 893 pp.

Tappe, D. T. 1941. Natural history of the Tulare kangaroo rat. *Journal of Mammalogy,* 22:117–148.

Teipner, C. L., E. O. Garton, and L. Nelson, Jr. 1983. Pocket gophers in forest ecosystems. *United States Department of Agriculture, Forest Service, Intermountain Forest and Range Experiment Station, Ogden, UT, General Technical Report* INT-154:1–53.

Tershy, B. R., A. Acevedo-G., D. Breese, and C. S. Strong. 1993. Diet and feeding behavior of fin and Bryde's whales in the central Gulf of California, Mexico. *Revista de Investigación Científica, Publicada por La Universidad Autonoma de Baja California Sur,* 1:31–38.

Tewes, M. E., and D. J. Schmidly. 1987. The neotropical felids: Jaguar, ocelot, margay, and jaguarundi. Pp. 696–712, in *Wild furbearer management and conservation in North America* (M. Novak, J. A. Baker, M. E. Obbard, and B. Malloch, eds.). Ontario Ministry of Natural Resources, Toronto, 1150 pp.

Thaeler, C. S., Jr. 1972. Taxonomic status of the pocket gophers, *Thomomys idahoensis* and *Thomomys pygmaeus* (Rodentia, Geomyidae). *Journal of Mammalogy,* 53:417–428.

Thaeler, C. S., Jr., and L. L. Hinesley. 1979. *Thomomys clusius,* a rediscovered species of pocket gopher. *Journal of Mammalogy,* 60:480–488.

Tomich, P. Q. 1964. The annual cycle of the California ground squirrel. *University of California Publications in Zoology,* Berkeley, 65:213–281.

Tomich, P. Q. 1982. Ground squirrels: *Spermophilus beecheyi* and allies. Pp. 192–208, in *Wild mammals of North America* (J. A. Chapman and C. A. Feldhamer, eds.). Johns Hopkins University Press, Baltimore, 1147 pp.

Toweill, D. E., and J. E. Tabor. 1982. River otter. Pp. 688–703 in *Wild mammals of North America* (J. A. Chapman and C. A. Feldhamer, eds.). Johns Hopkins University Press, Baltimore, 1147 pp.

Toweill, D. E., and J. G. Teer. 1980. Home range and den habits of Texas ringtails *(Bassariscus astutus flavus).* Pp. 1103–1120, in *Worldwide furbearer conference proceedings* (J. A. Chapman and D. Pursley, eds.). Worldwide Furbearer Conference, Inc. Frostburg, MD, 2:653–1551.

Trillmich, F., and K. A. Ono, eds. 1991. *Pinnipeds and El Niño.* Springer-Verlag, New York, 293 pp.

Trombulak, S. C. 1987. Life history of the Cascade golden-mantled ground squirrel *(Spermophilus saturatus). Journal of Mammalogy,* 68:544–554.

Tucker, V. A. 1966. Diurnal torpor and its relation to food consumption and weight changes in the California pocket mouse, *Perognathus californicus. Ecology,* 47:245–252.

Tuttle, M. D. 1976. Population ecology of the gray bat *(Myotis grisescens):* philopatry, timing and patterns of movement, weight loss during migration, and seasonal adaptive strategies. *Occasional Papers of the Museum of Natural History, The University of Kansas,* 54:1–38.

Tuttle, M. D. 1979. Status, causes of decline, and management of endangered gray bats. *Journal of Wildlife Management,* 43:1–17.

Tuttle, M. D. 1988. *America's neighborhood bats.* University of Texas Press, Austin, 96 pp.

Underwood, L., and J. A. Mosher. 1982. Arctic fox. Pp. 491–503, in *Wild mammals of North America* (J. A. Chapman and C. A. Feldhamer, eds.). Johns Hopkins University Press, Baltimore, 1147 pp.

United States Fish and Wildlife Service. 1994. *Dismal Swamp southeastern shrew* (Sorex longirostris fisheri) *recovery plan.* Hadley, Massachusetts. 49 pp.

Van Cura, N. J., and D. F. Hoffmeister. 1966. A taxonomic review of the grasshopper mice, *Onychomys,* in Arizona. *Journal of Mammalogy,* 47:613–630

Van Gelder, R. G. 1959. A taxonomic revision of the spotted skunks (genus *Spilogale*). *Bulletin of the American Museum of Natural History*, 117:229–392.

Van Vuren, D., and K. B. Armitage. 1991. Duration of snow cover and its influence on life-history variation in yellow-bellied marmots. *Canadian Journal of Zoology*, 69:1755–1758.

Van Wormer, J. 1969. *The world of the pronghorn*. Lippincott, Philadelphia, 191 pp.

van Zyll de Jong, C. G. 1972. A systematic review of the Neartic and Neotropical river otters (genus *Lutra*, Mustelidae, Carnivora). *Royal Ontario Museum, Life Sciences, Contribution*, 80:1–104.

van Zyll de Jong, C. G. 1979. Distribution and systematic relationships of long-eared *Myotis* in western Canada. *Canadian Journal of Zoology*, 57:987–994.

van Zyll de Jong, C. G. 1983. *Handbook of Canadian mammals. Part I. Marsupials and insectivores*. National Museum of Natural Sciences (Ottawa), 210 pp.

van Zyll de Jong, C. G. 1984. Taxonomic relationships of Nearctic small-footed bats of the *Myotis leibii* group (Chiroptera: Vespertilionidae). *Canadian Journal of Zoology*, 62:2519–2526.

van Zyll de Jong, C. G. 1985. *Handbook of Canadian mammals. Part II. Bats*. National Museum of Natural Sciences (Ottawa), 212 pp.

Van Zyll de Jong, C. G. 1991. Speciation of the *Sorex cinereus* group. Pp. 65–73, in *The biology of the Soricidae* (J. S. Findley and T. L. Yates, eds.). Special Publication No. 1, Museum of Southwestern Biology, Albuquerque, 91 pp.

Vaughn, T. A. 1982. Stephen's woodrat, a dietary specialist. *Journal of Mammalogy*, 63: 53–62.

Verts, B. J., 1967. *The biology of the striped skunk*. University of Illinois Press, Urbana, 218 pp.

Verts, B. J., and L. N. Carraway. 1998. *Land mammals of Oregon*. University of California Press, Berkeley, 668 pp.

Voigt, D. R. 1987. Red fox. Pp. 378–393, in *Wild furbearer management and conservation in North America* (M. Novak, J. A. Baker, M. E. Obbard, and B. Malloch, eds.). Ontario Ministry of Natural Resources, Toronto, 1150 pp.

Von Elsner-Schack, I. 1986. Habitat use by mountain goats, *Oreamnos americanus*, on the eastern slopes region of the Rocky Mountains at Mount Hamell, Alberta. *Canadian Field-Naturalist*, 100:319–324.

Vorhies, C. T., and W. P. Taylor. 1933. The life histories and ecology of jack rabbits, *Lepus alleni* and *Lepus californicus* ssp., in relation to grazing in Arizona. *University of Arizona, College of Agriculture, Agriculture Experiment Station Technical Bulletin*, 49:471–587.

Wadsworth, C. E. 1972. Observations of the Colorado chipmunk in southeastern Utah. *Southwestern Naturalist*, 16:451–454.

Wai-Ping, V., and M. B. Fenton. 1989. Ecology of spotted bat *(Euderma maculatum)* roosting and foraging behavior. *Journal of Mammalogy*, 70:617–622.

Walker, W. A., S. Leatherwood, K. R. Goodrich, W. F. Perrin, and R. K. Stroud. 1986. Geographical variation and biology of the Pacific white-sided dolphin, *Lagenorhynchus obliquidens*, in the north-eastern Pacific. Pp. 441–465, in *Research on dolphins* (M. M. Bryden and R. Harrison, eds.). Clarendon Press, New York, 478 pp.

Walkinshaw, L. H. 1947. Notes on the arctic hare. *Journal of Mammalogy*, 28:353–357.

Wallmo, O. C., ed. 1981. *Mule and black-tailed deer of North America*. University of Nebraska Press, Lincoln, 605 pp.

Washington Department of Wildlife. 1993. *Status of the western gray squirrel* (Sciurus griseus) *in Washington*. Washington Department of Wildlife, Olympia, WA, 38 pp.

Wassmer, D. A., D. D. Guenther, and J. N. Layne. 1988. Ecology of the bobcat in south-central Florida. *Bulletin of the Florida State Museum, Biological Sciences*, 33:159–228.

Watson, L. 1981. *Sea guide to whales of the world*. Dutton, New York, 302 pp.

Wayne, R. K., S. B. George, D. Gilbert, P. W. Collins, S. D. Kovach, D. Girman, and N. Lehman. 1991. A morphological and genetic study of the island fox, *Urocyon littoralis*. *Evolution*, 45(8):1849–1868.

Wayne, R. K., and S. M. Jenks 1991. Mitochondrial DNA analysis implying extensive hybridization of the endangered red wolf *Canis rufus*. *Nature*, 351:565–568.

Weigl, P. D. 1978. Resource overlap, interspecific interactions, and the distribution of flying squirrels, *Glaucomys volans* and *G. sabrinus*. *American Midland Naturalist*, 100(1):83–96.

Wells-Gosling, N. 1985. *Flying squirrels: Gliders in the dark*. Smithsonian Institution Press, Washington, DC, 128 pp.

Wemmer, C., ed. 1987. *Biology and management of the Cervidae*. Smithsonian Institution Press, Washington, DC, 577 pp.

Wetherbee, D. K., R. P. Coppinger, and R. W. Walsh. 1972. *Time lapse ecology, Muskeget Island, Nantucket, Massachusetts*. MSS Information Corp., New York, 173 pp.

Whitaker, J. O., Jr. 1963. A study of the meadow jumping mouse, *Zapus hudsonius* (Zimmermann), in central New York. *Ecological Monographs*, 33:215–254.

Whitaker, J. O., Jr. 1972. Food and external parasites of *Spermophilus tridecemlineatus* in Vigo County, Indiana. *Journal of Mammalogy*, 53:644–648.

Whitaker, J. O., Jr. 1980. *The Audubon Society field guide to North American mammals*. A. A. Knopf, New York, 745 pp.

Whitaker, J. O., Jr., and P. Clem. 1992. Food of the evening bat *Nycticeus humeralis* from Indiana. *American Midland Naturalist*, 127:211–214.

Whitaker, J. O., Jr., and W. W. Cudmore. 1987. Food and ectoparasites of shrews of south central Indiana with emphasis on *Sorex fumeus* and *Sorex hoyi*. *Proceedings of the Indiana Academy of Sciences*, 96:543–552.

Whitaker, J. O., Jr., and S. L. Gummer. 1992. Hibernation of the big brown bat, *Eptesicus fuscus*, in buildings. *Journal of Mammalogy*, 73:312–316.

Whitman, J. S., W. B. Ballard, and C. L. Gardner. 1986. Home range and habitat use by wolverines in southcentral Alaska. *Journal of Wildlife Management*, 50:460–463.

Whitney, P. 1976. Population ecology of two sympatric species of subarctic microtine rodents. *Ecological Monographs*, 46:85–104.

Wight, H. M. 1922. The Williamette Valley gopher. *Murrelet*, 3:6–8

Wilkins, K. T. 1984. Evolutionary trends in Florida Pleistocene pocket gophers (genus *Geomys*), with description of a new species. *Journal of Vertebrate Paleontology*, 3(3):166–181.

Wilkins, K. T. 1987. A zoogeographic analysis of variation in Recent *Geomys pinetis* (Geomyidae) in Florida. *Bulletin of the Florida State Museum, Biological Sciences*, 30:1–28.

Wilkins, K. T., and C. D. Swearingen. 1990. Factors affecting historical distribution and modern geographic variation in the South Texas pocket gopher *Geomys personatus*. *American Midland Naturalist*, 124:57–72.

Wilkinson, G. S. 1992a. Communal nursing in the evening bat, *Nycticeus humeralis*. *Behavioral Ecology and Sociobiology*, 31(4):225–235.

Wilkinson, G. S. 1992b. Information transfer at evening bat colonies. *Animal Behaviour*, 44(3):501–518.

Williams, D. F. 1978. Systematics and ecogeographic variation of the Apache pocket mouse (Rodentia: Heteromyidae). *Bulletin of the Carnegie Museum of Natural History*, 10:1–57.

Williams, D. F. 1984. Habitat associations of some rare shrews (*Sorex*) from California. *Journal of Mammalogy,* 64:325–329.

Williams, D. F. 1991. Habitats of shrews (genus *Sorex*) in forest communities of the western Sierra Nevada, California. Pp. 1–14, in *The biology of the Soricidae* (J. S. Findley and T. L. Yates, eds.). Special Publication No. 1, Museum of Southwestern Biology Albuquerque, 91 pp.

Williams, D. F. 1992. Geographic distribution and population status of the giant kangaroo rat, *Dipodomys ingens* (Rodentia, Heteromyidae). Pp. 301–328, in *Endangered and sensitive species of the San Joaquin Valley, California: Their biology, management, and conservation* (D. F. Williams, S. Byrne, and T. A. Rado, eds.). The California Energy Commission, Sacramento, 388 pp.

Williams, D. F., and H. H. Genoways. 1979. A systematic review of the olive-backed pocket mouse, *Perognathus fasciatus* (Rodentia: Heteromyidae). *Annals of the Carnegie Museum,* 48:73–102.

Williams, D. F., H. H. Genoways, and J. K. Braun. 1993. Taxonomy. Pp. 38–196, in *Biology of the Heteromyidae* (H. H. Genoways and J. H. Brown, eds.). Special Publication, American Society of Mammalogists, No. 10: 719 pp.

Williams, L. R., and G. N. Cameron. 1986a. Food habits and dietary preferences of Attwater's pocket gopher, *Geomys attwateri*. *Journal of Mammalogy,* 67:489–496.

Williams, L. R., and G. N. Cameron. 1986b. Effects of removal of pocket gophers on a Texas coastal prairie. *American Midland Naturalist,* 115:216–224.

Williams, S. L., and H. H. Genoways. 1978. Review of the desert pocket gopher, *Geomys arenarius* (Mammalia: Rodentia). *Annals of the Carnegie Museum,* 47:541–570.

Williams, S. L., and H. H. Genoways. 1980. Morphological variation in the southeastern pocket gopher, *Geomys pinetis* (Mammalia: Rodentia). *Annals of the Carnegie Museum,* 49:405–453.

Williams, S. L., and H. H. Genoways. 1981. Systematic review of the Texas pocket gopher, *Geomys personatus* (Mammalia: Rodentia). *Annals of the Carnegie Museum,* 50:435–473.

Wilson, D. E. 1973. Bat faunas: a trophic comparison. *Systematic Zoology,* 22:14–29.

Wilson, D. E. 1989. Bats. Pp. 365–382, in *Tropical rain forest ecosystems* (H. Lieth and M. J. A. Werger, eds.). Elsevier, Amsterdam, Netherlands, 713 pp.

Wilson, D. E. 1993a. Order Sirenia. Pp. 365–366, in *Mammal species of the world: A taxonomic and geographic reference,* second edition (D. E. Wilson and D. M. Reeder, eds.). Smithsonian Institution Press, Washington, DC, 1207 pp.

Wilson, D. E. 1993b. Family Castoridae. P. 467, in *Mammal species of the world: A taxonomic and geographic reference,* second edition (D. E. Wilson and D. M. Reeder, eds.). Smithsonian Institution Press, Washington, DC, 1207 pp.

Wilson, D. E. 1993c. Family Aplodontidae. P. 417, in *Mammal species of the world: A taxonomic and geographic reference,* second edition (D. E. Wilson and D. M. Reeder, eds.). Smithsonian Institution Press, Washington, DC, 1207 pp.

Wilson, D. E. 1997. *Bats in question: The Smithsonian answer book.* Smithsonian Institution Press, Washington, DC, 168 pp.

Wilson, D. E., and J. F. Eisenberg. 1990. Origins and applications of mammalogy in North America. *Current Mammalogy,* 2:1–35.

Wilson, D. E., and D. M. Reeder. 1993. *Mammal species of the world: A taxonomic and geographic reference,* second edition. Smithsonian Institution Press, Washington, DC, 1207 pp.

Wimsatt, W. A., ed. 1970–1977. *Biology of bats.* Vol. I, II, III. Academic Press, New York.

Winchell, J. M., and T. H. Kunz. 1993. Sampling protocols for estimating time budgets of roosting bats. *Canadian Journal of Zoology,* 71:2244–2249.

Winchell, J. M., and T. H. Kunz. 1996. Time-activity budgets of day-roosting eastern pipistrelle bats (*Pipistrellus subflavus*). *Canadian Journal of Zoology,* 74:431–441.

Winn, L. K, and H. E. Winn. 1985. *Wings in the sea: The humpback whale.* University Press of New England, Hanover, NH, 151 pp.

Wishart, W. 1978. Bighorn sheep. Pp. 161–171, in *Big game of North America* (J. L. Schmidt and D.L. Gilbert, eds.). Stackpole Books, Harrisburg, PA, 494 pp.

Wolff, J. O. 1980. Social organization of the Taiga vole (*Microtus xanthognathus*). *Biologist,* 62:1–4.

Wolff, J. O., W. D. Edge, and R. Bentley. 1994. Behavioral biology of the gray-tailed vole. *Journal of Mammalogy,* 75:873–879.

Wolff, J. O., and M. F. Johnson. 1979. Scent marking in taiga voles, *Microtus xanthognathus*. *Journal of Mammalogy,* 60:400–404.

Wolff, J. O., and W. Z. Lidicker, Jr. 1980. Population ecology of the taiga vole, *Microtus xanthognathus*, in interior Alaska. *Canadian Journal of Zoology,* 58:1800–1812.

Wolff, J. O., and W. Z. Lidicker, Jr. 1981. Communal winter nesting and food sharing in taiga voles. *Behavioral Ecology and Sociobiology,* 9:237–240.

Woods, C. A. 1993. Suborder Hystricognathi. Pp. 771–805, in *Mammal species of the world: A taxonomic and geographic reference,* second edition (D. E. Wilson and D. M. Reeder, eds.). Smithsonian Institution Press, Washington, DC, 1207 pp.

Wozencraft, W. C. 1993. Order Carnivora. Pp. 279–348, in *Mammal species of the world: A taxonomic and geographic reference,* second edition (D. E. Wilson and D. M. Reeder, eds.). Smithsonian Institution Press, Washington, DC, 1207 pp.

Wrigley, R. E. 1972. Systematics and biology of the woodland jumping mouse, *Napaeozapus insignis*. *Illinois Biological Monographs,* 47:1–117.

Yates, T. L. 1982. Moles. Pp. 37–51, in *Wild mammals of North America* (J. A. Chapman and C. A. Feldhamer, eds.). Johns Hopkins University Press, Baltimore, 1147 pp.

Yates, T. L., and D. J. Schmidly. 1977. Systematics of *Scalopus aquaticus* (Linnaeus) in Texas and adjacent states. *Occasional Papers, The Museum, Texas Tech University,* 45:1–36.

Yensen, E. 1991. Taxonomy and distribution of the Idaho ground squirrel. *Journal of Mammalogy,* 72:583–600.

Yoakum, J. D., and B. W. O'Gara. In press. *Ecology and management of the pronghorn.* Wildlife Management Institute, Washington, DC.

Yochem, P. K., and S. Leatherwood. 1985. Blue Whale—*Balaenoptera musculus*. Pp. 193–240, in *Handbook of marine mammals: The sirenians and baleen whales* (S. H. Ridgway and R. Harrison, eds.). Academic Press, London, vol. 3: 362 pp.

Young, S. P. 1958. *The bobcat of North America.* Stackpole Books, Harrisburg, PA, 193 pp.

Youngman, P. M. 1975. Mammals of the Yukon Territory. *National Museum of Natural Sciences (Ottawa), Publications in Zoology,* 10:1–192.

Zimmerman, E. G. 1970. Karyology, systematics and chromosomal evolution in the rodent genus, *Sigmodon*. *Publications of the Museum, Michigan State University, Biological Series,* 4:385–454.

Zimmerman, E. G., C. W. Kilpatric, and B. J. Hart. 1978. The genetics of speciation in the rodent genus *Peromyscus*. *Evolution,* 32:565–579.

Zwicker, K. 1989. Home range and spatial organization of the beach vole, *Microtus breweri*. *Behavioral Ecology and Sociobiology,* 25:161–170.

Mammalian Species
A series published by the American Society of Mammalogists, listed here in numerical order

1: *Macrotus waterhousii.* Anderson, S. 1969. 4 pp.

2: *Sorex merriami.* Armstrong, D. M., and J. K. Jones, Jr. 1971. 2 pp.

7: *Cynomys leucurus.* Clark, T. W., R. S. Hoffmann, and C. F. Nadler. 1971. 4 pp.

11: *Zapus hudsonicus.* Whitaker, J. O., Jr. 1972. 7 pp.

14: *Napaeozapus insignis.* Whitaker, J. O., Jr., and R. E. Wrigley. 1972. 6 pp.

15: *Neofiber alleni.* Birkenholz, D. E. 1972. 4 pp.

17: *Notiosorex crawfordi.* Armstrong, D. M., and J. K. Jones, Jr. 1972. 5 pp.

22: *Canis rufus.* Paradiso, J. L., and R. M. Nowak. 1972. 4 pp.

23: *Nycticeus humeralis.* Watkins, L. C. 1972. 4 pp.

25: *Cynomys gunnisoni.* Pizzimenti, J. J., and R. S. Hoffmann. 1973. 4 pp.

26: *Taxidea taxus.* Long, C. A. 1973. 4 pp.

27: *Sorex bendirii.* Pattie, D. L. 1973. 2 pp.

29: *Erithizon dorsatum.* Woods, C. A. 1973. 6 pp.

33: *Microsorex hoyi* and *Microsorex thompsoni.* Long, C. A. 1974. 4 pp.

34: *Sylvilagus bachmani.* Chapman, J. A. 1974. 4 pp.

36: *Geomys arenarius.* Williams, S. L., and R. J. Baker 1974. 3 pp.

37: *Canis lupus.* Mech, L. D. 1974. 6 pp.

40: *Didephis virginiana.* McManus, J. J. 1974. 6 pp.

42: *Phocoena phocoena.* Gaskin, D. E., P. W. Arnold, and B. A. Blair. 1974. 8 pp.

43: *Cryptotis parva.* Whitaker, J. O., Jr. 1974. 8 pp.

45: *Microtus breweri.* Tamarin, R. H. and T. H. Kunz. 1974. 3 pp.

46: *Microdipodops megacephalus.* O'Farrell, M. J., and A. R. Blaustein. 1974. 3 pp.

47: *Microdipodops pallidus.* O'Farrell, M. J., and A. R. Blaustein. 1974. 2 pp.

48: *Peromyscus attwateri.* Schmidly, D. J. 1974. 3 pp.

49: *Peromyscus pectoralis.* Schmidly, D. J. 1974. 3 pp.

52: *Cynomys parvidens.* Pizzimenti, J. J., and G. D. Collier. 1975. 3 pp.

55: *Sylvilagus transitionalis.* Chapman, J. A. 1975. 4 pp.

56: *Sylvilagus nuttallii.* Chapman, J. A. 1975. 3 pp.

59: *Onychomys torridus.* McCarty, R. 1975. 5 pp.

63: *Oreamnos americanus.* Rideout, C. B., and R. S. Hoffmann. 1975. 6 pp.

69: *Plecotus rafinesquii.* Jones, C. 1977. 4 pp.

70: *Peromyscus gossypinus.* Wolfe, J. L., and A. V. Linzey. 1977. 5 pp.

73: *Dipodomys stephensi.* Bleich, V. C. 1977. 3 pp.

75: *Ochrotomys nuttalli.* Linzey, D. W., and R. L. Packard. 1977. 6 pp.

77: *Euderma maculatum.* Watkins, L. C. 1977. 4 pp.

78: *Glaucomys volans.* Dolan, P.G., and D. C. Carter. 1973. 6 pp.

79: *Canis latrans.* Beckoff, M. 1977. 9 pp.

80: *Sciurus aberti.* Nash, D. J., and R. N. Seaman. 1977. 5 pp.

82: *Liomys irroratus.* Dowler, R. C., and H. H. Genoways.1978. 6 pp.

85: *Peromyscus californicus.* Merritt, J. F. 1978. 6 pp.

86: *Geomys pinetis.* Pembleton, E. F., and S. L. Williams. 3 pp.

87: *Onychomys leucogaster.* McCarty, R. 1978. 6 pp.

90: *Antilocapra americana.* O'Gara, B.W. 1978. 7 pp.

93: *Trichechus manatus.* Husar, S. L. 1978. 5 pp.

94: *Sigmodon fulviventer.* Baker, R. H., and K. A. Shump. 1978. 4 pp.

97: *Sigmodon ochrognathus.* Baker, R. H., and K. A. Shump. 1978. 2 pp.

98: *Parascalops breweri.* Hallett, J. G. 1978. 4 pp.

101: *Spermophilus spilosoma.* Streubel, D. P., and J. P. Fitzgerald. 1978. 4 pp.

103: *Spermophilus tridecemlineatus.* Streubel, D. P., and J. P. Fitzgerald. 1978. 5 pp.

105: *Scalopus aquaticus.* Yates, T. L., and D. J. Schmidly. 1978. 4 pp.

106: *Sylvilagus audubonii.* Chapman, J. A., and G. R. Willner. 1978. 4 pp.

118: *Peromyscus eremicus.* Veal, R., and W. Caire. 1979. 6 pp.

119: *Procyon lotor.* Lotze, J.-H., and S. Anderson. 1979. 8 pp.

120: *Castor canadensis.* Jenkins, S. H., and P. E. Busher. 1979. 8 pp.

121: *Myotis keenii.* Fitch, J. H., and K. A. Shump. 1979. 3 pp.

122: *Vulpes velox.* Egoscue, H. J. 1979. 5 pp.

123: *Vulpes macrotis.* McGrew, J.C. 1979. 6 pp.

124: *Lagurus curtatus.* Carroll, L. E., and H. H. Genoways. 6 pp.

125: *Brachylagus idahoensis.* Green, J. S., and J. T. Flinders. 1980. 4. pp

126: *Mustela nigripes.* Hillman, C. N., and T. W. Clark. 3 pp.

127: *Monodon monoceros.* Reeves, R. R., and S. Tracey. 1980. 7 pp.

129: *Condylura cristata.* Peterson, K. E., and T. L. Yates. 1980. 4 pp.

131: *Sorex tenellus* and *Sorex nanus.* Hoffmann, R. S., and J. G. Owen. 1980. 4 pp.

132: *Lasiurus intermedius.* Webster, W. D., J. K. Jones, Jr., and R. J. Baker. 1980. 3 pp.

133: *Enhydra lutris.* Estes, J. A. 1980. 8 pp.

135: *Marmota flaviventris.* Frase, B., and R. S. Hoffmann. 1980. 8 pp.

136: *Sylvilagus floridanus.* Chapman, J. A., J. G. Hockman, and M. M. Ojeda C. 1980. 8 pp.

137: *Myotis thysanodes.* O'Farrell, M. J., and E. H. Studier. 5 pp.

139: *Neotoma floridana.* Wiley, R. W. 1980. 7 pp.

141: *Ondatra zibethicus.* Willner, G. R., G. A. Feldhamer, E. E. Zucker, and J. A. Chapman. 1980. 8 pp.

142: *Myotis lucifugus.* Fenton, M. B., and R. M. Barclay. 1980. 8 pp.

143: *Sorex longirostris.* French, T. W. 1980. 3 pp.

145: *Ursus maritimus.* DeMaster, D. P., and I. Stirling. 1981. 7 pp.

146: *Clethrionomys gapperi.* Merritt, J. F. 1981. 9 pp.

147: *Microtus pinetorum.* Smolen, M. J. 1981. 7 pp.

149: *Myotis velifer.* Fitch, J. H., K. A. Shump, and A. U. Shump. 1981. 5 pp.

151: *Sylvilagus aquaticus.* Chapman, J. A., and G. A. Feldhamer. 1981. 4 pp.

153: *Sylvilagus palustris.* Chapman, J. A., and G. R. Willner. 1981. 3 pp.

154: *Alces alces.* Franzmann, A. W. 1981. 7 pp.

155: *Sorex dispar* and *Sorex gaspensis.* Kirkland, G. L., Jr. 1981. 4 pp.

156: *Martes pennanti.* Powell, R. A. 1981. 6 pp.

158: *Sigmodon hispidus.* Cameron, G. N., and S. R. Spencer. 1981. 9 pp.

159: *Microtus pennsylvanicus.* Reich, L. M. 1981. 8 pp.

161: *Peromyscus truei.* Hoffmeister, D. F. 1981. 5 pp.

162: *Dasypus novemcinctus.* McBee, K., and R. J. Baker. 1982. 9 pp.

163: *Myotis sodalis.* Thomson, C. E. 1982. 5 pp.

167: *Reithrodontomys megalotis.* Webster, W. D., and J. K. Jones, Jr. 1982. 5 pp.

168: *Tamias striatus.* Snyder, D. P. 1982. 8 pp.

169: *Reithrodontomys raviventris.* Shellhammer, H. S. 1982. 3 pp.

170: *Geomys personatus.* Williams, S. L. 1982. 5 pp.

172: *Lasionycteris noctivagans.* Kunz, T. H. 5 pp.

173: *Mephitis mephitis.* Wade-Smith, J., and B. J. Verts. 1982. 7 pp.

174: *Reithrodontomys fulvescens.* Spencer, S. R., and G. N. Cameron. 1982. 7 pp.

175: *Plecotus townsendii.* Kunz, T. H., and R. A. Martin. 1982. 6 pp.

176: *Oryzomys palustris.* Wolfe, J. L. 1982. 5 pp.

180: *Microtus chrotorrhinus.* Kirkland, G. L., Jr., and F. J. Jannett, Jr. 1982. 5 pp.

183: *Lasiurus borealis.* Shump, K. A., and A. U. Shump. 1982. 6 pp.

185: *Lasiurus cinereus.* Shump, K. A., and A. U. Shump. 1982. 5 pp.

189: *Urocyon cinereoargenteus.* Fritzell, E. K., and K. J. Haroldson. 1982. 8 pp.

190: *Monodelphis kunsi.* Anderson, S. 1982. 3 pp.

191: *Myotis auriculus.* Warner, R. M. 1982. 3 pp.

195: *Mustela erminea.* King, C. M. 1983. 8 pp.

200: *Felis concolor.* Currier, M. J. P. 1983. 7 pp.

208: *Idionycteris phyllotis.* Czaplewski, N. J. 1983. 4 pp.

209: *Pteronotus parnellii.* Herd, R. M. 1983. 5 pp.

210: *Synaptomys cooperi.* Linzey, A. V. 5 pp.

212: *Sorex ornatus.* Owen, J. B., and R. S. Hoffmann. 1983. 5 pp.

213: *Antrozous pallidus.* Hermanson, J. W., and T. J. O'Shea. 8 pp.

214: *Spermophilus elegans.* Zegers, D. A. 1984. 7 pp.

215: *Sorex fumeus.* Owen, J. G. 1984. 5 pp.

219: *Odocoileus hemionus.* Anderson, A. E., and O. C. Wallmo. 1984. 9 pp.

221: *Spermophilus beldingi.* Jenkins, S. H., and B. D. Eshelman. 1984. 8 pp.

223: *Microtus richardsoni.* Ludwig, D. R. 1984. 6 pp.

224: *Myotis volans.* Warner, R. M., and N. J. Czaplewski. 1984. 4 pp.

227: *Diphylla ecaudata.* Greenhall, A. M., U. Schmidt, and C. Joermann. 1984. 3 pp.

228: *Pipistrellus subflavus.* Fujita, M. S., and T. H. Kunz. 1984. 6 pp.

229: *Glaucomys sabrinus.* Wells-Gosling, N., and L. R. Heaney. 1984. 8 pp.

230: *Ovis canadensis.* Shackleton, D. M. 1985. 9 pp.

231: *Sorex pacificus.* Carraway, L. N. 1985. 5 pp.

232: *Dipodomys elator.* Carter, D. C., W. D. Webster, J. K. Jones, Jr., C. Jones, and R. D. Sutkus. 1985. 3 pp.

233: *Microtus oregoni.* Carraway, L. N., and B. J. Verts. 1985. 6 pp.

238: *Odobenus rosmarus.* Fay, F. H. 1985. 7 pp.

239: *Kogia simus.* Nagorsen, D. 1985. 6 pp.

243: *Spermophilus richardsoni.* Michener, G. L., and J. W. Koeppl. 1985. 8 pp.

247: *Peromyscus leucopus.* Lackey, J. A., D. G. Huckaby, and B. G. Ormiston. 1985. 10 pp.

250: *Mesoplodon stejnegeri.* Loughlin, T. R., and M. A. Perez. 1985. 6 pp.

253: *Scapanus orarius.* Hartman, G. D., and T. L. Yates. 1985. 5 pp.

255: *Dipodomys elephantinus.* Best, T. L. 1986. 4 pp.

257: *Reithrodontomys montanus.* Wilkins, K. T. 1986. 5 pp.

258: *Cystophora cristata.* Kovacs, K. M., and D. M. Lavigne. 1986. 9 pp.

261: *Blarina brevicauda.* George, S. B., J. R. Choate, and H. H. Genoways. 1986. 9 pp.

262: *Neotoma mexicana.* Cornely, J. E., and R. J. Baker. 1986. 7 pp.

266: *Bison bison.* Meagher, M. 1986. 8 pp.

267: *Microtus canicaudus.* Verts B. J., and L. N. Carraway. 1987. 4 pp.

268: *Spermophilus townsendii.* Rickart, E. A. 1987. 6 pp.

269: *Felis lynx.* Tumlison, R. 1987. 8 pp.

270: *Marmota vancouverensis.* Nagorson, D. W. 1987. 5 pp.

271: *Microtus longicaudus.* Smolen, M. J. 1987. 7 pp.

272: *Spermophilus variegatus.* Oaks, E. C., P. J. Young, G. L. Kirkland, Jr. and D. F. Schmidt. 1987. 8 pp.

273: *Thomomys bulbivorous.* Verts B. J., and L. N. Carraway. 1987. 4 pp.

274: *Spermophilus tereticaudus.* Ernest, K. A., and M. A. Mares. 1987. 9 pp.

280: *Lasiurus seminolus.* Wilkins, K. T. 1987. 5 pp.

281: *Ochotona collaris.* MacDonald, S. O., and C. Jones. 1987. 4 pp.

283: *Eumetopias jubatus.* Loughlin, T. R. ,M. A. Perez, and R. L. Merrick. 1987. 7 pp.

285: *Baiomys taylori.* Eshelman, B. D., and G. N. Cameron. 1987. 7 pp.

287: *Peromyscus crinitus.* Johnson, D. W., and D. M. Armstrong. 1987. 8 pp.

288: *Lepus townsendii.* Lim, B. K. 1987. 6 pp.

289: *Martes americana.* Clark, T. W., E. Anderson, C. Douglas, and M. Strickland. 1987. 8 pp.

291: *Choeronycteris mexicana.* Arroyo-Cabrales, J., and J. K. Jones, Jr. 1987. 5 pp.

293: *Tayassu pecari.* Mayer, J. J., and R. M. Wetzel. 1987. 7 pp.

296: *Sorex palustris.* Beneski, J. T., Jr., and D. W. Stinson. 1987. 6 pp.

297: *Chaetodipus baileyi.* Paulson, B. D. 1988. 5 pp.

302: *Ovibos moschatus.* Lent, P. C. 1988. 9 pp.

303: *Perognathus fasciatus.* Manning, R. W., and J. K. Jones, Jr. 1988. 4 pp.

304: *Orcinus orca.* Heyning, J. E., and M. E. Dahlheim. 1988. 9 pp.

305: *Phenacomys intermedius.* McAllister, J. A., and R. S. Hoffmann. 1988. 8 pp.

307: *Leptonycteris nivalis.* Hensley, A. P., and K. T. Wilkins. 1988. 4 pp.

310: *Neotoma albigula.* Macêdo, R. H., and M. A. Mares. 1987. 7 pp.

315: *Zapus trinotatus.* Gannon, W. L. 1988. 5 pp.

318: *Perognathus parvus.* Verts, B. J., and G. L. Kirkland, Jr. 1988. 8 pp.

319: *Phocoenoides dalli.* Jefferson, T. A. 1988. 7 pp.

320: *Chaetodipus hispidus.* Paulson, D. D. 1988. 4 pp.

322: *Spermophilus saturatus.* Trombulak, S. C. 1988. 4 pp.

323: *Dipodomys heermanni.* Kelt, D. A. 1988. 7 pp.

324: *Dipodomys californicus.* Kelt, D. A. 1988. 4 pp.

325: *Microtus townsendii.* Cornely, J. E., and B. J. Verts. 1988. 9 pp.

327: *Bassariscus astutus.* Poglayen-Neuwall, I., and D. E. Toweill. 1988. 8 pp.

328: *Neotoma stephensi.* Jones, C., and N. J. Hildreth. 1989. 3 pp.

329: *Myotis evotis.* Manning, R. W., and J. K. Jones, Jr. 1989. 5 pp.

330: *Neotoma micropus.* Braun, J. K., and M. A. Mares. 1989. 9 pp.

331: *Tadarida brasiliensis.* Wilkins, K. T. 1989. 10 pp.

332: *Myotis austroriparius.* Jones, C., and R. W. Manning. 1989. 3 pp.

336: *Delphinapterus leucas.* Stewart, B. E., and R. E. A. Stewart. 1989. 8 pp.

337: *Sorex trowbridgii.* George, S. B. 1989. 5 pp.

338: *Cratogeomys castanops.* Davidow-Henry, B. R., J. K. Jones, Jr., and R. Hollander. 1989. 6 pp.

339: *Dipodomys deserti.* Best, T. L., N. J. Hildreth, and C. Jones. 1989. 8 pp.

340: *Panthera onca.* Seymour, K. L. 1989. 9 pp.

349: *Nyctinomops femorosaccus.* Kumirai, A. and J. K. Jones, Jr. 1990. 5 pp.

351: *Nyctinomops macrotis.* Milner, J., C. Jones, and J. K. Jones, Jr. 1990. 4 pp.

352: *Ochotona princeps.* Smith, A. T., and M. L. Weston. 1990. 8 pp.

353: *Dipodomys ordii.* Garrison, T. E., and T. L. Best. 1990. 10 pp.

354: *Dipodomys panamintinus.* Intress, C., and T. L. Best. 1990. 7 pp.

355: *Microtus ochrogaster.* Stalling, D. T. 1990. 9 pp.

356: *Eptesicus fuscus.* Kurta, A., and R. H. Baker. 1990. 10 pp.

365: *Ammospermophilus interpres.* Best, T. L., C. L. Lewis, K. Caesar, and A. S. Titus. 1990. 6 pp.

366: *Ammospermophilus harrisii.* Best, T. L., A. S. Titus, K. Caesar, and C. L. Lewis. 1990. 7 pp.

367: *Ammospermophilus nelsoni.* Best, T. L., A. S. Titus, C. L. Lewis, and K. Caesar. 1990. 7 pp.

368: *Ammospermophilus leucurus.* Belk, M. C., and H. D. Smith. 1990. 8 pp.

369: *Dipodomys compactus.* Baumgardner, G. D. 1991. 4 pp.

371: *Spermophilus washingtoni.* Rickart, E. A., and E. Yensen. 1991. 5 pp.

372: *Spermophilus columbianus.* Elliott, C. L., and J. T. Flinders. 1991. 9 pp.

377: *Dipodomys ingens.* Williams, D. F., and K. S. Kilburn. 1991. 7 pp.

381: *Dipodomys nitratoides.* Best, T. L. 1991. 7 pp.

382: *Geomys attwateri.* Williams, L. R., and G. N. Cameron. 1991. 5 pp.

383: *Geomys breviceps.* Sulentich, J. M., L. R. Williams, and G. N. Cameron. 1991. 4 pp.

385: *Chaetodipus spinatus.* Lackey, J. A. 1991. 4 pp.

386: *Neotoma fuscipes.* Carraway, L. N., and B. J. Verts. 1991. 10 pp.

387: *Neurotrichus gibbsii.* Carraway, L. N., and B. J. Verts. 1991. 7 pp.

388: *Odocoileus virginianus.* Smith, W. P. 1991. 13 pp.

389: *Dipodomys microps.* Hayssen, V. 1991. 9 pp.

390: *Tamias amoenus.* Sutton, D. A. 1992. 8 pp.

393: *Ovis dalli.* Bowyer, R. T., and D. M. Leslie. 1992. 7 pp.

399: *Tamias dorsalis.* Hart, E. B. 1992. 6 pp.

403: *Dipodomys venustus.* Best, T. L. 1992. 4 pp.

406: *Clethrionomys californicus.* Alexander, L. F., and B. J. Verts. 1992. 6 pp.

411: *Tamias canipes.* Best, T. L., J. L. Bartig, and S. L. Burt. 1992. 5 pp.

416: *Sorex preblei.* Cornely, J. E., L. N. Carraway, and B. J. Verts 1992. 3 pp.

424: *Lepus alleni.* Best, T. L., and T. H. Henry. 1993. 8 pp.

425: *Lissodelphis borealis.* Jefferson, T. A., and M. W. Newcomer. 1993. 6 pp.

427: *Podomys floridanus.* Jones, C. A., and J. N. Layne. 1993. 5 pp.

428: *Myotis californicus.* Simpson, M. R. 1993. 4 pp.

431: *Aplodontia rufa.* Carraway, L. N., and B. J. Verts. 1993. 10 pp.

434: *Scapanus townsendii.* Carraway, L. N., L. F. Alexander, and B. J. Verts. 1993. 7 pp.

436: *Tamias cinereicollis.* Hilton, C. D., and T. L. Best. 1993. 5 pp.

439: *Ursus arctos.* Pasitschniak-Arts, M. 1993. 10 pp.

440: *Spermophilus lateralis.* Bartels, M. A., and D. P. Thompson. 1993. 8 pp.

442: *Lepus callotis.* Best, T. L., and T. H. Henry. 1993. 6 pp.

443: *Tamias palmeri.* Best, T. L. 1993. 6 pp.

444: *Tamias sonomae.* Best, T. L. 1993. 5 pp.

445: *Tamias ochrogenys.* Gannon, W. L., R. B. Forbes, and D. E. Kain. 1993. 5 pp.

448: *Mormoops megalophylla.* Rezsutek, M., and G. N. Cameron. 1993. 5 pp.

449: *Mirounga angustirostris.* Stewart, B. S., and H. R. Huber. 1993. 10 pp.

450: *Perognathus inornatus.* Best, T. L. 1993. 5 pp.

452: *Tamias ruficaudus.* Best, T. L. 1993. 7 pp.

457: *Lepus arcticus.* Best, T. L., and T. H. Henry. 1994. 9 pp.

458: *Lepus othus.* Best, T. L., and T. H. Henry. 1994. 5 pp.

461: *Tamias alpinus.* Clawson, R. G., J. A. Clawson, and T. L. Best. 1994. 6 pp.

463: *Perognathus amplus.* Best, T. L. 1994. 4 pp.

468: *Tamias panamintinus.* Best, T. L., R. G. Clawson, and J. A. Clawson. 1994. 7 pp.

469: *Tamias quadrimaculatus.* Clawson, R. G., J. A. Clawson, and T. L. Best. 1994. 6 pp.

470: *Lagenodelphis hosei.* Jefferson, T. A., and S. Leatherwood. 1994. 5 pp.

471: *Perognathus flavus.* Best, T. L., and M. P. Skupski, 1994. 10 pp.

472: *Tamias obscurus.* Best, T. L., and N. J. Granai. 1994. 6 pp.

473: *Perognathus merriami.* Best, T. L., and M. P. Skupski. 1994. 7 pp.

474: *Sciurus griseus.* Carraway, L. N., and B. J. Verts. 1994. 7 pp.

476: *Tamias merriami.* Best, T. L., and N. J. Granai. 1994. 9 pp.

478: *Tamias speciosus.* Best, T. L., R. G. Clawson, and J. A. Clawson. 1994. 9 pp.

479: *Sciurus niger.* Koprowski, J. L. 1994. 9 pp.

480: *Sciurus carolinensis.* Koprowski, J. L. 1994. 9 pp.

484: *Chaetodipus nelsoni.* Best, T. L. 1994. 6 pp.

487: *Nasua narica.* Gompper, M. E. 1995. 10 pp.

489: *Urocyon littoralis.* Moore, C. M., and P. W. Collins. 1995. 7 pp.

492: *Sciurus nayaritensis.* Best, T. L. 1995. 5 pp.

494: *Phenacomys albipes.* Verts, B. J., and L. N. Carraway. 1995. 5 pp.

496: *Sciurus arizonensis.* Best, T. L., and S. Riedel. 1995. 5 pp.

499: *Gulo gulo.* Pasitschniak-Arts M., and S. Larivière. 1995. 10 pp.

502: *Tamias senex.* Gannon, W. L., and R. B. Forbes. 1995. 6 pp.

509: *Spermophilus mohavensis.* Best, T. L. 1995. 7 pp.

510: *Myotis grisescens.* Decher, J., and J. R. Choate. 1995. 7 pp.

511: *Spilogale putorius.* Kinlaw, A. 1995. 7 pp.

515: *Lasiurus ega.* Kurta, A., and G. C. Lehr. 1995. 7 pp.

516: *Eumops underwoodi.* Kiser, W. M. 1995. 4 pp.

524: *Sorex arcticus.* Kirkland, G. L., Jr. and D. F. Schmidt. 1996. 5 pp.

532: *Arborimus longicaudus.* Hayes, J. P. 1996. 5 pp.

534: *Eumops perotis.* Best, T. L., W. M. Kiser, and P. W. Freeman. 1996. 8 pp.

535: *Cynomys ludovicianus.* Hoogland, J. L. 1996. 10 pp.

537: *Vulpes vulpes.* Larivière, S., and M. Pasitchiniak-Arts. 1996. 11 pp.

547: *Myotis leibii.* Best, T. L., and J. B. Jennings. 1997. 6 pp.

548: *Leopardus pardalis.* Murray, J. L., and G. L. Gardner. 1997. 10 pp.

551: *Eumops glaucinus.* Best, T. L., W. M. Kiser, and J. C. Rainey. 1997. 6 pp.

560: *Spermophilus bunnneus.* Yensen, E., and P. W. Sherman. 1997. 5 pp.

563: *Lynx rufus.* Larivière, S., and L. R. Walton. 1997. 8 pp.

564: *Neotoma cinerea.* Smith, F. A. 1997. 8 pp.

565: *Reithrodontomys humilis.* Stalling, D. T. 1997. 6 pp.

570: *Mustela frenata.* Sheffield, S. R., and H. T. Thomas. 1997. 9 pp.

578: *Herpailurus yagouaroundi.* Oliveira, T. G. de. 1998. 6 pp.

579: *Leopardus wiedii.* Oliveira, T. G. de. 1998. 6 pp.

586: *Tamiasciurus hudsonicus.* Steele, M. 1998. 9 pp.

587: *Lontra canadensis.* Larivière, S., and L. R. Walton. 1998. 8 pp.

591: *Marmota monax.* Kwiecinski, G. G. 1998. 8 pp.

595: *Arborimus pomo.* Adam, M. D., and J. P. Hayes. 1998. 5 pp.

599: *Stenella longirostris.* Perrin, W. F. 1998. 7 pp.

604: *Megaptera novaeangliae.* Clapham, P. J., and J. G. Mead. In press.

Photography Credits

Lois Alexander, University of Nevada, Las Vegas
  Page 18: *Sorex bairdi* (Baird's shrew)

J. Scott Altenbach, University of New Mexico (batmine@unm.edu)
  i: *Plecotus townsendii* (Townsend's big-eared bat)
  68, 77: *Leptonycteris curasoae* (southern long-nosed bat)
  76: *Choeronycteris mexicana* (Mexican long-tongued bat)
  83: *Myotis auriculus* (southwestern myotis)
  84: *Myotis austroriparius* (southeastern myotis)
  85: *Myotis californicus* (California myotis)
  87: *Myotis ciliolabrum* (western small-footed myotis)
  89: *Myotis evotis* (long-eared myotis)
  91: *Myotis grisescens* (gray myotis)
  94: *Myotis leibii* (eastern small-footed myotis)
  96, 96: *Myotis septentrionalis* (northern long-eared myotis)
  99: *Myotis thysanodes* (fringed myotis)
  101: *Myotis velifer* (cave myotis)
  102: *Myotis volans* (long-legged myotis)
  108: *Lasiurus ega* (southern yellow bat)
  111: *Lasiurus seminolus* (Seminole bat)
  115: *Pipistrellus subflavus* (eastern pipistrelle)
  120: *Corynorhinus rafinesquii* (Rafinesque's big-eared bat)
  123, 124: *Idionycteris phyllotis* (Allen's big-eared bat)
  126: *Antrozous pallidus* (pallid bat)
  130: *Nyctinomops femorosaccus* (pocketed free-tailed bat)
  131: *Nyctinomops macrotis* (big free-tailed bat)
  133: *Eumops perotis* (western mastiff bat)
  135: *Eumops underwoodi* (Underwood's mastiff bat)

Ronn Altig, Mississippi State University (altig@biology.msstate.edu)
  183: *Spilogale gracilis* (western spotted skunk)
  469: *Thomomys bulbivorus* (Camas pocket gopher)
  612: *Clethrionomys californicus* (western red-backed vole)
  669: *Zapus trinotatus* (Pacific jumping mouse)

American Society of Mammalogists, Mammal Slide Library / M. Andera
  639: *Microtus oeconomus* (tundra vole)

American Society of Mammalogists, Mammal Slide Library / BJ Betts
  440: *Spermophilus washingtoni* (Washington ground squirrel)

American Society of Mammalogists, Mammal Slide Library, James M. Sulentich
  494: *Perognathus alticola* (white-eared pocket mouse)

James Anderson, DeAnza College, Cupertino, CA
  456: *Sciurus nayaritensis* (Mexican fox squirrel)
  460: *Tamiasciurus hudsonicus* (red squirrel)

Scot Anderson, EarthViews
  385: *Tamias sonomae* (Sonoma chipmunk)

V. J. Anderson / Animals Animals (animals@capital.net)
  415: *Spermophilus brunneus* (Idaho ground squirrel)

Robert J. Baker, Texas Tech University, Lubbock, TX
  486: *Geomys knoxjonsei* (Jones's pocket gopher)

Roger W. Barbour
  20: *Sorex cinereus* (cinereus shrew)
  22: *Sorex dispar* (long-tailed shrew)
  62: *Parascalops breweri* (hairy-tailed mole)
  72, 72: *Mormoops megalophylla* (ghost-faced bat)
  79: *Leptonycteris nivalis* (Mexican long-nosed bat)
  83: *Myotis auriculus* (southwestern myotis)
  86: *Myotis californicus* (California myotis)
  92: *Myotis keenii* (Keen's myotis)
  95: *Myotis lucifugus* (little brown bat)
  97, 97: *Myotis sodalis* (Indiana bat)
  99: *Myotis thysanodes* (fringed myotis)
  102: *Myotis volans* (long-legged myotis)
  107: *Lasiurus cinereus* (hoary bat)
  112: *Lasionycteris noctivagans* (silver-haired bat)
  113: *Pipistrellus hesperus* (western pipistrelle)
  114: *Pipistrellus subflavus* (eastern pipistrelle)
  116: *Eptesicus fuscus* (big brown bat)
  117: *Nycticeius humeralis* (evening bat)
  121: *Corynorhinus rafinesquii* (Rafinesque's big-eared bat)
  122: *Corynorhinus townsendii* (Townsend's big-eared bat)
  126: *Antrozous pallidus* (pallid bat)
  129: *Tadarida brasiliensis* (Brazilian free-tailed bat)
  132: *Eumops glaucinus* (Wagner's mastiff bat)
  134: *Eumops perotis* (western mastiff bat)
  170: *Mustela frenata* (long-tailed weasel)
  185: *Spilogale putorius* (eastern spotted skunk)
  201: *Zalophus californianus* (California sea lion)
  230: *Leopardus wiedii* (margay)
  423: *Spermophilus mexicanus* (Mexican ground squirrel)
  489: *Geomys pinetus* (southeastern pocket gopher)
  492: *Pappogeomys castanops* (yellow-faced pocket gopher)
  496: *Perognathus amplus* (Arizona pocket mouse)
  547: *Liomys irroratus* (Mexican spiny pocket mouse)
  555: *Oryzomys palustris* (Marsh rice rat)
  557: *Reithrodontomys fulvescens* (fulvous harvest mouse)
  558: *Reithrodontomys humulis* (eastern harvest mouse)
  565: *Peromyscus californicus* (California mouse)
  568: *Peromyscus eremicus* (cactus mouse)
  569: *Peromyscus gossypinus* (cotton mouse)

573: *Peromyscus leucopus* (white-footed mouse)
582: *Peromyscus polionotus* (oldfield mouse)
585: *Ochrotomys nuttalli* (golden mouse)
595: *Sigmodon ochrognathus* (yellow-nosed cotton rat)
597: *Neotoma albigula* (white-throated woodrat)
599: *Neotoma cinerea* (bushy-tailed woodrat)
610: *Neotoma micropus* (southern plains woodrat)
630: *Microtus chrotorrhinus* (rock vole)
635: *Microtus montanus* (montane vole)
641: *Microtus pennsylvanicus* (meadow vole)
644: *Microtus pinetorum* (woodland vole)
657: *Synaptomys cooperi* (southern bog lemming)
667: *Zapus hudsonius* (meadow jumping mouse)
668: *Zapus princeps* (western jumping mouse)
692: *Sylvilagus palustris* (marsh rabbit)

Breck Bartholomew
474: *Thomomys talpoides* (northern pocket gopher)

George O. Batzli, University of Illinois, Champaign, IL
(g-batzli@pop.life.uiuc.edu)
616: *Clethrionomys rutilis* (northern red-backed vole)

Russell A. Benedict, University of Nebraska, Lincoln
25: *Sorex haydeni* (prairie shrew)
51: *Blarina hylophaga* (Elliot's short-tailed shrew)
173: *Mustela nivalis* (least weasel)

Scott R. Benson, National Marine Fisheries Service
269: *Stenella coeruleoalba* (striped dolphin)

Troy L. Best, Auburn University, AL
360: *Tamias canipes* (gray-footed chipmunk)
381: *Tamias rufus* (Hopi chipmunk)
522: *Dipodomys agilis* (agile kangaroo rat)
529: *Dipodomys elephantinus* (big-eared kangaroo rat)
542: *Dipodomys simulans* (Dulzura kangaroo rat)
545: *Dipodomys venustus* (narrow-faced kangaroo rat)

John W. Bickham, Texas A&M University, College Station, TX
(j-bickham@tamu.edu)
487: *Geomys personatus* (Texas pocket gopher)

Daryl J. Boness, National Zoological Park, Washington, DC
212, 212: *Halichoerus grypus* (gray seal)
215, 216: *Cystophora cristata* (hooded seal)

Jim Brandenburg/Minden (info@mindenpictures.com)
172, 172: *Mustela nigripes* (black-footed ferret)
697: *Lepus arcticus* (arctic hare)

Harold Broadbooks, Thousand Oaks, CA
358: *Tamias alpinus* (alpine chipmunk)
364: *Tamias dorsalis* (cliff chipmunk)
369: *Tamias obscurus* (California chipmunk)
373: *Tamias palmeri* (Palmer's chipmunk)
375: *Tamias panamintinus* (Panamint chipmunk)
376: *Tamias quadrimaculatus* (long-eared chipmunk)
387: *Tamias speciosus* (lodgepole chipmunk)

Illustration by Russell W. Buzzell, courtesy of Massachusetts Audubon
Society
626: *Microtus breweri* (beach vole)

Alan and Sandy Carey, Western Wildlife Photography, Bozeman, MT
227: *Puma concolor* (cougar)

Glenn D. Chambers, Columbia, MO
152: *Urocyon cinereoargenteus* (common gray fox)

Mark A. Chappell, University of California, Riverside
(chappell@citrus.ucr.edu)
394: *Marmota broweri* (Alaska marmot)
510: *Chaetodipus fallax* (San Diego pocket mouse)
704, 705: *Lepus townsendii* (white-tailed jackrabbit)

Ivar Christensen, Bergen, Norway
307: *Hyperoodon ampullatus* (northern bottlenose whale)

Herbert Clarke, Glendale, CA
518: *Chaetodipus spinatus* (spiny pocket mouse)

Jessie Cohen, National Zoological Park, Washington, DC
144, 145: *Canis rufus* (red wolf)

Mark Conlin/HHP
281: *Grampus griseus* (Risso's dolphin)

Stephen DeStefano
621: *Arborimus longicaudus* (red tree vole)

Robert C. Dowler, Angelo State University, San Angelo, TX
484: *Geomys breviceps* (Baird's pocket gopher)

Robert C. Dowler and Darin S. Carroll
561: *Reithrodontomys montanus* (plains harvest mouse)

Robert C. Dowler and Zane Laws
563: *Peromyscus attwateri* (Texas mouse)

Andrew N. Drake, Seattle, WA (adrake1366@aol.com)
iv–v: *Zalophus californianus* (California sea lion)
210: *Phoca vitulina* (harbor seal)
274: *Delphinus delphis* (short-beaked saddleback dolphin)

Kristina Ernest, Central Washington University, Ellensburg, WA
434: *Spermophilus tereticaudus* (round-tailed ground squirrel)

M. Brock Fenton, York University, Ontario, Canada
(bfenton@circus.yorku.ca)
659: *Dicrostonyx groenlandicus* (northern collared lemming)

Jeff Foott, Jackson, WY (jfoott@blissnet.com)
181: *Enhydra lutris* (sea otter)
211: *Phoca vitulina* (harbor seal)
391: *Tamias umbrinus* (Uinta chipmunk)
400: *Marmota olympus* (Olympic marmot)
526: *Dipodomys deserti* (desert kangaroo rat)

Richard B. Forbes, Portland State University, OR
(richardf@sbii.sb2.pdx.edu)
xvi, 431: *Spermophilus saturatus* (Cascade golden-mantled
   ground squirrel)
19: *Sorex bendirii* (marsh shrew)
32: *Sorex monticolus* (montane shrew)
42: *Sorex trowbridgii* (Trowbridge's shrew)
46: *Sorex vagrans* (vagrant shrew)
59: *Scapanus orarius* (coast mole)
60: *Scapanus townsendii* (Townsend's mole)
153: *Urocyon cinereoargenteus* (common gray fox)
167: *Martes pennanti* (fisher)
169: *Mustela erminea* (ermine)
176: *Gulo gulo* (wolverine)

191: *Conepatus mesoleucus* (western hog-nosed skunk)
224: *Nasua narica* (white-nosed coati)
229: *Leopardus pardalis* (ocelot)
231: *Herpailurus yaguarundi* (jaguarundi)
233: *Lynx canadensis* (Canada lynx)
296: *Phocoena phocoena* (harbor porpoise)
355: *Aplodontia rufa* (mountain beaver)
359: *Tamias amoenus* (yellow-pine chipmunk)
377: *Tamias quadrivittatus* (Colorado chipmunk)
382: *Tamias senex* (Allen's chipmunk)
384: *Tamias siskiyou* (Siskiyou chipmunk)
390: *Tamias townsendii* (Townsend's chipmunk)
403: *Ammospermophilus harrisii* (Harris's antelope squirrel)
404: *Ammospermophilus interpres* (Texas antelope squirrel)
431: *Spermophilus saturatus* (Cascade golden-mantled ground squirrel)
433: *Spermophilus spilosoma* (spotted ground squirrel)
441: *Cynomys gunnisoni* (Gunnison's prairie dog)
449: *Sciurus aberti* (Abert's squirrel)
452: *Sciurus carolinensis* (eastern gray squirrel)
454: *Sciurus griseus* (western gray squirrel)
467: *Thomomys bottae* (Botta's pocket gopher)
498: *Perognathus flavescens* (plains pocket mouse)
499: *Perognathus flavus* (silky pocket mouse)
508: *Chaetodipus baileyi* (Bailey's pocket mouse)
542: *Dipodomys spectabilis* (banner-tailed kangaroo rat)
571: *Peromyscus gratus* (Osgood's mouse)
583: *Peromyscus truei* (pinyon mouse)
586: *Baiomys taylori* (northern pygmy mouse)
588: *Onychomys arenicola* (Mearns's grasshopper mouse)
593: *Sigmodon fulviventer* (tawny-bellied cotton rat)
609: *Neotoma mexicana* (Mexican woodrat)
634: *Microtus mogollonensis* (Mogollon vole)
640: *Microtus oregoni* (creeping vole)
646: *Microtus townsendii* (Townsend's vole)
653: *Lemmus sibericus* (brown lemming)
699: *Lepus californicus* (black-tailed jackrabbit)

Karin A. Forney, National Marine Fisheries Service
279: *Lagenorhynchus obliquidens* (Pacific white-sided dolphin)

Carol Farneti Foster, Belize City, Belize
237: *Panthera onca* (jaguar)

Kathy Frost, Alaska Department of Fish and Game, Fairbanks
204: *Phoca fasciata* (ribbon seal)

William L. Gannon, University of New Mexico, Albuquerque
371: *Tamias ochrogenys* (yellowed-cheeked chipmunk)

Keith Geluso, University of New Mexico, Albuquerque
(kgeluso@unm.edu)
512: *Chaetodipus formosus* (long-tailed pocket mouse)
566: *Peromyscus crinitus* (canyon mouse)
578: *Peromyscus nasutus* (northern rock mouse)
579: *Peromyscus pectoralis* (white-ankled mouse)
649: *Lemmiscus curtatus* (sagebrush vole)

Kenneth N. Geluso
65: *Condylura cristata* (star-nosed mole)

Mickey Gibson / Animals Animals (animals@capital.net)
379: *Tamias ruficaudus* (red-tailed chipmunk)

Gilbert Grant, University of North Carolina, Wilmington
74: *Macrotus californicus* (California leaf-nosed bat)

I. F. Greenbaum, Texas A&M University, College Station, TX
(ira@bio.tamu.edu)
571: *Peromyscus keeni* (northwestern deer mouse)

William E. Grenfell, Jr., Granite Bay, CA (GrayOtter@compuserve.com)
37: *Sorex pacificus* (Pacific shrew)
43: *Sorex trowbridgii* (Trowbridge's shrew)
686: *Sylvilagus bachmani* (brush rabbit)

Bob Gress, Wichita, KS (wildtrek@southwind.net)
ii–iii, 328: *Cervus elaphus* (elk)
x,10: *Dasypus novemcinctus* (nine-banded armadillo)
xii: *Procyon lotor* (raccoon)
xxvi, 4, 5: *Didelphis virginiana* (Virginia opossum)
53: *Cryptotis parva* (least shrew)
63: *Scalopus aquaticus* (eastern mole)
105, 105: *Lasiurus borealis* (red bat)
140: *Canis latrans* (coyote)
142: *Canis lupus* (gray wolf)
149: *Vulpes velox* (swift or kit fox)
151, 151: *Vulpes vulpes* (red fox)
175: *Mustela vison* (American mink)
177: *Taxidea taxus* (American badger)
179: *Lontra canadensis* (northern river otter)
220. *Bassariscus astutus* (ringtail)
222: *Procyon lotor* (northern raccoon)
235: *Lynx rufus* (bobcat)
322, 332: *Odocoileus virginianus* (white-tailed deer)
326: *Pecari tajacu* (collared peccary)
330: *Odocoileus hemionus* (mule deer)
335: *Alces alces* (moose)
338: *Rangifer tarandus* (caribou)
339, 340: *Antilocapra americana* (pronghorn)
345: *Oreamnos americanus* (mountain goat)
349: *Ovis canadensis* (bighorn sheep)
352, 672: *Erethizon dorsatum* (North American porcupine)
388: *Tamias striatus* (eastern chipmunk)
409: *Spermophilus armatus* (Uinta ground squirrel)
416: *Spermophilus columbianus* (Columbian ground squirrel)
419: *Spermophilus franklinii* (Franklin's ground squirrel)
421: *Spermophilus lateralis* (golden-mantled ground squirrel)
427: *Spermophilus parryii* (Arctic ground squirrel)
429: *Spermophilus richardsonii* (Richardson's ground squirrel)
437: *Spermophilus tridecemlineatus* (thirteen-lined ground squirrel)
439: *Spermophilus variegatus* (rock squirrel)
444: *Cynomys leucurus* (white-tailed prairie dog)
445: *Cynomys ludovicianus* (black-tailed prairie dog)
457: *Sciurus niger* (eastern fox squirrel)
464: *Glaucomys volans* (southern flying squirrel)
485: *Geomys bursarius* (plains pocket gopher)
513: *Chaetodipus hispidus* (Hispid pocket mouse)
537: *Dipodomys ordii* (Ord's kangaroo rat)
549, 550: *Castor canadensis* (American beaver)
559: *Reithrodontomys megalotis* (western harvest mouse)
575: *Peromyscus maniculatus* (deer mouse)
589: *Onychomys leucogaster* (northern grasshopper mouse)
593: *Sigmodon hispidus* (hispid cotton rat)
602: *Neotoma floridana* (eastern woodrat)
637: *Microtus ochrogaster* (prairie vole)
674: *Lepus californicus* (black-tailed jackrabbit)
679: *Ochotona princeps* (American pika)
684: *Sylvilagus audubonii* (desert cottontail)
687: *Sylvilagus floridanus* (eastern cottontail)

Dan Guravich / Photo Researchers
147: *Alopex lagopus* (arctic fox)

Howard Hall/HHP (HHPH@aol.com)
242, 243: *Eubalaena glacialis* (northern right whale)
261: *Eschrichtius robustus* (gray whale)
264: *Tursiops truncatus* (bottlenose dolphin)
270: *Stenella frontalis* (Atlantic spotted dolphin)
300: *Physeter macrocephalus* (sperm whale)

Mike Hammill, Department of Fisheries and Oceans, Mont-Joli, Quebec, Canada (HammillM@dfo-mpo.gc.ca)
206, 207: *Phoca hispida* (ringed seal)

Richard R. Hansen/Photo Researchers
473: *Thomomys monticola* (mountain pocket gopher)

John D. Haweeli, New York, NY (jhaweeli@worldnet.att.net)
351: *Ovis dalli* (Dall's sheep)

John W. Haweeli
678: *Ochotona collaris* (collared pika)

Virginia Hayssen, Smith College, Northhampton, MA (vhayssen@smith.smith.edu)
535: *Dipodomys microps* (chisel-toothed kangaroo rat)

John E. Heyning, Natural History Museum of Los Angeles County
273: *Delphinus capensis* (long-beaked saddleback dolphin)

Alan Hicks, Wildlife Resources Center, Delmar, NY
607: *Neotoma magister* (Allegheny woodrat)

Michio Hoshino/Minden (info@mindenpictures.com)
xiv–xv: *Megaptera novaenangliae* (humpback)

Murray L. Johnson
620: *Arborimus albipes* (white-footed vole)
623: *Arborimus pomo* (Sonoma tree vole)

Douglas A. Kelt, University of California, Davis
523: *Dipodomys californicus* (California kangaroo rat)

Karl W. Kenyon, Seattle, WA
196, 196: *Callorhinus ursinus* (northern fur seal)

John M. Kipp, II, Severna Park, MD
308: *Mesoplodon bidens* (Sowerby's beaked whale)

David R. Klein
624: *Microtus abbreviatus* (insular vole)
703: *Lepus othus* (Alaskan hare)

Hal S. Korber
614: *Clethrionomys gapper* (southern red-backed vole)

Stephen Leatherwood/EarthViews
198: *Arctocephalus townsendi* (Guadeloupe fur seal)

Lynn and Paul Lefebvre, Gainesville, FL
650: *Neofiber alleni* (round-tailed muskrat)

Didier LeHenaff
337: *Rangifer tarandus* (caribou)

William P. Leonard, Olympia, WA (107746.156@compuserve.com)
472: *Thomomys mazama* (western pocket gopher)

C. K. Lorenz/Photo Researchers
189: *Mephitis mephitis* (striped skunk)

Lloyd Lowry, Alaska Department of Fish and Game, Fairbanks
208: *Phoca largha* (spotted seal)

Wayne Lynch, Calgary, Alberta, Canada
164: *Ursus maritimus* (polar bear)
214: *Erignathus barbatus* (bearded seal)

Rick D. Maiers, Winnipeg, Canada (MaiersL@dfo-mpo.gc.ca)
238: *Delphinapterus leucas* (beluga)

Jesus E. Maldonado, National Zoological Park, Washington, DC
41: *Sorex sonomae* (fog shrew)

Gary F. McCracken, University of Tennessee, Knoxville
128: *Tadarida brasiliensis* (Brazilian free-tailed bat)

Tom McHugh/Photo Researchers
435: *Spermophilus townsendii* (Townsend's ground squirrel)
519: *Microdipodops megacephalus* (dark kangaroo mouse)
605: *Neotoma lepida* (desert woodrat)

L. David Mech, U.S. Geological Survey, St. Paul, MN
143: *Canis lupus* (gray wolf)

Anthony Mercieca/Photo Researchers
187: *Mephitis macroura* (hooded skunk)

R. W. Murphy, Royal Ontario Museum, Toronto, Canada (drbob@rom.on.ca)
660: *Dicrostonyx hudsonius* (Ungava collared lemming)
662: *Dicrostonyx richardsoni* (Richardson's collared lemming)

David Nagorsen, Royal British Columbia Museum, Canada (dnagorsen@galaxy.gov.bc.ca)
401: *Marmota vancouverensis* (Vancouver marmot)

National Marine Fisheries Service
199: *Eumetopias jubatus* (Steller sea lion)

Michael W. Newcomer, Los Altos, CA (NewcWhales@aol.com)
263: *Steno bredanensis* (rough-toothed dolphin)

Flip Nicklin/Minden (info@mindenpictures.com)
244, 245: *Balaena mysticetus* (bowhead whale)
247: *Balaenoptera acutorostrata* (minke whale)
252, 252: *Balaenoptera musculus* (blue whale)
254: *Balaenoptera physalus* (fin whale)
257: *Megaptera novaeangliae* (humpback whale)
283: *Feresa attenuata* (pygmy killer whale)
284: *Pseudorca crassidens* (false killer whale)
285: *Globicephala macrorhynchus* (short-finned pilot whale)
288: *Orcinus orca* (killer whale)
292: *Delphinapterus leucas* (beluga)
293, 294: *Monodon monoceros* (narwhal)

Robert J. O'Brien, Portland State University, OR (obrienr@pdx.edu)
693: *Sylvilagus transitionalis* (New England cottontail)

Michael J. O'Farrell, Las Vegas, NV (mikeof@accessnv.com)
521: *Microdipodops pallidus* (pale kangaroo mouse)

R. Parker, courtesy of D. E. Brown
451: *Sciurus arizonensis* (Arizona gray squirrel)

James F. Parnell, Wilmington, NC
665: *Napaeozapus insignis* (woodland jumping mouse)

Donald L. Pattie, Northern Alberta Institute of Technology, Edmonton, Canada
34: *Sorex nanus* (dwarf shrew)

Dean E. Pearson, Missoula, MT
655: *Synaptomys borealis* (northern bog lemming)

B. Moose Peterson/WRP, Mammoth Lakes, CA (moose395@qnet.com)
35: *Sorex ornatus* (ornate shrew)
38: *Sorex palustris* (water shrew)
89: *Myotis evotis* (long-eared myotis)
140: *Canis latrans* (coyote)
155: *Urocyon littoralis* (island gray fox)
367: *Tamias minimus* (least chipmunk)
395: *Marmota caligata* (hoary marmot)
396: *Marmota flaviventris* (yellow-bellied marmot)
405: *Ammospermophilus leucurus* (white-tailed antelope squirrel)
407: *Ammospermophilus nelsoni* (Nelson's antelope squirrel)
410: *Spermophilus beecheyi* (California ground squirrel)
412: *Spermophilus beldingi* (Belding's ground squirrel)
424: *Spermophilus mohavensis* (Mohave ground squirrel)
448: *Cynomys parvidens* (Utah prairie dog)
458: *Tamiasciurus douglasii* (Douglas's squirrel)
462: *Glaucomys sabrinus* (northern flying squirrel)
501: *Perognathus inornatus* (San Joaquin pocket mouse)
503: *Perognathus longimembris* (little pocket mouse)
506: *Perognathus parvus* (Great Basin pocket mouse)
509: *Chaetodipus californicus* (California pocket mouse)
516: *Chaetodipus penicillatus* (desert pocket mouse)
530: *Dipodomys heermanni* (Heermann's kangaroo rat)
531: *Dipodomys ingens* (giant kangaroo rat)
533: *Dipodomys merriami* (Merriam's kangaroo rat)
536: *Dipodomys nitratoides* (Fresno kangaroo rat)
540: *Dipodomys panamintinus* (Panamint kangaroo rat)
544: *Dipodomys stephensi* (Stephens's kangaroo rat)
562: *Reithrodontomys raviventris* (salt marsh harvest mouse)
590: *Onychomys torridus* (southern grasshopper mouse)
603: *Neotoma fuscipes* (dusky-footed woodrat)
626: *Microtus californicus* (California vole)
631: *Microtus longicaudus* (long-tailed vole)
682: *Brachylagus idahoensis* (pygmy rabbit)
689: *Sylvilagus nuttallii* (mountain cottontail)

Robert L. Pitman, La Jolla, CA (Pitman@caliban.ucsd.edu)
266: *Stenella attenuata* (pantropical spotted dolphin)
267: *Stenella clymene* (Clymene dolphin)
272: *Stenella longirostris* (spinner dolphin)
275: *Lagenodelphis hosei* (Fraser's dolphin)

Robert L. Pitman, EarthViews
289: *Lissodelphis borealis* (northern right whale dolphin)
297: *Phocoenoides dalli* (Dall's porpoise)
303: *Kogia simus* (dwarf sperm whale)

John V. Planz
600: *Neotoma devia* (Arizona woodrat)

R. L. and V. R. Rausch, University of Washington, Seattle
28: *Sorex hydrodromus* (Pribilof Island shrew)
632: *Microtus miurus* (singing vole)
648: *Microtus xanthognathus* (taiga vole)

Lynn and Donna Rogers, Ely, MN (lrogers@northernnet.com)
vi: *Lepus americanus* (snowshoe hare)
xxiv, 158: *Ursus americanus* (American black bear)
136, 166: *Martes americana* (American marten)
161: *Ursus arctos* (brown or grizzly bear)
347: *Ovibos moschatus* (muskox)
399: *Marmota monax* (woodchuck)
696: *Lepus americanus* (snowshoe hare)

Mary Ann Rogers
477: *Thomomys townsendii* (Townsend's pocket gopher)

Leonard Lee Rue, Blairstown, NJ
652: *Ondatra zibethicus* (muskrat)

Luis A. Ruedas, University of New Mexico, Albuquerque (lruedas@sevilleta.unm.edu)
690: *Sylvilagus obscurus* (Appalachian cottontail)

Heinrich Schatz, EarthViews
305: *Ziphius cavirostris* (Cuvier's beaked whale)

C. Gregory Schmitt and Marshall C. Conway
701: *Lepus callotis* (white-sided jackrabbit)

D. R. and T. L. Schrichte, Honolulu, HI (TLSchricht@aol.com)
316, 320: *Trichechus manatus* (West Indian manatee)

Cecil Schwalbe, Tucson, AZ (cecils@srnr.arizona.edu)
12, 54: *Notiosorex crawfordi* (desert shrew)

Richard Sears, EarthViews
276: *Lagenorhynchus acutus* (Atlantic white-sided dolphin)
278: *Lagenorhynchus albirostris* (white-beaked dolphin)

Wendy Shattil/Bob Rozinski, Denver, CO (wshattil@compuserve.com)
418: *Spermophilus elegans* (Wyoming ground squirrel)
683: *Sylvilagus aquaticus* (swamp rabbit)

James H. Shaw, Oklahoma State University, Stillwater
343: *Bison bison* (American bison)

Gay G. Sheffield, Fairbanks, Alaska (Gay_Sheffield@fishgame.state.ak.us)
193: *Odobenus rosmarus* (walrus)

Steven R. Sheffield, Clemson University, Pendleton, SC
170: *Mustela frenata* (long-tailed weasel)

Larry M. Shults, Meeker, CO
194: *Odobenus rosmarus* (walrus)

Ronnie Sidner, University of Arizona, Tucson
130: *Nyctinomops femorosaccus* (pocketed free-tailed bat)

Lee H. Simons, Yreka, CA
17: *Sorex arizonae* (Arizona shrew)

Rob Simpson, Stephens City, VA (lfsimpr@lf.cc.va.us)
26: *Sorex hoyi* (pygmy shrew)
146: *Alopex lagopus* (arctic fox)

Jack W. Sites, Jr., Brigham Young University, UT
483: *Geomys attwateri* (Attwater's pocket gopher)

Norm Smith, Tucson, AZ (nsmith@ag.arizona.edu)
   362: *Tamias cinereicollis* (gray-collared chipmunk)
   592: *Sigmodon arizonae* (Arizona cotton rat)
   694: *Lepus alleni* (antelope jackrabbit)

Michael J. Smolen, World Wildlife Fund, Washington, DC
   491: *Geomys texensis* (Llano pocket gopher)

Brent S. Stewart, Hubbs-Sea World Research Institute, San Diego
   217: *Mirounga angustirostris* (northern elephant seal)

Robert E. A. Stewart, Freshwater Institute, Winnipeg, Canada
(StewartRE@DFO-MPO.GC.CA)
   205: *Phoca groenlandica* (harp seal)

Fiona Sunquist, Melrose, FL
   584: *Podomys floridanus* (Florida mouse)

Jack H. Tasoff, San Pedro, CA (jtasoff@earthlink.net)
   365: *Tamias merriami* (Merriam's chipmunk)

Tershy and Strong, EarthViews
   250: *Balaenoptera edeni* (Bryde's whale)

R. K. Thacker, Brigham Young University, Provo, UT
   149: *Vulpes velox* (swift or kit fox)

Merlin D. Tuttle/Bat Conservation International (batinfo@batcon.org)
   80: *Diphylla ecaudata* (hairy-legged vampire bat)
   104: *Myotis yumanensis* (Yuma myotis)
   119: *Euderma maculatum* (spotted bat)

John and Gloria Tveten, Baytown, TX (jltveten@earthlink.net)
   110: *Lasiurus intermedius* (northern yellow bat)
   514: *Chaetodipus intermedius* (rock pocket mouse)
   515: *Chaetodipus nelsoni* (Nelson's pocket mouse)
   524: *Dipodomys compactus* (Gulf Coast kangaroo rat)
   564: *Peromyscus boylii* (brush mouse)

R. W. Van Devender, Appalachian State University, NC
(vandevenderr@appstate.edu)
   6: *Dasypus novemcinctus* (nine-banded armadillo)
   23: *Sorex fumeus* (smoky shrew)
   29: *Sorex longirostris* (southeastern shrew)
   47: *Blarina brevicauda* (northern short-tailed shrew)
   49: *Blarina carolinensis* (southern short-tailed shrew)
   57: *Neurotrichus gibbsii* (American shrew mole)
   504: *Perognathus merriami* (Merriam's pocket mouse)

Beatrice Van Horne, Colorado State University, Fort Collins
   425: *Spermophilus mollis* (Piute ground squirrel)

James D. Watt, EarthViews
   248: *Balaenoptera borealis* (sei whale)
   310: *Mesoplodon densirostris* (Blainville's beaked whale)

Fred Whitehead/Animals Animals (animals@capital.net)
   301: *Kogia breviceps* (pygmy sperm whale)
   311: *Mesoplodon europaeus* (Gervais's beaked whale)

Stephen L. Williams, Baylor University, Waco, TX
   481: *Geomys arenarius* (desert pocket gopher)

Randall S. Wells (Chicago Zoological Society)
   304: *Berardius bairdii* (Baird's beaked whale)

Jerry O. Wolff, University of Memphis, TN (jwolff@memphis.edu)
   628: *Microtus canicaudus* (gray-tailed vole)

Franklin D. Yancey, II, Texas Tech University, Lubbock
   527: *Dipodomys elator* (Texas kangaroo rat)

Terry L. Yates, University of New Mexico, Albuquerque
   58: *Scapanus latimanus* (broad-footed mole)

Index to Scientific Names

Page numbers in *italics* indicate species information included elsewhere than in its own account. Page numbers in **boldface** indicate photographs located elsewhere than in their respective species account.

Alces alces, 334–336
Alopex lagopus, 146–148
Ammospermophilus
    harrisii, 402–403
    interpres, 404–405
    leucurus, 405–406
    nelsoni, 407–408, *532*
Antilocapra americana, 339–341
Antrozous pallidus, 125–126
Aplodontia rufa, 355–356
Arborimus
    albipes, 620
    longicaudus, 620–622, *623*
    pomo, 622–623
Arctocephalus townsendi, 197–199

Baiomys taylori, 586–587, *594*
Balaena mysticetus, 243–245
Balaenoptera
    acutorostrata, 246–248
    borealis, 248–249
    edeni, 249–251
    musculus, 251–253
    physalus, 253–255
Bassariscus astutus, 219–221
Berardius bairdii, 304–305
Bison bison, 342–343
Blarina
    brevicauda, 47–49, *51*
    carolinensis, 48, 49–51
    hylophaga, 48, 51–52
Brachylagus idahoensis, 681–683

Callorhinus ursinus, 195–197
Canis
    latrans, 139–141, *143*, *145*, *151*
    lupus, 141–143, *145*
    rufus, 143–146
Castor canadensis, 548–552
Cervus elaphus, **ii–iii**, 327–329
Chaetodipus
    baileyi, 507–508
    californicus, 508–509

Chaetodipus (continued)
    fallax, 510–511, *567*
    formosus, 511–512
    hispidus, 513–514
    intermedius, 514–515
    nelsoni, 515–516
    pencillatus, 516–517
    spinatus, 517–518
Choeronycteris mexicana, 75–76
Clethrionomys
    californicus, 612–613
    gapperi, 613–615
    rutilus, 616–617
Condylura cristata, 65–67
Conepatus
    leuconotus, 190–191
    mesoleucus, 191–192
Corynorhinus
    rafinesquii, 119–121
    townsendii, **i**, 121–123
Cryptotis parva, 52–54
Cynomys
    gunnisoni, 441–443
    leucurus, 443–445
    ludovicianus, 445–447
    parvidens, 447–448
Cystophora cristata, 215–216

Dasypus novemcinctus, **x, 6,** 9–11
Delphinapterus leucas, **238,** 291–292
Delphinus
    capensis, 272–273
    delphis, 274
Dicrostonyx, 658–664
    groenlandicus, 658, 659–660
    hudsonius, 658, 660–662
    richardsoni, 658, 662–664
Didelphis virginiana, **xxvi,** 3–5
Diphylla ecaudata, 80–81
Dipodomys
    agilis, 521–523
    californicus, 523–524
    compactus, 524–525
    deserti, 525–527
    elator, 527–528
    elephantinus, 528–529
    heermanni, *529*, 529–531
    ingens, 531–532
    merriami, 533–534

Dipodomys (continued)
    microps, 534–535
    nitratoides, 535–537
    ordii, *525*, 537–539
    panamintinus, 539–540
    simulans, 541–542
    spectabilis, 542–544
    stephensi, 544–545
    venustus, 545–546

Enhydra lutris, 180–182
Eptesicus fuscus, 115–117
Erethizon dorsatum, *167*, **352,** 671–673
Erignathus barbatus, 213–215
Eschrichtius robustus, 259–261
Eubalaena glacialis, 241–243
Euderma maculatum, 118–119
Eumetopias jubatus, 199–200
Eumops
    glaucinus, 132–133
    perotis, 133–134
    underwoodi, 134–135

Feresa attenuata, 282–283

Geomys
    arenarius, 480–481
    attwateri, 482–483
    breviceps, 483–484
    bursarius, 485–486
    knoxjonesi, 486–487
    personatus, 487–489
    pinetis, 489–490
    texensis, 490–491
Glaucomys
    sabrinus, 462–463
    volans, 463–465
Globicephala
    macrorhynchus, 285–286
    melas, 286–287
Grampus griseus, 280–282
Gulo gulo, 175–177

Halichoerus grypus, 211–213
Herpailurus yaguarondi, 231–232
Hyperoodon ampullatus, 306–307

Idionycteris phyllotis, 123–125

743

Kogia
    breviceps, 301–302
    simus, 302–303

Lagenodelphis hosei, 275
Lagenorhynchus
    acutus, 276–277
    albirostris, 277–279
    obliquidens, 279–280, *281*
Lasionycteris noctivagans, 111–112
Lasiurus
    borealis, 105–106
    cinereus, 106–107
    ega, 107–109
    intermedius, 109–110
    seminolus, 110–111
Lemmiscus curtatus, 31, 649–650
Lemmus sibiricus, 653–654
Leopardus
    pardalis, 228–229
    wiedii, 229–231
Leptonycteris
    curasoae, **68**, 76–78
    nivalis, *78*, 78–79
Lepus
    alleni, 693–695
    americanus, **vi**, 695–697
    arcticus, 697–698
    californicus, 699–701, *705*
    callotis, 701–702
    othus, 702–703
    townsendii, 704–705
Liomys irroratus, 547
Lissodelphis borealis, 280, *281*, 289–290
Lontra canadensis, 179–180
Lynx
    canadensis, 233–234
    rufus, 234–235

Macrotus californicus, 74–75
Marmota
    broweri, 393–395
    caligata, 395–396
    flaviventris, 396–398
    monax, 398–399
    olympus, 400
    vancouverensis, 401–402
Martes
    americana, **136**, 165–166
    pennanti, 167–168, *673*
Megaptera novaeangliae, **xiv–xv**, 256–258
Mephitis
    macroura, 186–188
    mephitis, 188–190
Mesoplodon
    bidens, 308
    carlhubbsi, 309
    densirostris, 310–311
    europaeus, 311–312
    ginkgodens, 312
    hectori, 313
    mirus, 313–314
    stejnegeri, 314–315
Microdipodops
    megacephalus, 518–520
    pallidus, 520–521

Microtus
    abbreviatus, 623–624
    breweri, 624–626
    californicus, 626–628
    canicaudus, 628–629
    chrotorrhinus, 629–630
    longicaudus, 630–632
    miurus, 632–633
    mogollonensis, 634–635
    montanus, 635–636
    ochrogaster, *594*, 637–638
    oeconomus, 638–639
    oregoni, 640
    pennsylvanicus, 641–642
    pinetorum, 642–644
    richardsoni, 644–646
    townsendii, 646–647
    xanthognathus, 647–649
Mirounga angustirostris, 217–218
Monodon monoceros, 293–294
Mormoops megalophylla, 71–72
Mustela
    erminea, 168–169, *171*
    frenata, 169–171
    nigripes, 172–173
    nivalis, *171*, 173–174
    vison, 174–175
Myotis
    auriculus, 82–83
    austroriparius, 83–85
    californicus, 85–86
    ciliolabrum, 87–88
    evotis, 88–90
    grisescens, 90–92
    keenii, 92–93
    leibii, 93–94
    lucifugus, 94–95, *96*, *104*
    septentrionalis, 96
    sodalis, 97–98
    thysanodes, 98–100
    velifer, 100–101
    volans, 101–103
    yumanensis, 103–104

Napaeozapus insignis, 665–666
Nasua narica, 223–225
Neofiber alleni, 650–651
Neotoma
    albigula, 596–598, *600*, *610*
    cinerea, 598–600
    devia, 600–601
    floridana, 601–603
    fuscipes, 603–604
    lepida, *567*, 604–606
    magister, 607–608
    mexicana, 608–609
    micropus, 609–610
    stephensi, 611
Neurotrichus gibbsii, 56–57
Notiosorex crawfordi, **12**, 54–55
Nycticeius humeralis, 117–118
Nyctinomops
    femorosaccus, 129–130
    macrotis, 130–131

Ochotona
    collaris, 677–678
    princeps, 678–680
Ochrotomys nuttalli, 584–586
Odobenus rosmarus, 193–194
Odocoileus
    hemionus, 329–331, *333*
    virginianus, **322**, 331–334
Ondatra zibethicus, 652–653
Onychomys
    arenicola, 588
    leucogaster, 588–590
    torridus, 590–591
Orcinus orca, 287–289
Oreamnos americanus, 343–346
Oryzomys
    couesi, 553–554
    palustris, 554–555
Ovibos moschatus, 346–347
Ovis
    canadensis, 348–350
    dalli, 350–351

Panthera onca, 236–237
Pappogeomys castanops, 492–493
Parascalops breweri, 62–63
Pecari tajacu, 325–326
Perognathus
    alticola, 494–495
    amplus, 495–496
    fasciatus, 497
    flavescens, 498–499
    flavus, 499–500
    inornatus, 501–502
    longimembris, 502–504, *519*
    merriami, 504–505
    parvus, 506–507
Peromyscus
    attwateri, 563
    boylii, 564–565
    californicus, 565–566
    crinitus, 566–567
    eremicus, 567–568
    gossypinus, 569–570
    gratus, 570–571
    keeni, 571–572
    leucopus, 572–574
    maniculatus, 575–577, *668*
    merriami, 577–578
    nasutus, 578–579
    pectoralis, 579–580
    polionotus, 580–582
    truei, 582–583
Phenacomys
    intermedius, 617–618, *619*
    ungava, 618–619
Phoca
    fasciata, 203–204
    groenlandica, 205–206
    hispida, 206–207
    largha, 208–209
    vitulina, 209–211
Phocoena phocoena, 295–296
Phocoenoides dalli, 297–298
Physeter macrocephalus, 299–301

Pipistrellus
 hesperus, 113–114
 subflavus, 114–115
Podomys floridanus, 583–584
Procyon lotor, **xii,** 221–223
Pseudorca crassidens, 283–284
Puma concolor, 226–228
Rangifer tarandus, 336–338
Reithrodontomys
 fulvescens, 556–557
 fulvous, *587*
 humulis, 557–558
 megalotis, 558–560
 montanus, *556*, 560–561
 raviventris, 562–563

Scalopus aquaticus, 63–65, *65*
Scapanus
 latimanus, 57–58
 orarius, 59–60
 townsendii, 60–61
Sciurus
 aberti, 449–450
 arizonensis, 450–451
 carolinensis, 451–453
 griseus, 453–455
 nayaritensis, 455–456
 niger, 456–458
Sigmodon
 arizonae, 591–592
 fulviventer, 592–593
 hispidus, *587*, 593–595
 ochrognathus, 595–596
Sorex
 arcticus, 15–16
 arizonae, 16–17
 bairdi, 18
 bendirii, 19–20
 cinereus, 20–21
 dispar, 21–22
 fumeus, 22–23
 gaspensis, 24
 haydeni, 24–25
 hoyi, 25–27
 hydrodromus, 27–28
 jacksoni, *27*, 28
 longirostris, 29–30
 lyelli, 30
 merriami, 30–31
 monticolus, 31–33
 nanus, 33–34
 ornatus, 35–36
 pacificus, 36–37
 palustris, 38–39
 preblei, 39–40
 sonomae, 40–41

Sorex (continued)
 tenellus, 41–42
 trowbridgii, 42–44
 tundrensis, *16*, 44–45
 ugyunak, 45
 vagrans, *32*, 46–47
Spermophilus
 armatus, 408–409
 beecheyi, 409–411, *455*
 beldingi, 411–413
 brunneus, 414–415
 canus, 415
 columbianus, 416–417
 elegans, 417–419
 franklinii, 419–420
 lateralis, 420–422
 mexicanus, 422–423
 mohavensis, 423–425
 mollis, 425–426
 parryii, 427–429
 richardsonii, 429–431
 saturatus, **xvi,** 431–432
 spilosoma, 432–434
 tereticaudus, *403*, *424*, 434–435
 townsendii, 435–436
 tridecemlineatus, 436–438
 variegatus, 438–440
 washingtoni, 440–441
Spilogale
 gracilis, 183–185
 putorius, 185–186
Stenella
 attenuata, 265–267
 clymene, 267–268
 coeruleoalba, 268–269
 frontalis, 269–271
 longirostris, 271–272
Steno bredanensis, 262–263
Sylvilagus
 aquaticus, 683–684
 audubonii, 684–685
 bachmani, 685–686
 floridanus, 687–688
 nuttallii, 689–690
 obscurus, 690–691
 palustris, 691–692
 transitionalis, 692–693
Synaptomys
 borealis, 655–656
 cooperi, 657–658

Tadarida brasiliensis, 127–129
Tamias
 alpinus, 357–358
 amoenus, 359–360
 canipes, 360–361

Tamias (continued)
 cinereicollis, 362–363
 dorsalis, 363–365
 merriami, 365–366
 minimus, 366–369
 obscurus, 369–370
 ochrogenys, 370–372
 palmeri, 372–373
 panamintinus, 373–375
 quadrimaculatus, 375–376
 quadrivittatus, 377–378
 ruficaudus, 378–380
 rufus, 380–381
 senex, 382–383
 siskiyou, 383–385
 sonomae, 385–386
 speciosus, 386–388
 striatus, *66*, 388–389
 townsendii, 389–391
 umbrinus, 391–393
Tamiasciurus
 douglasii, 458–459
 hudsonicus, 460–461
Taxidea taxus, 177–179
Thomomys
 bottae, 466–468, *478*
 bulbivorus, 468–469
 clusius, 470
 idahoensis, 470–471
 mazama, 471–472
 monticola, 473–474
 talpoides, 474–477, *477–478*
 townsendii, 477–478
 umbrinus, 479–480
Trichechus manatus, **316,** 319–321
Tursiops truncatus, 264–265

Urocyon
 cinereoargenteus, 152–154
 littoralis, 154–156
Ursus
 americanus, **xxiv,** 157–160
 arctos, 160–163
 maritimus, 163–164

Vulpes
 velox, 148–150
 vulpes, *148*, 150–152

Zalophus californianus, **iv–v,** 201–202
Zapus
 hudsonius, 666–667
 princeps, 668–669
 trinotatus, 669–670
Ziphius cavirostris, 305–306

Index to Common Names

Page numbers in *italics* indicate species information included elsewhere than in its own account. Page numbers in **boldface** indicate photographs located elsewhere than in their respective species account.

antelope, pronghorn, 339–341
armadillo, nine-banded, **x, 6,** 9–11

badger, American, 177–179
bat(s)
  big-eared
    Allen's, 123–125
    Rafinesque's, 119–121
    Townsend's, **i,** 121–123
  brown
    big, 115–117
    little, 94–95, *96, 104*
  evening, 117–118
  free-tailed
    big, 130–131
    Brazilian, 127–129
    pocketed, 129–130
  ghost-faced, 71–72
  hoary, 106–107
  Indiana, 97–98
  leaf-nosed, California, 74–75
  long-nosed
    Mexican, *78,* 78–79
    southern, **68,** 76–78
  long-tongued, Mexican, 75–76
  mastiff
    Underwood's, 134–135
    Wagner's, 132–133
    western, 133–134
  myotis
    California, 85–86
    cave, 100–101
    fringed, 98–100
    gray, 90–92
    Keen's, 92–93
    long-eared, 88–90
    long-eared, northern, 96
    long-legged, 101–103
    small-footed, eastern, 93–94
    small-footed, western, 87–88
    southeastern, 83–85

bat(s), myotis *(continued)*
    southwestern, 82–83
    Yuma, 103–104
  pallid, 125–126
  pipistrelle
    eastern, 114–115
    western, 113–114
  red, 105–106
  Seminole, 110–111
  silver-haired, 111–112
  spotted, 118–119
  vampire, hairy-legged, 80–81
  yellow
    northern, 109–110
    southern, 107–109
bear(s)
  American black, **xxiv,** 157–160
  brown, 160–163
  grizzly, 160–163
  polar, 163–164
beaver(s)
  American, 548–552
  mountain, 355–356
beluga, **238,** 291–292
bighorn sheep, 348–350
bison, American, 342–343
bobcat, 234–235
buffalo, American, 342–343

caribou, 336–338
cat(s)
  bobcat, 234–235
  cougar, 226–228
  jaguar, 236–237
  jaguarundi, 231–232
  lynx, Canada, 233–234
  margay, 229–231
  ocelot, 228–229
chipmunk(s)
  Allen's, 382–383
  alpine, 357–358
  California, 369–370
  cliff, 363–365
  Colorado, 377–378
  eastern, *66,* 388–389
  gray-collared, 362–363
  gray-footed, 360–361
  Hopi, 380–381

chipmunk(s) *(continued)*
  least, 366–369
  lodgepole, 386–388
  long-eared, 375–376
  Merriam's, 365–366
  Palmer's, 372–373
  Panamint, 373–375
  red-tailed, 378–380
  Siskiyou, 383–385
  Sonoma, 385–386
  Townsend's, 389–391
  Uinta, 391–393
  yellow-cheeked, 370–372
  yellow-pine, 359–360
coati, white-nosed, 223–225
cougar, 226–228
coyote, 139–141, *143, 145, 151*

deer
  caribou, 336–338
  elk, 327–329
  moose, 334–336
  mule, 329–331, *333*
  white-tailed, **322,** 331–334
dolphin(s)
  bottlenose, 264–265
  Clymene, 267–268
  common, 272–274
  Fraser's, 275
  killer whales, 282–284, 287–289
  pilot whales, 285–287
  right whale dolphin, northern, *280, 281,*
    289–290
  Risso's, 280–282
  rough-toothed, 262–263
  saddleback
    long-beaked, 272–273
    short-beaked, 274
  spinner, 271–272
  spotted
    Atlantic, 269–271
    pantropical, 265–267
  striped, 268–269
  white-beaked, 277–279
  white-sided
    Atlantic, 276–277
    Pacific, 279–280, *281*

747

elk, **ii–iii,** *327–329*
ermine, 168–169, *171*

ferret, black-footed, 172–173
fisher, 167–168, *673*
fox(es)
  arctic, 146–148
  gray
    common, 152–154
    island, 154–156
  kit, 148–150
  red, *148,* 150–152
  swift, 148–150

goat, mountain, 343–346
gopher. *See* pocket gopher(s)

hare(s). *See also* jackrabbit(s)
  Alaskan, 702–703
  arctic, 697–698
  snowshoe, **vi,** 695–697

jackrabbit(s)
  antelope, 693–695
  black-tailed, 699–701, *705*
  white-sided, 701–702
  white-tailed, 704–705
jaguar, 236–237
jaguarundi, 231–232

lemming(s)
  bog
    northern, 655–656
    southern, 657–658
  brown, 653–654
  collared, 658–664
    northern, 658, 659–660
    Richardson's, 658, 662–664
    Ungava, 658, 660–662
lynx, Canada, 233–234

manatee, West Indian, **316,** 319–321
margay, 229–231
marmot(s)
  Alaska, 393–395
  hoary, 395–396
  Olympic, 400
  Vancouver, 401–402
  woodchuck, 398–399
  yellow-bellied, 396–398
marten, American, **136,** 165–166
mink, American, 174–175
mole(s)
  American shrew, 56–57
  broad-footed, 57–58
  coast, 59–60
  eastern, 63–65, *65*
  hairy-tailed, 62–63
  star-nosed, 65–67
  Townsend's, 60–61
moose, 334–336
mountain beaver, 355–356
mountain goat, 344–346
mountain sheep, 348–351

mouse
  brush, 564–565
  cactus, 567–568
  California, 565–566
  canyon, 566–567
  cotton, 569–570
  deer, 575–577, *668*
    northwestern deer, 571–572
  Florida, 583–584
  golden, 584–586
  grasshopper
    Mearn's, 588
    northern, 588–590
    southern, 590–591
  harvest
    eastern, 557–558
    fulvous, 556–557, *587*
    plains, *556,* 560–561
    salt marsh, 562–563
    western, 558–560
  jumping
    meadow, 666–667
    Pacific, 669–670
    western, 668–669
    woodland, 665–666
  kangaroo
    dark, 518–520
    pale, 520–521
  mesquite, 577–578
  oldfield, 580–582
  Osgood's, 570–571
  pinyon, 582–583
  pocket
    Arizona, 495–496
    Bailey's, 507–508
    California, 508–509
    desert, 516–517
    Great Basin, 506–507
    hispid, 513–514
    little, 502–504, *519*
    long-tailed, 511–512
    Merriam's, 504–505
    Mexican spiny, 547
    Nelson's, 515–516
    olive-backed, 497
    plains, 498–499
    rock, 514–515
    San Diego, 510–511, *567*
    San Joaquin, 501–502
    silky, 499–500
    spiny, 517–518
    white-eared, 494–495
  pygmy, northern, 586–587, *594*
  rock, northern, 578–579
  Texas, 563
  white-ankled, 579–580
  white-footed, 572–574
muskox, 346–347
muskrat, 652–653
  round-tailed muskrat, 650–651
myotis. *See* bat(s)

narwhal, 293–294

ocelot, 228–229
opossum, Virginia, **xxvi,** 3–5
otter(s)
  river, northern, 179–180
  sea, 180–182

peccary, collared, 325–326
pika(s)
  American, 678–680
  collared, 677–678
pocket gopher(s)
  Attwater's, 482–483
  Baird's, 483–484
  Botta's, 466–468, *478*
  Camas, 468–469
  desert, 480–481
  Idaho, 470–471
  Jones's, 486–487
  Llano, 490–491
  mountain, 473–474
  northern, 474–477, *477–478*
  plains, 485–486
  southeastern, 489–490
  southern, 479–480
  Texas, 487–489
  Townsend's, 477–478
  western, 471–472
  Wyoming, 470
  yellow-faced, 492–493
porcupine, North American, *167,* **352,** 671–673
porpoise(s)
  Dall's, 297–298
  harbor, 295–296
prairie dog(s)
  black-tailed, 445–447
  Gunnison's, 441–443
  Utah, 447–448
  white-tailed, 443–445
pronghorn, 339–341

rabbit(s). *See also* hare(s); jackrabbits
  brush, 685–686
  cottontail
    Appalachian, 690–691
    desert, 684–685
    eastern, 687–688
    mountain, 689–690
    New England, 692–693
  marsh, 691–692
  pygmy, 681–683
  swamp, 683–684
raccoon, northern, **xii,** 221–223
rat(s)
  cotton
    Arizona, 591–592
    hispid, *587,* 593–595
    tawny-bellied, 592–593
    yellow-nosed, 595–596
  kangaroo
    agile, 521–523
    banner-tailed, 542–544
    big-eared, 528–529
    California, 523–524
    chisel-toothed, 534–535
    desert, 525–527